FOUR AGES OF UNDERSTANDING

FOUR AGES OF UNDERSTANDING

The First Postmodern Survey
of Philosophy from Ancient Times
to the Turn of the Twenty-first Century

JOHN DEELY

UNIVERSITY OF TORONTO PRESS
Toronto Buffalo London

© University of Toronto Press 2001
Toronto London Buffalo
Printed in Canada

ISBN 0-8020-4735-1

Printed on acid-free paper

Toronto Studies in Semiotics
Editors: Marcel Danesi, Umberto Eco, Paul Perron, and Thomas A. Sebeok

---

Canadian Cataloguing in Publication Data

Deely, John N.
   Four ages of understanding : the first postmodern survey of philosophy from ancient times
   to the turn of the twenty-first century

   (Toronto studies in semiotics)
   Includes bibliographical references and index.
   ISBN 0-8020-4735-1

   1. Philosophy – History. 2. Semiotics – History. 3. Postmodernism.
   I. Title. II. Series.

   B72.D43 2001   190   C00-932075-X

University of Toronto Press acknowledges the financial assistance to its publishing program
of the Canada Council for the Arts and the Ontario Arts Council.

University of Toronto Press acknowledges the financial support for its publishing activities
of the Government of Canada through the Book Publishing Industry Development Program
(BPIDP).

To Whom,
if not to those few who will read every word?

and to the living memory of Anthony Francis Russell

"Tony"

26 November 1922 – 1999 April 12
ally of spirit to each such reader

Aviso: Why Read This Book?

I came from my Parkview house to the Hispanic gathering in Jackson Park just in time for the food (having been able from the window to see when the time was right).

"Where have you been?" a lady unknown to me asked from across the table at which I took a seat.

"Writing a book," I replied, taking my first bite.

"Oh?" queried the stranger. "What about?"

"The history of philosophy" I said, taking another bite. Her face took on a quizzical look. "What are you thinking?" I asked, taking still another bite.

"Hasn't that already been written" she said, less a question than a hint I was wasting my time and, worse, the time of prospective readers who could already find what I had to say written elsewhere and, likely, better.

"Not so" I countered. "Besides, I have an angle."

"Then perhaps I shall have to read your book" she said; a polite comment, in a tone only half convinced. "When will your book appear?"

"Had the calendar not been wrong", I said, referring implicitly to matter discussed in chapter 5 of the alleged book, "it would have been in the twenty-first century. As it is, probably in the last year of this one. What a pity."

But you, dear reader, with the book in hand, haven't the need to ask when it will appear, though before further committing yourself you are likely indeed to want to know what possible "angle" could truly justify another – yet another – history of philosophy?

Well, I can tell you this much going in. Like any history, this book presents you with a large-scale hypothesis, or series of hypotheses ("more or less confirmed guesses", as a friend of mine might put it) about what happened in the past. But, in addition, because it is a philosophical history, the hypotheses presented are presented in the framework of a single unifying hypothesis about what bearing all this past has today for the immediate future of philosophy – for the history, that is to say, that someone else will have to write, even if for no other purpose than to set straight the story I am about to tell those of you who read on.

For it is an outrageous story. I tell you that philosophy as it has been taught in our American universities since their beginning in 1636 has mainly left out so many irreducibly key elements as to get the whole thing wrong, when it has not been made downright incomprehensible. And philosophy itself as a discipline of thought has suffered severely in consequence. For the probative details you have the book itself, an invitation to think for yourself long, deeply, and widely about the situation of human understanding as the twenty-first century of our era dawns.

Here is my bet. If you read this book through, you will come away convinced that what has claimed to be and been in fact the mainstream of philosophical thought in contemporary culture has turned into a side current, perhaps even a backwater. In the seventeenth century, modern philosophy, in order to develop, had to move pretty much outside the academy. In the late twentieth century, the philosophical establishment within the academy has become to philosophy's future what the judges of Galileo were to the future of science. That is how the story of philosophy will appear when our successors look back on the twentieth century. That is the bet. To call the bet you have only to read the book; and all the while yourself philosophize.

Contents at a Glance

Part IV POSTMODERN TIMES: The Way of Signs

Contents in Detail

List of Tables and Illustrations

Reconocimientos

Since early years I have been cursed or blessed with a habit of mind – a character defect it may be – that likes to turn over problems that have no solution, or at least no solution that can be provided outside of thought itself (if there). One day, after nearly two years of weekly seminars and intellectual visits with Mauricio Beuchot at the national university in México City in particular, the habit led to this book, begun on the 25th of February, 1996, and completed on the 20th of March of that same year – though ever since under more-or-less constant revision, in the course of which even undergraduate classroom discussions played a part (notably, the diagram on p. 231 below of "the Latin discussion of relation after Boethius" is thanks to my student Rick Hanson). It comes as a surprise to me still that, having grown up on the banks of the Rio Grande, so many years later I had to cross that river and go more than a thousand miles into México to reach the spot where the inspiration for this book found the circumstances for execution. In a casa rented from Alberto Diaz de Cosio, ceramista and friend, on the Privada de los Compadres, in Santa Maria Ahuacatitlan, Morelos, over the intense twenty-four days of its first draft, each night about 2300 hours Paco – Francisco Tellez Fernandez – would come from work and we would talk intensely, he, Teresita, and I, all in Spanish, sometimes resorting to as much as 50% or more of hypothesis, about the progress of the grand vision.

The revisions, perforce, since I had to return to my home in Dubuque, Iowa, two thousand miles the other side of the Rio Grande, had to be made from an outpost of that singular part of civilization we call "academia". When you live on the fringes, such a task is not easy, for it requires not merely the assistance of a research library (there is no other kind of library in fact; only good and inferior research libraries), but of a research library so excellent that it does not even exist in one place. Not even the legendary library of Alexandria, had it survived intact, would have been sufficient.

This is where friends come in. One of my best friends, Jack Doyle, is a virtual library. He seems always there with a source, an idea, not infrequently a stinging "to the contrary". Alongside this great scholar, it is my blessing to have also not one but two friends who not only have the temper and training of a true librarian, but who each hold the post of Director in academic libraries attached to institutions which over the years have had faculty who well knew that the life of the mind and the accumulation of library resources cannot be reduced to some shallow conception of teaching which changes with each passing fad and season. As a result, even though living on the fringes of the great research institutions which are the principal mainstay of human civilization insofar as that enterprise depends (and it depends centrally) on inquiry, I have had at my disposal institutional structures guided by minds and spirits that actually constitute what is central to the universe of discourse and life of the mind in its principal institutionalized setting.

And, even from an outpost, the great American program of interlibrary loan, supported by the crucial direction of such minds, such library directors, makes possible the revision to the point of publishability of a work as large in scope as this one. I want to take my readers on a journey across more than twenty-four centuries, with visits to every main surviving civilization on earth. To do it in any kind of a publically credible way required assistance, and Robert Klein, Library Director of Loras College, and Joel L. Samuels, Library Director of the University of Dubuque and Wartburg Theological Seminary combined, provided that assistance. Under them, I am indebted to their staff, particularly to the Loras interlibrary loan librarian DiAnn Kilburg, the public-services librarian Doug Gullikson, and the cataloging librarian Robert Schoofs.

As for critics and consultants in the work, my main debt is to Kenneth Schmitz, Ralph McInerny, Otto Bird, and Anthony F. Russell, proud author of *Logic, Philosophy, and History*, and as good a friend and intellectual colleague as ever has been the blessing of philosophers anywhere to have the companionship. I salute these allies in the work of the mind, especially Mauricio, Alberto, Paco, Teresita, Doyle, Klein, Samuels, Schmitz, McInerny, Bird, and Russell; and hereby acknowledge the indispensable contribution of all to the present work, with heartfelt thanks.

Preface: The Boundary of Time

Well if, as a matter of fact, all history is contemporary history, just as all sunshine is today's sunshine, yet which of the countless rays of the sun's light actually fall on us depends on where we stand in time and space, and since time in particular knows no rest, not even the relative rest of "staying in one place" as the earth on which we rest yet continually moves at $18^1\!/_2$ or so miles per second, let me, in order to give my reader a rest even in time, redefine for present purposes the boundaries of time as they bear on our common enterprise of creating a shared discourse, a discourse in which reader and writer alike are to have an active role, in which to consider some matters of philosophy.

The past is prologue to the present as the present is prologue to the future. That is a truism, but one the terms of which need redefining if we are to have a moment's rest in which to consider the matter of this book. What needs defining, or redefining, is not so much the term "prologue" as the terms "past", "present", and "future"; for they represent the divisions of time as a framework or measure for the pinpointing of events, and so have no fixity outside the very framework they provide. The "present", famously, is the boundary separating past from future, but the very boundary itself is notoriously shifting, for it moves as we try to state it, as in answering the question, "What time is it?", our answer works only to the degree that we allow it to lack precision. Were we to answer truly "Two o'clock", indeed, by the time we gave the answer, two o'clock would either not have arrived or already be past. As a practical matter, of course, our answer was good enough. But the theoretical and speculative point that it is impossible to state a present moment before that moment is past remains as the far more interesting point, ever deserving of consideration.

We need a broader notion of "present" than the instant joining past with future. The boundary of time that I would propose for the purposes of the present discourse is the lifetime of each of us brought together by the consideration of the matters written about in this book. As long as we, each of us, speaker and auditors, scriptor and lector, continue to live, we are entitled to speak of the "present". The present, then, as I am defining it here, is the exclusive preserve of the living. The boundary of time is then the separation of the no longer living from the not yet dead, on the one side, and the further separation of the not yet dead from the not yet living, on the other side. The already dead define the past. The not yet living define the future. The not yet dead define the present, the moment of our shared discourse.

By the device of these definitions, even though we are yet left with a shifting boundary both on the side of the past and on the side of the future, at least the interval between past and future, the present, is long enough for us to work some matters out and perhaps even contribute together to what will be the heritage of the past for those future inquirers who are not yet part of our present. I write for the present, the living, both in being and to come into being.

Now let us say that, at present (and we know what we mean), we are standing on the boundary of modern and postmodern times, and we are toward morning rather than toward evening on this boundary of a fourth age of human understanding to which the whole of previous speculative thought in its many rivers, streams, and hidden springs has conspired to lead us. I write for the purpose of illuminating that boundary, and from this point of view I make my selections from the countless rays of historical data all around us. To the extent that a history of philosophy, as one way of doing philosophy or even providing an introductory text (which it would be premature to call the present work), has among its purposes to help the reader understand the current intellectual situation – to give the reader some idea of how we got where we are, and where we might be going from here – then, for some foreseeable time to come, this is the best standpoint from which to write the history of philosophy. Probably I should rather say rewrite a history, for it is a question at once of new facts come to being and light together with new insights objectively rearranging the connections, and thereby the relevance and irrelevance, of old facts as well.

If there is one notion that is central to the emerging postmodern consciousness, that notion is the notion of sign. And for understanding this notion, nothing is more essential than a new history of philosophy. For the notion of sign that has become the basis for a postmodern development of thought was unknown in the modern period, and before that traces back only as far as the turn of the 5th century AD. Yet the context within which the general notion of sign was first introduced presupposes both the ancient Greek notion of "natural sign" ($\sigma\eta\mu\epsilon\hat{\iota}o\nu$) and the framework of Greek discussions of nature and mind which provoked the development of philosophy in the first place as an attempt to understand the being proper to the objects of experience. Not only does it emerge that the sign is what every object presupposes, but, in modern philosophy, the conundrum about the reality of the "external world", the insolubility of the problem of how in theory to get beyond the privacy of the individual mind, springs directly from the reduction of signification to representation. So here is one of the ways in which the four ages of this book can be outlined: preliminaries to the notion of sign; the development of the notion itself; forgetfulness of the notion; recovery and advance of the notion.

Tracing the development of the notion of sign from its beginning and against the backdrop of Greek philosophy yields an unexpected benefit by comparison with more familiar historical approaches. Every modern history of philosophy has been essentially preoccupied with the separating off from philosophy of science in the modern sense, especially in and after the seventeenth century. From this point of view, many of the continuing philosophical developments of the later Latin centuries tend to drop out of sight. It has become the custom to present modern philosophy, conventionally beginning with Descartes (17th century), simply as part and parcel of the scientific break with the authors of Latin tradition, and to treat the bringing of nominalism into the foreground of Latin thought by William of Ockham (14th century) as if that were the *finale* of Latin development.

This hiatus of two and a half centuries in the history of philosophy, however, effectively disappears when we make our way from ancient to modern times by tracing mainly the development of the philosophical notion of *signum*. From the High Middle Ages down to the time of Descartes we find a lively and continuous discussion of sign which, through a series of important if unfamiliar controversies on both sides of the thirteenth century, leads to a basic split in the closing Latin centuries. On one side stand those who think that the general notion of sign is an empty name, a *flatus vocis*, a nominalism, no more than a "relation of reason", an *ens rationis*. On the other side are those who are able to ground the general notion in an understanding of relation as a unique, suprasubjective mode of being, a veritable dual citizen of the order of *ens reale* and *ens rationis* alike, according to shifting circumstances.

Modern philosophy, from this point of view, appears essentially as an exploration of the nominalist alternative; and postmodern thought begins with the acknowledgment of the bankruptcy of the modern effort, combined with the determination pioneered by C. S. Peirce to explore the alternative, "the road not taken", the "second destiny" that had been identified in the closing Latin centuries but forgotten thereafter. Peirce's postmodern resumption of premodern epistemological themes produces a number of immediately dramatic and surprising results (beginning with the cure for the pathology dividing our intellectual culture between the *personae* of Dr. Jekyll and Mr. Hyde).

So derives the title for this work, *Four Ages of Understanding*: ancient Greek thought, the Latin Age, modern thought, postmodern thought. The book is a survey of philosophy in what is relevant to the "understanding of understanding" from ancient times to the present. It is intended both as a reference work in the history of philosophy and a guide to future research – a "handbook for inquirers" in history, philosophy, and the humanities generally, including historians and philosophers of science. The book also aims to aid in the classroom those professors willing to wean a new generation from the "standard modern outlines" of philosophy's history which serve mainly to support the post-Cartesian supposition that history is of next to no import for the doing itself of philosophy. Modern thought advanced by developing specializations; and within specialties, to borrow an observation from Stillman Drake, "each of us moves in a necessarily restricted circle and remains untouched by the labors of persons outside it on matters that are of no interest to us and our immediate associates." But when this kind of narrowness reaches such an extreme point that philosophy itself falls victim to specialization and overspecialization, its professors sometimes unable to tell the difference between logic and philosophy, signs and signifieds, it is time for an overall reassessment of the situation.

It is not enough to distinguish the history of philosophy from philosophy, philosophical from exegetic problems, if we do not at the same time realize that the history of philosophy *is* philosophy itself as so far actually realized in civilization. An exclusively synchronic development of philosophical problems generates mainly a blindness to one's own presuppositions and to the manner in which historical context shapes in essential ways contemporary consciousness – and unconsciousness – of basic philosophical problems. To see that there is more to be done is quite a different matter than proceeding as if nothing had been done before us. Only an inclusive historical approach has even a ghost's chance of restoring perspective and balance, of forcing the needed reassessment to a successful outcome.

My hope is that this book will help make it unconscionable for professors to continue to teach philosophy in the manner that has long become customary – as though the history counted for nothing, or provided only a side-show, especially that part of its history I make known in this book as the Latin Age, to which age, especially in its closing centuries (the period between Ockham and Poinsot or Descartes), we owe the general notion of sign taken for granted today insofar as it is a warranted notion and not a mere nominalism. Besides, the history of philosophy is not only philosophy itself as realized in civilization, but also a story, and a good one. Mates has suggested that to tell a story or even to criticize what others have said or done is incompatible with the search for truth in history. I couldn't disagree more, for it is on narrative that we live as distinctively human animals, and every good narrative has to have a beginning, a middle, and an end, however provisional. My aim has been to tell a "story of philosophy" somewhere near as well as it deserves to be told in order for something of the many truths at stake to come alive for those who happen to hear the tale – not the only one to be told, to be sure, but still a story of philosophy in the grand manner such a story requires to match its destiny. I have tried to equip the reader, as it were, with seven-league boots, making it possible to traverse twenty-four centuries in such a way as to obtain a vantage opening as far into the future of philosophy, I dare say, as at least the lifetime of anyone born by the time of publication of this book. The last word in any history is never spoken till the race itself is extinct, and not even then. So this is not a history for all time, but only for the first quarter or so, with luck the first half, of the twenty-first century; after which the postmodernism of which it speaks as harbinger will be spoken of rather with words of hindsight and Minerva, according to the saying of Hegel, that the owl of wisdom only flies toward evening.

John Dewey opened his 'Preface' of 1910 by observing that "An elaborate preface to a philosophic work usually impresses one as a last desperate effort on the part of its author to convey what he feels he has not quite managed to say in the body of his book. Nevertheless," he continued, reminding me of Poinsot's 'Preface' of

1631, which opened by citing from the book of 2 Maccabees 2.33: "There is no sense expanding the preface to the history and curtailing the history itself." So let me curtail this preface that the reader may pass directly to the history itself.

John Deely
Parkview, on the feast of St Augustine, as it happens
28 August 1998

FOUR AGES OF UNDERSTANDING

CHAPTER ONE

Society and Civilization:
The Prelude to Philosophy

What has long been called "philosophy" is obscure in its origins. So far as historical records go, philosophy is associated most specifically with the Greek language of the sixth century before Christ. The etymology of the name "philosophy" is not especially helpful: it is a putting together of the ancient Greek words for "lover" and "wisdom". To say, then, that philosophy is "love of wisdom" does not really get us very far. To get the beginnings of an idea of what the term "philosophy" means, let us look at what the earliest human beings called philosophers did that led to their being called "lovers of wisdom".

In the most general terms, the individuals credited with the introduction of philosophical thought into human civilizations were men who speculated on what constitutes the objects of human experience so far as those objects have or involve an existence or being independent of what we human beings may think, feel, or do. The philosophers, in other words, are those individuals who are credited with introducing into human thought the idea of reality, of something which is what it is on its own grounds, regardless of what further relations it may have to us or how it may appear in experience. Soon enough this thinking became reflexive, and raised the question of how might such a knowledge be possible in the first place. The original question led to a variety of theories about the nature of the cosmos, or *cosmologies*, as well as to views about being in general or *ontologies*, and eventually to the separation of scientific theory as such from philosophical speculation. The subsequent question led to various theories about the nature of knowledge, or *epistemologies*. Philosophical doctrines, it gradually became clear, are in some sense prior to and independent of scientific thought, and deal with the very framework itself of understanding and experience within which scientific pursuits about the sensible world are possible. As facts and theories become the coinage of scientific discourse, so ontologies and epistemologies become the coinage of philosophical exchange, two sides of the same coin, as we will see. Patently, discourse about being implies both epistemological and ontological issues, the understanding of the intertwining of which is pretty much the story of philosophy.

The association of philosophy with language is actually more profound than is commonly realized. Philosophy today is known to us primarily through works of prose, as distinct from poetry. And it has long been so. But in the beginning, philosophy and poetry were intimately intertwined. Pherecydes of Syros, who flourished in the sixth century BC (the most complete study[1] places his prime in 544/1BC), is reputed to have been the first to write in prose. More than one historian who has looked at these early materials of the formation of philosophy within ancient Greek civilization has been struck by what appears as almost a ratio: as science was at first a form of philosophy which struggled to free itself from the general, the speculative, the empirically unverifiable as such, so philosophy was at first a form of poetry which strove to free itself from mythology, animism, and metaphor as such. This fits well with Aristotle's view[2] that the work of Pherecydes belongs to that intermediate or transitional class of ancient authors who "do not use mythical language throughout". In any event, I am inclined to agree with West[3] that "it cannot be an accident that the three oldest prose books that have survived – Pherecydes, Anaximander, Anaximenes – were all expositions of the origin and nature of the world." The transition from poetry to prose did not happen overnight; but if one is to state critical views subject to dispute and demonstration there can be little doubt that prose is better suited to the task of doctrinal exposition than is poetry. So remarked Symonds in pondering the matter:[4]

> Zeal for greater rigor of thought was instrumental in developing a new vehicle of language. The time had come at length for separation from poetry, for the creation of a prose style which should correspond in accuracy to the logical necessity of exact thinking. Prose accordingly was elaborated with infinite difficulty by these first speculators from the elements of common speech. It was a great epoch in the history of European culture when men ceased to produce their thoughts in the fixed cadences of verse, and consigned them to the more elastic periods of prose. Heraclitus of Ephesus was the first who achieved a notable success in this new and difficult art. He for his pains received the title of σκοτεινός, the obscure; so strange and novel did the language of science [i.e., knowledge trying to achieve exact expression] seem to minds accustomed hitherto to nothing but metre.

And of course the change did not occur overnight. Far into antiquity, "like a pompous sacrificial vestment",[5] particular philosophic authors would continue to drag the hexameter "along the pathway of their argument upon the entities".

---

1 Schibli 1990: 2.
2 Aristotle c.348–7dBC: *Metaphysics* Book XIV, 1091b8.
3 West 1971: 5.
4 Symonds 1893: 11–12.
5 Ibid. p. 12.

Yet why philosophy, the struggle initially to come to terms with the notion of reality as something independent of the human, should originally have taken the form of poetic expression is interesting to ponder in its own right. I think the matter is bound up with the nature of experience itself as the original ground of human knowledge in structures of cognition shared with other animal life forms. Many animals, including human animals, live in society, and all social animals behave in a context of organization and hierarchy. But only human animals transform their social organization into civilizations, and only in the context of society thus transformed does philosophy appear. In this transformation and appearance language plays a central role, a role that bears looking at, for it will suggest an answer to the question of why poetic expression was the original philosophic form. (Reality was not merely discovered, we might say; it was celebrated!)

To begin with, it is vitally important to form a clear distinction between *language*, which is a species-specific human activity, and *communication*, which is a universal phenomenon of nature among all types of individuals, living and nonliving, plant and animal, human and nonhuman. All too often, indeed, normally, language and communication are confused. But the two are profoundly different. There are biological species that have no hearing. Yet because we and other animal species which catch our attention use sounds to communicate, we are prone to think of vocal communication particularly as "language", and to mistake the singing of birds, for example, or the barking of dogs, as some kind of language. Communication, however, is not language, although language can be *used* to communicate.

The phenomenon of language appears very late in the development of the universe, but at the very beginning of the development of the human species. Language, strictly speaking, is identified with a certain way of *modeling the world* in cognition. To see what is different about the human way of modeling, we have to understand, first, that every animal formulates its own model of the world, according to its own biological constitution and interests. Every organism comes to be within and depends upon the physical environment throughout its lifespan. Depending upon the channels of sensation, the organs of awareness, with which it is endowed, each organism becomes aware of certain aspects of its physical surroundings but not others. The organism is like a radio receiver, tuned to pick up certain signals from the environment but not others.

Moreover, again depending upon its biological constitution, each organism will react differently to the signals it does pick up. To some of them it will react positively, to others negatively, and to yet others indifferently. A hungry lion spying a sheep will be inclined to attack, kill, and eat the sheep. A lion who has just eaten its fill may spot a sheep and ignore it. A sheep spotting a lion we say "instinctively" fears the lion. The point is that the physical environment is one thing, the world as a particular organism is aware of it is something quite – not entirely, yet quite

– different. The former is the subjective or physical world, the world where things exist whether or not they are cognized. The latter is the objective world, the world as it is apprehended and organized within apprehension.

To begin with, the world of awareness includes only a small part of the physical environment. Furthermore, the world of awareness is organized differently than the physical environment is organized in its own being apart from the organism. The selectivity and species-specific network of relations according to which an organism becomes aware of its environment is called an *Umwelt*. "Umwelt" therefore is a technical expression meaning precisely *objective world*. In the objective world of a moth, bats are something to be avoided. In the objective world of a bat, moths are something to be sought. For bats like to eat moths, while moths, like most animals, are aversive to being eaten.

Each type of cognitive organism, we may say, has, so to speak, its own "psychology", its own way of "seeing the world", while the world itself, the physical environment, is something more than what is seen, and has a rather different organization than the organization it acquires in the "seeing". The world as known or "seen" is an objective world, species-specific in every case. That is what "objective" throughout this work principally means: to exist as known. Things in the environment may or may not exist as known. When they are cognized or known, they are objects *as well as* things. But, as things, they exist regardless of being known. Furthermore, not every object is a thing. A hungry organism will go in search of an object which it can eat, to wit, an object which is also a thing. But if it fails to encounter such an object for a long enough time, the organism will die of starvation. An organism may also be mistaken in what it perceives as an object, which is why camouflage is so often used in the biological world. So, not only is it the case that objects and things are distinct in principle, the former by necessarily having, the latter by being independent of, a relation to some knower; it is also the case that not all objects are things and not all things are objects.

The "psychology" or interior states, both cognitive and affective, on the basis of which the individual organism relates to its physical surroundings or environment in constituting its particular objective world or Umwelt is called an *Innenwelt*. The Innenwelt is a kind of cognitive map on the basis of which the organism orients itself to its surroundings. The Innenwelt, therefore, is "subjective" in just the way that all physical features of things are subjective: it *belongs to* and *exists within* some distinct entity within the world of physical things. The Innenwelt is part of what identifies this or that organism as *distinct* within its environment and species. But that is not the whole or even the main story of the Innenwelt. The subjective psychological states that constitute the Innenwelt do so not insofar as they belong to the subject they help identify, but rather insofar as they give rise to relationships which link that individual subject with what is other than itself, in particular its objectified physical surroundings.

These relationships, founded on, arising or *provenating from*, psychological states as subjective states, are not themselves subjective. If they were, they would not be *relationships*. If they were, they would not be *links* between individual and environment, but characteristics which separate and identify the individual from and within its surroundings. The relationships, in short, are over and above the psychological states. The relationships depend upon the subjective states; they do not exist apart from the individual. But they do not exist *in* the individual either. They exist *between* the individual and whatever the individual is aware of, and whatever the individual is aware of exists as *terminating* that relationship. A relation minimally involves three factors: that on which the relationship is founded or based, the relationship itself, and that at which the relation terminates. In terms of these three factors, the Innenwelt is the first factor viewed as giving rise to the second, while the Umwelt is the third factor viewed as terminating the second. The second factor, the relations themselves, or rather network of relations, is what constitutes the objective world as distinct in principle both from the subjectivity of the one possessing the Innenwelt and from the subjectivity of the things of the physical environment insofar as they exist apart from the particular network of objects known by this or that organism.

A concrete illustration should help make the point. The first time you visit a new city, you are easily lost. You have little or no idea of "where you are". Gradually, by observing various points of reference, the surroundings take on a certain familiarity. What started out as objects gradually turn into signs thanks to which you come to "know where you are". Soon enough, you are able to find your way around the new place "without even thinking about it". What you have done is to construct an Innenwelt which organizes the relevant physical surroundings into a familiar Umwelt. The cognitive components of an Innenwelt are called *ideas*, the affective or emotional components are called *sentiments* or *feelings*. The cognized components of an Umwelt are called *objects* – *objects signified*, as we shall see.

These remarks apply to all cognitive organisms, to all animals, including the human species. Each animal, depending on its channels of cognition, lives in an Umwelt more or less rich, more or less inclusive of various aspects of the physical environment. The cognitive process is twofold. First, the direct channels through which physical features of the environment are objectified are called *external senses*. The external senses are selective but not interpretive. When we speak of *sensation*, we are speaking primarily in terms of those features of the environment made known by external sense.

Second, in addition to external sense, there is the matter of the way in which the environmental features objectified are organized in awareness. This is a matter of internal sense rather than of external sense, and the organization added by cognition to sensations is what is called *perception*. Unlike sensation, which merely selects among environmental features those that can be objectified, as an AM radio selects among TV, FM, and other signals bombarding it, perception interprets what sensation presents. Perception ties sensations together to form the objects of experience, and what objects are within experience therefore is not wholly the same as – neither wholly the same as nor wholly different from – what the things are which, by physically acting upon the cognitive organism, activate its powers of sense.

The traditional scheme of perception,[6] refined but not gainsaid by scientific psychology, identifies the "five external senses" – sight, hearing, smell, taste, and touch – as feeding into "four internal senses" – the *synthetic or 'common' sense*, which relates external sensations to the same or different objects; the *memory*, which recognizes in sensations familiarity or novelty; *imagination*, which introduces into sensations alternative possibilities of organization – creating, for example, objective unities at variance with the material or physical unities given in the environment prior to or independent of the imagination; and the *'estimative power'*, which evaluates the sensations and imaginations according to the particular needs and interests of the organism – for example, as an object to be sought or an object to be avoided, for whatever reasons. When we speak of *perception*, we are speaking primarily in terms of the way sensations are incorporated into our experience of objects.

Through these various channels or avenues of apprehension of external and internal sense working together, thus, the Innenwelt and Umwelt develop as correlative structures, superordinate to and relatively independent of the physical environment as such. The Innenwelt is subjective, to be sure, but the Umwelt is objective; the Innenwelt is "private", but the Umwelt is "public". Two people have two ideas, but these ideas as psychological realities are but the foundations for a relation to an object; and while each person may have his or her own idea, that which the idea is *of* or *about* may well overlap or even be the same. Moreover, even when the object considered is the same between two people, they may well *feel differently* about that object. The Innenwelt gives rise to and sustains an Umwelt, and each Umwelt in turn gives rise to an indefinite number of possibilities for both communication and "misunderstanding".

I put this last word in quotation marks, because it introduces us to the distinguishing feature of the human Umwelt, to what further makes of a simple Umwelt a linguistic Lebenswelt: the human animal is the only animal which becomes aware of the difference between objects and things in terms of the difference between what is related to the knowing organism and what exists apart from or regardless of that relation.[7] Another way to put this is to say that the human animal is the only

---

6 This scheme, we may say, belongs to the tradition of what Peirce called "critical common-sensism" in philosophy, an expression which will come into its own over the course of the next sixteen chapters in particular.

7 We may say that an object which is also a thing exists both in relation to a knower and "in itself", provided that we understand that the expression "in itself" says no more than that the object in question has a dimension or aspect which exists apart from the relation whereby it is known. There is quite another meaning of "in itself", current in philosophy especially since about 1781, which refers to a supposed existent behind, but unknowable through or within, the appearances of sensation. Since this phantom "thing in itself" – "ding-an-sich", in the language by which this monster of intellectual imagination was foisted upon human thought – can be accessed neither within nor through sensory appearances, it is said to be unkowable "directly"; yet by being posited it is said to be known "indirectly". Of the "thing in itself" in this second sense Peirce (1905: CP

animal that is able to distinguish between *relations as such*, which cannot be sensed directly, and *related things*, which is what objects are as such. The human animal has the capacity, over and above sensation and perception, to consider objects as they are or might be apart from relations of sensation and perception, to consider objects according as they are or are not "in themselves", possessed of a being, for example, in the physical environment which is what it is (an undiscovered dinosaur bone, or a planetary system revolving around some other sun) quite apart from how we may think or feel about it, how we may evaluate or relate to it as an object should we happen to learn of its existence.

This capacity is what is meant by *understanding* in its difference from perception and sense. Such capacity is the origin of all that is distinctively human, as we shall see at length. Language is of a piece with understanding. Language is the ability to reorganize the Innenwelt in ways that are not tied to the biological constitution of the human organism, as are both sensation and perception. Sense, whether internal or external, has no possibility of becoming aware of anything that is not biologically proportioned and determined. The eye can see only differentiations of light or "color", the ear only differentiations of sound, and so forth; but the *range* of colors that will be visible or sounds that will be audible is determined by the physiological constitution of my body. Yet in the human Umwelt, not only can we consider physical objects and various possibilities for their organization, as can also a dog, a dolphin, a beaver, or a whale; we can further consider whether physical objects need be sensible, whether there might not be physical objects which are otherwise than what we perceive according to our own needs and wishes. Indeed, we can consider whether there might not be physical objects, such as gods or angels, which have no material body to sense or perceive.[8] Language thus is, at its root, just this possibility of considering things according to relations that have no bearing on our own biological constitution.

Thus the objective world of human beings, the human Umwelt, is unique among all the species-specific Umwelts of other animals in being singularly malleable – transcendent to biology. It is as if the objective world of the human being were a Tinkertoy set, which can be disassembled and reassembled as often and in as many different ways as we like. The human animal is *like* all other animals in living in an actual objective world or Umwelt; but the human animal is *unlike* all other animals (at least on this planet) in that its actual objective world admits of an indefinite

---

5.452) remarks that the would-be philosopher "has only to abjure from the bottom of his heart the proposition that a thing-in-itself can, however indirectly, be conceived; and then correct the details" in logical consequence of this abjuration, "and he will find himself to have become a Critical Common-Sensist." The reader should be advised that whenever the expression "in itself" occurs in this text apart from the context of explicit discussion of Immanuel Kant it is always in the first and never in the second of the two senses just discussed.

8 The Latins distinguished fictive from physical being, and included material and spiritual being as a subdivision of the physical order. See "The Term 'Physical' as Used by the Latins" in chapter 8, p. 382; and the further discussion in chapter 10, p. 475 note 110.

number of alternative possibilities, some of which can be actualized in turn. Thus human society is not only, like every society of animals, hierarchical; this hierarchy is *civil* as well, in that it can be embodied in different patterns of government agreed to by members of a given society, and it can be *changed* by further agreements, sometimes imposed by conflict. Although other animal societies engage in conflicts, these conflicts do not result in *constitutions* or *treaties*.

So different is the human Umwelt in this regard that it has sometimes been called by a different name. The early twentieth century philosopher Edmund Husserl spoke of it as a *Lebenswelt* or "lifeworld", and this term has come often to be used when speaking of the species-specific human Umwelt. Every Umwelt as constituted by perception is in principle finite and closed. But an Umwelt – the human Umwelt – as modified by understanding is finite only in fact; in principle, it is open to the infinite.

Thus, while every animal, including the human animal, lives within an Umwelt, only the human animal becomes aware of the difference between the "physical environment", understood as an ambience supporting and in part permeating all the Umwelts, and the Umwelt itself as an originally radically species-specific objective world. When, in the fourth century BC, the sophist Protagoras will propose "man", the *anthropos*, as "the measure of all things", of those that are that they are and of those that are not that they are not,[9] he speaks the truth of the human animal as a sentient biological organism, while revealing himself blind to the truth of the human animal as human, that is, as able to understand intellectually as well as to understand perceptually something of what surrounds each of us in our peculiar biological reality, alligator or human. What Protagoras will fail to grasp – the failure that will appear in retrospect to define "sophism" in the ancient world as it similarly defines the semiological would-be postmodernism of the closing decades of the twentieth century from the vantage of semiotic, as we will see – is precisely the difference between Umwelt as such and Umwelt as linguistically modified. For language does not supplant, destroy, or replace the perceptual modalities of the Umwelt; it precisely depends upon them and extends them, hence transforming them *only in part*, only aspectually, while leaving the biological *moyens* intact. Umwelt as Lebenswelt enables "man" in principle to measure all things, but only to the extent that the *difference* between all objects as such and some objects as also "things" is thematized and problematized. Then appears a difference to be understood between being and seeming, both of which "man" measures, but only of the latter *is* the measure. For every animal is the measure of what seems. That is what "animal" means.

If we assume that biological species come about by a process of evolution through which novelties are incorporated into the environment as subsequently regular features, we would have to say that human understanding or *language*, the

---

9 Protagoras c.444/1BC: fragment 1 in Freeman 1966: 125.

Tinkertoy structure unique to the human Innenwelt as underlying the human Umwelt or Lebenswelt, is an *adaptation* constitutive of our life-form. But when some new arrangement of apprehension is externalized or *coded* so as to be communicable to others, we have a case not of adaptation but of what has come to be called in biology *exaptation*, the application of evolutionary adaptations to new ends beyond that one or ones in terms of which the adaptations originally emerged.[10]

Language emerged as a new way of seeing or looking at the world. Communicated to another or others in this or that particular, language is *exapted* to communicate. In our species, one of the ways in which communication most readily comes about is through the use of vocal sounds, or *speech*. The use of sounds to communicate, however, is not the root of language. In fact, the use of sounds to communicate is entirely extrinsic to the nature of language. Many animals which have no linguistic capacity have ample vocal capacity. Speech is common in the biological world. The exaptation of language into speech is not common. It is species-specifically human, and only one of the "forms of embodiment" that language can take. Language can just as well be exapted in the form of writing or gesture. In terms of a given communication, any one of these – speech, writing, gesture – can be rendered equivalent.

From the point of view of external behavior, it is not always possible to tell when a given behavior is rooted in human understanding and when it is simply rooted in perception. Tools, for example, are the embodiment of relationships adapting a material structure to a purpose. Human beings pre-eminently make tools, but other animals make tools as well. Beavers build their dams, birds build their nests, gophers and rabbits construct their tunnels, monkeys wield their sticks, humans build their houses. But linguistic behavior goes beyond the embodiment of relations in material structures to express relations as signifying possibilities which exceed perception and sensation alike, possibilities which cannot as such be in any manner directly sensed. Any social animal can perceive dominance and subordination; but only a linguistic animal can express these relations in a constitutional form or restrain them by a code of law. Language, thus, mediates the transformation of social organization into cultural relations, and, through culture, the development of civilization.

Civilization, thus, as a social order promoting cultural creation,[11] can only occur in a society of linguistic animals. Wittgenstein's striking aphorism,[12] "If a lion could talk, we could not understand him", while quite obtuse, is yet doubly striking: it is striking for its confusion of language with speech, and it is striking for its

---

10 Gould and Vrba 1982. Here I could repeat an earlier formulation of the point at issue (Deely 1966: 172): "*Rooted* in a new way of seeing; *caused* by a new mode of adaptation: such is the fact of human emergence, the unique development gradual and substantial and immanent, yet in a radical cognitive modality transcendent" – transcendent, that is, of biology.

11 Hence the necessity of a distinction in principle between social life and cultural content so disastrously blurred in modern anthropology after Radcliffe-Brown. For the theoretical argument, I refer the reader to *The Human Use of Signs* (Deely 1994).

12 Wittgenstein c.1931–50: 223.

incomprehension of the nature of language as exapted into speech. Language, in its root, frees the individual and the group from an organization wholly tied to biological heritage, and opens the way to possible worlds alternative to what is here and now actually experienced. Such alternative possibilities are amply illustrated in the diverse civilizations of Sumeria, Egypt, Babylonia, Assyria, Persia, India, and China, all of which emerge from the mists approximately 6000 years ago. Each of the ancient civilizations appears clothed in religious mythologies and animistic explanations of what once passed for "history". In India, the *Vedas*, from whence we principally get Hinduism, trace back as far as i.1000/500BC. In India again, the Buddha lived c.563–483BC, whence his teaching spread to China and Japan. Lao-Tzu, from whom Taoism would eventually derive, lived c.604–517BC, and, also in China, Confucius c.551–479BC. It was an active period of human civilization.

Hinduism and Buddhism define, in religious terms, what is today called "the East" in contrast to the "West" of Judaism, Christianity, and Islam. The origins of the Jewish people begin to achieve clarity between c.1500 and 1000BC. The Jewish prophets appear around 800–700BC. From Judaism derive the two other principal Western religions, Christianity and Islam, the former in the first century AD, the latter in the early seventh century (Mohammed, AD570–632).

On the scene of civilization, that of Greece appears as a relative late-comer, somewhat after 1000BC. A vignette to illustrate the point: when Hecataeus of Miletus, a Greek historian and geographer of the sixth to fifth centuries BC, visited Egypt and made boast to the Egyptian priests of being able to trace his ancestry back fifteen generations to one of the gods, Herodotus reports[13] that the Egyptians took him to their sanctuaries where stood the statues of three hundred and forty-five high priests, each the male offspring of the one before, tracing back the three hundred and forty-five generations since *their* ancestral gods had walked the earth. Greece itself inherited from the Near Eastern centers of Babylonia and Egypt three millennia of civilization. In many respects Greece inherited much more than it initiated.

Nonetheless, the most determined effort of reason to find its own ground in experience for the explanation of phenomena took root in Greece, beginning (so far as written documents allow us to determine) in the sixth century BC. Arguments have been made, more or less speculative, never much convincing to those who go more by evidence than by "affinities" and "resemblances", that later Greek philosophers, including Pythagoras, Parmenides, and Plato, seem to have been influenced by Indian thought; and indeed the *Upanishads*, composed i.800/500BC, lay some claim to philosophy (although no body of thought developed in function of the understanding of a definite group of writings accepted as revelation can ever fully claim "philosophy" as its proper name). Nonetheless, the received view, not lightly arrived at, has been that the views of Thales, Anaximander, Anaximenes, Heraclitus, Anaxagoras, and Empedocles antedate Hindu philosophical writings and bear the

---

13 Herodotus a.425: *History*, Vol. 2, p. 143.

indigenous stamp of the Greek mind; and that this "indigenous stamp" is far more evident in Parmenides and Plato than any supposed Eastern "influence".

West has more recently argued[14] that "a period of active Iranian influence stands out sharply in the development of Greek thought, from c.500 to c.480BC", and that "for a century or so beforehand, milder oriental influences can be seen." Even though "afterwards, it is as if [the oriental influence] had been shut off with a tap", West believes that the influence in question[15] "was an ambrosia plant, that produced a permanent enlargement" where it touched "the sturdy stems of Hellenistic rationalism"; he even alleges[16] that "the *Bhadaranyaka Upanishad* alone throws more light on what Heraclitus was talking about than all the remains of the other Presocratics together". One recalls Bréhier's argument for an Indian influence on Plotinus.[17] For sure historians in these matters need to imbibe more deeply the difference between intersemioticity, which is reversible, and history, which is not.[18]

And through all the arguments of "influences" and "confluences", past and to come, what stands out is the distinctive growth of critical speculative thought in the ancient Greek language and culture to a measure and over a sustained period of time that is without parallel in any other ancient group, whatever their "influence", so far as the records survive. In this respect, Frankfort's classic anthology[19] of study of ancient Near Eastern documents as the spatio-temporal context, as it were, against which philosophy emerges in the ancient Greek language and culture still bears sufficient witness to the invention of sustained critical speculative thought as a unique contribution of the Greeks to the growth of human civilization. It was through the ancient Greeks that humankind at large was made aware and became aware of the difference between Umwelt and Lebenswelt; and the lesson is still being learned. For that is what philosophy has proved to be above all: the active influence within the human Umwelt to make its inhabitants aware of the openness in principle which distinguishes human inquiry from the social habits of animals limited to perceptual interpretations, and of the different methods of investigation necessary to resolve different types of questions.[20] The human Umwelt as open in principle to the infinite

---

14 West 1971: 239–40.
15 Ibid.: 241–2. In the early 5th century, West claims, "foreign contributions were no longer wanted; not because they were foreign to Greece, but because they were foreign to inquiry based on empirical data." Had what was really distinctive of the Greek origins of philosophy been *empirical data* rather the critical use of *speculative reason*, we should not have to wait another twenty-two or so centuries for scientific theory as such to separate itself off and independently establish itself vis-à-vis philosophical doctrine.
16 Ibid.: 201.
17 See the volume edited by Harris (1982), especially the careful survey therein by Wolters (1982: 293–308). See also Armstrong 1979: 22–8.
18 Kahn's response to West (Kahn 1979: 297–302), without using the term "intersemioticity", moves in precisely the right direction.
19 For example, see the collection, *The Intellectual Adventure of Ancient Man*, ed. Frankfort (1946), as well as various other works written by the authors who appear in this collection.
20 This last point regarding types of questions may be regarded as an anticipatory summary of much of chapter 11 below.

through language nonetheless tends in society, like any animal Umwelt, to close in upon itself and to mistake its ways for the only ways. Awakening and keeping alive in the human community the difference between animal Umwelt and human Lebenswelt, moving to realize the possibilities of human understanding by forging over the centuries a community of inquirers committed to achieving truth in bits and pieces now and ever more integrally in the long run has proved to be the profile of philosophy, its mission and task. That is what philosophy is; that is what it does.

Philosophy, we may say, emerges within civilization as that aspect or part of civilization through which understanding confronts within experience the other as other, confronts within experience the irreducibility of the objective world to my experience of it. This is why the first, though hardly the last and only, notion of "reality" is the notion of what is what it is prior to and independent of human thought and action. In the animal Umwelt, both in what it shares and what it lacks of the human Lebenswelt, there is no difference between objects and things, between sensation and perception. All is of a piece in experience, and of a piece with the animal itself as centering the Umwelt. The Umwelt as such, the objective world as such, is a kind of dreamland, however much it may include of the physical environment objectified through the channels of sense. To wake from this dream is to discover the Other in its otherness, that is to say, in its being in its own right as irreducible to my experience of it.

At the same time, only in and through the objective is the environment as physical, the order of things as such, what the philosopher Charles Peirce called "brute Secondness", encountered. Small wonder that the first philosophers, waking from the dream of purely animal life and imagination made human, found themselves constrained to use poetry in trying to shake themselves awake. For the discovery of reality in its initial sense of what does not reduce to our experience of it, but has a being, moreover, in its own right and independently of us, is perforce in many respects a rude awakening. As the philosopher Jacques Maritain so well noted, "the human being has many sleeps".[21] Philosophy has always to try not to become just another one of those somnolences.

---

21 "... il est pour l'homme plusieurs dormir" (cf. Jacques Maritain 1959: 2).

PART ONE

Ancient Philosophy

The Discovery of "Reality"

Likeness of Aristotle the Stagirite (384–322BC)
Engraved by Leonard Gaultier (1561–1641), from the title page of William du Val's 1629
edition in two volumes of Aristotle's *Opera Omnia* (Paris: Typis Regiis apud Societatem
Graecorum Editionum), in the Special Collections of Loras College Library

CHAPTER TWO

Philosophy as Physics

Beginning at the Beginning

Φύσις is the Greek word for nature. Nature was the Greek term for the environmental world which surrounds us, antecedes us, and upon which we depend. The Greek idea of a "science" or knowledge of nature, thus, is enshrined, down to this day, in the name "physics". To a large extent, this was the first name of philosophy. Interested in the realm of nature as a whole, the earliest philosophers took initially no special interest in one particular phenomenon of nature, the σημεῖον. There was good reason for this. One of the ways in which Greek civilization differed from Mesopotamian was in pushing divination from the center to the margins, and it is in the area of divination that we first encounter the σημεῖον[1] as a divinatory sign, including the verbal text of oracles. Philosophy concerned the assertion of the relative autonomy of which human thought is capable in the face of nature, not the befuddlement that normally accompanies the effort to construe oracles.

But a second sense of the σημεῖον as a phenomenon of nature did early attach itself to the Greek development of reason, namely, the medical idea of σημεῖον as a symptom from which the course of disease and cure might be projected, σημεῖον as diagnostic sign or medical symptom.[2] Of course the medical use of signs is entirely congenial to the development of human intelligence. And it is from this context that we find the most typical sense of σημεῖον in the intellectual culture of ancient Greece: as a natural phenomenon upon which reliable inferences can be based, or "natural sign". It is thence that the σημεῖον finds its way into the logic of Aristotle as the propositional content which provides us with the *locus* of truth and

---

1 According to Manetti 1993: 14.

2 Manetti (1993: 37) remarks that, "in contrast with doctors of today, who read signs in connection with the diagnosis of illness, early Greek doctors used signs in connection with prognosis", and makes reference on this point to the *Corpus Hippocraticum*. Manetti also notes (ibid.: 39) the common mythical origin of divinatory and medical practices, in that both were considered to be gifts of Apollo, and deems it striking "that the two earliest practices which begin sign-based knowledge should have been seen in their own time as having been originally connected".

inference:[3] "if the one proposition is stated, we have only a sign, but if the other is stated as well, a deduction".

Yet we must take care not to get too far ahead of our story. Even though *our* interest here, even at this earliest stage, may be the emergence of the theme of the *sign* as a general mode of being transcending the division of nature and culture, and of the *action of signs* as weaving the fabric of experience wherein natural and cultural being commingle to provide the pattern of human life, the fact remains that this theme does not appear at once, but only slowly; and hardly at all in the first age of philosophy. What first appears in the beginning is not the sign but that which presupposes the sign, namely, a world of objects, among which signs are regarded merely as a particular class – albeit a particularly privileged class, according to the saying of Aristotle:[4] "truth may be found in signs whatever their kind".

It is true that, within the world of objects of experience, the difference between objects which have and objects which do not have a being independent of the experience within which they are revealed is the first and most typical effect of a distinctively human action of signs. Apart from this action there could be no origin of "philosophy as physics", nor any transformation of animal Umwelt into the Lebenswelt of culture, where not only philosophy but eventually science will emerge as a cultural and linguistic achievement.

But it is only in the realization of the independent being of the world of nature that the beginning of philosophy takes form, not in the realization of what such a re-alization of being presupposes, not in the realization of what makes the experience of a universe independent of the finite mind possible in the first place. And the theories that were developed to explain the mind-independent dimensions of the objective world, as we will see, alone provide the conceptual tools necessary eventually to explain the sign, when human understanding finally, in the twilight zone between medieval and modern times, makes decisive the turn upon itself to ask in all earnest how is our knowledge of reality, even such as it is, so much as possible in the first place? At that moment the ancient discussion of being, especially as framed by the original categorial scheme of Aristotle and the development of that discussion among the Latin scholastics, becomes, improbably enough, indispensable to the success of the new quest, as we shall see. Yet there is no way Aristotle can be well understood entirely apart from Plato, nor Plato entirely apart from the presocratics. If that be true then, even to explain the sign, we need to tell the whole story of philosophy.

Both Aristotle and the Latins after him were fond of distinguishing between the sequence of events leading to the discovery of something (the *ordo inventionis*) and the more-or-less reverse sequence of thought whereby we explain the discovery in discourse (the *ordo disciplinae*). Were we simply to begin our history at the point where the general notion of sign emerges, we would begin not with the ancient Greeks but with the Latin Augustine in the fourth century AD. Were we to begin

---

3 Aristotle c.348–7BC: *Prior Analytics* II, 70a24.
4 Ibid.: 70a38.

our history at the point where it is realized that our experience of objects depends throughout on signs, we would begin not with the early Latins but at the dawn of modern times with the seventeenth-century Poinsot. Were we to begin our history at the point where it is realized that the universe of reality is itself already perfused with signs ahead of our experience of that world, we would not begin before Peirce's introduction of his new scheme of categories at the end of modern times. But that is not the way the matter unfolded historically, and it is *this* order, the *ordo inventionis*, that we wish to follow in this work, for the very good reason already indicated: even though the story of philosophy is much broader than the story of the discovery of the central role of sign in understanding and nature, so many of the conceptual instruments necessary eventually to understand the action of signs were forged in the laboratory of the history of philosophy that it is better not to separate the story of the sign from virtually the whole general history, at least on its speculative side. All the chapters to follow are dictated by this realization.

The human mind may not have begun its distinctive journey with the discovery of signs, but with the discovery of that in the objective world which the human use of signs alone and distinctively makes possible, namely, an order of being which is what it is independently of the human mind, an "order of natures" which is nonetheless given in the very experience whereby the mind becomes aware of objects. Yet to discover the sign not just as a type of sensible phenomenon but in general, the mind had to proceed (for reasons that will become apparent over the course of our narrative) in terms of that which presupposes the sign, namely, an objective world inseparable from nature, a "cosmos". The mind makes its way to the sign, as we shall see, only by first exploring the distinctively human consequence of the sign's activity without knowing it *as* a consequence of the sign's activity, namely, a mind-independent dimension within the world of objects constituting "nature". Like every other animal, the human animal begins using signs without knowing that there are signs; and even when the human animal, through its unique way of using signs, becomes aware that there are signs, this awareness is first and normally not in terms of signs according to their proper being, but rather only according to the being they have *within* the sensible dimension of the objective world which in fact the sign *founds* as a product, not of nature, indeed, in its physical being, but of nature as it assimilates to the experience of linguistic animals in particular – of nature in its anthroposemiotic dimension, we may eventually say.

Thus the story even of the sign begins with the discovery of nature as a reality prior to and in various ways escaping human purposes. The story of the sign, in short, is of a piece with the story of philosophy itself, and begins, all unknowingly, where philosophy itself begins, though not *as* philosophy. To proceed to tell the story of the sign in other ways is of course not impossible; but each such alternative approach leaves out too many of the pieces needed even for the effort of *re-telling* the story more succinctly when we turn around to explain what we have discovered – at least if we want to tell the tale in the most convincing and complete manner possible.

Our purpose in these pages, then, is to make the discovery which, we will argue, introduces postmodernity (the end of the story for now) clear and credible, and for this nothing less than a general history of philosophy will do. Even if we do not have to explore every theme of that history, we must yet explain all those themes that pertain to the presupposition of the sign's being and activity, in order to arrive at that being and activity with sufficient intellectual tools to make full sense of it as a theme in its own right. And those themes turn out to be nothing less or other than the very themes of ontology and epistemology forged presemiotically, as we might say, in that laboratory for discovering the consequences of ideas that we call the "history of philosophy". If the discovery of the sign began, as a matter of fact, unconsciously with the discovery of nature, then the beginning of semiotics was first the beginning of philosophy, for only as philosophy are the foundations of semiotics possible – even if semiotics is what philosophy must eventually become, as we shall see. Nothing begins where it ends; the best stories are told not from the middle; and, while the end of a tale may do much to illumine its beginnings, the end is hardly a substitute for the beginning.

In the case of the drama before us, the beginning lies between the seventh and the fifth centuries BC. In the Ionian city of Miletus, today a part of Turkey, today one of the richest trade centers of the Greek world, takes rise that distinctive tradition of human thought called philosophy. Here, in now modern Turkey, then modern Greece (but by c.599BC a part of Persia!), for the first time, the human mind leaves a clear record of seeking answers to the problems of the world and of society not from on high, but, so to speak, on its own level, in terms of our direct experience of nature and culture. Here for the first time emerged the idea of "natural law" as an order in the cosmos rooted in the nature of things rather than in the personal interests and wraths of supernatural beings.

Of these earliest Greek philosophers we have of their own writings mostly fragments – no works of Greek prose prior to Herodotus and no philosophical writings prior to Plato survive to us intact. Often the situation even in the ancient world was not much better, for the institution of libraries for the preservation of books comes about only later and gradually.[5] The earliest "books" were not conceived of as independent means of communication, but rather as a prop for spoken discourse and strictly subordinate thereto. Written discourse in the areas of what we would today call "philosophy" was, originally, not trusted or only grudgingly so independently of the spoken words of its author. One of the reasons for the fragmentary nature

---

5 Small wonder. It took a papyrus roll twenty-two feet long to accomodate a mere seventy pages of modern printed text. And in reading such a roll, it wound up backwards, requiring that it be re-rolled completely for the next reading. Given the fragility of the material, unnecessary unrolling and re-rolling was discouraged, which indirectly reinforced the tendency to rely on memory. Imagine the difficulties of storing large amounts of such "books", what we today call rather "scrolls" and, for excellent reasons, no longer use at all. Let me at least refer the reader to some basic works that will open anyone's eyes on the matter of early books and libraries: Kenyon 1951; Parsons 1952; Pinner 1958; and Reynolds and Wilson 1974.

of the evidence for the views of the earliest speculators "on the nature of things" was the neglect of what few manuscripts were produced as independent records. If a given "book" did not arouse interest within fifty years or so of its composition, it had almost no chance of surviving.[6] The thinker who first fully systematized the idea of a philosophy of nature or physics and introduced into its organization a well-thought-out scheme of causal influences was Aristotle, and to this day his reports on ancient views provide much of the intellectual context within which the earliest philosophers are evaluated. On the other side of this coin, I deem it not too much to say that, excepting Pythagoras (who has the singular interest of presaging the idea, not to come to fruition before Galileo and the birth of modern physics in the mathematical sense, of interpreting nature throughout on the basis of mathematics), a principal value of the so-called presocratic thinkers today, insofar as the most ancient development bears on the eventual understanding of sign in general, stems from the light they shed on the shape natural philosophy and metaphysics will receive at the hands of Aristotle.

Accordingly, while I have tried to draw on the best general studies of the presocratics[7] and the most recent monographs studying these thinkers for their own sake,[8] my own selection and treatment of the presocratics in this chapter is with an eye to the framing of later developments pertinent to our general history. As cross-references and suggestions for research along the way will show, our treatment is prospective of the dawn of the twenty-first century throughout.

"Monism"

Behind or below the appearance of nature's diversity there lies a single principle, one common "stuff". There is only to determine in what that stuff consists. Such is the undying idea of *monism*.[9]

Thales of Miletus (c.625–c.545BC)
Could anything better attest to the primacy of oral tradition in philosophy's opening age than the fact that he who is accepted by unanimous testimony to be the first philosopher neither has left us a single fragment nor is even known for a fact to have written anything at all? A conventional date for marking the beginning of philosophy

---

6 Even today, with institutionalized libraries, it is not unusual to find professional library staff in colleges and universities who cite "use" as a sufficient criterion for retention or weeding of volumes – "This book hasn't been checked out in thirty years; we should get rid of it". Of course such staffers should be fired; but often enough they become head librarians and find kindred spirits occupying the office of dean or president. Small wonder that great libraries, even today, are rare!

7 Notably Diels and Kranz 1951; Freeman 1966 and 1966a.

8 Notably the volumes in the Phoenix Presocratic Series of the University of Toronto Press, in particular, on Heraclitus (Robinson 1987) and Parmenides (Gallop 1984).

9 When the underlying stuff is identified with the divine nature itself, "monism" becomes "pantheism" – God is everywhere and all is God.

is 28 May 585BC, the date on which occurred an eclipse predicted by Thales.[10] What made this prediction remarkable was hardly the fact that it was largely based on access to Babylonian eclipse records kept for religious purposes, but rather the fact that, as Freeman would have it,[11] "Thales and his group, while using these data, introduced the scientific way of arranging them, drawing from them generalizations, which could in turn be applied". If we substitute here "doctrinal" for "scientific", as will appear, we have a more precisely defensible thesis on the "originality" of Thales. But let us not get ahead of the story.

Taking the year of the eclipse as the "prime" of Thales, thence is projected his birth at Miletus c.625BC and his death c.545BC.[12] Educated in Egypt and the Near East, it was he who is credited with introducing mathematical and astronomical science into Greece.[13] His principal idea concerning the constitution of the physical world was that water is the first principle, original form, and final destiny of all things. The most complete record we have of his thought is given by Aristotle in Book I of what is now called his *Metaphysics*:[14]

Of the first philosophers, most thought the principles which were of the nature of matter were the only principles of all things; that of which all things that are consist, and from

---

10 The dating of this eclipse is thoroughly discussed in Kirk, Raven, and Schofield 1983: 76n1 and 81ff.

11 Freeman 1966: 51.

12 "All these dates are equally artificial," Freeman comments (1966a: 55), "being based on the 'prime' at forty years of age which was fixed arbitrarily by Alexandrian chronologists at the most outstanding or easily-dated event in a man's life." Thus, once the "prime" or "acme" was determined, birth was simply projected backward by forty years and death forward by forty years – a very approximate system indeed, out of which our modern "time of flourishing", *floruit* (abbreviated to "fl."), comes, restricted to the comparatively sure date of acme or prime.

13 And thereby hangs a tale, told to us by Aristotle (c.335/4BC: *Politics* I, 1285b45ff.): "There is the anecdote of Thales the Milesian and his financial scheme, which involves a principle of universal application, but is attributed to him on account of his reputation for wisdom. He was reproached for his poverty, which was supposed to show that philosophy was of no use. According to the story, he knew by his skill in the stars while it was yet winter that there would be a great harvest of olives in the coming year; so, having a little money, he gave deposits for the use of all the olive-presses in Chios and Miletus, which he hired at a low price because no one bid against him. When the harvest-time came, and many were wanted all at once and of a sudden, he let them out at any rate which he pleased, and made a quantity of money. Thus he showed the world that philosophers can easily be rich if they like, but that their ambition is of another sort. He is supposed to have given a striking proof of his wisdom, but, as I was saying, his scheme for getting wealth is of universal application, and is nothing but the creation of a monopoly. It is an art often practiced by cities when they are in want of money; they make a monopoly of provisions."

14 Aristotle c.348–7dBC, 983b6ff. Naturally, Aristotle's reconstruction of Thales has been challenged, notably by Burnet (1930: 48–9). Freeman (1966a: 52), in her review of the situation, remarks simply: "On a point where Aristotle had to fall back upon conjecture [i.e., given the complete absence of any written lines whatever from the hand of Thales], nothing can be affirmed with certainty; but there are reasons for thinking that Aristotle's conjecture is the more likely", to which I would add as principal reason the proximity of Aristotle to the audial milieu and signosphere in which the thought of Thales was preserved!

which they first come to be, and into which they are finally resolved (the substance remaining, but changing in its modifications), this they say is the element and the principle of things, and therefore they think nothing is either generated or destroyed, since this sort of entity is always conserved, as we say Socrates neither comes to be absolutely when he comes to be beautiful or musical, nor ceases to be when he loses these characteristics, because the substratum, Socrates himself, remains. So they say nothing else comes to be or ceases to be; for there must be some entity – either one or more than one – from which all other things come to be, it being conserved.

Yet they do not all agree as to the number and the nature of these principles. Thales, the founder of this school of philosophy, says the principle is water (for which reason he declared that the earth rests on water), getting the notion perhaps from seeing that the nutriment of all things is moist, and that heat itself is generated from the moist and kept alive by it (and that from which they come to be is a principle of all things). He got his notion from this fact, and from the fact that the seeds of all things have a moist nature, and that water is the origin of the nature of moist things.

Some think that the ancients who lived long before the present generation, and first framed accounts of the gods, had a similar view of nature; for they made Ocean and Tethys the parents of creation, and described the oath of the gods as being by water, which they themselves call Styx; for what is oldest is most honourable, and the most honourable thing is that by which one swears. It may perhaps be uncertain whether this opinion about nature is primitive and ancient, but Thales at any rate is said to have declared himself thus about the first cause.

The abstract significance of Thales' thought lay not so much in his reduction of all things to water as in his reduction of all things to a single type of substance. The view that a single underlying principle accounts for the whole of the universe is called *monism*, and Thales gives us the first record of monistic philosophy.

The threadbare record of Thales' thought has left ample room for his posterity to flesh it out with tantalizing paradoxes, such as the one reported by Diogenes Laertius,[15] that "there is no difference" between living and dead;[16] or Aristotle's report, in his treatise *On the Soul*,[17] "that Thales came to the opinion that all things

---

15 Diogenes Laertius c.AD220: Book I "Thales" 35.

16 This seemingly outrageous view, however, had many echoes in the ancient world, e.g., the following remark by Empedocles less than a century and a half later (Freeman 1966: 52, fragments 8 & 9; an alternate English rendering together with the text of the Greek original can be seen in Inwood 1992: 213–14, fragments 21 & 22 in his numbering): "I shall tell you another thing: there is no creation of substance in any one of mortal existences, nor any end in execrable death, but only mixing and exchange of what has been mixed; and the name 'substance' (*Phusis, 'nature'*) is applied to them by mankind.

"But men, when these (*the Elements*) have been mixed in the form of a man, and come into the light, or in the form of species of wild animals, or plants, or birds, then say that this has 'come into being'; and when they separate, this men call sad fate (*death*). The terms that Right demands they do not use; but through custom I myself also apply these names". The same view can be found in Anaxagoras: see p. 25 below.

17 Aristotle c.330bBC: *On the Soul*, I, 411a8ff.

are full of gods", perhaps for the reason "that soul is intermingled in the whole universe". Such a view, Aristotle notes wryly, "presents some difficulties". For example:

> why does the soul when it resides in air or fire not form an animal, while it does so when it resides in mixtures of the elements, and that although it is held to be of higher quality when contained in the former? (One might add the question, why the soul in air is maintained to be higher and more immortal than that in animals.) Both possible ways of replying to the former question lead to absurdity or paradox; for it is beyond paradox to say that fire or air is an animal, and it is absurd to refuse the name of animal to what has soul in it.

Aristotle concludes by suggesting that this "opinion that the elements have soul in them seems to have arisen from the doctrine that a whole must be homogeneous with its parts"; that is to say, Aristotle is suggesting that the view that "there is no difference between living and dead" because all things are alive may be a logical consequence of monism as such.

While we may wish for a more complete record of Thales' thought, it is certain that his reputation was high in the ancient world. When Greece came to name its Seven Wise Men,[18] Thales topped the list.

Anaximander (c.610–545BC) and Anaximenes (c.580–500BC)

Thales' line of thought, the reduction of all things to a single principle, was brought to a higher level of abstraction by his pupil, Anaximander, c.610–545BC. Instead of water as the underlying being of the physical universe, Anaximander proposed a more abstract principle which he termed "apeiron", which translates roughly as the "indefinite". This *apeiron*, possessing of itself no specific qualities, develops by its inherent forces into all the varied realities of the world of experience. The many, thus, are but evanescent mutable aspects of the underlying and everlasting one.

But Aristotle points out a difference in the monism of Anaximander and that of his teacher, a difference that anticipates pluralist theories of the physical world:[19]

> The physicists have two modes of explanation.
>
> The first set make the underlying body one – either one of the three [to wit, water, air, or fire] or something else which is denser than fire and rarer than air – then generate everything else from this, and obtain multiplicity by condensation and rarefaction.[20]

---

18 Cf. Plutarch a.AD120.

19 Aristotle c.353BC: *Physics* I, 187a12ff.

20 Condensation and rarefaction, Aristotle notes (ibid., 187a 17–19), "are contraries, which may be generalized into excess and defect. Compare Plato's 'Great and Small' – except that he makes these his matter, the one his form, while the others [i.e., the early physicists] treat the one which underlies as matter and the contraries as differentiae, i.e., forms."

The second set assert that the contrarieties are contained in the one and emerge from it by segregation, for example Anaximander and also all those who assert that what is, is one and many, like Empedocles and Anaxagoras.

Anaximenes, fl.c.546BC, a student of Anaximander, simply returned rather to the type of explanation proposed by Thales, except that he substituted air for water as the underlying principle constitutive of all things. "Before the word came to denote atmospheric air," Kahn notes,[21] "*aēr* had meant 'mist' or 'vapor'; and Anaximenes must have chosen this principle because of its close association with the atmospheric cycle of evaporation and condensation. He appears to have taken that cycle as the paradigm for understanding physical change in general and explaining the origin of the world order: all things are derived from *aēr* by being condensed through cooling or by being rarefied through heating." There is room to wonder how much of a difference the substitution of "air" for "water" really amounts to.

"Pluralism"

Empedocles, c.495–c.435BC, and Anaxagoras, c.500–428BC, provide an interesting contrast of physical theories, both to one another and to their monist predecessors. For while they concurred in rejecting the idea that the whole diversity of nature can be reduced to a single principle, Anaxagoras posited an "infinite" or "innumerable" number of principles as requisite to explain the diversity of nature, while Empedocles thought that the four elements of fire, air, earth, and water, each irreducible to one another, would be sufficient in varying combinations to explain all further diversity in nature. By adding to the mixing of elements the forces of Love and Hate as causes, Empedocles also anticipated the dualist theories of physics.

Anaxagoras of Clazomenae (c.500–428BC)
Anaxagoras is reported as greatly influenced by the memory of Anaximenes, whose ideas so interested Anaxagoras in the heavens that he proclaimed the investigation of the sun, moon, and heaven as the object of his life. As to the constitution of the universe, Anaxogoras may be said to be the father of the idea that species are fixed, as evidenced by the rhetoric of his basic question:[22] "How can hair come from not-hair, and flesh from not-flesh?" Considering this question unanswerable, Anaxagoras advances to his basic conclusion:[23]

The Greeks have an incorrect belief on Coming into Being and Passing Away. No thing comes into being or passes away, but it is mixed together or separated from

---

21 Kahn 1979: 19.
22 Fragment 10 in Freeman 1966: 84.
23 Fragment 17 in Freeman 1966: 85.

existing Things. Thus they would be correct if they called coming into being 'mixing', and passing away 'separation off'.

Basing himself on Deichgräber,[24] Schofield, in one of the only books in English devoted wholly to Anaxagoras,[25] tells us that the lost book of Anaxagoras (so lost that not even its title can today be determined), the book which "rekindled hopes of philosophy in the breast of Socrates",[26] began with the famous words: "All things were together, unlimited both in multitude and in smallness", a statement which "contains in nuce the theme of his whole natural philosophy".[27] Aristotle has fleshed out the reasoning as follows:[28]

> The theory of Anaxagoras that the principles are infinite was probably due to his acceptance of the common opinion of the physicists that nothing comes into being from what is not. (For this is the reason why they use the phrase 'all things were together' and the coming into being of such and such a kind of thing is reduced to change of quality, while some spoke of combination and separation.) Moreover, the fact that the contraries come into being from each other led them to the conclusion. The one, they reasoned, must have already existed in the other; for since everything that comes into being must arise either from what is or from what is not, and it is impossible for it to arise from what is not (on this point all the physicists agree), they thought that the truth of the alternative necessarily followed, namely that things come into being out of existent things, i.e., out of things already present, but imperceptible to our senses because of the smallness of their bulk. So they assert that everything has been mixed in everything, because they saw everything arising out of everything.

---

24 Deichgräber 1933: 352, with n. 11.
25 Schofield (1980: 1) informs us that "it so happens" that "there is no authoritative book written in English that is devoted wholly to Anaxagoras", a gap his work presumably aims to fill. Yet in fact there is a rather large work by Gershenson and Greenberg (1964) which Schofield mentions only in the note prefacing his bibliography (p. 169), not even in his text, notes, or the bibliography itself, as one place, "a little old", to find "extensive bibliographies of Anaxagoras". Why we should not regard the work of Gershenson and Greenberg as in any way authoritative Schofield does not say. But we may guess that he takes umbrage at the fundamental challenge Gershenson and Greenberg level (Preface, pp. xxi–xxiv) against the work of Diels and Kranz which, since about 1879, when Diels first issued his *Doxographi Graeci*, followed in 1903 by his first edition of *Die Fragmente der Vorsokratiker*, have dominated and continue to dominate all presocratic studies other than Gershenson and Greenberg's substantial volume.
26 Schofield 1980: 1. Freeman (1966: 82; based on a remark in Plato's *Apology*) prefaces her presentation of the surviving Anaxagoran fragments with the remark that this book "was on sale at Athens for one drachma at the end of the fifth century". Prof. A. H. M. Jones (quoted in Kirk, Raven, and Schofield 1983: 257n2 infers on the basis of the price that the book must have been very short indeed, a manuscript "such as could be copied in well under a day."
27 Schofield 1980: 36.
28 Aristotle c.348–7bBC: *Physics* I, 187a27ff.

But things, as they say, appear different from one another and receive different names according to what is numerically predominant among the innumerable constituents of the mixture. For nothing, they say, is purely and entirely white or black or sweet, or bone or flesh, but the nature of a thing is held to be that of which it contains the most.

The ultimate cause of the mixing and separation in nature Anaxagoras assigned to Noûs or "Mind", infinite and self-ruling, mixed with no thing, alone by itself, all other things containing part of everything else:[29]

Mind took command of the universal revolution, so as to make (*things*) revolve at the outset. And at first things began to revolve from some small point, but now the revolution extends over a greater area, and will spread even further. And the things which were mixed together, and separated off, and divided, were all understood by Mind. And whatever they were going to be, and whatever things were then in existence that are not now, and all things that now exist and whatever shall exist – all were arranged by Mind, as also the revolution now followed by the stars, the sun and moon, and the Air and Aether which were separated off. It was this revolution which caused the separation off.

Athenians nicknamed Anaxagoras "*Nous*", but this seems in part to have been by way of irony, as a means of taunting him as to how seriously he took Mind, since, whenever it came to an actual phenomenon to be explained, he proposed explanations in exclusively material terms, and did so very well. (Mindful of this tradition, a later Greek playwright, Aristophanes [c.450–388BC] used the "revolution" or vortex of Anaxagoras in his play *The Clouds* to satirize Socrates' view of the god Zeus.) Anaxagoras thus arrived at an evolutionary conception of biological organisms (by recombinations of his fixed species), gave a correct explanation of eclipses, proposed a rational hypothesis of planetary formation, proposed that other celestial bodies are inhabited by animals like ourselves that "dwell in cities and cultivate fields as we do", considered the sun (still popularly deemed a god) to be a burning mass of stone (chips of which occasionally fall to earth, such as the large meteorite which crashed to earth at Aegospotami in 467BC) – all without any appeal to Mind whatever.

In exasperation, his enemies brought against him a formal charge of impiety for his views on the sun, which led to a death sentence. Anaxagoras preferred the sentence of death already levied, as he put it, on both his accusers and himself by nature: he fled Athens and lived out his life teaching philosophy to the age of seventy-three (when nature executed its sentence).

---

29 Freeman 1966: 84, fragment 12.

Empedocles of Acragas (c.495–c.435BC)[30]

Empedocles had been a student of the Pythagoreans, and had adopted their theory of the transmigration of souls. He saw all of nature in terms of attractions and repulsions, Love and Hate, acting on the four elements to bring about the development of all things. Endless combinations and separations brought about attractions and aversions resulting in the constitution of various things, and the interactions of these things in turn bring about nature and history.[31]

> Come, listen to my discourse! ... I shall tell you of a double process. At one time it increased so as to be a single One out of Many; at another time it grew apart so as to be Many out of One – Fire and Water and Earth and the boundless height of Air, and also execrable Hate apart from these, of equal weight in all directions, and Love in their midst, their equal in length and breadth. ... these things alone exist, and running through one another they become different things at different times, and are ever continuously the same.

> For from these (Elements) come all things that were and are and will be; and trees spring up, and men and women, and beasts and birds and water-nurtured fish, and even the long-lived gods who are highest in honour. For these (Elements) alone exist, but by running through one another they become different; to such a degree does mixing change them.

When Empedocles traveled, Freeman tells us,[32] "he was particularly welcome because of his medical knowledge, which led many to regard him as a seer, or even as a god". Among the mere 470 lines that survive from his writings are some tantalizing lines on the divine nature:[33]

> We cannot bring God near so as to reach him with our eyes and lay hold of him

---

30 Owens (1959: 417) points out that a "correct dating of Empedocles is of notable importance for understanding the history of Greek philosophy during the fifth century B.C.", because "the activities of Anaxagoras, Democritus, Gorgias, and others have to be kept in close chronological relation with the work of Empedocles." Lacking the linguistic competence in ancient Greek directly to enter the debate at the level of modifying its calendrical structure, I have followed what Owens (ibid.) describes as "a late dating for Empedocles, which for the most part has been accepted by historians", agreeing, for example, in the main with what Curd proposes (1998: "Chronology", pp. 15–18), in particular with her *caveat* that the arrangement settled upon is hardly the only one possible. So for the interest of readers, especially for ones who may be or become linguistically competent in the requisite fashion, I want to note my puzzlement at the silence of the literature in response to the close argument Owens has advanced (1959: 417–19) toward the conclusion that the correct span for the life of Empedocles is 521–461BC.)

31 Empedocles c.450BC: from fragments 17 and 21 in Freeman 1966: 53–5 (alternate translation with original Greek text in Inwood 1992: 217–18, in his numbering fragment 25 lines 16–20, 34–5; and fragment 26, lines 9–14.)

32 Freeman 1966a: 177–8.

33 Empedocles c.450BC: fragments 133 & 134, in translation of Bakewell 1907: 46. Cf. translation in Freeman 1966: 67; and in Inwood 1992: 253.

with our hands .... For he has no human head attached to bodily members, nor do two branching arms dangle from his shoulders; he has neither feet nor swift knees nor any hairy parts. No; he is only mind, sacred and ineffable mind, flashing through the whole universe with swift thoughts.

As to the whole of the cosmos, Symonds[34] has given us a translation redolent of later remarks of St Paul: "what *that* is, no eye hath seen, no ear hath heard, nor can it be conceived by mind of man." It is almost as though Empedocles took seriously what Anaxagoras professed about *nous*, and, in relation to the world, improved upon it in the bargain. At least so it seemed to Aristotle:[35] "Anaxagoras made both his homogeneous substances and his contraries infinite, as we saw, whereas Empedocles posits only the so-called elements". Aristotle saw Empedocles as at least arriving in the ballpark of truth about nature; for it was Aristotle's conclusion[36] that the principles required to make intelligible our experience of a changing physical world cannot be infinite yet must be more than one:

> for there cannot be one contrary. Nor can they be innumerable, because, if so, what is will not be knowable; ... also a finite number is sufficient, and a finite number, such as the principles of Empedocles, is better than an infinite multitude; for Empedocles professes to obtain all that Anaxagoras obtains from his innumerable principles ... This will suffice to show that the principles are neither one nor innumerable.

"Dualism"

Monism and pluralism were not the only ancient proposals for a scheme within which to render intelligible the phenomena of nature. Indeed, perhaps the most seminal and enduring scheme to emerge from these ancient mists was rather the idea that a binary logic suffices to explain the physical world. This idea usually goes by the name of *dualism*, the attempt to reduce the whole of reality to a simple dynamic interplay of two factors. The most celebrated of the ancient dualisms seems to have been introduced by Leucippus, who flourished in the fifth century BC. His view was fully developed and rounded out as a materialist philosophy by Democritus of Abdera, who was either the student or the associate of Leucippus.

Leucippus (c.470-390BC; fl.440–435BC)[37]
Leucippus came to Elea from wherever he originated, perhaps Miletus, sometime around 435BC, where he is thought to have studied under Parmenides' student, Zeno

---

34 Symonds 1920: 138; this is fragment 3 in Freeman 1966: 51.
35 Aristotle c.348–7b: *Physics* I, 187a23ff.
36 Ibid.: 189a12–19.
37 Many authors, notably Kirk, Raven, and Schofield (1983: 402) entitle him "Leucippus of Miletus". Others, equally distinguished, notably Freeman (1966: 90), entitle him "Leucippus of Abdera". But, as his birthplace is variously given in the records as Abdera, Elea, Melos, or Miletus, and nothing

of Elea. From Zeno, at least, he would have heard of the mathematical atomism of the Pythagoreans, since Zeno had directed the darts of some of his subtlest paradoxes against the Pythagorean doctrine of plurality.[38] Only a single fragment of Leucippus' direct teaching comes down to us: "Nothing happens at random; everything happens out of reason and by necessity".[39] We may suppose that Leucippus developed his doctrine of the Void, or empty space, as a way of making change and motion possible in the face of the Parmenidean doctrine of the Plenum or Sphere which is one and unchanging. In effect, Leucippus proposes that there is not one being which is unchanging but many, falling through a void; and by their collisions and conjunctions they constitute all things. Freeman[40] says of this original version of "atomic theory" that it

> intended to provide a final solution to the problems bequeathed by his predecessors on Being and Not-Being, Becoming and Passing-Away, Change, Motion, and the validity of sense-perception. It was designed in such a way as to solve the difficulties of the Milesians, to satisfy the propositions of the Eleatic school, and to incorporate what was valuable in the work of Empedocles and Anaxagoras.

Even though the author of this original atomic theory stands as "the most shadowy figure of early Greek philosophy",[41] it would be surprising were a synthesis so ambitious presented in a logic so simple to not long endure. As it happened, Leucippus had a disciple who saved philosophy's history from the chance of any such surprise.

Democritus (c.460–c.385/362BC)

Strictly speaking, with Democritus we are no longer in the period of the "presocratic philosophers", for he was a full contemporary of Socrates, although working at Abdera rather than Athens and not well known in Athens before the time of Aristotle's maturity. Yet because the atomism of Leucippus comes down to us only through Democritus, who was his pupil and intellectual heir, he is commonly presented along with Leucippus, who was a presocratic thinker. When Leucippus encountered Democritus and just how much time they spent together is not known. But meet they did, and Democritus was won over completely to the basic theory of the world of which Leucippus apprised him. Thence Democritus, by both spoken and written discourse, spread the views of Leucippus far and wide. His reputation as one of

---

decisive or even close to overwhelming has yet come to light as a basis for choosing, the choice in the present work is that choice is better left unmade in this particular.

38 See Tredennick's remarks in his "Introduction" (1930: p. xvii) to the Loeb Library edition of Aristotle's *Metaphysics*.
39 Translation from Freeman 1966: 91.
40 Freeman 1966a: 286.
41 Freeman 1966a: 285.

the most widely traveled of men in the ancient world led Clement of Alexandria (AD150–211/15) to accept as genuine the spurious passage[42] wherein Democritus himself is presented as saying, that "I have traveled most extensively of all men of my time, making the most distant inquiries, and have seen the most climes and lands, and have heard the greatest number of learned men; and no one has ever surpassed me in the composition of treatises with proofs". Whether the most widely traveled and most prolific of ancient philosophers or only one of the most, for a fact the popularity of the expositions of atomic theory made by Democritus represent the version according to which the doctrine Leucippus first had formulated came generally to be known. The elaboration of the epistemological basis for the atomic theory and its detailed application to the theory of perception, as distinct from the basic terms[43] and twofold principle of atomism, are generally[44] thought to be the contributions developed by Democritus over and above what he had received from the instruction of Leucippus.

Democritus ascribed to the atoms, the "uncuttable" ultimate units of matter or being, various shapes and a natural tendency downward, whence they fall of themselves through the void, combining and recombining as they encounter other atoms in their fall. The result of this movement in empty space is the world of experience, which is nothing but the various combinations and change of combinations of atoms that make up the diversity of the physical universe. The philosopher, realizing this, should pursue a life of good and noble actions done for their own sake, and nothing more.

Thus there exist only these two, Atoms and the Void, "both of which exist, Democritus says, the one as being, the other as not being".[45] Aristotle saw great merit in the theory of Leucippus and Democritus, calling it "the most systematic theory" and the "one that applied to all bodies".[46] He also saw it as making a significant theoretical advance over its predecessors:[47]

> none of the other philosophers made any definite statement about growth, except such as any amateur might have made. They said that things grow by the accession of like to like, but they did not proceed to explain the manner of this accession. Nor did they give any account of combination; and they neglected almost every single one of the remaining problems, offering no explanation, e.g., of action or passion – how in natural actions one thing acts and the other undergoes action. Democritus and Leucippus, however, postulate the 'figures', and make alteration and coming-to-be result from them. They explain coming-to-be and passing-away by their dissociation

---

42 Fragment 299, in Freeman 1966: 119.
43 See Freeman 1966: 90.
44 For the reasons reviewed in Kirk, Raven, and Schofield 1983: 404.
45 Reports Aristotle c.348–7bBC: *Physics* I, 188a22.
46 Aristotle c.355BC: *On Generation and Corruption* I, 325a.
47 Ibid.: 315b1ff.

and association, but alteration by their grouping and position. And since they thought that the truth lay in the appearance, and the appearances are conflicting and infinitely many, they made the 'figures' infinite in number. Hence – owing to the changes of the compound – the same thing seems different to different people: it is transposed by a small additional ingredient, and appears utterly other by the transposition of a single constituent. For Tragedy and Comedy are both composed of the same letters.

As we shall see in due course,[48] Aristotle's main reservation against the atomistic theory turns on his analysis of cause. From our present perspective, the one thing that marks rather discontinuity between the ancient Greek inquiry into nature Democritus envisioned and the physics of late modernity, is the splitting of the atom at Cambridge in 1932 by Cockcroft and Walton. For this led to the discovery through experiment of just what Democritus had thought by the name *atom*, "uncuttable", to deny, to wit, particles sub-atomic in character.

Mathematicism: A Theorem from Pythagoras

A theorem is an idea accepted or proposed as a demonstrable truth, often as part of a general theory. The "theorem from Pythagoras" I have in mind is not the famous geometrical truth that the square of the hypotenuse of a right triangle equals the sum of the squares of the other two sides, in honor of the discovery of which Pythagoras is said to have sacrificed an ox. What I have in mind is something much vaster, perhaps less a theorem than the germ of a theorem: the idea that somehow figure and number, geometry and arithmetic, in a word, mathematics, is essential to the constitution of the world. He left us no writings, but he left us this idea. In hindsight it strikes us as Pythagoras' main speculative idea.

He couldn't establish this grand theorem fully, but enough to deeply influence Plato – how deeply we cannot say, because, as we will see in the next chapter, Plato did not provide a written account of in what his esoteric thought on the world consisted. It was an idea that would not full come to flower for centuries. Passing over the murky numerological mysticisms that eddied here and there over the Latin centuries, we find the grand conception embodied in the mighty work of Galileo which set science irretrievably on a path distinct alike from that of the doctrines of philosophers and the dogmas of religious teachers. It was an idea that would grow into the physics of Newton, and ever after *physics* would no longer be natural *philosophy* but *mathematical* physics – what it remains today, the science more than any other that puts planes into the sky, satellites into orbit, probes into space, and determines whatever prospect there is of human beings taking up abode on planets besides "mother earth".

---

48 In chapter 3 below, "A Scheme of Causality", p. 64; and further paraphrasing Cartledge 1998: 3.

Pythagoras of Crotona (c.570–495BC)

The man responsible for the beginnings of a mathematical conception of the universe was above all, it would seem, some kind of a religious teacher; so it appears in hindsight fitting enough that he was a contemporary of the Hebrew prophets Haggai and Zechariah and of the Buddha, who would find his "enlightenment" about when Pythagoras would reach his prime. Called Pythagoras of Samos from his place of birth, he was also called Pythagoras of Crotona from the place in southern Italy where he founded his religious and philosophical school. And since birth is an accident, whereas achievement is personal, we prefer here the name that attaches to him from his choice of where to work. He held that every human being is made by God to acquire knowledge and to contemplate. His highly successful school was equally open to men and to women, with rules so strict it verged on being a monastery. Among the foods he prohibited were meat (probably out of consideration for the common ancient doctrine of transmigration of souls) and, curiously, beans.[49] Students in the school had to undergo a five-year initiation period before being fully admitted into the Pythagorean society, a practice which divided the students into *exoteric*, or outer ("probationary") students, and *esoteric*, or inner members.

The basis of the Pythagorean curriculum was mathematics. Indeed, the modern term "mathematics" seems to be a derivative of their school.[50] Pythagoras was famous for showing the reducibility of music to number, and for the specific theorem in geometry that bears his name. According to Diogenes Laertius, Pythagoras was the first to assert that the earth is round, and to assign to the physical world the name κόσμος, "cosmos". The very word philosophy seems to have been a coinage of Pythagoras,[51] and "philosopher" and "Pythagorean", in the sixth century BC, were sometimes used synonymously. He was unique among the early physicists in turning his eye away from matter to formal patterns of relation that could be expressed in mathematical terms, and declaring that these numerically regular relations and sequences were the true essence of the visible world.

---

49 Aristotle wrote a lost treatise *On the Pythagoreans*, according to which, as reported in Diogenes Laertius (c.AD220: lib. VIII, 34–5), "Pythagoras counseled abstinence from beans either because they are like the genitals, or because they are like the gates of Hades ... as being alone unjointed [i.e., the bean is the only plant without joints], or because they are injurious, or because they are like the form of the universe, or because they belong to oligarchy since they are used in election by lot."

50 Before the Pythagoreans, "mathema" had applied to the learning of any subject, not specifically to arithmetic, geometry, and allied investigations.

51 This according to a story that seems to go back to the 4th century BC, summarized as follows by Owens (1959: 31–2): "When asked who he was, he replied 'A philosopher', and explained the notion by comparing life to the Great Games. To these, some went to compete for prizes, others to sell wares, but the most fortunate were there as spectators. The speculative or theoretical (having in Greek the sense of 'contemplative') pursuit of truth is the life of the philosopher, and is the highest of all lives. This was considered by the Greeks to be the first use of the term 'philosopher' or 'lover of wisdom', and it implied in its Pythagorean setting that no man, but only God, is properly said to be wise."

A firm believer in reincarnation or "metempsychosis", Pythagoras claimed quite distinct memories of previous existences. He claimed one previous life as a courtesan, and another as a warrior in the battle of Troy. And he claimed once to recognize in the yelp of a beaten dog the voice of a deceased comrade. No ancient thinker was to exercise a greater influence on Plato.[52]

The Pythagorean Society survived Pythagoras himself for about three centuries; and his views on mathematics, as we have said, anticipated in crucial ways the transformation of the science of nature, physics, into the mathematical physics of today as it was initiated by Galileo and Newton. From our vantage point, even bearing in mind Aristotle's enduring point that mathematics can express only the formal causes of nature, leaving all else presupposed, the early Greek physicists appear almost as crude simpletons alongside Pythagoras.

Requirements and Dilemmas for a Philosophy of Being

Philosophy may have begun as physics or "philosophy of nature", but it was soon to over-reach those bounds in achieving the full amplitude of speculative understanding in what we will eventually come to see as *doctrina* rather than *scientia*. The dramatic expansion beyond the sensible will first come about in the work of Plato and, after him (yet in a wholly different fashion which will provide the main foundations for what philosophy will become in the Latin Age) Aristotle. Two thinkers from the presocratic period may be singled out in a special way as setting the stage for the later drama of philosophy as it was to play out in the opposed views of Plato and Aristotle and, through Aristotle especially, over the whole span of the Latin Age (or "medieval philosophy" – the age of philosophy "between" the ancient and the modern periods). These two key players were Heraclitus of Ephesus, in his prime about 504–501 BC, and Parmenides of Elea, in his prime about 475 BC.

Heraclitus the Obscure, of Ephesus (c.540–c.480 BC)
Heraclitus of Ephesus, a generation later than Pythagoras and a generation earlier than Parmenides, was also known as Heraclitus the Obscure, and with good reason, as shall appear. The story of his influence is as much a paradox as his doctrine. Being "a loner" in an audial age, he addressed no audiences, but, as if he had been transposed into the post-Augustinian culture of readers, he made his influence felt exclusively through the power of a written text. Then, ironically (history's special

---

52 Or perhaps a lesser one on the Latin Age in the particular of philosophical thought on the soul. Pomponazzi (1516: cap. 9, in finem, and elsewhere) spoke dismissively of "Pythagorean fables". The celebrated Latin Humanist Petrarch (1304–1374), writing in 1367/8 (p. 1155 of the Basil Latin text; cf. p. 92 of the Nachod English trans.), was considerably more acid. As regards the doctrine of metempsychosis (the transmigration or reincarnation of souls), he wrote, "I am amazed beyond belief that this idea could spring up in the head of any man, let alone a philosopher" ("... eius tamen est nota illa μετεμψύχωσις, quam in caput non dicam Philosophi, sed hominis scandere potuisse, supra fidem stupeo").

dish), his one book, even its title, was lost, so that he becomes known to our own, text-based age primarily through the reports of others rather than through his own text. Even Cratylus, his most famous disciple, apparently never talked with Heraclitus, but was converted to his views by reading rather than hearing! Shades of the future.

In the older readings, Heraclitus, like other physicists, sought for an order in change, a One within or behind the Many that would give stability and measure to the flux of reality. This he supposedly found in the doctrine of the λόγος. The Λόγος is that which transcends and governs over the process of change and everything that changes. So Freeman presents fragments 41 and 50:[53]

> He says: "Wisdom is one – to understand the Reasoned Purpose which steers all things through all things", and "Not me, but the Logos: first listen to *that*, and agree that 'All things are One' is Wisdom".

This was how he was read by the Stoics in the fourth century BC and by the Christians in the first century AD. But behold! A scholarly revolution. Burnet,[54] Surig,[55] and West,[56] have joined forces to demonstrate that there is no doctrine of *logos* in Heraclitus himself, that, as Kahn puts it,[57] "it is only with the Stoics that *logos* comes to be regularly used as an equivalent of *nous*."

So the question may be put: in reading Heraclitus, are we to understand the term λόγος as referring to Heraclitus's discourse and nothing else, or are we to understand it as referring beyond the discourse to the truth in things which warrants the discourse? To understand the Stoics, for sure, we will have to take the second route; but it may be that the first route is sufficient to understand Heraclitus himself. Nor will it matter to the immediate purpose at hand of understanding the presocratics as they provide the background and frame for what will happen to philosophy in the work of Plato and Aristotle. For this purpose we may pass over without any need to resolve the obscurity of the fragments on the point at issue. On this point it is enough for us to observe of Heraclitus the Obscure what Heraclitus is said to have observed of the Oracle at Delphi: he neither reveals nor conceals his thought, but signifies (*sēmaínei*).[58] Neither need we agree or disagree to pass along the suspicion of Luigi Romeo[59] that with Heraclitus "we are at the ἀρχή of semiotics" – an ἀρχή *in nuce*, albeit – "and in it Heraclitus is one of the thinkers climbing a lonely path, fencing only with Parmenides in an infinite world replete with interior and exterior signs".

---

53 From Freeman 1966a: 115–16; cf. Freeman 1966: 27, fragment 41; 28, fragment 50. Compare the translation, with facing Greek original, in Robinson 1987: 31 and 37.
54 Burnet 1930: esp. 142–3.
55 Surig 1951.
56 West 1971: esp. 124–9.
57 Kahn 1979: 308n64.
58 Or "indicates it through signs": see Romeo 1976 (in the 1986 reprint, see esp. pp. 226ff.).
59 Romeo 1976: 90 (in the 1986 reprint, p. 234).

For whatever may have been or not been the doctrine of λόγος in Heraclitus himself, he became from the beginning the philosopher of change as the only reality, the philosopher of process and becoming without end, the enduring point of reference on this view. The image that struck him to express the view combined both continuity and change, to be sure, but change first and foremost, with continuity only in the process whereby change continually occurs. "This ordered universe (*cosmos*)", declared Heraclitus,[60] "which is the same for all, was made neither by a god nor by man, but it ever was, and is, and shall be, ever-living Fire, in measures being kindled and in measures going out".

In less poetic terms, Aristotle put the view of Heraclitus as consisting in the proposition "that what is in movement requires that what knows it should be in movement; and that all that is depends on movement (herein agreeing with the majority)".[61] But the obscurity of Heraclitus did not arise from any points wherein he "agreed with the majority" in affirming the reality of motion and change. It arose from the extreme to which he pushed this seemingly evident point, and from the manner in which he expressed and appropriated the "majority view".[62] Among other sayings, Heraclitus was famous for the saying that "you cannot step into the same river twice".[63] His disciple Cratylus[64] was famous for criticizing this saying (fame came easier in the early days of philosophy), on the ground that you cannot step into the *same* river even *once*, for even as you step the river is flowing on! Aristotle considered that the Heracliteans reached this extreme pass owing to an overreliance on the testimony of sense:[65]

> The reason for this opinion is that while these thinkers were inquiring into the truth of that which is, they thought that which is was identical with the sensible world; in this, however, while they speak plausibly, they do not say what is true. ... And ... they held these views because they saw that all this world of nature is in movement, and that about that which changes no true statement can be made; at least, regarding that which everywhere in every respect is changing nothing could truly be affirmed. It was this belief that blossomed into the most extreme of the views above mentioned, that

---

60 Heraclitean fragment 30 in Diels-Kranz, my rendering. Compare the translation in Freeman 1966: 26; and the translation with facing Greek original in Robinson 1987: 25.

61 Aristotle c.330bBC: *De Anima* I, 405a27.

62 Aristotle c.335/4BC: *Rhetoric* III, 1407b12f.: "It is a general rule that a written composition should be easy to read and therefore easy to deliver. This cannot be so", however, "where punctuation is hard, as in the writings of Heraclitus. To punctuate Heraclitus is no easy task, because we often cannot tell whether a particular word belongs to what precedes or what follows it."

63 Yet see the cautionary commentary on these sayings in Robinson 1987: commentary on fragment 12, pp. 83–4; commentary on fragment 91a, pp. 139–41.

64 Thought to be an older contemporary of Plato with a prime somewhere between 450 and 400BC (latter half of the 5th century).

65 Aristotle c.348-7dBC: *Metaphysics* IV, 1010a1. One can but wonder if Aristotle would have considered the same regarding the skeptic reported by Avicenna (c.1024/1150: Tract. I, cap. 8, p. 58 lines 16–17), who gave the matter an epistemological turn while rolling Heraclitus and Cratylus into one with the saying "it is not possible to see something twice, nor even once" ("non est possibile aliquid bis videri, sed nec etiam semel").

of the professed Heracliteans, such as was held by Cratylus, who finally did not think
it right to say anything but only moved his finger....

Be that as it may, Heraclitus comes down to us as the philosopher who above all
held that *Panta rei, ouden menei*: "all things flow, there is nothing but change". This
formula does not actually survive in the fragments, but antiquity is unanimous in its
attribution to Heraclitus. In Book 11 of what has come to be called his *Metaphysics*,
Aristotle sanguinely opines that "perhaps if we had questioned Heraclitus himself":[66]

> ... we might have forced him to confess that opposite statements can never be true of
> the same subjects. But, as it is, he adopted his opinion without understanding what his
> statement involved. But in any case if what is said by him is true, not even this itself
> is true – viz. that the same thing can at one and the same time both be and not be. ...
> But if a true affirmation exists, this appears to refute what is said by those who raise
> such objections and utterly destroy rational discourse.

We shall never, this side of eternity, know in fact how Heraclitus would have responded to Aristotle on this point. What we can know at least is what was the question
Heraclitus raised to which Aristotle felt it necessary to respond, all the more necessary,
as we will see in the next chapter, in view of what Aristotle regarded as the wrong
response that had been made by the man under whom he first and mainly studied.[67]

Parmenides of Elea (c.515–c.450BC)
The dialectical antithesis to the view of Heraclitus was soon enough posited by Parmenides, in his prime about 475BC. Not *panta rei*, but rather *Hen ta panta*: all things
so are one that there is no place for change. With Parmenides we reach the boundary
of the original ancient development. He was an older contemporary of Socrates,
and Freeman[68] considers the Platonic dialogue titled *Parmenides* to "undoubtedly"
represent an actual meeting (though not a report thereof) that took place about 450BC.
A measure of Plato's respect for Parmenides may be gleaned from the fact that in

---

66 Aristotle c.330cBC: *Metaphysics* XI, 1062b. See further the discussion of *reductio ad absurdum*,
    "the reduction of an argument to absurdity", in chapter 4, p. 125 below.
67 "With some slight oversimplification" we can agree with Baird (in Baird and Kaufmann 1997: 17)
    "that Plato was convinced by Heraclitus that in this sensible world all things are in flux and, if this
    sensible world is all there is, no rational discourse is possible. This led Plato to the conclusion
    that there must be another world beyond the world of sense experience – a realm utterly free from
    change, motion, and time. At that point Plato was probably influenced not only by the Pythagoreans
    but also by Parmenides, the next great Pre-Socratic." Yes, but Aristotle was led rather to the contrary
    conclusion that, regardless of the question of reality beyond the world as sense experience reveals it,
    there must be another and truer way of understanding the world of sense experience itself than either
    Heraclitus, Parmenides, Pythagoras, or Plato was able to conceive. To this contrary conclusion, as
    we will see in the subsequent chapters, we owe the establishment of the framework of discursive
    knowledge within which first philosophical and then even scientific thought would best develop
    down to the present day, when finally we have turned to the question of how it is possible to signify.
68 Freeman 1966a: 140.

the dialogue of that name Parmenides instructs the young Socrates, in contrast with the usual dialogue pattern wherein Socrates always holds the upper hand.

The long-held view that Parmenides was roused to philosophize by the poet Xenophanes of Colophon (c.570–475BC), who had caused a furor with his declaration that the gods are myths and reality is but one, comprising both the world and God, is now dismissed as unlikely. Owens simply sees in Parmenides "the beginnings of metaphysics";[69] and indeed, as Symonds points out,[70] it was Parmenides "who gave utterance to the word of Greek ontology, τὸ ὄν, or Being, which may be significantly contrasted with the Hebrew I am." Not that τὸ ὄν cannot be found here and there in early Greek texts besides Parmenides, but that in Parmenides "being" becomes the interpretive horizon, a problem that will not begin to be explored in its foundations until Aquinas and certain of his commentators take up the question of "being as first known",[71] after which the question is forgotten until Heidegger in the early twentieth century.

But never underestimate the potential scope of scholarly revolutions. Curd[72] suggests that the "being" of Parmenides is not to be read, as it has almost always been, as what Aquinas will term *esse* ("existence") but rather as what Aquinas will term *essentia* ("essence") – "predicational" rather than "existential", in Curd's own way of speaking – and so as of a piece with the ancient pluralists, Anaxagoras and Empedocles among others, who, in this scholarly revolution, would become Eleatic familiars, as it were, rather than strangers.

The essentialist interpretation proposed by Curd has much to recommend it, notwithstanding its comparative philosophical poverty. For the older and common reading, no matter what chinks may be shown or made in its scholarly armor, retains the inalienable merit of being far more fundamental, inasmuch as predication presupposes the existence of the one predicating, no less than does any other form of cogitation. Curd would have us palm off to the later Melissus of Samos (c.481–c.401) the more profound aspects of the traditional view of Parmenides. But I think, without denying its interest, that the move is too facile by half; especially as the interpretation assigned to Parmenides himself is redolent rather of the saying that survives from Melissus:[73] "*If there were many things*" – which, except in the illusions of sense, there are not, for either Melissus or Parmenides – "each of them would have to be such as I say the One is".

Parmenides began from the common principle of the physicists: that nothing comes into being from what is not. But a being either is or is not. If it is, it cannot become something else, for in that case it would become what it is not, and something would come from what is not. And if it is not, it cannot come to be, for

69 So he entitles his chapter on Parmenides (Owens 1959: 56).
70 Symonds 1920: 12.
71 See chapter 7 below, esp. p. 341ff
72 Curd 1998 throughout.
73 Melissus of Samos c.441/40BC: εἰ γὰρ ἦν πολλά, τοιαῦτα χρὴ αὐτὰ εἶναι οἷόν περ ἐγώ φημι τὸ ἓν εἶναι. Fragment 8 in Freeman 1966: 49 (Greek from Kirk, Raven, and Schofield 1983: 398).

if it did, it would come into being from what is not. Therefore, all sense experience to the contrary notwithstanding, understanding tells us that motion and change of whatever sort must be an illusion.[74] Parmenides liked to image his idea of being as a sphere:[75]

> Like to the mass of a sphere on all sides carefully rounded,
> Everywhere equally far from the midst; for Fate hath appointed
> That neither here nor there should it either be greater or smaller.

On the mysterious side, anticipatory of a famous thesis of Renaissance followers of Thomas Aquinas,[76] Parmenides identifies being with thought: ... τὸ γὰρ αὐτὸ νοεῖν ἔστιν τε καὶ εἶναι. Freeman gives two renderings of this fragment: "For it is the same thing to think and to be",[77] and "That which it is possible to think is identical with that which can Be".[78] Gallop renders it:[79] "... because the same thing is there for thinking and being." Bakewell[80] cites the translation by Davidson:[81] "One thing are Thinking and Being".

In a fragment cited by Aristotle,[82] Parmenides easily challenges Heraclitus's right to hold the title of "the Obscure", saying "that of which there is more is thought". If Aristotle was of the view that the Heracliteans had relied too much on sense, he surely could not say the same of the Parmenideans. He expressed his estimate of the Parmenidean position rather as follows:[83]

> The first of those who studied philosophy were misled in their search for truth and the nature of things by their inexperience, which as it were thrust them into another path. So they say that none of the things that are either comes to be or passes out of existence, because what comes to be must do so either from what is or from what is not, both of which are impossible. For what is cannot come to be (because it is already), and from what is not nothing could have come to be (because something must be underlying). So too they exaggerated the consequence of this, and went so

---

74 Aristotle summarized the dilemma thus (c.348–7dBC: *Metaphysics* III, 1001b10): "But if there is to be a being-itself and a unity-itself, there is much difficulty in seeing how there will be anything else besides these – I mean, how things will be more than one in number. For what is different from being does not exist, so that it necessarily follows, according to the argument of Parmenides, that all things that are, are one; and this is being".

75 Compare this translation of fragment 8, lines 43–4, with that of Gallop 1984: 73: "From every direction like the bulk of a well-rounded sphere, / Everywhere from the center equally matched; for [it] must not be any larger / Or any smaller here or there." Cf. also Freeman 1966: 44.

76 See chapter 7 below, "After Creation, There Are More Beings But No More Being", p. 287.

77 Freeman 1966: 42, fragment 3.

78 Ibid.: 42n2.

79 Gallop 1984: 57.

80 Bakewell 1907: 13.

81 Davidson 1870: 5.

82 Aristotle c.348–7dBC: *Metaphysics* IV, 1009b30.

83 Aristotle c.348–7bBC: *Physics* I, 191a25.

far as to deny even the existence of a plurality of things maintaining that only what is itself is. Such then was their opinion, and such the reason for its adoption.

The Argument with the Sharpest Fang:
the Paradoxes of Zeno of Elea (c.495/490–c.430BC)

Misled or not, Parmenides yet begat some subtle offspring. If "an incisive argument is one which produces the greatest perplexity" and is hence "the one with the sharpest fang",[84] then the palm for incisiveness among the ancient philosophers must surely go to the Parmenidean Zeno of Elea (c.495/490–c.430BC), esteemed by Aristotle as the father of dialectic. This Zeno wrote a book of paradoxes based on the view traditionally attributed to Parmenides. What Turnbull says of Zeno as a character in Plato's dialogue *Parmenides* applies as well to the historical Zeno:[85] "Zeno's express purpose is to show, against those who ridiculed Parmenides' thesis of the One, that there is greater absurdity in the thesis of the Many." Nine of Zeno's paradoxes have come down to us. All make the same point that motion is impossible, an illusion of sense which understanding is obliged to disavow and dispel.

Consider the case of the apparently swift Achilles running to overtake a crawling tortoise. No matter how swiftly Achilles moves and how slowly the tortoise, if move they do, from one moment to the next they do not occupy the same point in space. Since, however, the point occupied by the tortoise at any given moment is *ex hypothesi* in advance of the point Achilles occupies, and since there are an infinite number of points separating these two specified points, we must either admit the futility of Achilles' catching the tortoise or endow him with the ability to traverse an infinite number of points in a finite time.

First Framing of the Contrast between Sense and Understanding

Yet the Heracliteans and the Parmenideans had well set up the classic opposition between intellect and sense that would occupy classical ancient thought and much of medieval thought (until the early moderns lost track of the means effectively to distinguish understanding from perception, and prepared the way for the shallow positivism and relativism that characterized much of philosophical thought in the closing decades of modernity's pursuit of the way of ideas, as we shall see). How Aristotle would handle this matter we must leave to the following chapter. Here suffice it to note that Parmenides no less than Heraclitus noticed the constancy of change in the world as revealed by sense; yet he was struck even more by the seeming contradiction the acceptance of such a revelation posed to the understanding, to the human intellect: how can what is not ever be, and how can what is ever not be?

Faced with seeming contradiction, which are we to believe, lowly sense or noble intellect? For Parmenides, as later for Plato, there can be no hesitation over such a choice. However paradoxical and unacceptable it may be to common sense and

---

84 Aristotle, c.353aBC: *Sophistical Refutations* 182b32.
85 R. G. Turnbull 1998: 4.

everyday life, the testimony of sense must be eschewed in favor of the intellectual vision that reality is one and unchanging. Permanence, not change, is hallmark of the "really real",[86] and the sphere – unchanging from whatever angle we view it – is the symbol thereof.

Heraclitus, by contrast, felt no such compunction. We do not know whether he so much as considered the question of how change is to be understood, how the notion of changeable being is to be rendered intelligible. What we do know is that he had no hesitation at all over affirming intellectually the testimony of sense, and affirming in change the hallmark of the "really real". Changing realities are the only reality was the conclusion he reached, and fire – ever changing from whatever angle we view – is the symbol for what is most real. The mind has but to affirm the testimony of sense, not in particular instances, as Heraclitus pointed out, but only globally, in order to reach understanding of "the nature of things".

Yet these views of the ultimate unity of reality were far from the only views entertained among these ancient first philosophers concerning the otherness of the world revealed by the senses. We must take note of yet other early physical views which have resonated through the centuries of the species-specifically human activity we call "philosophy" if our sketch of current knowledge of philosophy's early dawn is to be complete.

Summing Up

With this group of thinkers, the adventure of reason we still call philosophy was well and truly begun. Through many vicissitudes and conflicts with assertions of religious authority and revealed truth, in civilization as it has developed in continuity with ancient Greek thought there was finally no turning back to the earlier anthropomorphic and mythological forms as a substitute for abductive hypotheses and inductive verifications of ideas in experience. From the ancient monism of Thales to the postmodern pragmaticism of Peirce, through the Latin scholasticism of Thomas Aquinas, the rationalism of Descartes, and the empiricism of Locke, there has been a continuous experiment in pushing the boundaries of human understanding on its own ground and according to its own lights gained through experience. We have seen the beginning of the adventure. Let us move on.

---

86 The Hindu view expressed in the *Bhagavad-Gita* (i.499/199BC: 36) well expresses the conclusion Parmenides felt intellectually compelled to reach: "That which is non-existent can never come into being, and that which is can never cease to be. Those who have known the inmost Reality know also the nature of *is* and *is not*. That Reality which pervades the universe is indestructible. No one has power to change the Changeless."

CHAPTER THREE

The Golden Age:
Philosophy Expands Its Horizon

Three names define the Golden Age of ancient philosophy: Socrates, c.469–399BC; Plato, c.427–348/7BC; and Aristotle, 384–322BC. Plato was a student of Socrates. Aristotle, in turn, born when Plato was forty-three, became a student of Plato, and studied for some twenty years in Plato's Academy before founding his own school, the Lyceum. Like Pythagoras, both Plato and Aristotle had esoteric and exoteric teachings. But, by a perversity of history, in the case of Plato only the polished exoteric writings have come down to us, while in the case of Aristotle, since at least the time of Cicero (106–43BC), we have access only to the rough esoteric works, his lecture notes, as it were.

Socrates (469–399BC)

Of Socrates, beyond the fact that he was an actual historical figure, we know of his actual teaching very little, since he left no writings. He was fortunate to have had three pupils who wrote, Aeschines of Sphettus (fifth–early fourth century BC), Xenophon (445–355BC), and Plato.

From Aeschines (not to be confused with the fourth-century BC rhetorician) we have only fragments of seven dialogues, in each of which Socrates seems to have been the principal figure.[1] Aeschines portrays Socrates in a manner more or less consistent with the picture we get from Plato's early dialogues, but in some ways closer to Xenophon's portrayal.

The portrayal of Socrates we get from Xenophon is problematic. Xenophon, a general and an historian, wrote always from the point of view of a military leader, and with little depth of philosophy. His Socrates appears mostly as a figure idealized

---

1 The two main sources for what is left of Aeschines are Krauss 1911 and Dittmar 1912, conveniently discussed in English by Field 1967: 146–52. Chroust, however (1957: 1), considers that Aeschines ranks no better than all other sources ancient or later as secondary to Plato and Xenophon, the only Socratic sources to be truly regarded as primary.

in terms more of Xenophon's own ideas than of the ideas of Socrates which appear in Aeschines or Plato.

Plato's *Dialogues* give us by far the most complete portrait of Socrates that we have, but history has left us without the means to distinguish in Plato's work imagination from biography. The report of Diogenes Laertius[2] is perhaps a sufficient *caveat lector* ("Let the reader beware!"):

> They say that, on hearing Plato read the *Lysis*, Socrates exclaimed, "By Heracles, what a number of lies this young man has told about me!" For Plato had set down a great many things as sayings of Socrates which Socrates had never said.

Nor did Plato pretend to limit himself to fact in his use of Socrates as a figure in the *Dialogues*. Socrates under Plato's pen became a veritable literary device of twofold efficacy: he lent to Plato's views the color of a concrete life, at the same time clothing those views with the fame and authority surrounding the revered memory of Socrates in Athenian culture. Yet the consistency and richness of the character portrayed is principally responsible for the fact that Socrates continues and will continue to live in the minds of philosophy students as long as the works of Plato have readers.

The Sophists

By the time of Socrates' youth, Athens had been invaded by a group of teachers from the Greek colonies who went by the name of "sophist". They taught rhetoric, grammar, and logic for pay, and gradually acquired the reputation of having a greater interest in the pay than in the knowledge they professed. In the early days they were a vital if corrosive influence on the conservatism of Athens, a city which, despite its fame, was the city of origin of no great Hellenic thinker before Socrates, and after Socrates only of Plato.

The later attacks of Plato and Aristotle against the Sophists have been enough to ensure that the notion of Sophist given by Xenophon's Socrates is the one that has stuck: "those who sell their wisdom for money to any that will buy, men call sophists, or, as it were, prostitutes of wisdom". And indeed today "a sophist" is one careless of truth concerned to win in argument, and a "sophistic argument" is one put forward more because of the side it favors than the weight it bears – "promising to make the worse appear the better reason", as Aristotle is said to have accused the sophist Protagoras. "Political consultants" in today's democracies are the analogue of what sophists became in ancient Athens.

The complaint against the sophists, actually, was less that they needed money to live than that they were too often willing to tailor their teaching to the prejudices

---

2 Diogenes Laertius c.AD220: Book III "Plato" 35–6 (in Hicks trans. Vol. I, p. 309).

of those who would pay. It is a perennial problem, and the ill fate of the label in history should not blind us to the fact that the Sophists in the ancient world, even up to the end of the Roman Empire, were often honorable men who, as a group, played a vital intellectual and social role in ancient culture. Without them there would have been no Socrates. To the Golden Age the sophists gave the foundation.

Founder of Moral Philosophy and of the Search for Definitions

The focus of the first philosophers, as we have seen, was on the nature of the physical world, "the universe outside the mind". Of course they had, all of them, views on every subject. But the first really to concentrate on the universe within, not as a mystic or religious teacher, but as a thinker concerned to give intellectual foundations to ethical concerns, was Socrates. As Thales was the father of the philosophy of nature ("physics"), so Socrates was the father of moral philosophy ("ethics").

But in all of his inquiries, Socrates emphasized the importance of definitions, and this emphasis has surely been a permanent contribution to philosophical inquiry. A call for definition often shows that we do not really know what we are talking about, and it shows further that there is no other way to get clear even about our own views except by working out, as necessary, definitions of our terms. The theory of definitions would become an important point in the Neoplatonic school,[3] and thence throughout the Latin Age, as we will see. A brief passage from the *Meno* (86c) may serve to make the point:

> *Socrates:* As we are agreed that a man should inquire about that which he does not know, shall you and I make an effort to inquire together into the nature of virtue?
>
> *Meno:* By all means, Socrates. And yet I would much rather return to my original question, Whether in seeking to acquire virtue we should regard it as a thing to be taught, or as a gift of nature, or as coming to men in some other way?
>
> *Socrates:* Had I the command of you as well as of myself, Meno, we should not have inquired whether virtue is given by instruction or not, until we had first ascertained 'what it is'. But since you never think of self-control – such being your notion of freedom – but think only of controlling me and do control me, I must yield to you, for you are irresistible. And therefore it seems we have now to inquire into the qualities of a thing of which we do not as yet know the nature.

In the absence of a definition, the only way to avoid idle discourse is to proceed on the basis of an hypothesis as to the nature of the object under discussion:

> *Socrates:* Loosen the reins a little, and allow the question 'Whether virtue is given by instruction, or in any other way', to be argued upon hypothesis? Let me explain. ...

---

3 See, in chapter 4 below, "The Tree of Porphyry", p. 144ff.

As we know not the nature and qualities of virtue, we must ask, whether virtue is or is not capable of being taught, upon some hypothesis, as thus: what kind of spiritual good must virtue be in order that it may be taught or not? Let the first hypothesis be that virtue is not within the class 'knowledge', – in that case will it be taught or not? or, as we were just now saying, 'recollected'? For there is no use in disputing about the name. But is virtue taught or not? or rather, does not everyone see that knowledge alone is taught?

Meno: I agree.

Socrates: Then if virtue is a kind of knowledge, virtue will be taught?

Meno: Certainly.

Socrates: Then now we have made a quick end of this question: if virtue is of such a nature, it will be taught; and if not, not?

Meno: Certainly.

Socrates: The next question is, whether virtue is knowledge or of another species?

The Socratic Method

Perhaps simply as a result of Plato's dialogue form, perhaps as a result of his actual practices in teaching, Socrates is famous not at all for answers or theories in philosophy, but for the astute asking of questions which tend to undermine dogmatic frames of mind and to lead the one questioned along surprising paths. Often enough, the "Socratic method" in philosophy, as modeled in the *Dialogues*, is to inquire of the learner by a series of skilful questions which force him or her to discover that the knowledge of the subject matter under investigation is in fact already somehow in the learner's possession.

However, from his successful employment of the method, Plato draws from Socrates some remarkable conclusions. The soul, he concludes, by arriving at any truth, both proves itself immortal and shows that it possessed in a previous existence all the knowledge which inquiry in this life brings into mind: learning is but recollecting what was formerly known.

The theory and the method at once are illustrated in a famous passage from the *Meno* (81e), which it is best to quote at length, because the method of Socrates is best understood by observing it in action rather than by any verbose attempt to describe its process:

Meno: Yes, Socrates; but what do you mean by saying that we do not learn, and that what we call learning is only a process of recollection? Can you teach me how this is?

Socrates: I told you, Meno, just now that you were a rogue, and now you ask whether I can teach you, when I am saying that there is no teaching, but only recollection; and thus you imagine that you will expose me in a contradiction.

Meno: Indeed, Socrates, I protest that I had no such intention. I only asked the question from habit; but if you can prove to me that what you say is true, I wish that you would.

Socrates: It will be no easy matter, but I am willing to do my best for you. Suppose that you call one of your numerous attendants, whichever you like, that I may demonstrate on him.

Meno: Certainly. Come hither, boy.

Socrates: He is Greek, and speaks Greek, does he not?

Meno: Yes, indeed; he was born in the house.

Socrates: Attend now, and observe whether he learns of me or only remembers.

Meno: I will.

Socrates: Tell me, boy, do you know that a figure like this is a square?

Slave Boy: I do.

Socrates: And you know that a square figure has these four lines equal?

Slave Boy: Certainly.

Socrates: And these lines which I have drawn through the middle of the square are also equal?

Slave Boy: Yes.

Socrates: A square may be of any size?

Slave Boy: Certainly.

Socrates: And if one side of the figure be two feet long, and the other side two feet, how much will the whole be? Let me explain: if in one direction the space was two feet long, and in the other direction one foot, the whole space would be two feet taken once?

Slave Boy: Yes.

Socrates: But since this side is also two feet, there are twice two feet? – [There are.] – Then the square is twice two feet?

Slave Boy: Yes.

Socrates: And how many are twice two feet? Count and tell me.

Slave Boy: Four, Socrates.

Socrates: And might there not be another figure twice as large as this, but of the same kind, and having like this all the lines equal?

Slave Boy: Yes.

Socrates: And how many feet will that be?

Slave Boy: Eight feet.

Socrates: And now try and tell me the length of the line which forms the side of that double square: this is two feet – what will that be?

Slave Boy: Clearly, Socrates, it will be double.

Socrates: Do you observe, Meno, that I am not teaching the boy anything, but only asking him questions; and now he fancies that he knows how long a line is necessary in order to produce a figure of eight square feet; does he not?

Meno: Yes.

Socrates: And does he really know?

Meno: Certainly not.

Socrates: He fancies that because the square is double, the line is double?

Meno: True.

Socrates: Now see him being brought step by step to recollect in regular order.

(To the boy.) Tell me, boy, do you assert that a double space comes from a double line? Remember that I am not speaking of an oblong, but of a figure equal every way, and twice the size of this – that is to say of eight feet; and I want to know whether you still say that a double square comes from a double line?

Slave Boy: Yes [thereby proving indeed that he does not know geometry].

Socrates: But does not this line become doubled if we add another such line here?

Slave Boy: Certainly.

Socrates: And four such lines, you say, will make a space containing eight feet?

Slave Boy: Yes.

Socrates: Let us describe such a figure: Would you not say that this is the figure of eight feet?

Slave Boy: Yes.

Socrates: And are there not these four divisions in the figure, each of which is equal to the figure of four feet?

Slave Boy: True.

Socrates: And is not that four times four?

Slave Boy: Certainly.

Socrates: And four times is not double?

Slave Boy: No, indeed.

Socrates: But how much? – [Four times as much.] – Therefore the double line, boy, has given a space, not twice, but four times as much.

Slave Boy: True.

Socrates: Four times four are sixteen – are they not?

Slave Boy: Yes.

Socrates: What line would give you a space of eight feet – for that [namely, a doubling of the original two-foot line] gives a fourfold space, of sixteen feet, does it not?

Slave Boy: Yes.

Socrates: And the space of four feet is made from this half line [that is, the half line of one side of the square which is four feet per side]?

Slave Boy: Yes.

Socrates: Good; and is not a space of eight feet twice the size of this [the original square two feet on a side], and half the size of the other [the square four feet per side]?

Slave Boy: Certainly.

Socrates: Such a space, then [namely, a space of eight square feet], will be made out of a line greater than this one [of two feet], and less than that one [of four feet]?

Slave Boy: Yes; I think so.

Socrates: Very good; I like to hear you say what you think. And now tell me, is not this a line of two feet and that of four?

Slave Boy: Yes.

Socrates: Then the line which forms the side of the eight foot space [we are trying to create] ought to be more than this line of two feet, and less than the other of four feet?

Slave Boy: It ought.

Socrates: Try and see if you can tell me how much it will be.

Slave Boy: Three feet.

Socrates: Then if we add a half to this line of two, that will be the line of three. Here are two and there is one; and on the other side, here are two also and there is one: and that makes the figure of which you speak?

Slave Boy: Yes.

Socrates: But if there are three feet this way and three feet that way, the whole space will be three times three feet?

Slave Boy: That is evident.

Socrates: And how much are three times three feet?

Slave Boy: Nine.

Socrates: And what was to be the number of feet in the doubled square?

Slave Boy: Eight.

Socrates: Then the eight foot space is not made out of a line of three feet?

Slave Boy: No.

Socrates: But from what line? – tell me exactly; and if you would rather not reckon, try and show me the line.

Slave Boy: Indeed, Socrates, I do not know.

Socrates: Do you see, Meno, what advances he has made in his power of recollection? He did not know at first, and he does not know now, what is the side of a figure of eight feet: but then he thought that he knew, and answered confidently as if he knew, and felt no difficulty; now he feels a difficulty, and neither knows nor fancies that he knows.

Meno: True.

Socrates: Is he not better off in knowing his ignorance?

Meno: I think that he is.

Socrates: If we have made him doubt, and given him the "torpedo's shock",[4] have we done him any harm?

Meno: I think not.

Socrates: We have certainly, as would seem, assisted him in some degree to the discovery of the truth; and now he will wish to remedy his ignorance, but then he would have been ready to tell all the world again and again that the double space should have a double side.

Meno: True.

Socrates: But do you suppose that he would ever have started to inquire into or to learn what he fancied that he knew, though he was really ignorant of it, until he had fallen into perplexity under the idea that he did not know, and had desired to know?

Meno: I think not, Socrates.

Socrates: Then he was the better for the torpedo's touch?

Meno: I think so.

Socrates: Mark now the further development. I shall only ask him, and not teach him, and he shall share the inquiry with me: and do you watch and see if you find me telling or explaining anything to him, instead of eliciting his opinion.

Tell me, boy, is not this a square of four feet which I have drawn?

(graph 1)

Slave Boy: Yes.

Socrates: And now I add another square equal to the former one?

(graph 2)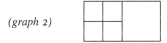

---

4 Guthrie translates "in numbing him like the sting ray"; the point of both translations referring to a fish of the region which gave an electric shock on contact.

Slave Boy: Yes.

Socrates: And a third, which is equal to either of them?

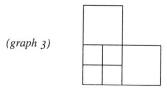

(graph 3)

Slave Boy: Yes.

Socrates: Suppose that we fill up the vacant corner?

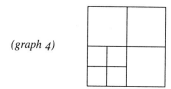

(graph 4)

Slave Boy: Very good.

Socrates: Here, then, there are four equal spaces?

Slave Boy: Yes.

Socrates: And how many times larger is this space [*graph 4*] than this other [*graph 1*]?

Slave Boy: Four times.

Socrates: But we wanted one only twice as large, as you will remember.

Slave Boy: True.

Socrates: Now, does not this line, reaching from corner to corner, bisect each of these spaces?

(graph 5)

Slave Boy: Yes.

Socrates: And are there not here four equal lines which contain this space?

Slave Boy: There are.

Socrates: Look and see how much this space is.

Slave Boy: I do not understand.

Socrates: Has not each interior cut off half of the four spaces?

Slave Boy: Yes.

Socrates: And how many such [cut-off half] spaces are there in this section [that is, in the interior square formed by the four lines of the half cut-off spaces]?

Slave Boy: Four.

Socrates: And how many in this [the original corner of *graph 1* above, which is the lower left space of *graph 3* and *graph 4*]?

Slave Boy: Two.

Socrates: And four is how many times two?

Slave Boy: Twice.

Socrates: So that this space is of how many feet?

Slave Boy: Of eight feet.

Socrates: And from what line do you get this figure?

Slave Boy: From this [the diagonal cutting the four original quadrants into half].

Socrates: That is, from the line which extends from corner to corner of the figure of four feet?

Slave Boy: Yes.

Socrates: And that is the line which the learned call the diagonal. And if this is the proper name, then you, Meno's slave, are prepared to affirm that the double space is the square of the diagonal?

Slave Boy: Certainly, Socrates.

Socrates: What do you say of him, Meno? Were not all these answers given out of his own head?

Meno: Yes, they were all his own.

Socrates: And yet, as we were just now saying, he did not know?

Meno: True.

Socrates: But still he had in him those notions of his – had he not?

Meno: Yes.

Socrates: Then he who does not know may still have true notions of that which he does not know?

Meno: Apparently.

Socrates: And at present these notions have just been stirred up in him, as in a dream; but if he were frequently asked the same questions, in different forms, he would know as accurately as anyone at last?

Meno: I dare say.

Socrates: Without anyone teaching him he will recover his knowledge for himself, if he is merely asked questions?

Meno: Yes.

Socrates: And this spontaneous recovery of knowledge in him is recollection?

Meno: True.

Socrates: And this knowledge which he now has must he not either have acquired at some time, or else possessed always? – [Yes.] – But if he always possessed this knowledge he would always have known; or if he has acquired the knowledge he could not have acquired it in this life, unless he has been taught geometry. And he may be made to do the same with all geometry and every other branch of knowledge; has anyone ever taught him all this? You must know about him, if, as you say, he was born and bred in your house.

Meno: And I am certain that no one ever did teach him.

Socrates: And yet he has these notions?

Meno: The fact, Socrates, is undeniable.

Socrates: But if he did not acquire them in this life, then he must have had and learned them at some other time?

Meno: Clearly he must.

Socrates: Which must have been the time when he was not a man?

Meno: Yes.

Socrates: And if there are always to be true notions in him, both while he is and while he is not a man, which only need to be awakened into knowledge by putting questions to him, his soul must remain always possessed of this knowledge; for he must always either be or not be a man.

Meno: Obviously.

Socrates: And if the truth of all things always exists in the soul, then the soul is immortal. Wherefore be of good cheer, and try to discover by recollection what you do not now know, or rather what you do not remember.

Meno: I feel, somehow, that I like what you are saying.

Socrates: And I too like what I am saying. Some things I have said of which I am not altogether confident. But that we shall be better and braver and less helpless if we think that we ought to inquire, than we should have been if we thought that there was no knowing and no duty to seek to know what we do not know; – that is a belief for which I am ready to fight, in word and deed, to the utmost of my power.

The Lessons of the Square

Plato seemed to think that this particular exchange made the point that the soul already knows what it seems to learn, and that from this situation we realize that the soul had a previous existence to its present bodily one. By taking on a body, the soul subjects itself to conditions of darkness and forgetting, a condition which philosophy remedies by teaching the soul to recollect what in fact it had consciously known in the previous existence and still carries within itself obscured and forgotten by the conditions of this life.

In the third century AD, Plotinus would make of this dubious mélange of weak abductions a whole philosophical program. By the end of the fourth century AD Augustine would demur (as a Christian he had to) from the inference of a pre-existence of the soul, on the grounds that the participation of the human soul through intelligence in the divine reasons would be enough to explain the learning Plato thought had to be but *recollecting*.

Yet not until the thirteenth-century work of the great Aquinas would the issue of the *Meno* be addressed on properly cognitive and epistemological grounds, in the doctrine of the *primum cognitum*, of the sense in which being provides the horizon of human understanding in its difference from the perceptions of sense.[5]

---

5 See the discussion of "The Problem of Being as First Known", chapter 7 below, p. 341ff.

Still, short of reading entire dialogues of Plato, there is no better way to get a direct glimpse and sense of the Socratic method than from the passage we have just completed.

The Gadfly

Socrates considered himself more a gadfly than a teacher. A "gadfly", literally, is any of the various species of fly that bite and annoy livestock. By transference or analogy, since Socrates' time, "gadfly" also means a person who, by persistent questioning, provokes, stimulates, or annoys. Socrates professed to know nothing, yet one thing he surely did know was how to ask pointed and disconcerting questions. Diogenes Laertius reports that a certain Chaerephon enquired of the Oracle at Delphi whether any man was wiser than Socrates. The oracle replied, "No one." Socrates explained this reply by pointing out that, if he knew nothing, and no one was wiser than he was, then no one else knew anything either. The oracle, in short, had neither revealed nor concealed but only signified that all men are ignorant.

Under the skillful and often barbed questions of a mind as quick as that of Socrates, such a pretense might to many discussants soon enough wear thin,[6] especially as the questions tended to reveal the incompleteness, contradictoriness, or absurdity of the views held by the one being questioned. And indeed the wide circle of questions that Socrates posed against the beliefs, prejudices, and certitudes of the Athenian people did eventually lead to a call for his death, and a sentence of death was actually rendered.[7] He had the chance to flee, but for reasons of his own preferred to surrender, to accept the poison cup of hemlock assigned him for annoying the livestock too long and too often. If his antagonists thought they had succeeded in putting an end to Socrates, history reveals few greater illusions.

Plato (c.427–347BC)

His student Plato saw to it that the death of Socrates was only a beginning. But Plato did not confine himself to the ethical concerns of individual behavior and the organization of the state – ethics and politics, as we say today – that primarily absorbed Socrates. Indeed, if we had only Plato's political views to go on, we might not admire him as much as we do. Some have professed to see in Plato's *Laws* a "prolegomenon to all future Inquisitions", inasmuch as there is "a fear of the abuses of freedom, and the conception of philosophy as the policeman of the people and the regulator of the arts" that runs throughout Plato's writings on politics. "Looking back over this body of speculation", one historian wrote in the year of Germany's invasion of Poland,[8] "we are surprised to see how fully Plato anticipated

---

6 In the c.391/360BC*Theaetetus* 150, Plato has Socrates admit that "the reproach which is often made against me, that I ask questions of others and have not the wit to answer them myself, is very just. The reason is that the god compels me to be a midwife, but forbids me to bring forth."
7 Circumstances of Socrates' trial and death are given in the three dialogues *Apology*, *Crito*, and *Phaedo*.
8 Durant 1935: 523.

the philosophy, the theology, and the organization of medieval Christianity, and how much of the modern Fascist state." More detailed philosophical argumentation of the point, with less excuse of a pressing influence of immediate events, has been made in a work of Karl Popper under the title, *The Open Society and Its Enemies*, which has been characterized as, and may be (the reader is recommended to form an opinion), "a travesty on Plato". Yet from the Christian Neoplatonism of Augustine in the early fifth-century AD will come the first full justification of the use of the police powers of the state to enforce religious orthodoxy.

True Being, Eternal and Unchanging

What is for sure is that to reduce Plato to a socio-political thinker is to deform his thought beyond anything that can remotely be justified. His pupil Aristotle understood him well on this point, and subsequently distinguished *human* understanding in terms of the fundamental difference between practical and speculative thought. "Practical" thought concerns such being as depends for its formation upon human thought and volitions. It begins with the individual's own behavior as "regulable" and in need of regulation ("ethics" in the narrow sense). But such thought expands to include the family and tribe ("economics", Aristotle called the expansion), and also the state ("politics", ethics in the full sense). "Speculative" thought, by contrast, though it admits of sub-specifications (as we will see) and can feed the growth of the practical, yet begins and ends with τὸ ὄν, being as that which precedes and forever eludes human dominion.

For Plato put all socio-political inquiries – all "practical thought" – in the larger context of the challenges to a theory of knowledge laid down by the early physicists, particularly the challenge posed by the opposed positions taken by Parmenides and Heraclitus on the nature of ultimate reality or being. In effect, the choice between Parmenides and Heraclitus turned on the question of what provides the true avenue to being: intellect or sense?

Between these two Plato hesitated not a moment. He opted for the intellect, and adapted the dialectic methods of Zeno of Elea and Socrates to champion the broadest and most definite of views as to the nature of reality. The loftiness of Plato's view may be gathered from the following passage of his *Republic*:[9]

> For he, Adeimantus, whose mind is fixed upon true being,[10] has surely no time to look down upon the affairs of earth, or to be filled with malice and envy, contending against men; his eye is ever directed towards things fixed and immutable, which he sees neither injuring nor injured by one another, but all in order moving according to reason; these he imitates, and to these he will, as far as he can, conform himself. Can a man help imitating that with which he holds reverential converse?

---

9 Plato i.391/360BC: *Republic* 500b–c, Jowett translation.
10 In the Hamilton-Cairns edition this expression "true being", τοῖς οὖσι, is rendered as "eternal realities".

Dialectic and Language

The true being upon which Plato sought to fix the eye of our mind was not of this world. For Plato, there were ideas and there were Ideas, or Forms. The ideas in our mind, that is, the individual cognitive states that belong to us as individuals, are not the Ideas of which Plato speaks; in them he has almost no interest. In linguistic communication he takes a much greater interest, because along with, and even prior to, mathematics it is the indispensable instrument of dialectic and, insofar, the key to philosophical knowledge.

But the main point that Plato seems concerned to make in this area is that philosophy can be entrusted to the spoken word alone, and cannot be written down. The strongest statement of this claim occurs in Plato's *Seventh Letter*,[11] where he says of "the subjects to which I devote myself" that "there is no way of putting it into words like other subjects", an ineluctable fact which "stands in the way of the man who would dare to write even the least thing on these matters":

> Hence no intelligent man will ever be so bold as to put into language those things which his reason has contemplated, especially not into a form that is unalterable – which must be the case with what is expressed in written symbols.

Or again:

> It is an inevitable conclusion from this that when anyone sees anywhere the written work of anyone, ... the subject treated cannot have been his most serious concern. ... If, however, he really was seriously concerned with these matters and put them in writing, then surely not the gods, but mortals have utterly blasted his wits.

Besides the "true doctrine" that "stands in the way of the man who would dare to write on such matters", it should be noted that there is Plato's elitist conviction that the study of philosophy should be restricted to the few also suited to rule the run of humankind. This conviction by itself stood in Plato's own way of composing a treatise on his esoteric teaching, according to the *Seventh Letter*,[12] and may have been more than half the reason for his dismissal of the written word:

> If I thought it possible to deal adequately with the subject in a treatise or a lecture for the general public, what finer achievement would there have been in my life than to write a work of great benefit to mankind and to bring the nature of things to light for all men? I do not, however, think the attempt to tell mankind of these matters a good thing, except in the case of some few who are capable of discovering the truth for themselves with a little guidance. In the case of the rest to do so would excite in

---

11 Plato a.347BC: *Seventh Letter* 341b–345.
12 Ibid.: 341d–e.

some an unjustified contempt in a thoroughly offensive fashion, in others certain lofty
and vain hopes, as if they had acquired some awesome lore.

So, a curious mixture. Not until the ninth-century rule of Charlemagne, within
the European framework of the so-called "holy Roman empire", would an idea of
common schools *begin* to take hold, and the tradition of liberal arts education in
the later middle ages would develop in the direction of education being seen as a
benefit, and finally a right and necessity, for all human beings. This development is
hardly complete, even today. (No university was founded within the vast civilization
of China until 1898.) But the direction of the development is clear. Plato may not
have held democratic views of education, but he was one of the first to see its
necessity from the beginning of human life to the flourishing of the individual
and, especially, the state. "By founding the Academy", Burnet thinks,[13] "Plato had
invented the university", even though we may think the full taking root of the
idea of a university as a cultural institution did not occur before the "high middle
ages". Of equal importance, if we look not only at the *Republic* but especially at
the *Laws* we will find that Plato has also "invented the secondary school",[14] and
that after him "we find such schools everywhere in the Hellenistic period, and the
Romans adopted it with other things", whence it becomes "the origin of the medieval
grammar school and of all that has come out of it since." If there is a single reason
why the civilization of Europe came to dominate the globe, it was not only because
of the establishment there of modern science. More fundamentally the reason was
that the institutionalized structures of university life, which made science possible
and welcome within a socially recognized "community of inquirers", had been put in
place by a tradition that required centuries to reach a critical mass of socio-cultural
coherence.

The authenticity of Plato's *Seventh Letter* is a subject of debate, and we may
be pretty sure that, though the weight of opinion currently seems in its favor, this
particular debate will never fully close. Nor need it; for much the same doctrine in
somewhat tamer tones is expressed by Plato in his *Phaedrus*, where the inability of
the written text to respond to readers' questions as a speaker could is underlined. The
Seventh Letter merely draws the furthermost consequences of the point. And, now
that Plato is so long dead, we are faced with the true finality of the pronouncement of
the *Seventh Letter*, be that pronouncement authentic or forged: "There is no writing
of mine on this subject" of the ultimate reality, "nor ever shall be".

In a perceptive essay on sign and language in Plato,[15] Helena Lozano-Miralles
observes that Plato responds to Heraclitean tradition in his dialogue *Cratylus*, where
he deals with the status of names; and to Parmenidean tradition in the dialogue
Sophist, where he deals with the status of false statements. There is also the matter

---

13 Burnet 1914: 311.
14 Ibid.
15 Lozano-Miralles 1988.

of the influence of Pythagorean tradition, which is harder to assess in the matter of "linguistic ideas" for want of "identification of a clear corpus". Yet all this serves mainly to remind us that theory of language is never Plato's main point, nor is there a likelihood, in any case, that Plato would have agreed that such "ideas", subjective states by any accounting, would "constitute the basis of semiosis".[16] Plato's main point is always *the Forms*, which are beyond language and human semiosis of any kind other than the final achievement of dialectic which enables the "spark" to leap from the realm of Forms and the Good to kindle in the soul the conflagration of philosophical understanding.

So it is more than an accident that[17] when Umberto Eco tries to advance the thesis[18] that "a general semiotics is nothing else but *a* philosophy of language", we find Porphyry to figure much larger than Plato, and Plato scarcely at all. When Manetti tries to claim a convergence unique in Plato, found nowhere else in antiquity until Augustine, where, be it only for a least briefest moment, the theory of signs as such intersects with the theory of language as such,[19] he is reduced to the absolutely passing occurrence of σημεῖον in the *Sophist* at 262a to say that a name is "a spoken sign" applied to what acts in contrast to a verb which is an expression applied to actions. From this single use of σημεῖον in the context not even of speech but of its parts, which occurs only in passing, never recurs, nowhere is thematized, and need not even be translated as "sign" to get the point of the passage,[20] Manetti tries to infer "the semiotic nature of Plato's conception of language" subsequently lost in antiquity. This is not so much a case of tight-rope walking without a net as it is of tight-rope walking without a rope. A butterfly touched on a twig; had the twig been its home, it would have stayed, but in fact it flew on to its home elsewhere.

Once a general conception of signs emerges in philosophy, centuries after Plato, it will indeed be possible to cast a backward glance over the rich literary remains of the Platonic *corpus* and divine there much that would have seemed to Plato of semiotic import had he realized the general role of the sign in the project of human understanding. But this is not at all how the landscape appeared to Plato

---

16 This idea that "linguistic ideas" or human language in any sense provides or constitutes the main basis or foundation of semiosis, we will see in chapter 16, is in fact a thesis strictly confined to late modern idealism in the development generally known under the label of "semiology" in its difference from semiotics. As late modern and contemporary developments, as we will see, "semiology" stems principally from the influence of the Swiss linguist Ferdinand de Saussure, while "semiotics" stems rather from the American philosopher Charles Sanders Peirce and, through him, from John Locke (for the name of the doctrine of signs) and from the Latin philosophical tradition insofar as it originated in Augustine and culminated in Poinsot on the matter of signification (for the notion of sign as a general mode of being verified both in nature and culture).

17 "Ab ipsa veritate coacta" as Aquinas once remarked of such a situation of hermeneutics: "the truth itself coerces the author".

18 Eco 1984: 4.

19 Manetti 1993: 56–7.

20 Jowett, for example, in his translation, rendered it "an articulate mark" without any loss of sense whatever to the thematic development proper to the dialogue.

in conceiving of language as an instrument of dialectic, along with and ultimately inferior to mathematics, in teaching those few humans capable of philosophy the true nature of the Good, which lies quite beyond the forms of language even in speech, and is finally seen only when, in Burnet's translation,[21] "a light is suddenly kindled as from a leaping spark, and when it has reached the soul it thenceforward finds nutriment for itself."

The Ideas of Platonic theory are the supra- or trans-sensible reality of which all that we behold with our eyes or touch with our fingers are but shadows and participations. Of themselves, the senses give us nothing of reality. To arrive at reality, we must use purely intellectual means, for only the intellect can give us a direct awareness of the Ideas, eternal and unchanging, which provide the measure by which truth can be determined. Justice, for example, is an Idea, eternal and unchanging, by the knowing of which alone it becomes possible to decide in the changing affairs of men when actions are just and when unjust. Only dialectic can reach the abstract level of true reality, but it must be used with great discipline and care. In introducing the citizens to dialectic, Plato warned in his *Republic*[22] that "they must not be allowed to taste the dear delight too early; that is one thing especially to be avoided":

> For young men, as you may have observed, when they first get the taste in their mouths, argue for amusement, and are always contradicting and refuting others in imitation of those who refute them; they delight like puppies in pulling about and tearing with words all who approach them.

Premature involvement in dialectic, thus, produces not philosophers but sophists:

> When the young men have made many conquests in argument and received defeats at the hands of many, they violently and speedily get into a way of not believing anything that they believed before, and hence ... philosophy has a bad name with the rest of the world. ... But when a man begins to get older, he will no longer be guilty of that sort of insanity; he will follow the example of the reasoner who is seeking for truth, and not of the eristic who is contradicting for the sake of amusement; and the greater consideration of his character will increase and not diminish the honor of the pursuits.

The Good

If there can be said to be one thing that most preoccupied Plato, it would be the Idea of the Good. In the *Republic*, Plato uses the image of a cave in which men see only shadows cast on the wall in front of them by a fire burning behind them to allegorize the situation of people in this life who rely on their senses to tell them what is. Only

21 Burnet 1914: 221. The remarks of von Fritz (1971: 412–13) on the non-mystical nature of this "leaping spark", against the Neoplatonists, are worth considering.
22 Plato i.391/360BC: *Republic* 539b.

by leaving the cave and entering into the light of day – the sun, which symbolizes the Good[23] – can human beings come to see things as they really are. That is to say, only by the right use of dialectic can the human being be led to see that the true nature of reality can be found only beyond the sensible world of material objects, in the realm of Ideas pure and simple, the Forms which sensible things imitate and participate but can never become. The conversion of the soul from becoming to the contemplation of being was the aim of dialectic, of education. A report from Burnet is illuminating:[24]

> Aristoxenos said that Aristotle "was always telling" how most of those who heard the lecture on the Good were affected. They came expecting to hear about some of the recognised good things, and when they heard of nothing but Arithmetic and Astronomy and the Limit and the One, they thought it all very strange.

"Let No One Without Geometry Enter Here"

What we know of the theory of the Forms or Ideas from the *Dialogues*, and of Plato's notion of dialectic rightly used, in the nature of the case, is only part of the story. Remember that the dialogues were not written for use within Plato's school so much as to popularize his views with outsiders. There was said to be on the portal of the school an inscription that reappears on the title page of Copernicus 1543: ἀγεωμέτρητος μηδεὶς εἰσίτω – "Let no one without geometry enter here".

It is easy to see why. If the true nature of reality is supersensible, then the objects of mathematical inquiry are much closer to reality than anything we can see or touch. Take any basic theory, say, that the interior angles of a plane triangle must equal one-hundred-and-eighty degrees. The triangle drawn on a blackboard or on paper is not the issue. However helpful it may be to the student in working out the theorem, it is fully beside the point of the theorem. The theorem concerns triangle in the abstract, which is the only place triangles actually exist. Not this or that triangle on paper, not this or that triangular figure seen with the eye or traced with the finger, but TRIANGLE pure and simple, the NATURE of triangle – what it is that makes a triangle be a triangle and not a square or a circle or anything else: THAT is the object about which the theorem holds. In fact, any visible or tangible triangular FIGURE is precisely not a triangle but a mere imitation of one. The only real triangle is the ideal triangle, the "Idea of triangle" (or type of triangularity), the object or focus of attention when we have in mind the thought of a triangle (that to which our thought relates us). Any given sensible representation of a triangle, or any figure we say is a triangular figure, is truly triangular only to the extent that it participates in the Idea of triangle as a mere token thereof. The accuracy of the representation or sensible figure is measured and judged by the nature of something that is never sensible: the

---

23 Remember the case of Anaxagoras, p. 27 above, who was sentenced to death for suggesting that the sun was not a god.
24 Burnet 1914: 221.

Idea of triangle. Moreover, not only is the sensible figure triangular just to the degree that it participates in the Idea of triangularity, but this participation can never be so complete that the sensible figure actually becomes TRIANGLE. It will never be more than an instance, a *token*, as Peirce would say, of the ideal *type* or Idea, TRIANGLE.

Similar remarks apply to number. Arithmetic concerns not sensible objects, albeit that we apply arithmetic ideas whenever we count things. Numbered things are not numbers, any more than triangular shapes are triangles. Mathematics much as Pythagoras thought of it was at the center of Plato's philosophy, and this role of mathematical thought is – and can be – only indirectly brought out in the verbal mode of the *Dialogues*. Here we run up against one of the greatest and perhaps irresolvable disputes in the history of philosophy: the role of mathematics in the understanding of the world. Like Pythagoras before him and Galileo, Newton, and Einstein after him, Plato seems to have believed that mathematics is the true language that God spoke in creating the universe, and only through mathematics can we finally come to know something of how the world in essence, not in appearances, really is. Aristotle faulted Plato for in effect putting mathematics in the place of philosophy, and saw it as a pernicious result of Plato's influence that[25] "mathematics has come to be the whole of philosophy for modern thinkers, though they say that it should be studied for the sake of other things."

The Relation of Aristotle to Plato
The one other major source of contemporary information we have on Plato's theory of Forms besides the dialogues is the writings of Aristotle. Alfred North Whitehead, who thought that Plato's "ἀγεωμέτρητος μηδεὶς εἰσίτω" maxim got it right, considered the rest of philosophy's history to be but a series of footnotes to Plato, of which Aristotle wrote the first.

---

25 Aristotle 348–7dBC: *Metaphysics* I, 992a30. Listen (with the mind's ear at least) to Turnbull (1998: 186f.): "... the picture I have drawn of the mature Plato, with its very heavy emphasis on the mathematical ground and character of the whole universe, justifies Aristotle's (in *Metaphysics* A) calling Plato a Pythagorean and makes it plausible that Plato's successor in the Academy, Speusippus, is being faithful to the mature Plato in making mathematics the key to philosophical understanding. That the issue of mathematics in the Academy after Plato's death was a major controversy is quite clear from Aristotle's *Metaphysics* M and N (and elsewhere).

"Though he does display eclectic tendencies, the great astronomer/geographer, Ptolemy [c.AD100–175], in his best known work does make use of major features of the mathematical Platonism that I have been describing. The *Almagest* [c.AD150] assumes that the 'fixed stars' travel together in their circumscribing sphere, that the earth is at its centre, that the several planets travel in circles, each with uniform velocity, and that the observed orbits of the planets can, given the exercise of ingenuity on Euclidian geometry, conform to the circularity and uniform velocity requirements. Despite a number of problems with the system, Ptolemaic astronomy stood up well for hundreds of years [until the early-16th-century work of Copernicus, in fact], providing for intelligible navigational guidance and calendar-making and giving human beings a sense of their place in the universe. Appropriately enough, its replacement went hand in hand with the development of the classical mechanics – another system that took mathematics as the key to understanding the universe."

But Aristotle, unlike Whitehead, did not think that Plato's guiding maxim got it right; he did not agree either with the theory of forms or with Plato's view of the mathematical nature of ultimate reality. As a result, to read Aristotle as a footnote to Plato is to repeat a main facet of the Neoplatonic experiment,[26] and to neglect the many ways in which Aristotle's thought cannot be correlated with that of Plato. In fact, these many avenues of divergence are far more important to understanding the course of the Latin Age and the eventual rise of science in the modern sense afterward than are the points of agreement. Be that as it may, we shall see that what is most interesting in the thought of Aristotle hardly reduces to what he thought was wrong with Plato's thought.

Aristotle is one of the important historical sources to learn about Plato, but he is the most important philosophical source to learn about Aristotle. So here we look to Aristotle rather to learn what Aristotle thought, not mainly to learn how what he wrote differed from or simply provides a critique of Plato. We must try mainly to see what Aristotle considered true and how he presented it on his own terms.

To understand Aristotle on his own terms is to understand an Aristotle as unknown to Alfred North Whitehead as he was to Whitehead's one-time collaborator, Bertrand Russell. For Aristotle's terms go so far beyond Platonic cosmology that it would be far more accurate to regard Plato as a prenote than to regard Aristotle as a footnote of whatever magnitude in a series however long. In fact, as Peirce would introduce postmodernity by seeing,[27] the history of science and philosophy from ancient times to the end of modernity largely consisted of a filling in of the details of the system of the world Aristotle had outlined. Not until the inner lining of knowledge itself became the focus of inquiry on a footing with, yet without sacrificing, the inquiry into outer nature (and indeed not until Peirce himself set his hand to the matter), will we encounter again such a system as that which Aristotle achieves.

Aristotle (384–322BC)

From the outset, Aristotle does not land so clearly on one side of the opposition of Heraclitus to Parmenides as Plato did. The idea that reality was to be found elsewhere than in the physical surroundings was not acceptable to Aristotle. He thought indeed that reality might be found elsewhere as well as in the sensible world. But he rejected the notion that reality might be found *only* elsewhere. He, more than Plato, took up directly the original challenge to discover the nature of the physical world, and his books titled the *Physics* express the core of his system. With Parmenides, he agreed that human understanding by intellectual means could reach a grasp of reality in unchanging aspects. But with Heraclitus he agreed that change is also something real, and that whatever reality may be, it must be found within, not just behind or beyond, the sensible. But how to respond to the saying

---

26 See chapter 4, p. 113ff.
27 Peirce c.1898: CP 1.1.

of Parmenides:[28] "For never will this be proved, that things that are not are"? In a nutshell, anticipating the medieval development of the theory of analogy, Aristotle's answer was that "being is said in many ways, not in one"; whence being may be said of being and nonbeing alike, but of the former as actual and the latter as potential.

What Philosophy Is Primarily Called On to Account For

To begin with, setting aside for the moment Parmenides' flat denial of change, Aristotle pointed out that neither the monists nor the dualists who accept change succeed in explaining it. The dualists *explain away* quantitative and qualitative or "developmental" change in favor of change of place (rearrangement of atoms) as the only "real" change. But what this change *consists in* they *presuppose* rather than explain. Thus, Democritus, whom Aristotle seems to regard as the most profound of his predecessors in proposing to explain the environmental world according to its proper being (whatever that might be), "explains" the coming to be, development, and movement of bodies on the basis of a rearrangement of atoms in space. But a rearrangement of atoms is an instance of local motion, or motion in space; and this is already an instance of *change*. Hence, the atomists beg the question: instead of telling us what change is, they tell us that change of position or place is the only real change.

But the monists do exactly the same thing. Whether they "explain" change in the sensible world by "condensation and rarefaction" or by the expulsion of opposites finite or infinite in number, they, too, presuppose rearrangement, movement, or change in place, rather than explain change. They too beg the question.

Heraclitus is, in a sense, even worse. He makes no effort at all *either* to explain away *or* to explain change. He simply affirms it. Change for him is the presupposition, not the experience to be explained, the *datum explanandum*. Change *is* reality, fire its best and clearest image.

Parmenides alone explains away change without presupposing any change. Democritus, the dualists, explain away all changes but one, movement in space, which they presuppose. Parmenides presupposes nothing. He points clearly and directly to the contradiction involved in *all* change, *any* change: nonbeing comes to be, being ceases to be. The case is no different than the square circle. If this be change, then change cannot be. Democritus, by contrast with Parmenides, is a piker. He *explains away* only qualitative and developmental change, while *presupposing* change of place as the basis of his explaining away. Heraclitus, by contrast with Parmenides, is a profligate. He explains nothing, but celebrates only change to infinity. Parmenides is intellectual sobriety itself: who cannot remove the seeming contradiction from the appearance of change has no right to affirm its reality, and the obligation to deny its possibility.

---

28   Cited by Aristotle (from Parmenides c.475BC) in XIV (c.348–7dBC) of his *Metaphysics*, 1088b36.

Possibility is the point exactly on which Aristotle seizes. His argument is as obvious as was Darwin's argument that the fittest survive, and equally unnoticed by those before and around him. Being, he noted, and nonbeing, have not only the full sense of unconfined actuality on the one hand and nothing at all on the other hand. They have also a partial sense: limited actuality in the case of being, and relative unreality in the case of nonbeing. The human infant is a potential geometer, but will have to mature and study to become a geometrician actually. The human infant is a potential adult, but actually only a child of four years. So we need not dive into a contradiction in affirming changeable being, we need only recognize that, to be changeable, a being perforce mixes potentiality with actuality, and conversely, in an ever-changing ratio. Every finite actuality gives rise to new and further potentialities, and every potentiality restricts and closes down some actuality or aspect of actuality.

With this distinction between the potential (relative nonbeing) and the actual (limited or relative being) made within the concept of being as unlimited or pure actuality *versus* the concept of nonbeing as what does not in any sense exist, Aristotle finds himself in a position to identify a common denominator of all change, without any need to explain change away absolutely (*à la* Parmenides) or even reductively and relatively to local motion (*à la* Democritus and the dualists or the dynamic pluralists and monists alike after Thales).[29] Change, says Aristotle, be it local motion or developmental or initiative, is "the act of a being in potency insofar as it is in potency." But to understand the interplay between potency and act in the reality of finite being, we need a sophisticated analysis of the varying respects under which a given being is from one point of view "actual" and from another "potential".[30] In other words, we need to examine and analyze the manner in which one being depends on other beings in being what it is.

---

29 They presuppose motion in space, then so construct their theories that all other change reduces to this. But real change, novelty in the universe, they explain away, reducing it to motion in space (or rearrangement of particles). For example (Aristotle c.355BC *On the Heavens* III, 305b1): "What the followers of Empedocles and Democritus do, though without observing it themselves, is to reduce the generation of elements out of one another to an illusion. They make it a process of excretion from a body of what was in it all the time – as though generation required a vessel rather than a material – so that it involves no change of anything."

30 In the Latin Age, as we will see, Aristotle's distinction between potency and act will become the basis for the distinction between creator as *ipsum esse subsistens* and creature as *esse participatum* or "finite being", the basis for understanding the transcendence of God as pure act to the world in which God is immanent as creator by imparting existence to those mixtures of potentiality and actuality we experience as "finite beings". But for this to happen the general distinction between potency and act as applicable to the whole variety of levels of actuality and potentiality within finite beings will first have to be transformed by St Thomas's radical argument (for example, in his *Summa theologiae*, Part I, Question 3, article 4, paragraph 2 of the body; Question 4, article 1, reply to the 3rd objection; etc.) that even the actuality of form, every form (that which gives specificity and determination to a being so as to make it "what it is"), is itself potency to the act of existence (*esse*, that is). See chapter 7 below.

The Datum Explanandum

What a successful philosophy of nature requires from the outset is an analysis of causality adequate to the phenomenon to be explained, namely, the intelligible possibility of change itself. In the case of the physical environment, we need to account not only for motion in space (change of place), but for the replacement of one individual by another (substantial change), and for the process of development whereby an individual both grows (quantitative change) and matures (qualitative change). As it turns out, not only "being" but also "change" and "cause" must be "said in many ways".

A Scheme of Causality Adequate to the Datum

A cause is that upon which something depends in being. If the something is an individual, there is not only the question of the cause of the generation, the *efficient cause*; there is also the question of what the individual is made out of, the *material cause*; and the question of what makes it to be this kind of individual (a horse, say, or a human being) rather than some other kind, the *formal cause*; and there is the question of how it develops from an initial to a mature state, from a seed to a full-grown organism of that type, the *final cause*. Were it only a question of moving things around in space, efficient causality in a diminished form – like a shove – would be enough. But to explain, along with beginning and ceasing to be, growth and development – quantitative and qualitative change as well as local motion – we need cause in this fourfold sense.

We shall see that when, in the later Latin Age, philosophers began to turn their attention more directly to so-called epistemological questions (that is to say, questions concerning the nature and extent of human knowing) than to the ancient ontological questions of physics, it was found necessary to introduce several refinements expanding the original fourfold to an eightfold scheme.[31] But for questions of physical as distinct from cognitive change, there is no need here to go into these elaborations, beyond noting their necessity, since details of this forgotten chapter of intellectual history we shall run across in due course. How the eightfold refinement comes about, where and why the refinements are necessary, we will see along the way, especially[32] when we come to discuss the action of signs ("Thirdness") in its contrast to interactions of environmental things as physical ("Secondness").

This scheme is clearest in the case of organisms, which indeed was Aristotle's principal interest; yet he considered rightly that it applies as well to all parts of the physical environment, inorganic as well as organic. The notions of efficient cause as the agency productive of an effect, of material cause as that upon which an agent acts to produce its effect, and formal cause as the unity of the effect as something distinct from the agent, are notions that do not normally lead to serious

---

31 See discussion and references to the Latin summaries given in chapter 15, esp. p. 633 nn73, 74.
32 See chapter 15, p. 632f.

misunderstandings. By contrast, the one type of causality in this original scheme that has proved the most problematic, or at least the most often misunderstood, is so-called "final causality", also called *teleology*.

Usually teleology is misconstrued as some force or pattern external to the organism, as when it is alleged that the final cause of grass is to provide food for cows, or that the final cause of cows is to provide steaks for restaurants. But this misunderstanding is gross and total. By "final cause" Aristotle meant originally no agency external to the organism, but the very pattern of growth and development that it typically exhibits – the relation of a substance in its initial state (from the moment of "generation") to that same substance in its mature state (or up to the moment of "corruption"); and this sense of "final cause" can hardly be denied. In modern biology, where later theological notions of teleology were confused with Aristotle's original notion of final cause, the original notion has been effectively reintroduced with the designation *teleonomy*.

A Lair for Later Nonsense: from Teleology to Teleonomy
Given the importance of terminology in philosophy, some rectification in particular of terms in the area of so-called "final causality" or "teleology" as original terms for the study of "goal-oriented" natural processes is in order. Ancient discourse about the heavens, indeed, up to the very end of the Latin Age and even into early modern times, was collectively a kind of indiscriminate mixture of unverifiable anthropomorphic assertions about celestial "influences" together with the compilation of detailed observations, calculations, and tables of actual movements traced by celestial bodies. Around the middle of the modern period, the latter sort of study came to eschew mythical, unverifiable, and especially anthropomorphic thinking about the heavens. Sober observers adopted the new term "astronomy" as the appellation for scientific celestial studies and abandoned the original umbrella term "astrology" to those persisting in the pursuit of imaginable connections between stars, planets, and human life as their primary concern.

The history of the term "teleology", by contrast, exhibits a different pattern. In the writings of Aristotle, the notion was proposed as a sober term referring to the developmental processes in substances, organisms in particular. Subsequently the term came to be used, or abused, as a label for facile claims by theologians (especially in the early to mid-modern period) to discern divine interventions and intentions in natural processes, including natural disasters (a practice of religious thought hardly new, but one which reached a kind of climax in the centuries immediately before Darwin). Whence in the very period when astronomy was dissociating itself from astrology, sober notions of teleology were entombed in excessive anthropomorphic thinking. As a consequence, by late modern times the very term itself, "teleology", carried so much baggage extraneous to its authentic use in Aristotle that it came to be discredited and abandoned as the scientific study of nature and organisms advanced.

But some natural processes, especially in the development of biological organisms, become virtually unthinkable other than as realizations of stages in natural patterns or "plans" (in von Uexküll's term). And so even the most hard-headed and positivistic of the late modern biologists found it necessary to follow Pittendrigh's lead and to re-open, around his newly coined term "teleonomy",[33] the sober debate launched, in fact (such noted historians of modern biology as Pittendrigh himself, followed by Mayr and others, to the contrary notwithstanding), by Aristotle's *Physics* and biology in the fourth century BC. Cutting through the typically modern anti-Aristotle rhetoric, we may say that the terminological move from "teleology" (abandoned to those given to excessively anthropomorphic thinking about nature) to "teleonomy" in the twentieth century (as the new term coined for reference to verifiably developmental processes occurring in nature) is an excellent and long overdue development, paralleling in the study of living beings the separation after the seventeenth century of "astronomy" as a scientific notion from the earlier umbrella use of "astrology" to cover indiscriminately mythological, religious, magical, and scientific notions about the heavens.

Chance Events

Part and parcel with Aristotle's doctrine of causality was his doctrine of chance. He is unique in the history of philosophy for having given the first coherent account of chance events, an account that will be elaborated on and incorporated into postmodern thought by Charles Peirce using the label of *Tychism*. For the Aristotelian account of chance will become all the more important after the discovery of evolution in the physical universe, when an explanation of how lines of causality come to deviate from their proper paths becomes crucial.

For Aristotle the chance event is not something uncaused simply speaking, but rather an event which results from the intersection of two or more independent causal lines. Each line of causality has its own proper causality, but when they happen to intersect the resulting event has no proper causality of its own. A meteor traveling through space has its path determined by quite a precise series of causes. The earth, in turn, revolving in its orbit, has its path determined by quite a precise series of causes. The paths may cross in such a way that the meteor collides with Earth. But the actual collision itself is a chance event, that is, an event determined by a series of causes external to itself. Again, a moth out looking for food and a bat out looking for food may happen to meet. Should they do so, the encounter is at the moth's peril, for moths are food to bats. The moth looking for food and the bat looking for food are two independent and intrinsically determined causal lines. But their intersection, turning this individual moth into food for this individual bat, was not something predetermined within either line. The intersection is a chance event, a matter of bad luck for the moth and good luck for the bat.

---

33 Pittendrigh 1958.

The chance event, thus, is neither unintelligible nor "uncaused" within the context of the interaction of substances, yet it has no *proper* cause, no intelligibility of its own except, as it were, externally, in relation to independent causal lines. Each of these independent lines of causality is intrinsically intelligible apart from the other and from the chance event; and they must intersect in order for the chance event to occur. The chance event thus is not uncaused, but it is caused only indirectly. Lying at and arising precisely from the intersection, the chance event lacks an intrinsic determinism; but it is nonetheless determined by the overall pattern of substantial interactions which make up the physical world.

Neither Monism Nor Dualism but "Trialism": The Triad of Act, Potency, and Privation (What is, What Could Be, and What Should Be Different)
Besides his elaboration of the notion of causality and his corollary explanation of chance, Aristotle also clarified the question of the number of factors or principles necessary to explain change as novelty in the universe. "Constrained as it were by the truth itself",[34] Aristotle noted that his predecessors who acknowledged change had appealed to contraries, that is to say, opposites, in their attempts to explain change. For example, a body passes from cold to hot, wet to dry, young to old, and so forth, all conditions or states which are mutually exclusive: a thing cannot be at one and the same time both wet and dry under the same aspect. Change always involves contraries, and contraries are conditions or states or characteristics which exclude one another, which come to be only by making the other cease to be. When a change occurs, something becomes what it was not, and what it was not it now is: it is no longer possible to avoid Parmenides.

Aristotle distinguishes *principles* from *causes*: a thing depends in its being on causes, but change proceeds from principles without a dependency in being. A thing depends in being on what it is, not on what it isn't; but what the thing isn't is presupposed for the possibility of the thing becoming other than what it now is. Principles constitute the intelligible framework or conditions of change; the actual factors productive thereof are causes. Thus, every cause is a principle as well, but not every principle is an actual cause. Contraries are the principles of change, for example, but only one of them is a cause in a given case. For "A" which has the property "C" of being healthy to become instead sick, the one condition or property "B" of sickness must displace the other. "A" must be lacking a state "C" in order to *change* to that state, but "A" does not depend in its being on what it lacks (otherwise it would not be).[35] What a being has or is, is a positive condition. What it has not or lacks is a negative condition, a condition of privation. This negative condition, however, is not a simple absence or lack. It is *the conditionally called for that could*

---

34 Aristotle c.348–7bBC: *Physics* I, 188b30.
35 Ibid.: 192a4: "Now we distinguish matter and privation, and hold that one of these, namely the matter, accidentally is not, while the privation in its own nature is not; and that the matter is nearly, in a sense, is, substance, while the privation in no sense is."

be but isn't yet, or isn't now. When we examine or analyze what is required for change to be possible, therefore, "we find in every case something that underlies from which proceeds that which comes to be".[36]

At this point Aristotle's famous distinction between potency and act must be introduced: a thing is not actually what it is potentially. The absence of a form is the privation which change presupposes. The way it actually now is, is the other contrary. And the thing itself actually now (a human being, say) what it could be otherwise (food, say, being digested in the belly of a lion) is the underlying third. The situation proceeds as follows.

A given individual with all of its characteristics exists in and through a constant interaction with its physical surroundings, the environment. In order to be an individual of a certain kind, as we have seen, there is present in act a substantial form giving unity and being to the individual, making it to be the *kind* of thing that it is. But, equiprimordially, there are present a whole series of accidental forms which at once typify and individualize the substance – make it this particular *individual* of that kind – insofar as it actually exists as part of the environment or "cosmos". Just as the essence of the individual is the substantial form or act correlated with the primary matter or potency which renders the individual liable to being replaced in being by other kinds of things, so this "composition" of potency and act is *itself* a potential whole respecting the actual individuating characteristics determined in turn by the environmental interactions through and on the basis of which the substance in question actually exists as a concrete particular occupying this space and time – not an abstract composite of flesh and bone but a concrete particular of *this* flesh and *these* bones. "Form" here, in both dimensions (the dimension of the substance as a kind of thing and the dimension of that same substance as an individual of that kind) is not a static Platonic introjection or participation of something in itself eternal and unchanging, remember, but is simply the actuality *correlated with* and *sustained on the basis of* the material dispositions which make the particular form and combinations of form possible here and now. Potentiality is not simply presupposed by act, it is that from which the act is educed and correlative with which the act is able to sustain itself (in the case of substantial form) or be sustained (in the case of accidental forms).

Now the dispositions of matter – the concrete potentialities of and within a given individual – are, taken collectively, as we will shortly say, "transcendentally relative", that is, both sustained and modified in and by the interaction which the individual sustains with its physical surroundings, an interaction which is constant. There is no moment of existence outside this interaction, and no moment of existence in which the material dispositions of the individual are not modified slightly or more than slightly by the forces acting upon it as an individual within the universe. But each change in bodily disposition, slight or extreme, produces a correlated change

---

36 Ibid.: 190b2.

in the complex of forms constituting the individual's actual being. That is to say, each change in bodily condition creates a disposition toward a complex of forms different from the actually constitutive complex prior to the change in disposition. As material dispositions incline the substance toward an actuality other than what it currently is, they create in that substance on its potential side, as the scholastics liked to say, an "appetite" or inclination for the substance to become other. Thus, in the course of bodily changes, an individual matures, ages, and, at the extreme of altered bodily dispositions, dies. The bodily changes essential to the maturation, say, are yet "accidental" in the sense that the individual survives throughout their series; but the series as a whole eventually combines with yet other environmentally induced "accidental" changes to so dispose the body that it eventually can no longer sustain even its present substantial form. The "appetite for form" in this extreme leads to the individual's replacement by yet other substances, which is what we call "death".

The mere absence of a form is not a privation. Blindness in a stone is not a privation. Such mere absence of a form not appropriate to the dispositions of the material complex in question is said to be a *negation*, a mere absence, not a privation. A *privation*, by contrast, is the absence of a form normally called for by the dispositions of matter proper to the type of individual. Thus blindness in a mature mammal is a privation, not a mere negation. But what is a negation under one set of circumstances can become a privation under another set of circumstances. Thus, as changes are introduced into the body through environmental interactions, the body is correspondingly inclined to the eduction and sustenance of new forms, new modes of actuality; and this inclination, insofar as it is resisted by other circumstances and dispositions, that is to say, insofar as it is in any measure unsatisfied, gives rise to a *privation* respecting what the disposed individual for the moment is not. Thus matter and form make the individual what it here and now is; but privation is required for what now is to become, through and as a consequence of new dispositions introduced into the material substance by environmental interaction, otherwise – whether substantially or accidentally or both. Thus the intrinsic *causes* of change are matter and form, but they are effective as causes only in combination with *extrinsic* causes bringing about new dispositions respecting which the individual is momentarily *deprived* of the correspondingly appropriate combinations of actuality, and the move to satisfy that deprivation is what constitutes the change – unceasing, as we have seen, just as the dependence of the individual on supporting physical surroundings is unceasing. The *causes* of change, thus, are manifold, and vary with the case; but the *principles* of change are always three: matter, form, and privation.

Causes may be indefinitely many, but principles are and need only be three. Empedocles failed to distinguish between causes and principles, and so posited an infinite number, rendering the world practically unknowable. Others of the early physicists posited too few principles. Neither monism nor dualism will do for an adequate philosophy of nature; the factors involved in a changing world of "mind-independent" or "physical" being are always and irreducibly three.[37] This is a truth that, as we will see, shall have to be discovered all over again when attention turns, at the end of the Latin Age and at the outset of Postmodern times, from the action of things in the physical environment to the action of signs in the environment of knowledge and culture, from the medieval universe of being and the modern universe of discourse considered separately to the two universes considered in their interpenetration.

Time and Space

Since Einstein, the treatment of time and space as a continuum has become a commonplace, if not a particularly well-understood one. It has to come as a surprise to the new student of Aristotle to learn that time and space for Aristotle exist in nature only fundamentally. Formally and actually time and space exist as the action of thought completes nature by creating in memory a series or network of relations which constitute the experience of time and space. Thus the "continuum of space and time" belongs neither to the order of being as it exists independently of the human mind nor to the order of what exists only as a consequence of human thinking, but exists rather objectively as one of the most intimate comminglings of mind and nature in the constitution of experience.

Let us begin with time, that ever mysterious "entity" in which we live out our lives. What is time? How does time exist? According to Aristotle, apart from any finite mind, there is in nature only motion and change and the finite endurance of individuals sustained by their various interactions, as we will shortly consider in more detail. Enter mind or consciousness. Now some object changes its position or "moves in space", and the mind remembers where the local motion began, sees the course of the movement, and notes where it terminates: the rabbit, for example, came out of that hole and ran behind that tree, where it is "now" hidden. The motion was not a "thing"; the rabbit is the "thing". The motion exists nowhere apart from the rabbit's actions – nowhere, that is, except in the memory of the perceiver which preserves as a continuous whole the transitory movement of the rabbit from its hole (the "before") to the tree (the "after").

Moreover, not all movements in nature are sudden, like a rabbit's dart. Many basic natural motions are regular and cyclical, like the rising and setting of the sun, the phases of the moon, the four seasons. By taking some such cycle, say, the passage from day to night and back, holding it in memory as a whole, and dividing it conveniently into segments, such as hours, minutes, and seconds, the mind takes what exists independently of the mind fundamentally, namely, movement, completes that existence by preserving in memory the "before" and "after" to constitute the interval "between" which the motion can now be said to have occurred, and, *voila!*, time. Thus time exists as the mind's completion of what occurs in nature only

---

37 See the discussion in the *Physics* I, 189a11ff.

as motion; but through this completion the mind provides for itself a frame of reference within which the duration of any particular thing can be measured. By referring erratic motions to regular motions, the "time" of the erratic motion can be determined. The mind-independent regularity selected by the mind for the purpose of the basic reference and preserved and divided in memory by a series of mind-dependent relations becomes both clock and time in the writings of Aristotle, whence his classic definition, preserved and well-understood by the Latins, yet as valid today as relativity theory: *time is the measure of motion according to before and after.*

And what about space? It, too, has a fundamental existence in the mind-independent aspects of the natural world, but acquires a formal and actual existence only through the activity of the mind in dividing up objectively, through a series of mind-dependent relations, the physical environment that is divided up according to physical differences among things through a series of mind-independent relations. Thus, the lion is really distinct from the pillar it is near, but "where" is it? To "the right" or "to the left" of the pillar. It is really "beside" the pillar (mind-independent relation), but whether this "really" is "to the right" or "to the left" depends on the orientation of the observer. Thus "being next to the pillar" may be a real relation, a physical feature of the environment. But "being to the right of the pillar" is a mind-dependent relation enabling us to orient ourselves with respect to mind-independent lions and pillars.[38]

Thus space, like time, exists "completively" (*completive*), through the activity of the mind preserving in consciousness relative positions in order to constitute for itself a "frame of reference" within which its actions and contemplations become oriented. Neither time nor space are purely mind-independent (though they are fundamentally physical) nor purely mind-dependent (though they are formally and actually constituted by mind-dependent relations): they are in fact an *objective mixture* of mind-dependent and mind-independent being necessary for the mind to know "where" and "when" things happen in the environment. Space is fundamentally "that which surrounds" any given body, but organized formally through mind-dependent relations; time is fundamentally the motions and changes of bodies in space, but completed by the mind through memory and organized formally through mind-dependent relations referring the irregular to the regular for purposes of measurement and orientation in duration.

Space and time, we will shortly see, thus enter into Aristotle's scheme of categories for discourse about mind-independent being as the categories, respectively, of "where" and "when". Newton did no better, and a little worse, by confusing the memorative work of the mind, which makes possible temporal measurement and spatial orientation alike, with what exists independently of the mind or "absolute"

---

38 In his doctrine of space, we should note, Aristotle subscribed under the term "plenum" to a notion of what Peirce termed rather "synechism" – a notion of continuity in nature, that there is no such thing as truly "empty" space, but only intervals devoid of some particular variety or other of material being and energy.

being. Einstein did about as well in realizing that time and space depend for their formal actuality on relations constituted by the mind on the basis of motions and positions of bodies independent of the mind. But what are we to make of those various and multiple "individual" things that move and interact to make up the physical environment?

Transcendental Relativity: Substance and Inherent Accidents

Here is Aristotle's answer, finally, to Parmenides. When we say that what is, is what it is, we need to understand that it is what it is not only actually but at the same time potentially. Things are *both* what they are now *and* what they could be under other circumstances. And, since circumstances are always changing, so is being. In the Latin Age, account would be taken of this fact by saying that the individual exists relative to its environment, and this ordering or "*transcendental relativity*" is part and parcel with the individual's being.

Aristotle's technical term for the individual being or existent was *substance*. Individuals, or substances, he pointed out, are involved in change at two levels. Sometimes there is change **of** individuals, and sometimes there is change of **individuals**. That is to say, sometimes the individual, while continuing to exist, undergoes changes; and other times the individual is destroyed by the changes it undergoes. When the individual survives whatever changes it undergoes, we are speaking of what Aristotle called *accidental* change. When the individual does not survive the changes it undergoes but is displaced by entirely new individuals (as when a man dies and the body immediately begins to be a mass of corrupting tissue), we are speaking of what Aristotle called *substantial* changes.

In every individual, there is not only the possibility of being otherwise in this or that particular, there is also the radical possibility of not being at all, of yielding up its stuff to the disposition of the universe in the maintenance of other beings. To potentiality in general Aristotle gave the name *matter*. To the potentiality of the individual to change in this or that particular Aristotle gave the name *secondary matter*; while to the radical potentiality of the individual to not be he gave the name of *primary* or *prime matter*.

Similarly, every individual is actually some kind of thing as opposed to another, a "member of a species", if you like. And every individual, however different it may be potentially, is actually some definite way here and now. To actuality in general Aristotle gave the name *form*. To the actuality of the individual according to type or kind he gave the name *substantial form*. To the actual characteristics and traits the individual has here and now he gave the name *accidental form*.

When the individual undergoes change, the subject of the change is the secondary matter of the individual. But when the individual itself ceases to be, the subject of the change is the primary matter, which now takes on some other substantial form(s). Hence the saying of the Latin scholastics: *corruptio unius est generatio alterius*, "the corruption of one thing is the generation of another". Substantial change takes place in the instant, while accidental change takes place in time.

The Categories of Aristotle

From this analysis Aristotle drew up his famous list of categories, by which he intended an enumeration of the various ways in which anything could be said to be. Something could be said to be in itself as a distinct individual in a species, in which case it falls into the category of SUBSTANCE. Or we could speak rather not of the individual but of that which belongs to the individual, in which case that of which we speak falls into the category of ACCIDENT, and this in a variety of ways. What we are speaking of may be an inherent characteristic or feature consequent upon its matter, in which case we are speaking of its *quantity*. Or we may be speaking of an inherent characteristic consequent upon form, in which case we are speaking of some *quality*. Or again we may be speaking of what belongs to an individual only with reference to something or someone else, in which case we are speaking of a substance in terms of its interactions with its environment or of the peculiar consequences of characteristics and interactions according to which a substance develops links to what it itself is not, namely, its surroundings. These links are strictly over and above the individualities linked, *intersubjective* when both sides linked exist as such in nature, but always at least *suprasubjective* in the being proper to them as such. Thus, we are talking about connections between individuals and their surroundings which reduce neither to the characteristics on which the connections are based nor to the environmental aspects at which the connections terminate. We are talking, in short, about whatever falls within the category of what Aristotle came to call *relation*.

The Category of Relation

Plato had no developed doctrine of relation; but there is every reason to think that he had a very clear grasp of the difference between intrinsic characteristics of a being, *esse in*, and relation as such, *esse ad*. If we grant Cavarnos's claim[39] that "for Plato a relation is always a peculiar characteristic: one which a thing has 'towards' another", then we may well suspect, from the number of passages in which the point comes up, that Aristotle was set to thinking about the matter from his studies with Plato.

Be that as it may, when Aristotle set about to thematize the point, that is to say, when he undertook to develop, explicitly and thematically, a doctrine of relations wherein would appear focally this unique feature of relation in an ontological scheme, some measure of the distance between Plato and Aristotle as systematic philosophers may be gathered from the extent of the difficulty that Aristotle had to overcome in order to establish something like the proper contour of this category of relation. The details of his difficulty acquire considerable importance for the Latin Age, as will appear when we there resume the difficulty.[40] We will see that, indeed, not until late in the Latin Age was clarity on the matter fully reached.[41]

---

39 Cavarnos 1975: 19; but see the whole discussion of Plato's texts, pp. 13–38.
40 See chapter 6, p. 227ff.
41 See chapter 9, p. 423 to end of chapter.

For the present context, it is enough to summarize the doctrine essential to the idea of relation as belonging to a category of its own. That doctrine may be briefly stated.

In common with all other accidents, relations require a subject, a physical individual – that is to say, a substance – to which they belong. But whereas the other accidents simply belong to that subject according to their subjective rationale (as size, shape, etc.), relations refer the subject in which they are based through a subjective rationale to yet some other subject, called the terminus of the relation.

Thus, two things can be "similar" or "the same" or "different" in shape or size, for example. Each of the two has its own shape, each has its own size. Neither the shape nor the size is a relation, and both the shape and the size are in the respective individuals. But the relations of similarity, sameness, or difference are only *founded on* what is *in* the related individuals. As such, the relations themselves are *over and above*, even though dependent upon, the subjective characteristics through or on the basis of which the two individuals are related. If, of two similar things, one is destroyed, the physical similarity ceases, even though the shape and the size of the one of the two not destroyed is unaffected by the destruction. For the one thing to have a size and shape it need only exist; but for that same thing to be similar or different respecting another, there must be another. Hence the relation properly speaking lies in the respect, not in the subjective characteristic which founds the respect when the environmental circumstances allow it.

When it is said that the basic categorial division for Aristotle is the distinction between SUBSTANCE and ACCIDENT, we may note, the assertion is 100 per cent accurate and, as the subsequent history of Aristotelianism Greek, Arabic, and Latin would prove, at least 50 per cent misleading. For, as we will shortly see, fully half of Aristotle's list of ten categories depend upon relation in its difference from those accidents which directly characterize or modify the substantial being of natural individuals. In this sense, the correct understanding of relation in its proper being as "over and above" the beings it relates may be said to be the principal key to understanding the Aristotelian categorial scheme as a whole.

Nonetheless, the differential status of relation among the accidents may be indicated even following the basic traditional division of (categorial) being into what exists "in itself" (*in se*) and what exists only "in another" (*in alio*), provided that we understand that to exist "in another" may be understood indirectly as well as directly (a fact conveniently illustrated through the Latin term "*in*" insofar as this term may be translated in the sense of "within", which is the direct sense of "dependence on another", or in the sense of "on the basis of", which is the indirect sense of "dependence on another"), as shown on the opposite page.

The Basic Categorial Scheme and Its Details
Not only the category of relation in particular, but the whole scheme of the categories in general was subjected to considerable analysis among the Latins. It came to be realized that fully half the categories in Aristotle's full list of ten – posture, where

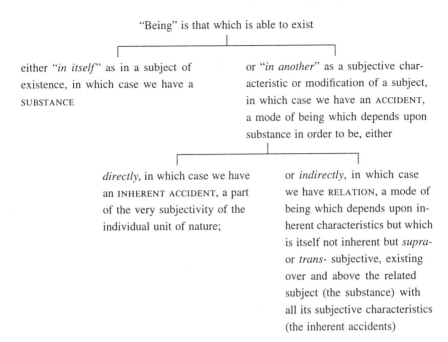

"Being" is that which is able to exist

either *"in itself"* as in a subject of existence, in which case we have a SUBSTANCE

or *"in another"* as a subjective characteristic or modification of a subject, in which case we have an ACCIDENT, a mode of being which depends upon substance in order to be, either

directly, in which case we have an INHERENT ACCIDENT, a part of the very subjectivity of the individual unit of nature;

or *indirectly*, in which case we have RELATION, a mode of being which depends upon inherent characteristics but which is itself not inherent but *supra-* or *trans-* subjective, existing over and above the related subject (the substance) with all its subjective characteristics (the inherent accidents)

"Being in Itself" versus the Two Senses of "Being in Another"

(location), when, and vestition (or external attachments) – were themselves varieties of the category of relation; while two more – action and passion (or undergoing an action) – considered substance in terms of (that is to say, relative to) its interactions and surrounding circumstances.[42]

Let us consider first the basics, then the details. A summary of the basis of the whole categorial scheme reduced to its bare and absolute essentials may be represented thus:

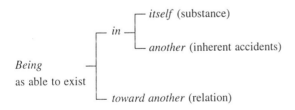

Being as able to exist

in
— *itself* (substance)
— *another* (inherent accidents)

— *toward another* (relation)

The Basic Scheme of the Categories of Aristotle:
"Esse In" ("Being In") vs. "Esse Ad" ("Being Toward")

---

42 This discussion gets highly technical, and it is not one we shall have occasion to take up in detail at any point. The interested reader can get a good sense of the discussion from Krempel 1952: chap. 20, p. 426ff., with plenty of technical leads to follow up on.

How, then, exactly, the nine categories of accident in counterpoint with the
one category of substance constitute a superstructure on this basic scheme may
briefly be described as follows. An individual may be considered in its proper
being as distinct from its surroundings insofar as it is able to exist in itself as
a unified center of characteristics, interactions, and relations, in which case we
are speaking of what falls in the category of *substance*. An individual may be
considered in itself according to the properties it has as a consequence of being
a material substance, in which case we are speaking of what falls in the category
of *quantity*. An individual may be considered again in itself but according to the
properties it has as a consequence of being a specific type of material substance,
that is, as a consequence of its form rather than its matter, in which case we are
speaking of what falls in the category of *quality*. An individual may be considered
as the origin of some behavior, in which case we are speaking of what falls in
the category of *action*. The individual may be considered as acted upon by some
other agent, in which case we are in the category of *passion*, that is suffering
or undergoing. (Thus action and passion are not the *relations* of cause and effect
but rather the foundations and terminations in subjectivity of those relations.) An
individual may be considered according to the way it positions itself (crouched,
upright, supine, etc.), in which case we have the category of *posture*. An individual may be considered according to its relation to surrounding bodies in the
environment, in which case we have the category of *where* or location. An individual may be considered in its relation to preceding events or individuals, in
which case we are concerned with the category of *when*. Or an individual may
be considered in terms of accoutrements it assumes for protection, decoration, or
whatever purpose, in which case we are speaking of what belongs to the category
of *vestition*.

The complete version of the "categorial scheme", then, may be set forth diagram-
matically (page opposite).

If we emphasize that the first five categories in this scheme enumerate what
separates the individual from its surroundings as a distinct individual, then we
are emphasizing the notion of *subjective being* or *subjectivity*. But if, instead, we
emphasize that it is only through interactions with its surroundings that the subjective
being or individuality of substance is able to maintain and develop itself, then we
are emphasizing the notion that subjective being even in its contrast with pure
relational being is nonetheless *transcendentally relative*, that is to say, is able to
exist and be understood only by the taking into account of what is other than itself.
The point of transcendental relativity is but further emphasized in the structure of
the categories of "vestition", "where", "posture", and "when"; and it is seen to
bear on substance itself as sustaining and originating the varieties of accident as
soon as we recall that the individual must be understood in terms of its compos-
itive principles, the agencies of its generation as well as of its sustenance, and,
as Aquinas in particular will argue centuries later in developing the doctrine of

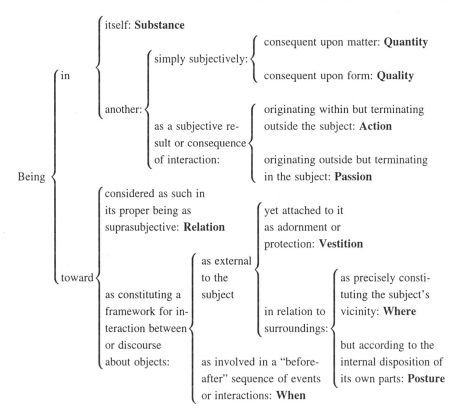

The Full Scheme of the Categories of Aristotle

creation,[43] in terms of the one-sided relation whereby all finite being depends upon God without God in turn having any dependency upon finite being.

General Purpose of the Scheme of Categories

Categorial schemes play an important role in the historical development of philosophical understanding, and therefore it is of the utmost importance to have a clear understanding of the purpose of Aristotle's scheme. It was the capstone, or finishing touch, in reply to Parmenides. Not content to note, in general, that being, that which is what it is, can be "said many ways", Aristotle goes on to enumerate specifically what those ways are. And the being he is talking about is precisely being as we find it in experience but as able to be apart from the experience through and in which we learn of it. The categories are the list of terms that can be predicated

---

43 See, in chapter 7 below, "The Reasoning of the Five Ways", p. 267ff; and the discussion of "Creationism vs. Evolutionism" in chapter 11, p. 506f.

"univocally" – that is, with a single sense – of features of the physical environment as such.

How Mathematics Applies to the Physical Environment

His doctrine of categories provides Aristotle with a way to explain the applicability of mathematics to physical objects without having to accept some version of a Pythagorean-Platonic doctrine that the intelligible objects of mathematics belong as such to the mind-independent order of physical being. As we have seen, material substances are complexes or "composites" of a variety and various levels of potentialities and actualities, in which the most fundamental level is the level of primary matter and substantial form. Now the accident of quantity follows immediately upon informed matter. Quantity is "the first accident of a material substance", as the medieval Aristotelians put it, and thus provides the mediating basis for all the other accidents, or characteristics, which accrue to material substances. The sensible environment, the physical world as we directly experience it, is precisely an interacting complex of such quantified individuals, material substances, individuals that occupy space. And the reason that the various components of the physical environment occupy space is that they have material dimensions or quantity, parts outside of parts.

Abstraction

One of the meanings of "abstraction"[44] is to focus on or consider one aspect of an object while leaving other aspects out of the consideration. This is exactly what the mind does, according to Aristotle, in constituting the objects of mathematics:[45] it considers the idea of a material substance as having dimensions in the abstract sense just defined – parts outside of parts, thus requiring an "occupation of space". Aristotle calls substance so abstracted "intelligible quantity", and considers it to provide the basis for mathematical investigations. Intelligible quantity can be considered under the aspect of its continuity or under the aspect of being divisible. As continuous it provides the basis for geometry; as discrete – divided by the mind into noncontinuous parts – it provides the basis for arithmetic. All further developments of mathematics stem from these two.

De-Fanging the Paradoxes of Zeno of Elea

The doctrine of quantity as the first accident of material substance, abstractable and

---

44 On the three general senses of this term that would develop among the Latins, see chapter 8, p. 380 below.

45 On this precise point, Peirce has a terminological suggestion that the term "presciss" be used to indicate that aspect of abstraction which focuses, for analytical purposes, on one or another aspect of objectivity, and that the term "abstraction" be reserved to designate the precise process of constituting the object of mathematics. I will largely adopt this suggestion, in passing, over the course of this work, as I did in *The Human Use of Signs* (Deely 1994). See, in chapter 7, the terminological note 125 on page 310.

divisible in thought, also provides Aristotle with an answer to Zeno's paradoxes.[46] The distance between any two points is potentially divisible in thought to infinity; but the distance itself is nonetheless finite and is not actually and physically so divided. Hence it is not physically impossible for Achilles to overtake the tortoise. It is only a question of a finite individual traversing a physically finite interval at a greater velocity than the other individual, and the fact that the mind can divide and subdivide this interval without limit does not affect the actual physical factors of the situation, which are mind-independent.

Physics, as the philosophical analysis of nature, is bound above all to explain how change is possible, not to explain change away. What Aristotle provided in the books of his *Physics* was precisely that, an intelligible framework to make understandable our experience of a world of sensible individuals constantly changing.

Preparing the Way for Galileo and Darwin: Celestial Matter
One fly in the ointment of Aristotle's physical theory was the heavens. According to the best observations then available, supported by certain religious or theological notions current in the ancient world,[47] celestial bodies did not seem to change except in place. Change of place alone, we have seen, was the kind of change which Democritus and other earlier physicists had tried to use to explain the generation and corruption of individuals on earth – "the sphere below the moon", as the ancients and the medievals spoke of the region where generation and corruption were known to occur. The best astronomical theory of the day, much of it worked out in Plato's Academy, postulated a series of spheres revolving around the earth at the center, carrying the planets and stars in their rotations.

Since these spheres and the bodies they carried gave no evidence of generation or corruption or any other kind of quantitative or qualitative change, Aristotle with most of the other ancients felt compelled to draw a hard and fast distinction

---

46 See chapter 2, p. 40.
47 Aristotle c.355BC: *On the Heavens* I, 270b1: "The reasons why the primary body is eternal and not subject to increase or diminution, but unaging and unalterable and unmodified, will be clear from what has been said to any one who believes in our assumptions. Our theory seems to confirm the phenomena and to be confirmed by them. For all men have some conception of the nature of the gods, and all who believe in the existence of gods at all, whether barbarian or Greek, agree in allotting the highest place to the deity, surely because they suppose that immortal is linked with immortal and regard any other supposition as impossible. If then there is, as there certainly is, anything divine, what we have just said about the primary bodily substance was well said. The mere evidence of the senses is enough to convince us of this, at least with human certainty. For in the whole range of time past, so far as our inherited records reach, no change appears to have taken place either in the whole scheme of the outermost heaven or in any of its proper parts. The name, too, of that body seems to have been handed down right to our own day from our distant ancestors who conceived of it in the fashion which we have been expressing. The same ideas, one must believe, recur in men's minds not once or twice but again and again. And so, implying that the primary body is something else beyond earth, fire, air, and water, they gave the highest place the name of aether, derived from the fact that it 'runs always' [*aither*, from *aei thein*] for an eternity of time."

between celestial matter, which is subject only to change of place (local motion),
and terrestrial matter, which, besides being subject to local motion, is subject to
increase and decrease both quantitatively and qualitatively and to generation and
corruption as well. Benedict Ashley has nicely shown[48] that, in this matter, Aristotle
was empirical to the point of compromising the foundations of his speculative system
for explaining change. In the Latin Age, Aquinas and a few other voices tried to point
out that this distinction was hypothetical more than it was observational, because
the distance of the heavenly bodies and the rate at which they develop may be of
such a scale that all the varieties of earthly change occur there as well but without
our so far having been able to detect them.[49] But these were lonely voices, left out
of account in the late Latin–early modern astronomical theories which made of the
Aristotelian hypothesis a dogma that prepared the way for the catastrophe of Galileo
at the hands of the Roman Inquisition. That is another story, but it is far from the
only one that later chapters will have to tell.

For the immutable celestial spheres were also what explained for Aristotle and
for the medievals why like can only beget like within a species population in the
normal course of things.[50] Since the spheres transmit to the earth their influences,
and these influences are unchanging, the changes in the sphere below the moon
too must follow a regular pattern. Whereas an environment changing sufficiently
radically would necessitate evolution for some and extinction for others, engendering
a process in which chance events would play perforce a crucial role, an unchanging
environment, by contrast, precludes any evolution of species and pushes chance
events to the margin of life's cycles.

This is sound biological doctrine by the most contemporary standards. But when,
in the seventeenth century, it was finally discovered that the celestial spheres did
not exist, and that the heavenly bodies were in principle of the same type as earthly
bodies, the distinction between celestial and terrestrial matter became untenable,
and with it the doctrine of the fixity of species. But by then, habits of thought were
so ingrained that many philosophers clung to the fixity of species with not so much
as a thought given to the fact that the main environmental support of the doctrine
had been proven a fiction. Of this story, too, we will see more in the course of
philosophy's history.

For the present, we need to mention one other factor important in Aristotle's
theory in ways that were quite at variance with the role it came to play in the later
debates over evolution: the Aristotelian doctrine of essence. As far as natural philosophy goes, this doctrine is of a piece with the Aristotelian doctrine of substantial
form. That is to say, "essence", as that which makes a being to be the kind of thing
that it is, is nothing other than the internal formal unity which makes the individual
to endure in time through all the series of "accidental changes" it undergoes from the

---

48 Ashley, "Change and Process" (1973).
49 See chapter 7, p. 263ff below; but esp. Aquinas c.1272/3: I.7 (cited in Deely 1973: 48).
50 See Thomas Litt, *Les Corps célestes dans l'univers de saint Thomas d'Aquin* (1963); Deely 1969.

moment of its generation to the moment of its demise or "corruption" (as Aristotle termed the terminating moment). To say that we "know essences", or are "able to know essences", in Aristotle's original scheme meant nothing more than that we can, through sufficiently careful and complete investigation, come to know the way things actually are in any given case.

But in the later Latin Age, this idea was developed in terms of an elaborate psychological theory of the process of abstraction. The mind was conceived, according to this theory, as disengaging from its matter the form itself *of the thing*, which was then held in its purity in thought ("form without matter", i.e., considered apart or abstracted from the material individual), the veritable "essence" according to which the thing was what it was. In the process of the elaboration of this theory over many generations and through many writers, the unchanging species of Aristotle's biology became a logical construct as well as (or instead of) a biological one. "Essences" became "unchanging" in quite a new, not wholly legitimate,[51] sense, as thinkers became accustomed to confusing logically constructed "essences" or ideal types with the substantial forms actually operative in nature. It became customary to project "what we know" back on to nature as "what essentially is".[52] This too was a major factor which prepared the way for the nineteenth-century discovery of evolution to be a disaster for philosophical tradition, one at least as unnecessary and counterproductive as was the trial of Galileo. But we must not get too far ahead of the story.

Organizing the Sciences

Along with his physical theory Aristotle was one of the first to try to provide an overall scheme for the organization of human knowledge in general. He did so by distinguishing human knowledge in terms of the type of object with which it was concerned. His first and most fundamental distinction was between *theoretical* and *practical* knowledge.

Understanding the Distinction between Speculative and Practical Knowledge

Theoretical knowledge, or "speculative thought", has for its object things which are what they are independently of human thought and action (or which will be what they will be when all human intervention is removed). Practical knowledge, or "practical thought", in sharp contrast, has for its object precisely those things which would not be *except for* human thought or action, things precisely as *under our control.*

Theoretical understanding, of course, may be applied to human affairs ("The speculative intellect becomes practical by extension", Aquinas would say). But the

---

51 See in chapter 14, p. 652, "Relations and the Knowledge of Essence", a discussion of what constitutes knowledge of essences.
52 This is still both relatively unknown and largely neglected territory in the history of philosophy, but an easy access to the flavor of the tale is the recent essay by Professor Coombs (1996) on "Modal Voluntarism in Descartes' Jesuit Predecessors".

distinction between theoretical and practical knowledge does not depend on our intention in acquiring the knowledge. It depends wholly on the type of object about which we have an understanding. What we *do* with knowledge of whatever type is up to us. But what *type* the knowledge belongs to is up to the object. For example, we can synthesize in the laboratory substances which do not exist in nature. This does not make substance in Aristotle's sense an object of practical knowledge. For whether a substance be made by art or by nature, that any substance involves matter, form, and privation, remains true as a conclusion of speculative knowledge.

And speculative knowledge does not only involve physics. The objects of mathematics provide yet another instance of speculative knowledge. The theorems of geometry or the equations of arithmetic, trigonometry, and calculus are true by reason of the objects with which they are concerned, not by reason of the intentions of the mathematician in working them out. An engineer may apply the speculative knowledge of geometry to the building of a bridge, but that does not make the knowledge he applies *practical*. What is *practical* is the bridge he builds and the applications he makes of geometry, but the geometrical knowledge itself, by reason of its object (as distinct from the engineer's objective), is theoretical.

Finally there is the branch of theoretical knowledge Aristotle himself called "first philosophy" or "theology", depending on his point of view at the time, but which later philosophers, especially in moderns times, have called rather *metaphysics*. It is an interesting tale.

"Metaphysics" by Any Other Name ...

Like all ancient manuscripts, the works of Aristotle were particularly subject to the vicissitudes of history. In the course of time, much was lost. The catalogue of Aristotle's works as we have it today seems to have been principally the work of Andronicus of Rhodes (c.100–25BC).[53] In organizing the writings at his disposal, he found certain works which dealt precisely with concepts which, while developed in Aristotle's physics, applied to considerations of substance which did not have material bodies, such as, notably, God, but also the Separated Intelligences or pure spirits which Aristotle had thought necessary to explain the revolution of the celestial spheres. Some notions developed in physics which seemed to apply to beings regardless of whether they were corporeal or incorporeal were certain aspects of the notions of causality, the notion of substance itself, the notion of essence as identical with form, and the most general notions of potentiality and actuality.

Andronicus grouped the writings concerned with such notions under a heading of his own devising, *Meta ta physica*, or *Metaphysics* – the works that come after the physics.

---

53 For something like the full story, see Laughlin 1995.

Aristotle's best student and immediate heir at age fifty to the Lyceum, Theophrastus[54] of Lesbos (372–287BC), had suggested that the master's works be studied according to the pattern of moving from the more to the less easily known. Indeed, Aristotle himself considered the proof of a "First" or "Unmoved" Mover (that is, of a purely actual intellectual being separate from the whole universe of matter and motion) to be a culminating consideration of his *Physics*; and he called the consideration of this "most divine being" *Theology* ("Discourse about God").

But Aristotle also considered reflection upon and systematization of the most general concepts discovered in physics but not restrictable to material objects to be the very work of giving foundation to philosophy as a whole, and this enterprise he called *First Philosophy*.

It was the writings that belonged to these two different considerations of Aristotle that Andronicus of Rhodes, from yet a third point of view, neither that of Theophrastus nor that of Aristotle, but that of an editor trying to arrange manuscripts in a suitable logical order, bundled or grouped together under the designation that was destined to stick, *Metaphysics*.

The "Unmoved Mover": Summit of Being in Aristotle's Speculative Scheme

Aristotle, unlike, for example, the later Neoplatonists,[55] but more like Plato, seems not to have placed much credence in what we call in retrospect the gods of paganism. His own conception of God was as a rather cold and removed being – cold, in that he (or It) was a completely self-absorbed activity of thinking; removed, in that this Self-Thinking Thought had no awareness of playing a part in the outside universe the Greeks called the cosmos. This "God" was the object of desire of the Separated Intelligences. We must also wonder if envy was not the best name for this desire; but in any event, the "love that moved the sun and other stars" as Dante immortalized it was nothing else than this desire of the Separated Intelligences to be as like to the Unmoved Mover as possible, out of which longing arose the eternal movement in perfect circles of the celestial spheres which, in turn, governed all comings-to-be and passings-away ("generations" and "corruptions") in the sphere below the moon.

Thus, note already that the "first" or "unmoved" mover hit upon toward the close of the books of the *Physics* is not at all an efficient cause of anything in the cosmos. He or It is not an agent acting upon anything outside his own Thought or Thinking, not even aware of anything outside. He "moves" the cosmos by the longing he engenders in the highest beings within that cosmos. These "highest beings" are, by comparison, finite; but we find in Aristotle no explicit notion of God as Infinite Being other than being unlimited from within by any potentiality, even though Aquinas and others later will see such a notion to be a consequent implicit

---

54 This name, meaning "one who speaks like a god", was given by Aristotle, and took so well that Theophrastus' original name is forgotten.
55 See the remarks from Gibbon 1788: 282–3, cited p. 143 below.

in the demonstration of "mover itself unmoved" with which the *Physics* of Aristotle concludes. Nonetheless, for Aristotle himself, the Unmoved Mover moves others not by any initiative from himself to the series of moved and moving movers, but by a longing arising within the highest beings involved in the cosmic series.

Outside the series entirely, he does not participate in it directly at all, but only indirectly through the longing of Separated Intelligences to be likewise perfect in autonomy, but imparting to the spheres and all within and below the spheres motion through their failure to achieve anything more than the shadow of such a perfection in the eternal return of each sphere upon itself in the cycles we experience as successions of day and night.

This God is, as Unmoved Mover, co-eternal with the cosmos. That is all. The First Cause is not "first" as initiating a series in which something else is "second". He – or It – is outside and apart from the series entirely. Only moved movers form a series; and that series, being eternal, has no first and no last. God is not so much a substance as the realization of the ideal of substance: a being able to exist in itself. All other substances exist in themselves, as we saw, only by interacting with other substances, and as long as they successfully sustain such interactions. Hence all other substances are, as the Latins will later put it, "transcendentally relative", that is, expressive even in their independent being of the environment surrounding them, which gives to their "independence" an indispensable context.

But the "substance" of the Unmoved Mover knows no such context. He alone is not a transcendental relative, a relative absolute being, but the one and only absolute being that is absolutely absolute.

Awareness of the existence of the Unmoved Mover is the highest achievement and moment of human consciousness. In achieving this awareness, the human intelligence mirrors in a feeble way the awareness of the Separated Intelligences who pass their whole existence in awareness of and futile longing to be like the Unmoved Mover. But there is no reciprocal moment in the awareness of the Unmoved Mover.

We will see in some detail how this notion of the Unmoved Mover is radically transformed in the conceptions developed by medieval Latin physics and metaphysics, and the crucial contribution Plotinus will make[56] to the development. But here it is enough to indicate that, with this notion of the Unmoved Mover, beyond and over against all movers caught up in the cosmic mechanism, we reach the summit of being in ancient Aristotelian speculative philosophy.

Practical Science

As to the other principal branch of Aristotle's tree of knowledge, what he called *practical thought*, the affairs which depend upon human initiative for their being divide into two main types: those which exist only within and as long as the very process by which they are made, and those which, as products of a humanly initiated

---

56 See "Toward the Idea of a Creative Source of Being" in chapter 4 below, p. 128.

process of production, survive as products after the process of bringing them into being has ceased. To evanescent products of the former sort, inseparable in their being from the very process through which they exist, he assigned the name *Ethics*. For example, justice, he thought, is a way of treating our fellow human beings. Justice and injustice exist in the treatment, not before or after, even though the *effects* of the treatment may endure in the attitudes and memory of the persons affected. To enduring products of the latter sort, those which survive as material embodiments of the activity through which they are brought into being, Aristotle assigned the general name of *Art*.

Subdivisions of Speculative and Practical Thinking
Both ethics and art admit of subdivisions, just as do physics, mathematics, and metaphysics. Physics, for example, subdivides into the study of the general principles of nature, study of the specific principles of living bodies, study of environmental phenomena or meteorology, study of extraterrestrial phenomena or astronomy, the study of subjective states of cognitive organisms or psychology,[57] and so on. Mathematics subdivides into arithmetic, geometry, calculus, etc. And metaphysics subdivides into ontology, epistemology,[58] etc.

Thus ethics, in Aristotle's view, was the study of human behavior according to how human nature can best flourish. He included under "ethics" the principles regulative of individual behavior, which is what we primarily mean by the term "ethics" today. But he also included under "ethics" the management of the family, which he called "economics", and the management of the state, which he called "politics". The development in our day of a study of "business ethics", thus, is a highly Aristotelian development. But he would have been critical of the way economics is studied today, and surely would have tried to remind politicians that they were called upon above all to implement in the public order the principles of moral philosophy.

The place of art in human life was large in Aristotle's scheme, for *art* in Aristotle's sense included not only pretty much of everything that we call "art" today, but a good deal more besides. Art in his sense extended to the whole realm of manufacture, architecture, and building of whatever type. It would not hurt the average factory

---

57 Our word "psychology" comes from Aristotle's term for soul (psyche), which, for Aristotle, was the substantial form or principle of living things, plants no less than animals. Thus psychology, in Aristotle's own context, was the study of all living forms, what we today have become accustomed to call rather "biology" since Lamarck (1744–1829) invented the term around the turn of the nineteenth century. The term "soul" has had a curious history since Aristotle. After Latin times especially, there has been a tendency to restrict its application to animal forms, or even exclusively to the human mind, as we shall see in the work of Descartes. But the next time you meet a vegetarian who tries to justify that dietary preference on the ground that we should not kill living beings, you might point out that plants have souls no less than animals and are therefore no less living! See the discussion of "medieval psychology" in chapter 7, p. 343, under the section on "Formal Object ...".
58 Sometimes called also "gnoseology"; but both these terms are of modern coinage.

hand or manager, for that matter, to consider that what they are involved in is – or should be – the creation of a work of art!

The Goal of Human Life

Moreover, even in Aristotle, there is a sense in which he thinks of ethics as a primarily individual affair. For the purpose of ethics is to guide the human being in reaching the goal of human life, which is happiness. But Aristotle's idea of happiness[59] is not easily distinguishable from Plato's ideal of the person "whose mind is fixed upon true being":

> The happy life is thought to be one of excellence. Now an excellent life requires exertion, and does not consist in amusement. And we say that serious things are better than laughable things and those connected with amusement, and that the activity of the better of any two things – whether it be two parts or two men – is the better; but the activity of the better is ipso facto superior and more of the nature of happiness. And any chance person – even a slave – can enjoy the bodily pleasures no less than the best man; but no one assigns to a slave a share in happiness – unless he assigns to him also a share in human life. For happiness does not lie in such occupations, but, as we have said before, in excellent activities.
>
> If happiness is activity in accordance with excellence, it is reasonable that it should be in accordance with the highest excellence; and this will be that of the best thing in us. Whether it be intellect or something else that is this element which is thought to be our natural ruler and guide and to take thought of things noble and divine, whether it be itself also divine or only the most divine element in us, the activity of this in accordance with its proper excellence will be complete happiness. That this activity is contemplative we have already said.
>
> Now this would seem to be in agreement both with what we said before and with the truth. For this activity is the best (since not only is intellect the best thing in us, but the objects of intellect are the best of knowable objects); and, secondly, it is the most continuous, since we can contemplate truth more continuously than we can do anything. And we think happiness has pleasure mingled with it, but the activity of wisdom is admittedly the pleasantest of excellent activities; at all events philosophy is thought to offer pleasures marvellous for their purity and their enduringness, ... and self-sufficiency ... must belong most to the contemplative activity. For while a wise man, as well as a just man and the rest, needs the necessaries of life, when they are sufficiently equipped with things of that sort the just man needs people towards whom and with whom he shall act justly, and the temperate man, the brave man, and each of the others is in the same case, but the wise man, even when by himself, can contemplate truth, and the better the wiser he is; he can perhaps do so better if he has fellow-workers, but still he is the most self-sufficient.

---

59 Aristotle c.335/4BC: *Nicomachean Ethics* X, 1177a2ff.

Though politics and business are part of Aristotelian ethics, therefore, the self-sufficiency of the individual, to the degree this is possible for the human being, achieved in the exercise of the highest faculty respecting its highest object, is the principal means by which the Stagirite[60] thinks that happiness can be achieved. He even reduced the point to a syllogism: "that which is proper to each thing is by nature best and most pleasant for each thing; for the human being, therefore, life according to intellect is best and pleasantest, since intellect more than anything else is the human being. This life therefore is also the happiest."[61]

Yet Aristotle had preceded this syllogism with some tantalizing remarks, of which much would be made in the Latin Age:

> Yet such a life would be too high for man; for it is not in so far as he is man that he will live so, but in so far as something divine is present in him, and by so much as this is superior to our composite nature is its activity superior to that which is the exercise of the other kinds of excellence. If intellect is divine, then, in comparison with man, the life according to it is divine in comparison with human life. But we must not follow those who advise us, being men, to think of human things, and, being mortal, of mortal things, but must, so far as we can, make ourselves immortal, and strain every nerve to live in accordance with the best thing in us; for even if it be small in bulk, much more does it in power and worth surpass everything. This would seem, too, to be each man himself, since it is the authoritative and better part of him.

The Instrument of All the Sciences

Finally, an extremely important development of Aristotle's thought, and one in which he seemed to take particular pride in being the first, was his work in what has come to be called *Logic*. Aristotle himself nowhere used this word. In fact, "logic" as a word seems to come to us rather from his competitors in the field, the Stoics, who, under the impetus provided by Zeno of Citium, c.336–243BC, missed by an historical eyelash being the founding fathers in this area (and provided, as we shall see, a main competition to the Aristotelian ideas on the division of the sciences that was to take centuries to resolve[62]). Aristotle himself spoke mainly of "Analytics", both pure ("Prior Analytics") and applied ("Posterior Analytics").

---

60 This appellation has been attached to Aristotle by reason of his birth in the Greek settlement of Stageirus in Thrace. Stageirus had been laid waste in the battles which had led to the conquest of Olynthus in 347BC by King Philip II of Macedon, father of a son who would become known to history as Alexander the Great. In 343BC Philip had hired Aristotle as Alexander's tutor, a role which he played for four years; but in 340BC Philip commissioned Aristotle to oversee a rebuilding and repopulation of Stageirus, and to provide the restored city with a set of laws. The city in turn commemorated its Aristotelian re-establishment by the declaration of an annual holiday. (Cf. Grote 1872: Vol. 1, 8.) It was common in ancient and medieval times for persons to be identified by their city of birth as a part of their name; but in the case of Aristotle, reference to him as "the Stagirite" had an exceptionally rich connotation.

61 Aristotle c.335/4BC: *Nicomachean Ethics* X, 1178a5.

62 See chapter 13 below, esp. p. 595ff.

This original development of logic came about as a consequence of Aristotle's realization that, regardless of the subject matter of his inquiry, in order to make progress and achieve any kind of clarity and order, there were certain principles he needed to apply. The study of these relatively context-independent principles is what has come to be called "logic", or the principles of organized investigation and presentation. To cover these principles, Aristotle wrote not one but a whole series of treatises over the thirty years between 360 and 330BC.

We will have occasion in the next chapter to look at these treatises in a little more detail,[63] but here we may describe them briefly. He wrote a treatise called *Categories*, dealing with the various fundamental types of terms, or *represigns*[64] (from "*signum + repraesentare*": "signs which represent without asserting"), that we *can use* to speak about "reality". He wrote a treatise *On Interpretation* (*Peri Hermeneias*), dealing with the specific type of interpretation peculiar to rational discourse, namely, the judgment expressible in a proposition or *dicisign* (from "sign + *dicere* or to say": "a sign which makes an assertion"). He wrote a treatise called the *Prior Analytics*, dealing with the form as such of sound reasoning, or validity – that is to say, the pattern according to which propositions are connected as premiss[65] to conclusion in an argument or *suadisign* (from "sign + *suadere* to recommend or advocate", "a sign which persuades, or gives a reason for what it

---

63 See "The Roots of Porphyry's Tree" in chapter 4, p. 144ff.
64 The traditional terminology for what are here named represigns, dicisigns, and suadisigns is simply "terms, propositions, and arguments". The rationale of the new terminology, largely derived from Peirce, is partially touched on below on p. 145; but for the technical details I refer the reader to Deely 1992b.
65 The reader may be immediately inclined to think this a misspelling of "premise", so let me establish from this first occurrence the usage that I will follow throughout this book, which has been influenced by Charles Peirce in the following way. "Premise" and "premiss" are, Peirce notes (1902a: CP 2.582), "two distinct words, recognized as such by older writers, but for the last century and more confounded. Premise is a legal word, derived from the French premise, ... Premiss is from the French noun premisse, and thence from the Low Latin praemissa, which goes back, as a substantive, to the early part of the thirteenth century. ... Propositio replaced it, when elegance was preferred to technical accuracy." Both words have come to be defined, in logic, as (ibid.) "[a] proposition, the consideration of which has logically affected, or contributed to the determination of, a conclusion of reasoning." However (1902a: CP 2.583), "the word 'premiss' became usual in the logical sense, in English, as early as Chaucer. In Wilson's [c.1525–81] *Rule of Reason* (1551) it does not occur, the phraseology there being like the following: 'The double repeate, whiche is a woorde rehearsed in bothe Proposicions, must not entre into the conclusion.' But in Blundeville's [fl.1561] *Arte of Logike* (1599) we read: 'A Syllogisme is a kinde of argument contayning three Propositions, whereof the two first, commonly called the premisses,' etc. In Watts's and other English logics it was spelt premiss and premisses. Johnson, however, in his *Dictionary*, gives premises in the plural and premiss in the singular, as distinct words, and remarks that the latter is little used in the plural outside of technical works. In such works the word spelt with two s's continued to be employed." Whence Peirce elsewhere concludes (c.1903: CP 2.253) that, "as to the word Premiss ... It is entirely contrary to good English usage to spell premiss, 'premise', and this spelling (whose prevalence is due perhaps to Lord Brougham, or at least chiefly supported by his insistence), simply betrays ignorance of the history of logic, and even of such standard authors as Whateley, Watts, etc."

asserts about what is represented"). He wrote a treatise called *Posterior Analytics*, concerning the relation of the form of reasoning to its content in determining truth about some event or occurrence in the world (more or less what we would today consider the province of "scientific method" and also "philosophy of science"). He wrote a treatise called *Topics*, concerned with the selection of sound opinions in the formation of public discourse and policies concerning matters in which certain knowledge (i.e., knowledge through proper causes) is not possible. And he wrote a tract on the false appearances of rational discourse, called *Sophistic Refutations*.

This group of writings covered the tools of rational discourse that Aristotle considered applicable to every investigation, regardless of subject matter. In medieval thought, study of the analytics came to be considered the proper introduction to philosophy as a whole, and it was in this sense, no doubt, that Andronicus of Rhodes placed these works first in his catalogue of Aristotle's writings. In the strict Aristotelian tradition, they were called not "logic" but the *Organon* or *Instrument of all rational discourse*.[66] It should be mentioned too that, in some ways more consistent than the Latin development of Aristotle's notion of Logic as the instrument common to *all* thought, it was the custom in the Arabic tradition of Aristotelian commentary to include the *Rhetoric* (composed c. 335/4BC) and the *Poetics* (c. 335/4BC) as part of the *Organon* itself. In Arabic tradition, rhetoric appears as the logic involved in practical knowledge and persuasion. Detailed study of this tradition[67] reveals that it has roots already in the sixth-century Greek school of Alexandrian Aristotelian commentary. Postmodern adoption of the term "suadisign" for argument and syllogism, therefore,[68] if taken sufficiently seriously, could prove to be a terminological move with wide theoretical implications and deep historical resonances, which could only enhance the impact of the move.

Demonstration, or Proof of a Point
The fact that the analytics of Aristotle are twofold needs to be carefully understood. He distinguished a "prior analytics", dealing with the pure form of discourse in abstraction from a further content or subject matter (what will be called in the Latin Age "formal or *summulae* logic"), from "posterior analytics", dealing precisely with the discourse as lending its logical form to the shaping of a particular subject matter (what will be called in the Latin Age "material logic"). But, since logical relations result not from what is as such but from what is thought to be, Aristotle was clear on the point that logic is never more than a heuristic tool of the inquiring mind. He never committed the late modern blunder of confounding logical form, either in

---

66 According to Coffey 1912: Vol. I p. 40, Diogenes Laertius was the first to use the term *organon* as a general title for Aristotle's logical works. But Laughlin 1995: 49 suggests that it was Andronicus himself who used the designation *organon epistēmē*. I have not had the opportunity to determine who, if either, is correct.

67 Black 1987: 34–94, esp. 59ff. See Black 1990, a later published form.

68 E.g., cf. Lanigan 1969; Black 1989.

itself or in any subject matter, with the structure of the physical world according to its proper environmental being.

Things as they are *thought to be* (objects as such) may or may not be the same in this or that respect with "things as they are". By getting clear about what we think, we put ourselves in a position to assess the consequences of what we think against further experience as revealing in what way and measure our thinking needs development, revision, or reversal vis-à-vis the universe of being. Logic, in short, pertains to the Umwelt precisely as rooted in a species-specifically human Innenwelt. By virtue of being thus rooted, logic places a restraint or check upon the arbitrariness of the linguistic sign exapted in communication.

At the level of outer expression or discourse, what we can say is actually unlimited. We can say the opposite of what we think, as in the lie; and we can claim to think what cannot be thought, as in the assertion that we have at home under glass, from fifteen different cities of the world, a collection of square circles. Moreover, in confused thought, we can hold to contradictions without realizing it.

But the constraining power of logic upon inward discourse, upon actual understanding as distinguished from spoken words (which may or may not convey such actual understanding), is always the same. Whether it be a question of material or merely of formal analysis, to whatever extent logic is applied to the point of revealing contradictions or of clarifying consequences of a given belief as necessary consequences, it reveals to us where there is and where there is not room for objection concerning any given point of understanding within the context of discourse within which the point is made.

The intellectual organization (or disorganization) itself *of a discourse* is the primary logical phenomenon. Even though logic perforce consists in the manipulation of intellectual symbols concerning objects in principle public, its function nonetheless pertains first of all to the signs of understanding as such underlying those objects, the inward side of discourse. What logic reveals *about the world* through speech to hearers of what is spoken (or through writing to readers of what is written) is, comparatively speaking, a secondary phenomenon. Logic, that is to say, applies only secondarily to signs exapted in communication with others, the outward side of discourse. Hence, Aristotle says:[69]

> All syllogism, and a fortiori demonstration, is addressed not to the spoken word, but to the discourse within the soul, and though we can always raise objections to the spoken word, to the inward discourse we cannot always object.

Aquinas, in his *Commentary on Aristotle's Metaphysics*,[70] will make the following observation relevant to this matter:

---

69 Aristotle, *Posterior Analytics* (c.348–7aBC), I, 10, 76b23–27. Cf. Avicenna in R. E. Houser 1999.
70 Aquinas c.1268: *In IV Metaphysicam* lect. 6, n. 6 (Busa vol. 4, p. 421).

it is impossible for anyone to actually adopt or believe the view that one and the same thing both is and is not in a given respect, even though some have attributed this opinion to Heraclitus. For while it is true that Heraclitus *said* this, yet it was not possible for him to *believe* what he said. Nor is it necessary that everyone has in mind or really believes everything that they say.

The logic in the proof of a point, then, appeals uniformly to inward discourse, even when it perforce makes use of outward speech. It is on this gap between inner and outer discourse, the fact that one can say anything regardless of what is actually being thought, that sophistic argument relies, both for its possibility and for its occasional rhetorical success.

The Place of Logic among the Sciences
A somewhat curious feature of Aristotle's logic is that he did not include analytics ("logic") anywhere in his scheme of human knowledge, his division of the sciences. He seemed to consider it neither speculative nor practical, but simply instrumental. As we will see, his silence on the matter opened the way to not a few centuries of controversy, beginning with the scheme of knowledge that would shortly be proposed by the Stoics. The following diagram may be helpful in getting an overall-view of this discussion of Aristotle's scheme for human knowledge:

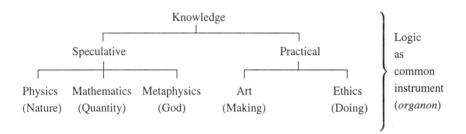

Aristotle's General Scheme of Human Knowledge and Logic

Looking Forward to Latinity, First Aspect

In summarizing the Golden Age, we may say that while no thinker in history has exceeded Plato in elegance of style and provocativeness of method, no thinker in history has exceeded Aristotle in synoptic vision and clarity of organization. Intellectually, ancient civilization effectively collapsed after Diocletian moved the seat of the Roman Empire from Rome to Nicomedia in Asia Minor around AD284. Half a century later, Constantine settled the capital in the city of Constantinople, which he built on the site that had been known for a thousand years previously as Byzantium.[71] Effective contact with Greek culture and language was lost when the so-called "Western Empire" – essentially what had originally been the Roman empire – went its own way of dissolution in subsequent centuries, gradually to take the definitively Latin form of medieval European civilization. Proficient knowledge of Greek became so rare in the West that what of the Greek writers was not available in Latin could not be studied. By this vagary, Plato dominated the early Latin Age through neoplatonic influences on Augustine, and Aristotle was not to become known till seven centuries later, when he finally became available in Latin largely courtesy of the Arabs.

Aristotle came as quite a shock to the Latin Christians. No one of the time had dreamed of the possibility of an entire world view rationally developed in all the major subject areas independently of any appeal to religious authority or divine revelation.[72] The first reaction was to censor the works, but saner minds soon made of the Aristotelian literary *corpus* the foundation of the newly emerging universities of the West. Aristotle's domination would continue to the end of the Latin Age. We will see this in chapters to come.

---

71 Actually, Constantine dedicated the new city on 11 May AD330, as *Nova Roma*; but even within his lifetime it came to be called "Constantinople", and so it went down in history, while yet "Byzantine" continued to be used for even the new civilization and art of the region. See chapter 5 below, p. 167.

72 There has not been space here to discuss the details of Aristotle's work in natural science, and of his many empirical investigations both of animals and of the constitution of states. But the student should sometime at least have a look at the contents of Aristotle's *Complete Works* which have survived to get a better sense of why it was made the foundation of the university curriculum in the West.

CHAPTER FOUR

The Final Greek Centuries and the Overlap of Neoplatonism with Christianity

The work of Plato and Aristotle was so successful that the Academy and the Lyceum that they had respectively founded became permanent institutions in Athenian life. Speusippus, rather than Aristotle, had succeeded Plato to head the Academy in 347BC, and was succeeded in turn by Xenocrates who was the head from 339–314BC. In 343BC Aristotle had founded the Lyceum, where his pupil Theophrastus succeeded him in 322BC. So successful were these schools as institutions that, in 307BC, a state decree was issued that required the approval of the Assembly for the future heads of these two philosophical schools.

Yet they were hardly the end of the ancient philosophical development. In this chapter we will look at further currents of development: cynicism, Stoicism, skepticism, Epicureanism, and the climactic development of the ancient Greek age, Neoplatonism. But note from the outset that the main importance of cynicism historically is the manner in which it fed into the Stoic development. And the main importance of skepticism, in the terms of our inquiry, is not simply that it is a view of knowledge as ever uncertain most congenial to the Epicurean reliance on atomistic theory in the area of epistemology, but rather, ironically, that, when it comes to preserving for us the theoretical debate that developed in late antiquity over the manner in which signs provide a basis for logical inference in the context of human discourse, the Stoic side of the argument has been preserved for us only by its enemies!

The theoretical component, as it were, of Epicureanism was especially weak. The theoretical writings of Stoicism have been mostly lost. As a result, the picture of these two schools that emerges from late antiquity is primarily in terms of so-called practical thought, their recommendations and views on the conduct of daily life, rather than in terms of their contribution to the epistemological development that will mainly interest us in later chapters.

The Founding of Stoicism

and, as Background Thereto, Cynicism

The first writings on logic came from the hand of Aristotle. But there was a second ancient development of logic, relatively independent, it would seem, that had a focus that was to prove significantly different from that of Aristotle. Whereas Aristotle focused on the proposition in terms of its makeup from parts which are not themselves propositions (the formation of dicisigns from represigns, as we might say[1]), and the makeup of arguments or "suadisigns" out of propositional or "dicisignificative" parts, the Stoic development of logic focused on the proposition or dicisign as a significant whole in terms of the possibility of combining dicisignificative wholes into yet larger wholes, still dicisignificative, wherein the original dicisigns would be interrelated as parts wherein the first implies the second, as indicated by the structure "If dicisign A then dicisign B". Propositions (or dicisigns) of this complex sort are commonly called "conditional", and Mates suggests that on the analysis of conditionals the Stoics made their analysis of the validity of arguments ("suadisigns") depend.[2] This alternative development of logic led to one of the more tantalizing controversies of late ancient thought in view of the Latin development that would follow – a controversy desirable to know yet always just beyond our capacity sufficiently to reconstruct as a consequence of the loss of essential records.

Zeno of Citium (c.336–260BC)

In the next to last year of the fourth century BC, that is to say, in or about the year 301, Zeno of Citium (c.336–260BC) founded what was to become a third major Athenian school at a location called ποικίλη στοά ("stoa poecile": "painted porch" or "picture porch"). This porch or "colonnade" was so called because it was decorated with pictures of the fall of Troy painted by Polygnotus (c.500–440BC, fl.480–450BC, called "the Homer of painting" by Aristotle) and his student Mikon. From this site the school went down in history as the Stoic school, or "Stoicism", its adherents the "Stoa" or "Stoics". Zeno had no love for youth, because he felt that immaturity, the natural state of youth, was incompatible with philosophy. He discouraged young men from attending his school, and when some came anyway, he would tell them that there is a reason why they had been given two ears and only one mouth: that they "may hear more and talk less".[3]

---

1 Of course, the characterization of propositional types and parts in function of the notion of sign here is deliberately anachronistic (see chapter 3, p. 88f. above), presupposing, as it does, first the insight not established until approximately the time of Poinsot (early 17th century), when it became possible to say that logic is wholly derivative from the being proper to signs, and second the attempt initiated by Peirce (late 19th century) to rethink the terminology itself of logic in light of this point. But the point of the anachronism is to keep in the reader's mind the theme in terms of the development of which we are principally considering the history of philosophy in its various parts.

2 Mates 1961: 93: "For example, at *Adv. Math.* VIII, 427–428, Sextus argues that since the Stoics have not agreed upon the truth-conditions for conditionals, and since they say that arguments are valid when and only when the corresponding conditionals are true, the Stoics have not agreed on a criterion for the validity of arguments, either. Neither De Lacy nor Bury shows any evidence of understanding this point."

3 Cf. Diogenes Laertius c.AD220: Book VII "Zeno" 23–4.

His own youth he had spent as a successful merchant, but had lost his fortune in a shipwreck on the Attic coast about 314BC. Reading Xenophon's *Memorabilia*, he became fascinated with the figure of Socrates, and, at the age of thirty, made himself a student of Crates the Theban, whom he perceived as like unto Socrates, and who had renounced his fortune in order to become a Cynic mendicant.

Cynicism (Antisthenes of Cyrene, 444–365BC)

"Cynicism" was not so much a philosophical school as it was a way of life in the ancient world, in many ways anticipatory of the desert anchorites who would become so numerous in Egypt in the early Christian centuries. The essential idea of cynicism was to reduce the needs of the body to their bare minimum in order to acquire for the mind a maximum of freedom; to this way of life Stoicism would add a distinctive body of philosophical doctrine, both speculative (in logic particularly) and practical. "Cynic" in this ancient context did not have at all the modern connotation of a person who believes that human conduct is motivated wholly by self-interest. The name accrued to the movement from the accident that the movement's founder, Antisthenes of Cyrene (444–365BC), had chosen as his lecture center a gymnasium called *Cynosurges* ("Dogfish") maintained for persons of low, foreign, or illegitimate birth. It was as a student of Socrates that Antisthenes had been inspired to adopt his ascetic ways[4] (although Socrates is reported to have jibed Antisthenes that his vanity could be seen through the holes of his cloak[5]).

Diogenes the Cynic (c.412–323BC)

Antisthenes' most famous pupil was Diogenes (c.412–323BC), a bankrupt banker from Sinope. Diogenes put into practice Antisthenes' doctrine of eschewing possessions and bodily comforts so completely, so ostentatiously, and so loquaciously that, even as a "street person", he became as famous in Greece as Alexander the Great. Reportedly the two actually met once in Corinth.[6] The great ruler came upon Diogenes lying in the sun, and announced his presence: "I am Alexander the Great King". Diogenes replied "I am Diogenes the dog". Alexander called on Diogenes to "Ask of me any favor you choose". Diogenes' request was that Alexander "Stop blocking the sun." After Diogenes, the Cynics became a religious

---

4 For example (from the *Phaedo* 64d): "*Socrates:* Do you think that the philosopher ought to care about the pleasures of … eating and drinking?

"*Simmias*: Certainly not.

"*Socrates:* And what do you say of the pleasures of love – should he care about them?

"*Simmias:* By no means.

"*Socrates:* And will he think much of the other ways of indulging the body – for example, the acquisition of costly raiment, or sandals, or other adornments of the body? Instead of caring about these does he not rather despise anything beyond what he needs?

"*Simmias:* I should say that the true philosopher would despise them."

Cf. Diogenes Laertius c.AD220: Book VI "Antisthenes" 2.

5 Diogenes Laertius c.AD220: Book VI "Antisthenes" 8.

6 Diogenes Laertius c.AD220: Book VI "Diogenes" 38; Arrian a.AD125: vii, 2.

order without religion, anticipating the mendicant orders of the thirteenth century in adopting begging as a way of life, sleeping in the streets and temples and teaching their doctrine that only virtue and internal freedom count.[7] Among Diogenes' more famous followers were Stilpo (380–300BC) and Crates of Thebes, the same Crates whom Zeno took as his first teacher in philosophy around 306.

Stoicism

In the five years after his initial apprenticeship to the Cynic way of life and thought under Crates, Zeno of Citium took time out to study at the Platonic Academy under Polemo (r.314–c.270/69), successor to Xenocrates (396–314BC); and as well to study with Stilpo of Megara (380–300BC), another student of Socrates once removed: Eucleides of Megara (c.450–374) had traveled to Athens to hear Socrates and returned to Megara stirring up rages of dispute. Ringing echoes of these disputes are said to have made Stilpo, about six when Eucleides died, a later disciple of Eucleides. At least Stilpo adopted the view (bringing him very close to Cynicism) that, since every philosophy can be contested, it is not in knowledge that wisdom lies but in so living as to be as independent as possible of reliance on anything external.

From reading Heraclitus, Zeno took the image of fire to represent the eternal law governing the world of change and representing the spark of the divine in man. He called it the λόγος ("logos"), or *Logos Spermatikos* – the "fertilizing wisdom of God". This Stoic Λόγος became one of the most enduring ideas of the ancient world. We find it in the writings of Philo of Alexandria (Philo Judaeus, c.30BC–AD50/54) described as "the first-begotten of God";[8] but most famously does the Λόγος appear in the opening of the Fourth Gospel around the close of the first Christian century. It matters not a whit to these later developments whether Heraclitus himself held a *logos* doctrine.

The Stoic Development

The Stoic philosophy rapidly developed into an endorsement of living a noble life of engagement in public affairs, and it is this aspect that is most popularly known today. Yet there was a significant and powerful speculative component to the actual Stoic development, and this dimension received as much or more impetus from an early disciple of Zeno as it did from Zeno himself.

Stoicism's Main Theoretician, Chrysippus of Soli (c.280–206BC)
At the Stoa an Asiatic Greek, Chrysippus of Soli (c.280–206BC), became Zeno's most famous follower and successor. Chrysippus was the most learned and prolific of

---

7 In this it must be said they wound up going to extremes of speech and example in flouting the social control of behavior through conventions. "A short meditation on the things dogs do in public", Armstrong suggests (1977: 118), "will show the direction which Cynic flouting of convention took."
8 See Philo a.AD54: "De confusione linguarum", ch. XXVIII, p. 89 (Greek), 90 (English).

the school, leaving behind him the incredible number of 750 books, none of which, even more incredibly, has survived in complete form. Of the most widespread and influential philosophy of the later ancient world we must piece together casual fragments to get even a glimpse of its doctrine.

The Stoic Organization of Life and Knowledge

In the area of public life or "practical knowledge", the Stoic doctrine called for men to participate in the affairs of the state, to undertake brave and noble deeds, and to maintain simplicity of life even in the midst of riches. Indeed, the most famous of the Stoics, apart perhaps from Chrysippus, was the Roman Emperor Marcus Aurelius (AD121–80), whose *Meditations* have survived as a classic of Stoic moral teaching. By acting nobly and rightly, the Stoics held, a human being participates in the divine *logos*, and justifies the spark of divinity within, which we call "intellect" or "reason".

On the speculative side, the Stoics developed independently a notion of logic somewhat at variance with Aristotle's ideas about the subject. For one thing, they did not go along with his "instrumentalist" notion of logic, but thought rather that it deserved and required its own place among the speculative sciences. For the Stoics were struck as much by the peculiarity of the subject matter of logic as they were by its pervasiveness: the "matter" of logic, they noted, not only exists everywhere in human thought, but it "exists" there in a rather remarkable way. In contrast with the things existing in our material surroundings, the objects logic deals with exist in a completely immaterial and intangible way, yet its bonds tie all men equally and everywhere. The reason is that all thought is bound by the laws of logic, and what makes an argument valid or invalid is as independent of the will of the one propounding the argument as are the movements of the moon and stars.

Through logic, or "rational philosophy", as the Stoics called it, as well as by great and noble deeds, human beings participate in the *logos*, the divine measure and proportion which rules all things. Thus, logic has a subject matter of its own every bit as much as does mathematics or physics, every bit as independent of human action, and one, moreover, of a singular subtlety. This subject matter which is peculiar and proper to logic they designated by a unique name, never successfully translated and, owing to the misfortunes of history which have lost to us all but fragments of the Stoic writings, not well understood today.[9] Logic, they said, is principally about the λεκτόν (*lekton*), the order which the mind finds in its own workings, just as the other sciences or types of knowledge are about the differing types of order that the mind finds elsewhere in the

---

9 Even in the Latin Age, details of the general Stoic positions mainly came to be known only after the recovery in 1529 of the reports contained in the turn-of-the-3rd-century writings of Sextus Empiricus; and Sextus was a skeptical enemy of Stoic doctrines in philosophy and logic. Nor has our situation in this particular much improved over that of the 16th-century Latins.

scope of human experience. Thus we arrive at a scheme of knowledge slightly variant from the original one that Aristotle had proposed less than a century before:[10]

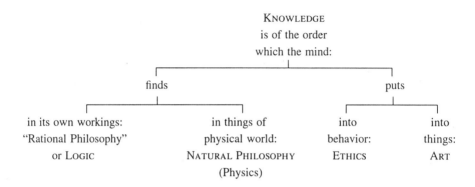

The Stoic View of the Place of Logic in the Scheme of Human Knowledge

The name "logic" reflects primarily this Stoic influence conceiving of *logos* as the immaterial order or pattern which the mind finds in nature and within its own workings as lekton as well, and which may be studied there according to its unique properties.

The Quarrel between Stoics and Peripatetics over the Place of Logic among the Sciences

But the Stoic way of conceiving the subject matter of logic leads to another question, which much exercised the ancient Stoics and Peripatetics (as the followers of Aristotle were called) and continued in Latin times: Is logic a science in its own right, or is it merely an instrument in the service of the other sciences? If it is both, how so exactly? As we will see,[11] this controversy found no satisfactory theoretical resolution until late in the seventeenth century, when a nonlogician, John Locke, off-handedly proposed a novel division of the sciences through which the ancient controversy (of which Locke may have had no knowledge at all) could be resolved.

Yet there was an even more important substantive controversy in the area of logic that developed between the Stoics and the followers of Epicurus, which we can only partially reconstruct in hindsight. But before giving an outline of this controversy, we must first glance over the main developments opposed to Stoicism.

---

10 At least here is the medieval report of the Stoic scheme, from the opening section (Book 1, reading 1, paragraph 2) of the *Commentary* by Thomas Aquinas (written c.1269) on the *Nicomachean Ethics* (c.335/4BC) of Aristotle.

11 Chapter 14 below, esp. p. 595ff.

Skepticism and Epicureanism

One of the strangest developments of the ancient world was hardly the development of a view of knowledge entirely skeptical of its results, but rather that such a view would find shelter and encouragement among those professing to be followers of Plato. Yet such is the turn events took before the Academy would be reclaimed by one of the most astonishing developments of antiquity, the movement known as "Neoplatonism".

The Origins of Skepticism

Pyrrho of Elis (c.365–275BC) traveled as far as India with Alexander the Great's army, and indeed he returned with a semi-Hindu outlook on life. His name has become synonymous with the most extreme form of skepticism. The tenth edition of Merriam-Webster's *Collegiate Dictionary* (1993), for example, describes Pyrrhonists as "extreme skeptics who suspended judgment on every proposition".

From his main proposition that "every reason has a corresponding reason opposed to it"[12] Pyrrho himself drew the most extreme consequences. He wrote no books, but his pupil Timon of Phlius (320–230BC) wrote a whole series of *Silloi* (Satires) which put Pyrrho's views into wide circulation. The core of his reflections seem to come down to this. Since certainty is unattainable, the wise man will seek not truth but tranquillity of life, and without fear of death; for just as life is an uncertain good, so is death not a certain evil. The myths and conventions of one's time and place ought to be accepted rather than contested, for tranquillity is thereby the more quickly reached and without fruitless controversy.

Through Arcesilaus (316–241BC), who became the head of Plato's Academy in 269 (the so-called "Middle Academy"), Pyrrho's views were brought into the mainstream. Given his position, of course, Arcesilaus was obliged to provide a Platonic vehicle for the skeptic views, and for this purpose, probably under Pyrrho's influence,[13] he used Plato's rejection of the reliability of sense knowledge. "Nothing is certain", he is reported to have said, "not even that".[14] In particular, reports Diogenes Laertius,[15] the followers of Pyrrho denied not only certitude. They

---

12 See the report in Diogenes Laertius c.AD220: Book IX "Pyrrho" 74–5.
13 Cf. ibid.; and see also Zeller 1870: 499ff.
14 Cf. Zeller 1870: 503. In his summation of skepticism (a.AD225b: *Adversus Mathematicos* VIII, 479–80), Sextus Empiricus argues the same point, but offers also a variant on the argument, either way thinking to win: "Many things are said which imply an exception; ... so also when we say that no proof exists we imply in our statement the exception of the argument which proves that proof does not exist; for this alone is proof. And even if it does banish itself, the existence of proof is not thereby confirmed. For there are many things which produce the same effect on themselves as they produce on other things. ... so too the argument against proof, after abolishing every proof, can abolish itself."
15 Diogenes Laertius c.AD220: Book IX "Pyrrho" 96–7.

deny, too, that there is such a thing as σημεῖον, a sign. If there is, they say, it must either be sensible or intelligible. Now it is not sensible, because what is sensible is a common attribute, whereas a sign is a particular thing. Again, the sensible is one of the things which exist by way of difference, while the sign belongs to the category of the relative. Nor is a sign an object of thought, for objects of thought are of four kinds, apparent judgements on things apparent, non-apparent judgements on things apparent, non-apparent judgments on things non-apparent, or apparent on non-apparent; and a sign is none of these, so that there is no such thing as a sign. A sign is not "apparent on apparent", for what is apparent needs no sign; nor is it non-apparent on non-apparent, for what is revealed by something must needs appear; nor is it non-apparent on apparent, for that which is to afford the means of apprehending something else must itself be apparent; nor, lastly, is it apparent on non-apparent, because the sign, being relative, must be apprehended along with that of which it is the sign, which is not here the case. It follows that nothing uncertain can be apprehended; for it is through signs that uncertain things are said to be apprehended.[16]

That such an attack on philosophy should come, in the name of philosophy, even for a period, out of the groves once trod by Plato is surely one of history's greatest ironies. And it shows something of the spirit of the time, as Rome was expanding to take over the Greek world.

Epicurus of Samos (341–270BC)

Insofar as the spirit skepticism embodied could be compatible with theory at all, it could be said that Epicurus of Samos (341–270BC) gave that new spirit a theoretical home – perhaps this is why Sextus Empiricus opposed even the Epicureans, so as to brook no check at all, even a friendly one, to trammel the full spirit of skepticism. Epicurus achieved this near-contradictory feat by effecting a remarkable stratagem. To begin with, unlike the Platonic Academy, he adopted from the first an epistemological paradigm compatible with an exclusive reliance on the workings of the senses. Then, in a jiu-jitsu flip of Platonism, he argued that for all knowledge *but* that of sense the conclusions of skepticism would apply. For of course, if the workings of the senses alone are to be trusted, all intellectual conclusions or even suggestions which go beyond the senses are ipso facto uncertain. But what is uncertain in going beyond sense may become certain if reduced back to sense, and, as we will see, for Epicurus, this is exactly the role the σημεῖον or "sensible sign" plays in knowledge: it points beyond itself, but in a manner that admits of eventual verification or rejection. Trust in sensation and rejection of the skeptical argument so far as it concerned the σημεῖον, thus, became the key to distrust in the "logical deductions" of putatively intellectual knowledge and the means to give the skeptical

---

16 "Causes, too, they destroy in this way", the text continues, then motion, then the possibility of learning, coming into being, good and evil – "the whole of their mode of inference can be gathered from their extant treatises", though Pyrrho himself left no writings.

spirit something it could never provide on its own, namely, a theoretical context in which to work.

Epicurus became enamored of philosophy around age fourteen, and left for Athens at age eighteen to study in the Academy. Among the ancients he found he preferred Democritus to Plato, and a free eclecticism to adherence to any one school. After a time he went to Asia, where he lectured on philosophy at Colophon, Mytilene, and Lampsacus. His listeners at Lampsacus, itself a remote city, were sufficiently impressed with the man that they raised a fund sufficient to buy Epicurus a house and gardens on the outskirts of Athens where he could live and establish a school.

If they did this to be rid of him, it seems an extravagant means. We can only conclude as the more probable hypothesis that they genuinely loved the man. In any event, in this house and garden, quietly teaching his pupils, participating in the customs of the city but keeping clear of politics, he lived up to his motto, *lathe biosas*, "live unobtrusively". Curiously, in the figure of Baldric, Archbishop of Dol from 1107 till his death in 1130, Bury gives us a thumbnail sketch of a Christian incarnation of the Epicurean ideal life. Baldric, Bury tells us,[17]

> was opposed to the fashionable asceticism; he lived in literary retirement, enjoying his books and garden, taking as little part as he could in the ecclesiastical strife which raged around, and exercising as mildly as possible his archiepiscopal powers.

It could have been Epicurus himself by a later disguise. In the seventeenth century's first half, Pierre Gassendi (1592–1655) would provide yet another such incarnation.

"Epicure" and Epicurism vs. "Epicurean" and Epicureanism[18]

The function of philosophy, Epicurus held, is not to explain the world but to guide the human being in the quest for happiness, and happiness is found in pleasure. That seems straightforward, but it is not. Today's dictionary defines the primary meaning of "epicure" as "one devoted to sensual pleasure", meaning especially food, drink, and sex; and the secondary meaning of "epicurean" as "relating to an epicure". And perhaps by his choice of the term "pleasure" to define the highest human good, together with his thesis that there is no life or existence for human beings beyond bodily existence, Epicurus condemned himself inexorably to being thus misunderstood at the level of popular culture and superficial history.

Yet a sharp distinction should be drawn between "epicure", as one given to the pleasures of external sense; and an "epicurean", as one who follows Epicurus

---

17 Bury 1912: 548.
18 The distinction drawn in this section is not one that is commonly invoked, with the result that "epicurism", which has little or nothing to do with philosophy, and "epicureanism", which has or should have everything to do with philosophy, have long since become inextricably entwined in common usage and are not likely to become untangled in any foreseeable future. Yet an epicure is *always and necessarily* a Sybarite, an Epicurean not so.

in pursuing the quiet contemplation of the reaches of reason while insisting on the greatest moderation in the indulgence of pleasures of external sense as the necessary means for making contemplative use of reason possible. The modern epicure can only feel cheated to discover that his namesake and model repudiated the epicurean way of life as commonly (mis)understood:[19]

> When, therefore, we say that pleasure is the chief good, we are not speaking of the pleasures of the debauched man, or those that lie in sensual enjoyment … but we mean the freedom of the body from pain, and of the soul from disturbance. For it is not continued drinking and revels, or the enjoyment of female society, or feasts of fish and other delicacies of a luxurious table, that make for the pleasantest life, but such sober contemplation as examines the reasons for choice and avoidance, and puts to flight the vain opinions from which arises most of the confusion that troubles the soul.

Like Aristotle and the Stoics, then, Epicurus in the end locates the highest good in the contemplative activity of understanding. They all agree that "happiness is activity in accordance with excellence," and "in accordance with the highest excellence", which will be the exercise of "the best thing in us".[20] But, whereas Aristotle and the Stoics could debate

> Whether it be intellect or something else that is this element which is thought to be our natural ruler and guide and to take thought of things noble and divine, whether it be itself also divine or only the most divine element in us,

Epicurus rather closed the debate by ruling that we need have no question or fear of anything divine, for such does not exist at the level of the human mind or soul. There are gods and they are immortal beings. But we humans are mortal all, through and through.

Freedom from Fear the Highest Wisdom
The wisdom which is the highest human good has nothing to do with the divine, but consists rather in the realization that we have nothing to fear. There is indeed a God living and immortal, and about this being we ought to believe[21] "whatever may uphold both his blessedness and his immortality." But this in nowise changes the fact that human beings are not gods and have no afterlife. Wisdom teaches us that "it is not possible to live pleasantly without living prudently, honorably, and justly; nor to live prudently, honorably, and justly without living pleasantly".[22] Nothing

19 From the letter from Epicurus (a.270BC, therefore) to Menoecus cited in Diogenes Laertius c.AD220: Book X, "Epicurus" 131–2.
20 Aristotle c.335/4BC: *Nicomachean Ethics* 1177a11.
21 Letter from Epicurus to Menoecus cited in Diogenes Laertius c.AD220: Book X "Epicurus" 123.
22 Ibid. 132.

more, for there is nothing more; nor is more needed, for this is enough. Tend your garden, and leave the world to tend itself. "God is not to be feared; death cannot be felt; the Good can be won; all that we dread can be borne and conquered": such are the maxims into which Epicurus is said to have once condensed his philosophy.[23] In his letter to Menoecus, such as we have it from the text of Diogenes Laertius,[24] Epicurus advises to

> Accustom thyself to believe that death is nothing to us, for good and evil imply sentience, and death is the privation of all sentience; therefore a right understanding that death is nothing to us makes the mortality of life enjoyable, not by adding to life an illimitable time, but by taking away the yearning after immortality. For life has no terrors for him who has thoroughly apprehended that there are no terrors for him in ceasing to live. ... Death, therefore, ... is nothing, either to the living or to the dead, for with the living it is not and the dead exist no longer.

Metrodorus (c.330–277BC) and the Belly

Epicurus' most famous pupil of the time, Metrodorus of Lampsacus, who died in 277BC, seven years before Epicurus himself, is reported[25] to have shocked and outraged Greece by the declaration that "it is indeed the belly, the belly and nothing else, which any philosophy that proceeds according to nature makes its whole concern." But in the context of Epicurus' acceptance of Democritus' teaching that the whole of the human being is a material arrangement, coarser atoms comprising the body and finer ones the soul, Metrodorus' outrageous statement is but a theatrical way of making Democritus' (and Epicurus') point that whatever "personal" existence we have begins and ends with the body that is "ours". "He who has a clear and certain understanding of these things", Epicurus advises,[26] "will direct every preference and aversion toward securing health of body and tranquillity of mind, seeing that this is the sum and end of a blessed life."

The Swerve

No account of Epicurus and Epicureanism would be complete without a mention of the extraordinary doctrine of the swerve: the sudden, uncaused deviation from uniform downward motion which individual atoms occasionally undergo. This random swerve results in collisions with other atoms causing them too to deviate from their uniform downward course, thus setting up a chain of actions and reactions which leave an element of indeterminacy in the otherwise completely determined motions of atoms in the void.

---

23 Cited in Murray 1927: 373.
24 Diogenes Laertius c.AD220: Book X "Epicurus" 124–5.
25 In Athenaeus, c.AD228: Book VII (p. 257).
26 Letter from Epicurus to Menoecus cited in Diogenes Laertius c.AD220: Book X "Epicurus" 128.

This doctrine is not to be found in the surviving fragments of Epicurus' own teaching. Testimony for it comes rather from two Epicurean philosophers, Lucretius (c.99–55BC)[27] and Philodemus of Gadara (c.110–c.40BC),[28] who became a philosophic mentor of the learned Roman orator and statesman, Marcus Tullius Cicero (106–43BC).[29] The doctrine is indeed a curious one. With the striking exception of Aristotle, discussed earlier,[30] most ancient philosophers tended to neglect the idea of chance in their physical doctrines. Epicurus, by contrast, seems to have given chance the strongest possible interpretation and made it central in his philosophy. For Epicureanism, the swerve in a given atom's path (when it is not caused by a collision with another atom, which would simply be a chance event externally caused in the manner explained by Aristotle) is the original chance event. The original chance events, the uncaused swerve of individual atoms, not only lack a proper cause. They lack any cause at all. There is not even an indirect cause for the swerve of the atom. Thus, the Epicurean doctrine of the swerve is the earliest record we have of a thinker proposing that there are such a thing as uncaused phenomena. The doctrine purports to introduce indeterminacy into an otherwise determined physical universe, and so make room for human free choices.

But Aristotle has already made clear in his accounts of causality and chance that indeterminacy and causality fit quite well together in an understanding of the universe, whereas the notion of something coming from nothing is another question altogether. Later philosophers in the Latin Age would show that something can come from nothing only on one of two assumptions: either on the assumption that the mixed potentialities and actualities that we call the physical world themselves depend upon and were created by a Pure Act which itself is unmixed with potentiality; or on the assumption that being and intelligibility are not convertible, that the physical world in its own right is ultimately incoherent for human thought. For understanding cannot make any headway except on the assumption that any given event provides the mind with material for an investigation which will uncover the relation of that event with yet other individuals and events which, together with intrinsic formal and material causes, explain why the phenomenon in question is the way that it in fact is.

The first of these two assumptions was explored by many Latins, Aquinas being but the most notable among them.[31] The second of these two assumptions was generally disregarded by the ancient Greek and medieval Latin philosophers for some very good and rather obvious reasons. What is the point of such an assumption? To assume that any given occurrence had no connection with causality warrants the one making the assumption to dismiss out of hand any investigation whatever, to

---

27 In his poem from the first half of the last century before Christ, a.55BC: *On the Nature of Things* Book 2, 216ff. (p. 113ff. in Rouse ed.).
28 Philodemus i.54–40BC: *On the Methods of Inference*, col. xxxvi, 13.
29 Cf. Usener 1887: 199–201.
30 Chapter 3, "Chance events", p. 66.
31 See, e.g., "The Reasoning of the Five Ways" in chapter 7, p. 267.

posit for inquiry regarding the event in question a complete dead-end. The Latins had a saying: "What is asserted gratuitously may be rejected with equal freedom" (*gratis asseritur gratis negatur*). There is no point of possibility of conversation on any point once the assumption in question is invoked. Bergson, we will see, invoked the Latin attitude on the question of evolution.[32]

Not until Hume, who replaces the idea of causal connections in nature with the idea of mere associations of objects in consciousness, would the assumption that there are natural events which have no causal connection whatever with other events be incorporated into the philosophical mainstream. With Hume, the compromising of the intelligibility of being in favor of such radical skepticism may be said to become a distinctive part of the modern heritage, definitively systematized in the work of Immanuel Kant, as we will see in chapter 13.

Even in modern science analogues of Epicurus' unintelligible, inexplicable "swerve" may be found. Such an idea may be found in astronomy associated especially with the name of Fred Hoyle, the proposal that new "background material" – mainly hydrogen atoms – constantly comes into existence in the present universe. The theory is widely known as the "steady state" theory of the universe, but Hoyle himself also calls it[33] the "continuous creation" theory. If this last name is intended to signify that God continuously creates such new material, then we have a situation not all that different from what Aquinas envisaged.[34] But unless the theory is directly invoking the dependency of the universe as a whole in its being on God as a Pure Actuality, an Existence Self-Subsisting, which is hardly a scientific theory in any modern sense, then the "continuous creation" view is on the same level as the swerve theory of Epicurus.

Again in modern science Heisenberg's "principle of indeterminacy", which is based on our inability at the microscopic level to determine velocity and position of a subatomic particle at one and the same moment, is sometimes interpreted as a proof that some events are uncaused. But the more common and more justifiable interpretation is simply that there are some events whose total causality escapes our knowledge, even though they are indeed fully caused from a sufficiently omniscient perspective, and we may hope at some future superior vantage gained in the progress of human inquiry to be ourselves in a position to trace out the exact lines of causality which now, either in themselves or in their intersection, elude us.

We must not get too far ahead of our story; but it is interesting to note that already in ancient thought the "swerve of the atoms" attributed to lost teachings of Epicurus anticipates a theme that will recur in modern science and philosophy, the idea, namely, that causality and chance are unconnected notions – an idea that Aristotle was the first to refute in the context of his own discussion of chance as framed by causality.

---

32 See chapter 11, p. 505ff.
33 Hoyle 1950: 122.
34 See below, chapter 7, p. 271f.; and chapter 11, p. 506f.

And of course we should not rule out the possibility that the testimony about the doctrine Lucretius himself propounded is defective. The standard treatment of Epicurus, relying on the testimony of Lucretius and Philodemus, explains that, since the natural motion of atoms is *downward*, without the swerve, which itself simply has no cause, atoms would never collide and no cosmos, consequently, would be formed. However, even supposing the natural motion of atoms to be downward, suppose further that this natural motion is of a different rate in different atoms. In that case, the "swerve", instead of being seen as simply "uncaused" and, insofar as a finite event, unintelligible, would be seen rather as resulting from a more rapid atom descending on a less rapid atom and striking it. When the strike would be, however slightly, off-center, the struck atom would "swerve" from its straight downward course according to the force of the impact, colliding in turn with another atom (or two), causing it also to swerve, and so on, in a more or less limited chain reaction of collisions each of which would be not *uncaused* but without a *proper cause* – that is to say, the swerve and the resulting collisions would be rooted not in simply but only in indirectly caused events, which is quite a different matter.

On this account, the Epicurean doctrine of the swerve would become conceptually a case subalternate to the general doctrine of chance events as Aristotle explained them. It may be that Epicurus had more sense and deeper understanding of the matter of causality and chance than his ancient witnesses or would-be modern and contemporary followers in the matter! Whether this further assumption be warranted I leave to the scholarly experts in ancient philosophy, and perhaps also to the future unexpected discovery of relevant ancient texts.

The Role of Sign in Epicurus' Thought

Though he based his philosophy on the ancient atomism of Leucippus and Democritus, Epicurus did not hesitate to discard or modify whatever from the original atomist doctrine he found incompatible with the reliability of sensation as the foundation of knowledge.[35] Of course, beyond sensation there is understanding, but understanding for Epicurus was only a name for the complex workings of sense itself, not a distinct cognitive power whereby the very natures or forms of the sensible might be grasped. Hence he rejected deduction as a valid form of reasoning and accepted only analogic inference based on sense experience.

Now natural signs, σημεῖα, were regarded in ancient Greece, outside the context of divination, in terms of natural phenomena, including notably medical symptoms, which serve to inform us of factual connections, as we have seen. Indeed, it was for just this reason, their connection in knowledge with truth and falsity, as we saw, that Aristotle connected them in his logic with the very content as such of propositions. Inferences from signs, not as propositional contents (for that would be intellectualism) but as sensible phenomena giving us reason to believe on the

---

35 I might recommend on this point the huge study of Bailey 1928: chs. 7 and 8 in particular.

basis of previous experience in their connection with something not immediately or as such sensed, then, would seem to give us a purely empirical foundation for our knowledge – exactly what the epistemology of atomism requires. The mechanics of sense perception for Epicurus amount to what has since come to be called a causal theory of perception, and its archetype can very well be seen in modern form in the classic work on meaning by Ogden and Richards.[36] The stream of atoms, not the object from which they stream, is what makes sense reliable: "neither the sound in the brass instrument that is struck, nor the sound in the mouth of the man who shouts, is heard but the sound which strikes our own sense",[37] and so on for each of the senses. So, when, on the basis of sense, we make an inference which carries us beyond sense, what we have done is not reach an intellectual idea capable of providing somehow its own justification, but simply framed a conjecture – made a judgment – the correctness of which, as Manetti well puts it,[38] depends upon "something which awaits confirmation", and so leaves open the way to error.

Now the sensations retained in memory and imagination as the basis for expectations tomorrow clearly form a mediating element between signs and what they signify for Epicurus. But the connection between these mediating "images", let us say, and the sounds whereby we express them in language, have nothing in common with the connection between the mediating images and the sensible objects whence they took rise in the first place. The latter connection is causal and insofar constant (which is why the senses are reliable at bottom), but the former connection is conventional and inconstant, varying between Greek and barbarian and even from place to place.

So even though the mind, in retaining and fashioning under its own power sensations formed under the action of sensibles, adds a "second movement" to the "first movement" of the senses' response to stimuli, this yet does not constitute, as Aristotle, for example, thought, a difference in kind between "intellectual" and "sensory" knowledge; for this "second movement" is itself no more than the formation of anticipations which will ultimately justify or vilify opinions the individual may make. It is sense *perception*, indeed, as opposed to *sensation* pure and simple. But it is not *understanding* irreducible to sense. Reducibility to sense, on the contrary, is just what makes perception reliable and opinion justifiable. Analogic inference, not deduction, is all that logic needs. And this provides us, exactly as Manetti advises, with nothing "sufficient to allow a common analysis and explanation" of the

---

36 Ogden and Richards 1923. Cf. the instructive analysis of the causal theory in the 1938 5th ed. of this work made by Oesterle 1944.

37 I take the argument of Epicurus from the report of it given by Sextus Empiricus in *Adversus Mathematicos* (a.AD225b) VIII 208. Later, we will see Aquinas make this very same point in arguing against there being images in sensation as such distinguished within perception: see chapter 7, esp. p. 318 (the discussion of 'formal object') and the section "Why Sensations Do Not Involve Mental Icons", p. 345. This would become a decisive point in the period of modern philosophy (see chapter 12 below, esp. p. 530ff. & 535).

38 Manetti 1993: 116.

inferential element, the σημεῖον or "sign", and the linguistic element through which we express inferences and discourse about where signs may lead and when they are justified. They remain, sign and language, two separate matters of investigation.

The Counterpoint of Stoicism and Epicureanism in the Last Greek Centuries

After the death of Epicurus in 270BC, the influence of his life and teaching continued to be felt throughout the ancient world. When Cicero asked, in the last century before Christ, "Why are there so many followers of Epicurus?",[39] Lucretius (c.99–55BC), in effect, gave answer in a poetic masterpiece, *De Rerum Natura* ("On the Nature of Things"), which stands as the most complete extant exposition of the Epicurean point of view. Down to the time of the Emperor Constantine (r.AD306–37) there were adherents who publically professed the Epicurean system, some degrading it to the level of epicure,[40] others faithful to the simplicity of the actual doctrine. Nonetheless, even in its purest form, Epicureanism stood polar opposite to Stoicism, the one urging a withdrawal from the tumult and cares of a public life, the other summoning to a profound involvement therein and summoning the performance of great deeds.

Both Stoicism and Epicureanism called for a simplicity of life, but the simplicity of the Epicurean life was inevitably compatible with softness, luxury, and withdrawal, while the simplicity of the Stoic called for strength and abstemiousness and involvement in public affairs. Stock[41] considered "the great lesson of Greek philosophy" to be "that it is worth while to do right, irrespective of reward and punishment and regardless of the shortness of life", and he rightly considered this "great lesson" to be a common achievement of the great schools of antiquity; yet, as he says, "this lesson the Stoics so enforced by the earnestness of their lives and the influence of their moral teaching that it has become associated more particularly with them." In the succeeding Latin Age the Epicurean influence as such would be comparatively negligible (until the Renaissance), but the Stoic influence would carry over,[42] along with the Neoplatonic influence, into the very formation of indigenous Latin thought, particularly through the work of Augustine.

The Stoic vs. Epicurean Polemic over Signs and Inference
Comparatively to the lofty development of speculative thought which marked especially the schools of Plato and Aristotle, at least in their founding, the picture that usually is drawn for us of the Epicureans and the Stoic schools alike is one

---

39 Cicero, *De Finibus* (45BC) I, 7.25.
40 Zeller (1870: 388n3) cites a report that, in the mid-2nd century BC, two Epicurean philosophers were expelled from Rome for the corruption of youth. Perhaps they were teaching *epicurism* rather than *epicureanism*.
41 St George Stock 1908: 4.
42 A superb overview is provided by Colish 1985.

of mainly practical thought, the application of philosophy to life. Yet this is not the whole story, and, the main primary sources all being lost, as long as they are lost,[43] we shall never know if this picture of Stoicism and Epicureanism as practical philosophies is truly just or only a matter of what Teilhard de Chardin once called in the area of physical anthropology (and paleontology generally) the "suppression of the peduncles". "Stoicism has been treated largely as a moralism", Rist concedes,[44] but only in order to argue that even what scant evidence we have shows "that at its best it was more than that."[45]

We know that there was a huge early development of Stoic logic only because some record of it has been preserved, as Mates puts it,[46] in "the accounts of men who were without exception opponents of the Stoics". These opponents were a certain Diocles Magnes[47] from the first century AD, whom we know only from the third century report of his *Synopsis of the Philosophers* as used by Diogenes Laertius to present the Stoic doctrine on logic; and the earlier contemporary of Diogenes, the famous Sextus Empiricus (c.AD150 – c.225), who, Mates warns us, we may expect has omitted from his account "any parts of the Stoic logic which he has found either too difficult or too good to refute", if such parts there be (which is, of course, unknown). Finally, there is the "report" of Stoic positions given by their opponent, the Epicurean philosopher Philodemus, whose exact dates are not known beyond the fact that he was contemporary with Julius Caesar, Cicero, Virgil, and Horace; therefore a denizen of the beginnings of the Roman Empire (as distinguished from the earlier Roman Republic) in the first century BC.

Philodemus, however, as an Epicurean, included the Stoics in his mid-first century BC tract *On the Sign and Inferences therefrom*, Περὶ σημείων καὶ σημειώσεων, only as part of a polemic designed to prove correct on all matters at issue the Epicurean position. The reading of this tract around 1883 during his short tenure at the Johns Hopkins University suggested to Peirce the coinage of "semiosis" as a contemporary term to name the action of signs. But what is fundamentally interesting about the tract of Philodemus (variously referred to by a Latin plural title, *De Signis*, or by the English title under which it was in fact published, *On Methods of Inference*, which omits the σημεῖον even in the singular) is the evidence it provides of a controversy rooted in the notion of sign, σημεῖον, toward the dawn of the Christian era, a controversy whose terms reveal that at this late period there did not exist in Greek philosophy a general notion of sign in which the two orders of nature and culture (linguistic communication in particular) are unified. The sign still belonged to the order of nature, language to the order of convention.

---

43 For who knows what decisive papyrus may turn up tomorrow on some archeological dig, or from some other totally imprevisible quarter? Such is the way of history, the anthroposemiotic access to what has gone before.
44 Rist 1969: 289.
45 His more recent anthology (Rist ed. 1978) offers yet further proof.
46 Mates 1961: 8.
47 "Diocles the Magnesian" in Hicks's 1931 translation of Diogenes Laertius c.AD220: see vol. II, 212.

As we might expect in a controversy between Epicureans and Stoics over the subject matter of logical inference, the Epicureans view everything in a-posteriori, experiential terms, the Stoics in a-priori terms of rational necessity. In the Stoic and the Epicurean analysis alike the σημεῖον is a material object or natural event accessible to sense, a *tynchánon*, in the transliteration of Manetti for a Stoic actual sensible referent.[48] To such an object a linguistic expression, *sēmaínon* in the Stoic logic, *onoma* in Epicurean, is mediately related; in the former case by what the Stoics call the *sēmaínomenon* or *lekton*, in the latter case by *prolepsis* (προλήψις, "preconception" or "anticipation").[49] Hence, within the agreement "about the validity of particular signs", this great theoretical difference emerges:[50] "while the Stoics considered an object to be a sign beginning from the consequent (or rather from what was referred to), the Epicureans considered it from the point of view of the antecedent".

To go beyond this firm general conclusion regarding this late Epicurean versus Stoic controversy at the present time is hardly possible for anyone relying on English but not deeply versed in the Greek language. For, in English, apart from Mates's own partial translation (of Sextus Empiricus a.AD225a), the best complete translation we have of Sextus Empiricus is Bury, the best translation of Diogenes Laertius is Hicks, and the only translation we have of Philodemus is that of Phillip and Estelle De Lacy.[51] Yet according to Benson Mates, generally regarded as the main expert in English on Stoic logic, Hicks did not understand the Stoic theoretical position well enough to translate Laertius' use of Diocles Magnes in a technically reliable way;[52] Mates says the same of Bury's translation of Sextus Empiricus;[53] and the

---

48 In the remainder of these remarks about this late Greek controversy, I will use the transliterations of Greek from Manetti 1993 in place of actual Greek.

49 Manetti (1993: 121), in what marks a decisive advance in the study of Epicurean philosophy, remarks, against the standard report of Epicurean theory of language (including the ancient reports in Sextus Empiricus and Plutarch, as Manetti points out on the preceding page): "To attribute to Epicurus a theory of language in which words refer directly to things, without the mediation of prolepsis, causes a contradiction with his doctrines of false beliefs. ... The existence of prolepsis as a mediating element between words and things allows for false assertions and assertions about things which do not exist." Contrast Manetti's graphic of the Stoic triangle of meaning (or "semiotic triangle") on p. 94 top with the Epicurean triangle on p. 120 bottom.

50 Manetti 1993: 128–9.

51 Actually Allan Marquand, who studied at the Johns Hopkins University with Charles S. Peirce in a logic seminar that was devoted in part to the study of Philodemus's text, made a translation of the text in connection with his seminar work; but this translation was never published. Perhaps it could be found and brought to print. As it is, we have only Marquand's own reflections from the seminar (Marquand 1883), in which is perpetuated the simplistic view that, for the Epicureans, to whose school Philodemus belonged, words refer directly to things rather than by the "mental" mediation of prolepsis (see note 49 above).

52 On Hicks, see Mates 1961: 2n4 *in finem*; 28n8; and the discussion on pp. 70–2, text and notes, esp. n55.

53 Mates 1961: see esp. p. 91; but passim. The main problem with Bury's translation Mates already stated in 1949 (298n30): that "everywhere, he does not distinguish between an argument and a conditional".

same again for the De Lacy work.[54] On top of this, from the way he aligns himself with post-Fregean logical writers, there is ample reason to suspect that Mates shares the strong late-modern bias against "Aristotelian logic" rooted in the nominalist reliance on material implication and the consequent reduction of logical analysis to a symbolic calculus.[55] This alignment might appear to put some taint of ideological suspicion on his own assessment of the early Stoic position.[56]

Yet despite the temporarily hopeless situation regarding English sources for reconstructing Stoic logic in the details of its uniqueness, we can yet say with definitiveness that in both the Stoic and the Epicurean cases the link between any theory of linguistic expressions and signs as such remains indirect and implicit. What Manetti remarks of the Stoics applies equally to the Epicureans, to wit,[57] they "do not reach the point of saying that words are signs (Augustine is the first to make such a statement)," and, in the particular case of the Stoics, "there remains a lexical difference between the *sēmaínon/sēmaínomenon* pair and *sēmeíon*".

Concerning this triad of terms, Eco had already remarked[58] that "the common and obvious etymological root is an indication of their relatedness"; so that perhaps we see in the *sēmaínon/sēmaínomenon* pairing some semantic drift in the direction Augustine will mark out as a unique path for philosophy to pursue in its Latin language development.[59] But this suggestion seems unlikely and, in any event, exceeds actual evidence from existing texts.[60] Much more obvious than any such imputed or implicit drift is the approximation to isomorphism between the

---

54 Mates 1961: 91–3.
55 The idea of so-called "material implication" in late-modern logic Peirce himself traced to the ancient Stoic controversy between Philo and Diodorus. Max Fisch, usually a reliable reporter on Peirce, in fact, traces "Peirce's Progress from Nominalism toward Realism" (Fisch 1967) in part on the basis of the change in his views on the Stoic controversy. While I think Fisch's characterization is generally accurate, on this precise issue Zeman (1997) has shown that the "progress" is more convoluted than it is linear.
56 At least there is a prima facie case that we have in Mates's discussion of Stoic logic a classic illustration of the Clever Hans fallacy, or "looking in the destination for what should have been sought in the source" (cf. Sebeok 1978a). "It is a startling fact that the Stoics were so consistent in the use of their technical terms and so sophisticated from the point of view of logic", Mates tells us (1949: 290n3), "that when the logical fragments are translated into English in the manner described, the results read like extracts from a text in modern logic." What then are we seeing in this result? More an actual ancient development or a confirmation of Mates's reliance on Łukasiewicz's account (1935) of Stoic logic? Fortunately, we have no need to decide this issue in the present work.
57 Manetti 1993: 98.
58 Eco 1984: 32.
59 Jackson (1972: 136) suggests exactly this: "instead of being novel, Augustine's use of 'sign' seems to be in agreement with the Stoic tradition". See following note.
60 We face with Jackson's suggestion a situation analogous to the one Rist describes respecting the contemporary writings about the last two of the four Stoic categories. "Despite the amount that has been written", he says (Rist 1969: 167), "it is not easy to conceal the fact that we have very little evidence indeed." As a curiosity for anyone to pursue, I would note that in the 4-volume Arnim collection of the Stoic fragments (Arnim i.1903/24), the *Index Vocabulorum ad Stoicorum Doctrinam Pertinentium, quae ab auctoribus Romanis e Graeco in Latinum sermonem translata sunt* has no entry under "signum" (IV, 174), nor, on the Greek side, does his *Index Verborum*,

Stoic *sēmaínon/sēmaínomenon* pair and the *signifiant/signifié* pair proposed by late modern semiology as the technical essence of "sign". [61] This similarity would also, and perhaps better, explain why Mates's version of Stoic logic proves so congenial to the logical theories of Frege and Carnap.[62]

Such speculations to one side, the present evidence from Greek antiquity requires us to hold that Augustine's eventual suggestion for sign as a general notion will mark the indigenous *point de départ* of philosophical speculation in the Latin Age, as we will see in due course.

Neoplatonism

The declining age of learning and of mankind is marked, however, by the rise and rapid progress of the new Platonists. The school of Alexandria silenced those of Athens; and the ancient sects enrolled themselves under the banners of the more fashionable teachers, who recommended their system by the novelty of their method and the austerity of their manners. Several of these masters, Ammonius, Plotinus, Amelius, and Porphyry, were men of profound thought and intense application; but, by mistaking the true object of philosophy, their labours contributed much less to improve than to corrupt the human understanding. The knowledge that is suited to our situation and powers, the whole compass of moral, natural, and mathematical science, was neglected by the new Platonists, whilst they exhausted their strength in the verbal disputes of metaphysics, attempted to explore the secrets of the invisible world, and studied to reconcile Aristotle with Plato, on subjects of which both these philosophers were as ignorant as the rest of mankind. Consuming their reason in these deep but unsubstantial meditations, their minds were exposed to illusions of fancy. They flattered themselves that they possessed the secret of disengaging the soul from its corporeal prison; claimed a familiar intercourse with demons and spirits; and, by a very singular revolution, converted the study of philosophy into that of magic. The ancient sages had derided the popular superstition; after disguising its extravagance by the thin pretence of allegory, the disciples of Plotinus and Porphyry became its most zealous defenders. As they agreed with the Christians in a few mysterious points of faith, they attacked the remainder of their theological system with all the fury of civil war. The new Platonists would scarcely deserve a place in the history of science, but in that of the church the mentions of them will very frequently occur.

Edward Gibbon (1777: 423–4)

Notionum, Rerum ad Stoicam Doctrinam Pertinentium have any Latin included under the entry for σημεῖον (IV, 128).

61 See chapter 16 below, p. 676f., and the discussion in the same chapter of "Signs without Objects", p. 681. Compare also Graeser's presentation (1978) of "The Stoic Theory of Meaning". For an astonishing problem in terms of the unity of the proposition the dyadic pairing under discussion might implicate, I refer the reader to Gaskin 1997.

62 See the table of "Comparison of Stoic Terminology with That of Frege and Carnap" in Mates 1961: 20.

As the lengthy epigraph introducing this section perhaps indicates, in the long history of philosophy, so-called Neoplatonism is one of the strangest chapters and strangest tales. It is intimately bound up with the religious and civil turmoils of the great sea-changes in Western religious thought and civilization that marked the centuries immediately on either side of the birth of Jesus Christ.

Platonism in general was the view that the sensible objects of experience are but participations or copies of Ideas or Forms which transcend experience entirely but are the objects of true knowledge which the intellect alone can reach through dialectic and reminiscence. Neoplatonism was this theory as modified in late antiquity to take account of Aristotelian criticisms of the theory and at the same time to accommodate various mystical notions of oriental religious beliefs associated, however indirectly, with Plato's acceptance of the transmigration or reincarnation of souls.

In particular, Neoplatonism developed a doctrine presenting the universe as an emanation from an ultimate indivisible source, the One, beyond being and nonbeing and any possible divisions of being, but from which in a series of emanations all divisions and levels of being originate, and with which the soul is capable of reaching a communion by turning within itself and following the appropriate methods or practices of asceticism and dialectic.

The Circumstances of Neoplatonism

Plato was about forty-three years old at the time that Aristotle was born. Aristotle was thirty-seven at the time of Plato's death at eighty-one. Whatever reservations and criticisms Aristotle had about Plato's views, their respective positions in the Academy and differences in age were such that Plato would hardly be the one fully to take account of Aristotle's critique. Aristotle lived another twenty-five years after Plato, dying himself at about the age of sixty-two.

Aristotle never accepted Plato's doctrine of Ideas. In its place, Aristotle developed a powerful and convincing theory of forms of his own. According to Aristotle's theory, the objects or "forms" of intellectual knowledge do not completely transcend the objects of sensory experience. They are, rather, initially drawn from within sensory objects and are fashioned by the understanding itself through a process of abstraction or "concept formation" wherein a counterpart of the form of the sensible thing itself is developed by the mind to provide, as a "quality" or psychological state of the knower, the basis for a relation of understanding terminating at the very sensible thing in the physical environment – but now apprehended under the aspect of intelligibility. In this way, for Aristotle, intellectual and sensory knowledge alike bear on the same world of experience, though in different modalities or ways.[63] At the same time, Aristotle was ambiguous about the nature of the human soul. The question raised by his philosophy was not what is the state of the soul when separated from the body, but whether the soul is capable of surviving the body's

---

63 See chapter 7 below, p. 309f.

corruption; and even to this question he did not leave an unequivocal reply. In this and in other ways Aristotle's philosophy was much less congenial than that of Plato to mystical and religious views of the universe.

Hence it was natural that, when the interest of the ancient cultures of Greece and Rome turned heavily in the direction of religious concerns, it was more to Plato than to Aristotle that they should turn, yet while hardly being able to ignore the work of Aristotle, especially in its criticisms of Platonic doctrine. This rethinking, then, of the philosophies of Plato and Aristotle in favor of Plato was the essence of Neoplatonism.[64] It was not a question of examining the two thinkers to reject the work of Aristotle in favor of Plato. No. It was question rather of showing that the two could be reconciled, could be shown in the implicatons of their respective doctrines more to agree than they in fact disagreed – agreed in particular more than Aristotle himself in his own lifetime had been able to realize. Far from being a hostile critic of Aristotle, Plotinus comes across in his writings rather as an interpreter sympathetic to Aristotle, who yet by his very sympathy was led to conclude that Plato in the end had got things "just about right". Corrigan[65] has effectively analyzed the intellectual process resulting in Neoplatonism as "a special kind of 'reconciliation'

---

64 "Platonism after the Stoics and especially Aristotle" is one way to describe Neoplatonism. This is what we would find were we to explore the work of Plotinus fully in its own right. Gerson (1994: xv–xvi) ends the first part of his introduction to his monograph on Plotinus by making precisely this point, and it needs to be borne in mind. "Porphyry tells us that the *Enneads* are full of concealed Stoic and Peripatetic doctrines", Gerson notes. The "many hundreds of references to Stoic doctrines" are "difficult to identify because the original texts are lost." These facts show "a fundamental feature of the *Enneads*: they are contributions to a rehabilitation or defense of Platonism against its opponents. The originality of Plotinus" consists overall "in appropriating distinctions and terminology that are Aristotelian and Stoic", then using these to reach "conclusions that frequently go beyond what could be called a plausible interpretation of Plato based on the writings of Plato or even on the oral tradition."

Here we confront again the problem of the esoteric doctrine of Plato. It is important to realize, Gerson emphasizes, that "Plotinus leans heavily on Aristotle for an understanding of what Plato's doctrines actually were." In particular, "Plotinus follows Aristotle" – and Plato himself, if the *Seventh Letter* is authentic (see p. 55ff. above) – "in holding that Plato had an unwritten doctrine of principles. Indeed, Plotinus appears to rely on Aristotle for understanding what that is. Some effort is expended in the *Enneads* in order to show that this unwritten doctrine is at least consonant with what appears in the dialogues. Finally, Plotinus will accept as authoritative an interpretation of Plato by Aristotle, an interpretation which Aristotle himself thinks leads a Platonic doctrine to shipwreck. Plotinus, however, will typically attempt to show that what Aristotle thinks is a disastrous consequence of a Platonic position is in fact true and even necessary. The alternative Aristotelian position is what ought to be rejected. And yet where Plotinus judges that Aristotle is really not in disagreement with Plato, he will quietly adopt Aristotle's terminology, distinctions, and even his explicit conclusions.

"In the light of the above, I have frequently begun my treatment of Plotinian doctrines with the reasons why Plotinus rejects the Aristotelian alternative. I have found this approach enormously illuminating. Plotinus is primarily a Platonist, not an anti-Aristotelian. But his Platonism is in many respects filtered through his struggle with Aristotle."

65 Corrigan 1996: 99.

between 'Plato' and 'Aristotle'" involving four basic stages "which might serve as a guideline for understanding what this might have meant more generally in early Neoplatonism":

> Reconciliation in this case would seem to mean, first, a statement more or less of what Aristotle's real position appeared to be; second, a recognition of the difficulties and puzzles implicit in that position as well as the potential richness for rational analysis; third, a critical analysis, extension, and development of the notion under discussion; and, fourth, a merging of the new point of view implicitly with what purports to be an interpretation of Plato [wherein, however] it is the *argument* which is meant to carry the day, not a previously determined allegiance. [The result, "Neoplatonism", is] an internal discourse or dialogue with an implicit interlocutor or interlocutors: that is, someone capable of understanding Aristotle ... and the nuances of ancient philosophy in a free and creative fashion.

Neoplatonism was the principal philosophical movement of that brief period when the cultures of Latin Rome and Greece existed as one Lebenswelt, from about 146BC to AD313, just before the seat of the Empire was shifted from Rome to Constantinople, and the Latin provinces were left to go their own way in philosophy, as we shall describe in the next chapter.

The Temporary Overlap of Greek and Latin Antiquity

146BC was the year in which Rome brought Greece fully under its military and legal control. It was a kind of cultural version of a "pyrrhic victory".[66] For when the military conquest had been achieved and Rome thought merely to assimilate the culture of Greece, what happened instead was that Greek intellectual culture overpowered the Roman mind. Despite Latin being the language of the Romans, Greek not only continued to be the language of "conquered" Greece, but became in effect the language of learning even in the capital and court of the Roman empire. Cicero, 106–43BC, well attested to the phenomenon:[67] "It was no little brook that flowed from Greece into our city but a mighty river of culture and learning."

Beginning with the first century, this was also the period when the conversion of that Empire in its enormous extent from Paganism to Christianity took place. So it was natural that philosophical thought at the time should find itself preoccupied with religious questions, and for this Platonism provided the readiest vehicle. In Plato's writings, the *Meno*, *Phaedrus*, and *Phaedo*, for example, form a kind of chain in

---

66 So called from Pyrrhus (318–272BC), the king of Epirus, who sustained such losses in defeating the Romans that he would have been better off not to have engaged them at all, and ultimately, despite the earlier victories, was destroyed by the losses his victory had cost him. Thus a victory in which the ultimate costs outweigh the immediate gains has come to be called a "pyrrhic victory".

67 Cicero, c.51BC: *De Re Publica* II, 19.

which the immortality of the soul is connected with the doctrine of Ideas and based on the ancient belief in transmigration (a belief which appears in the *Republic* and *Timaeus* as well).

And in these accounts the path of the soul's transmigration is connected with a doctrine of retribution – higher and lower states of reincarnation are determined by our conduct in this life. The *Republic* treats of the natural continuance or immortality of the soul as something indestructible; and the *Timaeus* treats of the human soul as derived from an immaterial and purely spiritual realm, either returning after death to a higher spiritual state, or descending into the lower life of an animal or worse. The *Theaetetus* contains a digression describing the soul's desire to fly away and be with God – "and to fly to him is to be like him". These are some of the more notable aspects of the original Platonism from which Neoplatonism, the "New Platonism", takes flight.

Philosophy, which started out as human understanding trying its wings in the project of assigning reasons for what we find going on in the world about us, which started out to discover the framework within which the human being can reach an understanding of itself and of the physical universe within which the human species appears among other animal forms, suddenly becomes a full-fledged vehicle of escape from everything that can be seen or touched. Originally turned outward to the reality of the physical universe as including the human soul, in Neoplatonism philosophy turns inward to find within the soul the sole path to reality.[68] Withdraw into yourself and look: there alone "the soul will see divinity as far as it is lawful".[69]

Yet this "turn within" was already intimated in Socrates' concern with the nature and definition of virtue, and further adumbrated in Plato's doctrine of forms. It is these intimations of an inward-looking philosophy in the work of Socrates and Plato that become full-blown in the "new Platonism" of late antiquity. Yet with Neoplatonism, we feel like the child who, with Platonism, was given a little kitten with big paws, never realizing from the paws that it would grow up into the mountain lion of Neoplatonism. We have the feeling that something has gone too far, something has gotten out of hand. The problem is not the examination of the universe within the human soul. Nor indeed is there any reason why that universe, especially in its moral nature, should be any less complex or extensive than the vast physical universe without the soul, the environment which provides the context within which human action, including its moral qualities, is realized.

The problem is with the separation of the two universes, the diremption of inner from outer, the pretense that the inner alone has claim on our understanding, and can be understood in its proper import without any regard for the outer world in its independent being, which is relegated wholesale to the order of becoming in

---

68 Rist does not tell us his rationale for his title, *Plotinus: The Road to Reality* (1967), but such a rationale would not be difficult to frame.

69 Plotinus, *Enneads* III. 4 (= i.AD255/63 #15).

contrast to being. The Neoplatonists, following the lead of Socrates and Plato, and further followed in the Latin Age by the Christian mystics, as we shall shortly have occasion to mention, were surely right in realizing that there is a sense in which even our surroundings, as ours, come to depend upon what is within ourselves. Yet this profound realization becomes one-sided when it is allowed to eclipse and shroud the profound independence which the physical realm also exercises in its sustenance of our being and provision of our possibilities of action and interaction. The philosophical problem is to account for neither inner nor outer in their separate "identity", but to account rather for that dynamic tension which maintains the boundary between the two as a permeable and labile boundary of interaction within the objective world of experience.

Science in the modern age will establish itself principally by concentrating on the physical dimension of the outer world; mystics of all ages will concentrate primarily on the inner world; but, as we shall see, not until the emergence of the Fourth Age of understanding in postmodern times will the action of signs be sufficiently thematized to account for the interdependencies of the two realms in the constitution of integral human experience, from mystical to scientific, sensible to intelligible, through the action of signs without which there would be neither self nor world to speak about.

Henology vs. Ontology

The central figure in the tale of Neoplatonism is, without a doubt, Plotinus (AD203–70). But there are many ancillary figures, and perhaps in this case we should mention first the somewhat mysterious figure of the third-century Ammonius Saccas (c.AD175–242). By some accounts a convert from Christianity back to paganism, Ammonius was a teacher both of Plotinus and of Origen (c.AD185–254), the first great Christian apologist. Plotinus, a Coptic Egyptian with a Roman name and a Greek education, studied with Ammonius at Alexandria for about eleven years before founding his own school at Rome around AD245. He came to be admired in the very highest circles of Roman society. The Emperor Gallienus (r.253–68) at one point considered sponsoring an attempt by Plotinus to restore the ruined city of Campania according to the plan of Plato's *Republic*. And it was the later Neoplatonist Aedesius, the successor to Iamblichus (died c.333), whose philosophical notions the Emperor Julian would rely on in the last attempt of a Roman Emperor to preserve the pagan religion of the ancient Republic, as we will see in the next chapter.

Porphyry (c.AD233–304) tells us that for his first ten years in Rome Plotinus gave oral expositions, some on the thought of Ammonias, but wrote nothing. This would place the earliest of Plotinus' writings around the year AD255, when the author was already fifty. Porphyry describes the writing fashion of Plotinus in a passage that helps one understand in a sympathetic way the difficulty, even obscurity, of the *Enneads*:[70]

---

70 Porphyry, c.AD300: *Life of Plotinus*, 8, pp. 29–31.

When Plotinus had written anything he could never bear to go over it twice; even to read it through once was too much for him, as his eyesight did not serve him well for reading. In writing he did not form the letters with any regard to appearance or divide his syllables correctly, and he paid no attention to spelling. He was wholly concerned with thought; and, which surprised us all, he went on in this way right up to the end. He worked out his train of thought from beginning to end in his own mind, and then, when he wrote it down, since he had set it all in order in his mind, he wrote as continuously as if he was copying from a book. Even if he was talking to someone, engaged in a continuous conversation, he kept to his train of thought. He could take his necessary part in the conversation to the full, and at the same time keep his mind fixed without a break on what he was considering. When the person he had been talking to was gone he did not go over what he had written, because his sight, as I have said, did not suffice for revision. He went straight on with what came next, keeping the connection, just as if there had been no interval of conversation between.

What actually comes down to us seems to be all that Plotinus wrote, but as it went through the editorial hands of Porphyry who fashioned a whole under the title of *Enneads* (or "Nines", six groups of nine treatises). The fifty-four treatises which make up this work Porphyry so arranged because both six and nine are perfect numbers; nine in particular[71] because nine, as the square of the trinity of complete harmony or three, is the perfect number. Scholars think that in fact Plotinus wrote forty-five rather than fifty-four treatises. But for this detail I refer the reader to the entry for "Plotinus" in the list of References at the end of this book, where the system of historical layering for all authors requires us to take the matter up.

Thus we owe to Porphyry the substance of what we know about the doctrine of Plotinus, the central figure and principal fount of Neoplatonism. His philosophical doctrine, varied by others but always around the central theme of the One, beyond being and nonbeing, the source and ambience of all that is, surrounding and within everything but itself nowhere, is the distinctive feature of the school. "His is an 'henology' not an 'ontology', an 'account of unity' and not an 'account of being'," is the way Leo Sweeney puts it,[72] in what ranks as one of the clearest and most concise introductory accounts of the philosophy of Plotinus in recent literature. As "ὄν" is the Greek term for "being", so "ἕν" (pronounced "hen") is the Greek term

---

71 MacKenna (in Grace Turnbull 1934: 11n.), in his translation, annotates Porphyry's remark that he has divided the writings of Plotinus "into six sets of nine, an arrangement which pleased me by the happy combination of the perfect number six with the nines", as follows: "In allusion to the Pythagorean theory that numbers are influential principles: three being the trinity is Perfect Harmony or Unity; twice 3 is the Perfect Dual; thrice 3 the Perfect Plural. This explains the use of 9 as a mystical number."

72 Sweeney 1961: 510. The term "henology" for "philosophy of the One", however, is not original with Sweeney but appears to be a coinage of Gilson 1948: 42 ("*énologie*" is the actual expression in Gilson's French text). See Aertsen 1992: 120n4.

for one. Whence, as "on+logos" gives "discourse about being or "ontology", so "hen+logos" gives "discourse about the one" or "henology".

The most instructive approach to Plotinus for our purposes in the present work, I think, is to develop this contrast between henology and ontology as it relates to logic. For, as we have already seen in dealing with the Stoics and will see much further in the chapters on the Latin Age, it is in the context of logic and the philosophy of nature that the doctrine of signs will eventually take form; and it will be the discussion of relation in Aristotle that will prove the principal seed from which the doctrine of signs will blossom. This approach will enable us to keep in the line of our main theme, whereas a fuller treatment of Plotinus' doctrine in its own right would lead us in a quite different direction, a path for another day.

The Question for Neoplatonism: Outward to Things or Inward to the Soul's Source and Origin? The "flight of the alone to the Alone"

We will see later in discussing Aquinas[73] that the medieval "philosophy of being" is rooted in a notion of the distinctive light of human understanding, according to which that which first falls within the grasp of a distinctively and species-specifically human awareness of the Umwelt is "being-as-first-known". It is at once the most primitive and the most comprehensive of all intellectual apprehensions, since it embraces in an undifferentiated, potential way all that experience and analysis will or even could reveal in the form of truths or fictions about the universe. Within this global grasp wherein the Umwelt is here and now presented to understanding under the totalizing relation of a whole to itself, according to Aquinas, the understanding or intellect forms its first concept in the experience of "this rather than that" which becomes, in judgment, "this is not that", and the "predicate" in this experience (the "not this" – or "not that") is the concept of *nonbeing*.

Plotinus wishes to focus our attention in the opposite direction from that which the mind moves in forming first the concept of "nonbeing" and consequently the judgment which grasps as the first principle of all further clarificatory discourse the principle that "one and the same thing cannot in one and the same respect both be and not be". He directs our consideration to what lies *prior* to the experience of difference, and prior even to the actuality of being-as-first-known, to the Source of everything that we call or experience as actuality in a world of "thises" that are not "thats":[74]

> Whoever beholds the One cannot say that It either is or is not such and such, for
> thereby the person would say that it is one of those beings which can rightly be termed

---

73 See "The Problem of Being as First Known" and "The Sequence of Primitive Concepts", in chapter 7, pp. 341ff. & 355f.; with further discussion in chapter 15, "The Peculiar Case of Firstness", p. 645ff.

74 From Plotinus i.AD263/68 #39: *Ennead* VI.8. 9. 37f., in the Greek text of Bréhier 1951: vol. 6, adapting a translation of this passage from Sweeney 1961: 513n21.

such and such, whereas It really is other than all such beings. Having seen that It is indeterminate, he can enumerate all the beings which come after It and then say that It is nothing of all of them.

This One is not the original global "being-as-first-known" of which Aquinas speaks, however, for *that* being is a virtual plurality, whereas the One of which Plotinus speaks is precisely both *before* and *beyond* all possible plurality and is the ultimate Source for everything that we experience as in any way different from anything else. To grasp the One, therefore, the soul must move from its first awakening not in the direction of nonbeing, that is to say, not toward the world of material objects and sense:[75]

> the soul travels the opposite way, it comes not to something else but to itself; and so when it is not in anything else it is in nothing but itself. But when it is in itself it is not alone and not in being, it is in That, for one becomes oneself not as entity but beyond entity by that intercourse. So if one sees that one's self has become this, one has it as a likeness of the Divine, and if one goes on from it, as image to original, one reaches the end of one's journey. And when a human being falls from the vision, that person wakes again the virtue within and considers all the order and beauty there, and is lightened and rises through virtue to Intelligence and through wisdom to the Divine. This is the life of gods and divine and blessed human beings: deliverance from the things of this world, a life which takes no delight in the things of this world, escape, in solitude to the Solitary.

In this "flight of the alone to the Alone" the human being discovers "the cause and power of a wise and intellectual life":[76]

> From the One comes Life and Intelligence because [the One is the source] of entity and being inasmuch as One. The One is simple and first, because the One is the principle and Source from which all things come. From the One comes primal motion, which is not in the One, and from the One comes also rest, of which the One has no need, for the One is neither in motion nor at rest, since the One has nothing in which to rest nor to which to move. Around what should the One move? Or to what or in what? For the One is the First. But the One is not limited, for by what could the One be limited?

How to Read Plotinus?
The manner by which the One gives rise to the universe is by what Plotinus calls "emanation". This conception is difficult to grasp save by metaphor: illumination "emanates" from a source of light, heat "emanates" from a source of heat, power

---

75 Plotinus i.AD255/63 #9: *Ennead* VI.9. 11. 35f.; cf. Sweeney 1961: 516.
76 Plotinus i.AD263/68 #32: *Ennead* V.5 in the Greek text of Henry and Schwyzer 1959: II, 5. 10. 10f.; adapting the translation of Sweeney 1961: 514.

"emanates" from a source of power, and so on. Plotinus envisions a cascade of beings emanating from the One which is beyond being, through pure intelligent spirits down through the embodied spirits of human beings to the nonbeing of matter itself, the source of evil in nature.

This central reliance on metaphor is what creates most of the difficulties in reading Plotinus. Aristotle had shown in his logic that without the principle of contradiction it becomes impossible to speak with clarity, and that he who would abandon the principle entirely would be unable to tell the difference between a man and a ship (a trireme, actually) or anything else. Sweeney suggests that there is a way around this problem, and that it lies in the difference between henology and ontology:[77]

> No one who has attentively read the *Enneads* can fail to realize that the principle of contradiction is not very operative or, at least, is not primarily operative there. Other principles influence the Greek author much more deeply as he worked out and expressed his position, and to these that principle is subordinated.
>
> This subordination seems inevitable if one reflects for a moment on the principle of contradiction. Such a principle has primacy in a philosophy of *being* for the simple reason that in such a philosophy being has primacy and that principle is a primal expression both of being and of its primacy. ... A philosophy is the intelligible re-presentation of the universe in light of what a philosopher conceives as genuinely real, and the basic principles will manifestly grow out of that conception of reality and be expressed in its terms.
>
> [Hence] where reality is differently conceived, the guiding norms are also different .... Plotinus is a case in point. His is not a metaphysics of being, which at best holds for him second rank. For him to be genuinely real is not to be being but to be one. ... the principle of being *seu* [or] contradiction[78] ... recedes into the background, as his frequent use of paradox perhaps indicates.

This is an ingenious if not entirely satisfying "solution" to the centrality of metaphor in the Plotinian explanation of the cosmos. Sweeney, by this maneuver, is able to bring everything together in Plotinus, beginning with the principle that "Whatever is real is one", proceeding to the principle that "Whatever is one, is also good", and concluding with the principle that "Whatever is prior is of greater reality than that which is subsequent". Thus the One, as prior to all division, is supremely Good. What emanates out from the One, being Other, is divided, and so both one and other than one. As one, the "creature" is good, but as other than one it partakes at the same time of evil; as dependent on the one it is a "creature", but as separated from the one it partakes at the same time of nonbeing. That creature closer to the one will have less of evil and more of good, hence is "higher" in a

---

77 Sweeney, "Basic Principles in Plotinus's Philosophy" (1961): 508–10.
78 Or – non-contradiction! See the discussion of "The Sequence of First or 'Primitive Concepts' consequent upon Being" in chapter 7, pp. 355–7.

priority of descent from the One. That creature farther from the One is "lower" in the descent, and matter itself is the lowest of all, the term and source of evil in a universe each of whose levels or "grades" of being marks a definitive step in a "hierarchy of being"[79] from the depths of matter to the heights of purely spiritual substances and beyond to the unknowable One from whom the hierarchical cascade of being proceeds and of which we know at least this much: that the emanation from the One of the multiplicity of grades of beings is a necessary procession.

In this way are to be found "at least three principles [– to wit: whatever is real is one; whatever is one is good; whatever is prior is of greater reality than the subsequent –] which appear primarily operative in Plotinus's thinking and which [unlike the principle of contradiction] are never violated or set aside".[80] That is no small thing, and enables Plotinus to speak with clarity after all, albeit a clarity different from what Aristotle considered clarity to be.

How to Interpret Ultimate Potentiality?

Good and Evil are two ideas that go together in experience and philosophy. Neoplatonism is commonly discussed beginning from Plato's Idea of the Good as the loftiest of the Forms. But at the other end of the hierarchy, as it were, the lowliest point of the universe is encountered in Plato's discussion of the creation of the universe, in the dialogue *Timaeus*, with the notion of "the receptacle" – in a manner, he says,[81] "the nurse of all generation". Plato summarizes the problematic as follows:[82]

> Wherefore the mother and receptacle of all created and visible and in any way sensible things is not to be termed earth or air or fire or water, or any of their compounds, or any of the elements from which these are derived, but is an invisible or formless being which receives all things and in some mysterious way partakes of the intelligible, and is most incomprehensible. In saying this we shall not be far wrong.

Here Plato retains to the end the split between the sensible world of forms in matter and the intelligible world of forms as such. In rejecting the idea that reality lies only in a suprasensible realm but includes also the sensible world as such, Aristotle rejects precisely this idea of a receptacle prejacent to and independent of the forms "received" in matter. In its place he posits his notion of "pure potentiality" or "prime matter", which has absolutely no existence independent of the substantial forms of material individuals but constitutes simply their intrinsic capacity to be transformed into other kinds of substances than they are here and now. Here and now may be an individual lion and an individual human being in an interaction:

---

79 The word "hierarchy" is used so freely in describing Plotinus' view of the universe that it comes as quite a surprise to realize that the term postdates Plotinus and comes rather from the 6th-century Pseudo-Dionysius. See Dominic O'Meara 1996: 66ff.

80 Sweeney 1961: 512.

81 Plato c.359–347BC, *Timaeus* 48d.

82 Ibid.: 48eff., esp. 51c.

the lion, hungry, has just leapt and sunk into the human his teeth and claws as the first step toward dinner. Other lions from the pride soon join in, and, by the end of the feast, of the human little remains but the bones, which in their turn may become fossils or simply reprocessed in other ways over the course of the universe's transformations. The flesh is on its way to being transformed into lion waste matter in one part and lion flesh in the other part. The same matter which had formerly received and sustained the substantial form of a human being is now receiving and being sustained by the substantial form of a lion.

But this flesh of the lion retains within its depths the capacity, in its turn, to be turned into the flesh of yet some other predator; and thence yet again into some other substance and series of substances in the unending process of transformations which we call the universe, the intelligibility of which we measure from within by means of what the Latins would term "transcendental relations", the very relations expressing the requirements in discourse for understanding the physical interactions through which material substances both sustain and transform themselves. Aristotle terms this potential dimension of material substance "prime matter", a purely intelligible dimension of substance real only in its correlation with substantial form and in no other way. The actuality of substantial form then becomes his *point d'appui* for locating reality at the very heart of the sensible world itself, distinguishing thereby the substantial form of material substance from the substantial form of substances – pure intellects – separated from matter. And implicit in this discussion is the distinction generally of the substantial forms of all finite existents from the reality of the Mover Itself Unmoved which transcends as Pure Act the distinction between potency and act which marks, the medievals would say, even the pure spirits whose forms are yet potential respecting the act of existence, even though a substantial form spiritual as such has no correlation with the prime matter which makes material substances transformable one into the other across the lines dividing natural kind from kind.

But the underlying potentiality out of which the individuals themselves arise, the "substrate" of substantial change (the "coming to be" and "passing away" of individuals), for Aristotle, against Plato, is not a "receptacle" but a finitizing correlate of substantial acts as not merely limited but transformable in the very specific kinds that they individually illustrate. Prime matter as "substrate" has no being in its own right, not even that of a pure formlessness, but only the relative being of a surpassable limit (thus differentiating material substance as such from spiritual substance as such) within which a form achieves specification of a mode of finitude according to which existence can be exercised. It is therefore the pure dimension within the natural individual or substance according to which the substantial form specifying the mode of existence exercised here and now is always replaceable by some other substantial specification dictated by the play of accidental changes overcoming the substantial dispositions necessary to sustain any given substantial form. Aristotle observed that a man cannot be said to have the potential to be a corpse, because the corpse would not be a man, and change requires continuity; but that does not change the fact that prime matter, from the point of view of the natural individual, is a "being-toward-death".

Potentiality, in sum, from prime matter all the way to subsistent intellectual forms existing not as instances of species but as species in their own right, is always relative to act, and can exist in no other way; whereas act is relative to potency only when the actuality in question is a limited or finite act. Thus nothing prevents act as such from existing as such in a pure form; and the analysis of change as a transition from potency to act leads by a sufficiently refined logical consequence to the notion of a pure act as existence itself, *ipsum esse subsistens*, the only source whence the action of causes becomes in the first place possible. "Pure Act" is Subsistent Existence, but "pure potentiality" has no existence save through the substantial actuality of which it expresses the limits as surpassable and replaceable. Prime matter is thus relative to substantial form, but only some substantial forms are relative to prime matter; and even in the case of those substantial forms that are correlative to matter, the correlativity belongs to them not as *act* per se but only as *finite* acts of *individual instances of specific kinds*.[83] (Hence will Aquinas conclude that substantial forms not correlative to matter, pure spirits, are not individuals *of a species* but are *each one a species* in its own right.)

Neoplatonism is commonly treated beginning with the Form of the Good, which leads to the One beyond being and non-being. But matter as the receptacle of forms leads to the notion of evil for Neoplatonism, and an analysis of the movement could as well start here, on the dark underside, as it were, of the doctrine of the Form of the Good. At least it can be said that Plotinus, in his effort to make a synthesis of Aristotelianism with Platonism, began precisely here with a revisiting of the difficult Aristotelian concept of prime matter as pure potency, developing the difficulties he identified in the direction of a restoration of the Platonic doctrine of the receptacle, a "surface as even and smooth as possible"[84] so as to make no impression of its own to mar the impressions made on it by the forms it receives. Plotinus begins apparently accepting Aristotle's doctrine that prime matter has no existence or nature of its own save in relation to form, a doctrine which led Aquinas, as other later Latins, to the view that God in creating the world acts "upon nothing", the only intelligible case where action presupposes nothing prejacent to itself, as we will see in chapter 7. But for Plotinus the acceptance becomes not a point of departure for the drawing of consequences directly so much as a point of departure for quite a different question with quite different consequences. Corrigan paraphrases the question Plotinus raises upon this point as follows:[85] "can we make sense of

---

83 There are not many modern studies of the contours of this recondite but crucial medieval discussion. The doctoral study of Collins 1947, esp. the chapter on "The Thomistic Polemic against Universal Matter", pp. 42–74, bears citing.

84 As Plato said in his *Timaeus* by way of analogy. Corrigan (1996: 115) puts the Neoplatonic position advanced from Plotinus in straightforward language: "matter *does* receive shape, but it is not itself shaped by this reception".

85 Corrigan 1996: 112.

the view that matter is potential *unless* we posit an underlying matter" – a matter, that is to say, more fundamental than that captured in Aristotle's doctrine of "prime matter", and very like that characterized in Plato's doctrine of the receptacle of forms – "which is none of the things upon it and yet all of them potentially?" In other words, that matter is "nothing in actuality" does not prevent it from being "something else" than actuality and independent of form as such in any sense, to which the giving of actuality through the reception of forms is presupposed,[86] namely, a prejacent receptacle, exactly as Plato had described in his *Timaeus*!

This reinterpretation by Plotinus of the ultimate nature of matter as potentiality ("prime matter") becomes, in this manner, the root of the conflict between Neo-platonism and the Latin Aristotelianism which would arise through the thought of Albert the Great and, especially, Thomas Aquinas after him in the interpretation of the Aristotelian doctrine of substance. The Plotinian reinterpretation is also allied to the Manichean views so attractive to the young Augustine who indeed saw matter and the body as the domain of evil, to the point of contemplating a divinity whence evil emanates in the material world even as goodness emanates in the spiritual world from a divinity purely good.

If we look to ontology rather than logic, then, Plotinus' insouciance toward the principle of contradiction would be rooted not in his mysticism, natural or supernatural, but precisely in his doctrine of being as never achieved in the becoming of forms in matter. But let us deal with the question in the most general terms possible. And in Neoplatonism, I think it is not ontology but the turning of the soul within itself as the source of all doctrine, ontological, epistemological, or logical, that is the central intuition, the decisive moment, the central meaning of "experience".

How to Deal with Contradictions?

We do not know what Aristotle would have said to Plotinus, since time prevented him from an opportunity to study or meet with Plotinus (Aristotle having been dead some five hundred and twenty-five years or so when Plotinus was born). Moreover, Aristotle never really considered the idea of viewing the Source of the universe in terms of what lay *prior* to any *primum cognitum*. His own philosophy, and that of those with whom he begged to differ, had always looked in the other direction, the direction of outer experience and the things revealed there, *posterior* to the experience of being. It was in this perspective that he formulated his famous *reductio ad absurdum* or "reduction to absurdity" of those who did not follow the principle of contradiction:[87]

> If all contradictories are true of the same subject at the same time, evidently all things
> will be one. For the same thing will be a trireme,[88] a wall, and a man, if it is equally

---

86 A view, as we will see, which the doctrine of *esse* developed in Aquinas absolutely precludes.
87 Aristotle 348–7dBC: *Metaphysics* IV, 1007b19.
88 A type of ship in the ancient world powered by three levels of oars.

possible to affirm and to deny anything of anything, – and this premise must be accepted by those who share the views of Protagoras. For if any one thinks that the man is not a trireme, evidently he is not a trireme; so that he also is a trireme, if, as they say, the contradictory is true. And we thus get the doctrine of Anaxagoras, that all things are mixed together; so that nothing really exists. They seem, then, to be speaking of the indeterminate, and, while fancying themselves to be speaking of being, they are speaking about non-being; for that which exists potentially and not actually is the indeterminate. ... for instance, if it is true to say of a man that he is not a man, evidently it is also true to say that he is either a trireme or not a trireme. If, then, the affirmative can be predicated, the negative must be predicable too; and if the affirmative is not predicable, the negative, at least, will be more predicable than the negative of the subject itself. If, then, even the latter negative is predicable, the negative of 'trireme' will be also predicable; and, if this is predicable, the affirmative will be so too. – Those, then, who maintain this view are driven to this conclusion, and to the further conclusion that it is not necessary either to assert or to deny.[89] ...

Again, either the theory is true in all cases, and a thing is both white and not-white, and being and not-being, and all other contradictories are similarly compatible, or the theory is true of some statements and not of others. And if not of all, the exceptions will be agreed upon.

It would seem to be on this last point – the possibility of the abandonment of the principle of contradiction only in respect of "some statements and not of others", with exceptions that "will be agreed upon" – that there will prove to be room for dialogue between Neoplatonism and the philosophy of being in the Latin Age. For what Plotinus has hit upon is the idea of taking the inward side of experience precisely as such, rather than its outward counterpart – the *Innenwelt* rather than the *Lebenswelt* – as his point of departure.

Intellectual Discourse vs. Mystical Experience

We will see something like this again at the origin of modern philosophy, when Descartes inspires the movement of Rationalism by turning away from the senses to find within his own mind the source of all truth and knowledge.[90] But Plotinus is in this respect much more radical than will be Descartes. For Descartes turns within still to deal with ideas and concepts directly expressible in intellectual discourse.

---

89 Aristotle 348–7dBC: *Metaphysics* IV, 1008a29: "Further, it follows that all would then be right and all would be in error, and our opponent himself confesses himself to be in error. – And at the same time our discussion with him is evidently about nothing at all; for he says nothing. For he says neither 'yes' nor 'no', but both 'yes' and 'no'; and again he denies both of these and says 'neither yes nor no'; for otherwise there would already be something definite. – Again, if when the assertion is true, the negation is false, and when this is true, the affirmation is false, it will not be possible to assert and deny the same thing truly at the same time. But perhaps they might say we had assumed the very thing at issue."

90 See chapter 12 below, p. 513ff.

Plotinus does not. He is interested in an experience, an experience that can only be called mystical, the contact of the human soul in an experience of the divine, and the cultivation and expansion within that soul of what it has of the divine. For "if one sees that one's self" has its humanity "as a likeness of the Divine", as Plotinus tells us in the text of the *Enneads* cited above,[91] "and if one goes on from it, as image to original, one reaches the end of one's journey", namely, the "life of man with God",[92] as the later Christian mystics would put it.

It is thus that the great attraction of Neoplatonism for the Christians will, so to say, emanate. The Christian revelation speaks of man as "made in the image and likeness of God", and the Christian religion teaches that the destiny of human beings is to be united with God through grace to spend all eternity in the contemplation of all reality through the "beatific vision", wherein the Divine Essence itself supplies to the soul the role of concepts, and God is seen as all in all.

As long as there is a tradition in the West and in the world of authors who will try to explain claims of direct experiences of God as transcending all of the world, there will be an interest in literature of the type that Plotinus generated in the school of Neoplatonism. Neoplatonic influence will be everywhere in the Latin Age, not so much as a philosophy (excepting the case of Scotus Erigena, which we will touch on shortly) as an atmosphere of mystical reverence and hunger for that "taste of divine things" of which mystics have always and will always speak. But an action on the human mind or soul initiated by God perforce transcends the proper sphere of what can be grounded in experience *as the measure of philosophical explanation*. Such an action may enter the sphere of human experience, to be sure; but it does so by definition and perforce from the outside. Philosophy may reckon the possibility of such action, and take account of its probabilities and apparent or possible consequences. But for thought to claim its origin in such a sphere, or to consist only or principally in such reflection, is to forfeit its claim as philosophical reason.

We would find the Neoplatonic mentality in Bonaventura (1217–74), "the Seraphic Doctor", Franciscan colleague of Thomas Aquinas at the University of Paris, in his doctrine of the primacy of will over understanding, because faith resides in the will, and to believe is more important than to understand.[93] We would find it especially in the Rhineland mystics around and just after the time of Aquinas – in the writings of the immortal Meister Eckhart (c.1260–1327, who was condemned by Church authorities in 1326 and probably escaped burning only by the grace of a natural death which came first), in the work of John Tauler (c.1290–1361) and Blessed Henry Suso (1295–1365); in Hildegard of Bingen (1098–1179), in Jan van Ruysbroeck (1293–1381) and the "Brethren of the Common Life"; in the letters and *Dialogue* of Catherine of Siena (25 March 1347 – 29 April 1380) and in the visionary reports, the *Revelations of Divine Love*, of her English recluse contemporary, Juliana

91 Plotinus i.AD255/63 #9: *Ennead* VI. 9. 11. 35f., more fully cited on p. 120 above.
92 See the work of this title by Moore 1956.
93 See especially Bonaventura's little classic (1259) translated as "The Journey of the Mind to God".

of Norwich (c.1342–c.1423); in the unknown author of the *Cloud of Unknowing*;[94] in
John of the Cross (1542–91) and Teresa of Avila (1515–82); and even to some extent
in the convent of seventeenth century Port Royale and the writing of Blaise Pascal
(1623–62). We would encounter a mentality essentially Neoplatonic also were we to
examine the cultures of the "East", India, China, and Japan – including the variations
on Hinduism and Buddhism and Taoism. Throughout these Eastern developments
there has been no rational counterpart in any development of philosophy proper;
and the effects on the culture as a whole have been somewhat devastating.

But, if reluctantly (for it would be an interesting way to go), yet necessarily, our
route does not much take us by those ways; for we are concerned in this book with
philosophy not as mystical experience but as able to develop explanatory concepts
making sense of the things of this world as we encounter them on that side of the
first experience of nonbeing to which the principle of contradiction no doubt applies.

Toward the Idea of a Creative God or "Source of Being"

Oddly, a principal development toward what will appear among the Latins as the
doctrine or philosophy of being came from this same Plotinus who rejected the
Aristotelian interpretation of the principles of reality and philosophical logic. For
by insisting that beyond the being of substance there is the One from which even
the self-sufficient being of substance (as existing or able to exist in itself) derives,
Plotinus seems to have been the first philosopher to introduce, or, perhaps better to
say, expressly to point toward, the notion of a cause of existence as such, rather
than simply of being in this or that respect.

The Aristotelian causal scheme, in which efficient or agent causality is primary
in the sublunary sphere (the environment as directly experienced, that is), always
presupposes something on which the agent acts. But in the *Enneads* of Plotinus, we
are introduced to the idea of existence as an act which is not the actualization of a
prior potentiality but that upon which all potentialities, realized or not, depend as
potentialities in order to be.

I have put this perhaps more clearly than the "henological" language of Plotinus
would itself allow. Yet the main point has been well brought out by the Plotinus scholar Lloyd Gerson[95] in observing that Aristotle "does not appear to have
considered that the existence of that which has already been generated [terrestrial
substances] or of that which is ungenerable [celestial substances] might be in need
of an explanation", while inviting us in a note[96] to "compare Plotinus's claim that,
despite the fact that the universe does not have a beginning in time, it does have a
cause of its existence." Thus, whereas the coming to be of a thing is the actualization
of prior potencies, and the passing away of things is a reduction of actualities back

---

94 Edited by Walsh 1981 (see under "Anonymous c.1380" in References). Rorem remarks (1993: 4)
    that the very title of this work is a phrase that the Pseudo-Dionysius coined.
95 Gerson 1994a: 18.
96 Ibid.: n. 27.

into potentiality, the *existence* of a composite thing is at once dependent on a cause or source outside the thing and *not* the actualization as such of a prior potency. "Causing existence", Gerson comments,[97] not being the "bringing about of a change", but the sustaining of that within which whatever change is in the first place possible, and that which every finite agent presupposes in order to be able to act in the sense of bringing about a change, then appears as "that for which there is no more appropriate term than 'creation'."

For the idea of creation, the Thomistic scholar Sertillanges reminded us,[98] reduces to the question of whether God acts "presupposing something, or presupposing nothing at all". Yet there will be this vast difference between the dependency of the universe in being on the One of Plotinus and on the Subsistent Existence we will find in the later analysis[99] of Aquinas: the One *necessarily* gives existence to the things outside and below itself; the Esse Subsistens of Aquinas is not so constrained, but *freely* creates, and is able to do so exactly because productive actuality is inferior in being to immanent actuality in which thought consists prior (whether logically or temporally) to any creation.

This distinction between act as immanent and productive, perhaps, a "henology" cannot reach, as an ontology can.[100] Be that as it may, and however obscurely, we seem to find first in Plotinus an analysis of the data of human experience thematically organized to indicate that the existence itself of things needs explaining as such.

To analyze change while presupposing existence is not enough. Aristotle's error in identifying being with substance Plotinus understood all too well, while his own error in identifying act with productive causality as presupposing potency had yet to be brought to light. Even so, we may chalk it up to history's penchant for producing ironies that the *Enneads* of Plotinus provide for the philosophers of being the second inkling of their central insight that, while all potency is correlative to some act, act need not be correlative of any potency but can exist immanently as unconstrained by any limitation from within. So it is not entirely surprising, but it is ironic, to find the philosophers of being bowing to the henologist[101] for raising consciousness to the point of considering being itself as finite on the side of creatures while infinite on the side of the creator. Not only Aquinas, but Scotus too, owes a debt to Plotinus, as does the Latin Age in general to Neoplatonism, as we must now pause to examine.

Neoplatonic Influences on the Latin Age

Both through the work of Plotinus himself in contemplating the existence of the cosmos, and with Neoplatonism in general as the end of the ancient world, history

---

97 Ibid.: 19.
98 Sertillanges 1945: 6–7.
99 See chapter 7 below.
100 This problematic was suggested to me by a reading of Ciapalo 1987, on learning that for Plotinus "motion primarily is cognition". Cf. the remarkable essay of Simon 1971.
101 Cf. Clarke 1952 and 1959. Some pretty serious controversy has developed around this point: cf. Gerson 1994: 233n11.

serves up one of her many ironies, delicious to those who have the taste. Here, in what to its principal protagonists was the last redoubt of ancient Paganism trying to rally and crush the invading and interloping of Christianity on the land of the gods, arose one of the permanent and potent influences on the indigenous development of the Latin Age.[102]

The anomaly of this situation became most concrete in the influence upon the Christian apologist Augustine, born fifty years after Porphyry's death, of the writings of the virulently anti-Christian Porphyry. Van Fleteren has captured the conflict in a few lines:[103]

> Porphyry, beyond all others, was the great anti-Christian of his time. He made explicit what was implicit in the Platonic tradition: the incarnation, God becoming man, was impossible since any fall into the material world involves a degeneration in being. It is against this background that Augustine theologizes about the incarnation as the way of purification for humankind. One of the ironies of Augustine's thought is that he understood the role of God incarnate in terms of the philosophy of a pagan who explicitly denied its possibility.

Pseudo-Dionysius and Other Unknown Authors of Christian Neoplatonism

There were many authors of this school who were of great influence in the Latin Age.[104] Some of the most influential texts were written by persons still unknown. For example, an author of whom we know no more today than that he was an Arabic writer of the ninth century, composed a work entitled *The Book of Causes*. This work was translated into Latin sometime after 1167 by Gerard of Cremona (c.1114–87), and was wrongly attributed to Aristotle. It became one of the two main Arabic antecedents to the development of the metaphysics of *esse* by Thomas Aquinas. We shall touch further on this work and its relation to Aquinas in discussing the twofold finale of Neoplatonism;[105] suffice it for the moment to note that according to Guagliardo, in the fifth chapter of his manuscript on the problem of metaphysics in the writings of Aquinas (interrupted by the author's death on 13 August 1995), "what St Thomas seems to take away from *The Book of Causes* is the ontological primacy of existence as first act, such that existence is what is most intimate to a thing once it has received it, since without existence the thing would be nothing."[106]

The anonymity of these medieval Neoplatonic authors was not always so innocent. Sometimes they availed themselves of the common medieval practice which

---

102 To gain some real idea of the scope of what I here pass off in a sentence, the reader should take the time to peruse at leisure the two volumes of Gersh 1986: *Middle Platonism and Neoplatonism. The Latin Tradition*.

103 Van Fleteren 1995: 22, from which I omit without indication only a quotation of Augustine which does not affect the point.

104 See Gersh 1986.

105 See p. 141 below, in this chapter.

106 Guagliardo 1995a: *An Introduction to the Metaphysics of St Thomas Aquinas,* ms. chapter 5.

we now consider (even if not they then) forgery, whereby a work is sent out under a famous name assumed by an unknown author in order to make more likely a reception for what he has written. An unknown Neoplatonist of probably the late fifth century wrote in this way an apocryphal work under the title *The Theology of Aristotle*, which worked its mischief chiefly through being translated into Arabic and presented as a genuine work of the Stagirite. By this work, Aristotle himself became a Neoplatonist.

The most famous of the Neoplatonic authors unknown in this dubious fashion presented himself in his manuscripts under the pen-name of "Dionysius the Areopagite". Thanks to the work of Stiglmayr and Koch at the end of the nineteenth century,[107] we know more today of this author's provenance than at any previous period. As we will see, though his personal identity has still not been determined,[108] his intellectual persona has turned out to be fundamentally that of the last great Neoplatonist, Proclus, thus involving us in a tale whose beginning and end are the same work viewed from within two different Lebenswelts, as we will remark shortly.[109] There is no doubt that the writings of this author have a merit in their own right. There is also no doubt that this intrinsic merit is not what explains the extent of their success. That is to say, there is no doubt that the writings would in no span of time have achieved anything remotely like their authoritative status and widespread influence over the medieval development of Greek and Latin Christian theology had it not been for the deliberate subterfuge under which they were put into circulation.[110] Frequently abstract and with little basis in sacred scripture beyond

---

107 Stiglmayr 1895, 1895a, 1900, 1909, 1928; Koch 1900.
108 The best guess so far, that by Stiglmayr 1928, seems to have proved untenable (Lebon 1930), yet remains (Pelikan 1987: 13) "tantalizing to ponder" for the further clues it provides toward a solution of the mystery, if solved it is ever to be.
109 See the discussion in this chapter of the "double finale" for Neoplatonism, p. 141 below.
110 "Now anyone who had been converted by a sermon of Saint Paul that has been cited almost from the beginning as the justification for doing apologetics as part of the task of theology could have been expected to describe in writing the nature of his conversion and the meaning of the true relation between Athens and Jerusalem. That he did so in the form of treatises in spirituality, rather than of treatises that were explicitly apologetic in methodology and purpose, only helped to confirm his status in the West, as it had in the East. What is surprising," concludes Pelikan (1987: 22), "at least in some ways, is not that some writings were eventually fathered on him, but that it took so long."
    Well, perhaps history had to wait first for Proclus, to provide a saddle for Neoplatonic philosophizing's Christian stalking horse! In any event, it remains that "the spirituality of Dionysius was accepted in the West because he was believed to carry authority" (ibid.); and the authority he was believed to carry, carry he did not. Yet by the time the false belief was exposed, so much authority had been invested in the Dionysian writings that this invested authority had become independent of its fallacious foundation. It is not just that pseudonymity succeeds if it manages to set down on paper what the "right people" will recognize as commonly received truth (ibid.: 23); there is also outright irony in the particulars of the case (ibid.: 21): "the hapless Pope Honorius was hereticized by the Third Council of Constantinople in 681, with repercussions that could still be heard in the debates over papal infallibility at the First Council of the Vatican in 1870. But Dionysius was rescued and given the position of what we must, somewhat anachronistically, call an 'apostolic father'."

the falsely claimed identity of the author as given in Acts 17:34, [111] once the false identification had been unmasked there was no escaping the conclusion of Luther[112] that the Pseudo-Dionysius "platonizes more than he Christianizes".

This pseudonymous author, who has influenced any person who has ever spoken the word or considered the notion of "hierarchy", wrote four principal works, *On the Celestial Hierarchy, On the Ecclesiastical Hierarchy, On the Divine Names,* and *On Mystical Theology*; in addition, ten letters of his authorship survive. These works, easily among the most influential of all sources drawn upon by authors of the Latin Age, we now know were composed between the fifth and sixth centuries, and we now think most probably by a Syrian desert monk of the sixth century. Whoever may have been the actual author, it was certainly not the long-dead first century Denys who was a companion to St Paul at the Athens Areopagus (the place in Athens where St Paul delivered his famous sermon "on the unknown God"), as the manuscripts we are discussing purport.

Yet the pious ruse was a spectacular success, first among the Greek Christians, then among the Latins.[113] Throughout their age, the work of this Pseudo-Dionysius was invested with the authority of St Paul himself, for[114] "it was believed that St Paul, who had communicated his revelations to his disciple in Athens, spoke through these writings." That the pseudo-Dionysius of the late fifth century came to be reverenced and commented upon by all the major Latin thinkers, then, was no small thing. This particular forgery, in matters of politics, religion, and theology, substantially molded the very shape of the Latin Age as an epoch of human civilization. Not till a thousand or more books were already written and the Latin centuries had reached the middle of the fifteenth century did it come to light that the authority of this Dionysius

---

See further Froehlich 1987 on the survival of the authority of the Dionysian writings after the unmasking of their author's fraud. One has to wonder if the enduring mystery of the actual individual identity of the author has not been a factor in the continued success of the writings as "authoritative"; it is as if the fraud, having only been half unmasked, were treated only halfway as forgery.

111   For a desperate attempt to claim a scriptural basis for the body of Pseudo-Dionysian doctrine, see Rolt 1920: 40–4. Far better to observe simply that (ibid.: 2) "these works have an added interest in the fact that ... neo-Platonism has strong affinities with the ancient philosophies of India". It may be that they find a "scriptural" basis there, in the large sense Griffiths claims (1980: 385), to wit, that "Neo-Platonism, as found in Plotinus and later developed by St Gregory of Nyssa and Dionysius the Areopagite, is the nearest equivalent in the West of the Vedantic tradition of Hinduism in the East". But that is not the question that interests philosophy as such in addressing the content of the pseudo-Dionysian, or any other, writings, as I had occasion to remark in passing above (p. 12) regarding the Upanishads as functions of the Vedic writings.

112   Luther 1520: 562, lines 8–11: "In 'Theologia' vero 'mystica' quam sic inflant ignorantissimi quidam theologistae, etiam pernitiosissimus est, plus platonisans quam Christianisans, ita ut nollem fidelem animum his libris operam dare vel minimam."

113   Pelikan (1987: 22), basing himself on the work of Stiglmayr (1895), remarks on "the almost immediate and almost complete success of the pseudonymity" of the present case.

114   This is the trenchant summary of Stiglmayr 1909: 17, from the more fulsome account in Stiglmayr 1900.

falsely so called was a theft, his name a forgery.[115] By the time the fraud[116] was unmasked, in short, the influence had become so extensive as to be irreversible. The pattern of thought from the writings of Pseudo-Dionysius and its development in a host of commentaries had been woven into the larger fabric of the whole Latin Age.

Were it not for this piously anonymous author, we could otherwise well not have the magnificent tract on the choirs of angels which Aquinas develops at length in the *Prima Pars*, the "First Part", of his *Summa theologiae*,[117] begun in 1266; for it was Pseudo-Dionysius who first informed us, or pretended to inform us, on a virtually "apostolic" authority believed to be such through most of the Latin Age, of the functions, names, and hierarchical arrangement of angels into three classes of nine "choirs": the Seraphim, Cherubim, and Thrones (who attend exclusively to

115 The main hero of this tale was the Renaissance Italian humanist Lorenzo Valla (1406–57), whom we shall have occasion to mention in passing in chapter 5, p. 204. More recent scholars try to put on a par with him in this matter Nicolas Cusanus (1401–64), an effort on which I have no comment. Rolt (1920: 1–2) advises that "the pious fraud by which he [the pseudo-Denys] fathered them [his writings] upon the Areopagite need not be branded with the harsh name of 'forgery', for such a practice was in his day permitted and even considered laudable". Well. I think more on the lines of Pelikan cited in the following footnote.

116 "Fraud": Dodds (1963: xxvii) glosses this use of the term à propos of the pseudo-Dionysian writing as follows: "It is for some reason customary to use a kinder term; but it is quite clear that the deception was deliberate." Deliberate, and elaborate, as Stiglmayr (1909: 13–14) trenchantly summarized: "it is plainly for the purpose of deceiving that he tells of having observed the solar eclipse at Christ's Crucifixion and of having, with Hierotheus, the Apostles (Peter and James), and other hierarchs, looked upon "the Life-Begetting, God-Receiving body, i.e., of the Blessed Virgin". The former of these accounts is based on Matthew 27.45 and Mark 15.33; the latter refers to apocryphal descriptions of the 'Dormitio Mariae'. For the same purpose, i.e., to create the impression that the author belonged to the times of the Apostles and that he was identical with the Areopagite mentioned in the Acts, different persons, such as John the Evangelist, Paul, Timothy, Titus, Justus, and Carpus, with whom he is supposed to be on intimate terms, figure in his writings." And Stiglmayr cites yet further indications (ibid., 15) of what he deems "fictions pure and simple, designed to strengthen the belief in the genuineness" of the forged writings.

Respect for the authors and the religious and theological development involved no doubt mandates the custom of using "kinder terms" than fraud and forgery; and some would argue forcefully that to speak of "fraud" and "forgery" in these matters is anachronistic. When it comes to pious matters of the early Latin centuries, many would argue for a generalization of Davenport's point (1916: 66) regarding the work of Pseudo-Isidore: "It was rather what we mean by legend than what we mean by forgery". There is merit in such reasoning, but in the end, I think, not much; and the polemics such reasoning leads to, the stories it justifies, suggest strongly that the refusal to apply the categories of fraud and forgery in these matters is misguided. When piety and fraud go hand-in-hand the piety does not lessen but augments the fraud, as drunkenness augments responsibility. I agree with the observation of Pelikan (1987: 11) that "it would seem more difficult than current conventional wisdom among theologians suggests to tell the difference between the 'pious fraud' of pseudonymity and just plain forgery." In outlining the "geography" of the Latin Age, we shall have again to touch on this matter: See chapter 5 below, "The Role of Mythology in the Shaping of the Latin Age", p. 193.

117 Aquinas c.1266: *Summa theologiae*, First Part, Questions 50–64 (which consider the being, life, and knowledge of angels); and Questions 106–114 (which consider the action of angels upon the material world of human experience). See the passing discussions in chapter 7 below, esp. p. 339, text and note 196.

divine worship); the Dominations, Powers, and Virtues (who tend to the general governance of the universe); and the Principalities, Archangels, and Angels (who have as their particular task attendance to specifically human affairs in the providence of God). We have Pseudo-Dionysius also to thank for many of the medieval ideas of ecclesiastical hierarchy, which the unknown author claimed as mirroring or miming the celestial hierarchy.

It is a rich field for historians and for theologians with an historical sense to mine, though few so far have truly shown heart for the task. Neither the theologians nor the ecclesiastical authorities are yet likely to welcome a deconstructive enterprise on the scale required to map and analyze the Pseudo-Dionysian effects wrought in Christian and civil consciousness between the appearance of these works late in the fifth century and their fifteenth century exposure as apocryphal legends. The problem is not one of motive, but of a task whose scale must intimidate the best-intentioned, and one for the execution of which not all the necessary tools are yet to hand. The roots of the problem go back to the beginning of the loss of Greek as a language of learning for the early medieval European peoples, whence grows the rhizomic influence of pagan Neoplatonism within Latin Christian religious thinking:[118]

> Since few Western readers were able or courageous enough to examine Dionysius in the original Greek, most of them sought the help of translations, paraphrases, comments, and commentaries that gradually constituted the Latin Dionysian corpus. At each stage a stratum of interpretation was added, which then influenced the next layer. Thus the influence of the medieval Dionysius cannot be appreciated from the Greek text and a modern translation, but only from these Latin translations and aids. Since many of them are not yet carefully edited or widely available,[119] the full picture of Dionysian influence requires much work.

So the pseudo-Dionysian effects stay at work today and tomorrow as part of the heritage of the cultural unconscious and archetypes peculiar especially to the post-Latin civilizations (but also to what lingers of the Byzantium of Constantinople in the Greek and Slavic peoples), both that of Europe itself and of those influenced significantly by Europe, which means (more and more each passing day) the globe of "Mother Earth". It is an amazing heritage. Indeed, Bede Griffiths, as we noted above,[120] recognizing that "Hindu tradition is not a philosophy but a theology", ventures the view that "Neo-platonism, as found in Plotinus and later developed by St Gregory of Nyssa [c.331–c.396] and Dionysius the Areopagite, is the nearest equivalent in the West to the Vedantic tradition of Hinduism in the East". It also appears as the most egregious surviving case from ancient times of the hypostatization of noumenal constructs (dismissed from philosophy by Kant as illegitimate

---

118 Rorem 1993: 237.
119 See the work of Chevalier 1937–50.
120 Griffiths 1980: 386 & 385, respectively. See the remarks in note 111 of this chapter.

expansions on the house of experience[121]), as we will shortly see in discussing the finale of pagan Neoplatonism and the question of the source from which the Pseudo-Dionysius seems principally to have forged his Christian imposture.

John Scotus Erigena[122] (c.AD810–c.877)

The writings of the Pseudo-Dionysius indirectly created – or at least brought to our attention – the only star in the night of Irish philosophy, "a man whose existence casts doubt upon the advisability of retaining the phrase 'Dark Ages' even for the ninth century".[123] Jean Potter describes Scotus Erigena[124] as "the most powerful philosophical intellect in Western Europe from the time of Augustine to that of Anselm", a judgment with which I would not disagree. Yet it was by the translation he made of Pseudo-Dionysius, rather than by his own original work, that he most significantly contributed to the Latin Age.

In 824 the Byzantine emperor Michael the Stammerer had sent to Louis the Pious (AD778–840), one of Charlemagne's successors (in 814) as a renewed Roman emperor,[125] a Greek manuscript of *The Celestial Hierarchy*. Louis turned this manuscript over to the monastery of St Denis, where, as in most places throughout Europe of that time,[126] few indeed could read Greek competently. A translation had been attempted about 838 at the hand Hilduin (c.775–855), abbot of St Denis from 815 and cousin of Louis the Pious. But Hilduin's translation was (by the standard of intelligibility) a thoroughly unsatisfactory job.

When, around 845, in Ireland, John Scotus Erigena (c.AD810–77) accepted an invitation to come to the Continent to teach in the celebrated Palace School founded by Charlemagne, he also accepted the request of Charles the Bald (823–77, son of Louis the Pious by his second wife, Judith, and King of France and the Spanish March since 843) to translate this manuscript. For almost alone in those Latin regions could Scotus Erigena actually read Greek.[127] The translation, completed by AD862,

---

121 Cf. Kant 1783, as touched on below in chapter 13, p. 559n29.

122 The name is often spelled "Eriugena", a version that is more correct in the sense that the "u" preserves the genitive "of" Ireland: John the Scot, born in Ireland; but it makes for a clumsy pronunciation in English today.

123 Durant 1950: 476. Apparently Durant was unaware that the expression "dark ages" originally designated the pre-Christian era in its entirety, but especially the zeniths of Greece and Rome. The expression was only reversed in the early Renaissance, when Greece and Rome came to be revered as the paradigms of civilization and learning, in contrast with the early Christian centuries when the Greco-Roman civilization in what became "Europe" collapsed along with its educational institutions. See part II, chapter 6, p. 213n1 for fuller discussion of this point.

124 Potter 1976: ix.

125 See chapter 5, p. 196.

126 For a scholarly study of the actual state of knowledge of Greek in the Latin West of the time, see the studies gathered in Herren and Brown eds 1988.

127 One of the curiosities of history: the schools maintained by the Church in Ireland continued the study of Greek long after the knowledge of that language had become virtually extinct in the rest of Western Europe. Both Alcuin and John Scotus Erigena had studied in Irish monasteries and we can only guess that it would be from there that Erigena brought the Greek that made him the

introduced into the heart of the Latin Age a quasi-official Christian theology painting the (quasi) Plotinian picture of a universe emanating out of God, passing through diminishing degrees and stages of perfection, and slowly returning by similar stages and degrees back to the deity. Revisions and alternative translations would soon enough appear; but Scotus Erigena provided the beginning of the Latin rebirth of Proclus in particular and Neoplatonic philosophy in general.

This idea of the going forth of things from God and their return to God through the Savior became the structure for the three parts of the *Summa theologiae* of Thomas Aquinas. But before that, and in a more literal transposition, it became the central idea of Scotus Erigena's own masterpiece of AD867, "On the Division of Nature" or *De Divisione Naturae*. But this familiar Latin title of the work was never used by Erigena himself, who always called it rather *Periphyseon*; and Jeauneau [128] goes so far as to cite the familiar Latin title as one "ill-chosen", in view of the fact that the reunification of nature with the divine is a theme of equal importance with that of its divisions in the finite order. Nonetheless, the familiar Latin title derives from the fact that Erigena's main distinction in this work was fourfold: nature which creates and is not created (God as source of all things), nature which is both created and creates (God's self-manifestation in creative ideas), nature which is created but does not create (the intelligible and sensible worlds), and nature which is neither created nor creates (all things as returned to God at the end of time). This work of Erigena's can be viewed as a valiant but futile effort in the short run (to judge by the schism of AD1054, by comparison to which the "Protestant Reformation" begun by Luther in 1517 was but a sub-species) to overcome the increasing divergence of thought between the Greek East and the Latin West. But this is a story whose conclusion remains to be written, and serious studies today[129] raise a suspicion that the importance of Erigena's work may well pertain more to some postmodern future than to its Greco-Latin past.

For Scotus Erigena's own presentation at its time ran into heavy weather. In 865 Pope Nicholas I demanded of Roman emperor Charles the Bald that he either send Scotus Erigena to Rome for trial of heresy, or at least dismiss him from the Palace School so that "he may no longer" give "poison to those who seek for bread."[130] In the thirteenth century his book was condemned by the Council of Sens (1225). Pope Honorius III, who in that same year described Scotus Erigena's book as "swarming with worms of heretical perversity", ordered that all copies should be burned. (In

---

marvel of the French court and imperial Palace School – and that gave to medieval Christendom the Pseudo-Dionysius. On this obscure subject, as McCormick (1994: 15–16) remarks, "the best efforts of accomplished historians" (see ibid.: 35n3) "have turned up only a few, fugitive traces". Jeauneau 1979 gives an idea of the tools Erigena needed in order to do his translation.

128 Jeauneau 1996: X.

129 See the essays in McGinn and Otten eds 1994. The collection by Martin and Richmond eds 1991, though not as unified as their title, *From Augustine to Eriugena*, might seem to suggest, well repays reading.

130 As reported in Guizot 1832: II, 388.

1277 Thomas Aquinas too was condemned; hardly a figure of significance in the period did not run into trouble on this score.)

There is a tale, alleged by William of Malmesbury (c.1095/6–1143), that Scotus Erigena, "a man of clear understanding and amazing eloquence", went to England in his later years, and there, at a monastery school, was stabbed to death with the iron pens of his students:

> He had long since, from the continued tumult of war around him, retired into France to Charles the Bald, at whose request he had translated the Hierarchia of Dionysius the Areopagite, word for word, out of the Greek into Latin. He composed a book also, which he entitled Περὶ φύσεως μερισμοῦ, or Of the Division of Nature, extremely useful in solving the perplexity of certain indispensable inquiries, if he be pardoned for some things in which he deviated from the opinions of the Latins, through too close attention to the Greeks. In after time, allured by the munificence of Alfred, he came into England, and at our monastery, as report says, was pierced with the iron styles of the boys whom he was instructing, and was even looked upon as a martyr; which phrase I have not made use of to the disparagement of his holy spirit, as though it were a matter of doubt, especially as his tomb on the left side of the altar, and the verses of his epitaph, record his fame.

The tale is rendered less credible by want of a motive. Whatever would provoke schoolboys to an attack so vicious? To what noble cause would it make the teacher a martyr? Perhaps Erigena tried to impose on his students his singular view that "no one enters heaven except through philosophy", an effort that could, even today, inspire undergraduates to murder. Martyr to philosophy or not[131] what is certain is that Scotus Erigena died around AD877, and that his name and work have become immortal in the annals of Neoplatonism.

Scotus Erigena, Natura Naturans, and Natura Naturata

Potter[132] considers it "inconceivable that a work of such intellectual power" as that of Erigena, "however alien to the mainstream of Latin Christian thought, should have been completely ignored". Yet the fact remains that all scholarly efforts to show a direct impact of Erigena's thought have failed when it comes

---

131   The tale is reported in Malmesbury i.1135–40: Book II, cap. 4, using the Giles trans. of 1847, p. 119; to which I have compared the Latin text of the Stubbs ed. of 1887, Vol. I, pp. 131–2, where the murder is described as follows: "… apud monasterium nostrum a pueris quos docebat grafiis ut fertur, perforatus, etiam martyr aestimatus est …". Trithemius (a.1516: 99a), puzzled as to the motive, comments simply: "Transpercé en effet de poinçons, je ne sais à l'instigation de qui, par les enfants qu'il instruisait, il brilla après sa mort par de nombreaux miracles." The singular view on the necessity of philosophy is taken from Scotus Erigena a.860: 64 (57, 15): "Nemo intrat in celum nisi per philosophiam". Suggestion of this view as motive for the stabbing is pure abduction. For a fully sober treatment of the tale as legend, see Cappuyns 1933: 252–69, esp. 256–60.

132   Potter 1976: xxiii.

to the specifics of the influence. Marenbon[133] concedes that "there is no convincing evidence that any of the outstanding thinkers" of the twelfth century, "such as Abelard, William of Conches or Gilbert of Poitiers, were influenced by John's work". At the same time, Marenbon rightly insists that the ninth and tenth century "multiplication of manuscripts" *Concerning Nature's Divisions* and the fact of the appearance of excerpts from it in various *florilegia* (the collections of quotations expressing dogmatic or ascetical views in concise form, popular throughout the "dark ages") is "ample evidence" of an influence of the work in Erigena's own day. Yet even Marenbon is able specifically to cite only Heiric of Auxerre (AD841–c.876) as "certainly" a disciple of Erigena while vaguely acknowledging that "most" of the other presumed followers "remain anonymous". For the rest, Marenbon relies for his case of "influence" on "glosses written in the margins of textbooks" (i.e., manuscripts used in the monastery schools of the day), while conceding that "it is not usually possible to be sure that a particular thinker composed glosses to a particular work and, if he did, to know which of the annotations in the various surviving manuscripts best represent his teaching".

Potter therefore suggests[134] that what we need to do is trace the "oblique influence" of *Concerning Nature's Divisions* "on scholastic metaphysics and mystical theology"; yet such a strategy is all too likely to go far afield.

I think the closest thing to such an "oblique influence" would be found rather were we to collapse Scotus Erigena's fourfold division of nature into the twofold division between *natura naturans* or "nature naturing" (nature as dynamic process, which would cover the first two of Scotus Erigena's divisions of nature) and *natura naturata* or "nature natured" (the various products or creatures of nature's fecundity, which would cover Scotus Erigena's second two divisions). This twofold division came into use in the Latin world around the turn of the thirteenth century, but was widely bandied about thereafter down to the end of the Latin Age, especially on the margins (inasmuch as the defining figures of the Latin mainstream more eschew than espouse the terminology when they give it mention),[135] down to the end of the Latin Age.[136]

Whence did this twofold distinction, so intriguingly parallel in central thrust to Scotus Erigena's fourfold division of nature, arise? Could it have been a simplification intended to express the thought of Scotus Erigena? There is no evidence to support such a prima facie plausible conjecture. The claim, cautiously and indirectly established by Siebeck,[137] that the distinction was introduced into the Latin world

---

133 Marenbon 1983: 71–3, "The Influence of Eriugena".
134 Ibid.: xxiii–xxiv.
135 See the survey of the broad occurrence of the terminology throughout Latin Europe from the 13th to the 17th century given by Weijers 1978.
136 Even then, in the 17th century, the terminology takes on a new life within modern philosophy when Spinoza adopts and transmogrifies it as a formula for the pantheism distinctive of his own philosophy.
137 Siebeck 1890: esp. 377.

by translations of Averroes's work has come to be more commonly and carelessly reported.[138] What has to be stressed in the situation of our present knowledge is that the distinction seems to have been introduced not by Averroes himself, but by the translators into Latin of the *Commentary* of Averroes on the *Physics* of Aristotle, which would make the terminology to be of specifically Latin origin dating from the early 1200s.[139] And this introduction of the terminology, within about three decades of the death of Averroes, was not direct and complete but partial: the translator uses the expression "natura naturata" and introduces into Latin the verb "naturare" under the form "naturatur" as a rendering of Aristotle's expression "φύεται".[140] Given the verb form, the formation of the present participle form *naturans* to contrast with the past participle *naturata* becomes an inevitable natural language formation.[141]

This apparent first appearance of the verb form presupposed in the *natura naturans/natura naturata* distinction has been labeled by Lucks[142] as "a rather cosmopolitan effect". The appropriateness of the remark is apparent from Renan's description of the context of the terminology's original dissemination:[143] "the circulated editions of Averroes' writings present only a Latin translation of a Hebraic translation of a commentary made on an Arabic translation of a Syriac translation of a Greek text"! Yet "naturare" itself as a new Latin verb, at least in the translation of

---

138 For example, in Grossman's "Introduction" (1981: 14–15) to the text of Dobroliubov's 1895 Russian poem, *Natura Naturans. Natura Naturata*: "The terms *natura naturans* and *natura naturata* were commonly used in the literature of natural philosophy from Averroes on, and notably in the work of Giordano Bruno (c.1548–1600) and Nicholas of Cusa (1401–1464). The ongoing discussion centered on the relation of God to the world, to nature. For Spinoza, God is the world-essence, the *natura naturans*. But existing in individual things God is also the *natura naturata*." Yet see how careless the "standard report" has here become! Grossman, perhaps following Windelband (1928: 344) tells us that the term occurs "notably" in Bruno and Cusa; yet in fact, one who examined the actual texts (Lucks 1935: 21) found that "Giordano Bruno does use the term, but only in passing", while "as for Nicolaus Cusanus: a diligent search through his *Docta ignorantia*, especially where he treats of the names for nature and God, failed to reveal the use of the term by this author."

139 The text cited by Siebeck 1890: 374, and by Lucks 1935: 14 following him, is from Averroes, *Comment. ad Aristotl. Phys.* II, 1, 11: "Necesse enim est, ut initium medicinandi sit ex medicina et non inducit ad medicinam, et non est talis dispositio naturae apud naturam; sed naturatum ab aliquo ad aliquid venit, et naturatur aliquid; ipsum igitur naturari aliquid non est aliud ex quo incipit sed illud ad quod venit. ... Hoc igitur nomen natura derivatur a nomine eius quod advenit sive quum dicimus ipsum esse naturatum; et hoc intendebat quum dixit: 'sed naturatum' etc., i.e., sed naturatum ab illo a quo generatur ad aliquid venit, et dicitur ipsum naturari aliquid."

140 Lucks 1935: 14–15: "... note that the verb *naturare* is used by the translator. Important too is the observation that just as the word, φύσις, is translated literally, *natura*, so the form φυόμενον, is rendered *naturatum*, and φύεται, *naturatur*."

141 Weijers (1978: 71) notes: "It may be that Michael Scot [fl.1200] created the active form *natura naturans*. At least, one first finds the expression within his *Liber introductorius* (in a context relative to the hope of engendering and to the power of God to modify natural infertility): *cum Deus sit natura naturans et ideo superet naturam naturatam* ['since God is nature naturing and therefore overcomes nature natured']."

142 Lucks 1935: 14.

143 Renan 1882: 52.

Averroes' *Commentary on Aristotle's Physics*,[144] correlates directly with Aristotle's Greek.

If the terminology is, let us say, Averroistic, at least as a product of Latin Averroism, even though not from Averroes himself, we need yet to consider whether, despite occurring in a period of renewed interest – at Paris, for instance – in the work of Scotus Erigena, it was not arrived at fully independently of Scotus Erigena's homologous but fourfold division. Though the story of the Latin translation of Arabic commentaries on Aristotle and other Arabic medical and "scientific" writings is a tangled one with many threads yet to be unraveled, the prospect of finding a major influence of Erigena among the commentators is not immediately promising. Lynn Thorndike's biography[145] of Michael Scot (?–c.1235), "the leading intellectual in western Europe during the first third of the thirteenth century"[146] and a chief one among those responsible for introducing works of Avicenna and Averroes to the Latin world, makes no mention of Scotus Erigena. Yet what medieval detective work in this area might uncover is a question too specialized for our further pursuit here since, in any case, it is this twofold division of Latin Averroism, rather than Scotus Erigena's fourfold division of nature, that has resonated over the later Latin centuries (from the thirteenth to the seventeenth), whence it has migrated to the present day, appearing most recently as the centerpiece in Robert Corrington's semiotic cosmology.[147]

The structural isomorphism between the putatively Averroistic distinction which *did* as such influence the Latin Age and Scotus Erigena's fourfold distinction which *seems not* as such to have influenced the Latin Age may provide some ground for a structural analysis mirroring something of Scotus Erigena's thought in lines of actual influence. Yet such an approach, structural in the sense which contrasts with diachrony, could still not properly be called even an oblique influence.

In the absence of quite new evidence, we must reconcile ourselves to maintaining as probable historical fact the very situation which Potter finds inconceivable, namely, that the Latin mainstream development practically ignored the work Scotus Erigena authored while devouring the work he translated of Pseudo-Dionysius. History is not always kind to what perhaps should have been. But then again, as we noted above, it may be a history yet to be written that will reveal the true import of Erigena's early attempt to integrate within a higher theological synthesis the Greek and Latin religious development.

The Finale of Pagan Neoplatonism
We jump (or jump back) to Proclus (AD410–85), last known author of influence and repute in the school of Greek Neoplatonism. We pass over much pagan tradition in

---

144 Lucks notes (1935: 15) that "the same verb, *naturare*," appears also in a section of the Latin translation of the *Commentary* by Averroes on Aristotle's *De Caelo*, where the section of Aristotle's text commented upon "does not contain the Greek verb φύεσθαι".
145 Thorndike 1965.
146 Ibid.: 1.
147 Corrington 1994.

between, notably Iamblichus (c.250–c.330); but there are no end of tempting byways, where here we are trying to cut a new main road, no more and no less. So we come to the author of a work titled the *Elements of Theology*, the one systematic exposition of a Neoplatonic metaphysics that has survived to our day. The work has an importance second only to the *Enneads* of Plotinus, though even Proclus' modern editor[148] concedes that the *Enneads* "stand on an incomparably higher philosophical level".

Proclus (AD410–485) and Pagan Theology

The title of Proclus's work proclaimed it as a "theology"; but it fulfilled that title in a twofold sense.

The first sense in which the work is a theology is a more or less idiosyncratic one:[149] for Proclus, the text we have from Plato is an inspired text, a *sacra scriptura*,[150] the given which it is our task only to interpret. The second and more interesting sense in which it is a theology is what gives the work its enduring interest as a classic of Neoplatonism, namely, its attempt to exhibit all the forms of true being as necessary consequences deriving in conformity with laws of succession from a single ἀρχή or principle, the One beyond being and nonbeing. Dodds puts the matter well. The value of Proclus is perhaps less that of a creative mind than that of one who systematizes the ideal Plotinus set forth of one comprehensive philosophy gathering into itself all the wisdom to be found in the ancient world. At least that is how Dodds, the late-modern editor of Proclus' main text, sees it:[151]

> The body of thought whose structure is anatomized for us in the *Elements of Theology* is not the creation of one individual or of one age; it represents the last result of a speculative movement extending over some five centuries. If we look at this movement as a whole we can see that its direction is throughout determined mainly by two impulses, one theoretical and the other practical or religious. On the theoretical side it reflects the desire to create a single Hellenic philosophy which should supersede the jarring warfare of the sects by incorporating with the Platonic tradition all that was best in Aristotle, in Pythagoreanism and in the teaching of the Porch. On the practical side we can best understand it as a series of attempts to meet the supreme religious need of the later Hellenistic period by somehow bridging the gulf between God and the soul; to construct, that is to say, within the framework of traditional Greek rationalism a scheme of salvation capable of comparison and rivalry with those offered by the mystery religions.

A Double Finale

Through the work of Proclus, Greek Neoplatonism meets a double finale. On the side of its defense of paganism and attempt to give a pagan "rationale of salvation", the

---

148 Dodds 1963: ix.
149 See the discussion in Dodds 1963: xii–xiii.
150 In the "renaissance", incredibly, Marsilio Ficino would revive this claim: see Gay 1966: I, 272.
151 Dodds 1963: xviii.

project failed and Proclus and his brethren sank into obscurity. But it now appears
that "the unknown eccentric", as Dodds calls him,[152] that "most mysterious of eastern
Fathers", as McGinn calls him,[153] the "genial forger", as Torrell calls him,[154] whom
we have come to know as Pseudo-Dionysius, arrived at his project by dressing up
precisely the work of Proclus in Christian guise and passing it off as the spiritual
and conceptual scheme of Paul's first century convert and companion. Dodds summarizes the work of Stiglmayr and Koch as having shown that Pseudo-Dionysius
reproduced "with a minimum Christian disguise the whole structure of Athenian
Neoplatonism", took over "practically the whole of its technical terminology", and
"followed Proclus slavishly in many of the details of his doctrine".[155]

When, in eleventh century Byzantium, there was a renaissance of Platonism,
Proclus was thought by some to be a pagan imitator of the Christian (pseudo)
Dionysius! It will be in the Latin world to which we are about to turn, however,
that the second finale, the Christian rebirth for Proclus and Neoplatonism, will be
especially achieved.[156] The work of Augustine and Pseudo-Dionysius had succeeded
in making Neoplatonic thought at home among the Latins. When, in 1268, William
of Moerbeke produced a Latin translation of the *Elements of Theology*, it was his
colleague and friend Thomas Aquinas who was the first unequivocally to recognize
that another work, *The Book of Causes*, attributed at the time to Aristotle, in fact had
been authored by some Arab philosopher on the basis of the *Elements* by Proclus.

Having realized the true provenance of *The Book of Causes*, Aquinas deemed
it important enough that he took the time in the busiest part of his life to write
a commentary thereon; and, Guagliardo notes,[157] "since neither Proclus nor the
author of the *Book of Causes* is a Christian", Aquinas "employs the writings of
Pseudo-Dionysius" (whom he, of course, called *beatus Dionysius*,[158] the "Blessed
Dionysius") to guide his evaluation of the works. So Proclus made the Pseudo-
Dionysius possible, and Pseudo-Dionysius, in return, prepared a way for Proclus to

---

152 Ibid.: xxvi.
153 McGinn 1994: 8.
154 Torrell 1996: 127.
155 Dodds 1963: xxvii–xxviii. "No other early Christian writer was so clearly influenced by a particular
      philosopher" as was Pseudo-Dionysius by Proclus, is how Osborn puts it (1967: 510).
156 Pelikan (1987: 24) avers that if it be true that "Dionysian spirituality and speculation may
      have been more influential in the West than in the East", that is "not primarily because of any
      disaffection toward it in the East, but because of the plethora of other works" – he mentions Origen
      and Gregory of Nyssa in particular – "embodying it", that is to say, embodying the Neoplatonic
      outlook and synthesis. Of course, this is to say little more than that the intellectual climate of
      Christian Byzantium, to the extent it became philosophical at all, was always dominated by
      Platonism rather than by Aristotelianism (cf. Cavarnos 1989), which comes close to saying that it
      underwent no substantial philosophical *development* properly so called, but constantly hearkened
      back to an older time when the obligations of the intellect to the finite being of what constitutes
      the physical surroundings remained shrouded in imagination and cultic practice.
157 Guagliardo 1995b: xii.
158 Aquinas c.1265–7: *In Dionysii de divinis nominibus*, opening line (Busa 4, p. 542).

live beyond and outside the paganism he preferred. If there be ironies in history, this surely must count among those that are notable. McGinn[159] is practising the art of understatement when he says that "Latin theology would have looked different in ways we probably cannot conceive without these writings".

Dying and behold we live. But death was the first and more immediate finale for pagan Neoplatonism; for while Proclus was conquering Europe in the guise of an early Christian more successfully than under his Aristotelian mask, in his own person not even his claimed communion with supernatural beings by fasting and purification[160] was able to save his philosophy and the school that gave it an institutional home. When, in 529, the emperor Justinian, by closing the Athenian academies, inadvertently symbolized the coming sterility in philosophy of the empire Diocletian had displaced from Rome, the Academy was solidly in Neoplatonic hands. And these hands were not Christian.

Let Gibbon, who provided the epigraph to our treatment of Neoplatonism,[161] provide now an epitaph for its pagan finale. This is an epitaph not on the work of any one author, but on Neoplatonism as an intellectual movement at the end of and as it belonged to pagan antiquity (for, as we have seen, besides this "pagan finale" there is also a "Christian rebirth" through the Pseudo-Dionysius). Here is Gibbon's description of the final situation of the pagan branch of Neoplatonism as a philosophical movement or development of Plato's school:[162]

> The surviving sect of Platonists, whom Plato would have blushed to acknowledge, extravagantly mingled a sublime theory with the practice of superstition and magic; and, as they remained alone in the midst of the Christian world, they indulged a secret rancour against the government of the church and state, whose severity was still suspended over their heads. About a century after the reign of Julian, Proclus was permitted to teach in the philosophic chair of the academy, and such was his industry that he frequently, in the same day, pronounced five lessons and composed seven hundred lines. His sagacious mind explored the deepest questions of morals and metaphysics, and he ventured to urge eighteen arguments against the Christian doctrine of the creation of the world. But in the intervals of study he *personally* conversed with Pan, Aesculapius, and Minerva, in whose mysteries he was secretly initiated, and

---

159 McGinn 1994: 10.
160 As reported in Bury 1923: I, 377. See further in Dodds 1963: xxv–xxvi. Of Proclus too could be said what Inge said (1934: iv) of Plotinus: "many who are not interested in philosophy will be stirred by the devotional earnestness of this pagan saint. But the value of his message to the world stands or falls with the truth of his conviction that thought and devotion, faith and reason, rationality and mysticism, are not enemies but allies. It is a tremendous act of faith; ... and many who are troubled by the decay of the old 'evidences' for the truth of religious dogma will perhaps feel that here they may find a resting-place above the high water mark."
161 Gibbon 1777: 423–4, cited p. 112 above.
162 Gibbon 1788: 282–3.

whose prostrate statues[163] he adored; in the devout persuasion that the philosopher, who is a citizen of the universe, should be the priest of its various deities. An eclipse of the sun announced his approaching end; and his life, with that of his scholar Isidore, compiled by two of their most learned disciples, exhibits a deplorable picture of the second childhood of human reason. Yet the golden chain, as it was fondly styled, of the Platonic succession, continued forty-four years from the death of Proclus to the edict of Justinian, which imposed a perpetual silence on the schools of Athens, and excited the grief and indignation of the few remaining votaries of Grecian science and superstition.

The Tree of Porphyry

Yet quite apart from the twofold, quasi-religious, interest of Neoplatonic philosophy which we have just examined (as the final redoubt of the pagan religion in ancient Rome, and as a principal influence on the development of theology in the Latin Age), there is one little work of Neoplatonism in particular which is of a more general and straightforwardly philosophical interest. This is the little treatise Porphyry (c.AD233–304) wrote (around AD271 and between his skirmishes as a general in the continuation of Plotinus's war against Christianity) as a letter to a friend, a Roman senator, to explain the five factors at play whenever we strive to formulate a definition of anything.

The tract came to be known by the Greek title of *Isagoge*, "Introduction", to the logical study of categories. In Latin, where it was read and studied all over Europe, the *Isagoge* was often called by the title of *Quinque Verba*, "The Five Words", because it had for its subject matter an exposition of the terms "genus", "species", "difference", "property", and "accident". This little tract was a jewel in the history of logic. It deserves study even today (though certain unnecessary overcodings with which the Latins embalmed the work need to be stripped away).

To appreciate the influence of the *Isagoge*, one must bear in mind that Aristotle's logical writings were the main body of Greek philosophy that passed into Latin translation at the beginning of the so-called "dark ages". The logical works, and the Aristotelian idea that logic is the indispensable instrument for rational progress in discourse regardless of subject matter, were thus at work in the medieval ferment of Latin thought even after Europe was thrown upon its own devices in matters of language and learning after the removal of the Roman Empire to the East in the fifth century.

The Roots of Porphyry's Tree

Aristotelian logic was also called "terminist logic", because it studied arguments in terms of relations among propositions as the component parts of arguments, and

---

163 That is, the statues of Pagan gods pulled down by order of the Christian emperors.

propositions as parts resolvable into relations of predication between terms. Thus, terms, propositions, and arguments (represigns, dicisigns, suadisigns, as we saw above)[164] formed the three principal parts or areas of logical investigation. Terms are linguistic signs which represent an object without making an assertion. Peirce, for this reason, would later call them by a Greek-derived name signaling this, "rheme", which in Latin would be *represign*.

In the middle ages, the study of terms was associated with what the Latins called "simple apprehension" or "simple awareness", that is, the awareness as distinct from and presupposed to any judgment about objects. The book of Aristotle dealing with terms, as we saw, was called the *Categories*, which meant the list of the most general or *generic* terms that can be applied univocally (that is, with the same sense in each application) to objects and aspects of objects encountered in our experience of the natural world. Thus, a natural individual, as we saw above,[165] Aristotle classified as a *substance*, and the characteristics of individuals he classified as an *accident*. Natural substances exist in themselves (*ens in se*), though dependently upon their environment and in interaction with other substances; but accidents exist dependently upon substances, either in them (*ens in alio*) or between them (*ens ad aliud*), precisely as those aspects of the individual whereby its own being is expressed and involved with its surroundings.

The so-called "accidents" of substance proved, upon fuller analysis, to be a various lot, ranging from quite incidental and chance features to stable and regular characteristics and intrinsic structural features without which the essential type of the individual would be different (this latter group of accidents, the stable and typical ones, were also called "properties"). The irreducible number of accidents generically considered was a subject of debate and to some extent dependent on the point of view adopted. As we have seen,[166] Aristotle's own most complete list included nine genera of accident: quantity, quality, relation, action, passion (or undergoing an action), posture, where (location), when, and vestition (or external attachments).

Following the study of terms and their properties Aristotelian logic turned to the study of terms precisely as functioning within the proposition, where they acquire further properties by virtue of being given a role whereby they no longer merely represent but make an assertion about the represented object. Propositions are linguistic signs which say something, and Peirce hence later called them *dicisigns* (from *signum*, to represent another, + *dicere*, to speak or to say). In the Latin Age, the study of propositions was associated with what the Latins called "judgment", that is, the complex awareness of an object formed by the expression of a definite opinion about it. The book of Aristotle dealing with judgments was called *Peri Hermenias*, "Concerning Interpretation". For some curious reason, this two-word Greek title was retained in Latin, but mistranslated as a single term, thus: *Perihermenias*. The

---

164 See "The Instrument of All the Sciences" in chapter 3, esp. p. 88.
165 In the section on "Transcendental Relativity" in chapter 3, p. 72.
166 "The Categories of Aristotle" in chapter 3, p. 73ff., esp. p. 77.

same work had a properly Latin title of two words quite well rendering correctly the original two-word Greek title, *De Interpretatione*, "On Interpretation".

Finally, the interrelation of propositions in the formation of arguments provided the focus of what Aristotle called *Analytics*, or logic proper. In analytics, arguments could be studied either from the standpoint of their form alone, which he called *Prior Analytics*, and which the Latins called "formal logic" or (very late) "minor logic". Arguments could also be studied from the standpoint of their subject matter as well as their form, which Aristotle called *Posterior Analytics* and the Latins called "material logic" or (again much later) "major logic". With "posterior analytics" logic shaded into philosophy and science proper. In his books of *Posterior Analytics*, Aristotle was concerned with the establishment of proofs or demonstrative arguments, arguments which state the *reason why* (or *propter quid*, as the Latins said) some situation or thing is the way it is, whence *suadisigns* (from *suadere*, to persuade).

But Aristotle also well recognized that many times we do not understand enough of the matter we are arguing about to construct such proofs. In the case of those not infrequent situations we are forced to rely on merely probable arguments, which state that "perhaps the reason is such and such", thus providing an hypothesis for further investigation or action. In the Latin Age, this type of reasoning was also called "induction", later "ascending induction" or "inductive ascent". Peirce, trying in part to remove the misunderstandings which the early medieval terminology had created among the moderns, called the process of reasoning to a hypothesis *abduction*, reserving the name "induction" (or, as a synonym, "retroduction") for reasoning involved in the testing of hypotheses.

The comparative evaluation of probable arguments Aristotle dealt with in a book he called *Topics*, that is, how to choose a good starting point for the construction and evaluation of probable arguments. And, finally, he wrote a work on how to detect and deal with flaws in arguments, or "fallacies", which he titled *On Sophistical Refutations*, that is to say, on the refutation of nice sounding arguments which yet depend on fallacies.

In his book on *Topics*, Aristotle introduced four key terms: definition, property, genus, and accident. These are the classification of *what can be said* about any given subject matter, and hence are called *predicables*. When we say of any X that it "is Y", we are giving either the definition of Y or are expressing about it a stable feature, a common feature, or a feature easily changed – that is, a property, genus, or "accident" (not to be confused with the broader sense of the term "accident" as the category contrasted to substance, which would include also what is here called a "property", i.e., a stable or necessary accident).

By "definition", here, Aristotle meant above all the essential definition, that is, the expression of the kind or type of thing under discussion, but also any accidental definition – in a word, any definition as such. Definition in the sense of essential definition is arrived at, on Aristotle's own account, by combining the genus with a difference constituting a specific type. So Aristotle's list of four "ways in which one thing can be said of another" implicitly contains five rather than four terms:

species or type, which corresponds to the essential definition; *genus* or essential element which the species shares in common with other types; *difference*, which, when added to the genus, establishes the unique kind; *property*, which expresses the being of a thing in a typical and regular way even though it is not part of the essence as such; and *accident*, which expresses, as it were, the individual uniqueness of a thing's history. This is why Porphyry lists five predicables rather than only four.

The Trunk of Porphyry's Tree

But of the object represented by any term, we can ask, "What is it?" Hence the subject of the predicables is a subject which concerns the definition of any term in relation to its object, what it signifies. In this way, as logic can be considered the introduction to the study of philosophy itself, so the study of the predicables appears as the introduction to the study of logic; for logic principally concerns the analysis of arguments, and arguments are formed through propositions, which in turn are formed from terms. The definition of terms is the key to the understanding of propositions formed on the basis of terms, just as the understanding of propositions is the key to understanding arguments in which these propositions are employed. Where X is a term, we must obviously know what X means or stands for, what it represents, before we can use X either in a proposition or in an argument.

Now the answer to the question "What is X?" always takes the form "X is Y", where Y conveys, necessarily, one or other (or some combination) of the following. Y must express either the essential definition of X, or something over and above that definition. If something over and above the essential definition, then it must express characteristics of the individual, either in the manner of a *property* or of an *accident* (a feature) easily changed. If the answer expresses the essential definition, it will express either the whole of that essence (*species*), or only part of the essence. If only part, that part must be either the common part (*genus*) or the differentiative part (*differentia*). (Note that, respecting Aristotle's categories, both "property" and "accident" belong to the class of "accidents" as opposed to "substance" itself.)

In this way, we readily see that the discussion of the predicables is nothing more nor less than the framework for any theory of definition, and definition is necessary on the face of it for any systematic use of terms in argumentation. Thus logic, as the study of argument forms, involves as part of its foundation the theory of definitions. And the theory of definitions is what the doctrine of the predicables establishes and explains: the form of the possible answers to the question "What is X", where X is a term standing for some object of thought, and where the answer "X is Y" predicates of X another term, Y, simple or complex, in an assertion about the nature or condition of X which purports to tell us the answer to our original inquiry.

Once it is understood that Porphyry has outlined the requirements for forming definitions of terms, it is easy to understand why he considered what he had written to be the *Isagoge* or *Introduction* to Aristotle's categories understood as the terms to be used in the formation of propositions and arguments. It is also easy to see why his treatise, given its brevity and comparative clarity, came to be widely used among the Latins as the introduction to logic as a whole.

An Example of Scholastic Commentary

The student should read Porphyry's text in the manner that the medievals themselves read it for the purpose of understanding and commenting upon it. The work should be broken down into its basic parts, and then the focal point of each of these parts needs to be identified. Because the work is so short, using the 1975 Warren translation of Porphyry's *Isagoge* into English, we may illustrate by means of it something of the manner of medieval commentary on a philosophical text.

Division and Analysis of the Text

The *Isagoge* divides basically into two major parts. First there is the definition of each of its five key terms (pp. 28–49). Then there is the comparative discussion of these key terms (49–62). In the discussion of *genus* (28–33), Porphyry distinguishes three senses, in order to focus upon "that predicated essentially of many things which differ in species" or kind (30). In discussing *species* (34–41), he establishes "what the genus is predicated of essentially and is itself predicated essentially of many things which differ in number" (35), that is, as individuals. In discussing *difference* (42–7), Porphyry again distinguishes several senses, in order to focus principally upon "strict differences [which] make something different in essence" or kind (42) and from which "divisions of genera into species arise and definitions are expressed" (43). In discussing *property* (48), Porphyry distinguishes four senses, but here his discussion becomes comparatively muddled. No one of the four finally emerges as clearly focal (or fully defensible), though "what occurs in the entire species, in it only, and always" comes the closest. In discussing *accident* (48–9), the focal definition is "what can belong or not belong to the same thing".

With these definitions in place, Porphyry proceeds to compare and contrast the focal meanings of the five key terms (pp. 49–62). How this comparative discussion is organized Porphyry fully explains in a paragraph inserted on page 55. No doubt it was at this point in the writing of his letter that the utility of such an explanation occurred to him (a little "out of order" logically speaking, as the creative process normally goes, which is more or less why drafts always improve by being revised and rewritten). A writer of the third century would not be in the position of a modern student, who, using a wordprocessing program on a computer, could simply insert a block of text at its most logical place. Using papyrus or some similar substance, an ancient writer would be considerably more constrained to insert an idea into a manuscript when and as the idea occurred, often without being able, for lack of materials, to redo the manuscript so as to situate the idea in its most appropriate place overall. In the present case, the paragraph beginning on page 55 would logically have belonged rather on page 49, as the introduction to the discussion of the "common characteristics of the five predicables". The problematic text in the paragraph in question opens as follows:

... each predicable differs from the four others. Since there are five predicables all together and each one differs from the other four, then if five is multiplied by four, the total number of differences becomes twenty.

This is plain enough. If we call genus 1, species 2, difference 3, property 4, and accident 5, then it is clear enough that each of the five can be compared and contrasted with the other four – 1 with 2, 3, 4, and 5; 2 with 1, 3, 4, and 5; 3 with 1, 2, 4, and 5; 4 with 1, 2, 3, and 5; and 5 with 1, 2, 3, and 4 – giving a total of 20 comparisons and contrasts, thus:

1 & 2	2 & 1	3 & 1	4 & 1	5 & 1
1 & 3	2 & 3	3 & 2	4 & 2	5 & 2
1 & 4	2 & 4	3 & 4	4 & 3	5 & 3
1 & 5	2 & 5	3 & 5	4 & 5	5 & 4

"But", Porphyry immediately adds, "this is not accurate", for the following reason:

When items in a series are counted in order, the twos always have one difference less because the difference has already been accounted for; the threes, two less; the fours, three less; and the fives, four less. The total number of differences becomes ten: four plus three plus two plus one.

In other words, just as the road from Dubuque to Chicago is the same as the road from Chicago to Dubuque, so a survey of that road carefully made will turn up the same features of the terrain whether the survey team begins in Chicago and ends in Dubuque, or begins in Dubuque and ends in Chicago. Thus, in our above table, the comparative discussion of 1 and 2 (genus and species) in the first column, thoroughly done, will achieve results finally isomorphic with the comparative discussion of 2 and 1 (species and genus) in the second column, and so on throughout the columns. Thus, shading the duplicate discussions in our original table of twenty differences, we see plainly, as Porphyry says, that "the total number of differences" to be comparatively discussed "becomes ten":

1 & 2	2 & 1	3 & 1	4 & 1	5 & 1
1 & 3	2 & 3	3 & 2	4 & 2	5 & 2
1 & 4	2 & 4	3 & 4	4 & 3	5 & 3
1 & 5	2 & 5	3 & 5	4 & 5	5 & 4

As Porphyry puts it,

We have already said how the difference differs from the genus when we say how the genus differs from the difference. It will remain for us to say how the difference differs from the species, the property, and the accident. The number of differences becomes three. In turn, we said how the species differs from the difference when we said how the difference differs from the species. We said how the species differs from the genus when we said how the genus differs from the species. Thus, it will remain for us to say how the species differs from the property and the accident. These differences are two. There will remain the explanation of how the property differs from the accident. For how the property differs from the species, the difference, and the genus was mentioned earlier in their differences from it. Since, therefore, we understand four differences of the genus from the others, three of the difference, two of the species, and one of the property from the accident, the total number of differences will be ten.

Outline of the Isagoge *as a Whole*
Thus, we get the following outline of the *Isagoge* as a whole (including the introductory paragraph, for which we save comment to the end of this discussion):

Praeteritio:[167] Deeper Issues Eschewed for the Purpose of Presenting the Simpler Notions
I. Definition of the Five Key Terms – 28–49
   A. Genus – 28–33
   B. Species – 34–41
   C. Difference – 42–7
   D. Property – 48
   E. Accident – 48–9
II. Comparative Discussion of the Five terms – 49–62
   A. *Genus* compared and contrasted with
      1. Difference – 50–2
      2. Species – 52–3
      3. Property – 53–4
      4. Accident – 54–6
   B. *Difference* compared and contrasted with
      1. Species – 56–7
      2. Property – 57–9
      3. Accident – 59–60
   C. *Species* compared and contrasted with
      1. Property – 60–1
      2. Accident – 61–2
      D. *Property* and *Accident* compared and contrasted with one another – 62

---

167 "Preterition" or "paralipsis": a rhetorical suggestion that, by deliberately concise treatment of a topic, much of significance is being passed over or left out. The purpose of the device is often to try to ensure that the listener will not forget about and will at some point be led fully to inquire into the matter mentioned in passing.

The most influential part of Porphyry's discussion, perhaps, stemmed from his discussion of the category of substance for the purpose of illustrating the interaction of species and difference. The constitution of the (as it came in later centuries to be called) hierarchy of natural being as resulting from this interaction became everywhere known among the Latins as "the Porphyrian Tree" (see below p. 153). Thus, Porphyry notes that "there is a highest genus beyond which there can be no other superior genus; there is a lowest species after which there can be no subordinate species; and between the highest genus and the lowest species there are some classes which are genera and species at the same time" (p. 35). This point holds for each of the ten categories, but it is natural to illustrate it first using substance, since all the other categories depend upon substance for existential instantiation.

To understand the interaction, one needs only to see how "the same differences understood in one way become constitutive and in another way become divisive" (p. 35). The notion of substance is the notion of an existing individual. Nothing in such a notion implies the possession of a body. Thus "bodily" is a difference which, if added to substance, *divides* the category of substance into the two species of material and spiritual substances, and *constitutes* under the genus of substance the species of *bodily substance*. To bodily substance, in turn, can be added the notion of "living". This difference *divides* bodily substance into the further species of animate and inanimate, and, together with bodily substance, *constitutes* the realm of living things.

Notice here that "bodily substance" is a species under substance, but a genus respecting its own division into living and inorganic. Thus "bodily substance" appears as an intermediate class: "The intermediate classes will be species of prior classes but genera of posterior classes", whereas only a "species which is predicated immediately prior to individuals will be a species only", that is, an *infima species*, a *lowest species* (p. 36).

Notice too how the difference works in dividing a genus into its species: the genus itself as lacking the difference becomes the subspecific contrast to the genus constituted through the addition of the difference. Thus the "tree" is positive along only one of its branches, and this progressive accumulation of positive differences in fact constitutes the "trunk" of the tree. The "infima species", or classifications not further divisible, are its branches, and the individuals under those lowest species the foliage or leaves of the tree.

Thus *animate bodily substance*, itself a species respecting bodily substance proximately and substance remotely, in turn can be divided by the introduction of the difference "sentient", resulting in plants, on the one hand (the negative branch: "non-sentient"), and animals, on the other.

Sentient living bodily substance, the positive branch, in turn can be divided by the difference "rational" into the (intermediate or sub) species of rational animals (the positive trunk) and brute animals (the negative branch: irrational animals). Eventually in the Latin Age the arrival at *rational animal* would come to be considered and presented as the end of the line on the positive side, on the ground that rational animal admits only of division into individuals. Thomas Aquinas would argue that this is so because it is the nature of animal to be composed of bodily parts, and such parts are intrinsically subject to corruption. Hence all animals, including rational animals, are mortal.

In Porphyry's day, however, and for many Latins as for Porphyry himself, there was still widespread belief in a plurality of gods – Zeus, Aphrodite, Mars, Neptune, and the rest – each of whom was, like human beings, endowed with a body, but, at the same time, unlike human beings, was immortal in that bodily form. Hence Porphyry regards "rational animal" not as an *infima species*, as is generally represented in later Latin and in modern logic texts, but rather as an intermediate class which can be further divided by the difference "mortal". Adding the difference "mortal" gives, in Porphyry's own text, two *infima species*: on the negative side, we get "immortal rational sentient living bodily substances", the pagan gods; and, on the positive side, we get "mortal rational sentient living bodily substances", human beings. But here, even on the positive side, just as in the later Christian medieval presentations of the tree shorn of gods, the "Tree of Substance" ends in individuals. Hence "mortal rational animal" and "immortal rational animal" constitute the lowest species respecting substance as the highest genus, and between the highest and the lowest in descending order we encounter inorganic bodies, living organisms, plants, and animals. The tree may be drawn schematically, as on the opposite page.

Similar trees can be constructed for each of the ten "highest genera" of finite being. Indeed, much of the development of natural philosophy in the second phase of the Latin Age consisted precisely in the development of just such "divisive and constitutive" differences as applied to each of the nine accidents. But a disaster for the philosophy of nature was anticipated in the assumption that the plan according to which the tree of substance was constructed could be applied to each of the variety of natural kinds we encounter in everyday life, together with Porphyry's sloppy and unfocused discussion of property as a predicable, in contrast to accident as a predicable. The anticipated disaster actually reached its climax with the work of Charles Darwin. The discovery of evolution is flatly incompatible with the theoretical notion that each of the "natural kinds" of birds and fishes, and so on, each genetic population of biology, as we might say today, is an *infima species* constituted by a *sic et non* (present or absent) difference. Indeed, not even the racial diversity of rational animals is adequately accounted for on such a basis.

But, contrary to what was assumed at the time, the Porphyrian "Tree of Substance" in its essential structure was not chopped down by Darwin's work and turned into firewood. Only a particular (and particularly rigid) application of it to the diversity of natural kinds was shown to be invalid.[168] Prepossessions of a

---

168 I have discussed this matter in a fullness of technical detail in a two-part article, "The Philosophical Dimensions of the Origin of Species", published in *The Thomist* XXXIII (January and April 1969), 75–149 and 251–342. A more accessible presentation I attempted later in brief form under the title "From Glassy Essence to Bottomless Lake" (Deely 1992).

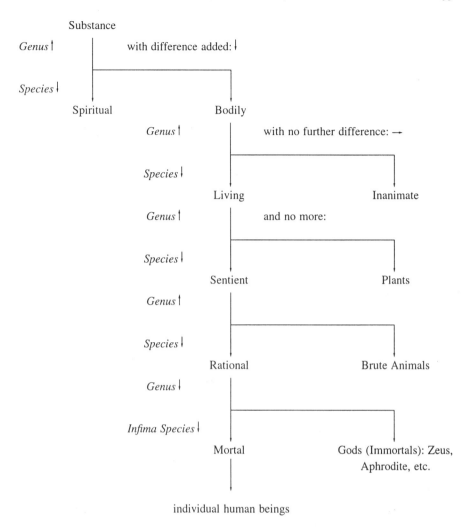

The Porphyrian Tree of Substances

time, nonetheless, often obscure for subsequent generations an earlier intellectual achievement, and this befell Porphyry's little classic. To the average student of late-modern times, the trunk of the Porphyrian tree survives not even in the ashes of memory. As postmodern philosophy recovers its proper scope, we may expect a renewed appreciation of what is enduring in Porphyry's accomplishment.

Porphyry's Achievement in the Isagoge
For the achievement of Porphyry in AD271 of providing the framework for any theory of the definition of terms remains as one of the permanent accomplishments of the human mind and one of the milestones in the history of philosophy. There

is no better link between the age of Greek philosophy and the Latin Age in the area of the epistemological development of philosophy as a whole down to our own epoch than this brilliant essay of Porphyry written to help a friend understand the categories of Aristotle. After all, anyone who strives to know "whereof they speak" draws perforce on the concepts outlined and brought to a not altogether stammering expression in the *Quinque Verba* of Porphyry.

The Famous "Praeteritio"

This brings us almost to the conclusion of our treatment of philosophy in its ancient or Greek phase. We may well note that a second main influence on the Latin Age of Porphyry's *Introduction* to logic sprang from the *praeteritio* in his opening remarks, where Porphyry outlined what he would *not* be discussing in the letter. This opening paragraph constitutes an aside wherein Porphyry explains that he is concerned with the "simpler notions" of what the predicables are, and not with the "deeper issues" of how exactly they exist. Thus he puts aside, "for example", the following investigations: "whether genera or species exist in themselves or reside purely and solely in things understood; whether, if they exist, they are corporeal or incorporeal; and whether they exist apart or within sense objects and in dependence upon them" (pp. 27–8).

For his immediate purpose Porphyry did indeed put aside these "profound questions", but by making such a point of it, he ensured that later authors would not let the matter rest. "A discussion too difficult and demanding to undertake now? What better bait to snare the commentator could there be?", asks McInerny,[169] observing that "it is difficult to find in the history of western thought a passage of comparable length that has had so vast an effect". Subsequent Latin authors, first Boethius, then the teachers of Peter Abelard,[170] and eventually William of Ockham, to name a few, took up precisely these questions, and out of their discussion arose the great medieval controversy over the nature and status of universals vis-à-vis particulars in our experience and understanding of objects. The controversy took on gale force, leaving the doctrine of *nominalism* to mark its passage.

In these two ways, then – by substantive contribution in the body of his essay and by speculative provocation in its introduction – Porphyry's modest "introduction to logic via the categories of Aristotle" lent impetus and shape to the indigenous development of philosophy in the Latin language.

Looking Forward to Latinity, Second Aspect: The Greek Notion of Σημεῖον as "Natural Sign"

But, as we pass to the Latin Age, perhaps the single most important thing to be noted, because it is what makes the Latin development, speculatively considered, a

---

169 McInerny 1990: 61.
170 See "The First Florescence of Nominalism" in chapter 6, p. 243.

truly *indigenous* development, is not any speculative influence that carried over from Greek philosophy through Neoplatonic or Stoic or any other channels of influence. What needs to be noted above all is the speculative *discontinuity* with which that age begins its indigenous development, and for this we need to focus our attention on an element of ancient thought that has never been central to any histories of ancient philosophy as thus far written.

We will shortly note in treating Augustine[171] that, when we look back from the present to those two ancient ages of understanding when the development of philosophy was carried first by the Greek language and then by the Latin, the general notion of sign amounts to the first Latin initiative in philosophy. Before the age of modernity began around the turn of the seventeenth century, the Latin Age as an organic whole ended in speculatively justifying the general notion of sign with the promulgation of which that age had begun, the general notion of sign we today take for granted as the badge of postmodernity.

In the ancient world, as might be considered indirectly indicated from the survey of its more prominent philosophical features we have just completed, the notion of "sign" was neither a central notion nor even the general notion that has become central (as we will see beginning with chapter 14) to establishing the contrast of postmodern with modern thought.[172] The notion of sign whereby Peirce, borrowing from the Latins, is able to mark the initiation of yet a fourth age of human understanding,

---

171 See chapter 6 below, p. 214ff.

172 The 1846 first American ed. of Liddell & Scott's *Greek-English Lexicon* enters three fields or ranges of usage under the entry for Σημεῖον (p. 1341). First: a mark by which something is known; a sign from the gods, an omen; a signal to do a thing; a standard; a device or badge; a signal, watchword, or warcry. Second: a sign or proof. Third: a point. The ninth English ed. of the same lexicon (p. 1593) expands upon these three ranges as follows. First: mark by which a thing is known; sign from the gods, omen; sign or signal made by flags to do a thing; standard or flag; landmark, boundary, limit; device upon a shield or figure-head upon ships; signet on a ring; watch-word, war-cry; a birthmark or distinguishing feature. Second: sign, token, indication of anything that is or is to be; in reasoning a sign or proof, an instance or example; a probable argument in the logic of Aristotle, an observable basis of inference to the unobserved in Stoic and Epicurean philosophy; in medicine symptom; shorthand symbols; critical mark. Third: a mathematical point, instant, unit of time.

In this threefold range, notice first the absence of any usage that pertains to a general theoretical discussion of sign. Notice further that the few examples of usage designating cultural phenomena as signs are examples of cultural items that function indexically, the way that medical symptoms function. Notice finally that the examples adduced from theoretical contexts of discussion are just those we have emphasized in Aristotelian, Stoic, and Epicurean logic.

In ancient Greek usage, thus, a sign appears at most as a type of phenomenon among and contrasting with other types, never in the theoretical guise of a general mode of being ranging across and into which enter all other types of phenomena, as Augustine will be the first to suggest and Poinsot the first finally to explain sign to be for the medieval Latin usage. Postmodern times begin only when the Latin conception is not merely recovered but its consequences are first developed and explored theoretically in the pioneering studies of Peirce. "From sign as an object among other objects to that which every object presupposes" is a fair summary of the semiotic trajectory along which philosophy traverses the centuries of speculation from ancient to postmodern times, the trajectory according to which we plot the "one long argument" which is the present work.

one as discontinuous with modernity in its epistemological thrust as modernity was from Latin times, is nowhere to be found in the original Greek florescence of philosophy. We have just noted this point on the celebrated authority of the Liddel and Scott *Greek-English Lexicon*,[173] but the point is perhaps even better illustrated by consulting the work of Cicero, who, after all, as we saw above, created the main original Latin version of the ancient Greek philosophical vocabulary, four centuries before Augustine will take up the pen. Cicero's use of the term *signum* in his Latin writings and translations from Greek reflects the same practical, naturalistic, and divinatory particular usages mirrored so many centuries later from ancient Greek writings in the Liddel and Scott *Lexicon*.[174]

Among the Greeks, we may close by noting that, when we look to usage in theoretical texts, the sign belonged all but exclusively to the natural world, and was regarded as belonging above all to the province of medicine and the forecasting of weather (or of science in the modern sense, we could say, had the Greeks clearly conceived of science in that sense), whence even though, as we saw in chapter 4, a notion of sign played a major role in the epistemological positions debated between the Stoics and Epicureans, the sign as conceived in and central to that debate was not "sign in general" as verified alike in cultural and natural phenomena but only "sign in particular" as instantiated in the class of natural, sensible phenomena. Whence too even that specific notion of sign crucial to the epistemological development of late Greek antiquity has played no major part in the traditional modern histories of ancient philosophy, although we have perforce had to highlight and showcase that debate in this first postmodern attempt at such a history.

The Greek term normally translated as "sign", σημεῖον ("sēmeîon"), is therefore inevitably misunderstood unless the reader of the translation is clued to the fact that this so-called "sign" is more like what we would call a *symptom* of disease, for example, or what the Latins would call a "natural sign", *signum naturale*, such as the "red sky in the morning" from which "sailors take warning", or the presence of milk in a woman's breast signifying a recent childbirth.

To our much later consciousness it may seem odd, but the Greek philosophers never conceived of the phenomena of culture as such (excepting only very specific, indexical instances or types of cultural creations, such as insignia and standards), including the species-specifically human exaptation of language to communicate (an exaptation itself commonly mislabeled as "language", as we noted in our opening chapter[175]), in terms of signification or the action of signs. The sign was viewed in the perspective of Greek philosophy and science principally, all but exclusively, as it manifested itself on the "nature" side of the "nature-nurture" dichotomy.

---

173 Note 172 preceding.
174 Compare the Liddel and Scott Σημεῖον entry with the entry "Signum" in Merguet's *Lexikon zu den Philosophischen Schriften Ciceros*, Vol. III, pp. 534–536.
175 See the discussion beginning on p. 5 above.

In this original perspective of understanding, the σημεῖον or "sign" pertains to human discourse only insofar as that discourse attains to an understanding of nature or speculative truth, in the *lekton* of Stoic logic or in the *proposition*, the *dicisign*, of Aristotle. Thus, whether in the medical tradition from Hippocrates (c.460–377BC) to Galen (AD129–c.199)[176] or in the logical traditions that develop after Aristotle first and later also Chrysippus (the Stoic line) and others,[177] the sign is thought of as encountered in the Umwelt only in sensible nature and, derivatively therefrom, at that singular juncture of human discourse where the understanding attains an object under the guise of being adjudicable as "true" or "false".[178] That such an attainment was species-specifically human was a firm opinion among the ancients; yet the ground of this attainment began to be thematically considered in its own right only in some of the more neglected aspects of the writings of Aquinas, as we will have occasion to see later.[179]

In passing from "natural sign" or σημεῖον to "sign in general" or *signum*, we may say, we first cross the frontier separating the Latin Age from the original Greek florescence of philosophy. Similarly, we will see that in the later forgetfulness of *signum* the thinkers of what will become the classical modern mainstream will establish a principal boundary separating modern times from the later Latin Age. And, later still, we will see that in the Peircean recovery of *signum* semiotics will establish yet another line of demarcation, a new frontier separating authentic postmodern thought from the various idealistic pretensions to surpass modernity, pretensions the hollowness of which is betrayed by their preservation of the epistemological and metaphysical essence of modern philosophy in conceiving of the sign as a vehicle exclusively arbitrary or linguistic in its construction. In this summary we have adumbrated the substance behind the title of our book, *Four Ages of Understanding*.

No doubt there will be a "fifth age", and beyond that yet others as new themes sufficiently vast emerge in awareness to define and govern new epochs in the development of human understanding. But, if the past history and gait of philosophical development are reliable indicators, that "Fifth Age" will not even begin to take form before the twenty-second century at the very earliest, more likely the twenty-fifth. By then, the notion of an "action of signs" and the dependency of objectivity on that action and the systems of signs it generates while interweaving the natural and the cultural, the speculative and the practical, will be so well established and so prominent at the forefront of popular consciousness that the time when "semiosis"

---

176 On this, see especially the work of Sebeok 1984c and 1996.
177 On this, see especially the work of Deledalle 1987.
178 See, e.g., in Aristotle, ch. 27 closing his *Prior Analytics*, 70a3–b38, where σημεῖον as a term recurs no less than eighteen times. I am grateful to Professor Deledalle, who marked for me and sent to me this text in the Greek in a correspondence dated 15 October 1996.
179 See chapter 7 below, esp. the section on "The Problem of Being as First Known", p. 341ff. I have also taken this matter up in a separate monograph, not historical but directly speculative, under the title *What Distinguishes Human Understanding?* (Deely 2000).

was a strange new word will seem a time positively neanderthal. Such is the pattern according to which the presuppositions that guide each age in its development are first formed and then taken for granted as the new generations of semiotic animals get on with the business of their life: for among intellectual beings, understanding is what distinguishes their life,[180] even as to perceive and act accordingly is the life distinctive of animals, or to take nourishment is the life distinctive of plants.

---

180 "Intelligere in intelligentibus est esse", as Aquinas might have said.

PART TWO

The Latin Age
Philosophy of Being

Likeness of John Poinsot (1589–1644)
Engraving by Herman Panneels (fl.1638–50) from the last year of Poinsot's life, published in 1645 on the antiporta page of the first posthumous volume of *Joannes a Sancto Thoma Cursus Theologicus* by Didacus Ramirez; discovered in the Vatican Library by Marco Forlivesi (1994)

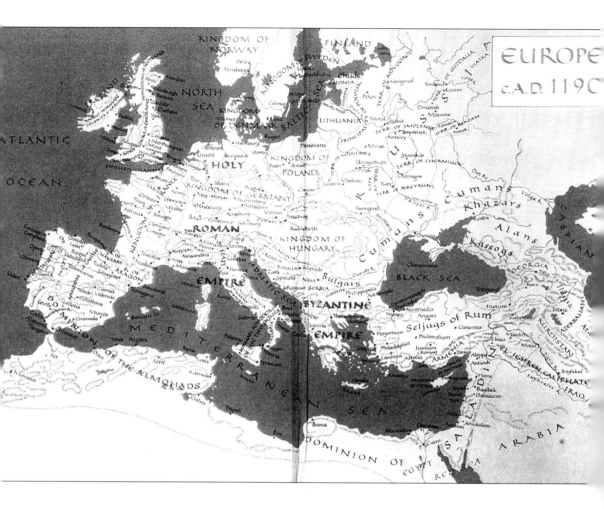

KINGDOM OF
NORWAY

FINLAND

Oslo
Tonsberge

NORTH

SEA

KINGDOM
OF DENMARK

KINGDOM OF SWEDEN

BALTIC SEA

LITHUANIA

ATLANTIC

OCEAN

Bremen

Hamburg

HOLY

KINGDOM OF GERMANY

KINGDOM OF
POLAND

Prague

Cracow

Vienna

Pressburg

Buda

Pesth

Russians

Minsk

Kiev

U S S I A

Moscow

Smolensk

TERR. OF SMOLENSK

TERR. OF CHERNIGOV

Chernigov

Cumans

Khazars

Alans

CASPIAN

ROMAN

EMPIRE

KINGDOM OF
HUNGARY

Cumans

SERBIA

Bulgars

Danube

BYZANTINE

EMPIRE

BLACK SEA

Kassogs

GEORGIA

Trebizond

Erzerum

ARAGON

CORSICA

ADRIATIC SEA

Rome

Naples

Salerno

Palermo

Messina

Nicomedia

Nicaea

Angora

Pergamum

Seljugs of Rum

Caesarea

MEDITERRANEAN

Iconium

Philadelphia

Laodicea

Attalia

ARMENIA

KURDISTAN

Mosul

Tabriz

AZERBAIJAN

MINION OF THE ALMOHADS

Tunis

SEA

Tripoli

Barca

Sirt

DOMINION OF

EGYPT

Cairo

Alexandria

Damietta

Jerusalem

Damascus

Tripoli

Tyre

ARABIA

RED SEA

CALIPHATE

IRAQ

Baghdad

CHAPTER FIVE

The Geography of the Latin Age

Political Geography: The Latin Lebenswelt

As the human mind needs a brain to function and the human body a place to be, so philosophy – or at least those who create the languages which express it – has a geography, a region where it comes to expression. In its first florescence on this planet, as we have seen, the geography and language of philosophy was more or less that of Greece, beginning with Ionia. Its second great florescence was to a great extent – not completely, but largely – isolated from the original Greek florescence, and found its expression in those nations of the West which inherited from Rome not its language of intellectual culture but its language of practical affairs, Latin.

When I was a student of philosophy, it always puzzled me where the so-called "Dark Ages" came from.[1] No one ever explained to me how exactly the medieval thinkers found themselves in the position of having practically to start all over again, to have to undertake a rather thoroughly indigenous philosophical development in the Latin tongue. How did it come about that Greek, the language of learning of the ancient world and the Roman Empire (stretching from the Bosporus at the extreme East to the shores of France and Britain, including Egypt and the coast of Africa) came to be lost to central Europe as all but a dim memory of philosophical inspiration? How did it come about that new institutions of civil life and learning had to be forged using a tongue that, in the ancient world, had served principally for military, business, and trade functions rather than for learning and intellectual growth?

As I look back on it, I'm not sure any of my professors (with one exception, and he never taught the introductory courses) really knew the answer to the question. It was just one of those dumb "brute facts" that make up history, while philosophy pretends to live in a timeless world of truths that lie above all that. I have since

---

1 For that matter, no one ever told me that the "dark ages", obviously not a term of compliment, had a fascinating history of its own, which I will have occasion to summarize in connection with the title of the following chapter: see below, p. 213n1.

learned that my professors were not exceptional in this regard. Even at the dawn of the twenty-first century, Christopher Dawson's observation from the middle of the twentieth century rings true:[2] "there is a gap of some five hundred years from the third to the seventh century in the knowledge of the ordinary educated person." Given such a gap, that "the real importance of this period is seldom appreciated"[3] is hardly surprising. Yet at the bottom of this very gap lie hidden the foundations of the indigenous Latin Age. Those foundations need to be exposed for anyone who would hope to understand the Latin period in the history of philosophy in something of its organic wholeness.

For in truth, of course, philosophers live in time as much as do otters and seals. Philosophers are born into an Umwelt and raised with its values. We need to recall here the lesson of our opening chapter, which applies to the making of Europe no less than it did to the making of Athens: that only gradually do thinkers wake to the possibilities of understanding which see in the world more than the present situation of human society. The transcendent, yet historical, possibility distinctive of human understanding is the capacity to envision the Umwelt in the light of alternative ways of connecting the past with the future. This is what makes the difference ultimately between the Lebenswelt as species-specifically human and the objective lifeworld or Umwelt as a generically common construct essential for the social life of any animal. Language, of course, is what ultimately makes this always possible difference sometimes actual. Language has the capacity of nullifying certain features of time, by connecting living generations with circumstances and peoples long dead, thereby expanding the horizon of consideration of future possibilities. Language provides for the mind eyes which can see beyond immediate social interaction. The Greek language had provided such vision for the ancient world. But in the cauldron out of which European civilization comes in its Latin guise, the Greek language had ceased to be an element. The transmission of culture in this crucial particular was interrupted, and a new organ of thought, new eyes for the mind, had to evolve.

From the point of view of the manner in which language elevates the mind's understanding, nothing is more important for a group that seeks to develop the specifically human possibilities of animal life than a philosophical language. For a philosophical language is precisely the use of language that most fully opens up the understanding to its own possibilities and reveals to it the difference between the

---

2 Christopher Dawson, "The Christian West and the Fall of the Empire", in Dawson 1954: 28–9. Marenbon has a fine essay addressing this very period, the opening centuries of the Latin Age, but he yields to tendentiousness in asserting (1983: vii) that: "No period in the history of philosophy is so neglected as the early Middle Ages." In fact, as Marenbon's own subsequent study (1991) of "later medieval philosophy" demonstrates, the title of "least known period" in the history of philosophy continues to be the late Middle Ages, that is to say (cf. Randall 1962: vi–viii), the closing rather than the opening centuries of the Latin Age, when the dramatic philosophical initiative that will come to be called "semiotic" (with which the Latin Age opens) is finally clarified in principle and reduced to its proper ground within the perspective of the philosophy of being.

3 Ibid.

world as an objective construct and the larger reality of a universe of being which makes even objectification possible in the first place. The Latin Age exemplifies the process, with features distinctly its own.

It is true that there were Latin figures, notably that of Cicero (106–43BC), who, in the century before Christianity dawned, were fully schooled in Greek philosophy and brought their learning into the heart of the Roman and Latin world. Who can forget or deny Montesquieu's salute to Cicero[4] as "the first of the Romans to make philosophy available beyond the circle of the learned and to detach it from the encumbrance of a foreign language". Yet Cicero and his circle were mainly rhetoricians, Roman aristocrats interested above all in statesmanship. They took up Greek philosophy not so much on its speculative side but, as Windelband summarized,[5] by "piecing together, from an essentially practical point of view, the different school systems which met their approval". Let Cicero speak for himself on the matter. "I am no mere translator of the Greeks", he tells us;[6] "besides presenting accurately the selected parts of their doctrines, I add thereto criticism and my own order of presentation."

And if the passage of time has sufficiently demonstrated that these Romans at the end of antiquity versed in Greek were not up to the speculative level of the Greek masters, yet their long-term service to Latin philosophy and education is not to be underrated; for they created some philosophical terminology that would eventually pass into the national languages of Europe. Could he have lived seven centuries, Cicero would have been amazed to discover that the contempt of the ruling class begun in his day for Latin compared to Greek works[7] was but the onset of a molting process whereby the imperial court itself would be transformed into a Greek satrapy once the seat of the empire had been moved from *Roma Antiqua* to *Nova Roma*, as we shall shortly see. But, could he have lived fourteen centuries, he would also have had the satisfaction of seeing his boast,[8] more or less idle in its day, become rather a true prophecy of the later Latin centuries, when "the Latin language, so far from having a poor vocabulary in philosophy, is actually richer than Greek."

Uniquely in the case of the Latin world, precisely because the conversion of the old Roman Empire into Christendom and the relatively autonomous intellectual development of the Latin West coincided so closely in time,[9] the establishment of a

---

4 Montesquieu, c.1709: I, 94: "Il est le premier, chez les Romains, qui ait tiré la philosophie des mains des savants, et l'ait dégagée des embarras d'une langue étrangère. Il la rendit commune à tous les hommes, comme la raison, et, dans les applaudissements qu'il en reçut, les gens de lettres se trouvèrent d'accord avec le peuple."
5 Windelband 1901: 161.
6 Cicero, 45BC: *De finibus* I.ii: "... nos non interpretum fungimur munere, sed tuemer ea quae dicta sunt ab iis quos probamus, eisque nostrum iudicium et nostrum scribendi ordinem adiungimus".
7 Ibid.: I.iii: "Ego autem mirari satis non queo, unde hoc sit tam insolens domesticarum rerum fastidium."
8 Ibid.: "ita sentio et saepe disserui, Latinam linguam non modo non inopem, ut vulgo putarent, sed locupletiorem etiam esse quam Graecam."
9 "Christianity," as Hamman puts it (1986: 1), "born in the East, developed above all within the confines of the Roman Empire, the frontiers of which it scarcely crossed." So it was that *theology*

philosophical language is bound up with the development of theology as a rationalization of religious belief and with the emergence of religion as an institutionalized cultural structure distinct from the state. This occurs among the Latins to a degree and in a manner unprecedented in the histories of previous civilizations, where religion was always wrapped up with and virtually inseparable from civil or state control. The emergence of Latin as a philosophical language in its own right was part and parcel of this development. The separation of the original Roman Empire into a Greek East and a Latin West led to a situation where the central religious institution of Christian civilization, the papacy, came gradually to be seen as one that could not be subordinated to the civil authority as such, not even that of the Roman emperor. The story is one of a contest for domination in which both sides lost. For, by the end of the Latin Age, neither had the state succeeded in gaining control of the church, nor had the church succeeded in gaining control of the state. This standoff was codified in the constitutions of states, and proved to be one of the decisive achievements of modernity. Here we can only indicate the outlines of the struggle insofar as they have a bearing on the climate of thought within which occurred the speculative developments of philosophy in the Latin Age.

As we make the transition from the Greek philosophical culture of ancient times to the Latin philosophical culture of the middle ages, therefore, what is needed above all is an intelligible picture of the manner in which a Lebenswelt was brought about wherein, from approximately the fifth century AD until the twelfth century, effective contact with the ancient philosophical culture created in the Greek language was lost. And, after the twelfth century, we need to have a picture of where the renewed contact with Aristotle came from, for it did not come from the Greek civilization called "Byzantium" into which the Roman Empire transformed itself after Constantine, but from another civilization entirely, the civilization of Islam that sprang from the life, work, and writing of Abū al-Qāsim Muhammad ibn ʿAbd al-Muttalib ibn Hāshim (AD570–632), usually shortened to Muhammad (sometimes "Mohammed", with other variants).

---

developed both in Greek and Latin, but among the Greeks its philosophical instrument remained predominantly Neoplatonic, with the result that *philosophy* developed mainly among the Latins, where Aristotle became dominant – no small factor in the eventual emergence of modern science, as the studies of Wallace best bring out. For the Latin peoples, Aristotle became "the Philosopher". For the Greek peoples of Byzantine rule, it was rather always Plato – or rather Neoplato, for they fell for the pseudo-Dionysian theological labyrinths in which dying Greece had met its first finale in philosophy (see above in chapter 4, "A Double Finale", p. 141). Beyond the frontiers of the Greco-Roman civilization, the civilizations of India, China, and Japan remained "officially" mired in the reincarnation myth (whether through the Vedas and Upanishads, the Buddha, or the Tao te Ching), the very myth that fell into increasing contempt among the Latins as philosophy grew. In these "praeter-Roman" civilizations the autonomous concerns of neither philosophical doctrine nor scientific experiment would be faced in any systematic way until globalization became inevitable through the technological successes of modernity. But how this will all work out on the level of religion remains to be seen.

The Separation of Roman Civilization into a Latin West and a Greek East
What we mean by the "middle ages", more accurately called the Latin Age in
Philosophy, is the period beginning about the fifth century, when an indigenous
Latin development began, and continuing up to the seventeenth century, when
Latin effectively gave way to the modern national languages as the mainstream
medium of intellectual thought and writing. One way at least to frame the story
of how the European nations came to be stranded philosophically in the Latin
language, I have found, is in terms of the first Christian Roman Emperor, Constantine (AD272–337, r.306–37), and the last Pagan Emperor, Julian (AD332–63,
r.361–3).

The overlap of the imperium through the reign of these two men is fascinating,
for all emperors prior to Constantine were pagan, while all emperors subsequent
to Julian were Christian. Beginning with the overlap of Christianity and Paganism
as the religion of the state in the reigns of Constantine and Julian, the careers of
the Roman emperors fall squarely into the pattern of sea-changes which separated
Europe, the original seat of the Roman Empire, from the Constantinople-based
remnant of that empire. This remnant was to last, steeped in the Greek culture but
philosophically stagnant, for yet another thousand years – the whole period in which
modern Europe took form, politically as well as philosophically.

Back to the Future: The First Christian Emperor
The fateful first step in the process of severing the Latin peoples from the Greek
heritage of ancient philosophy turns out to have been the moving of the capital of the
Roman Empire out of Rome. This was done by Diocles (AD245–313), or Diocletian,
as he called himself after the Roman army declared him Roman Emperor in 284.
He moved the capital from Rome to Nicomedia, a port city of modern Turkey on
the eastern arm of the Sea of Marmara, called today Izmit. Diocletian made this
move for military reasons, and appointed one of his generals, Maximian, to be his
co-ruler, with his capital near the Alps in the city of Milan. To succeed himself
and Maximian in due time Diocletian appointed as heirs-apparent Galerius, with
a capital at Sirmium, and Constantius Chlorus, with a capital at Trèves. The two
main emperors held the title of *Augustus*, while the heirs-apparent held the title of
Caesar. Diocletian directly ruled Thrace, Egypt, and Asia. His fellow-Augustus,
Maximian, ruled Italy and Africa. Galerius ruled the regions around the Danube
("the Illyrian Provinces"), and his fellow-Caesar, Constantius, ruled Gaul, Spain,
and Britain.

By this time, throughout the empire, Christianity had been broadly established
as a new religious sect competing with the ancient religion and gods of Rome.
Diocletian himself was a great statesman who proved himself beyond personal
ambition in freely resigning the imperial throne and refusing to return to it even
when later asked to do so. Yet he was the principal among the four rulers, and so
it is he who gets the blame for the worst of the ancient persecutions of Christians,

a persecution actually instigated by Galerius.[10] The decree of 302 was intended to suppress Christianity throughout the empire, but the persecution was actually most intense in the eastern provinces, and prepared the way for a later emperor, Constantine, to use the resentment of the great persecution to his military advantage.

The fourfold division of the empire into regions ruled by two principal and two subordinate emperors did not long survive Diocletian's abdication in 305. The retired Augustus Maximian had a son named Maxentius. The newly ascendant Augustus Constantius Chlorus had a son named Constantine. And neither of these ambitious young men was content to be passed over in the appointments for succession to the title of Augustus. A civil war soon broke out, in one of the crucial contests of which Constantine led his legions against Maxentius, who had the support of the praetorian guard of the city of Rome in the hope of restoring the ancient capital. It was during this campaign against Maxentius that Constantine declared himself a Christian, and instructed his troops to mark on their shields a cross. Now many of Constantine's troops were already Christians, and the others had long fought under the standard of a cross of light belonging not to Christ but to Mithras. By this brilliant instruction Constantine symbolically unified his army and, at the same time, as the troops of Maxentius fought under a pagan banner of the Unconquerable Sun, imparted to the dimensions of the battle as a whole an overarching religious symbolism.

The tactical nature of Constantine's declaration of Christianity is apparent from the circumstances that neither in personal deeds nor by accepting baptism did Constantine show himself to be a Christian in fact.[11] By declaring both for Christianity and for religious toleration, he was able to unite his troops in the face of his enemy, who was against both Christianity and toleration. Constantine had chosen a successful tactic. By 324 the last of his rivals for the imperial throne was executed, and the whole of the formerly Roman Empire was united in the person of Constantine.

---

10 Thus, before the custom of counting years from the birth of Christ had been adopted, many Christian communities, especially in the East, used a system reckoning from the age of martyrs, with the first year of Diocletian's rule, AD284, considered as the year 1. This system was happily abandoned, for it was just neither to Diocletian nor to the many martyrs who had suffered in the several earlier persecutions.

11 Between his nominal declaration of himself as a Christian in 312 and his actual baptism, a quarter of a century would elapse, during which Constantine did not become even a catechumen, that is (in the early Christian centuries), one who has formally requested and is actually receiving training in doctrine and discipline preparatory to baptism. By all the "church" rules of his day (for in his day, the Church was yet a congeries of local congregations), were any but a double standard applied to the one who was the emperor, far from his being accepted as the convenor of synods and councils (let alone of the first, and hence, arguably, most important, "general council"), the local church doors would have been closed in his face. Only when he considered death to be at hand did he accept to be baptized. A deathbed baptism was considered by many of the time to be a sure route to heaven, regardless of the previous conduct of life. And this was the theory that Constantine accepted, in an early, high-stakes anticipation of "Pascal's wager". And Constantine chose for the baptismal ceremony a bishop who adhered to the Arian view of the Trinity declared heretical by his own council of Nicea a decade earlier. The Greek church, by ignoring his conduct of life, tries to maintain the frankly ridiculous pretense that Constantine was a saint.

This rebirth of the unified empire Constantine hoped to symbolize and stabilize in the founding of a *New Rome*, *Nova Roma*, to be henceforward the capital of the realm. He chose for this new capital the site of ancient Byzantium, a beautiful and, militarily, all but impregnable location. Like Nicomedia, *Nova Roma* was on the coast of the Sea of Marmara, but it was also on the Bosporus, at the very boundary point separating Europe and Asia. The city was dedicated on 11 May, AD330.

Yet the new capital never quite acquired the symbolism Constantine had hoped for it. The name *Nova Roma* never took. Almost from the first, everyone called the new capital simply Constantinople, the city founded by Constantine. And what was deemed, and seemed at the time of the founding, to be a new beginning proved instead to be the beginning of the end, both of the ancient empire as Roman and of Greek as a language of living creation in philosophy, science, art, and culture. What the founding of Constantinople in 330 turned out to be was the inauguration of a nouveau-Greek civilization that lasted until the capture of the city by the Turks on 29 May, 1453, after which, down to the present day, *Nova Roma* came to be known as Istanbul.

After Constantine, the birth and residence of the princes succeeding to Constantinople's throne estranged them from the Roman idiom. Not only did the official name of the new capital never take, but even the manners, dress, and – especially – the proper language of the old capital was soon lost. As late as the reign of Justinian (r.AD527–65), the emperor still knew Latin and the court was bilingual. Justinian's codification of Roman law was made in Latin with a Greek translation. But after him, only the Greek version of the code was used and commented upon in the East. Before the death of the emperor Heraclius in AD641 the Latin tongue in Constantinople had passed into oblivion, only darkly preserved in the terms of jurisprudence and the ceremonial formulas of palace ritual. The eastern empire was now thoroughly separated from the West, the original empire; and the language and dominion of Rome had passed by the time of Charlemagne (AD742–814) to the control of the Franks and other peoples disdained by the Greek East as rude barbarians.

But how, in all this, did the unified empire under Constantine become again divided between Greek East and Latin West, and the Latin West lost to the control of the "Roman Emperor" of Greek Constantinople? It is a bloody tale, rooted in the methods of blood by which Constantine had consolidated his rule. His own son by his first marriage, Crispus, he ordered executed in 326. His second wife Fausta, daughter of Maximian, by whom he had three sons, he had executed about the same time. And then Constantine executed Licinianus, the son by his own sister Constantia of the last man before him to hold the imperial throne of the East, Flavius Licinius. Constantine's death was not the end but the continuation of this bloody tradition. And in the trail of blood the control of the West, the original Roman Empire, slipped from the hands of the occupants of Constantinople's throne. The tale is bound up with the last attempt to uphold the ancient pagan religion of Rome against the official establishment of Christianity as the religion of state under Constantine.

Forward to the Past: The Last Pagan Emperor

Constantine's will divided his empire among his three sons and two nephews. But first the army rejected the nephews, and then the eldest and the middle of the three sons were eliminated in military combat. By AD353 the remaining son, Constantius, was left sole emperor. But Constantius, in the year of his father's death, had had murdered all but two of the male relatives of his father. The two allowed to survive were Gallus, who was ill at the time of the slaughter and was expected to die shortly (he did not after all[12]), and his brother Flavius Claudianus Julianus, or "Julian", who was five. Why Constantius allowed Julian to live is unknown, but thereby hangs the tale of the last Pagan Emperor and of the loss of the Latin West to the Greek East.

Julian grew up in constant fear of his life. After all, his father, eldest brother, and male cousins were slain in the massacre that marked the transition of imperial rule from Constantine to his sons; and more recently his sole surviving brother had been slain in Milan. From that scene, after somehow persuading the emperor Constantius of the truth, which was that he harbored no political ambitions, he accepted happily, in 355, banishment to Athens. He had since age seventeen become fascinated with philosophy, and the idea of studying in the groves where Plato spoke elated him. But Athens was the fountainhead at this period not only of philosophy, but of pagan learning, religion, and thought in general. His experience of Christianity, even though raised in it theoretically, had practically speaking not been the best. He had, after all, experienced no beasts more ferocious than some men who called themselves Christians and claimed to be fashioning a Christian state. At Athens he was won over completely to paganism. Knowing the emperor as he did, Julian prudently kept his conversion secret.

Nonetheless, when Constantius after six months summoned him back to Milan, Julian surely had his apprehensions. Constantius had other things in mind. Not only were his rivals eliminated, but so practically speaking was his gene pool. Julian was the only male relation for the family to draw on, so Constantius gave him his sister Helena to marry and assigned him the government of Gaul. Julian proved an able governor and military commander. Inevitably Constantius became suspicious and tried to take from Julian his troops. Julian bade them go, but they rebelled and proclaimed him *Augustus*. Now the die was surely cast.

Constantius at his first opportunity marched his army westward to confront Julian. Julian advanced to meet him, at Sirmium pausing to announce publicly his paganism. It was the situation of Constantine marching against Maxentius with the religious symbolism reversed. But in November of 361, before battle could be joined, Constantius died of a fever near Tarsus. Julian marched on to Constantinople, where he ascended the imperial throne to become, at age thirty-one, Roman Emperor.

---

12 Constantius made up for this in 354, when he had Gallus beheaded in Milan.

To the luxury of the court Julian introduced the simplicity of a pagan philosopher, or, indeed, a monk. To the public, including some Christian bishops exiled by Constantius for not being Arian, Julian allowed full freedom of religion. But he himself worked to restore the pagan religion of Rome, and to his court he summoned the pagan philosophers to come and live as his guests. He wrote books and essays to justify his policies.

The final grand experiment in paganism was short lived. On June 27 of 363, on a military campaign in Persia, Julian was felled by a javelin. Ammianus Marcellinus of Antioch (c.AD330–c.400), a Syrian Greek who was among Julian's soldiers and later retired to Rome to write history, reports the deathbed scene:[13]

> Julian, lying in his tent, addressed his disconsolate and sorrowing companions: "Most opportunely, friends, has the time now come for me to leave this life, which I rejoice to restore to Nature at her demand ... having learned from the general conviction of the philosophers how much happier the soul is than the body. ..." All present wept, whereupon, even then maintaining his authority, he chided them, saying that it was unbecoming for them to mourn for a prince who was called for a union with heaven and the stars. As this made them all silent, he engaged with the philosophers Maximus and Priscus in an intricate discussion about the nobility of the soul. Suddenly the wound in his pierced side opened wide, the pressure of the blood checked his breath, and after a draught of cold water for which he had asked, he passed quietly away, in the thirty-second year of his age.

The soldiers made Jovian (c.AD331–64), Julian's captain of the imperial guard, emperor. He persecuted no one in his short reign, but he rediverted the support of the state to Christianity. Julian, remember, had come to Constantinople from the West. There continued to be emperors in the West, but after Julian all of them professed to be Christians, and the office became increasingly nominal, soon enough to disappear entirely as the formerly barbarian peoples from beyond the Alps began the sorting out of what would become modern Europe.

The Final Separation of East from West

The Prefect Sallust, who had declined the purple on Julian's death in June of 363, declined it again on the death of Jovian in January 364. After ten days the imperial diadem was settled on Valentinian (AD321–75). Thirty days after his own elevation he associated his brother Valens with him in the purple. To Valens he gave the seat of Constantinople and the praefecture of the East, the lands from the lower Danube to the boundary of Persia. For himself Valentinian took his seat in Milan and rule of the Western praefectures of Illyricum, Italy, and Gaul. Never were the East and the

---

13 Ammianus, c.AD363: xxv, 3 (Rolfe trans., vol. II, pp. 497, 501f.).

West united again in a single figure, and in the political complications that followed upon the death of Valentinian eleven years later, the empire in the West began its dissolution.

Valentinian died in November of 375, just one hundred and fifty days short of a twelve year reign. His death produced a complication. The son of his first marriage, Gratian, seventeen at the time, had already been invested with the purple. Yet conspirators at the deathsite plotted to have the second wife, Justina, present her infant son of four years, also named Valentinian, to the troops for investment by military acclamation with the titles and ensigns of supreme power. Gratian averted immediate disaster by accepting the choice of the army and recognizing Valentinian II as his co-ruler in the West.

The eastern emperor Valens perished in leading a military expedition at Hadrianople in 378. Gratian invested Theodosius as eastern *Augustus* in January of 379. In 383 Gratian was overthrown and slain in a revolt led by Maximus from Britain; but Maximus in turn overreached himself in 387 trying to overthrow as well Valentinian II. Theodosius marched from the East to Valentinian II's rescue and Maximus' death in 388.

The line of barbarians behind the imperial throne in the West who would eventually remove the imperial throne itself from the West began with the Frank, Arbogast, who assassinated Valentinian II in 392. Arbogast then illegitimately installed Eugenius as usurper of the throne of the West. Theodosius again marched westward, defeating Eugenius (394) and installing his eleven-year-old son Honorius as emperor of the West. Before he could return East, Theodosius grew sick and died at Milan on 17 January, AD395. His throne in the East passed to his elder son, Arcadius.

As the parting of the brothers Valentinian and Valens in 364 had marked the final separation of the ancient Roman Empire into an East, which would become a wholly Greek civilization, and a West, which would remain Latin, so this division of the old Roman world in 395 between the sons of Theodosius marked the final establishment of the empire of the East. This eastern, nouveau-Greek, empire survived under a continuous series of emperors from that date, AD395, until the taking of Constantinople by the Turks in 1453, a total of one thousand and fifty-eight years. The sovereign of that eastern and Greek empire "assumed, and obstinately retained, the vain and at length fictitious title of Emperor of the Romans; and the hereditary appellations of Caesar [for the heir apparent] and Augustus [for the present ruler] continued to declare that he was the legitimate successor of the first of men, who had reigned over the first of nations."[14] But the truth of the matter was quite otherwise than the Greek court insisted on pretending. The Latin peoples, barbarians in the eyes of the minions of Constantinople, were, even as Arcadius assumed the eastern rule, already in the process of throwing off completely the imperial rule devolved by Theodosius upon his son Honorius in 394.

---

14 Gibbon 1781: 378.

The Dissolution in Some Detail of Imperial Rule over the Latins, AD396–c.479
Honorius himself had not ended the first decade of his pusillanimous and disgraceful twenty-eight-year reign when, in 403–04, for protection against the Goths under Alaric (c.AD370–410), he moved the western capital from Milan to Ravenna, a city surrounded by marshes and with its own port for supply or escape. But who was to protect him against his sister?

Honorius's sister Placidia, widow of a barbarian king and a woman most remarkable, was, at the insistence of Honorius, remarried in 417, against her will, to Honorius's soldier Constantius. Yet she managed to have her new husband named by her brother co-ruler with him of the West. The son of Placidia and Constantius, Valentinian III, thus came in line to succeed the imperial throne. Constantius died in the seventh month of his reign, and Honorius followed shortly, leaving Placidia to rule the western empire for a quarter-century, first as regent for her son Valentinian III and then through him till her death in 450.

Valentinian III died five years after Placidia at the hand of an assassin, Petronius Maximus. The assassin himself, incredibly, was placed on the throne with the support of the senate and people of Rome. He lasted three months before a mob mangled him and cast his body into the Tiber. Avitus, Roman general appointed in Gaul by Maximus, was raised to the purple by the support of the Visigoths and their king, Theodoric, in 455. But the military and senate of Rome in October 456 compelled him to abdicate.

The forces behind the abdication of Avitus had been directed mainly by the Visigoth general Ricimer, who now found himself in a quandary, thus summarized by Previté-Orton:[15]

> Being a barbarian, he could not seize the crown himself; that would make the entire civilian population his enemies and incur the hostility of the Eastern Empire, his necessary ally against Vandal and [other] Visigoth [chieftains]. If he chose an able, warlike Emperor, he lessened his own power; if he took a nominee from the East, he could only count on half his submission; if he appointed an Italian puppet, his government lost credit in Italy and the support of the East. Trial was made of all these expedients.

He first made Majorian the emperor, a choice which the eastern emperor Leo sanctioned. Formal investiture was made at Ravenna in 457. But by 461 Ricimer, jealous of Majorian's ability and enraged by a peace signed by Majorian with the Vandal chief Gaiseric, forced Majorian, too, to abdicate. He tried now a puppet, commanding the senate to make Libius Severus a figurehead emperor for Ricimer's own rule. The life of this Severus expired as soon as it became inconvenient to his

---

15 Previté-Orton 1952: I, 97–8.

patron. Now Ricimer was reduced to petitioning a nominee from the East. Anthemius was made emperor of the West by the emperor of the East in Constantinople, and sent to claim his throne with a retinue of guards almost the size of an army. The senate and people accepted him, and Ricimer took the daughter of this new emperor in marriage, retiring to Milan. The situation in Italy gradually deteriorated to that of two armed camps.

Finally, in March 472, Ricimer advanced from Milan to a siege of Rome, proposing the replacement of Anthemius with Olybrius, a noble Roman. Rome resisted the change, but after three months of siege Ricimer gained entry to Rome, dragged Anthemius from concealment, had him murdered and Olybrius installed. Olybrius died after a reign of only seven months, but he had been preceded by Ricimer the previous August.

Leo, the eastern emperor, stepped in at this juncture by sending Julius Nepos to the western throne in 473. But Nepos arrived to find that Glycerius had already been made emperor by the military support of the Burgundian prince Grundobald. Grundobald, however, was unwilling to support Glycerius by civil war. For renouncing the scepter peacefully Glycerius was made Bishop of Salona. Grundobald returned to the Burgundian lands beyond the Alps. And Julius Nepos assumed the increasingly diminished western rule, making Ravenna his capital.

However, while in Rome, Julius Nepos had elevated the Pannonian Orestes to the titles of patrician and master-general of the troops. From this position Orestes, once Julius Nepos had moved to Ravenna, stirred his troops to armed revolt "against the obscure Greek who presumed to claim their obedience". Ravenna was an impregnable city. But rather than fight, Julius Nepos fled, on 28 August 475, to a disgraceful safety in his Dalmatian principality on the opposite coast of the Adriatic. There he lived an ambiguous exile for five years, when he was assassinated by the bishop of Salona – Glycerius, it will be remembered – who was then translated from the bishopric of Salona to the archbishopric of Milan. The troops of Orestes, however, did not wait out the five years, but, within months of Nepos' abdication-by-flight, had consented to the wish of Orestes that they declare his son, Romulus Augustulus, emperor of the West under the regency of his father. It was to prove the last link in the chain of western empire. Note the curious irony that this last emperor in the West bore the names of the founder of Rome and (in a diminutive form) of the founder of the Empire!

Before the end of the first year of Augustulus' reign, Orestes discovered that perjury and ingratitude are lessons that can be learned all too well, and often retort against their teacher. The alliance of barbarians which he had put together to oust Julius Nepos and instal Augustulus now demanded rewards in land amounting to a third of Italy, and, when Orestes rejected these demands as excessive, Odoacer (c.433–93), of the Hun tribe of Scyrii, formerly part of the troops of Attila (r.434–53), called to his confederates in all the camps and garrisons of Italy to extort by arms the just demands which their dutiful patience had been denied. Troops flocked to his standard, Orestes was executed, and the helpless Augustulus was reduced to dependency on the clemency of Odoacer. Captured in Ravenna in September 476, the boy emperor was put on a pension and relegated to a Campanian villa.

But Odoacer "had resolved to abolish that useless and expensive office" of emperor of the West. First he compelled Augustulus to submit to the Roman senate his resignation as emperor. Then he instructed the senate, whose unanimous consent he gained, to send a letter to the eastern emperor, now Zeno, requesting the termination of the imperial succession in the West, consenting that the seat of the universal empire be simply Constantinople rather than Rome, and requesting that Odoacer be invested with the title of Patrician and the administration of Italy as a diocese. Zeno ambiguously concurred,[16] and thus ingloriously ended – exactly when between 476 and 479 seems unknown – the Roman phase of the Roman Empire. Curiously, no one at the time fully saw in the event the 'fall of Rome', that is, the end of the Roman Empire among the Latins. It seems to have taken about a generation for the full magnitude of what had happened to sink in:[17]

> In obeying the Germanic king-patrician, whose Arianism they loathed, the Romans felt that they were loyal to their distant Emperor. What was even more important, Roman civilization, in spite of loss and deterioration, was still living in Italy and dominated by Catholic Christianity. The Arian Germanic patrician and tribesmen were still only an all-powerful garrison. The Senate, and far more the Pope and the Italian bishops, retained the moral guidance of the population and of its civil government. So though the Emperors had been replaced by barbaric Germanic kings in the West, the echo of the Empire's fall was deadened and its consequences mitigated and delayed by this persistent make-believe. None the less the truth could not but slip out. "The Western Roman Empire perished with this Augustulus", wrote Count Marcellinus in the next generation.

In effect, as of 479, the Germanic barbarians under Odoacer had conquered Italy, the Vandals under Gaiseric (AD428–77) had conquered Africa, the Visigoths had conquered Spain, the Angles and Saxons were conquering Britain, and the Franks were conquering Gaul. In the West the great Empire was no more, but all the pieces were in place for the formation of a new civilization; in the mix, in the center of the barbarian victory over the old Roman and new Byzantine civilization, the Latinized Church of Rome stood as "the representative of the old traditions of culture and as a bond of spiritual unity between the descendants of the conquered Romans and their barbarian conquerors."[18] As the denizens of the realm centered in Byzantium clung to Greek and abandoned Latin, so, remarkably, the denizens of the various barbarian realms which had displaced the old empire clung to Latin over their tribal tongues as part of their new spiritual heritage. The only learning in the new political

---

16 Compare the account in Vogt 1967: 250. See Martindale 1980; and Chastagnol 1966.
17 Previté-Orton 1952: 102.
18 Dawson 1932: 98. See also the general study of Dill 1958.

174   Part II   The Latin Age

realities was maintained in monasteries of the Church faithful to Rome, and Latin
was the language of those European centers, one and all.

The Onset of the Latin Age

The famous "middle ages", the Latin Age in philosophy, had begun. The turnabout
that the fourth century marked, the fifth century only confirmed. Taylor may well
insist[19] that "no date marks the passing of the ancient world and the beginning
of the Middle Ages"; but the processes of the transition were as rapid as they
were complex, and it is idle to maintain[20] that Augustine (AD354–430) "was not
mediaeval". A new civilization was in the making, Latin was to be its tongue, but
its peoples were shaped mainly by Germanic, Asiatic, and Slavic invaders who
settled and took control. Over the fifth century "these waves broke one after another
over the West: Vandals, Visigoths, Franks, Alamanni, Burgundi".[21] It was a time of
gestation, not merely transition. We may quibble with Jenks's designation[22] of these
mongrel strains of the newly forming Latin West as "Teutonic" communities, but we
can hardly dissent from his description of the period as "nursery of the Barbarian"
and "burial-ground of the Roman". For Augustine, it was hardly a burial ground. His
work became the intellectual cornerstone for the whole doctrinal development of the
Latin Age, for better or for worse, in matters of philosophy and theology alike. That
is what "Middle Ages" principally means: the time between the dominance of Greek
as the language of philosophy up to the time of Augustine, on one side, and the
emergence of the modern national languages as a vehicle of philosophical expression
in the seventeenth century and after, on the other side; in short, the Latin Age.

Odoacer (c.AD434–93) was the first barbarian to reign (r.476–93) openly and
legitimately in Italy. But what had happened, essentially, was that all the so-called
"barbarian" peoples from the northern frontiers of the empire had effectively made
their way inside, and when the administrative center of gravity of the empire shifted
East, what of Greek intellectual culture had penetrated the West shifted with it.
A new mix of peoples whose military and political world of practical affairs was
framed by the Latin language of the old empire was essentially left on its own to
forge a new civilization. "Divided from the East," remarks Hamman,[23] "the West
began its own history at the end of the fourth century and above all in the fifth." But
now "the East" is not India and China, it is the Greek-speaking peoples of the empire
once Roman, now Byzantine; and "the West" is not the religious whole of Judaism,
Christianity, and Islam, of which we spoke in chapter 1, it is the Latin-speaking
peoples of the old Roman Empire.

When the empire moved its capital east, its rulers little realized they were leaving
behind all the vitality of the future as well. Pelikan is fond of the aphorism "ex

19 Taylor 1911: 1.
20 Ibid.: 3.
21 Hamman 1986: 8.
22 Jenks 1898: v: "for want of a better name".
23 Hamman 1986: 7.

Oriente lux", "the light came from the East".[24] That may be and be that as it may; but, to extend the metaphor, in the intellectual world as in the physical world, as it happened not of necessity but in fact, the source of the light did not stand still but moved from East to West, and by the time the light was full shining in the civilization of the Latin West the civilization of the Greek East passed into the night of extinction. The great Lebenswelt of *Nova Roma*, for all its veneer of culture and Greek learning, insensibly settled down into the condition of an objective world more Umwelt than Lebenswelt, closed unto itself as if the human mind had no greater interpretive horizon than the relation of objects to itself. The animal endowed with language settled down to comport itself more like any other animal without language, and to live in a self-satisfied cocoon of its own making. Content with itself, the nouveau-Greek civilization of Byzantium closed on itself in thought as well as language, but not without launching some theological controversies which would signal the eventual break-up even of western Christendom, as dogmatic formulas became litmus tests of orthodoxy in the wake of Constantine's interference in religious affairs.[25]

A thousand years would pass before the civilization which had Constantinople for its imperial center would be vanquished by Islamic peoples. The theological

---

24 So he titles and so he makes the concluding words of the opening chapter of his splendid study of *The Spirit of Eastern Christendom (600–1700)* (Pelikan 1974: 1 & 7).

25 Hamman (1986: 5) has compared the relation between East and West during the crucial period of the so-called barbarian takeover of the Latin regions to "a one-way street", as follows: "In the course of the first centuries, Christianity had put down roots and developed within the political, economic, and cultural unity of the Empire. Christianity had found in Greek language and culture a means of expression, of unity, and of expansion. The principal Western theologians, Hilary, Ambrose, and Jerome, formed part of a spiritual elite which moved at ease in Greek culture. Ambrose, having been unexpectely named bishop, made his theological apprenticeship with the Greek masters Origen and Didymus the blind. Jerome and Rufinus opened the West to Greek exegesis and theology. This was, however, a one-way street, for there was not to be found in the East the same curiosity with regard to the West, even the Christian West. The imperial court established at Constantinople, instead of introducing Latin, was itself Hellenized. Only official documents and works of hagiography came to be translated into Greek. Augustine himself was little known in the East."

As early as the fifth century, "there was no longer an exchange between Eastern theologians and their Western counterparts", for the simple truth was that the Greeks had no interest in Latin thinkers, and did not even seem to think their language capable of developing the necessary vocabulary and distinctions to capture the religious dogmas the East, under the original stimulus of Constantine and Nicea, had seen fit to formulate as guidelines for action by imperial troops. Too bad that Augustine, who even in Trinitarian doctrine developed his thought independently of the East, in this one area of practical thought followed the Greek example and imported into the Latin world the horrible idea of providing (or at least trying to provide) theoretical justification for state control of individual conscience, writing, in the first decade of the fifth century (Brown 1967: 235), "the only full justification in the history of the early Church of the right of the state to suppress non-Catholics", and so laying himself open to Maisonneuve's charge (1962) that he was the first theorist of the later-medieval and early-modern institution (for the Protestant 'Reformers' too would adopt this Augustinian idea) of Inquisition. "Ex Oriente lux" indeed.

Not until Bayle 1686/8 would Augustine's rationale in this matter meet a full-scale challenge. And not until Powell 1960 would a philosopher of religion think to argue, in text as strangely written as it is unique, that the civil establishment of any church based on a claim of divine revelation runs contrary to natural law.

and religious heritage of Byzantium at that point would pass to Russia and the other Slavic peoples. But in science and philosophy there was virtually nothing to pass. No addition to human knowledge in these areas independent of theology and religious belief accrued under Byzantium, or if it did, it has yet to come to light.[26] No doubt the picture appears differently to those whose whole or main interest is in religion and theology. But even an investigator of such an orientation will find it necessary to take into account the harsh light which scholarship casts on the Greek civilization of Constantinople over the course of its history from the point of view of its political, philosophical, and scientific contributions to surviving civilizations.

Imperial Byzantium, "*the* Christian empire", as Pelikan emphatically puts it,[27] has been charged – too glibly, perhaps, but not without reason – with having broken Christianity in half over a vowel, and again over a word, in the process of destroying itself through having seen treason in every heresy. Let us try to get behind the facile formulae at least sufficiently to understand the eventual formation and philosophical development of a relatively independent Latin Lebenswelt.

The Breaking of Christianity over a Vowel

Constantine not only prepared the way for Christianity to become the official religion of the state, he also felt entitled to dictate its affairs. Luckily, as we have seen, the control of the Greek emperors perished in the Latin West. For one of the most decisive differences between the newly nascent Latin civilization and the senescent civilization Byzantium turned out to be is this: in the East the Church was subject to state control from the start, and the emperor at will raised and deposed its head, the Patriarch of Constantinople; in the West, the Church constantly managed to elude sustained state control, and its long-acknowledged head, the Bishop of Rome, managed overall to receive his election directly from his co-religionists rather than from any one civil ruler as such.

Under the original Roman Empire, Christianity had emerged first as an insignificant sect. Later it became sufficiently popular to constitute a perceived threat to the ancient religious beliefs of the empire and, as such, to merit persecution. Constantine, as we have seen, turned these persecutions to political and military advantage in the waging of civil war. Having won his wars, Constantine established Christianity as the favored religion of the state. Not content with this, he forced the newly official religion to adopt, in effect, propositional criteria of religious orthodoxy which could be made, in turn, guidelines for action by imperial troops. Under Constantine, and, as Kelly reminds us,[28] at Constantine's instance, occurs the transition of early Christianity from a diversity of local churches to a centralized doctrinal authority proposing a propositional criterion of orthodox belief. The transition was marked by the Council of Nicea and its Creed (AD325).

---

26 Cf. Tatakis 1949; Cavarnos 1989.
27 Pelikan 1974: 296.
28 Kelly 1968: 231.

Neither baptized nor even a catechumen,[29] the emperor Constantine took it upon himself to convene at Nicea in AD325, in the hall of one of his imperial palaces, what has come to be known as the first General Council of the Christian Church. The then-pope, Silvester I (r.314–35), not only had no participation in the planning of the council, but was prevented by illness from so much as attending. He was represented personally not even by Western bishops, but, if at all, only by two priests from Rome named Vitus and Vincentius.[30]On this last point, Ricciotti notes[31] that "none of the historians of the time who treat of the preparations for the council even mention the bishop of Rome."

The emperor Constantine himself, having convened it, both presided at this first council and joined in its debates, despite having declared a year previously by a letter[32] to Bishop Alexander of Alexandria, Egypt, and his priest Arius of Baucalis, that he considered the principal doctrinal (or, rather, dogmatic) matters before the council to be "problems that idleness alone raises, and whose only use is to sharpen men's wits".

Constantine's own main aim in convening this mother of all general councils – the beginning of "dogmatic formulae" – was the establishment of political union, with the determination of religious truth the means to this end.[33] His letter openly stated that if he "could induce men to unite" on the subject of "the ideas which all people conceive of the Deity", then "the conduct of public affairs would be considerably eased". So he did not appreciate disputes, as he put it (those who prefer understatement should love this), whose "cause seems to be quite trifling" and whose content derives from questions "entirely devoid of importance", in response to which hearers "should have kept silence". Yet out of these "idle problems" came the formulation of the Nicene Creed and the first official declaration of a Christian heresy, Arianism, the view that Christ was not consubstantial with, but only the first creature of, God. So began the history of Christian dogma, to which the Latin development of theology in the thirteenth century was one of the principal responses.[34]

---

29 See note 11 above in this chapter, p. 166.
30 This according to Sozomen i.443/50: *Ecclesiastical History* I, ch. xvii, "Of the Council convened at Nicaea on account of Arius" (pp. 33–4): "Constantine convened a synod at Nicaea, in Bithynia, and wrote to the most eminent men of the churches in every country, directing them to be there on an appointed day. ... Julius [a mistake for Sylvester], Bishop of Rome, was unable to attend on account of extreme old age; but his place was supplied by Vito and Vicentius, presbyters of his church."
31 Ricciotti 1953: 258.
32 Preserved in Eusebius c.339: ii, 64–72 (see esp. 63, 70).
33 Cf. Burckhardt 1880: 313ff., esp. 317: "In view of his own inward neutrality it was not difficult for him to keep the Church parties in suspense and not attach himself to any permanently. And so he allowed them to conquer in turn, and by energetic interventions provided only that he and his power should not be forgotten. ... This attitude his successors failed to understand, because they were themselves seriously concerned with the theological questions involved, and they left the party which they supported free to use violence and vengeance against its opposition."
34 See the various sections discussing theology as a discipline in chapter 7.

The central issue around which the council turned was whether Jesus in his divine nature as Λόγος was of the same substance or being ("consubstantial") with the Father, as expressed by the term HOMOOUSIOS; or subordinate to and only similar with the Father, HOMOIOUSIOS. The former position, championed especially by Athanasius (c.293–373), was adopted by the council and eventually established itself as the Catholic or orthodox view. The latter position comes down accordingly as "the Arian heresy".

It is easy to deride this dispute (surpassing even the lack of penetration exhibited in Constantine's letter to the principals, bishop Alexander and padre Arius) as a controversy over a single diphthong, as some historians, Gibbon most famously, vainly tried to do. But in fact this is one of those not infrequent cases in which the sounds and characters of language which approach the nearest to each other happen to represent the most opposite of ideas. The example of the present case became vital in the politics of the fourth, fifth, and sixth centuries, as can be seen from the ground that Arianism held: Gaul till the Franks under Clovis overthrew the Visigoths under Alaric II (r.484–507) in 507; Vandal Africa and Gothic Italy till Belisarius (c.AD505–65, the best general of the eastern emperor Justinian, r.527–65), temporarily recaptured these territories for Constantinople in the mid-sixth century; Spain till Recared changed the faith of the Visigoths there in 589).

When one recalls that Constantine later had himself baptized by one of the very bishops condemned in the Council of Nicea, one has to wonder what he thought he was accomplishing with this large-scale venture into territory about which he seemed to understand nothing. Not surprisingly, his interventions in ecclesiastical questions normally complicated them further. History can only say, and that very imperfectly, what did occur. We have no way of knowing what would have happened in these matters had Constantine, as emperor, not intervened. But we cannot help but wonder if the various questions that arose around Constantine "would not have been settled more speedily and completely had he not interfered with so many synods, councils, exiles, and despotic persecution", for the cogent reasons Ricciotti gives:[35]

> The Church with its internal vitality purely religious in origin had already overcome the most dangerous crises in the past as those of Gnosticism, Modalism, and the heresy of Origen. In Peter's house everything was put right by the occupants without the work of any Caesar appearing in the family as a major domo. No emperor had then called councils, exiled orthodox bishops like Athanasius and Eustathius, or preferred heretical ones like the two courtiers Eusebius of Nicomedia and Eusebius of Caeserea.
>
> One must say that the Council of Nicaea produced some good at least by giving a profession of faith. This is true. But this orthodox symbol was immediately subjected to a process of corruption as a result of the peculiar circumstances in which it was composed. ... If other ways had been followed, an orthodox profession of faith would

---

35 Ricciotti 1953: 291.

likewise have been obtained, but without the police methods, without persecution, without fratricidal quarrels, the sad consequences of which continued for many centuries.

Constantine, being the Caesar of his time, had no trouble giving to Caesar that which was Caesar's. His problem was in not understanding that there are things which are not Caesar's. "He considered it his duty far too often to go into the house of Peter to arrange things there. '*Ahi! Constantin …*'."[36]

Matters got even more extreme under Theodosius I, called "the Great", whose son Arcadius, as we saw above, embodied the final establishment of the empire of the East. For the great theological debates over the triune nature of God that preceded the Nicene Creed continued up to the Council of Constantinople (381), which completed the theological formula established in the Council of Nicea by extending to the Third Person of the Trinity the various opinions that Nicea had already settled on concerning the Second Person.[37] And in this interim the emperor Theodosius (r.379–95) entered, in the form of an Imperial edict dated 27 February 380, what can be seen in retrospect as an ominous adumbration of the more narrow, sectarian, and adversative use of the term "Catholic" as it came to dominate modern times in an opposition with "Protestant":[38]

It is our pleasure that all the nations which are governed by our clemency and moderation should steadfastly adhere to the religion which was taught by St Peter to the

---

36 Ibid.

37 So we arrive at the dogmatic formulation of the "Triune God". According to Kelly (1968: 102), the earliest application of the term 'triad' to the Godhead dates to c.181 in the *Ad Autolycum* text of Theophilus of Antioch (c.120–c.185/91), where he ventures that the three scriptural days preceding the creation of the sun and the moon "are types of the triad [τριάδος] of God and his Logos and his Sophia. In the fourth place is man, who stands in need of light – so that there might be God, Logos, Sophia, Man". Grant (1970: 53n3) argues that "this 'triad' is not precisely the Trinity, since in Theophilus' mind man can be added to it"; but the construction of Kelly is far the more interesting when we consider that to the Triune Godhead precisely, in the Christian dogma, is "man" added in the person of Christ.

38 From the *Theodosian Code* (Mommsen and Meyer ed. 1905: I.2, 834) XVI, 1, 2 (27 Feb. 380): "IMPPP. GR(ATI)ANVS, VAL(ENTINI)ANVS ET THE(O)D(OSIVS) AAA. EDICTUM AD POPVLVM VRB(IS) CONSTANTINOP(OLITANAE). Cunctos populos, quos elementiae nostrae regit temperamentum, in tali volumus religione versari, quam divinum Petrum apostolum tradidisse Romanis religio usque ad nunc ab ipso insinuata declarat quamque pontificem Damasum sequi claret et Petrum Alexandriae episcopum virum apostolocae sanctitatis, hoc est, ut secundum apostolicam disciplinam euangelicamque doctrinam patris et filii et spiritus sancti unam deitatem sub parili maiestate et sub pia trinitate credamus. Hanc legem sequentes Christianorum catholicorum nomen iubemus amplecti, reliquos vero dementes vesanosque iudicantes haeretici dogmatis infamiam sustinere nec conciliabula eorum ecclesiarum nomen accipere, divina primum vindicta, post etiam motus nostri, quem ex caelesti arbitrio sumpserimus, ultione plectendos. DAT. II KAL. MAR. THESSAL(ONICAE) GR(ATI)ANO A. V ET THEOD(OSIO) A. I CONSS." I have taken the English rendition from Gibbon 1781a: ch. 27, pp. 148–9, after comparing it both with the original Latin above and the English trans. of Pharr et al. 1952: 440; and the italics of the translation are mine.

the Romans; which faithful tradition has preserved; and which is now professed by the pontiff Damasus, and by Peter, bishop of Alexandria, a man of apostolic holiness. According to the discipline of the apostles and the doctrine of the gospel, let us believe the sole deity of the Father, the Son, and the Holy Ghost; under an equal majesty and a pious Trinity. *We authorize the followers of this doctrine to assume the title of Catholic Christians; and as we judge that all others are extravagant madmen, we brand them with the infamous name of Heretics*; and declare their conventicles shall no longer usurp the respectable appellation of churches. Besides the condemnation of divine justice, they must expect to suffer the severe penalties which our authority, guided by heavenly wisdom, shall think proper to inflict upon them.

Such a declaration, coming from an absolute head of state, should serve as a stark reminder of the importance both of subordinating the head of state to a constitutional law protecting the rights of citizens as human beings and of separating church from state in the affairs of civil life – a twin lesson still only imperfectly learned even today, and notwithstanding the evangelical exhortation not to give to Caesar the things which are God's (such as, pre-eminently, the conscience and thought of the individual human being in the working out of systems of belief). In the Latin Age, the Church maintained an overall independence of the State, while trying all the while to subordinate the State to itself. The contest was a standoff, but it was directly as a result of the many lessons learned that it became possible for modernity to arrive at the historical ideas necessary to institutionalize some separation of Church and State so that the idea of individual conscience might have some practical meaning in public life. Had the Latin Age not achieved this standoff, in this as in so many areas of public life today, there would be no "modern world".

The Further Breaking over a Word
When it is said that the Greek civilization of Constantinople broke Christianity in half a second time over a word, the accusation is not entirely just. The reference is to the word "and" added to describe the role of the Son in the procession of the Holy Spirit from the Father, the so-called *filioque* ("*and* the Son") controversy: the proposition that the Holy Spirit proceeds from the Father *and* the Son, not from the Father alone, or from the Father and Son unequally.

But this revision of the official Nicene formula did not arise in the East. It was initially proposed in AD589 by a Church council at Toledo, Spain, which made the original phrase of the Nicene Creed "*ex patre procedit*" read instead "*ex patre filioque procedit*". The Greeks protested. They insisted that the Holy Spirit proceeded from the Father alone, or at most from the Father *by* the Son, but certainly not from the Father *and* the Son. As it turned out, the addition to the Nicene Creed of the word *filioque* by a local Latin council kindled a flame of discord which burns until the present time, and became part of the occasion which eventually precipitated the separation of the then-unified Catholic Church into the Greek Catholic and the Latin Catholic churches, each of which charges the other with schism and heresy.

By what right, the Greeks in outrage demanded to know, could a Latin *local council* dare tamper with the official formulation arrived at in Greek and promulgated by a *general council*? (Nor, even setting the prideful outrage aside, is a good answer to the question obvious.)

When, at the turn of the ninth century, Pope Leo III (r.AD795–816) colluded with Charlemagne (AD768–814) to re-establish a western Roman Empire, an event we shall examine shortly below, it was Charlemagne who was to insist on the importance to faith of the Latin *filioque* formula which the Greeks resisted. Not until the eleventh century did the Vatican enter the *filioque* officially into the Latin creed. Yet, seeing that both the "homoousion" and the "filioque" controversies split Christendom for centuries, it is ironic that it was the first Christian emperor in the eastern "Roman Empire" who principally aggravated the Arian controversy, while the first Christian emperor in the reconstituted western "Holy Roman Empire" was the one who principally aggravated the filioque controversy.[39]

Philosophy in the Latin Age
Passing over the singular case of Augustine of Hippo, who "was to a far greater degree than any emperor or general or barbarian war-lord, a maker of history and a builder of the bridge which was to lead from the old world [of Greek philosophy] to the new" world of Latin philosophy,[40] which I postpone to the following chapter, it may be said that, in the West, under Odoacer's successor, or, rather, his displacer, Theodoric the Ostrogoth, the Latin Age of Philosophy begins in Italy – by yet another bloody tale.

When the empire of Attila the Hun had fallen apart on his death in 453, the Ostrogoths had entered the paid service of the Eastern emperors to drive all other barbarian peoples westward. Pannonia was their reward in land, but as insurance for their behavior the eastern emperor Leo had taken the son of the Ostrogoth king Theodemir to the court at Constantinople as hostage. This lad, Theodoric, had been born near Vienna two years after Attila's death. On his father's death in 475, Leo permitted Theodoric to become King of the Ostrogoths. Under Theodoric the Ostrogoths began to cause trouble for the empire, and Leo's successor Zeno conceived the scheme, some say under Theodoric's suggestion, of killing two birds with one stone by commissioning Theodoric to conquer Italy and replace Odoacer's rule with his own. In this event Zeno would recognize Theodoric as King of Italy and Patrician of Constantinople, while the lands of Italy would supply whatever needs the Ostrogoth still felt wanting from Pannonia and the new Ostrogoth territories along the Danube.

Theodoric invaded Italy. After five years of war Odoacer agreed to a compromise peace, and foolishly went with his son to a banquet with Theodoric at Ravenna. At

39 On how this latter controversy played out later in the Latin Age, see the "Footnote on the Greek Contribution to Latin Europe as Mainly Mediated by Arabic Islam" later in this chapter, p. 202ff.
40 Dawson 1954: 28.

this banquet Theodoric, with his own hand, slew Odoacer and Odoacer's son. In the court Theodoric established, the figure of Boethius came to the fore, and with Boethius the indigenous Latin Age of Philosophy began in Italy.

Anicius Manlius Severinus Boethius (c.AD475–524), after Augustine the most important transition figure from Greek to Latin philosophy, as we shall see,[41] was a man of noble Roman birth who loved books and learning, but took time out to serve Theodoric as minister, which proved to be a mistake. In the turmoil of Italian political life, Boethius was drawn perilously close to a treasonous conspiracy within the senate against the king, close enough, at any rate, that he was tried before Theodoric, adjudged guilty, and sentenced to death by garroting. The sentence was meted out on 23 October 524. For the next six hundred years, what Boethius had not translated of the works of Aristotle, Plato, and the other Greek philosophers – and even some of what he did translate – would be lost to the West[42] as it had to make its own way up all over again, and in the Latin language, to the levels of soaring intellectual vision for the human animal that the Greek language had first shown to be possible. Boethius, in other words, was the last figure of antiquity who had at his disposal both the full heritage of the Greek writings in philosophy and the linguistic skill and knowledge to re-express that heritage in the Latin language. The execution of Boethius by Theodoric, along with the baffling refusal by Augustine earlier to learn Greek, was the beginning of the so-called Dark Ages for Latin Europe.

The Proposal to Date Events from the Birth of Christ: The "Christian Calendar"

The beginning of the so-called Dark Ages for Latin Europe was also the beginning of the Christian calendar and the beginning of the great tradition of liberal arts education.

In 525 (about a year after Boethius' death by execution, thus), Dionysius Exiguus ("Dennis the Short", c.AD486–a.566) suggested that the year of Christ's birth be used as a new method of dating events (the supposed year, as it turned out, since his calculation proved to be a little off – perhaps less surprising than the fact that even the heirs of the subsequent scholars who exposed his error have yet to tell us full for certain in what year that birth occurred, though they tell us it was at least four

---

41 See "Boethius" in chapter 6, p. 224ff.

42 Tying the availability of Greek works to the Latin translations of Boethius alone, of course, is something of an oversimplification, in which the death of the learned figure of Boethius is made to stand as a symbol and synecdoche for the loss of access to the past in its Greek form. The specialist interested in the actual details behind such symbolic oversimplifications can consult Muckle 1942 and 1943. And it should be kept in mind that what was *translated* and so *theoretically* available is normally quite a different matter from what is *commonly known* or *in general use*. Even many of the works of Aristotle's logic that Boethius had translated were forgotten and effectively lost in the monastery libraries. When, around the time of Abaelard, interest in logic quickened across Europe and these forgotten manuscript translations were rediscovered, they led to a revival (c.1100–1200) sometimes called "the Boethian Age", before new and better translations made the newly rediscovered Boethian translations obsolete.

years BC!). The BC/AD system as used throughout the present book has become so accustomed with us that it is a bit of a surprise to discover that no one even thought of the system until the early sixth century. And it comes as a bit more of a surprise to discover that the proposal was not adopted by the Latin Church until the tenth century. The Moslem calendar is older than that. So do great events of a time fade from common knowledge and disappear into "the past".

The Origin of the Liberal Arts

The tradition of liberal arts education in the West is rooted in certain conceptions (and misconceptions) of Augustine, Boethius, Cassiodorus, and Isidore of Seville; but it was Cassiodorus (c.AD480–573), a contemporary of and noble Roman like Boethius, who first pulled the sources together so as to initiate this great tradition. Before touching on Cassiodorus, a particular earlier conception of Augustine bears remarking.

Augustine first conceived of the liberal arts as an intellectual discipline whereby the soul could in this earthly life attain and maintain a vision of God within itself. He got this conception from Plotinus[43] and, especially, from a now lost work of Porphyry circulated in Latin as *De regressu animae*, "On the return of the soul". When he later realized that this Neoplatonic Holy Grail was a natural impossibility, Augustine reshaped his conception to present the *artes liberales* instead as the intellectual weapons needed for Christians to appropriate truth wherever it might be found, which Augustine deemed to be the proper task of Christians.[44] This later, reshaped conception has proved to be the enduring educational ideal.

The First Medieval Source: Cassiodorus in Italy

The career of Cassiodorus ran parallel to that of Boethius, but with a longer course and happier end. Cassiodorus, too, served as a minister to Theodoric, in the capacity of secretary, a post he had also filled for Theodoric's predecessor, Odoacer, the first post-empire ruler of Italy, as we just saw. About 540 Cassiodorus withdrew from public life and proceeded to found two monasteries, in connection with which, about 544–5, he wrote a work called the *Institutiones divinarum et humanarum lectionum*, "an encyclopedia of sacred and classical learning". The second book of these "Institutes", dedicated to classical learning, discusses the "seven liberal arts" of grammar, rhetoric, dialectic, arithmetic, music, geometry, and astronomy, arranged under the headings of *trivium* for the first three and *quadrivium* for the last four. This sevenfold listing Cassiodorus took from Martianus Capella[45] (c.AD360–439?; fl.410–39); but Capella borrowed from many earlier writers, in particular Marcus Terentius Varro (116–26BC), in whose *Disciplinarum libri IX* the sevenfold "liberal arts" are already found enumerated and discussed.

---

43 E.g., *Enneads* I.3.1. (i.AD255/263#20) and III.8.2 (i.AD263/268#30).
44 See *De doctrina Christiana* II, 11.60 (PL 34, 63).
45 Capella i.410/29.

The disciplines constituting the *trivia* – logic, grammar (what we would now call "composition"), and rhetoric – were also later called *scientiae sermocinales*, the "discourse-based sciences", because they led to the mastery of the principles and practice of discourse, both inner and outer. The disciplines of the *quadrivia*, by contrast, were called the *scientiae reales* or "substantive sciences" because they concerned not discourse itself as an object but the objective theory (arithmetic and geometry) and application (in music and astronomy) of mathematics. Thus the "liberal arts" were the arts of mastering human discourse and the abstract thinking most distinctive of human understanding, as summarized in the accompaying diagram:

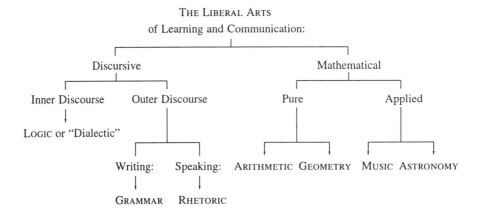

The Seven Liberal Arts

Over the many centuries separating the Latin Age from the present time, the notion of liberal arts education has never shifted from its discursive base in the "sciences" of Logic, Grammar or Composition, and Rhetoric; but the interpretation of the *quadrivium* has undergone more drastic metamorphosis.[46] The original four remaining "arts" can be regarded in one sense as a general metaphor for the university curriculum as a whole. But they can also be regarded, perhaps more accurately, as a nascent realization of the crucial role of mathematics in the structuring and advancing of the understanding of empirical subject matter generally, an early Pythagorean realization that found its first culmination in the Galilean Revolution inaugurating physics in the modern sense of mathematical physics early in the seventeenth century.[47]

This second book of Cassiodorus' *Institutes*, copied separately and expanded by anonymous scholars in the early Latin Age, became the basis for what came to be known, and still is known, as "liberal arts education". The main sources for Cassiodorus' notion of the liberal arts were Boethius, who had a division of

---

46 See Deely 1985b: "Semiotic and the Liberal Arts", *The New Scholasticism* LIX.3 (Summer),
    296–322, where the problem of "interdisciplinarity" is further addressed.
47 See chapter 11 below, esp. p. 493ff.

knowledge of his own adapted from Aristotle's division, differing from the original[48] mainly in speaking of "doctrinal" rather than "mathematical" speculative science, and in including under "doctrinal" astronomical and musical studies as well as arithmetic and geometry. Two important points to note in this scheme are, first, that "grammar" meant the *art of writing* with correctness and elegance; and, second, that "dialectic" meant a study of *logic*.

The Second Medieval Source: Isidore in Spain

The second main source in the early Latin Age for what became the tradition of liberal arts education came not out of Ostrogothic Italy but from Visigothic Spain, in the first three of the twenty books of the *Etymologiae* of Isidore of Seville (c.AD560– 636), covering I. grammar (again in the sense of composition or writing), II. rhetoric and dialectic (or logic), and III. arithmetic, geometry, music, and astronomy. In these books, Isidore follows Cassiodorus and Boethius in discussing the division or organization of human knowledge. Besides the one adapted from Aristotle, Isidore gives first what is in fact the Stoic division,[49] but, following Augustine who had mistakenly attributed the Stoic scheme to Plato, Isidore does the same. Arithmetic, geometry, music, and astronomy here are located under physics (an idea which Isidore mistakenly thinks comes from Plato; it would have seemed more appropriate to establish mathematics as a coordinate subdivision with logic under "rational philosophy"); rhetoric is coordinated with dialectics under the heading of logic; and ethics is divided, not according to individual, domestic ("economic" or "business"), and civil government, but according to the four cardinal virtues, prudence, justice, fortitude, and temperance.

On the Vitality of Mongrel Strains

Three things are particularly noteworthy about the tradition of liberal arts education as a heritage from the early Latin Age.

The first is that while Augustine, Boethius, Cassiodorus, and Isidore of Seville served as the principal *explicit* sources for all later discussions of the liberal arts (Alcuin of York, for example, in establishing Charlemagne's schools, used the Stoic division "of Plato" as his point of departure), the *implicit* conceptual source is a cross-fertilization of the two original schemes for dividing the sciences proposed by Aristotle and the Stoics in ancient Greek times. The synthesis of the two ancient classifications becomes complete in the so-called *didascalia* of the twelfth century, books introductory to the arts and philosophy. One of the most influential of these was the *Didascalion*, composed (i.1120–30) by Hugh of St Victor (1096–1141).[50]

---

48 Compare the original above, p. 91.
49 See above, p. 98.
50 The abbey of St Victor was founded by William of Champeaux in 1108, when Hugh was about twelve. We will shortly meet William of Champeaux as a champion of medieval (Platonic) realism and teacher of Peter Abaelard.

The second is that the "liberal arts disciplines" are alike distinguished by the type of objectivity according to which they are constituted: unlike scientific disciplines which investigate subject matters which have an existence prior to and in various ways independent of human understanding, the liberal arts disciplines in every case study a subject matter which depends for its very existence on the species-specific activity of the human mind. The liberal arts are alike concerned with an object of inquiry which depends on the mind itself for coming into being in the first place. They thus may be said to investigate the objective framework within which human inquiry becomes in the first place possible. To use the metaphor attributed to Hegel, any animal can see the blackboard; but in the liberal arts we are trying to "see the seeing". The disciplines constitutive of the liberal arts are "interdisciplinary" in that they concern the very framework within which disciplinary investigations become possible in the first place. This is true of the disciplines of the *trivium* and the *quadrivium* alike, but most fundamentally of the disciplines of the *trivium* inasmuch as even the learning of mathematics presupposes the learning of language; which leads to the third point.

The third point is that the original foundation of the liberal arts training in speaking, writing, and logic as the means indispensable to mastery of discourse, inner and outer, remains down to the present day as the core of the tradition of the liberal arts. Through all the variations that occur in educational fashion, and throughout the eventual inevitable expansion of the so-called "quadrivium" as knowledge grows over the centuries, this foundation has endured. Wherever an institution is devoted to the growth and communication of learning, so long as effective speaking, writing, and logical reasoning are prized, the tradition called "liberal arts education" remains alive and well.

The tradition of education in the "liberal arts", in short, like the Latin civilization itself that grew out of the wresting of control of the "western" Roman lands by the invading "Teutonic" or "barbarian" tribes that swarmed from the north, is a mongrel strain.

The Contribution of Islam to Philosophy in the Latin Age
The eastern empire not only left behind it the heartland of Europe and its original language. It soon enough lost Syria, Egypt, Sicily, North Africa, and Spain to the Moslems, to those who professed Islam. This subject opens a book in itself, but as our concern here is with an overview, it may suffice to note three things.

Where the Light Was When Europe Went Dark
The first of our three things to be noted is that, from about the eighth to the thirteenth century, the nations of Islam, not those of Europe or Byzantium, created the most vital Lebenswelt of human culture. The intellectual vigor of Moslem civilization in those years was the true successor to the spirit and learning of ancient Greece, with great centers of learning especially at Baghdad and, in Spain,

at Cordova and Seville. "Within four hundred years of its foundation," Southern summarizes:[51]

> Islam had run through phases of intellectual growth which the West achieved only in the course of a much longer development. So much has been lost that it is difficult to speak with any exactness, but it is certain that the Islamic countries produced a greater bulk and variety of learned and scientific works in the ninth, tenth, and eleventh centuries than medieval Christendom produced in any similar length of time.
>
> ... between the Latin and the Moslem worlds ... there was also an almost complete diversity of intellectual heritage. When the ancient world fell apart into its separate parts, Islam became the chief inheritor of the science and philosophy of Greece, while the barbarian West was left with the literature of Rome. ... Greek thought was taken over without a break from the schools of the Hellenic world into the courts and schools of Islam....

Philosophy in Islam found expression in the works of such men as al-Kindi, c.AD803–70; al-Farabi, c.878–c.950; Ibn Sina or Avicenna, 980–1037; al-Ghazali, 1058–1111; and Ibn Rushd or Averroes, 1126–98. Averroes used to refer to Aristotle as "the Philosopher", a title which came to be universally adopted among the Latins, for whom Averroes himself came to be referred to as "the Commentator".

The wealth of Greek culture survived in texts in Syria, both in Syriac and Greek versions. The Islamic heads of state appreciated and promoted learning among their peoples. From AD750 to 900, translations from every manuscript of Syriac, Greek, Pahlavi, and Sanskrit were made into Arabic. At the center of all this ferment were, in particular, the works of Aristotle, along with the works of Greek medicine by Galen and Hippocrates, mathematical works, and the astronomical work of Ptolemy, the *Almagest*, a name which attaches to that masterpiece·of mathematics applied to the heavens (*Mathematike Syntaxis*) from its Arabic version. But Aristotle was brought into Arabic translation by minds influenced heavily by Neoplatonic ideas, that is, by ideas which couched Plato in the interpretation of Plotinus and of Porphyry and which presented Aristotle as the author of the fifth century Neoplatonic treatise *The Theology of Aristotle*. This last work reconciled Aristotle with Plato, but only by turning both of them into Neoplatonists, which neither of them were. The Neoplatonizing tendency was accentuated as Moslem scholars sought to reconcile Greek philosophy with the Koran as the revealed word of God, something that, analogously, the European Christians, too, were inclined to do in their attempts to reconcile Greek philosophy with the Bible as the revealed word of God. In both cultures, Islamic and Latin, by the nature of the case, the influence of Aristotle was always most pure in his logical writings.

---

51 Southern 1962: 8.

One of the Most Astonishing Events in the History of Thought:
The Arab Mediation of Greek Intellectual Freedom to Latin European Civilization
The second thing to be noted is that it was not directly from Greece, still less
from Byzantium, that Europe in the Latin Age was put into contact with the ancient sources of scientific, medical, and philosophical learning. It was from the
literature of Islam translated from Arabic into Latin, especially from the centers of
learning in Moslem Spain, "a transplantation of books and ideas", Pelikan observes
approvingly,[52] "that has been called 'the most astonishing event in the history of
thought'."

And one of those astonishing events indeed it was. When, about the middle of the
twelfth century, Europe is awakened to almost the full range of Greek learning and
especially to the architectonic organization of rational inquiry set forth in the works
of Aristotle, it is to Islamic civilization that it owes its intellectual awakening, as if
Byzantium did not exist. From that influx comes alike modernity and postmodernity,
to the extent that both depend upon the structures of higher learning that we call
universities, which provide the principal mainstays of intellectual development as
we enter the twenty-first century.

For whatever reason, the Islamic heads of state in this period took a serious
interest in and promoted intellectual life and learning at the highest levels of the state.
They saw to it that, whenever new books were acquired in the progressive conquest
of Byzantine lands, these books were translated. Had this tradition continued, there
is no telling how far the growth of Islamic civilization would have gone, perhaps
even so far as to gestate the scientific revolution that will instead come from the
Latins, as we will see in chapter 11. But the trend was not to last.

Islam Beheads Itself
The final thing to be noted about philosophy in Islam was its ultimate extinction – not
in individual thinkers, of course, who continue to crop up in Islam as everywhere else,
but as a force in the shaping of the institutions and laws of the state and intervening in
any effective way between the religious teaching and the civil power of the state. In
orthodox Islamic society, government, law, and morality are all based by right upon
the religious creed as revealed in the Koran. As in orthodox Judaism, the texts accepted
as the basis of all life, civil as well as personal, prescribe so much in detail that little
room is left in principle for an exercise of a speculative reason that takes its warrant
from experience first of all by way of abduction, and its measure from deductions
drawn in the development of hypotheses always with an eye to inductive verifications
in a spiral of semiosis toward the infinite. In a word, the abdication in principle and
in detail of all judgment to the religious interpreters of sacred texts, for which Islam
as a civilization opted after the twelfth century, left no room for the development
in its tradition of the way of thinking called in postmodern times "pragmaticism".

---

52 Pelikan 1974: 273. The remark approvingly cited is from Southern 1962: 9. Compare the remark of
    Nasr 1996: 27, cited in n53 following. But for serious detail, see Badawi 1968.

This unfortunate turning point was marked principally by the writings of al-Ghazali – Abu Hāmid Muhammad ibn Muhammad at-Tūsī al-Ghazālī (1058–1111). Because reason depends upon sensation, he argued, we need a surer guide to truth than reason can provide. The civilization that relies on reason ends in universal doubt, intellectual bankruptcy, moral deterioration, and civil collapse, from all of which only reliance on the guidance of revelation can save us. So argued his famous book, the *Tahafut al-Falasifah*, *The Incoherence of Philosophy* (c.1095). Luckily for him, he of course knew exactly where alone the saving revelation was to be found. In his *Ihya Ulum al-Din*, *Revival of the Science of Religion*, he expounded and defended the Hadith (the traditions preserved by learned men of the Prophet's customs and conversations) and the Koran as containing the answers to every possible question of human concern and science.

After al-Ghazali would yet come "the Commentator", Averroes (1126–98), as before him had come the great Avicenna (980–1037). Averroes wrote a rebuttal of al-Ghazali under the title of *Tahafut al-Tahafut* (*The Incoherence of the Incoherence*). He argued powerfully for the necessity of reason to hold its own ground, and for the need to work out symbolic and allegorical interpretations of religious doctrine where scriptures literally taken run afoul of science. Yet not even Averroes' rebuttal managed to turn the tide.

Averroes seemed to argue not for a relative autonomy of faith and reason such as Aquinas would later promulgate, but for an absolute autonomy of reason under which faith provides superstitions necessary for the uneducated masses unable to rise to the intellectual paths of scientific and philosophical reason. Perhaps it was by going too far that he lost everything. In 1150 the Caliph at Baghdad had burned all the philosophical writings of Averroes under his power. In 1194 the Emir at Seville did the same, adding a ban on the study of philosophy and urging his subjects to burn whatever books of philosophy they might find whenever they might find them. Among the Latins the recondite commentaries of Averroes on Aristotle were prized and influential. But among his own people he became a prophet without honor.

Al-Ghazali had won a victory for which Islam continues to pay the price. For after him the civilization which had carried the torch of learning and speculation while Europe went dark, and which had passed that torch back to Europe at the cresting of the Latins' so-called dark age, itself went dark. The hermeneutics of Hadith and the Koran indulged that singular capacity of mind-dependent being to multiply relations upon relations in the justification of positions literally unjustifiable, just because they happened to occur in a context considered sacred by the people of the book and therefore to be adhered to literally, at whatever cost, by the device of an infinite semiosis in the service of closing, rather than opening, the mind.[53] It was

---

53 Could the point be made more unequivocally than in this sympathetically-intended summary of Nasr (1996: 27): "Viewed from the point of view of the Western intellectual tradition, Islamic philosophy appears as simply Graeco-Alexandrian philosophy in Arabic dress, a philosophy whose sole role was to transmit certain important elements of the heritage of antiquity to the medieval

not that way in Islam from the beginning. Too simplistic is the remark by Akhtar[54] that "ever since the first currents of Hellenic philosophy overwhelmed the simple literalism of the Muslim creed, Islamic 'orthodoxy' has never ceased to frown on the power of philosophy to plague its labours." The twelfth century clash between orthodoxy as represented by al-Ghazali and philosophy as represented by Averroes did not have to turn the way it did, and the Islamic culture under better sages (and political figures) may one day open again. But from the time of al-Ghazali well into the twentieth century and beyond, so in fact has Islamic culture turned: to the support of fundamentalist civilization where tradition does not suffer gladly nor far tolerate intrusions of independent reasoning.

The sense of the *relative* autonomy of rational thought in the sphere of human experience, so strong in parts of the mainstream of the Latin Age as arguably to constitute its distinctive heritage, thus came to be stifled in Islam, as it was throughout most of civilization except for first the early Greek and later the Latin predecessors to postmodernity. Islam fell into the same trap that all other institutionalized religious systems, East and West alike, have fallen into when their adherents gained control of the mechanisms of the state, the mistake of asserting the *absolute* autonomy of faith. What "absolute autonomy" in this context means is a religious belief articulated in propositions incapable of being proved (and, hence, incapable of being known to be true insofar as experience provides the means of rationally testing propositions) but asserted as necessarily accepted by anyone who is "saved" and as criterial for deciding whatever issues in whatever sphere of life to which the religious authority cares to extend itself, even through civil and police means.

Only this last move is fatal for philosophy. For once the "People of a Book" make this move, once absolute autonomy is accorded to the claims of religious authority "speaking for God", there is no longer any room for an interpretive scheme grounded elsewhere than in the cultural exegesis of the sacred text – no room, that is to say, for an interpretive scheme that cannot be subordinated to and adjudicated by a scriptural exegesis. This is a delicate point, a line not easy to draw, and in Islam, as in Judaism, the orthodox were not able to draw it. In AD784, a Persian poet was decapitated for asserting the superiority of his verses to those of the Koran; and in the 1990s we

---

West. If seen, however, from its own perspective and in the light of the whole of the Islamic tradition which has had a twelve-century-long continuous history and is still alive today, it becomes abundantly clear that Islamic philosophy, like everything else Islamic, is deeply rooted in the Qur'ān and *Hadīth*. Islamic philosophy is Islamic not only by virtue of the fact that it was cultivated in the Islamic world and by Muslims but because it derives its principles, inspiration and many of the questions with which it has been concerned from the sources of Islamic revelation despite the claims of its opponents to the contrary." In short, we face here all over again the confusion of those who would speak of "Indian philosophy" while relying on revelation, as discussed in chapter 1, and the confusions of Augustine and others in speaking of "Christian philosophy", as we will see in chapter 7. Philosophy is but a distinctive manner of intellectual exercise, neither Western nor Eastern, still less sectarian in the religious sense.

54 Akhtar 1996: 162.

have the case of a novelist placed under sentence of death, a "fatwa", for writing a book[55] that the Ayatollah Khomeini of Iran (c.1900–89) deemed insufficiently respectful of the Koran. (The Ayatollah is dead, but the *fatwa* remains in effect, and the affected author in hiding; perhaps till nature executes the *fatwa*?)

There are cases like that in the Latin Age. But the whole thrust of the civilization that comes out of Latin Europe, especially since 1648, has been to put a collar on the forces of inquisition and to develop the human possibilities of exploration and control of the physical world. The philosophy the Latin West developed has alone provided the intellectual framework justifying the relative spheres of faith and reason and the relative autonomy of the hermeneutic (or interpretive procedures) proper to each. Unless we wish to adopt an attitude of radical cultural relativism, maintaining that there is really nothing to choose between a civilization which has worked out a framework of relative autonomy for faith and reason and a civilization which rests on a framework of absolute autonomy for faith residing in the official spokesmen for the interpretation of the texts taken as divinely revealed who control by right and principle all public expression of thought and behavior within the state, this end-of-the-twentieth-century affair (even over an author supercilious to a fault by many accounts) is no mere matter of "journalism". Such an affair needs to be seen as a symptom of a profound philosophical and cultural problem rooted in the failure of some major currents of contemporary civilizations to recognize the coming of age of human understanding on its own ground of experience. This age includes, while remaining relatively autonomous with respect to, claims of religious authority as derived from divinely revealed texts and divinely sanctioned traditions. The symptomatic nature of the affair (what makes the "Rushdie affair", we might say, a σημεῖον not to be nominalistically glossed over) MacDonogh[56] in particular has tried to bring out by the symbolic device of asserting to have edited his book "in association with Article 19" of the United Nations Universal Declaration of Human Rights, which rejects the cultural relativism of absolute state autonomy, whether civil or religious, in the proposition: "Everyone has the right of freedom of opinion and expression; this right includes freedom to hold opinions without interference and to seek, receive, and impart information and ideas through any media and regardless of frontiers".

Insofar as failures of the type illustrated by "the Rushdie affair" remain embodied in structures of state power and government, we face an aspect of civilization which menaces what Maritain liked to call "the freedom of the intellect", by which he meant simply the right of the human individual to reach opinions through the experience of life and to express these opinions in judgments that may or may not be favorable to the dogmas asserted by authorities as obligatory or to the political preferences of a party in power. From this point of view, the literature that has grown up around the

---

55 Salman Rushdie, *The Satanic Verses* (London: Viking Penguin, 1988).
56 MacDonogh ed. 1993.

"Rushdie Affair"[57] takes on the larger significance of an importance for the long run, and is worth pondering. But above all should it be understood that what is at stake here is not an issue of "diversity", but a structural issue of the formation within civilization of institutions capable of sustaining inquiry, which is a matter quite distinct from psychological and sociological diversity and "individual preferences".

Like the separation of church and state in America as a modern achievement of practical thought, the achievement of the later Latins of a balance between faith and reason in the sphere of speculative thought is a monumental but precarious achievement of civilization, never won cleanly, for once and all, but achieved rather "inchmeal", as Levy said:[58]

> Reasonable people should have learned by now that morality can and does exist without religion, and that Christianity is capable of surviving without penal sanctions. The use of the criminal law to assuage affronted religious feelings imperils liberty ... [Blasphemy laws] are reminders too that the feculent odor of persecution for cause of conscience, which is the basic principle upon which blasphemy laws rest, has not yet dissipated.

Nor in full will it likely ever! But there is a great difference between a philosophical tradition which has so leavened civilization as to make such laws legal relics and areas of civilization which have remained impermeable to any such leavening and have resisted in principle the doctrinal development of any such tradition. (Nor should we forget the late-modern inverse secular counterpart of religious intolerance of freedom of the intellect such as we witnessed, for example, in the ill-fated experiment of the "Soviet Union". There is not only the problem of faith seeking to dominate or suppress reason; there is also the problem of reason seeking to eliminate even legitimate possibilities of belief. The thought-control mentality can operate through secular institutions no less than through religious ones, and this 'secular inversion' of the mentality represents in the early twenty-first century a greater challenge to the delicate experiment of balancing or "separating" church and state than does the religious original which inspired the Enlightenment experiment to begin with.) I think the leavening depends upon a recognition of the relatively autonomous spheres of "faith and reason", in the traditional phrase. The civil structure resulting from such a leavening in time is at each moment jeopardized by the new generations, which have not the historical depth to grasp how important it is to the human spirit that it be allowed to develop as the cutting edge of high civilization a community of inquirers. Yet it is on this development above all that a "scientific intelligence", as Peirce liked to say, the formation *over the centuries* of a "community of inquirers", depends.

---

57 A sampling: Brennan 1989; Appignanesi and Maitland eds 1990; Pipes 1990; Harrison 1992;
   MacDonogh ed. 1993; Levy 1993; Braziller 1994.
58 Levy 1993: ix, 579.

For a "scientific intelligence" depends precisely on a *community* of inquirers,[59] thinkers and researchers with both a confidence in the long run and an appreciation of the fact that present thought owes part of its meaning to what will be discovered and thought in the future – discovered not only by this but by succeeding generations in a semiosis, an action of signs, that opens to the infinite not mainly within the objective structures of mind-dependent being, but precisely as those structures interlace with another infinite entirely, the infinity of nature.

This was the infinity of what the medievals liked to call "real being" (in its staunch independence of the vagaries and wistful constructions of every finite intelligence) and "transcendental being" (in its capacity to instruct us as to the requirements existence as finite beings in a physical universe imposes upon us). The forging of such a community appears as a natural finality for the species of linguistic animal if we wish to flourish to the fullness of our own capacity as the animals who not only use, but also know, both that there are signs and that the action of signs alone provides the veins and arteries through which the lifeblood of intelligence can circulate.

The Role of Mythology in the Shaping of the Latin Age

The Latin Age was no more prone than any other to the inveterate dishonesty of individuals and social groups in pursuit of their various interests. But at a time when superstition loomed large and scholarship had but a tenuous footing, when the means of communication were frail and slow and the general level of learning low to nonexistent, fraud naturally had a larger stage on which to play.

There are those who object to the use of such terms as "fraud" and "forgery" in these matters, as we have already had occasion to mention in the remarkable case of Pseudo-Dionysius,[60] which had so great a shaping influence on the philosophy and theology of the Latin Age that not even the eventual exposure of the fraud could, after more than eight hundred years of influence, erase the mark. This was the case most important for philosophy; but it was far from the only case where "the edifice has subsisted after the foundations have been undermined". And if we refuse to speak of "fraud" and "forgery" in these affairs, we may as well abandon the very idea of critical history, with truth not far behind. Better to follow the saying of

---

59 It is no accident that a Chinese *individual* first invented gunpowder, another movable type; yet *nothing came of these discoveries* within the socio-cultural context of an "ancient" civilization that had to wait for "foreign influence" to establish in 1898 its *first university*, of which even the name (U. of Peking) is in jeopardy for nationalistic linguistic considerations, the very considerations that precluded universities in the first place as indigenous cultural flowerings.

60 Recall the discussion of "Neoplatonic Influences on the Latin Age" from chapter 4, p. 129; and in particular the discussion of the term "fraud" on its first occurrence in the main text, p. 133n116 in chapter 4 above, where we also discuss "forgery" as a term and the propriety of the application of such terms to the type of context we are considering, especially for the three cases of the Pseudo-Dionysian writings, the Donation of Constantine, and the False Decretals palmed off by Pseudo-Isidore.

Augustine:[61] "We are blessed not by seeing angels but by seeing truth"; and the truth is that the role of nonbeing in the Latin sense[62] in the shaping of the affairs of human civilization would not be easily overestimated, nor is civilization itself understandable, if we are not critically to evaluate the factors that go into the ongoing process of transforming the Umwelt of the human *animal* into the Lebenswelt of the *human* animal. For what Le Goff says of the civilization constituting the Latin Age, *mutatis mutandis*, holds true of every civilization before and since: "the society", he says,[63] "can only be understood if one shows how its material, social, and political realities were penetrated by symbolism and the imaginary world". Such late-modern philosophies as positivism and other variants which purported to present in formal logic and mathematical technique the sure avenue to every truth could gain a following only by a singular ignorance and ignoral of history, both in general[64] and in the Latin Age in particular.

The conditions of the seventh through tenth centuries made it natural that the medievals developed a special fondness for forging documents. There were forged gospels; forged decretals to serve as ecclesiastical weapons; forged mystical and religious writings to try to shape Christian belief; forged philosophical writings to gain a ready audience and wide influence; forged charters by which monks sometimes won royal grants for their monasteries; and forged charters to give some Cambridge colleges a false antiquity. Lanfranc, archbishop of Canterbury (c.1005–89), is even said by the papal Curia to have forged a charter to prove the antiquity of his see.

But two forgeries toward the end of the so-called Dark Ages, the eight-century "Donation of Constantine" and the ninth-century "False Decretals", had so fundamental a tenor and large a cast that they lent their content, like the pseudosophy and pseudology of Pseudo-Dionysius, to the shaping of the Latin Age as a whole. For between the Donation and the Decretals was sandwiched the restoration in the West of a Roman empire, not one in which the bishop of Rome was to be, like the patriarch of Constantinople, the emperor's domestic chaplain, but one in which the pope was to be sovereign in the realm of religion and possessed of a claim on the emperor's support should he choose to call upon him.

Like most powerful historical myths, these, used to re-establish in a new frame a Western Empire, took root from important actual historical circumstances, details of

---

61 "Non videndo Angelos beati sumus, sed videndo veritatem", entry #82 under "Veritas" in Lenfant 1665. The next entry is equally à propos: "Non aliunde sapiens Angelus, aliunde homo; aliunde ille verax, aliunde homo; sed ab una incommutabili sapientia et veritate."

The citations, however, are from Augustine's *De vera religione* of AD390/1, cap. 55, par. 110; and in the two editions of the work I was able to inspect (the Maurist ed. of 1700, tome I, col. 588 top, and the *Corpus Christianorum* ed. of 1962: 258) the term "angel" of the #82 entry occurs in the singular rather than plural form.

62 See particularly "Nonbeing in Latin Philosophy", in chapter 7, p. 350.

63 Le Goff 1988: viii.

64 See the discussion in chapter 15 below, esp. p. 726ff.

which became buried in the sands of time. How to pin down the growth of nonbeing from being in actual cases?

The Mythical Donation of Constantine

We have already examined the actual circumstances of Constantine's rise to power, of his founding of *Nova Roma* to seat the empire in the East, and of his slow-motion "conversion" to Christianity. The eleven years preceding his deathbed baptism are particularly difficult to understand. Of the killings he instigated in this last period of his life, Ricciotti remarks:[65] "it is difficult to find a reason. These acts, apart from being very unpleasant in themselves, are covered by the veil which we have already found in the life of Constantine.[66] The crimes [of the last decade of his life in particular] are in semidarkness and we can barely see the actual deeds and nothing of the motives for which they were committed, not even of the advantages of them to their author."

The actual facts as we know them from today's scholarly vantage, however, are not the "facts" as they impacted on the Latin world's development of its distinctive indigenous Lebenswelt, for better or for worse. For the actual events became among the Latins lost in the wrappings of a mythology powerful enough to affect decisively the shaping of the indigenous Latin Age of the West, particularly in the shape the contest between civil and ecclesiastical authority took among the Latin nations, despite the historical unreality of the Latin mythology as regards the actual fourth-century events in the constituting of the Greek East as seat of the ancient empire.

The being of history and the nonbeing of discourse at this point intersect to create what Llewellyn has described[67] as "a full historical and legal background to form the basis of papal government throughout the Middle Ages." For "considering the time of the composition of" the *constitutum Constantini*, as Ullmann remarks,[68] "it could have meaning only as regards the Eastern empire": "the real object" of the forgery "was the emancipation of the papacy from the imperial framework".

Let the facts be what they are. To them must be added the announcement, approximately four and a half centuries after the official opening of *Nova Roma*, in an epistle by Pope Adrian I (r.AD772–95) to Charlemagne, of the existence of the DONATION OF CONSTANTINE, "*Constitutum Constantini*",[69] a document of a legal significance hardly to be underestimated, purportedly dating from the fourth century. According

---

65 Ricciotti 1953: 273.
66 Ricciotti is referring to such matters as the early "biographers" of Constantine, who deliberately present his life in a favorable light by omitting mention of crucial facts (see the gloss on Eusebius c.339 in the References, p. 771), the attempt of the Eastern church to list him in the calendar of saints, and in general the bias to insist that the first emperor to become Christian must be regarded favorably by history.
67 Llewellyn 1971: 210.
68 Ullman 1962: 81. A teleology of history, then, would warrant (ideologically, not according to truth) this or any similarly aimed forgery: "*argumentum est ficta res, quae tamen fieri potuit*".
69 The basic text is presented in S. Williams 1964.

to this forgery, the first of the Christian emperors had come down with leprosy, and was both healed of the dreaded disease and purified in the waters of baptism by the Roman bishop Pope St Sylvester I (r.AD314–35). And never was a healer of souls or bodies recompensed more gloriously: the royal proselyte withdrew from the seat and patrimony of St Peter; he declared his resolution of founding a new capital in the East; and he resigned to the popes the free and perpetual sovereignty of Rome, Italy, and the provinces of the West – *"omnes Italiae seu occidentalium regionum provincias loca et civitates"*. This vast estate, in effect, the western Empire, was the pope's to do with as he pleased. What pleased him, in the person of Adrian's successor, Pope Leo III (r.AD795–816), as it turned out, was to re-establish in the West a new Roman empire, what would eventually (only after 1155 to be exact) be called the *Holy* Roman Empire.

The "Holy" Roman Empire

We deal here with one of the main pieces of the political geography of medieval Europe of which the student of philosophy should not be ignorant, because it contributed importantly to the frame within which the university world of high-medieval philosophy would soon begin to take form. This part of the story is rooted in the reign of Charlemagne (AD742–814), the most successful of the medieval kings. On Christmas day of the year 800 in the church of St Peter, Pope Leo III placed on the head of a Charlemagne kneeling in prayer a jewelled crown, and the congregation, which could hardly have so performed without instruction beforehand, thrice cried out according to the ancient ritual of the *senatus populusque Romanus* confirming a coronation, "Hail to Charles Augustus, crowned by God the great and peace-bringing Emperor of the Romans!".

The general plan for this coronation was familiar and welcome to Charlemagne, though there is reason to believe that the actual moment of the event came as a surprise to him. There is also reason to believe that the pope had well in mind on the occasion the potential power of the symbolism of a civil ruler who received his authority and crown from the Vicar of Christ; for such symbolism could not be unhelpful in future confrontations between throne and altar.[70] The so-established Roman Empire of Charlemagne was not wholly legal, but neither was it merely fiction. It rested on and reflected the military victories ceaselessly and relentlessly won by Charlemagne since he had become king in Germany in 771.

Charlemagne had also a great interest in learning. In 787, thirteen years before his imperial coronation, he had begun a series of initiatives in education, under the direction especially of Alcuin of York (AD732–804), whom Charlemagne brought to

---

70 When the occasion for such a coronation arose under the European circumstances of 1804, Pius VII was in the place of Leo III and Napoleon was in the place of Charlemagne. But, mindful of the potency of the earlier symbolism, Napoleon arranged for the coronation to be held not in Rome but in Paris. And, when the crucial moment for crowning arrived, to avoid any repetition of the old ambiguities, Napoleon took the crown and placed it on his head by his own hands. (Of course, his empire did not last as long as Charlemagne's either.)

Aachen in 782. These initiatives led to the first instance in history of something like a free and general education. Charlemagne imported first Alcuin, and then, under Alcuin's guidance, teachers from Ireland, Britain, and Italy.[71] By comparison with the centers of learning at the time in Constantinople, Baghdad, and Cordova, the network of Charlemagne's schools was feeble. But out of them would come in a few centuries the universities first of Europe and then of the New World, centers of learning and inquiry that would establish the frontiers of a postmodern community of inquiry as global. It was a question of getting an infrastructure in place, and the importance of such a contribution, Charlemagne's contribution, needs to be appreciated. All of this, Pope Leo III well understood, could only be consolidated and strengthened should Charlemagne hold the title of Roman Emperor. And according to the terms of the Donation of Constantine, this title was Leo's to confer. Pay attention to one of the best students of this dark historical moment:[72]

> Far be it from me to imply that Leo III made such use of the donation as to infer from it his right to restore the empire and its constitutional theory. By most of the critics this document is dated back to the beginning of the year 744; it was manufactured at Rome, probably at the Lateran, the very place where Leo was, at that time, beginning his career in the administration of the sacristy. It is more than likely, therefore, that there was something in common between the idea with which it is inspired and the conceptions of the Pope and his party with regard to the theoretical, or, at least, desirable, relations between the two powers [ecclesiastical and civil, in the year AD 800]. As may readily be imagined, such notions were not calculated to please Charlemagne. It is doubtful whether he had any very definite idea of the extent of the ancient imperial power. Times were changed, and not even so mighty a king as himself, not even the Byzantine successors of the true empire, could lay claim to an authority as absolute as that of a Trajan or a Constantine. In the West, especially, the military aristocracy – the forerunners of the feudal system – were a force to be reckoned with.
>
> In short, Christmas Day, 800, had been witness of a great and remarkable event, the full importance of which was not understood at the time. And this is not an isolated instance of the kind.

The idea behind the papal coronation was to restore the original Roman *imperium*, but with a decidedly new twist. The new twist, present from the beginning of schemes for the "restoration", was that the new western Roman Empire should be supported by and supportive of the Christian Catholic Church of Rome, and supportive specifically of the person and prerogatives of the bishop of Rome, the pope.

If the pope already held from Constantine rights over the whole of the West, then, in consecrating for the West a new emperor for the handling of civil affairs,

---

71 The backbone of the effort was monastic culture, particularly Benedictine monastic culture. See Leclerq 1961.

72 Duchesne 1898: 120.

the pope would only be acting within his rights. The new emperor, in turn, would hold his rights as emperor from his consecrator the pope. In Pope Leo's mind, the new entity would thus be a way to counter the subservience to the state which had characterized the eastern church from the time of Constantine. It would be the principal foundation stone on which the autonomy of the religious sphere in public life could be made practically to rest. The false donation of Constantine, in short, "expresses very clearly the conception of the new imperial régime which the Romans (and in particular the Roman clergy) adopted more and more definitely as time went on".[73] This is the conception of a benevolent, gracious, and protective sovereign, who would leave Rome and church affairs to the pope, who would reside far from Rome, but who would come to the aid of Rome if summoned for any special difficulty.

Of course, there was a problem. Not everyone, even at the time, accepted the forgery as genuine. The Greek monarch already had the title of Roman Emperor. However faint and fictive events had made that title in its substance by the time of the ninth century, the Greek monarch of Constantinople yet retained full, sole historic, and legal right to that title. Moreover, the ancient empire had considerably greater antiquity than the Church. Never in the past, not at any point prior to the surprise revelation of Pope Adrian I's letter, had the Church had or claimed any recognized authority to convey or transfer the title of Roman Emperor.

The involvement of the papacy in the new founding, the supposed refounding, clearly made of the new imperial entity a different animal from the imperium of pagan Rome. But the resistance to acknowledging this novelty lasted up to the reign of Emperor Otto I (AD936–73), crowned in 963. The word "holy", however, inserted into the designation of the refounded empire by Frederick Barbarossa in 1155, made the recognition of the novelty effectively explicit. The unhesitating embrace of the papal-sounding adjective by the states of the Latin civilization of the time, and of historians ever since, nicely underscores the novelty recognized.

In the political and diplomatic schemings of Charlemagne's time, the claim of the empire seated at Constantinople to the title coveted for Charlemagne was considered conveniently compromised by the fact a woman who had blinded her son and usurped his throne ruled as Empress Irene in Constantinople. Charlemagne himself took further advantage of this situation by proposing to Irene in 802 that marriage would duly serve dually to legitimize whatever might be dubious in either of their titles. But in this very year Irene's treasurer Nicephorus was crowned emperor by the patriarch of Constantinople in the church of St Sophia. Irene was banished to miserable exile on the isle of Lesbos, and Nicephorus as emperor forbade the patriarch of Constantinople to hold any communications with the pope, whom Nicephorus considered as the patriarch of Charlemagne.

---

73 Ibid.: 119. See Ullmann 1962: 44ff.

That Charlemagne's crowning contributed to the rift of the Latin and Greek churches over the *filioque*, however, was as nothing to the benefits the institution of the "Holy Roman Empire" brought the Latin world.[74] The title of Emperor newly conferred was far from an empty one; for the prince thus crowned ruled, by a combination of patrimony and conquest, in France, Spain, Italy, Germany, and Hungary. The empire newly titled thus had served to extirpate the last titular ruling claims of Byzantium over the West, and to adumbrate the contours of modern Europe.

Yet the line of family inheritance Charlemagne tried to establish for his empire came to nothing within a few generations. The degradation of the line may be signaled from the ridiculous epithets of the *bald*, the *stammerer*, the *fat*, and the *simple*, which were applied to the succeeding monarchs;[75] so that, after 888, the choice of Holy Roman Emperor became a matter of election, settled in Germany, even if consummated by a crowning in Rome. In the period between Charlemagne's death and the extinction of his line, Germany had become a federative republic. The seven most powerful feudatories of this republic – the king of Bohemia, the duke of Saxony, the margrave of Brandenburg, the count palatine of the Rhine,

---

74 The accumulating political grievances between the Greek East and the Latin West were reaching the critical mass that would result, in 1054 – two and one-half centuries plus four years after Charlemagne's ambiguous crowning in the illegal restoration of a western emperor – in the complete schism which has endured to this day. See the "Footnote on the Greek Contribution to Latin Europe …", p. 202 below.

75 There are infinite details to the story. In 813, four months before his death in 814, Charlemagne had raised to the imperial throne his son Louis "the Pious", an earlier division of the empire among his three sons Pepin, Louis, and Charles having been annulled by the death of Pepin in 810 and Charles in 811. In 817 Louis in turn divided the empire among his three sons, Pepin, Lothaire, and Louis "the German" (Ludwig, let us call him). When by a second wife he had a fourth son, Charles, later called "the Bald", Louis tried to annul the division of 817 to give Charles the Bald a share. This attempt led to a civil war in which Louis was defeated and jailed in 833 by his sons from his first wife. Lothaire treated his imprisoned father so badly that Pepin and Ludwig joined forces to restore Louis to the throne in 834. Pepin died in 838, and Louis made a new division of the empire among Lothaire, Louis, and Charles; but Lothaire began another war over this division. When his father Louis the Pious died in 840, Lothaire succeeded him as emperor by right of being the oldest surviving son, and immediately tried to reduce his brother Louis the German and half-brother Charles the Bald to the status of vassals, at which he was unsuccessful. In 843 the three brothers signed the Treaty of Verdun, which partitioned the empire of Charlemagne into what would become the modern states of Germany, France, and Italy. Ludwig ruled the first, Charles the second, and Lothaire the third – although Lothaire's region was much more complicated than the description of it as "roughly Italy" would suggest, and became, especially in the region of Lorraine, a battleground for centuries between Germany and France. In the period 877–88, Charles the Bald was succeeded in the rule of France by Louis II "the Stammerer", Louis III, Carloman, and, finally, Charles the Fat, under whom, around 884, by various accidents of time and death, the reign of Charlemagne became briefly reunited. But he was so ineffectual in resisting a Norse invasion of his realm that he was deposed and died in the same year, 888, ever after which the title of Holy Roman Emperor was decided by election. The hereditary line of Carolingian succession in France died out in 987. The Capetian dynasty, which began in that same year, lasted until the French Revolution of 1789.

and the three archbishops of Mentz, Trèves, and Cologne – gained the exclusive right to choose the emperor, while the actual crowning and anointing remained a prerogative of the popes up to and including the crowning of Frederick III as Holy Roman Emperor by Pope Nicholas V on 18 March 1452. But after that date, the Holy Roman Emperors rest their imperial title wholly on the choice of the electors of Germany. They forego as superfluous the papal crowning in Rome.[76]

Thus, even though the "Holy Roman Empire" never fully cohered after the death of Charlemagne – it was never holy, hardly Roman, nor quite an empire – it provided the framework within which the recognizably modern forms of European organization had begun to become visible already by the later ninth century;[77] and these forms in turn provided the context within which the university world of the twelfth and thirteenth centuries would establish itself. By the fourteenth century, the title of Holy Roman Emperor had a symbolic weight not fully supported by weight of arms, but potent on the stage and in the rituals of public affairs. The hereditary monarchs of Europe acknowledged the pre-eminence of his rank and dignity, making of him the first of the Christian princes and temporal head of the great republic of the West. Title of majesty accrued to him as to all kings, but only he came to dispute with the pope the highest prerogatives of creating new kings and assembling councils.

But our interest in the political geography of the Latin Age is only as backdrop to its philosophy, and for this it is enough to note in general that the heritage of the translation of the empire in the Latin world to Charlemagne continued in various guises to play a role in the political coherence of that Latin world all the way down to the seventeenth century. At that point, the beginning of modern times, yet another revolution – this time an intellectual and linguistic one – would bring an end to the Latin Age, with its philosophy of being and "way of things" in the sciences, by introducing a new Way of Ideas. This new way of ideas would both initiate and define the philosophical epoch of modernity even while science, in separating from the philosophy of being, would yet doggedly stick, in its naively realistic fashion, to its own version of the way of things.

The Mythical Decretals ("Decretales Pseudoisidorianae")
The document declaring the "donation of Constantine" was an eighth-century forgery pure and simple. But it was buttressed in the first half of the ninth cen-

---

76 The cultural institution of the Holy Roman Empire finally expired quietly in August 1806, when Francis II resigned the imperial crown without a successor; but by then it was a feeble medieval shadow in the full light of modernity.

77 When, in the 12th century, the Kingdom of Sicily claimed creation with the papal sanction of Anacletus II, it brought to ten the kings of the Latin world, the other nine being those of France, England, Scotland (these three only were more ancient than Charlemagne), Castile, Aragon, Navarre, Sweden, Denmark, and Hungary; and of these only the last was likewise involved with papal sanction.

tury, immediately after the refounding of a western empire, by a second forgery, a collection called the *Decretals*,[78] a volume destined to be placed open upon the altar[79] along with the Bible and the *Summa theologiae* of Thomas Aquinas during the deliberations of the Council of Trent (13 December 1545–4 December 1563).

This second forgery was assembled c.849 by a French cleric using the name "Isidorus Mercatus".[80] Along with a mass of authentic decrees by councils and popes, Mercatus neatly inserted a forged series of decrees and letters attributed to pontiffs from Pope Clement I (r.AD91–100) to Pope Melchiades (r.AD310–14). The collection was designed to show that the consent of the pope was required by the oldest traditions and practice of the Christian church for any bishop to be deposed, any council to be convened, and in general for the decision of any major issue. The *Decretals* also confirmed the representation of Pope Sylvester I as having received full authority, both sacred and secular, over the whole of western Europe in the "Donation of Constantine" so recently publicized by Pope Adrian I.

So by the end of the ninth century were in place what appeared to Enlightenment eyes of the eighteenth century as "the two magic pillars of the spiritual and temporal monarchy of the popes".[81] Down to the seventeenth century – the very end of the Latin Age – various popes cited the *Donation* and the *Decretals* as authentic documents to prop Vatican policies as occasion warranted. By the time the true status of the forgeries had been adequately determined, the institutions and events pointing toward the Western ideal of a separation of church and state were so far advanced in the social and political consciousness of the European peoples that what would have been important in the ninth, tenth, or even twelfth centuries no longer made any difference. Not even the unmasking of the forgeries could undo their effects, quite more extensive and largely at variance with what anyone could have foreseen in the beginning, for the development of modern civilizations.

The Fate of the Forgeries
The first challenge to the *Donation* was made in a private lawsuit introduced by a Sabine Benedictine monastery in 1105. The forgeries, in an adequate environment of free information, would not be that difficult to demonstrate. Many of the inauthentic

---

78 Pseudo-Isidore c.AD849. See Hinschius 1863; further Davenport 1916 (a work whose value is restricted to those unable to read anything but English, I might note); also Ullmann 1962: ch. 6., p. 167ff., esp. 180–4.

79 So Leo XIII 1879: 190: "the Fathers of Trent made it part of the order of the conclave to lay upon the altar, together with the code of Sacred Scripture and the decrees of the Supreme Pontiffs, the *Summa* of Thomas Aquinas, whence to seek counsel, reason, and inspiration." See the remarks of Villien on the book of decretals cited in note 82 below, p. 202.

80 Hinschius 1863: CCI–CCIII sets April 847 and 853 as the outside dates, deeming 849 the most probable.

81 Gibbon 1788a: 292. There was, of course, also a "third pillar", at least for the spiritual primacy, conveniently downplayed by hostile Enlightenment critics, to wit, the primacy of Peter as first "bishop of Rome" and the unbroken line of succession of popes after him as occupying the same "see".

documents, for example, cited scripture in the translation of Jerome (c.AD347–419), who was not even born until Pope Melchiades, alleged author of the citations, had been dead already for twenty-six years.

Yet the real beginning of the end for the imposture did not come until Lorenzo Valla set his pen to the matter in 1440. His contemporaries marveled at a boldness that, in the context of the times, appeared to many eyes as on or across the border of sacrilege. Yet such was the evidence and such its presentation (if we may compress into a single statement the scholarly details of the retreat of eight centuries' accumulation of credulity in the wake of Valla's criticism) that even the advocates of the Roman court came eventually to cede the case. The Council of Trent was near the far boundary in time of the success of the forgeries as such, though, Villien reports,[82] not till the early nineteenth century was the matter ceded by all parties.

"Fraud is the resource of weakness and cunning", no doubt.[83] Descartes would use this argument at the dawn of modern times to prove that "God is not a deceiver", and make of this conclusion the *fundamentum inconcussum veritatis*, the "unshakable foundation of truth", in his new philosophy. "For although the ability to deceive may perhaps be regarded among us men as a sign of intelligence," Descartes noted, "the will to deceive must undoubtedly always come from malice, or from fear and weakness, and so cannot belong to God."

Even so, it was thus that the will and intelligence of men prepared the ground, first, through the creation and application of the forgeries, for the final separation of Rome, Italy, and the whole of Europe from the ancient empire that Constantine had translated into Greek and moved to the East; and second, through the exposure of the forgeries and outrage over their past use, for the establishment of a distinction such as had never previously taken hold between civil and ecclesiastical authority in the practical creation of a public space for private conscience.

A Footnote on the Greek Contribution to Latin Europe as Mainly Mediated by Arabic Islam

Not until the last fifty years or so of Constantinople's existence as a Christian city, before it fell in 1453 to Turkish arms and its new destiny as Istanbul, would Byzantium contribute directly to the intellectual life of the West in philosophy, and

---

82 Villien 1911: 221: "Quand," in the sixteenth century, "commença l'assaut donné par les protestants, ceux-ci ne furent jamais seuls à la besogne. Après le calviniste du Moulin vinrent les catholiques Georges Cassandre et Antoine le Comte que les centuriateurs de Magdebourg se bornèrent à copier. Pendant quelques temps, il est vrai, des catholiques: le jésuite Torrès, le franciscain Malvasia, le cardinal d'Aguirre lui-même, se firent les champions chevaleresques du pseudo-Isidore contre les centuriateurs luthériens et le calviniste David Blondel, mais d'autres catholiques, l'Espagnol Antonius Augustinus, archévque de Tarragone, Baronius, Bellarmine, du Perron, Labbe, Sirmond, de Marca, Baluze, Papebrock, Noris, Noël Alexandre, luttaient contre les apocryphes, avec les Van Espen, les frères Ballerini, Blasco et Zaccaria. Si, au XIX⁰ siècle encore, le faussaire trouva des défenseurs dans Dumont et l'abbé Darras, l'unanimité des savants, sans aucune distinction de patrie ou de religion, proteste contre le malheureux succès de cette déplorable fourberie."
83 Descartes 1644: 203. See "The Unshakable Foundation of Truth" in chapter 12, p. 517.

then mainly by the flight of scholars and manuscripts, especially to Italy. There, in Renaissance Italy, the reintroduction of knowledge of the Greek language and the first Latin access to the full range of Plato's works, known to medieval Europe previously only through part of the *Timaeus*, brought about an explosion of interest in Platonic philosophy. It began with the lectures of Gemistus Pletho (c.1356–1450) in Florence and was institutionalized by Cosimo de Medici with his support for the establishment there of the Platonic Academy. Marsilio Ficino (1433–99), as head of this enterprise from 1462, prepared the first complete translation of Plato from Greek into Latin, a manuscript completed c.1470 and published in 1484.

In this period an important factor was the move of John Bessarion (1403–72) from Constantinople to Rome. By the first quarter of the fifteenth century, Constantinople was in clear military danger from the Turks. Yet the Latin West would offer no assistance to the eastern capital as long as the Greek church, divided from the Roman church officially since 1054,[84] remained divided. As a prelude to the military rescue of Constantinople, then, Pope Eugenius IV convened in 1438 a general church council at Ferrara, attended by the Byzantine emperor John VIII, the patriarch Joseph of Constantinople, and a large retinue of metropolitans, Greek bishops, monks, and scholars. One of this retinue was the learned John Bessarion, archbishop of Nicea, who played a leading role in the deliberations to follow.

Eight months into this council a plague broke out in Ferrara, and in 1439 the council was moved to Florence. Some scholars date the beginning of the Renaissance in Italy from the influx of learned Greeks that came to Florence with that council. In any event, the council succeeded in reaching agreement on a proclamation of unification. On the *filioque* clause that had so agitated Charlemagne against the Greeks, as the Greek prelates against the Latins, the conciliar participants decided that the version of a formula declared acceptable to the Greek representatives of Constantinople, *ex Patre per Filium procedit*, could be accepted as synonymous

---

84 In that year, Michael Cerularius (c.1000–59), patriarch of Constantinople since 1043, convened a council representing the whole of eastern Christianity, in response to a bull of excommunication issued against him by the papal legates in July 1054. These legates had been sent to Constantinople to discuss reunifying the Greek and Latin churches, in the wake of an earlier letter from Pope Leo IX to the patriarch demanding that he recognize papal supremacy on pain of presiding otherwise over "an assembly of heretics, a conventicle of schismatics, a synagogue of Satan". The emperor received the legates, but Cerularius denied their competence to deal with the issues between patriarch and pope. When Pope Leo IX died in April 1054 and no pope was promptly elected to succeed him, the legates lost patience and deposited on the altar of St Sophia in Constantinople their fateful bull. The council convened by Cerularius formally condemned the bull of the legates and "all who had helped in drawing it up, whether by their advice or even by their prayers". From that response dates the full and formal schism of eastern from western, Greek from Latin, Christianity. A short three years later, on 2 September 1057, Cerularius as patriarch of Constantinople solemnly crowned Isaac Comnenus as emperor of the (eastern) "Roman" Empire. Bury (1911: 236n64) sums up the rest of the story: "This powerful and ambitious prelate, Michael Cerularius, aimed at securing for the Patriarch the same headship of the Eastern Church and the same independent position in regard to the Emperor, which the Pope held in the West. [The emperor] Isaac deposed him" in 1058 and sent him into exile, where he died the following year.

with the formula adhered to by the Latin representatives of Rome, *ex Patre Filioque procedit*. On 6 July 1439, the council was able to issue a decree, publically read in Greek and in Latin, reuniting the two churches.

But when the emperor and his retinue returned to Constantinople to announce the joyous news, civil war broke out. The people and clergy of Constantinople repudiated the decree, and for the next fourteen years this strife raged. Gregory III, who had succeeded to the patriarchate of Constantinople in 1443, was driven into exile by 1450 for supporting the union (or reunion). The antiunion clergy, representing the Greek majority, urged the sick to die without sacraments rather than receive them from the hands of any "Uniate" priest.

Bessarion quickly deserted this sorry mess. When the lower clergy and people of Constantinople repudiated the decree the Council of Florence issued in 1439 to heal the *filioque* schism and to resolve related matters, he moved in disgust to Italy, where the pope made him a cardinal. He brought with him a trove of Greek manuscripts, and was himself a living vehicle of Greek philosophy. Lorenzo Valla (1406–57), the great literary scholar (called a "humanist" at that time) who adorned the Naples court during the reign (1435–58) of King Alfonso the Magnanimous, called Bessarion *latinorum graecissimus, graecorum latinissimus*, "the most Greek of all the Latins, the most Latin of all the Greeks".

The weight of Valla's accolade is better appreciated in light of the fact that this was the same Valla who had exposed in 1440 as a forgery the *Constitutum Constantini*, or "Donation of Constantine", discussed earlier in this chapter, according to which the first Roman emperor to profess Christianity had transferred to Pope Sylvester I early in the fourth century the secular dominion over all of western Europe.[85] Valla too it was who first unmasked as *Pseudo* the Dionysius whose writing the earlier Latins had revered as a participation of philosophy in the apostolic work of St Paul.[86]

The learned Cardinal Bessarion himself made for the Latins a new translation of Aristotle's *Metaphysics*; but it was as a disciple of Gemistus Pletho that he emerged as the leader of Platonic forces in the intellectual controversies of the time. Aristotle's domination of philosophy in Italy ended with Bessarion. Bessarion gave his library as a bequeathment to Venice, the most Byzantine of the Italian cities, where today it exists as a jewel in the Biblioteca Marciana. How high the fortunes of Platonism rode in the Italy of John Cardinal Bessarion's time may be glimpsed from the fact that, just a year before his death, in the 1471 conclave of cardinals, Bessarion narrowly missed election to the papacy.

Meanwhile, nineteen years earlier, and fourteen years after Bessarion's migration

---

85 See "The Fate of the Forgeries", p. 201 above. Actually, the falsity of the "donation" had already been exposed in 1433 by Nicholas of Cusa, in a work titled *De concordantia Catholica* written for the Council of Basel as part of its effort to reassert the supremacy of the councils over the popes. But it was the devastating historical and linguistic criticism that Valla made of the document that proved more decisive for a full settlement of the question.

86 See chapter 4, p. 130f.

to Rome, Constantinople was made a Turkish capital in 1453 by the forces of Mohammed II (whose mother had been Christian), the Sultan of Turkey from 1451 to 1481. After the Council of Florence, the *Cambridge Medieval History* reports,[87] a Byzantine noble was known to declare that he would rather see the Turkish turban at Constantinople than the red hat of a Roman cardinal, perhaps a snide gibe at the great Bessarion. In 1453 this noble gentleman got his wish.

We need not enter the debate whether the political entity of Byzantium "deserved to die". Indeed, much of the art, theology, and religious orientation of the Byzantine civilization in fact survives, in Russia and in the Slavic cultures. But after the conquest of Constantinople, the "New Rome", millions of southeastern European Christians were drawn into Islam, and routes of commerce and political influence were changed beyond imagining. The migration of Greek scholars to Italy and France that had begun in 1397 was greatly accelerated, enriching Italy especially with salvage of the Greek civilization. For better or worse, Byzantium had finished its role and yielded its place as a living polis. The Rome of Caesar and Augustus, in the end, did not survive its transplanting from *Roma Antiqua*, for *Nova Roma* was no more. Mosque had supplanted cathedral, Istanbul Constantinople. The main heirs in matters of philosophy were the original lands of Latin Europe, a linguistic community whose philosophical development we must now explore from its early separation from the Greek civilization to the collapse of that civilization and beyond, to its own dissolution into modernity.

Intellectual Geography: Seeing Latinity Whole

It needs to be said that the absence of a proper outline for the Latin Age in philosophy as a whole has long been a major obstacle to appreciating especially the later works of the period, and particularly their relevance to the controversies over signs which mark the end of modernity and the dawn of a postmodern era in philosophy. For, as we shall see, though little notice of the fact has been heretofore taken by minds absorbed in other speculative themes, yet it was the general notion of sign, more than any other single notion, perhaps, that marked the beginning and launched the indigenous development of Latin philosophy.

The Hodge-Podge Standard Treatment in Late Modern Times
The accustomed treatment of the Latin Age up till now, in introductory and advanced presentations alike, has been misleadingly presented both in its title and in its extent. Customarily labelled "medieval philosophy" the standard coverage of the period extends (in a hodge-podge selection of writings) from Augustine to William of Ockham (d.1349/50),[88] though in one notable case to Nicolas Cusanus (d.1464).

87 Vol. 4: 620f.
88 John Marenbon, a Fellow of Trinity College, Cambridge, authored an admirable pair of volumes titled respectively *Early Medieval Philosophy (480–1150): An Introduction* (Marenbon 1983) and

Tachau, in a ground-breaking study,[89] has shown that Scotus's distinction between so-called intuitive and abstractive awareness (*notitia intuitiva/notitia abstractiva*) provides the initial frame for the shift of emphasis from being to discourse in the later Latin centuries.[90] I am sure that this work will contribute to bring about a change in the treatment of late Latin authors that is long overdue. For in the standard coverage heretofore, Latin authors after Ockham are given only the most superficial treatment when they are not completely ignored. As a result, in standard modern treatments of its history, philosophy is supposed to "begin again" with Descartes or shortly before with Francis Bacon (1561–1626),[91] who shared the passion of Descartes for a new beginning together with an ill-considered jettisoning of Latin tradition as such.

It is true that Étienne Gilson succeeded in showing that Descartes depended on the terminology of the late scholastics, an achievement hailed by more than one scholar as initiating a new era in Cartesian studies. Yet even the studies of late Latin authors in relation to Descartes are likely to miss (and so far have in fact missed) the most unique theme within the Latin development (as certainly did Descartes himself![92]), which is that of the being proper to signs, the one theme that the Latin

---

Later Medieval Philosophy (1150–1350): An Introduction (Marenbon 1987). But what happened in philosophy between Ockham and Descartes, between (except for Descartes), let us say, 1350 and 1650? Was it a desert, as we will see Matson claim as we open chapter 8 below and as Marenbon's titles might be construed to imply? Or were these centuries rather a luxuriant rain forest of tropical exuberance in the development of philosophy, as any reading that penetrates the surface of the later Latin texts without succumbing to the "nose of wax fallacy" reveals? Marenbon is typically modern in remaining silent on the point, while suggesting subtly or not-so-subtly by the titling of his volumes that he has introduced his readers to the full extent of the Latin Age so far as it demands the attention of historians of philosophy at least (if not that of those philosophers who have no need of history given their superior lights and analytic capabilities). When, in 1991, he had the opportunity to issue in paperback a new edition of his 1987 hardback work, Marenbon (1991: xii), aside from some bibliographical notes and items, saw need for no more than "the correction of a number of minor verbal and typographical errors", leaving intact the standard modern outline of in what consists "medieval philosophy". So much for his conception (ibid.: 191) of "the very conditions of disciplined thought".

89 *Vision and Certitude in the Age of Ockham: Optics, Epistemology, and the Foundations of Semantics* (Tachau 1988).

90 "… the notion of intuitive cognition was still inchoate when Scotus adopted it, and subsequent medieval readers credited him with its invention. If their attribution is not precisely accurate, it is indicative of the fact that virtually everyone who employed the terminology to the mid-point of the fourteenth century took Scotus's definition as his starting point." "Despite the difficulties presented by his innovation in grafting intuition onto the process induced by species, the dichotomy of intuitive and abstractive cognition was rapidly and widely adopted by Parisian trained theologians. Within a decade of the Subtle Doctor's death, its acceptance on the other side of the English Channel was also ensured. That is not to say that his understanding was uniformly employed; nor, indeed, that all who employed the terminology of intuitive and abstractive cognition considered Scotus's an adequate delineation of the modes of cognition; nevertheless, the history of medieval theories of knowledge from ca. 1310 can be traced as the development of this dichotomy" (Tachau 1988: 70, and 80–1).

91 Parkinson 1993: 5–6; Deely and Russell 1986.

92 The thesis established in detail in my *New Beginnings* volume (Deely 1994a).

Age begins on its own and not by way of resuming themes received from Greek thought.

And the fact remains that, when it came to assembling "the most comprehensive anthology of writings in western philosophy in print",[93] the Oxford University Press in 1998 accepted, for the ancient and medieval coverage, a collection that ends with William of Ockham, and jumps from there to Descartes before resuming the coverage down to the present. This is in conformity with the standard outline of the history of philosophy and of medieval philosophy that is taught in the schools and accepted by the professors.

Of course there are individual scholars, John Doyle and Ken Schmitz and a hundred more, increasingly many of them, who have come to realize the "standard outline" has long falsified the picture, especially on the side of the Latins, and should not longer stand. Yet stand it does at the frontier of the twenty-first century, as the Oxford Pojman volume, together with Marenbon's *Later Medieval Philosophy* volume written from the perch of a Fellow of Trinity College, illustrates. So too the Yale reprint in paperback of Marcia Colish's masterful 1977 study of *Medieval Foundations of the Western Intellectual Tradition* still announces as the telling conclusion of its title: *400–1400*. So the question stands: how should the "standard outline" be revised, not in infinite detail, but as a broad working outline?

Time may be a good partner in advancing the development of a subject-matter that has once been well outlined, as Aristotle claimed,[94] but the situation of teaching medieval philosophy in late-modern times bears witness rather to Aristotle's inverse point[95] that in the absence of such an outline progress in the area tends toward a standstill. Infinite details to bog down in are always there. What is needed is an abduction, a leading hypothesis, to bring the details into a larger picture. What is needed is a reliable outline within which the details make sense and interest.

A Proper Outline

Yet for all its conspicuous absence in today's academy, a proper outline of the Latin Age, long overdue, is not difficult to draw. The development of philosophy in Latin after the late-fifth-century fall (or, rather, evaporation) of the Roman Empire in the West is an indigenous, multi-faceted, and highly organic development which divides naturally into two main periods or phases.

The *first period* extends from Augustine (AD354–430) in the fifth century, who introduces the general notion of sign as a theme for development alongside others, to Peter Abaelard (1079–1142) and John of Salisbury (1115–80) in the twelfth. In this interval, the logical treatises of Aristotle and such related Greek writings as

---

93 From the jacket copy for Pojman ed. 1998 (essentially repeated in the opening line of the editor's "Preface").
94 Aristotle c.335–4BC: *Nicomachean Ethics* 1098a20–5.
95 Ibid.

Porphyry's *Quinque Verba* (the *Isagoge*) were the only works of Greek philosophy surviving in translation from the Greek. Over this interval, philosophy in its own right (that is, as relatively unmixed with theology) developed around mainly logical and methodological questions.

The *second period* extends from Albertus Magnus (1193–1280) to Francis Suárez (1548–1617) and John Poinsot (1589–1644), when the full range of Aristotle's writings, along with such influential Arabic commentaries as those of Avicenna and Averroes, provided the newly emerging universities with the substance of their curriculum across the full range of philosophical subject matter – including those areas we now see as specifically scientific. Hence the great emphasis in the second phase on philosophy of nature or "physics" in the original Greek, and especially Aristotelian, sense.

Outside central Europe, which maintained the high-medieval tradition of more or less subordinating philosophy to theology ("handmaiden to theology", *ancilla theologiae*, was the metaphor actually used,[96] to unexpectedly baneful long-term effect), this emphasis developed into a special focus, especially in the Italian schools, on the place in nature of the human species. This development survives vestigially in many college and university curricula as courses variously labeled "philosophy of man", "philosophy of human nature", "philosophy of the human person", "philosophical anthropology", and the like. *In the Italian peninsula*, this specificity of focus led to advances in medicine and to a preparation of the ground for the framing of nature's details in mathematically calculable terms which climaxed in the work of Galileo and the establishment of sciences in the modern sense.[97] *In the Iberian peninsula*, the focus led rather to a concentration on social, political, and religious questions more in direct continuity with the theological emphases of the central European "high middle ages", although in logic and psychology breakthrough developments took place especially in the areas we now recognize generically as epistemological and specifically as semiotic.

Thus, just as in the first period of the Latin Age there was a concentration on methodological tools (the "liberal arts") and concepts of logic, so in the second period there was a concentration initially on the substantive matters of natural philosophy broadly treated so as to provide also the foundations for ethics and metaphysics (these two subjects, according to the customs and *Weltanschauung* of the period, were treated thematically more within theology than within philosophy itself). There was also a concentration in the second period (under the dubious rubric, "material logic") on the expansion of logical questions to include the whole of what is called today philosophy of science, epistemology and criteriology, as well as much of ontology.

---

96 Perhaps from Peter Damian (1007–72), a monk of the eleventh century who was also the figure principally responsible for the idea of purgatory taking hold at the level of popular culture.

97 The work of William Wallace in recent years (1977–92) has been particularly rich in showing the theoretical connections of Galileo's work to the larger nascent scientific Lebenswelt of his time.

Worthy of special mention is the fact that, in the last two Latin centuries,[98] intellectual foundations were laid in the university world of the Iberian peninsula for the development of international law and for dealing with the general problems of cultural conflict and assimilation. Here the landmark names are Francisco de Vitoria (1492–1536), whose work helped frame the imperial legislation for Spain's New World territories; and Francisco Suárez (1548–1617), with his rethinking of natural law. In the areas of social and political philosophy, as well as ontology and theory of knowledge, the scholastic faculties of the principal universities of Portugal and Spain in the fifteenth, sixteenth, and seventeenth centuries left behind a vein of pure philosophical gold, which has only begun to be mined.

Anticipating the Two Destinies[99]

To this later, substantive period belong the works of the Conimbricenses, Araújo, Poinsot, and other forgotten Latin Hispanic philosophers whose insight into the foundations of the theory of knowledge in terms of the role of signs in human experience anticipated the development of what is now coming to be recognized as the postmodern phase of contemporary philosophy. From our point of view today, in fact, Poinsot, as the author of the *Cursus Philosophicus* of 1631–35, appears alongside Francisco Suárez, as author of the *Disputationes Metaphysicae* of 1597, in providing what Jack Miles described[100] as "one of the two great seventeenth-century summations of medieval philosophy".

For the classical modern authors, as for those whose study of the early-modern period is made in terms of the classical (or "canonical" authors), Suárez was the textbook philosopher. Through his *Disputationes Metaphysicae* was the philosophic thought of the Latin Age filtered into modern European learning. He was generally taken to be, at the time, a faithful expositor of Thomas Aquinas.[101] In the early decades of the late-nineteenth-century Thomistic revival, however, many heated debates arose over the question of Suárez' reliability as a guide to the views of Thomas Aquinas. These debates were generally and decisively settled in the negative.[102]

But fidelity to St Thomas was not Suárez' principal concern, and his contribution to philosophy on other grounds is equally beyond question. Still, as far as concerns

---

98 This is the period of coalescence of what Gracia (1992, 1993) has well termed "Hispanic philosophy".

99 The reference is to chapter 9 below, p. 411.

100 Miles 1985. From the point of view of the classical modern development, however, as Miles goes on to note, while Suárez "remained the textbook philosopher of Europe long after Descartes had given philosophy a new *point de départ*, Poinsot, by contrast, was nearly without intellectual issue until he was rediscovered in this century by Jacques Maritain." For details, see Deely 1986 and 1995. This latter essay is basically about the work of Etienne Gilson and Jacques Maritain in relation to Poinsot.

101 "Thomism as formulated by the Jesuit Suárez was universally taught and finally supplanted the doctrine of Melancthon, even in the universities of Protestant countries" (Bréhier 1938: 1).

102 See chapter 11, p. 500f.

the question of what is and is not consistent with the views of Aquinas in philosophy, as Nuchelmans well put it,[103] the *Cursus Philosophicus* of John Poinsot presents itself as an exemplar "of the powerful tradition to which he belonged and wholeheartedly wanted to belong". Fidelity to St Thomas was a principal concern of Poinsot. In contrast with the procedure of Suárez, Poinsot made this concern *co-ordinate* with the exercise of philosophical reason, a co-ordination exhibited in the literary forms of his *Cursus Philosophicus*.[104] Thus, as we will see in part in later chapters, the study of the work of Poinsot provides an essential corrective to the historical influence of Suárez on the early moderns. The synthesis of his *Cursus Philosophicus* proves an indispensable resource to any historian of philosophy on two counts: first, for understanding the intellectual situation in philosophy at the time that modern thought broke with the Latin Age to establish the autonomy of a scientific approach distinct from the doctrinal approach proper to philosophy; second, for understanding the speculative links which tie later Latin developments to main themes centrally definitive of the postmodern development of philosophy pursuing the way of signs as alternative to the modern way of ideas.

Language and the Ages of Understanding

A further point. This problem of properly outlining the Latin Age is related to a fact which, in my estimation, has not been taken note of to the extent that it needs to be. I have in mind the fact that the major changes in philosophical epochs happen to correspond in general with the major linguistic changes in Western civilization: the natural macro-units for the study of philosophy would appear to be the major changes in the situation of the natural languages.

This correlation of linguistic change and philosophical ages, in fact, is illustrated in the major divisions of the present book. The period of Greek philosophy extends from the sixth-century BC pre-Socratics to the end of the dominance of Greek as the language of learning at the end of the original western Roman Empire in the fifth century AD. At that moment, as we have seen above, the Latin-speaking peoples were thrown back on their own resources. At that moment, the indigenous development of philosophy from a Latin linguistic base began, and unfolded over the next eleven hundred or so years along with the various ramifications of European civilization itself.

Not until the seventeenth century would a linguistic sea-change again occur, this time as the emergence of the European national languages to displace Latin as the principal medium of mainstream philosophical discourse. Modern philosophy, not coincidentally, rises against Latin scholasticism on this tide of the emerging natural languages. The postmodern period, again, coincides with a breakdown of the modern national linguistic compartmentalizations, as a new global perspective begins to emerge beyond national differences of language.

---

103 1987: 149. See also the remarks of Thomas Merton (1951: 334).
104 See Deely 1985: 417–20.

This time, however, with the onset of postmodernity, the emerging perspective is based not on a unity of natural language, as in the previous three epochs, but on the achievement of an epistemological paradigm capable of taking into account the very mechanisms of linguistic difference and change as part of the framework of philosophy itself. This movement, the postmodern development, is coming to be based especially in the work of the American philosopher Charles Sanders Peirce, as we will see, with its leading premiss that "the highest grade of reality is only reached by signs".[105] As we will also see, this foundational thrust of Peirce's work takes up again themes in logic and epistemology that developed strongly in the last two centuries or so of Latin thought.

But lest we get too far ahead of the story, let us turn at once to the development itself of philosophy in the Latin Age. In a one-volume survey of philosophy, we cannot undertake to cover all the topics and figures indicated in our outline of the Latin Age. To tell, in a single volume, something like a complete story linking the past with the concerns of postmodernity, particularly in discourse analysis, we shall have to concentrate on a few key figures and themes. But even a beginning student deserves to have a synoptic view of philosophy's development, while any student who may decide to go on in philosophical or historical studies – the kind of student to whom the present work is especially addressed – deserves to be made aware in advance of some of the major landmarks that can reliably be made use of in undertaking advanced investigations.

---

105 Peirce 1904a: 23.

CHAPTER SIX

The So-Called Dark Ages

Three "set-ups" in particular from the ancient world determined how philosophy would be put into play in the Latin Age. The first was the "praeteritio" of Porphyry, which would occasion the famous "controversy over universals". The second was the difficulties Aristotle experienced in getting clear about the uniqueness of relation as a category of philosophical thought and mode of being both objective and physical, which would occasion Boethius's introduction into the Latin mainstream of the distinction between transcendental and ontological relation. The third was the novel introduction by Augustine of Hippo of the general idea of sign as superior to the division of being into natural and cultural.

The first two set-ups were alike transmitted to Latinity through the work of Boethius as translator and commentator. But the third was indigenous to the Latin Age, and, by a slow development of centuries, prepared the way for the eclipse of modernity in the new concerns of postmodernity with the nature of human discourse. As we will see, then, it is this third, neglected theme, the one most proper to the Latin Age, in fact, that brings together all its concerns and that carries its development right up to the edge of modern times; for, as we will see, it is in reaching an understanding of the being proper to sign that the Latins best resolved together the controversy over universals and the controversy over the status of relation as a mode of being. Each of the "set-ups" proved to be but one face of a three-sided problem, the problem of sign as the universal instrument of learning and communication – the key to the problem the moderns would pose in terms of the nature and extent of human understanding, but could not solve, as we will see.

Augustine of Hippo (AD354–430)

Augustine of Hippo, AD354–430, need not have been part of the Dark Ages, but he chose to be by his disinterest in learning Greek. The so-called "Dark

Ages",[1] we have seen, did not actually begin in Europe until after the execution of Boethius in 524, when there were almost no figures left in the West with the education to make them capable of dealing with texts in the Greek language. Augustine lived well before this time. The knowledge and use of Greek was all around him. But in his *Confessions* of the year AD397, Augustine tells us that he disliked and neglected the study of Greek,[2] and he candidly owns that he read the Platonists in a Latin version.[3] The evidence, as Brown put it in his masterly biography,[4] compels us to regard it as "most unlikely that Augustine spoke anything but Latin":

> Between the exclusively Latin culture into which he had been so successfully educated, and any pre-existing 'native' tradition, there stretched the immeasurable qualitative chasm, separating civilization from its absence. What was not Roman in Africa could only be thought of by such a man in Roman terms. Augustine will use the word 'Punic' to describe the native dialects which most countrymen would have spoken exclusively, and which many townsmen shared with Latin. This was not because such men spoke the language of the ancient Carthaginians. Rather Augustine, an educated man, would instinctively apply this, the traditional, undifferentiated term, to any language spoken in North Africa that did not happen to be Latin.[5]

---

1 The expression needs some background to be appreciated. In the early through middle Latin centuries, the expression referred to the Greek and Roman times prior to the spread of the "light" of the gospel – hence to the "dark ages" of pagan false worship. But in the Renaissance the riches of Greco-Roman intellectual culture began to be recovered and appreciated on their own. At that moment the period of late antiquity, that is to say, the early Christian centuries, when, as far as the Latin peoples were concerned, the old Greco-Roman civilization was collapsing and their educational system along with it, appeared rather as the time of night and barbarism. Renaissance authors then rhetorically reversed the interpretant of "dark ages" (for details, see esp. Mommsen 1942) to refer to the centuries required to rebuild an intellectual culture – the Latin centuries between the collapse of the western Empire and the Italian Renaissance, more or less – as by comparison with which the height of Greco-Roman learning appeared rather as an age of light. The success of this Renaissance rhetorical reversal is evidenced by our chapter title and by the general usage of the expression "dark ages" today. I add the qualifier "so-called" to distance myself from the anti-scholastic bias of the Renaissance humanists who effected this discursive feat; and I would restrict the reference of the principal expression to the centuries between the death of Boethius and the establishment of the universities, which proved to be for human civilization the single greatest transforming institution, the principal support, along with libraries, for the formation and development across the centuries of what Charles Peirce would call the "scientific intelligence of a community of inquirers".
2 Augustine AD397: *Confessions* i, 14.
3 Ibid.: vii, 9.
4 Brown 1967: 22.
5 Brian Stock (1996: 4) would have us believe that sometime "after 410" Augustine "acquired greater expertise" than the knowledge of Greek exhibited "in his early writings". But that is to say almost nothing, and, to diminish even this minimal claim, Stock in the same sentence alludes to the fanciful quality of the claim in describing the matter as "a subject of speculation", where "speculation" does not mean the knowledge of being Aristotle called "speculative", but rather something more like "wishful thinking", in that each contributor to this particular "subject of speculation" has proposed

Probably no thinker of the Latin Age, not even Aquinas, surpassed Augustine in profundity and range of thought. Deep as was the genius of Augustine, his learning, in contrast, as Gibbon pointed out in a startling *obiter dictum*,[6] was in one undeniable sense superficial: that of being confined to the Latin tongue. Precisely in this restriction he anticipated the Dark Ages, as so much else of the Latin Age. For it seems that it was the initiatives of Augustine, more than any other single figure, that were to define the issues for 1100 or so years of the indigenous intellectual development most properly called simply the Latin Age.

The First Latin Initiative in Philosophy: Sign in General

To trace the influence of Augustine is to tell the whole story of Latin times, in theology as well as in philosophy, including the Protestant side of the Reformation after Luther posted his ninety-five theses in October of 1517. Even in the trial of Galileo the thought of Augustine was a principal player.

Here we will look mainly at but two of Augustine's many works,[7] the two wherein he principally proposes his seminal and provocative notion of *signum* which, as we will see, more than any single notion, serves to demarcate the uniqueness of the Latin Age in philosophy as a total whole.[8] The first of these works is Augustine's

---

for Augustine a degree of competence in Greek that the speculator, as Courcelle made note (1950: 11n3), "finds convenient" for his own purposes. On this thin subject the reader may consult mainly Courcelle 1943: pp. 149–223 of the 1969 English trans.; Altaner 1967: 129–53; and Courcelle 1968: 149–65. Despite the later date of Stock's writing, he in fact has nothing more to go on for his claim of improved expertise in Greek on the later Augustine's part than had already been taken into account by Brown (1967: 271), who described Augustine's ignorance of Greek as "the great lacuna of Augustine's middle age", a "'splendid isolation', that would have momentous consequences for the culture of the Latin church". In particular, to this "great lacuna" we owe the beginnings of what would culminate in the seventeenth-century work of Poinsot as the first establishment of a unified foundation for the notion of *signum* Augustine introduced as a general mode of being to which in communication nature and culture relate as species.

Aware of the gap in his learning created by his inability with Greek, Brown tells us (ibid.) that "only after 420, when confronted with a Pelagian, Julian of Eclanum (384–454), who claimed to [and did in fact] know the traditions of Greek theology far better than he did, would he try to refute his critic by a shrewd if essentially superficial comparison of a few texts in the original Greek with their translation." This polemical exercise hardly cancels the fact that, to the end, as Brown put it (1967: 271), "Augustine remained a cosmopolitan *manqué*", a crippled participant in the Greek dimension of the mixed Greek and Latin culture of his passing era; yet he proved a harbinger in his writing of the coming Latin Age when philosophy would indigenously develop anew in the Latin language, without the help one would have expected from the Greek schools and libraries ruled over by Constantinople even after Justinian in 529 closed the philosophy academies in Athens.

6 Gibbon 1781a: 431.

7 The complete works of Augustine are only now appearing in English under the editorship of John E. Rotelle (Hyde Park, NY: New City Press), and will fill 46 volumes when the set is complete.

8 Philosophy in the Latin Age will become much more a text-based tradition of reading than had been Greek philosophy, which, as we glimpsed earlier (chapter 2, p. 20f.), relied more on oral tradition than on the clumsy written scrolls intended mainly to aid spoken discourse. By the Latin Age, books in the modern format of bound pages ("codices", as they were originally called, ancient "books" being scrolls) were coming into use (a new development from the early Christian centuries,

De magistro, which he wrote in 389; and the second is the *De doctrina Christiana*, on which he worked from c.396 to 426. (Having written books I and II and two-thirds of book III in 396–7, he then, after a hiatus of three decades, finally completed book III and wrote book IV in 426.) For of his grand story we have space to follow only one of the many threads that extend all the way from the late fourth century to the dawn of postmodern times – the thread, namely, that most pertains to Peirce's formulation in 1867 of the categories within which the human use of signs as such takes place. Following this thread in its entanglement with the various principal medieval themes of philosophical reflection we will see enables us to make along the way a new determination of the "middle ages", one that fills in the standard gap between Ockham and Descartes in the currently received outlines of the history of philosophy.

This is one of the really surprising discoveries from recent work in philosophy, the fact that the idea of *sign* as a general notion, which we today take more or less for granted, did not exist before the fourth century AD, when it appeared in the Latin language as a proposal in the writings of Augustine.[9] With Augustine we encounter for the first time the general idea of the sign as applicable equally to natural phenomena like clouds and cultural phenomena like words or buttons. Thus was launched in philosophical tradition a line of speculation that was both the first of the Latin initiatives in philosophy and the one that took the whole of the Latin Age to reach maturity.

Indeed, the scope of this general notion of sign was not much clarified before Aquinas in the late thirteenth century,[10] about when the *locus* of the notion in the phenomenon of relation (already made for natural signs by the ancient Stoic tradition, be it noted) was also determined in the work of Roger Bacon.[11] The foundations of the general notion, however, were not determined successfully before John Poinsot in the early seventeenth century.[12] The name for the philosophical study taking such a notion as its base was not proposed before the end of the seventeenth century in the work of John Locke, who suggested the name "semiotics" from the Greek

---

in fact), and Augustine was a major player in laying the foundations of the transition from oral to reading culture. So it is worth noting (Stock 1996: 7) that Augustine's way of approaching questions concerning reading is "through the theory of signs. He is the first to have proposed a relationship between the sender, the receiver, and the sign (normally a word), which subsequently becomes a standard feature of medieval and modern theories of language. In the application of his ideas on speaking to reading, the role of signification remains unchanged: the sender is replaced by the text and the receiver by the reader. Other triads involving sending, receiving, and appropriate intermediaries account for a variety of mental activities, including thinking about what has been heard or read."

9 As we have seen, this conclusion is the report of those who have investigated the matter with some claim to Greek along with Latin, namely, Umberto Eco and his students. See Eco et al. 1986; Manetti 1993.

10 See "The Problem of Sign in Aquinas", chapter 7, p. 331.

11 See, in chapter 8, "The First Attempt to Ground the General Notion", p. 365ff., esp. "Losing Sight of the Type in a Forest of Tokens", p. 367.

12 See "The Vindication of Augustine" in chapter 9, p. 430.

term for sign, σημεῖον ("sēmeîon").[13] And the actual undertaking of such a study to understand the action and role of signs in the full extent of human knowledge and experience did not occur before the work of Charles Peirce around the turn of the twentieth century.[14] The notion of sign as proposed by Augustine, in short, is relevant, directly or indirectly, to all four of the ages of understanding so far: to Greek philosophy by transcendence of restriction to nature; to Latin philosophy for its foundation; to modern philosophy by its neglect; and to postmodern thought by its centrality.

Augustine is famous for many things, such as the dubious full-scale elaboration of the theological notion of "original sin". He called it a *felix culpa*, a "happy fault", in that there would not otherwise have been the need for a redemption of mankind, and hence no Redeemer. Perhaps his notion of *signum* as a general notion was a kind of "happy fault" as well, a result precisely of his ignorance of the Greek language. For in ancient Greece (leaving aside divination traditions and their links with Mesopotamian cultures) there had been much written about the notion of σημεῖον, both by philosophers and especially by the physicians and students of medicine. But what these ancient authors seem to have been talking about, virtually without exception, as we saw in Part I, was not Augustine's general notion of *signum*, but only what was called in Latin times *signum naturale*, "natural sign". These are signs which have a physical relation to their significate apart from our experience of them as signs, such as a complexion indicating the proximate approach of death, the lactation of the female breast indicating childbirth, the pawprint of a passing animal, a fever indicating physiological disorder, and the like.

Signs in this sense, σημεῖα, in no way belonged to the realm of human culture, the sphere of the σύμβολον or "symbol", still less to the realm of ὀνόματα, the names which make up the system of human language within the cultural sphere. In other words, for the Greeks, there was no general notion of sign bridging nature and culture. There was only a specific notion of sign, determinately restricted to phenomena of nature and to health and disease in the body. The first ones from whom I received report of this discovery are quite clear on the point:[15]

> One must realize that Greek semiotics, from the corpus Hippocratum up to the Stoics, made a clearcut distinction between a theory of verbal language (ὀνόματα) and a theory of signs (σημεῖα). Signs are natural events acting as symptoms or indices, and they entertain with that which they point to a relation based upon the mechanisms of

---

13 See chapter 14, "The Scheme of Human Knowledge", p. 590ff.
14 See chapter 15, "The Recovery of *Signum*", p. 611ff.
15 Eco et al. 1986: 65. Compare Meier Oeser 1997: xvi: "Voraugustinisch war das Zeichen (σημεῖον) im eigentlichen, d.h. seiner Definition entsprechenden Sinn, wie auch nimmer es konkret gefaworden sin mag, Mittel der Inferenz. Erst mit der von Augustinus formulierten Zeichendefinition verbindet sich der Anspruch, alle Arten von Zeichen, die natürlichen Indizes ebenso wie die willkürlich eingesetzten Zeichen, zu bestimmen. Und es ist dieser augustinsiche Begriff des *signum*, von dem die scholastische Tradition ausgeht und auf den sie sich, affirmativ oder kritisch, stets beziehen wird."

inference ('if such a symptom, then such a sickness'; 'if smoke then burning'). Words stand in quite a different relation with what they signify. This relation is based upon the mere equivalence or biconditionality which appears also in the influential Aristotelian theory of definition and tree of Porphyry which springs from it.

It was Augustine who first proposed a 'general semiotics' – that is, a general 'science' or 'doctrine' of signs, where sign becomes the genus of which words (ὀνόματα) and a theory of signs (σημεῖα) are alike equally species.

With Augustine, there begins to take shape this '*doctrina*' or 'science' of *signum*, wherein both symptoms and the words of language, mimetic gestures of actors along with the sounds of military trumpets and the chirrups of cicadas, all become species. In essaying such a doctrine, Augustine foresees lines of development of enormous theoretical interest; but he suggests the possibility of resolving, rather than effects a definitive resolution of, the ancient dichotomy between the inferential relations linking natural signs to the things of which they are signs and the relations of equivalence linking linguistic terms to the concept(s) on the basis of which some thing 'is' – singly or plurally – designated.

There is no reason to think that Augustine was aware that, in Greek philosophy, there was no such thing either as a linguistic sign or as sign in general, but only natural signs.[16] Had he known this, he would almost certainly have thought and written differently than he did. As it was, he enjoyed not only creative genius but also naive innocence of a rustic in casting forth onto the sea of ideas the notion of sign as superior to the division of being into what is independent of and what depends upon the mind, a distinction otherwise central to the whole Latin Age of philosophy under the labels of *ens reale* and *ens rationis*. What sort of a peculiar creature must a sign be that it cannot be restricted to one or the other side of this divide, but can, in one and the same vehicle, pass from one to the other order of being, carrying the user of signs with it, and creating in the bargain the problem for those users to tell the difference between reality and fiction?

But the whole idea of philosophy was born in the attempt to discern reality. To confuse reality with fiction is a diversion and distraction. The point is not to confuse the two, but to reach reality and express it for what it is with a precision of language and speech. *Ens rationis*, constructs of the mind, are indeed necessary to this end, as in logic. But otherwise they hold little interest to the philosopher who sets as his goal the *being*, the *real* being, of the things that are. The implication of the proposal that there is a real being, the sign, which is as at home in fiction as in reality did not even begin to sink in to the Latin mind when it was first proposed.

---

16 Every general statement risks oversimplification; yet without general statements, made as responsibly as we can make them, there can be no intellectual advance. We have already made note of the singular exception of Plato's use of σημεῖον (see chapter 3, p. 57 above). Jackson (1972: 116) reports a similar singularity in Origen (c.AD185–c.254). Moreover, general statements, unlike categorical universal assertions, are not falsified but illustrated by true exceptions. So qualified should be the understanding of the statement to which this note appends.

Even Augustine himself, in making the proposal, had quite other things in mind, namely, the supersensible truths of divine revelation and the illumination of the mind by the Teacher who speaks within.

The Illumination Theory of Knowledge

This last point is crystal clear in Augustine's dialogue with his out-of-wedlock son Adeodatus. The text of this dialogue, entitled *On the Teacher* ("De Magistro", written about 389), divides neatly into two parts. In the first part Augustine leads Adeodatus in Socratic fashion to the realization that signs are omnipresent in our experience, and that without them experience and knowledge itself are removed. Then, having reached this point, he wheels about, as it were, and just as surely forces Adeodatus to realize that, were there no illumination from within the mind of one who inquires, signs would avail for nothing whatever in knowledge and life. This illumination from within the mind alone enables us to see things as they are, signs and other objects alike (*signa et res*), so that only the Truth which speaks within the soul, which Augustine identifies with Christ, the only Teacher, not the use of signs as such, is able to instruct the human soul. Nor was this "wheeling about" a mere display of rhetorical and dialectical mastery of the subject matter. It revealed one of the most permanent and profound ambivalences in Augustine's thought; for the very man who introduced to the world *signum* as a general notion, the very man who Todorov and Manetti tell us[17] proposed a general "semiological" system based on communication, was the very man who stands unmistakably (in the minds of those who study the whole of his writings, and do not merely rape them for the sake of a thesis to be defended[18]) as a man "for whom communication was always an inscrutable mystery".[19]

Augustine's "illumination theory" of knowledge is Neoplatonic in inspiration, but ideally suited also to the temperament of a man who made the inner life of prayer and self-examination his centre. After this work of Augustine, the question *De magistro* (especially how teaching is possible) became a standard exercise in the scholastic disputations of the medieval university which every professor was obliged to conduct as part of their teaching duties. In Augustine's own case, he has told us some thirty-seven years later, as his life neared its end,[20] that the dialogue "on the teacher" had no more purpose than to show that God alone, and God in the person of Christ, teaches the human being in such a way that *knowledge* results. At this defining moment, Markus remarks,[21] "Augustine does not feel called upon even to allude to the theory of signs", even though that theory had occupied the bulk of the dialogue. He introduced to the Latins and to philosophy the sign as a theme, but he himself was never to thematize it.

---

17 Todorov 1982: 47; Manetti 1993: 167.
18 "Thesis hodie defendenda ...", as the later scholastics would have said.
19 In the words of Augustine's most learned modern biographer, Peter Brown (1967: 349).
20 Augustine, AD426/7: *Retractationum libri duo* I. 12.
21 Markus 1972: 71.

The Scope of Signs in Knowing

By the seventeenth century, what was indisputable in Augustine's original point had been largely reduced to the fact that there are signs within the mind as well as signs external to the mind, and that the latter depend upon the former in order to function within cognition. Yet Augustine himself never posited "signs within the mind", and in his own evaluation of the role of "the teacher" dismissed even the signs outside the mind save for what use Christ might choose to make of them when teaching within. There is irony in these circumstances, to be sure.[22] For Augustine elsewhere in his writings developed a profound doctrine of the *verbum interior* or *verbum mentis*, the "interior word" or "word of the mind", in his doctrine of the Trinity especially. (Nor is this the only place we will encounter a crossing of the theological doctrine of the Trinity with the philosophical doctrine of signs in the Latin development of both doctrines.[23]) Markus is no doubt correct in opining that Augustine's doctrine of the word as spoken by the soul had only to be effectively integrated with his doctrine of the word as spoken by the mouth in order to advance the whole doctrine of signs dramatically. But we look in vain to Augustine for any such synthesis. It simply did not occur to him, did not lie on his line of intellectual and spiritual march.

Later on it would be different. The sign would no longer be a mere prospective general theme, but actively thematized. By then, it would be considered *selbstverständlich*, "obvious", that there are signs within the mind, and that these are our psychological states, whether affective or cognitive; and the cognitive states in particular came to be called generically "formal signs". The signs outside the mind exist in the order of sensible phenomena, whether natural or cultural, and they came to be called generically "instrumental signs". The dependency of the instrumental sign on the formal sign in order to function within awareness is a physical, that is to say, an effective or actual, dependency. But every sign consists in the three-cornered *relation itself* connecting the sign at one and the same time to the mind and to the object signified. The sign strictly and formally as such does not consist in the basis of the sign relation, which may exist outside the mind as a feature of some sensible

---

22 The irony is perhaps best pointed out in the work of Meier-Oeser 1997: 33: "Diese 'Pejorisierung des Zeichens' durch Augustinus, dem das Zeichen zugleich im wesentlichen seinen Stellenwert im scholastischen Diskurs verdankt, bleibt späterhin virulent. Zwar wird sie dort wirksam ausgeschaltet, wo, wie besonders im späten Mittelalter, das *verbum mentis*, der geistige Begriff, selbst als Zeichen par excellence erscheint. Aber die zeichenkritischen Momente der augustinischen Auffassung merkieren stets eine Gegenposition, welche das Zeichen aus dem Bereich der mentalen Präsenz und Unmittelbarkeit herauszuhalten bemüht ist; eine Position, die gerade von zahlreichen 'neuzeitlichen' Autoren der frühen Neuzeit vertreten wird."

Yet the point is clearest in Markus 1972: 80: "the *verbum quod foris sonat* is the sign of the *verbum quod intus lucet*, but of this latter Augustine never speaks as a sign; and yet this is, in his view, the 'word' most properly so called. Its relation to 'words' as normally understood, to the significant sounds uttered when we speak, is left somewhat obscure." Overcoming of this obscurity is the whole story of the coalescence of semiotic consciousness in the Latin Age.

23 See, e.g., chapter 9 below, p. 441; and p. 244n89, in this chapter.

object or inside the mind as an idea. Hence the physical dependency within semiosis of signs outside the mind on signs inside the mind – of objects as signs on ideas as signs – is not a logical dependency of the sort that would make the signs which have a foundation outside the mind any less *signs* than those which have their foundation in thought and feeling, *for relation itself as a mode of being is indifferent to the subjective status of its foundation.*

But this ingenious solution gets us more than a thousand years ahead of our story.[24] In the short term, the medieval Latins were much more fascinated with Augustine's notion of God as an Illumination at the center of the soul than they were with the implications as such of his general notion of sign. Perhaps, had they been in a position to realize how novel and original Augustine's supposition of sign as a generic notion really was, the Latins would have looked more quickly and fully into its possible foundations.

But the "superficial learning" which was Augustine's linguistic lot by temperament and choice had become, unchosen, the general lot of the Latins. Even those who would prefer things otherwise had little room for say. Not until we reach Ludwig Wittgenstein (1889–1951), an author in the first half of the twentieth century[25] of the theoretically contrary works, *Tractatus Logico-Philosophicus* (1922) and *Philosophical Investigations* (1938–46),[26] will we encounter again such a combination of native genius and ignorance of forebears as was to be found in Augustine (although the narrow scope of Wittgenstein's writing hardly bears comparison with the vistas of Augustine!).

The Original Interest in Signs

Going into the fifth century, in any case, what interested Augustine was not the full investigation of his highly novel notion. Having no means to appreciate its novelty, he could afford to take it for granted in pursuit of what more interested him, as, after him, would many centuries of the Latin Age. His interest in the notion of sign lay in the fact that it provided us ways of reconciling the book of nature with the books of the Scriptures, through both of which, as far as Augustine was concerned, God speaks to our minds and hearts. All this becomes clear in his masterpiece *On Christian Doctrine, in Four Books*, "De doctrina christiana libri quattuor", which was on his mind[27] over at least twenty-nine of the later of his seventy-six years of life. In this work he stands as the first figure in philosophical history to enunciate what will come to be called, after Peirce's work inaugurating postmodern philosophy, a semiotic point of view.

---

24 Cf. Poinsot's *Tractatus de Signis* (1632a), book II, question 1, 236/42–237/16, question 5, 271/22–42. But the turning-point comes in Aquinas: see chapter 7, p. 335ff. below.

25 And coincidental namesake of the Russian marshal (Adolf Peter, 1769–1843) who, in the final alliance against Napoleon's French empire, led an army that Napoleon met and defeated in battle at Montereau on 18 February 1814.

26 See chapter 13, p. 582 below.

27 See, e.g., Kannengiesser 1995; Jackson 1972.

Book I on Christian Doctrine

Augustine opens book I of *On Christian Doctrine* with the distinction between signs and things. He will devote book I to the consideration of things, he tells us, and book II to the consideration of signs. A thing, we learn in chapter 2 of book I, is what has so far not been made use of to signify something. A clear awareness of the profound difference in principle between an *object* (which as such represents itself in awareness, and so necessarily involves a relation to a knower) and a *thing* (which has its being independently of a relation to a knower whether or not it has such a relation, and so is *also* an object *when* it has such a relation) has not yet become part of philosophy's patrimony. The medievals are still on the way of things, still in hope of isolating in thought and expressing in language a pure "reality" over against and in every respect transcendent to the knower. But they have as well what should never be lost, a keen sense of our contact in awareness and community in nature with a surrounding physical environment which commands our respect and provides the keys to many mysteries.

Book II on Christian Doctrine

In chapter 1 of book II we learn that a sign is anything perceived which makes something besides itself come into our awareness. With this definition, at a stroke, Augustine proposes the sign as superior to the division of being into natural and cultural: any material structure, whether from nature or art, which, on being perceived, conveys thought to something besides itself functions as a sign.[28]

But soon a very curious thing happens. Augustine has begun by enunciating in its full scope a semiotic point of view. Now we will see a treatment of things in terms of their signifying function, he tells us. And to give us an idea of how extensive such a treatment will have to be, he introduces a whole series of distinctions to cover virtually the complete range of signifying phenomena: natural vs. conventional significations; signification as it functions in animal cognition vs. signification as it functions in human cognition; the signification of words and the signification of groans; the signification of flags and the signification of fires. But all too soon we find that he has distinguished all these phenomena only in order to *exclude* them from further consideration as going beyond the limits of his immediate purpose.

Just as Augustine first proposed the general notion of sign not in order to explain or justify it but as one tool toward the accomplishment of another project, so too he begins this second book with distinctions that establish the more general semiotic point of view and sweep over the horizon of prelinguistic, linguistic, and postlinguistic phenomena of signification only for the sake of background to the narrow identification of the specific case of conventional signs instituted by God. The words of scripture and the sacraments of the Church, it turns out, not the sign

---

28 This definition is reiterated on p. 1316, col. b of the *De Dialectica* of 387, possibly but not certainly authored by Augustine, where the sign is defined as "anything which shows itself first to the sense and then indicates something beyond itself to the mind".

in its proper being and the perspective proper to it, is not the only thing, but the *focal* thing, in Augustine's interest. The context in which Augustine proposed his definition helps in understanding both its originality and its shortcomings.

A Notion Pregnant with Problems

Without challenging the more basic proposition that the sign has a way of being superior to the contrast between natural and cultural being, medieval thinkers will yet soon find Augustine's proposed general definition of the sign to be too narrow. Aquinas[29] will find it too narrow on two grounds. The first (although he goes back and forth on this, as we will see in chapter 7) is that angels too communicate by signs and yet, being without bodies, the signs the angels make use of in discourse with one another cannot be of the sort Augustine identifies with the sign in general. The second ground is that human beings, too, Aquinas will say, in the use of intellectual concepts, employ signs which cannot be wholly reduced to perceptions.[30]

Amplifying, in effect, upon this last point of Aquinas, first Duns Scotus (c.1266– 1308), then William of Ockham (c.1285–1349) and logicians after him, will precede the work both of the Conimbricenses (1606, 1607) and of Poinsot (1632a) in finding Augustine's definition too narrow because it applies neither to concepts nor to percepts as such. Yet both concepts and percepts, ideas and images in the mind, nonetheless perform in awareness the essential function of the sign, which is to stand in cognition as representing another than itself.[31]

When one thinks of a horse, one is directed first of all not to the subjective psychological or mental state without which one would not be thinking of a horse, but to a certain type of object capable of being instantiated physically in perceptually accessible ways. But it is not the fact of being perceptually accessible that makes the horse an object. There need be no horse present in perception for one to think of a horse. One can indeed think of an object in principle incapable of being perceptually instantiated in its proper being, such as God or an angel, to use ready-made medieval examples. Still less is it the fact of being perceived by sense that makes the concept

---

29 See "The Problem of Sign in Aquinas", chapter 7, p. 331.

30 This last point will become a focus of discovery at the foundation of Husserl's *Logische Untersuchungen* at the end of modern times (1900–1), but Husserl will not see the point in terms of the sign-function of ideas; and hence, when he converts his insight into a methodology under the name of "Phenomenology", his work becomes but an extension of modern rationalism trapped within the boundaries of the modern idealist paradigm, rather than a work of semiotic.

31 The point of how one understands the "minimal sign function", so to say, is technical and important. Here suffice it to note, from Poinsot's *Treatise on Signs* (1632a: 217/28–41), the following: "that in the definition of sign 'represents' is taken strictly and most formally for that which represents in such a way that it does not manifest in any way other than by representing, that is to say, a sign so stands on the side of the object of the representing that only in the representing is it devoted to that object and does not manifest the object signified in any other way than by the representing.

"Whence one *excludes* many things that represent something besides themselves and [yet] are not signs, and *concludes* that a sign must be more known and manifest *in the representing* than the significate, so that in being and knowable rationale the sign-vehicle is dissimilar and subsidiary to what it signifies" – through the triadic relation which the representation provenates.

or idea of horse a sign, for the concept or idea of horse is precisely that subjective or psychological state *on the basis of which* one is here and now thinking of horse and not of whale or dolphin.

Neither subjective state nor object need be perceived in order for the subjective state to be precisely that on the basis of which something other than itself (some object, that is to say) is brought into one's awareness, and for the object to exist precisely as that which is signified on the basis of some subjective state. Subject and object are correlated as that to whom and that which is signified, but the mediating third effecting the correlation is precisely a relation over and above either having *its* foundation or basis indifferently inside the mind (as a subjective condition or state) or outside the mind (as a material structure of sense perception).

Hence, what is truly essential to the being and function of a sign is not that it be something perceived, as Augustine's definition would require, but merely that it be an element of awareness bringing into further awareness something besides itself, something that it itself in the awareness is not. Augustine's definition, in logical terms, is defective by reason of being too narrow. It leaves out a part of what is to be defined.

The Strength of Augustine's **Signum**

The shortcoming or weakness in Augustine's proposed general definition, at the same time, is precisely its strength in terms of his special interest in the words of scripture and the sacraments of Christian life, for both of these signs directly involve the senses. For just as the words of scripture are, in their visible and audible aspects, material structures which, on being perceived, convey thought to something other than the noises heard or marks seen, so too are the sacraments perceptible materials which, as "sacred vessels", convey to the soul something beyond. As "an outward sign instituted by Christ to give grace", a sacrament is a manifest species of Augustine's sign.

This fact, together with Augustine's authority as next to last[32] of the four great Fathers[33] of the Latin church, readily explains the inclusion of Augustine's definition

---

32 Quasten 1950: "Boniface VIII declared (1298) that he wished Ambrose [c.340–97], Jerome [c.340–420], Augustine [354–430] and Gregory the Great [c.540–604] known as *egregii doctores ecclesiae*. These four Fathers are also called 'the great Fathers of the Church'. The Greek Church venerates only three 'great ecumenical teachers', Basil the Great [c.330–c.379], Gregory of Nazianzus [c.330–89/90], and [John] Chrysostom [c.345–407], while the Roman Church adds St. Athanasius [c.295–373] to these three, and thus counts four great Fathers of the East, and four of the West."

33 The early Christian writers, both Greek and Latin, who, between the death of the last Apostle, John, and the death of Augustine and beyond, formed the early consciousness and doctrinal or theological development of Christianity are often called, generically and loosely, the "Fathers of the Church". Augustine was also one of the last Christian Latin writers taken – if indeed was even he – with any general seriousness in the world of Byzantine theology, which looked down upon the Latins as a cultural and – especially – theological inferior. The classification of Latin "fathers" outside the Greek world (e.g., Tixeront 1920) extends much further, to include authors as late as Isidore of Seville

of *signum* in Peter Lombard's *Sentences* (c.1150), the compilation of patristic views (an "anthology", as we would call it) which became the basis of theological studies in the medieval university from the twelfth century till the end of the Latin Age.[34] (Indeed, as we will shortly see,[35] a *Commentary on the Sentences of Peter Lombard* became, in the later Latin centuries, the equivalent of today's Ph.D. dissertation, whence the proliferation of such commentaries in the medieval libraries.)

The fourth book of Lombard's *Sentences*, wherein Augustine's definition is incorporated, became the focus of what is in effect the "high semiotics" of the Latin Age, namely, sacramental theology as it developed continuously right down to the present day and even across the post-Reformation denominational lines of competing Christian sects. Protestant denominations no less than Catholicism consider Augustine to be their own. For that specifically religious phase of historical theoretical semiotic development, as for many others,[36] Augustine stands astride the split of Renaissance Christianity into Catholic and Protestant as a kind of governing figure over the thinking of both sides. Quite apart from his failed attempt to give a precise definition for his proposed general notion of sign (a failure demonstrated in the later Latin critiques of his proposed definition of sign in general as too narrow), the influence of Augustine's original *general proposal itself* resonates no less in the treatises of Protestant authors such as Timpler (1604, 1612), Keckermann (c.1607), and Scheibler (1617) than in those of Catholic authors such as the Conimbricenses (1605), Araújo (1617), and the *Tractatus de Signis* of John Poinsot (1632).

But the very dates of these authors show how slow was Augustine's novel proposal to mature in its theoretical possibilities. On the philosophical side of the powerful idea he has introduced, he himself had nothing further to say. He leaves to his Latin posterity instead "a constantly alive, burning and inevitable problem".[37] This flame does not always burn bright. But even when it only smolders and provides little more than smoke, as when we enter the thicket of nominalism,[38] it proves enough to demarcate a continuous trail from the first to the last of the Latin centuries. Here, with the first step on that trail, we begin our journey to postmodernity.

Boethius (c.AD480–524)

When Boethius, in 523, was tried before King Theodoric and sentenced to death for treason, he spent his time on death row writing one of the universally loved masterpieces of Latin philosophy, *De consolatione philosophiae*, "On the Conso-

---

(c.AD570–636). But Augustine, being confined in his consciousness to the Latin language, may be considered also the first of the medievals. As we will see, Charles Peirce occupies an analogous position (but wholly within philosophy) as a last of the moderns and first of the postmoderns.

34 On Lombard, see in this chapter p. 249 below.
35 P. 250 below.
36 See Sullivan 1963.
37 Beuchot 1986: 26.
38 See chapter 8, "The Thicket", p. 394 below.

lation of Philosophy". This work explored the metaphysical labyrinth of chance in history intertwined with human destiny, of divine foreknowledge of events and human responsibility for actions chosen, of time and eternity. In the exploration, Boethius gave himself to reconcile divine perfection and omnipotence with the evident disorders in both the moral and the physical governance found in the world of experience. On 23 October 524, his executioners, taking no notice of his work finished or unfinished, strangled him with a cord till his eyes bulged in their sockets and beat him the rest of the way to death with clubs. Boethius was a Christian, yet scarcely a line in this book could not have been written by one of the great stoics, Zeno of Citium himself, Epictetus (c.AD50–130), or Marcus Aurelius (AD121–180), as if this one man, Boethius, symbolized the passing of the torch of philosophy from pagan to Christian times.

Boethius On the Trinity *and the Division of Speculative Knowledge*
Around the year 520 Boethius had written a book in which he tried his hand at assimilating and advancing a major speculative foray undertaken just over a century earlier by Augustine. For this work he used a somewhat more prolix title than the simple *On the Trinity* title that Augustine had used. He titled his work *Quomodo trinitas unus deus ac non tres dii*, "How it is that the trinity is one god and not three gods". Weisheipl calls this work "anomalous and almost anachronistic".[39] In the twelfth century the work was the subject of numerous commentaries, but in the following century we know only of the one commentary upon it, which Thomas Aquinas wrote c.1257/8. The title would hardly suggest it, but from this work Aquinas[40] derives some basic ideas on how the human understanding constructs from the materials of experience the objects of the theoretical sciences, physics, mathematics, and metaphysics.[41] In *physics*, the understanding focuses on being as it can neither be nor be thought apart from matter. In *mathematics*, the understanding considers what can be thought but cannot be apart from matter – substance quantified as prior to all other sensible characteristics, "intelligible matter".[42] While in *metaphysics*, the understanding considers being as it can both exist or be and be thought apart from matter.

Nor is the work of Boethius in this area limited in its actual influence to the early medieval period. In the early twentieth century, building on both Aquinas and Boethius, the French philosopher Jacques Maritain produced one of the masterpieces of late-modern epistemological theory. His work titled *Distinguish to Unite, or The Degrees of Knowledge*,[43] resumes and updates the theory of Boethius and Aquinas

---

39 Weisheipl 1974: 134.
40 Aquinas c.1257/8, *In librum Boetii de Trinitate expositio*.
41 This section of Aquinas's commentary on the *De Trinitate* of Boethius has been excerpted and competently translated into English as an independent treatise by Armand Maurer under the title *The Division and Methods of the Sciences* (Maurer trans. 1958).
42 See p. 78 above.
43 Maritain 1932 (French original ed.), 1959 (authorized English trans. from 4th French ed.), 1963 (7th and final French text).

in this area. In particular, Maritain refined under the notion of "physics" three distinct investigative modalities: physics in the ancient and medieval sense, which has as its rule, or resolves its considerations into, the intelligible aspects as such of material objects; strictly empirical science, which has for the rule and resolution of its considerations the observable or sensible aspects of material objects as such (further subdivided into empiriometric and empirioschematic); and physics in the modern sense, "mathematical physics", which informs the observations of empirical science with a mathematical content of intellectual imagination rather than a content either of intelligibility as such (as in the physics of Aristotle) or of a narrative of sensory observations.

Boethius' Terminology for Aristotle's Difficulties with Relation

But it was in his translation of Aristotle's difficulties in getting clear about the distinctive or unique character of relation as a mode of being that Boethius made the most decisive contribution in the long run to the problematic of a general notion of sign that Augustine, in all innocence, had bequeathed to Latin philosophy. This problematic, one of the slowest to mature among the Latins, as has been said, is also the one that carries over directly into the postmodern period. The reason is that it affords the intelligible substructure in terms of which the action of signs reduces to being in such a way as to demonstrate the thesis advanced in passing in the course of Maritain's work just mentioned: there need be nothing to prevent a philosophy of being from being at the same time a philosophy of mind.[44] We will see this in due course. Here let us look at the Boethian translation of Aristotle's difficulties.

By 510 Boethius had translated and commented upon the *Categories* of Aristotle. By this work, he set the terms according to which the whole tangled medieval discussion of relation would develop, and by which the problem raised by Augustine's posit of signs as superior to being divided into mind-independent and mind-dependent would eventually be resolved. In particular, it was from Boethius that the pair of expressions, *relatio secundum dici* ("relation according to the way being must be expressed in discourse") and *relatio secundum esse* ("relation according to the way relation has being"), eventually *transcendental* vs. *ontological* relation, were put into play. The former expression, "relation according to the way being must be expressed in discourse", Boethius fashioned to account for Aristotle's first two attempts to define relation,[45] which turned out to apply equally to substance and the inherent ac-

---

44 Maritain 1959: 66; 1963: 388.
45 Aristotle, c.360BC: *Categories*, ch. 7, 6a36–9: Πρός τι δὲ τὰ τοιαῦτα λέγεται, ὅσα αὐτὰ ἅπερ ἐστὶν ἑτέρων εἶναι λέγεται, ἢ ὁπωσοῦν ἄλλως πρὸς ἕτερον· ("Those things are called relative which, being either said to be of something else or related to something else, are explained by reference to that other thing."). And again at 6b6–9: πρός τι οὖν ἐστιν ὅσα αὐτὰ ἅπερ ἐστὶν ἑτέρων εἶναι λέγεται, ἢ ὁπωσοῦν ἄλλως πρὸς ἕτερον· οἶον ὅρος μέγα λέγεται πρὸς ἕτερον· ("So it is with all other relatives that have been mentioned. Those terms, then, are called relative, the nature of which is explained by reference to something else.")

cidents as such. The latter expression, "relation according to the way it has the being proper to itself", he fashioned to apply only to Aristotle's second attempt to define relation as a phenomenon restricted to intersubjective instances of physical being.[46]

Aristotle's Difficulties

In the discussion of the Aristotelian categories as Boethius presented it and the medievals took it up, as with Aristotle himself,[47] what was essayed in the categorial list had little to do with linguistics and everything to do with the variety of ways in which physical being is found to exist in our experience independently of human society. Whatever truly exists in nature as an individual, we saw above, Aristotle classed as a *substance*. Whatever exists in nature as some modification or characteristic of an individual, however important, Aristotle classed as an *accident*.

Among the accidents (some, but by no means all, of which can come and go without destroying the individual they modify and characterize at a given time) Aristotle counted *relations*. In order to include relation in his list as a *distinct* category, Aristotle had to formulate for relations a definition which would cover all and only relations – a definition which would be neither too narrow nor too wide. In this effort he encountered a major difficulty: just as the accidents of substance ultimately have to be explained in terms of the ability of substance to sustain them, so substance itself ultimately has to be explained in terms of the ability of the environment to sustain individuals (in terms of the "principles and

---

The difficulty in understanding the terminology Boethius created reached legendary proportions in Neoscholastic circles after Krempel (1952: 394). Remarks on substance by Boethius himself such as McInerny cites (1990: 102n13) raise the question whether there is not an unclarity in the terminology because Boethius himself only confusedly grasped the difficulty to which his terminology conveyed a prospective solution.

46 *Categories*, ch. 7, 8a28–34: εἰ μὲν οὖν ἱκανῶς ὁ τῶν πρός τι ὁρισμὸς ἀποδέδοται, ἢ τῶν πάνυ χαλεπῶν ἢ τῶν ἀδυνάτων ἐστὶ τὸ δεῖξαι ὡς οὐδεμία οὐσία τῶν πρός τι λέγεται· εἰ δὲ μὴ ἱκανῶς, ἀλλ' ἔστι τὰ πρός τι οἷς τὸ εἶναι ταὐτόν ἐστι τῷ πρός τι πως ἔχειν, ἴσως ἂν ῥηθείη τι πρός αὐτά. ὁ δὲ πρότερος ὁρισμὸς παρακολουθεῖ μὲν πᾶσι τοῖς πρός τι, οὐ μὴν ταὐτο γέ ἐστι τὸ πρός τι αὐτοῖς ἔναι τὸ αὐτὰ ἅπερ ἐστὶν ἑτέρων λέγεσθαι. ("Indeed, if our definition of that which is relative was complete, it is very difficult, if not impossible, to prove that no substance is relative. If, however, our definition was not complete, if those things only are properly called relative in the case of which relation to an external object is a necessary condition of existence, perhaps some explanation of the dilemma may be found. The former definition does indeed apply to all relatives, but the fact that a thing is explained with reference to something else does not make it essentially relative."). For extended discussion of the definitions and their English translations in terms of the conceptual content at stake, see Deely 1985. (In modern English the intellectual situation in this area has actually deteriorated. Since 1963, the Ackrill translation of the *Categories* – Aristotle c.360BC – has gained currency over the older Edghill translation, the newer normally having the presumption of improvement over the older, provided the sponsoring press is sufficiently reputable. But in this case, alas, for the reasons combed in detail in Deely 1985: 472–9, esp. 473n114, we can only await the day when Ackrill's translation in turn suffers the fate of Edghill's, hopefully at the hands of a translator with philosophical sensibilities considerably superior to what Ackrill displays.)

47 See above p. 73f.; and *pace* Trendelenburg (1846) and those who took up his lead in trying to see in the categories only the grammar of the ancient Greek language.

causes and sustaining conditions of existence", in medieval terms). In other words, in actual existence, every substance and every accident is maintained by realities of circumstance and being other than itself. So it appears that "relation" is not a *distinct* category of physical being, but rather a condition which applies to physical being in every category, including and beginning with substance. How then is relation to be conceived of as a *distinct category*?

To resolve his problem Aristotle proposed, in answer to this question, a distinction:[48] "the fact that a thing is *explained* with reference to something else does not make it *essentially* relative." Relation *as a distinct category*, then, would comprise all and only those features of being whose very essential conceivability involves being toward another, those features of being which cannot, even by an abstraction, omit reference toward.

An individual is conceivable apart from knowing who were the parents. A size is conceivable apart from conceiving what sort of thing might be that size. And so on. But a relationship in the categorial sense is inconceivable except in terms of something other than itself: a son or a daughter as an *individual* may be thought of without giving any consideration to the parents, but an individual *son* or *daughter* is inconceivable apart from consideration of a parent as well. For the parents make the offspring be as a *daughter or son*, even though the daughter or son as an individual exists independently of the parents who procreated. Of course the individual is procreated; but the procreator's existence is not part of the procreated individual's essence. But the offspring is not only procreated as a matter of fact. As *offspring* the whole essence of the individual consists in its relation to its procreators, even though as an *individual* in its own right it has an essence which is more than and here and now independent of that relation.

Thus the classical medieval definition of relation as "that whose *whole* being consists in a reference or being toward another"[49] is intended to convey Aristotle's idea of relation as verifiable under a distinct category of physical being.

Transcendental Relation

To memorialize Aristotle's unwelcome realization that even those types of being which are not relations in this sense (namely, individuals and whatever characteristics of individuals there are besides relations, such as quantity, quality, and the rest) are yet relative in their existence and in their possibilities for being explained, the medievals after Boethius circulated a distinct name: *relatio secundum dici*, "relation according to the requirements of discourse about being". Boethius had introduced this terminology into his translation of and commentary upon Aristotle's book of Categories, *In categorias libri quattuor* (c.AD510).

There is then a profound sense of relativity in medieval discourse *which applies to every category* of accident as a subjective characteristic and to substance itself

---

48 Aristotle c.360BC: *Categories*, ch. 7, esp. 8a28–34
49 "sunt illa, quorum totum suum esse se habet ad aliud".

as the subject of existence. The Latins recognized a relativity that reaches to the very pillars and foundation of finite being in its own order. Following Boethius, they called this radical ontological relativity, the relativity of all subjective being as such, *relatio secundum dici*, "relation according to the requirements of bringing being to expression in discourse". But they later also called this sense of relation, which applies to the explanation of the whole of nature, *relatio transcendentalis* (transcendental relation), after the qualification "transcendental" became the accepted medieval term for any notion that applies to more than one category.

Categorial Relation

In contrast to this transcendental relativity there is the sense of relation which applies *only to the single category* of relation (i.e., which designates only what is relative in its very definition *as well as in* its possibilities for explanation and conditions for existence), which Boethius termed *relatio praedicamentalis*, that is, "predicamental" or "categorial" relation. *Praedicamentalis* was a Latin expression that applied both to category (of being) and to predicate (of a sentence). Later thinkers have inferred from this fact that there is more linguistic involvement in the ancient scheme of categories than Aristotle saw or the medievals came to realize. But for the medievals themselves this terminology reflected no more than their understanding of Aristotle's scheme of the categories as identifying those senses in which being, when "said differently", could yet be said (hence "predicated") in a single sense ("univocally") among a variety of tokens or instances of a type of being.

Purely Objective Relations

After Boethius, Avicenna made explicit for the Latins the idea of a relation formed wholly in thought – "non formatur nisi in intellectu". On top of the realization that relations consist purely in referrals, the suspicion soon took root that referrals may only *seem* sometimes to be independent of perception or discourse. This suspicion took nurture from the medieval development of logic as a science of relations obtaining among things *as they are thought of*, as distinct from things (and relations among things) as they are in themselves indifferent to human thought.

Categorial relations are supposed to be relations among things existing independently of our thought of them. Logical relations exist only in and as a result of our thought, and hence can obtain even among imaginary or mistaken beings. Hamlet was not a happy-go-lucky fellow, even though he is fictitious. These latter relations the medievals called *relationes rationis* or "relations of reason" ("mind-dependent relations"), not because only rational animals formed them, but because only rational animals could become aware of them and make them an object and instrument of study in their own right.

Moreover, inasmuch as logical relations could not exist apart from thought, such relations were neither transcendental nor predicamental (i.e., categorial). The question arose almost at once in medieval debate whether the whole idea of relation as a category had not been an objective confusion, mistaking a referral *made by thought* for a mode of being *existing in nature* independently of thought. In other words, in the medieval debate over the notion of relative being, the dispute centered on whether in the physical world there were only transcendental relations, categorial relations being in reality only comparisons made by the mind – *relationes rationis* or "mind-dependent relations" – in the consideration of objects.[50]

The Ontological Peculiarity of Relations Anywhere

The translations of Boethius and Avicenna's work carried the discussions of the Latin Age in the area of relation more or less to this point. The fact that categorial and rational relations share alike a common "essence" or definability as something whose whole being consists in a reference to another was not a point of central interest in the original medieval debates over relation, either to Boethius or to his immediate successors in the discussion. In general, the medieval mainstream focused immediately on the differences between physical being (*ens reale*) and logical being (*ens rationis*), and on the problem of universals, which first appeared in the guise of *nominalism*, as we shall shortly see, the view that general conceptions (such as Augustine's proposal of *signum*) are nothing more than mind-dependent relations.

Nonetheless the point did not escape notice entirely that, if there are relations in the world *as well as* in thought, then relations in thought are unique among mind-dependent beings in having as their positive essence exactly the same positive structure as their mind-independent counterparts.[51] Not much was made of this point before Aquinas made it central to the intelligibility of the Christian dogma of God as triune, but the medievals did have from Boethius an expression to designate relation in its indifference to the distinction between mind-independent and mind-dependent being, namely, *relatio secundum esse*, "relation as such according to the way it has being". The point of this expression was that relation was a relation (according to

---

50   Aquinas reports this debate as carried on not only among the Latins of his time but also earlier among the Arabic Aristotelian commentators: see Aquinas c.1265/6: *Quaestiones disputatae de potentia*, q. 7, art. 9c (Busa 3, p. 246). See the summary of the issue at the end of the Latin Age in Poinsot 1632a: *Tractatus de Signis*, Second Preamble, "Whether there exist on the side of mind-independent being relations consequent upon intrinsic forms". Krempel (1952: 489f.) traces the real–rational relations distinction to Simplicius (c.AD490–560) on the Greek side and Avicenna (AD980–1037) on the Arab and Latin side.

51   A fictional individual with his or her various characteristics, as fictional, is precisely *not* what a physical individual *is*, namely, something having an existence and being apart from a relation to cognition. But a relation, whether real or fictive, as a relation, in either case has an existence or being over and above its subjective foundation, source, or ground, and hence *is* in either case what as a relation it is in the other case. The distinction between fictional and real, thus, is *central* to the idea of substance and its inhering accidents, but *marginal* to the idea of relation. The distinction between real and fictional individuals is drawn on the basis of the nature of substance, as part of its very conception. But the distinction between real and fictional relations is not drawn at all on the basis of the nature of relation. The distinction between real and fictional is not part of the very conception of relation, but is *applied* to that conception extrinsically, from the point of view of whether the terminus of the relation is purely objective or physical as well.

the way it had being) regardless of whether its being emanated from a concept in the mind or from a material characteristic of a physical individual. Hence eventually relation viewed under this singularity came to be called "ontological relation".

But since this was not a point at the center of medieval concerns at the moment of its peripheral realization, unfortunately, *relatio secundum esse* was not an expression the medievals generally undertook to refine and ramify. They did not, for example, develop any one-word synonyms for *secundum esse* comparable to their stipulation of "transcendental" as an equivalent for *secundum dici*. The most serious attempt to translate *relatio secundum esse* into a national language settled on the designation "ontological" as the translation of "secundum esse", a choice lacking in neither justification nor difficulties,[52] but still the expression best suited to convey the singularity at issue.

But within the medieval mainstream, by the time thinkers began to realize the general philosophical and particular epistemological importance of the point highlighted in the expression "relatio secundum esse" for the justification of Augustine's general posit of sign as generic to nature and culture, with which the Latin Age began, that age was effectively over and the classical mainstream development of philosophical modernity had well and truly begun ignorant (in its mainstream authors[53]) of the belated Latin realization.

Accordingly, we leave the discussion of relation at this point more or less where Boethius himself left it, a stage of development which may be briefly indicated in the form of the following diagram incorporating Avicenna's explicitation:

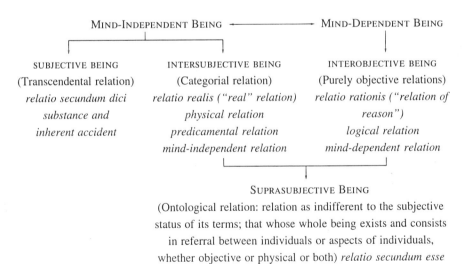

MIND-INDEPENDENT BEING ⟷ MIND-DEPENDENT BEING

SUBJECTIVE BEING	INTERSUBJECTIVE BEING	INTEROBJECTIVE BEING
(Transcendental relation)	(Categorial relation)	(Purely objective relations)
relatio secundum dici	*relatio realis ("real" relation)*	*relatio rationis ("relation of*
substance and	*physical relation*	*reason")*
inherent accident	*predicamental relation*	*logical relation*
	mind-independent relation	*mind-dependent relation*

SUPRASUBJECTIVE BEING

(Ontological relation: relation as indifferent to the subjective status of its terms; that whose whole being exists and consists in referral between individuals or aspects of individuals, whether objective or physical or both) *relatio secundum esse*

The Latin Discussion of Relation after Boethius and Avicenna

52 See Deely 1985: 463–5, 472ff.
53 As documented in Deely 1994a and to a great extent in chapter 10 below.

How the discussion moved beyond this point will appear in later chapters. But first we must mark the tunnel leading from the breakup of the original Roman Empire after Diocletian and Constantine to the indigenous development of the Latin philosophy and civilization associated with the much later "Roman Empire" irenically or ironically termed "Holy".

The Tunnel to Latin Scholasticism

The closest thing to a truly dark period in the so-called dark ages runs from the execution of Boethius in 524 down to the eleventh century work of Anselm, Abaelard, and Peter Lombard. During this period what was left of ancient Roman educational structures in the western Empire crumbled to dust, and the nascent monastery and clerical schools took time to gestate a new educational blooming.

Yet even this dark tunnel had the vestigial illumination of Neoplatonic influences overlapping the Christianization of Europe, as we saw in chapter 4,[54] especially in the avid circulation of the writings of the supposed companion of St Paul at the Areopagus thanks to the ninth century translation by John Scotus Erigena. Nor can we lightly esteem the turn-of-the-century initiatives in education under Charlemagne, managed by Alcuin of York,[55] even though the course of the tenth century saw such turmoil that even "the advances of the Carolingian renaissance were imperilled and seemed on the verge of annihilation."[56]

The annihilation did not come about, and the combination of Carolingian and monastic achievements proved indeed to prepare the way, at the end of the "tunnel", for the taking clear form of "scholasticism", that marvelously sophisticated method for the logical analysis of texts that became the hallmark of higher education and university life in the mature centuries of the Latin Age.

Lights at the End of the Tunnel: Anselm of Canterbury (c.1033–1109), Peter Abaelard (c.1079–1142), Peter Lombard (c.1095–1160)

The so-called Dark Ages would end when the translations of Aristotle coincidentally inundated Latin Europe with a program of understanding that extended rational discourse to all parts of the universe. At the end of the Latin Age, fully empirical and mathematical sciences were far enough along to end all reliance on textual authority. The book of nature had begun to be read in its own right, the tradition of Aristotelian commentary had overstayed its welcome, and there was a general and

---

54 See esp. p. 130ff.
55 See chapter 5, p. 196ff.
56 Gilson 1925: 29: "Le Xᵉ siècle est une époque de troubles profonds et d'obscurcissement au cours de laquelle les résultats acquis par la renaissance carolingienne sont remis en question et semblent même sur le point d'être complètement anéantis."

healthy feeling that it was time to put the books of Aristotle aside and let thinkers get on to other things.

But in the Dark Ages thinkers had had little on which to exercise powers of reason other than logic itself and the various texts of revelation. Habits of careful empirical observation are hard to develop and harder to sustain without social and institutional support. In general, it is easier to read than scientifically to observe. And the arrival from the Arab world of the complete works of Aristotle gave to the Latins a whole world of nature to read and think about in which reason as a doctrinal exercise could aspire to leave no corner unexplored. It was no wonder that the Latins turned their well-honed logical skills to the texts of Aristotelian philosophy and to the exposition of the natural world it revealed. The result, of course, would be "scholasticism", probably the most highly sophisticated set of methods for the intellectual analysis of the content of a written text that had ever been devised.

Two thinkers in particular personified the highest development of logic over the course of the so-called Dark Ages: Anselm of Canterbury, sometimes called "the first scholastic", and his younger contemporary, Peter Abaelard. As Anselm was the older as well as the more typically medieval of the two, let us look first at him.

Medieval Philosophy at Its Christian Extreme

Anselm was a philosopher of the most sectarian sort. His concern was not to seek the reasons for phenomena but to seek the reasons for religious faith. Not that reason was his starting point and faith his goal. Just the opposite. Faith was his starting point and the rationalization of what faith accepts his goal. Hence his motto: *fides quaerens intellectum*, "faith seeking understanding", not *intellectus quaerens fidem*. For him, it would seem, Christian faith was the absolute presupposition not merely for understanding theology, but equally for philosophy – for understanding anything worth understanding. He believed in Jesus as the Son of God and he believed in God as the Creator and Source of all things. Not surprisingly, his two most famous works deal with his two highest beliefs. In *Cur Deus homo*, "Why God Became Man", he sought to give the reason for the incarnation; and in the *Proslogion* he sought to give the reason why one is able to doubt the existence of God only insofar as one is a fool – not, that is to say, stupid necessarily, but one who, regardless of "I.Q." rating, says "No!" to the reality of God. In the bargain Anselm wrote a tract to prove the existence of the object of our universal ideas as absolute standards rooted in the divine nature itself. Here is one of the clearest realizations of the meaning of "realism" in the Middle Ages: not that material things exist as knowable but that the objects of universal ideas exist independently of our minds. It is one step short, if that, of Plato's "Ideas" become Christian.

The controversy over universals is better illustrated and makes more progress in the work of Anselm's slightly later contemporary, Abaelard. But no one left a more lasting mark on the thought of subsequent generations than did Anselm with his famous argument claiming to prove from our idea of God that God necessarily exists. Immanuel Kant (1724–1804) called this form of argument the "ontological argument". The name is singularly inapt, but it has stuck; and the argument so (mis)named recurs again and again in slightly varied form over the centuries. Anselm's original formulation is still the most intriguing. His title as the "father of the ontological argument" is his greatest claim to fame in philosophy, and is the aspect under which we shall consider him here.

The Ontological Argument

The original text in which Anselm presents his argument is entitled the *Proslogion*. Composed late in the eleventh century, the section of text introducing the nucleus of Anselm's argument is brief, approximately three pages in length, divided into four chapters, after which come yet twenty-two more chapters. "Chapter 1. A rousing of the mind to the contemplation of God", however, is not so much a part of the actual reasoning about God as it is a pious or rhetorical exhortation of the soul to itself and to God to confirm by understanding what the soul holds in belief, to harness whatever understanding might be possible to the service of fortifying that belief.[57] The remaining three chapters lay out the famous argument aiming so to harness the understanding as to make it justify the belief from which the argument begins:[58]

Chapter 2. That God Truly Exists

Well, then, Lord, you who give understanding to faith, grant me that I may understand, as much as You see fit, that You exist as we believe You to exist, and that you are what we believe you to be.

Now we believe that you are something than which nothing greater can be thought ("aliquid, quo nihil majus cogitari possit"). Or can it be that a thing of such a nature does not exist, since, according to the Psalmist,[59] 'the Fool has said in his heart, "There is no God".'

But surely, when this same Fool hears what I am speaking about, namely, "something than which nothing greater can be thought", he understands what he hears; and what he understands is in his mind, even if he does not understand that it actually exists. For it is one thing for an object to exist in the mind, and another thing to understand

---

57 Especially in modern times, commentators on Anselm's argument have dealt with it as intellectual play, which is fair enough in modern terms. But Mauricio Beuchot (see esp. "Naturaleza del argumento Anselmiano" in 1993a: 27ff.), in his treatment of both the modern approaches and the original perspective or approach of Anselm himself, quite rightly points out that, in Anselm's own case, there was no question at all of intellectual play, but rather of "putting into play an understanding compromised by religious faith", and compromised so radically as to leave no room for intellectual play undertaken just for its own sake. Anselm regarded reason, or human understanding, much as did the Moslems after al-Ghazali (p. 188 above), as having no standing or autonomy apart from the divine revelation of religious truth which provides for understanding its necessary and only legitimate context of exercise (except, of course, Anselm did not regard the Koran as revealed truth, but only the Bible).

58 Text from Anselm of Canterbury, *Proslogion* cap. II–IV (c.1077–8a: 227–9).

59 Psalm 13.1, 12.1.

that an object actually exists. Thus, when a painter plans beforehand what he is going to execute, he has an idea in his mind, but he does not yet think that it actually exists because he has not executed it. However, when he has actually painted what he has conceived, then he both has it in his mind and understands that it exists because he has now made it.

Even the Fool, then, is forced to agree that something-than-which-a-greater-cannot-be-thought exists in the mind, since he understands this expression when he hears it, and whatever is understood is in the mind.

And surely that-than-which-a-greater-cannot-be-thought cannot exist in the mind alone. For even if it exists solely in the mind, it can be *thought* to exist in reality independent of that thought as well, which is greater than existing in thought alone. If, then, that-than-which-a-greater-cannot-be-thought exists in the mind alone, this one and the same that-than-which-a-greater-*cannot*-be-thought is that-than-which-a-greater-*can*-be-thought, which is obviously impossible.[60] Therefore there can be no doubt that that-than-which-a-greater-cannot-be-thought exists both in the mind and in reality.[61]

Chapter 3. That God Cannot Be Thought Not To Exist

And certainly this being, God, so truly exists that it cannot be even thought not to exist. For something can be thought to exist that cannot be thought not to exist, and this is greater than that which can be thought not to exist. Hence, if that-than-which-a-greater-cannot-be-thought can be thought not to exist, then that-than-which-a-greater-cannot-be-thought is not the same as that-than-which-a-greater-cannot-be-thought, which is absurd. That-than-which-a-greater-cannot-be-thought, then, so truly exists that it cannot even be *thought* not to exist. And you, Lord our God, are this being. You exist so truly, Lord my God, that you cannot even be thought not to exist.

And this is as it should be. For if some intelligence could think of something better than you, the creature would be above and would judge its creator, which is completely absurd.

In fact, everything else there is, except you alone, can be thought of as not existing. You alone, then, of all things, most truly exist; you, therefore, of all things, possess existence to the highest degree. For anything else than that-than-which-a-greater-cannot-be-thought does not exist as truly, and so possesses existence to a lesser degree.

---

60 Recall the problem of "How To Deal with Contradictions?" from chapter 4, pp. 120 & 125ff. above.
61 There is also a problem at this point which seems not to have occurred to Anselm or to any of the many commentators on his argument over the years, namely, this: since the point of his argument turns on the singularity of its object, that-than-which-a-greater-cannot-be-thought, and this object, to escape self-contradiction, *if thought*, must be thought as really existing, yet it need not be thought, and often is not, for not everyone at all times is actually thinking about God. But *to have to be thought* is greater than what can either be thought or not be thought. Therefore that which is *really*, and not just *in thought*, something-than-which-a-greater-cannot-be-thought cannot be an object which can sometimes be thought, sometimes not thought. I will return to this point and expand upon it in concluding the discussion of Anselm in the text above.

Why then did the Fool say in his heart, "There is no God", when it is so evident to any rational mind that you of all things exist to the highest degree? Why, indeed, unless because he was a stupid fool?

Chapter 4. How "The Fool Said in His Heart" What Cannot Be Thought

How indeed has he said in his heart what he could not think? Or how could he not think what he said in his heart, since "to say in one's heart" and "to think" are one and the same? But if he really – nay, rather, *since* he really[62] – *both* thought (because he said in his heart) *and*, because he could not think, did not say in his heart "There is no God", there is more than one way in which something is "said in one's heart" or thought.

For in one sense, a thing is thought when *the word* signifying it is thought. But in another sense a thing is thought when *the very object* which the thing is is understood. In the first sense, God can be thought not to exist. But God cannot be thought not to exist in the second sense.

No one, indeed, understanding what God is, can *think* that God does not exist, even though he may *say* in his heart the words "There is no God", either by depriving them of signification or by giving them some peculiar signification.

For God is that-than-which-nothing-greater-can-be-thought. Whoever really understands this, understands clearly that this same being so exists that not even in thought can it be said not to exist. For whoever understands that God exists in such a way as to be that-than-which-a-greater-cannot-be-thought cannot think of him as not existing.

I give thanks, good Lord, I give thanks to you, since what I believed before through your free gift, I now so understand through your illumination that if I did not want to believe that you existed I should nevertheless be unable not to understand that you do exist.

Anselm, at this point, is rather pleased, for he finds that he has outdone himself. He discovers that he has not merely confirmed or fortified belief in God's existence, as he had hoped; he now finds that he has actually succeeded in making unbelief impossible. A bad day for atheists, the day Anselm penned his *Proslogion*; for the day they read that text will be their last as an atheist! Or so Anselm thought.

A contemporary of Anselm's named Gaunilon, using as a pen-name "The Fool", wrote to Anselm what he considered to be a rebuttal of this argument.[63] The "Reply of the Fool" was more than double the length of the three chapters containing the nucleus of the original argument, and Anselm's "Reply to the Fool"[64] was three times longer still. And so it has gone on for centuries, with whole books being

---

62 Since the Psalmist says he did, and the inspired writers of scripture can tell only truth.

63 Gaunilon c.1079: *Liber pro Insipiente adversus S. Anselmi in proslogio ratiocinationem auctore Gaunilone Majoris Monasterii monacho* ("Book on behalf of the Fool against the reasoning of Anselm, written by Gaunilon, a monk of the Major Monastery").

64 Anselm c.1079: *Liber apologeticus contra Gaunilonem respondentem pro insipiente.*

written on either side of this "many-faced argument",[65] so that by now a section of a good-sized library could be filled with books and essays discussing the ontological argument, pro or con. Indeed, in one of the very recent contributions to this ongoing discussion, Charles Hartshorne has put together at least two books[66] on Anselm's behalf that run together over six hundred pages.

Suffice it to note here that, in his reply to Gaunilon, Anselm quite correctly pointed out that Gaunilon had missed the key point of the whole argument, namely, the uniqueness of the object on which the argument turns. If, in place of the definition of God as "the being greater than which nothing can be conceived", we substitute the positive concept of "the most perfect being", the logic of the argument loses its force. A being of this or that type can be most perfectly conceived without necessarily being conceived as existing. If we conceive of God simply as "the most perfect being", whether that being yet exists remains an open question. But if we conceive of God as "the being greater than which nothing can be conceived", the question whether that being yet exists, far from being an open question, is rather a question that, by being asked, shows that the questioner has failed to understand the definition he or she has professed to accept. To use Descartes' later example, a questioner would be mad to say that he or she has conceived of a triangle, and now wished to inquire whether it had three sides. For existence is to a being greater than which nothing can be conceived as having three sides is to a triangle. To challenge the original argument by changing the definition of the key term without realizing it, therefore, is a sign of confusion, or, to put it in Anselm's terms, the mark of the fool.

Dixit insipiens in corde suo, non est Deus, "The fool says in his or her heart, 'there is no God'." The statement is from a psalm that Anselm, like every other medieval monk, chanted every day in the monastic choir. He had therefore a lot of time to ponder the remark if he so wished, and wish he did. Why would the fool say such a thing? Anselm's argument, thus, is a pious meditation recast in probative form.

Now Anselm well appreciated the importance to intelligent discourse of knowing what it is whereof we speak. So he made as his first move the assignment of a definition to the term "God". Is there an underlying common meaning of the word "God" that a fool or a wise man or anyone in between invokes when the word is employed? Anselm thinks that there is indeed such a universal meaning. Everyone would agree that God is the-being-greater-than-which-nothing-can-be-thought.

If one demurs, the argument cannot proceed. Let us therefore grant the definition to see where it leads. In my mind I can imagine a most perfect island, without knowing whether an island corresponding to my imagining actually exists. But a perfect island is a particular kind of thing. Whatever particular kind of thing I think

---

65 The title for Hick and McGill's 1967 collection subtitled "Recent studies on the ontological argument for the existence of God".
66 Hartshorne 1962 and 1965.

of, I can think of other particular kinds of thing more perfect in this or that respect. But God is not one kind of perfect thing among others. God exceeds that perfection of all particulars in all respects. I do not have a positive idea of God. I know only that God is that than which a greater cannot be conceived in any respect. As an object of thought, therefore, God is a unique object.

The argument of Anselm turns on that uniqueness.[67] The logic of the argument does not hold for every variety of uniqueness or perfection. It holds in one case only, the case of the being greater than which nothing can be conceived.

Now this being, not some other, if I conceive it as not existing, I have failed to conceive it. For to exist in thought is greater than not to exist in thought, but to exist actually is greater than to exist only in thought. In order to ask if God exists, God must already exist in thought, or my question could not be asked. But if God exists in my thought as that than which nothing greater can be conceived, then God must also exist actually; otherwise God is not that than which nothing greater can be conceived. So, by granting that I mean by God that-greater-than-which-nothing-can-be-thought, when I ask the question, "Does God exist?", or make the assertion, "There is no God", I at one and the same time affirm and deny that I am thinking of that than which a greater cannot be thought. Since it is foolish to contradict oneself in speaking, especially when speaking philosophically, Voilà! we have the answer to our question. How is it that the fool is able to say in his or her heart that there is no God? Because, indeed, he or she is a fool, at one and the same time affirming and denying the same object in the same respect. By the term "God" I mean the greater than which nothing can be conceived. Yet by the question or the denial I implicitly reject what the term I am using signifies, thus revealing my folly.

Writing in 1266, two hundred and forty-two years after the first appearance of Anselm's argument, Thomas Aquinas rejected the ontological argument on two grounds.[68] His first ground was that perhaps not all would accept Anselm's definition of the term "God", "seeing that some have thought that God was a body".[69] This cursory dismissal of Anselm's "definition" of the term "God" as "that than which none greater can be conceived" could be an unfortunate consequence of the fact that Aquinas may well have known Anselm's argument only in truncated form as transmitted through one of the late *florilegia*, the fragmentary dogmatic and ascetical

67 Compare the similar case with Descartes' arguments in philosophy in chapter 12, p. 513ff.
68 See his *Summa theologiae* I, quest. 2, art. 1, "Whether God's existence is self-evident", obj. 2 and ad 2.
69 "... forte ille qui audit hoc nomen, *Deus*, non intelligit significari aliquid quo majus cogitari non possit, cum quidam crediderint Deum esse corpus" (I.2.1 ad 2). Indeed, the unfortunate David of Dinant went so far as to opine that God is in fact *prime matter*, the ultimate potentiality out of which all radical transformations of bodily substances take place, a view that Aquinas uncharacteristically characterizes as *stultissimus*, "most foolish" (I.3.8c.). But Anselm already knew from revelation that fools deny God. So this part of Aquinas's rebuttal is perhaps not to the point, since it was not a question of whether there are fools, but of why they deny God; and Aquinas no less than Anselm would allow that the view of God as being a body or material potency of any kind shows enough confusion to allow the holder of the opinion to qualify as a fool.

or ethical anthologies of early Christian writers compiled and circulated from as early as the fifth century in the East up to the time of St Thomas. Thus, it needs to be borne in mind that, as above noted, in addition to the three chapters of the *Proslogion* cited above, there are (besides the preamble and chapter one) twenty-two subsequent chapters which elaborate precisely the meaning of the expression "that than which none greater can be conceived",[70] and are thus in a sense a continuation or fuller development of the basic proof. The "short form" of the argument, thus, is a nucleus rather than a nub.

What would Aquinas have had to say of Anselm's definition of the term "God" had he seen the full elaboration, and had he seen it as the sequel to Anselm's prior discourse on the essence of divinity, the *Monologion*? Would Aquinas still have so summarily dismissed Anselm's attempt at definition? Perhaps not; but then again, in view of his own approach to the question of how to attach existential import and meaning to the term "God",[71] perhaps yes. Yet there is no denying that the thirteenth-century *Commentary* of Aquinas on the sixth-century treatise *On the Divine Names* authored by the Pseudo-Dionysius voiced conclusions redolent of the eleventh-century sentiments Anselm expressed in his *Monologion*, or "discourse on the essence of divinity":[72] "Whoever investigates something incomprehensible should be satisfied if he reaches by way of reasoning a quite certain conclusion that it exists, even if he is not able to penetrate by understanding the manner of this necessary existence." And what could equal the incomprehensibility and ineffability of "that which transcends in its existence the existence of all things"? If, therefore, the highest exercise of understanding and reason leads to the comprehension that the source of existence is incomprehensible because, in contrast to everything from which our experience and reasoning begins, what it is has no distinction from the fact that it is, "the foundation of one's certainty is not shaken in the least" by one's coming to comprehend that the manner in which the source of existence knows the things which exist, the very things from which we by reasoning arrive at the knowledge of the necessary existence of that source, is incomprehensible. For "who

---

70 "Id quo majus cogitari non potest"; "id quo majus nequit cogitari"; "idipsum quo majus cogitari nequit"; "aliquid quo majus cogitari non potest".

71 See chapter 7 below, esp. p. 266ff.

72 Anselm of Canterbury, *Monologium* cap. LXIV (c.1076: 210): "Videtur mihi hujus tam sublimis rei secretum transcendere omnem intellectus aciem humani: et idcirco conatum explicandi qualiter hoc sit, continendum puto. Sufficere namque debere existimo rem incomprehensibilem indaganti, si ad hoc ratiocinando pervenerit ut eam certissime esse cognoscat; etiamsi penetrare nequeat intellectu, quomodo ita sit: nec idcirco minus his adhibendam fidei certitudinem, quae probationibus necessariis, nulla alia repugnante ratione asseruntur; si suae naturalis altitudinis incomprehensibilitate, tam ineffabile, quam id quod supra omnia est? Quapropter si ea, quae de summa essentia hactenus disputata sunt, necessariis rationibus sunt asserta, quamvis sic intellectu penetrari non possint, ut et verbis valeant explicari; nullatenus tamen certitudinis eorum nutat soliditas. Nam, si superior consideratio rationabiliter comprehendit incomprehensibile esse, quomodo eadem summa sapientia sciat ea quae fecit, de quibus tam multa nos scire necesse est: quis explicet quomodo sciat aut dicat seipsam, de qua aut nihil, aut vix aliquid ab homine sciri possibile est? Ergo si non eo quod seipsam dicit, generat Pater, et generatur Filius: *Generationem ejus quis enarrabit?* (Isaiah LIII, 8)."

will explain how he knows or expresses that highest source about which the human being knows either nothing or next to nothing?", Anselm queries plaintively in those pseudo-dionysian tones which won the sympathy of Aquinas for "negative theology", in no small part,[73] through his assumption of the authenticity of their source.

In any event, Aquinas rejected the claim of probative force for Anselm's line of reasoning on a second and more fundamental ground: even granting the word God to mean something than which a greater cannot be thought, the consequence of this definition is not that God *actually* exists but only that we are (rightly or wrongly, as must be further determined) *thinking* of God as actually existing.[74]

This brings us to the very problem that we noted above[75] as not having occurred either to Anselm or to any of the many promoters of the ontological argument since Anselm, namely, the problem that not only is it greater to exist in both thought and reality than to exist in thought alone or in reality alone, but to exist as not able not to be thought is greater than to exist as sometimes able to be thought and other times not.[76] Thus, the point of the ontological argument turns on the singularity of its object, that-than-which-a-greater-cannot-be-thought. This object, to escape self-contradiction, *if thought*, must be thought as really existing. But it need not be thought, and often is not, for not everyone at all times is actually thinking about God. But to have to be thought is greater than what can either be thought or not be thought. Therefore that which *really*, that which *in itself*, and not just in thought, is something-than-which-a-greater-cannot-be-thought cannot be an object which can sometimes be thought, sometimes not thought. Therefore Anselm's argument does not have for its object a *really existing* something-than-which-a-greater-cannot-be-thought, but only an object which, if thought, must be *thought* as really existing,[77] but which, at the same time, manifests that it is not *really* that-than-which-a-greater-cannot-be-thought, for whatever is really that-than-which-a-greater-cannot-be-thought cannot sometimes be thought and other times not.

And the point can be pressed even further. If God *really* is that-than-which-a-greater-cannot-be-thought, then God must exist as a self-subsisting thought (which is actually what both Aristotle and Aquinas, with differing degrees of completeness, succeeded in showing), and is never as object of our thought directly present as such – that is, as God "is in the existence proper to God"[78] – even when we thematically focus upon that-than-which-a-greater-cannot-be-thought. For that-than-which-a-greater-cannot-be-thought, as an object of our thought, need not

---

73 See chapter 7 below, p. 276f.
74 Aquinas c.1266: *Summa theologiae* I.2.1. ad 2.
75 Note 61, this chapter, p. 235.
76 Had it occurred to him, Descartes could have martialled this point in support of his contention that the idea of God is innate in the soul from its first moment of existence, and has only to be fully realized in consciousness to be seen for what it is, the mark of the Workman upon His work.
77 See Aquinas on God's knowability in the *Summa* I.3.4c, cited below in chapter 7, p. 282.
78 *Deus ut est in se*.

always be thought, whereas that-than-which-a-greater-cannot-be-thought, as really existing, cannot fail to be thought. Whence, no matter how the ontological argument is couched, it fails to touch on the real existence of God, at which it is aimed, but concludes only to something which holds for our situation as finite thinkers.

Mortimer Adler came to the University of Dubuque sometime in the 1970s as part of a lecture tour on "How To Think about God". Subsequently he published a book on the subject in which the first part claimed to be based on Anselm and the second part (which someone failed to proofread) based on Aquinas. Overall the book was actually not all that great, but the point of the first part captured the situation exactly. If we are to think clearly about God, we must indeed think of God as existing actually and not merely in thought. But clear thinking on our part is not sufficient to prove, even in the unique case of God, that God actually exists. For that, appeal must be made rather to the nature of actual existence, whence, if at all, some proof or other may be derived.

Descartes, as mentioned above, later would compare the situation to that of a triangle. Existence is to God as having three sides and three angles is to a triangle. As we cannot think of a triangle unless we think of it as having three sides and three angles, so we cannot think of God unless we think of God as actually existing. But this argument makes the point of Adler and Aquinas, not the one Descartes or Anselm before him hoped to make.

Arguments for the existence of God based on the world of actual existence Kant called "cosmological arguments", and again the name stuck, this time, at least, with some aptness. The most famous of these, too, come from the middle ages. But let us wait till we come to Aquinas to consider the cosmological argument,[79] for his is the classical formulation of how our experience of a changing world can so

---

79 See the *Quinque Viae* discussion in chapter 7, p. 267. The influence of Kant in this matter is very peculiar, almost rising to the level of history's worthy ironies. Having misnamed the "ontological argument" (by applying to its point of departure a term, "ontological", the original denotation and connotation of which alike had little to no suggestion of the ideal order), he now proceeded, in effect, to do something similar for the proofs which begin, for Aquinas, from an encounter within experience with the physical aspects of the environment in sensation recognized as such by intellectual analysis and then taken as starting points for a reasoning that develops the internal dimension of intelligibility grasped within the experience of physical being as subjectivity objectified or cognized discursively to the point of manifesting with necessity the ground for affirming the existence of a physical subjectivity which is not sensible and has *for its essence* existence (in contrast to all directly experienced beings, which manifest a difference between what they are and the fact that they but happen to be existing here and now). Technically, what Aquinas considered the "first and more manifest way" fell under Kant's rubric of "cosmological". The proof from efficient cause (Aquinas's "second way") Kant called "physiotheological", a designation whose sole merit is having passed into an oblivion almost as great as the one from which it should never have emerged. In any event, since Kant had no way of recognizing the emergence within the objectivity of experience of material aspects of the subjectivity of the physical environment (as we will see in chapter 13), he correspondingly had no way to understand the proper opposition of arguments of the "cosmological type" to arguments of the "ontological type", with the result that Kant's discussion, as Collins (1954: 503) gently puts it, "does not systematically dispose of all possible metaphysical proofs, as he claimed it to do". It is the whole story of the modern period in miniature: "the narrow

be conceptualized as to lead to an affirmation and understanding of what the word "God" ought to mean insofar as it is used correctly to designate an existence beyond the order of all finite existing beings.

Peter Abaelard (c.1079–1142)

Abaelard cut his teeth on the question of universals, beginning about 1103. Along the way, something else got cut as well. Abaelard is one of the few philosophers as fabled in the halls of romance as in the halls of philosophy.

c.1117–1142: Héloïse (c.1098–1164) and Abaelard

Around 1117 he was hired to tutor a young woman named Héloïse, an orphan whose parents have left no trace, except that she was the niece of Fulbert, a canon of the Paris cathedral of Notre Dame,[80] who admired and respected her intelligence and love of learning. He commissioned Abaelard to be her tutor. Abaelard claims to have maintained "the utmost continence" up to the time he met Héloïse,[81] but as it happened they learned together the ways of the flesh, and she became pregnant.

He offered to marry her, but the only way to an intellectual career in those days lay in the Church, and marriage would block that path unless she subsequently agreed to become a nun, in which circumstance the marriage could be forgiven Abaelard by church authorities. She preferred to be his mistress in secret, which would have left the way to advancement open. By now they had an infant son, Astrolabe. Abaelard insisted on a secret marriage instead, which would also keep open the way to advancement.

But Fulbert preferred his dignity to Abaelard's career opportunities, and made the secret marriage known. Héloïse publicly contradicted her uncle with whom she was again living, and Abaelard, to save her from Fulbert's abuse, put her in a convent. This was too much for Fulbert. With some kinsmen he entered Abaelard's room at night and "cut off those parts of my body whereby I had done that which was the cause of their sorrow."[82] Fulbert was ruined by the deed, but so was Abaelard, and

---

historical scope of his study of the philosophical sources" (to borrow Collins's formula) allowed him to dismiss as unthinkable what in fact he merely had failed to think through.

80 Not to be confused with the slightly earlier Bishop Fulbert (AD960–1028), called by his fond pupils the *Venerabilis Socrates*. This slightly earlier Fulbert founded, about 1006, the great cathedral school of Chartres, the most renowned in France before Abaelard. To this school, before the end of the 11th century, came such scholars as John of Salisbury (1115–80), William of Conches (c.1080–1154), Berengar of Tours (c.1000–88), and the great logician and subtle theologian Gilbert of la Porrée (1070–1154), making it the light of Europe in the generation after Abaelard, just as, in the generations before, the Palace School founded by Charlemagne (first at Compiègne, then at Laon) had reached a height of glory *under* Charles the Bald (AD823–77 – reigning as Charles I King of France from 840–77, and as Charles II Holy Roman Emperor from 875–7), but *mainly because of* the work of Scotus Erigena discussed in chapter 4, p. 135.

81 From Abaelard's autobiography, circulated c.1133 under the title *Historia calamitatum mearum* ("the story of my calamities"), ch. 5. For the circumstances and purpose of this little work, see Sikes 1932: 25f.

82 Ibid., ch. 7.

oppressed by the spectre that "the tale of this amazing outrage would spread to the very ends of the earth", as indeed it has, from 1119 to this day.

For Héloïse it was Abaelard or no one. She took the veil, and reputedly[83] proceeded to write to Abaelard over the next quarter-century some of the most amazing love letters in all of literature. For Abaelard, of course, choice was gone. It was neither Heloise nor anyone else. He became a monk of St Denis.

In the Wrong Place at the Wrong Time
Let us move on to the intellectual side of Abaelard's life. Here too he was unfortunate, again the wrong man at the wrong time. Abaelard was the greatest genius of his time, of astounding originality in logic and dialectic. The wealth of his originality has still to be mined.[84] Why? Because just at the time that he produced his mature works, the flood of Aristotelian translations began, and the logic and philosophy of Aristotle crowded the logic of Abaelard from the Latin stage. He reminds me of the fate of Abel Gance, one of the great directors of films in the silent era. Toward what proved to be the end of that era, Gance produced his masterpiece, a seven-hour epic which requires three screens and the accompaniment of a full orchestra. But just as the film was ready to open, the first "talkie" was released. Everyone crowded to the talkie, and Gance's film opened to an empty house, closed unnoticed, and nearly passed into oblivion.[85]

The "Problem of Universals" and the First Florescence of Nominalism
It is at the time of Abaelard that the *praeteritio* of Porphyry,[86] although earlier developed in the work of Boethius,[87] really seizes center-stage in medieval philos-

---

83 The oldest manuscripts known for these letters (c.1120–41?) date from the 13th century, translated from Latin into French around 1280 by Jean de Meung (i.1240/60–1305). They are a brilliant and undying piece of romantic literature from the Latin Age. Though their authenticity has been challenged, the strong probablility that they are genuine (Gilson 1938: 36) has recently been reinforced by the analysis by Mews (1999: 143) of a second, earlier set of letters (i.1114/17?) apparently by the same authors, which would be (ibid: 5) "the love letters Peter Abelard composed in order to seduce Heloise when he was teaching at the cathedral school of Notre Dame".
84 For example, the "glosses on Porphyry" translated by McKeon (see n. 93 below) in 1929 became available in published form only in 1919; and the first complete edition of the Parisian manuscript of Abaelard's main work on logic, his *Dialectica*, presumably from the third and final redaction by Abaelard i.1135/7 (De Rijk 1970: xxii), was first published in 1956 under De Rijk's editorship. Here are great opportunities for young graduate students willing to master Latin and able to philosophize.
85 Almost half a century later, the canisters of Gance's masterpiece were discovered and restored as far as possible by Steven Spielberg, who put on the film as Gance had tried, full orchestra and all. *Napoleon* played to packed houses in Los Angeles (where I got to see it), New York, and Chicago. I hope I live to see complete critical editions of Abaelard's work.
    And of course every analogy limps. The diversion to the full range of Aristotelian writings hardly compares to the shallow talkie that did in Gance's *Napoleon*. The point remains that Abaelard's work deserves a thorough revisitation.
86 See chapter 4 above, n. 167, and text at p. 154.
87 Indeed, McKeon remarks (1929: 204) that Abaelard's "gloss on Porphyry" (see n. 93 below) could also be called a commentary on the commentaries of Boethius on Porphyry from c.509–10, for Abaelard's discussion of the universal "derives much from Boethius".

ophy. The earlier work of Boethius devoted about 60 per cent of the discussion to the utility of logic, the remainder to universals. By contrast, Abaelard devotes 80 per cent of his discussion to developing the intricacies of the problem of the universal. "Whether genera or species exist in themselves or reside purely and solely in things understood; whether, if they exist, they are corporeal or incorporeal; and whether they exist apart or within sense objects and in dependence upon them":[88] these became now the burning questions of the age, and led to the first florescence of a plague that would reappear after Ockham, and has been with us ever since, the doctrine of *nominalism*. In its first florescence, nominalism appeared in the work of Jean Roscelin (c.1050–1120), sometime before 1092. He taught that universal terms such as genus, species, and the like have no proper signification of their own. He used an unforgettable expression to describe universals: *flatus vocis*, "a snorting or fart of the voice" – empty air. Only individual beings exist, all else are mere "names", *nomina* (whence the designation *nominalismus*, "nominalism"). For Democritus there were atoms and the void; for Roscelin, individuals and names.

But Roscelin extended his doctrine to a sensitive issue. The civilization of Islam was by this time nearing the height of its power. Teachings of Christianity and teachings of Islam had come into conflict in Spain in particular, where the level of intellectual culture in Moslem centers was very high and familiarity with Aristotle quite intimate. One of the things taught by the *Koran* was that there is but one God, Allah. The Moslems regarded the Christian doctrine of the Trinity as a heresy, contrary to the Koranic teaching on the unity of Allah. Nor did the early Christians have ready answers to the Moslem question of how three Persons can yet be one single God. The question is indeed difficult.[89]

---

88 Porphyry c.AD271: *Praeteritio*, pp. 27–8.

89 The historically and theoretically most credible explanation, a rational abduction surpassing the monumental labor even of Augustine's classic *De Trinitate* (i.399/422–6), may be the one Aquinas worked out, which may help to explain why the legend persists that the first of his two major theological syntheses, the *Summa contra Gentiles*, had as a principal intention the intellectual equipment of missionaries especially but not exclusively to Moslem lands (see the discussion in Torrell 1996: 104–7; and see below, chapter 7, p. 263n33). Taking his point of departure from the unique feature of relation according to which it consists not in subjectivity but suprasubjectivity, Aquinas argued that the interior life of the one God consists in a pure communion or communication of Persons which, as distinct, are subsistent relations having one common foundation or ground in the single divine nature or "essence" or "substance" (a pure Act of Being without intrinsic limitation or specification by potentiality, Subsistent Existence, as we will see – pp. 272 & 282ff. below), the one "Godhead" (as Meister Eckhart, the younger contemporary of Aquinas and fellow disciple of Albertus Magnus, put the point). Centuries later, the last of the great Latin followers of Aquinas, John Poinsot (writing indeed under his Latin *nom de plume* and *nomen religiosum* of Joannes a Sancto Thoma), expressly basing himself on Aquinas's insight in this area, will see in the uniqueness of relation the solution also to the problem of how the sign can be superior to the difference between mind-independent being and mind-dependent being, *ens reale* and *ens rationis*, reality and fiction. On this view, the ontological understanding of communication at all levels – from that which occurs between inorganic substances on up to the communion of the Divine Persons in the inner life of

Roscelin did not help. "God", he said, is a *flatus vocis* we apply to the Three Persons, each of whom is individually the true reality. "Trinity", too, then, is a *flatus vocis*. We have from Roscelin's own hand no record of his views. But we do know that Anselm, as a leading ecclesiastical figure of the time, held for the reality of universals in the sense Roscelin was denying. And we do know that Roscelin was summoned in 1092 before an episcopal synod at Soissons and given the choice of retractation of his views or excommunication for them. Roscelin retracted on whatever points the ecclesiastical synod was insistent, but apparently held to his basic nominalistic doctrine. Later in his teaching career (Gilson suggests[90] that it was probably at Loches in France) Roscelin had Abaelard for a pupil.

Around 1103, William of Champeaux (c.1070–1121) began to teach at the cathedral school of Notre Dame in Paris. William of Champeaux had been a student of Roscelin, but he held polar opposite views on the question of universals, much closer to Anselm's *Monologion* and Plato's doctrine of Ideas. It was William's misfortune that early in his teaching days (around 1108) the young Abaelard enrolled as a student in his course. According to Abaelard's report – for again, as with Roscelin, we have no records from William of Champeaux's own hand – this William out-Platoed Plato, holding not merely that individuals participate in the true Forms of reality, but that the whole of each universal Idea enters into each and every individual. All humanity is in every man.

Abaelard brought Aristotle's criticisms of Plato's theory of ideas down to earth. He had a field day drawing out logical consequences and antinomies in William's views, and he did so openly before the class. All humanity in every individual? Then every individual is in every individual, too. The student Abaelard under William of Champeaux's attempt at tutelage leaves us a picture of a somewhat conceited and boastful youth, insolent, so self-conscious of his talent as to think nothing of trampling without respect on the teachings and sensitivities of his masters and his peers. This picture is not so different from the one Pierre Bayle painted in 1696:[91] Abelard "was at first [William's] Beloved Disciple, but it did not continue long; the Professor had too much trouble to answer the Subtle Objections of that Disciple, not to conceive Vexation and Hatred against him". And both pictures are confirmed by William of Champeaux's later action. About a year after William retired from

---

the Godhead, and at all levels between (God with human beings, human beings with God, with one another, with animals, with plants or "nature in general"; nonlinguistic animals with humans, with one another, with the environment; even plants with the soil, with one another, as happens in infections, where surrounding plants develop antibodies, etc.; the various planetary, stellar, and galactic dependencies) – depends on the same feature of relation which justifies Augustine's posit of sign as a general notion. We will see this in due course; but for now we must not run further ahead of the story.

90 Gilson 1944: 238.
91 From the entry "Abelard" in the 1710 English edition of Bayle's celebrated *Dictionnaire historique et critique* of 1696, advertised as having "many Additions and Corrections, made by the Author himself, that are not in the French Editions" (London: Printed for C. Harper et al.), Vol. I: 19. (The cited passage, however, is in all the editions.)

teaching to establish the Abbey of St Victor in 1108, his successor and appointee at Notre Dame proposed to yield his teaching post to Abaelard. William of Champeaux vetoed the idea.[92]

Rejecting both realism in the medieval sense (Platonism) and nominalism, what did Abaelard himself propose? The question in my opinion remains an open one, on which an adequate doctoral dissertation needs to be written. Some say he held views no different from those of his later contemporary, John of Salisbury (1115–80). John of Salisbury settled the question simply with a doctrine that has come to be known as *conceptualism*: the mind recognizes the same or similar characteristics in different individual objects and conveniently gathers these differences into one mental concept or idea, which provides the meaning for the universal or general term, the spoken sound or written character string with which the concept is then associated.

But I think Abaelard was subtler than this.[93] So-called conceptualism is more sophisticated than the crude original nominalism we have in the reports of Roscelin's views, perhaps, but conceptualism and nominalism are hardly exclusive of one another. John Locke held exactly Salisbury's solution. Let Charles Peirce make our point:[94]

> Many philosophers call their variety of nominalism, "conceptualism"; but it is essentially the same thing; and their not seeing that it is so is but another example of that loose and slapdash style of thinking that has made it possible for them to remain nominalists. Their calling their "conceptualism" a middle term between realism and nominalism is itself an example in the very matter to which nominalism relates.

The claim of nominalism is that there is no direct referent, no proper significate, for general terms on the side of the object. This claim is hardly met by pointing out that such terms depend in their meaning on a subjective ground in the mind. That is quite beside the point.

In its most extreme form, nominalism claims that linguistic sounds are correlated with individual physical things and nothing more, a kind of linguistic dualism (there are words, there are things, and there is nothing besides). The view is naive and indefensible, but it has been held. A more sophisticated nominalism would bring in a third factor, recognizing that the difference between a mere sound or mark as

---

92 Abaelard's other old teacher, Roscelin, somewhere around 1120 tried to have Abaelard indicted for heresy on the basis of Abaelard's book *On the Divine Unity and Trinity*. One might say Abaelard knew how to burn his bridges. In 1140, the pope himself is said to have burned his books.

93 See Abaelard a.1118#1, "The Glosses of Peter Abailard on Porphyry", trans. in McKeon 1929: 208–58. The translation is sufficiently intelligible to convince the reader of the importance and subtlety of Abaelard's view, but unfortunately not intelligible enough to enable an understanding of those views. At least it is impossible to entertain the illusion that McKeon's translation makes the original in any measure superfluous.

94 Peirce 1909: CP 1.27.

physical and that same sound or mark as linguistic needs to be accounted for, and can be accounted for only by positing a third factor in the individual employing the sound or mark in discourse.

But the problematic arises from the side of the referent, the object signified: what is *its* status, a question hardly answered by invoking the connection of dependency between words as spoken or written and psychological states within the users of language. For, as we have already had occasion to note in passing, these states themselves, what Aristotle called the "passions of the soul", already exhibit the essential character of signs in making present another besides themselves.[95] Physical sounds apart from the passions of the soul could not be words, but as words they signify through, rather than to, those *passiones*.

The Possible Nominalistic Character of Augustine's Proposal of Signum

The point may be illustrated by Augustine's original proposal of *signum* as a general notion. The famous medieval dispute over *nominalism*, all unwittingly, Augustine presaged with his begging of the question of how to overcome the ancient dichotomy between the causal relations linking natural phenomena to the things of which they are signs and the imaginary relations linking cultural phenomena to the things of which *they* are "signs". For if it is not sufficient to propose a common term for diverse phenomena in order to establish or reveal a nature truly common within the diversity, we can see that, without facing the question (without realizing it), Augustine left to his posterity the question of whether any general doctrine of signs or "semiotics" would not be a mere nominalism.

John of Salisbury is reported to have complained about the problem of universals that "one never gets away from this question. The world has grown old discussing it, and it has taken more time than the Caesars consumed in conquering and governing the world." I have not been able to track down the report; but I did find Salisbury complaining[96] of his old professors and friends that "they remained involved in and occupied with the same questions whereby they had used to stir their students", but "did not seem to have progressed as much as a hand's span." His is the typical complaint of the man of affairs about the philosophers. Sometimes it is just. But in this case it would have helped if the complainer had understood the true dimensions of the problem. For John of Salisbury, merely being a man of affairs is not excuse enough; for his ability as a philosopher was considerable, and it was up to him to make time enough in his affairs sufficiently to realize those abilities in matters upon which he chose to venture public comment.

Abaelard, however, saw quite clearly that the "problem of universals" considered in relation to the problem of the being proper to signs opens up the whole vista of the problem of nonbeing, even though we do not find that he himself would explore that vista by tracing, as we will see Poinsot finally do four centuries later, the dependence

---

95 See p. 222 above.
96 John of Salisbury 1159: 100.

of understanding upon sense to its root in the action of signs, and the possibility of the action of signs to its root in the singular being of relation whence the sign derives its constitutive indifference to subjective provenance.[97] For once it has been recognized that there is signification within language as well as in the world of nature,[98] in other words, once we recognize that the sign in its being transcends the "opposition" or difference between the orders of language (and there through culture generally) and physical nature, we need to take account of a surprising consequence:[99]

> For when the subjects existing in nature are destroyed, if someone speaks the name "rose" or "lilly", even though the things named no longer exercise a signification, yet the signification within the understanding is not reduced to nothing, because the understanding continues to signify whether the thing exists or does not exist any longer.

The signification nature achieves in the world of things is transitory, whereas that which the understanding achieves through language endures. But for this, nonbeing needs to be seen in its oppositional complementarity with being. As we will see, this is exactly what Aquinas will achieve in his understanding of the terms *ens reale* and *ens rationis*.[100] Yet the problem is already clearly indicated here in Abaelard's writing, and it is a profound semiotic problem indeed.

The Sic et Non *(c.1122) of Peter Abaelard and the* Sentences *(c.1150) of Peter Lombard*

We pass over Abaelard's amazing *Dialogue between a Philosopher, a Jew, and a Christian* because it is unfinished and we do not know where Abaelard wished to take it. Too bad not only that it was left unfinished but also that the author did not add a Moslem to the dialogue, to give us a fuller picture of the situation of his time. Perhaps it was a little early for the Latins to take seriously this third variety of Western believer.

---

97 See chapter 9, "The Vindication of Augustine", p. 430ff. At the same time, without pushing the problem of the being proper to signs to a fundamental resolution in terms of the *type itself* "signum", Abaelard introduces a number of distinctions and reversals of point of view concerning the problem of distinguishing various *tokens* of signs that, without advancing the fundamental problematic of the possible unity of a doctrine of signs, are quite important in their own right and further testify, were such testimony needed, to the rich field for future workers that his texts provide. Some of these subordinate semiotic points were first indicated by Eco et al. (1986), and have been further fleshed out in the work of Meier-Oeser 1997: 43–50.

98 Abaelard himself (i.1135/7: 111) puts the point conversely: "Est autem significare non solum vocum, sed etiam rerum".

99 Abaelard, a.1118#1: "Rerum ... significatio transitoria est, intellectus vero permanens. Destructis enim rebus subiectis, si quis hoc nomen proferat 'rosa' vel 'lilium', licet rerum quas nominabit, significationem iam non teneant, significatio intellectuum non vacuatur, quia sive res sit, sive non, intellectus semper constituuntur."

100 See chapter 7, "Nonbeing in Latin Philosophy", p. 350ff.

Abaelard's Sic et Non

But there is no passing over Abaelard's *Sic et Non*, a collection begun perhaps as early as 1122, and worked on possibly as late as 1142. The first mention of it is in a letter sent in 1140 to St Bernard of Clairvaux, always Abaelard's nemesis, from William of St Thierry.[101] Thierry advises Bernard of a suspicious book secretly being circulated by Abaelard among his partisans. How did it influence the Latin Age, since it disappeared thereafter from history until 1836, when Victor Cousin (1792–1867) found a manuscript copy in a library at Avranches?[102] One can only suspect that the influence came through the sanitized *Sentences* of Peter Lombard, who was a student of Abaelard and called the *Sic et Non* his breviary.

What was the *Sic et Non*? The title means "Thus, and To the Contrary", "Yes and No". It posed 157 questions, including ones bearing on the fundamentals of Christian belief. Under each question, arranged in two columns, were contrary or contradictory quotations (sometimes from the same source) on the same point at issue, drawn from the Bible, the Fathers of the Church, and pagan classics. The oppositions were too naked. Even the insouciant Abaelard did not dare to put the book into open circulation at the time.

Lombard's Sentences

In 1150 a similar work appeared, the *Sententiarum libri IV*, "Four Books of Opinions". Peter Lombard presented the compilation in a less tendentious array. What he did was to take materials from "his breviary", the *Sic et Non*, and reorder them in a manner congenial to the religious orthodoxy of the time, "based", as O'Meara says,[103] "upon the concatenation of articles in the creed." The term "sententiae" is usually transliterated rather than translated when the work is referred to in English, and combined with the editor's name so as to give the impression that he were the author, thus: *The Sentences of Peter Lombard*. But the "sentences" in this title means "opinions"; and the opinions are not those of Lombard, but are selections taken from the writings of the Fathers of the Church – those early Christian writers, as we have already had occasion to mention, who, from the first century to the death of Augustine and after, had formulated and shaped the religious and doctrinal consciousness of the Christian church. The four books, thus, are an anthology of the views of these writers, but an anthology conscientiously constructed to channel even conflicting opinions toward the support of orthodox conclusions. By substituting this conscientiousness for the contentiousness of Abaelard's *Sic et Non*, even while using much of the same materials, Lombard ensured a favorable reception for his work. In place of the consternation Abaelard loved to engender, Lombard's presentation was received with grateful enthusiasm.

---

101 In Cousin ed. 1836: clxxxvii.
102 The scholarly story of this discovery from Cousin's time to the present is best told in the "Introduction" to the critical edition of *Sic et Non* by Boyer and McKeon 1976–77: 1–6.
103 O'Meara 1997: 54.

For the need for such a work was enormous. The social organization of the Latin West had reached a kind of saturation point which made the crystallization of a structure of higher learning inevitable. As Aristotle's literary corpus provided a rational content for that structure on the part of philosophy, so the anthology of Lombard performed a similar service on the side of religious thought. And as the logically refined tools of intellectual criticism were put to work on the analysis of and commentary upon the works of Aristotle, so these same tools were put to work in the same way on the compilation of views Lombard had assembled. These views, remember, crystallized the faith and aspirations not of individual men, but of representatives of the development of the Christian consciousness of a believing community. The manner in which Abaelard on his own inclined to present them invited wrath. Yet the need for some kind of summary compilation such as Abaelard first had effected was enormous.

In Migne's nineteenth-century edition of the Fathers, the *Patrologiae Cursus Completus* fills an entire wall with books floor to ceiling. The *Series Latina* alone (customarily abbreviated PL, for *Patrologia Latina*) runs to two hundred and twenty-one large volumes, and the *Series Graeca* (or PG, for *Patrologia Graeca*) adds one hundred and sixty-six more volumes equally large. Imagine the enthusiasm for a work purporting to distill this enormous mass of three hundred and eighty-seven volumes down into one or two volumes of "the essential passages" for ready consumption. This was the situation of Lombard's *Sentences*. So popular was Lombard's work that Roger Bacon (c.1220–92), self-styled as "the only seer in the country of the blind",[104] captiously complained that it had replaced the Scriptures.[105] But the acceptance of Lombard's work triumphed at the time over such objections. The *Sentences* became the staple for graduate work in theology, and the way to get the medieval doctorate was by writing a *Commentary on the Sentences*. Whence, including one by Thomas Aquinas and two by Duns Scotus, such *Expositiones* or *Commentariae in IV libros sententiarum* accumulated in the later centuries of the Latin Age. Over four thousand have actually been counted surviving in European libraries.

Without Aristotle, without Lombard, the medieval universities would have taken shape about when they did anyway. But how their curricula would have been shaped in that case we could only guess. As it was, they took the philosophical shape of the Aristotelian system and the theological shape of the *Sentences* of Peter Lombard. It could have been otherwise; but in either case it was not a bad beginning.

---

104 *Obiter* in Maloney 1988: 12.
105 This remark may be a little unjust to Bacon, yet one cannot avoid thinking that, had it been his
      Opus Maius or *Opus tertium* in the place of Lombard's *Sentences*, Bacon's complaint on the score
      would have gone unvoiced. See chapter 8 below, p. 365.

CHAPTER SEVEN

Cresting a Wave: The Second Stage

To say that the later Latin Age is inaugurated by the advent of something like the complete *corpus* of Aristotle's works in translation risks an exaggeration in the student's mind of the influence of this work on the creativity and genius of the period. Had Aristotle remained unknown, there would still have been a flowering of this period. Anyone who thinks that the principal authors of the period can be reduced to the influence of ancient sources is on a dead-end trail. What counts with minds of genius is always what they do with their sources, and to this end the knowledge of the sources is but an aid and an abetment.

Moreover, the "Aristotle" introduced to Latin Europe was not the pure Greek Aristotle who once walked the streets of Stagira and frequented the groves of Plato's Academy. He was something much more complex, a Greek who was introduced through the prism of a thousand minds and at least four cultures, two of them older,[1] one of them younger,[2] than the present Christian culture and civilization of Latin Europe. Already in the period of Abaelard and Lombard, Arabic and Jewish philosophers were influencing Christian thinkers in Spain. When the door of translations opened the way for Aristotle into the Latin world, he did not enter alone. Along with him entered, from ancient Greece, Hippocrates and Galen, Euclid and Ptolemy; from the world of Hispanic Judaism, Moses Maimonides; from the Moslem world, al-Kindi, al-Farabi, al-Ghazali, Avicenna, Ibn Gabirol, and Averroes. And that is only a token list.

Still, we have only one volume within which to work, so we will confine ourselves to a few thinkers whose works establish landmarks. And, to make even this limited purview manageable, we will present these few landmark thinkers under speculative themes which accomplish a threefold expository goal. We will explore the Latin Age according to themes which were important to the self-understanding of the time, but which serve also to provide a synoptic view of the period as a whole, and to manifest its relevance to the present and immediate future of philosophy so far as such things can be foreseen.

---

1 Jewish and Greek culture.
2 Islamic culture.

Albertus Magnus (c.1201–1280)

The first medieval to survey all the major works of the man known among Latins as "the Philosopher", and so to comment upon them as to assimilate them to the Latin Age, was Albertus Magnus, c.1201–80, "Albert the Great". There is no exaggerating the greatness of this man. If we substitute for the word "prince" the expression "philosophical scientist" and the name "Albertus Magnus" for "Charlemagne", to Albert may be appropriated an observation once made of Charlemagne:3 "The appellation of *great* has been often bestowed and sometimes deserved, but ALBERTUS MAGNUS is the only philosophical scientist in whose favour the title has been indissolubly blended with the name." After his death, the Roman Catholic Church declared him, as well as a saint, patron of natural sciences. His worthiness for this title can be suggested, perhaps, from such a detail in his writing as his discussion of conditions of egg-formation under which would be produced a crow that was not black.4 On the literary legacy of Albert the Great, as also in the case of Abaelard, much valuable work remains to be done. Athanasius Weisheipl, after his masterly biography of Aquinas, intended to produce a comparable landmark on Albert, teacher of Aquinas. Some of the groundwork of this project we have,5 and while death has ensured that we will not have the finished product, Weisheipl's colleague and friend, the great Galilean scholar William Wallace, has taken up the work6 and we may yet hope in our time for such a masterpiece as Weisheipl would have fashioned.

With Albert begins in the West that reading of the book of nature in earnest and systematized observations that will gradually separate out empirical science from the speculative doctrines of Aristotelian physics. When combined with mathematical techniques in the time of Galileo, the development will result in the most powerful tools for extending human control over the physical world that have ever been devised in the history of civilization, thanks to science made capable "of walking solely with the legs of rational experience and mathematics and of traveling far and everywhere, into the heavens and the invisible structures of terrestrial matter".7 But it would be some centuries before the kind of empirical interests for which Albert was so suited by temperament would become institutionalized and socially supported. And by then other names would be more prominently associated with the establishment of empirical research, including some from among that tribe of Franciscans who, in Albert's immediate experience, tended to consist of "ignorant men who would fight by every means the employment of philosophy".8

---

3 Gibbon 1788a: 302.
4 See Wallace 1980.
5 Weisheipl 1980a, b.
6 See as illustration the "Albertus Magnus" special issue of *The American Catholic Philosophical Quarterly* 70.1 (Winter 1996), guest-edited by Wallace.
7 Redondi 1983: 329.
8 As reported in Gilson 1922: II, 9. Albert's contemporary, Roger Bacon, c.1214–92, the most famous medieval scientist, naturally (inasmuch as he was a Franciscan) reciprocated this ill-feeling. But

It was under Albert the Great that Thomas Aquinas (c.1224–74) received his intellectual formation. Of this great master Torrell[9] remarks that his "Neoplatonism, marked by Avicenna and Pseudo-Dionysius, gave rise to a family, and if we cannot say that the whole school of Cologne is Albertinian," we can at least "say without question that the Neoplatonism of that school is Albertus Magnus's legacy – as was also the Thomism that departed from it little by little."

"The Splendor of the Latins"

If there were one defining figure for the whole of the later Latin Age – actually there were at least three such – that one would be Thomas Aquinas. It was from his work above all that the Latin Age comes to be characterized as the age of the philosophy of being. For while philosophy in this period was focused initially on things, the order of *ens reale* as exercising an existence independent of human thought and action, yet the great Aquinas so adjusted the focus that the very notion of "thing" became a transcendental, that is to say (speaking within the context of a distinctively medieval development of philosophy[10] foreclosed in the modern period, yet essential

---

these two should have been natural allies. In general, the Franciscans in England regularly produced – and much more so than Albert's own order, where Albert was more *sui generis* – men of a scientific temper against whom Albert's generalization was most unjust.

9 Torrell 1996: 313.

10 I say "distinctively medieval" because, although founded indeed on various remarks of Aristotle in his text of c.348–7bBC, we know since the work of Pouillon 1930 that the first systematic thematization of the content of those ancient *obiter dicta* was essayed during the infancy of Aquinas, c.1225/8, by Philip Cancellarius, and this theme of the "transcendental properties consequent upon being" was taken up thereafter by the main medieval authors, including Thomas's principal teacher, Albert the Great. The distinctiveness of the contribution of Aquinas to this philosophical theme has been studied especially by Aertsen (in a series of works, but especially Aertsen 1996). Our interest in the present context, as will appear, is mainly the bearing of the doctrine of the transcendentals on the semiotic doctrine of ontological relation and on the subordination of the notion of "being as such" or "*ens commune*" to the prior notion of *ens primum cognitum*; though we should also note Doyle's article (1997) showing the decadence of the transcendental theme in Kant, where ontological relation is reduced to logical relations (*entia rationis*), as we will see in chapter 13.

Here is one of those many junctures where we risk getting too far ahead of our story. Yet let it be noted that when an author such as O'Meara (1997: 191, 188) writes of "the idealist distinction of transcendental and categorical" (because after Kant "transcendental" became a term for "the analysis of active human subjectivity"), one has to think that his early years of philosophy at River Forest went for nought, that only his later years of theological study in Europe remain in his mind. Among the merits of his book is the reminder it gives us of just how far medieval studies have to go in recovering the organic unity of the Latin Age and the pivotal role Aquinas played in gestating that unity at a level deeper than confessional allegiance. The distinction in question, contrasting (in more than one way) what characterizes the content of all the categories with the content proper to each category (the content constitutive of the categories, we might say, insofar as being contracts to finite modes) is far older than modern idealism in any form (let alone the late Kantian form). Not only was it hardly idealist in its original formulation (neither on the side of subjectivity as transcendentally relative, nor on the side of objectivity as indifferent to the distinction between physical and objective relations), but no scheme of categories "idealist" in the modern sense can accommodate the ancient sense or medieval development of the several facets of "transcendental" features of being encountered within experience. Indeed, with something like the full story told,

for semiotic), a property convertible or coextensive, in Aquinas' philosophy, [11] with being, truth, goodness, unity, and – perhaps, for this is a disputed question[12] – beauty.

This adjustment necessitated a radical development of the philosophical doctrine of analogy, that is to say, the account of how one and the same word can be used in related but different senses in discourse. This doctrine of analogy pretty much began its philosophical life in the Stagirite's reply to the Parmenidean One doctrine that "being is said in many ways"; but we find the discussion resumed in Aquinas's writings at a much higher level than anything to be found in Aristotle. We will see that precisely for want of an understanding of the foundational implications of Aquinas's doctrine of analogy and his corollary doctrine of the transcendental "properties" of being, most of his late-modern followers, in their battle against Descartes and the idealism in general that became the hallmark of modernity, fell into that trap (native to the way of things) of proceeding "as if a philosophy of

---

the appropriation of the term "transcendental" by Kant appears as something of a temporary aberration in the process of being corrected as postmodernity resumes the semiotic themes so strongly sounded in the closing Latin centuries. "Transcendental" characterizes the involvement of subjectivity beyond itself not only in the human case, and uniquely in the human case only as understanding is unique, which is not by restriction to an Umwelt but by transforming Umwelt into Lebenswelt, which would not be possible, as we will see in chapter 13, were the cognitive transcendence of "active human subjectivity" such as Kant analyzes it to be.

"In the semeiotic theory of the nineties" Deledalle (1992: 293–4) was of the opinion that "there will be no ground, except inside the sign-action, far away from Being and without any relation to Being", that "there will no longer be any substance, but only relations, productive of objects within a system of signs in process." But in speaking thus he shows once again the incapacity of late-modern idealism to realize the distinctive perspective of the doctrine of signs as no longer tied to either side of the old *ens reale / ens rationis* distinction. To be locked into a perspective restricted to the latter branch of this distinction has been the characteristic of modernity, even as near-exclusive preoccupation with the former branch of the distinction characterized ancient and medieval concerns. Whatever may be said of any philosophy "transcendental" in a primarily modern sense or of "the semeiotic theory of the nineties" insofar as it betrays unbroken ties with the epistemological paradigm defining modernity, the semiotic development of the doctrine of signs in the definitively postmodern perspective and paradigm of epistemology proper to itself guarantees that the twenty-first century belongs to a new age of understanding. Begging the reader's indulgence for getting so far here ahead of the story, let me resume the main narrative.

11 The *locus classicus* out in which Aquinas develops his distinctive doctrine of the "transcendental properties of being", the *"transcendentalia"* or simply *"transcendentales"*, is Aquinas c.1256/9: *Quaestiones Disputatae de Veritate*, the body of question one (= q. 1 *corpus*; in Busa ed., vol. 3: 1). See the diagram of this text, in which Aquinas derives the transcendentals of medieval tradition from within being-as-first-known, in chapter 15, p. 648 below. There are further discussions of the transcendentals in various places throughout the writings of Aquinas. In this present book, I shall have occasion to take up more detail of the doctrine of the *transcendentalia* also in chapter 9 below, p. 424n37.

12 "Most scholars hold that the medievals incorporated the beautiful into the list of transcendentals", Aertsen observed in 1991: 145–6; but, against this late-twentieth century consensus, he further observes that "the general picture of thirteenth-century thought about the beautiful is that it is not a new, separate transcendental, but that it is to be discussed within the framework of the good". Cf. Kovach 1974. And far is this from the only disputed question: cf. Wolter 1946: 100, notably.

being could not also be a philosophy of mind",[13] and quite missed the problem of being-as-first-known, as shall appear.

Even when due allowance has been made for the fabrications and exaggerations endemic to hagiography as a literary genre, it is clear from the events of Aquinas's life that from childhood his mind and spirit were fixed on reality such as it could not be contained within the confines of the material universe, however boundless or eternal that universe might be in time and space. It is not only that he spent his life as a friar and a teacher of theology. The transcendence of his vision is the heart of his philosophy.

Aquinas vis-à-vis Aristotle and Lombard

Aristotle had concluded his *Physics* with a demonstration, as he thought, of the existence of a series of pure intelligences, bodiless spirits or, as he said, "separated substances",[14] that were the cause of the circular motion of the heavens. Above this series of Intelligences, however, and responsible even for their motion by the attractive power which evoked their love, hovered the First Mover, the source of "the love that moves the sun and [other] stars", a self-subsistent thinking, and the *final* cause of all that moves, down to the rocks and mud of earth.

Aristotle saw this "First Mover" as a self-absorbed thinker, not even aware, perhaps, of the universe he moved, and certainly not involved with the details of that universe at the level of the generations and corruptions that go on below the sphere of the moon, toward the center of the universe where all its least noble elements are gathered in the making up of the earth and all that is part of the earth. Having been the first thinker of record to raise the notion of cause above the notion of "efficient" or agent cause, perhaps we should not be surprised that Aristotle came to think of the "Prime Mover", the "Mover that moves without being moved", in terms of the highest form of distinguished causality, and in terms of thought rather than of transitive action. Be that as it may, for a certainty he never conceived of the need for the universe to have a cause of its "being as such", a cause of existence. For even the faint suggestion of such a notion, unheard of among the ancient "physicists", the ancient world would have to wait for Plotinus, and his "henology" or "philosophy of the One" beyond being (and "non-being");[15] and, after that, for the medieval Latins who would take up this question – not only after Aristotle and the Neoplatonists, but after, also, the Arabic thinkers who, like the Latins, knew little to nothing of Greek (they had relied on Christians in their midst from Islamic conquests of regions previously under Byzantine control to make the translations into Arabic of the Greek heritage),

---

13 Maritain 1959: 66; 1932: 388: "comme si une philosophie de l'être ne pouvait être aussi une philosophie de l'esprit".
14 Not "separable substances", that is, substantial forms able to exist apart from matter but one time or sometimes embodied in it, but "separated substances", i.e., substances whose nature it is to exist as disembodied forms.
15 See chapter 4 above, p. 128ff.

but who knew much of the thought of Aristotle as well as of Plotinus and the others who succeeded Aristotle in contemplating the matter of a "cause of the cosmos".

Only with these Latins of the "High Middle Ages", Thomas Aquinas in particular, is the relation of the universe to its "Creative Source" decisively clarified according to its most radical philosophical intelligibility: as the making of something where before (to speak through a spatial metaphor) there was nothing at all, *creatio ex nihilo*, "creation out of nothing" – the realization that God in giving to creatures an existence in their own right presupposes nothing whatever on the side of the creature as *that upon which* He acts; so that the creation depends in the whole of its being upon the divine existence which, in turn, depends upon nothing at all. There is God, the infinite perfection of existence, which can be participated in finite ways.

The rendering actual of that participability as extrinsic to God is the act of creation, and the sustaining of such participation is of a piece with creation. But the participability and the participation are simultaneous in and with the creative act. "Participability", thus (despite the grammatical form of the *"-ability"* suffix to the noun-form signifying "able to be participated"[16]), is not a potentiality properly speaking; for it has no existence *in God*, and no existence *outside of God*. "Participability", the "potency", exists only *as actualized*. That is to say, "participability", or "imitability", has "being" *only* as intrinsic to and specificative of an *actual creature*, something that exists "in fact".[17] The world, thus, is really related to God as dependent upon the divine existence, but God has no relation of dependency at all upon the world to which the divine existence gives being according to the intrinsic limitations and specificities which make of the creation a plurality of beings.

For the rest, in the scattered texts that came to be called Aristotle's "metaphysics",[18] but which Aristotle himself thought of merely as, from one point of view, "discourse about god" ("theology"), or, from another point of view, as a discourse aimed at bringing together the loose ends of physics ("first philosophy"), Aristotle was concerned above all with sorting out and pulling together the various notions of physical science which appeared to have a wider application than the world of matter in motion. These notions could be used, perhaps, to flesh out and explore a notion of *being as such*, superior to the division between celestial and terrestrial matter, material substances and separated intelligences, primary and secondary movers. But Aristotle had not thought of the situation fully in that way. He had not thought of it as "metaphysics". He had thought of the matter merely of investigating the foundations and consequences of physics, lead where that may.

---

16 I.e., "participable" (= "able to be participated").

17 This is why contradictory notes cannot constitute an essence: it is not because God is not omnipotent that a square circle cannot exist, but because the pure intelligibility of being cannot be realized in a finite mode which negates itself. It is a limitation neither *in God* nor *outside of God*, except in the creation itself which requires to be intelligible in order to participate in limited ways with the unlimited understanding of the divine life.

18 Recall "Metaphysics by Any Other Name" in chapter 3, p. 82.

Aquinas was half-inclined to pick up where Aristotle had left off, for he saw that Aristotle had mistaken much about this "First Mover". Nor was it merely the Greek Aristotle of ancient Athens that Aquinas contemplated, as we have seen, but the "multicultural Aristotle" that came to the Latins by way of the influence of Plotinus, Augustinian thinkers, and the "gentile" Arabic thinkers of Islam. But first, as a student of the newly nascent theology, before any public thought of Aristotle in any shape or form, Aquinas had to deal with Lombard's *Sentences*.

The Idea of Theology as Sacra Doctrina *to Displace "Christian Philosophy"*
The Latin world had changed a lot since the days of Augustine. Philosophy in the time of Augustine had been regarded not so much as an intellectual discipline as a way of life and, as we saw, Neoplatonism even developed some pretensions to being a 'way of salvation'. In this climate, as thinkers who developed their ideas within the framework of ancient pagan beliefs were pagan philosophers, so those who thought within the framework of the new Christian beliefs were Christian philosophers. To be a *Christian* philosopher meant simply (it is quite a lot, actually) to be a Christian who *thinks about philosophical questions and problems*, just as to be a *pagan* philosopher meant simply to be one who thinks about these same issues but without the added dimension of a specifically Christian framework of beliefs and concerns.

But a Christian *philosopher* is one thing, a Christian *philosophy* quite another; just as a cultural context for philosophical (or scientific) thought is one thing, the philosophy (or science) quite another, whatever the liaisons and reflections there may be that develop historically between the two. But just this, the formal lights distinguishing different activities of human thought and different dimensions within the same activity, is what Aristotle made up for in the approach of Plato and what Augustine could not receive from his Neoplatonist guides in philosophy.[19]What Augustine received instead was "a philosophical spiritualism"[20] from which he went on to an acceptance and unmatched defense of the religious spirituality he found in the gospels and early Christian church. Neither his time, his temperament, nor his tools were oriented to the task of distinguishing for the work of human understanding a relative autonomy respecting religious belief on one side and the role of sense perception on the other.

In fact, for all his considerable genius and originality in the intellectual development of Christian doctrine, Augustine's stance was typical of patristic thought, as Neoplatonism was typical of the Greek religious thought of Byzantium and the pagan thought, Greek and Latin, of Augustine's day. This, then, was the style of thought

---

19 As a result, says Maritain (1959: 300), "to ask St. Augustine for a philosophical system is to claim for philosophy and its proper light something that really comes from the light of the most exalted Christian wisdom, faith and charity." The whole of chapter 7, "Augustinian Wisdom", of this work by Mariain, pp. 291–309, is given over to an examination of the subject matter of the present section.
20 In Gilson's phrase (1960: 232).

inevitably embodied in the assemblage of writings made by Peter Lombard under the title of *Sentences*, despite the framework of Aristotelian logical thinking within which these early Christian authors were summarized, organized, and interpreted. It is quite a coincidence of history that, in the Latin Age, Lombard's anthology of patristic thought and Aristotle's "system of the sciences", highly refined and developed through commentaries both of ancient Greek and more recent Arabic origin, became available together at just the moment when, especially at Bologna and Paris,[21] what we have come to call universities were also forming. And at just this time too a young genius sallied forth from the Aquino castle of Roccasecca to join the intellectual fray.

Lombard's *Sentences* were barely a century old when Aquinas studied them and was compelled, in order to win his academic spurs, to write upon them a thorough *Commentary*. This he did well and truly enough, but the result was something unusual. By the result here I do not mean the substantial commentary on the sentences that he produced. I mean the conclusion Aquinas reached that the *Sentences* were not suitable for the purpose to which they had been put in the universities, namely, that of providing beginning students with an acquaintance with theology.

Now what could Aquinas have had in mind? Today, roughly since the 1960s, we distinguish *religious studies* from *theology*, and students today know only of departments of religious studies, which may or may not include formal courses in theology. That distinction did not exist in Aquinas's day. Indeed, the new disciplinary notion then was precisely that of theology, a notion to whose final form Aquinas did so much to contribute.

Theology for Aquinas was the use of human reason in the service of the mysteries of faith, and the mysteries of faith all go back to God. Scripture and tradition are materials for theologians to use, because they convey the mysteries to us; but it is up to the theologian to give these materials a rationalized form, using indeed the autonomously valid intellectual tools of logic and philosophical reason (the proper achievements of human understanding in its own sphere, let us say), while centering their use no longer on human experience as such but on how the God to whom all faith is directed through revelation in its twofold form of sacred scripture and Christian tradition can be said to permeate that experience. That God, the Christian God, became incarnate in the person of Jesus, to be sure, and it is only through the Savior that all things are able in fact to return to that Source from which they have issued. But the structure or framework for the proper study of theology, the use of reason in the service of understanding divine things, is the going forth of the universe from God in creation and the return of the universe to God through the Redemption.[22]

---

21 See Haskins 1957.

22 Torrell 1996: 43 glosses this point with the observation that, for St Thomas, the profound reason
    for this plan lies in the idea that the act of creation mirrors externally the interior procession of the
    divine persons: "If we do not remember the biblical affirmation of God as the Alpha and Omega of

Moreover, this structure has to be formally unified in order to meet the requirements of fully thematic or *systematic* knowledge (and indeed the "theology" formulated by St Thomas is sometimes termed "systematic theology" in contrast to "patristic theology" or "biblical theology"; but, in the mind of St Thomas, such uses of the term theology would have been metaphorical at best, at worst equivocal). For what was new in the conception of St Thomas was the idea of the possibility of a new *scientia* (a new *doctrina*, as we might rather say[23]) beyond the specific types of knowledge that can be established by human reason functioning in its own order as the understanding of a rational animal dealing with the structure and causes of the surrounding environment and of our own physical being as organisms endowed with awareness and feelings. St Thomas was not one of those who, like Augustine or Anselm, thought that it was sufficient to refer the basis of our reasoning to the articles of Christian faith and writings of a sacred scripture. To the contrary, he recognized with Aristotle the possibility of a whole structure of rational knowledge divided into

---

all that is visible and invisible, this plan may seem only a rather flat assertion. We do not perceive all its depth until we grasp the organizing *ratio* that gives it its intelligibility. Thomas sees the *ratio* in the fact that the creation – the emergence of creatures from God, the first principle – finds its explanation in the fact that even in God there is an 'emergence of the Principle', which is the procession of the Word from the Father. The divine efficacy that works in the creation is thus related to the generation of the Word, just as the formal cause of the grace that will permit creatures to return to God is linked to the spiration of the Holy Spirit. More precisely and fully, we might therefore say that the divine missions *ad extra* are explained according to the order of the processions of the divine persons *ad intra*." Torrell further notes that "in this way of conceiving things, the entire universe of created beings, spiritual and material, thus appears animated by a deep dynamism that" – whence, he concludes (in a flight of thinking more wishful than deductive) – "when the time came, would without difficulty permit the integration of historical becoming into theological reflections."

23 The medievals, following Aristotle, used the terms "doctrina" and "scientia" interchangeably to designate the disciplined use of reason to develop systematically a formally unified knowledge of some subject matter. The rationale of such a systematic development was precisely the formal aspect under which the subject matter in question was thematically unified. So, for example, the study of the human being as "a physiological system" would give rise to one body of knowledge, the study of the same subject matter as "capable of free acts" would give rise to another, the study of the same subject matter again "as influenced by emotion" another, and so on. In medieval terms, each of these studies would have the same "material object", but each would attain that object and unify the investigation of that object under a different formality, and it is this formality which gives rise and unity to different "sciences", that is, prospective bodies of knowledge, by providing, even within one and the same material object, distinct "formal objects". Later on, we will see, in the passage from the Latin Age to modern philosophy, it became necessary to distinguish between "science" in the modern sense of a body of knowledge whose various propositions or theses refer directly to what can be subjected to falsification by empirical means and "science" in the philosophical sense of a body of knowledge whose various propositions or theses refer directly to the understanding as able to attain to a knowledge of being which is not reducible to sense perception but depends for its verification within experience upon intelligible necessities analytically isolated within a consistent network of discourse. What is important to note at this juncture is that, when St Thomas refers to a "science", he is doing so in the Aristotelian sense of a formally unified and systematically developed investigation, which sense is prior to and compatible with the modern distinction between "science" (*scientia*) and philosophy or theology (*doctrina*), and the distinction of all three from the "dogma" of proclamations primarily authoritative.

various sciences according to the subject matter and manner of study which was perfectly valid in its own right and the conclusions of which could not be gainsaid by or dictated by religious belief and authority. The idea of a "Christian philosophy", so strong in the Fathers of the Church and after them even down to the present day, may yet be said to have formally died in the writings of Aquinas with his distinction of "sacred doctrine", that is, theology (*sacra doctrina* or *theologia*), from every branch and type of experimental, mathematical, and philosophical science, even if only to be replaced by something finer.[24] And never forget that, for Aquinas, reason, human understanding, is free only in the line of truth; so that, if there can be confessional abuses imposed on reason, indeed, this does not mean that reason is "free" to abuse confessions of faith in its turn:[25] "For just as matters of religious belief cannot be demonstratively proven, so too opinions contrary to religious belief cannot be demonstratively shown to be false, but they can be shown to be unnecessary"; whence their categorical assertion "belongs not to philosophy but to an abuse of philosophy".

---

24 Among the 20th-century writers who have tried to defend the idea of "Christian philosophy", only Maritain seems to have awakened in the end fully to the consequences of what St Thomas wrote as the opening question with 10 articles for his *Summa theologiae*. His witness is the more valuable because, of all those propounding the cause of a "Christian philosophy", from 1931 onward (see Maritain 1932a, 1935: esp. ch. 2; also 1938) he was recognized on all hands as the most competent spokesman. Yet the words on the subject from his last year of life and last book (Maritain 1973: 507) were these: "Ici une petite parenthèse: je viens d'employer le mot 'mystique naturelle', et j'en ai usé bien souvent, parce que, lorsqu'on est pressé par la recherche, on se sert des mots qu'on a sous la main. Mais si digne d'attention que soit la chose, le mot en question ne vaut rien. Je me suis creusé la tête pour en trouver un meilleur; ce que je voudrais proposer, c'est 'la mystique du regard du soi' ou, plus brièvement, 'la mystique du miroir', par opposition à 'la mystique de l'union d'amour à Dieu' ou 'la mystique du feu'. Le même problème se pose avec le mot 'philosophie chrétienne', que j'ai aussi employé bien souvent, et qui ne vaut rien non plus; ce que je propose à la place, c'est 'la philosophie comme plénièrement telle' ou 'la philosophie allant de l'avant', par opposition à 'la philosophie comme simplement telle' ou 'la philosophie trébuchante'."

    And his closest intellectual associate of his final years, Heinz R. Schmitz, in the "Préface" he wrote for this volume under the *nom de plume* of Ernst R. Korn (ibid., xvii), considered the point salient enough to mark it with a paragraph of his own, which I cite in part: "Si aujourd'hui il propose de la désigner par un autre mot, c'est d'abord parce que le nom de philosophie chrétienne évoque trop l'idée d'une philosophie non pas libre, mais liée par on ne sait quelles convenances d'ordre confessionnel. Il y a cependant une raison plus profonde pour changer le vocabulaire sur ce point. C'est que le terme de 'philosophie chrétienne' risque de masquer aux yeux de notre esprit que nous avons affaire ici, non plus à la philosophie parvenue à sa pleine maturité, à la *philosophie comme plénièrement telle*. Dans le fond, ce qui est en jeu ici est bien plus qu'un changement de vocabulaire."

    We can only wonder what comment would be made on the new proposal by Bréhier first of all, and secondly by Gilson.

25 Aquinas c.1257/8: *Super Boetium De Trinitate*, q. 2, art. 3c (Busa 4, p. 525): "si quid autem in dictis philosophorum invenitur contrarium fidei, hoc non est philosophia, sed magis philosophiae abusus ex defectu rationis, et ideo possibile est ex principiis philosophiae huiusmodi errorem refellere vel ostendendo omnino esse impossibile vel ostendendo non esse necessarium. sicut enim ea quae sunt fidei non possunt demonstrative probari, ita quaedam contraria eis non possunt demonstrative ostendi esse falsa, sed potest ostendi non necessaria."

What would distinguish "sacred doctrine" from both philosophical doctrine and from science in the modern sense was precisely the formal rationale or light under which it attained its object, namely, the light of faith accepting a divine revelation. Such a science was necessary, Thomas posited, because the final destiny of the human being with God after death is something known only by divine revelation, not by any natural investigation or means. Such a science was possible, he posited, because he accepted that we do in fact have a revelation from and by God of this eternal destiny of the individual human being. And such a science was indeed a science, that is to say, a prospectively unified and thematic area of investigation, because it studied all things under the aspect of something "revealed or able to be revealed" to human understanding by God.[26]

Moreover, this new science of theology is not only distinct from the philosophical and experimental sciences – all *doctrina humana*, as we might say – for the very same reason that these various sciences are distinct from one another (their formal objects, as we have seen[27]), but it is also superior to them for a twofold reason. Theology takes its principles not only from logic and experience but also and primarily from the word of God; and theology is not confined to being either speculative (pertaining to the knowledge of being as it exists independently of human thought and action), as is the case with physics, mathematics, or metaphysics, or practical (pertaining to the knowledge of being as it exists dependently upon human thought and action), as is the case with art and ethics, but extends itself to both orders of being as creatures of God.[28] Yet just as speculative knowledge alone is distinctively human knowledge and this knowledge "becomes practical" by being applied to things prospectively under human control, so theology is more speculative than it is practical because it extends first to God as revealed and then to the things revealed by God about the creation. Whence, just as speculative knowledge is superior to practical knowledge in the philosophical and scientific order, so theology is superior to speculative and practical knowledge alike in the order of philosophy and science. So is the

---

26 Aquinas, *Summa theologiae* I.1.4c: "Quia igitur sacra doctrina considerat aliqua secundum quod sunt divinitus revelata, secundum quod dictum est art. 3, omnia quaecumque sunt divinitus revelabilia, communicant in una ratione formali objecti huius scientiae" ("Because, therefore, theology considers materials according as they are divinely revealed, as was said in the preceding article, anything whatever that can be divinely revealed shares in the single formal rationale of the object of this science").

27 "Diversa ratio cognoscibilis diversitatem scientiarum inducit", as St Thomas put it himself at the opening of his *Summa theologiae* (I.1.1c: "a diverse rationale of knowability brings about a diversity of systematized human knowledge").

28 Ibid. I.1.4c: "licet in scientiis philosophicis alia sunt speculativa, et alia practica, sacra tamen doctrina comprehendit utramque; sicut et Deus eadem scientia se cognoscit, et ea quae facit" ("although human disciplines of knowledge are either speculative or practical, yet theology embraces both the speculative and the practical; just as God knows by one and the same knowledge himself and the things which he makes"). Similarly, as we will eventually see (in chapters 9 and 13 below), the doctrine of signs is not restricted to the speculative or the practical order but extends to both, yet for a very different reason: not because it draws on a light superior to human understanding but because it provides the means whereby speculative and practical understanding alike is achieved.

groundwork laid for the notion of theology as "queen of the sciences", and the notion of philosophy as "handmaid of theology" ratified.[29]

But – and this is the decisive point – what is new about the idea of theology in the writings of Aquinas is the fact that religious thinking within confessional confines is sharply distinguished from the philosophical use as such of reason which is not confessional; and theology is at the same time itself elevated to a doctrinal or "scientific" status within those same confines by the application to it of the Aristotelian idea of *scientia* as the thematically unified and systematically developed knowledge of a given subject matter critically based on the pertinent principles and causes. A systematic discourse about God as revealed – *theos* + *logos*: such was what Aquinas conceived theology to be:[30] "For all things are treated in sacred doctrine under the rationale of God, either because the things considered belong to God himself, or because they are ordered to God as beginning or end."

This framework is not at all well represented in the four books of patristic opinions assembled by Peter Lombard (anymore than it is in the patristic writings themselves or in the collection of books of the Bible). To be sure, all the elements and pieces are there, but scattered and disjointed over a thousand pages, with many repetitions, detours, and backtracks thrown in the student's way. Aquinas thought that the *Sentences* needed done to them what Louis Napoleon III (1808–73) thought the boulevards of Paris needed: a widening and straightening so one could get where one wanted to go.[31] The *Summa theologiae* of Thomas Aquinas is that "widening and straightening" of the intellectual boulevards of Christian thought for which the

---

29 This expression, "philosophy is the handmaid to theology" (*"philosophia sit ancilla theologiae"*), well expresses St Thomas's idea of the use theology must make of the principles of logic, philosophy, and science in order to give a rational structure to the understanding of the content of revelation: "theology uses such principles as subordinate and ancillary instruments" ("utitur eis tanquam inferioribus et ancillis").

30 *Summa theologiae* I.1.7c: "Omnia autem pertractantur in sacra doctrina sub ratione Dei; vel quia sunt ipse Deus; vel quia habent ordinem ad Deum."

31 And, of course, in the case of Paris, get a clear cannon-shot off against unwelcome visitors. Buckley strongly suggests (1987: 43) that something of this nature followed upon the eventual success of Thomas's plan: "Lombard had held medieval theology together, presenting a common series of texts upon which vastly different theological structures could be built. The *Sentences* gave all the theologians of the Middle Ages, irrespective of the color of their convictions, a common language and a common tradition within which the conflicting theologies of Duns Scotus, William of Ockham, Durandus of St. Pourçain, and Thomas Aquinas could contact and speak intelligibly with one another. The *Sentences* provided for the Middle Ages what Catholic theology has never been able to regain: a focus or a unity precisely within dispersion, a common series of theological statements, a vocabulary and a common intellectual tradition which allowed substantial disagreements, and an irreducible pluralism with a shared culture. ... [O]pting for the work of Aquinas over the Lombard's ordered assemblage of texts from the Fathers of the Church which were the common possession of all Christians", Buckley argues, introduced a "factional schism within Catholic theology" that would parallel "the sectarian divisions which were increasingly polarizing Christianity" through the various Protestant reforms of the 16th century and after.

This is an interesting observation, and perhaps helps to understand the turn from "theology departments" to "religious studies" departments with the late-20th-century return to a more ecumenical spirit among Christian denominations.

Sentences of Peter Lombard demonstrated the need. The *Summa theologiae* was conceived and executed in Aquinas's mature mind as the introductory textbook of theology to replace the *Sentences*.

Well, he died before he was quite finished. Diligent disciples completed the *Summa* from his notes, in what is called the "Supplementum" or posthumous completion of the third and final part of the work; but who knows how Aquinas himself would have adjusted and integrated the notes and manuscripts used by his students in forming this "supplement" that appears to this day as the conclusion of his master work? After his death, early enthusiasts for his plan of theology actually tried to use the *Summa theologiae* in place of the officially mandated *Sentences*, but the authorities of the time would not tolerate the effort.[32] Not until the sixteenth century would the work begin to be used as Thomas had planned, beginning at least with Cajetan's 1497–9 lectures at Pavia. The cardinal Thomas de Vio Cajetan had sufficient ecclesiastical and academic stature that when he replaced the *Sentences* with the *Summa* there was no one to gainsay him. After Cajetan in Italy, professors in Catholic universities elsewhere, especially in the Iberian peninsula, followed suit; and this move contributed greatly to the strong identification of Aquinas with "Catholic" as opposed to "Protestant" thought over the centuries since, notwithstanding the fact that Thomas himself, like Augustine before him who escaped such a partisan fate, lived and wrote at a time when the terms "Catholic" and "Christian" were wholly synonymous, before the adversative sense that came to attach to "Catholic" in opposition to "Protestant" in the wake of Luther.

Cosmology in Aquinas
The whole *Summa*[33] was constructed on the image of an "eternal return", a cyclical cosmos. Of course, for the Latins, the "cycle" was the Christian one of innocence,

---

32 From the *Acts* of the Provincial Chapter of the Roman Dominican Province held in Perugia in 1308 (Kaeppeli and Dondaine eds 1941: 169): "Item volumus et ordinanums firmiter observari quod lectores et bacellarii legant de Sententiis et non de summa Thome".

33 Besides the *Summa theologiae*, Aquinas had also written, i.1259/65, a second huge *Summa contra gentiles*. Oddly, the intention of this work has become subject to extensive debate (Torrell 1996: 104–7). The once common, clean, and simple story that the work was intended to aid missionaries to Spain in convincing Moslems of the truth of the Catholic faith turns out to be a legend dating only from about the 16th century. Why not simply see the work as a case of Thomas making for himself and any reader interested his first review of the whole horizon of intellectual controversies that appeared to one of his time professing the Christian faith? He might well have done this, given the place of the work in the chronology of his literary career, as preparatory to the massive task he would undertake shortly, namely, that of commenting on nearly whole of the philosophical *corpus* of Aristotle in order to show its consonance (and the consonance of the work of human understanding in general, even at its own level of a doctrinal development independent of confessional allegiance) with the confessional allegiance of a Christian as such.

Both works, in any event, both *Summae*, are masterpieces, but the *Summa theologiae* has the added virtue of being the one writing in which Aquinas most maturely spoke his own mind, and it has become customary, when referring to "the *Summa*" of Aquinas without qualification, invariably to mean the *Summa theologiae* unless context makes very plain otherwise; and normally the context to the contrary is explicitly supplied by the custom of always referring to the *Summa contra gentiles*

fall, and return through redemption; but underlying this was the ancient secular image of a cyclical cosmos such as Aristotle had envisaged, and which was the cosmological image for a long time to come. At the same time, no one had better than Aquinas distanced himself from the dogmatic conclusions others had allowed themselves to fall into by taking that cosmological image of an unchanging cycle of natural developments for certain fact. In the *Summa* itself, both these points – the image of the cosmos as cyclical, and the assertion that the details of that image are more of the nature of hypothesis than fact – appear fairly early, in a passage where Aquinas is talking not at all about faith but about the use of human understanding vis-à-vis natural phenomena sometimes to develop hypotheses about the reasons for those phenomena and sometimes actually to explain natural phenomena through natural causes:[34]

> In seeking to provide an explanation for some datum, reason can be employed in either of two ways.
>
> First, it can be employed so as to establish sufficiently the reasons for the fact, as in natural philosophy there seem to be reasons sufficient for demonstrating that the movement of the heavens is of a uniform velocity.
>
> But reason can also be employed in another fashion, which does not establish reasons for the fact, but which shows instead that explanatory hypotheses proposed are congruous with the fact to be understood, as illustrated in astronomy, where the theory

by its full name or by the contraction *Contra gentes*. I follow these customs here. As the Mexicans almost always mean "Mexico City" when they say "Mexico" without qualification, and not the *state* of Mexico within the *country* of Mexico, so when the Thomists say "the *Summa* of St Thomas" they almost always mean the *Summa theologiae* and not the *Summa contra gentiles*.

34 I. 32. 1. ad 2 – references to the *Summa* are always by part, indicated by Roman numerals as I, II, or III for the *Prima pars*, the *Secunda pars*, and the *Tertia pars*, respectively. Part II of the *Summa* has a major subdivision, indicated as I-II (for *Prima pars Secundae partis*, sometimes shortened to *Prima Secundae*) or II-II (for *Secunda pars Secundae partis*, or *Secunda Secundae*). A reference to any of these parts is then further specified by arabic numerals after the Roman numeral. The first arabic numeral indicates a Question number within the Part. A second arabic numeral indicates an Article number within the Question. The article reference, if further specified, will be: either to the *body* of the article, indicated by a small letter "c" (for *corpus*, "body"); or to an *objection* which precedes the body of the article, sometimes preceded by the abbreviation "obj." (for "objection" – there are about 10,000 of these over the course of the whole work); or to a *reply to an objection*, indicated by the expression "ad" (from the Latin *ad*, "toward" or "reply to", an answer directed toward the specific objection numbered). Within each article, the statement of objections preceding the body of the article concludes with a brief "proof text" from Scripture or the Fathers, with its source clearly indicated. (This so-called "proof text", however, does not merely counter or balance the negative tone of the objections. It functions heuristically to suggest to the thoughtful reader an anticipation of the subtleties that Aquinas will deem necessary to reach a truer view of the matter under discussion.) Whence the customary reference form for citing the *Summa*: PART, QUESTION, ARTICLE, SUBDIVISIONS OF ARTICLE (OBJECTIONS, BODY, REPLIES).

Within this form, O'Meara usefully notes (1997: 65), the Articles "are the basic investigative unit of the work", and there are well over 4,000 of these investigative forays undertaken within the organizing framework of the 611 "Questions" posed over the threee "Parts".

of eccentrics and epicycles is proposed on the ground that the sensible appearances of the heavenly movements can thereby be saved, that is, accounted for.[35]

This latter type of explanation cannot suffice to *prove* anything,[36] however, for it may well be the case that these appearances could be equally well saved within the framework of other theories.[37]

The example in the second paragraph of this text was a poor choice on Aquinas's part, no doubt, as the reason for the apparent "uniform velocity" of the heavens is the rotation of the earth on its axis, a cause of which the medievals were ignorant; and the cause which they assigned, the relatively greater perfection of the celestial bodies such that they could change in no way except by uniform rotation in place, proved to be a fiction. But this poor choice of an example to illustrate the possibility of reason assigning a proper cause for a given phenomenon should not be allowed to take away from the actual point of which there were, even in medieval times, better and indeed definite examples. This is the point that it *is* sometimes possible to assign the proper cause for a natural phenomenon. It would have been better had Aquinas made this point using an example that time has not discredited, such as Aristotle's or Gregory of Nyssa's true and proper explanation of why eclipses happen, namely, as a result of the casting of a shadow by an intervening body. More recent examples would be Salk's vaccine against polio, or the dramatic series of applications of human intelligence which enabled the Apollo 13 crew to turn its mission from complete to only partial failure.

Yet even the poor choice of example makes yet another point: in Aquinas the physical image of Aristotle's universe is preserved, even though he quite well sees it for what it is, as the rest of the cited text makes clear (and even in citing the example of uniform motion as supposed to have been properly explained he says no more than that this *seems* to be an example of the point, not categorically that it *is* an example; yet there is no getting around the fact that an example actually categorical would have been preferable).

This last point of the text of Aquinas, that the cosmological image of the universe that we have inherited from Aristotle and his followers is to be kept distinct in principle from features of natural process for which proper causes have been identified and assigned, Aquinas had also made earlier, and, be it said, more efficaciously, in his *Commentary* on Aristotle's work *On the Heavens*. There, commenting in the

---

35 Supposing these factors, then the heavens would move as they in fact do. If X, then Y; but Y, therefore possibly X: if the "possibly" is removed, we commit the logical fallacy of "affirming the consequent". This fallacy is avoided only when the antecedent is the *only possible* reason for the consequent, or when the consequent is qualified as by "possibly" or "therefore there are grounds for holding that the antecedent might be the case", etc.
36 Except mayhap the cleverness of the reasoner. It is the problem of Peircean abduction.
37 As first Copernicus (c.1514, 1543), then Galileo (1610, 1613, 1623, esp. 1632, 1638), then Newton (1687), later Einstein (c.1920), to be followed by yet unknown others, amply demonstrate.

second book on the attempts by Eudoxus and others to account for the appearance
of occasional shifts in the regularity of observed planetary movements, he said
unmistakably:[38]

> The suppositions proposed by none of these men are necessarily true. For although
> by granting such suppositions the appearances would indeed be saved, it is still not
> necessary to say that they are true suppositions, because it is possible that the ap-
> pearances could be saved with respect to the stars and planets according to some other
> explanatory scheme not yet conceived of by men. Notwithstanding, Aristotle employed
> suppositions of this sort as though they were true so far as the character of the celestial
> motions is concerned.[39]

Shortly before his death Aquinas took ill and ceased to write. Hagiography reports
that he was granted a vision, in the light of which he is reported to have said that his
work now appeared to him "as so much straw". I have often wondered if the vision
was not a revelation that the universe was not a cyclical but an evolutionary one, thus
wrecking the image on which the plan of the work had been based; but of course
the speculation is gratuitous. (And even an evolutionary view can be reconciled
with the plan of the *Summa* if we adopt the suggestion of O'Meara[40] to "best
imagine the course of the *ST* not as a circular return but as upward spiral", consistent
with the Neoplatonic conceptions imbibed in medieval thought from Augustine and
Pseudo-Dionysius.) What is certain is that Aquinas stopped writing and shortly died.
What is also certain is that Aquinas had planned that his work supplant the *Sentences*
as the basic introductory text in theology, and that this dream was never realized
till well after Aquinas had left this earthly scene. As we noted, not till the dawn of
the sixteenth century was the *Summa* actually used in a classroom, by Thomas de
Vio Cajetan, as Aquinas had planned.

The Subject of Theology and the Existence of God; the "Metaphysics of Esse*"*
Now the very first question Aquinas poses as the starting point for theology is the
question of what is its subject matter. And he answers God, and all else as related
to God as beginning and end. The second question he asks is whether this subject
matter is real or imaginary, that is to say, does God really exist? There is only

---

38 Aquinas c.1272/3: *In libros de coelo et mundo*, book II, lectio 17, n. 451 (Busa 4, p. 36):
   "illorum tamen suppositiones quas adinvenerunt, non est necessarium esse veras: licet enim talibus
   suppositionibus factis, apparentia salvarentur, non tamen opoetet dicere has suppositiones esse veras;
   quia forte secundum aliquem alium modum, nondum ab hominibus comprehensum, apparentias
   circa stellas salvantur. aristoteles tamen utitur huiusmodi suppositionibus quantum ad qualitatem
   motuum, tanquam veris." For a fuller context of discussion of these texts, see Deely 1965/6, 1969;
   and Deely and Nogar 1973.
39 And so in a few centuries would the ecclesiastical judges in the case of Galileo.
40 O'Meara 1997: 57–8; cf. also 75: "although he [Aquinas] had little inkling of a world shot through
   with development and evolution, ... his understanding of causality would have led him to appreciate
   ... an independent world of finite beings intricately emerging in time ...".

one procedure of reasoning by which we can hope to arrive at an answer to this question, Aquinas says. This is the procedure of reasoning from what we experience to what must be the case for that experience to be as it is. But it will not do to tell "a likely story". The kind of reasoning which merely proposes hypotheses to "save the appearances" will not do here; for, as we saw, this kind of reasoning as such never proves anything but merely provides, at best, fruitful hypotheses as a basis for further research. The question here is one we want to answer with a "yes" or a "no", not with a "probably" somewhere between. But for any given effect there is always a proper cause – that is, given an effect, there is always a cause prior to it on which its immediate condition of being depends.[41]

The question of whether God exists, therefore, so far as it is a reasonable question, comes down to this. Are there any phenomena in our experience which could not be as they are unless God exists?

Be careful to understand the question strictly. We are not asking here about amazing phenomena or alleged miracles, mystical experience or anything of the like. The question concerns ordinary phenomena, ones that we can thoroughly analyze to the point of seeing intellectually the variables involved, so that when we say "this could not be unless", we are expressing an *intelligible necessity* and not mere rhetorical ignorance, an ideological preference, or a determined wish. "Intelligible necessity" is the operative qualification: we are looking for a situation that is intelligible *not just on an hypothesis*. We seek, rather, a situation, if such there be, that, viewed under the proper analysis, immediately and directly reveals *as its only alternative* the existence of God.

Quinque Viae: *The Reasoning of the "Five Ways"*

Aquinas considers that there are several features of our experience of the world which can so be analyzed as to reveal to us the intelligible necessity of affirming that God exists. He enumerates five such: the phenomena of motion, agency, possibility and necessity, grades of perfection, and cosmic order. It would not appear that Aquinas considers this an exhaustive list, but merely an illustrative one. From the items on this list, at least, he tells us, it is possible to construct an analysis which leads us from what we certainly experience to an intellectually certain affirmation of the existence of God as the basis for or necessarily involved in that experience. He calls this a demonstration *that* something is the case ("demonstratio *quia*"). From effects we reason to the cause. Other times we go from causes to effects ("demonstratio *propter quid*"). But for this procedure of *propter quid* reasoning the cause has to be something that is on our own level of being, something finite, something bodily.

---

41 For example, when an airliner crashes, the federal agency responsible for air-traffic safety immediately launches an investigation. They do not try first to determine *whether* there was a cause for the crash, and if so, what; they proceed directly to try to find out *what* was the cause, full well knowing that there is always a cause for everything that occurs.

ad p^m q^o dd. q. intellualit~ pcede~ n attribut~ sci^e
die q. ipa n rocinet~ f~ qa predcdo d'
pncipijs ad gclõef. f~ qa ei^9 gfcdr̃õ
rõcinacio e intelluali gsid'rõu ppicissĩa

5 z gclõef ei^9 pncipijs. ad f dd. q dj e
   f õe; intellõm c^latũ q̃m ad gpe'foe. n au
   f intellõm ir̃latũ cu ipe scipm intelligẽ—
   do gpedat. e u'o f õe; intellõm
   uiatoris q̃m ad gg^oe; q^a gg^ofcut~ qd e

10 n au q̃m ad gg^oe; q^a gg^ofcut~ õn e. a beatis
   au gg^ofcut~ z̃ qd e. qa uidẽt ei^9 eeã;.
   z t̃n fcã die n e folu d'fba d̃o. f~ z
   d' alijf q̃ intellõm huãn e f fcat uie
   n excedẽt q̃m ad qd e gg^ofcedũ d'eif.

15 ad tt̃iũ dd. q fcit~ f dcm e huãa gsid—
   rõ q̃m ad fui t̃nũ q^odãm^o ptigẽt. ad
   ãglicã gg^oe;. n f f eq^altatẽ f~
   f z̃dã affeloe;. un dco. dĩ: uz. c. d' di.
   no. q aũe mlõrũ guolutõe ad un

20 f digẽ habite intellũb; eq^alib; ãglif
   z q̃m aũab; e p̃u z pol̃. ad quat̃ũ dd.
   q gg^o e fid; maxi^e ptom; ad intellõm n e~
   ea rõif ineftigõe ao accipem^9.
   f~ fciplici accep^e intellf tenem^9. dicim~

25 aũ ea n intellig^e i q̃m ir̃tllf eor plenari—
   ã gg^oe; n l̃t. q qd nobif i p̃mũ
   repm^tit~.

Cod. autogr. f. 101va 1—27 = Q. 6 a. 1 q. 3 ad 1—4

Handwritten passage from Thomas Aquinas
c.1257/8: Q. 6, art. 1, q. 3, ad 1–4
(Busa 4, p. 537)

Transcription of passage

Ad primum ergo dicendum quod intellec-
tualiter precedere non attribuitur scientiae divinae, quasi ipsa non ratiocinetur procedendo de
principiis ad conclusiones, sed quia eius ratioci-
natio est intellectuali consideratione propin-
quissima et conclusiones eius principiis.

Ad secundum dicendum quod deus est
supra omnem intellectum creatum quantum ad
comprehensionem, non autem supra intellectum
increatum, cum ipse se ipsum intelligendo com-
prehendat. Est vero supra omnem intellectum
viatoris quantum ad cognitionem, qua cognoscitur quid est, non quantum ad cognitionem, qua
cognoscitur an est. A beatis autem cognoscitur
etiam quid est, quia vident eius essentiam. Et
tamen scientia divina non est solum de deo, sed
de aliis quae intellectum humanum etiam
secundum statum viae non excedunt quantum
ad quid est cognoscendum de eis.

Ad tertium dicendum quod, sicut supra
dictum est, humana consideratio quantum ad
sui terminum quodammodo pertingit ad angel-
icam cognitionem, non secundum aequalitatem,
sed secundum quandam assimilationem. Unde
Dionysius dicit 7 c. De divinis nominibus quod
'animae multorum convolutione ad unum sunt
dignae habitae intellectibus aequalibus angelis,
in quantum animabus est proprium et possibile'.

Ad quartum dicendum quod cognitio etiam
fidei maxime pertinet ad intellectum. Non enim
ea rationis investigatione accipimus, sed simpli-
ci acceptione intellectus tenemus. Dicimur autem ea non intelligere, in quantum intellectus
eorum plenariam cognitionem non habet; quod
quidem nobis in praemium repromittitur.

The reply to the first argument is that systematic knowledge of divine things is said to
develop intellectually not in the sense that it
proceeds by reasoning from principles to conclusions, but in the sense that what the process
of reasoning by which it advances is closest to
is intellectual consideration and [the drawing
of] conclusions from its principles.

To the second argument the response is that
God is above every created mind as regards
comprehension, but not beyond uncreated understanding, since God comprehends himself by
understanding. He is beyond all understanding
in this life as regards a knowledge by which is
known what He is, yet not as regards a knowledge that He is. Yet the blessed in heaven know
also what He is, because they see His essence.
And yet divine science is not only about God,
but also about other things which do not surpass
human understanding as regards what is known
of them even in this life.

To the third argument I answer that, as was
said above, the terminus of human awareness
pertains in a certain way to the awareness of angels, not according to an equality, but according
to a certain assimilation. Whence Dionysius
says in chapter seven of his work *On the Divine
Names* that "souls by a turning of many things
to one achieve an intellectual understanding
equal to that of angels insofar as this is proper
and possible for souls".

The answer to the fourth argument is that
even knowledge by faith pertains in the highest
way to understanding. For we do not accept that
knowledge from investigation by reason but we
hold it by a simple acceptance of understanding.
Yet we are said not to understand the truths of
faith inasmuch as the understanding does not
have an exhaustive awareness of them; which is
indeed the further reward promised to us.

Passage as it appears in Decker ed. 1965:
212/26–213/20

Translation of passage

Aquinas proceeds to fashion his famous "five ways" (the *quinque viae*) of show-ing *that* God exists. These are the most famous of the "cosmological arguments" for the existence of God, and Aquinas thinks that, in contrast to any possible form of the "ontological argument",[42] they have the advantage of actually proving what they claim to prove.

Since the procedure of successfully reasoning to the affirmation that "God exists" as a true conclusion must be in every case the same, perhaps it will be enough, for present purposes, to follow this reasoning along what Aquinas describes as the *prima et manifestior via*, "the first and more manifest way". The more manifest way will be to begin a thematic reflection from whatever phenomenon of experience and observation so pervades our consciousness that we know of no exception to it. We want to begin with a phenomenon that extends as far as our awareness of the sensible universe extends. The phenomenon in our experience that best fits this requirement is the experience of motion, of objects in motion. And motion, as the most obvious example of change in general, remember, was first defined by Aristotle in the definition that Aquinas accepts:[43] motion is the act of a being in potency insofar as it is in potency, technically; or, somewhat more simply (but not over simply), motion is a transition from a state of potentiality to an actual condition, from a potential to an actual situation.

The phenomenon of movement in space is one phenomenon in our awareness of the universe, one "transition from potency to act", that is all-pervasive. Compara-tively speaking, the other items on the list of possible points of departure for the discursive development of probative arguments presuppose some structure in our experience, presuppose an Umwelt already formed. But motion we experience from the first as that through which an Umwelt is formable in the first place. It provides the materials out of which an Umwelt is fashioned, and not merely a phenomenon that we experience from within an Umwelt, which is the case with each of the other four items on our fivefold list of prospective points of departure.

There would have been in the mind of Aquinas another consideration for seeing the primacy of motion in constructing a *quia* reasoning to the existence of God: motion transcends the distinction between celestial and terrestrial matter.[44] The heavens and the earth are alike in manifesting local motions. Thus, throughout the entire universe, it can be said that whatever part of a thing changes is made to change by some other agency, either by another part of itself or by something external to itself. For one and the same thing in one and the same respect cannot be at one and the same time agent and patient.

---

42 Recall our remarks on the historical origins of this terminology (chapter 6, pp. 234 & 241, esp. n79), and on the singular ineptness of the designation "ontological argument": but one has to choose one's fights, and on this one, principally but not exclusively verbal, I here pass. The interested reader may find in Collins (1954: 501ff.) a cogent discussion of the objectionableness of the terminology from Kant that has nonetheless become part of the heritage of modern philosophy.

43 See chapter 3 above, p. 63.

44 See chapter 3, p. 79.

A "moved mover" is the first term that needs to be taken along the way. We need to understand what is meant by a "moved mover". A moved mover is a subject of motion which, while causing motion in something else, requires yet something else again to explain its own motion; a moved mover is an actual cause which, in causing something else to undergo a transition from potency to act, itself undergoes such a transition in its own being. Aquinas is then able to point out that when you explain the motion of one moved mover by another, as is normally the case in natural explanations *propter quid* (as when you explain the dent in the car by the rock that hit it), the further question can always be raised: yes, the car was dented when the rock struck it; but who or what caused the rock to fly in this direction? And so on.

One moved mover well explains another as far as a specific effect or phenomenon is concerned. But no matter how far we pursue explanations within such a series, there is always another "Yes, but ..." to be raised. Suppose the series infinite. Yet for exactly the same reason and in exactly the same way, what is true of each finite segment or part of the series is true also for the series as an infinite whole. Any explanation made in terms of a moved mover always requires completion by yet another moved mover. It is not that an infinite series of moved movers is impossible. If the universe is eternal, then the series of moved movers which make up the universe is infinite, but intrinsically incapable of fully explaining itself nonetheless. Whether eternal or finite in time, Aquinas points out, the universe is created in this sense of being dependent in its being through every "here and now" moment past, present, or to come.[45]

Be the series of moved movers infinite or be it finite, there is only one possible way to complete it as a *fully intelligible* series of moved movers, and that is by postulating that *outside the series*, and *simultaneous with the whole of the series*, there exists a cause of motion which is not itself moved. This is how Aquinas defines an "unmoved mover": an actual cause which, in causing something else to undergo a transition from potency to act, itself undergoes no such transition. So the *whole order* of "moved movers", that is to say, the entire universe of interacting finite beings, the combined orders of transcendental and ontological relatives, as we might also say, is set in contrast to the singularity and uniqueness of an "Unmoved Mover", one in being and essence, a cause of "motion" which, being purely actual, itself in imparting existence or *esse* ("creating") under finite modes (that is to say, in enabling there to be changing being of whatever mode and type insofar as it is actual), undergoes no transition from potency to act.

An "Unmoved Mover", in short, proves to be a Source of actuality which precludes intrinsic limitation by potency; a Source of actuality which admits no transition from potentiality, a Subsistent Act of Existence independent of any intrinsic correlation with a specifying limit. Purely actual, the Unmoved Mover which

---

45 See further discussion of "creationism" in chapter 11, p. 506f.

the intelligibility of change here and now requires us to posit as a simultaneously concurring cause in any case whatever of movement or change anywhere in the universe, regardless of whatever other reasons for the change are *also* involved, knows no diversity within itself, at least not the kind that bespeaks potentiality for change as a transition from potency to act. The consequence of this condition of supreme actuality unconditioned from within Aquinas calls "the divine simplicity", to which we yet must assign further names in order to appreciate the reality of the Creative Source of all being, a Source beyond being and nonbeing as falls within our understanding

The next forty-one Questions of the First Part (or "Part I") of the *Summa* are spent exploring the meaning of such a conception, after which, at Question 44, Aquinas begins to treat of God's creation, the cause of evil, and the various levels of physical creation, from angels down to earthly creatures. In Part II he treats of human beings as made in God's image, first in general (I-II), and then as regards the virtues in particular, both theological and philosophical, so to speak (II-II). Part III treats of the Redemption, or the return of the universe to God through the salvation of humankind.

The Divine Names and "Negative Theology":
"Of God We Can Know Only That He Is and What He Is Not"
The first "name of God" for Aquinas is that to which the proof from motion concludes: Pure Act, or *Ipsum Esse Subsistens*, an Unmoved Mover because he knows within himself nothing whatever of the potentiality which is presupposed to change and constitutive of it from within. Yet because we are able to know "in this life" only through the formation of concepts and the formation of concepts is based on the experience of sensible changes, our knowledge of God proves to be of a rather paradoxical sort. We can know of God, by demonstration, *that* he exists, but, beyond that, insofar as our concepts are multiple and his being is simple, we know more *what he is not* than we do what he is. What he is, is pure act, self-subsistent existence. What he is not is mixed act, changeable, potential, diverse, transitional.

But the formula "We know of God that he is and what he is not" leads to astonishing abuses, sometimes circulated in the name of St. Thomas, when it is not adequately understood. Later on in the history of philosophy, Immanuel Kant will introduce his readers to a radical distinction between "what appears" and "what is in itself". What appears is what we can know; what is in itself is what we cannot know and is intrinsically and forever unknowable. Any construal of the statement of Aquinas that we can know of God that he is and what he is not along the lines of the later Kantian distinction between knowable phenomena of experience and unknowable things-in-themselves would be worthy of contempt were it not for the intrinsic difficulty of the matter at issue.[46]

---

46 See the discussion in chapter 13 below, p. 573n60.

For Aquinas, the idea of knowing that something is in such a fashion as to preclude in principle *all further* knowledge whatever of what it is that is would be laughed out of court. When Aquinas says that "God is unknowable", he means simply that multiple concepts, without which our knowledge cannot maintain itself, cannot express the unity of the divine being as it exists in itself. For in itself *there is no difference* between essence and existence in God, not because God "has no essence" (one might equally well say he "has no existence"), but because in his unique case and uniquely *his essence is his existence*. He has an "essence", all right, that is to say, He Is; he even is "something", namely, what the universe of finite being is not, namely, multiple. We cannot know what God is as he is, but we can know that he is as the truth of a proposition that there exists and must exist concurrent with every moved mover an Unmoved Mover without which neither motion nor any finite being could be. And that is a starting point for yet further affirmations, for the reaching of yet further "propositional truths". For example, by contrast with finite being, therefore, we may say that this Unmoved Mover is an "Infinite Being", but we must beware of dichotomies.

It begins to seem as if dichotomies will never do. I suspect this is so, although there is no doubt they have their place and can sometimes express a decisive truth, as when a woman proves pregnant or not. The dichotomy of knower/known, however, will not do, we have seen; the dichotomy of sign/signified will not do, we are seeing, for the sign relation is triadic not dyadic; now we are seeing that the "that something is" versus "what something is" dichotomy will not do either, even when it comes to such understanding of God as can be eked out by human understanding.

The "that he is" in the proposition "we can know of God that he is" turns out to be multiple. We can know "that he is" where "is" carries the sense of "actual existence" or *ens reale*; but we can know also "that he is" a number of other things as well: that he is simple; that he is being; that he is one, that he is good; that he is true – that he is all the *transcendentalia* but in a subsistent mode rather than a conceptual one, and various other things as well: no deceiver, faithful, everlasting. Where does it end?

How could it end? We are talking of the knowledge of God. Even if we restrict ourselves by some impossible device of method to only "getting it right", our knowledge cannot end regarding this object. There is not some bare minimum knowledge of God which we can achieve, beyond which there is only an Empty Nothing. That is knowledge of God conceived on the model of the Kantian "thing-in-itself", a blunder of the first order. When it is said that we cannot know of God "what he is", all that is meant is that since our knowledge of God is attained through concepts and God does not have a diversity of rationales within his being but only existence (or *esse*, if you must), therefore our knowledge of God is always external to his proper being.

But so is our knowledge of his existence, of course. As we will see, for St Thomas, the "existence" of God in the proof that "God exists" is the truth of a proposition, not the object of an experience. Mystical experience is said to be exactly the *actio Dei in anima*, the "action of God upon the soul", exactly as ordinary experience is said to be the *actio sensibilis in sensu*, the "action of the sensible upon the sense". And either that is indeed what mystical experience is, or there is no mystical experience other than the confused claims of self-deluded pathetics.[47]

God is one, not many; that is to say, he is not diversified from within by a variety of rationales, as are substances with their variety of accidents. That being so, since we can know him "in this life" only by a variety of concepts, we cannot know *what he is*. But we can indeed know a great deal and a great many things *about* him – that he is real, not a figment of human construction within the understanding without counterpart in the physical order; that he is good, not in any way lacking or deprived of existence; that he is one, not in any way specified and limited from within; that he is true, not in any way capable of being deceived; that he is ... and so on, in a semiosis as unlimited as God is infinite.

That is the meaning of the assertion that of God "we can know only *that* he is". We have no empty "that" covering an unknowable "what", but a "that" so full it exceeds our capacity to express "what" it reveals, *especially* according to the unity proper to the divine existence of pure actuality. "What" expresses for the human understanding a simple intelligible, that is to say, a category – substance or an accident, whether subjective or suprasubjective (as in the unique case of relation). But God is not "simple" in the way that even what falls in the category of substance is simple; for a substance is yet transcendentally relative, dependent on accidents in order to be, and God is not even that.

That is why, in the formula "We can know of God that he is and what he is not", it is vain to seek "a shadow of agnosticism or of semi-agnosticism", as Maritain says.[48] But let Aquinas speak for himself on the point:[49]

There is a twofold consideration in the names we attribute to God: on the one hand are the perfections themselves signified, such as goodness, life, and the like; on the

---

47 See Maritain 1959: 2nd part *in toto*; and 1973: 507, the "petite parenthèse" cited in Para. 1 of n24, p. 260 above.

48 Maritain 1959: 229. St Thomas applies to the agnostic or quasi-agnostic view of human knowledge of God (speaking specifically against the claims on the point of Moses Maimonides, 1135–1204, the principal Jewish thinker of the Latin Age) that it is a view "[quod] non sit usquequaque verum" (Aquinas c.1265/6: *Quaestiones disputatae de potentia*, q. 9. art. 7c. [Busa 3, p. 258]): "nam et dionysius dicit, quod 'negationes sunt maxime verae in deo; affirmationes vero sunt incompactae'. non enim scimus de deo quid est, sed magis quid non est, ut damascenus dicit. ... quamvis hoc non sit usquequaque verum, nam sicut dicit dionysius, 'sapientia et vita et alia huiusmodi non removentur a deo quasi ei desint, sed quia excellentius habet ea quam intellectus humanus capere, vel sermo significare possit; et ex illa perfectione divina descendunt perfectiones creatae, secundum quamdam similitudinem imperfectam'. et ideo de deo, secundum dionysium, 'non solum dicitur aliquid per modum negationis et per modum causae, sed etiam per modum eminentiae'."

49 Aquinas c.1266: *Summa* I.13.3 (Busa 2. p. 202): "in nominibus igitur quae deo attribuimus, est duo considerare, scilicet, perfectiones ipsas significatas, ut bonitatem, vitam, et huiusmodi; et modum significandi. quantum igitur ad id quod significant huiusmodi nomina, proprie competunt deo, et magis proprie quam ipsis creaturis, et per prius dicuntur de eo, quantum vero ad modum significandi, non proprie dicuntur de deo, habent enim modum significandi qui creaturis competit."

other hand is the mode of the signification. As regards that which such names signify, the perfections properly pertain to God, and they pertain more properly than to the creatures [from which they have been abstracted], and they are said of God with logical priority. But as regards the mode of signifying, the names are not properly said of God: for they have this mode of signifying which pertains to creatures.

Of God, in short, we can and do know many things.[50] That he exists is only the starting point, the necessary starting point, however, if we are to have any chance of steering clear of the shoals of illusion. For God is no more *noumenon* than he is *ding-an-sich*. The *quinque viae* of St Thomas are not a matter of illegitimately adding a wing to the house of experience; they are precisely the discovery within the house of experience of the foundation of all experiences, actual and possible, sane and insane, of *entia realia* and *entia rationis* alike.

The appearance to the contrary notwithstanding, the distinction between knowing that God is and not what he is, is not a dichotomy but a trichotomy. For when we learn of God that he exists, we also learn that he is not nothing, an *ens rationis*, and that he is not therefore a fiction of understanding; and we learn therefore *something of* "what he is", not according to his proper existence (which is simple) but according to the lights which make our experience intelligible, namely, our concepts (which are plural). For we learn that this God who exists is the source of being, not of evil as the absence of being; is the source of truth, not the failure in grasping being which is error; is one, not the multiplicity of beings given in sensible experience; and so on, in an "unlimited semiosis", as we have said.

And where did Aquinas learn all this? Well, to a great extent he figured it out for himself, but it cannot but be one of the embarrassments or ironies of history that he learned it best apparently from the pen of a fraudulent authority, the famous or infamous Dionysius the Areopagite.[51] In the treatise "On the Divine Names" of Pseudo-Dionysius is expressed better than anywhere else in the combined Greek and Latin literature, if we except only the commentary of St Thomas upon this

---

50 Cf. Maritain 1959: 229, italics added: "For we know with certain knowledge, more certain than mathematical knowledge, that God is simple, one, good, omniscient, all-powerful, free ... [this is Maritain's own ellipsis, not an editorial omission of text], we are more certain of the Divine Perfections than of our own heart. This formula ['We do not know what God is'] signifies: 'We do not know of God what he is' in the sense that we do not attain in itself the quiddity of God, we do not know in what the deity itself consists. For when we attribute to God one or another predicate [including 'existence as signified', be it remarked], it is not His essence formally seized as such that we attribute to Him; *it is a perfection which is certainly contained in that essence, but which we can only conceive as it exists elsewhere*," namely, within our world of sensible experiences. "Indeed, that a predicate be attributed to God is itself a result of our inadequate way of conceiving. In him there is no duality of subject and predicate. To know Him as He is could only consist in an absolutely simple vision" wherein God himself in his own being would displace the concepts whereby we know 'in this life'. In the afterlife of the soul which attains union with God ('in heaven'), says St Thomas, just this is what occurs.
51 See the remarks of Aquinas c.1265/6 cited in n48 above.

treatise, the realization that in knowing that God is (whatever we realize that he
is, beginning with "real" and advancing) we also know what he is not, namely,
any of these things we know he is in the way that we learned of the things in
question (existence, unity, truth, goodness, ...) as matter of experience, but *that he
is all of these things in a higher way* than either our experience can reveal or our
concepts can directly express, the so-called "threefold way" of simple affirmation
(*via affirmationis:* there is good in creatures), qualified denial (*via negationis:* good
is not in God in the way that good is in creatures), and eminent affirmation (*via
eminentiae:* good is in God in a higher way than is possible for creatures or than is
possible for our understanding fully to grasp).

So the movement, explicitly or implicitly, whereby grow the symbols expressive
of any true knowledge of God is always threefold, not twofold: (1) there is first
the affirmation "that God is" whether simply or in this or that way; (2) then there
is the denial that his existence or being or goodness or life or whatever perfection
has been affirmed in the judgment "that God is" is realized in any of the ways
that we encounter its realization in sensible things; and (3) finally there is the third
movement, the realization that since it is true "that God is" but also true "that God is
not" in any of the ways of which we have direct experience of perfections, therefore
any perfection of which it is true "that God is" in that way must be true according
to a higher realization than our understanding can express and true within a perfect
simplicity of existence and being which likewise exceeds our means of expression.
So we know of God that he is good, for example, and what he is therefore not,
evil, for example; but *how* he is good we are at a loss to comprehend. We know
only that he is and that he is not in the way that anything directly experienced is.
"So we understand that God is above and beyond [*supra*] all things", St Thomas
tells us[52] in the exposition he was required to make in view of the authority the
author of the original text enjoyed before his imposture had been forced into the
light; "above and beyond not only the things that are, but also the things that we
are able to understand."

When one reads the "Commentary upon the Divine Names", one feels the reverence the commentator has for the author.[53] But one also feels something different in
the atmosphere of the commentary. It does not read quite like any other writing of
Aquinas. There is no doubt of the authenticity of the commentary. But there is also
no doubt that the text commented upon, to a degree that no other text manifests in
the Aquinian *corpus*, extracts from St Thomas a need to express himself at times in

---

52 Aquinas c.1265–7, *Super librum Dionysii de divinis nominibus*, cap. 7. lect. 4. (Busa 4, p. 572):
   "mens nostra ... cognoscit deum esse non solum super omnia quae sunt infra ipsam, sed etiam
   supra ipsam et supra omnia quae ab ipsa comprehendi possunt. et sic cognoscens deum, in tali statu
   cognitionis, illuminatur ab ipsa profunditate divinae sapientiae, quam perscrutari non possumus.
   quod etiam intelligamus deum esse supra omnia non solum quae sunt, sed etiam quae apprehendere
   possumus, ex incomprehensibili profunditate divinae sapientiae provenit nobis".
53 Indeed, Pelikan (1987) notes that Aquinas in the course of his other writings cites the
   Pseudo-Dionysius some 1700 times.

ways that are comparatively forced, ways that are not fully his own preferred ways of speaking. It is an imponderable question: would Aquinas have commented as deferentially upon this text as he does had he known that the identity of the author of the text was a false identity? We can only guess. My guess is that he would not have commented so deferentially, if he would have commented at all, which I deem doubtful. Had Aquinas known what Luther knew, he would have dismissed this "Dionysius" much as Luther did.[54]

Even though barely more than two and a half centuries separate Luther's dismissal from Aquinas's reverence, a full two of those centuries mark the period during which the false identity assumed by the author of the Pseudo-Dionysian texts ensured that their content would become so fully assimilated to the thinking of the Latin Age as to be all but indistinguishable from that part of it concerned with "the names of God". Would the texts have achieved this measure of assimilation and appropriation simply on their own merits, unassisted by the false authority under which they so long commanded the closest attention? It is indeed an imponderable question. On the one hand, the authenticity of the texts as belonging to the mainstream of mystical writings is undeniable, whoever was their author. On the other hand, since no other text from this mainstream, not even the classics of John of the Cross, have ever achieved the command of such widespread attention, careful reading, and reverent exposition, can one conclude otherwise than by thinking that, in the end, not all but only the greater part of the success of the Pseudo-Dionysian writings represents ill-gotten gains? The ideas stand on their own, certainly; but it was not "on their own" that they laid claim to universal attention in the formative Latin centuries.

In any event, when all is said and done, the famous "negative theology" associated with the influence of the Pseudo-Dionysian writings above all turns out to be in some ways the most positive knowledge of all, for it gives us truly if inadequately something of the truth about God, creator of all things, who can neither deceive nor be deceived, unlike we who know him "through a glass darkly" or, as the fraudulent Denys might say, or rather not say, "apophatically".

For St Thomas Aquinas, "theology", even "negative theology", is not the highest wisdom; it is only, within the framework of his suppositions, the highest exercise of human understanding discursively exercised. It is higher than philosophy, assuming its supposition true, because it accepts its starting point in the fashioning of propositions from material that is supposed to be divinely revealed, and not merely from experience as that from which even our most intellectual concepts arise and to which they recur. But in the *discursus* of theology, reason and logic remain just what they are even in philosophy. For theology as a "sacred doctrine", *sacra doctrina*, the existence of God is a matter of faith. But insofar as theology employs discourse it draws upon the resources proper to philosophy and which philosophy alone can provide. Here, in the order not of religious dogma but of philosophical doctrine

---

54 Cited in chapter 4 above, p. 132.

even impressed for the service of dogma, the existence of God is not only a matter of faith but of debate and, St Thomas thinks, of possible demonstration. What faith believes thus has or can have a twofold aspect respecting human understanding. Sometimes reason can also demonstrate what faith believes, and other times faith believes what reason can only show to be free from internal contradiction, to be "not impossible". Dogmas of faith can sometimes be, under other auspices, doctrines of philosophy. But doctrines of philosophy *as such* can never be dogmas of faith, and there are dogmas of faith which can never be doctrines of philosophy, namely, when what is claimed as revealed exceeds what it is possible for human understanding to demonstrate on the grounds of experience. But, even then, philosophy has the right to examine whether what is claimed to be revealed is incompossible with what experience does truly show, that is to say, with what philosophy can actually demonstrate from experience; and, were the answer to be affirmative, St Thomas would say that either there has been a mistake in the understanding of the revelation, or the revelation is falsely so called.

For God knows all that a human can know and more, for God knows himself and all the ways in which the divine existence can be imitated in finite ways and existentially participated from without; whereas the human understanding can know only the finite imitations themselves and participations of the divine existence we call the universe or world of nature, together with the fact that all finite being depends upon the infinite existence of God which, precisely because within it there is no diversity of rationale (God's essence *being* God's existence), exceeds our capacity to understand. Cajetan spoke for Thomas and the whole Thomistic tradition when he said:[55]

> ... in God there is only one formal nature or rationale, and this is neither exclusively absolute [transcendentally relative] nor exclusively relative [ontologically], neither purely communicable nor purely incommunicable. ...
>
> We fall into error when we proceed from the absolute [the transcendental relative] and [the ontological] relative to [conclude that] God [is one or the other, either or both], because the distinction between absolute and relative is conceived by us prior to God; in consequence, we try to place God in one or other of these two members of the distinction. In point of fact, the matter is totally different. The divine nature is prior to being and all of its differences: it is *above* being, *beyond* unity, etc.

Hence the "esse divinum" cannot be expressed in human language according as it is apart from its creation, but only as it is above its creation as source and exemplar

---

55 Cajetan 1507: I, q. 39, art. 1, n. 7: "... est in Deo unica ratio formalis, non pure absoluta nec pure respectiva, non pure communicabilis nec pure incommunicabilis; ...
   Fallimur autem, ab absolutis et respectivis ad Deum procedendo, eo quod distinctionem inter absolutum et respectivum quasi priorem re divina imaginamur; et consequenter illam sub altero membro oportere poni credimus. Et tamen est totum oppositum. Quoniam res divina prior est ente et omnibus differentiis eius: est enim *super ens* et *super unum*, etc." See further the discussion in chapter 9, p. 424n37.

thereof. But as exemplar it is diversified in rationales, that is to say, "possible essences"; in itself there is no diversity, only a single "essence" which *is* existence. "Being" is said *from* the act of existence, but from the actual existence of finite things of experience, "beings" in whom to be is something more than what they are. But in God to be is not something more than what he is, for what he is and to be are the same. So, of our names for God, being is the first and the most proper, insofar as it is the name most closely derived from and associated with the experience of existence; yet God remains beyond our experience of existence because there is no "what" in the case of God that can be known apart from the fact that he is; and yet at least one late-modern author in the Thomistic line argues forcefully that "person" among the divine names deserves a privileged, perhaps highest, position in the "hierarchy".[56]

We learn through philosophical discourse (whether within or outside of the *discursus* of any theology, including Christian theology) of a unique and necessary case in which, unlike everything of which we have direct experience, what a being is in no wise differs from the fact that it is. This fact, moreover, is not a sensible fact, not a *datum* of experience; it is a *factum*, an achievement of understanding, something constructed by the mind itself that yet expresses a truth that is independent of the construction. The fact in question is a *factum*, not a *fictum*. What it expresses belongs to the order of *ens reale*, not *ens rationis*; but what it expresses of that order of *ens reale* concerns not something intrinsic to the order of finite entities as finite but rather something upon which those finite entities actually experienced are seen to depend here and now and under every aspect according to which they enjoy any existence at all, not only real existence but even possible or imaginary existence; for error no less than truth formally taken belongs to *our* "real existence" at least, and our real existence falls under the dependency of an existence participated, an existence other than what participates it, an existence that is – no less than that of any other finite being – as distinct from "what" we are as the infinite being of God *is not* distinct from what he is.

So through all the "names of God" there runs a common thread. In the world of experience, we encounter various perfections of creatures. Upon analysis, we see that some of these perfections imply at the same time limits, such as "a beautiful face". The language that expresses these perfections cannot be applied with propriety to God. But other perfections, such as life or intelligence, while we experience them in limited ways, upon analysis have no intrinsic and necessary implication of imperfection. The language that expresses these perfections can with propriety be applied to God.[57] "God talk", thus, can either fall between mere metaphor and

56 Maritain 1959: 231–6.
57 Aquinas, c.1266, in his *Summa* I.13.3 ad 1 (Busa 2, p. 203), replies to the following objection:
   "Omnia enim nomina quae de Deo dicimus, sunt a creaturis accepta. Sed nomina creaturarum
   metaphorice dicuntur de Deo, sicut cum dicitur *Deus est lapis*, vel *leo*, vel aliquid huiusmodi. Ergo
   omnia nomina dicta de Deo, dicuntur metaphorice"; to which he replies as follows: "ista nomina" –

confused nonsense, as when we speak of God in any terms that involve or imply a body in what they signify as well as in how they signify; or it can be clear and distinct and correct as far as it goes, which is never "to the heart of the matter", to the divine existence as constituting the divine essence. "And so, when this name 'wise' is said of a human being, the name in a certain way circumscribes and comprehends the thing signified", St Thomas says by way of illustrating the point;[58] "but this is not what happens when the name 'wise' is said of God, for in that application the name leaves the thing signified as uncomprehended and exceeding the signification of the name".

Even existence, the "to be" or *esse* which is the very essence of God, on being affirmed in a proposition, answers only the question whether God is, without reaching to the question of what he is, because even this affirmation proceeds according to a distinct rationale of the human understanding, and this rationale is foreign to the surpassing simplicity of the divine existence. If there is a God, then he must be one, living, intelligent. ... The "if" part of this hypothetical dicisign must be answered affirmatively in order for the "then" part to constitute a genuine knowledge, a knowledge, that is to say, which bears upon the way things are independently of how we think or desire them to be. In this sense, it is the beginning of the doctrine of the "divine names", the articulation of words which are true concerning God even though they do not express the manner of existence according to which he does not participate but simply is existence. The *quinque viae*, the discursive contexts which establish the fact of an existence constitutive of or rather identical with itself and the source of all else that is in various modes of dependency, addresses the "if" clause, to turn it into a "since". But just as the "then" follows upon the "if", so the "since" has consequences. And the tracing out of these consequences, the development of these consequences in discourse, constitutes the doctrine of the divine names, "God talk" in the sense that transcends wishful thinking, pious nonsense, and blabbering confusion. It is not the most common strain of discourse we encounter in everyday life.

So the paradox giving rise to the much abused notion and name of "negative theology":[59]

---

good, wise, living, intelligent, person, etc. – "quae proprie dicuntur de Deo, important conditiones corporales, non in ipso significatio nominis, sed quantum ad modum significandi. Ea vero quae metaphorice de Deo dicuntur, important conditionem corporalem in ipso suo significato".

58 Aquinas c.1266: *Summa* I.13.5c. (Busa 2, p. 203): "et sic, cum hoc nomen sapiens de homine dicitur, quodammodo circumscribit et comprehendit rem significatam, non autem cum dicitur de deo, sed relinquit rem significatam ut incomprehensam, et excedentem nominis significationem. unde patet quod non secundum eandem rationem hoc nomen sapiens de deo et de homine dicitur. et eadem ratio est de aliis. unde nullum nomen univoce de deo et creaturis praedicatur, sed nec etiam pure aequivoce, ut aliqui dixerunt."

59 Aquinas c.1265–7: *Super librum Dionysii de divinis nominibus*, cap. 7. lect. 4. (Busa 4, p. 572): "cognoscitur deus per cognitionem nostram, quia quidquid in nostra cognitione cadit, accipimus ut ab eo adductum; et iterum cognoscitur per ignorantiam nostram, inquantum scilicet hoc ipsum est deum cognoscere, quod nos scimus nos ignorare de deo quid sit."

God is known through our cognition, because whatever falls within our awareness we understand to be derived from him; and at the same time God is known through our ignorance insofar as this is what it is to know God, namely, to know that we do not know of God what he is.

Aquinas makes the point in his own name with an equal or greater clarity:[60]

> From the fact that our understanding is not proportioned to the divine substance, this very thing which is the substance of God stands beyond the boundaries of what our understanding can attain, and so is unknown by us; and for this reason that is the highest point of human understanding of God, that one knows that one does not know God insofar as one knows that what God is exceeds every aspect of God that we do understand.

And what aspects of God do we understand? Well, we know that since he exists, and if we are careful with our use of language, we can say that "he" is a number of things, based on our experience of being. For example, because the name "being" applies simply and with logical priority to substance, insofar as the simple is the cause of the complex, we can say of God that he is "the first simple substance".[61] We can also say of him that he is "the first cause".[62] So begin to unfold "the names of God", that is to say, the determination through analysis of the terms of human language that can be truly and properly applied to God even if they cannot be applied to God in accordance with his essence, precisely because his essence has no distinction whatever from his existence, and his existence has intrinsic to it no diversity of rationale corresponding to the diversity of rationale according to which our words, including our "names of God", differ from one another. But note carefully that the progression of the divine names presupposes as its starting point that God exists. For otherwise the names of God are empty nominalisms, *entia rationis sine fundamento in re* ("purely objective beings with no foundation in what is apart from our thought"). If God exists, then we can say of him x, y, and z, but not a, b, and c, etc. That is why one way of looking at the *quinque viae* is in terms of beginning the pro-

---

60 Aquinas c.1265/6: *Quaestiones disputatae de potentia*, q. 7. art. 5. ad 14 (Busa 3, p. 244): "ex quo intellectus noster divinam substantiam non adaequat, hoc ipsum quod est dei substantia remanet, nostrum intellectum excedens, et ita a nobis ignoratur: et propter hoc illud est ultimum cognitionis humanae de deo quod sciat se deum nescire, in quantum cognoscit, illud quod deus est, omne ipsum quod de eo intelligimus, excedere."

61 Aquinas, c.1252/6: *De ente et essentia*, cap. 1 (Busa 3, p. 584): "quia ens absolute et per prius dicitur de substantiis, ... substantiarum vero quaedam sunt simplices ... sunt enim causa eorum quae composita sunt, ad minus substantia prima simplex, quae deus est."

62 Ibid. (Busa 3, p. 585): "quia omne quae, quod est per aliud, reducitur ad illud quod est per se sicut ad causam primam, oportet quod sit aliqua res, quae sit causa essendi omnibus rebus, eo quod ipsa est esse tantum. ... et hoc est causa prima, quae deus est."

cess of making the names of God real names by converting the hypothetical "if" from which they flow into a categorical "since" upon which they follow as real consequences.

Let us look a little more fully at the "if" clause converted into a "since ...". In other words, let us look a little more closely at the philosophical conclusion of the discourse which makes of our knowledge of God, such as it is and insofar as it is correct if inadequate, a knowledge pertaining to the order of *ens reale* in contrast to the mansions of *ens fictum*. In other words, let us examine at more length the beginning of our knowledge of God "that he is", but without forgetting what Aquinas called the most important point about our knowledge of God in every particular and in its totality: that no matter how successfully we multiply our points of knowledge "that God is" this and that and the other, no one of these points nor any totality of such points amounts to a knowledge of what God is *as he is in the identity of his essence as pure actual existence*. We catch, in certain of the divine names, indeed *something* of "*what* he is"; but these somethings never add up to "what he *is*", for that perforce and forever exceeds the grasp of a finite understanding, even one open to the infinite. For to be open is one thing, to enclose another.

Ipsum Esse Subsistens

Very early in his theological discussion of the divine being Aquinas's central philosophical intuition, animating the whole of his *Summa* and personal thought, at least as the principal authors of Neothomism have succeeded in revealing it to us, comes to the surface of his text. God (the unmoved mover), Aquinas tells us, does not have an essence in the way that other things (moved movers) do:[63]

> Because *esse*, "to be", is the actuality of every form or nature; for goodness or humanity isn't signified in act except insofar as we signify it to be. It is therefore necessary that whatever actuality of being be compared to an essence which is distinct from it [be so compared] as an act to a potency. But since we have been able to show that there could be nothing potential in God,[64] it follows that the essence in God is not something which is other than his *esse*.

He adds a line of Heraclitean fire and Stoic Λόγος:[65]

---

63 Aquinas c.1266: *Summa* I.3.4c. (Busa 2, p. 189): "quia esse est actualitas omnis formae vel naturae, non enim bonitatis vel humanitas significatur in actu, nisi prout significamus eam esse. oportet igitur quod ipsum esse comparetur ad essentiam quae est aliud ab ipso, sicut actus ad potentiam. cum igitur in deo nihil sit potentiale, ut ostensum est supra, sequitur quod non sit aliud in eo essentia quam suum esse. sua igitur essentia est suum esse."

64 See Aquinas c.1266: *Summa* I. 2. 3., the proof that the universe of finite beings depends upon the simultaneous existence of an Unmoved Mover.

65 Aquinas c.1266: *Summa* I.3.4c. (Busa 2, p. 189): "quia sicut illud quod habet ignum et non est ignis, ist ignitum per participationem, ita illud quod habet esse et non est esse, est ens per participationem."

For just as that which is on fire but is not fire is ignited by participation, so that which has *esse* and is not *esse* is being by participation.

Nor could Aquinas be clearer about how far removed is God from what our eyes see and our fingers touch, even though, as the Source of what is most actual in the physical world, God is at the most intimate heart of all things in their sustenance of existence:[66]

> "To be" is said in two ways: In one way it signifies the act of being; in the other way it signifies the making of a proposition, which the mind formulates by applying a predicate to a subject. In the first of these two ways of understanding "to be", we cannot say that we know the existence of God, but only in the second way. For we know that this proposition which we form about God, *God exists*, is true; and this we know from his effects,[67] as was said above.

So Aquinas, well versed in Aristotle's doctrine that demonstration "is addressed not to the spoken word but to the discourse within the soul",[68] vindicates the claim of Augustine that "God is more truly thought than expressed, and exists more truly than he is thought."

At first we were able to conclude to the necessity of a cause on which the universe depends in its totality, a cause which is at each moment simultaneous with the interactions of moved movers, not far, perhaps, from the Unmoved Mover of Aristotle's *Physics*. But now with such refinement of that primitive discovery as Aristotle never made or began to make, we see clearly that *this* Unmoved Mover is no one in an essentially subordinated series, such as Aristotle envisaged. *This* Unmoved Mover is no self-absorbed Thought unaware of the details of the world which it moves. For *this* Unmoved Mover is *Ipsum Esse Subsistens*, the Source apart from which nothing, no least detail or most trivial aspect of the physical universe, at any point of time or eternity, is or moves in any way at all. We are able to see, in short, that existence as involving motion, possibility and necessity, and so forth, is the proper effect of God. Finite beings require something upon which to act. God, imparting existence, "acts" presupposing nothing at all.

We are able to see, also, a definitive resolution to the ancient question of whether there is one God or many gods, "monotheism" versus. "polytheism". *Ipsum Esse*

---

66 Aquinas c.1266: *Summa* I.3.4 ad 2 (Busa 2, p. 189): "esse dupliciter dicitur, uno modo, significat actum essendi; alio modo, significat compositionem propositionis, quam anima adinvenit coniungens praedicatum subiecto. primo igitur modo accipiendo esse, non possumus scire esse dei, sicut nec eius essentiam, sed solum secundo modo. scimus enim quod haec propositio, quam formamus de deo, cum dicimus deus est, vera est. et hoc scimus ex effectibus, ut supra dictum est."

67 First and most manifestly, but far from exclusively, the movement of bodies in space, as we saw (above, p. 270).

68 See "Demonstration, or Proof of a Point" in chapter 3, p. 89 above.

Subsistens, an "Existence Subsistent of Itself", being without potentiality, cannot be restricted in such a way as to have an "equal" other. For being is either self-subsistent or by participation. If self-subsistent, it is a pure actuality without a restriction from within which limits it to a determinate realm of finite nature. In that case it is the One source whence existence by participation is extrinsically possible. But if a given being is by participation then that being is not God, however lofty in a comparative scale of finite beings a given individual might be by various standards. For plurality requires restriction of each from within, and this is precisely what the divine nature, as self-subsistent *esse*, precludes.

"God Is More Intimate to Created Beings than They Are to Themselves"

The doctrine of Aquinas in point of assigning a clear and explicit meaning for the term "creation" is one of the more remarkable achievements of human understanding. We have seen that Aristotle did not seriously consider the question of a "beginning" of the world in any sense, and that not until the One of Plotinus, "beyond being and nonbeing", do we encounter a glimmering of this notion of a Creative Source for the things of the world. Yet even the Plotinian notion of a "creative Source" of finite being is short of the idea of creation as Aquinas spells it out, for the God of the *quinque viae* is not simply a creative source but a purely actual infinite existence which depends in giving existence to finite beings on nothing whatsoever outside itself. Hence there is no necessity in the creative action.

Unlike the One of Plotinus, the God of the "proof from motion" is involved in no necessity through which it communicates existence to whatever begins to be as distinct from the infinite existence of God. In Aquinas, a direct consequence of his first argument to the conclusion that God is an "unmoved mover" or "pure act of existence without intrinsic limitation by any potentiality" is that not merely the whole order of finite beings as such is dependent upon God but that every detail within that order is dependent upon God in exactly the same way and for exactly the same reason: the argument concludes to an irreducible distinction between that which *is* its own existence (God) and that which merely *has* an existence contracted to a terminating "nature",[69] a boundary of potentiality beyond which it (any creature) cannot go without losing its hold on existence. For if we prescind from the difference between spiritual and material substances and speak simply of the difference between created and uncreated being, there are but two ways of "having an essence".[70] One is the way in which God has an essence, namely, as identical with his existence, which precludes his being defined because language requires a diversity of rationales in order to form a definition of anything and there is no such diversity of rationales in the divine being. The other way of having an essence is the case where the essence

---

69 "Habet esse, et non est suum esse" is one of the formulas used by Aquinas himself (*Summa* I.7.2c: a created form "has existence, and is not its own existence").
70 Compare Aquinas, c.1252–6: *De ente et essentia*, cap. 4 (Busa 3, p. 586).

is other than that which exists, in which case the existence of the thing is received, limited, and held within the bounds of the nature of the one receiving it.

The argument does not go back in time to a "beginning", nor is it merely a question of a "source" from which things somehow "proceed". It is a question of "something out of nothing", a proposition unintelligible *within* the order of moved movers, but taken by Aquinas to be precisely expressive of the relation *between* God and creatures which is a real relation of dependency on the side of creatures but a purely free relation of divine choice on the side of the God who shares in whatever limited way the actuality of existence which is proper to himself alone. Nor is the "existence" which God in the creative act gives an isolated or individual possession of each substance isolated unto itself, but rather is it (as we have seen the doctrine of transcendental relative requires in any case) an existence which involves an order among created things, a complex of ontological relations and interactions without which the substances could not sustain themselves. Action follows upon being, and the "action" insofar as the being is more or less than a knowing being is *transitive* action, that is to say, *interaction*.[71]

The common teaching in neothomistic circles is that the idea of God as "author of all things" in the Christian Scriptures is the actual source, historically speaking, for the idea of creation. This assertion has been explicitly related to the history of philosophy before Aquinas in a learned lecture on the subject by Kenneth L. Schmitz:[72]

> Within the philosophical tradition that stems from the Greeks the question of origin has received extensive and intensive consideration. At no time did it receive more consideration than in the high middle ages. Matthew of Aquasparta, a younger contemporary of St. Thomas, has left us a summary of philosophical positions on the question which he has found in the philosopher Averroes. The latter had reduced the philosophical positions on the question to five. First, things are said to come to be through the discovery or disclosure of latent forms (attributed to Anaxagoras). Second, things may be said to come to be through the orderly arrangement of separate elements (attributed to Empedocles). Third, through the bestowal of forms (attributed to Plato and his followers). Or fourth, from a giver who is either separate from the things (attributed to Avicenna) or somehow joined to them (attributed to Themistius). Or fifth and finally, things may be said to come to be by being led forth from potency into act (attributed to Aristotle). None of these five positions hold that things are created from nothing, nor is one able to come to this knowledge from experience alone.

---

71 Aquinas c.1265/7, *Super librum Dionysii de divinis nominibus*, cap. 7. lect. 4. (Busa 4, p. 573): "ipsa divina sapientia est omnium causa effectiva, inquantum res producit in esse et non solum rebus dat esse, sed etiam esse cum ordine in rebus, inquantum res invicem se coadunant in ordinem ad ultimum finem."

72 Schmitz 1982: 12–13.

Only the concluding statement here merits argument. If Averroes' survey is correct and Matthew of Aquasparta's summary accurate, we can indeed conclude that the doctrine of creation out of nothing, *creatio ex nihilo*, is not to be found in the philosophical literature prior to Aquinas. But if the proof from motion offered by Aquinas is indeed based on our experience of the world and is indeed a valid line of argument, then it is of a certainty possible to come to the knowledge that creatures have their restricted existence from the unrestricted existence of God and that there is nothing which God in imparting restricted existence presupposes by way of either potentiality or actuality outside of his own existence in order to bring about that order of moved movers ("restricted existences") which is what Aquinas calls creation.

In other words, the idea of creation as the dependency in being of whatever exists in intrinsically limited ways on the existence of God as intrinsically unlimited, the idea, that is to say, of "creation out of nothing", can indeed be arrived at from experience alone and is so arrived at least implicitly by anyone who considers valid the proof from motion. For what the proof from motion ends by concluding implies precisely the consequence that God in giving existence to creatures acts presupposing nothing at all of existence on the side of what he creates:[73]

> For since God is existence itself by essence, it follows that created existence is the proper effect of God, just as to light on fire is a proper effect of fire. But this effect God causes in things not only when they first begin to be but for as long as they continue to be, just as light is caused in the air by the sun as long as the day lasts. For however long, therefore, a being has existence, for just that long is God present to that thing according to the manner in which it has existence. For existence, the act of being, is that which is most intimate to each thing, and that which is most profoundly intrinsic to each thing; for existence is what is formal in respect of everything which is within anything, as was made clear above. Whence of necessity God is present within all things, and this intimately.

Existence is the point at which God is present to the world; but outside of what exists there is only – nothing at all. Later on[74] Aquinas will explain that it is in certain respects more proper to say that things exist in God than it is to say that

---

73 Aquinas c.1266: *Summa* I.8.1c. (Busa 2, p. 194): "deus est in omnibus rebus, non quidem sicut pars essentiae, vel sicut accidens, sed sicut agens adest in quod agit. oportet enim omne agens coniungi ei in quod immediate agit, et sua virtute illud contingere. unde in vii physic. probatur quod motum et movens oportet esse simul. cum autem deus sit ipsum esse per suam essentiam, oportet quod esse creatum sit proprius effectus eius; sicut ignire est proprium effectum ignis. hunc autem effectum causat deum in rebus, non solum quando primo esse incipiunt, sed quamdiu in esse conservantur; sicut lumen causatur in aere a sole quandiu aer illuminatus manet. quandiu igitur res habet esse, tandiu oportet quod deus adsit ei, secundum modum quo esse habet. esse autem est illud quod est magis intimum cuilibet, et quod profondius omnibus inest, cum sit formale respectu omnium quae in re sunt, ut ex supra dictis patet. unde oportet quod deus sit in omnibus rebus, et intime."
74 I.8.3 ad 3.

God is present within all things; nevertheless, the presence of God within all things, not as part of their nature nor as one of their characteristics or circumstances but as the source of the whole of the existence they have correlative with the essence or potentiality making them be – by specification and restriction – the kind of being that they are (human, alligator, stellar, etc.), "as an agent is present to that within which it acts",[75] is a pure truth of reason, and therefore of philosophy and *doctrina intellectiva*, even if its clearest enunciation historically was in fact in the context of the attempt by Aquinas to establish a *sacra doctrina* specifically Christian beyond the boundaries of philosophy. The doctrine of creation out of nothing, I think we must say, may to be sure be utilized as an *ancilla theologiae*; but in that case (in order for it *to be* that) the conclusion in question must be by a logical priority a conclusion of philosophy, for the very reasons just considered. Not only may one arrive at this knowledge by abduction from experience alone, but that is precisely how Aquinas presents it in his *prima et manifestior via*.

The presence of God to and within all beings, of course, is precisely the central doctrine of Neoplatonism. Outside Plotinus (AD203–270), we find it also in the *Bhagavad Gita* (i.499–199BC) and the *Tao Te Ching* (i.550–399BC). If these early "sacred works" are read in the light of the philosophical doctrine of Aquinas as it follows from his first proof of the existence of God, they appear as profound meditations on the manner in which the creature capable of thought and reflection should appreciate the existence of all things within the knowledge and love of God and try to realize this appreciation in his or her manner of conducting everyday life. All that is lacking in these works, the *Gita* in particular, is the understanding that "having existence" (as distinct from "being existence") is not an illusion to be overcome but a privilege to be exercised. The "dualism" of God and creatures is not an illusion, *"Maya"*, but a consequence of the difference between what *is* existence and what *has* existence; in other words, of the difference between what is purely actual and what exists as a mixture of potency and act, of the difference between God and creature.

"After Creation, There Are More Beings but No More Being"

Forms are required for things to be this and that, to explain the diversity of the world; but existence is always on loan from God *and cannot be borrowed elsewhere*. The ultimate actuality of those forms in all their diversity, curiously, is not their own. In this singular case, the case of the existent as such, more singular by far than Anselm's object of thought "than which a greater cannot be conceived", none but God *possesses* what all others *share*; and all others *share* what God alone *possesses*.

"After creation", the Thomists of the Renaissance liked to say, "there were more beings, but no more being";[76] and now we see why: one there is that exists without

---

75 I.1.8c: "sicut agens adest ei in quod agit."
76 "Post creationem, sunt plura entia sed non plus ens." We could be Heideggerian and capitalize this last "b" ("e" in the Latin); but why bother? The point is compatible with Heidegger's thought,

borrowing, and all other existence, even in giving rise to the formal perfections which define and diversify being, are on loan from that one. Whence it follows that God is present in all things, not as a part of their essential or accidental subjective constitution, but "as an agent is present to the one in which it acts",[77] wholly present everywhere to all things,[78] for the existence of created being is his proper effect "as to ignite is the effect proper to fire".[79] Just as a thing burns only so long as there continues to be fire, so does a thing exist just so long as the action of God continues with respect to it.

All existence is from God, yet from that truth either that God is all or that all is God does not follow. As Aquinas put it,[80]

> By saying that God alone is existence, we need not fall into the error of those who have said that God is that universal existence whereby each thing whatever is formally. For the existence which is God is of such a condition that there can be no addition to it, whence through its very purity it is and distinct from every other existence.

Hinduism, Buddhism, and Taoism used to be accused of "pantheism", of holding that God is all in all. To this charge recent protagonists in the debate have introduced a new term: not pantheism, they say, but *panentheism*, is the truth about being and reality. God is all in all, but yet he transcends all. The divine being constitutes every being, yet all beings together do not exhaust the divine being. However many beings there are, however long the cosmic process emanates and transforms beings into beings, never is the divine transcendence exhausted. God is all in all, but always more than all. The retention of the transcendent dimension combined with the affirmation of the immanence of God as constitutive of all things is what defines panentheism and distinguishes it from pantheism.

Pantheism was clearly anathema to the existential doctrine of Aquinas; but panentheism no less, clever as it is as a new stage in the historical dialectic of human discourse. For what the doctrine of Aquinas precludes is not only the reduction of divine transcendence to immanence in the cosmos, but rather and more profoundly the making of the being of God constitutive of the being of things. One could frame this as a consequence of his distinction of essence from existence, but this distinction was not original with him. Closer to original with Aquinas rather was the idea that God has an essence which consists in existence, and closer still to original with

---

but is no part of that thought, and to use fashionable devices to create an impression otherwise is mischievous.

77 I.8.1.c.
78 I.8.4.
79 I.8.1.c.
80 Aquinas, c.1252/6: *De ente et essentia*, cap. 4 (Busa 3, p. 586): "nec oportet, si dicimus quod deus est esse tantum, ut in illorum errorem incidamus, qui deum dixerunt esse illud esse universale, quo quaelibet res formaliter est. hoc enim esse, quod deus est, huius condicionis est, ut nulla sibi additio fieri possit; unde per ipsam suam puritatem est esse distinctum ab omni esse."

him was the explicit awareness of the consequences of affirming the denial of a distinction of essence and existence in the unique case of God. The preclusion of the claim of panentheism is a consequence mainly of the fact that in every being whose essence is other than existence *something is added to existence*, and it is *this addition* which prevents the identification of the formal being of creatures with the reality of God:[81]

> For God is not some finite existent, but transcends the totality of such existents, and for this reason when, through understanding or any other cognitive modality, we become aware of existents, by none of those cognitive modalities through which we become thus aware is God known. Again God is interior to all things causally, yet even so he is nothing of what is in those things constituting them as finite: and for this reason, whatever is cognized in existing things whether by intellect or sense or whatever modality, in all of the things that are known God too is known in a certain way, namely, as cause, yet for all that he is known from none of them as he himself exists.

Neither in Aristotle nor anywhere else in previous tradition is there anything to compare with this discussion of Aquinas. In the Thomistic revival initiated by the 4 August 1879 encyclical *Aeterni Patris* of Pope Leo XIII, a number of leading figures emerged: Mercier (1851–1926), Maréchal (1878–1944), Gilson (1884–1978), and Maritain (1882–1973) from France; Lonergan (1904–84) from Canada; Rahner (1904–84) from Germany. Of this group, Gilson and Maritain in particular insisted on the primacy of *esse* in the metaphysics of Aquinas, and I think even my brief remarks above are sufficient to indicate that they were right in their emphasis, even though this is by far from the whole of Aquinas (there is no way to reduce all the vast range of propositions and doctrines expressive of Aquinas's mind as a series of corollaries to the primacy of *esse*[82]). It remains that the metaphysics of *esse* in

---

81 Aquinas c.1265–7, *Super librum Dionysii de divinis nominibus*, cap. 7. lect. 4. (Busa 4, p. 572): "deus enim non est aliquid existentium, sed supra omnia existentia et ideo, cum per intellectum et alia praedicta [opinio, phantasia, scientia, tactus, nomen, etc.], cognoscantur existentia, nullo praedictorum per cognitionem alicuius existentium deus cognoscitur. rursus deus est omnia in omnibus causaliter, cum tamen nihil sit eorum quae sunt in rebus essentialiter: et ideo, quidquid in rebus existens cognoscatur vel intellectu vel sensu vel quocumque praedictorum modorum, in omnibus istis cognitis, quodammodo cognoscitur deus, sicut causa, cum tamen ex nullo cognoscatur sicut est."

82 Gilson created a school with many members who could only be described as "single-issue Thomists". Everything was judged by whether a given author allegedly did or did not grasp, to their satisfaction, the "primacy of *esse*" in the thought of Aquinas. But the thought of Thomas ranged over many more issues than those that can be reduced to the metaphysics of *esse* or the metaphysics of anything else. To exclude from the "authentic tradition of St Thomas" all those thinkers after him who explored the foundations, implications, and applications of the thought of Aquinas to questions not corollary to the metaphysics of *esse* amounts to ideological folly. What began as an important insight, the "intuition of being", as Maritain somewhat counterproductively labeled the issue, thus ended gradually as a stifling "single-issue Thomism" orthodoxy sapping much of the vitality of the Thomistic revival in the United States and Canada.

Aquinas is among the most distinctive and foundational of his insights, as far beyond the act/potency doctrine developed in Aristotle's writings as the starship *Enterprise* is beyond the shuttle *Challenger*.

A Note on the Distinction between Essence and Existence
The doctrine of the "act of being" (*actus essendi*) is so strong and highly developed in Aquinas that when, toward the mid-twentieth century, the philosophical movement called "existentialism" came along, Thomists with some glee and legitimacy could lay claim to the movement, to being the "true existentialists". Yet of course those who originated the late-modern movement called Existentialism[83] neither saw themselves as followers of Aquinas nor were particularly interested in Aquinas. And, as would later happen with the Neothomist attempts to equate the *Sein* of Heidegger with the *actus essendi* of St Thomas, the partisans of St Thomas were able to advance their cause only by missing what was central to the insight and actual concern of their putative late-modern *manqués*. In the case of the modern existentialists, what had caught their attention was more the Latin *non-ens* ("*ens rationis*") than anything like the Thomistic *esse*; in the case of the Heideggerians, the focus of insight was rather the being proper to things existing as known and cathected (affectively integrated within the Innenwelt) than the *esse* proper to *ens reale* that was the focus of insight for Neothomism. (The "nose of wax" fallacy need not be confined to students of the *Latin* scholastics!)

Such misunderstandings are inevitable and normal in the historical development of philosophical discourse. I doubt that the same can be said of the neothomistic claims that Aquinas discovered the distinction between essence and existence, that before Aquinas we encounter on this point only what Burrell[84] calls "the pre-history of the distinction of existence from essence", which has been the neothomistic position through most of the twentieth century.[85] Whatever the "prehistory" of this distinction may have been, if indeed there was such a prehistory, St Thomas clearly did not think that the history could begin with his work. In his own opinion, not only could the distinction already be found expressly in the work of Boethius and Aristotle before him; but it was also his opinion that in Boethius the distinction is presented correctly as a *self-evident truth*, that is to say, a truth which anyone who thinks about the matter will more or less instantly see, a truth that needs little more than to be formulated in order for any participant in the discourse to understand it and have to agree with it. Besides his two commentaries on Boethius, where Aquinas makes his understanding of the mind of Boethius plain on the matter,[86] he

83 See below, chapter 13 p. 578f.
84 Burrell 1986: 20.
85 Details of the story are provided by McInerny 1990.
86 Aquinas, c.1257/8: *Super Boetium De Trinitate*; and c.1259: *Expositio in librum Boethii de Hebdomadibus*. See the contemporary commentary by McInerny, 1990.

had already said the same earlier, in fact in one of his earliest and most important speculative treatises in philosophy, when speaking wholly in his own name:[87]

> And because what a purely spiritual intelligence is, as has been said, is the same as or identical with its form as an intelligence, for this reason its quality or essence is that very form, and its existence received from God is that by which it subsists in the physical world. And on this account some say that a substance of this kind, to wit, a spiritual substance, is composed from that by which it exists and that which it is, or from that which is and an act of existence, as Boethius puts it.

Material substances are composites of matter and form, this is their whole essence. Spiritual substances have no matter, yet they do have potentiality respecting existence, just as do material substances. And this is precisely because, as was said as early as Aristotle[88] (much earlier too, I am sure, though we lack for texts): what a thing is and that it is are different.

In discussing the problem of how we come to know what something is, Aristotle distinguished between "being" and "substance", and distinguished between definitions which tell us what a substance is, what would later come to be called "real definitions", and definitions which told us only what words mean, what would later come to be called "nominal definitions". For nominal definitions as such he had no scientific use, because "one can signify even things that are not", whereas science concerns only things that are. Hence, the first question science must answer is whether a thing exists, and only then what is it, which smacks suspiciously of a distinction between existence understood in terms of "being" and essence understood in terms of "substance" framed in the technical context of Aristotle's discussion of what constitutes scientific demonstration.

Now Aristotle, in this context, considered that "to know what something is and to know the explanation of the fact that it is are the same", that is to say, he considered that the knowledge of the causes which made the thing be in this or that way to be the same as to know what the thing is insofar as it is a real thing. Definitions for scientific purposes of mastering the order of *ens reale* answer to substances which are real beings, not to names which are indifferent to what is or is not. But he saw the difference between "being" which does not fall in a genus and "substance" which does; and he confined "definition" to the latter, even though he did not consider nominal definitions to be definitions for the purposes of science. And he saw quite clearly that, as he himself put it, "what a man is and that a man is are different";

---

87 Aquinas c.1252/6: *De ente et essentia*, cap. 3 (Busa 3, p. 586): "et quia, ut dictum est, intelligentiae quiditas est ipsamet intelligentia, ideo qualitas vel essentia eius est ipsum quod est ipsa, et esse suum receptum a deo est id, quo subsistit in rerum natura. et propter hoc a quibusdam dicuntur huiusmodi substantiae componi ex quo est et quod est vel ex quod est et esse, ut boethius dicit."

88 Aristotle c.348–7aBC: *Posterior Analytics* II.

292 of Part II The Latin Age

that is to say, the substance of man, being a real substance, admits of real definition, but the being of any given man need not be real.

According to Burrell, as we took note,[89] this remark of Aristotle's pertains to the prehistory rather than to the history of the distinction between essence and existence. According to Aquinas, however, this remark of Aristotle's is to be understood in the very terms of the distinction between essence and existence and therefore as part of its history – or at least that is the light in which he himself saw Aristotle as having made the remark, as he expressly tells us in his explanation of what Aristotle has said at this point:[90]

> What is that which a man is and a man's existence are not the same: the reason they are not the same is that only in the case of the first principle of being, which is being essentially, is actual existence and its whatness one and the same; but in the case of all these other beings which are beings through participation [in the being which is essentially existence] the existence of the being and the essence of the being are necessarily unidentical. And this is also the very reason why one and the same demonstration cannot show both what something is and that it is.

And of course, if Aquinas understood Boethius correctly, and was further correct in agreeing with Boethius's identification of the difference between essence and existence as belonging to the category of truths that need only be enunciated to solicit recognition and agreement from mature and serious participants in the discourse, then he would also be right in understanding Aristotle to have seen the distinction in question and to have taken note of it insofar as it had a bearing on the technical discussion which he had undertaken.

But in that case what was unique or original about Aquinas's metaphysics was not that it began by discovering something that many others had seen all along, but rather in the realization that the causal analyses philosophers had made up until now had all alike presupposed existence in their analysis of the effects and types of causality. What was original with Aquinas was the singling out of existence as such, the act of being as that with respect to which all forms are potential, as *itself* an effect to be accounted for *as* effect, and not simply presupposed to the action of various other types of causes explaining this or that formal effect in the order of finite beings. Of course, as soon as the point has been made, the realization dawns that existence is not merely a formal aspect of being, but that which every formal aspect presupposes in order to exercise its formality, in order to specify finite being in this or that way, as of this or that type. So as an *effect* existence is a universal

---

89 Burrell 1986: 20

89 Burrell 1986: 20

90 Aquinas c.1270/1: *In libros posteriorum analyticorum* II. lect. 6. n. 3 (Busa 3, p. 303): "aliud est quod quid est homo et esse hominem: in solo enim primo essendi principio, quod est essentialiter ens, ipsum esse et quidditas eius est unum et idem; in omnibus autem aliis, quae sunt entia per participationem, oportet quod sit aliud esse et quidditas entis. non est ergo possibile quod eadem demonstratione demonstret aliquis quid est et quia est".

effect, the one effect without which there are no other effects. As the one effect without which there are no other effects to consider, existence then appears as the one effect proper to the creative activity of God – the handwriting of God in the form of created beings, let us say. The "dependency in being" which Aristotle rightly saw as the essence of causality is now understood not in terms of the various types of dependency we can presciss[91] *within* the order of finite beings interacting, but is generalized rather as the specific and distinctive dependency of the *entire order of finite beings interacting*, the "ordo universi" as such in its totality, seen in relation to its creative source as that which makes possible in the first place interactions among finite beings, namely, existence, "like light in the air from the influence of the sun".[92]

It was not the "discovery" of an obvious truth which would occur and had occurred to practically everyone in every age of philosophical understanding who had reflected on the difference between truth and error, fact and fancy, what could be and what is – namely, that whether something is does not answer the same question or pertain to the same aspect of reality as what is that something if it is – that marked the originality of Aquinas in the area of thought about existence. Not at all. What marked his originality was casting one term of that obvious distinction in a heretofore unreflected light, by considering precisely that aspect of "being" which does not fall within any genus, namely, its existence, in the perspective of the proportion of effect to cause.[93] And this novel perspective was not something Aquinas arrived at gradually, but something he expressly stated in his earliest writings, perhaps even more clearly than in the much later *quinque viae*:[94]

> That actual existence should be caused by the form itself or by the essence of a thing (I am talking about an efficient cause) cannot be the case, for the reason that in that case some particular thing would be its own cause and would produce itself in being, which is an impossibility.[95] So every particular thing whose actual existence is other than its nature has that existence from another. And because everything that depends

91 See the terminological discussion in note 125, p. 310 below.
92 Aquinas c.1252/6: *De ente et essentia*, cap. 3 (Busa 3, p. 585): "sicut lumen in aere ex influentia solis".
93 One finds this point in Aquinas early as well as late, as we shall shortly see. On the late side, however, particularly clear is the c.1266 treatment in the *Summa* I.45.5. and I.104.1.
94 Aquinas c.1252/6: *De ente et essentia*, cap. 3 (Busa 3, p. 585): "non autem potest esse quod ipsum esse sit causatum ab ipsa forma vel quiditate rei (dico sicut causa efficiente) quia sic aliqua res esset sui ipsius causa et aliqua res seipsam in esse produceret, quod est impossibile. ergo oportet quod omnis talis res, cuius esse est aliud quam natura sua habeat esse ab alio. et quia omne, quod est per aliud, reducitur ad illud quod est per se sicut ad causam primam, oportet quod sit aliqua res, quae sit causa essendi omnibus rebus, eo quod ipsa est esse tantum. alias iretur in infinitum in causis, cum omnis res, quae non est esse tantum, habeat causam sui esse, ut dictum est. patet ergo quod ... esse habet a primo ente, quod est esse tantum. et hoc est causa prima, quae deus est. omne autem quod recepit aliquid ab alio est in potentia respectu illius, et hoc quod receptum est in eo est actus eius. oportet ergo quod ipsa quiditas vel forma ... sit in potentia respectu esse, quod a deo recepit; et illud esse receptum est per modum actus."
95 It involves a contradiction.

on something else reduces to that which is essentially as to a first cause, there must needs be something which is the cause of the actually existing of all things by virtue of the fact that it itself is existence and nothing else. Otherwise an open infinity of causes results, since every thing which is not actual existence alone would need a cause for its actual existence, as was said. Whence it appears that … every particular being has its existence from a first being which is pure existence. And this pure, self-subsisting existence is the first cause which is God. For everything which receives something from some other is in potency with respect to that other, and this which is received in the receiver is its act. Whence it follows that essence itself or form … is in potency respecting the actual existence which it receives from God; and that actual existence received is received in the manner of act.

The doctrine is the same, from one end of the writings of Aquinas to the other end. Compare the early text just read to another written by Aquinas just as he was about to begin his *Summa theologiae*:[96]

The act of existence itself is the boundary act participable by all beings, but existence itself participates in nothing beyond itself. Whence, if there be anything which is itself existence subsisting, which is what we say of God, we say that self-subsistent existence does not itself participate of anything beyond its pure existence. There is no comparable rationale at work in the case of other subsisting forms which have to participate respecting existence as a potency respecting act; and so they are able to participate in something other than themselves by reason of being in a certain manner in potency.

The pretension that St Thomas discovered the difference between essence and existence is no older than the twentieth century, but over the course of the decades of that century it led to some pretty strange posturing. Aristotle made it the condition of a science which wanted to understand reality that it answer first respecting an object it sought to investigate the question *whether that object exists* apart from the mind's consideration. Yet Phelan[97] would have us believe that "in the world of Aristotle there was no *esse*." The effort to maintain that Aquinas was the first to discover the difference between essence and existence leads those engaged in it to remarkable conclusions more reminiscent of the modern idealism they oppose than of the way Aquinas presents the distinction between essence and existence as an ancient heritage of philosophy and a common heritage of anyone who begins to

---

96 Aquinas c.1265/6a: *Quaestio disputata de anima*, art. 1. ad 2 (Busa 3, p. 376): "ipsum esse est actus ultimus qui participabilis est ab omnibus, ipsum autem nihil participat; unde, si sit aliquid quod sit ipsum esse subsistens, sicut de deo dicimus, nihil participare dicimus. non autem est similis ratio de aliis formis subsistentibus, quas necesse est participare ad ipsum ut potentiam ad actum; et ita, cum sint quodammodo in potentia, possunt aliquid aliud participare."
97 Phelan 1957: 118.

think on the matter of the contrast between physical being objectified and purely objective being, the point of origin of distinctively human awareness. Phelan is led so far as to tell us "*that* God is is not mysterious" because "it can be demonstrated". By contrast, "*that* creatures are is indeed a mystery", although "*what* a creature is is not mysterious" because "it is conceivable".

Something is backward here. To where has experience disappeared in these bizarre assertions? We experience creatures, not as creatures, of course, but as fellow finite beings with whom we are caught up in essential interactions, our "transcendental relatives", we might say at this point. We experience in every loss and every death around us the difference between what things are and whether they are. If we are lucky, we may figure out that there is a God, or someone may be able to set out for us in a way that we can grasp its "rational necessity". The actual existence of this God, in such a case, remains something asserted, "the truth of a proposition", as Aquinas put it. What a creature is is very mysterious, not because it is conceivable but because of our direct experience of being as finite. And the existence of God is even more mysterious, because our experience, outside of mysticism, does not attest to *that* existence directly. Experience does not directly attest to infinite existence as it does attest to the finite existence of our transcendental relatives in the family of finite being; at best – again, outside of mysticism – what experience does is provide, through our interactions with the finite beings surrounding us, the intellectual materials which imply the reality of an infinite existence, and hence from which we can conclude to that reality with propositional truth.

What is backward, I would suggest, in the neothomistic fairytale, is just what McInerny put his finger on in a book that will prove more important to history than it did to its day: "The difficult thing is not, as Existential Thomists put it, to isolate or segregate *esse* from essence" and then by a singular vigilance protect our minds from introducing into *esse* (*ut exercitum* or *ut significatum*?, quaerit Advocatus Diaboli) any hint or suspicion of dreaded 'essentialism'. "*Au contraire*", expostulates McInerny.[98] "The heart of the matter is to establish that there is one in whom they are *not* distinct. *That* is the achievement." To which I can only add: *D'accord*.

The achievement Aquinas won by casting a common distinction in the light of the proportion required between effects and proper causes, and finding that between existence and particular causes such proportion was wanting, was the achievement of reaching a position from which it is possible to see or "demonstrate" that, notwithstanding the difference between essence and existence in the whole of our direct experience of being, this very experience implies the reality of one and only one being in whom essence and existence are not distinct but one and the same,

---

98 McInerny 1990: 253; the last italics only are added to the text.

a being *the essence of which* is existence and, as a result (speaking from the only
point of view that we can speak, namely, that of our understanding), supremely
perfect:[99]

> Although God is existence and nothing besides, this hardly means that the other
> perfections and noble qualities are wanting to him, but means rather that he possesses
> all of the perfections which exist in all the categories of finite existence. Because
> he possesses all perfections he is said to be "simply perfect" or "perfect without
> qualification", as both Aristotle and Averroes as his commentator say in Book V
> of the *Metaphysics*. But he has those perfections in a more excellent way than any
> things possess them, because in him they are entirely unified, whereas in finite beings
> the perfections are scattered. And the reason perfections in God are one is because
> they all belong to him according to his undivided act of existence; just as were
> someone able to effect the activities of all qualities through one single quality he
> would have all qualities in that one quality, so God contains in his own existence all
> perfections.

The consequent discovery that participation (that is to say, the exercise of an act
of existence which is no part of one's essential structure as a particular instance
of the possible kinds of finite being) presupposes potentiality within the very actuality of formal structures as formal is what excludes the divine existence from
constituting the formal being of creatures, as proponents of Hinduism, Buddhism,
and Taoism came generally to teach. This is the insight that leads Aquinas to define
essence, particularly substantial essence, as the last (or first) potentiality in the
line of participability respecting existence as the ultimate actuality of all forms.
The "being of creatures" thus stands outside the divine being by reason of being
intrinsically composed according to a diversity of rationales or "possibilities", which
the divine simplicity excludes; and yet the being of creatures is completely dependent
upon the divine being as the only source whence existence, as not derived, can be
derived. Under this existential dependency the full range of causal interactions then
has its play in determining what possibilities of the finite order – what possible
participations of the divine perfection – shall be, become, and pass as historically
actual; and the "immanence" of the creative action at the inmost being of all that
procession of becoming and passing away is yet formally no part of that which is
being finitely.

---

99 Aquinas c.1252/6: *De ente et essentia*, cap. 4 (Busa 3, p. 586): "quamvis sit esse tantum, non oportet
quod deficiant ei reliquae perfectiones et nobilitates, immo habet omnes perfectiones quae sunt in
omnibus generibus. propter quod 'perfectum simpliciter' dicitur, ut philosophus et commentator in
v metaphysicae dicunt. sed habet eas modo excellentiori omnibus rebus, quia in eo unum sunt, sed
in aliis diversitatem habent. et hoc est, quia omnes illae perfectiones conveniunt sibi secundum esse
suum simplex; sicut si aliquis per unam qualitatem posset efficere operationes omnium qualitatum,
in illa una qualitate omnes qualitates habet, ita deus in ipso esse suo omnes perfectiones habet."

Let Thomas make this final point himself:[100]

> And so when we say that an essence is a being, if someone thinks that therefore an essence is caused by some being, either by itself or by some other, the thought process has gone awry, because it was not in this manner of conceptualization – the manner, namely, in which something subsisting in its actual existence is a being – that essence was said to be being, but rather was essence said to be being as that by which something exercises actual existence. Whence to ask how an essence itself is by something is to go awry. The proper question to ask is how something else is through an essence.

For essence has no being except through the existence which exercises it. How could it? For essence is a formal perfection, and all forms are potential respecting actual existence! Yet it is essence – not existence, but that through which existence realizes and exercises itself finitely, that which specifies and limits the finite exercise of existence – that gives intelligibility to what is in the actual world of nature and interacting beings. Essence explains the limits as well as the capacities of finite beings, and guides accordingly (*"forma dat esse"*) their comings and goings both accidental and substantial through the play of causal interactions within the constraints of formal structures.

Theology as a Systematic Exercise of Reason
Theology in the cultural milieu shaped by Aquinas was a pressing need, and what was pressing about it was quite specific to the cultural situation defining the end of the so-called "dark ages". The translation of Aristotle's scientific and philosophical writings into Arabic in the ninth century had compelled Moslem thinkers to struggle to reconcile Islamic teaching and Greek philosophy. The same thing had happened in Spain to the community of Hebrews in the twelfth century, inspiring ibn Daud (c.1110–c.1180) and Maimonides (1135–1204) to seek a harmony between Judaism and Hellenic philosophy. So now, at the turn of the thirteenth century in central Europe, the arrival in Latin dress of Aristotle surrounded by a phalanx of Arabic commentators impelled Christian thinkers to try their hand at assimilating Greek science and metaphysics. Scriptural authority was little help, for the Arabs had their own scriptures, and Aristotle was invulnerable to such an appeal, being both long dead and older than either the Christian or the Islamic scriptures (as least the ones specifically so). Christian thinkers were forced, in such a cultural situation, either to abdicate or to use the language and tools of reason. In other words, they were

---

100 Aquinas c.1256/9. *Quaestiones disputatae de veritate*, q. 21. art. 4. ad 4. (Busa 3, p. 125): "et ideo cum dicimus: essentia est ens; si procedatur sic: ergo est aliquo ens, vel se vel alio; processus non sequitur, quia non dicebatur hoc modo esse ens, sicut aliquid subsistens in esse suo est ens, sed sicut quo aliquid est. unde non oportet quaerere quomodo ipsa essentia aliquo sit sed quomodo aliquid alterum sit per essentiam."

forced to develop a theology, as distinct from exegesis, patristics, or anything we would today call "religious studies". And form a theology they did.

It is not that there was no theological reasoning before Aquinas's century. Of course there was. Indeed, more than one of the early patristic writers were skilled practitioners of Greek philosophical concepts, to mention nothing of the speculative genius displayed by Augustine in his *De Trinitate* of the early fifth century. But these writings without practical exception were of an apologetic and pastoral bent, which presupposed the Christian standpoint in such a way and to such an extent as virtually to deny philosophy any proper autonomy outside the sphere of religious orientation. They were imbued through and through with the spirit of *parti pris*. Taking sides was the name of the game; partisan spirit its élan. Below the intellectual vigor of these writings were the array of "practical" or "pastoral" writings of a strictly ecclesial, liturgical, or sacramental orientation.

With Aquinas, religious thinking becomes something more than a mere partisan expression and appropriation of "pagan philosophy". Religious thinking, to begin with, was made to respect thinking simply so called; for human understanding was recognized by Aquinas to have a proper autonomy and sphere of exercise, which, if not neutral respecting divine revelation (for Aquinas considered that all truth pointed in the direction of the divine origin of thought and being), was nonetheless not subject to mere dictates of authority either, but only to evidence in the light of which even authority could be countered as abusive. Recognition of and the demanding of respect for the "rights of reason" were what distinguished the religious thinking of Aquinas and made his theology, even though based on and presuppositive of Christian revelation, a "science" which could draw on without distorting the achievements of human understanding in the speculative and practical spheres alike. By distinguishing the proper spheres of religious belief and philosophical understanding, Aquinas was able to erect a framework for systematic thinking within which reason would keep its due, and hence within which intellectual dialogue would in principle be possible between faiths and across cultures. In time, the delicate plants of science, distinct from philosophy and theology alike, for the seeds of which Aquinas's main teacher Albert showed such keen sensitivity, would find room for their normal development within Aquinas's synthesis of philosophical doctrine and Christian religious dogma.[101] That grace presupposes and perfects nature was Aquinas's motto across the boards, and nowhere more than in the affairs of the intellect.

Aquinas's metaphysics of *esse* is the foundation of his theology, insofar as theology is an edifice of contemplative reason expressed in discourse in the light of faith, as is clear from the very organization Aquinas gives to his *Summa*. But

---

101 A number of needless debacles would obscure this fact for centuries, as we will glimpse in chapter 11; but the greatest of the followers Aquinas found among the later moderns, Jacques Maritain, would show this to be true in his epistemological masterwork, *Les Degrés du Savoir*, discussed briefly in chapter 6, p. 225f. above.

theology in Aquinas's sense no longer plays in today's culture the role it did for so many centuries, in no small measure as a consequence of what he achieved. In a "religious studies" department today, there would be no thought of displacing Lombard (that is, patristics). "Theology" would be, at best, a co-ordinate study alongside scripture and patristics. More probably theology would be a subordinate study in many places considered dispensable, as in the lecture I attended by a Presbyterian who rhetorically challenged a largely Dominican audience in Chicago to explain how anyone could put as much trust in reason as Aquinas did and still expect to be saved. There is reason why Rahner, Schoonenberg, and others today respectfully differ from Aquinas as to the central subject matter of theology, and think that an anthropocentric theology would better fit the Christian mission today. But this is a philosophy text, and we have not the time or space to go off on this fascinating theological cross-road.[102]

The Human Soul and Mortality

One of the great controversies in which Aquinas participated concerned the interpretation of Aristotle's books *On the Soul* ("De Anima"). Averroes construed the Stagirite's text to say that there is but one Mind for all human beings, and that as a pencil ceases to write when the author sets it down, so the individual human at death ceases to participate in the one same *Intellectus Agens* which uses each of us in our turn as its pencil. Consciousness continues, but it is not *our* consciousness that continues – it never was. Other interpreters granted not even this much to immortality. They saw in the Stagirite a doctrine on this score not much different from Epicurus: as the soul of a dog recedes back into the potency of matter when the dispositions of the body (the organization of secondary matter) are no longer able to sustain it, so too with the soul of a human when the body becomes sufficiently indisposed. Ask not where are yesteryear's snows; they are back in the potency of matter where they yesterday came from, and whence tomorrow they will be called when conditions in the environment are again right.

Aquinas thought that Averroes had the better argument in thinking that Aristotle's text required in the individual human being the active presence of a power of understanding which could not be explained at the level of organic powers such as those on which the senses depend. But he thought that Averroes' denial that this *intellectus agens* was a faculty of the individual human nature was wrong. As he explained at the end of the year 1270 in his *De unitate intellectus*, "On the Unity of the Intellect against the Averroists", nature, any nature, is complete within itself at the level of substance. This is what it means for an individual to *subsist*. If human nature in the activity of understanding gives proof of being able to grasp an object (such as being) which transcends the restrictions of time and place that mark every material object as such, then that nature in its root – that is to say, the soul – must

---

102   Writing strictly as a philosopher, I think I have shown (Deely 1996) there are good grounds in Aquinas himself for such a change of focus. But Rahner hardly needs my assistance.

itself have an immaterial dimension which is not educed from the potency of matter but is capable of surviving when the body corrupts.

At this point the medieval arguments in favor of the capacity of the human soul to survive the destruction of the body (by reason of a nature irreducible to bodily correlation) took a turn anticipative, as it were, of the modern materialist doctrine introduced by Pierre Jean Cabanis (1757–1808) in the first[103] of twelve *mémoires* collected together and published in 1802 under the title of *Rapports du physique et du moral de l'homme*. Cabanis, a physician as well as a philosopher, proposed the idea that the brain is the organ within the body specialized for the production of thoughts, as the stomach is specialized for digestion, the genitals for reproduction, the eyes for seeing, and so forth. Long before, it is true, the physician and philosopher Alcmaeon of Croton (fl. early fifth century BC) had first identified the brain as the central organ of consciousness in his treatise *On Nature*. But for Alcmaeon, the brain was still the rational soul's bodily instrument, not the embodiment of the rational mind (or "intellect") as the eyes embody the power of sight or the stomach the function of digestion.

Against this appealing modern doctrine that brain embodies rational human thinking as eyes embody sight Aquinas raised in advance some interesting considerations. For the brain, like any bodily part, is material, and therefore, like everything material (every bodily part), is extended in space. Therefore it is not possible that specifically human thought has the brain as its adequate producing cause. For specifically human thought is often self-reflective, that is, capable of turning back wholly upon itself. In self-reflection, the mind's activity of thinking and the object of thought coincide. This would not be possible if thinking were, like perception, intrinsically involved with matter. It would be a case of a finger scratching its own tip. For the first accident of whatever is involved with matter is quantity, the having of parts outside of parts.[104] And any quantified power, that is to say, any cognitive power *directly* exercised through a bodily organ, would be precluded by the very extension of that organ from a complete turning back on itself – from perfect or self-reflection, such as we experience in ourselves when we examine our consciences. Nonlinguistic animals, whose souls are wholly educed from matter, are incapable of such complete or perfect self-reflection. At most they are capable of an imperfect reflection whereby one sense power corrects or supervises and supplements another power subordinate to it. Any given sense power can reflect or "turn back" upon another, lower power; but, being intrinsically quantified, such a power cannot turn back upon itself – any more, again, than a finger, being a quantified body, can scratch its own tip.

This intrinsic restriction by the conditions of extended matter is why the range within which vision can occur is limited, and so on with hearing and the other sense powers of the body. Sense powers have an upper and a lower limit beyond which

---

103 Written, apparently, in 1796.
104 See the question of "How Mathematics Applies to the Physical Environment" in Aristotle, chapter 3, p. 78 above.

their awareness cannot go, however powerful they may be within that range.¹⁰⁵ Only powers which participate in the human understanding exhibit (and only through that participation) a capacity to expand to the infinite, to being material and immaterial, finite and infinite. And the human understanding itself, in grasping being as its object, grasps something which precisely transcends the material world and oversteps the boundaries of the interactions of material substances.

It follows, therefore, that as the human understanding or mind is capable of an activity which transcends the limits of matter, the root principle of that activity, the rational soul, must be capable of surviving the destruction of the body. *Ab esse ad posse valet illatio*: "from what is actual to what is possible is a valid inference". Action follows from being, so what acts independently of matter must exist independently of matter. Thus Aquinas concluded to the natural immortality of the human soul: the activity of understanding shows in its exercise a transcendence of the limitations inherent in quantified, that is, material, substances; therefore it has an existence which is not restricted to its bodily condition. The intellectual soul, the human soul, depends on sense for the object but not for the exercise of understanding. But what acts independently of the bodily organs can exist independently of those organs. Hence, the death of the body, uniquely in the human case, is not the end of the soul, not the disappearance of the individual back into the generalized potency of matter.¹⁰⁶

---

105 Cajetan reduced this argument to a trenchant formula: *intus existens prohibet extraneum et obstruet illud*, "what is of a material nature limits and obstructs what can be grasped externally"; which amounts to an abstract generalization of the concrete formula found in many places and formulations in Aquinas himself (e.g., c.1265/6a: *Quaestio disputata de anima*, art. 2c [Busa 3, p. 371]): "quae est receptiva omnium colorum, caret omni colore".

106 The argument was not available to Aquinas, but it is the one from the late 20th century that best expresses the point of the arguments that were available to him. Human language has no bodily organ. If you ask, "What language were you born speaking?", meaning "language" in the vulgar sense of the species-specifically human modality of language exapted to create linguistic communication, not only is the answer "None", but the underlying adaptation, "language" in the species-specifically human sense of a modeling system that is not directly and completely tied to biological constitution, as discussed in chapter 1 of this book, does not even depend on vocal cords or voice. In México we had a friend deaf and dumb from birth, Francisco el Mudo he was known as, with whom we carried on elaborate communication of the most distinctive and irreducibly linguistic sort without a word being spoken in any sense reducible to what dictionaries contain. Of course one needs a brain to see, but that does not make of the brain an eye. Similarly, one needs a brain to understand, but that does not make of the brain the understanding. Thomas's point is subtle, and the absence of any intrinsic genetic determination in the formation of one natural language (Latin vs. Greek, English vs. Spanish, etc.) over against the others (the many external determinants are beside the point) makes of natural language as understood semiotically the best "empirical" referent for the type of argument for individual human immortality that Aquinas is trying to make. But, of course, the force of the argument depends also on his doctrine of substance and of essence as specifying the natural abilities and powers proper to a being as natural constitutives of "what it is", as well as on his doctrine of *esse* as communicating to the formal powers the whole of their reality as exercising a reciprocal causality with *esse* (making it the *esse* of a human being, say, rather than the *esse* of a gopher or slug, etc.). Outside of this framework of distinctions, the point of the argument for the immateriality of the intellect as manifesting an

For the strict Aristotelians the conclusion posed a problem. For matter and form, potency and act, are strictly correlative. Hence the human soul, as the form of a body, must be reducible to the potency of the matter it actuates, exactly as is the soul of the nonlinguistic or "brute" animals. So much later would argue Pietro Pomponazzi (1462–1525), first at Padua (1495–1509), then at Bologna (1512 till his death). He embodied his reasoning in the book he published in 1516, *De Immortalitate Animae*, "On the Immortality of the Soul", where Aquinas is cited as the "decos latinorum", "the splendor of the Latins".[107] Pomponazzi's contemporary, the celebrated Cajetan (1469–1534), after an earlier sermon of unmatched arrogance[108] in which he proclaimed against the blindness and folly of Pomponazzi, later[109] humbly recanted his views and professed immortality knowable only by the light of faith.

Well, the question of immortality is a perennially interesting one, in which each of us has an eventual stake. The trouble with this debate, from a pragmaticistic point of view, is that there is after all only one way to subject it to the test of experience, and once having done that, the experimenter proves incapable of writing up a report. "Near death" experiences will hardly do. Close but no cigar. It is real death that is required.

Short of that, it can certainly be said that, whatever may be the case with the individual soul, strict Aristotelians, among whom Cajetan on this question came to include himself, have undoubtedly failed on this score to understand the doctrine of *esse* central to Aquinas in his distinction from (indeed, his transcendence of) Aristotle.[110] For *esse*, the act of being, comes to the supposit, the individual as a complete whole or unit of being. And the soul of that supposit, even be it *also* the form of a body, if it be a soul capable of an activity transcending the limitations of prime matter, would assuredly be capable of existing apart from the body it informs. For Aquinas the human being is a substance, indeed, and the human soul is the form of a body, indeed; but the rational soul is not *only* the form of a body, it is *also* the subject of an act of existence proper to itself which it communicates to the body as long as the dispositions of the body permit. After that, the soul continues on to its destiny.

---

exercise of existence which goes beyond the capacity of the bodily organic structures to fully account for can hardly be felt. For the point of the argument is not an *isolated* point, but a culminating one sustained by the whole framework of his anthropology, natural philosophy, and metaphysics of *esse* together.

107 Pomponazzi 1516: cap. 4, opening par.: "latinorum decus Diuus Thomas Aquinas" ("the splendor or glory of the Latins, the Divine Thomas Aquinas", or "St Thomas Aquinas", although "Divus" is a bit stronger than "Sanctus"); cf. p. 286 of the 1948 Hall/Ransdell English trans.

   Such an accolade used in appreciation of Aquinas in the Renaissance would have been in the line of the Latin practice of calling Aristotle "the Philosopher", Maimonides "the Rabbi", and Averroes "the Commentator".

108 Delivered before Pope Julius II on the First Sunday of Advent, 1503.

109 See the remarks in note 154 of this chapter, p. 324 below.

110 Cajetan on immortality is extensively studied in Schmitz 1953, and on the general doctrine of *esse* in Reilly 1971.

As able to exist apart from the material structures and organs of the body, the soul is said to be "immortal"; but as the form for a body the soul so existing is *incomplete* in its substantial nature. In its own right, therefore, the human soul existing as such is a very peculiar "substance", indeed. It is an incomplete substance, whole only when and as informing a body, but existent even when deprived of doing so, namely, from death on.[111]

And because it has a spiritual nature, it retains always a core of independence which transcends and eludes every external force, every probe from without of its innermost tendencies and secrets at the personal core of this intelligent being we call "human" as a moral creature. At this spiritual and intellectual center, from which the being properly called human emanates, reside what Aquinas called "the secrets of the heart" ("*occulta cordium*"), the innermost intentions which constitute the moral life of the individual mortal which can be known as they are to God alone, and which no force external to the soul itself can finally determine. These secrets of the heart are the ultimate fruit of human liberty, the womb of individual destiny, hidden behind the eyes and face and manner, at which others may guess but God alone can know as judge.[112]

The human soul is thus not the form of an angel. It is not a *separated* substance, but a *separable* substance, and an incomplete one at that. Aquinas's thought on this matter was surrounded by a considerable network of orthodox belief: the belief that the soul has no pre-existence but is directly created by God at the appropriate moment as form of its body and, at one and the same time, as so participating *esse* as to continue in existence when the body has corrupted;[113] the belief in the Second Coming, at which time there will be "a new heavens and a new earth", with the souls of the dead restored to bodies in glorified form – no longer subject, that is, to the corruptions and wants of flesh as we know it.

On many of these tenets of religious belief philosophy is and must be silent (the bad example of Neoplatonism notwithstanding). But there is no gainsaying what becomes intellectually possible as intelligible in the light of Aquinas's interpretation of Aristotle's philosophy of nature, based on his own metaphysics of *esse*.

---

111 Thus, Aquinas saw in the philosophical doctrine of the natural immortality of the soul a kind of preamble to or adumbration of the orthodox Christian theological teaching about the eventual *resurrection of the body* and its reunification with the soul in a glorified form at the "parousia", the end of time.

112 See, e.g., the *De veritate* (c.1256/9), Q. 8, art. 13.

113 The interested reader should study without fail the c.1265/6a work of Aquinas *Quaestio disputata de anima*, "Disputed Question on the Human Soul", in its totality, though I may note that article 2 (Busa 3, p. 370) directly addresses the question of the act of being or existence (*esse*) proper to the soul and why the human understanding as a distinctive or "species-specific" cognitive power may presuppose but cannot itself act through any bodily organ as such; and that article 14 in particular addresses directly the question of "the immortality of the human soul, and whether it is immortal" (ibid., p. 386), as article 15 addresses the question "whether the human soul separated from the body is capable of understanding" (p. 387).

The "Preambles to Faith"

And making intelligible in the context of philosophy propositions of religious belief or faith was a main objective of theology as a rational undertaking. This objective later became explicit in the project of establishing what came to be called the *praeambula fidei*, the "preambles to belief". These were the rationalizations of experience and the world which would make of Christian belief a congenial, transcendent extension of what reason is able to know and to prove on its own grounds:[114]

> So therefore in the development of theological doctrine we can make use of philosophy in three ways. First, for the purpose of demonstrating matters which are conducive to faith ["praeambula fidei"], which one believing ought to have knowledge of, such as the truths about God provable by natural reason – that God exists, that God is one – and other truths of this kind, whether about God or about creatures, which are proved in philosophy, and which faith presupposes. Second, for calling attention to natural phenomena which suggest or bear some resemblance to truths which are held on faith, the way Augustine in his book on the Trinity draws many parallels from teachings of philosophy to illustrate the Trinity. Third, for resisting assertions advanced contrary to faith either by showing them to be false or by showing them to be gratuitous.

For Aquinas was a firm adherent of the view that truth can be only one. There cannot be something true in revelation which truly contradicts what we know to be true in experience. The task of theology is to deal with the details of the unity of truth as revealed directly by God in the world of culture through the Church and scriptures, on the one hand, and as revealed by God indirectly in the world of nature through experience and reason, on the other hand.

Philosophy, as distinct from theology, is concerned only with truth as it can be discerned through human experience. But it is impossible in the nature of the case, Aquinas thought, that if philosophy proceeds carefully, thoroughly, and well, it will come up with conclusions incompatible with what we know from the Christian revelation. This was a point on which Aquinas was passionate. When Siger of Brabant (c.1235–81), in the 1269–70 scholastic year, composed his "Questions on the 3rd book of Aristotle's *Treatise on the Soul*" (*Quaestiones in Tertium de Anima*) defending as correct an interpretation of Averroes' interpretation of Aristotle that

---

114 Aquinas c.1257/8: *Super Boetium De Trinitate*, q. 2. art. 3c (Busa 4, p. 525): "Sic ergo in sacra doctrina philosophia possumus tripliciter uti. primo ad demonstrandum ea quae sunt praeambula fidei, quae necesse est in fide scire, ut ea quae naturalibus rationibus de deo probantur, ut deum esse, deum esse unum et alia huiusmodi vel de deo vel de creaturis in philosophia probata, quae fides supponit. secundo ad notificandum per aliquas similitudines ea quae sunt fidei, sicut augustinus in libro de trinitate utitur multis similitudinibus ex doctrinis philosophicis sumptis ad manifestandum trinitatem. tertio ad resistendum his quae contra fidem dicuntur sive ostendendo ea esse falsa sive ostendendo ea non esse necessaria."

was incompatible with Christian belief,[115] Aquinas in rebuttal was relentless, ending thus:[116]

> Behold our refutation of these errors. The position is not based on documents of faith but on the reasons and statements of the philosophers themselves. If, then, there be anyone who, boastfully taking pride in his supposed wisdom, wishes to challenge what we have written, let him not do it in some corner, nor before children who are powerless to decide on such difficult matters. Let him reply openly if he dare. He shall find me here confronting him, and not only my self, but many others whose study is in truth. We shall do battle with his errors, and bring a cure to his ignorance.

The "Christian Philosophy of St Thomas Aquinas" of which Gilson likes to speak was in fact his theology. Reasoning guided by the light of the revelation of a specific believing community is precisely what Aquinas considered theology to be. That is why Maritain, at the end of his life, after many and eloquent attempts over years to defend the notion, ended by abandoning the expression "Christian philosophy", and rightly so, as, after all, an inapt designation.

Free Will and Freedom of Choice

A "preamble", not to religious belief, but to the possibility and intelligibility of morality, was in Aquinas' mind the philosophical doctrine of the freedom of the will, the capacity in the human being within limited contexts of thought and behavior to exercise freedom of choice in determining aspects of the individual's destiny in time. This doctrine is not of a piece with the doctrine of the natural immortality of the human soul as an incomplete substance in its own right (a "substance" insofar as it is able to exercise existence independently of the body, "incomplete" insofar as its complete exercise of existence is not independent of the body but precisely as form of the body), but is yet closely related thereto.

So-called "free will" is a form of appetite or desire, a movement which carries the soul out from itself toward the acquisition or possession of a recognized good. The

---

115 Sometimes Siger is charged with the theory of "two truths", that is to say, with teaching that a proposition could be true in philosophy but false in theology and vice-versa, but this charge is an injustice to Siger. His teaching was merely that reason and philosophy lead to some conclusions which actually contradict what we know to be true by revelation, but that in those cases we should not consider the conclusions true. The "two truths" theory itself would be formulated by his Averroist descendants in the time of Pomponazzi (1462–1525).

116 Aquinas 1270: *De unitate intellectus contra Averroistas* (Busa 3, p. 583): "haec igitur sunt quae in destructionem praedicti erroris conscripsimus, non per documenta fidei, sed per ipsorum philosophorum rationes et dicta. si quis autem gloriabundus de falsi nominis scientia, velit contra haec quae scripsimus aliquid dicere, non loquatur in angulis nec coram pueris qui nesciunt de tam arduis iudicare; sed contra hoc scriptum rescribat, si audet; et inveniet non solum me, qui aliorum sum minimus, sed multos alios veritatis zelatores, per quos eius errori resistetur, vel ignorantiae consuletur."

key term here is "appetite", *appetitus*, a technical term of philosophy in the Latin Age signifying an inclination to act. Thus "appetite" is the intrinsic inclination of a being to act, an inclination which arises directly from and expresses its substantial nature according to circumstance. Appetite is, if you like, the transcendental relation of finite being to action. Thus "appetite" exists in all beings, cognitive or not, as the very inclination of a being to respond according to its nature to its circumstances. A stone held in the hand of a person standing on a planetary surface exists in circumstances which incline it to fall should the hand let go. The same stone cast into the sun will vaporize. The falling and the vaporization alike are expressions of the *appetitus* proper to the stone. Appetite as the simple inclination to action of any being as such the scholastics, Aquinas in particular, termed *natural appetite*, which they distinguished from the inclination to action which arises within a being only as a consequence of its being aware of something. The inclination to act based on or arising from awareness they termed rather *elicited appetite*. The inclination to grow in a living substance is a natural appetite; the hunger that grows in an animal is likewise a natural appetite. But what makes the hunger, say, among the largest majority of late-twentieth-century Americans (allegedly 91 per cent of families in 1997, for example) take the form of a desire to eat turkey on the last Thursday of November is a natural appetite channeled and specified by elicited appetite. Elicited appetite is an inclination to act that is consequent upon and mediated by cognition.

Hence there will be as many elicited appetites as there are varieties of cognition. In this way Aquinas, following Aristotle rather closely on this point, distinguishes *voluntary behavior*, which is common to human beings and all other animals, from *free acts* which are possible only (and only occasionally) for linguistic animals. In order to make this point here, let us anticipate in a summary form, as it bears on the question of *appetitus*, the discussion of sense-perception and species-specifically human apprehension we will take up in detail below under the rubric of "being as first known".[117] Only linguistic animals have a modeling system or "cognitive map" (an *Innenwelt*) that is not restricted to the sense-perceptible aspect of the physical surroundings. As a consequence, only linguistic animals have an elicited appetite, an inclination to reach out to the surroundings, that is not restricted to the sense-perceptible aspects of those surroundings but precisely sets them against an interpretive horizon of infinite semiosis, an action of signs which goes beyond the horizon of material being to see, prospectively at least and in principle, temporal actions in the light of eternity and finite goods against the background of infinite desire. Maybe the linguistic animal becomes often enough a religious animal because of these same considerations or factors; be that as it may, the elicited appetite consequent upon intellectual cognition is exactly what is meant, according to Aquinas, by the "freedom of the will". In his own words:[118] "tota ratio libertatis ex modo

---

117 See in this chapter "The Problem of Being as First Known", p. 331ff. below.
118 Aquinas, *De veritate* (c.1256/9), q. 24 "De libero arbitrio", art. 2 "Utrum liberum arbitrium sit in brutis", *corpus*.

cognitionis dependet" ("the whole rationale of freedom of choice is a function of the manner of awareness"). We may illustrate the central distinctions in a simple diagram.

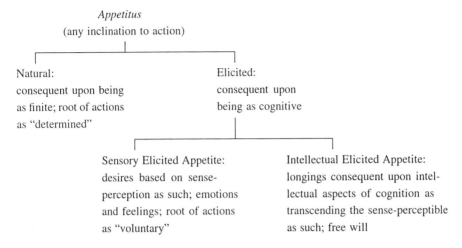

"Free Will" as Part of the Scheme of Appetites

Humans and other animals alike experience desires and inclinations consequent upon their awareness of things, and actions based on such awareness are in all cases "voluntary actions". But free acts, in distinction from voluntary acts, arise not only when an intellectual awareness results in an inclination to do something, but when in addition that intellectual awareness itself is reflexively mediated so that the lack of determination to sensible aspects as such of desired objects actually and expressly becomes a factor in the realization (or frustration) of the very inclination itself.

One may become aware of the need to relieve oneself, a "call of nature" indeed and a natural appetite. But the "becoming aware" of this call brings into play also elicited appetite, and a house-broken dog, for example, will voluntarily defer the satisfaction to appropriate circumstances, as will a socialized human animal. But the voluntary deferment cannot be sustained indefinitely. Eventually nature will insist on having its way; and if "appropriate circumstances" have not arisen by that point, a disaster, more or less minor, will ensue.

The same limitations apply whether the elicited appetite is sensory or intellectual: both voluntary and free actions may elect a path that nature through circumstance will eventually make into a "dead-end". In such cases the culmination of voluntary and free actions alike is frustration of the elicited appetite by the limitations of the organism's very nature; and no one will bring this fact more clearly to light than will the Victorian "rational animal" Sigmund Freud (1856–1939) late in modern times. But the basic framework in which the possibility and limits of freedom of choice become intelligible, a "freedom" without which the very ideas of "morality" and "responsibility" become antinomic, has nowhere been outlined more clearly than in the writings of Aquinas. His honorific title as the "Light of the Latins" is earned by his investigations into many areas of philosophy and religion, but perhaps none moreso than his exposition of the very possibility and intrinsic limitations, both internal and external, of human freedom.

The Starting Point of Metaphysics

The doctrine of being in Aquinas, or rather, the doctrine of the act of being, *esse*, makes of the problem of metaphysics in his writings a different but hardly totally different matter than was the case with Aristotle's "first philosophy". Aristotle, in the text that survives under the title of *Metaphysics*, spoke of "the science he was seeking" to determine the object of. Well, to that quest Aquinas was finally confident that he had brought a successful outcome. What Aristotle tentatively sought Aquinas definitely found.

In the later Latin Age, the competing interpretations of Avicenna and Averroes over the object of metaphysical knowledge drew the lines explicitly followed by the greater part of the medieval Latins:[119] Averroes had taught that metaphysics was concerned only with spiritual beings, the "separated intelligences" and ultimately the God who moved the heavens, whereas Avicenna had taught that metaphysics is concerned rather with an object established by a more generic or "most common notion" of being under which fall both material and spiritual substances and even God – the view, in broad strokes, that would be passed to the moderns at the close of the Latin Age through the work of Suárez.

In this crowd, Aquinas stood out by the fact that his own position could not be neatly traced to the Avicenna-Averroes controversy, although his highest respect for these Arab philosophers may be seen from the positive treatment he gives in assimilating their ideas to his own thought in the two earliest writings we have from his pen.[120] Nowhere does Aquinas take his stand in terms of that controversy as such. He does not allow the terms of the question to be posed for him, but follows the lead of Aristotle in requiring strictly that the terms of the investigation be taken from the requirements of the subject matter. His position finally is certainly *closer* to that of Avicenna; but for Thomas, God does not fall *under* the concept of "common

---

119 A classic study in this area is that of Zimmermann 1966.
120 In a non-polemical, expository manner, Aquinas set forth his own understanding, in the first treatise, the c.1251 *De principiis naturae*, of main ideas from Averroes (the treatise covers the three principles of change [matter, form, and privation] and the four causes of change [material, formal, efficient, and final] and the different way in which each of the causes and principles is to be understood by analogy); and in the second treatise, the c.1252/6 *De ente et essentia*, he set forth his understanding of main ideas from Avicenna (concerning the understanding of essence, in itself, in its relation to *ens reale*, and in its relation to the logical intentions of genus, species, difference, property, and accident). Though both were certainly composed prior to 1256, Torrell (1996: 349) favors the relative priority assigned here.

being", *ens commune*, which metaphysics develops, but *outside* it as principle and cause – exactly as he tells in the text which Aertsen[121] chooses to conclude his excellent article on method and metaphysics in Aquinas: "It pertains to one and the same science to investigate the proper causes of a (subject-) genus and the subject itself".[122] His position is more complex than that of his influential predecessors, therefore, Greek and Arabic alike, more original than a position that can be mainly traced to such classic sources of Latin philosophical thought; and indeed is bound up with the distinctively medieval development of the doctrine of the transcendentals as common properties "convertible" with being because permeating "being as first known", as we have already had occasion to note.

As a result, the attempt to specify exactly what is the object of specifically metaphysical thinking has occupied a good deal of Thomistic scholarship in the late-modern period. The basic issue by the end of modern times had come to be framed in terms of a question as to whether the concept of "being as such" (*ens inquantum ens* or *ens commune*) is arrived at by a process of *abstraction*, a traditional teaching at least as old as Cajetan and as recent as Maritain;[123] or is the object of metaphysics arrived at rather by a singular judgment, the so-called *negative judgment of separation*, which is the source of the notion of "being as such".

The "Three Degrees of Abstraction"
According to the doctrine of the "three degrees of abstraction", the *first degree* occurs when the mind forms the concept which presents to it the intelligible object of *mobile being* by unifying the objects of experience under the formal rationale of being able neither to be nor to be thought apart from matter, and proceeds to draw out the properties and consequences of what has thus been conceived. This object can be further specified according as one concentrates on the sensible manifestations or instantiations of what falls under this concept to develop the properly empirical sciences or *sciences of observation*,[124] or on the intelligible content proper to this concept, which yields the traditional physics of an Aristotelian type.

In the *second degree* of abstraction, the mind focuses on the quantified or extended aspect of sensible objects and unifies this aspect under a concept which presents the object of *intelligible quantity*, which as such cannot exist apart from matter but can be so thought, and out of which thinking develops the various mathematical sciences, beginning with arithmetic (quantity as divided into numerable sections or "parts") and geometry (quantity as continuous, yielding figures and shapes etc.).

---

121 Aertsen 1989: 418.
122 "eiusdem autem scientiae est considerare causas proprias alicuius generis et genus ipsum:" Aquinas c.1268/72: *In duodecim libros metaphysicorum Aristotelis expositio*, "Proemium" (in Busa 4, p. 390).
123 Maritain 1959.
124 There are many important and fascinating details in the notion of the basic sub-specific distinction possible within the first degree of abstraction which I pass over, referring the interested student to the brilliant treatment in Maritain and a few others.

Finally, in a *third degree of abstraction*, the mind prescisses[125] within experience those aspects of objects which both can be and be thought apart from matter, unifies these considerations in a concept of being as such ("being as such need not be material"), and proceeds with the exploration of the content and consequence of such a concept.

The first thing to be noted about this terminology has been well said by Armand Maurer,[126] namely, that the key term, "abstraction", is not to be understood here in a linear way, as if mathematical abstraction lays hold of a subject simply more abstract and general than that of natural philosophy, and metaphysical abstraction of one simply more abstract and general than mathematics.

The key to understanding the threefold "degrees", in fact, lies precisely in the manner in which the object attained in each relates to existence: in the first degree, the objects analyzed retain throughout the denotation of capacity for existence in the material order of being as *ens reale*; in the second degree the objects analyzed denote formally a purely mind-dependent objective existence restricted to the order of *ens rationis*; whereas in the third degree it is a question of objects denoting again the order of *ens reale* but now in its full amplitude of physical being which can be spiritual as well as material – *ens reale*, that is, thought in the full amplitude of its possibilities and extending to the first principles and causes of finite being as existentially dependent upon a purely actual or "existential" source.

The "Negative Judgment of Separation"

According to the doctrine of the "negative judgment of separation", the way that Aquinas in fact arrived at his concept of being as such was by realizing the consequence of the proof of the unmoved mover in physics and of the immortality of the soul in psychology, the consequence, namely, that *not all being is of this kind*,[127] to wit, subject to the conditions of matter and spatial motion. By this "negative judgment", the notion of "being" is "separated" from necessary embodiment in material conditions, and the two notions of being, material being and immaterial being, are by this act "united" in a single, new concept of "being as such", that is, being as able to be realized in material and spiritual substances alike.[128]

---

125 Since most readers of this work in manuscript flagged this word as a typographically incorrect form of "precise", it is clear that a terminological note here is necessary by way of clarification. My usage here is influenced by the remark of Peirce 1905a, CP 5.449: "If we desire to rescue the good ship Philosophy for the service of Science from the hands of lawless rovers of the sea of literature, we shall do well to keep prescind, presciss, prescission, and prescissive on the one hand, to refer to dissection in hypothesis, while precide, precise, precision, and precisive are used so as to refer exclusively to an expression of determination which is made either full or free for the interpreter [in removing vagueness from the use of an expression]. We shall thus do much to relieve the stem 'abstract' from staggering under the double burden of conveying the idea of prescission as well as the unrelated and very important idea of the creation of *ens rationis* ... but which gives mathematics half its power."

126 Maurer 1958: xxi–xxiii.

127 "Non enim omne ens est huiusmodi" is the actual expression of Thomas in his *Commentary* on the *Metaphysics* of Aristotle.

128 This doctrine, as developed especially in the writing of the Italian cleric Deandrea (1957), was

This manner of doctrinal expression has an interesting history. In the classical Latin phase of the development of Thomistic thought, as just mentioned, the manner of speaking of Cajetan established itself. In the Neothomistic modern phase of "revival" of a development of Thomistic thought, but now in the dominant national languages and so outside of Latin (but, of course, drawing on Latin sources and applying all the tools of modern scholarship to the illumination and evaluation of those sources), two scholars, Louis-Bertrand Geiger and J. D. Robert, independently and more or less simultaneously,[129] attached a special significance to the terminology of the final version of the opening of Aquinas's "reply" to Question 5, Article 3, of his commentary on the *De Trinitate* of Boethius.

The surviving manuscripts of this particular work from Aquinas's hand had been edited at least since 1880, with the various redactions of the just-mentioned opening preserved, in the work of Uccelli.[130] Now, however, in 1947, the argument was made that since Aquinas had gone through several versions before settling upon his opening statement, a special significance ought to be attached to the terminology Aquinas finally settled upon, since it was obviously achieved only after considerable effort at precision; and this terminology spoke of attaining the object of metaphysics not through an "abstraction" but through a judgment of "separation". Since, in the original Latin epistemology, abstraction begins in the so-called "simple awareness" of the mind's first act, whereas judgment occurs rather as a second act of the mind bearing on actual existence, it seemed reasonable and perhaps more than reasonable to think that what had happened through these several redactions was that Aquinas "was progressively realizing", as Maurer later put it,[131] "the eminently existential character of the subject of metaphysics". These authors seemed to forget or not to have understood the importance of the fact that the question of the manner in which the objects distinguishing the speculative sciences relate to existence is already a firm and constitutive part of the doctrine of degrees of abstraction.

Since this all came at the very time when the mania for making Thomism "existential" was reaching a crescendo, the newly emphasized comparison of the aborted beginnings of Q. 5. Art. 3. with the one Aquinas finally settled upon "led some to see a radical shift in Thomas's thinking, one fraught with significance for the way we understand the speculative sciences, particularly metaphysics."[132] But in

---

taken up and further developed by a group of Dominican scholars affiliated with the Aquinas Institute School of Philosophy in the 1950s and 1960s, particularly in a doctoral dissertation by Anthony Schillaci (1961). By reason of various cumulatively incredible circumstances, this dissertation, though passed, was never properly finished nor published in any form. It is not so easy any more to get away with founding a school of thought on unpublished research materials, so I myself undertook to present a summary version of the Schillaci thesis, which in fact Schillaci himself used in class and recommended for publication (Deely 1967). But my version of the presentation in that publication, like Deandrea's notes, is only marginally historical.

129 See Geiger 1947 and Robert 1947.
130 Besides Uccelli 1880, a more recent discussion of Thomas's autograph and the alternative attempts at opening can be found in Decker ed. 1965.
131 Maurer 1958: xxiv.
132 McInerny 1990: 136. See also the whole of ch. 5 in McInerny's book, p. 148ff. The most exaggerated of all the "existentialist" views within Neothomism traces its lineage to the work of

the way of this interpretation lies the plain fact that the terminology of the opening of Q. 5. Art. 3. of his commentary on Boethius's *De Trinitate*, for all his care in arriving at it, does not appear to have had in St Thomas's own mind the transcendent importance over the circumstances of the difficulties within the commentary itself that the existential neothomists tried to assign to it; otherwise we must attribute to inattentiveness or carelessness, two traits that have never been ascribed to the later work of Aquinas, the fact that, in writings subsequent to this commentary, Aquinas does not strictly maintain the terminology of "separation" there introduced, while he does speak in other ways that remain consistent with that terminology.

The Compatibility of the Two Doctrines

Which of these approaches is the "correct" one for arriving at the notion of being as such? In fact, it is hardly necessary to choose between them. Schillaci, as a proponent of the negative judgment, made a good case for the view that, as a matter of historical fact, Thomas Aquinas did arrive at his notion of *ens inquantum ens* on the basis of the twin proofs of the Unmoved Mover in physics and the radically spiritual nature of the intellectual soul in "rational psychology". But supposing this as a matter of historical fact, it would yet be a mistake to conclude from this that the concept *must*, or *can only*, be reached in this way. For indeed it would follow from Aquinas's doctrine of the self-reflexivity of the soul that the experiential materials necessary for performing an "abstraction" such as Maritain describes, or for formulating the same judgment expressed by Aquinas in his *Commentary* on the *Metaphysics of Aristotle*, could be garnered quite independently of the supposedly necessary "proofs" of a bygone era, simply through a reflective stance.[133]

   In fact, Schillaci, following the lead of Deandrea,[134] was able to show that the point of the language of separation found in the commentary on the *De Trinitate* of Boethius can indeed be verified over the range of Aquinas's writings; but this in no way contradicts or invalidates the language developed *also* from the range of Aquinas's writings to speak of the three speculative sciences in terms of varying types of abstraction. Between the threefold distinction of the commentary on the *De*

Owens (1963, 1968), with the claim that a prescissive focus on *esse* even among sensible existents already suffices to ground metaphysics (Knasas 1990). Authors in this line fail to notice that their arguments work only insofar as their focus leads to the postulation of an immaterial source for the *esse* of material beings, which is to beg the question of the validity of metaphysical knowledge as both Aristotle and Aquinas posed it: until we know that there is more to reality than the existence of material substances, we have no basis for a philosophical doctrine of being that goes *beyond* physics. From this point of view, an "immaterial source of *esse*" is no different than a "source of motion itself unmoved": "metaphysical knowledge" is not what *leads* to the conclusion, but rather what *follows from* it.

133 Indeed, this surely seems to be demonstrated in Maréchal's *Le point de départ de la métaphysique* (1922), in the work of Bernard Lonergan (1965), and in so-called "transcendental Thomism" of the 20th century generally. Norris Clarke (1992) has even derived the materials from the "experience of community", which would also follow as possible from Aquinas's doctrine on the soul. A highly accessible presentation of the reflective standpoint as *A Path into Metaphysics* has been recently published by Robert Wood (1990).

134 Schillaci 1961: see the remarks in n128 above.

Trinitate of Boethius, together with other uses of a resonant terminology scattered throughout Aquinas's writing, on the one hand, and the three degrees of abstraction formulated by Cajetan and Poinsot in the Latin Age, on the other hand, there is, as Maritain put it,[135] "a terminological difference with not a glimmer of difference in doctrine".

The Question of Analogy

Closely related to the just-discussed problem of the object of knowledge with which metaphysics begins is the *doctrine of analogy*. This doctrine undertakes to explain the proper nature of the unity of the concept by which being as such is presented objectively. When "being is said in many ways", what is expressed through the saying when it is true and not rather "mindless chatter"? Curiously, though the term "analogy" runs all through Aquinas's writings when this or some kindred question comes up, he himself never pulled his various contexts of usage together into a unified treatise. Aquinas left the materials for a doctrine of analogy, but he did not explicitly formulate it as anything like a separate treatise.

Moreover, the question of analogy is not merely a technical problem. We confront here an essential characteristic of natural language, a universal semiotic phenomenon, namely, the fact that human discourse is rife with only imperfectly controllable relations among different uses of words. The same phenomenon is exhibited in the so-called "transcendental" concepts mentioned above, linguistic expressions conveying a content that cannot be stipulatively restricted to any one category of existence. But if we confine ourselves to the writings accomplished by Aquinas himself, his main interest in the doctrine of analogy is in the context of the divine names, where the philosophy of being reaches its outermost limit, the outermost limit of human understanding.

Analogy in the Texts of St Thomas Aquinas: A Function of Naming

So it is not surprising that the discussion of analogy in Aquinas finds its roots in the observation by Aristotle in the fourth and seventh books of his "first philosophy" that "being is said in many ways"; for the philosophy of Aquinas, as we have seen, is before all else a philosophy of being, and of being understood in terms of the ultimate actuality of all the forms of being which is itself accordingly capable of no further participation, namely, the act itself of being, existence. As grace presupposes nature, so for Aquinas theology presupposes the intelligibility of being and the intellectual tools whereby that intelligibility is rendered actual and brought to expression in human discourse, both the "inward discourse" and its "outward expression" (the exaptation of language to communicate, as we have said) in the formation of a linguistic community, upon which all else in religion, as in civilization generally, depends, in the main. In other words, for Aquinas, theology is unthinkable apart from philosophy of being, but the philosophy of being cannot be thought only in terms of

---

135 "Il y a une différence de vocabulaire, il n'y a aucune différence de doctrine": Maritain 1947: 39, penultimate para. of n. 14. See also Leroy 1949.

theology without betraying its proper nature as human understanding. "Ecumenism", for Aquinas, is rooted first in the commonality of human understanding, and only through that in faith, just as grace does not supplant but perfects human nature. Philosophy is prior to theology, if not in ultimate importance as wisdom, yet as that without which theology degenerates into ideology and fideism and religion becomes in spite of itself a degenerate Lebenswelt indistinguishable in function, for all its difference in content, from the closed Umwelt of the nonlinguistic animals.

Now this brings us to a very interesting matter, and that is the lack of terminological isomorphism between the language of ancient Greek philosophy and the language of medieval Latin philosophy in the matter of what mainly interests Aquinas under what he calls *analogia* or *analogice dictum*, "analogy" or "spoken analogically", which is the matter of the fact that "being is said in many ways". For Aristotle does not at all speak of ἀναλογία in this context, but rather of πλεοναχῶς λέγεσθαι. This last is the Greek expression that the Latins render *multipliciter dicitur*, "said in many ways", for which St Thomas offers as a synonym *analogice dicitur*, "said analogically". The notion that transliterates from Aristotle's Greek as "analogia", by contrast, is nothing more than the proportion of relations in mathematics. The analogy that Aquinas is interested in, however, is not that of a science restricted to the order of *ens rationis*, purely objective being; he is interested in a sense of "analogy" that applies directly to the knowledge of *ens reale*, "physical being objectified". In other words, the "many ways" in which being can be spoken, to which Aristotle never applied the Greek transliterate counterpart of the Latin "analogia", is precisely what Aquinas begins by extending the notion of ἀναλογία to; and he does so precisely to draw "God talk" within the purview of his doctrine of being:[136]

> A proportion can be spoken of in two ways. In one way, a proportion is a definite relation of one quantity to another; and in this way of speaking double, triple, and equal are different types of proportion. In another way, any relation of one thing to another can be called a proportion, and in this way of speaking there can be a proportion of creatures to God, insofar as they are related to him as effect to cause, and as potency to act; and in this way of speaking a created intellect can be proportionate to knowing God.

So the ancient Greek doctrine of ἀναλογία becomes the Latin doctrina of *analogy*; but in the Greek it concerns mathematical relations, whereas in the Latin it is extended to cover any relations whatever among objects, and physical relations

---

136 Aquinas c.1266: *Summa* I.12.1. ad 4: "proportio dicitur dupliciter. uno modo, certa habitudo unius quantitatis ad alteram; secundum quod duplum, triplum et aequale sunt species proportionis. alio modo, quaelibet habitudo unius ad alterum proportio dicitur, et sic potest esse proportio creaturae ad deum, inquantum se habet ad ipsum ut effectus ad causam, et ut potentia ad actum, et secundum hoc, intellectus creatus proportionatus esse potest ad cognoscendum deum."

of effect to cause in particular. This becomes the heart of Aquinas's doctrine of the knowledge of God that is possible within the orbit of philosophy, or, what comes to the same thing, possible for human understanding as such:[137]

> The knowledge natural to us takes its origin from sense, whence our natural knowledge can extend only so far as it can be led by sensible things. But from sensible things our understanding cannot reach so far as to attain to a seeing of the divine essence, because sensible creatures are effects of God that do not adequate the divine causal power. Whence from the knowledge of sensible things the whole power of God cannot be known, nor consequently can his essence be seen. But because sensible things are his effect depending upon a cause, we can be led from them to know that God is; and to a knowledge of those things about him which are necessary for him to be the first cause of all beings exceeding all of his caused things. Whence we know of him his relation to creatures, to wit, that he is the cause of all of them. And we know the difference of creatures from him, to wit, that he is not anything of those things which are caused by him; and that the creatures caused by him are not separated from him because of his deficiency, but because the transcendent unity of his perfections so far surpasses the multiplication of perfections in finite beings.

So our "names of God", say, "good", gain their primary meaning from experience of sensible beings; and when we apply them to God they retain this primary meaning through which now we discourse not about a sensible but a supersensible being concerning which we understand that he is himself good and the cause of the good we experience, while being good – capable of excellence in operation – in a way that is in the line of but beyond the reach of any excellence of operation that we can directly experience.

So we see that in St Thomas the doctrine of analogy is entirely an epistemological doctrine, not an ontological one. That is to say, it is a doctrine about our knowledge of things and use of language to express that knowledge to others; it is not as such a doctrine about the things that are independently of our knowledge, a doctrine of being. We name things as we know things and in no other way. When the knowledge is confused, the naming is confused. But when the knowledge is based on one thing, good experienced, let us say, or being experienced, or again truth experienced, and so

---

137 Aquinas c.1266: *Summa* I.12.12c: "naturalis nostra cognitio a sensu principium sumit, unde tantum se nostra naturalis cognitio extendere potest, inquantum manuduci potest per sensibilia. ex sensibilibus autem non potest usque ad hoc intellectus noster pertingere, quod divinam essentiam videat, quia creaturae sensibiles sunt effectus dei virtutem causae non adaequantes. unde ex sensibilium cognitione non potest tota dei virtus cognosci, et per consequens nec eius essentia videri. sed quia sunt eius effectus a causa dependentes, ex eis in hoc perduci possumus, ut cognoscamus de deo an est; et ut cognoscamus de ipso ea quae necesse est ei convenire secundum quod est prima omnium causa, excedens omnia sua causata. unde cognoscimus de ipso habitudinem ipsius ad creaturas, quod scilicet omnium est causa. et differentiam creaturarum ab ipso, quod scilicet ipse non est aliquid eorum quae ab eo causantur; et quod haec non removentur ab eo propter eius defectum, sed quia superexcedit."

on, and the name is applied to another thing that we do not experience yet know *that it is* existing, and existing as good, being, true, and so forth, then *what* is signified is signified as being true of creatures *and* true of the cause of creatures, the creator; but *the mode* of the signifying is inseparable from *the mode* in which the perfection signified is directly experienced, that is to say, as diversified in creatures which are *more unlike* God than like him yet still *partial or limited reflections or icons* of their ultimate existential source. *What is signified* is the same in creator and in creature, but it is signified adequately in application to the creature and inadequately in application to the creator. So *what is signified* is *partly the same* in the two cases and *partly different*, but the difference is what makes the application to the creator an *analogous* use of whatever the term be – existence, being, one, true, good, and so on. Nor can the difference be removed, because to remove it we would have to change the conditions under which we know.

The creature is known first, not as creature but simply as "something", some being. In the creature are experienced directly perfections and imperfections. Thus the notion of perfection itself comes from experience, and is multiplied (or differentiated) also by experience. Those experiences in which perfection and diversity of perfections are learned directly remains the primary reference point for the concept of perfection and perfections. When these concepts are applied to what is known to exist in the truth of a proposition (namely, that there is a being whose very essence is to exist, and that as cause of the existence of all beings whose essence is distinct from their existence, since existence is what gives final actuality to all formal perfections in that which exists, this *ipsum esse subsistens* is therefore perfect in uniting in itself all that is perfect in creatures in divided ways), the truth of that proposition is also augmented by our coming to understand what was implied in its original, primarily existential application. So we know of God *that he is*, but also *that he is one, that he is good, that he is creator*, and so on, by a strictly logical development that has experience as its referential ground but God known or objectified as its term.

Now we see the importance of Aquinas saying that we know the existence of God through the making of a proposition, not through direct experience. In late-modern philosophy, a huge literature will develop arguing over whether existence is a predicate. In the Latin Thomistic tradition, later authors introduced a simple distinction between existence as exercised and existence as signified. "Existence" as a predicate *signifies* existence as *exercised*. Our only direct experience of existence (always setting aside the matter of mystical experience as defined above[138]) is the existence of sensible things. Here we directly encounter *existence as exercised*, and from this experience we formulate the concept of existence. This concept has for its object not a sensible thing but *existence as signified*, the idea of something which exercises an act of being, something which is or possesses an *actual exercise of*

---

138 See p. 273f. in this chapter.

existence; and this concept can be applied to sensible things (as when we think of a friend, rightly or wrongly, that he has not died yet) or to spiritual things (as when we judge, rightly or wrongly, that there are purely spiritual substances). And it is just such an application, as we saw above,[139] that occurs in the *quinque viae*. And now we see how the doctrine of the divine names follows from the discovery in discourse of the reality of the divine existence as subsistent existence, as existence which is the very essence of that which exists – a pure existence knowable by us in philosophy only through the truth of a proposition. We can now see expressly what was true of the truth of that proposition all along: the knowledge "that God exists" already was an instance of knowledge through analogy. So it is hardly surprising to realize that all the names we can truly form of God are likewise analogous uses of language.

Thus, we see how the doctrines of the knowability and unknowability of God, in the thought of Aquinas, are reconciled through his notion of analogy. The point is so central to his thought that it is possible to multiply the citation of texts practically without limit from the range of his writings. I was tempted at this point simply to let one of his late-modern followers speak on his behalf in terms of making a summary of the point; for no later author has stated the situation better than Maritain,[140] standing as he did at the far boundary of modernity and the frontier of postmodernity, well cognizant the while of the great Latin tradition in metaphysics the moderns had all but succeeded in obliterating. But not even the incomparable Maritain brings together in a single text the point of Aquinas that we are able to know God through creatures for the very same reason that God is aware of creatures through himself, and that the reason why some of the words we both invent and learn over the course of our life experience are more applicable to God than are others is because some reflect more directly what is true of being as such even though all of them reflect directly limited beings, that is to say, existence formally diversified through the essential structures which are what distinguish the being of creatures from the divine being in whom all diversity is reduced to the single surpassing perfection of existence itself subsisting; so that "knowledge in God is the same as

---

139   See p. 283 in this chapter.

140   The text I am thinking of is Maritain 1959: 251: "In the case of metaphysics, analogy constitutes the very form and rule of knowledge. God is not attained in virtue of His incommunicable nature and selfhood, according to the indivisibility of His pure and simplest essence, but only according to that which is shown in His reflections (reflections that, by the way, are truthful) and in the analogical participations which things proportionate to our reason offer us of Him. His essence is not attained as such [no more, to repeat, than his existence], but only inasmuch as creatures, by their very nature, speak of it to our understanding. Thus, not only is the mode of knowing human, but, in addition, the object itself as proposed to the mind and made the term of knowledge (*sub ratione primi entis*) is taken as He condescends, so to speak, to human reason in the mirror of sensible things and by the analogy of being. Metaphysics is poised at the summit of the created world, and from that vantage point, it looks upon the inaccessible entrance toward which all created perfections converge – but without seeing Him in Himself. It grasps His purest light only as it is broken up in the multiplicity of these perfections."

to exist as knowing",[141] and so on for all the other perfections whose intelligible core does not of itself imply the limited conditions under which we experience and from which we abstract (or presciss) that intelligibility and give it expression in the diversity of our conceptions:[142]

> Nor can it be said that whatever is said of God and of creatures can be predicated completely equivocally, because unless there were some agreement of creature to God according to reality, the divine essence would not be the exemplar of the creatures; and so by knowing his own essence God would not know creatures. For the same reason we would not be able to arrive at a knowledge of God from created things; nor would there be any reason why any one of the names suited to creatures should say something more of him than does any other, because in equivocal sayings whatever name is stipulated makes no difference,[143] from the fact that none of them expresses an agreement in reality. Whence it must be said that neither wholly univocally nor wholly equivocally is the name of knowledge predicated of the knowledge of God and of our knowledge, but according to analogy, which expresses no more than a relational similarity.

We know that we know, but that to know is other than the fact that we are; whereas in the case of God, we know that for him to be is to be knowing, and since knowing is his very existence he knows everything that does or could imitate that existence in finite ways; and we, for our part, knowing some of those finite ways, come to know something of God – both that he is, and that he is not knowable in the way that creatures are knowable. Knowing that he is and that he is infinitely knowable, it is not surprising that we can develop a doctrine of divine names without ever exhausting the object so progressively expanded within our awareness. For no matter how much or how little we come to know or think we know, we know always that he is more than whatever we have been able to conceive or will be able to conceive.

So we can see how God can be said both to be a being and to be above being and nonbeing. God is a being insofar as our term "being" is taken from our experience of actually existing things and applied therefrom, by analogy, as we have seen, to the case of the being for whom to exist is the essence, *ipsum esse subsistens*. But

---

141 Aquinas c.1256/9: *Quaestiones disputatae de veritate*, q. 1. art. 2c. (in Busa 3, p. 17): "ita scientia est idem quod esse scientem in eo."

142 Ibid.: "nec tamen dici potest quod omnino aequivoce praedicetur quidquid de deo et creaturis dicitur, quia nisi esset aliqua convenientia creaturae ad deum secundum rem, sua essentia non esset creaturarum similitudo; et ita cognoscendo suam essentiam non cognosceret creaturas. similiter etiam nec nos ex rebus creatis in cognitionem dei pervenire possemus; nec nominum quae creaturis aptantur, unum magis de eo dicendum esset quam aliud; quia in aequivocis non differt quodcumque nomen imponatur, ex quo nulla rei convenientia attenditur. unde dicendum est, quod nec omnino univoce, nec pure aequivoce, nomen scientiae de scientia dei et nostra praedicatur; sed secundum analogiam, quod nihil est dictu quam secundum proportionem."

143 That is, all are equally irrelevant – or relevant – because none says anything that has a bearing on the referent.

insofar as "being" names finite being capable of ceasing to exist, then God is not a being but beyond being and nonbeing. So St Thomas, with due deference to the Neoplatonists, can say that[144] "according to the truth of the matter, the first cause is above being, in that it is the infinite act of existence itself; while being is that which participates in the act of existence finitely."

Finally, we should note that Aquinas, in developing his doctrine of analogy as far as he does with an eye to his principal interest, which is the explanation of how there can be a true and valid philosophical discourse about God, is careful to point out that this extreme use of analogy at the far frontier of human understanding is consonant with other, more ordinary, examples of analogy within human discourse. His perhaps favorite example is the quite earthy one of a healthy organism. A healthy organism, he notes, produces healthy urine. The healthy organism is the cause of the urine, urine an effect; yet as effect it is a sign of that which produced it. Should the sign reveal that the producing organism is not healthy, some medicine may be called for. The medicine now hopefully will play the role of cause, whose effect will be health – the restoration of health – in the organism; and the proof of the success or failure of the medicine will be the next urine the organism produces. "Health", thus, is said directly of the state of the organism, but, on the basis of or "from" that usage, "health" may be applied secondarily – *analogously* – to such related other things as medicine and urine. But *these* are "healthy" only by reference to the organism as "healthy". So Aquinas provides us with a rule which, at least as he presents it himself, is proposed as holding for all analogous use of language without exception, whether we are talking about finite being or about God, and if about God whether we are speaking metaphorically or about perfections that exist more properly in God than we experience their existence in creatures:[145]

---

144 Aquinas 1272: *In librum de causis*, lect. 6 (Busa 4, p. 511): "secundum rei veritatem causa prima est supra ens in quantum est ipsum esse infinitum, ens autem dicitur id quod finite participat esse, et hoc est proportionatum intellectui nostro cuius obiectum est quod quid est ut dicitur in iii de anima". Cf. Guagliardo et al. 1996: 51–2.

145 Aquinas c.1266: *Summa* I.13.6c. (in Busa 2, p. 203): "in omnibus nominibus quae de pluribus analogice dicuntur, necesse est quod omnia dicantur per respectum ad unum, it ideo illud unum oportet quod ponatur in definitione omnium. et quia ratio quam significat nomen, est definitio, ut dicitur in iv metaphys., necesse est quod illud nomen per prius dicatur de eo quod ponitur in definitione aliorum, et per posterius de aliis, secundum ordinem quo appropinquant ad illud primum vel magis vel minus, sicut sanum quod dicitur de animali, cadit in definitione sani quod dicitur de medicina, quae dicitur sana inquantum causat sanitatem in animali; et in definitione sani quod dicitur de urina, quae dicitur sana inquantum est signum sanitatis animalis. sic ergo omnia nomina quae metaphorice de deo dicuntur, per prius de creaturis dicuntur quam de deo, quia dicta de deo, nihil aliud significant quam similitudines ad tales creaturas. ... sic nomen leonis, dictum de deo, nihil aliud significat quam quod deus similiter se habet ut fortiter operetur in suis operibus, sicut leo in suis. et sic patet quod, secundum quod dicuntur de deo, eorum significatio definiri non potest, nisi per illud quod de creaturis dicitur. de aliis nominibus, quae non metaphorice dicuntur de deo, ... huiusmodi nomina non solum dicuntur de deo causaliter, sed etiam essentialiter, cum enim dicitur deus est bonus, vel sapiens, non solum significatur quod ipse sit causa sapientiae vel bonitatis, sed quod haec in eo eminentius praeexistunt. unde, secundum hoc, quantum ad rem significatam per

in all the cases of names which are applied to different things analogously, all the applications must needs be made with respect to one thing, and so must it needs be that that one thing be contained in the definition of all. And because the rationale which a name signifies is a definition, as is said in Book IV of the *Metaphysics*, the analogous name in question necessarily applies first to that thing whose definition is included in the definition of the others, and secondarily or consequently to the other things [whose definition includes other considerations as well], according to the order in which they are more or less proximate to that first thing.

So, for example, the health which is said of an animal falls within the definition of health which applies to medicine: a medicine is called "healthy" insofar as it causes health in an animal; and the health said of an animal falls likewise within the definition of health which applies to urine, which is said to be "healthy" insofar as it provides a sign of the animal's health.

So the names applied to God metaphorically apply first to creatures rather than to God, because said of God they signify nothing other than resemblances to the creatures in question. ... So the name "lion" applied to God signifies nothing more than that God goes about his works as fiercely as a lion goes about his. And so it is clear that according as such [metaphorical] terms are applied to God their signification cannot be defined except through that which is applied to creatures. Concerning other names which are said of God not metaphorically ... these names apply to God not merely causally but also essentially, ... without this in any way gainsaying the fact that, as regards the stipulated or conventional meaning by which the name signifies, such names are applied by us first to creatures, which are what we primarily know. Whence too even the names of perfections which creatures have from God as their cause and which belong more eminently to the divine being than they do to the finite being of creatures and in this sense apply with ontological priority to God yet retain the mode of signifying which belongs to the perfections as found in creatures, as we explained above.

That is the doctrine of analogy we find primarily in Thomas Aquinas's own writings reduced to the main point that even in the case of names applied properly if "supereminently" to the divine existence, it is the acquisition of signification by these names within the context of sensible experience that remains regulative. And the reason why we can know God is the same as the reason why God can know creatures: because they are finite and partial imitations external to God of the perfection found infinitely and wholly internal to the purity of the divine *Esse Subsistens*.

About ten years before he undertook his *Summa*, in Q. 2. Art. 11 of his *Quaestiones Disputatae de Veritate* written between 1256 and 1259, Aquinas had added a distinction between an "analogy of proportion" and an "analogy of proportionality". The former occurs when we speak by analogy of two different things which yet belong to the same order, as "health" said of an animal, of medicine, and of urine.[146] The latter, an "analogy of proportionality", occurs when we speak by analogy of two things belonging to entirely different orders, for example, one to the order of *ens reale* and the other to the order of *ens rationis*, or one to the order of created being and the other to the order of uncreated being, where there is an absence of proportion between the two things talked about.[147] In such a case we speak of a parallelism of relations, of a ratio, in effect, as constituting the ground of the analogy; and only in this latter way can we speak analogically of God and creatures, and even then with some further qualifications.[148] This is what Cajetan will invoke as justifying his claim that there is a uniquely metaphysical analogy of what he calls "proper proportionality" and that only this analogy has claim to the status of a doctrine of first philosophy.

But in between this text of the *Disputed Questions on Truth* Q. 2. Art. 11 and the text of the *Summa* Q. 13. Art. 6 examined above came the *Commentary on the Divine Names* of c.1265/7, written just before or partially overlapping the writing of the First Part of the *Summa*. There he was reminded again from Pseudo-Dionysius of the simpler trick of the "threefold way" of simple affirmation followed by qualified negation followed by an affirmation of eminence:[149] not only can no perfection that intrinsically implies limitation (like "good muscle tone", which presupposes body) be affirmed of God, but even any perfection that has no intrinsic link with limitation, such as living, intelligent, good, being (even though we encounter it in experience according to limited manifestations), cannot be simply affirmed of God in

---

146 Aquinas c.1256/9: *Quaestiones disputatae de veritate*, q. 2. art. 11c. (in Busa 3, p. 16): "quaedam convenientia inter ipsa quorum est ad invicem proportio, eo quod habent determinatam distantiam vel aliam habitudinem ad invicem, ... sicut ens dicitur de substantia et accidente ex habitudine quam accidens ad substantiam habet ..."

147 Ibid.: "convenientia etiam quandoque attenditur non duorum ad invicem inter quae sit proportio sed magis duarum ad invicem proportionum. ... sicut nomen visus dicitur de visu corporali et intellectu, eo quod sicut visus est in oculo, ita intellectus in mente."

148 Ibid.: "quia ergo in his quae primo modo analogice dicuntur, oportet esse aliquam determinatam habitudinem inter ea quibus est aliquid per analogiam commune, impossibile est aliquid per hunc modum analogiae dici de deo et creatura; quia nulla creatura habet talem habitudinem ad deum per quam possit divina perfectio determnari. sed in alio modo analogiae nulla determinata habitudo attenditur inter ea quibus est aliquid per analogiam commune; et ideo secundum illum modum nihil prohibet aliquod nomen analogice dici de deo et creatura. sed tamen hoc dupliciter contingit: quandoque enim illud nomen importat aliquid ex principali significato, in quo non potest attendi convenientia inter deum et creaturam, etiam modo praedicto; sicut est in omnibus quae symbolice de deo dicuntur, ut cum dicitur deus leo, vel sol, vel aliquid huiusmodi, quia in horum definitione cadit materia, quae deo attribui non potest. quandoque vero nomen quod de deo et creatura dicitur, nihil importat ex principali significato secundum quod non possit attendi praedictus convenientiae modus inter creaturam et deum; sicut sunt omnia in quorum definitione non clauditur defectus, nec dependet a materia secundum esse, ut ens, bonum, et alia huiusmodi."

149 Recall the discussion from p. 275f. above. Compare also the analysis by McInerny (1996: 113–15) of the *De veritate* text in question.

the manner that we affirm it of creatures. Thus, I exist and God exists; but existence is not exercised in God in the manner that it is exercised in my being; existence in God is exercised in a manner that transcends my understanding but is nonetheless actual existence. This method, always remembering the distinction between perfections whose very definition or concept implies limitation and perfections whose very definition or concept does not imply limitation even though our direct experience of them is limited, achieves the same results more simply than does the application of the distinction between "proportion" and "proportionality" to the case of analogy.

The bottom line, then, is that analogy as Aquinas treats it is a doctrine about how we use words to express what we know, and transfer words from one meaning to another in order to illumine related things and to develop their connections in discourse. Aristotle called it "equivocation by design". Aquinas called it "analogy". Pure equivocation, of course, is the use of two terms in two entirely unrelated senses, like the "bark" of a dog and of a tree. Terms used in the same sense, like "animal" said of a human being and of a chimpanzee or of a cat, both Aristotle and Aquinas called "univocal". But when one term is brought into relation with another term in such a manner that the meaning of the first term is made relevant to the understanding of the other, then we are in the domain of analogy: the bark of a dog and the bark of a tree have this much in common, that they both sometimes provide protection; in this sense the two terms otherwise equivocal can be rendered analogous through a prior reference to "protection" (or in some other way).

Notice too that in the matter of the divine names, the ways of speaking about God, Aquinas notes that whether we are talking about perfections ontologically prior in God or mere imaginary resemblances fashioned by the mind to give to the being of God some intelligibility relative to the being of creatures, as when Augustine likens God to "a pure eye, because he sees all", in either case *our knowledge*, the development and expression of which is what analogy primarily concerns, goes from creatures to God. In this precise particular, the heart of the matter, it makes no difference that we find, paradigmatically, that existence is "more proper", that is to say, "ontologically prior", in God, whereas "fierceness" is clearly an operational property proper to lions and only said of God metaphorically.

Regardless of the ontological situation, whether the relations involved are mind-dependent or mind-independent relations does not matter.[150] What makes a use of terms analogical for Aquinas is the placing of the definition of one term within what is understood of the definition of some other term. It is an activity of thought in relation to the objects of thought, and ranges across the whole field of objects to which thought extends: from the pure potentiality of prime matter which, because it cannot be directly experienced, Aquinas pointed out, is known only *by analogy* to what we do directly experience, all the way to the pure actuality of God which, because it cannot be directly experienced, Aquinas pointed out, is known only *by*

---

150 McInerny 1996: 9–10 puts it this way: "Thomas is noting that there are inequalities, orderings *per prius et posterius*, among things talked about that do not affect our way of talking about them."

analogy; in between these two extremes are included the intermediate cases, such as that in which "bark" is seen in the light of protection, or medicine and urine in the light of "health". As a late-modern Scotist put it,[151] "clearly the order of the being of things, the order of knowing them, and the order of designating them do not agree". Thomas could not agree more. Analogy pertains to the use of vocabulary whereby a philosopher is able to sort out these competing differences. It is, we might almost say, that part of the doctrine of signs which pertains to the critical use of intelligence in science and philosophy and to what Peirce will call "the ethics of terminology"; but that would get us too far ahead of the story.

Analogy in Thomistic Tradition: A "Concept of Being"

I hope the reader has found the doctrine of analogous names just set forth straightforward and clear, for that is how it appears in the limpid Latin texts of Aquinas himself. After Aquinas, within what would become his own school of commentators, for a long time nothing in particular happens respecting his doctrine; although outside of that specific intellectual line I have already remarked that not enough study of Scotus has been done to know if indeed his doctrine of being is as antithetical to that of Aquinas as the superficial contrast between analogous and univocal terms would make it seem; for we now see that there is nothing in a term as such that makes it analogous, but only its deployment within the field of our apprehensions. "Being" is an analogous term not by reason of any properties of its letters or their combination but because it is "said in many ways", because it is something verified proportionally in quite different things, namely, "existence in this or that capacity" or even, in the restricted case of finite existents, a "capacity for existence" with all the variety that implies. "Being" is an analogous term because, in short, with respect to this character string "being", a *cultural code* has been established: within and through the exaptation of language to communicate, a "universe of discourse" has been created specifically for the purpose of revealing what was implied in Aristotle's discovery that there was something in human experience ("being" he is said to have called it, though he spoke no English) which is verified within each category but which cannot be confined within any category, and so is and must be "said in many ways".

So it is not without interest to discover that the first author formally to attempt a unification of the texts wherein Aquinas deals with the subject he terms "analogy" was an author who happens also to have been vehemently opposed to the success in philosophy of the writings of Duns Scotus, as he was to the success in religion of Martin Luther. Thomas de Vio Cajetan (20 February 1469–10 August 1534), christened "James de Vio", took "Thomas" as his "name in religion" on joining the Dominican order in 1485, at the age of sixteen. He was destined to become known most commonly after his place of birth, Gaetanus. This is the man known to history as "Cajetan", the cardinal of the Catholic church once considered for pope

---

151 Shircel 1942: 19.

who failed in his attempts to tame Luther but whose commentary on the *Summa* of
St Thomas is enshrined in print to accompany the best edition of that masterwork
that has ever been prepared over these last eight centuries, the one commissioned
by Pope Leo XIII and completed between the years 1888 and 1906.

To understand Cajetan, like every man, it helps in some ways, if not in all, to
consider his times, and Cajetan's were turbulent indeed. He was the first, as was said,
to undertake to thematize the notion of "analogy" in terms of its role in the thought
of St Thomas, but it would seem that his doing so was ill-fated by the importance
attached in his milieu to the renewed knowledge of Greek language that had come
to Italy especially in large measure as an unexpected side benefit, as we have seen,
of the Islamic conquest of the city of Constantinople in May of 1453. Cajetan was at
the forefront of those who came quickly to recognize the overwhelming importance
the knowledge first of Greek, and later of Hebrew and other Semitic languages, was
bound to acquire for scriptural studies and hence, eventually, for theology itself. It
is to his credit – so many things fall to his credit and discredit, it is astonishing that
as yet no proper biography has been written – that he pressed at the highest levels
of university and ecclesiastical life for the renewed study of Greek. So – what can
we say – why should not history strike yet another of its stunning ironies in making
his very appreciation of Greek Cajetan's downfall as the expositor of the theme of
analogy in the Latin of Aquinas?[152]

Cajetan under the best of circumstances inclined to be arrogant.[153] You can still
feel his *hauteur* radiating between lines of his *Commentary* on the *Summa*, or from
the whole of his sermon of 1503 on human immortality.[154] Weisheipl,[155] who would

---

152 Ashworth, in a "superior" review (1999: 215f.) of McInerny's magistral summary (1996) of his
long years of reflection on the theme of analogy and the relation under this theme of the doctrines
expressed in the writings of Aquinas and Cajetan, reminds us that Cajetan is related to other
writers than Aquinas, then petulantly rebukes McInerny for ignoring both these writers and the
"good deal of work" that "has been done on all this historical material since 1961". We may
presume that both these neglects are overcome in Ashworth's own encyclopedic report (1998:
414) that "logicians and theologians developed a theory which divided words into three sorts
[to wit, univocal, equivocal, analogical], independently of context." Assuming the accuracy of
the report, McInerny's "neglect" of the works in question may be no more than the shadow of
his clear illumination of the fact that to speak of "sorts of words", analogical ones especially,
"independently of context" is, for Aquinas, a linguistic delusion (an "ens rationis formaliter,
materialiter sumptum").
153 The experience of Luther recounted in his *Acta Augustana* supports the general picture. Cajetan,
Luther reported (1518: 275), "although he said, and now even glories in it, that he would act
toward me as a father and not as a judge, I could not detect any such paternal attitude, except one
which was sterner than any court of justice".
154 Cajetan 1503; a view he came more and more completely to retract in a series of writings tied
to the years 1509a, 1519 (see Romans ch. 9), 1527 (see ch. 22), and 1534 (see ch. 3), when
he came categorically to assert, with no apologies for or mention of his polemics of 1503, that
no philosopher ever has or could, as a "*praeambulum fidei*" or any other way, demonstrate the
immortality of the individual human soul, although he considered such immortality to be a truth
known by divine revelation.
155 Weisheipl 1967; see also Mandonnet 1905.

have known, if anyone of the last modern generations had known, what influences shaped Cajetan's approach to St Thomas, passed over in silence the question of Cajetan's intellectual formation, which gives us a measure of how much work remains to be done in the area. Be that as it may, Cajetan seems to have imbibed, if not the love of Plato, at least something of the traditional Byzantine attitude of the superiority of the Greek language for the treatment of speculative problems. This attitude returned to Rome from Constantinople with the expatriation there of John Cardinal Bessarion, dead when Cajetan was but three, yet a giant presence still, as we can imagine, in the Rome and "College of Cardinals" of Cajetan's mature years; for Cajetan browbeats his Latin peers as "abusers of language"[156] for not following the regulative usage of the Greeks in the matter of analogy, leaving it unsaid or perhaps unnoticed that the primary abuser on the point was Thomas Aquinas himself.[157] Cajetan, for his own part, will indeed take the Greek usage as regulative when, in 1498, he sends forth his to-be-famous work entitled *The Analogy of Names*. The title was felicitous if the doctrine flawed; but the flaw in the doctrine revealed itself soon enough in his letter of 1509 that has come down in history under the more ominous title "the concept of being"; for it is not *as a concept* that being is analogous, it is rather as a *way of speaking* involving necessarily and irreducibly more than one concept derived from experience.

But why should Latin usage conform to Greek usage, unless Greek usage is somehow superior, somehow "regulative". The Byzantines had always considered it so, and their theology developed accordingly, followed by their civil censures. The very idea is not incredible. It is simply false. No one familiar with linguistics today would subscribe to such a notion as a historical language superior *in general*, true as it might happen to be in some particular areas on some particular points. The question that interests us here is whether *analogy as Aquinas thought of it* is just one of such areas or points. There is no doubt that Aquinas does not use *analogia* in a manner isomorphic with Aristotle's use of the Greek ἀναλογία. The only author I know of who has approached the texts of both authors in exactly this light concludes that, on the basis of a detailed comparison of the texts,[158]

> we would have to say that where Thomas is talking of analogous names, names analogously common to many, Aristotle speaks of things said in many ways, with reference to one and the same nature, and not equivocally. Rather than chide Thomas [for an abuse of language], we should perhaps draw some such conclusion as the following. When Thomas speaks of analogous names he does not mean to echo a linguistic expression of Aristotle's, since in the texts which occasion talk of analogous names in Thomas's commentary Aristotle uses such phrases as 'said in many ways in reference to one'. Aristotle clearly means to contrast that kind of talk with univocally

---

156 "Abusiva tamen locutio est", is how he puts it in his commentary on the *Summa*.
157 See the detailed discussion in McInerny 1996: 21ff.
158 McInerny 1996: 33–4.

common and equivocally common terms. Thus, *what* Thomas and Aristotle are both talking about is the same, but they do not *label* it in the same way. There is no fixed relation between Aristotle's use of the Greek term [ἀναλογία] and Thomas's use of the [Latin] loan word [*analogia*].

Yet even the expression "loan word" concedes too much in Cajetan's misguided direction. It is not a question of a term "on loan"; it is a question of the development of a terminology appropriate to expressing the problem as Aquinas sees it. And Aquinas did not speak Greek nor read it well enough to comment directly on Greek texts; nor have we clear evidence that Cajetan knew Greek well enough to justify his browbeating of the Latins in this matter. For certainly his subsequent exposition of what was supposed to be "the mind of the divine Thomas" (*ad mentem D. Thomae*) went far enough astray.

In bare essentials, Cajetan distinguishes (following Aristotle) the two extremes of words applied to different objects but with exactly the same sense, as "human being" said of every student in a class, which are *univocal* terms; and words apparently the same but which apply to objects in completely diverse senses, as "bark" of a dog and of a tree, which are *equivocal* terms. Between these two extremes are words which are used with *different but related senses*, and this is the case of *analogous terms*. So far so good.

However, the case of analogous terms is not simple, and there are many discussions of subdistinctions of metaphor under the heading of "analogy" in Latin authors. The case of metaphor Cajetan calls the *"analogy of improper proportionality"*, passing over expanded discussion as irrelevant to his interest (and despite its very clear interest for the doctrine of the divine names), Cajetan remarks little more than that terms may have senses related through a similarity in their objects which is extrinsic and accidental to the nature of the objects, as "a bright sun" and "a bright smile", a "smiling girl" and a "smiling meadow".

Cajetan calls the case where what is really in the referent of one of the related terms is attributed to the referent of the other on the basis of a causal relation between the two, *"analogy of attribution"*. For example, words may be related in sense because what they apply to are related through causality, as "healthy" said of an organism and of urine the organism produces. Health is in the organism intrinsically, but in the urine only as reflecting that health. Or we speak of a "healthy environment", because, like medicine, it tends to promote health in the organism.

Now Cajetan comes to his main thesis. When words have related senses as a result of a property which is intrinsic and essential to the objects designated by each, the result is what he calls *"analogy of proper proportionality"*. This alone is what Cajetan titles the analogy of being. Two things quite different, a frog, say, and a meteorite, yet both exercise existence. "Being" said of anything actual expresses something intrinsic to that thing, and yet the being is differentiated according to the form or type of thing that exercises it. Being then becomes a matter of a proportion, a *proportio ad esse* or "proportion to existence", a powerful and attractive notion, not least of the attractions of which is that it returns *analogia* to the primary use of ἀναλογία in the ancient Greek writings, which is that of a mathematical proportion, "two is to four as four is to eight": as a frog exercises existence in its own way as a frog, so does a man exercise existence in the way proper to a man.

But the "fly in the ointment" appears especially in Cajetan's identification of the lowest level of analogy, what he calls "analogy of inequality". A fly and a human are both animals, both beings. "Animal" said of both is said in the same sense, that is, univocally. A man is an animal in just the sense that a fly is an animal: both are capable (in Thomistic terms) of receiving the impressions of the forms of other things in such a way as to cognitively relate to those things as physical elements of the environment become and made part of an objective world or Umwelt. But both are beings, too. And in the "hierarchy of being", a fly is *lower* than a human being. Therefore, however they may be "equal" as animals, as "beings" they are related as lower and higher. Therefore, whatever the logician might think and say, the philosopher, who prefers wisdom over mere logic, has to say that fly and human as "animal" are not equal but unequal. Animal, in such a case, that is to say, with reference to the hierarchy of being, is not a univocal term as logic would have it but an analogous term, a term analogous "by inequality". What logicians see as univocal terms appear in the superior wisdom of philosophy as terms analogous by analogy of inequality, inequality in being.

That then there are absolutely no such things as univocal terms seems not to have occurred to anyone. At least I have not seen this made as a point in the literature. Now this may seem on the face of it ridiculous, and I think it is; but there is more, as usual, to the situation than meets the eye. One needs to realize, for example, that "body" was regarded by the Latins, by Thomas himself, as an "equivocal" term as between qualitatively immutable celestial bodies and terrestrial bodies subject to generation and corruption. So Cajetan with his "analogy of inequality" was giving voice to and linguistically marking a conception much broader and more "in the air" of his time than any narrow reading of logical texts and doctrines would reveal. His idea is not ridiculous, at least not in the immediate way that might appear to a sufficiently ignorant postmodern reader. Yet it is wrong, as is always the mischief wrought by philosophers when they concoct a doctrine that mysteriously renders them *Übermenschen*, "supermen", superior to the requirements of logic in the manner that binds lesser minds.

The problem lies in the idea that "being", because it turns out that it must be "said in many ways", is an *intrinsically* or *irreducibly analogous* term; for no term is "intrinsically" anything apart from contexts of application. The key to the problematic, I suggest, lies in the fact that we experience many different things existing in many different ways, and we experience the need to somehow bring all this diversity under a common designation for conveniences of discourse, to be sure, but also for the purpose of a discourse which can express the truth about things as a matter of philosophical doctrine. When we reach the conclusion that "not all being is material", we indeed express a judgment that, as Aquinas remarked, precludes physics, whether in the ancient sense or in the modern sense, from the status of "first philosophy", for if not all being is material then being cannot be adequately understood in physics however completely we come to understand and even dominate the world of bodies in motion, any more than relation can be adequately understood if we restrict our perspective to the reality of relation as it exists independently of the mind.

The judgment of separation, the abstraction of "being" as a concept presenting an object not restricted to the material or to the spiritual order but capable of verification in both orders, makes it possible to unify the knowledge of the diversity of beings in an understanding of "being as such", thereby providing a subject of possible thematic investigations so specific and distinctive that the unity of the science (or rather the doctrinal unity, as we should say in the wake of modernity) so constituted is ensured. The unity of a true philosophical knowledge, however, as Schillaci said,[159] "is not a rigid set of restrictions but an organic 'oneness' like that of a living thing in that it permits the science to come into existence, to contact and assimilate reality, to develop according to its own nature and to reach the end of that nature." If we may conclude in this respect that a metaphysics that does not come to treat of God has not reached its natural finality, we may claim with all the greater ferocity that a metaphysics that claims God or even "esse" *ut exercitum* for its proper object has misunderstood itself in so radical a way as to have betrayed its nature. Between these two extremes lies the idea of being and the realm of *ens commune* that idea constitutes under the discursive heading of "analogy". Within that realm lies the meaning and possibility of metaphysics, one of the features distinctive of the human Lebenswelt in its difference from the perceptual Umwelt of the animals without language.

Beyond the Analogy of Names and Concept: "Analogy of Being"
Cajetan set the terms of the subsequent discussion of analogy within and beyond the Thomistic tradition. Some have claimed to find grounds for dissatisfaction with Cajetan's presentation as a faithful expression of the thought of St Thomas expressed early in no less an authoritative voice than that of Sylvester Ferrariensis (c.1474–1528). In his *Commentary on the Summa Contra Gentiles*, written i.1508/17 and first published in 1524, now published to accompany that work of Aquinas in the critical Leonine edition as Cajetan's commentary accompanies the Leonine *Summa*. McInerny[160] grants that "on the points where Sylvester has offered his independent view, a basis is provided for a bifurcation in subsequent interpretations", but he thinks that "it would be wrong to say that Sylvester presents us with a clear alternative to Cajetan's interpretation"; for in his work what we find, after all, are "not so much different interpretations as different emphases: the basic outlook of Cajetan is retained." Thus, to whatever extent Ferrariensis did or did not early point

---

159 Schillaci 1961: 511.
160 McInerny 1961: 30. See the whole of section 2, "Sylvester of Ferrara", pp. 23–31.

out something of the rather different tenor of Aquinas's own treatment of analogy from that set forth by the learned Cajetan, it remained the voice of Cajetan that continued to be heard and attended to within and beyond Thomistic circles over the subsequent centuries, including the late-modern Neothomistic revival.

But in Neothomistic circles, not universally, though quite broadly, the renewed discussion of analogy took an even more radical turn away from the actual presentation of Aquinas. Dissatisfaction with Cajetan was everywhere expressed,[161] yet nowhere for quite the right reasons – the main reason being that he had distorted St Thomas by failing to understand the lexicological and accompanying syntactic differences that accompanied the transliterate pair *analogia*/ἀναλογία. These differences are in themselves without any necessary significance for philosophical doctrine. But Cajetan made them significant by (mis)taking the two words as names for the same phenomenon in the two languages, contrary to fact. As a result, the doctrine of *analogia* in Aquinas and the doctrine of *analogia* in Cajetan are not the same doctrine. Even though the doctrines of Cajetan and Aquinas partially overlap, as do the respective Latin and Greek terms, nonetheless, because his thought moved away from the overlap in the direction of the Greek syntax rather than in the direction of the rather different Latin syntax developed in the wake of the doctrine Aquinas himself synthesized, the net result in Cajetan was an attempt to outline a scheme of analogy in which it was argued that corresponding to the term itself "being" that must be used in different ways there is a single *concept itself* that is analogous. And so the criticism of Cajetan began mainly along the line that he had "essentialized" being, that in reducing being to a concept he was "too formalistic" – in a word, that he had missed the point of *esse* in the thought of St Thomas.

What was needed, it came to be thought, was not a logical doctrine of analogy nor a doctrine of the concept of being as analogous but a doctrine of *being itself* in its full "extramental reality" as analogous. Just as we saw in dealing with the transcendentals that there can be, as Poinsot put it,[162] "a twofold understanding of truth, the one in being, the other in knowing", so why might there not be a twofold doctrine of analogy, the one in knowing and yet another, more fundamental one in being itself? Why not an *analogy of **being itself***, not of the term "being" or of the concept being, but an "analogy" in the very order itself of *ens reale*? This is what the late-modern Neothomists came to postulate in the works of Przywara, Geiger, and Fabro,[163] to name a prominent few.

But there is no parity in the two cases. And even if we remember the origin of the very term "hierarchy",[164] yet there is an even more sure giveaway. The authors in question, in order to develop their "analogy of being", "very often use the style

---

161 The effort of Klubertanz (1960) is worth mentioning here, and well repays study; as does the work of Phelan 1941; Montagnes 1963: esp. 126–58; and Marc 1933 and 1933a.
162 Poinsot 1643: 590: "est duplex acceptio veritatis, alia in essendo, alia in cognoscendo, seu alia transcendentalis, alia formalis."
163 Przywara 1962; Geiger 1953; and Fabro 1961.
164 See chapter 4 above, p. 122n79.

and manner of speaking which was used by the Platonists, which had ceased to be customary" among those who moved in Thomas's circle.[165] The "development" in question amounts to a recrudescence of Neoplatonism in the very heart of Neothomism,[166] without the excuse of the false authority of the Pseudo-Dionysius. When the epistemological doctrine of analogy actually found in the writings of Thomas is transformed by some late-modern alchemy into an ontological doctrine as such, we are back to the situation of attributing to objects as known a status and relations which belong not to them otherwise than as known, without, however, being any longer able to tell the difference between which order of being we are dealing with, since we have conflated everything into a doctrinal milieu that is no longer that of Thomas, but once again that of a Christian Neoplatonism, now in the wake of distinctively modern idealism.

There are analogies in being as experienced and understood, but *ens reale* is not an analogy, it only *requires* analogy to be brought within the orbit, however imperfectly, of human understanding. Those who make of *being itself* an analogy perforce "have to resort to the style and manner of speaking of the Platonists"[167] without the excuse of having to preserve "sacred and divine dogma by concealing it from the eyes of the infidels",[168] as Aquinas generously wrote to excuse Dionysius, not knowing that he was going out of his way to protect a common (or uncommon) thief.

---

165 Appropriating for the occasion the observation of Aquinas c.1265–7, *Super librum Dionysii de divinis nominibus*, Prooemium (Busa 4, p. 542): "accidit etiam difficultas in praedictis libris ex multis: primo, quidem, quia plerumque utitur stilo et modo loquendi quo utebantur platonici, qui apud modernos est inconsuetos."

166 E.g., Foote 1940: "It is because things really are analogous that the universe presents itself, a unity, attractive to intellect, and penetrable by knowledge which excels science. It is because things are analogous that mind can course up and down the grades (the 'steps') of perfections – where univocal unities would be futile – can freely range transversely from category to category. By analogies man can go from himself, the being he knows best, far down to the truth, the goodness, the beauty of all inferior creation, which is ordered to him; he can rise to know something of what it means to be a creature without matter. Finally, since beings are analogous to Being [there we encounter early the magical capitalization later to become so familiar in contexts where existential Thomists try to expropriate for their wholly foreign purpose the Heideggerian *Sein*], from the existence and perfections of finite things, man can have knowledge of the transcending excellences, the very subsistence of God".

Pure Neoplatonism unconscious of itself. Of course, that is to begin, not to end, a story. For the idea of "participation", central to two of Aquinas's *quinque viae*, is precisely an originally Platonic doctrine which becomes central for the metaphysics of *esse*, precisely because, as St Thomas puts it (c.1265/6: *Quaestiones disputatae de potentia*, q. 3. art. 7c. [Busa 3, p. 202]), "ipsum esse est communissimus effectus primus et intimior omnibus aliis effectibus; et ideo soli deo competit secundum virtutem propriam talis effectus"; and "ubicumque est virtus divina, est essentia divina", because of the indistinction whereby the divine essence is the divine existence. But this particular story of Thomism and Neothomism I here have place only to mention, not to enter upon. See the intriguing beginning in A.F. Russell 1987.

167 Aquinas c.1265–1267, *Super librum Dionysii de divinis nominibus*, Prooemium (Busa 4, p. 542): "plerumque utitur stilo et modo loquendi quo utebantur platonici".

168 Ibid.: "ut sacra et divina dogmata ab irrisione infedelium occultaret."

Throughout his work, as Henle best and most completely showed,[169] Aquinas fought against the confusion and conflation of our ways of knowing with the ways of existence exercised by natural beings. To salvage what Neoplatonism made of being it was necessary to speak of divine rather than human ideas, a concession Aquinas generously made to the Pseudo-Dionysius only because he took him at his word for who he was.[170] To play the same game today without the same excuse is to risk betraying the heritage Aquinas worked so hard to leave through his commentaries on the philosophers and his reverence toward the scriptures alike.

The Problem of Sign in Aquinas

The problem of sign as it crops up in the writings of Thomas Aquinas marks a watershed in the Latin development of Augustine's philosophical initiative, and of course we can see in retrospect that any doctrine of analogy such as Aquinas developed would be a subalternate part of a general doctrine of sign. Here come to the surface of conscious attention all the tensions latent in Augustine's original proposal. After Aquinas, much of the best speculative energies of thinkers over the three and a half centuries remaining to Latin as the mainstream language of philosophical development will be expended, with an increasing clarity of focus, in the working out of these surface tensions.

In his quite early writing, his "doctoral dissertation" of commenting on Lombard, composed between 1254 and 1256, Aquinas manifests awareness of a problem with Augustine's proposed formula for defining sign in general. Yet he so expresses himself that the reader must conclude that, whatever the problem, the young Aquinas is not ready to reject outright the Augustinian formula which restricts signs to relations grounded in sense-perceptible vehicles of signification. He is not himself poised to formulate a unified doctrine of signs, a full-scale semiotic.

Here, in the *Commentary on the Sentences of Peter Lombard*, Aquinas distinguishes the term "sign" according to a primary usage, which denotes something sense-perceptible founding a relation of signification,[171] and he says that, at most, it is only by a kind of secondary usage that something which does not fall under

---

169 Henle 1956.
170 Aquinas c.1265–7, *Super librum Dionysii de divinis nominibus*, Prooemium (Busa 4, p. 542): "haec igitur platonicorum ratio fidei non consonant nec veritati, quantum ad hoc quod continet de speciebus naturalibus separatis, sed quantum ad id quod dicebant 'de primo rerum principio' verissima est eorum opinio et fidei christianae consona." – "nor is this rationale for belief of the Platonists consonant with truth insofar as it contains separated species of natural relations, but as regards that which it leads them to say of the 'first principle of things' it is true indeed and the opinion they express is consonant with Christian faith."
171 i.1254/6, *In IV Sent.* dist. 1, q. 1, art. 1, quaestiunc. 2, ¶32 (Busa 1, p. 417): "Signum importat aliquod notum quoad nos, quo manuducimur in alterius cognitionem. Res autem primo nobis notae, sunt res cadentes sub sensu, a quo omnis nostra cognitio ortum habet. Et ideo signum quantum ad primam sui institutionem significat aliquam rem sensibilem, prout per eam manuducimur in cognitionem alicujus occulti. Et sic MAGISTER accipit hic signum", and with him the young Aquinas.

the senses might be called a sign.[172] Whence he concludes, for example: effects of intelligible causes are not signs of their causes; only effects of causes falling within the order of sensible phenomena are signs of their causes.[173] Again: the concepts involved in the communications among angels are called signs only figuratively or metaphorically.[174]

But it is not only the young Aquinas who speaks in this way. In some of his very last writing in his *Summa theologiae* Aquinas virtually repeats the early view:[175]

> The name and definition of a thing is taken principally from that which belongs to the thing primarily and essentially, not from that which belongs to it through something else. Now a sensible effect, being the primary and direct object of man's knowledge (since all our knowledge springs from the senses), by its very nature leads to the knowledge of something else. Intelligible effects, by contrast, are not such as to be able to lead us to the knowledge of something else except insofar as they are manifested by another, that is, by sensible things. Thence is it that things offered to the senses are primarily and principally called signs, as Augustine says in Book II *Of Christian Doctrine*, where he writes that "a sign is something that, beyond the impression it makes on sense, makes something else enter cognition". But intelligible effects do not have this rationale of sign except insofar as they are manifested by some signs.[176] And in this way, too, some things which are not sensible are yet said in a certain way to be sacraments, namely, insofar as they are signified by sensible things.

Even a careful student of Aquinas, unless that reader were focused systematically on the problem of sign in his writings, could easily seem justified in taking Aquinas's apparent acceptance of Augustine's proposed definition of sign as an

---

172 Ibid., ¶33: "Contingit autem aliquando quod magis notum quoad nos, etiam si non sit res cadens sub sensu, quasi secundaria significatione signum dicatur." His discussion here, based on the second book of Aristotle's *Ethics* (1104b4), anticipates the kind of interpretant that will be called by Peirce "emotional".

173 ¶35: "dicendum quod in rebus intelligibilibus fit processus ab his quae sunt notiora simpliciter, sicut patet in mathematicis. Unde ibi effectus non sunt signa causarum, sicut in sensibilibus."

174 ¶36: "dicendum similiter de locutione angelorum, quod fit per ea quae sunt notiora simpliciter. Unde non possunt proprie dici signa, sed quasi *transumptive*." "Transumptive" is also an English word, defined in the OED as figurative or metaphorical.

175 c.1273, *Summa theologiae* III.60.4 ad 1 (Busa 2, p. 862): "unumquodque praecipue denominatur et definitur secundum illud quod convenit ei primo et per se, non autem secundum id quod convenit ei per aliud. Effectus autem sensibilis per se habet quod ducat in cognitionem alterius, quasi primo et per se homini innotescens, quia omnis nostra cognitio a sensu initium habet. Effectus autem intelligibiles non habent quod possint ducere in cognitionem alterius nisi inquantum sunt per aliud manifestati, idest, per aliqua sensibilia. Et inde est quod primo et principaliter dicuntur signa, quae sensibus offeruntur, sicut Augustinus dicit in ii de doct. christ., ubi dicit quod 'signum est quod praeter speciem quam ingerit sensibus, facit aliquid aliud in cognitionem venire.' effectus autem intelligibiles non habent rationem signi, nisi secundum quod sunt manifestati per aliqua signa. et per hunc etiam modum quaedam quae non sunt sensibilia, dicuntur quodammodo sacramenta, inquantum sunt significata per aliqua sensibilia."

176 By some sensible effects with which they are entangled in human experience.

adequate general definition. It would be enough, for example, to cite as Aertsen does[177] the apparently categorical statement from Aquinas's *Disputed Question* concerning communication among angels, to receive the impression that the matter was settled:[178]

> A thing cannot be called a sign, properly speaking, unless it be something from which one arrives at an awareness of something else as if by discoursing;[179] there is accordingly not a sign in the case of angelic communication, because angelic knowledge is not discursive, as we saw in the previous question. And for this reason too signs in the case of human beings are sensibles, because our knowledge, which is discursive, arises from sensible things.

But the problem with Augustine's formula, not even in the writings of Aquinas, is as simply and easily resolved as the texts cited so far make it appear. To see the actual complexity of Aquinas's thought on this matter, a more careful attention is required, and a more systematic examination of the writings. The reader in this matter cannot, it turns out, afford to be focused, like Aquinas himself, on problematics other than that of the sign thematically taken as such according to its proper being and action – at least not without running the risk of being misled, like Aertsen, into reaching a premature conclusion. For when other considerations are put aside or subordinated to the problem of the being and action proper to signs, and the writings of St Thomas are thematically perused in this light, even though he did not write them in this light (even though, that is to say, he did not write a systematic *Tractatus de Signis*), the problem with Augustine's formula begins to appear as insurmountable.

Consider the following remarks. First, from the *Disputed Questions on Truth*, q. 9, art. 4, the reply to objection 5:[180]

> Even though in our experience of material objects whose effects are more known to us than are the causes a sign is something posterior in nature, nevertheless, that it be prior

---

177 Aertsen 1988: 230, text and notes.
178 Aquinas c.1256/9, *Quaestiones disputatae de veritate*, q. 9. art. 4 ad 4 (Busa 3, p. 60): "dicendum, quod signum, proprie loquendo, non potest dici nisi aliquid ex quo deveniatur in cognitionem alterius quasi discurrendo; et secundum hoc, signum in angelis non est, cum eorum scientia non sit discursiva, ut in praecedentibus habitum est [q. 8. art. 15]. Et propter hoc etiam in nobis signa sunt sensibilia, quia nostra cognitio, quae discursiva est, a sensibilibus oritur."
179 That is, by passing from the one thing as known first to the other as known after and because of the first.
180 Aquinas c.1256/9, *De veritate*, q. 9, art. 4 ad 5 (Busa 3, p. 60): "Ad quintum dicendum, quod quamvis in naturalibus, quorum effectus sunt nobis magis noti quam causae, signum sit id quod est posterius in natura, tamen de ratione signi proprie accepta non est quod sit vel prius vel posterius in natura, sed solummodo quod sit nobis praecognitum: unde quandoque accipimus effectus ut signa causarum, sicut pulsum signum sanitatis; quandoque vero causas signa effectuum, sicut dispositiones corporum caelestium signa imbrium et pluviarum."

or posterior in nature does not belong to the rationale of sign properly understood, but only that it be something logically prior.[181]

Whence not only can effects become within experience signs of causes, but so transitively can causes become within experience signs of effects; for, as we will see,[182] the relation constitutive of any sign as such cannot be reduced to any relation of cause *or* effect.

Second, even in the earlier text (the reply to the previous objection 4) cited by Aertsen as if settling the matter of Aquinas's view of sign, the cited passage is immediately followed by a second statement which reveals a kind of schizophrenia within the thought of Aquinas about the sign. He contrasts sign *"properly speaking"* ("proprie loquendo") with sign *"in general"* ("communiter dicere"):[183]

> Only something from which we are led to the cognition of another discursively can be called a sign, properly speaking; and from this point of view there is no sign for an angel, since the knowledge of angels is not discursive, as was established in the preceding question. And from this point of view too signs for human beings are sensible objects, because our knowledge, which is discursive, arises from sensible things. But, in general, we can say that anything whatsoever known on the basis of which something else is known, is a sign; and from this point of view a concept can be said to be a sign of whatever is known through it. And so angels do know things through signs; and so too does one angel speak to another through a sign, namely, by means of a specifying form or concept in the actuality of which the understanding of the one angel is rendered directed or ordered to that of the other angel.

But in this light,[184] "proprie loquendo" seems almost to say "loosely speaking" or "according to an unreflected way of putting the matter"; while "communiter"

---

181 *Praecognitum:* that is, a sign must be something which precedes the signified in knowledge logically, whether or not it so precedes temporally. This point will become crucial, we will see (especially in the discussion of sense qualities in chapter 12, p. 522ff.), in the semiotic analysis not only of icons within perception and intellection, but also in the analysis of sensation prescissively considered, where common and proper sensibles prove no less related by sign relations than one perceived object to another, or any object perceived or understood to the organism cognizing it; so that the whole of our awareness, from its origins in sense experience to its loftiest constructs of understanding, proves to be a web of sign relations.

182 See chapters 9 and 10 below; and see also Poinsot 1632a: Book I, Question 2, 137/8 n. 4.

183 Aquinas c.1256/9: *Quaestiones disputatae de veritate* q. 9. art. 4. ad 4 (Busa 3, p. 60): "signum, proprie loquendo, non potest dici nisi aliquod ex quo deveniatur in cognitionem alterius quasi discurrendo; et secundum hoc, signum in angelis non est, cum eorum scientia non sit discursiva, ut in praecedenti quaestione est habitum. et propter hoc etiam in nobis signa sunt sensibilia, quia nostra cognitio, quae discursiva est, a sensibilibus oritur. sed communiter possumus signum dicere quodcumque notum in quo aliquid cognoscatur; et secundum hoc forma intelligibilis potest dici signum rei per ipsum cognoscitur. et sic angeli cognoscunt res per signa; et sic unus angelus per signum alii loquitur; scilicet per speciem, in cuius actu intellectus eius fit in ordine ad alium."

184 Compare Poinsot 1632a: 225/17–26, and 226/8–45.

seems almost to say "strictly speaking" or "from the point of view of a scientific consideration of the matter".

Yet other texts buttress this opposition. Again from the *De veritate*, this time q. 4, in reply to a seventh objection to the effect that[185] by as much as an effect is posterior, so much the more does it have the rationale of a sign. The example cited to support the objection is crucial:[186]

> But a spoken word is a final effect issuing from the understanding. Therefore the rationale of sign belongs more to it than to the concept of the understanding; and likewise too the rationale of word, which is imposed from the manifestation of the concept.

Aquinas introduces at this point remarks implying some distinctions concerning the concept of the relation of cause to effect that will not be fully clarified for a long time after him,[187] framing his answer accordingly:[188]

> The rationale of sign belongs by natural priority to an effect before it belongs to a cause when the cause is related to the effect as its cause of being, but not when related to the effect as its cause of signifying. But when an effect has from the cause not only the fact of its existence, but also the fact of its existing as signifying, in that case, just as the cause is prior to the effect in being, so is it prior in signifying; and for this reason the interior word possesses a rationale of signification that is naturally prior to that of the exterior word.

Perhaps even more intriguing is the lead Aquinas throws out in passing in the fourth of his *Quaestiones Quodlibetales*,[189] when he distinguishes spoken words from what is understood by them: "the spoken word is a sign only and not what is signified; but what is understood is both sign and signified, as is also the thing."

Clearly, over the years, whatever he said in his doctoral dissertation, Aquinas moved far beyond a simple-minded contrast of a "literal" to a "figurative or

---

185 "Quanto effectus est posterior, tanto magis habet rationem signi."
186 "Sed verbum quod est in voce, est effectus postremus ab intellectu progrediens. Ergo ei magis convenit ratio signi quam conceptui mentis; et similiter etiam ratio verbi, quod a manifestatione imponitur."
187 See, for example, chapter 15, p. 631ff.
188 c.1256/9, *De veritate*, q. 4. art. 1 ad 7 (Busa 3, p. 25): "ratio signi per prius convenit effectui quam causae, quando causa est effectui causa essendi, non autem significandi, sicut in exemplo proposito accidit. Sed quando effectus habet a causa non solum quod sit, sed etiam quod significet, tunc, sicut causa est prius quam effectus in essendo, ita in significando; et ideo verbum interius per prius habet rationem significationis quam verbum exterius, quia verbum exterius non instituitur ad significandum nisi per interius verbum."
189 Aquinas, c.1269–72, *Quodlibetum quartum* q. 9. art. 17 (Busa 3, p. 461 col. 1: 019 QDL n.4, q. 9. art. 2c.): "Dependet ergo unitas vel diversitas vocis significativae, sive complexae, sive incomplexae, ex unitate vel diversitate vocis vel intellectus; quorum unum, scilicet vox, est signum et non signatum tantum; intellectus autem signum et signatum, sicut et res."

metaphorical" use of the term "sign" as it applied to psychological states in contrast with overt behavioral manifestations of those states, and as it applied in some generic, common sense to both. John Poinsot, the only classical Latin author to systematically study the writings of Aquinas from a semiotic point of view and to synthesize the results of that study in a formal *Tractatus de Signis*, resolved the schizophrenia we have pointed out by pointing out in turn that Aquinas himself never undertook to author a treatise on signs as such but contented himself with commenting on various aspects of the doctrine of signs as they impinged on various other concerns which Aquinas had taken as his thematic focus in this or that discussion. As a result, in his various remarks, depending on the focal theme of the particular discussion, one or another aspect of the action of signs would be in the foreground of Aquinas's attention, and he would make his remarks accordingly. Only in this way can the schizophrenia of the writing about sign be overcome:[190]

> In order to make clear the mind of St. Thomas on this question, one must reckon with the fact that sometimes he speaks of a sign precisely as it exercises the office of representing another besides itself, and in this way of speaking he concedes to the formal sign [the icons of perception and understanding, as we will see] the rationale of a sign simply. At other times St. Thomas speaks of signs which, as things objectified and first known, lead us to something signified, and in this usage he teaches that a sign is principally found in sensible things.

The schizoid appearance of the texts, then, is nothing more than a by-product of the absence in the writing of an explicitly semiotic point of view systematically employed throughout. What the schizophrenia signaled (or "symptomatized"), it turns out, was an ultimate disquiet on the part of Aquinas, not with the general notion of sign as put in play by Augustine, but with the formula proposed by Augustine to express that general notion in a definition. Aquinas, in the end, had no problem with the general notion itself (like Augustine, he knew almost nothing of Greek, nor does anything suggest that it occurred to him that there was no general notion of sign in Greek philosophy). His problem was with the definition Augustine had proposed for it, yet a definition he was initially inclined to adopt both because of its consonance with our first impressions about the action of signs within our experience as human beings and because of the weight of authority and respect which the name of Augustine had come to carry in Latin tradition by the time Aquinas undertook his studies.

As the problem of metaphysics in the writings of Aquinas can be seen enigmatically compressed in the formula from his *Commentary* on Aristotle's *First Philosophy*, "*non enim omne ens est huiusmodi*" ("yet not all being is of this material kind"), so the problem of sign in the writings of Aquinas might be likewise compressed in

---

190 Poinsot, *Treatise on Signs* (1632a), Book II, question 1, 225/16–25.

a saying paraphrastic of his *Commentary* on Peter Lombard's *Sentences*, apropos of Augustine's definition of sign in general in *On Christian Doctrine*:[191] *non enim omne signum est huiusmodi* ("yet not all signs are of the order of perceptible objects").

We become aware of signs, says Aquinas, in the objects presented by sense. Only later, if ever, do we come to realize that the psychological states which transform sensations into objects of perception and understanding are able to bring about this transformation, and so give structure and meaning to our experience of objects in their difference from sensations, only because these states themselves, the *passiones animae* ("passions of the soul") mentioned by Aristotle in his work *On Interpretation*, are already themselves signs in the first place. Sensible objects at first seem to be but things; but, as we learn more and more of their connections with other objects, both in the world of nature and in the world of culture, these objects become more and more significant. But the ideas in the mind by which we think these objects, the thoughts by which we say how things appear to us and to be apart from us, these *are* signs from the beginning.

In his *Disputed Questions on Truth*, Aquinas elaborated.[192] Signs for us are sensible objects because human knowledge as discursive originates from the senses. But it can be said more generally that a sign is anything known in which something other than itself is presented, and this is the case with an intellectual concept in presenting the intelligibility of any object, or with a percept presenting the desirability or undesirability of any object. Thus the ideas and images, the thoughts in our mind, which alone transform physical sounds or marks into signs, are the cause of both the existence and the exercise of the signification, for example, of linguistic signs.

The words of human language, apart from the thoughts and habit structures binding the human community together through conventions and customs, fall back to the status of mere physical phenomena, of sounds and marks without significations. But within the context of human social interaction, these same sounds or marks are elevated at once to the level of signifying sounds and marks. Their becoming associated with and participation in the ideas and feelings of the ones discoursing is what brings about the transformation. Thus, not only the being of linguistic elements as signs, but also their actual exercise of signification, can be seen to depend on thought as cause. "And therefore the interior word, the thought or idea, has the rationale of sign more fundamentally than does the spoken or written word."[193] In this way angels, no less than human beings, know things through signs, and through signs speak to one another.[194]

---

191 See *Commentary on the Sentences of Peter Lombard* (c.1254/6), Book IV, dist. 1, q. 1, quaestiunc. 2.

192 See the *Disputed Questions on Truth* (c.1256/9), q. 4. art. 1 ad 7, q. 9. art. 4 ad 4 & ad 5.

193 Ibid.: 4. 1. ad 7: "et ideo verbum interius per prius habet rationem significationis quam verbum exterius." The point is expanded upon under the topic of the dependency of the instrumental on the formal sign in Poinsot's *Tractatus de Signis*, 1632a: 271/22–42.

194 Ibid.: 9. 4. ad 4: "Et sic angeli cognoscunt res per signa, et unus angelus per signum alteri loquitur."

"A little less than the angels you made him, and a little more than the beasts."
As the angels apprehend objects always in their intelligibility, so human beings
sometimes do too. Humans are like the angels in being able to know something of
what things are. But like the beasts and unlike the angels, human beings first know
objects not according to what they are but only according as they act here and now
on the senses. The human animal first forms an Umwelt. Unlike the beasts which
have no intellectual apprehension, but unlike the angels which have no power of
sense perception, the human being *becomes aware* that the objects related to the
perceiver and the perceiver's interests *also* exist in the physical universe with an
independence of that perception and those interests. This awareness, the inchoation
of a semiotic consciousness, as we will see in the chapters of Part IV, is the beginning
of philosophy, science, and morals – of civilization as distinct from social interaction.
It is the difference in principle between the Umwelt of animals and the Umwelt as
human, between society and culture, between Umwelt and Lebenswelt.

There is a distinctively human use of signs which overlaps both the knowledge of
angels and the awareness of animals. And this distinctively human use Augustine's
definition fails to capture. Augustine says what is true of the sign as it is found
among brute animals and among human animals as well. But of the sign as it is
found among human animals but not among brute animals, his definition misses the
point.

As to signs among angels, what shall we say? It is not merely that Augustine's
original definition of sign left the case out, it is the question of whether the case is
really a case. Are there angels? In Aristotle's cosmology, the mathematical model
of revolving spheres first developed by Eudoxus and later brought to such perfection by Ptolemy, interpreted as a physical model, provided inferential grounds
for postulating the physical existence of "separated intelligences", that is to say,
intelligent, living substances which never had and never will have a body. *Separated*
intelligences, that is to say, intellectual substances which are pure forms and not
the form of a body. In the Latin Age some saw this as a philosophical proof of
the existence of angels, others argued that the angels whose existence is spoken
of in the revealed scriptures have nothing to do with the "separated intelligences"
postulated to move the celestial spheres. But in either case, separated intelligences
and scriptural angels have in common that they are understood to be intellectual
substances of a purely spiritual or wholly immaterial nature, living forms without
and apart from matter. Human souls, if immortal, are *separable* substances, but as
actually separated they are *incomplete*, being spiritual forms indeed (hence immortal)
but yet forms created to animate bodies, a fact which Aquinas saw as one of the
'verisimilitudes from the order of nature of something taught by the faith',[195] in this

---

195 Aquinas c.1257/8: *Super Boetium De Trinitate*, q. 2. art. 3c (Busa 4, p. 525): "cum in imperfectis
    inveniatur aliqua imitatio perfectorum, in ipsis, quae per naturalem rationem cognoscuntur, sunt
    quaedam similitudines eorum quae per fidem sunt tradita"; whence philosophy can be used within
    theology "ad notificandum per aliquas similitudines ea quae sunt fidei".

case the doctrine of the resurrection of the bodies in the formation at the end of time of the "new heaven and new earth", the *parousia*.

Now from the doctrine of angels we are arriving at a notion of a use of signs that transcends the cognitive activity of the brutes and even that of humans, although not entirely; and yet the philosophical grounds on which were postulated of old substances of the sort angels would be have long since in the main turned to sand. Yet it is not necessary determinately to establish the actual existence of angels in the order of *ens reale* in order to make use of them in the development of hypotheses or "thought experiments" that determinately bear on that order. The case is not at all like that of the existence of God, where, unless it be determinately established that he *is* as an actual existent all other proofs "that he is" good, "that he is" one, and so on, are mere "noumena", empty conceptual constructs. For we are not trying to establish an actual science of angels. That they be mere hypotheses is enough,[196] as long as that supposition is coupled with the determinate judgment that material being does not exhaust reality. Maritain gives an interesting illustration of the point:[197]

> It is impossible for human science to know determinately the behaviour of a corpuscle at each instant. For human science observes and measures things with the aid of material instruments and in virtue of physical activities, and can only see an electron by jogging it with light. But suppose a pure spirit, who knows *without material means* (and so, no longer by means of empiriological concepts) the behaviour of this corpuscle at each instant; such a spirit would see that the principle of causality applies strictly and in its full ontological sense. The hypothesis of a pure spirit has no meaning for the physicist. But if it had no meaning for a metaphysician, there would be no metaphysics.

But let us return to the time of Aquinas. See how tardily, we can say from that time, are the philosophers of being arriving at the problematic rooted in the human use of signs! And in this arrival even the angels, be they merely beings of intellectual imagination (for no brute animals could dream them up), have played

---

196 Cf. Maritain 1959: 220–1: "It is impossible to say that the possible existence of pure spirits implies any contradiction. For the notions of spirit, knowledge, love, far from implying existence in matter, of themselves imply immateriality. That pure spirits do exist in fact," he goes on to argue, we have "some well-founded indications of the natural order", indications which turn out to be dialectical, not probative, be it noted. "But even if this existence be taken as simply possible, metaphysics is not dispensed from considering its discoverable laws. He who has not meditated on the angels will never be a perfect metaphysician", and the theological tract on the angels inspired by the extravagant and detailed pseudo-descriptions of the infamous Pseudo-Dionysius, at least as it is found in the *Summa* of Aquinas, "virtually contains a purely metaphysical treatise concerning the ontological structure of immaterial subsistents, and the natural life of a spirit detached from the constraints of our empirical world." Such "knowledge as we can thus acquire of pure created spirits", Maritain concludes, belongs determinately to "intellection by analogy" and to what we know from direct experience of the structure of finite being in its contrast to the infinite being of God wherein *esse* is the *essentia*.

197 Maritain 1959: 191.

a role that is actual if only historically. We move in the history of philosophy not in the order of knowledge already in hand to be clarified, what the medievals called the *ordo disciplinae* ("order of exposition"). Historical development reveals more the opposite, the order of discovery, or *ordo inventionis*, where hypotheses ("abductive guesses") play an indispensable part. Practically everything seems to get discovered ahead of the sign, and all of it comes to bear eventually on the speculative requirements for rendering an account of what the being proper to sign is once one becomes aware of it and of its ubiquituous role in knowledge, experience, and reality.

Take, as an illustration, the problem of analogy, which, we saw above, seems to be what is at the forefront of the problem of metaphysical knowledge when we ask how is it possible to speak of "being" as a unified subject of inquiry, what is that psychological condition or state, the *passio animae*, on the basis of which being as such becomes an object of human understanding. Being as such is not a thing but a distinctively human object of understanding in the light of which we are able to come to understand the objective structure of experience as an interweaving of mind-independent with mind-dependent elements, and thence further the created character of the physical world as "dependent in being" regardless of whether or not it has always existed and will always exist. For it is in this light that we come to understand that God is *Ipsum Esse Subsistens* and that the physical universe throughout is by consequence *ens per participationem essendi*. In the light of this distinctive object we can thematize the difference between objects and things, and between finite and infinite things. In this light, the light of being, we are able to ask about God and the world, and dispute whether there are angels and whether there is life after death. Neither a concept nor a thing, being as such as an object is unique precisely because its internal unity is not that of a substance nor that of an accident, but of a nature which transcends substance and accident to enable us to see both as beings, and to see being itself as "able to be said in many ways". The analogy of being presupposes, on the side of our knowledge, distinctively human discourse which makes the analogous unity of being as such possible in its own right as objective. To every objective state over and above sensation as such there corresponds, not in particular (one-to-one) but generically, a subjective state, an Innenwelt, on the basis of which that objective state is maintained in awareness. To every Umwelt there corresponds an Innenwelt. But the sign is what mediates the two. What is *this* being which is neither subjective nor objective in *its* proper being, restricted neither to nature nor to culture in its functioning?

The problem of analogy, in this light, suddenly appears as but a fragment of the much larger problem of the role of signs in knowledge, a species-specifically human case of the use of signs, truly enough, which even the angels have helped historically to identify, but a "species" under a "genus" nonetheless (a "token under a type", as could also be said), the "genus" (or should we say "genius") *signum*. This is why Heidegger speaks of the problem of being in terms of a unity that being exhibits *prior* to the categories; and why he sees in Cajetan's doctrine of analogy, as also in Aquinas's doctrine of the transcendentals,[198] attempts to get at the fundamental problem which yet are not attempts sufficiently clarified in principle. For the problem lies deeper still than any awareness of diversity, and goes to the possibility for beings to appear in *any* guise in the first place, particularly as "things", apparently independent objects within experience. Whence the clearing within which objects stand as things, real or apparent? So the knowledge of being may depend on the prior action of signs; but being must become known before signs can become known, and the investigation of the action of signs must await the establishment of the reality of what is acting, if the science is not to be empty. And what comes first *before or into our awareness* is not a sign as such but being as a distinctive object, the "formal object", as we may now say, distinctive of understanding as species-specifically human.

The Problem of Being as First Known

Well, you can see that it is beginning to look as if Aquinas left to posterity mainly problems! This is why he figures so large in any adequate introduction to or history of philosophy, because, although as a theologian he was concerned to give Christian answers to questions, he never let his answers stand in the way of the further questions always to be raised by human beings as thinkers, Christian or not. He lived by the motto Peirce suggested many centuries later: "Do not block the road of inquiry!" As a theologian he provided answers, but he never let his theological role stifle the spirit of the philosopher in him which breathes where it will. As a philosopher, he raised more questions than any theologian could hope or credibly pretend to solve. This is why his writings live through the centuries long after most theologians' tomes have fallen to dust and even after "departments of theology" have given way to "departments of religious studies". Like being itself, Aquinas stands as a transcendental figure, unable to be fit without remainder into any one category. He was theologian and more than theologian, mystic and saint; but he was also philosopher and more than philosopher. He was a human thinker of the first order.

Among his enigmatic bequeathments was his notion of *ens ut primum cognitum*, "being as the object distinctive of human understanding", which reappears in post-modern times most clearly with Heidegger's *Seinsfrage* ("Being-question") but, as we shall see,[199] also earlier, if at first glance more obscurely, as the Peircean category of "Firstness". This notion was not of being as providing the object of metaphysics, *ens inquantum ens* ("being-insofar-as-it-is-being"). Still less was it the *ens mobile et sensibile* ("changeable being") of physics. Nor was it the *individuales materiales et sensibiles* ("material and sensible individuals") which are the common object of the sensations of all the animals, the common material out of which each species of

---

198 See chapter 15, p. 648, where the derivation of the transcendentals from within being-as-first-known is diagrammed.
199 See "The Peculiar Case of Firstness" in chapter 15, p. 645.

animal constructs its species-specific objective world. In the Neothomistic revival,[200] I am sure that no greater mistake was made than the assumption by some of its principal figures that *ens ut primum cognitum* ("being as the object distinctive of human understanding") could simply be equated with *ens reale sensibile* ("sensible physical[201] being"), or at least with mind-independent being as such (*ens reale*) first given by sense, and that is the end of it. They thought there was no need to pause, nothing here to pause over, so that they could move on from there to what really interested them, the "being" which metaphysics has as its object, "being as such".

Along the way they ran afoul of Heidegger, and the end of the modern era. The dispute between realism and idealism at a stroke was superseded, and the champions of realism, locked in a struggle to the death with modern idealism, awakened to find that their problematic had died with the modern age. For the requirements of postmodernity, their preoccupations were not wrong but too narrow; their polemics were not misguided but out of date; their positions were not too dogmatic but insufficiently fundamental.

With Heidegger, who never pretended to be a Thomist but simply a philosopher in his own right, and with some success, philosophy for the first time in its long history was forced to begin systematically to thematize, directly and clearly, the profound problematic of *ens ut primum cognitum*. Intimately bound up with the problem of the sign which Peirce had thematized only slightly earlier, the combined works of these two men ignorant of one another – Charles Peirce in America and Martin Heidegger in Germany – more than any others, effected the overthrow of the epistemological paradigm which defined modernity and began that new epoch of philosophical thought and history which we designate, for want of a better name, "postmodern". Postmodernity, we shall see, is that immediate future of philosophy upon the exhaustion of the energies which gave life to the philosophical problems and preoccupations of the mainstream figures who, after and along with Descartes,

---

200 I don't know of a single important figure in the late-modern Thomistic revival who accepted for himself the label "Neothomist". Maritain and Gilson rejected it with particular vigor. But here it is not a question of how they thought of themselves, but of where they appear in history and how that place should be named. I doubt that Porphyry or Proclus thought of themselves as "Neoplatonists", any more than Gilson or Maritain thought of themselves as "Neothomists". Still, the "Neoplatonists" were the Platonists who belong to a definite historical epoch after Plato, with its distinctive preoccupations and problems. Just so, the "Neothomists" were the Thomists of the revival of Thomism called into being by Pope Leo XIII's 1879 encyclical, *Aeterni Patris*. This revival was distinctively concerned to vindicate, against the modern idealist doctrine that the mind knows only what the mind itself makes, the rights of the Thomistic doctrine that the mind is capable of a grasp of things as they exist in reality. This was the modern meaning of "realism", as also of the post-Aquinian "scholastic realism" that Peirce identified as belonging to the distinctive essence of pragmaticism in its difference from pragmatism and modern philosophy generally (Peirce 1905: CP 5.423; discussed in chapter 15 below, "Pragmaticism Is not Pragmatism", p. 616ff.). The Thomists who were preoccupied with the claims of modern idealism, and especially who championed realism against that idealism, are, as a historical group and intellectual movement of the 19th and 20th century, the "Neo-Thomists".

201 See the gloss below on "The Term 'Physical' as Used by the Latins", p. 382 in chapter 8 below.

defined the first age of philosophy within the national languages which succeeded
Latin as the vehicle of intellectual culture.

So it is interesting that, from within the very perspectives of Neothomism itself,
not only did Maritain himself wind up rejecting the name "Christian philosophy"
as proper to philosophy-come-of-age and as fully itself, but the name his close
intellectual associate and literary executor prefaces Maritain's last book by suggesting as best to replace this designation is one from which, at this point of
history, the influence of Heidegger cannot be dissociated:[202] "If philosophy is called
theo-philosophy, 'philosophy of God', from its most sublime intitulation,[203] yet it
prefers the name of *Seinsphilosophy*, 'philosophy of being', because this latter name
is redolent of its lowly origins together with its highest object."

But we must not get too far ahead of the story. Our immediate concern is to make
clear what the problem of being-as-first-known was as it appeared in the works of
Aquinas.

The "Formal Object" of Latin Scholasticism (Peirce's "Ground"[204])

A little "medieval psychology" is needed at this juncture in order to understand the
main analytical point around which turned the problem of being as first known for
Aquinas. The medievals had a discipline of psychology, but it was both broader
than what we call "psychology" today and had a quite different focus.[205] Medieval

---

202 Korn 1973: xxiv–xxv: "Si de son nom le plus sublime, la philosophie est appelée *théo-philosophie*,
elle préfère le nom de *Seinsphilosophie* parce que celui-ci lui rappelle ses humble origines en
même temps que son objet le plus haut: la déité qui est l'être même subsistant." Korn's preference
as expressed here is supported by Black's remark in the following note.

203 What Korn has in mind in speaking thus had been noted slightly earlier in his text (Korn 1973:
xxiv n. 34): "Don't forget that metaphysics, in the writings of Aristotle and Aquinas, bears the
name of *theology* insofar as it is a knowledge of divine things", always keeping in mind Aquinas's
distinction between theology as founded on revelation and theology as a part of philosophy.
But Black reminds us (1987: 406–7) of what should be taken as a cautionary tale in this area:
"Philosophers as a whole have often been tempted to make philosophy into the image of its loftiest
objects. Through this act of *hubris*, they set their sights on a worthy, but perhaps unattainable,
ideal, and in its relation to that ideal, all less exalted goals inevitably pale by comparison. But
if we reject this sort of philosophical *hubris* as inappropriate, if we opt instead to acknowledge
the limitations of the philosopher as a human subject, if we realize that these limitations are not
confined to the outward and corporeal aspects of human existence, but that they pervade the
speculative life as well – then we will be obliged to alter radically this philosophical ideal. Perhaps
ironically, ... the Arabic philosophers have provided us the wherewithal to accomplish such a task.
For they have shown us the multiplicity of rational and quasi-rational processes that we have at
our disposal."

204 See chapter 15, p. 641; and the discussion of "primary iconism" in Eco 2000: 103–22.

205 I might mention that Timothy Gannon (1904–91), who founded the Department of Psychology at
Loras College in 1956, devoted the last year of his life, fighting against the clock of a terminal
cancer, to writing a history of psychology from the Greeks to the present day, concentrating
especially on the establishment of psychology as a modern academic and scientific discipline after
Wundt (1832–1920). For such a task, his prior training in philosophy was indispensable. For not
only is psychology the latest scientific step-child of philosophy, but psychology as an established
academic discipline has so far indulged the fantasy that history is unimportant in a science, with

psychology was not concerned with what we call today "psychological states" so much as with the intelligible structure of the soul as capable of performing operations of cognition, appetition, locomotion, and nourishment. (Thus even plants fell within the medievals' notion of psychology!) In their "rational psychology" (*de anima rationali*), they were interested in distinguishing and enumerating the various "powers" or "capacities" the soul had for knowing. Through how many distinct channels does the soul achieve cognitive contact with the environment, and how are these channels made to work together or cooperate in the revelation and construction of the objects of experience?

The Latin philosophers, taking a cue from Aristotle, developed a unique and powerful analytic tool for dealing with such questions, the notion of the *formal object*, which they defined as whatever is directly and essentially attained by a power and by reason of which whatever else is attained is attained. Thus, the formal object of sight is *differentiated light* ("color", but color in this sense). Because the eye is sensitive to differences in light, it can *therefore also* see shapes, positions, movements, sizes; but take away the light and everything disappears.[206] The eye sees nothing. The formal object of hearing is sound. Because the ear is sensitive to a range of tonal differences, it can hear sirens and symphonies as well as public lectures in philosophy. But suppress sound waves and the ear hears nothing.

By this means, the Latins were able to distinguish in the soul a hierarchy of cognitive and affective powers, as well as locomotive ones. The list, like that of Aristotle's categories, was a matter of some dispute. But the school of Thomas Aquinas generally identified an interplay of ten formally distinct cognitive channels[207] which together establish the objective world on the basis of the physical interactions which directly activate the senses. Of these ten powers, nine were common to human animals and other higher animal forms.[208] The nine common to all higher animals are the following. First, the five external senses of sight (having differentiated light for its formal object), hearing (with the formal object of sounds), smell (with odors for its formal object), taste (with the formal object of flavors), and touch (with the formal object of the textures of bodily surfaces).[209] Over and above these, in

---

the result that most practitioners of psychology know little of their provenance and less of the limitations of a thorough present-mindedness. In this climate, Gannon's book, *Shaping Psychology* (1991), provides a unique and much needed overview of psychology today, or, as he put it in his subtitle, a view of "How we got where we're going".

206 Neothomist authors took sometimes to calling external sense "infallible", meaning by this no more than that a given external sense power responds only to an actual stimulus, and in its response attains directly nothing other than its formal object. The point is valid, but the terminology is hopeless.

207 With the *caveat* entered in p. 347n217 of this chapter below.

208 This is an interesting and underdeveloped topic. See Deely 1971.

209 Today, it is generally recognized that temperature constitutes a formal object distinct from texture; and there are other scientific refinements possible upon the basic scheme. But all such refinements rely implicitly on the analytic technique by which the scholastics grounded the basic scheme of cognitive sense powers in the first place.

hierarchical order, are a "common sense", that is to say, a synthetic sense,[210] which has for its formal object the combining of the input of the five external senses to make of their input a unified field; memory, which recognizes in present sensory stimuli features of past stimulation; imagination, which puts together sensations and memories in ways that will serve the interests of the organism; and a *vis aestimativa* or estimative power, which evaluates the perceptual situation overall in terms of what is to be sought after and what avoided here and now.

Why Sensations Do Not Involve Mental Icons

The school that developed on the basis of the writings of Aquinas was somewhat unique in consistently and forcefully denying that there were any mental *images* involved in sensation as such. Their reason for this denial was quite fundamental. The objects of sensation, being objects physical and material, are on the same level as the external sense powers, which have a physiological structure and are activated by specific physical stimuli.[211] Not only is it the case that sensation is the action of the sensible on the sense ("*actio sensibilis in sensu*"), but, as an immediate consequence, logically speaking, it is also the case that actual sensation is of the singular individualities that make up the environment as here and now stimulating the sense powers.[212] Since the object, inasmuch as it provides physical stimuli to the sense power,[213] is here and now present to the sense as part (like the sense itself) of the physical environment, and since the object as sensory stimulus and the sense power stimulated are on the same level without any disproportion to be overcome, to posit a sense image is entirely superfluous.

Aquinas is about as emphatic and clear on the point as is discursively possible. Maritain[214] pins on it the basis of realism itself in philosophy. Well before Ockham got the credit for inventing shaving, so to speak, Aquinas in his work used the so-called "Ockham's razor"[215] – the idea that theoretical entities should be posited as

---

210 Not to be confused, therefore, with "common sense" as signifying the sound practical judgment that is independent of specialized knowledge or training.

211 The specific aspect of a stimulus conveyed through a physical action of environment on sense organ the Latins called *species impressa*, "an impressed form of specification", a term of much mystery and dispute, which meant in the end little more than the aspect of a stimulus according to which it causes, say, a "C" chord to sound rather than a "D" chord; or a surface to appear "green" rather than "crimson red", etc.

212 Aquinas, 1267/8, *In II de anima*, lect. 12: "sensus secundum actum sunt singularium quae sunt extra animam".

213 The qualification, "inasmuch as", is crucial, for example, in the case of a dead star which yet exists currently in its light rays. See Maritain's discussion of the point (1959: 118n1); and also the excellent discussion in a classic of late modern Neothomism, Cahalan 1985: esp. ch. 10.

214 Maritain 1959: 118n1.

215 Quite curiously, another of history's tasty ironies, the phrase for which Ockham gets everywhere credit and fame in modernity nowhere occurs in his actual writing (Thorburn 1918). Yet the very phrasing occurs commonly in the writings of Aquinas and other Latins who both preceded Ockham and showed a better grasp of what is simple and what complex in natural phenomena, particularly as relating to cognition. Even though alternative versions of the formula do occur in Ockham, and

seldom as possible: *entia non multiplicanda sunt praeter necessitatem* ("explanatory hypotheses which explain the same phenomenon with the postulation of fewer factors are to be preferred") – to show as superfluous the doctrine that Ockham and other late Latins would teach in holding that external sense attains its object only in an image formed by the mind.

Why Perceptions Do Involve Mental Icons
In the case of the powers of internal sense, the situation is quite different. To perceive a sound as *a police siren*, to perceive an *ambulance* from a white surface with a red pattern, to respond to a *danger* from a falling rock, all this requires an active interpretation of environmental stimuli on the side of the organism. The organism forms a *perception* or *image*, on the basis of which it relates to a pattern of sensory stimulus as an object of experience (such as "a rock falling toward me"). Here there is a disproportion between the stimulus as such and what is perceived as object. Moreover, the stimulus may be misperceived, it may be interpreted as something which is actually not even there in the environment where perception indicates it to be (as in the case of a misperceived or mislocated sound, for example).

The sensory stimulus, thus, provides an objectified selection here and now of aspects of the physical surroundings sustaining the organism through a whole range and series of interactions, and far the greater part of these interactions form no part of the sensation as such; but the transformation and objective arrangement of these "sensed" aspects into what are experienced as objects within an Umwelt to be sought, avoided, or safely ignored is the work of the perceiving organism, not of the objects perceived. A sensation is always of something physically there; but the object perceived in consequence of that sensation is not always something physically there, but mayhap only objectively in the main. The organism may be psychotic, schizophrenic, or merely mistaken in what it mainly perceives through and on the basis of what it senses.

For both these reasons – to remove the disproportion between stimulus and response, and to supply for the presence of the perceived object as perceived – "ideas", psychological mental constructs, concepts (which the Latins called generically *species expressa*, "expressed specifying form", that is, a form of consciousness which directs awareness to this rather than that) must be formed on the side of the perceiving organism as the basis for its cognitive, affective, and/or motor response to the object perceived. Thus sensory images occur in perception, but not in sensation.

The argument here anticipates, more or less completely, the famous notion of "Gestalt" that would be introduced into scientific psychology in the early decades of the twentieth century through the work of Max Wertheimer (1880–1943) and

---

are invoked again and again (see Tornay 1938: 9), there remains the irony that the actual wording of what has come everywhere to be called "Ockham's razor" (for example, the version that Peirce cites – 1903b: CP 5.26) is found as such in Aquinas and earlier authors, and never in Ockham's own text.

Wolfgang Köhler (1887–1967).[216] The field of perception reveals objects in a way and according to properties that cannot be derived from a mere summation of its purely sensory components. For sensations, analytically prescissed and considered as such, are physical relations caused by physical stimuli and resulting in relations of awareness or apprehension based on the stimulation and terminating in the source of the stimulation. Perceptions also found cognitive relations as terminating in the sensory stimulus, but by adding to or wrapping that stimulus within an interpretation which transforms it into an object of experience ("a cognitive type") which may or may not be real, and may or may not exist in the physical world the way it is perceived to exist objectively.

With the Latins' breakdown of objectivity into the three levels of understanding, perception, and sensation, the last of which necessarily involves physical relations to which the first two add various cognitive relations of the organism's own devising, only some of which are also physical, we can see, quite clearly, that the Latins are explaining the Innenwelt to which an Umwelt or objective world corresponds under a quite different terminology and according to a methodology distinctive of their period.

Ens Primum Cognitum: *Species-Specifically Human Apprehension*

Now over and above the nine cognitive powers common to higher animals, the human animal has a species-specific cognitive capacity, what we called in the opening chapter "language" as distinguished from communication and speech. The medievals called this capacity *intellect* ("intellectus"), human understanding as more than perceptual interpretation of sensory objects.[217] Both the reasons requiring the positing of ideas in the internal senses apply here. But on what basis or ground are we justified in positing intellect as a cognitive power distinct from and superordinate to, say, the estimative power of animals? What, in other words, is the formal object, the "ground", of understanding?

It was in this context, as we have seen, that Aquinas posed the problem of being as first known. The human understanding, or "intellect" (*intellectus*), as the name

---

216 Wertheimer 1912; Köhler 1929. See the discussion in Gannon 1991: 76, and esp. "Gestalt Psychology", 100–3. In late-modern philosophy, Wittgenstein, flailing about to escape the nominalistic fly-bottle of his own mind, would introduce his famous "duck-rabbit" (borrowed from Jastrow 1900) to argue the inadequacy of the modern sense-data approach to phenomena of perception. But Wittgenstein mistook the "aspect-seeing" or "seeing-as" phenomenon for something a-typical of perception (c.1931–50: II, 195), simply because everyday objects appear to us normally in an unambiguous fashion. He thus missed the main point of the argument for the difference between sensation and perception as such. See the discussion in Monk 1990: 507–16.

217 For simplicity's sake, I am going discuss "intellect" here in general terms, without going into the further details of how, in Aquinas's thought, the species-specifically human power of understanding is further differentiated within its own order. The most interesting of these internal differentiations, perhaps, is the manner in which Aquinas is able to point out a specifically intellectual capacity for memory that cannot be reduced to the internal sense power of memory. This *intellectual memory*, thus, belongs to the rational or "intellectual" part of the soul as such and participates in the mode of knowing proper to intellect which is able to consider being in itself as capable of existence apart from the perceptual world to which the animal without intellect – without language – is restricted.

for a distinctive faculty or cognitive capacity species-specific to human beings, presupposes and requires a distinct formal object, something that it attains by an apprehensive grasp no other power is capable of making. Otherwise it is superfluously posited, an empty name for what is accurately described by the language of internal sense.[218]

Being as first known, thus, is precisely the original awareness of human understanding in which is contained, "confusedly", says Aquinas (that is, in an incompletely differentiated manner), *everything* which it is subsequently possible for us actually to learn from experience, including the existence of God. Even the notion of "being as such" is but a prescission that takes place within the orbit, the horizon, of being-as-first-known. And Aquinas holds this view from the very earliest days of his writing.[219]

I think what this "being as first known" consists in for Aquinas is precisely the seeing of the Umwelt as a whole in relation to itself as something not fully reducible to our experience of it. Out of this notion of an "existence in itself" develops the awareness of the physical environment in its difference from the objective world as such, the awareness of obligations to treat other things as more than mere conveniences for ourselves, the awareness that not everything that exists belongs to what our senses reveal. In short, out of this awareness develops the Umwelt as *Lebenswelt*, the species-specifically human world where philosophy, science, history, literature, morality, and all the rest that makes enculturated society different from the social world of brute animals takes form. Neither a particular concept nor a particular object, being-as-first-known is the intellectual light or clearing within which mere *objects* of perception, which as such consist in their relations to us as knowers, are transformed even within the objective order into *transcendental things* – that is to say, those features of the environment, whether or not objectified, which exercise and participate in an existence in their own right *apart from* our perceptions and derived from the same source, whatever that might be, on which the physical universe as a whole depends.

In other words, I think that the contemporary Thomist scholar Vincent Guagliardo got it exactly right when he wrote that being as first known in Thomas Aquinas is the condition for the human use of signs, "and provides an alternative to the approach of either idealism or empiricism, both of which trivialized the question of being":[220]

> In this context being is not reducible to the human intellect. But neither is it known without the human intellect, so that being is not simply reducible to sensible things either. Being, then, has a peculiarly semiotic quality: knowable only to an intelligent being (thus excluding animals) as the properly human way of knowing but not referring

218 This is exactly what Hume thought. See "Sense and Understanding" in chapter 12 below, p. 535ff.
219 See the *Commentary on the Sentences*, I, dist. 8, q. 1, art. 3c.
220 Vincent Guagliardo 1993: 51.

(at least in its primary instance or meaning) to the human knower but to otherness. In this primal phenomenon – as Heidegger saw – being "negatives", i.e., expresses an elemental "not", which allows the semiotic chain of meaning to develop beyond any mere "here" or "now", "this" or "that" of the things of experience, as well as to develop beyond the knower in his/her state of any actual knowing, opening up the realm of further possibility, further semiosis. All this is to say that "being" is foundational to both the things known and the human knower who knows, to any determinate object or interpreting subject. If this be the case, then being serves as the condition without which there would be no anthroposemiotics,

that is to say, no distinctively human involvement with signs, and hence no metaphysics, no "doctrine of analogy", or any other philosophy either.

Listen to Aquinas himself on the point:[221]

> The activity of understanding is twofold. There is the activity wherein it grasps what something is, which is called the grasp of indivisibles. And there is the activity wherein it composes and divides what it grasps. In both phases there is something foundational.
>
> In the first activity, indeed, there is something which first falls under the conception of understanding, namely, what I call being. Nor can anything be conceived by this first operation of the mind unless being be understood.
>
> The second activity, that of composing and dividing, too has something that comes naturally first, namely, the principle that *it is impossible for one and the same object in one and the same respect to simultaneously be and not be.*[222] For no one can understand anything according to this second activity unless this principle be understood. And this principle depends on the understanding of being.

Now you begin to see how much more the expression "philosophy of being" signifies than merely the metaphysics of *esse* and the discovery that *Ipsum Esse Subsistens* (God as the Self-Subsistent Act of Existence) is the ground of the physical universe as an interplay of finite existents. All that is fine, but it all tells but one side of the story. Besides the universe of *ens reale* and *entia realiter existens* (physical and physically existing beings), there is also the universe of discourse within and out of which the physical universe and God as the physical ground of the universe

---

221 Aquinas, *In duodecim libros metaphysicorum Aristotelis expositio* (c.1268/72), IV, lect. 6, n. 10 (Busa 4, p. 421): "cum duplex sit operatio intellectus: una, qua cognoscit quod quid est, quae vocatur indivisibilium intelligentia: alia, qua componit et dividit: in utroque est aliquod primum: in prima quidem operatione est aliquod primum, quod cadit in conceptione intellectus, scilicet hoc quod dico ens; nec aliquid hac operatione potest mente concipi, nisi intelligatur ens. Et quia hoc principium, impossibile est esse et non esse simul, dependet ex intellectu entis …: ideo hoc etiam principium est naturaliter primum in secunda operatione intellectus, scilicet componentis et dividentis. Nec aliquis potest secundum hanc operationem intellectus aliquid intelligere, nisi hoc principio intellecto."

222 How much more compact is the Latin: "impossibile est esse et non esse simul". Refer to the earlier discussion from Aristotle on "How to Deal with Contradictions", chapter 4, pp. 120 & 125f.

are arrived at derivatively from the experience of objects as more and other than the physical surroundings as such. And within this universe of discourse, the objective world, not outside and independent of it, history and revelation occur: whether the sacred histories of the "people of a Book", as the Moslems say, or the secular histories of human achievement and conquest through various civilizations; and whether "sacred revelations", wherein a believing community forges its identity around the understanding of the word of God, or secular revelations of the species-specific diversity of objective worlds forged out of the common physical environment and revelation of the environment itself according to its own laws and preobjective possibilities.

The metaphysics of *esse* gives us to understand the ultimate nature and structure of the physical environment as a participation of being. But the common ground on the side of the human Innenwelt out of which this understanding grows is the same ground out of which the sacred and secular histories which belong to the human Umwelt as a Lebenswelt grow. That ground, according to Aquinas, is being-as-first-known. The primary division of being for the Latins was into "real being", *ens reale*, and "purely objective being", *ens rationis*, which they also called "non-being", *non ens*. But now it turns out that what is independent of the human mind and nonbeings that the mind constructs both belong as objects discovered within being-as-first-known. Out of this discovery develops the set of concepts which make all intellectual analysis possible in the first place (the "sequence of primitive concepts", as we will shortly discuss.[223])

Nonbeing in Latin Philosophy

Let me begin here with a brief summary. For Aquinas, *ens* is the term best designating the start of species-specifically human experience. From the initial grasp of being will be articulated the whole of our experience as human experience. And the first division of being, that is, the first contrast given in our experience of the world, is the contrast within *ens* between real being, as what exists independently of the mind (*ens reale*, or mind-independent being), and nonbeing (*non ens*, more commonly termed *ens rationis* by reason of the framework of Latin preoccupation with getting at *ens reale* through what exists consequently and dependently upon the mind's own workings).

Non ens, "non-being", is an initially puzzling designation. But the more common designation for what is being distinguished, *ens rationis*, appears in hindsight, at least from outside the medieval framework of preoccupations, as a positive misnomer, since the designation has in fact created no end of misapprehensions among later students of medieval thought. Let us try to sort out the apprehensions and misapprehensions.

Literally, and in the standard modern readings, *ens rationis* "obviously" means

---

223 See p. 355 below.

in English *being of reason* (*ens* "being" + *rationis* "of reason"). And yet, according to the psychology or life-science developed by the Latin scholastics, all the animals with powers of internal sense (and therefore capable of perception) form "beings of reason" in the course of structuring through experience their awareness of the environment, even though such animals of course have no reason – *ratio* – in the sense of *intellectus*, or understanding. But one must go below the surface of the Latin texts to realize this.

On the surface, the scholastic authors explicitly deny that brute animals as well as rational animals form "*entia rationis*". That is because they are considering *entia rationis* not in terms of their mere functional presence within perception and conception ("materialiter", in scholastic parlance), but solely in terms of their critically controlled and recognized presence within understanding ("formaliter", in scholastic parlance). Brute animals and internal sense *formally* do not fashion "beings of reason", that is, they make use of mind-dependent relations without knowing that there are such relations. But *materially* they do indeed fashion mind-dependent structures, the very structures out of which "beings of reason" *would be* fashioned had they the cognitive capacity to recognize the difference between objects and things. Not to see this subtle point, however, is to miss one of the potentially most important contributions of the Latin Age to the possibility of developing a doctrine of signs.

Instead of perpetuating the misunderstandings latent in the translation "being of reason", let us simply translate *ens rationis* as *mind-dependent being*. Hence *ens rationis* or "mind-dependent being" itself can be divided as follows (now let us forget for a moment that we have just repudiated the standard rendering, for the sake of emphasizing through paradox the point of our repudiation). On the one hand, there are *perceptual beings of reason*, to wit, *entia rationis* formed by brute as well as human animals. In this subject the medievals typically took almost no interest. On the other hand, there are *conceptual* or *intellectual beings of reason*. Among these the Latin schoolmen recognized the possibility of distinguishing several different kinds or sub-species, but the only kind in which they were really interested was something that they called *second intentions*.

What was meant by a "second intention" is fairly straightforward. Whenever you know something, insofar as you know it, it becomes an object of thought or awareness. In so becoming, that object acquires as such, as existing for awareness, certain characteristics, such as predicability. That is, you are able to *predicate* things only of what exists as known. Predicability, thus, would be a second intention: something can be the subject of a proposition, actual or prospective, only insofar as someone is thinking about it. So, second intentions generically are the characteristics that things acquire as they exist in intellectual awareness.

Characteristics that things have independently of awareness, "outside" of the mind, as it were, or "in nature", the Latins called *first intentions*. But the further characteristics these same things acquire as they come to exist within the mind are second intentions. And specifically, these second intentions include the ideas or concepts corresponding to the five words of Porphyry – genus, species, difference, property, accident.[224] Moreover, these second intentions, among the many kinds of mind-dependent being which could be distinguished, were the kind the scholastics were principally focused upon as the subject matter of logic. Logic, as they were interested in it, was above all the order that the mind, in and through its own workings, introduces into things in order to know reality. This objective ordering subordinating fictions to reality, or trying to, is what was meant by "second intentions".

In contrast to the physical order, where relations depend upon accidents of substances, in the objective order (the order of things as known) there is no limit to the formations of relations upon relations upon relations, to infinity. Yet all such relations piled on relations are called "second intentions" rather than third and fourth and fifth intentions and so on, not only because they can go on to infinity, but because "they all pertain to a cognized object as such, and to be cognized is always a second state of a thing"[225] insofar as *habens esse* ("exercising actual existence"), or being a physical existent, is regarded as "first", and what pertains to a thing as *habens esse* is considered to constitute the order of "first intentions".

This contrast between relations in the physical order which depend upon actual characteristics of actual individuals (upon "subjective accidents of substances" in Aristotle's terms) and relations in the objective order which are not tied to actual subjective characteristics but may be founded upon whatever other relations happen to exist within a given cognition was the reason why Aristotle, and the Latin logicians after him, rejected arguments which led to an infinite regress. An infinite regress is actually possible only in the mind, because only in the mind can relations be founded upon relations. So any argument that involves an actual infinite regress, to the extent that it involves one, is an argument that has lost touch with the order of physical being as something to be explained through proper causes. For proper causes are found only within the physical interactions of finite substances, and these, as finite, are always determinate within the order of moved movers. Hence the Latin adage, *regressus ad infinitum absolute repugnat*, "an argument involving an infinite process is self-defeating".[226] For the whole point of the contrast between "second" and "first" intentions is to gain a critical control of mental constructs so as to be

---

224 The "five words" we discussed in detail at the end of chapter 4, "The Tree of Porphyry", p. 144ff.; and keep in mind that the Aristotelian category of "accident" includes the Porphyrian predicables difference, property, and accident, all three.

225 Poinsot 1632: 292a33ff.

226 This adage, not only by the Latins but by Aristotle himself and the ancient Greek Peripatetics, is constantly invoked in such a way – e.g., in the *quinque viae*, as we have seen – as to suggest strongly that something about their philosophical context made this adage seem much more *Selbstverständlich* than it appears to modern or postmodern eyes, as I found out when I undertook to investigate its basis for *The Human Use of Signs* (Deely 1994). That was when I came to realize that the physical impossibility of relations as such providing the basis for yet other relations in the order of *ens reale*, while this presents no problem within the order of *ens obiectificatum*, is the ground of the adage. Considering how much is at stake on its truth, it may seem surprising that extensive accounts of its import are hard to come by. It is a rich field for further research, to be

able rightly to order them to the goal of distinguishing what is independent of the mind – reality in this sense – from what the mind makes up. First intentions occur in the field of physical interactions as precluding an actual regress to infinity. But second intentions, in their own order, can actually be multiplied to infinity. Only their subordination to the order of first intentions keeps an explanation on the trail of physical being. Should that subordination be lost, for whatever reason, thought begins to wander off into the labyrinth of its own mind's making. The functional equivalence of real and unreal relations comes to the fore, and there is no longer any check to discriminate between what might be and what is the case.

This nice simple picture is complicated slightly by the fact that second intentions, too, can become part of the "actual existence" exercised by things. For example, a man becomes a judge, a priest, or a teacher. That is to say, certain relations of power and responsibility are based on his existence as a physical organism (he must be in order to be made a judge), and these relations with which he is invested by society (as such mind-dependent relations) amount to new characteristics which individuate him within human society. Nonetheless, these new characteristics belong to him, even to his very existence exercised, only as it is exercised not only subjectively but also in the objective order. According to their being in the terms of the *ens reale/ens rationis* distinction, they are cognition-dependent characteristics; yet they belong to the judge in his actual *objective* existence as a functioning member of society.

The better Latin logicians recognized this anomaly, that the line separating first intentions from second intentions, insofar as it involved the being peculiar and proper to relations, was not and could not be a hard and fast line drawn in particular cases once and for all. But the anomalous aspect of the first/second intention distinction was not along their line of primary interest. They let it pass. In this way, the philosophy of being lost much of its potential for augmenting human understanding, as we will have occasion to see in more detail when we return to this topic in chapter 10 below.[227] Here, suffice it to say that in letting pass unexplored this little inconvenience to their "realistic logic" the medievals, in effect, dropped out of their consideration the Umwelt in its proper being as distinguished from the being of the physical environment. They also lost at the same time the analytical capacity to take adequate account of that primary form of reality which experience is as the result of belonging not simply to the biological race of rational and linguistic animals, *homo sapiens sapiens*, but to the specific cultural group of Christian, Moslem, Jew, Hindu, Buddhist, New Age, or what have you. Each group, by foregoing the analysis of this small inconvenience, was left free to consider their Umwelt as perfectly natural, the others as unexplained, perhaps unexplainable, deviations from the real.

Just how much larger the world of being-as-first-known is than the world of supposed reality (*ens reale*) may be seen from the following schema:

---

sure; the entry "Infinite process" in Deely 1994 will I hope provide a starting point for some future researcher.

227 See the discussion in chapter 10 beginning at p. 468 below.

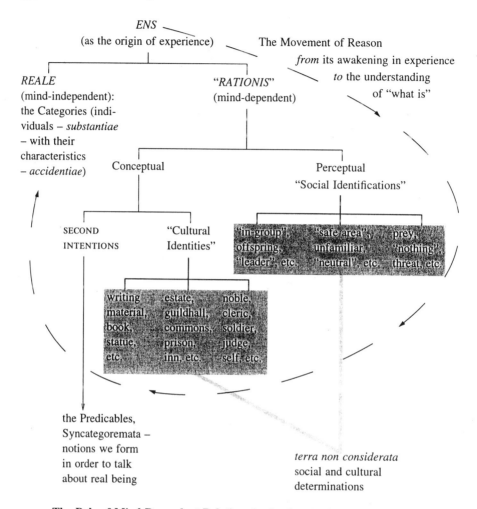

The Role of Mind-Dependent Relations in the Structuring of Experience

But let us not conclude simply on a note of what the Latins missed after Aquinas, that, even in order to know being, we must wrap it in nonbeing. Let me at least say enough to show why they had the temptation so to narrow their scope in the first place. By focusing on the "order to *ens reale*", the Latins were able to show how the human mind comes to equip itself with the conceptual tools necessary for the possibility of science as we understand it today, precisely as it developed over the later Latin centuries and burst upon the scene of modernity to occupy and continue to hold the central place in Western civilization,[228] notwithstanding the tergiversations of modern philosophy.[229]

---

228 See "Science Comes of Age", chapter 11 below, p. 487ff.
229 See chapter 13 below, "The Strange Case of Dr Jekyll and Mr Hyde", p. 540ff.

The Sequence of First or "Primitive Concepts" Consequent upon Being

"Being as first known" is not so unlike the "blooming buzzing confusion" that William James (1842–1910) reflected upon.[230] For Aquinas, and in his school after him,[231] the Latins saw quite well that the *primum cognitum* was not an abstract genus of logic, but a primitive apprehension of the intelligibly knowable as such in a confused and indistinct or quasi-potential manner, according to the everywhere accepted maxim, *anima est quodammodo omnia*: "the soul" – the human mind – "is in a certain way all things", as it is able to know being in its transcendental amplitude. Understanding, they reasoned, proceeds naturally from potency to act, or rather from the imperfect to the (relatively) perfect. The proportionate object of such a progression must likewise be something confused and imperfect. And, inasmuch as the more distinct as such is more perfect than the confused, the notion of being as manifested in any particular object of awareness has a more confused – a more "potential" – intelligibility as indistinctly mingling every character actually found or findable in that object.

This "being", as the most primitive of intellectual apprehensions,[232] is given to understanding by the senses, to be sure. But it can hardly be confused with the concrete physical object insofar as that object is a physically individual existent, or complex of individual existents, an *ens reale*. For "being as first known" is also the richest of all objectifications, embracing every particular intelligible object in the amplitude of analogy, albeit according to a totally confused and undistinguished awareness (such as the much later formation of a notion of "being as such" helps to dispel). Thus material entities as particular beings are experienced "factually" only because being has been previously grasped in a way that is very different from conceptualizations of the logical order. This is the meaning of the saying of Aquinas, "being is what first falls under human understanding" (*"primo in intellectu cadit ens"*).

Out of this primitive awareness, which is bound up with and transformative of perception as well as sensation from within, there arises, in the course of changes experienced (movements, etc.), and by way of opposition to being, the idea of *non-being*, as we have seen. In the earliest phases of apprehension, this idea originates via the senses, supported by feelings of "disappointment", out of the basic awareness of differences in the sensibly varying situation, the universe in motion – perhaps out

---

230 James 1911: 50, where he attributes the expression to "someone".

231 The most extended discussion of being-as-first-known, *De Primo Cognito*, in the school that developed out of the writings of Aquinas seems to be that of Poinsot 1633: *Philosophiae naturalis prima pars* (*Part I of Natural Philosophy*), Quaestio 1, "De Scientia Philosophiae et Ordine Cognoscendi" ("On Philosophical Knowledge and the Order of Knowing"), articulus 3, "Utrum magis universale, atque adeo ipsum ens ut sic, sit primo cognitum ab intellectu nostro" ("Whether the more universal, and therefore being itself as such, is primarily known by human understanding"), Reiser ed. vol. II, 20a2–33b38. In the References at the end of this work I list this treatise separately as 1633a.

232 The "prima ratio cognoscibilis seu primum cognitum formale respectu nostri intellectus", as Poinsot formulated it (1633a: q. 1, art. 3).

of experiences of opposition in particular. The polarity from experience of "what is" and "what is not" provides the understanding with the first materials for a judgment: that "being is not non-being", or, as Aquinas once more concretely formulated the primitive possibility, "this is not that" (*hoc non est illud*).

In this very act of comparison, the understanding grasps (again for the first time) *distinction*. Just so, in the course of experience, being and nonbeing, *ens reale* and *ens rationis*, create each other as elements of experience. They are not absolutes, they are correlates; and, as in experience so correlated, they provide the basis of all further distinctions. This new grasp, in turn, enables yet another new grasp, grasp in judgment of the first principle of intelligible discourse, which – in its turn – provides the ground of endless further judgments of a logical kind. This first principle of intelligible discourse is exactly as Aquinas described it in the text above cited,[233] and is called (see the humor in this) by some *the principle of contradiction* and by others *the principle of non-contradiction*. But at least both agree on exactly what is the content of this principle: that it is not possible to both be and not be at the same time in the same respect, "*impossibile est esse et non esse simul*", as we saw.

As the direct outcome of the judgment that being is not non-being, the principle of contradiction participates in the non-alternative, therefore necessary, character of that prior judgment. Understanding, unable, on the inward side,[234] to affirm and deny the same thing under the same aspect, has manifested to it by the senses likewise that entities are one way or another but not both in a given aspect, giving rise to the notion of being undivided or *unity*. But what is experimentally undivided in itself is given, in and by that very experience, as divided from others. So arises (intellectual) grasp of *plurality*, of many beings each of which is itself one.[235]

At this stage, finally, tautological judgment (a judgment true by virtue of logical form alone) and the recognition of *identity* ("every being is what it is") becomes possible. Only then does the recognition of an "outside world" as such, that is, a world outside of our subjectivity and beyond our Umwelt (i.e., independently existing in respect of our being as knowers),[236] become possible as well.

---

233 Aquinas, *Commentary on the Metaphysics of Aristotle* (c.1268/72), IV, lect. 6, n. 605, more fully cited on p. 349 above.

234 In words we can say anything; but Aquinas thought like Aristotle on this point (Aristotle, *Organon*, c.348–7aBC: 76b24–7): "demonstration is addressed not to the spoken word but to the discourse within the soul, and though we can always raise objections to the spoken word, to the inward discourse we cannot always object". Often you can actually see someone say what they clearly do not think, just to preserve their position (or pride) in an argument.

235 See the reply to the 15th objection in q. 9, art. 7, of his *Quaestiones disputatae de potentia*, where Aquinas (c.1265/6, in Busa 3, p. 258) provides a near-complete summary exposition of this discussion.

236 It may not be premature to note that this recognition sets the human use of signs (or "anthroposemiosis") apart in principle from the use of signs brute animals make ("zoösemiosis") as such. As it might be said, and as Jacques Maritain did say (1942: 9): "In its most perfect function, which is not to manufacture ideas but to judge, the understanding seizes upon existence exercised by things."

These seven elements, then – being, non-being, distinction, contradiction, unity, plurality, identity – are the foundation for the notion of "truth as conformity".[237] Their sequence, being the same for all in its necessary features, is what lays the ground of possibility for intersubjective agreement in the linguistically communicable results of judgments as well. We have here, so to speak, the intellectual infrastructure of cultural reality in its difference from the purely social world. Idealism in the modern sense (that the mind knows only what the mind itself makes) is precluded in the setting of such an analysis "by the fact that the knowing subject is discovered" – or, more exactly, discovers itself – "only within a world of change subject to the law of contradiction".[238] This law of contradiction itself, moreover, along with the transcendentals and other logical concepts, "such as 'something', 'identity', 'non-identity', 'agreement', 'disagreement', 'characteristic', 'relation', and 'connection'," is rooted, as Strasser well says,[239] "in our concrete dealings with beings. The elementary rules of logic owe their compelling force to our habitual knowledge about the identity, unity, inner indivision of being and its difference from other beings. In other words, the logical evidences are based upon, or, rather, arise out of, a certain experience of being as being".

The "Way of Things", the Philosophy of Being, and Single-Issue Thomism
So the Latins followed the path that they did at the time they did, focusing not on the *primum cognitum* itself and as such, but on the way *from* what "first falls into understanding" *toward* the world of nature and things of the physical environment, quite simply because of what they considered to be most needed at the time. They were interested in reality, precisely in the ancient sense with which Greek philosophy had begun. They wanted to find the way to understand the order of being existing independently of the human mind, and they wanted to develop the tools necessary to clear a path to that understanding.

They did not think of themselves as preparing the way for a whole new "age of understanding", but that, in part, is precisely what they were doing. Had they not pursued the course that they did, modern science would not have become a cultural possibility in the West. As they themselves saw it, they were pursuing the way of wisdom, insofar as wisdom has the function of knowing the "rationale of being and non-being", as Aquinas himself put it, "and the notions following therefrom".[240] As

---

237 The basis for the prior possibility of such conformity being something else again, as Heidegger (1943) was first to point out, in an essay all the more important for coming in the wake of Kant's elaborate explanation of why any such conformity could be no more than a mere appearance, a "phenomenon" in the invidious sense he so well managed to attach to the final ontological impoverishment of that term.

238 Ashley 1973: 291–2.

239 Strasser 1963: 263. Cf. Aquinas, *Commentary on the Metaphysics*, V, lect. 11, n. 912 (in Busa 4, p. 436). And see the diagram of Aquinas's notion of the implicit content of the *primum cognitum* in chapter 15, p. 648.

240 Aquinas (c.1269/72) *Summa* I–II, 66, 5 ad 4: "Cognoscere autem rationem entis et non entis, et totius et partis, et aliorum quae consequuntur ad ens, ex quibus sicut ex terminis constituuntur

the heirs of modernity in its scientific achievements, not even the postmoderns are in a position to gainsay the Latins on this point! Each epoch, in developing its own insights and possibilities for understanding, proves also to be preparing the way for a succeeding age.

"Being" is larger than "thing". But how to find, from within being, which includes ideas no less than things, the path to things as such is no mean achievement. Modern science insofar as it treads the way of things today owes much to the Latins. Modern philosophy, by contrast, originally conceived as of a piece with the origins of modern science, actually wound up on another path entirely. And by wholly losing sight of the transcendental aspect of things, modern philosophy made of the way of ideas a cul de sac, a dead-end. The way of things, it turns out, is not incompatible with the philosophy of being. But the way of ideas, in failing to realize that ideas are signs, rendered itself incompatible both with philosophy of being and with the aspirations of science to understand the physical environment of animal life. Dr Jekyll, the scientist in the modern sense, soon discovered within his own breast Mr Hyde, the philosopher in the modern sense.

But this again gets us ahead of our story. Here let us simply note that the Latin Age, as the epoch of the philosophy of being, gave rise to the famous metaphysics of *esse*, indeed, but was much more than simply that metaphysics. It would, for example, be hard to deny Gilson's charge against Cajetan that he missed the point and the boat on the metaphysics of *esse*. But, as I hope has become clear, there is much more to Aquinas as well as to the Latin Age than this single issue. Aquinas, in representing the Latin Age, left a lot of boats to miss. It is to Cajetan's credit that the *primum cognitum* was one of the boats which he, unlike the Neothomists, did not entirely miss. There are rich but difficult texts in this matter to be mined over the tradition of commentators on Aquinas's writings, not only in Cajetan, but in Poinsot and Soto and perhaps elsewhere. The one of our contemporaries who was doing the most promising pioneering work in this area, Vincent Guagliardo, died in 1995 at the age of fifty-one, his work just beginning to bear published fruit. His last major essay[241] is one of the best places to begin to think about this problem of the *primum cognitum* in relation to the doctrine of signs.

Thomism after Thomas

If there is a single issue on which the membership in the school of Thomas Aquinas should be decided, given the breadth and diversity of topics treated in his writings, that issue should be more of a general historical nature than any one specific doctrinal issue. There most certainly was a 'Dominican School' that developed over the later Latin centuries around the work of Aquinas, as one of the three

---

principia indemonstrabilia, pertinet ad sapientiam, quia ens commune est proprius effectus causae altissimae, scilicet Deus."
241 Guagliardo 1995.

dominant currents of Renaissance scholasticism. On the existence and members of this school the first court of judgment to take into account must be the collective opinion that the centuries have formed; and indeed the earliest period, the immediate decades following the death of Aquinas, have hardly been studied.[242] But by the early fifteenth century, and continuing to the middle of the seventeenth century, a major current of Latin commentary upon and development of the thought of Aquinas clearly emerged, what we may justly call the period of "classical Latin Thomism", in contrast to the late nineteenth century revival of Thomism outside the Latin language commonly designated Neothomism.

Certainly not all in the original historical school stand on a level of equal eminence. The *Princeps Thomistarum*, "First of the Thomists", so called because it was he who began what turned out to be the major Latin tradition of Thomistic commentary, was Joannes Capreolus (c.1380–1444). Three decades after Capreolus's own death and a century and a decade after the death of Aquinas, Thomas de S. Germano brought to publication in 1483/4 the *Libri IV Defensionum theologiae Thomae Aquinatis*, which was a manuscript Capreolus had developed as an extended defense of the intellectual positions taken by Aquinas in relation to his own work as a professor assigned to teach the *Sentences* of Peter Lombard.

With Capreolus begins the Latin line of major authors who published in a capacity of expounding and developing the thought embodied in the various writings of Aquinas. That line, distinguished and long, will continue unbroken for a little more than two centuries, to the end of the Latin Age. The most eminent of the lineage can be easily listed.

Thomas de Vio Cajetan (1468–1534) and Ferrariensis (c.1474–1528) are authors whose writings we have had occasion to mention above in discussing analogy.[243] Francisco de Vitoria (1492–1536) upheld the view of Aquinas that grace presupposes nature by developing (largely against major Protestant reformers) the doctrine of human rights as consequences of human nature prior to and independent of questions of divine grace and religious confession, and a doctrine of international law based on the conception of universal human rights. Dominic Soto (1494–1560), a part of whose historical role we will have occasion to explore in a later chapter,[244] also contributed greatly to understanding the philosophical dimensions and basis of law within a state. Melchior Cano (1509–60), whom Soto succeeded in a Chair at Salamanca, has a reputation confined all but exclusively to theological areas, and in particular to the matter of the critical, scientific evaluation of the sources on which

---

242 The lack of detached work in this area makes all the more valuable the pioneering study developed under the direction of James Weisheipl, namely, Roensch 1964: *Early Thomistic School*. Haldane (1998) designates this period as "the first Thomism" and the period of the major Latin commentators as "the second Thomism", but departs from this terminology to call the modern revival begun in the late 19th century not "the third Thomism" but rather (a needlessly hyphenated) "Neo-Thomism".

243 See, in this chapter, p. 323f. and p. 328f., respectively.

244 See chapter 8 passim, but esp. p. 408ff.

theological thought principally depends and of the manner in which theological thought draws upon those sources. In this matter, his beautifully written and highly original study *De locis theologicis*, published in 1563 within three years of its author's death, marked a major stage in the development of theology as a scientifically critical discipline, and adumbrated the emergence of a branch of theology that came to be called in modern times "fundamental theology". Domingo Bañez (1528–1604), a confessor and adviser to Teresa of Avila and next to last of the major Latin Thomistic authors, is best known for his role in developing the Thomistic side of the huge controversy between Jesuit and Dominican theologians that exploded near the beginning of the seventeenth century and became so intense that within a few years of his death the discussion was shut down by papal order;[245] but in

---

245 The heat of this controversy is suggested by the increasingly severe series of papal sanctions leveled against those participating, the first in September 1607, another in December 1611, another in May 1625, and yet another – this one effectively shutting the dispute down as a public affair – in August 1641. Indeed, at the time, the very organization of written treatises in theology had to be modified to accommodate the sanctions (see Deely 1985: 433n.44). By late-modern times, these papal strictures from the first half of the seventeenth century had long since fallen into desuetude. Jacques Maritain (1966: 14, 32), one of the few modern authors seriously to revisit the terms of the ancient controversy, considered that the Bañezians had the better side, but were hobbled in their arguments by reason of being "'Cyclopean' Thomists", that is to say, followers of St Thomas not yet "become conscious of non-being and of its formidable role in reality", hence with an eye "fixed solely on the perspective of being" and not ready because not even aware of the need to "open onto the avenues of non-being windows as large as those open onto the avenues of being" and to traverse in thought "paths of non-being" every bit "as difficult as those of being". (So we might make the perhaps obvious point that one need not be a Thomist to adhere to a Cyclopean ontology; that is found also in Suárez [1548–1617] and Wolff [1679–1754], after all, and quite a few others. Late-modern positivism was a whole movement founded on a reductivist Cyclopeanism.)

This particular blindness on Bañez's part goes far toward explaining his out-of-hand dismissal of the then-developing controversy over the being proper to sign, in which nonbeing plays an essential and constantly hovering role, which we will discuss in chapter 8. For the few pronouncements Bañez makes in the matter suggest that he did not grasp the main issues involved in the threefold distinction of signs/objects/things within experience (Bañez 1599: 104): "No dejaré advertir in esta lugar cuán impropiamente hablan algunos modernos cuando dicen que los conceptos mentales son signos de las cosas, a las cuales expresan y en sí mismas representan formalmente. En efecto, también según la propiedad de la lengua latina, la razón de signo y de significar tiene representación imperfecta en sí respecto de la cosa representada. Pues ciertamente si alguien expresamente enseña alguna verdad, ineptamente diríamos que la ha significado. Pues quien significa no hace la cosa presente de manera íntegra. Y, y que las voces representan a los conceptos mentales no expresa y formalmente, sino que son ciertos instrumentos que no se adecúan a la perfección de la cosa significada, por ello propiamente se dicen signos y que significan. Mas, sin embargo, los conceptos mentales, ya que contienen toda la perfección de la cosa representada en ellos mismos formalmente en un ser inteligible, por ello no se han de llamar signos, sino imágenes expresas de las cosas. Como también el Verbo en las cosas divinas es ciertamente imagen del Padre, pero no su signo. Más aún, también en las cosas humanas el hijo de un hombre es imagen del padre, que representa al padre y, sin embargo, no significa al padre, ya que en lo que representa no se considera que representa algo distinto de si mismo, ya que lo representado por la misma razón de semejante está en la naturaleza para el mismo hijo. Así también el concepto, al representar a la cosa, ya que la representa en cuanto formalmente se contiene en el ser inteligible en el mismo concepto, no se dice que representa algo distinto de sí mismo concepto, no se dice que representa

Neothomistic circles he has been lionized mainly for his exceptional appreciation of the role of *esse* in the thought of Aquinas, as expressed in his *Commentary* of 1584/8 on the First Part of the *Summa*, where he emphasizes, against his fellow Thomists, that, "it is not just the last act," as Beuchot summarized the teaching, "but both the first and the last. That is, *esse* not only completes a being, but makes it possible for there to be a being at all".[246] After Bañez comes John Poinsot (1589–1644), who

---

algo distinto de sí mismo, sino que representándose representa la cosa contenida en si mismo. Estas cosas han sido dichas a causa de los varones doctos, aunque a veces hablen como la mayoria y sientan como la minoria. Pues también Santo Tomás a veces no hable con tanto rigor."

Cyclopean Thomism indeed!

246 Beuchot 1998: 648. The statement Beuchot thus so concisely summarizes reads in Bañez himself (1584/8: *In I.3.4*, p. 141) as follows: "Et quamvis ipsum esse receptum in essentia composita ex principiis essentialibus specificetur ab illis, tamen in eo quod specificatur nullam perfectionem recipit, sed potius deprimitur et descendit ad esse secundum quid, eo quod esse hominem, esse se angelum, non est perfectio simpliciter. Et hoc est quod saepissime d. Thomas clamat, et Thomistae nolunt audire: quod esse est actualitas omnis formae vel naturae, sicut in hoc articulo in ratione secunda dicit et quod in nulla re invenitur sicut recipiens, et perfectibile, sed sicut receptum et perficiens id in quo recipitur: ipsum tamen, eo ipso quod recipitur, deprimitur, et ut ita dixerim, imperficitur." – "And although actual existence itself is received in a composite essence and specified by the essential principles, nevertheless, it receives no perfection from the fact that it is specified, but is rather deprived and brought down to an existence in a certain respect, by the fact that to be a man or to be an angel" – that is to say, by the fact that a substance, be it material or spiritual – "is not a perfection simply speaking. And this is what S. Thomas so loudly and frequently proclaims and the Thomists want not to hear: that existence is the actuality of every form or nature, as he says in the article in the second argument, and that existence is not found in any thing as what is doing the receiving and what is perfectible, but as received and perfecting that in which it is received: yet it itself, by the very fact of being received, is deprived [of its fullness], and, as I might say, rendered imperfect."

Llamzon (1966: 12), who has made an English translation of the section of Bañez's *Scholastica commentaria* concerning I.3.4 (but without following the structure of the text "in all its technicalities"), inadvertently reveals in his preface to the translation exactly the point on which the extreme partisans of existentialist Neothomism met shipwreck. After rightly pointing out, with Bañez, that, for St Thomas, "in a finite being, *esse*, though extrinsic to the creature's essence, is yet the most internal to it of all the principles," he goes on to say (I add the italics) that "essence relates to esse *only as a limit*". But that is precisely to deny to form everything *specific* to it; because "to limit" is a function common to every form of finite being *without exception*. If that exhausts the function of form in finite being (and anyone inclined to think that surely Llamzon must be eccentric in missing so obvious and fatal a point is free to consult the Neothomist allies Llamzon accurately cites without me having to repeat their citation here), we would have to conclude that finite *existence itself* is what specifies this individual as an alligator, that as a termite, and that as a human being. But, of course, that is not merely to insist on the primacy of *esse*, it is to assign to *esse* the function that Thomas (and everyone else, including Bañez himself) assigns to *essentia* as formal. Thomas did not achieve distinction by denying what everyone else agreed to, but by seeing that very agreement in a light that showed that *esse* considered as a proper effect has no cause as such in the finite order, as we said above in our "Note on the Distinction between Essence and Existence", p. 290.

When Thomas Aquinas cites approvingly the ancient adage that *forma dat esse*, indeed he does not mean that *esse* flows from the form *as from the source*; what he means is that form specifies which finite channel the current of *this individual* existence must flow in, and it does it from within by the actuation it receives from the *actus essendi*. Essence, as distinct from existence, indeed gets whatever reality it has from *esse*; but the reality it gets is not only that of a *finite* form, a limit; it

took in Latin the name *Joannes a Sancto Thoma*, and with whom the continuous Latin line of the classical Thomist commentators came to an end. As Capreolus was *princeps*, so Poinsot is *ultimus*, fixed forever in history, as Maritain justly said, [247] as "the latest and most mature of the geniuses who explained St Thomas" in the Latin line. As we will see over our next two chapters, Poinsot figures even more prominently than Aquinas himself in bringing the Latin Age to close with a successful resolution of that main speculative problem with which Augustine had (so inadvertently) both opened and defined that age.

Within the Latin line or "school" of Thomism, pre-eminence has long and justly been accorded to three members. Through the range, depth, and distinctiveness of their work, Cajetan and Poinsot have earned this status. Also for depth and distinctiveness, but over a narrower range, Bañez ranks as one of the pre-eminent three.

It is almost time to consider some new names to add to the list, not of the classical Latin commentators, to be sure, for that is a time definitively past, a role closed, but from the authors of the Neothomistic revival of the turn of the twentieth century. Who the names will be from the "New Scholasticism" of the nineteenth and twentieth centuries is probably clear enough from what has already been said. It should also be clear from what has been said that the truest judgment in this whole matter has been expressed in the words of Maritain. "Philosophy lives on dialogue and conversation", he said;[248] "to continue the conversation with congenial and clear-sighted companions of the stature of Cajetan, Bañez, and John of St. Thomas is a privilege of the genius of Thomas Aquinas and of his grace-given mission". For "the development of St. Thomas' doctrine in the works of the commentators is a fascinating process to which not enough attention has been given".

Into the Abyss

In Aquinas's fundamental criticism of Augustine's definition of sign can be seen the flames of the "constantly alive, burning and inevitable problem" Beuchot noted[249] as Augustine's principal bequest to posterity in the matter of what we now call "semiotics". This is the name used after Locke and Peirce. But the medievals referred to the subject area in their own technical argot as the *doctrina signorum* or "doctrine of signs", an expression also adopted by both Locke and Peirce as a synonymous amplification of "semiotics" as a proper name. We have also seen that much, though

---

is rather that of a finite *form*, a specification according to which existence can be exercised and does exercise itself in this rather than that finite way.

247 Maritain 1953. v. Cf. Ramirez (1924. 806). "Jean de Saint-Thomas est regardé à juste titre comme l'un des plus grands théologiens thomistes. Ses contemporains, d'une voix unanime, l'appelèrent un second Thomas, brillante étoile en face du Soleil (saint Thomas d'Aquin); et toujours, on le plaça en compagnie de Cajetan et de Bañez, aux côtes de l'Ange de l'École."

248 Maritain 1953: v.

249 Beuchot 1986: 26 (see chapter 6, p. 224).

not all, of the thought of Aquinas is bound up with matters that either depend on the problem of the sign, or are so closely kin thereto as to defy satisfactory outcome unless they can be reworked in the light of a doctrine of signs – such problems as the *ens ut primum cognitum* (being-as-first-known) and the *analogia entis* ("analogy of being").

Yet beyond his rejection of Augustine's definition as inadequate to express the general notion of sign according to its proper being, Aquinas, unfortunately (for it would be most interesting to have seen his mind directly at work on the problem), never focuses his attention directly on what exactly is it that the most general definition of sign expresses or applies to, insofar as *signum* says something common to sensible objects and psychological states alike. Aquinas leaves open the question of the possible nominalistic character of Augustine's proposal,[250] even though clearly in the case of his writings he did not consider the doctrine of signs to be a nominalistic doctrine. Indeed, it is plain from his work that he had little use for theories of a nominalist variety, and he was never tempted to adopt one as his own in any area outside the one area he preferred to avoid entirely, the area of empty discourse, or even discourse which deliberately avoids clarity about its content.[251]

Aquinas himself, in short, left the problem of the being proper to signs still to be confronted head-on. But he had a contemporary who did not so leave the problem. And thereby hangs a largely untold tale of the closing Latin centuries.

---

250 See "The Possible Nominalistic Character of Augustine's Proposal" in chapter 6, p. 247.

251 It is hard to imagine what he would have thought of the later Wittgenstein's attempt to turn the whole of philosophy into a nominalism; or of the attempt of Derrida to make free association under individual cleverness the rule for guiding judgments in philosophy.

CHAPTER EIGHT

The Fate of Sign
in the Later Latin Age

We are near the end of the thirteenth century, still a full three centuries from the clear onset of modernity, and with nearly six centuries to cross before reaching the frontiers of postmodern times. How to cover the closing three hundred years of the Latin Age? We could follow the well-beaten traditional path of carrying our discussion of the Latins beyond Aquinas only as far as Scotus (c.1266–1308) and Ockham (c.1285–1349), then jump with a single bound to Descartes (1596–1650) and classical modern philosophy. Established academic custom would more than justify such a procedure: it sanctions it. But what justifies the established custom?

In the first place, why should we go along with the blatant nonsense which still tries to pretend that the three closing Latin centuries are "a philosophical desert"[1] when they are not? And why follow a path so well traveled when it requires us to miss whatever sights there might be along the way? For even deserts have their beauty. And the truth is that the closing Latin centuries are more like a dense tropical rain forest than a desert. It is easier to get lost in them than to find a way through, but that hardly justifies those committed to exploring the land from simply flying over them without a stop.

Besides, even if we have to find a completely untraveled route, we already have a number of clues from philosophical tradition that suggest there is a path through (rather than around or over) the forgotten centuries of late Latinity. And we have clues as well suggesting where the path lies. Why not let the "constantly alive, burning and inevitable problem" bequeathed by Augustine to the Latin Age show us the way? All we have to do is trace out the growing Latin awareness of the problem of how to justify the general notion of sign, and we will find that it is enough – enough to get us over the closing Latin centuries without the aid of the familiar paths, and enough to provide us with intellectual sustenance and plenty of sights to make the journey interesting in the bargain.

---

1 This is the statement made by Matson in the second volume of his prestigious 1987 work titled *A New History of Philosophy*, II, 253. But this "new history" is mistitled, for it tells anything but a new tale. It is classic late modern, and nothing but.

So let us leave the desert and air routes to those who prefer familiar paths. In the spirit of philosophy itself, and with a bow to Robert Frost,[2] let us go instead by a road much less taken. Let us rather strengthen the hand of those few since Descartes to introduce philosophy without pretending that modernity, in a historical vacuum, sprang full blown from the mind of Zeus. The game is worth the candle, for we shall find that by exploring a new way in preference to going the established way, we will arrive among the first able to understand the interpretive horizon of postmodernity.

Roger Bacon (c.1214–1292)

We need not go beyond Aquinas's lifetime to find our first missing link in the chain of thinkers connecting the Latin Age to modern times and beyond, to the semiotic concerns of postmodernity. Roger Bacon, fully contemporary with Aquinas, was the first author to leave a record of looking for the ground outside of language itself for the uniquely Latin general notion of *signum*. Bacon, born about ten years before Aquinas, also outlived him by eighteen years. Though none of the early Latins had doubted that the emperor – "blessed Augustine", as Bacon called him – indeed had clothes,[3] none had yet thought to wonder where exactly the garments lay hidden.

The First Attempt to Ground the General Notion

Roger Bacon was the first, so far as we know at the moment, to try to lay out the ground on which could be shown to stand a general definition of sign adequate to the general notion with the proposal of which Augustine had opened the Latin Age. In fact, Bacon failed to demarcate the needed foundation for the general notion we have seen the Latins everywhere presume. But honor lies in the undertaking, for it is no disgrace, but normal, to fall short in the first attempt at a grand speculative philosophical enterprise, especially for a man confessedly more interested in the practical applications of knowledge than in its doctrinal underside.

A Man of Details

Bacon, in addressing the matter of the being proper to sign directly in a treatise titled *De Signis,* which he had made part of his *Opus Maius*, looked directly into the

---

2 I have in mind Frost's poem from the *Atlantic Monthly* of 1915, "The Road Not Taken": "Two roads diverged in a yellow wood, / And sorry I could not travel both / And be one traveler, long I stood / And looked down one as far as I could / To where it bent in the undergrowth; // Then took the other, as just as fair, / and having perhaps the better claim, / Because it was grassy and wanted wear; / Though as for that the passing there / Had worn them really about the same, // And both that morning equally lay / In leaves no step had trodden black. / Oh, I kept the first for another day! / Yet knowing how way leads on to way, / I doubted if I should ever come back. // I shall be telling this with a sigh / Somewhere ages and ages hence: / two roads diverged in wood, and I – / I took the one less traveled by, / and that has made all the difference."

3 That is, knew what he was talking about.

abyss that Augustine had presumptively treated as solid ground. This *Opus maius*, Bacon's "Larger" or "Greater Work", he had assembled from his writings of many years after the election of Pope Clement IV in February 1265, in hope of getting that pope's direct backing for his scheme for the overhaul of Christian education. Bacon wanted more attention paid to the books of scripture and to the book of nature, with less attention paid to the newfangled theology. He thought the Christian world needed more observation of the environment and less commentary on Aristotle.

He sent the *Opus maius* to Clement together with a synopsis he called the *Opus minus*. And he followed up the transmission of these two works to Clement by sending him, by special messenger, yet another grand summary he titled the *Opus Tertium*, including along with it a lens with which he urged the pope to make some personal experiments in optics. But Clement died in November 1268, and, beyond a general interest, we have no idea what he really made of Bacon's writings.

Bacon was fond of an idea he ran across in the work *De disciplina scholarium*, attributed to Boethius. In the *Compendium of the Study of Theology* which Bacon composed in his last year of life (1292), he paraphrased Boethius thus:[4] "Who spurns trifles little by little falls to the depths". It might have been Bacon's motto for his conception of the intellectual life as a whole, for the entirety of his work was dedicated to the proposition that the most minute of the empirical details of nature are of the utmost importance for human understanding. In this he was to prove surely right, though the vindication would take centuries.

Bacon, self-styled as "the only seer in the land of the blind", was understandably bitter about the failure of his contemporaries to give his work the recognition he deemed it to deserve. Being "a man with an itch for self-expression",[5] he was filled with sentiments that, as Maloney put it,[6] "clearly could not have endeared him to his superiors and many of his peers". In particular, Bacon did not like the notion of theology as it was being developed by Aquinas and others,[7] while his more mundane interest in the relevance of things which we would today call scientific and natural was being ignored. More than this, he thought that the new theology was off on a wrong track entirely. Here[8] Bacon anticipates something of the contemporary rationale for displacing departments of theology with departments of religious studies:

> Although it ought to be recognized that the principal focus of the work of theologians ought to be on the sacred text, ... yet theologians have been principally occupied for

---

4 Bacon 1292: ¶45; and see also ¶23.
5 Southern 1962: 56.
6 Maloney 1988: 8.
7 In his *Compendium studii philosophici* (c.1272)—a work described by Easton (1952: 69–70) as "nothing but a scurrilous attack upon his contemporaries in every rank of society"—Bacon dismisses the translation work of William of Moerbeke, the translator Thomas Aquinas personally preferred to rely on for Latin versions of Aristotle's Greek, as the worst of all the translated texts available, which reveals to us more of Bacon's bile than of Moerbeke's ability. See Maloney 1988: 129n72.
8 Bacon 1292: ¶17.

the past fifty years with *questions*,[9] which is clear to all from the treatises, *summae*, and horseloads[10] composed by many.

Losing Sight of the Type in a Forest of Tokens

When, however, Roger Bacon decided in his senectitude to make one last try at producing an acceptable response to those who had many times called on him to "write something useful for theology",[11] he followed all too closely the example of "the book of the blessed Augustine *On Christian Doctrine*".[12] Just as Augustine had passed over the broad range of signifying phenomena in order to focus on the sacraments of the Church and the words of scripture, so Bacon in this work considers the broad range of signifying phenomena only with an eye to its application to the study of the sacred text. By succumbing to the temptation to pander to a need for linguistic theory as something the theologians could not avoid, he risked betraying the insight which marked the progress from his early *Sumule dialectices* (c.1245) to his *De Signis* of 1267: the realization that the traditional approach (after Aristotle's *De Interpretatione* and Boethius) of distinguishing words from all other signs and then focusing on language alone needed to be rethought from the ground up in the light of a general semiotics or doctrine of signs.[13]

Bacon begins chapter 1 of his *Compendium of the Study of Theology* with the observation that "in order to conceive the truth of signs it is first necessary to say a few words about the notion of signs". But instead of proceeding to expose the general notion, he plunges at once into a forest of varieties of signifying[14] which more beg the question than illuminate the general notion as such.

This was a pity, for Bacon had shown in his treatise *De Signis* of 1267, inserted as part of the *Opus Maius*, that he knew better. In his opening sentence of *De Signis*, he addressed squarely the unanswered question raised by Augustine's general definition:[15]

---

9 He is referring to the structure, or literary form, that was being developed for the writing of theology, as we discussed in chapter 7, p. 248n34. Maloney (1988: 120n4) expands upon the point with regard to Bacon. But see how enduring the "question" format as a literary device in philosophy was to prove to be, right down to the last century of the Latin Age. See the quotation from Doyle on this point cited in chapter 9, p. 421 below.

10 "honera equorum".

11 Which must have been irritating, for this is what Bacon considered himself to have been doing all along.

12 Bacon 1292: ¶25.

13 As Maloney rightly says (1988: 23), "Semiotic considerations in the *summulae* tradition rested squarely on Aristotle's *On Interpretation* 2 as transmitted by Boethius". See Maloney 1983 for fuller discussion of Bacon's insight.

14 See Meier-Oeser 1997: 54ff., where Bacon's classification of signs is reduced to a wonderfully clear diagram. And on this point of clear presentation of the classifications of sign made by various authors across the Latin Age, together with the bringing to light of yet further texts and authors to be studied in the context of semiotic, Meier-Oeser's study is without peer.

15 Bacon c.1267: ¶1.

> Sign is in the category of relation, and is said [to be] essentially relative to that for
> which it signifies, since it posits that significate in act when the sign itself is in act,
> and in potency when the sign itself is in potency.

Meier-Oeser, in addressing this point in his marvelously detailed study of signs
over the Latin Age,[16] observes that the assignation to the sign of a relational status
was a common tradition; but such a general observation conceals the point of
assigning sign to the *category* of relation in the specific context of the Aristotelian
understanding of the doctrine of categories prevailing in the milieu within which
Aquinas and Bacon wrote. Otherwise it becomes difficult or impossible to understand the doctrinal significance of the fact that, writing in the Latin milieu 365 years
later, John Poinsot – the first, as we shall see, successfully to answer the general
question posed by Augustine's notion – dismisses exactly the view Bacon propounds
in an opening sentence of his own *Tractatus de Signis*. The sign in general, he
remarks,[17] includes both signs given by nature and signs created by society, "and
for this reason cannot be as such a categorial being or a categorial relation", because
whatever pertains to the categories belongs determinately and restrictively to what
is given by nature, as Aquinas, following Aristotle, had explicitly remarked.[18]

The rebuttal is definitive. Bacon's attempt did not reach deep enough. Even so, it
has the merit of being an attempt, the merit of reaching to the real problem behind
Augustine's glib proposal. The proposal was that the sign possessed or exhibited
a general mode of being, verified equally in natural and cultural phenomena. The
problem is that such a proposal has to be justified, if not by Augustine, at least by
someone. What is needed is an explanation of how such a common mode of being is
possible, a mode of being which transcends the division between natural and cultural
being, being as it exists prior to and independently of the mind's working, and being
as it exists objectively not only in but partially or wholly as a result of the mind's
working. Anything, even self-contradictory propositions, can be asserted.[19] Anyone,
including Augustine, can assert that the sign has a general mode of being superior to
its particular or specific instances. But what is gratuitously asserted can with equal
freedom be denied. Whence, unless someone can *justify* what Augustine has asserted,
unless someone can explain how such a general mode of being indifferent to the
circumstances differentiating natural and cultural phenomena as such is possible in
the first place, it may well be that Augustine's proposal is a mere nominalism, a
flatus vocis, a chimaera or fiction of discourse with no more substance than Sherlock
Holmes or leprechauns.

---

16 Meier-Oeser 1997: 51–3.
17 Poinsot 1632a: 117/28–118/8. See chapter 9 below, esp. pp. 427 and 431ff.
18 See Aquinas's *Disputed Questions on the Power of God* (c.1265/6), q. 7. art. 9; and the discussion
   in Deely 1985: 472ff.
19 See the discussion of demonstration in chapter 3 above, p. 89f.; and the discussion of "How to Deal
   with Contradictions" in chapter 4, p. 125f.

The Problem of the "Nose of Wax"

As we move beyond Bacon in the Latin milieu, the language of the scholastics becomes more and more dense. One of the main reasons, if not the main reason, for the neglect of this period in the standard outline of philosophy that prevailed over the nineteenth and twentieth centuries is precisely the fact that the Latin of the mainstream philosophical discourse develops a technical terminology from the thirteenth century onwards that is shared by all the authors of all the schools. As a result, this terminology becomes in effect a "ground-cover" so thick as to be almost impenetrable to visitors from the future, such as ourselves. The humanists of the Renaissance ridiculed the scholastic Latin as "barbaric", but that was only a rhetorically effective way of saying that they were not interested in the speculative subtleties the scholastics had developed. The truth is that the scholastic Latin, as Peirce saw so clearly and remarked so forcefully, is a scientific language, not a literary one; and the whole complaint of the humanists comes down to this fact. They attacked and ridiculed the Latin of scholasticism for exactly the same reason that Charles Peirce would make it the basis upon which to formulate an ethics of terminology for the progress of philosophy in postmodern times.[20]

But Peirce was an intellectual worker of exceptional insight. While I think that his later views on the matter of the scholastics (for early in life he naturally shared the prejudices of the air he breathed, only later critically rejecting them) are likely to be those that prevail in the longer run, we will see that in the twentieth century, time after time, the best and most careful scholars investigating the area of the doctrine of signs among the later Latins fail to penetrate beyond the literal appearances to arrive at a deep understanding of the basic doctrinal issue concerning the sign: does the sign indeed have a general mode of being that transcends and unites through the action of signs the otherwise distinct realms of nature and culture, and if so, how is such a mode of being even possible in the first place?

Instead of grasping this issue and following its development, we will see that such later twentieth century scholars as undertake to penetrate again this past terrain follow instead the patterns of the ground cover, the literal appearances of the superficially common terminology. Instead of penetrating behind the appearances to the fundamental doctrinal issue of the being proper to sign as exhibited in whatever variety or type of sign, the investigators instead follow the derivative and secondary issue of how does this or that author divide signs into different categories. In this way, the question of the being proper to signs eludes their grasp, and they can only point to literal appearances to justify scholarly conclusions which miss the central matter-at-issue. We see this process at work here in Meier-Oeser's discussion of sign as relation in Bacon. We will see it again and again in the scholars he relies upon who try to situate the work of Poinsot at the end of the Latin doctrinal development of semiotics in relation to other writings of this milieu.[21] And we see it in Meier-Oeser's

---

20 See chapter 15 below, p. 662ff. in particular.
21 See chapter 10 below.

own analysis where he says[22] that for Poinsot the relation constitutive of the sign as such fundamentally "is something real" ("etwas Reales ist"[23]), where the text of Poinsot that he cites to support this conclusion says rather that the relation in question "*can be* real" ("realis esse potest"[24]). *Can be*, not *is*: for when the circumstances

---

22 I go here to the penultimate concluding paragraph of his generally excellent and detailed historical analysis of texts on "the metaphysical status of the sign-relation" (Cap. IV, Section "D. Der metaphysische Status der Zeichenrelationen", in Meier-Oeser 1997: 192–235).

23 Meier-Oeser 1997: 235.

24 Poinsot, *Tractatus de Signis* (1632a), Book I "On the Sign in Its Proper Being", Question 3 "Whether the relation of sign to signified is the same as the relation of sign to cognitive power", 160/34 (= Reiser I 667b50); for Poinsot assumes on this point the prior analyses he had made of the circumstances under which the possibility for a mind-independent to be real (that is to say, actualized, or actually exercised) will be realized or not, analyses whose bearing he had made explicit in the main conclusion of the immediately preceding Question 2, "Whether the sign-relation in the case of natural signs is mind-independent or mind-dependent", by pointing out (137/9–14) that "the relation of a natural sign" – whether instrumental and exterior to the mind or formal and interior to the mind's own workings – "to its significate by which the sign is constituted in being as a sign, is mind-independent and not mind-dependent considered in itself and by virtue of its fundament and *presupposing the existence of the terminus and the other conditions for a physical relation*". See further, therefore, the two "Preambles" to the independent edition of the *Tractatus* we refer to as Poinsot 1632a, esp. the Second Preamble, Art. 2 "What is required for a 'categorial' relation", and, within art. 2 esp. 90/41–91/29, which boils down to the point most crucial for the doctrine of signs (91/26–27), to wit, that "a physical relation has a mind-independent fundament with a coexistent terminus". In the case of a thought of a physically nonexistent (whether no longer or never existent) object, the representamen or "formal sign" has a fundament which need not be itself objectified in order to exist, but, in that case, the suprasubjective relation in which the being constitutive of the thought *as a sign* consists is precluded from being intersubjective unless in discourse two or more thinkers are considering the same object; in which case the intersubjectivity is one of community in discursive objectivity only (rather than between knowers and the subjectivity which is known or discoursed about as well).

   The more usual case of a mind-dependent relation is that wherein the relation wants for a mind-independent fundament, which is what Poinsot explicitly and exclusively remarks at this point in the Preamble (see the terminological note25 following this note). But the more remarkable case, of far greater interest for the doctrine of signs, and constituting, to borrow the striking expression of Teilhard de Chardin on a related point, "the sharp exacerbation to the point of disclosure" of what is most at the heart of the doctrine, is the case where the requisite sort of fundament for a physical relation of sign to object signified is not wanting but the relation's being physical in this regard is yet precluded by the want of physical existence in the terminus signified (even though a physical being for the sign relation can yet be realized in the constitution of a discursive community, as remarked) – the case that comes up in Question 2 of Book 2, cited above (137/9–14).

   This is perhaps the single most important one of many related points in Poinsot's doctrine of signs which cannot be garnered simply by a literal reading of the text at this or that passage, but which must be brought together by the reader in considering the text as a whole, an inevitable deficiency of the text generated, as I tried to indicate in first discussing the problems of its presentation as an independent tractate (Deely 1985: 404), by Poinsot's placing it first in the context of previous discussions rather than first on its relatively independent footing. His doctrine of the sign as an irreducibly triadic ontological relation indifferently "real" or "unreal" according to circumstances escaped the notice of his contemporary readers so far as we have yet been able to examine them, and it continues to escape the critics contemporary of the 1985 independent edition of his *Treatise* so far as they insist on approaching the work exclusively in the historical terms of existing terminology, sources and influences, an approach which cannot but founder on the "nose of wax" fallacy.

prevent the relation from being "real" in the Latin sense, it will be exercised, if at all, only objectively.[25]

In this difference of assertion lies the whole fate of the doctrine of signs as a unified theory, as a vindication rather than a qualified rejection of the original general proposal inherited from the work of Augustine. For in this difference lies the whole doctrine of Poinsot at the end of the late Latin development that the being proper to sign consists neither in mind-independent nor in mind-dependent relation determinately but in ontological relation as able to be either or both depending on surrounding circumstances, the context of the actual exercise of signification *hic et nunc* in any given case. It is not that the scholars in question are not good scholars. They are very good scholars. Not every rock is a fossil bone; and not everyone who has held a fossil bone saw what they were holding.

The literal appearances are always necessary to indicate to us when a scholastic author is discussing problems related to the sign, and they are generally sufficient, but only to the extent that nothing original is being said by the text. They are hardly sufficient to tell us what answer to the general question of the being proper to all signs, *if there is one*, is being given when an author cloaks his answer in the same terminology used by other authors who have actually not addressed the general question, or who have failed to arrive at an answer, or who have answered it otherwise than it is being answered in the given text. So it is that, whatever the difficulty, we must penetrate below the ground-cover to the underlying architectural semiotic proper to the work, be it the work of Roger Bacon, John Poinsot, or anyone in between. This is the problem the scholastic philosophical vocabulary must be made to yield up in the matter of the doctrine of signs in general, and it is no easy task; for precisely their common, technical vocabulary creates in its literal appearances the famous problem of the "nose of wax",[26] to wit, the hermeneutic problem of sorting through the consequences of the fact that the later great scholastics each make use of the seemingly same authorities and vocabulary – but to make or support points not merely different, but often in conflict or contradiction with one another.

There is nothing wrong with the approach as far as it goes; it is just that it does not go to the central doctrine of Poinsot's text, with the result that all those relying on the method inevitably wind up deforming the doctrine while vainly justifying the deformation with an appeal to the literal appearances, the words as marks on a page underinterpreted in their crucial character as sign-vehicles, as *repraesentamina*.

25 An "objective relation", thus, in the doctrine of signs, corresponds actually neither to the Latin *relatio realis* nor to the Latin *relatio rationis*, nor even to the Latin *relatio secundum esse*, although this last expression comes the closest, for an objective relation is necessarily ontological no matter what the circumstances of its realization. Poinsot's doctrine, in requiring such a notion in order to be understood, once again forces the reader beyond the literal appearances of the traditional terminology he employs perforce, but to which he too much restricts himself, we can say in hindsight, viewing the situation from the vantage of having, with the help of Jacques Maritain before all others, recovered his doctrine from the lost depths of the late Latin history to which it initially sank.

26 See chapter 10, p. 464f.

Augustine gave us a general notion of sign as an assertion, and some divisions of sign to work with. He also gave us a specific definition of sign which can be verified but not in the general sense or case he proposed. In effect, he proposed a classification of signs in conformity with his definition of sign, but he failed to realize that the general notion his divisions were meant to illustrate and his definition tried to express were incompatible. His definition and divisions alike were too narrow for the general notion of sign that he had originally proposed. Later scholastic authors would multiply the divisions of sign and the standpoints from which divisions would be made. But what has to be kept in mind is a tricky point that Augustine, and most Latins after him, did not keep in mind, the point specifically that any classification of signs – such as sacraments as signs, or words of scripture as signs, or smoke as a sign – presupposes a definition of what a sign is. Classification and definition express of a term the same content but from two different points of view. The definition expresses the term's comprehension, the division its range of applicability.

Had Augustine been a bit more of a logician, he might have seen right off that his definition was too specific to suit his general notion, since it cut off the class of signs within the mind. Since, however, it had not occurred to Augustine that the "words" within the mind signify no less than spoken and written words, and indeed do so more fundamentally, he did not notice the exclusion. Aquinas had pointed this out, and Bacon here in his *De Signis* (quite independently of Aquinas, we may presume), points it out as well:[27]

> A sign however is that which, offered to sense *or to understanding*, designates something to the understanding itself; because *not every sign is offered to sense as the common description of sign supposes*, but [can be] something offered to the intellect alone.

Yet, as anyone who has wrestled with the matter soon comes to realize, the task of reaching a definition satisfactory to guide serious intellectual investigation is among the most difficult tasks with which doctrinal progress in philosophy has constantly to wrestle.

The Mote in Augustine's Eye and the Beam in Bacon's Own

In making his point that the definition accepted by the Latins from Augustine was too narrow, Bacon unwittingly makes his corrected definition also too narrow in another direction. For although Bacon's definition allows for the case where something imperceptible by a sensory faculty can also be a sign, at the same time, as Maloney points out,[28] Bacon's own formulation "requires that the interpreter have an intellect and thereby precludes animals from being able to communicate among themselves by signs, which Bacon clearly does not intend." For, if he does intend it, he not

---

27 Bacon c.1267: ¶2, italics added.
28 Maloney 1988: 130n91.

only flies in the face of all experiential evidence, but contradicts himself later in the same text:[29]

(7) Turning now from natural signs to signs ordained for signifying by the mind and receiving the rationale of sign from an intention of the mind, such signs are twofold: One is from the mind with a deliberation of reason and choice of the will, whether according to custom or as a neologism, and of this sort is a sign instituted by the understanding, such as [the signs] of language and idiomatic expressions and the circle of grapes and things displayed for sale in the windows of shopkeepers positioned to be signs not only representing others but [representing also] themselves, such as bread and other edibles in a display window, and similarly weapons and reins and tools and all things of this sort which are set forth as the sign of a sale according to all the diversity of professions and of the mechanical arts.

(8) *Another sign created by the mind is one which comes about without deliberation of reason* and without voluntary choice, based neither on convention nor on a considered proposal, but arising as it were suddenly and instantaneously and by a kind of natural instinct and impulse of nature and from a naturally acting power. *Such are all the expressions of brute animals* and many of those of rational animals as well, such as the groans and sighs of the sick, many cries of astonishment and of sorrow and exclamations and many such things which suddenly and without deliberation issue from the rational mind moved by the sensible part.

Bacon sees the mote in Augustine's eye, but not the beam in his own.

Moreover, as Maloney also points out,[30] "having broadened his definition of a sign to include concepts as signs, he never pursues the point further. Nor does he list them as an example in one of his classes of natural signs."

Bacon clearly recognized that in the matter of signs what was needed was a new point of departure, and to his great credit he never ceased casting about for that new point of departure, even though he never hit upon it.[31] Like Thomas Edison, who, asked how he felt about the failure of 4000 chemical combinations that didn't do what he was looking for, answered that he felt pretty good because he had succeeded in identifying 4000 places not to look, Bacon pressed on in his investigation of signs. Unfortunately, where he had been on the right track in 1267, by the time he adapted his *De signis* in 1292 to provide the substance of his *Compendium of the Study of Theology*, he was moving in the wrong direction. He was multiplying the details of the general notion without having sufficiently clarified the understanding of just what it was of which he was multiplying instances. And since distinctions of reason can be multiplied to infinity, as we saw above,[32] it soon became impossible to tell, in

---

29 Bacon c.1267: ¶s 7–8, italics added.
30 Maloney 1988: 131n91.
31 Cf. ibid.: 19.
32 See chapter 7, "Nonbeing in Latin Philosophy", esp. p. 352f.

the forest of Bacon's classifications of signs, which were real and which imaginary trees. He had in effect, as we put it earlier, lost sight of the type in creating his forest of tokens.

The Uniqueness of Sign Relations

It is a pity that, after 1267, Bacon never went over again the opening ground of the *De signis*. For there were in the *De Signis* so many of the key pieces in the puzzle of the doctrine of signs, it would seem that only his impatience to get on to applications of the doctrine prevented him from better seeing what was finally required for its foundations. Not only did he see that the general notion of sign required a definition that included the "passions of the soul", but he also had some grasp of a key twofold fact that would not be definitively clarified for a very long time after him: that the relation of signification constituting the sign as such is a notion at once irreducibly triadic (that is, involving the three terms of sign-vehicle, signified, and interpretant) and irreducibly distinct from relations of causality as such, even in the case of so-called "natural" signs such as smoke or footprints.

The following text,[33] read through postmodern eyes, appears as a kind of anticipation of the distinction[34] between "Secondness", the realm of physical interaction and 'brute force', and "Thirdness", the realm of sign-relations as such, in the scheme of semiotic categories Peirce will finally introduce in 1867:

> The third kind of natural sign, however, is found universally as an effect in respect of its cause, as a footprint is a sign of an animal and smoke is a sign of fire. And many such examples are gathered. For an effect is posited more to be a sign with respect to the cause than conversely, since an effect is more known to us and a sign has to be more known to us than a significate, because through an awareness of a sign we come to a cognition of a significate. And there is nothing untoward in the fact that relations of cause and caused and of sign and significate are found in the same things, since according to the order of nature one thing is the cause of another without having a comparison of themselves with a knowing power, but solely from the [dyadic] fact of their comparison or relation with one another. By contrast, relations of sign and significate and of the one to whom the signification occurs are applied through a relation or comparison to the mind apprehending [that is to say, triadically].

Interpretant or Interpreter?

It is true that Bacon seems to have identified the third term of the sign relation with a person, an interpreter, an all but universal blunder in authors prior to Peirce

– not to mention, less excusably, posterior authors[35] – who treated the subject of signs:[36]

> although there be a voice or a circle of grapes or something else actually imposed in respect of something and instituted for the same so far as it might represent and signify to another, nonetheless, if there be not someone for whom the significate is actually signified the sign is not a sign in act but in potency only. For it is one thing to be actually imposed for signifying to whomever that is possible, quite another thing to be a sign in act.

But note that Bacon's wording on the point is sometimes sufficiently abstract at least to point in the direction of the depersonalized notion of the *interpretant* rather than an interpreter, as Peirce would finally say in giving a 'logically proper name' to the third term of the sign relation. Such an abstract formulation appears, for example, in the following passage from Bacon's text:[37]

> This verb "I signify" more essentially and principally respects that [relative] to which something is acquired, [and] this is a situation or matter signified rather through a dative than through an accusative. And for this very reason the thing relative to which the sign signifies is not referred to except accidentally, which is the way something knowable is referred to [the prospect of] knowledge.

To newcomers to the questions about signs, Peirce's distinction between "interpretant" and "interpreter" always seems baffling. But, as we will see in later discussion,[38] in fact this distinction is crucial to understanding the action of signs as that follows upon the being proper to them. Failure to grasp the point that the third term in the relation constitutive of sign need not be a person blinded logicians for centuries, including throughout the Latin Age, to the fact that the problem of language and "reality" is not a question simply of "words", "concepts", and "things", but of signs and their significates as mediating the difference between objective and physical reality at all levels and in all the dimensions both of Umwelt formation and of the species-specifically human transformation (or "opening up") of Umwelt into Lebenswelt (never more than partially achieved, be it noted!).

The Originality of Bacon's Work on Sign
Bacon made it a point of pride that, as far as he was concerned, his basic thought on signs was original and not derivative from reading Augustine's *On Christian*

---

35 See chapter 17, p. 730, text and note 179.
36 Bacon c.1267: ¶1.
37 Ibid.
38 Especially in chapters 15 and 17.

Doctrine.[39] But he shows no signs of having realized that, were it not for Augustine, there would be no general notion of signs in the Latin language for him to be thinking about. It could have been otherwise. But it appears that as a matter of fact the Latins were the first to have the notion of sign as a general notion and that Augustine – perhaps because of his ignorance of Greek – was the one who proposed that notion. After Augustine, anyone using the Latin term *signum* in a general sense was indebted to Augustine, consciously or not, willingly or not, as anyone using the term "hierarchy" is indebted to the Pseudo-Dionysius.

If Bacon had better understood his provenance, he would better have understood the scope of the problem he thought to resolve with the single opening sentence of his *De Signis*. Like Martha in the gospels, he was too busy about many things; and he also missed the one thing necessary. He was the first, it seems, actually to touch on the foundation stone of the doctrine of signs. But, not realizing what he had his hands on, he left the stone lie mostly buried, where it would yet remain for some three and a half centuries.

Joannes Duns Scotus (c.1266–1308)

Three men dominated the closing Latin centuries, Thomas Aquinas (c.1224–74), Duns Scotus (c.1266–1308), and William of Ockham (c.1285–1349).[40] Around the works of these men formed schools of thought which drew partisan and doctrinal lines establishing frontiers so recondite that it often requires years of study really to understand "what's the shooting about".

An example may serve to make the point. Writing near the very end of the Latin Age, three hundred twenty-four years after the death of Scotus, at the conclusion of his main discussion on the nature and conditions required for relations existing in the physical environment, Poinsot raises a technical question which, he tells us, serves to point up the principal difference between the Thomists and the Scotists as it had emerged over the past three centuries:[41]

> But you might ask concerning that condition of a mind-independent and categorial relation, namely, that the extremes be mind-independently distinct, whether it is required that they be distinct on the part of the things, that is, of the extremes materially, or

---

39 Bacon 1292: ¶25; discussion in Maloney 1988: 22–4.
40 Aquinas died about to turn 50 – just old enough, by his own reckoning, to turn metaphysician. Duns Scotus was eight at the time, and would live only 34 years longer. Ockham was already 23 when Scotus died, and lived yet another 31 years. By chronology, Ockham should have been by far the most metaphysical of the three. In fact, he was by far the least, especially where it came to recognizing the requirements experience imposes on any theory which seeks to explain human knowledge.
41 From his *Ars Logica* of 1632, q. 17, art. 2, 579b35–580a28. This is part the discussion which forms the Second of the two Preambles to the independent edition of his *Tractatus de Signis*, 1632a: 92/26–93/14.

whether it is required that they be distinct not only materially but also on the part of the rationale of their foundation, so that the proximate fundament of the relation is also mind-independently distinct from the relation.

The response to this inquiry is that in this lies the difference between the schools of St Thomas and of Scotus. For Scotus, in Book I of his *Commentary on the Sentences of Peter Lombard*, dist. 31, q. 1, requires only a distinction between the things which are the extremes, not between the rationales of founding. St Thomas requires both, as is clear in the *Summa theologiae*, I, q. 42, art. 1, where on this ground he denies that there is an ontological relation of similarity and equality between the divine persons independently of our minds, because the foundation [of relations of similarity and equality] is the same in each of the persons, to wit, the divine essence, by reason of which they are alike; it would be the same if one whiteness existed in two stones. The reason for this is taken from Cajetan and the other interpreters commenting on q. 42, art. 1, because in these relatives [i.e., in the case of ontological relatives that are reciprocal] the material extremes are referred because the rationales themselves of the founding are referred; for it is because the whitenesses are similar that the white things are similar. Whence if, on the contrary, the whitenesses are not similar, because there is only one whiteness, the white things themselves could not be similar in whiteness, because they are the same, since, by hypothesis, there is only one and the same whiteness. But if they are similar, it will be in something else, not in the formal rationale itself of a white thing. But it is enough to have insinuated this concerning this difficulty, for it is a difficulty that looks more to the theologians and the metaphysicians.

To a beginning student today, as to many a professor, such a "clarification" is completely bewildering, and may help to explain the neglect of these later centuries when the discussion of "special questions" had become so refined; it should also point out why this period is more like a dense rain-forest than a desert where nothing grows!

In Search of the Fundamental Ground
Fortunately, in the development of the doctrine of signs, while these various recondite subtleties are hardly irrelevant, at the same time, neither are they necessary to the grasp of the central issues and alternatives which demarcate the fundamental ground. By sticking closely to our problem we may hope to make our way through without disappearing forever into some remote underbrush of philosophy. For the basic insights and development of terminology that went into the answering at last of Augustine's tacit question cut across the divisions of the later Latin schools, and are more a common property than the outcome of one or the other school as such.

When, at the end of modernity, Charles Peirce broke ranks with his peers by insisting on the importance of previous philosophy, and particularly of the late Latin scholastic period, he found more of value to the establishment of his semiotic among the Latins than in any single place, and we will see why. And though his prodigious studies ranged far and wide, so buried were the most relevant contributions that, in general, he was able to get no farther than Scotus in his recovery operations. Yet it is fascinating to note how much overlap resulted in the final conception of the being proper to signs in the semiotic of Charles Peirce and in the final answer to Augustine's question that emerged in Latin thought.[42] It is not only that Peirce and Poinsot drew on much of the same Latin sources. It is especially the objective requirements of the sign that determine the final outcome or "shape" of the fundamental doctrine to which the sources are but landmarks along the way.

Working on the Beam from Roger Bacon's Eye

It is Scotus who begins to make up for the fact that Bacon, even after broadening his definition of sign to include concepts, never pursued the point. Like Bacon, Scotus was a Franciscan friar. So it may be not a coincidence that the first definition of *signum* that we find in Scotus is a definition of sign exactly mirroring the defective version of Bacon just discussed:[43]

> To signify is to represent something to the understanding; what therefore is signi-
> fied is the object conceived by the understanding. But whatever is conceived by the
> understanding is conceived under some distinct and determinate rationale, because un-
> derstanding is a kind of act, and accordingly the mind distinguishes what it understands
> from something else. Everything that is signified, therefore, is signified under a distinct
> and determinate rationale.

Passing over for a moment the fact that Scotus has here, inversely to Augustine, too narrowly defined the action of signs (for we will see with Fonseca[44] that it is an error easily and without loss corrected), notice the conclusion Scotus draws: "therefore what is signified is the object conceived by the understanding". That is to say, thought is what makes the sign the vehicle of the object, what enables a person to connect a sign with a thing; for the sign makes thought evoke the image or idea of the thing and thereby go to the thing itself (if it exists). Thought goes to the thing *insofar as the thing is thought, that is, objectified, cognized or known*, and hence to the actually existing thing when what is thought also exists subjectively ("physically"), as may or may not happen to be the case.

Intuitive and Abstractive Awareness

Here becomes relevant to the doctrine of signs the distinction Scotus introduces between what he calls *intuitive* and *abstractive* cognition or knowledge. This terminology is everywhere adopted but differently interpreted after Scotus. Tachau[45]

---

42 See Beuchot and Deely 1995 for the detailed discussion, and Deely 1994c for commentary on why the detailed discussion is important.

43 Scotus a.1308b: *Super libros Elenchorum*, q. 15, no. 6; in Wadding ed. 1639: vol. 2, 22a.

44 Chapter 9, p. 412ff.

45 Tachau 1988: 81, a work which I would particularly recommend for the interested student.

has observed that, so widespread does the use of this terminology become, the history of theories of knowledge in the Latin Age after AD1310 "can be traced as the development of this dichotomy."

The semiotic import of this distinction derives from the sign-character of thought in just the manner Scotus calls attention to it. Intuitive cognition terminates at an object as acting upon the senses here and now, that is, in the immediate surroundings of the physical environment. Recalling the Thomistic argument on the superfluousness of positing psychological states of a mental character (ideas or images, *species impressae* or *conceptus*) at the level of sensation,[46] Poinsot is able to point out that sensation, as analytically prescissed and considered in its own right, is capable only of cognition as intuitive.

Perception and understanding, insofar as they are dependent upon and continuous with sensation, will, by virtue of that continuity, also be capable of intuitive awareness or knowledge. But both perception and understanding will be capable not only of intuitive awareness but also of abstractive awareness. The reason is that the relations of the mind to the environment in the case of perception and understanding are sustained not only by the input of sense but also by the ideas or icons the mind itself forms as the basis for yet further cognitive relations to what is objectified. Perception and understanding achieve an awareness of an organism's surroundings not merely as things in the environment act upon organs of external sense but precisely as objects are correlates of perceptual images and conceptual ideas. Aspects of the environment objectified in sensation are but raw materials in the formation of perceptual and conceptual objects. Sensations are only a part, albeit a fundamental part, of objects perceived; and they may not even pertain at all to what is understood as such.

We see then that what is objectified in sensation is one thing; but objectification, in perception and understanding alike, goes beyond sensation to create a total objective world that exists correlative to the Innenwelt comprising sensations plus perceptions, and intellections. Sensation is restricted to the objectification of some proportionate parts only of what is there in the physical surroundings. Perception rises above this to create an awareness of what might or could be there on this or that interpretation of sense or this or that recollection of what past experience has taught in relation to what sense presents. Understanding rises even higher to the consideration of pure possibilities and the consideration of subjective structures of physical being independent of all finite cognition. Intuitive awareness is restricted to aspects of objects physically present and active upon sense here and now. Abstractive awareness knows no such restriction, but reaches beyond the present to objects and aspects of objects that need not be present here and now and that may or may not have a subjective existence at the time of their consideration. In abstractive awareness, apprehension terminates not at the physical environment as such but at the objective

---

46 See "Why Sensation Does Not Involve Mental Icons", in chapter 7, p. 345.

world, the Umwelt, as in principle distinct from the physical environment. Hence in abstractive awareness illusion first becomes possible, and therewith error, both perceptual and intellectual.

Because abstractive awareness terminates in the objective world as such and not just in the objective world as physical (except insofar as sensation is at work), to the extent that abstractive awareness transcends intuitive awareness it enables us to consider the nonexistent as if it did exist. In perceptual judgments this is not simply the situation of either error, illusion, or wishful thinking. It is also the situation that makes possible strategy and cunning among animals. But in intellectual discourse as depending on the awareness of the difference between *objects*, which exist as known but sometimes may or may not *also* exist as things, and *things*, which exist as belonging to the physical environment but may or may not exist as known or apprehended, the significance of abstractive apprehensions becomes much greater still. For this possibility of recognizing the difference between objects as such and objects as things enables understanding alike to create myths and to consider the existence of physical realities beyond the range of our biological senses. Through abstractive awareness human understanding is able to consider a possible future in which actual things might be different, and an actual present in which possible things are not only sensible.

The Three Meanings of Abstraction
Abstractive awareness, thus, while no longer a familiar philosophical concept, is yet not a recondite one. It is one of the three uses to which the term "abstraction" and its derivatives were put in the Latin Age.[47]

First, abstraction was used by the Latins in exactly the sense Locke would speak of in the late seventeenth century as the manner in which general ideas of perception are formed, namely, by focusing attention on one aspect of an object, say, the color or the shape of an apple, and leaving out the rest so as to arrive at a general notion of "red" or "round". Abstraction in this sense the Latins recognized as common to all higher animals and not restricted to "rational" or human animals.

Abstraction was used in a second sense among the Latins to describe the psychological process whereby the intellect draws from the materials of sense perception the intellectual essence or intelligibility of the objects of sense. Some Neothomist authors came to call this process "ideogenesis", understanding "idea" in a restricted intellectual sense contrasted with the images of sense-perception. In the writings of Boethius and after, as we saw in the last chapter,[48] abstraction in this second sense became the basis for one of the great medieval theories concerning the organization of the sciences.

---

47 The first two senses are older in the Latin Age. They are discussed in the texts of Aquinas in some detail in "Animal Intelligence and Concept-Formation" (Deely 1971). For the root of this discussion in Aristotle, see "Abstraction" in chapter 3 of this book, p. 78.
48 See chapter 7, p. 309 above.

But the third sense of "abstraction", abstractive awareness in contrast to intuitive awareness, which dominated the later Latin Age and remained prominent in early-modern philosophy (for example, the terminology is still found in Spinoza, 1632–77), came to be all but forgotten as the modern period reached its later stages. Yet this third sense was in many ways the most interesting, and is surely the most important for semiotic. Abstractive awareness in this third sense referred to the manner in which cognition transcends the limits of its strictly sensory origin and ground, to some measure alike in both perception and understanding. Peirce will introduce the very concept again in the context of reviving the doctrine of signs toward the turn of the twentieth century, and it may help at this juncture to mention his description of the process of abstraction presupposed as giving to the signs "used by a 'scientific' intelligence, that is to say, by an intelligence capable of learning by experience", their distinctive character:[49]

As to that process of abstraction, it is itself a sort of observation. The faculty which I call abstractive observation is one which ordinary people perfectly recognize, but for which the theories of philosophers sometimes hardly leave room. It is a familiar experience to every human being to wish for something quite beyond his present means, and to follow that wish by the question, "Should I wish for that thing just the same, if I had ample means to gratify it?" To answer that question, he searches his heart, and in doing so makes what I term an abstractive observation. He makes in his imagination a sort of skeleton diagram, or outline sketch, of himself, considers what modifications the hypothetical state of things would require to be made in that picture, and then examines it, that is, observes what he has imagined, to see whether the same ardent desire is there to be discerned. By such a process, which is at bottom very much like mathematical reasoning, we can reach conclusions as to what would be true of signs in all cases, so long as the intelligence using them was scientific. The modes of thought of a God, who should possess an intuitive omniscience superseding reason, are put out of the question. Now the whole process of development among the community of students of those formulations by abstractive observation and reasoning of the truths which must hold good of all signs used by a scientific intelligence is an observational science, like any other positive science, notwithstanding its strong contrast to all the special sciences which arises from its aiming to find out what must be and not merely what is in the actual world.

In science, abstraction of this sort leads to the development of instruments for the detection and handling of aspects of the universe of which we could never become directly aware by the unaided senses alone. Abstraction also leads to the formation of hypotheses which enable us to know how to use such instruments, and suggests what instruments to build in the first place in order to test inductively whether the theoretical entities posited as possibly or probably existing have indeed an existential status.

---

49 Peirce c.1897: CP 2.227.

In philosophy, in the case of the existence of God, for example, as Aquinas pointed out, abstractive awareness enables us to raise the question of existence even though the object is so abstract that not even instruments extending our senses in any way or degree can touch the existence into which we inquire. Yet in thought, as Aquinas put it, in the proposition "God exists"[50] we are able through discourse to argue about and through judgment to touch upon the truth concerning the very existence of God and of other extensions of the physical universe not accessible to sense or to perception. Such less extreme examples of abstractive awareness as the case of knowledge of the soul, or of the understanding itself, are cited in the semiotic of John Poinsot, along with the most extreme example of abstractive awareness in thought about God.[51] Many examples could be added from modern science, from the discussion of phlogiston, which turned out not to exist, to the discussion of quarks and antimatter, which perhaps do.

The Term "Physical" as Used by the Latins

As an aside, the reader should take note of the following. This prospectively infinite reach of human understanding is what lay behind the medieval fondness for the formula that "the intellectual soul is capable of becoming all things" ("*anima est quodammodo omnia*", to quote exactly). The infinite reach of understanding is also behind the use, little understood today, by some of the best Latin authors of the term "physical" to apply to whatever exists in the order of being as it exhibits an existence independent of the finite mind.[52] In modern usage, "physical" tends to be a synonym for "material", in contrast to "spiritual". But in Latin philosophy, "physical" extends equally to material and spiritual substances and to the *esse divinum* itself, even to the discussion of grace among the theologians.[53] Modern ignorance on this point means that the student should note that "*physica*" among the Latins can be extended also to spiritual being insofar as such being is cognition-independent. An angel would be no less "physical" than a rock.

Scotus on the Dynamics of the Sign

Anticipation too can be found in Scotus for Peirce's point that the interpretant of a sign, even when an interpreter is involved, is yet always something distinct from the interpreter, and that the semiotic triad of sign-vehicle/interpretant/object is not

---

50 See chapter 7, p. 283.
51 Poinsot, *Tractatus de Signis*, Book III "Concerning Modes of Awareness and Concepts", Question 1 "Whether Intuitive and Abstractive Awareness Differ Essentially in the Rationale of Cognition", 291/12–42, esp. 291/19–26.
52 In the translation of *ens reale* as "mind-independent being", the hyphenated expression is short for "whatever is capable of existence in the order of being as it exhibits an existence independent of the finite mind"; and the qualification "finite" on the term "mind" is also essential to the correct understanding in English of the Latin *ens reale*. We will have occasion to develop this point further in chapter 10 below, p. 475n110.
53 By way of example, see Poinsot 1637: 38.

a static one but a stage in a process where what is a sign at one stage can be an interpretant or object at another stage, and so on ad infinitum:[54]

> To utter a [linguistic] sign does not reduce to the emission of a breath thus or so, but it is a sound so pronounced and articulated as to be a spoken word, and the imaginable word which corresponds thereto is the mental word, which is something formed in act by the memory.

Scotus repeats, moreover, Aquinas's point that there is an overlap in the human use of signs with the use of signs among angels, but with this difference that can be seen from Scotus's text: that telepathy, impossible for the human, is normal for the angel:[55]

> One forms a vocal sound for the purpose of signifying and declaring that which is understood. But that vocal sound is not formed immediately by the understanding insofar as it is understanding; the audible sound is formed by some power mediating the understanding, such as the vocal chords. This fact is an imperfection of human understanding. If therefore a word were produced or formed as expressive of that which lies hidden in the understanding, and the production of this word were by virtue of the very understanding itself of the one understanding, it would not be any the less a sign.

The Semiotic Web

But perhaps most tantalizing is the anticipation we see Scotus give to the notion of signs as a system. For once the being proper to signs has been attained, the notion of signs as a system prepares the way for an appreciation of the inevitable analytic shift to the action of signs (or *semiosis*, as we shall see Peirce call it),[56] and to an exploration (by means of signs) of the role of signs in experience and knowledge as a whole. For signification does not occur as an isolated act, but as something sustained by a vast network, a network that will prove as vast ultimately as the universe itself:[57]

> Even though there is a great controversy over the spoken word, whether it is a sign of a thing or of a concept, notwithstanding, and granting, in short, that that which is properly signified by the voice is a thing,[58] there are nevertheless many signs ordered

---

54 Scotus, *Reportata Parisiensia* (c.1302–3), lib. 1, dist. 27, q. 2, n. 8; in Wadding ed. 1639: vol. 22, 334b.
55 Scotus c.1300: *Opus Oxoniense*, lib. 1, dist. 27, q. 3, n. 14; in Wadding ed. 1639: vol. 10, 370b.
56 For *agere sequitur esse*, "action follows upon being".
57 Scotus c.1300: *Opus Oxoniense*, lib. 1, dist. 27, q. 3, n. 19; in Wadding ed. 1639: vol. 10, 377b–378a; italics added.
58 Here "thing" must be understood transcendentally, specifically as transcending the distinction between object strictly and thing strictly, so that it is well borne in mind that whatever is a thing in principle may *also* be an object, and conversely.

to the same significate (to wit: the letter, the voice and the concept), just as there are many effects ordered to the same cause, no one of which is the cause of the other, as is clear from the case of the sun illuminating many parts of the medium. ... And just as one can grant that a more proximate effect is *in some way* a cause in respect of a more remote effect, *not properly*, but on account of that priority which obtains among such effects respecting the cause; so can one grant of many signs ordered to the same significate that one is *in some way* a sign of the other, because it provides the understanding of that other, since the more remote would not signify unless the more immediate in some way signifies first, and nevertheless the one is not on this account *properly* the sign of the other, just as we saw in the case of cause and causing.

Here for the first time we see discussion of a hierarchy of signs, not as "sacred" signs are superior to "profane" signs, for example, but as all signs are at work within a system. We begin to get a picture of the network, the "semiotic web", of signs that sustains human understanding and constitutes every Umwelt. If indeed the spoken sign is a sign of a thing, it signifies the thing "in a dative case" indirectly, that is, through or on the basis of thought, "by means of the concept". And what the concept has for its content – and therefore as the terminus of the relation it founds over and above the knower – is the thing itself insofar as it is thought.

Notice that Scotus says, at the beginning of the above citation, that "in short, ... that which is properly signified by the voice is a thing". The spoken sign signifies, simply, not the thing *as such*, but the *conceived thing* or *object signified* coincident with some environmental features at least insofar as sensations enter into the object as conceived here and now. And in the word's achieving this signification of its object or "thought thing" a whole hierarchy of semiotic functions is involved. An individual letter is *in a way* a sign of the word; the word is *in a way* a sign of the concept (that is, of the interpretant). But this last is *properly and directly* a sign of the thing signified, as also are the written and spoken words through or on the basis of the concept, which illuminates the medium of understanding to which each of them belongs. Scotus also puts it this way:[59]

Whether the things signified, the objects, exist or not, the concepts remain unaffected as signs thereof. It follows from these considerations that a name essentially signifies its object in the same way whether that object is also a thing, or whether it is only

---

59 Scotus a.1308a, *In Perihermenias, opus secundum*; in Wadding ed. 1639: vol. 1, 586a–b. But since in this case I have taken a little more liberty with the Latin in view of discussion to come than is normally permitted a translator, I particularly owe it to the reader in this case to give Scotus's own words in place of my speaking for him. For though a translator always puts words in the translated author's mouth which the translated author never used, it is not to the same measure in all cases. Here, in any event, are Scotus's own words: "sive res sit, sive non, similitudines univoce sunt signa illarum. Ex istis sequitur, quod nomen essentialiter significat rem, sive res sit, sive non sit, quia rem repraesentat secundum quod similitudo ejus in anima est, et est signum".

an object; because the concept represents its object according as it is a likeness which exists in the soul, and which gives rise to the relation according to which it is a sign.

Duns Scotus vis-à-vis Roger Bacon and Thomas Aquinas

Scotus, then, picks up exactly Aquinas's point that intellectual concepts or ideas, too, are signs, and signs more fundamentally than are spoken words. But we have to suspect that Scotus picked up the point not from Aquinas but from Roger Bacon. And the reason for thinking this is not simply that Bacon and Scotus were both English Franciscans, but mainly that if Scotus had picked up the point from Aquinas he would have so expressed it as to include percepts as well as concepts, images as well as ideas, as we will see in Poinsot.[60] Perhaps, too, he would have been careful to say precisely why the point did not apply to sensation, since Thomas, as we saw,[61] was above all clear on the superfluousness of ideas and images at that level of the initial, pervasive cognitive stimulation in sense. Scotus did none of this. He began instead with a statement about signification which would have limited the use of signs to human animals (and angels), which is exactly how Bacon defined the sign in his *De Signis*.[62] All of this, well short of conclusive proof, yet gives some reason to think that the primary influence on Scotus in developing the point Aquinas had made more than eleven years before Bacon's *De signis* was not Aquinas but Bacon.

Yet see how far beyond Thomas Aquinas and Roger Bacon alike has Scotus advanced the doctrine of signs overall. It is clear why Scotus was Peirce's favorite among the Latin writers whose acquaintance he had been able to make. Not since the beginning of the Latin Age has there been an author who pushed as far as Scotus along the way of signs from within a philosophy of being. What for Aquinas had been a point made in passing subordinate to yet some other point has become in Scotus, rather, a point of departure for developing for its own sake and in its own line the realization that intellectual concepts are among the most fundamental of the signs in the human use of signs. Yet the human use of signs, "anthroposemiosis", involves percepts or images and sensations as well as concepts. The involvement of percepts and sensations distinguishes the human use of signs from the case of angels. The involvement of concepts distinguishes the human use of signs from that of nonlinguistic animals.

William of Ockham (c.1285–1349)

We come to the third defining figure of the later Latin Age. No Latin writer, with the possible exception of Suárez (who agreed with Ockham as he disagreed with Scotus and with Aquinas on the fundamental points propaedeutic to the doctrine of signs) more influenced modernity, down to its twilight. The huge two-volume work

---

60 Poinsot 1632a: Book II, Question 2, esp. 247/22–4.
61 Chapter 7, "Why Sensations Do Not Involve Mental Icons", p. 345.
62 See p. 372f. above.

on Ockham by Marilyn McCord Adams, a classic by size alone, fondly reduces the "of Ockham" to a modern last name: *William Ockham*.[63] As Aquinas was the "glory of the Latins", so Ockham can perhaps be said to be the "inspiration of the moderns".

Ockham did not inspire by his writings a doctrinal school in quite the way as did both Scotus and Aquinas. The grouping around Ockham is a looser grouping, with Ockham at the head not as an authority to be expounded but more as a *primus inter pares*, a "first among equals" in a congeries of authors united mainly in their agreement to do away so far as possible with abstract entities and adhere closely to the reality of things as individuals, deemed the only reality.

As in the High Middle Ages Aristotle was called "the Philosopher", Averroes "the Commentator", and Maimonides "the Teacher", so in the later centuries, as Sylvester of Ferrara ("Ferrariensis") was sometimes called the "First of the Thomists", because he began the traditions of Latin commentary upon the writings of Aquinas, Ockham was everywhere considered "First of the Nominalists", in this case not because there had been no nominalist doctrine before him but because he was the first to make its development a mainstream Latin current. So Ockham was not "first" in a chronological sense, but he was rather "first" in the sense of "foremost": the title *Princeps Nominalistarum* in his case bears almost the sense of "Prince of the Nominalists" (as in "Prince of Darkness" for matters epistemological).

The Second Florescence of Nominalism

Now what was nominalism? The student in hope of a ready answer should listen at once to the greatest of the medieval historians of the twentieth century:[64]

> Here we enter upon a poorly understood doctrinal terrain, one that is extremely complex and of which one knows at least this much going in, that the term "nominalism" does not at all suffice to define it.

We have seen already a first florescence of nominalism under Roscelin, in the time of Abaelard.[65] There the term meant that only individual things as such exist, and that the terms we utter in speaking generalities or making universal statements are so much wind, a kind of fart of the mouth (*flatus vocis*). In nominalism's second and more enduring florescence the nominalists became much more sophisticated about their handling of terms. But that only individuals in the strict sense exist, that is to say, that there are apart from thought only subjects of existence ("substances")

---

63 The title for McCord Adams 1987. This innovation of McCord Adams so well fits the late-modern customs of naming that it is likely to stick. Here, nonetheless, I will keep to the more correct traditional usage.

64 Gilson 1944: 657: "Nous pénétrons ici sur un terrain doctrinal mal connu, extrêmement complexe et dont on sait du moins déjà ceci, que le terme de nominalisme ne suffit aucunement à le définir."

65 See "The 'Problem of Universals' and the First Florescence of Nominalism" in chapter 6, p. 243 above.

with their subjective modifications ("inherent accidents"), and nothing over and above individual substances apart from thought – this remained the heart of the commitment. *Esse*, we may say, so far as it expresses *ens reale*, means *inesse*.

In the original florescence of the dispute, the nominalism of Roscelin was pitted against the realism of William of Champeaux, who, recall, "out Platoed Plato". But in the florescence under Ockham, the dispute was against what in the later middle ages was called "moderate realism" to contrast with the extreme Platonic realism of the earlier time. Moderate realism, which was the position of both Aquinas and Scotus, held that concepts in our mind are capable of expressing in thought relations that really connect us with the actual situation of the physical universe. Let us go by Peirce's characterization of the dispute in this second florescence, for it is accurate:[66] "the question between nominalists and realists relates to thoughts, that is, to *the objects which thinking enables us to know*". Clearly the objects which thinking enables us to know include but, at the same time, are more and other than the mere physical individuals that reliance on sensation is alone able to reveal.

There was no question that much of what we objectify beyond the physical individuals accessible as such through sensation is not "real". Of course, even the philosopher's stone of ancient alchemy that would turn any metal into gold, or the Fountain of Youth for which Ponce de Leon (1460–1521) searched the Americas, were real *as ideas* – that is, they were actual psychological states of actual historical individuals. And the *objects* those actual individuals sought were not real, as it proved. The dispute does not concern a truism about thoughts being real even when their objects are illusory, nor the commonplace that there are illusions.

The dispute turns on the very nature of objectivity itself. But what about those objects of thought that do turn out to be real, even though they were not sensed in advance, such as the planet Uranus which was first predicted and then discovered? And how is it that even mythical objects sometimes influence public events before their unreal status is discovered, as Galileo could testify, or the witches at Salem? And what about "the laws of nature, and that property of gold by which it will yield the purple of Cassius", Peirce asks us. Are they "no more real than the philosopher's stone"?

If you understand the terms of the controversy, then, the question between the nominalism of Ockham and the so-called "moderate" realism of Scotus and Aquinas is, in its nature, susceptible of but two answers: yes or no, without a between: "Are the laws of nature, and that property of gold by which it will yield the purple of Cassius, no more real than the philosopher's stone?"[67]

It must not be imagined that any notable realist of the thirteenth or fourteenth century took the ground that any "universal" was what we in English should call a "thing",

---

66 Peirce 1909: CP 1.27. The use of italics is my own.
67 Peirce 1909: CP 1.27; the citation preceding the note number is from the text; the following extract is from the note on p. 9 of CP 1.

as it seems that, in an earlier age, some realists and some nominalists, too, had done; though perhaps it is not quite certain that they did so, their writings being lost. Their very definition of a "universal" admits that it is of the same generic nature as a word, namely, is: "Something so fashioned as to be suitable for predication of more than one."[68] Neither was it their doctrine that any "universal" itself is real. They might, indeed, some of them, think so; but their realism did not consist in that opinion, but in holding that what the word signifies, in contradistinction to what it can be truly said of, is real. Anybody may happen to opine that "the" is a real English word; but that will not constitute him a realist. But if he thinks that, whether the word "hard" itself be real or not, the property, the character, the predicate, hardness, is not invented by men, as the word is, but is really and truly in the hard things and is one in them all, as a description of habit, disposition, or behavior, then he is a realist.

Thus, the question was whether all objective properties, laws of nature, and predicates of more than an actually existent subject – all that exists in thought not as a subjective state but as its publically communicable content – are, without exception, mere figments or not.

Ockham's Problem with a Doctrine of Signs: There Are No "Generals"

Even without going further into the details of the matter, you can see that, from the point of view of the doctrine of signs, we are going to have problems with Ockham. For a sign *consists* in a triadic relation over and above the three individual terms it connects. But, for Ockham, there are no relations over and above the individuals that exist. The *mind* may make such connections, just as *the mind* could make up the Fountain of Youth and the Philosopher's Stone. The mind can do many things.

This is a problem for semiotic, because, remember, we are seeking to explain or ground Augustine's general notion of sign. But now it turns out that there is nothing to ground. The word *signum*, like any other term beyond a proper name like Julius Caesar, names primarily a mental construct. But the original question was how can the sign so exist as to be indifferent to the distinction between *ens reale* and *ens rationis*.

Perhaps we had the question wrong. Ockham would so claim. There is no being proper to signs in general. There are only particular signs, tokens without an authentic, a "real", type. Some of these individual signs are from nature, like smoke. Others are from the soul, like concepts or names or groans. But as to what they signify, that is, as to the connection between the individual thing we call a natural sign and the individual thing we call a conventional sign, that connection is

---

68 The text is corrupt at this point, reading as follows: "Quod natum optum est praedicari de pluribus"; for which I substitute from CP 2.367 (1901) "quod aptum natum est praedicari de pluribus", and translate accordingly.

always from the mind, if Bacon was indeed right in pointing out that sign relations are always distinct from causal relations.[69]

"The Only Difficulty There Is in Understanding Ockham"

Perhaps you can see from this challenge to the basic question why Gilson would say[70] – I used to think, until quite recently, that he had said this tongue in cheek; but I see clearly now that he did not, and why – that "the only difficulty there is in understanding Ockham" is his notion of concepts as "natural signs". For by his teaching as a nominalist, the concept is simply an individual characteristic, a subjective state confirming its bearer in his or her distinct identity as an individual. It can no more connect one individual with another than any other individual characteristic. The whole point of an inherent accident as such is to distinguish and individualize, to characterize subjectivity. The shape of my nose is not the shape of your nose, unless mayhap we are Siamese twins bound at the nose. Of course I may *compare* your nose's shape with someone else's, and so *make* a relation *between* the two. But that is the work of the mind, not something physical or real. In reality there is only your nose and my nose, yours belonging to you and mine belonging to me.

So too with concepts. You have yours and I have mine. So how do they present to us a common object of discourse for understanding, or a common object of perception when we hear the same siren or try to escape the same fire? For that matter – and this goes to the heart of Gilson's point – in the absence of real relations, how can one speak about "natural signs" at all? If the nominalist is not to play Anselm's fool by showing that he does not understand what he himself is saying, he will not speak about "natural signs" at all. For on nominalist terms the relation constituting a sign is in every case the same: a mind-dependent being, a construct of the understanding without any counterpart as such, actual or even possible, on the side of what is signified. Every sign, insofar as it involves suprasubjectivity, let alone actual intersubjectivity, is and must be, on nominalistic terms, an empty objectivity, so to say a "*flatus mentis*".

For that matter, furthermore, what do concepts do anyway? It is as if Ockham were to announce to you, "I have an idea". And when you asked "What about?", he answered, "About? It's not *about* anything. It's just an idea." "Yes", you say, "I know. But what is it an idea *of?*" "Why does it have to be *of* or *about* something?", is Ockham's peevish reply; "Why can't it just be an idea? The trouble with you is you don't appreciate individuality. You think everything has to be hooked up with something else, and it doesn't. An idea in your mind is no different from a nose on your face. The only thing it is hooked up with is you."

---

69 See "The Uniqueness of Sign Relations" above in this chapter, p. 374.
70 Gilson 1955: 491.

A Terminological Advance Marred by Conceptual Incoherence
As you may imagine, there is more to be said on the problem around which this imaginary dialogue turns. But let us take a break from a conversation that for the moment seems to be going nowhere in order to consider another of history's ironies.

Ockham and his followers adopt an understanding of being which excludes relations other than those fashioned by the mind in making comparisons and, as a further consequence, implies that *flatus vocis* is an appropriate designation both for sign in general and for natural sign in particular insofar as there is an issue concerning the mind's capacity to express in discourse an understanding of anything that is what it is independently of our grasp of it beyond a "brute secondness" of individual sensations. But they neither develop nor advert to these further consequences. Instead, they adopt the terminology of "natural sign" as a proper label for concepts, and supplement this adoption within a few years by a further twofold proposal. They propose "formal sign" as a new designation for concepts as so-called natural signs, and they propose that what Augustine had defined as a sign, namely, some sense-perceptible object which leads to an awareness of another than itself should be called simply an "instrumental sign".[71]

So we are treated to another recurrence of irony in the development of ideas. If it is not history's favorite dish, it is yet served up so often that the historian with no taste for it will have a hard time digesting the doctrine of signs as a theme that as much or more than any single other totalizes the indigenous development of the Latin Age. When we are told that with Ockham the concept of sign becomes central to the treatment of logic[72] and that it is after him that a distinction of modes of representation becomes integrated into the understanding of signification itself,[73] it is not obvious on the surface of the development that all this has taken place within a further determination of the speculative context of philosophical thought that makes the existence of sign in general a *flatus vocis*. What is said by the followers of Ockham, and what they are themselves focused upon, brings at first blush a new clarity to many issues in the discussion; but the new clarity comes at a hidden price. The clarity of the central focus leaves disguised and hidden at the periphery the fundamental denial implied in the central doctrine constitutive of nominalism as a

---

71 The choice of "instrumental" to designate signs as defined by Augustine is particularly obscure. Indeed, even the choice of "formal" for the characterization of (cognitive) psychological states as "signs" receives little clarification – at least as presented in the present work – before Fonseca (see, e.g., p. 412 below). **Why** was this term "instrumental" chosen for the sign which begins its existence in the role of an object or quality accessible to sense? From what context was the denomination taken? Contrasted to what? Though I have several colleagues who profess (intuitively) to know, they are unable to convince me. I do not know. Another subject in need of some doctoral dissertations. We can at least note that the idea of "instrumentality" in the Latin context was much richer than the mechanical overtones the term would receive in modern times, when the notion of causality came to be more or less restrictively identified with what Aristotle had identified as the "agent" or "efficient" cause. The instrumental sign is hardly that!
72 Meier-Oeser 1997: 114.
73 Ibid.: 119.

distinct philosophical school or position. In this particular case, this would be the denial of the possibility of there being a unified subject matter for semiotic inquiry, of there obtaining a mode of being which is verified – here as formal, there as instrumental, now as natural, then as conventional, in this instance intentional, in that instance unintended, and so on: a mode of being essential to the sign in the sense that all signs partake of it, even in the differences which make of them this or that variety from the point of view of the circumstances of the action of signs and of the classification of signs that it is possible to make.

The new terminology distinguishing "instrumental" from "formal" signs has the appearance of advancing the traditional criticisms offered earlier by Aquinas and Scotus in discussion of Augustine's definition, by fixing it in a clear and simple terminology. Thus, the sign as *proposed* by Augustine was one thing – a general mode of being whose particular instances as such are verified equally and indifferently in nature and in culture. But the sign as *defined* by Augustine was something much more restricted – anything which, on being perceived by sense, brings into awareness something other than itself. This restrictive formula is now said to apply only to a particular class of signs, called now "instrumental". But the concept expressed in this restricted definition is deemed *too narrow* in view of the fact that it excludes "entities" (or aspects of entities), namely, psychological states, which perform the essential or "minimal" sign function of bringing along with themselves an awareness of something other than themselves, yet without being themselves objects perceived through external sense. These latter "mental states" as fulfilling the minimal sign function are not instrumental signs, clearly. To them Augustine's specific definition, in contrast to his generic proposal, does not apply. Let us call them "formal signs", in contrast to "instrumental": interior in contrast to exterior signs.

Now as a matter of fact, the earlier criticisms which had made the point of the instrumental/formal distinction without terminologically marking the point, had been formulated in the writings of Aquinas and Scotus, and even Bacon, in order to advance an epistemolgical perspective incompatible with nominalism, namely, the perspective of scholastic realism. But by not coupling their new terminology with any critique of the general notion of sign, while at the same time continuing to use the term "sign" as if it were a common designation, the nominalists (with seeming innocence[74]) masked, both from themselves and from their opponents, the conceptual equivocations upon which their terminology depends.

How Politics Lent to Nominalism a Factitious Following
There is a further complication of issues around the work of Ockham and the subsequent major development of nominalism. Much larger and more immediate than the discussion of signs is the whole series of questions constituting the "conciliar controversy", the controversy which erupted in consequence of a head-on clash between

---

74 For they seemed to have neither intention nor realization of the intellectual sleight-of-hand in which they were engaged.

the highest civil and the highest ecclesiastical authority of medieval Christendom. This particular clash arose between Louis of Bavaria and Pope John XXII. First John tried to assert his authority over the question of who could or should be Holy Roman Emperor. Then Louis tried to assert his authority over the question of who could or should be Pope. The role of a general church council in the resolution of this clash was the principal "theoretical" issue which absorbed and focused Ockham's intellectual energies and those of his most important followers. In this titanic struggle the questions over formal and instrumental signs were assuredly of a quite secondary or even tertiary concern, narrowly focused and narrowly pursued, it seems, within the context of classroom logic.

Probably it would not be too much to say that the various circumstances of his life which led Ockham to become entangled in a thicket of concerns pertaining much more to theological and practical than to speculative thought within philosophy, and to enter into a bog of practical, political, and theological machinations where life and liberty were at stake, proved overwhelming. Perhaps it is no more than a small wonder that the incoherence of nominalism with the idea that the function of concepts is to present what they themselves are not in awareness passed unnoticed as a small detail in nominalist writings overall.

Whatever the reasons, finally, it remains that the inexplicability of the fact that concepts cannot be without making us aware of something besides themselves unless relations be admitted as suprasubjective modes of physical being (that is, as modes that need not be themselves objectified in order to be) is not something that caught the notice of the Ockhamites. Passing in silence over the question of the legitimacy of Augustine's posit of sign as a general mode of being, the Ockhamites simply resume with a renewed fierceness the earlier criticism of Augustine's definition of sign as restricted to sensible objects and not applying to ideas, and fix the point of the criticism in the adoption of a new terminology. So it comes about that, shortly after Ockham, we find the Latins distinguishing between *instrumental signs*, to which Augustine's classical definition of sign applies, and *formal signs*, to which Augustine's definition does not apply because they are not sensible objects before and in order to be signs. Formal signs are the concepts or ideas within the mind. Instrumental signs are sensible objects insofar as they signify something other than themselves.

The grounds for some such distinction are quite clear independently of nominalism. Insofar as the terminology can be regarded as fixing the criticisms of Augustine already found in Aquinas, Bacon, and Scotus, the distinction in question can be regarded as a terminological advance, and so the scholastic realists generally tried to interpret it. But the irony is that, *on nominalist grounds, this distinction does not fix the earlier criticisms* as superficially appears, but belongs to another line of thought entirely. In the nominalist line, the proposed terminology should not be regarded as a distinction between two types of sign at all, but rather as a distinction between one group of realities, so-called instrumental signs, which really are signs, and another group of realities, so-called formal signs, which (if instrumental signs are signs) are not really signs at all, let alone "natural signs". The inner logic of their own position does not immediately appear to the nominalists. The aspect of an apparent terminological advance in the traditional discussion is what first catches all eyes. Only gradually, as we will see in chapter 9, do subsequent thinkers making use of the new terminology come to realize that the seeming distinction may be rather an equivocation, a use of one word, "sign", with two completely different meanings. For formal and instrumental signs can be two species of the genus *signum* only if there is such a thing as sign in general. And precisely this possibility is what nominalism denies. Hence the title of our previous section introducing the new vocabulary: a terminological advance marred by a conceptual incoherence.

We began the story of the Latin Age with Augustine, and we saw that his proposal of sign in general constituted a primary speculative initiative distinguishing that age from anything to be found in the age of Greek philosophy. Indeed, the treatment of Augustine's proposal in the hands of later Latin thinkers has provided one of the principal paths in our story of the indigenous development of the Latin Age up to this point. But now we are led to consider that Augustine's ignorance of Greek may have been the occasion simply for a major Latin blunder. A path that up to this point had seemed to lead us along a fairly straightforward development of scholastic realism now suddenly takes a sharp turn into the thicket of late-medieval nominalism, where the dominant issues, moreover, have little to do with anything like a disinterested pursuit of speculative truth sought for its own sake within philosophy. Moreover, if we consider the social and political side of Ockham's thought, we find so much that is sympathetic to modern times that we gain a strong inkling of why modern historians of philosophy have generally tended to end the serious treatment of the Latin Age with the study of Ockham.

But the fact of the organic development of a foundation for a unified doctrine of signs – semiotics in the very sense postmodernity will begin by resuming – belies the common teaching that the epistemological and ontological development of the Latin Age followed a path that ends in the nominalist thicket. Only the fact that historians of philosophy have not had the tracing out of this path after Augustine as a principal interest has allowed this organic development as it moves beyond the nominalist thicket to remain hidden in the modern telling of the story of philosophy's history. There is no avoiding the thicket in any reasonably complete history of philosophy in the Latin Age. But neither is there any real justification for ending the story there. On the contrary, the most fundamental issues of ontology and epistemology are at stake in the discussion of Augustine's proposal of sign as a general notion, and once this discussion has been engaged, we find that the path of the Latin development not only leads into the thicket but also continues beyond it.

Indeed, once we trace the path of signs through the thicket as best we can, we find that it emerges all the more clearly on the other side, and leads to a decisive culmination of semiotics in the seventeenth century. In the previously neglected *Treatise on Signs* published in 1632 by John Poinsot (1589–1644), we not only find a theoretical justification for what Augustine had posited, but we find also a definitive rejection of the idea that signs can be identified with any particular class of sensible entities. We find also that this *Tractatus* of Poinsot does not appear out of nowhere, like an aureole fallen from the skies. It takes form rather as a critique and summation of the indigenous Latin discussions of *signum* after Augustine, including the nominalist turn those discussions take in and beyond the thicket.

We will see that the path of the sign leads us through writings of authors in the last two Latin centuries that have been all but neglected by every major modern historian of philosophy. We will see also that these neglected writings are essential to understanding the Latin Age as an organic whole in the history of philosophy, especially insofar as that age derives anything of its indigenous character vis-à-vis the heritage of ancient Greek thought from the speculative initiatives of Augustine. And we have already seen that the notion of sign must be counted as one of the most influential and fundamental of Augustine's initiatives which have shaped the Latin development in philosophy. But to get beyond the thicket we must first negotiate it. Let us take the plunge, if only for the sake of reaching the other side.

The Thicket (i.1349/1529)

I have already suggested that part of the reason for the thicket along the path of speculative thought in the area of epistemology and semiotics at this point in Latin history lies in the fact that there was at this period a considerably larger and denser thicket of conflicting interests that grew up along the way of practical thought within Ockham's lifetime. The events constituting this larger thicket overall are more germane to the history of theology than to the philosophical development that principally interests us, inasmuch as they feed directly into the circumstances which would germinate the "Protestant revolt" from papal authority within Latin Christendom. Yet indirectly, they created at the same time a climate within which speculative interests that might well not have flourished on their own merits were able to "piggy-back", as it were, on political interests to gain a footing and acceptance that would significantly affect the currents of mainstream philosophical development over the three-and-a-half or so centuries remaining to the Latin Age.

As an aid in understanding how nominalism achieved a significant popularity in spite of its speculative weaknesses, accordingly, and as a concrete illustration of how political events and personalities can influence the sociological success of theories within philosophy relatively independently of their speculative merits, the thicket within which Ockham's nominalist theories take root is one of the more fascinating of the many historical diversions in the long story of philosophy; and the side aspect of some logical terminology bearing on semiotic which arises under the cover, as it were, of this thicket, far from being marginal, will prove central to our tale.

A Thicket within the Thicket, 1309–1417:
The Papacy, First at Avignon and Then in Schism

A fateful year in Ockham's life was 1325. He was already forty-three, and a fugitive from papal power when, in that year, Sciarra Colonna placed on the head of Louis of Bavaria the imperial crown of the Holy Roman Empire. Few acts better symbolized how effectively the long Vatican effort directly to subordinate the civil European powers to papal authority had come to an ignominious end with the flight of Pope Clement V nineteen years earlier from Rome to Avignon to gain the protection of the King of Naples from the King of France on one hand and from the Roman populace on the other. It was Ockham's peripheral role in the cataclysmic events of this so-called Avignon papacy or "Babylonian Captivity" of the popes that mainly brought him to the center stage of Latin thought in the fourteenth century. His writings have managed to hold much of the historical limelight long after the initial reasons for the attention paid to them have vanished.

When, in that same year, 1328, Ockham visited Louis in Pisa offering to exchange the defense of his pen against the theory of papal supremacy in return for the defense of Louis's sword against any authorities seeking to return Ockham to the papal prison for trial of heresy, Louis accepted the exchange with delight. Whether the trade of the wine of Paris for the beer of Munich was a good one, we know at least that, from then until his death, Ockham never dared to venture beyond the sphere of imperial protection, not even during the two years by which he outlived Louis.

The drama of the Avignon papacy had begun when Ockham was twenty-four years of age, with the flight of Clement V from Rome in 1309. Ockham's championing of the conciliar movement – the claim that general councils should be regarded as superior to popes – lent great popularity to the whole of his work. Particularly popular, as you may imagine, was Ockham's argument that expression of opinion should be everywhere free, short of the spreading of deliberate falsehood. His view on this point anticipated "Dr Jekyll", our metaphor in chapter 13 below for the rise of modern science and academic freedom. But his nominalistic epistemology anticipated rather the pathological Mr Hyde, as we shall see. And it was the aspect of Ockham's writing called the *via nominalia*, presciently called the *via moderna* at Oxford, that took root with many contemporary teachers of logic among whom the formal/instrumental sign distinction came to be circulated.

We enter here upon a tangled tale. Even though it is but a sidelight or backdrop to our principal investigation, it might be well to mark the principal trees of this particular forest for the reader's ease of passage. The following table, then, sketches the so-called "papal schism".

The Papacy at Avignon, 1309–1377

To appreciate the sociological power of the events in which the work of Ockham had come to be caught up and placed near the center, let us backtrack a little in our historical diversion. The quarrel of Louis of Bavaria was with the same pope who

Popes at Rome	Popes at Avignon	Popes established by Councils
	1309 Clement V moves papal court from Rome to Avignon.	
	1316 John XXII	
	1334 Benedict XII	
	1342 Clement VI	
	1352 Innocent VI	
	1362 Urban V	
	1370 Gregory XI	
1378 Gregory XI moves his court to Rome, dies, Urban VI elected.	1378 Cardinals reconvene in Anagni, declare Urban's election invalid, elect as pope Clement VII, who sets up his court at Avignon.	
1389 Boniface IX succeeds Urban VI.		
	1394 Benedict XIII	
1404 Innocent VII		
1406 Gregory XII		
		1409 Cardinals convene Council of Pisa, elect Alexander V.

considered Ockham a heretic, Pope John XXII. The beginning of that quarrel dated back only to around 1314, when one group of electors had chosen Louis of Bavaria to be German king and Roman emperor, another group had chosen Frederick of Austria, and the future Pope John XXII tried to reserve choice between the two to the papacy. Louis and Frederick preferred to settle the matter by war, and Louis won in 1322, thereupon considering himself to be the (Holy) Roman Emperor. Now Pope John XXII ordered that he renounce this title until and unless he, the pope, should confer it. When Louis refused, John XXII issued a bull of excommunication in 1324, and interdicted any region from recognizing Louis as their king. But Germany by this time considered John XXII to be an ally of France, and stood by Louis in his title of both German king and Roman emperor.

These emperors had customarily been crowned in Rome, something that Louis did not achieve until six years after his excommunication, and then, as we have mentioned, only at the hands of a Roman nobleman, Sciarra Colonna, not at the hands or by the consent of the absent Pope John XXII. In fact, Sciarra Colonna himself, along with his whole family, had a quarrel with the papacy. The Colonna quarrel went back considerably farther than that of Louis with John XXII, and may be said to be part of the root of the whole affair of the papal "Babylonian Captivity"

Popes at Rome	Popes at Avignon	Popes established by Councils
		1410 John XXIII elected.
		1414 John XXIII convenes Council of Constance.
1415 Gregory XII offers Council of Constance his resignation in exchange for the council's accepting to be first reconvened under his authority.		1415 Council deposes John XXIII, accepts authority and resignation of Gregory XII.
1417 Martin V resumes the tradition of a Roman papal court.	1417 Benedict XIII denies the authority of the Council and continues to assert his papal title, but retreats to the safety of his family stronghold in Valencia.	1417 Council of Constance deposes Benedict XIII and elects Martin V.
	1423 Benedict XIII dies without a successor. End of Avignon line.	

The Thicket within the Thicket: The "Papal Schism"

at Avignon. The Colonna quarrel had reached dramatic proportions in 1297, when Pope Boniface VIII (r.1294–1303) deposed and excommunicated Cardinal Pietro Colonna and Cardinal Jacopo Colonna, and the two had responded by issuing a manifesto placed on the altar of St Peter's appealing *from* the Pope *to* a general church council. At the same time they allied themselves with King Philip IV of France against the pope and against his supremacy in civil affairs. Not until a member of the Colonna family would be crowned Pope Martin V toward the end of 1417 would this deeper and more encompassing quarrel be well and truly ended, as we will see. But we must not get ahead of the story.

In December of 1301 Pope Boniface issued a bull against King Philip of France, which tells the story in its very title: *Ausculta fili* ("Listen, Son"). The bull provoked the French king in turn to summon, in April 1302, the first States-General in French history, in which all three "estates" or classes – nobles, clergy, and commons – supported the temporal power of the king against the pope. In October the pope convened a council at Rome, which issued the bull *Unam Sanctam*,[75] concluding

---

75 For a full text of *Unam Sanctam* in English trans. see Thatcher and McNeal 1905: 314–17.

that, in all things: "We declare and define and pronounce that it is necessary for salvation that all men should be subject to the Roman pontiff".

King Philip replied through the convening of two assemblies, one in March and one in June 1303, which called for the deposition of Boniface from the papacy by a general church council. Boniface declared in reply that only a pope could call such a council. He then proceeded to prepare a decree of excommunication against Philip and an interdict upon France as long as it should continue to accept Philip as king.

But before the pope could issue the decree and interdict, a band of some two thousand mercenaries, led by Sciarra Colonna and William Nogaret, invaded the papal palace at Anagni and sequestered the pope, demanding (27 September, 1303) that he resign. There is even a story, credited as "of considerable trustworthiness" by Guizot,[76] that Sciarra struck the pope in the face and wanted to kill him when Boniface persistently refused to resign.

After three days of this abusive captivity, in any event, the people of Anagni, led by the Orsini clan, freed the pope from his captors and restored him to the Vatican. There he died on 11 October, at the age of seventy-five. Boniface's successor took the name of Benedict XI (r. 1303–4). He excommunicated Sciarra Colonna along with others involved in the outrage against Boniface, and was dead within a month, apparently of poisoning by Ghibellines, another Italian faction.

King Philip of France supported for election as Benedict XI's successor the archbishop of Bordeaux, Bertrand de Got, and de Got was in fact elected pope on 5 June of the following year, 1305. Notwithstanding the support Philip had given him for his election, the new pope sought safety alike from Philip and from the Roman families by physically moving the papacy from Rome to a territory protected by the King of Naples. The territory was Avignon. The pope was Clement V, who thus became the first of seven, later nine, Avignon popes.[77]

In moving from Rome to Avignon, Clement hardly suspected that he was laying the groundwork both for the greatest crisis in the leadership of the Church itself and for the catapulting onto the center stage of European attention the thought of a Franciscan friar which, on the speculative merits of his epistemological theories alone, might otherwise have fallen shortly into oblivion. But that twofold consequence was exactly what history held in store for the Latins.

---

76 Guizot 1869: I, 479.
77 The line of Avignon popes traces as follows: Clement V (r.1305–14); John XXII (r.1316–34); Benedict XII (r.1334–42); Clement VI (r.1342–52); Innocent VI (r.1352–62); Urban V (r.1362–70), who made an effort to return the papacy to Rome in October 1367, but resettled it at Avignon in September 1370; and Gregory XI (r.1370–78), who returned the papacy to Rome in November 1377 and there died in March 1378. Once the "great papal schism" opened in the very year of Gregory XI's death, a "second Avignon line" began with the pope, or antipope, Clement VII, succeeded in 1394 by Benedict XIII. But with the end of the papacy, or antipapacy, of Benedict XIII, whether by the deposition decreed by the Council of Constance in 1417 (which Benedict rejected) or by his death in 1423 (which he had to accept), no more popes chose Avignon for their principal residence.

When Clement died in 1312, the electoral conclave convened to choose his successor was disrupted by a mob which burned down the building in which the conclave was being held and called for the death of all Italian cardinals, who understandably scattered. A subsequent conclave, convened at Lyons under the protection of French troops, eventually (in 1316) elected John XXII to succeed Clement.

The new pope was a man of severe discipline in public affairs and ascetic austerity in private life. His intellectual eye had been caught by Ockham's application of nominalism to theology. He summoned Ockham to the papal court to be tried for "abominable heresies", and there we find Ockham in 1328, imprisoned or threatened with imprisonment at Avignon with two Franciscan companions. The three escaped and sought the protection of Louis of Bavaria, king of Germany and Holy Roman Emperor, as we have seen.

There was another motive worth mentioning which would have inclined the fugitive Franciscan friars to seek the protection of Louis. In 1323, one year before Pope John XXII had excommunicated Louis of Bavaria, John XXII had officially intervened in the famous Franciscan controversy of the time over the poverty of Christ by issuing the bull *Cum inter nonnulla*, which branded as heresy the view that Christ and the Apostles had refused to own property. The condemned view was one championed by many Franciscans as part of their special dedication to poverty. These proponents of "the poverty of Christ" had already flocked to the support of Louis against the pope. Buoyed by such support among others, Louis had responded to his excommunication by himself issuing in 1324 a call for a general council to try for heresy this man "John XXII, who calls himself pope".

Marsilius of Padua (c.1290–1343) and John of Jandun (c.1275–1328) showed up in Louis's court to lend their support to him against the pope. These were two famous University of Paris professors who had authored a book entitled *Defensor Pacis*, "Defender of the Peace". This work argued that a general council of the Church should be summoned by the emperor rather than the pope, and that the election of a pope should be subject to the emperor's consent, rather than the other way around. This was the context in which Louis began, in 1327, his march to Rome for an imperial coronation. He arrived on 7 January 1328, and on the 17th, to the acclaim of the populace, Sciarra Colonna (d.1329) placed the Imperial Crown on Louis's head.

Pope John XXII responded from Avignon by proclaiming a crusade against Louis. Louis issued in reply an imperial edict deposing the pope, and he convened a committee of Roman clergy and laity that, on 12 May 1328, named Peter of Corvara as Pope Nicholas V.[78] This antipope was but a shadow of the "papal schism" shortly to come. Within two years this Nicholas renounced his claim and was led, begging

---

78 This temporary pope, or antipope, Pietro Rainalducci from Corvara, is not to be confused with the slightly later Tommaso Parentucelli (1397–1455), who would reign 1447–55 as Pope Nicholas V, a papacy glorious forever by reason of having the vision and applying the means to found the Vatican Library.

for pardon, before John XXII. John granted him pardon but put him in prison for the rest of his life. No doubt a similar fate awaited Ockham when, in that same year, 1328, he became for the emperor a hired gun in theological matters in exchange for the emperor's protection in ecclesiastical and civil matters.

Thus, by the time of Ockham's death at mid-century, Christian thinkers of the late fourteenth and early fifteenth centuries found their attention demanded by a complex of the greatest practical problems threatening the very existence of the Christian Lebenswelt. The death of Gregory XI in March 1378, shortly after he had restored the papacy to Rome, brought the practical diversion to its climax, but only to precipitate another crisis, which would end in 1417 with the election by the Council of Constance of a Colonna to be Pope Martin V. In this council, which opened on 5 November 1414 and successfully resolved the Great Schism of competing popes on 17 November 1417, a leading role was played one of the greatest of Ockham's followers, Pierre d'Ailly (Petrus de Aliaco, 1350–1420), churchman and "Eagle of France".

So when we discern later, in the shadows of our thicket, the figure of Pierre d'Ailly taking a hand in shaping the terminology for the distinction between formal and instrumental signs,[79] it will be well understood that this was at the time hardly the central feature or principal focus of his attentions. The thicket is not only epistemological and semiotic, but ecclesiastical, civil, and sectarian as well. The return of the papacy from Avignon to Rome in 1378, instead of restoring peace and order to affairs ecclesiastical and theological, soon precipitated instead the so-called "great papal schism", which became the main preoccupation of d'Ailly and indeed of the period.

The Papacy in Schism, 1378–1417

On the death of Gregory XI, a small Roman conclave, terrorized by a mob of Romans surrounding the Vatican and threatening to kill all non-Italian cardinals if an Italian, preferably a Roman, were not elected pope, voted (on 8 April 1378) fifteen to one to place Bartolommeo Prignano, Archbishop of Bari, on the papal throne. Prignano took the name of Urban VI.

French cardinals gathered in Anagni, and on 9 August declared the election of Urban invalid. Even the Italian cardinals joined them, and on 20 September, the entire College of Cardinals proclaimed Robert of Geneva to be the true pope. This Robert took the name of Clement VII and residence at Avignon, while Urban VI remained resident at Rome.

St Catherine of Siena (1347–80), the Dominican nun who had fought so hard to end the "Babylonian Captivity", as she had called the Avignon papacy, sided with Prignano as Urban VI against Robert as Clement VII. Robert she called a Judas. St Vincent Ferrer (1350–1419), a Dominican friar, sided with Clement VII, and called Urban VI a Judas for not stepping aside. From the vantage of a secular historian,

---

79 See p. 405 below.

Gibbon wryly notes:[80] "It is singular, or rather it is not singular, that saints, visions, and miracles should be common to both parties."

We have not space or motive to follow all the details of this "great papal schism", which lasted the thirty-nine years from 1378 to 1417 (or 1423, which was when the last claimant to the Avignon papal line died without issue). But its main outline as pertinent to our story may usefully be sketched. On the Roman side, there were, including Urban VI, a succession of four popes involved in this schism. Urban VI was succeeded in 1389 by Boniface IX; Boniface in 1404 by Innocent VII; and Innocent in 1406 by Gregory XII, whose papacy survived in his own mind until his death in 1423. On what we may call the "second Avignon side", there was a succession of only two popes: Clement VII was succeeded in 1394 by Benedict XIII. To fill out the picture, we need to mention a third line of popes (or second line of antipopes) launched by the Council of Pisa, convened in 1409 by a bipartisan group of cardinals renegade from the then two competing popes, Roman Pope Gregory XII and Avignon Pope Benedict XIII. These bipartisan cardinals created first Pope Alexander V (r.1409–10), and then Pope John XXIII (r.1410–14). This last antipope convened the Council of Constance in 1414, which was reconvened in 1415 by Roman Pope Gregory XII. It was this council that first deposed John XXIII, accepted the resignation of Gregory XII, deposed Benedict XIII, and elected Martin V in conclusion.

The ideas of William of Ockham and Marsilius of Padua that a general council should choose and govern the pope were applied to the competing papacies of Roman Pope Urban VI (r.1378–89) and Avignon Pope Clement VII (r.1378–94) in a work entitled *Epistola concilii pacis* ..., written and circulated in 1381 by Heinrich von Langenstein (c.1325–97), a German theologian on the faculty of the University of Paris. This book became a focus of pressure on the competing popes to resolve an intolerable situation. Gregory XII invited Benedict XIII to a conference. Benedict offered to resign if Gregory would resign. Gregory refused. Cardinals who abandoned Benedict joined with cardinals who abandoned Gregory to call the Council of Pisa, which opened on 25 March 1409. This council summoned both Benedict and Gregory to appear. Both refused. The council declared them deposed, and named the Cardinal of Milan as Pope Alexander V, with instructions to the new pope to call another general council by May of 1412.

But, since Pope Gregory XII and Pope Benedict XIII refused to recognize the Council of Pisa, Pope Alexander V became not the new pope but the third concurrent pope. When he died the following year (1410), his cardinals elected Baldassare Cossa (1350–1416), who had been papal vicar of Bologna under Boniface IX (r.1389–1404), to succeed Alexander V. Cossa took the name of Pope John XXIII.[81]

---

80 Gibbon 1788b: 296n76.
81 This same name, Pope John XXIII, was taken again in late-modern times by Angelo Giuseppe Roncalli (1881–1963), when he was elected pope in 1958. This late-modern John XXIII convened the Second Vatican Council in 1962.

Pope (or Antipope) John XXIII convened the Council of Constance on 5 November 1414. This was to prove the largest council in Christian history, and the most important since Nicea in 325. On 5 April the council issued its decree, *Sacrosancta*:[82]

> This holy synod of Constance, being a general council, and legally assembled in the Holy Spirit for the praise of God and for ending the present Schism, and for the union and reform of the Church of God in its head and its members ... ordains, declares, and decrees as follows: First, it declares that this synod ... represents the Church Militant, and has its authority directly from Christ; and everybody, of whatever rank or dignity, including also the pope, is bound to obey this council in those things that pertain to the faith, to the ending of this Schism, and to a general reform of the Church in its head and members. Likewise it declares that if anyone, of whatever rank, condition, or dignity, including also the pope, shall refuse to obey the commands, statutes, ordinances, or orders of this holy council, or of any other holy council properly assembled, in regard to the ending of the Schism or to the reform of the Church, he shall be subject to proper punishment ... and, if necessary, recourse shall be had to other aids of justice.

On 29 May the council deposed Pope John XXIII. He accepted the decree. Pope Gregory XII now made the council an offer. If the council would agree to being reconvened and legitimated by his authority, he, Pope Gregory XII, would then resign. This was agreed and accomplished with Gregory's resignation on 4 July 1415. On 26 July 1417, the council deposed the one remaining of the three popes, Pope Benedict XIII. He did not accept the decree, though most everyone else did (Pedro de Luna died at ninety years of age, six years after the deposition which he rejected, in his family stronghold near Valencia, still Pope Benedict XIII in his own mind). On 17 November the electoral committee of the Council chose Cardinal Oddone Colonna to be pope. He took the name of Pope Martin V, and all of Christendom excepting the tiny circle of Pedro de Luna accepted his reign.

Well does Peirce note[83] that "the great outburst of nominalism in the fourteenth century ... was connected with politics, the nominalists being generally opposed to the excessive powers of the pope and in favor of civil government, a connection that lent to the philosophical doctrine a factitious following."

A Thin Layer of Logic within the Thicket:
A New Terminology Migrates from Paris to Iberia ...

You can see that, with Ockham, the path of the sign has taken a turn into a thicket which is a veritable semiotic jungle. Let us take hold at this point of logic to gain an Ariadne's thread to lead us within this jungle to a point where our path at least becomes again clear.

---

82 English trans. of the decree "Sacrosancta" issued by the Council of Constance in April 1415, cited from Ogg 1908: 393.
83 In his "Lessons from the History of Philosophy", 1903a: CP 1.17.

Peirce notes of Ockham[84] that he always writes of a mental conception "as a logical term, which, instead of existing on paper, or in the voice, is in the mind, but is of the same general nature, namely, a sign." This seems to have been enough to agitate his followers at the University of Paris interested in logic to pursue with singular ferocity the critique made by Aquinas, Bacon, and Scotus of Augustine's definition of sign as too narrow.

Recall that in the text of Augustine's original definition two elements appeared as essential. The first was that the genus of sign was a material structure accessible to sense; and the second was the differentiative factor of making something other than itself, *aliquid aliud*, come into awareness. Both these elements came under the microscope of later-medieval analysis, and both were found wanting. But it was the first element in Augustine's definition, according to which a sign is a sense-accessible structure, as we have seen, that was the first to be challenged.

Already in Aquinas we have seen reservations expressed on this point. Aquinas explained that Augustine was speaking only from the point of view of what is true for intelligence precisely considered as dependent on the senses for its material object, and not from the point of view of intelligence as such. From the point of view of intelligence as such, neither in the case of God, nor in the case of the angels as pure spirits,[85] can we say that there is an essential dependence on sense-impression. And even in the case of human understanding, the case of intelligence as species-specifically human, where intellectual concepts do have an extrinsic dependence upon and make essential use of perceptual materials, the intellectual content as giving rise to a relation of understanding provides us with an instance of signification that is not directly tied to a sense-accessible structure either on the side of the subjectivity of the knower (the concept as a psychological state) or on the side of the object understood in its intellectual dimension transcendent to perception as such. As we saw, these reservations of Aquinas were repeated independently, and more pointedly repeated, both by Bacon and (especially) by Scotus.

Against the background of the powerful clarification and amplification of the semiotic status and role of psychological states in the activity of human understanding provided in the earlier work of Aquinas, Bacon, and Scotus, what we find still later at the University of Paris is a group of professors of logic enamored of Ockham who take up yet more pungently the earlier established line of criticism. The nominalist logicians make no enquiry into the being proper to sign as such. What they do, in the context of logic as a kind of discourse analysis, is emphasize that the essential function of the sign seems to be fulfilled by the bringing into awareness of an object

---

84 Peirce 1871: CP 8.20.
85 This is true even if we suspend judgment on the actual existence of angels and consider them as pure possibles, which is one of the reasons why Maritain, as we saw in chapter 7, was motivated to say that "he who has never contemplated the possible existence of angels will never be a metaphysician".

other than the sign-vehicle, regardless of whether the vehicle of that awareness be itself sensed or even sensible.

For these later Latins have come to consider the essential function of the sign to be transparently realized by the "passions of the soul" (*passiones animae*), whether conceptual or emotional. Thus, "passions of the soul" amount to the very phenomena that would be, in effect, rediscovered in modern times by Franz Brentano (1838–1917) under the designation of "intentional", a term Brentano frankly borrows from the Latin Age in the writing of his 1874 classic, *Psychology from an Empirical Standpoint*. Among the scholastics,[86] the terminology of "intentionality" was introduced from the translation of the late twelfth century *Commentary* of Averroes on Aristotle's *Treatise on the Soul*. Thereafter this terminology came to be widely (though not universally) used as a short-hand way of indicating the essential relationality of psychological phenomena. The terminology of intentionality was highly developed, however, only in the last Latin centuries; and the appropriation of it made by Brentano for modern use proved to be only superficially in line with the late Latin idea – more thoroughly developed around the terminology of "formal signification" anyway – that thoughts in the mind and feelings in the heart make present objects other than themselves, without those objects having first to make impressions on external sense. (For, in the analysis made for the purpose of Brentano's appropriation, the meaning of the Latin-derived term "physical" is thoroughly reinterpreted in line with the idealist assumption underlying modern empiricism and rationalism alike, which reduces signification to representation in the case of mental states and so makes of the objects of direct experience wholly constructions of the mind's activity[87]).

Nonetheless, whether we look at late Latin epistemological developments through the terminological optic of intentionality or through the more mainstream optic of formal signification, a consensus of late Latin authors emerges to the effect that, as the post-Aquinian medieval Parisians put it, Augustine was mistaken when he included in his definition of sign "being an external sense-accessible structure"; for the essentially relational structure consequent upon psychological states manifests the action proper to signs without being external to the organism as sign-user.

Criticizing the First Part of Augustine's Definition

The Ockhamites incorporated the conclusion of this argument into a discussion which they made the basis for a revision of Augustine's definition. A sign, they said, is "anything known that serves to make present in the awareness *aliquid aliud*" –

---

86 See Beuchot 1994; Deely 1975.

87 The reduction of signification to representation is the speculative essence in matters epistemological of the transition from the Latin Age to the mainstream development of the classical Modern Period from Descartes to Kant, a story that will be told in chapters 9, 12, and 13 below. For detailed analysis of the late-modern idealist interpretation of the "mental/physical" distinction as it bears upon the understanding of Brentano's 1874 text, see "Semiotic and the Controversy over Mental Events" (Deely 1978b).

something other than itself, regardless of whether that *praecognitum*[88] be itself an object of sense or not. Signs, accordingly, they concluded, may be divided into two fundamental classes. If the sign has for its vehicle a sensible object, that is, a material structure accessed as such by sensation, then it should be called an *instrumental* sign. But if the sign has for its vehicle a psychological structure which is not outwardly sensed, but merely felt or experienced inwardly, and, by being so felt or experienced, serves to make present some object, then it should be called a *formal* sign.

No one knows when this exact terminology was proposed. Doyle at one point thought he had found the original stipulation in Giles of Rome (1243–1316), and said so in print.[89] He had based his abduction on the manner in which the Conimbricenses had referred to Giles. But even Homer nods. When, having made his announcement, Doyle tracked down the Conimbricenses' remark to Giles's actual text, he was reminded again of Gilson's adage, "Check your references!". The Conimbricenses had misled one of the best and most careful medievalists of the late twentieth century.

The closest we have come so far to tracking the introduction of this terminology is in the studies and textual redactions by Ludger Kaczmarek of the work of Petrus de Aliaco (1350–1420), usually mentioned in scholarship today under the national-language version of his name, "Pierre d'Ailly".[90] In d'Ailly's *Destructiones Modorum Significandi (secundum viam nominalium)*, "Destructions of the Modes of Signifying (following the path of the nominalists)", from around 1396, we find not *signum formale* and *signum instrumentale*, but at least *significare formaliter* and *significare instrumentaliter*. Meier-Oeser, in the fullest discussion of the historical details in this matter yet made,[91] thinks that the actual terminology in question does not come about till after (and because of) Soto, but he cites in particular only Fonseca's work of 1564 to illustrate the point,[92] which leaves matters where they stood in 1982.[93] So here is matter for probably more than one excellent doctoral dissertation in the history of philosophy.

For the moment the best we can say, until more work has been done in the thicket, is that somewhere, probably at Paris among the nominalist logicians who felt allegiance to Ockham, the argument criticizing the first part of Augustine's definition had crystallized in the form of a new terminological proposal to fix the point, a proposal which itself underwent some evolution before becoming definitively settled in the nominal "formal/instrumental" marker, possibly only after Soto, and

---

88 I.e., concomitantly known, but with a logical priority. See chapter 7, 334n181.

89 Doyle 1984: 571.

90 This d'Ailly is the same "Eagle of France" whose *Imago mundi* of 1410, by its prediction that the Atlantic could be traversed in a few days with the luck of a fair wind, encouraged Columbus in his dreams of discovery. Columbus made over 1000 notes in his personal copy of d'Ailly's book, as can be seen either in the original preserved in the Biblioteca Columbina or in the facsimile edition published by the Massachusetts Historical Society in 1927.

91 "Die Unterscheidung von *signum formale* – und *signum instrumentale*", in Meier-Oeser 1997: 238–51.

92 Meier-Oeser 1997: 246–7.

93 Deely 1982: 52ff.

in the Iberian rather than the Parisian milieu.[94] According to this argument, what is essential to the sign is not how it is experienced, whether by sensation or feeling or purely intellectually,[95] but that it make present something more than itself, something other. In Augustine's definition, according to this argument, considered in respect of *signum* in general, the first part of the definition is not generic but extraneous, whereas the second part, "aliud ex se faciens in cogitationem venire" ("from itself making another to come into thought"), contains the whole essence.

The "whole essence", in the context of medieval thought, cannot be expressed simply, but only through a genus and a difference. By about 1400, the argument had developed to the point of asserting that the proper genus of sign is not "something sensible" but merely "anything cognized"; while the differentiative factor is simply "making present in cognition another".

What the Criticism Accomplished and What It Left to Be Accomplished
This second part of the definition had yet to come under the philosopher's microscope. But one step at a time. The introduction of the terminology *signum instrumentale* to cover only the sign as Augustine's definition applies, and *signum formale* to include those yet more fundamental signs which Augustine's definition

---

94 Important background for Soto's Parisian studies can be found in Villoslada 1938.
95 In the c.330BC text of Aristotle, *De Interpretatione* 16a3–8, on which the medieval logicians leaned so heavily, and which states that spoken words are signs of the passions of the soul, the Latin phrase *passiones animae*, "passions of the soul", could, in itself, be interpreted to include feelings as well as thoughts. In the strict context of Aristotle's text, there is no doubt at all that he was referring to psychological states which are cognitive and not to affective states, although Kretzman (1974) has seen fit usefully to labor the point in scholarly fashion. But of course there are affective *passiones animae* as well as cognitive ones. And the same considerations that apply to the cognitive states which compel the recognition that they are signs apply also to the consequent affective states, if for no other reason than that they participate in the irreducible order of the cognitive states to an objective other superordinate to the one feeling as well as knowing. That *amor transit in conditionem objecti*, that "love penetrates the status of the known as such", is an adage of the scholastics that has yet to be fully incorporated into the perspective of epistemology and *Umweltstheorie* (among pioneering works in this regard, as throughout the whole area of epistemology and semiotics, Poinsot has proven a seminal influence on those few late modern writers cognizant of his rich *Cursus Philosophicus* of the early 17th century: see Maritain 1951, 1953a, 1954; Forlivesi 1993).
   It does not do to point out that, in the Greek, Aristotle does not say that spoken words are signs of the passions but symbols (*symbola*), and in another way symptoms (*semeia*), because the Latins were working from Latin texts, and these said signs (*signa*). Had it not been for Augustine's ignorance of Greek, all this disputation might not have come about. But what was Boethius' excuse? It is clear that, once introduced, the general notion of sign proved so convenient that it was without a second thought taken up on all hands. (Even Markus, who, if anyone, should know better, says in the course of his analysis of the ancient Greek, pre-Augustinian authors [1972: 66, italics added] that, "in general, *no one would dispute* that words are signs"; so we are left simply to marvel why "for no writer" [ibid.] "is reflection on language carried on in terms of 'signs'.")
   The final authority in all these matters, after all, is not some text but experience, against which the text is read and in light of which subsequent authors are led to expand, contract, or abandon the original. In the case of extending the *passiones animae* to include feelings among signs, this is exactly what happens with Peirce's "emotional interpretant".

left out, was a worthy advance along the way of signs. It brought a little more into the open the inevitable choice of facing the "burning and inevitable" problem Augustine had innocently posed, either to resolve it satisfactorily or to abandon the general notion of sign.

The main thrust of the newly established terminological distinction, whatever its specific authorial and textual origin, is clear: signs in their vehicle may be either material or psychological – physical or psychical, in Peirce's terms – while remaining equally signs in either case. With this distinction, semiotic consciousness, initiated with Augustine's proposal that the sign transcends the distinction between nature and culture, is brought to a new level: the sign transcends not only nature and culture, but also the distinction between inward and outward experience.

But how this is possible? What *is* the sign *such that it is able* to achieve this double transcendence over nature and culture, and inner and outer? The question remains to be addressed. In other words, the second part of Augustine's revolutionary definition, the truly differentiative element constituting the sign, namely, that it is relative to something other than its vehicle, remains to be examined in detail. There is so far nothing to indicate that this phase of the historical development begins in the thicket, though of course no one knows what surprises await there till it has been more fully cleared, especially over the seventy-five years separating the birth of Soto (1495) from the death of d'Ailly (1420).

Out of the Thicket

What we can say is that, before 1529, we are well across the thicket and the trail is clear again. For in that year, Domingo de Soto, who did his graduate work at Paris among the nominalist professors of Montaigu, has published at Alcalá his *Summulae*, or "Introductory Logic" text. After this publication we find the distinction between formal and instrumental signifying on everyone's lips.[96] Going into the thicket, the way of signs from Augustine to Aquinas, Roger Bacon, and Scotus was fairly clear. Here on the other side of the thicket the way is clear again, from Soto to the end of the Latin Age in Poinsot's *Tractatus de Signis* (of 1632). Looking back into the thicket from this point where the trail again becomes clear we see only shadowy shapes, d'Ailly principal among them, dominated by the figure of Ockham at the thicket's nether boundary.

By some measures the thicket is not all that large. D'Ailly is born the year of or the year after Ockham's death, and only seventy-five years separate the birth of Soto from the death of D'Ailly. Moreover, there are quite likely scholars, such as Professor Angelelli at the University of Texas, Austin, perhaps Meier-Oeser and Kaczmarek, too, in Germany, and Spade at Indiana, who can see considerably farther and more clearly into the thicket than I have been able to report here. The work is in

---

96 Cf. Soto 1570: lib. 1, cap. 2, lect. prima, 3rb–5ra. Meier-Oeser reports simply (1997: 246): "Die unmittelbare Quelle dieser Bestimmung des *signum instrumentale* sind Sotos Ausführungen zum *instrumentaliter significare*".

progress, so clearing the thicket is only a matter of time. But in the meantime, there are 1206 years separating the completion of Augustine's *On Christian Doctrine* from the publication of Poinsot's *Treatise on Signs*, which is the first work successfully to justify Augustine's posit of *signum* as a vehicle enabling communication over the divides separating nature from culture and inner from outer experience. From the death of Aquinas in 1274 to a resolution at last in 1632 of the "burning and inevitable problem" handed to the Latins by Augustine's ignorance of Greek, the thicket obstructs only about half (180 of the last 358 years) of our journey along the way of signs.

Domingo de Soto (1495–1569) and the Path Beyond the Thicket

Dominicus Soto stands as a key transition figure in the story of sign over the last Latin centuries. His importance stems not from any theoretical contribution he developed on his own, but from his success in importing the Parisian discussions of sign into the Iberian university world, where these discussions took a much deeper root and more profound turn. While a graduate student in Paris Soto imbibed the elevation to terminological status of the distinction between inner states as "formally signifying" and outwardly perceived material structures as "signifying instrumentally". On returning to Iberia as a professor of logic and philosophy, he put this distinction into broad circulation through the vehicle of writing what proved a highly successful introductory logic text,[97] the opening sections of which incorporated the definitions of terms and framework of distinctions concerning *signum* that he had absorbed from his Paris graduate studies.

Soto called his logic text a *Summulae*. In using this title he conformed to the fashion of the period, which was to use the title from the hugely successful *Summulae Logicales* of Peter of Spain (c.1210–77), completed c.1245.[98] Peter's treatment of logic had come to be universally regarded as the classic model for a common teaching of logic in the Latin world at the elementary level. Hence, all elementary logic texts had come to be called *summulae* books.

If we consider the whole of Europe, there is no comparing the success of Soto's *Summulae* with that of Petrus Hispanus. But if we consider the confines of the Iberian world, the success of Soto's work after 1529 may be said to have come close. As a result of the popularity his book came to enjoy within the Iberian academic Umwelt, the framework of the discussion about signs that he had imported from Paris became

---

97 First published in 1529, this text went through many subsequent editions.
98 A Petrus Hispanus, Petrus Juliani of Lisbon, was elected pope on September 15 of 1276, taking the name of John XXI. If this Petrus was indeed the author of the *Summulae*, which is commonly taught but far from certain (see d'Ors 1997), this election marked an unusual distinction among professors of logic. In the following year (20 May 1277), unhappily, the pope in question, author of the *Summulae* or not, was killed by a falling ceiling.

the framework within which signs were discussed throughout the Iberian university world. In the hundred years following the publication of Soto's *Summulae*, disputes about *signum* became almost daily events in the Iberian schools, and the terminology of the distinction between some entities called signs as formal and other entities called signs as instrumental came to be everywhere bandied about.

The problem with this terminology, as above remarked,[99] is that it at best glosses over and at worst conceals a serious theoretical equivocation. One can interpret it as a consolidation of the scholastic realist critiques of Augustine made by Aquinas and Scotus. Or one can consider it rather in the framework of the nominalist doctrine that there are no general or common modes of being, no relations existing apart from the activity of mental comparisons of actual individuals. Thus, in itself, the terminological point is not necessarily an advance in the understanding of *signum* first proposed by Augustine, since it can just as easily be made in the context of a flat rejection of Augustine's proposed general notion as a mistake, a *flatus vocis*.

It seems clear enough in Soto's work that he himself regarded the distinction in the line of a consolidation of the earlier critique of Augustine's definition of sign, particularly as found in the writings of Thomas Aquinas, of whose school Soto considered himself a member. Thus Soto, like Aquinas and most of the Latins before Ockham, combined a critique of the wording of Augustine's specific definition proposed for sign with an acceptance of Augustine's general notion itself of sign as a mode of being verified equally in natural and cultural phenomena. But by not addressing directly and in systematic detail the question of *how* such a mode of being indifferent to the difference in objectivity between mind-dependent and mind-independent being is verified in the case of the sign as such, Soto himself makes no advance beyond approximately the point that the foundational discussion of semiotics had reached going into the thicket.

Thus, Soto enjoys the importance of being a main transitional figure in our story, the conduit, as it were, by which the distinction between formal and instrumental signification reached the Iberian peninsula in the early 1500s, and the one who, by making the discussion of this distinction widespread, helped force the hand both of the scholastic realists and of the nominalists over the fundamental issue of semiotics. The root of the problem appeared differently from the different sides, but facing up to the root issues on both sides could only be a question of time, as individual thinkers realized more and more of the logical consequences of the ideas involved, and shared their growing realization in an ongoing series of published writings.

On the side of the scholastic realists, those who would continue the Latin tradition of accepting Augustine's *signum* as really being what it purported to be – a general mode of being of singular versatility in weaving the fabric of what we call experience – it was incumbent to show one of two things.

---

99 In the section on terminological advance introducing "The Thicket", p. 392 above.

In the strongest case, they would have to show how a univocal application, an application of the same word in the same sense, could be made of the term "sign" in such expressions as "formal sign" and "instrumental sign". To make this strong showing, they would have to address a central question. What is the type of which formal and instrumental signs are tokens? Indeed, what is the type of which *all* signs, natural and conventional no less than formal and instrumental, are tokens? What is the type of which *every* distinction among signs is a token? Or, to put the question in more typically Latin terminology, what is the universal of which every particular sign is an instance?

But perhaps there is after all no type, but only an analogous grouping of phenomena which, for various reasons, we call "signs". This would be a weaker case on which the scholastic realists could fall back. Perhaps there is, after all, no underlying unity among signifying phenomena, but only a family resemblance, some kind of an analogous unity expressed by the term *signum*. While there are universals, types of tokens, perhaps after all *signum* is not to be counted among them. That Augustine was mistaken and made a false posit, thus, could still be compatible with scholastic realism.[100]

On the side of the nominalists, too, there was a central question waiting to be addressed. It was not the question of whether Augustine had blundered. An affirmative answer to this question could be assumed *ex hypothesi* by any nominalists who once raised the question (which, explicitly at least, they generally seem not to have done). The central question for nominalism would be more hypothetical. Since there is no general mode of being corresponding to the word "sign" (since there is no general mode of being corresponding to any term), what is the advantage in speaking of various sorts of *sign* at all? Should we not rather identify one group of concrete individuals or characteristics as signs and call all other groups by another name? And which group of particulars, and why, is best and most properly labeled *signum*? The two leading candidates would be words on one side and ideas on the other.

Soto did not himself put the questions this way. But the reception his work received created a climate in which the eventual putting of these questions became inevitable. We may say, accordingly, that the importance of Soto in our story is twofold. First, by the popular success of his *Summulae* within Iberia, he created a climate and established the framework of discussion in terms of which the semiotic controversies of the climactic final century go forward. Second, he gives a clear boundary to the thicket: from Soto to the end of the Latin Age, the way of signs again becomes a clear path of development easily followed, at least as easily as the path up to the thicket.

---

100 It is thus, for example, that Rasmussen (1980, 1982, 1983) finds, and quite legitimately so, something more in Wittgenstein's later work than a mere apotheosis of modern nominalism. The problem, however, is that Wittgenstein never reached an understanding of the stronger case for scholastic realism which can be made in this and other epistemological areas, perhaps as a consequence of his neglect of historical figures who developed the Latin (or any other) issues.

CHAPTER NINE

Three Outcomes,
Two Destinies

After Soto and the Parisian nominalists, what remains to be considered in the subjection to scrutiny of Augustine's proposal is the second part of the definition of sign, the heart of the matter, the crucial "reference to" or "standing for another". On this discussion hangs the fate of Augustine's assumption that there is a *signum* "in general", that there is communication over the divide between physical nature and the human Umwelt, and between Innenwelt and Umwelt, and that the vehicle which shuttles across and transcends this divide is the sign according to a being proper and unique to itself, whence its action springs according to circumstances.

The First Outcome: Pedro da Fonseca (1528–1599)

Given the great ferment that had been generated by the prominence Soto had achieved in the Iberian world, the author who more that any other seems to have been responsible for bringing about the focus that led to the successful resolution of the problem of sign as Augustine had launched it was the Portuguese Jesuit Pedro da Fonseca. An author as perspicacious as Luigi Romeo considers Fonseca to be the first classical author of semiotic.[1] But this judgment needs to be qualified in view of Fonseca's doubts about the unified nature of the sign as an object of inquiry,[2] the key question on which the speculative fate of Augustine's posit hangs.

We enter here into *terra incognita*. The reader at this point should ask (Oh! for Finnish! where gender is not distinguished in pronouns!), should I say "him" or "her" self, and in what order? In any event, the reader needs to ask self-reflexively whether that reader in question has ever heard of Pedro da Fonseca, or even Petrus Fonsecus, prior to reaching this point on this page? If not, then let me remark that the point is that René Descartes, of whom the reader has almost assuredly heard, did. If so, then let me remark that most readers of the English speaking world at

---

1 Luigi Romeo, "Pedro da Fonseca in Renaissance Semiotics: A Segmental History of Footnotes", *Ars Semeiotica* II.2 (1979): 190ff.
2 In his *Institutionum dialecticarum* of 1564, Liber I, caput VII.

the turn of the twenty-first century have not heard of Fonseca, for the very good reason that most (nearly all) histories of philosophy circulated in this Lebenswelt over the last two centuries would have no mention of him, his work, or his school. Passing over "why", suffice it to say the exegesis to follow may be of what Fonseca might have intended to say, and certainly (in my mind) ought to have said; but that it is "only a guess", as clearly and modestly made as the circumstances allow. Sherlock Holmes never guessed; but I am of the school of Peirce, which arrives at the truth only by guessing, and even at that only over the long run. What follows, therefore, should be read as my abduction – a term I like for the criminal flavor it lends to philosophizing – of how best to fill in the gap in the current "histories of philosophy" between Ockham and Descartes.

Let us begin. Let us make, that is to say, a guess at the riddle of why the historians have been silent on the interval separating Ockham from Descartes.

As the principal professor of philosophical studies at the University of Coimbra, Fonseca not only wrote major works of his own, but he also organized the team of thinkers there whose work came to be known collectively as the *Cursus Conimbricensis*, usually referred to as the "Conimbricenses". Of particular interest to our present exploration was the publication in 1564 of his *Institutionum dialecticarum libri octo*. Essentially a summulist logic text, this work was read far and wide in the Latin world, having gone through some fifty-three editions by the year 1624.

It was Pedro's work, in fact, far more profoundly than Soto's, that prepared the final fate of *signum* in the Latin West vis-à-vis modernity. Above all he admired Duns Scotus, whom he closely follows. But he begins by correcting in his working definition of sign the restriction of the action of signs to the orbit of human understanding that would follow as a consequence of the way both Bacon[3] and Scotus[4] had defined it. In place of intellect, Fonseca says that to signify is more broadly "to represent something *to a cognoscitive faculty*".[5]

An Appearance to the Contrary Notwithstanding ...

Fonseca seems at first as if he embraces eagerly the new terminology instituted (or at least presented by Soto as if) to pinpoint the effective criticism Aquinas and especially Scotus had made in bringing to the fore the manner in which concepts function as signs more primordially than any objects of the Umwelt, including natural signs of the environment such as smoke or such pre-eminent cultural signs as words:[6]

Formal signs are similitudes or certain forms (*species*) of things signified inscribed within the cognitive powers, by means of which the things signified are perceived. Of this sort is the similitude which the spectacle of a mountain impresses upon the eyes,

---

3 See "The Beam in Roger Bacon's Eye", chapter 8, p. 372.
4 See "Working on the Beam from Roger Bacon's Eye", chapter 8, p. 378.
5 Fonseca, *Institutionum dialecticarum libri octo* (1564), I, 34.
6 Fonseca 1564: lib. I, cap. VIII.

or the image which an absent friend leaves in another's memory, or again the picture one forms of something which he has never seen. These signs are called "formal," because they form and as it were structure the knowing power.

Instrumental signs are those which, having become objects for knowing powers, lead to the cognition of something else. Of this sort is the track of an animal left in the ground, smoke, a statue, and the like. For a track is a sign of the animal which made it: smoke the sign of an unseen fire: a statue finally is a sign of Caesar or someone else. These signs are called "instrumental," either because through them as instruments we signify to others our ideas; or because just as an artist must move his instrument in order to shape his material with it, so must powers able to know first perceive these signs in order to know anything through them.

Hence may be gathered the most striking difference between instrumental and formal signs: since indeed formal signs do not have to be perceived by us in order for us to come to an awareness of the thing signified by the perception they structure; but unless instrumental signs are perceived, they lead no one to an awareness of anything.

Too glib had been the Ockhamite designation of concepts as *signa naturalia* along with all those phenomena of human experience which seem to have a connection with what they signify antecedent to and independent of social interaction. Many questions worthy of discussion are begged in this cross-classification of natural signs – here within the mind and there outside – as eventually came to light.[7] Fonseca saw this, yet he made his reservations known with too much delicacy and indirection for even some of his best admirers to catch. As had happened with Augustine's original proposal of *signum*, it seems, so the new terminology was everywhere adopted by the Latins without due regard for the difficulties it concealed. This glossing over of a fundamental difficulty can be illustrated from the lecture course given on the logical doctrines of Fonseca by Professor J. B. Bosserel at the University of Graz, Austria, in 1615. Bosserel gives the following summary of Fonseca's discussion of signs in the *Institutes* of 1564:[8]

> To signify means to represent something to a being able to know, as, for example, to the sense, the imagination, the understanding. Signs are divided into two groups. The first comprises formal and instrumental signs. The formal ones are similitudes, like images of things signified that exist in cognitive powers, through which the things signified are apprehended, as, for example, the resemblance of a friend. In order that these signs may be known, it is not necessary to see the eyes through which one sees the signs. Instrumental signs are those which are represented to cognitive powers as soon as they are recognized by them, and also when they lead to the recognition of other things, as the footprint of an animal, smoke, or wrinkles in the forehead.

7　See, in the 1985 edition of Poinsot's *Treatise on Signs*, p. 27 n. 13, if you wish to follow up this point.

8　Bosserel 1615.

The second group contains natural and conventional signs. Natural signs are those which signify the same thing to everybody, such as moans and laughs. Conventional signs are those which signify through, as it were, a socially structured human intention, such as words and letters, as well as those which have entered the usage of all people,[9] such as ivy and cypress.

Note that natural signs can also be formal, but not all of them. For a concept and a moan are both natural signs, yet a moan is not formal, but instrumental.

... Again the Ghost of Nominalism to Haunt Augustine[10]

Yet a careful reading of Fonseca himself reveals some dis-ease. For along with his adoption of the formal/instrumental terminology to express a division of signs based on their function in experience relative to the cognizing organism, with the implied restriction within that division of the classical Augustinian definition to the one class of instrumental signs only, Fonseca introduces as well some profound reservations as to whether in fact these two types of "signs" really have a common basis. They are both *called* "signs", but so is the protective outer layer of a tree trunk and the sound of an alarmed dog *called* "bark".

Fonseca is not as blunt as this. His remarks are subtle and indirect, subjunctive in mood, as it were. But he quite clearly wonders at the level of murmuring if Thomas and Scotus didn't perhaps somehow get it all backwards in thinking that psychological states are semiotic phenomena more fundamental than words, statues, pictures, and footprints in the sand. The designation of concepts as *formal signs* is not a fully settled usage, he admonishes, "nor is it clear that they are with full propriety said to represent" objects other than themselves; whereas it is fully clear that instrumental signs represent through a linkage with other objects.[11]

Whether he is showing the influence of Ockham or not, he certainly expresses[12] what Ockham should have said about the situation in the light of his nominalism: "Perhaps the Divine Augustine defined sign the way he did precisely because it covered everything that settled ways of speaking would really want to call signs", and

---

9 How fragile proves "the usage of all people": it is today all but forgotten in common culture, even of the schools, that Bacchus wore a wreath of ivy to express the then-belief that this plant could prevent drunkeness, or that the early Christians transferred the symbolism of ivy to typify, through its ever-greenness, everlasting life; forgotten too is the ancient, once-common, dedication by the Romans of the cypress tree to Pluto, god of the underworld, land of the two rivers of death, because a cut cypress tree does not grow again. Whence the cypress tree was associated with cemeteries, its wood once commonly used for coffins, and twigs of it were often placed in Greek and Roman coffins. (At the other end of the scale, in another key of history's ironies, the wood for cupid's arrows was thought to be cypress wood!)

10 Recall from chapter 6 "The Possible Nominalistic Character of Augustine's Proposal", p. 247.

11 Fonseca 1564: lib. I, cap. VIII: "priora illa" – scil., *signa formalia* – "nec admodum usitate nominantur signa, nec satis proprie dicuntur repraesentare: haec vero posteriora" – scil., *signa instrumentalia* – "maxime".

12 Ibid.: "Unde D. Augustinus quasi complexus omnia, quae populari sermone signa dicerentur, hoc modo signum definivit: Signum est, quod et seipsum sensui, et praeter se aliquid animo ostendit."

not through any blunder, as the Latins considering the matter, ever since Aquinas, have so far led themselves to imagine.

The new terminology made so popular through Soto's *summulae* was not, after all, that much more to Fonseca's liking than the summulist movement itself, which he expressly tells us has departed too far from a true and careful reading of Aristotle.[13] Fonseca's attitude toward the specifically Latin development of logic creates a suspicion that the formal/instrumental division is not in Fonseca's mind truly his own, that he is rather reacting to and attempting to assimilate to his own more conservative and more Greek thought elements that have become so widespread in the Latin milieu that they have to be dealt with, like it or not.

Fonseca Anticipating Modernity: The Reduction of Signification to Representation in the Order of Formal Signs

In line with such reservations, we further find in Fonseca an explicit attempt to identify the precise role of representation in signification. And he finds that, in the case of the formal sign, the two are not distinct. He thinks that the relation of representation to signification in the case of a formal sign is one of identity, one wherein the two are equated:[14]

> To signify is nothing else than to represent something to a cognizing power. But since everything that represents something is a sign of the thing which it represents, it happens that whatever signifies something is its sign.[15]

Now the cat gets out of the bag. Fonseca's text is so nuanced that it cannot be read as coming right out to say and specifically deny that there is really a common notion, or, rather, a common mode of being that unites these two kinds of signs. What the text does is imply what Suárez will later explicitly say: that what formal signs do is merely represent, while instrumental signs add to this representation, through their dependency on formal signs, an actual signification of something other than themselves.

In other words, instrumental signs are that class of entities properly said to signify in representing and properly called signs. Formal "signs" are properly said only to represent and are properly called similitudes or likenesses, "such as the image that

---

13 Ibid.: "Preface".
14 Fonseca 1564: lib. I, cap. VIII.
15 "Atque ut alte, et a capite significandi modos, repetam, Significare nihil aliud est, quam potentiae cognoscenti, aliquid repraesentare. Cum autem omne, quod aliquid repraesentat, sit signum rei, quae repraesentatur, efficitur, ut quicquid rem aliquam significat, sit signum eius." Romeo (1979: 194) translates this: "In order to trace the modes of signification back to their most remote origin, 'to signify' is simply to depict something to a cognoscitive being. Everything representing something is a sign of what is represented, hence whatever represents something is at the same time a sign"; and this is a good translation, but it does not sufficiently emphasize to my mind the equation Fonseca makes between *repraesentat* ("represents") and *significat* ("signifies"), where Poinsot will deny an equation.

a perceived mountain impresses upon the eye".[16] Clear in Fonseca's text is the notion that the formal sign, improperly called "sign", is a subjective structure, an idea of the mind insofar as it is a psychological or subjective state characterizing an individual.[17] The instrumental sign, too, is a subjective structure, but one that is extramental and hence one that, through its dependence on the formal sign, carries the mind to something other than itself through a (suprasubjective) relation. This relation, however, results *from the mind relating* sign to signified. In the case of the formal sign, such a relation does not obtain. The formal sign is simply whatever objective content the mind is aware of in a given cognition. The formal sign *is* the concept, the intramental or "psychological" subjective determination itself, the "species". Hence, the formal sign is a mere representation, a "similitude", while the instrumental sign adds to this representation, and dependently upon it, a relation between itself as an object and *some other* object as signified.

If, therefore, we wish to speak exactly and according to the truth of the matter, we would speak not of formal and instrumental *signs*, but of formal *representations* and instrumental *significations*, and only the class of sense-perceptible objects will properly and strictly be called *signs*. I think there is no difference between Fonseca's early subtlety and Suárez's later bluntness: words signify, concepts represent.

Consider Fonseca's final statement of the difference between formal and instrumental "signs".[18] Formal and instrumental signs, he says, finally differ in this, that formal signs are neither usually nor with exactitude called signs. What formal signs do, exactly speaking, is represent. Instrumental signs, by contrast, are the only things that, exactly speaking, signify. It is for this reason that instrumental signs alone are called signs in established usage, and for this reason too that Augustine defined sign in the fashion that he did. It was not a definition too narrow, but an exact definition.[19] For in the case of formal signs, signification differs not a whit from representation; and instrumental signs are signs only dependently upon formal signs. True, the so-called instrumental signs add a relation whereby one object is connected to another object. But these relations are a result of the dependence of the instrumental upon the formal. Hence, insofar as they introduce a distinction or difference between the instrumental and the formal sign, they do so by adding something proper to the mind alone, namely, the formation of relations, suprasubjective connections or *nexi* between *apprehended* things. Formal signs only represent. Instrumental signs depend upon formal signs. Whatever instrumental signs do over

---

16 Fonseca 1564: I, 8: "Huius generis est similitudo, quam mons obiectus imprimit in oculis."

17 Ibid.: "Dicuntur autem haec signa formalia, quia formant, et quasi figurant potentiam cognoscentem."

18 Ibid.: "Differunt etiam hac ratione, quod priora illa nec admodum usitate nominantur signa, nec satis proprie dicuntur repraesentare, haec vero posteriora, maxime." The import of the text I find clearer in the Portuguese rendering of Ferreira Gomes (1964: I, 37): "Diferem também pela razão de que os primeiros nem são habitualmente chamados sinais, nem com grande exactidão se diz que significam; mas estes ultimos significam ao maximo."

19 Ibid.: "Unde Divus Augustinus quasi complexus omnia, quae populari sermone signa dicerentur, hoc modo signum definivit."

and above representation they do as a consequence of their mind-dependent status, not of themselves. Instrumental signs work wholly in function of formal signs, and, at the level of formal signs, there is no difference between "to represent" and "to signify". Whatever difference instrumental signs add they do not add as signs but as functions of formal signs, that is to say, of concepts.[20]

For Fonseca, therefore, the extension of the notion of sign to concepts in the mind is not an advance but an improper application of the term. Either we should not call concepts signs or we should call extramental signs something else. The expression "sign-function" did not occur to him, though it would do nicely. What he was focused upon was not an improved terminology for what Augustine had termed "signs" but an appreciation of the fact that what Augustine had termed "signs" does not square with terming concepts "signs". And, from the point of view of this preoccupation, it can be truly said that what was defective had not been Augustine's definition, as some later Latins came to suppose, but his idea of sign as a general mode of being indifferent to nature and culture.

Fonseca, thus, did not see the terminology of formal and instrumental signs as consolidation of the critiques of Aquinas, Bacon, and Scotus, but as a muddying of the waters, an obfuscation of the fact that those critiques themselves were misguided, and misguided by accepting Augustine's groundless general proposal rather than his solid definition. When we speak of formal and instrumental signs, therefore, we are not speaking of two species under a common genus, for there is no genus common to the two. The word "sign" in the two expressions is an inexact way of speaking, a misleading use of language, a *flatus vocis*. Exactly speaking, there are mental representations and verbal significations, and only the vehicles of the latter can properly and exactly be called *signs*.

Here indeed, about one thousand one hundred and thirty-eight years after the fact, is the burning and inevitable problem burst fully to flame. Here is the challenge that any good Greek philosopher might have hurled at Augustine immediately on reading *On Christian Doctrine*.[21] Fonseca, in suggesting a denial of a unified object at the base of the doctrine of signs, is denying the possibility of a general account, theory,

---

20 Which would fit in nicely with Eco's attempt to *replace* signs with sign-functions (see chapter 17 below). For if formal signs are not properly called signs, and instrumental signs, insofar as they add to formal signs "relations to something other", do so not from themselves (i.e., from their being as signs) but from their being as dependent upon formal signs (concepts), then indeed are they better described as *sign-functions* than as *signs*. This gets us ahead of ourselves in the historical development, and makes quite another terminological point than the one preoccupying Fonseca; but it helps us to appreciate what is to come.

21 A reviewer of the manuscript for this work responded at this point with some indignation: "On what basis would 'a good Greek philosopher' challenge the 'ignorant' Augustine? Simply on the basis of an absence of a doctrine of signs?" I should have thought the ground of the challenge evident at this point: *On Christian Doctrine* proposes the σύμβολον of human language to be a σημεῖον, whereas in Greek thought the two are as opposed as nature and nurture, convention and necessity, symptoms of disease and lies proffered as proofs.

  "It seems to me that the ambivalent character of Augustine's *signum* may be put as follows", the reviewer continued: "The issue becomes clear only now: a realistic theory of signs is an

or doctrine of signs. He gives the picture of a man pressured by the development of thought and terminology in the summulist tradition to envisage in the Latin environment of his times the specific possibility of a semiotic. But he resists the prospect and in the end rejects and denies the possibility. "The possibility of a philosophical doctrine of signs", we can imagine him saying, "is not a real one. Augustine, as an accidental by-product, as it were, of his failure to learn Greek, has drawn you Latins into an illusion, a dream, and it is time to wake up."

The stage is set for a denouement. Instead of a single outcome, a long slow development from the launching of Augustine's proposal in the fifth century to its climactic justification at last in the seventeenth century, we find instead with Fonseca explicitly, as with Ockham implicitly, the whole slow development of the earlier Latin centuries challenged as a speculative blunder. There will be not one destiny for Augustine's unknowingly novel proposal but two, the one repudiating, the other vindicating, the notion of *signum* with which the Latin Age was born.

Here in Fonseca, from the point of view of semiotic, we might almost say modernity is hatched, for classical modern philosophy was founded on the reduction at the level of ideas of signification to representation, as we will see. Here is the first formal proposal that, when it comes to the ideas and images formed in cognition by the mind itself, the two – representation and signification – are one and the same. The proposal comes seventy-seven years before the *Meditations on First*

---

impediment to the liberation of the sign into its own nature and modality, hence into the possibility of a postmodern semiotics." But this is a strange clarity indeed, for whence this "realistic theory of signs"? There is precious little "theory" of sign in or before Augustine. Before him, there is only the observed fact that events in nature warn us of what is occurring (symptoms of disease) and what is to come (signs in nature and divination). That is not theory, but at most theory-laden observation, quite a different animal. Yet the reader seems to think that *Augustine*, not the ancients, is the one who has saddled us with "a realistic theory of signs", for the report continues: "That is, the Augustinian insight flagged the notion of sign but in such a way as to impede its proper development." Yet this is ridiculous, for the Augustinian insight, or error, was to see in sign a general mode of being that can be specifically verified equally and indifferently in natural and in cultural spheres alike. If the interpretation of Manetti, following Eco, is correct, Augustine flagged the notion of sign so as eventually to dissociate it from nature, by signaling that it is words, not events, that actually signify. That line of inference leads to modern idealism or to semiology – to which (they being "birds of a feather", as we will see in chapter 16) is a matter of indifference. I do not think at all that Augustine's soaring insight took flight from any intuition on his part for "a realistic theory of signs". If Augustine's insight as presented and contextualized in the present work is correct, what Augustine flagged (without knowing it, since he was ignorant of Greek) was the "realistic theory of sign" *implicit in the Greek usage of the term* σημεῖον, with the consequence of showing that *any realistic theory of sign as such* would impede, not to say preclude, the proper and natural development of the doctrine of signs (see chapter 18 below, if an "envoi" can be considered a chapter).

So the Augustinian insight did the very reverse of flagging the notion of sign "in such a way as to impede its proper development"; it flagged the notion rather in such a way as to (for the first time of which we have clear record) begin to start to commence to open the way to its proper (postmodern) development. So would I answer the reviewer's plaint that "It seems to me that, if I am right, we could have been told this more clearly before [ms.] p. 280".

Philosophy of Descartes, seventy-three years before Descartes' *Discourse on the Method of rightly conducting one's reason and seeking truth in the sciences,* and sixty-four years before his *Rules for the Direction of the Mind.* Words may signify, but concepts only represent.

Fonseca has already sent abroad to the Latins the very message on this point of Suárez, the Latin author for whom the mainstream early moderns will have the readiest ears in the period of formation of classical modern philosophy. For to distinguish signification from representation both at the level of formal signs and at the level of instrumental signs requires a doctrine of real relations, and Suárez will assure the classical early moderns that, just as they suspect, any such doctrine is mistaken.[22] As Scruton will publicly object to Eco exactly three hundred ninety-six years after the publication of Fonseca's *Institutiones,* there is no science of buttons, no way that clouds signify rain in any sense univocal with the way that the word "rain" signifies.[23]

Reversing the Earlier Criticism of Augustine

Thus appears in Fonseca – somewhat contrary to the obvious sense of his own words in the mind of a casual reader (a circumstance not unusual in the development of philosophical doctrines by any means) and assuredly contrary to the semiotic development the influence of his work will otherwise further in spite of everything – an effort to promote continued acceptance of St Augustine's definition of the sign as a correct general definition, that is, one valid for all cases *properly* called sign in a unified sense. The Augustinian definition obviously applies to instrumental signs – sense-perceptible realities which function subsequently as signs. Hence, if indeed the definition is truly a full definition of signs, then the possibility of treating ideas under a doctrine of signs is foreclosed.

The point to concentrate on, Fonseca thinks, is not some chimerical unity between interior and exterior signs, but rather on the differences in exterior signs between what is natural and what is not. The distinction between natural and conventional signs, he thinks, is not a dichotomy but a trichotomy:[24]

> Conventional signs are those which signify by deliberate intention and as if by a kind of compact. Such signs are of two types. For some signify as the result of stipulations, such as the words by which men converse, or the letters by which absent parties communicate; others, however, signify as the result of customs and traditions of use, in the way that items displayed in a shop signify what is for sale. And of those signs which signify by stipulation, there is again a twofold signification, proper and improper.

---

22 Suárez 1605: disp. 1, par. 6; cf. Poinsot 141/12–142/13.
23 Roger Scruton, "Possible Worlds and Premature Sciences", *London Review of Books* (7 Feb. 1980), 14. Eco (1984a) provided an adequate response.
24 Fonseca 1564: lib. I, cap. IX.

... Indeed practically all words have an improper signification as a result of adaptation and change in use, through metaphor, catachresis, metalepsis, or metonymy.

Was the Definition Wrong, or Was It the General Proposal That Was Ill-Conceived?

You can see that things are moving toward a climax. Something has to give, either Augustine's definition or his more general proposal. The question of whether *signum* is a nominalism can no longer be avoided. What is clear at this point is that there is a growing complexity of considerable interest, and not without its antinomies, in the Latin understanding of signs. The definition of sign is becoming unsettled in several ways. The division of signs is ramifying and intersecting in unexpected ways, ways that have consequences for the very attempts at definition.

Fonseca, naturally, wants things to go the way he thinks the truth requires. And the truth requires that the indigenous Latin *summulae* tradition be brought to heel, before things get further out of hand. In his mind, exactly what is needed is a return to the Philosopher. For Fonseca was not bound by the "superficial learning" of Augustine. He knew that the famous *De Interpretatione* I, 16a3–8 did not say that spoken words are *signs* of passions of the soul, but symbols (*symbola*). He knew that Aristotle did not say that these passions of the soul are *signs* of things or objects, but likenesses (*nomoiômata*). And he knew that Aristotle did not say that spoken and written symbols are alike in being signs of the passions, but in being symptoms of them (*sêmeia*). Symbols, likenesses, symptoms; nowhere signs. The word, as the Latins used it, did not exist. Augustine has created a phantom of the mind, a phantom of his own *opera*.

Fonseca knew that the semiotic triangle the Latins had everywhere relied upon, especially in the development of the *summulae* logics, was paper over an abyss. For there is no such notion as Augustine's *signum* in Aristotle, or anywhere else in what we have from Greek philosophy. The Latins had been duped by the Greek-ignorant proposal of Augustine. If, now that Greek had been recovered, the Latins were to look anew at the text of Aristotle, they would see that they had been led down a garden path. They would discover for themselves that the way of signs is a road to nowhere, for at the end of the Latin path they would discover the illusion of the doctrine of signs.

Fonseca's Stratagem

Not only for this single purpose, of course, but for a whole broad range of considerations such as only a man of learning could conceive, Fonseca organized that team of Latin researchers who, like himself, were learned in Greek, for the purpose of commenting not on some half-Arab, half-Latin surrogate for Aristotle, but on the Greek Aristotle himself. Among his chief collaborators were Emmanuel de Goes (1542–1597), Cosmas de Magelhães (1551–1624), Balthasar Alvarez (1561–1630), and Sebastian de Couto (1567–1639). The work of this remarkable team is what has come down to us as the five-volume set of commentary on Aristotle called the

Conimbricenses,[25] the last volume of which, the one that principally interests us here, was brought to publication by de Couto. Let Professor Jack Doyle here take over the story, for no one knows this part of it better than he:[26]

"Conimbricenses" is the name of a group of Jesuit professors of philosophy at the University of Coimbra during the latter half of the 16th century. It is also the name given to a five-volume set of philosophical commentaries on Aristotle which they edited and published between 1592 and 1606. The last volume to appear was a logic, entitled *Commentarii Collegii Conimbricensis et Societatis Jesu. In universam dialecticam Aristotelis Stagiritae. Secunda Pars.*

Coming out in 1606, this volume followed a logic, spuriously attributed to the Conimbricenses, which had been published in 1604 at Frankfurt, Cologne, Hamburg, and Vienna. This spurious logic, which in fact was based on notes taken twenty-five years earlier by a Jesuit student at Coimbra, was denounced by the Conimbricenses themselves as both fraudulent and inaccurate. Their own work, appearing first at Coimbra and then, in 1607, with a Greek text of Aristotle added, at Lyons, was intended to set the record straight. For the most part it did just that, although I can attest from my own examination that its disjointed and frequently cryptic style, its numerous printing errors, and its principal editor's tendency to write usually in the editorial first person singular, look like signs of haste in its production. Despite that, however, the work overall is excellent, and even though it might have been designed by a committee, it is anything but a camel.

The Conimbricenses' project was in the form of Aristotelian commentary. To be more exact, it was commentary *per modum quaestionis*. The Logic in the Lyons edition is a good example of this at its best. Through two main parts, the *Conimbricenses* have reviewed individual treatises of the *Organon*. For each treatise, they give the Greek of Aristotle, translate it into Latin, summarize its philosophical doctrine, and then comment on it by raising *questions* which it had occasioned among the Scholastics of the 16th and earlier centuries. Their scholarship, as regards Greek, Latin, philosophy, and the Scholastic tradition before them is quite evident. Evident also is the genuine character and depth of their own philosophical interest.

The particular work with which I am concerned is the *commentary* on Aristotle's *De Interpretatione*. More precisely, my concern is with the first chapter of that commentary. Entitled *De Signo* ("On the Sign"), it runs over sixty pages in quarto.

The die was cast. The "burning and inevitable problem" Augustine handed the Latins at the outset of their historical age, "constantly alive" throughout that age, as Beuchot said and as we ourselves have seen, had soon, one way or another, to be laid to rest. Either it would flare to light a new Age of Understanding, or it

---

25 Stegmuller 1959: 95–7 goes into the attribution of each volume to its respective editor; further scholarly sources on the matter are indicated by Doyle 1998: 18n6.

26 Doyle 1994: 567–8. See also Stegmuller 1959: 95–8; Sommervogel 1891.

would be extinguished once and for all. Fonseca hoped for a *requiescat in pace*. He counted on his Coimbra colleagues for the interment.[27] He did not live to see his disappointment.

Second Outcome: The Conimbricenses (1606, 1607)

The Conimbricenses were members of the faculty of the University of Coimbra at the time John Poinsot was an undergraduate student there. The last mention of Poinsot in the Coimbra archives is on 8 May 1606, as "having attended the first-year theological lectures". If Fonseca thought that the work the Conimbricenses undertook in 1592, seven years before his death, would result in a setting of the Latin record straight on the subject of signs along the lines he envisaged in his *Institutions*, had he lived to see their treatise *De Signo* it may have been for him something of a rude shock.

The Second Part of Augustine's Definition

There is no telling, at least to my knowledge, whether it was directly from suggestions of Fonseca or only indirectly and more on their own that the Conimbricenses took the tack that they did. But it was to prove the decisive one. By decisive here I mean the turn to face directly the problems raised by the second part of Augustine's original definition, according to which a sign is distinguished by always bringing into awareness something other (*aliquid aliud*).

That this part of the foundational problem of semiotics came only gradually to the foreground of the Latin discussions is a matter of historical record. Augustine's original definition of *signum* stood as long as it did precisely because it accommodated the "common sense" tendency to identify signs with sense-perceptible objects. In doing this, it also accommodated the notion that, among the objects of our experience, some are signs, others merely objects. Even the expansion of the notion of sign to include interior or psychological states did not definitively rule on the question of whether signs are, as it were, a permanent class to which certain things belong but not others.[28]

Yet the sign-vehicle, be it a material structure accessible to outward sense or a psychological structure of inward experience, requires always the conveyance of a content distinct from itself as object signified. This essential link to a content formally distinct from the vehicle conveying that content pertains to the distinctive feature constituting any sign as such, regardless of what things are to be included under the heading of sign. So much is this so that we may say that, among all the authors, ancient as well as medieval or modern, who have treated of signs the one

---

27 The depositing of a dead body in the earth or in a tomb.
28 Consider the curious remark reported in Collis 1954: 26–7. In the first contact of the Spaniards with the Maya in 1517, having sailed from Cuba to Catoche, Mexico, at the top of the Yucatan, Bernal Diaz remarked of the natives that "it was impossible to converse with them except by signs."

point of common agreement that emerges across all the discussions is that a sign, *whatever else it may be*, is, in every instance, something relative, *aliquid relativum*.

When they finally got around to looking closely at this part common to the whole variety of competing descriptions of phenomena cited as "signifying", the late Latins found themselves in an especially privileged position. They were not only the heir of the ancient Greek discussions of relation. This ancient discussion had been given in Latin what would prove to be a decisive new twist by the Boethian translations of Aristotle's work on the categories, according to which (at least so thought the Latin Aristotle) we speak of being as thought to exist in its own right. I am referring here to the Boethian coinage of the expression *relatio secundum dici*, "relation according to the requirements of expressing being in discourse", also called "transcendental relation", which we discussed at some length in chapter 6. At this point it would be well to review that discussion.[29]

Resuming the Ancient Discussion in Latin Terms
Try to get the key terms as reasonably clear in your mind as you can.

Remember that everything has to be explained in terms of something besides itself: this is all that "transcendental relation" means. The expression "transcendental relation" is not quite literal, because what it names are subjects of existence with their subjective characteristics, not relations as such.[30]

But one among the many things to be explained is what exists not as or within an individual, but with its whole being between other things: this is what "relation" or "pure relation" or "relation as such" signifies.[31] A relation as such may exist in the environment or in thought. When it exists in the environment it is called a "physical relation", also a "mind-independent relation".[32] When it exists in only thought it is called a "mind-dependent relation".[33] Mind-independent or physical relations, because they belong to the category of real being, are also called "categorial relation" or "praedicamental[34] relation". Thus "categorial relation", "physical relation", and "mind-independent relation" are synonymous terms.

"Ontological relation"[35] is the term used to express the fact that a relation may have a source in nature or in thought, but in either case the relation as such remains a pure relation. And, finally, "objective relation" simply means a relation existing as known, as an object of awareness, regardless of whether it exists in nature *as well* as in thought or *only* in thought. Thus, a mind-independent relation may or

---

29 See p. 227ff. in chapter 6.
30 See chapter 6, p. 228f.
31 See chapter 6, p. 227.
32 See chapter 6, p. 229.
33 See chapter 6, p. 229f.
34 "Praedicamentum", remember, being the Latin term for "category" considered in relation to linguistic expressions univocally predicable or "able to be said" of objects which have as well subjective existence and being. See chapter 6, p. 229 above.
35 See chapter 6, p. 230f.

may not be an objective relation, and an objective relation may or may not be a mind-independent relation. The same for an ontological relation: it may or may not be known. If known and mind-independent in its circumstances, the relation will be objective as well as physical; if not, the relation will be purely physical.

With these terms refreshed, let us take up the discussion of relation at the point where the Latins themselves focused on it in passing from the so-called Dark Ages to the so-called High Middle Ages of Aquinas and Scotus. The dispute, remember,[36] centered on whether in the physical world there were only transcendental relations.[37]

---

36 See chapter 6, "Purely Objective Relations", p. 229f.
37 A reviewer of the manuscript at this point remarked that "the discussion of 'transcendental relation' seems to reduce 'real' relation to physical categories, thus bypassing the mediaeval discussion of 'transcendentalia' in precisely their trans- or meta-physical scope, all but two of them (*ens, res*) being 'extrinsically' relational but not thereby necessarily physical". So one has to realize that the discussion of the term "physical" among the Latins (see chapter 8 above, p. 382) needs further clarification. I expand the text of the following paragraphs to try to make clear why the notion of "transcendental relation" is synonymous with the subjective categories of physical being (substance and its inherent accidents), in sharp (but overlapping, and therein lies the difficulty) contrast with the *transcendentalia*, the so-called "transcendental properties of being", which, like relation itself, exceed the subjective order without being reducible to fictions, to purely objective *entia rationis*.

But what needs to be noted here is that the rationale of what came to be called, after Aquinas (notably c.1256/9: *Quaestiones disputatae de veritate*, q. 1c, as we saw in chapter 7), the "transcendental properties of being" or *transcendentalia* is *neither* that of the *relativum secundum dici seu relatio transcendentalis*, the "transcendental relative", *nor* that of the *relatio secundum esse*, the "ontological relation", for both of these pertain to the expression of *ens primum cognitum* as restricted to special modalities, the modalities of subjectivity and suprasubjectivity. The *transcendentalia* or "transcendental properties of being", by contrast, pertain to the expression of *ens primum cognitum* not as it contracts to distinct modalities of this or that kind but according as it enfolds all the beings of experience in common or general modalities which, as "general" or "common", pertain to all beings insofar as they are capable of existence. And just as beings are capable of existence according to both subjective and suprasubjective modalities, so the transcendental properties of being in general follow upon not one or the other but upon both of these rationales of possible existence.

Insofar as a being has a rationale of existence, regardless of whether the rationale in question be subjective (*esse in*) or intersubjective (*esse ad*), a being is said to be, in general, "a thing", *res*, just as it is said to be "a being", *ens*, insofar as it exercises a rationale of existence. And any being considered in terms of the rationale according to which it exercises existence, whether the existence exercised be subjective or suprasubjective, is said to be "one thing", *unum*. And this one thing, if contrasted to anything or everything other than itself, is said to be "something", *aliquid*, that is to say, "other" (*aliud*) than what makes up the rest of the world (*quid*), or "something other". Finally, any one being can be considered in relation to any other being in terms of desire, whence it is said to be "good", *bonum*; or in terms of cognition, whence it is said to be *verum*, or "true" (which can be further subdivided as providing the basis for what is known, as consisting in what is known, or as the expression of what is known [cf. Poinsot 1643], which in turn raises the possibility of being mistaken, and the whole question of nonbeing, as we have seen).

So the classical transcendentals, *ens, res, unum, aliquid, bonum, verum, involve* the rationale of transcendental relation *and* the rationale of ontological relation but *do not reduce to either* of these two rationales. The *transcendentalia* express something different: just as "transcendental and ontological relation" together express the totality of special rationales according to which being as first known can be contracted to and further subdivided within the orders of what is and what is not

According to one side in the controversy that developed after Boethius, categorial relations, supposedly physical, are not so. That is a mistake. There are no physical relations. So-called categorial relations are, in reality, only comparisons made by the mind, *relationes rationis*, in the consideration of objects. As thoughts they are real, but as what is *signified* by thought, as objective, they are *purely* objective, that is to say, objective without any mind-independent counterpart, *without* any intrusion of physicality within the objectivity. This last was a view which, as we have seen, came widely to be held among those later Latins who came to call themselves "*Nominalistae*", that loose confederation of thinkers that came to be especially (but not exclusively) associated with the work of the fourteenth century scholastic William of Ockham.

The Thomists and the Scotists made up the two other main schools of late-medieval thought, the Latin Age from the fourteenth to the seventeenth century. They held, on the contrary, that so-called "relations of reason" (or mind-dependent relations) are indeed *essentially* relative but are yet distinct from any being essentially relative in a categorial sense. The reason was clearly stated by Aquinas:[38] "only things independent of the soul pertain to the categories". Yet what *is* essentially relative in a categorial sense is indeed *essentially* relative, that is to say, based upon but not reduced to some *other* category of *inherent* or *subjectively modifying* characteristic or "accident". So, since both mind-dependent and mind-independent relations have the same essence of a suprasubjective "being toward" over and above their subjective foundation, basis, or ground in an object (or subject, if the object happens to be a physical individual as well as a cognized one), only circumstances external to the relation itself determine whether the relation itself belongs *hic et nunc*, "here and now", to one or the other order.

A given relation, "predicate", say, may be such that it can only belong to the objective order, not by reason of its essential nature, that is to say, not by reason of being a relation according to the way it has being, but simply by reason of some

---

independent of the activity of the finite mind (while ontological relation as a special rationale has the further function of explaining how these two orders interpenetrate in experience as a consequence of the unique general property of being that attaches to signs as ontologically relative, making the distinctive action of signs, "semiosis", possible, as we are in the process of seeing in this and the following two chapters), so the "transcendental properties of being" express the general rationales according to which being as first known permeates and overflows all the contractions to specific or special modes. I hope this sufficiently clarifies the point which caused the reviewer to raise objection.

38   Aquinas c.1265/6: *Quaestiones disputatae de potentia*, q. 7, art. 9c (Busa 3, p. 246): "in nullo autem praedicamento ponitur aliquid nisi res extra animam existens. nam ens rationis dividitur contra ens divisum per decem praedicamenta, ut patet v metaph. si autem relatio non esset in rebus extra animam, non poneretur ad aliquid unum genus praedicamenti, et praeterea perfectio et bonum quae sunt in rebus extra animam, non solum attenditur secundum aliquid absolute inhaerens rebus, sed etiam secundum ordinem unius rei ad aliam, sicut etiam in ordine partium exercitus, bonum exercitus consistit. ... oportet ergo in ipsis rebus ordinem quemdam esse; hic autem ordo relatio quaedam est. unde oportet in rebus ipsis relationes quasdam esse, secundum quas unum ad alterum ordinatur."

circumstance extrinsic to that essential nature which prevents the given instance of relation from being realized independently of cognitive activity. But another given relation, "offspring", say, is such that it can belong to the subjective order as well as the objective order, not as a subject, of course, but as dependent upon and really characterizing a subject – really being an offspring of that individual regardless of whether the fact is known, not known, or denied. Neither substance nor any inherent accident, neither a subject of existence nor any of its subjective modifications, has this indifference to the distinction between the order of what is, and the order of what is not, capable of existence independently of the cognitive activity of organisms in particular or some finite mind in general. For though there can indeed be fictional substances and fictional subjective characteristics of substances, yet these are, *as fictional, essentially* relative, which is *not* what they would be were they not fictional. Non-fictional being may have the character of *esse in* or *esse ad*, depending upon whether the real being in question is a subject, a subjective characteristic, or an intersubjective (so a-fortiori suprasubjective) characteristic; but a fictional being as such has only the character of an *esse ad*, a being relative to some discursive activity apart from which it would have no *being* at all. All fictional beings are *entia non realia* and as such pure relations; but some non-fictional beings as well are pure relations and as such *entia realia*. So *entia realia*, the realm of the categories, includes relations and more than relations; but *non ens*, the realm of fictions, includes nothing more than relations.

The categories in mainstream medieval thought are only those univocal ontological rationales according to which instances of physical being, whether subjective or suprasubjective, in order to be understood, must be thought. Categorial relation, even though relative in its very definition (as is also any relation formed in and by thought, any *relatio rationis*), cannot yet be reduced to any "relation of reason" because we find in our experience of objects relative aspects which are not invented by us, that is, essential relativities which are discovered and not created.[39] Contemporary examples would be the order in a marching column of army ants, which is something over and above the individual ants as such; or the revolution of the planets around our sun rather than *e converso* (a point on which the medievals themselves were notoriously confused, well illustrating the essential and functional equivalence between categorial and rational relations as objective relations).

In chapter 6 we have already called attention to the early discovery that categorial and rational relations share alike a common "essence" or definability as something whose whole being consists in a reference to another.[40] And we pointed out there that no one at the time took special note of this discovery because attention was focused elsewhere. In the early medieval debates over relation, the center of interest was on *differences* between physical being (*ens reale*) and logical being (*ens rationis*). The early Latins noticed this point of similarity unique to the case of relation as a curiosity

---

39 Cf. Poinsot 1632a: 86/6–19.
40 See "The Ontological Peculiarity of Relation" in chapter 6, p. 230f.

– curious enough to make of it passing mention, but nothing more. The expression they used to designate relation in its indifference to the distinction between mind-independent and mind-dependent being, we saw, was *relatio secundum esse*, though several centuries later "ontological" was proposed as a one-word translation for "secundum esse" to parallel "transcendental" for *secundum dici*. No synonyms or short versions of this expression were ever developed among the Latins, because the point was never generally thematized. By contrast, a Latin stipulation was introduced to make "transcendental" an equivalent for *relativum secundum dici*.

But now we have reached the point in the discussion of sign among the Latins where the pertinence of the development of these points concerning the theory of relation to the foundations of the doctrine of signs begins to be apparent. We have reached the point where the whole previous discussion of relation over centuries suddenly becomes directly relevant to the contemporary controversy (I mean contemporary to the Conimbricenses, Araújo, Poinsot, and the other Latins of the time).

For once attention began to focus on the differentiative part of Augustine's definition as revised to include psychological as well as physical vehicles of signification, the Latin authors were forced to begin to address directly the import of the sign as a relative being. Since a sign, in every case, imports "something relative to something else", *aliquid stans pro alio*, what precise meaning is to attach to the "relative to" (the *stans pro*) in the semiotic case, the case of the sign as such?

Focusing the Controversy over Signum
Given the terms of the medieval development of the notion of relative being, the Latin discussion at this turn could be given a very precise sense: Is the sign to be identified with a being relative in the transcendental sense (*secundum dici*) or in the ontological sense (*secundum esse*)? For once it is understood that the whole of the physical universe is relative at least transcendentally (i.e., in its explainability) and sometimes perhaps ontologically as well (i.e., in its very definition), then it is also clear that anything relative must be relative in at least one of these two senses. The sign precisely as such is a relative being, to be sure; but every being that is relative is so either transcendentally only or ontologically as well. Which is the case for the sign? Very soon, we will see that the late Latin discussion of sign actually came to be stated in just these terms.[41] But, as a matter of historical fact and as we have painfully seen, only slowly and with much preliminary groping was this level of clarity in principle reached.

Whether the Latin author who initiated the turn of the discussion in this direction was Pedro da Fonseca himself or not, the Hispanic Aristotelian school he inspired most certainly did begin to frame the discussion of sign in these terms of the classical

---

41 Poinsot, *Tractatus de Signis* (1632a), Book I, *Concerning the Sign in Its Proper Being*, Question 1, "Whether a Sign Is in the Order of Relation", 117/18–23.

Latin discussion of relation since Boethius, but especially after Aquinas.[42] Compared to the writings after the Conimbricenses, earlier discussions of sign which speak mainly in terms of categorial relation (such as the 1267 *De Signis* of Roger Bacon) appear as hopelessly naive. How far the Conimbricenses had advanced in realizing the perspective of semiotic can be seen in the following remark: "There is nothing which leads to the cognition of anything else which cannot be reduced to some sort of sign".[43]

Unfortunately, two points confused the developing discussion as first Fonseca and now the Conimbricenses influenced it. Natural signs, such as clouds or smoke, seemed to belong to the order of physical being, whereas conventional signs, such as words or monuments, seemed rather to be *entia rationis*, mind-dependent beings. Transcendental relatives pertained to the physical order, while rational relatives pertained to the logical or cultural order. Hence, as we saw, Fonseca opined that "formal" signs are perhaps not signs in the same sense as "instrumental" signs.[44] And we find that the Conimbricenses, citing as their principal predecessors in this view Alexander of Hales (1185–1245) and Peter of Ledesma (d. 1616), identify signs as being or being like transcendental relatives in all cases. That is, they identify a sign as consisting mainly and essentially in the foundation for a given sign relation. This foundation is a physical structure in the case of natural signs and a cultural construction in the case of conventional signs.

The discussion in the Conimbricenses' text moves in a direction which is not quite the one Fonseca had envisaged, but somewhat contrary thereto. Fonseca, recall, had moved in the direction of denying sign-status to the concept, and so denying that sign as a general mode of being can be verified within as well as outside the mind. By contrast, the discussion of the Conimbricenses affirms that, after all, there is indeed a unified subject matter for semiotic inquiry, a common meaning behind the general term *signum* that extends to the *verbum mentis*, the concept, and the *verbum vocis*, language, as well as to natural objects, σημεῖα. The unified subject matter consists in the different ways in which relations can be founded in the structures of subjective being.

But the price for unification of the doctrine of signs along the lines drawn by the Conimbricenses is enormous. For if this position is correct, then the whole view of sign as consisting in a true relation, a suprasubjective mode of being as such,[45] and an irreducibly triadic one at that, has been mistaken. What a sign consists in rather is the foundation from which a relation provenates, a *relatio secundum dici*; it does not consist in the relation itself so provenating, a *relatio secundum esse*. In other

---

42 Conimbricenses 1606, 1607: *De Signo*. See Doyle 1994 for a magnificent though brief summary.
43 Conimbricenses 1607: q. 2, art. 3, p. 27.
44 Fonseca 1564: lib. 1. cap. 8. See p. 415ff., esp. 416, above.
45 A *relatio secundum esse*, a relation according to the way relation has being, an ontological relation; in contrast to transcendental relation, a *relatio secundum dici*, which consists in the various factors which are necessary to bring into consideration for the purpose of understanding the status of any individual being or event in its subjectivity within the physical surroundings.

words, the general mode of being in which sign consists is as such part of the order of subjectivity. It does not as such rise above or stand outside that order; it is of a piece with it – *illi imbibita*, "assimilated thereto" or "part and parcel thereof", in Poinsot's memorable designation.[46]

But if the sign does not consist in a true relation, it is difficult or impossible to see how it can serve as the medium of *communication between* two or more individuals of whatever species or type. For the transcendental relation knows, in Peirce's terms, only the "communication" of brute force or Secondness, that is, physical interaction. And even though a transcendental relation may *give rise to* a true relation as suprasubjective, suprasubjectivity by itself (we will see this with Kant) is not enough to guarantee *communication*. Communication requires *actual intersubjectivity*, and the only thing that guarantees actual intersubjectivity within the order of experience as involving cognition is not mind-dependent relation (which is suprasubjective but not necessarily intersubjective) nor even categorial relation (which is intersubjective as well as suprasubjective but not necessarily objective, that is to say, not necessarily involved within cognition). No. The only thing that guarantees intersubjectivity as a possibility realizable within cognitive experience is the *indifference* of relation according to its suprasubjective rationale to the exercise of existence based on nature alone, cognition alone, or nature and cognition together. Ontological relation is neither categorial relation nor purely objective relation but the possibility of both or either. Transcendental relation is neither categorial relation nor any objective relation, it is rather the objectification of subjective being as knowable.

By going the Conimbricenses' route, the doctrine of signs is unified, but the sign is destroyed in the process. Augustine has won, but, on the Conimbricenses' accounting, his victory proves pyrrhic. Maybe even the hopes of Fonseca to defeat the general notion would have been sufficiently satisfied by the awarding of victory on these terms!

Well, since the sign is triadic, it is fitting that there should be three endings to the Latin story that began with Augustine and took more than a thousand years to tell. We have seen the denouement of Fonseca and Ockham: Augustine's idea was an illusion. We see now the denouement of the group Fonseca founded in part, as we may harbor suspicion, to help settle the matter: Augustine's idea was no illusion, but it was not what he thought it was either; for the sign is not beyond the order of subjectivity, but part and parcel thereof. The third outcome is perhaps the most satisfying one: Augustine's proposal was a stroke of genius, for, without knowing how, he had put his finger on the manner in which the universe, at every level, from the divine being down to the slime mold and below, brings about semiosis, that is to say, an action of signs, from which follows whatever communication transpires among finite beings whenever it occurs – what the later moderns would more obscurely identify under the heading of "evolution".

---

46 *Tractatus de Signis*, Second Preamble, art. 2, 92/25.

The Vindication of Augustine: John Poinsot (1589–1644)

In a tale as long as this we can afford to be brief in the conclusion. For so many aspects of the story have had to be told along the way that by the time we have reached this point we can well dispense with long preliminaries and "cut to the chase".

Augustine of Hippo began the medieval semiotic development with a question disguised in the form of a proposition: Does the sign as the means of knowing have a being which transcends the divide between nature and culture? John Poinsot ended the medieval development with the answer to this question that explicitly justified Augustine's original implicit proposal. Poinsot's *Treatise on Signs*, essayed in the very year of John Locke's birth (1632), provided semiotic inquiry, to guide its investigations, for the first time with the thematic realization of a unified subject matter involved with, but also outside of, the subjective order.

Poinsot answers the question bequeathed by Augustine of how the ancient dichotomy between the causal relations linking natural phenomena to the things of which they are signs and the imaginary relations linking cultural phenomena to the things of which *they* are "signs" is overcome in the being of the sign. For the being proper to a sign consists, in every case, of neither a transcendental nor a categorial nor a rational relation, but simply of an ontological relation (a *relatio secundum esse* as expressing the single definable structure common to relation regardless of the circumstances extraneously further differentiating the realization of this structure as categorial or "rational", physical or objective, at a given moment).

Poinsot had the advantage of the whole Latin tradition of discussion of relative being to draw on. But what was decisive was that he had the insight of how to apply the many distinctions of that tradition to the question so as to get a resolution. He saw at once that if all being is relative, but either subjectively so in the rationale of transcendental relativity or suprasubjectively in the rationale of ontological relativity (and in the latter case indifferently to the question of whether the source of the relation under varying circumstances be thought or nature), then the question of the being proper to every sign as such all but answers itself by the very terms in which it has now been posed.

The Standpoint of Semiotic

In effecting his answer to the profound question of how the being of sign is able to bridge nature and culture, thought and being, Poinsot begins his *Treatise* with exactly the point that Augustine's famous and first attempt at a general definition of sign had presupposed. Instead of simply stating what a sign is, Poinsot asks rather what a sign must be in order to function in the way that we all experience it to function, namely, as indifferent to the distinction between real and imaginary being, truth and falsehood, or as conveying indifferently cultural and natural objects.[47]

---

47 *Tractatus de Signis*, Book I, Question 1, 117/18–119/9.

To answer this question,[48] Poinsot distinguishes sharply, as had Soto, between *representation* and *signification*. This distinction becomes his basis for differentiating between signs and objects: an object may represent itself, but a sign must represent another than itself. Thus, representation is involved in the being proper to a sign as the foundation for the relation of signification, but the signification itself always and necessarily consists in the relation as such, which is over and above that characteristic of a material being or psychological state of an organism upon which the relation itself is founded.

Signification is opposed from the outset to whatever exists as an individual material entity or aspect thereof, that is, to subjective being in its entire extent. Signification is always something over and above its foundation in some individual being or material object, something superordinate thereto, something of its very nature *intersubjective*, either actually or prospectively. Signs act through their foundation, but the actual sign as such is not the foundation but the relation which exists over and above that foundation linking it as sign-vehicle to some object signified.

This object signified, in turn, may or may not also be an existing thing, that is to say, it may or may not have as a dimension of its being an indifference to whether or not it is signified (inasmuch as it may *also* happen to exist apart from the signification).[49] But this further dimension and status of the object, exactly as Scotus said, is a matter of indifference to the sign as such. For the sign as such consists purely and simply in the *relation between* sign-vehicle and object signified, effected as such through an interpretant, an actual or prospective observer, as we might say. This relation is not affected intrinsically by the conditions which affect the subjective status in reality of the object signified in any being it may happen to have apart from the signification.[50]

Thus, *things* are fundamentally distinct, in Poinsot's semiotic, from *objects*, in that the former do not necessarily while the latter do necessarily involve a relation to a knower. Things may or may not also be objects, and objects may or may not also be things. But every object signified exists as such as the terminus of a sign relation. Whatever exists as a thing has a subjective structure, that is to say, a structure indifferent to being or not being known. But whatever exists as signified has an objective structure as terminus of a relation founded upon and correlated with[51] some subjective structure of being, such as the psychological reality of a concept in the mind or the physical reality of a spoken, written, or gestured word. Signs mediate between objects and things by giving

48 Ibid.: 119/10–124/39.
49 Cf. Poinsot 1632a: Book III, Questions 1 and 2; Raposa 1994.
50 Cf. Book I, Question 4, 166/1–180/7.
51 The correlation with the fundament gives to the terminus its objective status as extrinsic formal cause, something that does not belong to it simply and formally as terminus, but only as terminus *opposed* to ("obicitur") the concept or feeling as fundament.

rise to objects as significates[52] and by the partial objectification of things in sensation.[53]

Whence objects participate in the indifference of sign relations to being based in cultural or natural constructions, and sign-vehicles are distinct from signs as the foundations of relations are distinct from the relations they found. The foundation as such belongs to subjective being, whereas the relation as such is always suprasubjective. So is the object as such which terminates the relation, even though nothing prevents this object from coinciding materially with some actual structure of subjective being – again, either natural or cultural.

Reaching the Type Constituting Whatever Token

Previous medieval criticisms of Augustine's original attempt to define sign in general, brought from the University of Paris to the Iberian university world, notably by Dominic Soto in the early sixteenth century, had gone no further than to distinguish between signs whose relation to the object signified was founded on physical structures of subjectivity accessible to outer sense (the case of so-called *instrumental* signs, to which alone Augustine's definition applies), and signs whose relation to the object signified was founded on psychological structures accessible to inner sense and understanding (the case of so-called *formal* signs). Despite the novelty of the terminology, the reasoning itself of Soto and his Paris masters, when it was not nominalistic, amounted to nothing that could not already be found explicitly in Scotus and Aquinas. One of Poinsot's contemporaries, Francisco Araújo, made express note of this point: "What Soto says amounts to what we find in Aquinas".[54]

By contrast, the work of Poinsot advanced the discussion dramatically. The originality of Poinsot's advance is underscored by contemporary testimony. In the inventory of Latin opinions provided by Araújo's synoptic presentation of Latin discussions of sign up to 1617, Poinsot's solution to the problem of sign is conspicuous by its absence.[55] That is to say, as of 1617, the solution on which Poinsot was already at work and would propound in his *Tractatus* of 1632 had yet to be propounded. Poinsot showed that the vaunted distinction between formal and instrumental signs circulated throughout Iberia after Soto was in fact a consideration secondary to the primary consideration of the being proper to the sign as such consisting in a pure relation according to the way relation has being.[56]

---

52 Cf. Book I, Question 1, 122/17–123/25; Question 3, 161/24–34; Question 5, 195/18–29.
53 See Book I, Question 6, esp. 209/34–47, 210/25–32, 211/29–213/7; and Book III, Questions 1 and 2.
54 Araújo 1617, lib. iii, q. 2, art. 2, dubium 1: "in idem incidit dictum Magistri Soto".
55 Araújo 1617: the series of four "*Dubitatur*" following the treatment of first intentions. In *Dubitatur I* Araújo gives his own view that there is not a single rationale for natural and conventional signs but only "an analogy of two concepts", as is also the case for "signs whose signifieds exist and signs whose signifieds don't exist", which, however, leaves the doctrine of signs in essentially the circumstances assigned to it by the Conimbricenses.
56 Poinsot 1632a: *Tractatus de Signis*, Book II, Question 1, 223/1–229/38.

For signs are called "formal" or "instrumental" not according to what is proper to them as signs but only according to the representative aspect which in the sign belongs to the *foundation* of the sign relation rather than to the *relation itself* in which the sign as such exists in its actual signification.[57] The same point applies, however, to the other main traditional division of sign into natural and conventional. Like the division of signs into formal and instrumental, this division, too, into natural and conventional is made not from the point of view of that which constitutes every sign as such, but from the point of view rather of that subjective or "absolute" characteristic of some individual which makes of that individual the foundation for a relation in the essential sense of existing over and above its subjective ground. Yet what constitutes every sign as such is an ontological relation triadic in character (which may be either rational and purely objective or categorial – physical as well as objective – depending on circumstances, and even sometimes one and sometimes the other, also depending on circumstances). And this relation is always suprasubjective, sometimes intersubjective, never subjective. Hence, it cannot be identified with any *term* in the sign relation, not even that term from which the sign-relation primarily performs its function as *vehicle* for the presentation of something (namely, the signified object) which neither the sign vehicle nor the sign relation itself is. Never identified with any one term, in fact, the sign as such *consists* in the uniting or nexus of the three terms – sign-vehicle (that from which representation is made), interpretant (that to which representation is made), object signified (that which is represented). "By the one single sign-relation which constitutes the proper being of the sign," Poinsot says,[58] are the three terms of sign-vehicle, object signified, and prospective observer brought into unity.

The line of argument is as novel as the conclusion to which it leads, a conclusion which, like Darwin's positing of natural selection and many a great thesis of science and philosophy, seems obvious once it has been stated. Since rational and categorial relations have the same essence or definable structure of essential relatives which, as such, exist dependent upon some subjective foundation but as superordinate to that foundation, it matters not whether the foundation be a material structure or a psychological structure or the quasi-unconscious habit structure of a convention: in

---

57 Poinsot 1632a: Book I, Question 3, 163/28–36, italics added: "this division of signs into instrumental and formal presupposes in the signs themselves diverse manners of stimulatively moving and representing to the cognitive power, specifically, as an external object or as an internal form; *yet this is related presuppositively to the rationale of sign*, whereas the most formal rationale of a sign consists in being something substituted for a significate, whether as an object external or as representable within the power." See also Book I, Question 2, 142/16–145/28, esp. 143/21–144/5; Book II, Question 5, esp. 271/22–42.

58 Book I, Question 3, 154/25–9: "Si vero consideretur potentia ut terminus in obliquo attactus, sic unica relatione signi attingitur signatum et potentia, et haec est propria et formalis ratio signi." – "If indeed the cognitive power", that is, that to which representation is made, what Peirce will later generalize under the term *interpretant*, "is considered as a term indirectly attained, then the object signified and the power are attained by the single relation in which the sign has its formal and proper rationale."

whatever case, the foundation as such does not constitute the sign formally, the sign in its proper being as sign.

And whether the foundation gives rise to a categorial relation or a mind-dependent relation makes no difference to the fact that the relation to which it gives rise is what constitutes the sign formally as a sign. *This* relation is in either case an ontological relation in contrast to a transcendental relation. Moreover, whether the circumstances surrounding the relation in which the sign consists make that relation to be purely objective or physical and categorial as well as objective is a matter of indifference to the sign as such, precisely because and inasmuch as this distinction (whether the sign relation is purely objective or physical and categorial as well as objective) normally depends on circumstances extrinsic to the signification. Thus, a dinosaur bone recognized as such functions as a natural sign vehicle, even though the objective relation to which it gives rise here and now, which would be categorial if the dinosaur were alive, is purely rational in the circumstance of the dinosaur's now not existing.

With this identification of signs with pure relations as such medieval semiotic reaches its highest point of development. The question of whether signs can be identified with any definite class of things able to exist subjectively, whether as physical or as psychological realities, is definitely answered in the negative. In every case, the sign as such, consisting in the relation between sign-vehicle and object signified, is something suprasubjective and invisible to sense. Those "things" or perceived objects which we call signs, such as traffic lights, barber poles, words, and so on, are not, technically speaking, *signs* but the *vehicles* of signification. The actual *signification itself* consists in the relation between the vehicles and the knowability of their objective content. Similarly, those psychological states such as images or concepts called by the later medievals "formal signs" are not technically speaking signs but the *vehicles* of signification.

A New Definition of Signum

At this stage of discussion a new definition of signs may be said to be implicit: a sign is that which any object presupposes. Any subjective structure, whether physical or psychological, is never a sign strictly speaking but merely something which *can* *enter* into a sign relation, either as its foundation (as sign-vehicle) or as its terminus or ground[59] (as or "within" an object signified) or as its interpretant (as that to which the significate is presented through the sign-vehicle), or as now one, now the other, in an unending process of developing and changing significations. The being in which the sign, properly and formally speaking, consists is never some object as such, nor is it any subjectivity as such. The being in which the sign properly and formally consists is rather each strand in the network of real and unreal relations in function of which whatever objects appear exist as objects (as nodes or termini in the network of relations) in the first place.

---

59 See, in chapter 15, the discussion of "Ground", p. 641ff.

The medieval distinction between "things" as what exist whether or not known and "objects" as whatever exists as known appears in Poinsot's synthesis as mediated by "signs" as a third term of the distinction. For things cannot become fully objects except through psychological states and conditions. And psychological states and conditions cannot exist as such save through giving rise to relations indifferently categorial or imaginary ("rational" in the broadest sense of mind-dependent). These relations founded upon psychological states have as their terminus objects indifferently *also* physical (such as the planets and stars and whatever of the physical universe happens to be known at any given time) or *merely* objective (as in the case of leprechauns, dragons, and Dracula). In either case, the "objects signified" hold their place among the many objective features constituting the world of experience, a mixture of "nature" and "culture". These objects known, in their turn, become signs of one another as new relations among them are imagined or discovered. And so, in the end, the universe as a whole, in terms of medieval semiotic theory, exactly as Peirce later projected,[60] comes to be "perfused with signs, if it does not consist exclusively of them". For now we see that there are signs and there are signifieds, and that whatever is signified can itself become a sign in relation to other objects signified!

One Further Augustinian Heritage: Grammatical Theory and Modistae as a Minor Tradition of Latin Semiotics

Beginning in the later years of the lifetime of Aquinas, various thinkers, known in retrospect as "modists" ("modistae") from their emphasis on the influence of syntax on significations within discourse, tried to establish the notion of "grammatical universals" at work in language, "speculative grammar", as they called the quest. I do not want to go into great detail, not because "the modistae were stupid", as a famous scholar in semiotics once said of his reason for dismissing them in favor of a major allotment of time to Aquinas instead, but because in the end their development contributed little or nothing of major significance to the understanding of sign in general that finally emerged from the mainstream philosophical and logical discussions of the Latin Age. Perhaps such a denouement was to be expected from the detailed nature of their work entirely tied to that grand part of the order of *ens rationis* familiar to schoolchildren as "grammar". Still, their idea for a *grammatica speculativa*, a "speculative grammar", caught the imagination of no less a postmodern figure than Charles Peirce himself, and is reflected at every point in the late-modern essays[61] on "generative grammar". It might have come to something; it just didn't in fact, and there may be (I suspect there are) reasons in principle for the failure.

---

60 Peirce 1905–6: CP 5.448n.
61 I say "late-modern", in contrast to the seminally postmodern efforts of Peirce, because the end-of-the-20th-century notions of "generative grammar" have the pure flavor of Cartesianism, as we will see in chapter 17.

What could be a more obvious point of departure in attempting to develop a theory of signs than human language, far and away the most important system of significations day to day. Well, there are actually a number of major considerations which militate against this as a good idea; but being a bad idea is not necessarily proof against its being tried. And nothing so determines the specifically linguistic conveyance of significations as does the grammar, the syntax, the specific organization of a given natural language. Indeed, the arts of language identified in the *trivium* (logic, grammar, and rhetoric) had come to be known as *scientiae sermocinales*, "the word-based sciences", we might perhaps say.

By one of history's famous ironies, the attempt to visualize a science of signs from the irreducibly anthropocentric and narrow base of the *scientiae sermocinales*, grammar in particular, since this has a controlling role in the more permanent (written) expression of both logic and rhetoric, came to a head around 1260–80, the very years in which Aquinas wrote the materials that Poinsot would undertake to synthesize as the first theoretically unified semiotic or doctrine of signs. The effort, naturally enough, took for a master the sixth century work of Priscian ("Priscianus Caesariensis", fifth-sixth century AD), the prolific and important Latin grammarian whose stature was hardly diminished by his having done his work in the high prominence of the imperial context of Constantinople. He came to exercise over the Latin Age an influence equal to and in some respects surpassing that of Donatus,[62] whose *Ars Minor* (a.AD349) was a staple of the period and on into modern times. Priscian's main work, the *Institutiones Grammaticae*, or "Grammatical Foundations", in eighteen books,[63] exists in a thousand medieval Latin manuscripts. The first sixteen books, which treat of morphology ("De accidentibus"), are often copied separately and given the collective title of *Priscianus Maior* by the Latins. The last two books treat of syntax, and are called the *Priscianus Minor*; but it should be noted that these

---

62 Aelius Donatus (c.AD310–380) was, if not the first, at least the second most important grammarian of the Latin language. St Jerome (a.AD347–419/20), who created the Latin Vulgate Bible, in fact, was one of his pupils. His *floruit* is assigned to a.AD354–463 (Holtz 1981: 15–16). We know that Jerome as a teenager went to Rome for study with Donatus, already famed (c.AD363), and that his work had been consulted since c.AD350; so perhaps we might take p.AD349 as the approximated date for the complete *Ars Grammatica* (actually *Ars Donati Grammatici Urbis Romae, Ars Minor + Ars Major I–III*: see Holtz 1981: 583), a.AD349 for the four-times-shorter *Ars Minor* (17 pages in the Holtz edition vs. 71 for the *Donatus Major*), which has provided the basis for fundamental Latin grammars down to the present day. The larger work pays more attention to syntax, the lesser to the inflected forms or morphology of Latin. Donatus also treated of subjects that Priscian did not touch, notably tropes, figures of speech, barbarisms, and solecisms.

63 For reference purposes, let us estimate a composition date of c.526/7, using i.515/540 as the *floruit*, and c.AD480–c.560 for the span of Priscian's life, for the following tentative reasons. We think that Priscian was born in Algeria in the late 5th century, so let us say c.AD480. Educated in the school of Theoctistus, we know that he taught at Constantinople under Emperor Anastasius I (r.AD491–518), delivering a panygeric for him c.AD512. Since the *Institutes* (or *Foundations*) are a work of maturity and many years, we cannot go too far wrong assigning them to the middle *floruit* of an author of whom we *know* no more than that he was born in the 5th century and died in the 6th, adding the notion that individuals involved in his type of work tend to continue in it to the end or near the end, and that seldom do human individuals exceed one hundred years of life.

last two books constitute nearly a third of the whole of the *Grammatical Founda-tions* (the "Institutions"). What would eventually attract the modistae to Priscian in particular was that his familiarity with Greek gave to the *Foundations* some of the characteristics of a comparative grammar, while at the same time it provided a basis for the study of the "logic of language", a "speculative grammar", as noted above.

Now the interpretation of the *trivium* disciplines of grammar and rhetoric in particular as *scientiae* found little to no support in the Aristotelian and Thomistic currents of the Latin mainstream. Poinsot, for example, dismisses them from the consideration of his *Cursus Philosophicus* in two lines,[64] by reason at worst of their not being sciences at all (in view of their having to rely on a method which is purely descriptive rather than probative), or at best of their object having a purely conventional structure which, so far as it links up with anything of nature, pertains rather to logic.

So one has almost to wonder if the progress of semiotic consciousness might not actually have been impeded by the fact that the first ones to embrace the idea of a the-matically organized *scientia signorum*, "science of signs", were not the mainstream thinkers influenced by Aristotle above all after the twelfth-century translations, but rather those oriented toward the older Stoic and Augustinian paradigm for Christian wisdom out of which, it will be recalled, the "liberal arts" tradition of both the *trivium* and *quadrivium* sprung.

Now the greatest champion of retaining the Augustinian paradigm of Christian thought developed on the basis of Stoic and Neoplatonic influences, against the de-velopment of an alternate paradigm based rather on the new Aristotelian influence as championed by Albert and Aquinas, was a contemporary of Thomas Aquinas, Roger Kilwardby (c.1215–79), also a man of great learning and of enormous influence in ecclesiastical and university affairs particularly in England, where he rose to the post of archbishop of Canterbury in 1272 and thence to cardinal in 1278. Despite his being a fellow Dominican with Thomas Aquinas, that the work of Aquinas had in its time a more sophisticated or powerful foe is doubtful. When, in 1277, bishop Stephen Tempier of Paris issued his celebrated, or infamous, condemnation involving views of Thomas, his brother bishop Robert Kilwardby of Canterbury issued a parallel condemnation of his own, during one of his visits to Oxford University. It was a landmark event, all right, but one of those which mainly mars the intellectual landscape of the time it helps to define.[65]

---

64 Poinsot 1632, Q. 27 "On the Unity and Distinction of Sciences" Art. 1 "Whence from the rationale of the knowable derives the specific unity and diversity of sciences", 826b40–4: "Rhetorica autem et Grammatica vel non sunt scientiae, quia non procedunt demonstrative, vel non sunt rationales, sed sermocinales." See also ibid. Q. 1. Art. 4, 277b5–11.

65 Gilson (1955: 385–427) devotes a whole part and three chapters to "The Condemnation of 1277", which he sees as the end of scholasticism's golden age; and he notes in particular (p. 410) that "The very fact that the theology of Duns Scotus is often mistaken for a voluntarism is due to his desire not to teach a single one of the condemned theses". So we have another large-scale instance (cf. the remarks in the first paragraph of n245 of chapter 7, p. 360 above) of how the very structure

Now Kilwardby appeared in his Umwelt as formidable a figure intellectually as he was politically. He did not by burying his head in the sand defend the old paradigm which made no distinction between philosophy as a pure work of human understanding and theology as a work of human understanding elevated by the light of divine revelation and sometimes too (but neither necessarily nor always) by mystical experience. To the contrary, whether "he was more zealous than correct"[66] or not in doctrinal matters philosophical, he made himself fully master of the new learning, so that when he spoke and acted firmly in favor of the then-long-established Augustinian paradigm of "Christian philosophy" (for he was a great influence at Oxford University in particular, and took an especial interest in Merton College, which had been founded there by one of his friends two years after Kilwardby arose to the archibishopric of Canterbury), he did so while integrating into that traditional paradigm the sources of the "new learning" that Albert, Thomas, and others, as we have seen, were taking in such a radically different direction.

In particular, it was Kilwardby's view that not just logic but all three of the trivium's disciplines fall outside the Aristotelian division of speculative and practical sciences. The problem, as he envisaged it, was not that grammar (or "composition"), rhetoric, and logic are not in their own right sciences. The problem was that these

---

of Latin texts in theology and philosophy was sometimes affected for the worse by authoritative "condemnations" issued in the name of a dogmatic authority but bearing upon matters well within the boundaries of philosophical freedom to explore. In pointing out these unpleasant facts along the way, I risk creating for at least some readers a serious misunderstanding. It has long been the custom, especially in Neothomistic circles, to present the impact of Christian belief and medieval theology upon the doctrinal development of philosophy in a wholly positive light, as transformative decisively of basic concepts and issues. And indeed, whether it be the freeing of the idea of creation from the necessary emanation Plotinus posited or the appreciation of the peculiarity of the being proper to relation in contrast to all that constitutes physical subjectivity in the reflections on the Trinity which found their way through Aquinas and Poinsot especially into the heart of the doctrine of signs, the positive influences are there and are decisive.

But plenty of authors have emphasized this side of the medieval development. Much of the work that still needs to be done is precisely the result of a largely one-sided emphasis, and a *parti pris* tendency to sweep under the rug the embarrassments of history which has so far largely intimidated scholars from reassessing *in toto* the Pseudo-Dionysian and Pseudo-Isodorean and related frauds which entered illegitimately into the very pattern and fabric of the Latin heritage, and discouraged even the competent few from facing squarely the consequences and addressing the implications both doctrinal and historical of experiments in the manipulation and control of inquiry.

As usual, Jacques Maritain stands out from the crowd (1970: 257–400, "Un regard sur l'histoire", esp. 303–43) in pointing expressly to the kind of problem and historical reassessment I have tried at various points along the way to indicate the need for; but if the lessons of history in these matters had been more learned and explored and less denied and ignored, perhaps we might not have had to see such a grand-scale secular repeat of them under the great empire of the Soviet Union between its official founding on 30 December 1922 and its official dissolution on 26 December 1991; and perhaps too, though this may be wishful thinking, had Communism not chosen in secular form the route of inquisition that the religious wars of Europe had otherwise discredited we would not have seen its large-scale continuation in the politics of late-modern China. What needs to be learned better and understood more deeply is the lesson that the road of inquiry cannot be blocked without damage to the human good, and that is why so often in this work I point to attempts at and the ill consequences of such blockage.

66 So opines an authority as great as Weisheipl (1967a: 533).

"sciences", the *sermocinales*, have for their object signs rather than things (harking back to the division between signs and things introduced by Augustine in his *Doctrina Christiana*, as we have seen). He was also a great admirer of Priscian, and wrote commentaries on the grammatical works of both Donatus and Priscian.

The Case for a "Science of Signs" in Kilwardby Adscriptus

The earliest and strongest statement we have proposing – hardly executing, as Poinsot would finally accomplish, but yet explicitly proposing – a *scientia signorum*, a "science of signs",[67] comes out of a manuscript dating to Kilwardby's early intellectual prime in the form of *Commenti super Priscianum Maiorem*, "A Commentary on Priscian Major". The work in question was written probably c.1250, and almost certainly i.1230/70.[68] Since Kilwardby was known to have written a commentary on *Priscianus Minor* and this commentary on the *Maior* contains many points of doctrine set out by Kilwardby elsewhere in his writings, notably in the celebrated *De Ortu Scientiarum* of this same period, it is not surprising that in the manuscript collections which come down to us the *Commenti super Priscianum Maiorem* is ascribed, including by at least one contemporary ascription, to the hand of Kilwardby himself.

Nonetheless, the work is not signed as such, and the one scholar who has made it his business to establish authenticity and inauthenticity in the case, Osmund Lewry,[69] has cast doubt on the authorship of this manuscript, so that its authorship must be considered at this point as strictly unknown. It *may* have been by Kilwardby himself; it certainly was *ascribed* to Kilwardby. Since the work of Lewry, a number of serious scholars, such as Ashworth[70] or Meier-Oeser,[71] have taken to referring to this work in terms of the "Pseudo-Kilwardby"; but this is a great mistake. We have here an *anonymous* author, not a *pseudonymous* one. There is clearly a great and important difference between an author who deliberately assumes an authorial name and a work which is mistakenly by others ascribed to a name.

This difference between an author who assumes a false name, which can be done for a variety of reasons, including innocent ones, and an author who has a name falsely ascribed to him by accident, becomes all the more important when, as we saw with the twin cases of Pseudo-Dionysius and Pseudo-Isidore (which, to say the least, assumed a fundamental importance for the Latin Age), an author assumes another's identity precisely in order to cloak the writing with attention and respect it might not otherwise receive. The present case of "Kilwardby Adscriptus" is the case of an innocent error at most. Pseudo-Dionysius and other like misrepresentations are

---

67 But in the medieval sense of "science", which had not yet been distinguished from but was used synonymously with philosophical knowledge as *doctrina*, a point we shall discuss in its proper place.
68 According to Pinborg 1975.
69 See Lewry 1975; also Lewry 1981.
70 Ashworth 1998: 413.
71 Meier-Oeser 1995: 603; 1997: 65–72.

anything but innocent. It is not a small thing to create even a prima facie linguistic parity between an innocuous "Pseudo-Kilwardby" and an anything but innocuous "Pseudo-Dionysius" or "Pseudo-Isidore".

For this reason I want to suggest that this custom of referring to a "Pseudo-Kilwardby" be rejected before it becomes established, and that we should speak rather of *Kilwardby Adscriptus*, a "so-called Kilwardby", an author who made no pretensions to being someone he was not nor even adopted a pen name, but who appears simply to have been misclassified (if he was misclassified) in the manuscript catalogues; and who appears also properly to belong in the theoretical family of works kindred in spirit to the authentic works of the man under whose name the mistaken classification has been made, under the form of a text that "reflects a middle stage"[72] on the way to the modistae and "speculative grammarians" proper.

The author of the Kilwardby Adscriptus text (be he indeed Kilwardby or, instead, some poor soul lost in the mists of *temps perdu*) discusses the idea of a general "science of signs" only for about thirty-two paragraphs (seven pages) in the Fredborg et al. edition of his Priscian Major commentary, before going off in the direction that would lead to the not very distant (or great) future of the modistae and "speculative grammarians".[73] But in this brief opening section of his text he makes in passing two points that will eventually, and independently, come to loom large in the mainstream philosophical thematization of the doctrine of signs. The first is that he sets his proposed science within the Stoic triad of speculative ("*natura communiter dicta*"), practical ("*voluntas cum eligentia*"), and rational ("*ratio*") science, just as we will eventually see Locke do[74] in coining the name "semiotics" for the doctrine of signs. The second is that he proposes the division between sign and signified as a division of being itself. The points deserve comment in turn, beginning with the second.

Of the second point we may observe that too soon did he propose his division. Its prematurity in the climate of speculative development doomed its immediate acceptance. For such a division to succeed as a division of *being* in the late Latin context, it would first have to have been shown in a thematic and systematic way how the objects of experience depend throughout upon sign-relations in their constitution as known. And for this demonstration not merely some terminological distinction such as that proposed between formal and instrumental signs would be adequate, as we have seen; one would have to have arrived at the far more fundamental understanding of this (or any other) division of signs in terms of relation as a general mode of being at once superordinate to all subjective foundations and indifferent to provenance from nature or mind in the constituting triadically of the being proper to every sign as such. And the achievement, speculatively and historically, of *this*

---

72 Pinborg 1975: 6+.
73 The classic contemporary study remains that of Bursill-Hall 1972; see also Bursill-Hall, Ebbesen, and Koerner eds 1990.
74 In chapter 14 below.

fundamental tracing of the roots of the doctrine of signs to the unique feature of the being proper to relation (*relatio secundum esse*, that is) which is the source of the possibility of an action of signs transcending or rather interlacing the distinct orders of σύμβολον or ὀνόματα (as synecdoche for the realm of culture) and σημεῖον (as synecdoche for the realm of nature) through the variegated, ever-shifting realizations of the being proper to *signum* – this was the unique privilege of John Poinsot.

Of the first point, we may observe that when the Kilwardby Adscriptus text proposed, alongside natural philosophy (or physics) and moral philosophy (or ethics), a *scientia de signis*, the author was indeed anticipating most or all of Locke's conclusion for the *Essay concerning Humane Understanding* of 1690. But because he made his proposal partly aside from the mainstream development of Latin philosophy and especially without preceding or accompanying it with the necessary clarifications in principle of the relations among proper and common sensibles and between concepts and objects as all being thoroughly sign relations, the historical privilege of naming the new perspective thematically proposed would remain open and, in the end, fall rather to Locke.

It is just as well. For the new perspective, as we shall further see, is not a "science" in the sense that modernity would appropriate but rather a "doctrine" in the sense that has always among the Latins distinguished philosophical knowledge in what is proper to it. Like all the developments of human understanding, the coming to the fore of this new perspective appropriating "science" for its name would take place over a long interval of critical discourse. But in the end we are better off. For we now clearly see – or at least will be in a position to once we reach chapter 17 – that, so far as the sign is at issue, the development of understanding in question was a doctrinal one, not a scientific one; and, hence, that we should speak, as Sebeok well remarked,[75] rather of a "doctrine of signs", a *doctrina signorum*, than of a "science of signs", a *scientia de signis*. And it was for this doctrine that Locke proposed the name that has stuck: σημιωτική, in Latin "semiotica", in English "semiotics".

Consequent Clarifications

But we anticipate (the results of chapters 14 and 15 in particular). As yet, as of the seventeenth century, the point we have currently reached in making this "backward glance" or *Blickwendung* over the text of Kilwardby Adscriptus, the new doctrine has received, in fact, no name of its own beyond the generic Latin philosophical one of *doctrina signorum*. Locke has not yet equated the English rendering of this expression with σημιωτική, and the Kilwardby Adscriptus proposal for a *scientia signorum* has been ignored. But Poinsot has now demonstrated, against all nominalistic interpretations, the unity of the doctrine soon-so-to-be-named *semiotica* through his showing that the general being constitutive of the triadic sign relation is that of relation strictly and properly so called, ontological relation or *relatio secundum esse*.

---

75 Sebeok 1976: ix and ff. Commentary in Deely 1978, 1982a, and related articles.

In achieving this watershed advance, Poinsot brought into new clarity a number of points in the doctrine of signs which had been widely discussed among the late Latins debating questions concerning the nature or being proper to signs. The root insight into the possibility of "semiosis" as the action following on the being proper to signs Poinsot indeed found in Aquinas.[76] But in Aquinas the point was illuminated by sustained reflection on, or buried in a discussion of, the Trinity, the question of how three Persons can be consistent with the notion of God as One. To realize and to point out explicitly the broader implication for the phenomenon of communication in the fact that sign relations share in common with all relations, whether physical or cognitive and purely objective, the property of being in principle superordinate to their foundations, and hence always prospectively intersubjective, was a move Aquinas himself never made. Poinsot's broader application of this insight drawn from a text of Aquinas was unprecedented, as the long and chequered history of discussion of that same text sufficiently manifests.[77]

Poinsot emphasized that, besides what they share in common with all relations, the relation in which a sign consists also exhibits a feature irreducible and unique to the sign, namely, triadicity or "Thirdness", that is, the involvement always of three terms.[78] This conclusion, though widely shared among the late Latin authors and all but explicit as early as Roger Bacon, remained much in need of clarification even after Poinsot's unequivocal treatment of the point. Indeed, the third term of the sign-relation as such did not receive a name of its own prior to Peirce's introduction of the term "interpretant", as we shall see in chapter 15.

But Poinsot's *Treatise on Signs* not only came at the very end of the medieval Latin development,[79] it came so late that the interests of modern Europe were already turned elsewhere. And both its novelty and decisive clarification of previously discussed insights was largely hidden from readers' view by the conservative design of the philosophical and theological volumes into which Poinsot had so skillfully incorporated semiotics as if it were nothing unusual, whereas in sober truth it implied a rethinking of the whole notion of knowledge and experience and even "tradition".

Poinsot wrote – in this retaining for his work the fundamental cast of the medieval thinker – with an eye to ordering new insights relative to past achievements as the dominating Latin context, particularly as expressed in the writings of Aquinas. This is an attitude of mind at least as difficult to relate to for postmodernity as it was for modernity.[80] The novelty of a discovery taken on its own terms held almost no

---

76 Poinsot 1632a: *Treatise on Signs*, Second Preamble, art. 2, 93/17–96/35.
77 See the survey in the *Tractatus de Signis*, "Second Preamble on Relation", Article 2 "What Is Required for a Categorial Relation", the "Resolution of Counter-Arguments", 93/17–96/36, which shows that the Thomistic commentators generated more bafflement than agreement in their exposition of this text. Further in Deely 1988: esp. sect. G, p. 82ff.
78 Poinsot 1632a: Book I, Question 3, 153/1–159/22, esp. 154/25–9.
79 Beuchot 1980.
80 See the discussion of "The Method and Literary Forms of the *Treatise on Signs*" in the 1985 Deely edition of Poinsot 1632a, pp. 417–20, esp. 418n27.

fascination for the truly medieval writer. That he found in Aquinas the fundamental account of why relations are indifferent to their subjective ground was everything for Poinsot. The originality of his ingenious application of this previously obscure insight to clarify the foundations of the general notion of sign, something neither Aquinas nor anyone else before him had accomplished, was comparatively nothing in Poinsot's eyes, a mere detail to be brought to the fore within a vast philosophical synthesis worked out before him. Never mind that it implied a reworking of that synthesis from its foundations in human experience as the source and measure of discursive rationality.

Poinsot's *Treatise on Signs* was no doubt the most stunning of the outcomes of the Latin discussions of the notion of *signum* launched by Augustine. For Poinsot's work points to the realization that Augustine's was the most original notion separating the onset of indigenously Latin philosophy from all that had gone before in Hellenic thought. Yet this decisive implication of Poinsot's *Tractatus* passed without immediate notice, perhaps even in its own author's mind, into the grave of Latin history.

But like a vampire which enters the grave to sleep but not to die, Augustine's continually living problem in fact cannot be put to rest. It lies too close to the center of distinctively human existence, and the time of its further unfolding would inevitably come. At the end of modernity, when every strategy to escape the impasse to which the reduction of signification to representation in pursuing the modern "way of ideas" had failed, Poinsot's solution to the ancient problem of the sign was rediscovered by one of the most restless of the many thinkers to become entangled in the coils of modernity's commitment to idealism, Jacques Maritain. In the early 1900s,[81] he began a long series of fundamental reflections which, little by little, brought the lost solution closer and closer to the light. Finally in 1985, in the context of contemporary semiotic developments, Poinsot's work received its first full display in an independent edition.[82] It was just in time for postmodernity's full morning light.

The End of the Story in Latin Times and Its Opening to the Future

The story of medieval semiotics, in sum, opens with the positing of the first notion of "sign" in the contemporary sense made by Augustine in the fifth century. The story develops through a complex and rich discussion of the foundational notions involved therein. This development reaches its highest point in Poinsot's resolution of the main problem raised by Augustine's notion of sign: the problem of how there can be a being common to signs as involved in natural phenomena and signs as involved in the phenomena proper to culture.

After Poinsot, the Latin discussion of signs continued among Latin authors even up to the nineteenth century. But this discussion no longer affected or formed part

---

81 Details in Deely 1986.
82 The 1985 Deely edition of Poinsot 1632a.

of any mainstream. The change would not have been evident to those living and writing at the time. But in hindsight, there is no mistaking that the once-mainstream currents that had fed the growing of a semiotic consciousness among the Latins swirled off into side channels and became little more than intellectual eddies of a dying age. These eddies were intricate, interesting, and for a time after Poinsot appeared to increase; but in fact the whole development was leading off to one side of what was to become philosophy's next mainstream development.

And none after Poinsot have been brought to light so far who rose to the understanding of the manner in which grasping the essential type of the sign rendered all possible identifications of sign tokens definitively subordinate.[83] Latin authors such as Mastrius and Bellutus in the Scotist school,[84] Comas del Brugar among the Jesuits,[85] Makowski in Poland,[86] continue to treat of signs as if the terminological distinction between "formal" and "instrumental" signs were the main point at issue, or the most illuminating theoretical concern. In fact, as we have seen, so far is this distinction from the heart of the matter that even nominalists, who effectively destroy the general notion of sign, can be found paying lip-service to the distinction. And Meier-Oeser shows[87] that even this discussion after Poinsot increasingly moved in the direction Fonseca had indicated, to wit, that of making all signification instrumental, reducing concepts to representations directly known as objects – the key to modernity as "rationalism" and "empiricism", as we will shortly see.

---

83 This remains as unhappily true of scholars today in reviewing the critical edition of Poinsot's *Tractatus* as it did of his contemporaries in reading it. Meier-Oeser (1997: 215) says that "Diese Stelle ist für Deely's Poinsot-Interpretation von zentraler Bedeutung" – but instead of referring to the central doctrine of the triadic relation constituting sign being an ontological relation indifferent to provenance, he is referring to the fact that the literal appearance of the words "de signis et notitiis" occurs in earlier authors as well around Poinsot's time, concluding that thereby is belied Poinsot's originality of doctrine! Meier-Oeser's work in this regard is reminiscent of Krempel (see my remarks on Krempel in Deely 1985, passim) for a combination of historical thoroughness in attention to detail with doctrinal obtuseness in appreciating what is at issue conceptually and as a matter of philosophical doctrine. And we will see in passing in chapter 10, p. 465ff., a handful of other critics succumbing to what we have termed this "nose of wax fallacy".
84 A later contemporary of Poinsot, Bartholomaeus Mastrius (1602–73), whose name in Italian life was Bartolomeo Mastri (see Crowley 1948), dealt with the sign in three places: the formal/instrumental sign distinction is discussed in his *Disputationes in Arist. Stag. libros De Anima* of 1643 (pp. 380–404, d. 6, q. 3, "De intellectione ac verbo mentis") and in his *Disputationes in Organum Aristotelis* 1646 (pp. 4–11, Institutiones, pars I, tr. I, "De terminis ac eorum affectionibus"; and 239–91, d. 2, "De vocibus et communibus earum affectionibus"); in his *Disputationes in quartum librum Sententiarum [Petri Lombardi]* of 1664 (pp. 1–11, In IV Sent., d. 1. q. 1 "De natura et essentia sacramenti in genere") he discusses the "practical sign", as was customary in those times. Cf. Poinsot 1667: Q. 60, "De Sacramentis", Art. 1, esp. Dubium Primum, Secundum, et Quintum; Art. 2, esp. Dubium Primum.
85 Comas del Brugar 1661. This work, for its date astonishingly traditional in the cosmological images it relies on, is yet notable for achieving some advance in the semiotic organization of logic. See the discussion in Deely 1988.
86 See Makowski 1679: 278; biography in Hajdukiewicz 1974.
87 Meier-Oeser 1997: "Der Zeichenstatus der Konzepte", pp. 251–62; also ch.VI, pp. 337ff.

Even so, given the history, one would have expected to find Neothomistic authors who picked up the loose ends of semiotic in the Latin Age and reintroduced the sign to modernity. But such is not the case. Generally, when the neoscholastics treated of signs at all, their preoccupation with the realistic aspect of Latin philosophy led them into a diversion. Understanding neither the nominalist origins of the formal/instrumental sign terminology nor the foundational issues that terminology glossed over, these authors managed to delude themselves into thinking that they had found in the distinction of formal from instrumental signs some kind of short-cut to scholastic realism.[88] Yet in fact it was not the doctrine of formal signs but the doctrine of sensation as independent of icons, together with the doctrine of relations as mind-independently real, that formed the heart of scholastic realism, as Peirce well saw. And indeed, with the just-mentioned exception of one little-noted but radical aspect of Maritain's reflections on sign, it is only in contemporary semiotic development as it stems principally from the work of Charles S. Peirce that anyone picks up the threads of medieval semiotics to resume the discussion pretty much from the point where modern thought prematurely foreclosed the mainstream Latin development. As medieval semiotics began with one of the last of the Fathers and first of the medievals, so contemporary semiotics begins with one of the last of the moderns and first of the postmoderns. In these terms, semiotics may be said to represent the main thrust of postmodern thought insofar as this designation has a positive content and a relevance to previous philosophy.

But to appreciate how a new development of a semiotic consciousness is the main thrust of postmodernity, we need first to look at the modern interlude – or perhaps, for reasons that shall appear, I should speak of "the modern underside of philosophy in an age of science". For Poinsot's *Treatise on Signs* comes from the press only the year before the 1633 condemnation of Galileo, bracketed on one side by the 1631 appearance of Descartes' *Rules for the Direction of the Mind* and five years later by the same author's 1637 *Discourse on Method*. The "modern period" has barely begun when quickly philosophy comes to play Mr Hyde to Dr Jekyll as the figure of science reading the book of nature in observational and mathematical terms. For while the protagonists of the nascent science in the modern sense are convinced they are finding ways and means to advance together the understanding and control of nature, the protagonists of philosophy become convinced rather that scientific necessities are and cannot be other than shadows and projections of the mind's own workings.

---

88 A discussion of late-twentieth-century authors who tried to reduce the doctrine of signs to a mere abutment of realism in the controversy with idealism can be found in Deely 1976: 15 and 1978a. Exactly why the doctrine of formal signs by itself – that is, divorced from a larger context of a doctrine of signs as grounded in the ontological peculiarity of relation and the doctrine of sensations as logically prior to the involvement of icons in cognition – is useless in such an abutting role is discussed in Deely 1994a: 83n38. But the reasons can already be gleaned from what is said in chapter 7 above concerning the *primum cognitum* in general (p. 341ff.) and the role of mental icons in sensation and perception in particular (pp. 345–7).

For want of a doctrine of signs modern philosophy takes an epistemological turn that leads the mind into and upon itself. The moderns can find there neither windows nor doors opening unto the realm of any mind-independent being such as the ancients and the medievals, together with the founders of modern science, had fancied themselves to discern. The modern period proves to be one of the shortest of the Ages of Understanding so far, and with reason; for it provides us with by far the strangest tale of any length in the long history of philosophical discourse. The ancient way of things expanded in medieval times to a philosophy of being; but that expansive vista contracts in modern times to a "way of ideas" which knows no outlet. The scientific Dr Jekyll and the philosophical Mr Hyde emerge together from the shadows of the passage between the Latin Age and the modern interlude to postmodernity.

CHAPTER TEN

The Road Not Taken

Stating the Question

A great thinker is, willy-nilly, a man of his time. Whether he looks forward or backward in his thought, he does so inevitably through the filter of contemporary eyes – his own. And what he sees is perforce tinted by that filter of experience. Breathing the air of his period, he cannot help but imbibe something of its aspirations, whether to further them or to oppose them, as the case may be. Before leaving the Latin Age for the fresh pure air of modernity, let take a last closer look at the case of the semiotic of John Poinsot, to consider in the light of its details the mainstream modern development to follow.

In short, let us pause for a chapter on the frontier of what will become the "modern period" of mainstream philosophical development, to consider not only what was but what might have been. With the work of Poinsot we have reached what is effectively the farthermost boundary of Latin philosophy as a mainstream development. The seeds of what will come to be called "rationalism" are already germinating in the thought of Descartes, and the development of "empiricism" will not be far behind; but both of these developments, we will see, are germinated in the triumph of the representative theory of concepts over the significative theory that climaxed in the *Tractatus de Signis*. After Poinsot, especially, it would appear, in Jesuit authors – who, after all, largely dominated European university life over the early-modern period – more and more the doctrine of signs was turned in the Fonsecan direction of a reduction of the notion to "instrumental signification" dependently upon concepts which only represent – which are objects first of all. Thus, with the work of Poinsot, we are already astride the boundary that will separate the modern period of mainstream philosophical development from the scholasticism which was the mainstream, as including a Thomistic current in particular, of the Latin Age.

Let us take a last look at that frontier before crossing it, by casting upon it a prospective light under which the early-modern development has heretofore never full been viewed. Since the source of our light lies on the Latin side of the boundary, and played no part in the actual development of the modern mainstream, as we will see in subsequent chapters, we will leave this chapter as the conclusion of our treatment of the Latin Age, even though what we will illuminate are precisely the philosophical doctrines of the early-modern mainstream development. Leaving out the momentous modern achievements in scientific thought proper and in the social and political spheres of "practical philosophy" to consider only the metaphysical or, more properly, epistemological doctrines proper to modern philosophy, the reader may find the light unusually stark – "jaskrave", as they say in Ukraine for a light which leaves the distinctions between where the light is and not exceptionally sharply marked, and almost forces one to squint at what it illumines.[1]

Poinsot, we have just seen, was the first thinker fully to vindicate the Augustinian proposal of sign in general from the charge of nominalism. We may say that, in achieving this, he succeeded in locating the beginning point of the way of signs in the uncovery of a point of view which transcended the would-be realism common to ancient Greek and Latin thought, while yet continuing in a line justificative of the aspirations of the nascent modern science of mathematical physics and experimental development of observations. The newly established standpoint, that proper to the development of a doctrine of signs or (as it will eventually come to be called[2]), "semiotic", differs from the standpoint of previous philosophy by bringing equally into focus the mind-dependent and mind-independent aspects of the objective content of experience, and by revealing that experience to consist of an irreducible interpenetration and interweave of the workings of the physical environment with the workings of the mind itself.

But the discovery and establishment of this standpoint in Poinsot's *Tractatus de Signis*, we know in hindsight, was destined to be utterly eclipsed by the dramatic events surrounding the work of Galileo and by the attempts in their wake of Descartes and others to establish new foundations for philosophy in the analysis of ideas construed as themselves the objects of direct experience, something that the semiotic standpoint consistently precludes from the moment it is realized. The mainstream development of modern philosophy was destined to overlook the way of signs, and to take instead the way of ideas, a way which would lead with the inevitability that logical consequence has in the realm of ideas to a most unsatisfactory outcome, namely, the repudiation of the hope of modern science (continuous with the ambition of Greek and Latin philosophy) to understand the actual world in the being proper to its physical surroundings as antecedent to and in some basic sense independent of our individual opinions and thought processes.

---

1 A colleague of Ukrainian descent, Dr Roman Ciapalo, suggested to me the analogy, adding that the story thus told "makes you feel like throwing away your Copleston", meaning, I take it, not that there is anything wrong with Copleston's account in its individual details, but rather that the manner in which those details are illustrative of the standard outlines of the history of philosophy in what relates to medieval and modern thought proves hopelessly inadequate to the actual story of philosophy once semiotic is brought into play.
2 See chapter 14 below.

Since our project is to understand the actual course and state of philosophy, we are obliged to trace the road actually taken in its history; but nothing prevents us from pausing at this fork in that road to consider the modern landscape in the light most proper to the end of the indigenous Latin development, the light that first revealed the way of signs which it would be the destiny only of *post*modernity actually to travel and explore in detail. In other words, nothing prevents us from making a survey of the situation of early-modern philosophy as it *would have* appeared to contemporary eyes familiar with the finally established requirements of the doctrine of signs, in order to contrast that same situation as it appeared to contemporary eyes fixed rather on exploring the newly defined way of ideas. In fact, the discovery of the way of signs is, as we move into the second quarter of the seventeenth century of our actual history, about to fall into oblivion. But that does not prevent us, as travelers of the mind, from surveying an alternative counterfactual to history's actual course, yet in itself possible and indeed superior speculatively to the epistemological paradigm which modern philosophy would find enshrined in the Kantian synthesis a mere century and a half from the vantage which the close of the Latin Age has afforded us.[3] It is not a question of changing past history, but of changing future history.

Thus, the reflections of this chapter turn around two thinkers of the same age, but placed now in a peculiar light – "jaskrave", as we have said. The one thinker, René Descartes (1596–1650), normally apparent in the foreground of early-modern philosophy, we relegate rather to the background. The second thinker, John Poinsot (1589–1644), born seven years and dead six years before Descartes (1596–1650), normally missing entirely from the standard recountings of early-modern philosophy, we take here as our foreground figure. We already know from our last chapter[4] that Poinsot was the author of the first successful attempt theoretically to unify the subject matter of semiotic inquiry. We know also[5] that, excepting only Suárez, with whose work alone in this matter the early moderns had thorough acquaintance,[6] Poinsot was the author of the most complete authoritative synthesis we have of Latin philosophy and theology in its final stage of development as an indigenous, linguistically homogeneous tradition. So there is plenty of reason for pausing at this point to undertake some imaginative reconstruction of the speculative situation at the end of the Latin Age, before passing on to consider the quite different and, in philosophy at least, quite antithetical developments that would soon define the actual modern mainstream development.

---

3 Here is the advantage an explorer in the world of ideas has over one in the physical environment. The traveler in space, confronted with a fork in his journey, may, like Robert Frost on the occasion of his famous poem (Frost 1915) which provided the title for our chapter, look "down one as far as I could to where it bent in the undergrowth"; yet must he remain "sorry I could not travel both and be one traveler". In the world of ideas, nothing prevents us from traveling the road the moderns neglected, even while taking full cognizance of the road they did in fact travel.
4 See chapter 9, "The Vindication of Augustine", p. 430ff.
5 See chapter 5, "Anticipating the Two Destinies", p. 209ff.
6 See "The Boethius of Modernity" in chapter 11 below, p. 500f.

As the way of signs would be rediscovered in the late-nineteenth-century work of Peirce,[7] so work of Poinsot in this area would be rediscovered in the early twentieth century by Jacques Maritain.[8] But what these twin rediscoveries at the frontier of postmodernity would alike reveal is a speculative outlook far more congenial to the historical achievements of science in the modern sense[9] than anything to be found, ironically, in the lineage of philosophy in the modern sense!

The present chapter has as its purpose to propound a single heuristic thesis or point: that an integral understanding of the Latin Age in terms of *signum* as its unifying theme provides a way of looking at modern philosophy that is very different from the received opinions concerning modern and medieval philosophy alike, a way of looking which profoundly affects our understanding of the contemporary situation in philosophy and the shape of its immediate future. Instead of looking from the work of Descartes to the line of mainstream modern development that followed upon it in the two streams of classical rationalism and empiricism synthesized by Kant, as we will undertake to do in our next three chapters, we are in this chapter instead undertaking to survey the horizon of mainstream Latin thought as it existed at the time that Descartes undertook his work, in order to see how full and good a use Descartes – and, after him, all the classical moderns – made (or failed to make) of the Latin resources available in principle at the dawn of modern philosophy, especially as regards the professed main modern interest, namely, the nature and extent of human understanding.

What comes into view as soon as one effects such a shift in standpoint as has just been proposed is actually quite surprising. For it turns out that there were important speculative developments of the Latin tradition under way, especially in Iberia, of central relevance for the contemporary postmodern context of discourse analysis and culture studies in general. Of these developments Descartes had no knowledge,[10] and the Cartesian influence screened them out of subsequent mainstream development as modern philosophy moved from Latin to the natural languages.[11] In particular, our shift of standpoint reveals that more than a century of late Latin development anticipated John Locke's proposal for a philosophical "doctrine of signs", or "semiotic", which would give us a sort of logic and critique of knowledge different

---

7 See "The Common Sources for the Semiotic of Charles Peirce and John Poinsot" in Beuchot and Deely 1995.

8 On the relation of Maritain to Poinsot specifically in the matter of semiotic, see Deely 1986.

9 See esp. Maritain 1959, *The Degrees of Knowledge.*

10 In defense of Descartes' ignorance of the rapid development of semiotic within the Iberian peninsular university world, it should be noted that the principal authors responsible for this development were Dominican writers, and that the reading of Dominican writings was interdicted at La Flèche, the Jesuit college where Descartes received his principal intellectual formation.

11 The point here made is far more general than my particular line of argument in the present chapter, as can be seen, for example, from a reading of Doyle 1994 or Wells 1994.

from what the mainstream of modern thought presaged,[12] while at the same time providing exactly what the moderns wished for, namely, a new starting point for the philosophical enterprise as a whole rooted directly in the experience of each of us more than in the authority of ancient figures.

The "shift from 'Scholasticism' to 'Modernity', many would say, has its echo in our present shift from 'Modernity' to 'Postmodernity'."[13] But few indeed have been aware that the echo in question resonates with specific anticipations of what is to come after modernity as a development based not on a unity of natural language (as in the epochs of ancient, medieval, and classical modern philosophy) but on the achievement of an epistemological paradigm forged from the realization that "the highest grade of reality is only reached by signs",[14] a paradigm capable of taking into account the very mechanisms of linguistic difference and change as part of the framework of philosophy itself.

A story must be told before it can be believed or disputed, and I have come to think that the story of the closing centuries of Latin scholasticism's contribution to the understanding of mind that modernity bungled is a story neither believed nor disputed precisely because it has not yet been truly told. Descartes and Poinsot, contemporaries in the glorious seventeenth century, are alike, seen from our vantage today, doorways to the past – to the twelve hundred years of Latin philosophy in Poinsot's case; in that of Descartes, to the three hundred and fifty years of modernity's determined effort to present itself as the once and future truth owing nothing to history. But it is not the grand vistas of past history open through the work of these thinkers that interests us here. Our focus in this reflective chapter is on the coevality of Poinsot and Descartes, the overlap of these two thinkers in that magic moment when, at once, modernity was gestated and postmodernity presaged – the former in Descartes' starting from ideas as such construed as objects, the latter in Poinsot's starting from ideas as such construed as signs and objects as such as signifieds. For by taking this latter point of departure, Poinsot was able not only to synthesize the Latin past, but to give it a future bearing beyond modernity itself, a bearing on the shaping and substance of the postmodern era nascent today.

By comparison with Descartes, Poinsot's contribution to the seventeenth century search for a new beginning in philosophy is difficult to access. In his *Rules for the Direction of the Mind* of 1628, Descartes proposed, as the necessary solution to the muddle of the Latin past, adoption of a new method without which "the pursuit of learning would, I think, be more harmful than profitable".[15] "By 'a method'", he explained,[16]

---

12 See chapter 14 below, "Locke Again: The Scheme of Human Knowledge".
13 Natoli and Hutcheon 1993: viii.
14 Peirce 1904a: 23.
15 Descartes 1628: 17.
16 Ibid.: 16.

I mean reliable rules which are easy to apply, and such that if one follows them exactly, one will never take what is false to be true or fruitlessly expend one's mental efforts,[17] but will gradually and constantly increase one's knowledge till one arrives at a true understanding of everything within one's capacity.

As to the writings of the ancients, insofar as they contain, by virtue of the natural light, scattered glimmers of the Cartesian method, they perhaps deserve to be read, "but at the same time there is a considerable danger that if we study these works too closely traces of their errors will infect us and cling to us against our will and despite our precautions".[18]

In other words, what is proposed as novel in the Cartesian system is the system itself, in particular the method of analysis of objects into their simplest components, buttressed by methodical doubt maintained at each step of the way. Adoption of the Cartesian approach, moreover, is recommended as necessary from the outset if "the pursuit of learning" is not to be (as by implication it has perforce always heretofore been) "more harmful than profitable".[19] Thus, as Descartes would later confess in his *Discourse on Method*:[20] "when I cast a philosophical eye upon the various activities and undertakings of mankind, there are almost none which I do not consider vain and useless." The historical dimension of philosophy seemed to Descartes the very paradigm case for dismissal in the search for truth. Whereas Aristotle's meditations on first philosophy (c.348–330BC) led Aristotle first to consider the views of his predecessors, the *Meditations on First Philosophy* of Descartes (1641) would lead Descartes first to dismiss his predecessors – as he had so frankly told us to expect in his earlier *Discourse on Method*.[21]

The desire for a new approach to philosophy that characterized the birth of modern philosophy in the seventeenth century, moreover, was not something vague and general, but quite specific. The moderns knew both what they were looking for and where they expected to find it. Descartes spoke for the entire period in his twofold assertion[22] that "the most useful inquiry we can make at this stage is to ask: What is human knowledge and what is its scope?", and that the task for such

---

17 Hence Descartes' assurance to Mersenne in his letter of February 1637 (cited from Stoothoff 1985: 109; cf. Kenny ed 1970: 30) that his method "consists much more in practice than in theory" and "extends to every kind of subject-matter". The requisite rules, of course, Descartes set himself to supply, and with the hindsight of three centuries I can confidently report to you that, while Descartes' various discourses in this area are still widely read by philosophy students, they have nowhere served for the complete rebuilding of the edifice of human knowledge that Descartes envisioned for them. The issuance of "promissory notes" in philosophy, still popular in analytic circles today, may be said to have been begun by Descartes; but the last three hundred years tend to discredit the practice when history is made a part of its consideration.
18 Descartes 1628: 13.
19 Ibid.: 17.
20 Descartes 1637: 112.
21 Ibid.: 114–15.
22 Descartes 1628: 31.

inquiry is "to seek to encompass in thought everything in the universe, with a view to learning in what way particular things may be susceptible of investigation by the human mind."

Poinsot's approach to the problems of philosophy, including those pertaining to the nature and scope of human knowledge, was in almost every respect contrary to that of Descartes (and of the moderns to follow). To begin with, he did not think that there was any sure and easy method, old or new, that would lead to the infallible discovery of philosophical truth. For him, experience provided no short-cut or substitute for studying the works of those who had gone before, and the method for doing this was to reduce the arguments to be found in previous authors to their logical core and express this core in strict logical form as the means whereby alone hidden assumptions and unsound premisses could be brought to light.[23] Hence, he rejected Descartes' view[24] that "ordinary dialectic is of no use whatever to those who wish to investigate the truth of things", though he agreed completely with Descartes in repudiating those who prescribed the forms of dialectic as a means for taking, "as it were, a rest from considering a particular inference clearly and attentively".[25] The forms of dialectic, for Poinsot – the necessary aspect of even probable syllogisms – are merely the preliminary instrument for positioning ourselves to adjudicate what is philosophically sound or unsound in the views of another, ancient or modern.

The disagreement between Poinsot and Descartes over method extended also to the object of our knowledge. Poinsot was not a reductionist. He did not believe that higher orders of difficulty in knowledge could be reduced to complex arrangements of ultimately simple objects, so that the complex could be deduced from the simple merely by a careful observation of the proper ways in which simple objects combine to form complex wholes.[26] Poinsot accepted rather a doctrine of substance according to which ontological unities in nature do not ordinarily correspond and can seldom be made to correspond in one-to-one fashion with objective unities represented in knowledge, as Cajetan before him had best clarified in the maxim that objects divide differently than do things.[27] Knowledge, for Poinsot, consisted essentially in

---

23 See Poinsot's "Prologus Totius Dialecticae, Praeludium Primum: quo proponitur dialecticae disputationis exercitium et praxis", in the *Artis Logicae Prima Pars* (1631), 3a1–5a3 (=*Tractatus de Signis*, "First Prologue: Wherein is set forth the exercise and practice of dialectical disputation", 10/1–13/12).

24 Descartes 1628: 37.

25 Ibid.: 36.

26 In this regard too (see chapter 12, p. 512 below), Leibniz even more than Descartes would supply the maxim neatly spearing the spirit of the modern quest for a method, with his proposal to supplant logic with an *ars combinatoria* (a "combinatory art"). The holy grail of *Calculemus!* – "Let us calculate!" – would ever provide the modern hope for resolving disputes beyond the capacities of any discursive logic.

27 Cajetan 1507: *Commentaria in Summam Theologicam. Prima Pars*, q. 1, art. 3, where he enunciates the principle that differences among things are quite another matter than differences among objects, which Poinsot takes up as one of the fundamental principles of the doctrine of signs: see the

the establishment, for any given case, of a correspondence in relationships between objective representation and ontological reality, allowing in particular for objective states of affairs which have no physical counterpart existing apart from their representation.[28] To know the truth in any given case is critically to determine which pattern of objectivity we are dealing with in this or that aspect of experience.[29]

In other words, Poinsot was a quintessential scholastic, at the very moment historically when the maze-like complexity of the results arrived at by the scholastic method and the rhizomic multiplicity of authorities established in the scholastic line were experienced by most as a stifling burden more trouble to learn than it was worth.[30] Scholastic logic, the entry into the system of philosophy in the mainstream university curricula against which Descartes and the moderns rebelled, demanded seven years' study in Poinsot's university, three in formal or "summulist" logic and four in so-called "material" logic, which was the study of logic as an instrument not

---

Tractatus de Signis, Book I, question 2, 149/41–151/21, question 4, 187/28–190/23 and n. 33 thereto, p. 187; esp. Book II, question 1, 235/36–236/46, question 5, 270/37–271/21. See also Cajetan's comments on q. 28, art. 1 of this same part of the Summa, partially cited in n. 18, p. 95 of the Tractatus de Signis.

28 Poinsot 1635: 77b26–78a24 (cited in Book I, question 4 of the Tractatus de Signis, n. 35): "In the object of a power the focus of attention is not formally mind-independent or entitative reality, according as the object has being in itself, but the proportion and adaptation to the power. This proportion indeed as it subjectively exists in a thing must be mind-independent; but in terms of the relation to the power, that it exists subjectively in the thing itself is not what is regarded, but rather that it exists objectively relative to the power in question – although on other grounds, if the power itself respects only mind-independent being [as the external senses], it will also require a mind-independent being in the object, not as existing, but as related to the power. For existence is always in an order to itself and subjectively, whereas to a power it always pertains objectively. Whence a mind-dependent being, although in itself it has subjectively no reality, can still be the object of an act of understanding and specify that act by reason of an objective proportion which it takes on in an order to the understanding when it has a real fundament and is conceived on the pattern of mind-independent being. For then it can perfect and specify the understanding by a mind-independent perfection, not one innate to itself or existing in itself, but one borrowed and appropriated from mind-independent entity, on whose pattern it is objectively conceived, as we have said in the Logic 2. p. q. 1. art. 3 [Reiser ed., 265b44–266b12]. Thus, even though reality and the character of being belongs to mind-independent and mind-dependent being analogically, and not simply in the same way, nevertheless, objectively it can be found in a mind-dependent being simply in the same way as in a mind-independent being, because, presupposing a borrowing from mind-independent being and from its fundament, the very proportion and adaptation to a cognitive power which alone pertains essentially to an objective rationale is there, for the mind-dependent being is truly and properly coapted, so that it terminates a true and proper act of understanding exactly as do other objects." The same basic notions hold for the higher powers of purely sensory life, as Poinsot shows in Article 3 of the First Preamble to the Treatise on Signs.

29 The Latin context in which Poinsot is concerned to synthesize his views, the landscape he surveys in the area we call epistemology, is rich beyond imagining. "Like some great philosophical Indies, it now lies in wait for its Columbus", wrote a current Marco Polo of studies in Latin philosophy (Doyle 1984: 121. See also Doyle 1987, 1988, and 1990).

30 Nor did scholastic analyses bearing on the case of Galileo, discussed in the next chapter, do much to sustain the credibility of the scholastic approach. Whatever the merits of Poinsot's speculative views in the matter of human understanding, the practical matter of his couching them unreservedly in the traditional academic forms of late Latin scholasticism all but guaranteed their immediate destiny – which was to pass into oblivion.

merely for restating arguments in form but for adjudicating therewith the truth of their contents.[31]

Imbued with the deepest respect for tradition, Poinsot felt charged with a double mission: not only to advance the truth, but to do so in a way that carried with it the whole of past truth. Simonin has described the dilemma well:[32] "Poinsot is determined to let no new achievements be lost, and to profit from the final developments of a scholasticism which had exhausted itself in the plenitude of its refinements."

Finding a Focus

If, therefore, we are to find from Poinsot a contribution to the modern demand for a new beginning in philosophy, it will be hidden among the plenitude of refinements made in the final developments of scholastic philosophy, the mainstream philosophy of the Latin Age. There may of course be more than one such contribution in the vast synthesis of Poinsot's *Cursus Philosophicus*. But the most promising area in which to look would naturally concern the nature and extent of human knowledge. For Poinsot was inevitably a man of his own time as well as a figure of tradition. He worked from one of the most vital centers of seventeenth-century university life, was cognizant of all the currents of modernity,[33] and breathed in spite of himself the atmosphere (the "signosphere", we might almost say[34]) of the period.

It is no accident that Latin scholasticism, along with the peripheral currents which would replace it as mainstream on the Continent and in England, had undergone in its later development a shift in emphasis from ontological questions to questions of epistemology, as we would call them today. In this regard, the decisive influence on Poinsot's thought came from the University of Paris, where his predecessor at Alcalá, Dominic Soto, had done his graduate study.[35] At Paris, Soto had been steeped in the controversy begun by followers of Occam over the adequacy of Augustine's classical definition of sign, enshrined in the fourth book of Lombard's *Sentences*

---

31 This was the manner in which the Latins developed the difference between Aristotle's books of "prior analytics" (formal logic) and "posterior analytics" (scientific demonstration). See "The Instrument of All the Sciences" in chapter 3 above, p. 87ff.

32 Simonin 1930: 145.

33 That Poinsot clung to discredited empirical beliefs of the ancients (Lavaud 1928: 416–17) or knew nothing of the works of Galileo and Descartes (Simon 1955: xix) are myths that need to be exploded, as pointed out in the "Editorial AfterWord" to the *Tractatus de Signis* (Deely 1985: 399–404, esp. n. 8 p. 403). Suffice it here to point out that the structure Poinsot finally gave to his *Cursus* as published, both in what it omits in natural philosophy and what it incorporates in logic, is inexplicable except on the assumption of Poinsot's intimate awareness of the philosophical trends developing in Italy and central Europe.

34 Since "atmosphere" here is a metaphor for the cultural air, which is always a matter of signs.

35 An excellent brief summary of the general historical context, based on the many works of Muñoz Delgado, and on Ashworth 1974, 1978, is provided in Angelelli 1992, esp. sect. 3, "From Montaigu to Alcalá and Salamanca". But this is an area which would well reward the study of gifted graduate students.

as the focus for sacramental theology, according to which a sign is something which, on being perceived by sense, brings into awareness another besides itself. The Parisian logicians developed at length a point that Aquinas had qualified in passing in a number of contexts but never thematized,[36] the point that this definition from Augustine is too narrow, because intellectual notions and phantasms alike – in a word, concepts and percepts, ideas and images – function precisely to bring into our awareness something that they themselves are not. And not only, for example, is it the case that an idea of a dog is not a dog, but also is it the case that a dog thought of may or may not be a dog existing. Nascent here is not merely the dyadic distinction emphasized by the Paris logicians between signs as vehicles of awareness themselves sometimes perceptible and sometimes not, but, more fundamentally, a triadic distinction among concepts as psychological states, objects as apprehended terms of cognitive relations, and things existing physically whether or not objectively. But the immediate focus of the controversy in Paris was on the question of whether the sign is rightly defined when being perceptible to sense is made part of its definition; and to this question the decisive answer was made in the negative.

From this answer arose a new definition of *signum* as *anything* which brings into awareness what it itself is not,[37] and a corresponding new division into signs which perform the act of signifying only on condition that they are themselves objective terms of apprehension, hereafter called *instrumental signs*, and signs which perform the act of signifying without themselves being objects first apprehended as such, hereafter called *formal signs*. The actual coinage of this terminology, as we saw,[38] historians have yet to attribute to a specific individual. What seems certain is that the terminology was in use in participial form and adverbially in Paris by the time Soto studied there, and it is certain that Soto introduced the terminology and the controversy into the Iberian university world early in the sixteenth century, where

36 Hence, in commenting on these various contexts spanning the professorial career of Aquinas – c.1254/6a: the *Commentary on the Sentences of Peter Lombard* IV, dist. 1, q. 1, quaestiunc. 2; c.1256/9: the *Disputed Questions on Truth*, q. 4, art. 1 ad 7, q. 9, art. 4 ad 4 and ad 5; c.1269/72: the *Questions at Random*, q. 4, art. 17; c.1266–1273/4: the *Summa theologiae* III, q. 60, art. 4 ad 1 – and synthesizing their import, Poinsot concludes only that "it is more probably the opinion of St. Thomas that a formal sign is truly and properly a sign in the very same sense that an instrumental sign is a sign" (*Artis Logicae Secunda Pars*, Q. 22, Art. 1, "Utrum sit univoca et bona divisio signi in formale et instrumentale", 694b1–4; =*Tractatus de Signis*, Book II, Question 1, 225/11–14). Recall our review of this sequence of texts in the writings of Aquinas made in chapter 7 above, p. 331ff.
37 As Peirce might have put it in 1906–7, Augustine had provided no more than "a ragged-outlined notion of what we call a sign" as "the word is ordinarily used"; whereas what is needed is "such a definition as a zoologist would give of a fish, or a chemist of a fatty body, or of an aromatic body. – an analysis of the essential nature of a sign, if the word is to be used as applicable to everything which the most general science of sēmeio´tic must regard as its business to study" (from "The Basis of Pragmaticism in the Normative Sciences" of 1906 and "Pragmatism" of 1907 in Houser et al., *The Essential Peirce Volume* 2 [1998], pp. 388 and 402–3, respectively).
38 See chapter 8, esp. 390n71 & 404ff.

it became, over the next century, as Poinsot testified[39] and we ourselves saw in chapters 8 and 9 above, a matter of daily dispute in the Iberian universities.

The problem, as Poinsot saw the situation, was that Soto had introduced this discussion of sign into the Iberian curriculum in a disruptive fashion. For he had made the discussion of signs a part of the opening chapters in his introductory logic text or *Summulae*,[40] and this example had been followed by other Iberian professors, giving rise to "a vast forest of intractable questions and a thorny thicket of sophisms" which have served mainly "to burden and abrade the minds of students, causing no little harm".[41] For "the grasp of beginners is not proportioned to these questions about signs" – "swarming with so many and extraordinary difficulties"[42] – which, "for the slower wits", have "raised a fog".[43] Poinsot's solution to this problem was to remove "the metaphysical and other difficulties from the books *On the Soul* which the ardor of disputants has caused to intrude into the very beginning of the *Summulae* books" and "to publish separately, in place of a Commentary on the books *On Interpretation*" a "treatise on signs and modes of awareness".[44] This treatise cannot be appropriately introduced – introduced, that is, without causing undue confusion and perplexity – until mind-dependent being and relation have first been thoroughly treated, for the reason that it is on these two notions, and especially the notion of relation,[45]that successful "inquiry concerning the nature and definable essence of signs principally depends".[46]

---

39 Poinsot 1632a: 194/39–40.
40 Soto 1529, 1544.
41 Poinsot's 1631 "Preface" to the *Artis Logicae Prima Pars*, p. 1 (=*Tractatus de Signis*, "To the Reader of 1631", 5): "immensam inextricabilium quaestionum silvam et spinosa sophismatum dumeta excidere curavimus, quae audientium mentibus onerosae et pungentes utilitatis nihil, dispendii non parum afferebant".
42 Poinsot's 1640 Preface to the second separate edition of his *Artis Logicae Secunda Pars*, as reprinted in R I, p. 249 (=*Tractatus de Signis*, "To the Reader of 1640", 35): "... tractatum de signis, pluribus nec vulgaribus difficultatibus scaturientem, ne hic iniectus aut sparsus gravaret tractatus alio satis per se graves ..."
43 Ibid.: "... fateor sic me ista tractasse, ut accuratioribus oculis haud quaquam praeluxisse praesumam, at nec tardioribus offudisse caliginem, ..."
44 Poinsot's 1640 Preface to the second separate edition of his *Artis Logicae Secunda Pars*, R I, p. 249 (=*Tractatus de Signis*, "To the Reader of 1640", 35): "Quod in prima Logicae parte promisimus de quaestionibus pluribus, quae ibi tractari solent, hic expediendis, plane solvimus, excepto quod iustis de causis tractatum de signis, pluribus nec vulgaribus difficultatibus scaturientem, ne hic iniectus aut sparsus gravaret tractatus alio satis per se graves, seorsum edendum duximus loco commentarii in libros Perihermenias simul cum quaestionibus in libros Posteriorum, et pro commodiori libri usu a tractatu Praedicamentorum seiunximus."
45 Because mind-dependent being – all the structure of objectivity fashioned by the mind itself in Umwelt formation – reduces to a variety of relation. This point will come sharply into focus in the discussion, in chapter 15 below, of "Relations and the Knowledge of Essences", p. 652ff., esp. 655.
46 Poinsot, *Artis Logicae Secunda Pars* (1632), remarks "super libros Perihermenias", 642a22–24 (=*Tractatus de Signis*, 38/21–39/4): quaestiones istae de signis "nunc autem in hoc loco genuine introducuntur, post notitiam habitam de ente rationis et praedicamento relationis, a quibus principaliter dependet inquisitio ista de natura et quidditate signorum."

Here we see one of the best illustrations of the manner in which the work of Poinsot attempts what Simonin[47] called "a synthesis of irreconcilables": "On the one hand, Poinsot is determined to let no new achievements be lost", while, "on the other hand, he is determined further still ... to arrange his work in its totality according to the pattern and methods of long-standing tradition." Poinsot does not disagree with Soto's emphasis on the importance of a doctrine of signs. "Since the universal instrument of logic is indeed the *sign*," he tells us,[48] "the very foundation of the exposition of logic goes unexamined" until and unless the project of a doctrine of signs has been completed. Moreover, as the unfolding of his treatment of the questions on relation and mind-dependent being as they pertain to the doctrine of signs makes clear, in Poinsot's view, interpretation is an activity coextensive with the life of the mind.[49] Hence a *Treatise on Interpretation*, strictly and properly so-called, cannot be restricted to the logical interpretation of terms and propositions, but must extend itself to the instrument of interpretation as such, whether logical or otherwise, and this instrument is the sign. Thus, in view of the full requirements of philosophical tradition, the proper place for a consideration of signs in their full amplitude is not merely in connection with or as part of a traditional commentary on Aristotle's *De Interpretatione*, as Poinsot's Coimbra teachers and others in the milieu had essayed. The proper treatment of signs must *take the place of*, must be made *instead of* and *supplant entirely* the traditional commentary.[50]

This solution is brilliant as far as it goes. "One sees there quite clearly the eye and hand of an exceptional artist", as Simonin says of Poinsot's treatment of logic in general (1930: 145). But, "whatever sympathy one may have for the attempt, it seems equally clear that it was not destined to develop and fulfill itself normally." Why not? Because more is at stake than a mere question of respecting the pattern of long-standing tradition.

The very determination to let no new achievements be lost itself *guarantees* that the pattern will have to be modified. It is only a question of how far one is to go with such modification. By insisting on *the minimal modification of tradition possible consistent with what has been newly achieved*, Poinsot no doubt places at the same time the maximum emphasis on the already achieved, which was his set and constant purpose. Whereas Descartes embodied in his work the modern spirit

---

47 Simonin 1930: 145.

48 "... commune siquidem Logicae instrumentum est signum, quo omnia eius instrumenta constant, idcirco visum est in praesenti pro doctrina horum librorum ea tradere, quae ad explicandam naturam et divisiones signorum ..." ("Super libros Perihermenias", in *Artis Logicae Secunda Pars*, 642a615–21; =*Tractatus de Signis* 38/13–19).

49 See 466n71 below.

50 It is plain that to *replace entirely* the traditional commentary with a treatise on signs is radically different from making the treatment of signs *a part of* a traditional commentary *or introduction to* a traditional commentary focused on logical interpretation. See Deely 1988: 55–6.

loving novelty for its own sake and valuing the newly discovered in principle over the already known, Poinsot embodied in his work exactly the opposite spirit of valuing the integrity of established truths equally with the importance of new discovery. He consequently paid heed to the importance of relating newly discovered truths to what has been established, and had no use for pursuing the lead of new consequences apart from a rather full regard for the landmarks provided by past connections.

It is here, I think, that Simonin[51] rightly sees in Poinsot "a synthesis of irreconcilables". The consequences of new truths inevitably lead beyond, as well as bear relations to, the boundaries of what has already been discovered. By emphasizing the boundaries of the already discovered, Poinsot risked having newly discovered truth, in effect, become camouflaged in the landscape of the already known. This, in fact, is exactly what happened with his *Treatise on Signs*.[52]

Moreover (and this is a point to which Poinsot had hardly given sufficient reflection), the fixity of the pattern itself of long-standing tradition is not something given once and for all. The "most natural place" for the treatment of signs at the time of Poinsot's confrontation of the problem generated by Soto's *Summulae* vis-à-vis Latin philosophical tradition in general and Thomistic tradition in particular would not remain the "most natural place" once his separate publication of a foundational *Treatise on Signs* had successfully reduced the doctrine newly established to its proper perspective and unity. For such a treatise, by its very success, would inevitably alter the situation.

At the time he undertook to write his own *Tractatus* on the subject of sign, Poinsot expressly held the opinion that the treatment of signs in the courses introductory to the philosophy curriculum (that is, the courses of 'minor', 'formal', or 'summulist' logic) was bound to appear eclectic and confused, disruptive of the order of traditional introduction without commensurate gain. The problem, *then*, that is, at that point of the doctrine's development, was to systematize the treatment of signs and to discover the unity proper to the problematic of *signum* providing the foundations for interpretation in general, and logical interpretation in particular. As a research matter, this was a subject for advanced study, not introductory courses.

But if this problematic of sign could be systematized and the unity and treatment proper to it assimilated, the problems constituting it could then be presented clearly and in their proper relation to logical studies – and to other studies insofar as they are 'sign-dependent'. *At that point* a new historical situation would have been created. Now it would be possible to make a consideration of sign part of the introduction without creating confusion and resorting to eclecticism, because it would no longer be the case that the underlying problematic had not been thought out and presented independently in its proper unity. This new situation would therefore require a change in the pattern of traditional introduction, but now the change would be

---

51 Simonin 1930: 145.
52 See Deely 1985: 447n76 and esp. 461n97.

integrative rather than disruptive – it could effect the commensurate gains that clarity and a higher order of synthesis in the subject matter offers to beginning students.

In fact, exactly this is what happened with a logic by Michael Comas ("Miguel Comas del Brugar") published at Barcelona in 1661. Comas, expressly basing his treatment not on questions of pedagogical preparedness but on the requirements proper to the order of doctrine – and, *expressis verbis*, on Poinsot's work in this area – provided a kind of anticipation of the Peircean project of deriving even the traditional concerns of formal logic and syllogistic directly from the prior consideration of the sign in its proper being (further specified as this and that kind of sign – in the case of logic as then conceived, 'second intentions'). In other words, Comas uses Poinsot's arguments on the nature of signs in relation to traditional logic to begin the treatment of that very logic, especially for beginners, with the discussion of signs; and Comas does this in a way systematically derived from Poinsot's *Tractatus de Signis*. Comas's derived way of introducing the discussion of sign into the beginning treatment of logic offered an alternative both to the way that Poinsot had chosen and to the way chosen by Soto that Poinsot had criticized. The alternatives pursued by Poinsot and Comas alike repugned the confused eclecticism of Soto's approach. But, compared to one another, the opposition of the ways of Poinsot and Comas is sequential, not repugnantial. What we have here is a detail illustrative of the evolution of intellectual culture consistent with long-standing tradition. Today's graduate seminars have a way of shaping even the most traditional among tomorrow's introductory textbooks for undergraduates. Had the model provided by the logic of Comas del Brugar been adopted beyond the Pyrenees, who knows what the impact might have been in the European theatre. As it happened, we will never know.

If Poinsot's concern for integrating new achievements according to the pattern and methods of long-standing tradition represents a synthesis of irreconcilables by its failure to account sufficiently for the requirements of evolution in intellectual culture and for the manner in which symbols grow, this is precisely because, as Simonin also notes,[53] "Poinsot's work reveals itself as a work of transition". There are ample reasons for suspecting that Poinsot realized he stood at some kind of boundary of the Latin development, and felt charged with the task of preserving a record of its integrity down to the utmost refinement of its developments. He perhaps made a conscious choice to sacrifice the natural development of his own work in favor of preserving for future generations the landscape and organic texture of philosophy in the Latin Age. "Understood in this way", as Simonin suggests,[54] "and given its place in the development of history, the work of Poinsot acquires a particular significance, and perhaps an especial interest, at a time", such as the present one, "when one rediscovers the flavor of an ancient style."

---

53 Simonin 1930: 145.
54 Ibid.: 146.

Adjusting the Focus: Understanding What We Have Found

The reader needs distinctly to weigh and consider duly what we have discovered at this point. While there is no doubt that Poinsot's treatise on signs stands as a new achievement in one of the final developments of the plenitude of refinements of Latin scholasticism, in view of the modern development and beyond, that is hardly its principal interest. What is most striking to realize is that this treatise on signs proves, on Poinsot's handling, to stand also as a definitive fulfillment of Descartes' proposal[55] that we must "seek to encompass in thought everything in the universe, with a view to learning in what way particular things may be susceptible of investigation by the human mind" if we are to answer that "most useful inquiry we can make at this stage", namely, what is the nature and extent of human knowledge? Locke would later set the same ideal or goal for modern philosophy. "We shall then use our understandings right," he advises,[56] "when we entertain all objects in that way and proportion that they are suited to our faculties, and upon those grounds they are capable of being proposed to us". In other words, Poinsot found within the resources of Latin tradition an answer to the modern question concerning "in what way particular things are susceptible of investigation by the human mind". The answer lay in the doctrine of signs.

There are two ways we can look at Poinsot's achievement on the point. We can consider his doctrine of signs specifically within the context of his *Cursus Philosophicus Thomisticus*, or we can consider the *Tractatus de Signis* as a virtually autonomous treatment that can be evaluated on its own as an independent whole establishing the sign as the key to a philosophy of experience. Looked at either way, even though his treatment of the sign was so skillfully balanced and qualified by his artistic integration of it into the traditional treatment of logic that this deep tendency escaped the notice of his contemporary readers, Poinsot turns out to have provided us with nothing less than a new starting point for the philosophical enterprise as a whole – a veritable "new beginning", as I argued at length in an earlier book for specialists in the history of early-modern philosophy.[57]

The Tractatus de Signis *Viewed from within*
the Cursus Philosophicus Thomisticus

Let us consider the novelty of Poinsot's work within the context of his *Cursus Philosophicus* as a whole. The first part of the *Cursus* consists of the treatment of logic, first according to its form, then according to its informing an actual subject matter by way of providing proofs and establishing probabilities. True to his admission that the question of the sign goes to the foundations of the subject matter of logic, we find that the opening two and a half chapters of the first of the

---

55 Descartes 1628: 31.
56 Locke 1690: 30.
57 Deely 1994a.

introductory logic or *Summulae* books introduce definitions and divisions of all the terms that will form the subject of the discussion in the *Treatise on Signs* replacing a Perihermenias ("On Interpretation") Commentary in the Second Part of logic. Here, in these opening two and half pages of the *Cursus Philosophicus*, Poinsot manages to list, without discussion, all the terms and distinctions originally used by Soto to introduce into the Iberian university world the substance as well as the fruits of the Parisian controversy whereby the definition of the sign proposed by Augustine in the fifth century and used ever since among the Latins is relegated to the subdivision of signs as "instrumental", and a broader definition is proposed in its place as one comprehensive enough to cover "formal" signs as well – comprehensive enough to apply to everything which the doctrine of signs must cover, as Peirce would later say.[58] Thus, in Poinsot's day, the doctrine of signs, to be established on its own grounds, will cover the same materials as the opening chapters of the traditional introductory logic text, but at a deeper level and reorganized according to a different point of view, which Poinsot calls simply that of a *doctrina signorum*.

Nor is this all. Remember that Poinsot spoke of "the metaphysical and other difficulties from the books On the Soul" as needing special resolution from the systematic perspective of the *doctrina signorum*. In my 1985 edition of Poinsot's *Tractatus de Signis* as an independent work, I included as Appendix B the complete table of contents from the *Cursus Philosophicus*, both as it appears in Reiser's edition and in the form of a Synoptic Table displaying the whole in an organizational chart. If one glances at that appendix, one finds that it is nothing less than the final conclusions of natural philosophy traditionally viewed that become the starting point of the newly demanded *doctrina signorum*. The reason is that the formal sign, which, remember, is identified with the products of perceptual and/or conceptual cognitive acts, usually called *species expressae* by the natural philosophers, does not come up for discussion in the traditional natural philosophy until the treatment is reached of material being which is both living and cognizant, and this is at the very end of the order of exposition. What is last in exposition, however, is first in discovery: with the *doctrina signorum* Poinsot professes to have discovered the means of accounting for the origins and structure of experience as irreducible to subjective being, whether physical or psychical.

Dramatically enough, he traces the basic insight of the *doctrina signorum* to Aquinas's treatment of the Trinity as a community of persons, and to Cajetan's interpretation in particular of the notoriously difficult text in the *Summa Theologiae* wherein St Thomas says that the Persons of the Trinity are able to subsist as purely relative beings because of what is unique to relation among all the modes of physical being, namely, that it exists suprasubjectively according to a rationale – the rationale of "being toward" – which is indifferent to the fact of being exercised independently of being cognized or known. In other words, every physical being

---

58 See n37, p. 456 above.

which exists either in itself or in another exists subjectively and must, as such, exist whether or not it is known to exist by some finite mind, that is to say, whether or not it exists objectively as well as physically. But relation, in order to be what it is, exists not subjectively but as an intersubjective nexus or mode, and for this it *makes no difference* whether *the relation* obtains physically as well as objectively or only in the community of knowledge. In either case, whether it exists only as known or physically as well as objectively, a relation exists in exactly the same way: over and above subjectivity. By contrast, substance and accidents exist subjectively only when they are not pure objects of apprehension. Indeed, purely as objects apprehended, they are not subjective existents but relative objects *patterned after* what are not relative, namely, physically existent substances with their accidents, which, Poinsot points out, is precisely why there are mind-dependent relations but not mind-dependent substances or mind-dependent accidents other than relations.[59]

In other words, as *isolated* in this or that respect, physical being is determinately subjective, but in whatever respect reality enjoys *communion*, in that respect it is determinately *suprasubjective* and as such can be maintained in cognition alone, in physical being alone, or in physical being and in cognition alike. Hence in the case of the Trinity, Aquinas argues, a diversity of persons subsistent as *relations* is consistent with the unity of God as pure existence subsistent in itself, *ipsum esse subsistens*.

In the case of the *doctrina signorum*, the application of Aquinas's point about the being proper and unique to relation as a mode of being is much humbler and, philosophically, quite independent of the theological doctrine that the interior life of God consists in a communion of three (ontologically relative) persons. By all accounts, Poinsot points out, signs are *relative* beings whose whole existence consists in the presentation within awareness of what they themselves are not. To function in this way the sign in its proper being must consist, precisely and in every case, in a relation uniting a cognitive being to an object known *on the basis of* some sign vehicle. What makes a sign formal or instrumental simply depends on the sign vehicle: if it is a psychological state, an idea or image, the sign is a formal sign; if the sign vehicle is a material object of any sort, a mark, sound or movement, natural or artificial, the sign is an instrumental sign. But whether the sign is formal or instrumental, natural or conventional, is subordinate to the fact that, as a sign, the being whereby it exists is not the subjective being of its vehicle (psychological or material, as the case may be) but the intersubjective being, prospective or actual, of a relation irreducibly triadic.[60]

---

59 Poinsot, *Artis Logicae Secunda Pars*, Q. 17, "De Praedicamento Relationis", Art. 2, "Quid requiratur, ut aliqua relatio sit praedicamentalis", 581b24–582a16 (=*Tractatus de Signis*, Second Preamble, Art. 2, 96/1–36).

60 *Artis Logicae Secunda Pars*, Q. 21, Art. 3, "Utrum sit eadem relatio signi ad signatum et potentiam", 664a49–b2 (=*Tractatus de Signis*, Book I, Question 3, 154/28–30): "unica relatione signi attingitur signatum et potentia, et haec est propria et formalis ratio signi".

Many centuries later, Peirce would resume this point under a clearer terminology: every sign, in order to function as a sign, requires an object and an interpretant, and hence consists in a triadic relation. But the point itself – that the *doctrina signorum* has in reality a unified subject matter for investigation as a consequence of what is unique to the being of relation in general, namely, a status of indifference to provenating from nature or mind – while debated intensely among the Latins, is found thematically established not in Soto, the Conimbricenses, or Araújo,[61] but in Poinsot. For the first time, a definitive resolution is effected of "the possibility", originally suggested by Augustine,[62] "of resolving … the ancient dichotomy between the inferential relations linking natural signs to the things of which they are signs and relations of equivalence linking linguistic terms to the concept(s) on the basis of which some thing 'is' – singly or plurally – designated". Natural and conventional signs are alike signs because they are alike constituted by triadic relations as such irreducible to subjective being and as such indifferent to their status as provenating from mind or nature.[63] This definitive resolution is effected within the *Cursus Philosophicus* of John Poinsot.[64]

In effecting his resolution, as we saw in chapter 9, Poinsot writes in a typically "medieval" fashion. All the Latin scholastics of his time use the terminology of *relatio secundum esse* and *relatio secundum dici*, *relatio realis* and *relatio rationis*, *relatio praedicamentalis* and *relatio transcendentalis*,[65] confirming Eco's remark[66] that "medieval materials at first glance normally appear to be stubborn repetitions of

---

61 Cf. Beuchot 1980.
62 Eco, Lambertini, Marmo, and Tabarroni 1986: 65.
63 "The conclusion derives from that distinguished doctrine in Cajetan's *Commentary on the Summa theologica*, I, q. 1, art. 3, that the differences of things *as things* are quite other than the differences of things *as objects* and in the being of an object; and things that differ in kind or more than in kind in the line of things can differ in the line of objects not at all or not in the same way. And so, seeing that the rationale of a sign pertains to the rationale of the knowable [the line of thing as object], because it substitutes for the object, it will well be the case that in the rationale of object a mind-independent natural sign and a stipulated mind-dependent sign are univocal signs; just as a mind-independent being and a mind-dependent being assume one rationale in their being as object, since indeed they terminate the same power, namely, the power of understanding, and can be attained by the same habit, namely, by Metaphysics, or at least specify two univocally coincident sciences, as for example, Logic and Physics. Therefore in the being of an object specifying, stipulated and natural signs coincide univocally.

   "So too a cognitive power is truly and univocally moved and led to a thing signified by means of a stipulated sign and by means of a natural sign." (*Artis Logicae Secunda Pars*, Q. 22, Art. 5, 715b37–716a16; =*Tractatus de Signis*, Book II, Question 5, 270/38–271/12).
64 See the *Artis Logicae Secunda Pars* (1632), Question 21, "De Signo Secundum Se", Articulus 3, "Utrum in signo naturali relatio sit realis vel rationis", 635b10–663b25, esp. 658b30–659a39 (=*Tractatus de Signis*, Book I, Question 2, 135/1–152/7, esp. 141/12–142/13), together with Question 22, "De Divisionibus Signi", Art. 5, "Utrum sit bona divisio in signum naturale et ad placitum et ex consuetudine", 715a33–719a15, esp. 715b37–716a16, and Art. 6, "Utrum signum ex consuetudine sit vere signum", 719a17–722a37, esp. 720a39–b26 (=*Tractatus de Signis*, Book II, Question 5, 269/1–277/12, esp. 270/37–271/12, and Question 6, 278/1–283/32, esp. 280/15–43).
65 See, e.g., the analytically fragile but textually massive presentation of Krempel 1952.
66 Eco et al. 1986: 64.

a common archetype or model, differing not at all or at least not perceptibly". The forest stands out from the trees, but how make the differing trees stand out within the forest? Scholars skilled in the literal appearances have, on precisely literal ground, failed utterly to see the uniqueness of Poinsot's doctrine.[67] These scholars have failed to imbibe the medieval adage that "the authorities have a nose of wax". As Eco and his collaborators[68] said of the *topos* of *latratus canis*, so must it be said of the *topos* of *signum*: "beneath literal appearances, every time the *topos* is cited, one has grounds for suspecting that a slight or more than slight shift of perspective has taken place". Nowhere more than in the matter of the *doctrina signorum* do we find that, among the Latin authors, "concealed differences stand out against the background of seeming repetitions – differences of the sort promising to reveal the heart of systems in reality very different."

In the case of his *Tractatus de Signis* vis-à-vis the *Cursus Philosophicus* as a whole, at least two further points need to be noted if we are fully to appreciate in this context Poinsot's contribution to the seventeenth century search for a new beginning in philosophy.

From Sensation to Intellection: The Scope of the Doctrina Signorum
Not only does the *Treatise on Signs* cover the very materials that make up the opening three chapters of the *Summulae* books, that is, of the traditional *Cursus Philosophicus* as a whole, but one needs to realize that these opening materials of the *Summulae* books concern *the simplest elements of the primary form of cognitive life*, namely, concepts as the forms of, as providing the structure for, simple awareness. In Poinsot's *Libri Summularum* themselves, that is, the *Artis Logicae Prima Pars* of 1631, concepts are envisioned primarily in the narrow sense as restricted to ideas in the understanding or intellect (*species expressae intellectus*). This point I did not emphasize sufficiently in my Second Semiotic Marker on Poinsot's text,[69] since it

---

67 Looking exclusively from the perspective of formal logic in the traditional Latin sense, Muñoz Delgado (1964: 14, 22) expressed a certain puzzlement or even exasperation over the preference among French and American researchers for the work of Poinsot over that of Soto, a view naturally enough echoed in students of Muñoz Delgado's work such as Ashworth and Angelelli. Indeed, Ashworth (1988, 1990) not only takes her orientation from Delgado's opinion, but seeks to establish it independently by appeal to literal appearances "as one of the few philosophers who has actually read some of the sixteenth-century authors to whom Poinsot was indebted" (not, apparently, Araújo, nor the contemporary studies of Araújo's work by Beuchot 1980, 1983, 1987: see Ashworth 1990a). She enters waters which, at least at the time, surpassed her capacities to navigate, ending with the shipwreck proclamation that in Poinsot nothing is to be found which does more than repeat Dominic Soto's views. The claim is indefensible, but it does serve to signal the difficulty of the material. No period better than the later Latin period verifies Gracia's thesis (1992: 332) "that the history of philosophy must be done philosophically" in order to be intrinsically helpful to the philosopher. The "nose of wax" is to scholars of late Latin philosophical writings what the Bermuda Triangle is to sailors – or what Romeo made the Oracle at Delphi out to be; for we encounter in this late Latin period, in effect, texts which neither reveal nor conceal, but only signify.
68 Eco, Lambertini, Marmo, and Tabarroni 1986: 65.
69 See the 1985 edition of Poinsot's *Tractatus*, p. 19.

was written mainly to help the reader anticipate the departure from the established tradition that Poinsot would make in returning to treat this matter of the concept more broadly from the standpoint of the *doctrina signorum* proper *in place of* the traditional Perihermenias commentary, which restricts itself to the concept narrowly conceived, that is, to ideas as opposed to images.[70] For in returning to treat this matter from the standpoint of the *doctrina signorum* envisaged fully as such, Poinsot is at pains to establish with his opening sentence that it can no longer be concepts in the narrow sense that are at issue, but precisely concepts in the broadest sense as including the psychological life of animals as well, or, if one prefers, of human beings not only specifically as rational but generically as animals:[71]

> The question holds as much for a concept of the understanding, which is called an expressed specifier and word, as for an expressed specifier of perception or imagination, which is called an icon or phantasm. How does the definition of a formal sign, which is a formal awareness and which of itself and immediately represents something, apply to these?

However, seeing that the *doctrina signorum* resumes and recasts the whole doctrine of *phantasiari*[72] or perception and *intelligere* or human understanding from the natural philosophy of cognitive organisms in reshaping the foundations of logic as such still does not reveal the full scope of the *doctrina signorum* as it bears on the understanding of experience. Not only intellection and perception are dependent on signs for the total structure of their objective apprehensions but sensation as well. As if to emphasize the role of signs in cognitive life, not merely according to the narrow conception of interpretation worked out in the traditional commentaries

---

70 *Artis Logicae Prima Pars* (1631), 6b2–13 (= 16/40–17/2 in the separate edition of the *Tractatus de Signis*): "Nec est inconveniens, quod de simplicibus et his, quae pertinent ad primam operationem, agatur in Logica bis, quia, ut notat S. Thomas 1. Periherm. lect. 1., de dictionibus simplicibus sub alia consideratione agitur in Praedicamentis, scilicet ut significant simplices essentias, sub alia in libro Perihermenias, scilicet ut sunt partes enuntiationis, sub alia in libris Priorum, scilicet ut constituunt ordinem syllogisticum." See following note.

71 *Artis Logicae Secunda Pars* (1632), Q. 22, Art. 2, "Utrum Conceptus Sit Signum Formale", 702a44–b4 (=*Tractatus de Signis*, Book II, Question 2, 240/1–242/2, where the passage is extensively annotated): "Procedit quaestio tam de conceptu intellectus, qui vocatur species expressa et verbum, quam de specie expressa phantasiae seu imaginativae, quae dicitur idolum vel phantasma, quomodo illis conveniat definitio signi formalis, quod sit formalis notitia, et quod seipso et immediate aliquid repraesentet." In the face of such a text, even apart from Poinsot's further discussion of the role of signs in external sensation and the life of brute animals, which we shall consider shortly, it is fatuous to conjecture (Ashworth 1988: 132) "that Poinsot would not have gone beyond the standard debate as to whether *interpretatio* meant an utterance or an assertion".

72 I.e., the genus of knowing common to brute and rational animals over and above sensation: see Poinsot, *Philosophia Naturalis Quarta Pars in Tres Libros de Anima*, Quaestio VIII, "De Sensibus Internis", Art. 2, "Quid sint phantasia et reliquiae potentiae interiores, et in quibus subiectis sint", 252a38–265a46, discussed in editor's n. 2 at 240/4 in the *Tractatus de Signis*. See also Deely 1971: 55–83.

on the *De Interpretatione*, but according to the broadest and fullest conception of cognition established in the traditional commentaries on the *De Anima*, Poinsot expressly frames his concluding question "Concerning the Sign in Its Proper Being" to establish "Whether the true rationale of sign is present in the behavior of brute animals and in the operation of the external senses".[73]

The importance of such a question in the context of the search by Poinsot's contemporaries for a new beginning in philosophy cannot be overemphasized. Even though Descartes turned radically away from sensation in *his* attempt to re-establish a foundation for philosophy, that attempt was soon countered in the work of John Locke and the empiricists after him, who turned precisely to external sense in *their* attempt to renew philosophy's foundation. Whether we regard sensation as the foundation of knowledge and core of experience or merely as a superficial point of departure from which to turn to inner experience, either way, the matter of sensation became central to the modern search for a new beginning in philosophy.

Whereas the philosophers of what was to become the modern mainstream distinguished between primary and secondary qualities of objects, Greek and Latin philosophers had distinguished rather between proper and common sensibles; and of course it is the latter – the traditional – viewpoint that Poinsot works with in his *Cursus Philosophicus*. Bearing on the same subject matter, the two viewpoints are not unrelated. In chapter 12, we will investigate in considerable detail the comparative consequences of adopting one or the other of the two standpoints.[74] For the present chapter, therefore, it may be enough to note that the standpoint of the Latin scholastics, as Poinsot takes it up and reshapes it according to the requirements of the *doctrina signorum*, provides the materials for an analysis which demonstrates that the qualities of sensation sustain among themselves relations in strict accordance with the defining characteristics of the type of relation in which signification consists.[75] Though it did not occur to Peirce to overthrow the modern approach to sense qualities on the grounds that Poinsot advanced,[76] it was nonetheless by holding the so-called secondary qualities harmless in his category of Firstness while underscoring the semiotic character of the so-called primary qualities in his category of Secondness, Peirce tells us,[77] that he arrived at his idea for Pragmaticism:

---

73 *Artis Logicae Secunda Pars*, Q. 21, Art. 6, "Utrum in brutis et sensibus externis sit vera ratio signi" (=*Tractatus de Signis*, Book I, question 6).

74 See chapter 12, "The Qualities Given in Sensation: A Comparison of Modern and Medieval Treatment", p. 522ff.

75 Poinsot, *Artis Logicae Secunda Pars*, Q. 21, Art. 6, "Utrum in brutis et sensibus externis sit vera ratio signi", 686a13–688a28, esp. 687/34–42 (=*Tractatus de Signis*, Book I, Question 6, 205/34–209/32, esp. 208/34–47).

76 See, in chapter 12 below, the comparison of Poinsot and Hume under the heading "Sensation along the Way of Signs versus Sensation along the Way of Ideas", p. 530ff.; and see in chapter 15 the remarks on this point in note 7, p. 613.

77 Peirce 1907: 422, in Houser et al. 1998.

[For] arguments may turn upon such a quality ... for the reason that its meaning has structure. ... Accordingly, two such qualities, say, for example, hardness and specific heat, could not be interchanged, as we have supposed the feelings of blue and red to be interchanged, without considerable (in fact, without enormous) disturbance of the general condition of nature, as well as of a revolution in chemical physics, and other physical theories.

And this is exactly to argue for the validity of sensation and for the dependence of understanding upon sense in terms of the defining characteristics of the type of relation in which signification consists, especially that characteristic whereby a relation of signification, through its subordinate status in the sign-vehicle respecting the object signified, guarantees that a semiosis which is not degenerate leads us through the sign to an awareness not merely of something *other* but also of something *more*. The contexts are different, but the intellectual anticipation is clear. The role of the sign first at the sensory origins and foundations of awareness and only then in the perceptual and intellectual superstructures of awareness is what Poinsot undertakes to envisage in removing the discussion of *signum* from the traditional terminist perspective and recasting it in a unity and perspective proper to itself, exactly as Peirce will later do in positing pragmaticism as the way through the Kantian phenomenal veil.

The *Treatise on Signs*, then, for all Poinsot's conservative concerns and commitment to tradition in the very sense that post-Cartesian Europe will reject, is of its very nature a radical work: it takes up again the then-traditional point of entry into philosophical study (formal logic), and reshapes that point of departure according to an understanding of the fundamental activity of mind – namely, awareness as such – which makes of that activity a branch of the doctrine of signs. We have here, in the heart of Poinsot's determinedly traditional *Cursus Philosophicus Thomisticus*, nothing less than the doctrinal beginnings of a revolution in philosophy, a revolution profoundly in sympathy and tune with the modern search for a new beginning in philosophy, yet infinitely sounder in its consequences and infinitely more in tune with the requirements of critical common sense for philosophy. Even from within his tradition, Poinsot's *Tractatus de Signis* constitutes a new beginning in philosophy, where the concerns of logic and those of natural philosophy, epistemology and ontology, are joined through their common origin in the action of signs within intellection and, more generally, within experience.

The Foundation of the Perspective Proper to the Doctrina Signorum, *i.e., Its Point of Departure*
As we saw in chapter 7, the philosophical tradition indigenous to the Latin Age, as it culminated in the work of Aquinas and the school that developed after him down to the end of the Latin epoch, had a very clear focus: being. If there is one name that exactly characterized that development overall it is surely the philosophy of being, capacious enough to encompass development of dogma in the religious

sphere without stifling the doctrinal development proper to philosophy as such, while incubating at the same time the development that would emerge decisively in this time of Galileo, Poinsot, and Descartes as science in the modern sense of the word. In this regard, we had occasion, as early as chapter 6, to note in passing Maritain's remark[78] that the medieval preoccupation with developing a philosophical grasp of the order of being as it exists independently of the finite mind should not blind us in hindsight from realizing that a philosophy of being, according to the plenitude of its possibilities, must also be a philosophy of mind, *une philosophie véritable épistemologique*, as we might perhaps say, in line with Sebeok's observation[79] that epistemology marks "the midmost target" of the study of the action of signs (insofar as existing terminology can serve to mark a development not envisioned at the time that the vocabulary of modern philosophy, to which the term "epistemology" belongs, was fashioned). The first demonstration of this utmost possibility of the philosophy of being was no doubt the explicitation by Aquinas of unity, truth, goodness, plurality ("something", *aliquid*), and even thing as transcendental properties convertible with being itself.[80] But this was something incidental to the central medieval preoccupation. It remained for later thinkers, beginning especially with Poinsot, to show how Aquinas's notion of being as "first known" contained thematically the possibility of establishing a doctrinal standpoint that transcends the division of being into what is (*ens reale*) and what is not independent of the experience (*ens rationis*) within which it becomes known. Just the establishment of such a doctrinal standpoint, one that is superior to the opposition of *ens reale* to *ens rationis*, is the opening gambit requisite for a development full and proper to a doctrine of signs.

Recall from our earlier discussion[81] how being, the proper object of intellect as sound is of hearing or color of sight, is that with the grasp of which understanding begins, and being as first known (*ens ut primum cognitum*) divides first into being as it is and being as it is not independent of our cognition, *ens reale* and *ens rationis*.[82] Each of these further divides in turn: *ens reale* into substance and accident, *ens rationis* into negation and relation, on the other hand.[83] The study of substance

---

78 Chapter 6 above, p. 226 at note 44.

79 Sebeok 1991: 2.

80 See above, chapter 7, p. 253, text and note 10; chapter 9, 424n37.

81 See chapter 7, especially the sections on "The Problem of Being as First Known" and "Nonbeing in Latin Philosophy", pp. 341 & 350, respectively.

82 "Primum enim quod in intellectu cadit, est ens; secundum vero est negatio entis; ex his autem duobus sequitur tertio intellectus divisionis (ex hoc enim quod aliquid intelligitur ens, et intelligitur non esse hoc ens, sequitur in intellectu quod sit divisum ab eo)". Aquinas c.1265/6, *Quaestiones disputatae de potentia* q. 9, art. 7 ad 15 (in Busa 3, p. 258).

On the order of primitive concepts from being as first known to the point where correspondence truth can be asserted, see above, "The Sequence of First or 'Primitive Concepts' consequent upon Being" in chapter 7, p. Of course, 355ff.

83 In my article on first philosophy (Deely 1987: 8) the text on this point erroneously is printed as "negation and privation" instead of "negation and relation".

and accident as including the accident of mind-independent relation as a physical mode was the work of natural philosophy, but the study of negation and relation as mind-dependent objective modes had no comprehensive study. As a result, in working up to the doctrine of signs, Poinsot had to go to great lengths to show the consequences of a fundamental point that had come to light as early as Boethius's work on Aristotle[84] but had previously been little noted, as if it were some kind of anomaly with but marginal interest, the point, namely, that both negations and relations as mind-dependent beings share with mind-independent relation the common rationale of a "being toward", in contrast with all other modes of mind-independent being, which share as such the rationale of subjectivity or "being in" (*esse in se* in the case of substance, *esse in alio* in the case of accidents other than relation formally considered). But, in the main Latin development, the only focus in the study of *ens rationis* as such had been established in the distinction between "first" and "second intentions", inasmuch as the latter relations – second intentions – were taken to provide the subject matter for formal logic.[85]

The distinction between so-called "first" and so-called "second" intentions appears so straightforward that only the best of the Latin logicians saw much need to make their students aware of the considerable subtleties required to understand its full implications. But this was only a particular example, as we saw in chapter 7,[86] of their unfortunate general custom of passing over without note the considerable complexity of the order of *ens rationis* as a whole adequately considered, to say nothing of the role of *entia rationis* in the structuring of perception as such (*phantasiari*) in its distinction from and possible independence of (in brute animals) human understanding or "reason" *tout court*. Unfortunately, it is just these neglected complexities that are of much greater importance to the *doctrina signorum* than the distinction itself as taken to provide the focus for formal logic. For example, as Poinsot notes, "a first intention can also be found in the case of mind-dependent beings, as are many negations and privations and extrinsic denominations".[87] Thus,

---

84 See the section on "The Ontological Peculiarity of Relations Anywhere" under the treatment of Boethius in chapter 6, p. 230f.

85 *Artis Logicae Secunda Pars*, q. II, art. 2, 291a26–48 (=*Tractatus de Signis*, First Preamble, art. 2, 59/19–60/6): "But this formality of a second intention is called 'second intention' according to the difference from a first intention, as if a second state or condition of an object were being expressed. For an object can be considered in two states: *First*, as it is in itself, whether as regards existence or as regards definable structure. *Second*, as it is in apprehension, and this state of existing in cognition is second in respect of the state of existing in itself, which is first, because just as knowability follows on entity, so being known follows on that being which an object has in itself. Those affections or formalities, therefore, belonging to a thing according as it is in itself are called first intentions; those belonging to the thing according as it is known are called second intentions. And because it is the task of Logic to order things as they exist in apprehension, therefore of itself Logic considers second intentions, the intentions which coincide with things as known."

86 Recall the extended discussion of first and second intention in particular, pp. 351–4 above.

87 *Artis Logicae Secunda Pars*, Q. 12, Art. 1., 464b24–8 (=*Tractatus de Signis*, First Preamble, Article 2, 58n2): "... etiam in entibus rationis potest inveniri prima intentio, sicut sunt multae negationes et privationes et denominationes extrinsecae".

social and cultural roles and personality structure, though mind-dependent creations, *yet belong to the order of first intention.*[88] Again, "One second intention can even be materially subtended and accidentally denominated by another second intention, and so a second intention assumes the manner of a first intention in respect of the second intention to which it is subtended." Whence a *processus in infinitum*, useless in principle for explaining things at the level of physical causality,[89] is perfectly possible within the objective order,[90] and, as Peirce best pointed out,[91] is the normal condition in the action of signs within cognition – normal, because it is a consequence of the very nature of a sign as anything which determines something else (its *interpretant*) to refer to the same object and in the same way as does it itself, thus creating the three-way link or relation between sign-vehicle, interpretant, and object-signified (or significate) as the "terms". of the semiosis; with the understanding that the relation as a whole is dynamic or "transitive", such that each element, according to circumstance, can become in turn the sign-vehicle, *ad infinitum*, in an open spiral of ever-growing semiosis, by the fact that each new sign-vehicle acquires its status by leading to *something more* (when it is not degenerate, but sometimes even when it is, for the involvement of understanding

---

88 In the *Tractatus de Signis*, see 60/15–35 in the First Preamble, Article 2, and Book I, Question 2, 141/28–142/13, and n. 32 p. 150, at the end.

89 Such is the classical foundation for the rational demonstration of the existence of God from our experience of the world in Aquinas c.1266: Prima Pars, q. 3, art. 3. Cf. Poinsot, *Artis Logicae Secunda Pars*, Q. 17, Art. 2, 584b40–586a48, esp. 585a24–b11 (=*Tractatus de Signis*, Second Preamble, Article 3, "First Difficulty", 102/37–105/13, esp. 103/12–39).

90 *Artis Logicae Secunda Pars*, Q. 2, Art. 2, 292a33–293b12 (=*Tractatus de Signis*, First Preamble, Article 2, 61/31–62/18): "It follows secondly that although a first intention absolutely taken must be something mind-independent or belonging to something in the state of being independent of objective apprehension (for otherwise it would not be simply first, because that which is mind-independent always precedes and is prior to that which is mind-dependent), yet nevertheless **it is not contradictory that one second intention should be founded on another. In such a case, the founding second intention takes on as it were the condition of a first intention in respect of the other or founded intention, not because it is simply first, but because it is prior to that intention which it founds**.

"For since the understanding is reflexive upon its own acts, it can know reflexively the second intention itself and found upon that cognized intention another second intention; for example, the intention of a genus which is attributed to animal, can, as cognized, again found the second intention of species, inasmuch as the intention of genus is a kind of predicable species. And then this founded second intention denominates the founding second intention as prior, by reason of which circumstance it is said that the genus formally is a genus and denominatively is a species. This is something that frequently happens in these second intentions, to wit, that one of them is in itself formally of a certain type, but is of another type as known denominatively. Nevertheless these are all said to be second intentions, even though the one second intention is founded on another second intention, and there is not said to be a third or a fourth intention, because they all belong to (or coincide with) the object as known, but being known is always a second state for a thing. And because one second intention as it founds another takes on as it were the condition of a first intention in respect of that other founded on it, so even that intention which is founded is always said to be second."

91 Cf. Peirce 1902b: 2.303.

with sense guarantees an at least marginal existential component in every human use of signs[92]).

In view of this situation, it is not surprising that Poinsot devotes one of the longest questions in his *Tractatus de Signis*[93] to showing that the action of signs requires for its explanation the extrinsic formal causality of objective interaction – what Peirce calls "ideal" causality (but also confuses with final causality)[94] – which can be found in nature wherever there is an assimilation through representation of one thing to another in guiding future outcomes.[95] And, as if to underscore the point, Poinsot devotes the following question[96] to showing why the Aristotelian four causes of material interaction do not explain the action of signs. Equally fascinating is Poinsot's demonstration that brute animals as well as rational animals fashion and deploy mind-dependent structures of objectivity which they make use of in adapting the world to their own interests and needs. This analysis of so-called *entia rationis* materially formed and employed in the use of signs by animals without language is one of the most important elements in the preambles to Poinsot's *Tractatus de Signis*, bound up with his argument that percepts as well as concepts are formal signs. Animals, remarked Maritain,[97] make use of signs without knowing that there are signs; Poinsot shows further (what amounts to the same, but at a more sophisticated and technical level of doctrinal exposition) that animals make use of mind-dependent relations without knowing that there are mind-dependent relations.[98]

---

92 Eco (1990: 28 and 38) makes two important glosses regarding "infinite semiosis". First, "In structuralistic terms, one could say that for Peirce semiosis is potentially unlimited from the point of view of the system but is not unlimited from the point of view of the process. In the course of a semiosic process we want to know only what is relevant according to a given *universe of discourse*." Second, "Semiosis is unlimited and, through the series of interpretants, explains itself by itself, but there are at least two cases in which semiosis is confronted with something external to it. The first case is that of indices. ... indices are in some way linked to an item of the extralinguistic or extrasemiosic world. The second case is due to the fact that every semiosic act is determined by a Dynamic Object. ... We produce representamens because we are compelled by something external to the circle of semiosis."

93 *Artis Logicae Secunda Pars*, Q. 21, Art. 4, "Qualiter dividatur obiectum in motivum et terminativum", 670a18–679b53 (=*Tractatus de Signis*, Book I, Question 4, 166/1–192/14).

94 See the "Excursus on Peirce and Poinsot" in the Editorial AfterWord to the *Tractatus de Signis*, 492–8, esp. 493–4.

95 See "Semiotics and Biosemiotics: Are Sign-Science and Life-Science Coextensive?" (Deely 1991); and chapter 6 of *Basics of Semiotics* (Deely 1990a), 83–104. Also Deely 1997 & 1998.

96 *Artis Logicae Secunda Pars*, Q. 21, Art. 5, "Utrum significare sit formaliter causare aliquid in genere efficiendi", 679b14–685a33 (=*Tractatus de Signis*, Book I, Question 5, 193/1–203/32). See Deely 1991.

97 Maritain 1957: 53.

98 See Poinsot, *Artis Logicae Secunda Pars*, Q. 2, Art. 4, "Per quam potentiam et per quos actus fiant entia rationis", 301a1–306b45, esp. 301b33 302b4, where he explains precisely that "sensus interni ... repraesentare possint id, ad cuius instar formatur aliquod ens fictum, quod est materialiter formare entia rationis", and 305b19–28 (=*Tractatus de Signis*, First Preamble, art. 3, 65/1–76/45, esp. 66/47–68/31, and 74/39–48); Q. 22, Art. 2, "Utrum conceptus sit signum formale", 704a11–41 (=Book II, Question 2, 246/13–247/21). Cf. "Idolum. Archeology and Ontology of the Iconic Sign" (Deely 1986d).

My concern here, however, is not only to show how the *doctrina signorum* brings into a more comprehensive focus the many complexities of the problematic of mind-dependent being which were left in the background and on the margins of traditional logical and ontological analysis. My concern for the moment is mainly to show exactly how the *doctrina signorum* within Poinsot's *Cursus Philosophicus* relates to *ens reale* and *ens rationis* as terms distinguished within the intellectual grasp of *ens ut primum cognitum*, "being as first known". For, as Poinsot himself remarks,[99] the doctrine of signs begins – that is to say, achieves the standpoint proper to itself – with the establishment of the notion that the sign as such, precisely because it consists in a relation, transcends our experience of the objective contrast between *ens reale* and *ens rationis*, between what does and what does not reduce to our experience of it.

The point is simple, the move based on it is dramatic. Yet the text conveying this feat[100] is framed with so many technical complexities from the analysis of relation as a mode of being, complexities presupposed to the discussion of *signum* as Poinsot is concerned to situate the discussion, that Poinsot's best modern students have missed its ultimate thrust,[101] although once just barely.[102] Let me extract from the tangle the key assertion,[103] and then try to explain its import:

> we speak here of ontological relation (of relation according to the way it has being) not of categorial, that is, determinately physical, relation; because we are discussing the sign in general, as it includes equally the natural and the social sign. Hence the general

---

99 *Treatise on Signs*, Book I, Question 1, 117/28–118/6, included in the quotation in the following note.

100 *Artis Logicae Secunda Pars*, Q. 21, "De Signo Secundum Se", Art. 1, "Utrum signum sit in genere relationis", 646b16–45 (=*Tractatus de Signis*, Book I, Question 1, 117/18–118/18): "*Quaerimus ergo, an formalis ista ratio signi consistat in relatione secundum esse primo et per se, an in relatione secundum dici seu in aliquo absoluto, quod fundet talem relationem.*

"Quid sit autem relatio secundum dici et secundum esse, relatio transcendentalis et praedicamentalis, dictum est in q. 17. de Relatione [art. 1. et 2., = *Tractatus de Signis*, Second Preamble, art. 1 & 2, 80/1–99/42]. Et loquimur hic de relatione secundum esse, non de relatione praedicamentali, quia loquimur de signo in communi, prout includit tam signum naturale quam ad placitum, in quo involvitur etiam signum, quod est aliquid rationis, scilicet signum ad placitum. Et ideo praedicamentale ens esse non potest nec relatio praedicamentalis, licet possit esse relatio secundum esse iuxta doctrinam D. Thomae 1. p. q. 28. art. 1. explicatam eadem q. 17 [esp. 580a32–582a16, = *Tractatus de Signis*, 93/17–97/36], quod solum in his, quae sunt ad aliquid, invenitur aliqua relatio realis et aliqua rationis, quae relatio manifestum est, quod non sit praedicamentalis, sed vocatur relatio secundum esse, quia pure relatio est et non aliquid absolutum importat."

101 See the editor's note on the text of the *Tractatus de Signis*, Book I, Question 1, at 117/22.

102 Maritain alone in recent times begins to penetrate Poinsot's foundational doctrine in what is original to it, yet never quite cuts fully to its core: see Deely 1986, esp. 120–2.

103 *Artis Logicae Secunda Pars*, Q. 21, Art. 1, "Utrum signum sit in genere relationis", 646b26–45 (=*Tractatus de Signis*, Book I, Question 1, 117/28–118/18). See the extended discussion of the point that conventional no less than natural signs consist in the being proper to relation at *Artis Logicae Secunda Pars*, Q. 21, Art. 2, "Utrum in signo naturale relatio sit realis vel rationis", 658b30–659a39 (=*Tractatus de Signis*, Book I, Question 2, 141/12–142/13.

discussion involves no less even signs – to wit, stipulated signs as such – which are mental artifacts.[104] And for this reason, the rationale *common* to signs cannot be one which pertains exclusively to the order of physical being, not even that of a physical relation as such.[105] By the same reasoning, the common rationale of all signs could indeed be that of ontological relation as such, i.e., of relation according to its most proper character as suprasubjective (prescinding from the status of that on which the relation is founded or from which it provenates – mind-independent in the case of objective relations which are also physical, mind-dependent in the case of objective relations which are purely objective), according to the point made by St Thomas in the *Summa theologiae*, I, q. 28, art. 1, and explained in our Preamble on Relation – to wit, that only in the case of these things which exist toward another is found some mind-independent relation and some mind-dependent relation,[106] which latter plainly is not categorial, yet is called a relation according to the way it has being (an ontological relation), because it is purely a relation and does not import anything absolute.

Put as simply and straightforwardly as possible, Poinsot is saying here that the *doctrina signorum* must take its departure from a standpoint which transcends the division of being into *ens reale* and *ens rationis*.[107] This explicit realization is what sets his *Tractatus de Signis* apart within the *Cursus Philosophicus* and within Latin tradition as a whole as a virtual demand for a new beginning in philosophy, a beginning in terms of which the division of being into categories, for example, needs to be justified anew in terms of an experiential starting point;[108] and, we may

---

104 I.e., which are mind-dependent beings, objective creations of the mind itself which, lacking all subjectivity, have no being apart from the workings of thought. See the extended discussion of the point that conventional no less than natural signs consist in the being proper to relation at *Artis Logicae Secunda Pars*, Q. 21, Art. 2, "Utrum in signo naturale relatio sit realis vel rationis", 658b30–659a39 (=*Tractatus de Signis*, Book I, Question 2, 141/12–142/13.

105 See Poinsot 1632: Logica 2. p. q. 14. art. 1., *"Quid sit praedicamentum et quid requiratur ut aliquid sit in praedicamento"* ("What a category is and what are the conditions for anything's belonging to a category"), Reiser ed., 500b36–501a2: "Since the distinction of the categories was introduced for this, that the orders and classes of diverse natures might be set forth, to which all the things that participate some nature might be reduced, the very first thing to be excluded from *every* category is mind-dependent being, for being that depends for its existence on being cognized (mind-dependent being) has not a nature nor a true entity, but a constructed one, and therefore must be relegated not to a true category, but to a constructed one. Whence St Thomas says (in q. 7, art. 9 of his *Disputed Questions on the Power of God*) that only a thing independent of the mind pertains to the categories" (cited in n. 10 to Book I, Question 1 of the *Tractatus*, p. 118).

106 See the *Artis Logicae Secunda Pars*, Q. 17, "De Praedicamento Relationis", Art. 2, esp. 580a30–582a16, but also 578a24–579a34 (=*Tractatus de Signis*, Second Preamble, Article 2, esp. 93/17–96/36, but also 89/21–91/28). See further Q. 2, "De Ente Rationis Logico", Art. 1, "Quid sit ens rationis in communi et quotuplex", 287a10–32, 288a25–39; Art. 2, "Quid sit secunda intentio et relatio rationis logica et quotuplex", 291b1–46; Art. 4, "Per quam potentiam et per quos actus fiant entia rationis", 303b8–304a5 (= *Tractatus de Signis*, First Preamble, Article 1, 51/37–52/5, 53/32–45; Article 2, 60/7–44; Article 3 [sic], 70/24–71/19).

107 See Deely 1977, and 1980: 82–6.

108 Note 16 to 86/22 in the 1985 publication of Poinsot's *Tractatus de Signis* was intended to clarify this implication of Poinsot's work, but proved instead to be the single greatest occasion of

even say, a beginning which can be ignored only by aborting the fullness of the possibilities yet open to the philosophy of being as a living philosophical tradition.

To begin with, what is called *ontological relation* or *relation according to the way it has being* is called, in Poinsot's Latin, *relatio secundum esse*, a designation, we saw above, which derives from the work of Boethius in the early sixth century.[109] Within the Thomistic tradition, the *secundum esse* relative became a *terminus technicus* that had achieved a very high degree of precision thanks to the commentaries of Cajetan, Soto, and Araújo, among others. Categorial or physical relation, *relatio praedicamentalis seu relatio realis*,[110] fits the definition of *relatio secundum esse*, but so does mind-dependent relation or *relatio rationis* fit the definition.

---

misunderstanding in the contemporary discussion of Poinsot (Bird 1987: 106–7, followed by Ashworth 1988: 134–6). Accordingly, I found it necessary to clarify the point at some length (Deely 1988: 56–87, esp. 56–69), and this clarification has been incorporated into a much expanded version of note 16 for the electronic version of the *Tractatus de Signis* released by Intelex Corporation in 1992.

109 See, in chapter 6, "Boethius' Terminology for Aristotle's Difficulties with Relation", p. 226 above.

110 Here I need to repeat more forcefully the point made in chapter 8 above (p. 382) about the term "physical" as used by the Latins. The translation of *relatio realis* as "physical relation" has been the second greatest occasion of misunderstanding in contemporary discussion of the 1985 edition of Poinsot's *Tractatus de Signis*. "'Physical beings' will not do for *entia realia*", D. P. Henry states (1987: 1201), "since theological entities are for Poinsot non-physical (indeed meta-physical) but nevertheless real"; whence Henry deems this a "quite inappropriate" translation of a key term, a criticism in which he is joined by Furton 1987: 767 and Ashworth 1988: 145, who also objects on the ground that "there are places in which the type of real being picked out may well include spiritual beings".

The objection stems from ignorance of the details of the philosophical vocabulary in Poinsot's tradition, to be sure, but it also serves to emphasize the need mentioned above to go beyond the literal appearances in reading the authors of mainstream Latin tradition. In this particular, nonetheless, I was surprised to learn that it is apparently little known among contemporary renaissance Latin scholars that, beginning with Aquinas himself (e.g., c.1269: *Sententia libri ethicorum* I, lect. 1, n. 1), the term "physical" extends equally to material and spiritual substances, including the *esse divinum* ("Essentia Dei physica consistit in cumulo omnium perfectionum in gradu infinito et in summa simplicitate, ita ut, quamquam perfectio a perfectione differt plus quam ratione ratiocinante, non distinguantur tamen inter se nisi ratione ratiocinata cum fundamento in re imperfecto" – Gredt 1936: vol. II, thesis XXXII). Thus Poinsot, in the 1637 first volume of his theological *Cursus*, disp. 8. art. 6. ¶8 (but in vol. II of the modern Solesmes ed., p. 38b), speaks of divine grace as producing a "specialem modum praesentiae realis et physicae respectu Dei", flatly contradicting Henry's assertion that theological entities for Poinsot are non-physical.

The division of *ens reale* into spiritual and material substances, in the Thomistic tradition, is precisely a division (a sub-division) in the order of physical being – the order, that is to say, of being as existing independently of objectification in finite cognition. "Ens physicum" and "ens reale" alike designate this order of being throughout its extent, whence the synonymy drawn upon in the 1985 *Tractatus de Signis* translation is inaptly singled out by the reviewers for criticism. A reliable modern guide to the technical Latin usages in Poinsot's tradition can be found in the 2-volume text entitled *Elementa Philosophiae Aristotelico-Thomisticae*, written by the learned Benedictine philosopher-scientist, Joseph Gredt, exactly according to the traditional plan of Poinsot's *Cursus Philosophicus*, but updating the material of natural philosophy pertaining to experimental science (psychology, biology, physics, etc.) and addressing the problems under more current headings: see the "Editorial AfterWord" to the *Tractatus de Signis* (Deely 1985),

Now the sign is a peculiar being because our experience of it can be reduced neither to the categories of *ens reale* nor to the experiential and reflexive contrast of *ens reale* with *ens rationis*. Our experience and use of *signum* conveys with equal facility phenomena of nature, such as lead us to anticipate a storm, and phenomena of culture, such as lead us to anticipate a ceremony.

Poinsot emphasizes a twofold point which sets the Thomistic development of *signum* apart within Latin tradition. The reason that *signum* must be identified with *relatio secundum esse* is, first of all, because relation in this precise sense designates the only ontological rationale (*ratio entitatis*) which, alone and uniquely, can be found verified in each of the opposed orders of *ens reale* and *ens rationis*: this much is already clear in the cited text, with its explicit demand that the *doctrina signorum* begin at a point beyond, or prior to, the distinction between *ens reale* and *ens rationis*. The uniqueness of the action of signs that follows from this, however, Poinsot uniquely developed, a point on which we would effectively not hear again until Peirce will take it up late in the nineteenth century.

The second point is more subtle. Even though others in Poinsot's tradition had identified the sign-relation with *relatio secundum esse*, they had not seen how this identification implied a unified subject matter for the *doctrina signorum*. Sometimes relations are mind-independent, as in the case of natural signs, sometimes relations are mind-dependent, as in the case of conventional signs: this much everyone saw. What Poinsot further saw was that this opposition of natural to conventional signs does not preclude the relation constituting *either* type of sign from being sometimes mind-dependent and sometimes mind-independent.

In the case of natural signs, a natural sign formally as a sign functioning here and now is mind-dependent when the conditions required for the relation to be mind-independent are not realized. As Poinsot put it, "relatio signi naturalis ad suum signatum ... realis est ... supponendo ... conditiones relationis realis", alias rationis – "the relation of a natural sign to its significate is mind-independent when the circumstances required for a relation to be physical are realized"; otherwise, even the relation of a natural sign is mind-dependent,[111] that is (*as* a relation; or *the relation itself in its proper being*) purely objective.

In the case of conventional signs, the foundation for the sign-relation consists "in the extrinsic denomination whereby the sign-vehicle is rendered imposed or appointed for signifying by common usage", inasmuch as "it is through this imposition that something is habilitated and appointed to be a stipulated sign, just as it is through some natural sign-vehicle's being proportioned and connected with a given significate that there is founded a relation of the sign to that sig-

p. 461n97. Originally published in 1899, Gredt's work went through 7 editions in the author's lifetime, and there have been at least 5 posthumous editions, of which I have drawn primarily on the 1961 posthumous edition by Zenzen.

111 *Tractatus de Signis*, Book I, Question 2, 137/9–15. Araújo is even more explicit on the point, as reported in Beuchot 1980: 52–3.

nificate." But this original foundation does not prevent that same conventional sign from becoming habituated within a population, and by this means becoming transformed into a sign relatively natural, signifying as such by a mind-independent triadic relation and no longer merely by a mind-dependent one.[112] Thus, just as circumstances can dictate that a natural sign be realized as such through a mind-dependent relation, so circumstances can bring it about that a conventional sign be realized through a mind-independent relation.[113] And mind-independent relations based on habit constitute signs not only in the order of conventions among human animals, but also in the order of interactions between human beings and other animals or among animals themselves. In Poinsot's terse summary, "not all custom is a human act, but all custom can found a natural sign", including the individually influenced social habits which constitute customs among nonlinguistic animals.[114]

In other words, the status of *signum* as ontologically relative is not as much that of a genus respecting natural and conventional signs as its determinate species as it is an existential condition which can be realized in the mind-independent and mind-dependent orders indifferently according to the role of the fundament together with the circumstances which surround the sign but do not constitute it within cognition as a sign. For only a triadic relation can constitute a sign as such. Whether this relation will be mind-dependent or mind-independent is determined not only by the role of the fundament engendering the sign relation, but also by the circumstances under which that fundament operates in generating the relation. Thus, if the fundament of a sign-relation is a pure stipulation taken as such *prescinding from any custom which has grown up around the stipulation*, then the resulting

---

112 *Tractatus de Signis*, Book II, Question 6, 280/26–43: "when speaking of human custom, even though it proceeds from a free cause and so is denominated a free effect, nevertheless, the formal rationale of signifying is not any free deputation, but the very frequency and repetition of acts, and this signifies naturally, because it is not a moral deputation, that is to say, it is not an extrinsic deputation which denominates only morally, but the intrinsic performance of acts and their frequency and multiplication constitutes the customary sign. Therefore a signification attaches to that sign naturally, even as multiplied free acts generate a habit as a natural and not as a free effect, because the very multiplication of the acts does not function freely relative to generating the habit, so neither does the multiplication of acts function freely relative to the signifying resulting from the force of the repetition of the acts, even though these acts in themselves [i.e., singly taken] may be free."

113 According to Beuchot's report, therefore (1980: 47), we have here an important difference between Poinsot and his two main forebears, Soto and Araújo: "Por eso prefiere la de Soto, quien divide primariamente el signo en natural y convencional y, como subdivisiones del natural, el perfecto y el imperfecto o consuetudinario. Así, al ser imperfecto, no tiene significición real, sino de razon, teniendo fundamento en la costumbre, que imita a la naturaleza."

114 *Artis Logicae Secunda Pars*, Q. 22, Art. 6, 720a39–b2 (=*Tractatus de Signis*, Book II, Question 6, 280/15–23: "generaliter loquendo consuetudo non solum invenitur in hominibus, sed etiam in brutis naturali instinctu operantibus. Unde ... et ita non omnis consuetudo est actus humanus et [omnis consuetudo] fundare potest signum naturale". Detailed analysis of the "scholastic psychology" of nonlinguistic animals is made in Deely 1971; of the lability of customary signs, see Deely 1978a.

sign will be a conventional sign constituted by a mind-dependent relation. If the fundament of a sign-relation is a natural feature or characteristic of an object, or a psychological condition or state (a concept, be it an idea or an image) – *and the terminus of the sign-relation (the object signified) also exists physically*, then the resulting sign will be a natural sign constituted by a mind-independent relation. But the *signum*, whether here and now verified under a determinately mind-independent relation or under a determinately mind-dependent relation, is realized according to the same rationale in either case and in both cases, to wit, the rationale of a triadic "being toward" which as such transcends subjectivity in every case and renders objects signified univocal in their being as objects regardless of differences in their status as things physically existing.

This singular ability of the sign to pass back and forth between the orders of mind-independent and mind-dependent being with rationale unchanged (precisely and uniquely because, as sign, it is an exercise of the ontological rationale of relation) gives the *doctrina signorum* the singular capacity to explain both the possibility of correspondence truth and the reason why truth as correspondence is needed as a critical check upon experience as constituted from within by a texture of relations commingling real and unreal objects, natural and conventional signs, deceits as well as wisdom. The doctrine of signs has a unified subject matter to investigate precisely because the rationale which constitutes any given sign is the same regardless of the circumstances of its occurrence, even though the circumstances of its occurrence will locate the sameness now as resulting primarily from nature, now as primarily from cognition, usually as an admixture of the two orders as together constituting experience. The very fact that the same being of the *relativum secundum esse* is realized in the diversity of all signs as the common ground of the action proper to signs explains the difference between the objective order as such and the subjective order of physical being, including psychological subjectivity.

Poinsot is not only re-explaining the opening chapters of his traditional *Cursus Philosophicus* in terms of the bearing thereon of the last chapters which conclude it (and therewith the traditional *Cursus Artium*), chapters from the tradition of commentary on the *De Anima*; he is also explaining the nature of experience and the experiential origins of the traditional doctrines of logic and the categories of natural philosophy. But his concern is not to emphasize all this inasmuch as it is material assuredly new. On the contrary, his concern is to control, balance, qualify, and restrict by the total concerns of Latin tradition the *doctrina signorum* that more recent concerns and refinements of Latin tradition have forced to the foreground.

The question we have now to ask is what would have to be made of this doctrine newly systematized were it free to follow on its own terms its deep tendency and enter history on its own terms, rather than under the terms imposed upon it by a traditional superstructure developed largely oblivious to its own foundations as a sign-dependent structure? In other words, how does the *doctrina signorum* appear when viewed no longer in the context of Poinsot's *Cursus Philosophicus Thomisticus* (and hence, indirectly, as a commentary on Thomas Aquinas), but rather as a pure philosophical possibility and doctrine in its own right?[115]

The Tractatus de Signis *Viewed in Terms of Its Own Requirements for Philosophy*

The first thing to be said about Poinsot's *Treatise on Signs* viewed on its own has been said by the grand old man of Peirce scholarship, Max H. Fisch:[116] "within its limits, it is the most *systematic* treatise on signs that has ever been written". What Poinsot has presented in his thematization of the sign is a thoroughgoing demonstration that the action of signs is what gives structure to our sensations, perceptions, and understanding, both practical and theoretical – in a word, to our experience as a whole. If this is true, a philosophy based on experience must be based on the sign, and a philosophy of signs must be a philosophy of experience even in order to be and to remain, beyond that, a philosophy of being. If philosophy begins with experience, then philosophy begins with signs and remains dependent upon the action of signs in its farthest developments. Philosophy can know objects which are more than signs and, through such objects, something of things as well in their own being, as can science; but nothing of this can come about without signs or other than through the action of signs critically controlled and adjusted by understanding, both comparative and reflexive.

Viewed in terms of its own requirements for philosophy, therefore, Poinsot's *Tractatus de Signis* has the same consequences that we have seen it to have for tradition: it requires a re-examination of philosophy's starting point, exactly as the moderns demanded; and a recognition that that starting point is rooted in the action of signs which determine the nature and extent of our knowledge, which the way of ideas blocked from the view of the moderns. "Poinsot's semiotics", wrote Sebeok,[117] "expands our comprehension not only of communication, but in countless ways of

---

115   In other words, what would happen were we to put to the *Cursus Philosophicus* and existing tradition as a whole the proposal Poinsot put explicitly only to the logicians of his day? I paraphrase 38/11–19 of the *Tractatus de Signis*:

> Nevertheless, because these matters are all treated in those books by way of interpretation and signification, since indeed the universal instrument of awareness is the *sign*, from which all its instruments are constituted, therefore, lest the foundation of the expositions of philosophy itself go unexamined, the project of the present work is to treat of those things concerning the nature and divisions of signs insinuated in the works of traditional philosophy, but which have been reserved for special treatment here. (Sed tamen, quia haec omnia tractantur in his libris per modum interpretationis et significationis, commune siquidem cognitionis instrumentum est signum, quo omnia eius instrumenta constant, idcirco visum est in praesenti pro doctrina horum librorum ea tradere, quae ad explicandam naturam et divisiones signorum in libris traditionalibus insinuata, huc vero reservata sunt.)

116   Fisch 1986: 180.
117   Sebeok 1986b: 15.

what is communicated, and it suggests possibilities for finding a unity for knowledge that may have seemed lost forever after Descartes."[118]

In the end, once the traditional terms of its discussion have finally been understood, the most surprising thing about Poinsot's *Tractatus de Signis* is how modern it clearly was in the context of its original composition in sharing and vindicating the modern aspiration for a turn to experience and a reading of the book of nature on its own terms within experience. At the same time, by eschewing instead of sharing the modern presupposition that ideas are objects – indeed, by showing that the very nature of sign as ontologically relative precludes its intramental occurrence under the guise of object directly apprehended, the most surprising thing about Poinsot's *Tractatus de Signis* is how postmodern it clearly is (and foundationally so) when translated into the context of semiotic development at the dawn of the twenty-first century.

History has its accidents, but in this case it has also its confluences. The year in which Poinsot brought his *Tractatus* to publication was the year in which John Locke was born. At the age of fifty-eight, Locke, in fathering the second of the two great traditions which defined the development of modern philosophy, concluded his famous *Essay concerning Humane Understanding* by proposing that the answer to the modern question posed by Descartes in launching the rationalist tradition, and posed anew by Locke himself in launching the empiricist tradition, should perhaps be sought instead by launching another tradition, a line of reflection based on "*semiotic* or *the doctrine of signs*".[119] Neither Locke himself nor any of his successors in the modern period tried out this "way of signs". Instead, as history

---

118 A striking instance of what Greimas once described as "intersemioticity", this remark of Sebeok echoes a passage from Maritain's masterpiece (1959: 66–7) undertaking to reconcile the growth of science in the modern sense with the epistemological tenets of philosophy of being, an undertaking largely based on Maritain's understanding of the unified doctrine of signs precisely as first set forth by Poinsot: "If workers are not wanting, if unreasonable prejudices (due above all, it seems, to a morbid fear of ontological research and of all philosophy ordered to a knowledge of things – as though a philosophy of being could not also be a philosophy of mind) do not turn them back from the study of the only philosophy that claims to face the universality of the extramental real without at the same stroke pretending to absorb all knowing into itself, it might well be hoped that we will see a new dawn break upon a new and glorious scientific era – putting an end to misunderstandings engendered in the realm of experimental research by the conflict between Aristotle and Descartes – in which the sciences of phenomena would finally achieve their normal organization, some, physics above all, undergoing the attraction of mathematics and continuing their remarkable progress along this line, others, biology and psychology especially, undergoing the attraction of philosophy and finding in that line the organic order they need and the conditions for a development that is not merely material, but truly worthy of the understanding. Thus there would be a general redistribution springing from the natural growth of the sciences of phenomena, but one that would also suppose – and this point is quite clear – the supreme regulation of metaphysical wisdom.

"The divine good of intellectual unity, shattered for three centuries now, would thus be restored to the human soul."

119 After treating the moderns in their own right, we will be in a position to expand this sentence into chapter 14, "Locke Again: The Scheme of Human Knowledge".

amply recorded, the "way of ideas" was pursued by modern philosophy down to its classical systematization in the *Critiques* of Immanuel Kant, a Pyrrhic victory if ever there was one.

As we will see in chapter 14, Locke's proposal, when it was considered at all, was rejected out of hand – for example, by Leibniz, in his *New Essays concerning Human Understanding* (1704), on the grounds that natural phenomena and conventional signs have no common denominator, because the latter are arbitrary and the former not; and that a distinction one of whose parts – semiotic – virtually absorbs the other two – physics and ethics – is defective.[120] Fraser, in his 1894 edition of Locke's *Essay*,[121] has only disparagement for "this crude and superficial scheme of Locke" wherein it is proposed that the study of signs as providing the means for speculative and practical knowledge alike may hold the key to understanding aright the nature and extent of human knowledge.

As the modern period in philosophy reached its end, a more judicious assessment was made by Charles Sanders Peirce. But this we will have occasion to see at length when we reach chapter 15. Here it is enough to observe that Locke's proposal for semiotic, once seen against the backdrop of Poinsot's *Tractatus de Signis*, surely appears as one of history's confluences within the *Zeitgeist* of the seventeenth century, revealing as it does that the very problem exercising modern thought in its rejection of Latin immersion in Aristotelian philosophy of nature was the problem on which Poinsot brought all the resources of Latin tradition to bear, namely, the problem, as Locke put it,[122] of "the way and proportion that objects are suited to our faculties, and upon those grounds they are capable of being proposed to us". This task, in Descartes words,[123] is one which "everyone with the slightest love of truth ought to undertake at least once in his life, since the true instruments of knowledge and the entire method are involved in the investigation of the problem". That Peirce should have come to be regarded in the twentieth century as the father of semiotics, as in the seventeenth century Descartes was of rationalism and Locke of empiricism, is, by contrast, rather more of an accident, the historical accident whereby the highest development of Latin thought on the doctrine of signs after Ockham fell into oblivion, and the Iberian influence on university life, except as filtered through Suárez, became lost to modern times.

As the contemporary development enters a postmodern age, this particular accident of history, at least, is being redressed. And in this particular we have learned enough to now see clearly that, when it comes to the doctrine of signs, what Whitehead once credibly alleged[124] is credible no longer, namely, that:

---

120 Cf. Winance 1983: 515 – "c'est dans la tradition de Peirce, Locke, et Jean de Saint-Thomas que la logique peut devenir une sémiotique qui absorberait l'épistémologie et même la philosophie de la nature."
121 Vol. II, p. 463 n. 1.
122 Locke 1690: 30.
123 Descartes 1628: 31.
124 Whitehead 1925: 39.

a brief, but sufficiently accurate, description of the intellectual life of the European
races during the succeeding two centuries and a quarter up to our own times is that
they have been living upon the accumulated capital of ideas provided for them by the
genius of the seventeenth century.

The problem with Whitehead's assertion is that, in the area of the doctrine of signs,
the accumulated capital of ideas provided by the genius of the seventeenth century
was primarily Hispanic, and by dint of circumstance (not excluding some deep-
rooted prejudices) was effectively not available to the European races to draw upon.
Whitehead's observation is, in equal parts, sufficiently accurate and sufficiently
inaccurate. This chapter has dealt with the part that is inaccurate. If the intellectual
life of the European races during the past three centuries had indeed been living
upon the complete capital of ideas laid up in the seventeenth century, Peirce would
not be regarded by anyone as the father of semiotic tradition but as one of its
late systematizers, perhaps in a position respecting semiotic tradition comparable to
the position in which Poinsot found himself respecting Latin tradition in logic and
natural philosophy, or Thomistic tradition in theology.

What is certain is that philosophical doctrine as it developed in the later Latin centuries in the area of what we today call "epistemology", or the theory of knowledge,
has an intrinsic relevance to the modern concern to grasp the true nature and grounds
of human understanding; and, beyond that, to see understanding itself in relation
to the action of signs on which understanding thoroughly depends – especially, as
we will see in chapter 14, as the suspicion was voiced by Locke under the name of
semiotic. Locke's concern, anticipated by Poinsot, has been taken up today through
the work of Charles Sanders Peirce, whence it bids fair to become the mainstream
postmodern development as philosophy, along with the rest of civilization, moves
into the twenty-first century.

Conclusion

The independent publication of Poinsot's *Tractatus de Signis* in 1985 indeed had
the merit, among others, as Santaella said,[125] "of making evident that the doctrine
of signs proclaimed by Locke did not have to wait two-hundred years to rise
in the bosom of Peirce's complex and monumental work". Yet Peirce does not
provide the only proof in contemporary philosophy of the value of Poinsot's work
to philosophy's future. Jack Miles, in preparing copy for the release by the University
of California Press of the 1985 autonomous edition of Poinsot's *Treatise on Signs*,
wrote: "That Poinsot's diagnosis of the course of western philosophy was superior
to – or at the very least clearly distinct from – the alternative diagnosis of Descartes
and of all modern philosophy is proven, Deely argues, by the re-emergence in our

---

125 Santaella 1991: 155.

day of Poinsot's questions as semiotic." I would stand by Miles's formulation, but add in support of it here the following concluding observations, before we return to a tracing of philosophy's actual path in crossing the frontier separating the Latin Age from what would become the mainstream modern development.

If we put Poinsot's claim that the doctrine of signs transcends in its starting point the division of being into *ens reale* and *ens rationis* into contemporary terms, what is being asserted is that semiotic transcends the opposition of *realism* to *idealism*. Not until Heidegger in the contemporary period do we encounter such a claim among the philosophers. Heidegger at least recognized that "this problem [of the unity of being prior to the categories] was widely discussed in medieval ontology especially in the Thomist and Scotist schools," and although he did not think that the medieval discussion succeeded in "reaching clarity as to its principles", neither did Heidegger know of Poinsot's work in this particular, nor of Aquinas's neglected doctrine of the *primum cognitum*. Correspondence truth both Poinsot and Heidegger recognized; but with his doctrine of signs Poinsot was achieving within the Latin tradition the first systematic clarification of the ontological foundations in relation for the possibility of truth as a conformity knowable in the structures of objectivity between thought and things, the very clarification Heidegger called for as late as 1943 in his essay *Vom Wesen der Wahrheit*, "On the Essence of Truth".

The difficulty and originality alike of Poinsot's work derive, in short, from his recognition that *the first concern* of anyone who would seek to explain signs, the universal means of communication, must be to pay heed to "Aristotle's *problem of the unity of Being* [as that which is experientially first in human understanding] as over against the multiplicity of 'categories' applicable to things".[126] The experience of signs and of the escape from the subjectivity of the here and now is as fundamental in its own way as is the experience of things in terms of the data which provide experimental justification for the scheme of the categories, as is clear from the fact that the derivation of the categories from experience is itself a function of the use we make of signs in developed discourse.[127]

Nor can we omit to mention specifically in Poinsot's case that peculiarity of late Latin texts which typically gives rise among modern readers to what we have called the "fallacy of the nose of wax". For Poinsot was a man of the Latin Age, a "medieval man"; and such men were in the habit, "opposed to modern habits", as Eco best noted,[128] of attributing retrospectively to their authorities, their favored *auctores*

---

126 "Und wenn schliesslich *Hegel* das 'Sein' bestimmt als das 'unbestimmte Unmittelbare' und diese Bestimmung allen weiteren kategorialen Explikationen seiner 'Logik' zugrunde legt, so hält er sich in derselben Blickrichtung wie die antike Ontologie, nur dass er das von Aristoteles schon gestellte Problem der Einheit des Seins gegenber der Mannigfaltigkeit der sachhaltigen 'Kategorien' aus der Hand gibt" (Martin Heidegger, *Sein und Zeit* 1927: 3).

127 See the gloss on Poinsot's *Artis Logicae Secunda Pars*, Q. 17, Art. 1, "Utrum a parte rei dentur relationes, quae sint formae intrinsecae", 577a10–28 (=86/9–22) in the 1985 *Tractatus de Signis*, Second Preamble, Article 1, p. 86 n. 16, especially as expanded in the electronic edition on the basis of Deely 1988.

128 Eco 2000: 416n22.

("*auctoritates*"), what in fact they were seeing in original fashion. The obverse of this habit in their late modern (and postmodern) readers gives rise, as we have seen, to an excess of credulity respecting the literal appearances of a text, wherein the camouflage of the sparse terminology defeats the readers' interpretive efforts, miscasting, as it were, the role of the reader; and what is original remains concealed in the translation to the modern reading, which reveals instead only "a wasteland of repetitions", as we have seen it alleged. Different habits of different ages, at this particular boundary, have produced "the result that it is always difficult to understand to what extent [a medieval author, especially later ones] assumed positions contrary to", or simply different from and novel respecting, "earlier tradition".[129]

Yet the task is not impossible. In the case immediately before us, we can say that Poinsot's contribution to the seventeenth-century search for a new beginning in philosophy, albeit unnoted and unheeded at the time, was nothing less than to show in detail what that new beginning, the turn to the "book of nature" read through experience, might best consist in so far as concerned the future development of philosophy in the doctrinal order: namely, a setting out in earnest along the way of signs. It was a contribution destined to be overlooked in its day, but privileged to enter into the history of semiotic development anew at a later time, the time when the exploration of the way of signs would be, for the first time, thematically undertaken. By this accident history achieves another confluence, and the last of the Latins joins the last of the moderns to initiate a postmodern era in philosophy, where experience and the being proper to it become the central occupation of philosophy in exploring the way of signs.

But we must remember that, in terms of our survey of philosophy's history, all that has just been said, however true, yet describes the shadow or ghost of a road not taken. Having looked down this road as far as we could to where it bends in the undergrowth of the early twenty-first century, let us return to the other, perhaps not just as fair,[130] yet having for sure the better claim in being the way actually trod by that small army of thinkers who gave us the modern world. It is time to consider the Way of Ideas in that kind of detail that only historical actuality can provide.

---

129 Ibid.
130 The allusion is to Frost 1915: 223, from chapter 8, 365n2 above.

PART THREE

The Modern Period

The Way of Ideas

Likeness of John Locke (1623–1704)
Engraved in 1713 by George Vertue (1646–1756), after a 1697 painting by Gottfried Kneller (1646–1723); from the frontispiece to the sixth edition in three volumes of *The Works of John Locke* (London: printed for D. Browne et al., 1759), in the Special Collections of Loras College Library

CHAPTER ELEVEN

Beyond the Latin Umwelt: Science Comes of Age

Questions Only Humans Ask

The objective world of the human being is as much a selection of physical stimuli and reorganization of the features of the environment thus made objectified or known as is the objective world of any animal. This situation is by force of circumstance, a simple consequence of the fact that we are biological organisms with sensory organs that detect some things and not others, and with a biological nature that finds some things in the environment suitable and desirable and others not. Thus, we live first of all in a world which is determined in its objective structure, on the one side, by the interaction of material objects with our organs of sense and, on the other side, by our nature as organisms suited for some things more than for others.

Like all higher organisms, this so-called "nature" according to which we have preferences and requirements in relation to the physical environment around us is not something that has no flexibility at all. Social animals learn from one another, and in this way discoveries or preferences of one individual can, through learning and assimilation, become characteristic of a group. For example, in the human case, ants are one of the features of the physical world quite suited to meeting part of the nutritional needs of our bodies. Among the readers of this book, there are probably few who have eaten ants, and fewer still who eat ants as a regular thing. Why not?

There are, after all, other human communities which relish eating ants as a great delicacy. The story is told of one of the early front-rank anthropologists that he used to enjoy having American friends over to his New York apartment for a fairly lavish dinner which would invariably delight the taste buds and pique the curiosity of his guests. "What is this? It's delicious!" was a frequent early remark at these occasional gatherings. But the anthropologist would mysteriously refuse to tell until coffee after the meal. Then, in order to observe and record the reactions, he would reveal what his guests had reveled in with such gustatory delight. These reactions were frequently quite extreme, not unusually to the point of illness and vomiting.

So it is with all the higher social animals. They develop patterns of preference in the fulfillment of their needs, so that the Umwelt or objective world in which they live admits of some variety and interest. Yet this variety is wholly constrained in its outer limits by physiology and biology: the animals cannot become aware of anything in the environment which is not proportioned to action on their channels of sense perception, and they cannot meet their needs by eating types of food that fall outside the range of what their bodies are capable of assimilating and transforming into their own flesh.

But in the case of human animals, the factor of language introduces an element of unprecedented flexibility into the Umwelt. Suddenly we have an animal which is able to relate to things on the basis of a whole new set of considerations. The human animal discovers in the objects that it perceives a dimension of existence-in-itself, and marks this difference with a peculiar use of sounds and marks which is what ordinarily is meant when the term "language" is used. But, as we noted in the opening of this book, this use of language to communicate through sounds and marks is in fact an exaptation not an adaptation, a secondary employment of language not the primary one. Primarily language consists in a way of seeing the world that is able to conceive of possibilities in the arrangement of objects that does not reduce to their relation or possible relation to the needs and interests of the human being as an organism. This way of seeing the world is capable of considering the relation of objects to themselves as well as the place such objects may have in the physical environment as that environment is something existing not merely distinct from but in principle other than the objective world from within which the various possibilities of existence are considered in the first place.

As a consequence of this unique way of seeing objects, the Umwelt becomes, uniquely for the human being, a starting point for investigations which can discover things that could never be discovered by simple sensation and sense perceptions organized on the basis of sensation in terms of biological needs and interests further specified and structured by learned patterns subspecific to a particular society. Thus, the human Umwelt comes to be populated with objects that exist in no other animal's Umwelt, and that cannot, moreover, be communicated as such across species lines.

If you want to gain an appreciation of the difference between language and communication, try finding out from your dog or cat where he has been the next time he disappears for a day or two. You will have no trouble communicating with the animal at the level of perceptions and feelings. But language is the exaptation of perceptions and feelings in relation to a consideration of the way things are or might be independently of perceptions and feelings. Language structures a communication about objects based on a grasp of relationships that can be detached from their immediate foundations in perception and redirected to other aspects of objects independent of their immediate presence in perception. To let your dog know that you are glad to see him will be no problem. But when you get to the point of asking where he's been you will find out the difference between language and communication.

Of course, given language, it can be exapted to communicative uses in speech and writing. But *this* communication, linguistic communication, presupposes a difference in the fundamental way of cognizing the world. Without the underlying difference, communication between animal individuals cannot rise above the perceivable sensory aspects of the sounds used in communication. Your dog understands well the tone and feeling that accompany your words. But the words as words, as relating to objects in their proper being as objects distinct from whatever relation they happen to have in perception here and now – this level of meaning escapes the dog completely, and forever will.

The question of how it stands with being, How are things really?, arises only among linguistic animals, only among human beings. And by exapting language into the external forms of speech and writing, or gestures, for that matter, we can communicate to our conspecifics, to individuals of our own species, our own doubts or convictions about the way things "really are". Unfortunately, nothing guarantees that we will be right in particular cases, and few things are more difficult, even in limited cases, than determining how things "really are". But hope springs eternal in the human breast. And there is plenty of reason both for hope and for despair in this area, given the history of the species.

Reasonable Questions Philosophy Cannot Answer

The human use of signs is marvelous indeed. How did it happen that an animal confined to the surface of the earth came to know the distance of the earth from the sun? How did it happen that this animal came to know that, all sensory appearances to the contrary notwithstanding, the earth does not stand still while the sun revolves around it but, quite the reverse, revolves around the sun at the astonishing speed of about eighteen-and-a-half miles per second, while both sun and earth *further* are in motion relative to the other stars, in one of countless galaxies? How does it happen that, if the earth is moving so rapidly through space, there are days when the air is completely calm? And so on.

Even though all such questions arose initially within philosophy, as we saw earlier in visiting through Thales the shores of ancient Greece, philosophy is powerless to arrive at answers to such questions. This has led some in modern times, such as Bertrand Russell (1872–1970), to conclude that philosophy consists in raising questions that are, at the time, unanswerable. As long as they remain unanswerable, they continue to be philosophical questions.

But, over the centuries, human beings discover more and more ways to expand their investigations of the cosmos, and questions that were once unanswerable later on become answerable. At that moment, *science* is born in its difference from philosophy. Science is the study of answerable questions, while philosophy is the raising of questions beyond the horizon of our present ability to give answers. For this reason philosophy is the mother of all the sciences, and each of the sciences, one by one, go their independent way as soon as human beings reach the level of intellectual maturity to begin to get answers to the types of questions that constitute that science.

How Is Philosophy Different from Science?

This view of the difference between science and philosophy is true as far as it goes. But it does not express the whole of the difference, or even what is most important to it. There is a further difference between questions which admit of answers but *in principle* cannot be answered directly by experimental means, and questions which can be so answered. In the Latin Age, the one term *scientia*, "science", was used for all of human knowledge in its intellectual form. Nonetheless, the Latins also had a term for the discursive knowledge proper specifically to the former sorts of question: *doctrina*. Little by little in the modern period, the term *scientia* became assimilated more and more to the latter sorts of question, that is to say, questions for which the only possible answer must be derived from experimentation. And that is the situation today. Science is a word that only philosophers still try to apply to philosophy. The time for giving this up is long past, but old habits die hard in human cultures.

In any event, the modern period was the time in human history when the distinction between science and philosophy came to be firmly established in the human Lebenswelt. It is the distinction between questions directly answerable by empirical means and questions that must be answered by thought itself at its own level of objectification as irreducible to the objectifications of sense. This difference between philosophical doctrine and scientific theory is not an opposition, but a distinction and difference between complementary theoretical enterprises. Science cannot develop without being based on assumptions whose validity can be adjudicated only with recourse to the doctrinal arguments proper to discourse within philosophy. The "first philosophy" of Aristotle as a reflection on the principles, methods, and even results of scientific investigation remains as a more fundamental form of inquiry than science itself. But such inquiry can in no way substitute for science or adjudicate its results in advance. It took the three centuries or so of modernity for the human mind to grasp this point with any clarity.

Today we see clearly that the object of science, while transcending perception, always concerns and essentially depends upon what can be directly sensed within perception. By contrast, the object of philosophy concerns, among other things, rather the framework as such of understanding according to which whatever is sensed and perceived is interpreted intellectually. A story told about Hegel's approach to the teaching of an introduction to philosophy may help illustrate the point. Philosophy differs from the natural sciences, he is said to have explained, in that its object has to be constituted anew each time we philosophize, while the objects investigated by natural science already have in part a fully determined being in the rocks and stars of the physical environment. To get the point across, he would then ask his students whether they could see the blackboard. Of course they could, and breathed a sigh of relief that perhaps the going in this class was not going to be as rough as rumored. On noting their assent, Hegel then advised them they were therefore in a position to begin doing science. But now for philosophy. "You see the blackboard", he affirmed. "Now", he said, "we begin our first question in philosophy. Can you see the seeing?" The students' relief at the earlier question at once disappeared, and they knew the course would not be so easy after all. The object philosophy seeks to investigate is like that: it exists determinately only in the thinking, not prior to and independently of it. It can be understood; it cannot be perceived by sense.

This object is not reducible to language, but is nonetheless accessible only through language. Debating whether the atom can be split, the scientist can ultimately resort to an experiment *demonstrando ad sensus*, "demonstrating by sensible effects". Debating whether God exists or what the nature of signs is, such that they can be used to debate about objects which depend upon material conditions (such as atoms), or spirits, which by nature would not depend upon matter (especially in the case of God), the philosopher never has the privilege of falling back upon such a "crucial experiment" to indicate likelihood among probabilities.

From first to last, philosophy has only a *demonstratio ad intellectum*, an "appeal to intelligibility", whereupon to rest its case. Science is the domain of experiments. The domain of philosophy is intellectual doctrine as irreducible to what can be manifested as decisive in an empirical frame. There are many areas in the development of hypotheses and the elaboration of frameworks for the testing of hypotheses where, to be sure, philosophy and science overlap. But ultimately there is always the difference between *scientia* as what can in some important measure be reduced to a crucial experiment *demonstrando ad sensus*, and *doctrina* as a body of thought sensitive to its own implications and striving for consistency throughout, while achieving explanations (however provisional) at a level beyond what can be empirically circumscribed in unambiguous ways.[1]

Some of the questions which philosophy is powerless to answer religion, too, is powerless to answer. But coming out of the Latin Age, this fact was, to say the least, not fully appreciated by the proponents of religion. The word "doctrine" in the Latin Age was used not only for specifically and irreducibly philosophical theories but also for the linguistic formulations of religious beliefs. And when religious doctrine tries to lay claim to knowledge that can be truly established only by scientific or by philosophical discourse, serious trouble is only a matter of time. Doctrine in the philosophical sense is not and can never be dogma in the religious sense.

The Quarrels between Faith and Reason

Now this is an aspect of the development of philosophy on which we have not dwelt over-much in this book, although we have had occasion to mention along the way various "condemnations" suffered at the hands of Church authorities, such as that of John Scotus Erigena in the ninth century or that of Roscelin late in the eleventh century.

---

1 On the contrast of *doctrina* with *scientia* in the modern sense, see the terminological entry "Doctrine" in the *Encyclopedic Dictionary of Semiotics* (Deely 1986a), and appendix I, "On the Notion 'Doctrine of Signs'", in *Introducing Semiotic* (Deely 1982: 127–30).

The story of condemnations of philosophers by religious authorities is a very long one, requiring several volumes of its own to be told properly. Scarcely a single major thinker of the Latin Age, including Thomas Aquinas himself, was not condemned by religious authorities at one time or another. More than one civilization has been destroyed by inappropriate and improper assertion of religious authority. Islamic civilization essentially beheaded itself around the time of Averroes, and has never to this day recovered that freedom of thought required for intellectual vitality and life.[2] In the Latin twilight, at the dawn of modern times, just as science was making its first major moves to separate its domain from that of the philosophers, our own civilization came close to doing the same.

There is also another side to the story, ways in which religion has expanded the range of human inquiry. Great as were the achievements and academies of ancient Greek philosophy, it was the Latin "middle ages" of Christian civilization that gave to the world the system of universities. The university, as it has increasingly provided a focus for support of research to ground "teaching", more than any single institution, has transformed civilization by giving the development of inquiry an institutional framework. However much the Latin Age owed to the Greek heritage, the university was nonetheless an indigenous Latin development; and it was this development that germinated the "modern world", in particular its great institutions of ongoing learning and science. The religious atmosphere in which the Latin Age began impacted expansively on poetry,[3] rhetoric,[4] and natural theology[5] right from the outset. Whatever conflicts there have been, there has also been, on the face of it, something quite positive in the contribution the religious faith gave to at least some thinkers by temperament inquirers; for it enabled them to move "scientific intelligence" beyond isolated, individual genius into a framework of developing community. Yet not even this fascinating tale is the road I want to follow now.

Every highway has its own advantages. By tracing the history of philosophy as an intellectual doctrine, rather than as the story of how modern science came to establish itself, we have taken a less well-mapped route through the Latin Age. The single most properly defining event of this route was the landmark introduction of the notion of sign, the notion definitive in terms of the Latin philosophical culture as such and as a whole, as we have seen. By following this route, we have pointed the way for better understanding contemporary developments. But we also missed some of the most exciting and notorious events of the last Latin century when the modern national languages began to displace Latin as the mainstream medium of intellectual discourse, events that introduced the modern age. Let us take at least a glance back at these well-mapped events along the common route.

---

2 See "The Contribution of Islam to Philosophy in the Latin Age", in chapter 5 above, p. 186.
3 Taylor 1911.
4 Cameron 1991.
5 Pelikan 1993.

The Condemnation (21 June 1633) of Galileo Galilei (1564–1642)

If we had to pick one event as the defining event of the outset of modernity, probably the best choice would be the condemnation of Galileo for teachings deemed contrary to the revealed Word of God. The consequences to Galileo's person from this event were so comparatively mild that I am tempted to concentrate rather on the case of Giordano Bruno (c.1548–1600), who illuminated the beginning of the "age of reason" with flames. After eight years imprisonment by the Inquisition, first at Venice (23 May 1592–27 February 1593), then at Rome, Bruno was, for heresy, bound to an iron stake and burned on a pyre in the Piazza Campo de' Fiori, on 19 February 1600, at the age of fifty-two.[6] Indeed, on the fateful Friday, 22 May 1592, when he was arrested by agents of the Inquisition, Bruno was preparing to leave Venice for Frankfurt, presumably to oversee the printing of his manuscript *On the Composition of Images, Signs, & Ideas*, completed the year before, "the most outspoken and intransigent of the works published in his lifetime, at least from the viewpoint of Roman Catholic Orthodoxy"[7] in Italy of the time. But the simple fact is that it was the milder and more reasonable case of Galileo which permanently inflamed the indignation and imagination of scientific people everywhere.

Galileo was condemned on 21 June 1633, one year after Poinsot published his *Tractatus de Signis*. Descartes, learning of the condemnation, immediately rushed to his publisher to withdraw from production his just completed treatise *Le Monde* ("On the World"). Poinsot, even though well connected with the highest Church authorities of the time, skipped the publication of his own treatise on astronomy and apparently destroyed all the manuscripts.

Now what was the Galileo controversy all about? If you are really interested, and I suggest that perhaps you should be, an excellent starting point would be to read *Galileo, Science, and the Church* by James Langford.[8] And if you are *really* interested, then the richest source of properly philosophical, and not merely cultural, lessons to be learned from the case is perhaps contained in the ongoing studies of William A. Wallace and his colleagues (1977–92). Wallace was a member of the papal commission which reopened the Galileo case in this century and concluded with a formal acknowledgment by the Church of its blunder. The whole situation has been reviewed in detail by Annibale Fantoli[9] since the conclusion of that commission. Although his large study does not change the overall outline one gets from Langford, the wealth of scholarly detail and the tracing of the reluctant steps of official retrenchment over the more than three centuries from the trial to the present is well worth the reading. The case the inquisitors thought to have closed in 1633 turned out to be the opening of a case not closed yet, one wherein the erstwhile judges have themselves become defendants on trial by history.

---

6 In 1889, a statue to Bruno was erected on the spot of his burning.
7 In the description by Higgins and Doria 1991: xxxv.
8 Langford 1992.
9 Fantoli 1996.

Well what was the issue in the Galileo case? To reduce it to a simplest bottom line,[10] it was a question of who knows better than God and his official representatives on earth how the heavens work? The Scriptures plainly tell us that the sun moves around the earth.[11] From unanswerable arguments in Aristotle also, we know the earth to be motionless at the center of the universe. Galileo, on the contrary, is trying to tell us that it is the sun that is the motionless center and the earth that moves. This claim is contrary to all experience as well as contrary to the revealed word of

---

10 And I skip over the messy details of Tycho Brahe's alternative hypothesis to Copernicus which fit the data as well without requiring the rejection of traditionally established positions in cosmology, theology, and scriptural exegesis, because this "alternative" has proved in the hindsight of history to be exactly what Galileo deemed it to be at the time: *multi passus extra viam* – a waste of everyone's time. Even so, the definitive observational proof that Galileo needed for his position, namely, the detection of stellar parallax (an apparent circular movement of a nearer star against the background of farther stars mirroring the orbital motion of the earth on which the observer stands) required better telescopes than the time could devise, and had to wait well over a century, by which time the overthrow of the Ptolemaic model had already been thoroughly achieved on several independent grounds.
   Galileo was unable conclusively to demonstrate the conclusions he wanted to advance as being, in his judgment, the facts of the matter about the solar system; even so, his argument was that the weight of the evidence, the *pondus considerationis*, inclined the sufficiently sophisticated participant in the controversy toward his view. Many have tried to argue that this lack of conclusive demonstration at the time on Galileo's side mitigates or somehow makes less damaging the certainty of the religious authorities in their own theological and hermeneutic conclusions, which all today concede were in fact ill-founded in all that concerned the case (even though, as it were, invisibly so at the time), but which yet were made the basis for severe action against Galileo and censure of his work. How this can be effectively construed as mitigating has always been a mystery to me.
   The slow retrenchment on the part of the religious authorities over the centuries succeeding Galileo's trial seems mainly to reveal how hard it can be for religious authority to come to terms with the fallibilism that is built into the human condition by the role of nonbeing even in the knowledge of being, as we saw in chapter 7, even under the circumstances of a civilization moving in the direction of building religious tolerance into its civic and legal constitutions as part of the "normal" condition of everyday life. This growth of appreciation for the doctrinal requirements of intellectual freedom is the line of development that distinguishes the derivatives of European civilization even during but especially after the "Latin Age". We are fortunate that the Galileo case concerned not philosophy as much as science, which has the advantage of the *demonstrationes ad sensus*; otherwise the Galileo case might have become for Christian civilization the seventeenth century analogue of the twelfth century case of Averroes over which, by siding with the "conservative" views of al-Ghazali (the muslim counterpart of that time to Cardinal Bellarmine in Galileo's time), the properly intellectual development within the then-glorious Islamic civilization was in effect derailed, as we discussed in chapter 5.
11 For example: Josue 10:12–13, "Josue prayed to the Lord, and said in the presence of Israel, 'Stand still, O sun, at Gabaon, O moon, in the valley of Aialon!' And the sun stood still, and the moon stayed, while the nation took vengeance on its foes". Again, Psalms: "The Lord is king, in splendor robed; robed is the Lord and girt about with strength; And he has made the world firm, not to be moved" (92:1); God "fixed the earth upon its foundation, not to be moved forever" (103:5); "He has pitched a tent there for the sun, which comes forth like the groom from his bridal chamber and, like a giant, joyfully runs its course. At one end of the heavens it comes forth, and its course is to the other end" (18:6–7). Again Ecclesiastes 1.5: "the sun rises and the sun goes down: then it presses on to the place where it rises". The creationists have a weak case against evolution compared to the case the 17th-century fundamentalists had against the heliocentrism proposed by Galileo and Copernicus.

God. (See the accompanying diagram of the competing systems.) Now who is to be believed, God in his infallible revealed word or Galileo in his fallible human voice? But not only that. If God says one thing and Galileo another, shouldn't Galileo be silenced? Should any Christian be allowed to challenge the revealed Word of God? Is this not dangerous for the good of souls?

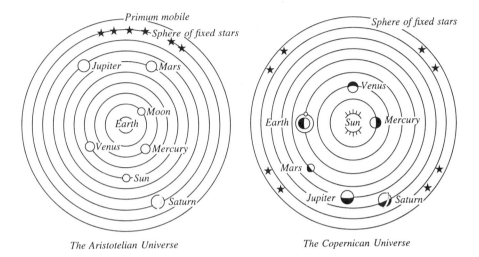

The Aristotelian Universe   The Copernican Universe

Representation of the Ptolemaic-Aristotelian and the Copernican Systems in the Time of Galileo (after Langford 1992: 26 and 38)

It is worth remarking that the "condemnation of Galileo" was not as wholly sectarian an affair as is often presented. The ignominy attendant upon the Roman condemnation of Galileo should not be used to divert attention from the fact that the main Protestant leaders of the time, standing on scriptural grounds, were more hostile to Copernican astronomy than were the generality of clerics in Rome. We are dealing here with a "climate of the time", not some Roman aberration. Martin Luther (1483–1546), in 1539, had been as plain as anyone about what to make of the Copernicus (1473–1543) whom we find now, less than a century later, inspiring Galileo:[12]

> People give ear to an upstart astrologer who strove to show that the earth revolves, not
> the heavens or the firmament, the sun and the moon, as if someone moving by carriage

---

12 Entry no. 4638, dated 4 June 1539, in Luther 1531–46: 412–3: "De novo quodam astrologo fiebat mentio, qui probaret terram moveri et non coelum, solem et lunam, ac si quis in curru aut navi moveretur, putaret se quiescere et terram et arbores moveri. Aber es gehet ikunder also: Wer do wil klug sein, der sol ihme nichts lassen gefallen, das andere achten; er mus ihme etwas eigen machen, sicut ille facit, qui totam astrologiam invertere vult. Etiam illa confusa tamen ego credo sacrae scripturae, nam Iosua iussit solem stare, non terram."

or by ship thought himself to be stationary and the land and trees to be moving. But the case is more like this: One who wants to appear clever cannot go along with what everyone seems to observe; he must come up with something different. So this clever soul, who wants to turn the whole of science of astronomy upside down. Yet even in those difficult matters I put my faith in the Sacred Scriptures, for Joshua commanded the sun to stand still, and not the earth.

Melancthon (1497–1560), the principal intellectual of Lutheranism, likewise regarded the circulation of the views of Copernicus as reprehensible. Writing in 1549,[13] thus eighty-four years before the infamous Roman condemnation, Melancthon pronounced it "a want of honesty and decency to assert such notions publicly, and the example is pernicious". The relatively greater "scientific freedom" in the development of astronomy in the Protestant lands at this period stemmed not from principle but from the lack of coordination provided by a centralized religious authority. That was what made the difference in Italy. And a main pressure on the Vatican officials to take a fundamentalist conservative line on interpretation of scripture at this period was precisely the blossoming Protestant Reformation, leaders of which all stressed the literal plain meaning of the sacred text. To preserve any hope of overcoming this latest splintering of Latin Christendom, it behooved the Roman authorities to adopt in scriptural matters so far as possible the interpretations most congenial to "the separated brethren".

When, in 1615, the Carmelite Friar Paolo Antonio Foscarini (c.1565–1616) published in Naples a booklet attempting to show how the Bible might be read consistent with the astronomy of Copernicus, he shortly received from Cardinal Robert Bellarmine (1542–1621) a letter, dated 12 April 1615, urging him to "consider whether in all prudence the Church could encourage giving to Scripture a sense contrary to the holy Fathers and all the Latin and Greek commentators". On 5 March of the following year, the Vatican Congregation of the Index presented Foscarini with a deathbed present in its decree "that the book of the Carmelite Father, Paolo Antonio Foscarini, be prohibited and condemned, and that all other books likewise, in which the same is taught, be prohibited, as this decree prohibits, condemns, and suspends them all respectively". The Congregation gave as the reason for its decree "that this opinion may not spread any further to the prejudice of Catholic truth".[14]

The point I like to make about the Galileo case, however, is that both sides proved wrong. Read for yourself the official statement of condemnation from that famous Wednesday morning, 22 June 1633, delivered by the "cardinals [Borgia, d'Ascoli, Bentivoglio, Scaglia, Barberino, Zacchia, Gessi, Verospi, Barberini, and Ginetti] of the Holy Roman Church, Inquisitors-General by the Holy Apostolic See specially

13 Melancthon 1549: 216f.
14 See Favaro ed. 1890–1909: vol. XII, 171f. for Bellarmine's letter; XIX, 323 for the Index decree.

deputed against heretical pravity throughout the whole Christian commonwealth"
as the "final sentence against you":[15]

> Invoking therefore the most holy name of our Lord Jesus Christ and of His most glo-
> rious Mother, ever Virgin Mary, by this our final sentence, which, sitting in judgment,
> with the counsel and advice of the Reverend Masters of sacred theology and Doctors
> of both Laws, our assessors, we deliver in these writings, in the cause and causes at
> present before us between the Magnificent Carlo Sincori, Doctor of both Laws, Proctor
> Fiscal of this Holy Office, of the one part, and you Galileo Galilei, the defendant, here
> present, examined, tried, and confessed as shown above, of the other part:
>   We say, pronounce, sentence, and declare that you, the said Galileo, by reason of
> the matters adduced in the trial, and by you confessed as above, have rendered yourself
> in the judgment of this Holy Office vehemently suspected of heresy, to wit, of having
> believed and held the doctrine that the Sun is the center of the world and does not move
> from east to west and that the Earth moves and is not the center of the world, which
> doctrine is false and contrary to the sacred and divine Scriptures; and [having believed
> and taught] that an opinion may be held and defended as probable after it has been
> declared and defined to be contrary to the Holy Scripture;[16] and that consequently you
> have incurred all the censures and penalties imposed and promulgated in the sacred
> canons and other constitutions, general and particular, against such delinquents.

What can we say of all this, beyond recalling as a fact now generally granted that
neither the sun nor the earth is at or near the center of the universe? We are not really
sure today that there is a center. Repeated arguments have been made on behalf of
the Inquisitors to the effect that Galileo was guilty at the time of making assertions he
could not prove – as if the accusers of Galileo by contrast were resting their case on
quite provable assertions. Yet how does it improve or vindicate or render palatable
the false certainty of the Inquisitors concerning what was "of Faith" to note that

---

15 See Favaro ed. 1890–1909: XIX, 402–6, for the original of the Santillana trans. (1955: 306–10)
from which I draw. That three of the ten judges did not sign the final decree as delivered went
unremarked until 1864, and stands to this day as one of those "human facts" whose motivation is
unfathomed.

16 Earlier in their final declaration the judges in the case had referred back to the Copernican
condemnation of 1616, in which two propositions, submitted for judgment on 19 February, were
adjudged on 24 February as follows (Favaro ed. XIX, 321). Of the proposition that *The Sun is the
center of the world and hence immovable of local motion* it was ruled that "All that is said in this
proposition is foolish and absurd in philosophy, and formally heretical since it explicitly contradicts
in many places the sense of Holy Scripture, according to the literal meaning of the words and
according to the common interpretation and understanding of the Holy Fathers and the doctors of
theology." Of the proposition that *The earth is not the center of the world, nor immovable, but
moves according to the whole of itself, also with a diurnal motion*, it was ruled that "All that is said
in this proposition receives the same censure in philosophy and that in regard to theological truth it
is at least erroneous in faith". These stale judgments they now freshly applied to the matter at hand,
which was no longer Copernicus but directly Galileo.

not until 1728 did Bradley record an aberration of starlight that gave the first direct evidence for the revolution of the earth around the sun? Or to note that not until 1818 was Bessel able so to correct and organize Bradley's data as to factually establish parallax, the apparent motion of the star theoretically required by motion of the earth? This hardly changes the circumstance that Galileo was found guilty of heresy on a question that could not legitimately be made subject to such a judgment. Redondi's impassioned and scholarly effort (1983) to construct an alternative history, in which the "true reason" for the condemnation of Galileo proves not at all the question of the relative motion of sun and earth but rather Galileo's espousal of an atomistic theory of sense qualities incompatible (implicative heretically) with the theology of the Eucharist as then understood, is likewise so much sand in the eyes vis-à-vis the text of the official condemnation. The larger point of the Galileo case, surely, is much more prospective than retrospective.[17] The larger point is not some secret workings of the past, but that there are limits to religious authority and to the understanding of all doctrines, theological as well as philosophical. The problem of finding out more clearly where and what those limits are has been the principal story of modern times as the epoch of civilization in which science established itself as distinct from philosophy and theology (as medieval times saw the establishment of theology as distinct from philosophy, and ancient times the realization of philosophy as distinct from mythology, a long painful growth from childhood toward a maturity that largely yet eludes the species wishfully styled "sapiens").

In the excitement of the time they thought they were only doing philosophy in a new way, a finally "enlightened" way. Now that the novelty has matured we can see that indeed they were establishing rather a whole new dimension of human understanding, science in contrast to philosophy and theology. The principal contribution of the seventeenth century to human civilization was not directly philosophical, that is, it was not in the line and order of philosophical doctrine as such. It was rather in the separating off from philosophy of the proper sphere of reason applied to the experimental study of the physical environment according to the being that environment has independently of our thoughts and emotions, including religious beliefs and sacred texts. As one of the main achievements of the Latin Age can be said to be the establishment of the distinction and boundary between dogmas of religious orthodoxy and the doctrinal exercise of human understanding in theology as formally distinct from philosophy, so the modern period can be said to have achieved an establishment of the distinction and boundary between even philosophical doctrines and the formally distinct experimental exercise of understanding in the formation and testing of hypotheses properly called "scientific" in contrast to

---

17 "As they returned to their homes after the Congregation's session", Fantoli notes (1996: 427), "for the cardinals and officials of the Holy Office the 'Galileo affair' was by now a closed chapter. They had no suspicion that the true 'Galileo affair' was instead beginning right on that very day 22 June 1633 and that their names would pass to posterity not only as judges of the tribunal of the Holy Office but also and above all as the accused, destined to be called innumerable times in the centuries to come before the much more severe tribunal of history."

philosophy and theology alike, as well as to religious belief or faith. What in the time of Augustine was yet one grand mélange of reason, faith, and politics was gradually being sorted out in the intellectual culture of the developing civilization into distinct if compenetrating spheres of theology, philosophy, and science in the cognitive order and the distinct if compenetrating spheres of church (religious authority) and state (civil authority) in the practical order of the organization of everyday life.

How the Latin Age Came to Be as Lost to Modernity as Was Greek Antiquity to the Latin Age

Part and parcel of this separation of science from both philosophy and religion, however, was the larger rejection of the study of written texts as a proper way to acquire knowledge about the world. The writings of Aristotle, which the religious authorities had met with condemnations and attempts to suppress as heretical when they were first introduced into the Latin West in the twelfth century, had been turned by the time of Galileo into an authority of almost intolerable dimensions. You can see this plainly if you read the *Commentary* of Cardinal Cajetan on the First Part of the *Summa* of Thomas Aquinas. There, ignoring the explicit warnings Aquinas elsewhere gives against the certainty of the Ptolemaic and Aristotelian astronomical doctrine of heavenly spheres (some of which we saw in chapter 7[18]), Cajetan weaves the doctrine of the heavenly spheres into the substance of the presentation of the so-called "five proofs" for the existence of God (*quinque viae*). He thereby compromised uselessly whatever probative force the "ways" might actually have had in the text upon which he comments.

The tradition of commentary on the works of Aristotle, begun in Aquinas's generation, had extended itself to theology, as we saw,[19] on the basis of the books of the so-called *Sentences* in which Peter Lombard had arranged his selection of the patristic writings. The commentary tradition had become the principal medium of intellectual discourse in all spheres ever since[20] – remember the "horseloads" derided by Roger Bacon. In the beginning, each author would comment on many, sometimes all, of the works of Aristotle. As time went on, certain works and certain parts of works came to stand out as especially problematic, and authors would concentrate their attention on these "special questions", omitting the more general commentaries altogether.[21] By the time of Galileo, the commentary tradition had transformed itself into a series of independent works on special topics. But underlying the whole intellectual enterprise were still the Aristotelian writings, within which alone was provided the framework which made the *quaestiones* fully intelligible.

---

18 See p. 263ff. above.
19 See p. 223f. above.
20 See end of p. 366, text and note 9; and p. 421 above.
21 See Chenu 1964: 220ff., for the description of the early Latin Aristotelian commentary tradition. One can compare this with the structure the late tradition assumed in the "Synthetic Index and Synoptic Table" of Poinsot's 1631–5 *Course of Philosophy* presented in Deely 1985: 352–75 (= Poinsot 1632a: Appendix B).

The Boethius of Modernity: Francisco Suárez (1548–1617)

As Boethius at the turn of the sixth century provided practically the only access Latinity would have to Greek thought for the next nine centuries, so (for quite different reasons, however) Suárez, ably seconded by Fonseca and his Conimbricenses, became nearly the sole channel by which Latin philosophical doctrines influenced the shaping of the modern philosophical mind. As a result, among other things, the hard-won doctrine of signs disappeared from modern thought.

When, in 1597, Francisco Suárez published the volumes of his *Metaphysical Disputations* ("Disputationes Metaphysicae"), he created a sensation. He had been the first to put aside completely the text of Aristotle and write instead a book of metaphysics according to his understanding of the requirements of the subject matter.[22] This was exactly what Aquinas had done, remember,[23] but without such immediate success, in writing his *Summa theologiae* to replace the commentary approach based on Peter Lombard's patristic anthology with a theological work organized thematically according to the logical demands of the subject matter.

But the world was more ready for such a pushing aside of authority by the time Suárez wrote. His work on metaphysics caused a sensation, not only because it followed a thematic logical arrangement rather than an authoritative one, but also because it prefaced each topic of discussion with what appeared to be an exhaustive survey of the opinions of all previous authors on the subject. Gilson remarks[24] that to read the *Disputationes Metaphysicae* of Suárez is to feel oneself present at the judgment seat of the previous four hundred years of Latin philosophy.

No wonder these handy volumes came to occupy a place on the bookshelf of every intellectual in Europe. Just as Lombard had reduced to a handy volume the hundreds of volumes of writings of the Church Fathers, so Suárez had reduced to a manageable proportion the thousands of volumes of writings of the Latin philosophers and theologians in the principal area where philosophy has any claim to independence from empirical studies as such. The founding figures of modern philosophy showed their appreciation by deferring to the authority of Suárez on all questions of what had the Latins taught in philosophy, while turning their own attention to the exciting new project of establishing the study of the world independently of an exegesis of texts, sacred as well as secular. It was the death of Latin scholasticism, for textual exegesis was the method by which scholasticism as a distinct historical form had been defined and created.

---

22 See Ferrater Mora 1953; Gilson 1952: 97; and of course Suárez himself, who tells us (1597: disp. II, Vivès vol. 25, p. 64): "a textus Aristotelici prolixa explicatione abstinendum duximus, resque ipsas, in quibus haec sapientia versatur, eo doctrinae ordine ac dicendi ratione, quae ipsis magis consentanea sit, contemplari" in Gilson's summary paraphrase: "the subject matter of the *Disputationes* is not the text of Aristotle's *Metaphysics*, but the very things (*res ipsas*) with which metaphysical knowledge is concerned".
23 See chapter 7, pp. 258–63, esp. 262.
24 Gilson 1952: 99.

But the moderns, it must be said, went too far. First, their reliance on Suárez was not as well founded as the impression created by reading Suárez alone would give one to believe. When, in the late nineteenth century, Pope Leo XIII mandated a revival of Thomistic studies, so far had the knowledge of things medieval deteriorated that hardly anyone knew any longer how to deal with the Latin manuscripts. For those who wanted to bring to this "Thomistic revival" the best tools of philology and critical textual scholarship developed since the pioneering work in the renaissance by Lorenzo Valla and his contemporaries, the case of Aquinas was exceptionally difficult. If you look inside the front and back cover of Weisheipl's 1974 biography and study of Aquinas, you will find there reproduced actual manuscript pages written in Aquinas's own handwriting, similar to what we have reproduced here in chapter 7 (pp. 268–9). It is completely illegible. An average of four years' training in paleography was required to bring a well-motivated scholar learned in Latin to the point where he or she could begin to start to commence to read Aquinas's manuscripts. That is why the matter of producing a critical edition of Aquinas's works, the so-called "Leonine Edition", drags on. The first volume appeared in 1882, and volumes are still appearing. The set is not yet complete.

Now Ignatius of Loyola (1491–1556), in establishing the Jesuits, had recommended to them that they take Aquinas as their master in theology. So you can imagine that, when the Jesuits responded to the papal call at the end of the nineteenth century to revive the thought of Thomas Aquinas, they were inclined to approach his writings through the eyes of the greatest interpreter their order had produced. That was Francisco Suárez. In the early decades of the twentieth century really interesting debates raged over the interpretation of Aquinas by Suárez. Those debates are now long forgotten, but their upshot was to establish beyond the shadow of a doubt that, however great an intellectual Suárez may have been in his own right (and he was great indeed), he was not at all reliable as an expositor of the philosophical thought of Aquinas. In particular, on the crucial subject of signs and relations, his presentation of Aquinas was fully deformed. The views of Suárez in this area were those of Fonseca, not at all those of Aquinas.

The views of Fonseca, remember,[25] reduced ideas as signs to representations, making no difference between objects and ideas, because the difference depended on the doctrine of mind-independent relations. This doctrine as Aquinas and his school had developed it both Fonseca and Suárez rejected as false. This proved to be a crucial point. Beginning with Hobbes and Descartes, continuing in an unbroken line through all the mainstream modern authors – Locke, Berkeley, Hume, Spinoza, Leibniz – and culminating in the synthesis by Immanuel Kant of the two principal modern currents (Rationalism and Empiricism) in his work of *Critiques*, the view was adopted that ideas as representations and the objects we directly experience are one and the same.

---

25 See "Anticipating Modernity" in chapter 9, p. 415ff.

We will look at the implications of this doctrinal rejection in more detail. But before we do, we need to give some consideration to the second most defining event of modern times after the work and condemnation of Galileo. That is the controversies that surrounded and followed the publication by Charles Darwin of *The Origin of Species* in 1859.

The Debates around Charles Darwin (1809–1882) and **The Origin of Species** (1859)

You would think that a history lesson as traumatic to the community of believing Christians as Galileo had provided would have been enough, but once is almost never enough in such matters. In the England of 1859 it was no longer possible to have the author of a scientific book brought before a religious tribunal and tried for heresy. But if it had been, Charles Darwin would have found himself the Giordano Bruno of the later part of the nineteenth century. Humankind too often fears admitting how little we actually know about the universe, and people generally are reluctant to recognize that the objective world of things as known, in which we have no choice but to live, is not the same as the actual universe of reality in its fullest extent. Not even the disappearance of the eternal, unchanging heavens under the blows of Copernicus (1473–1543), Tycho Brahe (1546–1601), Galileo (1564–1642), Kepler (1571–1630), Newton (1642–1727), and others had been enough to prepare human culture at large for the inevitable discovery that species are not fixed and immutable but evolve.[26]

The medieval doctrine of transcendental relations, long forgotten by Darwin's time, and never circulated among the moderns at any time, also should have helped here. You remember Aristotle's discovery that even the subjective parts of substance and substance itself have inscribed in their being a certain relativity which is part and parcel of their intelligibility.[27] A hand is not an arm or a body, but a hand cannot be understood solely except by being thought in relation to an arm and ultimately a torso as well. And so it is with the whole of finite being, without exception. Nothing in the observable universe can be understood solely on its own terms, but only in relation to other things besides, things which the thing we seek to understand is not. Every finite being, in short, is *transcendentally relative*, that is, depends upon an environment both to be and to be understood.

And so it is with organisms above all. Every species is relative to that part of the physical world on which it depends for sustenance. If the circumstances bearing on that dependency change, the organism too must change. It must find a new way or a new place to get sustenance. The alternative for the individual is death, for the species extinction.

---

26 See "Preparing the Way for Galileo and Darwin" in chapter 3, p. 79ff.
27 See, in chapter 6, the sections on "Aristotle's Difficulties", p. 227, and "Transcendental Relation", p. 228.

We have records of fossils that go way back before we knew what fossils were. Albert the Great discussed some specimens that we would now call fossils. But in medieval times they were anomalies, that is, objects of awareness which possessed too little context for us to know what to make of them. The modern world had begun to provide that context. Just as Aristotle had used the military expeditions of Alexander the Great as occasions to have brought to him specimens of plants and animals and constitutions and laws of states from far and wide for the purpose of making comparative studies, so on an even vaster scale after Columbus were brought back to Europe ever more and diverse specimens of plants, animals, and fossils for the people interested in those things to study and classify.

Little by little, it became apparent that none of the existing schemes of classification of living forms based on the assumption of the fixity.of species could accommodate the data. By this means, "evolution" began first to establish itself, not so much as a theory or problem, but as a kind of necessary background concept or summary expression of the realization, gradually secured through human experience, that nothing in the universe seems exempt from radical transformation. The fundamental "fact" of evolution is the physical record of past occurrences different from present ones for which no logical construct can be substituted but upon which whatever logical constructions we make about the past must themselves rest. There is no way to "save the appearances" of nature and assume that the universe in general and our planet in particular has not undergone an evolution.

But if action follows upon being, and all being is transcendentally relative, it would follow that the whole of nature exists in and through process. The world into which Darwin led us was the world of the changes which take place in the interaction of the diverse kinds of cosmic entities, and of the relations of interdependence which obtain between the various levels of the cosmic interaction when there is no fixed environmental structure apart from those changes and levels to keep the organization static over time. In other words, the world into which Darwin led us was simply the physical universe as we had been living in it all along, but under the objective misapprehension that it had a static rather than a dynamic order. Evolution as a theory simply objectified and brought into the human Lebenswelt an awareness of features of the physical surroundings which had been there all along but previously not as part of the objective world.

Probably you have all seen a film wherein the growth of a plant, which is quite slow to direct sensory observation, is made to appear at high speed, so that the slow, all but imperceptible transformations of growth in the actual environment appear as dramatic and rapid transformations in the film. Sir Julian Huxley challenges us in imagination to construct such a film of the physical universe, and picture it run at high speed:[28]

---

28 Huxley 1953: 28.

With a hundredfold speeding up, individual lives become merged in the formation and transformation of species. With our film speeded up perhaps ten thousand times, single species disappear, and group radiations are revealed. We see
an original type, seized by a ferment of activity, splitting up and transforming itself in many strange ways, but all the transformations eventually slowing down
and stabilizing in specialized immobility. Only in the longest perspective, with a
hundred-thousand-fold speedup, do over-all processes of evolution become visible –
the replacement of old types by new, the emergence and gradual liberation of mind, the
narrow and winding stairway of progress, and the steady advance of life up its steps of
novelty.

The data of common-sense observation, even over the span of written history,
are not enough to reveal directly to our eyes the story that the fossil record, the
geological layers of the rocks, and the light from the stars and galaxies, reveal to
our minds. Evolution is the most striking independent confirmation of the Latin
philosophical doctrine of transcendental relation that one could imagine. Compared
to this story told by the book of nature, all the stories of all the revolutions and
changes in human history reveal a comparatively unchanging world. Just as the
senses seem to reveal a sun that moves and an earth that stands still, so do these
same senses seem to reveal individuals that are born and die but species that continue
without end. But just as the senses, empowered by new instruments which extend
their reach and guided by new intellectual hypotheses which tell the eye where to
look, reveal a quite different universe from that of a stationary earth, so too do the
senses, empowered by data accumulated from aeons of time past and guided by the
understanding of a world today which no longer produces its evidences in the same
way, reveal a quite different universe from that of an unchanging earth.

There was a time for this universe as we know it when the stars were not yet.
Before there could be planets there had to be stars; and before life, planets of a
suitable sort. But prior to modern times the world had been conceived principally in
terms of space. Aristotle remarked that, in his day, Plato stood alone in thinking that
time had a beginning.[29] Christianity added a dimension of history, but only insofar
as history involves the Christian view of the human species and its salvation. But
it is no longer possible to maintain that the physical world today is basically as it
always was. The dimension of human history but extends prehistory, that is to say,
the history of nature itself in its physical unfolding. Listen to Loren Eiseley:[30]

It would come as a shock to those who believe firmly that the scroll of the future is
fixed and the roads determined in advance, to observe the teetering balance of earth's
history through the age of the Paleocene [c.65–58 million BC]. The passing of the
reptiles had left a hundred uninhabited life zones and a scrambling variety of newly

---

29 Aristotle c.348–7bBC: *Physics* VIII, 251b11ff.
30 Eiseley 1958: 7–8.

radiating forms. Unheard-of species of giant ground birds threatened for a moment to dominate the earthly scene. Two separate orders of life contended at slightly different intervals for the pleasant grassland – for the seeds and the sleepy burrows in the sun.

The range of environmental conditions presupposed for the possibility of our type of organism extends far beyond the vision or direct experience of any of the beings currently living within that range. By our best determinations so far, the creation of that environment required billions of years. It was built up gradually by an incalculable multitude of interacting forces that first made living beings possible and afterward included living things, step by step creating a hierarchy of living forms in which the lower and simpler supported the higher and more complex.

For all the difficulty of measuring past occurrences from their traces in stone (transcendental relations fossilized, as it were), for all the dependency of knowledge of the past on interpolations, assumptions, extrapolations, and analogies, Raymond Nogar (fondly called by his students "Cosmic Ray" when he wasn't around to hear) used to say,[31] "the broad, overall picture of the succession of organic forms in space and time is too heavily documented by cross-checking and convergence of materials to be rejected by the objective observer", where "objective observer" simply means an observer who takes account of all that is available to us in objectified form – as known, that is – of the physical environment within which this little bubble of our Lebenswelt is maintained and into which we try to assimilate ever more of the surrounding physical through scientific objectifications grounded ultimately in what our bodily senses first and constantly reveal.

The philosophical import of evolutionary theory to philosophy requires no more than this: a present world with features different from those of times past. The first philosopher to see and say this full clearly was Henri Bergson.[32] What choice does the mind interested in nature have, he asks? Once it has been established that the world today differs in its physical structures and forms of life from the world of the distant past, and this yet again from the world of a still more distant past, there are but two possibilities. Either the present state of the world is connected to the previous states of the world by a continuous chain of causalities, or it is not so connected. If it is not so connected, then the relation between past and present can be ascertained only by consulting the mind of God, to which we have no access. If it is so connected, then it is only by ferreting out and following those various causal lines of natural interactions that we can gain whatever *understanding* may be possible of why the world changed in the ways that it did and why today it is the way it is. It is a choice between developing our understanding of the world through causes or abandoning all hope of understanding.

To this calm Bergsonian observation the opponents of the idea of evolution have consistently thrown up the same passionate reply: "But we do have a direct access

---

31 Nogar 1963: 63.
32 Bergson 1909: 29–30.

to the mind of God, through the Bible! And the Bible tells us that God created the world. Therefore evolution is false."

"Creationism" vs. "Evolutionism"

This is among the most enduring, baffling, and empty of the controversies of all of history, to say nothing merely of modern times, whence it continues to rage around us[33] long past its time.

In 1945, Antonin Sertillanges, an excellent philosopher – not a great one, but a very, very good mind – wrote an entire book, *The Idea of Creation*, on just this question. This book should have shown everyone once and for all that this celebrated controversy is a nominalism, empty air delivered in withering blasts. For "there is nothing to prevent us from seeing in evolution, instead of a substitute for creation", which it could hardly be anyway, "simply another perspective on the manner in which the creative fact is bound up with the facts of nature."[34] But not everyone read Sertillanges, and, anyway, he wrote in French, a language most proponents of "creationism" don't know.

But the doctrinal language that he spoke was pure Thomas Aquinas, from whom Sertillanges took the idea for his book. In the time of Aquinas, it was believed that the Bible taught that the world had a beginning. Aristotle taught, quite explicitly to the contrary, that the world was eternal. This, indeed, was one of the several reasons why the medieval church authorities tried to chop off Aristotle's head as soon as it appeared in Latin, by condemning his work and forbidding that it be read.

Thomas Aquinas, who clearly read Aristotle and thought for himself besides (you would have expected that, as a saint, he would have paid a little more attention to the church authorities), commented on this controversy by pointing out that the question of God's creation of the world has no least connection with the question of whether the world is eternal or had a beginning in time. Creation is not a question of *when* the world exists but a question of *how* the world exists. And any system of interacting finite beings, statically or dynamically conceived, can be shown to be possible only on the assumption of an infinite being who imparts to them at each moment, and sustains them at each moment in, actual existence.[35] The idea of creation reduced to its essential content is not the idea of a beginning in time but of a dependency in being, a *dependentia in esse*.

This is what Sertillanges repeated to his modern contemporaries in 1945. Creation is purely and simply a question of does God act presupposing something besides Himself, or presupposing nothing at all? That is a metaphysical question, not a scientific one. Evolution, by contrast, is a scientific, not a metaphysical, question; and still less one that can be decided by religion.

---

33 See, e.g., the news article "Dumping on Darwin" (Lemonick 1996).
34 Sertillanges 1945: 128.
35 Of course you recognize here the reasoning from the *Summa theologiae* which we discussed in chapter 7 above, p. 267ff.

There are some matters that can be decided by neither philosophy nor religion, and the question of whether the world as a matter of fact changes over time in its basic structures and specific features is one of them. If you want to know how the world changes in its physical being over time you have to go out, gather the evidence capable of revealing this, and not refuse to look at that evidence. Aristotle can tell you that if the environment on which the earth depends does not change, then neither will the earth. But Aristotle cannot tell you whether the environment on which the earth depends changes or not. For that you have to look at that environment. To babble philosophy or to quote scripture contrary to what you find in the physical evidence is inane. Said rightly Sertillanges:[36]

> Whoever does not see that has not grasped the essential import of the notion of creation. He has restricted and anthropomorphized the notion beyond what is permissible. Once that has been pointed out, moreover, we are free to return calmly to the biblical conception of an initial creation after or beyond which is a divine repose.
>
> We henceforth know well that one can conceptualize this repose in any of three forms: as sanctioning the fixity of beings in their genus and species; as giving them over to their progressive unfolding through time; or, finally, as imparting to the latent psychism with which it has endowed them the responsibility for temporal creations more and more exuberant.
>
> One is free to choose, awaiting further evidence. But it is to be fervently hoped that after so much vain quarreling, we Christians will cease bringing forward unjustified censures respecting this doctrine of evolution, to which, under one form or another,[37] the future seems certain to belong.

The legitimate argument of the "creationists", therefore, is not against the idea of evolution but against those particular versions of evolutionary theory propounded by persons who so misunderstand the nature of the case and so confusedly grasp the ideas they propound as to think that it is enough to show that there has been an evolution to show that there is no God. Such was the actual case of the Soviet cosmonaut who went outside his space capsule and looked around, then equated the failure of his eyes to detect God with a proof that God does not exist.

John Dewey (1859–1952) and "The Influence of Darwin on Philosophy"
John Dewey is one of the most revered names in American philosophy, especially for his reform programs for education. Around the turn of the twentieth century he published an essay entitled "Darwin's Influence upon Philosophy".[38] This essay was the text from one of the lectures in his course of public lectures given at Columbia University in the winter and spring of 1909 under the heading of "Charles Darwin

---

36 Sertillanges 1945: 142.
37 Under the second one of the three forms, as it turns out.
38 Dewey 1909.

and His Influence on Science". It was particularly successful. When, in the following year, he incorporated this essay as the opening in an anthology of his essays with the title modestly modified to "The Influence of Darwinism on Philosophy", he gave the collection as a whole its name from that part. In his title, of course, "Darwin" was a metaphoric symbol, a synecdoche, in fact, for evolution.

As a student who had taken three years of philosophy classes exclusively in Latin using the commentaries of Aquinas on Aristotle as a primary textbook so far as practical, I can still remember my dismay, as a young professor in Rensselaer, Indiana, in 1967, on reading this essay of Dewey's over lunch hour. More than dismayed, I was outraged. How could a man of such prominence and influence make such ignorant statements about Aristotelian and medieval philosophy and get away with it? So incensed was I that I sat down to write an accurate account of the impact of evolution on philosophy of nature in the Latin tradition, a long essay published in two parts, the first of which appeared in January 1969.

Well, the essay has not been as successful as was Dewey's (though I still have hopes for the long run). But I have no doubt that Ashley was fully correct when he pointed out[39] that, in fact, the removal of the celestial spheres from consideration (that is, the destruction of the idea of the heavens as an unchanging and ruling cause of earthly generations and corruptions) has freed the philosophy of nature as the Latins had conceived of it to develop in its own line.

But my point here is that, by the time Dewey wrote his essay, it could have the success it had because no one any longer knew or cared about the actual Latin doctrines on the philosophy of nature or on anything else. In other words, though my own particular background prevented me from seeing it at the time, Dewey's essay was less of a philosophical piece than a symptom – σημεῖον – of how far from Latinity the modern world had moved in less than three centuries. The house of cards was ready to fall of its own weight. It had to, for there was no more substance to sustain it. Science had come of age, but it was high time for philosophy to reassert itself and claim its own domain.

I didn't know it at the time, but just such an event was well underway. Its principal vehicle was a huge body of writings that had been left behind by one of Dewey's erstwhile teachers, Charles Sanders Peirce. By comparison with Peirce, not only Dewey but all the other names in American philosophy, with the possible exception of Josiah Royce (1855–1916) and, in more limited respects, William James (1842–1910), are strictly second-rate. But Peirce had violated the unwritten rule and pact which was the bond of late modernity: *Thou shalt not read the Latins*, for they had nothing to say of worth.

Peirce doubted the wisdom of this closed-mindedness toward the past, and went his own way, for which he paid a high price, including the sacrifice, as it turned out, of a stable academic career. But the time was ripe. Modernity was languishing. And

---

39 Ashley 1973.

what Peirce rediscovered through the Latins was precisely the doctrine of signs. It was the beginning of Postmodern times, for Heidegger and a number of others were onto the same trail, though none so expressly as Peirce himself. He was the last of the moderns and first of the postmoderns, as we shall see.

But first we have to look at the moderns themselves and the philosophy they produced, as much from scratch, almost, as the first Latins after Boethius, though, as mentioned, for very different reasons.

Science and Academic Freedom: The Achievement of Modernity

Let us leave the debates of those who think with their eyes and throw around words devoid of any clarified sense or any genuine content of historical understanding to those who wish to continue them, and return to the lesson for philosophy that the modern period above all has taught.

Just as there are religious questions which it is impossible for philosophy to resolve and that must be left to the freedom of the individual conscience of the various believers, and just as there are questions that religious authority cannot resolve because they belong properly and truly to the realm of intellectual proof and reason, so there are scientific questions which neither philosophy nor religion can resolve. These questions must be left to the competence of those who are willing actually to study nature with their senses and with instruments that extend the senses and to devise hypotheses suitable to what those observations and investigations reveal. Neither science, religion, nor philosophy can substitute the one for the other, and every experiment in doing so has led to disaster. Bruno, as mentioned above,[40] gave a shining example of this lesson in 1600.

The best part of modernity went in to understanding just what was it that such an example proves. With the assistance of Galileo and Darwin especially, though there were many lesser figures with illustrative dramas as well, the lesson has been precariously learned. I say "precariously", because there are always those at work to undermine the institutional forms in which particular lessons of history, even the most salutary ones, have come to be embodied; and there is nothing in history to say that they may not one day succeed. The fact that Islam lost its culture of intellectual freedom in the twelfth century did not mean that it lost its sword. The achievements of liberty are always precarious, and more than one creative individual from each of the great fields of the mind – philosophy, literature, science, religion – has died in consternation to prove the point.

But to the modern period above all goes the palm for the establishment of science in the modern sense and the vindication of its proper rights against both the philosophers who thought their methods sufficient to study all of nature adequately and the religious leaders who thought their reading of divine truth sufficient to enable them

---

40 See p. 493 above.

rightly to decide who, from among either the philosophers or the scientists, should be allowed to air their views, and to what extent. This has been no small achievement, and one to be preserved by every means possible. Insofar as something so important as the freedom of the intellect can be reduced to an institutionalized form within civilization, the word "tenure" names this achievement of modern thought within the university, for those who understand the meaning of the word and the historical moment it expressed. The soul of a university is the promotion of a community of inquirers. When that promotion ceases, there and to that extent the university dies. Plato's Academy gave birth to the idea. The Latin Age gave birth to the institution. But the Modern Age brought the university to the early edge of maturity. To postmodern times falls the task of understanding that the institutionalization of inquiry within human society under the name of university is not enough if the path of inquiry is not kept open.

CHAPTER TWELVE

The Founding Fathers:
René Descartes and John Locke

Henri Bergson used to speak of a "natural geometry of the human intellect" in order to explain the resistance of people to seeing the development of things in time. Whether there is such a "natural geometry" or not, it is certain that Descartes, in founding modern philosophy, had an aversion to history, and considered it in general an obstacle to philosophical understanding. Philosophical understanding, thought Descartes, could only be obtained by a mind turning within itself, away from the senses, where the mind might find, in the soul itself, an absolute certitude which could then become the foundation for building anew, stone by stone, a sure edifice of human knowledge in which there would be no need or room for doubt and mere probabilities. Shades of Plotinus, but with a difference, the difference of seeking a foundation precisely expressible in rational, not metaphorical and mystical, terms.

The most famous adage of modern philosophy, perhaps of all philosophy, comes from Descartes: "*Cogito ergo sum*", "I think therefore I am".[1] There is a tale told

---

1 Have a look at how Spinoza (1663), whom Gilson, himself a great scholar on Descartes, called "an incomparable commentator", explains the "ergo sum": "what we must note here, above all else concerning this foundation, is that this formula, I doubt, I think, therefore I am, is not a syllogism in which the major premiss is omitted. For if it were a syllogism, the premisses would have to be clearer and better known than the conclusion itself, therefore I am. And so, I am would not be the first foundation of all knowledge. Moreover, it would not be a certain conclusion. For its truth would depend on universal premises which the Author had previously put in doubt. So I think, therefore I am is a single proposition which is equivalent to this, I am thinking."

In the first of his last four books, Maritain (1966: 800–4) proposed a far more radical interpretation of the *Cogito*, distinguishing "philosophy" from "ideosophy" and denying to Descartes the very right to be counted as a philosopher. He begged his readers not to dismiss the claim as "the whim of a crazy old man", with reason, I thought at the time. Yet since, one of Maritain's readers, Peter Redpath (1997), has taken up the point and made it the thesis of a sustained scholarly and hermeneutic effort to vindicate by elaborating, in effect, Maritain's assertion (1966: 803) that "a lineage of idealist origin, which from mutation to mutation more and more radically impugns extra-mental reality and the absolutely first foundation of philosophical knowledge," – which I would take to be the absence of icons in sense cognition and the termination at being of understanding – "cannot be called a philosophical lineage". Whether this effort to show that, in the case of

– I know not if it be true – that Descartes met his actual death, not in the court of Queen Christina of Sweden (1626–89, r.1644–54) on 11 February 1650, of a cold that became pneumonia, as traditionally taught, but in a Paris restaurant. Celebrating with friends his escape from that court under the guise of death, he responded to a waiter who asked if he would like coffee, "I don't think ...", and before he could get the "so" out of his mouth, he was gone.

But there is another adage of modern philosophy, not so well known, but actually more expressive of the true essence of modern philosophy. It comes not from Descartes, but from Leibniz: *Monads have no windows.*[2] That is, each unit of being is possessed of its own representations of the world, and these representations, not the world, are all that the individual can know or will ever know – though fortunately one can rest secure in the knowledge, which can be sufficiently derived from the representations one does have, that there is a Great Monad, God, who sees to it that all the private representations of the various monads are coordinated and in harmony – a divinely "pre-established harmony", thus, as the Leibnizians put it.

René Descartes (1596–1650)

René Descartes was a man with a mission. He felt that this was a mission directly from God, as it had been revealed to him in a dream – in fact, three consecutive dreams – on the night of November 10, 1619, while he was staying near the German city of Ulm.

The Dreams of Descartes
He tells us that the dreams involved the seventh ode of the fourth-century AD Roman poet, Decius Magnus Ausonius (c.AD310–c.395), which opens: "Quod vitae sectabor iter?" – "What road shall I take in life?" And he interpreted the dreams to mean that it was his task to provide a new foundation for the sciences based on the example of mathematics, the one study that, even in his youth, he "delighted in above all" and marveled that "nothing more exalted had been built upon such firm and solid

---

Descartes (Redpath 1997: 20), "it is more helpful to consider him as a rhetorician and poet, and as a continuator of a long standing tradition of learning of the classical *rhetor*, rather than as a philosophical innovator" will ultimately succeed or not, if the tale of Descartes' death related in the text above be true, then Redpath well includes in his series of alternative categories for the classification of Descartes that of *magus*, "sorcerer" or "magician".

But I feel obliged to say, pace Maritain, that Descartes cannot finally be dismissed from the ranks of philosophers. If "in the last resort the question is always, 'What is real?'", as Burnet well said (1914: 11) and Maritain would agree, then "no matter what the answer given may be, where that question is asked, there we have philosophy"; and how is it to be denied that Descartes asked this question, however unanswerable in the end (and in spite of his deepest intentions) the supposition of his method – the modern supposition that sensation terminates in ideas – renders the question. My guess on that last point is that Maritain concurs.

2 "Les Monades n'ont point de fenêtres, par lesquelles quelque chose y puisse entrer ou sortir" (Leibniz 1714: ¶7). Neither windows nor doors nor any other manner of ingress or egress, therefore!

foundations".[3] His opinion of philosophy at the end of his studies is one with which many students everywhere can sympathize:[4]

> Regarding philosophy, I shall say only this: seeing that it has been cultivated for many centuries by the most excellent minds and yet there is still no point in it which is not disputed and hence doubtful, I was not so presumptuous as to hope to achieve any more in it than others had done. And, considering how many diverse opinions learned men may maintain on a single question – even though it is impossible for more than one to be true – I held as well-nigh false everything that was merely probable.

The Methodological Doubt

Now what is the method of mathematics? To begin with a proposition fully and clearly understood and to proceed to derive therefrom by foolproof deductions a series of other propositions. It was Descartes' mission to find a way to enable philosophy to proceed in similar fashion. To this end he hit upon the *method of universal doubt.*

By doubting everything that can be doubted, he will persist in regarding everything that admits of the least probability of error as if it were completely false, until such time as he dies, presumably, or he finds something which admits of no doubt whatever. Obviously, one of the first things, if not the first thing, to fall before such an onslaught of doubt is anything to do with the senses, beginning with the physical world and including his own body. That such an extent of doubt is "unreasonable" in practical terms he freely grants; but the point of the doubt is not practical, it is purely speculative. Remember the methodological principle: to hold whatever is *in any least degree* susceptible of doubt as if it were completely false. He is thrown back completely, he finds, on the speculative resources internal to his own mind.

Fortunately for him, such a doubtless situation soon arises. The case of his own existence as a thinking being proves to be a situation which admits of no least measure of doubt. For though he be deceived in everything, yet in order to be deceived he must be. Notice, however, the restriction of the proof: it proves the existence of a thinking being, not of a being with a body. And it is certain because the mind sees clearly and distinctly that thinking, erroneous or not, directly involves existence.

Voilà, the way to pattern philosophy after mathematics: as long as I stick to what I clearly and distinctly conceive, and assent only to what immediately follows therefrom with equal clarity, I cannot err.

The Proof of God's Existence and the Foundation of Knowledge

Now I see with immediate clarity, runs the argument of Descartes, that every effect must have an adequate cause, and that this cause must contain at least as much

---

3 Descartes 1637: 114.
4 Ibid.: 114–15.

perfection as that which it produces. And I find in myself the idea of God as a supremely perfect being. Since this idea exists, it must have a cause:[5]

> The nature of an idea is such that of itself it requires no formal reality except what it derives from my thought, of which it is a mode. But in order for a given idea to contain such and such objective reality, it must surely derive it from some cause which contains at least as much formal reality as there is objective reality in the idea. For if we suppose that an idea contains something which was not in its cause, it must have got this from nothing; yet the mode of being by which a thing exists objectively or representatively in the intellect by way of an idea, imperfect though it may be, is certainly not nothing, and so it cannot come from nothing.

Could it be my own mind which causes the idea of God? Not at all. For I have found my mind to be subject to error and doubt. But the representation of a supremely perfect being exceeds what I find my mind to be, and exceeds therefore what my mind is capable of producing. Therefore my idea of God must be produced by something outside of me. But this cause can be none other than God himself, because only God possesses actually the fullness of perfection represented in my idea of God. I now realize that I could not have the idea of God were it not that God himself both existed and implanted this idea in my soul, "the mark of the workman upon his work".[6]

It is a remarkable argument. Let us look at a formulation of it in Descartes' own words:[7]

> reflecting upon the fact that I was doubting and that consequently my being was not wholly perfect (for I saw clearly that it is a greater perfection to know than to doubt), I decided to inquire into the source of my ability to think of something more perfect than I was; and I recognized very clearly that this had to come from some nature that was in fact more perfect. Regarding the thoughts I had of many other things outside me, like the heavens, the earth, light, heat and numerous others, I had no such difficulty in knowing where they came from. For I observed nothing in them that seemed to make them superior to me; and so I could believe that, if they were true, they depended on my nature in so far as it had any perfection, and if they were not true, I got them from nothing – in other words, they were in me because I had some defect. But the same could not hold for the idea of a being more perfect than my own. For it was manifestly impossible to get this from nothing; and I could not have got it from myself since it is no less contradictory that the more perfect should result from the less perfect, and depend on it, than that something should proceed from nothing. So there remained

---

5 Descartes, *Meditations on First Philosophy*, 1641: 28.
6 Ibid.: Meditation 3. From this we might extrapolate how Descartes would view the 20th century development called (esp. after Whitehead 1929; Hartshorne 1948, 1962, 1972) "process philosophy": "that I", he writes (ibid.), or anything else in the world, if such there be, "have many potentialities that are not yet actual, this is all quite irrelevant to the idea of God, which contains absolutely nothing that is potential".
7 *Discourse on Method*, 1637: 127.

only the possibility that the idea had been put into me by a nature truly more perfect than I was and even possessing in itself all the perfections of which I could have any idea, that is – to explain myself in one word – by God. To this I added that since I knew of some perfections that I did not possess, I was not the only being which existed (here, by your leave, I shall freely use some scholastic terminology), but there had of necessity to be some other, more perfect being on which I depended and from which I had acquired all that I possessed. For if I had existed alone and independently of every other being, so that I had got from myself what little of the perfect being I participated in, then for the same reason I could have got from myself everything else I knew I lacked, and thus been myself infinite, eternal, immutable, omniscient, omnipotent; in short, I could have had all the perfections which I could observe to be in God. For, according to the arguments I have just advanced, in order to know the nature of God, as far as my own nature was capable of knowing it, I had only to consider, for each thing of which I found in myself some idea, whether or not it was a perfection to possess it; and I was sure that none of those which indicated any imperfection was in God, but that all the others were. Thus I saw that doubt, inconstancy, sadness and the like could not be in God, since I myself would have been very glad to be free from them. Besides this, I had ideas of many corporeal things capable of being perceived by the senses; for even if I were to suppose that I was dreaming and that whatever I saw or imagined was false, yet I could not deny that the ideas were truly in my mind. But since I had already recognized very clearly from my own case that the intellectual nature is distinct from the corporeal, and as I observed that all composition is evidence of dependence and that dependence is manifestly a defect, I concluded that it could not be a perfection in God to be composed of these two natures, and consequently that he was not composed of them. But if there were any bodies in the world, or any intelligences or other natures that were not wholly perfect, their being must depend on God's power in such a manner that they could not subsist for a single moment without him.

Here we encounter the ghost of our old friend Anselm of Canterbury, fresh in from the eleventh century. Descartes' version of "ontological argument" has become perhaps as famous as the original.

Surely in no philosophy is God more central than in that of Descartes. Apart from the idea of God, according to Descartes, we can only inevitably drown in a sea of doubt, for it turns out that even my idea of myself as thinking, which at first blush *appeared* to be the starting point for all certain knowledge, now, on more complete analysis, turns out itself to be derived from my idea of God. For I think of myself as an imperfect being; but I could only arrive at this idea by a contrast with the idea of a perfect being, a contrast I had made without realizing it in the earlier, confused stages of my thinking. The true starting point of all knowledge, though heretofore I was not able to realize it, is the idea of God implanted in my soul from the beginning of my existence.

Here the argument cuts to something deeper than simply another variant on an ontological argument, suggesting something of the complexity of the cultural situation which led Redpath to his radical departure from the common run of Cartesian commentary. Certainly no works of the standard Cartesian canon suggest anything as radical as what Redpath has undertaken to vindicate in his trilogy so far.[8] But we do not have to go the whole distance with Redpath in writing Descartes out of the brotherhood of philosophers to realize that Descartes nonetheless is saying, as it were, between the lines, that the early medieval Augustinian tradition (mixing, it will be recalled, mysticism, sectarianism, and Neoplatonism under the misbegotten label of "Christian philosophy"), as embraced in the lifetime of Aquinas by his confrere on the Paris faculty, Bonaventure, had gotten the matter of the distinctiveness of human understanding more right than had Aquinas with his difficult, even elusive account of the *primum cognitum* we examined at such length in chapter 7. Far more than Anselm with his presaging of Descartes' argument from the idea of God to the reality of God, Bonaventure is the precursor of the central doctrine Descartes would have us embrace concerning the origin and character of truly human apprehension:[9]

> Since nonbeing is the privation of being, it does not come into our understanding except through being; but being does not come to us through something else because everything which is understood is understood as nonbeing or being in potency or being in act. If, therefore, nonbeing can be understood only through being and being in potency only through being in act, and if being signifies the pure act of being, then being is what first comes into the intellect and this being is pure act. But this is not particular being, which is limited because mixed with potency; nor is it analogous being because that has only a minimum of actuality because it has only a minimum of being. It remains that the being in question must be divine Being.
>
> Strange, then, is the blindness of the intellect, which does not consider that which it sees first[10] and without which it can know nothing. The eye, concentrating on various

8 Redpath 1997, 1997a, 1998.
9 Cousins 1978: 96–7, translating from Bonaventura 1259: 82, ¶s 3–4: "Volens igitur contemplari Dei invisibilia quoad *essentiae unitatem* primo defigat aspectum in ipsum *esse* et videat, ipsum esse adeo in se *certissimum*, quod non potest cogitari non esse.... Cum autem *non-esse* privatio sit essendi, non cadit in intellectum nisi per *esse*; *esse* autem non cadit per aliud, quia omne, quod intelligitur, aut intelligitur ut *non ens*, aut ut *ens in potentia*, aut ut *ens in actu*. Si igitur *non ens* non potest intelligi nisi per *ens*, et *ens in potentia*, non nisi per *ens in actu*, et *esse* nominat ipsum purum actum entis: *esse* igitur est quod primo cadit in intellectu, et illud *esse* est quod est actus purus. Sed hoc non est *esse* particulare, quod est esse arctatum, quia permixtum est cum potentia; nec *esse* analogum, quia minime habet de actu, eo quod minime est. Restat igitur, quod illud *esse* est esse divinum.
    "Mira igitur est caecitas intellecus, qui non considerat illud quod prius videt et sine quo nihil potest cognoscere. Sed sicut oculus intentus in varias colorum differentias lucem, per quam videt cetera, non videt, et si videt, non advertit; sic oculus mentis nostrae, intentus in entia *particularia* et *universalia*, ipsum *esse* extra omne genus, licet primo occurrat menti, et per ipsum alia, tamen non advertit. Unde verissime apparet, quod 'sicut oculus vespertilionis se habet ad lucem, ita se habet oculis mentis nostrae ad manifestissima naturae' [Aristotle, c.348–7bBC: II, 1]; quia assuefactus ad tenebras entium et phantasmata sensibilium, cum ipsam lucem summi *esse* intuetur, videtur sibi nihil videre; non intelligens, quod ipsa caligo summa est mentis nostrae illuminatio [Psalm 138.11], sicut, quando videt oculus puram lucem, videtur sibi nihil videre."
10 The 1953 Boas translation, p. 35, has at this point (for "illud quod prius videt"): "that which is its primary object".

differences of color, does not see the very light by which it sees other things; and if it does see this light, it does not advert to it. In the same way, the mind's eye, concentrating on particular and universal being, does not advert to being itself, which is beyond every genus, even though it comes to our minds first and through it we know other things. ... Thus our mind, accustomed to the darkness of beings and the images of the things of sense, when it glimpses the light of the supreme Being, seems to itself to see nothing. It does not realize ...

The "Fundamentum Inconcussum Veritatis": That God Is No Deceiver

But now I find that from this idea of God, recovered methodically out of the clouding of sense and doubt and restored to its primacy in my apprehension, I am able discursively to draw other truths, the very ones sought for in order that my knowledge (even of sensible nature) might be brought to rest on sure foundations. For it is incompatible with the goodness and perfection of God that God should allow me to fall into error provided that I use my God-given powers of understanding and will rightly. And that means above all that I must never allow my will to assent to or to seek anything which my understanding does not clearly and distinctly conceive. For it is "the very fact that God is not a deceiver, and the consequent impossibility of there being any falsity in my opinions which cannot be corrected by some other faculty supplied by God, [that] offers me a sure hope that I can attain the truth" even in matters where I at first encounter doubt and uncertainty.[11]

Thus the idea of God, all powerful and all good, perfect, which I find within my soul, even more than my own existence, becomes the *fundamentum inconcussum veritatis*, the "unshakeable foundation of truth" and the *primum cognitum intellectus*, the point of departure for human knowledge as human; and the goodness of God becomes the guarantee that my reason when used correctly will lead, even in conjunction with sense, to yet other truths:[12]

when I turn my mind's eye upon myself, I understand that I am a thing which is incomplete and dependent on another and which aspires without limit to ever greater and better things; but I also understand at the same time that he on whom I depend has within him all those greater things, not just indefinitely and potentially but actually and infinitely, and hence that he is God. The whole force of the argument lies in this: I recognize that it would be impossible for me to exist with the kind of nature I have – that is, having within me the idea of God – were it not the case that God really existed. By 'God' I mean the very being the idea of whom is within me, that is, the possessor of all the perfections which I cannot grasp, but can somehow reach in my thought, who is subject to no defects whatsoever. It is clear enough from this that he cannot be a deceiver, since it is manifest by the natural light that all fraud and deception depend on some defect.

---

11 Descartes 1641: 55.
12 Ibid.: Meditation 3, 35.

God, being supremely perfect, cannot be a deceiver on pain of contradiction:[13] this is the metaphysical foundation on which the certainty of human knowledge rests whenever it achieves a clear and distinct conception, "because every clear and distinct perception is undoubtedly something, and hence cannot come from nothing, but must necessarily have God for its author."[14]

Descartes says it forty or fifty different ways, but the unshakeable foundation of truth for him comes always back to the same point: not to the "Cogito ergo sum", as vulgarly taught even among Cartesians, but to the realization that God is and can be no deceiver. This quality unique to God, namely, incapacity for deception (to be One who "can neither deceive nor be deceived") and not anything proper to the thinking self as a finite being other than being a creature of this God, is the ground for our confidence in human knowledge when it is reached by the right use of our critical powers. Being a creature of God, insofar as I use my freedom as my Creator intended it to be used – to wit, in the line of good – I participate in a limited way in the unlimited capacity of my Creator to preclude deception:[15]

> Absolute certainty arises when we believe that it is wholly impossible that something should be otherwise than we judge it to be.[16] This certainty is based on a metaphysical foundation, namely that God is supremely good and in no way a deceiver, and hence that the faculty which he gave us for distinguishing truth from falsehood cannot lead us into error, so long as we are using it properly and are thereby perceiving something distinctly.

What about the universe outside myself besides God? What about its real, not merely possible or probable, existence? What about my body and other people? The answer remains the same:[17] "... the very fact that God is not a deceiver, and the consequent impossibility of there being any falsity in my opinions which cannot be corrected by some other faculty supplied by God, offers me a sure hope that I can attain the truth even in these matters."

The Rationalist Tradition

At this point I leave you to go read Descartes for yourself, for enough has been said already to give you a clear idea of the meaning of the term *Rationalism* as it applies to those modern thinkers who followed Descartes along this Way of Ideas. Rationalism is the view that reason is in itself a source of insight and truth superior to and independent of all sense perception – independent, that is, in the strongest possible sense of having no need whatever of the senses in the derivation

13 Ibid.: Meditation 4, 43.
14 Ibid.
15 Descartes 1644: 290.
16 This first sentence of the extract is interpolated into the English translation from the 1647 Picot French translation approved by Descartes himself.
17 Descartes 1641: Meditation 6, 55.

of its proper content or in the establishment of the foundations, even if not all the particulars, of rational knowledge. To see this view develop in action, you can read, for example, the *Ethics Demonstrated in Geometric Order* (i.1662/76) by Benedict Spinoza (1632–77), or the *Monadology* (1714) by Gottfried Wilhelm Leibniz (1646–1716).

And remember this, from the all-too-brief previous chapter: much of what was going on in the modern period concerned not so much philosophy itself as the determined effort of science to investigate the book of nature in observational terms and to interpret it mathematically. This effort survived the symbolic disaster through which Galileo had come to stand for intellectual oppression by religious authority, and had by his fate galvanized intellectuals everywhere to fight for freedom of expression for ideas with a ferocity such as had never obtained before in history.

You may catch something of the flavor of this battle and of the meaning of its watchword "enlightenment" (so difficult to comprehend by those who, being heirs to the victory, simply *take for granted* the fruits) from the circumstances which prevented the publication of Spinoza's *Ethics* within his lifetime. All was not sweetness and light, even within the ranks of those agreed on rationalism. In the summer of 1675, we find Spinoza writing the following to a friend nervous about receiving copies of his new book:[18]

> I was on the point of leaving for Amsterdam, to see to the printing of the book I wrote you about [his *Ethics*]. While I was occupied with this, a rumor was spread everywhere that a book of mine about God was in the press, and that in it I strove to show that there is no God. Many people believed this rumor. So certain theologians – who had, perhaps, started the rumor themselves – seized this opportunity to complain about me to the Prince and the magistrates. Moreover, the stupid Cartesians, who are thought to favor me, would not stop trying to remove this suspicion from themselves by denouncing my opinions and writings everywhere.
>
> When I learned this from certain trustworthy men, who also told me that the theologians were everywhere plotting against me, I decided to put off the publication I was planning until I saw how the matter would turn out.

The book never came out in Spinoza's lifetime, which ended on the 20th of February 1677; but it did toward the end of that very year, thanks to the good offices of friends. The book opens with a lengthy version of ontological argument for the existence of God, and concludes that knowledge and love of God is the greatest human good. That may seem a strange book for the theologians of the day to oppose, but wait until you find out[19] what, for Spinoza, the love of God consists in; and, at the same time, what the knowledge of God basically informs us about the world outside of God.

---

18 From Letter 68 in Gebhardt 1925: IV, 299; trans. cited from Curley 1988: 401.
19 From your own reading of his writing, not in this book.

So there is much more to the story of modern philosophy than simply the doctrinal content on which we here have to concentrate. But whatever else is to be said of the philosophy of Descartes and the colleagues it inspires over the modern centuries, you can see that it proceeds blithely unaware of the carefully developed Hispanic Latin distinction between *representation*, in which an object may present itself, and *signification*, in which an object or a concept can only present something other than itself. In equating ideas with objects represented, here at the very beginning of modern thought, the late Latin notion of concepts as formal signs in the tradition of Aquinas and Poinsot is rendered impossible. But, of course, the tradition begun with Fonseca and furthered by a host of Jesuit writers in the first modern century after him of denying that "formal signs" are really signs (because they are direct objects of representation) is at the same time rendered triumphant. From this point of view, modern philosophy can be said to have its origins in the abandonment of the first coalescence of semiotic consciousness achieved over the centuries of discourse on the question linking Augustine with Poinsot. The priority of signs to objects becomes lost to view, and objects of experience become not a partial revelation of surrounding nature and culture but a screen separating the mind from things.

Of course, ideas are what they are and remain such regardless of a philosophical theory. In that sense, it makes no difference at all what we think about ideas. But that is not the point. The point is to gain an understanding which expresses accurately the nature of a given object under investigation. So this much we can say going in: if the doctrine of signs was correct in assimilating to the notion of *signum* ideas as well as words and natural phenomena – *if*, I say – then Descartes with his theory of ideas is on a wrong track, and so is the whole of rationalism after him in maintaining the representative theory of ideas.

John Locke (1632–1704)

John Locke was born in the very year that the *Tractatus de Signis* vindicating Augustine's heritage was published. He was five years old when Descartes published the *Discourse on Method*, and nine when the *Meditations on First Philosophy* appeared. He was eighteen when Descartes died. France gave Descartes a state funeral, a unique event in the history of philosophers, and a measure of the fame which attended Descartes' name by the time of his death. Thus, Locke grew up hearing about the views of the famous René Descartes, and of course about the doctrine of the idea of God as an innate idea, that is to say, an idea in the mind or soul from the first instant of its existence.

Locke himself was a physician by training. Everything he did related to and depended on the senses. Real life, he found, is far from certainty. To proceed as Descartes recommended, even in thought, would make medicine and life itself impossible to comprehend. Locke devoted himself over a long period of years to work on a book on the nature and extent of human knowledge in which he hoped to show the truth of the matter, which is (so he held) that all knowledge is from the senses and that Descartes was completely mistaken in holding that any idea at all, including the idea of God, is innate. So was born *An Essay concerning Humane[20] Understanding*, the great work which was to define the terms of the epistemological debate within classical modern philosophy between *Rationalism* as it took rise from the work of Descartes and what would be called *Empiricism*. As Descartes initiated rationalism, so Locke, with his *Essay*, would initiate empiricism. (Not that he had no predecessors,[21] but that the mainstream classical modern development would take place as a "rationalist-empiricist" dialectic centered on the Cartesian – equally the Fonsecan and Suárezian – notion of idea as self-representing object; and the "empiricism" of this dialectic began with the work of Locke.)

The rest of modern philosophy would be the story of the development of these two currents in counterpoint, and of Immanuel Kant's attempt to make a synthesis of the two, especially in his *Critique of Pure Reason*. Hegel would make a valiant attempt at rejecting the whole debate and giving it new terms, but, for various reasons, without great success. After that, rationalism and empiricism would continue to play out their string under various guises, most prominently as "phenomenology" and "analytic philosophy", respectively, in the twentieth century. But until Heidegger in the European tradition preceded by Peirce on the English-speaking side went to the heart of the matter, classical modern philosophy sunk ever deeper into the solipsism[22] of its underlying assumption, making it ever more plain to all that the paradigm of knowledge from which both rationalism and empiricism took their point of departure could not afford a solid footing for the enterprise of "understanding understanding".

It was forty years after Descartes' death and fourteen years before his own that Locke brought out the first edition of his great work. He divided it into four books, and the first one he directed dead against the notion of innate ideas. "I shall set down the reasons that made me doubt of the truth of that opinion," he tells us genially,[23] "as an excuse for my mistake, if I be in one; which I leave to be considered by those who, with me, dispose themselves to embrace truth, wherever they find it."

It seemed to Locke that the whole content of human understanding reduces to the ideas we get from sensation, and the ideas we get by reflecting on the operations of our own mind in receiving and working with the materials of sensation. "These, when we have taken a full survey of them, and their several modes, combinations,

---

20 So was the term "human" spelled in Locke's day.
21 Notably Francis Bacon (1561–1626) with his *Novum Organum* of 1620 – see Deely and Russell 1986.
22 Solipsism, from the Latin *solus* + *ipse* (or *ipsius*), "the self alone" (or "of one's self alone"): hence any view that the self can know directly nothing but its own modifications or the products of its own mental workings; in the extreme the view that only the existence of the self can be known of a certainty.
23 Locke, *An Essay concerning Humane Understanding*, Book I, ch. 2, sect. 1.

and relations, we shall find to contain all our whole stock of ideas; and that we have nothing in our minds which did not come in one of these two ways."[24]

The Qualities Given in Sensation: A Comparison of Modern and Medieval Treatment

Somewhere along the way, probably indirectly from the Italian cleric Gassendi (1592–1655), Locke picked up the distinction between so-called *primary* and *secondary* sense qualities, that is to say, between sense qualities without which a material body seems to be unimaginable (hence *primary*, or essential to the very notion of bodies) and sense qualities which we can imagine a body existing without (hence *secondary*, or inessential to the notion of bodies, and hence candidates for the category of mental constructs or phantoms of the mind's own workings). This distinction had originally been proposed by Democritus in connection with his atomism. Gassendi, himself a latter-day Epicurean and skeptic in matters of knowledge, would have been familiar with this fact.[25] Yet, while the distinction itself was not indigenous to modern times, only after Locke did it emerge as a defining characteristic of a whole period rather than a single school of philosophy. Galileo (1564–1642), likewise an admirer of the ancient atomic theory of nature, had seen the distinction in question as part and parcel of the new physics, not the physics of Aristotle which had been based on sensible matter, but a new physics, a mathematical physics, which cut below the apparent sensible qualities of bodies in motion to deal with the quantified substantial base all sense qualities presuppose.

For Aristotle, such a base was indeed real, but required an abstraction to presciss as such.[26] Considered in itself, this base of "substance quantified" provided both an "intelligible matter" as the object of pure mathematics and the reason why applied mathematics holds good for things in the physical environment, all the way from the number of sheep in a herd to the weight that a bridge will support and the amount of lift required to raise a body into the air. Yet substance quantified is not the whole of substance, but an abstraction from experience. It did not and could not provide

---

24 Ibid. Book II, ch. 1, sect. 5.
25 Probably too Gassendi would have been attracted by his skepticism to the sophistic relativism in matters cognitive that this ancient atomistic theory had been put by Protagoras. So the question of whether the distinction in question was originally an attempt at formulating a genuine philosophical doctrine subsequently diverted into a sophistic ploy to justify in advance (as it were) an urbane Humean skepticistic relativism, or originally an expression of relativistic skepticism that Democritus on his own thought could be rehabilitated into an intellectually respectable tool for dismantling an indeed troublesome problem at the intersection of epistemology with ontology, cannot be closed entirely. Windelband (1901: 60n1), nonetheless, thinks that the latter alternative is the likely one: "It is extremely improbable that the solution of the problem through the subjectivity of the sense-qualities, which is found in Democritus, was presented already by Leucippus [Democritus' teacher in the matter of atomism, be it remembered], and therefore before Protagoras, who is universally regarded as the founder of the theory." In either case, the proposed solution would have been attractive to Gassendi!
26 See "How Mathematics Applies to the Physical Environment" and "Abstraction" in chapter 3, p. 78.

an adequate standpoint for the analysis of anything like the totality of the world as experienced, since experience *begins* precisely with the interactions of material substances through the accidents mediated but not constituted by quantity.[27]

The modern resuscitation of the ancient distinction between sense qualities which are primary and those which are secondary, thus, roots ultimately in a disagreement over the essence of material substance, an aspect of the break between moderns and Latins into which Locke himself never directly looked. Is the essence of material substance a mixture of actualities and potentialities submitted first to extension in space and thence further to a whole series of qualities and relations making up the heterogeneity of individuals interacting to constitute the physical world, or is the whole essence of material substance already constituted by extension in space, all else being a kind of dream of thought and illusion for those who think?

Descartes had already opted for the latter position, and marked it terminologically with his division of being into "thinking thing", *res cogitans*, and "extended thing", *res extensa*. Whence comes the quintessentially modern dualism of *mind*, including humans, angels, and God, on the one hand, and *body*, including all bodies in motion, on the other hand. Whence too comes the basis for the metaphor which came to dominate the scientific imagination of the eighteenth and nineteenth centuries, the idea of "world as machine" and of "man as machine"[28] insofar as the human mind is involved with body.

But though the terminology fixing the point for popular consciousness came from Descartes, the idea itself traces back to Pythagoras,[29] especially through Plato,[30] and was fixed at the dawn of modern times principally in the work of Galileo:[31]

> Philosophy is written in this grand book, the universe, which stands continually open to our gaze. But the book cannot be understood unless one first learns to comprehend the language and read the letters in which it is composed. It is written in the language of mathematics, and its characters are triangles, circles, and other geometric figures without which it is humanly impossible to understand a single word of it; without these one wanders about in a dark labyrinth.

And since quantity is to be taken as not the first accident but the whole essence of material substance, it follows[32] "that tastes, odors, colors, and so on" – all the sensible features of bodies called "proper" by the Latins – "are no more than mere

---

27 Recall the various other subjective characteristics of material individuals besides substance, and the one intersubjective characteristic without which the subjective being of substance itself within an actual environment would be untenable: see chapter 3, "Transcendental Relativity", p. 72, and "The Categories of Aristotle", p. 73ff.

28 The very title of the 1748 classic of scientism and materialism by Julien Offroy de La Mettrie (1709–51): *L'Homme machine*.

29 See chapter 2, p. 32.

30 See "Let No One Enter Here without Geometry" in chapter 3, p. 59.

31 Galileo Galilei, *The Assayer* (1623): 237f.

32 Ibid.

names so far as the object we place them in is concerned, and that they reside only in consciousness", here meaning the subjectivity of the knower.

Thus, the modern distinction between primary and secondary qualities, in being taken up by Locke, simply received a new and wider currency. What had begun as a specialized distinction based on a reconceptualization of the object of physics in mathematical terms became, through Locke's work, a part of the patrimony of empiricism as well as of rationalism – a common patrimony of modern philosophy.

The Latins had followed Aristotle in speaking rather about *proper and common sensibles* to discuss the content of what enters awareness through the channels of exteroception. The moderns choose now to speak instead of *primary and secondary qualities*, partly, as we have seen, in solidarity with the realism of modern science, its concern to know what is in nature independently of human beings. Yet a more careful consideration still might be worth our while. What is at stake with these distinctions, with these two different ways of speaking? How are they the same and how are they different? Or are they merely two different ways of saying the same thing, equally valid from their respective points of view?

What Is at Stake?: Preliminary Statement

To begin with the first of these questions, we can say that a great deal, in a certain sense everything, is at stake in this issue. For even though Descartes turned radically away from sensation in his attempt to re-establish a foundation for philosophy, precisely that attempt is what is being countered by the empiricists in *their* attempt to renew philosophy's foundation. Thus, whether we regard sensation as the foundation of knowledge and core of experience, à la Locke, or, à la Descartes,[33] regard it merely as a superficial point of departure from which to turn to inner experience, the matter of sensation becomes central to the establishment of modern thought in its distinctive character.

The Common List of Sense Qualities

Given the biological constitution of *Homo sapiens sapiens*, it is not surprising that philosophers have been able to agree on a basic list of sensible characteristics or qualities presented objectively in experience, even across the divide that separates the Latin Umwelt from the Umwelt of the moderns. Their complete list of the contents of sensation is virtually identical: color, shape, size, solidity, texture, rest or motion, position, number or plurality, odor, flavor or taste, sound, warmth or coolness.

But when it comes to assessing the epistemological import and ontological status of the items on the list, agreement rapidly dissolves, beginning with the question of

---

33 And don't forget Plotinus!

which items in the list are the basic ones and which the comparatively derivative ones.

How Modern and Premodern Treatments Mainly Differ

The modern philosophers distinguished within the list between what they termed *primary and secondary qualities* of objects. The *secondary* qualities they considered to be color, odor, taste, sound, and warmth or coolness in particular, and to be the comparatively derivative items – derivative, that is to say, from the mind's response to bodies more than from the bodies themselves.

The Greek and Latin philosophers, basing their analysis on the notion of formal object (as that which a given cognitive ability alone reveals or makes known[34]), distinguished quite differently, between what they called *proper* (or 'special') and *common* sensibles. They considered the *proper* sensibles, the sense qualities revealed through a single channel, to be color, odor, taste, sound, and texture or relative warmth, and considered them to be the basic items, *not* the comparatively derivative ones, because all other items in the list of sense qualities depend upon the proper sensibles in order to be attained or "cognized".

Moreover, note that the moderns speak of *qualities*, which, for the Latins, must be inherent in objects, either really or apparently. That is just why the moderns called some "qualities" primary and others secondary: because the former they considered to be, and the latter not to be, "really" qualities of the objects perceived. So just what the Latins considered fundamental in sensation, the moderns considered illusory.

And here recall the Latin difference of opinion over whether sensation involves mental images.[35] For the moderns, as for the Nominalists and Suárez, the so-called sense-qualities are precisely that: mental images. But for Aquinas and perhaps for Scotus that is gratuitous, completely unwarranted. And if *no* sensibles strictly taken (considered, that is, at the level of sensation analytically prescissed by an analysis in terms of formal objects[36]) are pure creations of the cognitive organism, none of them on the list can be as such classed as illusory.

The answer to our first question, then ("What is at stake with these two different ways of speaking – the modern discourse about 'primary and secondary sense qualities' versus the ancient and medieval discourse about 'common sensibles and proper sensibles'?"), gives us also a partial answer to our second question ("How are these two discourses similar and how are they different in their substantive content?"). For in seeing that much is at stake in adopting one or the other point of view, we see also that there are indeed general similarities and differences in the points of view from which the two lists are drawn up. But to get any answer to our third question concerning the comparative validity of the two standpoints, a thorough detailed evaluation of the similarities and differences is indispensable.

---

34 See the discussion in chapter 7 above, p. 343ff.
35 Chapter 7, p. 345.
36 See "The 'Formal Object' of Latin Scholasticism" in chapter 7, p. 343.

What Is at Stake: The Bottom Line

If the moderns are right in deeming the proper sensibles to be phantoms of the mind, and the premoderns are also right in deeming the common sensibles to be known only through and on the basis of the proper sensibles, then, a chain being no stronger than its weakest link, we have no way of precluding the suspicion that, even though a world of bodies be unimaginable without the primary qualities, these qualities too, and bodies along with them, may be phantoms of the mind. Voilà the "problem of the external world"! It arises, not out of nothing, not out of language gone on holiday, but, very precisely, out of one particular *analysis* of the list of qualities given in sensation.

Are the Standpoints Equally Valid?

Wilson has pointed out[37] that "early modern figures" key to the emergence of rationalism and empiricism as the modern mainstream developments "did not put much weight on the special/common sensible issue in maintaining that only a subset of the apparent qualities are, as we perceive them, really in the objects". Perhaps so much the worse for them. Let us see, for assuredly "the relation between the common/special [i.e., common/proper] sensible distinction and the objective/subjective [i.e., primary/secondary] quality distinction is", as Wilson notes without developing the point, "a complex and interesting one". Just this relation and contrast of the two sets of distinctions is what I want to explore here.

The two distinctions – proper/common sensibles vis-à-vis primary/secondary qualities – are in one sense parallel, in another inverse. They are *parallel*, in that the modern list of qualities taken collectively matches the Latin scholastic list of sensibles. They are *inverse*, however, in that the qualities listed as primary in the modern list match the common sensibles, which, in the scholastic list, are dependent on the proper sensibles and so are secondary; while the proper sensibles, which are primary in the scholastic list, match the qualities listed as secondary and dismissed as illusory in the modern list.

The inversion results from the standpoint according to which the two traditions distinguish the sensible characteristics or qualities of objects given in perception. The scholastics drew their distinction, as it were, unselfconsciously, from a point of view that is closest to what Peirce called "phaneroscopy", but that we would more likely today call "phenomenological". This point of view had no name among the Latins, who simply considered that they were being experiential.

The moderns (ironically, set as they are on a path which leads inexorably to idealism) at first drew their distinction from an adamantly realist point of view: the primary qualities are those which hopefully will prove to be mind-independently present in objects, while the secondary qualities are those supposed easily con-

---

37 Wilson 1992: 210n42.

structed and inscribed in objects by the mental activity of the perceiver. But as events soon proved, the hopeful realism of the modern distinction was hopelessly misguided.

Berkeley (1685–1753) and Hume (1711–1776) Showing the Consequences of the Modern Standpoint

Bishop Berkeley (1685–1753), an "empiricist" of a most extraordinary sort, explicitly pointed out that the two kinds of qualities as understood in modern philosophy are interdependent in experience in such a way that there is little ground for alleging a difference in status for the two vis-à-vis a supposed order of mind-independent being:[38]

> They who assert that figure, motion, and the rest of the primary or original qualities, do exist without the mind, in unthinking substances, do at the same time acknowledge that colours, sounds, heat, cold, and such like secondary qualities, do not, which they tell us are sensations existing **in the mind alone**, that depend on and are occasioned by the different size, texture, and motion of the minute particles of matter. This they take for an undoubted truth, which they can demonstrate beyond all exception. Now if it be certain, that those original qualities **are inseparably united with the other sensible qualities**, and not, even in thought, capable of being abstracted from them, it plainly follows that they exist only in the mind. But I desire any one to reflect and try, whether he can, by any abstraction of thought,[39] conceive the extension and motion of a body, without all other sensible qualities. For my own part, I see evidently that it is not in my power to frame an idea of a body extended and moved, but I must withal give it some colour or other sensible quality which is **acknowledged** to exist only in the mind. In short, extension, figure, and motion, abstracted from all other qualities, are inconceivable. Where therefore the other sensible qualities are, there must these be also, to wit, in the mind and nowhere else.

If we employ the terminology of the moderns from the standpoint the Latins, Berkeley's argument can be stated yet more forcefully. The sensible qualities of the objects of experience are so linked in experience that the supposed primary qualities are only known and attained through and on the basis of the qualities supposed secondary. Hence, if the latter are constructed by the mind, there is no basis left whatever for alleging the former not to be.

---

38 Berkeley, *A Treatise concerning the Principles of Human Knowledge* (1710), Part I, sect. 10, p. 45.
39 Lacking the explicit analytical tool provided by the notion of formal object, Berkeley here speaks of perceptual abstraction alone. But when the distinction between understanding and perception is drawn on the grounds implicit in Aristotle and explicit in Aquinas and other Latin authors, the intellectual idea *as opposed to* the perceptual image of an extended body ("intelligible matter", as the scholastics called it) is not only possible but also the basis for explaining mathematics. See the sections on "How Mathematics Applies to Nature" and "Abstraction" in chapter 3, p. 78.

Nor was this point lost on David Hume (1711–76), who exactly makes it in his own way:[40]

> It is universally allowed by modern enquirers, that all the sensible qualities of objects, such as hard, soft, hot, cold, white, black, &c. are merely secondary, and exist not in the objects themselves, but are perceptions of the mind, without any external archetype or model, which they represent. If this be allowed, with regard to secondary qualities, it must also follow, with regard to the supposed primary qualities of extension and solidity; nor can the latter be any more entitled to that denomination than the former. The idea of extension is entirely acquired from the senses of sight and feeling; and if all the qualities, perceived by the senses, be in the mind, not in the object, the same conclusion must reach the idea of extension, which is wholly dependent on the sensible ideas or the ideas of secondary qualities.

Spelling Out the Bottom-Line Consequence of the Modern Standpoint as the Origin of the Problem of the External World

Students of philosophy today can hardly see or hear the word "philosophy" without associating it with people who wonder if they are really there and who can't tell whether they are dreaming or experiencing others. What these same students don't realize is that this seemingly inevitable association is actually a product mainly of modern philosophy, a consequence that is inevitable only in light of the modern doctrine that ideas are self-representing objects.

By the point in *An Enquiry concerning Human Understanding* where Hume goes on to show that the distinction between primary and secondary qualities supposed as representing respectively mind-independent and mind-dependent being is without foundation in the way of ideas, he had already given his reader in its explicit thematic form the famous "problem of the external world":[41]

> By what argument can it be proved, that the perceptions of the mind must be caused by external objects, entirely different from them, though resembling them (if that be possible) and could not arise either from the energy of the mind itself, or from the suggestion of some invisible and unknown spirit, or from some other cause still more unknown to us? ...
>
> It is a question of fact, whether the perceptions of the senses be produced by external objects, resembling them: how shall this question be determined? By experience surely; as all other questions of a like nature. But here experience is, and must be entirely silent. The mind has never any thing present to it but the perceptions, and cannot possibly reach any experience of their connexion with objects. The supposition of such a connexion is, therefore, without any foundation in reasoning.
>
> To have recourse to the veracity of the supreme Being, in order to prove the veracity

---

40 *An Enquiry concerning Human Understanding* (1748), 154 para. 15.
41 Hume, 1748: Part 1, sect. 12, p. 152, paras. 11–13.

of our senses, is surely making a very unexpected circuit. If his veracity were at all concerned in this matter, our senses would be entirely infallible; because it is not possible that he can ever deceive. Not to mention, that, if the external world be once called in question, we shall be at a loss to find arguments, by which we may prove the existence of that Being or any of his attributes.

Whence "reason", Hume concludes,[42] "can never find any convincing argument from experience to prove, that the perceptions are connected with any external objects."

Sensation in the Perspective of the Doctrine of Signs

Contemporaneously with the founding fathers of classical modern philosophy, Poinsot, in his *Tractatus de Signis*, had taken up the standpoint on sensation of the Latin scholastics in order to incorporate that standpoint into the doctrine of signs. Viewing sensation from the standpoint of semiotic was neither the way in which Aristotle had first conceived it, nor yet a fully established way of treating the matter, even though there were others of Poinsot's Umwelt who had moved in this same direction. Fully reconceptualized according to the requirements of the doctrine of signs and constituted as a semiotic standpoint, it turns out that the point of view in question is readily, while the modern resumption of the ancient atomistic standpoint is but marginally, compatible with the doctrine of signs.

For the standpoint in question, that of Aristotle reconceptualized within semiotic or the doctrine of signs, it turns out, distinguishes among two types of sense data in a way that is *neither* realist *nor* idealist in the modern sense. In contemporary terms, this standpoint thus newly thematized is not in the first place ontological nor even epistemological, but rather *experiential*, as we have mentioned, much in the sense that late-modern philosophers, after Husserl (but trying to shrive away Husserl's idealist twist[43]), have come to thematize as "phenomenological".[44]

For the question answered in older tradition with the distinction between proper and common sensibles concerns the relation of environmental things to the channels of sense through which and on the basis of which these things become aspectually and in part objectified. Some aspects of the physical environment, namely, the proper sensibles, are objectified, cognized, or known through a single channel of sense only. Other aspects are assimilated to experience through more channels than one, namely, the common sensibles.

---

42 Ibid.: para. 16.
43 See, e.g., Spiegelberg 1965; Langan 1996: 13–19, 37–124.
44 I have not thoroughly considered the matter, but it might be that a strict application of rules 5 through 7 of the "Ethics of Terminology" (see chapter 15 below, p. 662ff.) would oblige us to prefer "phaneroscopical" to "phenomenological" in this matter. Quite apart from any "ethical" consideration, however, the modern idealist twist Husserl imparted to the term "phenomenology" may well prove eventually to result in that term's being supplanted by "phaneroscopy" as a lexicographical item in the later mainstream development of postmodernism.

The modern distinction between secondary and primary qualities begs the question of which qualities are the comparatively more fundamental by ignoring the role of sensation in experience and supposing straight off that we can say in advance what is real and what is not – precisely the point on which Berkeley called the early-modern bluff to devastating effect. Instead of showing what was real and what ideal, the modern approach gave away the game by having adopted a standpoint consistent with showing everything in sensation to be ideal.

By contrast, the Latin scholastic distinction among sense qualities is drawn in a way that allows for a rational discourse and decision concerning the ontological status of objects experienced in terms of the physical aspects of their being. Following Aquinas on this point, Poinsot further saw that this way of distinguishing among sense qualities is the only way that the social construction of the objective world in and through formal signs maintains continuity with and partially incorporates the physical environment as such in its character as something prejacent to every Umwelt.

From the standpoint of contemporary consciousness, what Poinsot in his *Treatise on Signs* proves able to show, in effect, is that the requirements of a doctrine of signs are consonant with the nascently experiential standpoint of the scholastics, but definitely incompatible with the would-be realist stance of the moderns. For the modern stance begs the question of the physical status of sensed things, which experience must rather provide the basis for deciding, if decided it can be. That is why the modern distinction leads, in spite of itself, and as Berkeley and Hume soon manifested, to modern idealism.

Sensation along the Way of Signs vs. Sensation along the Way of Ideas
In this area it is instructive to compare Latin thought in the person of Poinsot with modern thought in the person of Hume. To Hume's claim[45] that "no man, who reflects, ever doubted, that the existences, which we consider, when we say, **this house** and **that tree**, are nothing but perceptions in the mind", Poinsot answers, to the contrary,[46] that the view that external sense (as distinguished from perception as the further work of internal sense – *phantasiari* – and of understanding) attains as its object an image produced by the mind is more than merely subject to doubt. A sufficiently thorough analysis[47] proves the view in question to be finally incoherent[48]

---

45 1748: 152 para. 9.
46 *Tractatus de Signis*, Book III, Question 2, "Whether a Concept Is a Formal Sign", esp. pp. 309/47–312/6, with cross-references to the books commenting on the *De Anima*, namely, Poinsot's *Philosophiae Naturalis Quarta Pars* of 1635, Q. 6, Art. 1, "Whether It Is Necessarily the Case That an Exterior Object Be Present Physically in Order to Be Sensed", 170a38–177a47, esp. 172b13–173a30, and Art. 4, "Whether the External Senses Form an Icon or Expressed Specifying Form In Order to Cognize", 192a18–198a16, esp. 195a5–46. Lengthy citations from these cross-referenced texts are incorporated in the critical apparatus of the 1985 Deely edition, q.v.
47 See *Tractatus de Signis*, Book III, Question 2, 310/37–312/6.
48 "Implicat" is the term Poinsot uses.

in terms of sense experience as such,[49] as well as in terms of the rational analysis of sense experience.[50] If sensation and perception were alike involved with mental icons, Hume would have a case. But, for want of sufficient technical analysis, the appearance of his case amounts to sophism.

Sense experience is defined by contact with physically present aspects of objects. We can imagine or remember an absent object, but we can feel the resistance only of what is present here and now. Between an object acting physically on an organ of external sense and that organ itself as a physical attribute of the organism there is no disproportion, as there is between a perceived object and the sensory stimuli taken as basis for the perception.

Yet ideas or images are required only to supply presence for an object otherwise absent, or to supply the proportion between what is perceived and what is sensed. Neither of these reasons for supposing an image at work within cognition apply to the case of external sensation. Hence, the supposition of images in the case of external sense is gratuitous, simply without warrant.

Rational analysis of sense experience thus confirms what brute experience seems to testify: sensation is concerned with physical aspects of objects present here and now in the environment. There are simply no grounds for holding that external sense, prescissively distinguished as such within perception and understanding, attains as its proper object an image produced by the mind itself.

How far apart the Latin and the modern mainstreams had drifted in this area – or, perhaps we should say, how exclusively the early moderns received Latin tradition through the filter of Suárez – becomes apparent from Poinsot's further remark that his conclusion on this matter (which we may note was at variance with Ockham and the nominalists no less than with Suárez and Hume) "is the more common one among those competent to treat of the question".[51] So much for Hume's "no man who reflects has ever doubted".[52]

Notice in particular, at the present juncture, that Poinsot grants, in what he considered to be a contrary-to-fact conditional argument (a *reductio ad absurdum*), that *if* sense were to know in an image, then indeed would there be an insoluble "problem of the external world". And he grants this, as it were, anticipating Hume's very terms:[53]

---

49 "Probatur a posteriori", in Poinsot's terms.
50 "Probatur etiam a priori" is Poinsot's expression for this point.
51 Poinsot, *Treatise on Signs*, 1632a: 310/8–9.
52 The whole of Book III of the *Tractatus de Signis* is devoted to these and related issues concerning experience of physical aspects of objects, insofar as our perceptions and conceptions involve sensation.
53 Poinsot, *Tractatus de Signis*, Book III, "Concerning Modes of Awareness and Concepts", Question 2, "Whether There Can Be an Intuitive Cognition, either in the Understanding or in Exterior Sense, of a Thing Physically Absent", 312/2–6. See the extended commentary on this crucial point in Deely 1994a: 83n38.

But if the object exists in something produced by itself as in an image or effect, it will not be seen immediately, but as contained in the image, while the image itself is that which is seen.

Hume argues in his *Enquiry*[54] that *since* "the mind has never any thing present to it but the perceptions", meaning the images the mind itself makes, "and cannot possibly reach any experience of their connection with objects", *therefore* "the supposition of such a connexion is without any foundation in reasoning." Poinsot argues that *since* the mind deals in sensation not with images but with physical relations grounded in physical interactions of brute force, *therefore* the supposition of images at the sensory core of experience is without any foundation in reasoning.

The hypothetical consequence that *if* sensation were of images *then* we would have no experience of a connection with external objects, which Hume considers a conclusive direct proof of the insolubility of the "problem of the external world", Poinsot takes as an indirect dialectical proof (a *reductio ad absurdum*) of what Latin tradition had established along several independent lines of direct argument, namely, the superfluousness of *species expressae* (ideas or images) in external sense (sensation) as such, and the gratuitousness of supposing or positing them there in the first place.

Thus, the very basis from which Hume concludes, in his *Enquiry concerning Human Understanding*,[55] that reason "can never find any convincing argument from experience to prove, that the perceptions are connected with any external objects", is the same basis from which Poinsot developed rather, in his *Treatise on Signs* and in his psychology, convincing arguments showing that perceptions are connected with external objects precisely through the action of aspects of the physical environment on external sense analytically distinguished and taken as such within the activity of perception and understanding as a global whole.

We find here an interesting and particularly instructive illustration of how the same material of experience, even while providing in its sensory component something of a common measure for the comparative soundness of differing views, can be transformed differently in the hands of different philosophers.

Samuel Johnson (1709–1784) Filling the Shoes of the Fool
This is a point poorly understood by those who criticize philosophical theories without understanding that sensation, to the extent that it provides a common measure within perception for the evaluation of philosophical doctrine, does not function in the direct way that experimentation does in the testing of a scientific theory. Samuel Johnson, for example, confronted with the problem of responding to Berkeley's view that matter does not exist because "everything in the universe is

---

54 1748: sect. 12, Part 1, p. 152 paras. 11–13.
55 Ibid.: para. 14.

ideal", reacted with unforgettable alacrity. According to Boswell's report,[56] Johnson, "striking his foot with mighty force against a large stone, till he rebounded from it", said of Berkeley's view: "'I refute it thus'."

That would be fine had it been a question of scientific theory, but for a philosophical doctrine Johnson quite missed the point. Rocks, trees, houses, and stars remain just what they are in common experience for any philosophical theory. What changes is not what is given in sensation, but how that given is to be understood.[57] No kicking of stones, or throwing stones, or even hitting Berkeley – or Hume – over the head with a stone, will serve to disprove the theory of sensation as terminating in mental constructions as such. It is not a question of whether there *is* brute secondness, but of *how* brute secondness is to be interpreted. To answer this question, discourse is necessary – not physical blows.

The Semiotics of Sensation
Crucial to Poinsot's discussion of sensation is his demonstration of how the Latin scholastic standpoint on sensation assimilates to the *doctrina signorum*. The scholastic way of distinguishing provides in this instance the materials for an analysis which results in the conclusion that the manner in which the common sensibles presuppose the proper sensibles is in strict accordance with the defining characteristics of the type of relation in which signification consists. I cite the most trenchant passage:[58]

> *Wherefore we respond simply* that sense cognizes the significate in a sign in the way in which that significate is present in the sign, but not only in the way in which it is the same as the sign. For example, when a proper sensible such as a color is seen together with a common sensible, such as a profile and movement, the profile is not seen as the same as the color, but as conjoined to the color, and rendered visible through that color, nor is the color seen separately and the profile separately; so when a sign is seen and a significate is rendered present in it, the significate is attained there as conjoined to the sign and contained in it, not as existing separately and as absent.

The importance of the point that the analysis of sensation establishes a grounding of cognition in real physical relations *which are at the same time sign relations* emerges from the following considerations.

If indeed experience begins with sensations, as empiricists claim, and sensations are an irreducible mixture of common with proper sensibles, the latter of which are related to the former as sign to signified; and if the formation of sensations as perceptions requires, as all agree, the formation of images by the mind on the basis of which the sensible qualities are further presented *as* this or that; and if the under-

56 *The Life of Samuel Johnson*, 1793: entry for 6 Aug. 1763.
57 See "Berkeley's Idealism and Dr Johnson's Stone" in chapter 13, p. 549.
58 Poinsot, *Tractatus de Signis*, Book I, Question 6, "Whether the true rationale of sign is present in the behavior of brute animals and in the operation of the external senses", p. 208/34–47.

standing of what is perceived[59] also requires the elaboration by the mind of ideas or concepts in order for what is objectively perceived to be understood in this rather than that manner (not to mention understood at all); and if, in Peirce's formula,[60] as Aquinas, Scotus, the Conimbricenses, Poinsot, and others of the Latin milieu had argued, "all thought is in signs", meaning that all concepts – all images and all ideas – are related to their objects as signs to significates, and every thought must be interpreted in another thought; then indeed the whole of experience, the being proper to it, from its primitive origins in sensation to its elaboration in perception and further development in understanding, all experience from its lowliest origins in sense to its highest attainments in theoretical understanding, is a continuous network, tissue, or web of sign relations.

If that be so, then the doctrine of signs – the thematic elaboration of the role of signs in the constitution of knowledge and experience as the only path we have to the apprehension of objects and the truth about things – is not something peculiar or marginal to the philosophical enterprise but rather something central to it and at its core, however long it takes for individual philosophers and philosophy itself to reach that realization as part of its general history.

Comparative Evaluation of the Modern and Premodern Standpoints

The difference in the modern viewpoint and the older traditional one, thus, turns out to be very far indeed from two different standpoints, each legitimate from its own point of view. For the modern distinction not only begs several questions. It also misses the point of sensation as analytically prescissed from perception and understanding alike, even granting that both the higher levels depend on sensation for their base:[61]

> In the object of a cognitive power the focus of attention is not reality as formally mind-independent or entitative, according as the object has being in itself, but the proportion and adaptation to the power. This proportion indeed as it subjectively exists in a thing must be mind-independent; but in terms of the relation to the power, that it exists subjectively in an actual thing is not what is regarded, but rather that it exists objectively relative to the power in question – although on other grounds, if the power itself respects only mind-independent being [as is the case with external

---

59 Motion, say, as a point of departure for considering the question of whether a being transcendent to the material order might not be required in order for the perceived fact of physical motion to be possible in the first place (cf. Deely 1994: Gloss 33, esp. p. 155); or as a point of departure for differentiating between projectiles and falling bodies, etc.

60 Peirce 1868a: CP 5.253.

61 John Poinsot, *The Fourth Part of Natural Philosophy, Concerning Animate Being* (1635), Quaest. II, "On the properties of the soul in general", Art. 3, "Whether powers are specified and distinguished through acts and objects", Reiser ed. vol. 3, 77b26–44; cited in the modern edition of the *Tractatus de Signis*, pp. 190–1, n. 35.

senses prescissively taken], that power will also require a mind-independent being in the object, not as existing, but as related to the power. For existence is always in an order to itself and subjectively, whereas to a power it always pertains objectively.

And this question of levels within cognition, too, as conceived by modern empiricism, bears a closer look.

Sense and Understanding

At first Locke's doctrine of the dependency of understanding on external sense sounds no different than what was taught by Aristotle and Aquinas. How is the maxim everywhere subscribed to by the empiricists of modernity, "There is nothing in the understanding which was not first in the senses", any different from the motto subscribed to by the Latins, "*Nil est in intellectu quod non prius fuerat in sensibus*"? The maxims indeed are nominally the same; but the thrust of the maxim as the empiricists understood it was to affirm the continuity of experience to the point of denying the difference in kind between sense and understanding, or at least to make the content of knowledge valid only for the sensory. "Human understanding" tended to become simply the name for a more complex organization by human beings of the essentially same sensory materials organized by brute animals.

In Locke himself this was a conjecture:[62]

> It suffices me only to have remarked here, that perception is the first operation of all our intellectual faculties, and the inlet of all knowledge in our minds. And I am apt too to imagine, that it is perception in the lowest degree of it, which puts the boundaries between animals and the inferior ranks of creatures. But this I mention only as my conjecture by the by.

But shortly in Hume, as, before Locke, already in Thomas Hobbes (1588–1667), that there is difference only in degree between human and other animals became a dogma:[63]

> Next to the ridicule of denying an evident truth, is that of taking much pains to defend it; and no truth appears to me more evident, than that beasts are endowed with thought and reason as well as men. The arguments are in this case so obvious, that they never escape the most stupid and ignorant.

No sophisticated formal object with an ability to presciss aspects of macroexperience here:[64]

---

62 Locke 1690: *Essay*, Book I, ch. 9, sect. 15. Cf. Deely 1987: iii–vi.
63 Hume 1739/40: *A Treatise of Human Nature* (1739–40), Book 1, ch. 3, sect. 16.
64 Ibid., continuing the previous statement.

536 Part III Modernity: The Way of Ideas

We are conscious that we ourselves, in adapting means to ends, are guided by reason and design, and that it is not ignorantly nor casually we perform those actions which tend to self-preservation, to obtaining pleasure, and avoiding pain. When, therefore, we see other creatures, in millions of instances, perform like actions, and direct them to like ends, all our principles of reason and probability carry us with an invincible force to believe the existence of a like cause. It is needless, in my opinion, to illustrate this argument by the enumeration of particulars. The smallest attention will supply us with more than are requisite. The resemblance betwixt the actions of animals and those of men is so entire, in this respect, that the very first action of the first animal we shall please to pitch on, will afford us an incontestable argument for the present doctrine.

This doctrine is as useful as it is obvious, and furnishes us with a kind of touchstone, by which we may try every system in this species of philosophy [the species of modern empiricism]. It is from the resemblance of the external actions of animals to those we ourselves perform, that we judge their internal likewise to resemble ours; and the same principle of reasoning, carried one step further, will make us conclude, that, since our internal actions resemble each other, the causes, from which they are derived, must also be resembling. When any hypothesis, therefore, is advanced to explain a mental operation, which is common to men and beasts, we must apply the same hypothesis to both; and as every true hypothesis will abide this trial, so I may venture to affirm, that no false one will ever be able to endure it.

In this the way for Darwin was made by one measure easier and by another measure harder. The way was made easier in that it lessened the gap that had to be explained in the "origin of man". But the way was made harder in that the gap had been lessened on specious grounds.

For Hume and the later empiricists had no glimmer of understanding of the Latin doctrinal methodology for the determination of differences in cognitive levels through the analysis of formal objects,[65] and hence they had no glimmer of the irreducible difference between understanding and perception on which rationalists, when they did not simply take the difference for granted, could rightly insist as demonstrable in a variety of ways. The most important was achieved by Edmund Husserl (1859–1938) toward the end of the modern age, when he made his demonstration of the transcendence of sensory data achieved in intellectual intuition[66] the basis for the last vital phase of modern rationalism under the banner of his idealistically conceived *phenomenology*.

The Nature of Ideas
It would be hard to imagine a wider divide than that between one man who founded even the knowledge of God on sensation, as Locke did, and another who founded even the knowledge of sensation so far as it can be trusted on the idea of God and

---

65 See chapter 7 above, p. 343. Cf. also Deely 1966: 152#4; Deely 1971: 56–83, esp. 65–6 & 82–3.
66 See his *Logical Investigations* of 1901–2.

the divine goodness as found in the soul prior to all sensation, as Descartes did. Yet, for all his opposition to and difference from Descartes on the origin and ground of human knowledge, there was one particular on which Locke and Descartes found themselves in all but perfect agreement,[67] and that was on the nature of ideas.

On this point Locke declared himself up front. For with the "idea of an idea" Locke opens his *Essay*, and on this "idea of idea" – to wit, the idea of ideas as the objects directly experienced – he bases the whole of his discussion until his concluding chapter. In that chapter, as we shall see, he will call into question not only his own work and that of Descartes, but, by implication, the whole mainstream development of classical modern philosophy which continued to use this same "idea of idea" as a representation within and fashioned by the mind itself, a representation taken as alone providing the direct object of thought and experience whenever we experience anything or reflect about what we have experienced:[68]

> I must here in the Entrance beg pardon of my Reader, for the frequent use of the Word *Idea*, which he will find in the following Treatise. It being that Term, which, I think, serves best to stand for whatsoever is the Object of the Understanding when a Man thinks, I have used it to express whatever is meant by *Phantasm, Notion, Species,* or whatever it is which the Mind can be employ'd about in thinking.

By combining a representative mention of the variety of terms left over from the discussion of ideas in Latin Age with the blanket inclusion of "*whatever* it is which the mind can be employed about in thinking", Locke signaled clearly enough his intention in this passage. He aimed "to replace the theory-loaded terms of the schools" not with "a more or less theory-neutral" term,[69] but rather with a single-theory-specific term that would supplant, in the context of modern empiricism, the all too poly-theory-laden scholastic usage which, by· that time, outside the Iberian Umwelt, hardly anyone could any more be bothered to try and untangle.[70]

Although several of the terms on the scholastic list were applied most specifically to the analysis of intellectual cognition, in the mainstream Latin renaissance traditions of natural philosophy all of these terms would apply, in modern parlance, to the psychological states involved in the cognitive behavior of any biological organism, any animal. But in seventeenth century England particularly, the focus was on social and political theory and the struggle against the Catholic kingdoms opposed to Protestant England, rather than on continuing the centuries-old, arcane,

---

67 I say "all but", for Locke, alone among the mainstream moderns, maintained a modest reservation, which will provide our subject in chapter 14 below.
68 Locke 1690: "Introduction" to the *Essay*, para. 8.
69 This is what Tipton tries to suggest (1992: 97).
70 The Latins had, by Locke's time, about a dozen synonyms for "whatever it is which the mind can be employed about in thinking", each with its own nuances and overtones of analysis, as exemplified in the following list (which is not exhaustive): "repraesentatio", "species", "conceptus", "idea", "notitia", "intentio", "verbum", "idolum", "phantasma", "phantasia", "imago", "proles mentis".

and authority-ridden debates between Scotists, Thomists, and Nominalists, such
as continued in Iberia. And even on the Continent, where the taste for matters
metaphysical was much greater than in England, the temper of the times, as we
saw in Descartes, was to start all over again, and to do so without regard for
the full context of Latin thought, rather than to trouble any further with the heritage of Aristotelian commentary and theological discourse modeled on that same
tradition.[71] Even such Protestant authors as tried to extend the Latin dialogue on
these important questions across the frontiers of modernity were completely ignored in the modern mainstream. Who today has even heard of Timpler (1604,
1612), Keckermann (c.1607), and Scheibler (1617), among others? Yet their day
will come.

The Common Heritage of Modern Times (c.1637–1867)

What a strange thing history is. What a monument to Aristotle's complaint[72] that
the philosophers generally either account for *chance* in ways that remove it from
intelligibility or neglect to take any account of or allow any room in their explanations for chance events, even though chance events are clearly important in the
constitution of the world[73] and in the affairs of men.

From the point of view of striking coincidences, there are many parallels between
modernity and the Latin Age.

Just as Augustine had the resources but preferred for reasons of his own to cut
himself off from the Greek sources all around him, to be followed by subsequent
generations of Latins who had no alternative but to follow his lead ignorant of
the true Greek situation, so Descartes had the resources but preferred for his own
reasons to brush aside the Latin sources all around him, to be followed by subsequent
generations of moderns who willingly followed his lead of preferred ignorance
regarding the true state of the larger Latin situation.

Just as those who came after Augustine had as their only real window unto and
conduit from Greek thought the work of the single author Boethius, so those who
came after Descartes had as their only real window unto and conduit from Latin
thought the work of the single author Suárez, the Boethius of modernity.

---

71 Descartes neatly set the theologians aside from his own work with a feint of modesty (1637: 114):
   "I revered our theology, and aspired as much as anyone else to reach heaven. But having learned
   as an established fact that the way to heaven is open no less to the most ignorant than to the most
   learned, and that the revealed truths which guide us there are beyond our understanding, I would not
   have dared submit them to my weak reasonings; and I thought that to undertake an examination of
   them and succeed, I would need to have some extraordinary aid from heaven and to be more than a
   mere man." Whereas even a mere man could full well take on the philosopher's task, since he need
   no more than the resources of his own mind without regard for anything outside, since all outside
   depends upon sense, which is doubtful, and so may be treated as if it were completely false.
72 Aristotle c.348–7bBC: *Physics* II, esp. 195b31ff.
73 See "The Framework of Evolutionary Science" in Deely 1965: Part I, 102–30, esp. 110ff.; and De
   Koninck 1937.

Perhaps the most striking parallel of all is that each of two ages began from a blind assumption. The Latin Age began with the blind assumption that Augustine's proposal of *signum* was a solid idea and not an empty nominalism. Yet it took all the centuries of Latinity to realize main consequences of the proposal, to discover the difficulties with the original formulation, and finally to uncover the actual ground of what had been proposed through a dawning understanding of the uniqueness of relation as a mode of being suited by nature to be equally at home in the physical environment and in the surroundings of culture, the universe of things and the universe of thoughts, to be mediator between all realms in the peculiar "convertibility" of being and true with unity and good. The modern age began with the blind assumption that Descartes' proposal of ideas as consisting in representations was a solid starting point. The unfolding of the consequences of this assumption in the works of successive thinkers would define modernity and give it a distinctive cast of speculative unity beyond all the differences of the otherwise opposed positions and schools. So, as the sign gave to the Latin Age an indigenous and overall unity through all its controversies, the idea as object representing itself gave to modern times *its* indigenous and overall unity.

But the moment a later generation would begin to think that their experience of communication was real, the moment they began to think of that experience of communication as a proper starting point for philosophy, the remaining days of classical modern thought were numbered. For with the substitution of experience of real relations for ideas as the starting point, and the belief in communication as the guiding notion for developing the consequences of that point of departure, postmodernism had begun. Spring steals up on winter, at first all unnoticed, then carries the day. For if ideas were indeed what Descartes and Locke and the mainstream moderns took them to be, all genuine *experience* of communication could only be, in Kantian terms, a "transcendental illusion".

CHAPTER 13

Synthesis and Successors: The Strange Case of Dr Jekyll and Mr Hyde

In December 1885, almost nineteen years after the obscure birth of philosophy's postmodern era in the publication of the "New List of Categories" by Charles Sanders Peirce and eight years before his own demise, Robert Louis Stevenson (1850–94) penned in effect an unwitting epitaph for philosophy's modern period. The celebrated story-teller cast the epitaph in order to relate the "strange case of Dr Jekyll and Mr Hyde". As its title provides the epitaph, so the story itself provides the metaphor for what proved to be, after Galileo, the strange indeed relation into which philosophy entered with the new development of experimental and mathematical sciences. Both together – the new science and the new philosophy – thought to think anew the world. But, as intellectual events of the modern period forced ever more to the fore the final consequence of the shared epistemological assumption concerning sensation on which the rationalists after Descartes and the empiricists after Locke based their otherwise competing strategies for determining the compass of human understanding, the incompatible personalities of the two enterprises, science in the modern sense and the philosophy styled modern, made it ever more clear not merely that their partnership could not long survive, but that one at least of them had taken an irreversibly pathological turn. Stevenson's book was a work of psychological fiction, a riveting tale that symbolizes as well, if we let Dr Jekyll stand for science, the strange outcome of philosophy in its modern guise.

Dr Jekyll Sets Up Shop. The Scientific Side of Modernity: Coming to Terms with Nature

Once entered upon the way of ideas, it proved difficult for philosophers to advance in the project of giving a foundation to studies of the universe outside the human mind. This was ironic. For on its scientific side the glory of modernity was to find out, or seem to find out, more and more about the physical environment which is not species-specific but common to all the animals. For the first time, one species of animal, the human animal, had established, or seemed to have established, various means for the *critical control of objectification*. This was the process of determining what was merely part of the Umwelt as purely objective in depending for its existence *wholly* or *principally* upon mind, and what was part of the Umwelt as physically objective as well. The *physically* objective is objective, to be sure (for only the known can lead to the unknown), but links the Umwelt from within experience with a larger physical environment. The objective realm of experience, viewed under this distinction within objects, provides clues and paths whereby, with the help of instruments to extend the range and strengthen the capacity of our senses together with hypotheses to guide the use of those instruments, it becomes possible to extend indefinitely our understanding of and increasing control over the circumstances of the physical world.

The Copernican Revolution

We discovered that the earth was not at the center of the universe but one among several planets in a "solar system", a system with the sun at its center. The discovery is called in history the "Copernican Revolution", because Copernicus (1473–1543) was the one to devise a heliocentric system most proximate to the time that convincing proof was developed that the sun did not revolve around the earth. But we found that neither was the sun the center of the universe as a whole. We discovered that Jupiter had moons, the sun had spots, Saturn had rings; and, in the late twentieth century, as part of the same ascending arc of scientific discovery through the deployment of hypothesis-guided instruments, we discovered that Saturn, after all, was not the only planet with rings. We discovered that space and time form some kind of continuum with the very fabric of the universe, wherein the very mass of bodies creates the distortions of space responsible for the mysterious phenomenon we call "gravity", the measurement of a body's duration varies with the speed at which the measurement is taken, and the observation of celestial phenomena distant from earth provide us with a window into the landscape of the past of the universe. We discovered that we are not observers from outside nature's system but participants in that system both when and as we observe it, are perhaps even its means of "getting to know itself".

The Darwinian Revolution

We discovered that the earth was not a static body with life on it, but that life and the planet supporting it form together one total system. Within this system the planet provides the conditions that sustain life, but the living forms also change the conditions of the planet itself, so that the forms of life prevalent at one period of planetary development create conditions which, at one and the same time, make new forms of life possible and the old forms no longer possible. This discovery, or realization, is called the "Darwinian Revolution", because it was Charles Darwin (1809–82) who first proposed both an idea that living things evolve and a statement of a mechanism, "natural selection" (the fact of the differential survival of the life forms born into each biological generation). This mechanism is so obviously at work in the world of life that it needed only to be formulated in the climate created by the accumulation of fossil and exotic living plant and animal forms from all parts and periods of the earth in order to become at once accepted as the heuristic basis for the reorganization of scientific research in its totality. For the accumulation of forms had made it impossible for all but the dogmatic and scriptural fundamentalists to cling to the ancient idea that species never change.

In the wake of the Darwinian Revolution we found that the giant rain-forests of the tropical regions are not just wild exuberances of exotic flora and fauna but perform a previously unobjectified function for the planetary system as a whole comparable to the functions that the lungs perform for our individual body. We found that it is not enough to conquer existing diseases, because the causes of disease are themselves organic and therefore themselves constantly evolving. So medicine had to become research-based, not just to discover more of what the situation is, but to keep ahead of the game, because the situation itself is always evolving new things – new organic forms of life – to be discovered. Medieval Europe had the Black Plague, but never AIDS or Ebola.

The Freudian Revolution

Most disconcerting of all, we discovered that the "rational animal" really is an animal, that the human psyche has roots as deep as its ancestry, and drives as powerful as the roots are deep. Much of behavior is not a matter of choice, but the expression of patterns of action in which the rational (the *potentially* rational) individual is caught up by virtue of being an organism of a specific type with a biological heredity constitutive of that type. There is not only the conscious mind, but a depth of many layers of preconscious, half-conscious, and long forgotten experiences yet at work within the psyche upon which the conscious mind depends and upon which it draws in perceiving the world the way the individual actually does. This congeries of insight was called the "Freudian Revolution", because Sigmund Freud (1856–1939) was the first convincingly to demonstrate that the channel by which the species is propagated, sexuality, is also a channel by which the individual is linked to a larger world of past and future than reason left to itself would ever dream of in the ordinary compass of an individual life.

Freud's pupil, Carl Gustav Jung (1875–1961), would show that this past and larger psyche englobing the individual sphere of consciousness, wherein controlled reason puts itself to work, is not only biological but, in the human case, symbolic as well, with archetypal patterns and myths of racial consciousness at work unconsciously shaping some of the constructs even of reason and morality.

The Philosophical Side of Modernity: Abandoning the Way of Texts

On the side of philosophy, the whole point of abandoning Latin Aristotelianism in particular and Latin tradition in general had been to free up the philosophical mind to concentrate on the methods and results of the new sciences, to give the new ways of thinking and new ways of exploring nature foundation, intellectual justification, and perhaps even to find their philosophical counterpart for getting an understanding of the world both deeper and more secure than anything either the Greeks or the Latins had been able to achieve.

No one gave a thought to the great debate going on in the Hispanic Umwelt, even as Descartes wrote and Locke was born, over whether ideas as representations were themselves primarily objects or merely the foundation for relations constitutive of signs; for if the latter, then the representative aspect of the idea exists objectively only through the relation by which that idea serves, from its first moment and for as long as it endures in the psyche at any level, merely to provide the basis whereby the individual is linked to aspects of the total reality of the universe other than the individual himself or herself or itself.

Instead, Descartes, and every major modern after him down to Hegel, simply accepted that ideas are primarily objects, and gave themselves over to the effort of how to get beyond ideas to the world of nature in the exploration of which the whole of modernity was interested. Their main concern, at the outset of this project, was to get free of the shackle of being required to frame every discovery, every hypothesis, and every experiment concerning nature in the terms dictated by exegesis of the cultural object constituted of some pre-existing traditional text, be that text sacred (as with the Bible), secular (as with Aristotle or Aquinas), or religious (as with the Fathers and Peter Lombard's anthology of the views of the Fathers).

The way of textual exegesis as the way to understanding nature had been tried in every civilization known to history. Every culture had its sacred scriptures, and every culture had its clerical or priestly class who had claimed to be able to see in and explain from those scriptures the rules of human conduct and the secrets of the universe. First the Arabs and then the Latins had gone farther and achieved greater success with this method than had any previous culture, precisely because they had not confined their exegesis to sacred texts but had included also the scientific and philosophical, the "secular", writings of the ancient Greeks.

But the religious leaders in the Arab world had cut off the secular development and asserted total hegemony for exegesis based on sacred texts alone. Religious leaders in the West had never gotten that far, though not a few had surely tried. They had, for all the later Latin centuries, encouraged both the sacred and the secular exegesis, but, as Galileo discovered, the secular exegesis was to be finally governed by the sacred exegesis, and the use of observation and experiment to interfere with this religious domination was not to be suffered lightly.

Well then, said the modern philosophers, let us do away with all exegesis as the method of intellectual thought, certainly for science, but why not for philosophy as well? After all, even the Arabs and the Latins had relied on ancient Greece. But what had Greece relied on? Certainly not authoritative texts of philosophy or science, for, apart from the traditions of poetry (and divination), there were none. Why not abandon the way of texts and follow the example of ancient Greece? Why not try to look at nature itself for ourselves? Some even tried to call on the authority of Aquinas to support the revolt against authority, for the

Glory of the Latins himself had said, citing Boethius on the point, that the argument from authority is the weakest argument that is possible in philosophy. Let science, then, use observation, experiment, and mathematics to discover the secrets of nature; and let philosophy turn away from the texts to see by its natural light, the light of reason, what the truth may be. Let us start over from there.

So was born modernity as rebellion. It was a reaction against, a rejection of, the ways of the past, especially the use and abuse of authority as the measure of all things, even the things of the mind.

So far so good. And then one of history's delicious ironies. In the case of modern philosophy, the abandonment of the textual exegeses of scholasticism opened the floodgates for the very tidal wave that scholasticism, in its own time, had managed to contain. As Peirce put it,[1] after Descartes, in the very wake of his work,

> there was a tidal wave of nominalism. Descartes was a nominalist. Locke and all his
> following, Berkeley, Hartley, Hume, and even Reid, were nominalists. Leibniz was
> an extreme nominalist, and Rémusat, who has lately made an attempt to repair the
> edifice of Leibnizian monadology, does so by cutting away every part which leans at
> all toward realism. Kant was a nominalist; although his philosophy would have been
> rendered compacter, more consistent, and stronger if its author had taken up realism,
> as he certainly would have done if he had read Scotus. Hegel was a nominalist of
> realistic yearnings. I might continue the list much further. Thus, in one word, all
> modern philosophy of every sect has been nominalistic.

On the scientific front there was almost no down-side to the modern revolution. Men and women of science went from victory to victory in the study of nature, from Galileo's discovery of spots on the sun and moons around Jupiter to the experiments with lightning by Benjamin Franklin (1706–90), to the harnessing of electricity in artificial light by Thomas Edison (1847–1931), to the discovery of radium by Marie Curie (1867–1934) and the discovery of a vaccine against polio by Jonas Salk (1914–95).

Enter Mr Hyde: The Problem of the External World as the Schizophrenia of Modernity

On the philosophical front, however, as we saw in chapter 12,[2] there proved to be a problem right from the start. The new method had no trouble getting the rationalist experiment of modern philosophy off the ground. The problem was getting back. Descartes, remember, began by rejecting our only direct connection with the physical

---

1 Peirce, "Lessons from the History of Philosophy", 1903a: CP 1.19.
2 See esp. the "Origin of the Problem of the External World", chapter 12, p. 526 & 528f.

environment. Sense perception certainly does fool us sometimes, and therefore, in the implementation of methodological doubt, must be set to one side. But unless we can subsequently recoup the loss, we are left in thin air.

The First Attempt to Prove There Is an External World

Watch Descartes himself try to finesse the problem, at the end of his *Meditations on First Philosophy*. This was one of the principal works that launched modern metaphysics on the way of ideas, the work wherein Descartes thought to establish the existence and goodness of God as the source and rule of all truth in ideas:[3]

> It remains for me to examine whether material things exist. And at least I now know they are capable of existing, in so far as they are the subject-matter of pure mathematics, since I perceive them clearly and distinctly. For there is no doubt that God is capable of creating everything that I am capable of perceiving in this manner; and I have never judged that something could not be made by him except on the grounds that there would be a contradiction in my perceiving it distinctly. The conclusion that material things exist is also suggested by the faculty of imagination, which I am aware of using when I turn my mind to material things. For when I give more attentive consideration to what imagination is, it seems to be nothing else but an application of the cognitive faculty to a body which is intimately present to it, and which therefore exists.
>
> ... I will go back over all the things which I previously took to be perceived by the senses, and reckoned to be true; and I will go over my reasons for thinking this. Next, I will set out my reasons for subsequently calling these things into doubt. And finally I will consider what I should now believe about them. ... [For] now, when I am beginning to achieve a better knowledge of myself and the author of my being, although I do not think I should heedlessly accept everything I seem to have acquired from the senses, neither do I think that everything should be called into doubt.
>
> ... On the one hand I have a clear and distinct idea of myself, in so far as I am simply a thinking, non-extended thing; and on the other hand I have a distinct idea of body, in so far as this is simply an extended, non-thinking thing. And accordingly, it is certain that I am really distinct from my body, and can exist without it.
>
> Besides this, I find in myself faculties for certain special modes of thinking, namely imagination and sensory perception ... [and] it is clear that these other faculties, if they exist, must be in a corporeal or extended substance and not an intellectual one; for the clear and distinct conception of them includes extension, but does not include any intellectual act whatsoever. Now there is in me a passive faculty of sensory perception, that is, a faculty for receiving and recognizing the ideas of sensible objects; but I could not make use of it unless there was also an active faculty, either in me or in something else, which produced or brought about these ideas. But this faculty cannot be in me,

---

3 From Meditation 6 of Descartes' *Meditations on First Philosophy* (1641), "The existence of material things, and the real distinction between mind and body".

since clearly it presupposes no intellectual act on my part, and the ideas in question are produced without my cooperation and often even against my will. So the only alternative is that it is in another substance distinct from me – a substance which contains either formally or eminently all the reality which exists objectively in the ideas produced by this faculty (as I have just noted). This substance is either a body, that is, a corporeal nature, in which case it will contain formally and in fact everything which is to be found objectively or representatively in the ideas; or else it is God, or some creature more noble than a body, in which case it will contain eminently whatever is to be found in the ideas. But since God is not a deceiver, it is quite clear that he does not transmit the ideas to me either directly from himself, or indirectly, via some creature which contains the objective reality of the ideas not formally but only eminently. For God has given me no faculty at all for recognizing any such source for these ideas; on the contrary, he has given me a great propensity to believe that they are produced by corporeal things. So I do not see how God could be understood to be anything but a deceiver if the ideas were transmitted from a source other than corporeal things. It follows that corporeal things exist.

There is the first attempt in modern philosophy to prove the existence of a world outside our minds. But notice what makes such an attempt necessary. By going the way of ideas, Descartes has chosen a speculative path according to which there is nothing about ideas themselves which makes them link up with something beyond the subjectivity of the knower, in sharp contrast to the way of signs, according to which the very existence of an idea presupposes sensation (rooted wholly in physical relations unmediated by ideas), to which the addition of ideas as giving rise to interpretive relations serves only to reinforce the carriage of the knowing subject beyond subjectivity and places the subject in a situation in part prospectively and in part actually intersubjective. But along the way of ideas, cognitive states (ideas) have their whole existence from the knower as modes of the knower's consciousness; and even sensations produce and terminate in ideas, mental images (in contrast to the subjectivity of environmental things as acting on the senses here and now). In Aristotelian terms, ideas are quite simply *inherent accidents*, that is to say, individual or subjective characteristics. Were ideas primarily signs, the case would be different, for signs belong not to the class of inherent (or "subjective" accidents) but to the class of relations (or "suprasubjective" accidents). Relations, as accidents of substance, are singular in that of themselves and by their very nature they exceed subjectivity and establish links, actual or prospective, with what the individual having the idea is not. But ideas, in Descartes' speculation, are not primarily signs. They are primarily objects. They are representations which present themselves, according to their various contents, it is true. But that these contents are not merely modes of the self, like the ideas themselves are, is something that has to be proved. Moreover, it turns out that this is something that can be proved in only one single case, the idea of God.

Thus Descartes' argument, like that of Anselm, has a logic that applies only to a single case.[4] This restricted application of the argument is what makes it necessary for Descartes to make every subsequent existential consideration in his system, including the matter of his own body and the external world of other selves and bodies, depend on what he has learned about the divine existence, and in particular the fact that "God is no deceiver". In the Cartesian perspective on the way of ideas, on such a thread hangs the external world.

Locke's Stand on the Problem

Locke considered the making of our "belief" in the world of sense to depend utterly on a single speculative thread that has nothing whatever to do with the senses to be a preposterous and unacceptable situation. It can be said that he launched empiricism as a counter-movement to rationalism out of his complete dissatisfaction with Descartes' handling of everything that pertained to the senses. But Locke too accepted the way of ideas as the path empiricism must follow. He considered that the primary qualities of bodies are the link between our ideas and the physical environment, for in representing these qualities our ideas are representing something which really is in the things behind the mental images of sensation as the stimulus of the mind's forming the images.

But we have already seen that the primary qualities are known dependently upon the secondary qualities. So if the secondary qualities are fictions of the mind's own making, and the primary qualities depend with logical necessity on the secondary qualities in order to be present before the mind, we have in fact no way to justify our belief that the primary qualities represent qualities really in the things themselves. To know that, we would have to be able to compare the two, to compare the ideas directly with the things. But only the ideas, never the things themselves, are present in our awareness. So how can we compare them? This is a slight detail which seems not to have occurred to Locke.

What to Do with Common Sense?

As a man who put stock in common sense,[5] Locke had never for a moment doubted the existence of the world of bodies. But common-sense belief is one thing, a philosophical justification of that belief quite another. In philosophy, it is necessary either to justify what common sense holds, or to abandon it. The mainstream modern philosophers saw no other way but the way of ideas, and on that way there is no question that the common-sense view of the physical world – that it exists, we are aware of it in our perceptions, and we deal with it in our activities everyday – needs some revision, whether

---

4 See chapter 6 above, p. 238.
5 Locke 1690: Book IV, ch. 8, sect. 2: "nobody will so openly bid defiance to common sense, as to affirm visible and direct contradictions in plain words; or if he does, a man is excused if he breaks off any farther discourse with him." Compare Aristotle on this point, "How to Deal with Contradictions?", in chapter 4, p. 125 above.

Locke realized it or not. Locke's acceptance of the equation of objects experienced with ideas, however, proved to be the Achilles' heel in his desire, by the doctrine of .empiricism, to restore common sense to philosophy and the external world to science.

So let us pause upon our way to give a tip of the hat to the sole figure who appears on the early-modern scene with an attempt to get at the root of the problem, the founder of the "Scottish School of Common Sense Philosophy", Thomas Reid (1710–96). Beginning with his *An Inquiry into the Human Mind on the Principles of Common Sense* of 1764, Reid proposes, against his modern colleagues in general and Berkeley and Hume in particular, a philosophy of mind that "is an essentially semiotic theory".[6]

Reid's valiant effort to establish principles of common sense in modern philosophy, viewed in the light of earlier Latin developments in epistemology, had one great shortcoming which, uncorrected, could only doom the effort. While Reid rejected the proposition that we directly know only our own ideas, which is the bedrock of modern epistemology, he did so without having a way effectively to discriminate between sensation and perception as such. Hence, he made his case for direct knowledge of physical things so strong as to be unable to deal as a matter of principle with the fundamental difference between perceptual objects in their objective constitution through relations and perceptual objects in what they have of a subjective constitution as things accessible in sensation.

Reid has much to say that enriches our understanding of the semiotics of sensation. Yet his analysis leans on the modern distinction of primary and secondary qualities; and it further lacks explicit means to integrate sensation within a semiotics of understanding. For just as in perception Reid's philosophy lacks the essential sophistication of an equivalent of the notions of formal sign and even formal object, this same weakness extends to his doctrine of "conception", of intellection as distinct from the perception of sense. Reid shared the modern prejudice against Latin philosophy before the work of Descartes. A pity, for had he looked there he would have found the materials necessary to vindicate his call for a return to principles of common sense in philosophy.

As it is, even though he does not achieve the status of a culminating or transitional figure in philosophy's history, Reid "was, as it were, the one man of the eighteenth century who stood up and said 'the emperor has no clothes on'."[7]

The mainstream call for anything like a return to common sense remained that of Locke in his founding of empiricism, with the claim that the senses are the origin of all we know. Yet his followers along the mainstream way of ideas did not fail to notice that, in this regard, Locke with empiricism had done no better than Descartes with rationalism in restoring to modern philosophy a contact with the down-to-earth realm of material objects and everyday common sense.

---

6 Henle 1983: 156.

7 Ibid.: 167. For the 21st century, Eco (2000: 133; cf. 1990: 36 and passim) seeks "to revive … a standpoint of common sense" as "a venerable philosophical concept" of "maximum usefulness" in developing semiotics.

Bishop Berkeley's Idealism and Dr Johnson's Stone

Listen to the good Irish bishop of the Church of England, George Berkeley (1685–1753), in honor of whose visit to Newport, Rhode Island, around 1732, perhaps, is named the home city of the main campus of the University of California (though, if so, habitually mispronounced). From this man, as a young lad of twenty-five, first spoke the clearest consistent voice expressive of the ineluctable destination of the way of ideas. Two other voices would try to mitigate this consequence, that of Hume and that of Kant. But neither could suppress the disappearance from human consciousness of all direct contact with a world of material bodies in motion such as the new sciences fancied themselves to be about.

Berkeley's voice is deservedly first, for in his work alone is the evaporation of the material world under the sun lighting the way of ideas both recognized and accepted:[8]

> It is indeed an opinion strangely prevailing amongst men, that houses, mountains, rivers, and in a word sensible objects have an existence natural or real, distinct from their being perceived by the understanding. But with how great an assurance and acquiescence soever this principle may be entertained in the world; yet whoever shall find in his heart to call it in question, may, if I mistake not, perceive it to involve a manifest contradiction. For what are the forementioned objects but the things we perceive by sense, and what do we perceive besides our own ideas or sensations; and is it not plainly repugnant that any one of these or any combination of them should exist unperceived?

The world was outraged. Dr Johnson, as we saw,[9] kicked a stone to prove this wrong. He might as well have kicked Berkeley, or bashed in his head with the stone. A novice in logic can tell you that brute force can silence a person, but it cannot win an *argument*. The attempt to argue by such means has even been raised to the indignity of a fallacy formally named: the fallacy *ad baculum*, "the appeal to the stick". Beating someone over the head will not do. Only reasons well and consistently construed to prove a point can carry an argument. And these were all on Berkeley's side. All that Dr Johnson had to show for his proof was a sore toe and demonstration to the world that, when it came to philosophy, he was a fool.[10]

The Skepticism of David Hume

David Hume (1711–76) well understood that Berkeley had the better of the argument, and so much the worse for common sense. Nor, being an empiricist, did he think that Descartes' "proof" of the world of bodies was worth the time of day. Yet

---

8 Berkeley 1710: *The Principles of Human Knowledge*, Part 1, sect. 4.
9 Chapter 12, p. 532.
10 Recall "Anselm's Fool in Samuel Johnson's Shoes" from chapter 12, p. 532f.

he did not think that it was necessary to go so far as to outright deny the existence of a world of bodies, the "external world". It would be quite enough to confess and maintain a thoroughgoing skepticism on the matter, even while going about the gentlemanly occupations of eating and drinking and everyday life. What the way of ideas really showed, he thought, was that no one need take philosophy all that seriously.

A skeptic, Hume tells is, is nothing more nor less than the man who has gotten to the bottom of the way of ideas and makes no bones about it. A skeptic is the man who has plumbed the depths of modern philosophy and found it wanting from any point of view that could remotely be called that of a "plain man of common sense":[11]

> There is not a greater number of philosophical reasonings, displayed upon any subject, than those, which prove the existence of a Deity, and refute the fallacies of Atheists … The Sceptic is another enemy of religion, who naturally provokes the indignation of all divines and graver philosophers; though it is certain, that no man ever met with any such absurd creature, or conversed with a man, who had no opinion or principle concerning any subject, either of action or speculation. This begets a very natural question; What is meant by a sceptic?
>
> . . . .
>
> I need not insist upon the more trite topics, employed by the sceptics in all ages, against the evidence of sense; such as those which are derived from the imperfection and fallaciousness of our organs, on numberless occasions; the crooked appearance of an oar in water; the various aspects of objects, according to their different distances; the double images which arise from the pressing one eye; with many other appearances of a like nature. These sceptical topics, indeed, are only sufficient to prove, that the senses alone are not implicitly to be depended on; but that we must correct their evidence by reason, and by considerations, derived from the nature of the medium, the distance of the object, and the disposition of the organ, in order to render them, within their sphere, the proper criteria of truth and falsehood. *There are other more profound arguments against the senses, which admit not of so easy a solution.*
>
> It seems evident, that men are carried, by a natural instinct or prepossession, to repose faith in their senses; and that, without any reasoning, or even almost before the use of reason, we always suppose an external universe, which depends not on our perception, but would exist, though we and every sensible creature were absent or annihilated. Even the animal creation are governed by a like opinion, and preserve this belief of external objects, in all their thoughts, designs, and actions.
>
> It seems also evident, that, when men follow this blind and powerful instinct of nature, they always suppose the very images, presented by the senses, to be the external objects, and never entertain any suspicion, that the one are nothing but representations

11 Hume 1748: *An Enquiry concerning Human Understanding*, Sect. XII: of the Academical or Sceptical Philosophy, Part I.

of the other. This very table, which we see white, and which we feel hard, is believed to exist, independent of our perception, and to be something external to our mind, which perceives it. Our presence bestows not being on it: Our absence does not annihilate it. It preserves its existence uniform and entire, independent of the situation of intelligent beings, who perceive or contemplate it.

But this universal and primary opinion of all men is soon destroyed by the slightest philosophy, which teaches us, that nothing can ever be present to the mind but an image or perception, and that the senses are only the inlets, through which these images are conveyed, without being able to produce any immediate intercourse between the mind and the object. The table, which we see, seems to diminish, as we remove farther from it: But the real table, which exists independent of us, suffers no alteration: It was, therefore, nothing but its image, which was present to the mind. These are the obvious dictates of reason; and no man, who reflects, ever doubted, that the existences, which we consider, when we say, this house and that tree, are nothing but perceptions in the mind, and fleeting copies or representations of other existences, which remain uniform and independent.

So far, then, are we necessitated by reasoning to contradict or depart from the primary instincts of nature, and to embrace a new system with regard to the evidence of our senses. But here philosophy finds herself extremely embarrassed, when she would justify this new system, and obviate the cavils and objections of the sceptics. She can no longer plead the infallible and irresistible instinct of nature: For that led us to a quite different system, which is acknowledged fallible and even erroneous. And to justify this pretended philosophical system, by a chain of clear and convincing argument, or even any appearance of argument, exceeds the power of all human capacity.

By what argument can it be proved, that the perceptions of the mind must be caused by external objects, entirely different from them, though resembling them (if that be possible) and could not arise either from the energy of the mind itself, or from the suggestion of some invisible and unknown spirit, or from some other cause still more unknown to us? It is acknowledged, that, in fact, many of these perceptions arise not from any thing external, as in dreams, madness, and other diseases. And nothing can be more inexplicable than the manner, in which body should so operate upon mind as ever to convey an image of itself to a substance, supposed of so different, and even contrary a nature.

It is a question of fact, whether the perceptions of the senses be produced by external objects, resembling them: how shall this question be determined? By experience surely; as all other questions of a like nature. But here experience is, and must be entirely silent. The mind has never any thing present to it but the perceptions, and cannot possibly reach any experience of their connexion with objects. The supposition of such a connexion is, therefore, without any foundation in reasoning.

To have recourse to the veracity of the supreme Being, in order to prove the veracity of our senses, is surely making a very unexpected circuit. If his veracity were at all concerned in this matter, our senses would be entirely infallible; because it is not possible that he can ever deceive. Not to mention, that, if the external world be once called in question, we shall be at a loss to find arguments, by which we may prove the existence of that Being or any of his attributes.

This is a topic, therefore, in which the profounder and more philosophical sceptics will always triumph, when they endeavour to introduce an universal doubt into all subjects of human knowledge and enquiry. Do you follow the instincts and propensities of nature, may they say, in assenting to the veracity of sense? But these lead you to believe, that the very perception or sensible image is the external object. Do you disclaim this principle, in order to embrace a more rational opinion, that the perceptions are only representations of something external? You here depart from your natural propensities and more obvious sentiments; and yet are not able to satisfy your reason, which can never find any convincing argument from experience to prove, that the perceptions are connected with any external objects.

. . . .

Thus the first philosophical objection to the evidence of sense or to the opinion of external existence consists in this, that such an opinion, if rested on natural instinct, is contrary to reason, and if referred to reason, is contrary to natural instinct, and at the same time carries no rational evidence with it, to convince an impartial enquirer. The second objection goes farther, and represents this opinion as contrary to reason: at least, if it be a principle of reason, that all sensible qualities are in the mind, not in the object. Bereave matter of all its intelligible qualities, both primary and secondary, you in a manner annihilate it, and leave only a certain unknown, inexplicable something, as the cause of our perceptions; a notion so imperfect, that no sceptic will think it worth while to contend against it.

So came about one of history's great ironies: that modern empiricism, introduced to vindicate the views of the "plain man of common sense" against the dream of Descartes, ended up, of all the philosophies in history, the one most removed from and contemptuous of "common sense". When, in the late nineteenth and early twentieth centuries, Neothomist authors entered the lists to combat modern idealism, one of their principal concerns was to show how a restored metaphysics faithful to the principles of a philosophy of being really would achieve what Locke and then Reid had in vain attempted, namely, a continuity with common sense.[12]

---

12 One of the earliest works in this regard was also the most notable: Reginald Garrigou-Lagrange, *Le sens commun, la philosophie de l'être et les formules dogmatiques*, the first edition of which appeared in 1909 (Paris: G. Beauchesne), with a 4th "revised and enlarged edition" appearing in 1936 (Paris: Desclée de Brouwer). In between, the task of critically clarifying a sound continuity between an intellectual core of "common sense" and the speculative and practical dimension of properly philosophical knowledge was taken up also by Jacques Maritain. Beginning in 1920, in the first of a projected seven "fascicules" or small volumes spelling out the *Éléments de Philosophie*, of which only the first two were completed, Maritain devoted a key section of the first volume, *Introduction générale à la philosophie* (Paris: Librairie Pierre Téqui, 1920), to the theme of "philosophy and common sense". The most definitive edition of this work can be found in vol. II of the 15-vol. *Jacques et Raïssa Maritain Oeuvres Complètes* (Fribourg: Éditions Universitaires Fribourg Suisse, 1987), 11–272, esp. 130–9, "La philosophie et le sens commun". This work was

But the one thing that the early moderns had never been able to consider was an alternative to the way of ideas. They had never realized that, in going the way of ideas, they were in fact making a choice between two ways of starting philosophy anew by taking human experience itself as the starting point. One of these ways did not necessitate the break with common sense and the separation of intelligibility from mind-independent being. For the realization that between the way of signs and the way of ideas there is a decisive alternative was a realization that had emerged as such principally within a region of Latin discourse, the Hispanic Umwelt of Iberia, with which the British and Continental philosophical worlds of this time had little concourse. And the realization had emerged too late, practically speaking, to impact modernity. By 1632, the repudiation of Latin philosophical texts continuous with the age-old traditions of philosophy previous to science was already set, the way of ideas already adopted as the way of the immediate future.

Of course, any one of the early moderns might independently have hit upon the way of signs. But in fact none of them did so. In every beginning lies the end. The moderns were finding soon enough that they had no choice but to give up the idea of the mind's being able to grasp being in its transcendental amplitude, and under that light, little by little, to understand physical nature through empirical means. The men of science, the men of philosophy came to conclude, were dupes of their own enthusiasm. They were not, and could not be, doing what they thought they were doing. The embodiment of modernity as philosophy was not the scientific Dr Jekyll. The embodiment of modernity as philosophy was the pathological Mr Hyde.

Immanuel Kant: The Synthesis of Rationalism and Empiricism
And yet those scientists were doing *something*, and it was marvelous by any standard. If not what they seem and deem themselves to be doing – namely, advancing in knowledge of the subjective constitution of the physical environment – then what? For science was what modernity had been all about. For the sake of freedom to develop a scientific philosophy had modern times begun. Yet, speculatively speaking, Berkeleyan idealism and Humean skepticism were a disaster for science. For they pulled the epistemological rug out from under what the scientists were hoping to do, had thought themselves doing. With Berkeley and Hume the modern world of scientific objectivity had been conjured away by modern philosophy. Thanks a lot. Surely a way of understanding the situation better than this could be found along the way of ideas.

---

translated into Spanish, Portuguese, Korean, Hungarian, Italian, Japanese, and Czech; and into English by E. I. Watkin as *An Introduction to Philosophy* (1930), which appeared in many editions over the following decades. Maritain undertook a more detailed exposition of his central points on this subject in his 1932 classic, *Les Degrés du Savoir*. The translation based on the 4th French ed. under the supervision of Gerald Phelan, *The Degrees of Knowledge* (New York: Scribners, 1959), remains the most authoritative English version; see there his discussion of "Realism and Common Sense", pp. 82–111.

Such was the conviction of Immanuel Kant (1724–1804), born in the city of Königsberg (now Kaliningrad) on 22 April 1724 and associated with its university from 1775 till his death on 12 February 1804. Höffding reports[13] that "his name was really Cant, but the philosopher changed the C into a K, to prevent its being pronounced like S." His report has been disputed,[14] yet whether we think of "cant" as "to speak in technical jargon" or "cant" as in "can't know anything as it is independent of mind", the name fits; and the original spelling Höffding alleged well suggests to an English speaker how the "Kant" variant should best be pronounced.

In the eighteenth century, the distinct establishment of "science" and "philosophy" as two notions, the one concerned with experiment and the mathematization of sensible appearances, the other concerned with doctrine in the intellectual sense of the clarification and systematization of questions not resolvable by scientific means, was still far from completion. In fact, had Kant died and the manuscript for his book of 1781 gone unpublished, he would be thought of today, if at all, as a scientist rather than as a philosopher; for previous to 1775 he had published only one treatise, and that a short one, on a problem of physics. As it is, he is known rather as the Master of Modernity in philosophy, the mightiest of the thinkers who established themselves along the way of ideas.

Yet not even he, in the end, could escape the inevitable. For ideas have their consequences, however long it may take the psychology of human beings to work them out. In this case, what had to be worked out was the consequences of a definite "idea of ideas" as self-representing objects, not merely as self-representing objects, but as providing even in sensation the terminus of cognitive activity. Thus, even when Kant reintroduces relations into knowledge whereby objectivity itself is opposed to subjectivity (known set "over against" knower) as the terminus of a relation is opposed to its subjective provenance, these relations as cognitive yet have no outlet whence to become, besides suprasubjective, *inter*subjective as well.

---

13 Höffding 1900: II, 32; following Borowski 1804.
14 Cassirer 1921: 12–13: "Concerning the origins of his family Kant says, in a letter written in his old age [13 October 1797], that his grandfather, whose final residence was Tilsit, came from Scotland. ... Objective scrutiny has not substantiated this testimony, at least in the form in which Kant gives it; it has since been established that Kant's great-grandfather was already living as an innkeeper in Werden, near Heydekrug. The statement by Borowski, his first biographer, that the family name originally read 'Cant', and that Kant himself first introduced the now customary spelling of the name, has also proved incorrect; as far as the name can be traced through documentary evidence, we encounter it in the version 'Kant' or 'Kandt'. It is possible, therefore, that the statement concerning Scottish descent, which Kant must have received from an old family tradition, is wholly without foundation. In any case, no one has so far been able to prove it with any adequate degree of certainty." So it is of some interest to find that the Oxford *Dictionary of Surnames* lists "Cant" as "English and Scots", and concludes its entry (Hanks and Hodges 1988: 92) as follows: "A family by the name of Cant, who held land at Masterton, near Dunfermline, are descended from Flemish cloth merchants of the 15th century. The German philosopher Immanuel Kant (1724–1804) was the grandson of a Scots immigrant to Königsberg, where he lived all his life." Whether Hanks and Hodges here are confirming Borowski or challenging Cassirer is a loose end I leave for some one to tie!

For in the Kantian scheme, objects as appearing are not *indifferent* to including environmental physical being as such (indeed, necessarily doing so in sensation as distinct from perception and understanding but continuous therewith in direct experience, as Aquinas and Poinsot argued[15]), for "original input" from environment to cognitive power, in Kantian terms,[16] "is not characterizable at all". In the Kantian scheme, appearances are *opposed* to the thing-in-itself as what is known to what is unknowable. Whence the ineluctable farthermost consequence of this "idea of idea" from which the way of ideas takes its departure is solipsism, the enclosure of the mind within the products of its own workings, the making of consciousness both the womb and the tomb of thought.

Newtonian Science

By training and temperament, Kant was a man of science. The work of science he admired above all was the *Principia Mathematica Philosophiae Naturalis* (1686–7) of Sir Isaac Newton (1642–1727), in Kant's day the best account yet conceived by the human mind of why the stars and planets behave as they do. Nor did this account present itself as some "likely story". It showed well and truly how, given this and that, the rest naturally followed. In other words, the key to the power of Newton's book lay in its mathematical expression of the observations the astronomers had accumulated in order to be able to *predict* the further actions of heavenly bodies (such as eclipses and the return of comets) and their consequences (such as tides). Indeed, Pierre-Simon Laplace (1749–1827) thought the system of Newton, with the few adjustments that he, Laplace, had made, could trace out for all time to come the patterns that celestial bodies would trace in the skies of earth. The line of Newton's work was the principal source of the eighteenth- and nineteenth-century conception of the universe as one grand machine.

But what made everything possible, what lay behind all the great advances of the works of science, was the idea of *necessity*, the idea that things in nature, if one looks deeply enough, follow one another in ways that could not be otherwise. For every phenomenon there is a reason, or complex of reasons, and the work of science is to find and express those reasons, those necessities. This idea of necessity was what the rationalists considered their home ground.

Consider Kant's notion of substance as an example:[17]

---

15 Poinsot 1632a: Book III, Question 2.
16 Collins 1999: 147.
17 *Thoughts on the True Estimation of Living Forces* (1747), 8. This was Kant's first published work. It is worth noting that in this early work, with the notion of substance cut loose from all reference to experience, Kant is able to *deduce* from *his* notion of the individual substance conclusions which Aristotle only *abduced* (or hypothesized) of the physical universe or "world" as a whole, such as that it has no "place" where it exists (no "*ubi circumscriptivum*", in the categorial parlance of the Latin scholastics), and "other propositions, which are not less remarkable, and which capture the understanding so to speak against its own will". (It would be hard to find a better capsule summary of modern philosophy.)

Since every self-sufficient being contains within itself the complete source of all its determinations, it is not necessary for its existence that it stand in relation to other things. Substances can therefore exist, and yet have no outer relation to things, nor stand in any actual connection with them.

Contrast this notion with the original Aristotelian idea of substance,[18] or with the Latin notion of substance[19] as a relative center of unity and action, which, through its action, struggles so to dominate both the internal systemic requirements and the external environmental structures as to maintain itself in existence. When the empiricists, from Locke on, challenge the notion of substance, it is principally the modern rationalist conception with which they do battle, a notion of substance from which both intrinsic and extrinsic relativity have been abstracted, leaving a "substrate" able to exist only in a rationalist's dream.

From Dogmatic Slumber to Idealist Consciousness

So Kant was a rationalist through and through, and he was a man of scientific bent. When he read Hume, he was not converted to empiricism or to skepticism, but he was, as he put it, awakened from a "dogmatic slumber". Now what was this slumber from which Hume had awakened him? According to Gilson,[20] the following sentence[21] by Hume "was the very one that aroused Kant from his dogmatic slumber":

> there are two principles which I cannot render consistent, nor is it in my power to renounce either of them, viz. that all our distinct perceptions are distinct existences, and that the mind never perceives any real connexion among distinct existences.

But if that be the case, then what Kant was awakened to was little more than a realization of the consequences of the rationalist doctrine on substance.[22] If perceptions come only from the senses, where there is no grasp of necessity, but only of conjunctions and associations of objective phenomena, then where does the necessity upon which science relies come from? Kant's answer is that the necessity of science is not in nature but is introduced into the perceptions of sense by reason. He took for his subject matter the very subject matter "of the knowledge that survives erroneous

---

18 See "Transcendental Relativity" in chapter 3, p. 72ff.
19 See the discussion in chapter 6, p. 228, and chapter 9, p. 423.
20 Gilson 1952: 122.
21 From the appendix to Hume's *Treatise of Human Nature*, 1739–1740: 636.
22 Hegel well perceived the central role of Kant in revealing what was truly inescapable about the way of ideas, what rendered empiricism ineffectual in trying to bring the rationalist movement "down to earth" and "back to the senses". Hegel wrote (in 1802: 374): "Hume's and Locke's reflective way of philosophizing, more thoroughly and systematically worked out on German ground and soil, becomes German philosophy."

beliefs and illusory appearances",[23] and he found that it was not what the ancients or the medievals had thought it to be, namely, mind-independent being, but rather, through and through, mind-dependent being, albeit objective, rather than *merely* subjective, as many of his modern idealist forebears had more or less expressly come to hold. Yet, as we will see, his success in restoring a relational structure and objectivity to knowledge did not in the end move him beyond the trajectory toward solipsism emerging ever more clearly, through the work of thinker after thinker, as modernity's distinctive intellectual physiognomy, as we will see.[24]

Reason has certain patterns or "molds" ("a-priori forms", as Kant calls them) according to which it shapes and presents the contents of all possible experiences. The patterns are a-priori, that is, they are prior to all actual experience. Actual experiences presuppose that the individual first exist; they are a-posteriori, after the fact. Before the fact come the regulative forms of understanding, not the forms of nature which give it its subjective constitution prior to and independent of our experience, which can never be known to us. In seeing necessities in experienced objects, we are seeing not what belongs to actual nature but only what comes from

---

23 Collins 1999: xiii.
24 "Like the captives of Philippi", Stevenson says of Jekyll's transformation into Hyde (1885/6: 65), "that which stood within ran forth." We may agree completely with Arthur Collins (1999: 14) that "Kant's thinking needs no modernization and has immediate application to our own philosophical problems". But the reason for this situation is just the opposite of what Collins would have us think. Collins (p. xiv) thinks that since "Kant's radical subjectivisim is not a commitment to the mental status of objects of apprehension", this is enough to move his work beyond idealism *tout court*, to make of his work a veritable "basic anti-idealistic philosophy".

Here is Collins's argument. Both Descartes and Locke identified the objects of immediate experience with ideas as subjective mental states. Kant, to the contrary, separates the objects of immediate experience from the mental states of subjectivity and gives them a relational, necessary structure as truly objective and "public", in the restricted sense of being opposed to the subjective mental states on the basis of which they exist suprasubjectively as objects. This warrants concluding that Kant's thinking can be "liberated from idealistic interpretation".

Here is why the argument fails. The contrast Collins draws between the subjectivism of Descartes and Locke, on the one side, and the objectivism of Kant, on the other side, is accurately drawn as far as Collins draws it. But the contrast in this particular is not enough to efface the deeper idealist bond. For the "essence of idealism" is not that "the things we immediately apprehend in experiences are realities that exist in our own minds" as mental states thereof, *pace* Collins (p. xiv); but that whatever we apprehend *in all that we apprehend of it* is a product, whether directly (as "ideas" in the mind) or indirectly (as "objects" terminating ideas-based relations), of our mind's own working. That the things we immediately apprehend in all that we apprehend of them the mind itself makes (be they regarded à la Kant as objectively opposed to the subject, or be they regarded à la Descartes as subjective modifications of the one knowing), in contrast with whatever it be that exists or may exist independently of those workings: that is the true essence of modern idealism. Poinsot neatly skewered this central point early (1632a: 312/3–6) in what were to prove the formative years of the classical mainstream development. With idealism's central tenet so understood, no liberation of Kantian thought is possible – as a matter of principle. Kant's philosophy needs no modernization because it is quintessentially modern, root and branch. If the implications of Kant's thought are unacceptable in the framework of postmodernity, that is precisely because of their thoroughly modern character.

the requirement of our own minds. As Kant himself later summarized the matter in his *Critique of Judgment*:[25] "The faculty of knowledge from a-priori principles may be called pure reason, and the general investigation of its possibility and bounds the critique of pure reason."

The mind forms its objects of apprehension under the stimulus of things. But the mind itself, purely out of its own resources, makes of these objects of perception *scientific* objects by introducing into them necessities which scientific investigation is able subsequently to discover and express. Hence Kant's famous formula: "Gedanken ohne Inhalt sind leer, Anschauungen ohne Begriffe sind blind" – concepts without percepts are empty; percepts without concepts are blind.[26]

Thus, Kant is able to preserve the necessities needed for science. But he preserves the needed necessities only as properties belonging to the *phenomena*, the objects of our direct experience and awareness as created by our minds. He divorces the necessities sharply and entirely from the "things-in-themselves" which lie *behind* the phenomena and *somehow* (by means in principle ungraspable by the human mind) provoke the mind to their formation. Thus, the actual entities of the physical environment in their proper being and their means of acting upon the conscious self are never as such in any measure revealed *in* or *through* the phenomena. Even the so-called "noumena", when spoken of in contrast to the "phenomena", belong not to the realm of "things in themselves" but to the same realm as the constructed appearances; they are the *intelligible dimension* as such of the sensible phenomena as the mind constructs them.

This distinction between "noumenon" and "ding-an-sich ("thing-in-itself") is an important technical distinction of Kantian philosophy that is not always understood even in the Kant literature, where "noumenon" and "thing-in-itself" are often

---

25 Kant 1790: I, 3.
26 Kant 1787: 75: "If the *receptivity* of our mind, its power of receiving representations in so far as it is in any wise affected, is to be entitled sensibility, then the mind's power of producing representations from itself, the *spontaneity* of knowledge, should be called the understanding. Our nature is so constituted that our *intuition* can never be other than sensible; that is, it contains only the mode in which we are affected by objects. The faculty, on the other hand, which enables us to *think* the object of sensible intuition is the understanding. To neither of these powers may a preference be given over the other. Without sensibility no object would be given to us, without understanding no object would be thought. Thoughts without content are empty, intuitions without concepts are blind. It is, therefore, just as necessary to make our concepts sensible, that is, to add the object to them in intuition, as to make our intuitions intelligible, that is, to bring them under concepts. These two powers or capacities cannot exchange their functions. The understanding can intuit nothing, the senses can think nothing. Only through their union can knowledge arise."

   Whence it is ironic that Jakob von Uexküll, the great pioneer of zoösemiosis, took his original inspiration for the animal Umwelt, precisely a world without concepts, from the Kantian theory of mind; for surely in a wholly logical world the study of the purely perceptual intelligence of animals would have been rather the inspiration for the jettisoning of Kantianism in the philosophy of mind. History, as we have seen, has its ironies. Consult "Jakob von Uexküll" in Deely 1990: 119–24; and compare the discussion of the relation of understanding to sense intuition in Poinsot 1632a: Book II, Questions 1 and 2.

equivalated under the general heading of "unknowable", an equivalation for which Kant himself bears much responsibility.[27] In principle, noumenon and ding-an-sich, though both limit concepts on the knowable, set their "limits" in quite different manners, are "unknowables" in quite different ways. For the noumenon is the non-referential concept of an intelligible content, whereas the thing-in-itself is a limit concept which one needs to posit in order to preserve the restriction of cognition to appearances ("phenomena") and do away with the claims of traditional physics and metaphysics. Thus, as Collins aptly puts it,[28] were there "no noumena at all," within the Kantian system "the reality of things-in-themselves cannot be supposed to be threatened."

Kant himself stresses the rejection of traditional metaphysical claims to a knowledge of real being; but it is quite important to realize that what he has rejected in fact is the whole tradition of natural philosophy from Aristotle's day to his own. What Aristotle called ὄν and the Latins called *ens reale* they deemed knowable antecedently to mind's activity and categorized it accordingly. Over against *ens reale* they set *ens rationis*, also knowable but only consequently upon and produced by the mind's activity. Kant set this ancient notion of *ens reale* over against the "appearances" of experience, and categorized it as an empty unknowable, the realm of the *ding-an-sich*, "thing in itself". The "noumenon" he also set over against the "appearances", but this time on the side of the very constructive activity of the mind itself responsible for the appearances.[29] Throughout the construction process in which knowledge of experience arises and consists, the world of things-in-themselves lies completely and forever beyond the horizon of human knowledge. This thesis was of the essence of his first edition of *The Critique of Pure Reason*.

Removing Scandal from Philosophy: The "Only Possible Proof" of
an External Reality

Now Kant considered it "a scandal to philosophy and to human reason in general" that "the existence of things outside us (from which we derive the whole material of knowledge, even for our inner sense) must be accepted merely on *faith*".[30] He considered further that his epistemological system provided the means of removing this scandal. So, in 1787, when he brought out the second edition of this master

---

27 See, e.g., Cassirer 1921: 216–7; or Kant himself, 1783: §33 [sic]: "... also in der Tat auf Dinge an sich selbst (noumena) zu gehen scheinen ....".

28 Collins 1999: 30.

29 The "noumenon" as such is empty, therefore, not only for a completely different reason than is the "thing in itself", but also on the opposite "side", so to speak, of the appearances in their contrast with "the things themselves unkowable in themselves" (Kant 1783: §33): "the concepts of the understanding seem to have a deeper meaning and import than can be exhausted by their merely empirical use, and so the understanding inadvertently adds for itself to the house of experience a much more extensive wing, without ever observing that it has transgressed with its otherwise legitimate concepts the bounds of their use."

30 "Preface to Second Edition" (1787) of the *Critique of Pure Reason*, trans. Norman Kemp Smith [New York: St Martin's Press, 1956], 34 n. a.

work, he considerately provided, both in the text itself and in the preface,[31] the explicit removal of all the grounds implicit in the first edition of 1781 on which "anyone thinks good to doubt" the existence of things in a physical environment surrounding us.

Now in what did the "only possible" (as Kant modestly termed his procedure) strict "proof of the objective reality of outer intuition" consist? The proof turns on acceptance of the separation of knowledge of the fact *that* environmental things exist, on one side, from, on the other side, even the hope of knowledge of *what* those existing things are in their own right (are, that is to say, in *their* actual existence and nature apart from *our* internal representations). That the environmental outer things are not themselves in any direct manner objectifiable (and hence remain unknowable in their intrinsic constitution and essence as things) is highlighted in this "proof" by the fact that the existence Kant alleges for them is identical with that aspect of inner experience which provides "the *empirical consciousness of my own existence, which is determinable only through relation to something which, while bound up with my existence, is outside me*".[32]

In Kant's conclusion, we see that the existence of things in the physical world has not been encountered directly and grasped as exercised by the things on their own side, not even aspectually:[33]

> this latter [i.e., the in itself unknowable thing] must therefore be an external thing distinct from all my representations, and its existence must be included in the *determination* of my own existence, constituting with it but a single experience such as would not take place even inwardly if it were not also at the same time, in part, outer.

Kant's proof of the existence of an external world has derived that existence as a necessary postulate accompanying the empirical experience I have of my own existence. It remains only my own empirical existence that I experience directly, but it is not "my own existence" in the simple subjective sense of Descartes; for with Kant the "empirical self" of experience is itself *already an objective construct*, already a complex terminus of mental activities through and thanks to which all objectivity obtains in opposition to the subective, "over and against" it. "Since we do not create the objects we represent in our perceptual experience", as Collins summarizes Kant's argument (I think exactly),[34] but only what we know of them beyond existence, "we have to suppose that they are really out there." The outer perceived reality, "the existence of which Kant says he *proves*, is not posited or inferred or believed in or imagined";[35] but – and only here do we reach the crucial

---

31 Preface, n. a, pp. 34–5; text p. 245ff.: "THESIS. *The mere, but empirically determined, consciousness of my own existence proves the existence of objects in space outside me.*"
32 Ibid., 35, Kant's italics.
33 Kant 1787: Preface to 2nd ed., 36.
34 Collins 1999: 142.
35 Ibid.: 2.

point – neither is it *known* beyond the fact *that* it is. That fact, for Kant, is not in any way a starting point. It is rather a limit, an absolute limit, the frontier of the unknowable; and that is the ultimate essence of modern idealism in all its guises, the quintessence, which Kant merely distills. However much he may repudiate details in the Cartesian conception of consciousness, he embraces the background assumption that the mind by its own activity presents whatever is directly known in objects of experience. The phenomena are a veil, a curtain, indeed, which neither opens nor can be opened; so that (exactly) the (apparently) "shared empirical world *is* the world".[36]

Remember the distinction from Fonseca and Suárez between concepts which merely represent and words which, through their dependency upon concepts, acquire relations to and among concepts thanks to which the words function as signs. Signs, then, differ from concepts in involving relations; but the relations they involve come from the concepts. Concepts represent, words signify; but they signify dependently upon concepts, and this relation of dependency whereby words signify objects is a creature of the mind's thinking: it is a mind-dependent being. Relations as distinct from subjective characteristics consist in objects terminating the constructive activity of the cognitive subject as knower, and further in comparisons the mind makes among objects, nothing more.

Kant in effect takes over this notion that all objective relations are creatures of the mind's activity but reattaches them now directly to the concepts. Concepts as elements of subjectivity are transcendental relatives but they *give rise to* objective relations through and in which the experience of the world and the self is constituted and consists. This is an important, if not a decisive, point:[37] mind-dependent being is an objective, not a subjective, mode of being. With Kant knowledge is no longer the simple "possession of idea" it tended to be with Descartes and Locke. Knowledge, and with it experience, is made through and through relational, suprasubjective and not merely subjective in its terminus. Cognition is, we may say, "object oriented" (in just the sense that Brentano will introduce in less than a century as "intentional"[38]). And objectivity is not simply "representations framed by the mind" but the complex terminus of relations based on mental representations formed by the mind in part through sensations received in space and time. But the problem is that all objective relations remain *omni ex parte* products of the mind's activity. Their *termini*, the objects experienced or known, are subjective mental states. No. Subjective mental

---

36 Collins 1999: 183n1.
37 For the fact that the objectivity of mind-dependent being was neglected among the moderns before and rediscovered by Kant does not alter the fact that the point was not only well-known among the Latins but centrally thematized for semiotic in Poinsot's dead-born treatise on signs a century and a half before Kant wrote.
38 Brentano 1874. The scholastic roots of Brentano's notion of intentionality are well known, and were noted in passing above (see chapter 8, p. 404). Not so well appreciated is the fact that Brentano twisted this notion to fit exactly the idealist doctrine that defined the mainstream development of modern philosophy, as also noted above (chapter 8, p. 404n87).

states may be involved, but their involvement is as founding and provenating relations to objects; and the objects are public, not private. Collins argues[39] that this suprasubjective character of objects, which he calls "public" as opposed to private, and the distinction it presupposes between mental states as private and objects as public though mind-dependent is what separates Kant from idealism and makes him, in fact, a "realist" of a (special) sort. This of course is true insofar as some given variant of idealism reduces all phenomena to mental states in the sense of "subjective" that is opposed to "objective". But the "public" character of objects here is irremediably compromised by the fact that the relations to the objects known owe their whole existence to each mind doing the experiencing or knowing. The relations do not have that ontological status whereby, as we have seen, they are able to pass back and forth between experience and nature, according to circumstances external to the relations themselves. They are purely objective, grounded purely in the mind's own working. They create, then, only an apparent intersubjectivity, and only insofar as each human mind works according to a same "mechanism" for generating appearances. Only some representations terminate in illusions; but none terminate in mind-independent being, ever.

Kant has restored relations to concepts as such, then, and even objectivity to suprasubjectivity, setting in this way a great distance between himself and his Cartesian (or Leibnizian) forebears, but not in the way required for even occasional instantiations of true *intersubjectivity* among knowers, or between knowers and things of nature. He has not restored relations to concepts as such in the way that Poinsot showed to be necessary in order for concepts to be themselves signs in the first instance and the relations of concepts to be the sign relations par excellence in which all other sign relations beyond those naturally determined among the data of sense are participations and extensions. For sign relations are ontological, that is to say, indifferently mind-dependent or mind-independent according to circumstance. But the objective relations Kant thematizes are determinately mind-dependent in every case and circumstance. He has objective relations, but only and purely objective relations. His system precludes relations that are simultaneously physical *and* objective, or first only objective and then also physical, or first physical and then only objective or also objective; for there is no room for that indifference essential to

---

39 "Were we to accept, mistakenly, the equivalence of 'mind-dependent' and 'mental'," notes Collins (1999: 165), "we would think that all appearances are mental. But Kant never deviates from the view that outer objects, the appearances that conform to the Categories, are enduring and thus not mental. However, even if we made the mistake of identifying the domain of appearances with mental reality, we would thereby exclude things-in-themselves from that domain altogether, for things as they are in themselves are by definition not mind-dependent. Therefore, even if that mistake were allowed, it would not support Amerik when he finds a 'mentalist character' in Kant's conception of reality. In this book, I have sought to establish that Kant makes room for nonmental objects and for mental representations, but not for mental objects of knowledge," in the sense that science and everyday experience attain objects that are not illusions. This is excellent internal exegesis of the Kantian texts, but it does not suffice to remove Kant from the tradition of idealism or the ultimate trajectory of solipsism which marks the path of all the moderns to Hegel, as we will see.

the being of relation as ontological (*secundum esse*) whereby it can move according to circumstance back and forth between the realm of things in themselves and things as known, inhabiting either or both realms indifferently. There can be no ontological relation in Kant, for there can be no category at all of mind-independent being other than, as we have seen, the unknowable and empty one of "thing-in-itself", *ding an sich*. The external world is even more unknowable in the philosophy of Kant than was God in the philosophy of Aquinas.[40]

The heart of Kant's alleged proof of the external world is not at all an inference from sense data (such an alleged inference as Hume had already shown to be, along the way of ideas, useless in this matter). It is not through an intellectual intuition that I become conscious "that I myself exist *as determined in time*".[41] The certainty of the existence of things outside me is reached simply as a *concomitant* or *necessary counterpart* of an inner intuition which is sensible, namely, the inner intuition wherein "I am conscious that I myself exist as determined in time",[42] while "the determination of my existence in time is possible only through the existence of actual things which I perceive outside me"[43] *in* but *not constitutive of* the phenomena. This consciousness is posterior to "the *intellectual consciousness* of my existence, in the representation 'I am', which accompanies all my judgments and acts of understanding",[44] for "the reality of outer sense, in its distinction from imagination, rests simply on that which is here found to take place, namely, its being inseparably bound up with inner experience, as the condition of its possibility."

Kant has described here, in short, as the core of his proof, a particular instance of what we saw characterized among the Latins as a "transcendental relative",[45] in full contrast to the pure relation in which the sign consists, and through which is achieved the triadic form of signification as an ontological relation:[46]

> an expression expressing a transcendental relation – which is nothing else than a relation according to the way subjective being must be expressed in discourse – does not convey relation from its principal significate, but something absolute, upon which some relation follows or could follow. For if it does not convey something subjective, it will not be transcendental, that is, ranging through diverse categories, but will look to one category only. Whence a transcendental relation is not a form adventitious to a subject or absolute thing, but one assimilated to or imbibed with it, yet connoting something extrinsic upon which the subject depends or with which it is engaged, as, for example, matter relative to form, a head relative to the headed, a creature relative to God; and so transcendental relation coincides with relation according to the way being

---

40 See chapter 7, p. 254ff.
41 Kant 1787: preface, p. 36n; italics added.
42 Ibid.
43 Kant 1787: 245.
44 Ibid.: preface, 35n.
45 See the discussion in chapter 3, p. 72; chapter 6, p. 228; and chapter 9, p. 423.
46 Poinsot, *Tractatus de Signis*, 90/13–36.

must be expressed in discourse. And some[47] erroneously divide relation according to the way it has being into transcendental and categorial. This is a wrong division, because a transcendental relation is in the absolute entity itself and does not differ from its [subjective] being, and so its whole being is not toward another, which is required for a relation to be ontological, to be a relation according to the way it has being.

Representations as transcendental relatives, whether they be inner or outer representation, are *involved* in the sign but *never constitute it* in its proper being. From the point of view of a doctrine of signs, missing in Kant's analysis is what the sign adds over and above representation, for what the sign adds is not relation as determinately objective but relation as indifferently objective and/or physical; in other words, relation as ontological. Missing, as a consequence, is the account of how representation is made to function within signification in a *strictly subordinate* capacity. Missing, in short, is the necessary completion of transcendental relativity (the relative *secundum dici*) by ontological relativity (the relative *secundum esse*), together with the understanding that transcendental relativity actually obtains only in an existential codependency with a complex of ontological relations physically realized and *knowable* as such.

Moreover, this twin realization *has* to be missing in Kant's analysis. For what was common to the rationalists and the empiricists alike in going the way of ideas was the denial that there is such a thing as mind-independent or physical relations. And this common assumption is incorporated in the Kantian synthesis of the two modern currents of epistemological development. It is of the essence of the way of ideas that ideas be construed as objective representations, and that whatever relations are consequent upon them are wholly of the mind's own devising, "pure objectivities", as we might say. Everywhere in the modern literature the word "relation" is used. But the mainstream modern authors use the term only in two senses – the sense either of what the Latins called "transcendental relation", which is a quasi-metaphorical designation for the subjectivity of things as able to exist individuated in their own right; or of what the Latins called "relation of reason", which is a *comparison* made by the mind of two or more things. Never in the modern literature is the word "relation" used in the sense of categorial or – still less – ontological relation.

From outside the way of ideas, the unknowability Kant postulates on the side of the things environmentally existent is no more than the projection of a logical consequence of his typically modern background assumption that apprehensions without exception terminate directly in representations formed by the mind. This assumption, however, not the nature of mind, reality, or experience, is the root of the famous problem of the external world as the characteristic problem of modern philosophy.

---

47 Poinsot refers here principally to Suárez.

From the point of view of the Latin tradition, which makes a distinction between representation and signification, this assumption is erroneous in a twofold way. First, when ideas are analyzed in the perspective of this distinction, which presupposes the reality of relation, it emerges that the representations formed by the mind as such (perceptions or concepts, images or ideas, *species expressae*) never terminate apprehension, but provide rather (and only) the basis upon which the mind is related to objects.[48] In this provision of the fundament of a sign relation, the concepts of the mind contribute as *sign-vehicles* (as participating in the extrinsic formal causality proper to objects as that on which cognitive powers depend) to the termination of apprehension at an object.[49] Peirce will call the sign-vehicle a *representamen*,[50] because it is a representative factor serving to found relations terminating in the presentation of an object other than itself.

Second, much as the critical realists in Maritain's line argued toward the end of the modern period, representations formed by the mind do not constitute that sliver of objectivity which external sense contributes to the objective totality of experience in the giving of a constant physical embodiment to perceptual and intellectual representations. The environment itself does that, precisely as constituting a realm of "things-in-themselves" knowable as such, and precisely through its action on the organism inasmuch as the sense organs of that organism exist at the same level and in proportion with the material objects acting upon them to produce awareness of the environment in its proper being *as* acting here and now.[51] On the aspectual objectification of the physical environment itself in this action rests the whole possibility of a human use of signs through which science and philosophy alike are able to know more than the mind's own workings.

"Second Copernican Revolution" or Vindication of Mr Hyde?

Of the three propositions which, taken together, express the elements of the common sense view of the physical world that empiricism in Berkeley and Hume rejected in toto – that (1) it exists, that (2) partially *in its own being as physical* it enters into our awareness through sense perception, and that (3) we deal with it in our activities every day – Kant, by synthesizing rationalism and empiricism into a single theory on the basis of their common assumption, considers that he has restored the first and the third elements: that such a world exists, and that we deal with it in our everyday activities. But the second point, that we are aware of that physical world itself in our

---

48 In Poinsot's words (*Tractatus de Signis*, opening remarks, 116/16–17, 117/14–19: "the rationale of something manifestative or representative ... is found *in a sign* both with an order to another ... and with a dependency ... as upon a measure."

49 See Poinsot 1632a: Book I, Question 4, esp. 173/38–180/7; and Appendix C, esp. 380/10–26, and, in the expanded Appendix C of the electronic edition (Charlottesville, VA: Intelex Corp., 1992), Article 6.

50 See chapter 15, p. 640 below.

51 Recall the argument "Why Sensations Do Not Involve Mental Icons" from chapter 7, p. 345.

perceptions, remains for him part of the Grand Illusion of earlier philosophy and of modern science insofar as it has not been informed by modern philosophy. In Dr Jekyll, the "man of science", whether he realizes it or not, there lives and breathes the psychotic[52] Mr Hyde.

Kant called his removal of the second only of the three propositions or elements of the common-sense view a "Second Copernican Revolution". Better to call his position "the vindication of Mr Hyde". For, having come to the scene of this revolution from a long way off, and by a route that never crossed Kant's ken, we are in a position to see what Kant has done rather dramatically differently than he himself saw it. Let us re-read the paragraphs in which Kant celebrates his synthesis of rationalism and empiricism by comparing his method with the inspiration of Copernicus. When Kant's writing is read in the light of the contrast between the ontologically and the transcendentally relative as the Latins developed that contrast along the way to an understanding of sign as transcending all such oppositions as noumena/phenomena, nature/culture, outer world/inner world, the true achievement of the *Critique of Pure Reason* would appear to lie in its demonstration that the unconscious choice of the way of ideas over the way of signs at the outset of modernity was bound to lead to the dead-end of solipsism. The blunder of modernity was not at all made by Dr Jekyll in thinking to come to know more and more of physical nature itself. The blunder was made rather by Mr Hyde in making the assumption that what the mind first and exclusively knows is a representation as such that the mind itself makes. By choosing the way of ideas, in short, the moderns committed themselves to a speculative debacle.

How so?

Suppose it is the case that there are relations over and above all the modes of subjective being, that these relations as such are indifferent to whether their ground be one time in nature and another time in thought, and that these relations as such enter into the sign in a peculiarly irreducible way – triadically – by revealing an object which may or may not be a thing *to* someone *on the basis of* some sign-vehicle.

The modern way of ideas begins by denying this supposed fact. So, if this is a fact, then the whole development of modern philosophy according to the way of ideas is the working out of a network of logically implicated counter-factual proposals. In this case, what Kant has effected, in making a synthesis of the two main schools that have developed in this manner, amounts to the making explicit of some inevitable consequences of the failure to incorporate the truth about relation into the theory of knowledge. And, from this point of view, of particular interest is the verification again in Kant's philosophy of the inherent tendency of the modern philosophical mind toward solipsism.

Here is what Kant says à propos of Copernicus:[53]

---

52 Psychosis: a fundamental lasting mental derangement characterized by defective or lost contact with reality.

53 *Critique of Pure Reason*, preface to 1787 2nd ed., p. 22.

Failing of satisfactory progress in explaining the movements of the heavenly bodies on the supposition that they all revolved around the spectator, he tried whether he might not have better success if he made the spectator to revolve and the stars to remain at rest.

From the point of view according to which we are now viewing Kant's situation, this just-quoted remark reduces the Copernican hypothesis down to a question of alternate suppositions concerning which was the primarily real and which the primarily unreal relation. What Kant here states well illustrates the functional equivalence of the two types of relation within an objective scheme.

Kant continues:

A similar experiment can be tried in metaphysics as regards the intuition of objects. If intuition must conform to the constitution of the objects, I do not see how we could know anything of the latter a priori [i.e., how there could be necessity in certain connections between objects not reducible to the merely apparent necessity of customary association alone postulated by Hume]; but if the object (as object of the senses) must conform to the constitution of our faculty of intuition, I have no difficulty in conceiving such a possibility.

So far, we have no quarrel with Kant. The objects of our senses must indeed conform to the constitution of the sense faculties: objects can affect the eye primarily only as differentially reflecting light, and so on for each sense. Moreover, we have also seen[54] that there is a sense in which an external sense can be called a "faculty of intuition", since its operation alone requires the here-and-now presence in physical being of its adequate object. This is but to say, in the Latins' terms, that powers are transcendentally related to their objects, and that, in the case of sensation, physical interaction by itself alone suffices to explain the objective union attendant upon the physical influence (categorial relation) here and now of a physical object upon a passive sensory organ.

But at this point possible agreement with Kant ends for anyone holding for the reality of relation as above described. For as cognition develops out of the passivity of sense through the active formation of concepts by internal sense (imagination, memory, natural instinct of various kinds), the transcendental relation of power to object is superseded by an ontological relation of sign (concept as formal sign) to signified (object as made naturally present in cognition as extrinsic specifier). This reversal and subordination of the internal subjective means of objectification to external specifications initially introduced through the senses is not possible from within the modern tradition. For such reversal and subordination can only come about through the intervention of relation as an ontological rationale mediating the

---

54 See the discussion of "Intuitive and Abstractive Awareness" in chapter 8, p. 378ff.

connection between concepts and their objects in perception and understanding, and between organism and environment in perception's sensory core.

Hence, the decisive determination constitutive of his would-be Second Copernican Revolution comes when Kant extends the primacy of transcendental relation over the means of knowing both to the active process of concept formation and to the actual function concepts perform as means of objectification. Kant has no choice but to make this move, given the constraints of the modern assumption about the nature of ideas. To do otherwise than he here does, he would first have to abandon the way of ideas. If sensory intuitions are to become known, "I cannot rest in these intuitions", Kant tells us, "but must relate them as representations to something as their object, and determine this latter through them". That is, *I* relate them, not *they are related*; I *determine the object* through the relations my mind creates (albeit a-priori as well as a-posteriori), not the relations *determined by the signified* convey the mind through the concept as sign-vehicle to the awareness of what is signified.

Kant may be said to be the first in the modern tradition concerning the difference between a relation and its subjective foundation to have seen, with a clarity and depth comparable – but one-sided and inverse – to that found in Poinsot's *Treatise on Signs* at the end of the Latin Age, the true requirements of the problem. He sees the dilemma, that is, but, assuming as alternative to "the way of things" only the way of ideas, sees but one way out. Let me speak – not for Kant, yet with him – to show how the assumed dichotomous alternative within a trichotomous situation determines what Kant concludes:[55]

> *Either* I must assume that the concepts, by means of which I obtain this determination [of what has been given in intuition], conform to the object [in which case the concept as it functions in cognition is ontologically relative, and is measured by the object as sign by signified], *or else* I assume that the objects, or what is the same thing, that the experience in which alone, as given objects, they can be known, conform to the concepts [in which case the concept, even as it functions formally as a pure means of cognition, is only transcendentally relative].

To the question "Whether the formal rationale constitutive of a sign as such consists, primarily and essentially, in an ontological or in a transcendental relation", the Latin Age had already demonstrated that only two systematically conceived answers are possible. In this respect, the *Critique of Pure Reason* by Immanuel Kant and the *Tractatus de Signis* by John Poinsot together symbolize the realization

---

55 Kant 1787, Preface, p. 22, italics added. Kant's ignorance of the way of signs as alternative to the way of ideas mapped by the Latins in arriving at the ground for Augustine's *signum* he announces clearly, if unwillingly, in his "Preface" to the original edition of the *Critique of Pure Reason*, where he modestly advises us concerning his book that "there is not a single metaphysical problem which has not been solved, or for the solution of which the key at least has not been supplied". We will hear just such pompous blather again in connection with the first book of Wittgenstein (see below, p. 582, text at n87). As modern thought grows old, it sends modesty on holiday.

in philosophical literature of the alternative consequences for human understanding of the way of ideas, which makes of ideas a transcendental relation, versus the way of signs, wherein the idea itself functions as idea only through generating an ontological relation.

According to the *Tractatus*, concepts (being natural signs formal in type) as they function in cognition are ontologically relative. As such, they sustain the convertibility of being with truth expressed in the medieval doctrine of the transcendentals.[56] But in the *Critique*, concepts, even as functioning in actual cognition, remain primarily transcendental, that is to say, mentally or psychologically subjective, in their relative being. As a result, they compromise the transcendental character of truth in the medieval sense of "transcendental truth" (the character of truth as founded independently of any finite mind) and its convertibility with being. The real and the rational are no longer coextensive in principle, for the real is no longer in any measure accessible to reason, to perception, or to sense.

How, then, do we communicate? We don't. We only seem to. But because our minds all function according to the same scheme of categories, our internal representations, like those of Leibniz's monads arranged by God in a pre-established harmony, will necessarily be the same in type. And here Kant works out the second great scheme of categories after Aristotle's original one; but as Aristotle's scheme purported to be expressive of the order of mind-independent being, Kant's scheme can only pretend to be one of mind-dependent being, albeit the necessary expression thereof; for within the terms of the Kantian scheme, the mind knows and can know only what it constructs according to its own inner rules and forms in constituting the phenomena. His categories apply *only* to phenomenal/empirical experience *in contrast to* the empty unknowable of the things in themselves. But this alleged empty unknowable was, through understanding based on sensation, the very *locus* of the categories in the philosophy of Aristotle among the Greeks and Aquinas among the Latins.

But now, under the terms of the Kantian revolution, under the epistemological paradigm Kant would have us accept, the bubble of each individual's consciousness can only be burst in death. It cannot otherwise be pierced or penetrated. We can see the world only from within, as an animal sees its Umwelt. The sign relation which opens that Umwelt to the possibility of understanding its difference from the physical environment, its partial incorporation of the physical environment, and its transformation into a Lebenswelt wherein civil society, philosophy, literature, science, the arts, and all that distinguishes the exercise of human understanding and feeling in its difference from closed animal perceptions: the sign relation in this sense has no place in the critical philosophy of Kant. The whole of ancient and medieval philosophy, on the modern accounting, along with science itself, was all along never doing what it thought it was doing, namely, pondering and investigating the world

---

56 See chapter 7, p. 253, text and note 10; chapter 9, p. 424n37.

and mind as part of nature. No, all along, all that was being done, all that anyone could or can do, is to wander down the corridors and examine the constructions of their own mind – suprasubjective albeit, "objective" and not merely "subjective", but closed in principle to actual *cognitive intersubjectivity* by the fact that the only correlate to the subjective representation founding the "relation to an object" is the terminus as and only as produced by the activity of the mind itself within which the relation provenates. Not only are the "things-in-themselves" of the physical world precluded from participation in the terminus of such relations; so equally are the "things-in-themselves" of other knowers precluded, even though these last in their turn are constrained to provenate a "veil of appearances" on the pattern of our own. Whether this is contrary to actual experience, of course, depends entirely on what experience *is*. If experience is as Kant analyzes it to be, then (*pace* Collins and the anemic "realism" his thin band would envisage as possible even after Kant[57]), whatever the advances have been since Leibniz, they do not change the "bottom line". If, on the contrary, experience is a texture of relations precisely indifferent ontologically to their subjective provenance, then the "bottom line" is that the very appearances themselves participate in the very mind-independent being of the things which include the knower as part of the environmental world known in part and in principle each time a sense is activated by a stimulus (which is constantly, as the doctrine of transcendental relation early established).

Each one of us may wonder what lies before our experience or beyond that experience; but the very experience itself must have a structure different from that which Kant envisages and presents us with analytically in his *Critiques*, or one can never know being, "what is". Kant's is a world in which there is ample room for faith, inasmuch as knowledge of the physical world, along with everything else concerning the world external to the subjective–objective polarity of individual consciousness, has been excluded. But his is the world of modern philosophy. For modern philosophy, it is not Jekyll who can be cured but Hyde who must conquer.

Vico's Prognostication

Kant called his philosophy a "second Copernican revolution", but there is room to think that Copernicus would have been revulsed by the comparison. Copernicus was the first Copernican revolution, and Galileo was the second. Nor was Kant a third; for his two predecessors in this revolutionary line were concerned with what they took to be the reality of nature in just that sense that Kant, invoking the name of Copernicus, would have us deny as accessible to human understanding.

One does not find the name of Giambattista Vico (1668–1744) very often, if at all, in indices to studies of Kant. And yet perhaps one should. Like Kant, Vico was a great admirer of Isaac Newton. And, also like Kant, he thought through his own work to bring into consciousness the fundamental truth that even the great Newton

---

57 See Collins 1999: esp. 173ff., for details on the identity of this truly 'light brigade'.

had not yet seen, the truth that the human mind after all is suited to a knowledge only of its own creations. The medieval Latins envisioned the mind as an embodied intelligence open to the infinite because able to grasp being, as we have seen. They even had a maxim to this effect: *anima est quodammodo omnia*, "the mind in knowing extends to the whole of being", a maxim derived from the work of Aristotle and redolent of the doctrine of being's transcendental properties.

But this aim and ambition, modern philosophy was coming to say, had been an aberration, a consequence of a profound misunderstanding of the role of sense in knowledge. Little by little, according to Vico's diagnosis, the truth would come to light:[58]

> In the night of thick darkness enveloping the earliest antiquity, so remote from ourselves, there shines the eternal and never failing light of a truth beyond all question: that the world of civil society has certainly been made by men, and that its principles are therefore to be found within the modifications of our own human mind. Whoever reflects on this cannot but marvel that the philosophers should have bent all their energies to the study of the world of nature, which, since God made it, He alone knows; and that they should have neglected the study of the world of nations, or civil world, which, since men had made it, men could come to know. This aberration was a consequence of that infirmity of the human mind by which, immersed and buried in the body, it naturally inclines to take notice of bodily things, and finds the effort to attend to itself too laborious; just as the bodily eye sees all objects outside itself but needs a mirror to see itself.

The Kantian "critical philosophy", in this context, appears as a providing finally of just that mirror by which at last the eye will see itself, and find in the reflection the only truth that it is possible, after all, for the human mind to find: the truth of its own reflection in the objects of its knowledge. And that is what becomes the truth, at least the truth of philosophical modernity: acceptance of the proposition that, at the level of understanding, whatever the mind knows in what the mind knows of it the mind itself makes. The proposal is there for us to evaluate, to criticize and accept in one form or another, or to criticize and fundamentally reject as we will see Peirce do. A scheme of categories of the modes of mind-independent being may not be enough; but a scheme of categories that rules out such being entirely simply will not do. What is needed is a scheme of categories capable of synthesizing and expressing the interpenetration of constructions of understanding and structures of nature within human experience as the locus of objectivity.

A first attempt at that in the wake of Kant's work was quick in coming, through Hegel's thinking. The attempt proved abortive, it would seem,[59] but an attempt it

---

58 Vico 1744: ¶331.
59 Provisionally, at least, for present purposes, I am inclined to accept Peirce's evaluation of Hegel's doctrine of categories (see chapter 15, p. 645n102), and discuss here only the root of his disagreement

was. Had the attempt succeeded, the very history of modern philosophy itself would need to be written very differently. But the coils of modern idealism wound tight and deep, and the first attempt at overcoming Kant proved to be but an interlude in modernity's death from strangulation by those coils, a slow death which is still taking place all around us as far as philosophy is concerned. That interlude, a prelude to Peirce, is what remains to be explored to bring closure to the modern period of the history of philosophy.

Georg Wilhelm Friedrich Hegel (1770–1831)

After Kant came Hegel. Of course there was Fichte (1762–1814) just before Hegel; Schelling (1775–1854) and Arthur Schopenhauer (1788–1860) along with him; after him Ludwig Andreas Feuerbach (1804–72), Friedrich Wilhelm Nietzsche (1844–1900), and Gottlob Frege (1848–1925). But the last true giant encountered far down the way of ideas is Hegel, and he already had one foot off the path. Hegel's *Phenomenology of Spirit* (1807), to a lesser extent his *Encyclopedia of the Philosophical Sciences* (beginning in 1817), already signals a paradigm shift bound to come, a rebellion from the acceptance of the unacceptable limits which Kant – by synthesizing rationalism and empiricism on the basis of their common assumption of ideas as representative objects, and of objects as head to toe of the mind's own making – had placed as shackles on the human understanding.

Hegel began in 1801 as a *Privatdozent* at the University of Jena. In 1807 he left Jena to become editor of the *Bamberger Zeitung*, but government censorship of the press drove him from this post in exasperation after only one year. He moved to Nuremberg as headmaster of a *Gymnasium* in 1808, married Marie von Tucher there in 1811, at the age of forty-one. The first volume of his *Science of Logic* (*Wissenschaft der Logik*) was published at Heidelberg in 1812, the second volume in 1816. He followed his book there the year of that second volume, becoming the first professor of philosophy at the University of Heidelberg. In this post he published in the following year his *Encyclopedia of the Philosophical Sciences*. On 22 October 1818, at the invitation of the Prussian minister of education, he took the chair of philosophy at the University of Berlin that had been vacant since Fichte's death in 1814. This chair would not be vacant again until Hegel's death in 1831.

In 1821 Hegel published his *Philosophy of Right*. He devoted half his preface to the denunciation of Jakob Fries (1773–1843), a poor soul who had been dismissed by the state from his professorship at Jena and declared an outlaw by the police for having published in 1816 a work *On the German Confederation and the Political Constitution of Germany* that was unacceptable to those in power. In 1831, the year of Hegel's death, he appealed to the British parliament to defeat the Reform Bill

---

with Kant over the doctrine of the *ding-an-sich* as unknowable. Hegel's notion of being may have been inadequate at best, but by bringing it into play with nonbeing in the experience of becoming he had at least moved decisively outside the line of Cyclopean ontology mentioned in passing above (chapter 7, p. 360n245).

to strengthen democracy in England. The authoritarian spirit, unfortunately, would prove all too alive and well in the political parts and influence of the philosophy of Hegel. Yet it can hardly be said – indeed the claim would be a travesty – that his "Absolute Spirit" would contribute to the inspiration of Hitler (1889–1945) and the animation of the Third Reich, both because the thinking of Hitler and his circle never rose to anywhere near the level of Hegel, and because in the thought of Hegel the term "absolute" has a special and even technical sense. His "dialectic" would inspire Marx (1818–83). But even if, through Marx, we come to Lenin (1870–1924) and Engels (1820–95) and the historical creation of the communist state, still with us as the menace of late-modern China, how justly can Marx be saddled with the excesses of Leninism/Stalinism? And still less justly can Hegel be saddled with the excesses of National Socialism. If his is "a philosophy of history", it is yet of a history that never occurred.

From his commanding post at the University of Berlin, after 1827, the *Jahrbücher für wissenschaftliche Kritik* was the organ of his school, destined to become the most influential philosophy in the history of post-Kantian Europe. Hegel's death came suddenly, on 14 November 1831, over the week-end at the beginning of the fall term; the cause, originally diagnosed as cholera, is considered unknown. His students pored over his notes and their own to assemble four more books not quite Hegel's own: *Aesthetics*, *Philosophy of Religion*, *Philosophy of History*, and *History of Philosophy*. It was not a lesser reprise of the Dark Age practice of Pseudo-Dionysius all over again, for the student involvement was acknowledged from the outset; but the announcement of the publication as by the "Circle of Friends of the Eternal One" suggests more than a little of the legendary spirit. Even so, time would play its part. The quadruple publication was almost, but not quite, the end of philosophy's modern era: it was a harbinger of the turn from ideas to experience in a fuller sense which would allow for signification in its irreducibility to and priority over representation, and so cross over the line to open philosophy's next era.

As difficult a thinker as Kant, but greater, Hegel sees at once the contradiction in saying that we can know *that* something is, but can in no way further develop this initial knowledge.[60] In his criticism he goes for Kant's jugular. He is alone

---

60 In fact, this was the very problem Aquinas had faced in the quite different context of human understanding developing from its origins in sensation a valid conceptual knowledge of God as an actually existing object of thought wholly inaccessible to sense. His conclusion was that anything that can be known to exist can further be known to have definite characters, even when we cannot know those characters in the manner in which they are actually exercised on the side of the known; but in that case – human understanding of the existence of God as the sole being whose essence is existence – the "unknowability in itself" stemmed both from the disproportion between knower and known and from the dependency of the human knower on sensation as the ultimate source of real relations in the development of conceptual knowledge, an 'unovercomable' yet still relative (because, as we saw in the Latin doctrine of the divine names in chapter 7 above, there is no limit to the conceptual growth of valid knowledge according to which it can be validly asserted "that God is" this, and this, and this, etc.) 'unknowability' quite sharply opposed to the Kantian posit of absolute unknowability wholly fixed as a limit. So, as we saw in the discussion of sense qualities in

among the moderns in reasserting the reality of relation, and the convertibility of being and truth in the coextensiveness in principle of intelligibility with being. But he thinks to work out an ideal categorial scheme from which it will be possible by a principally deductive thought to arrive at the details of the natural world. He has still one foot in the way of ideas. Heidegger pinpoints the problem:[61] "when Hegel at last defines 'Being' as the 'indeterminate immediate' and makes this definition basic for all the further categorial explications of his 'logic', he keeps looking in the same direction as ancient ontology", meaning away from the *primum cognitum* as the 'yet insufficiently considered'.

Even so, when we look at modern philosophy from its national-language beginnings in the seventeenth century up to its culmination in Kant's *Critiques*, Hegel by comparison marks a confused but decided call for a new beginning, some *via nova et alternativa* – a new line of exploration, alternative to the way of ideas, with his dialectic triad of being/nonbeing/becoming. For the first time in almost two hundred years, the common assumption of modern times underlying and necessitating its constant proclivity toward solipsism and subjectivism – a proclivity, be it said, in spite of itself yet from the outset – is put into question. Hegel even tries to revive the history of philosophy, though his lectures on the medievals look emaciated in the light of the knowledge that has been gained since Gilson's early work on Descartes, or even in comparison with the early-modern summaries of Suárez, which

---

both chapters 7 and 12, the principal key to "realism" in the thought of Aquinas remains the doctrine of sensation as consisting in a physical interaction of environmental beings that excludes from its essence mental images or icons, in contrast to perception and intellection (or "understanding") alike.

That is why, even in the one place where, according to a philosophy of being, "unknowability" becomes an insuperable factor in the growth of understanding, it is not as a fixed, unpassable limit, but as an ever shifting one according both to context and to individual intellectual ability. For where being provides the intellect's distinctive object and sensation provides the intellect with an irreducible direct contact with the order of *ens reale*, an imperfect knowledge of what something is is implied and contained in the simple perspective of ascertaining the fact ("*quia*") that something is as a matter of methodological principle of the knowing. In other words, in any case, including that of God, wherein a thing is known not by its essence in itself but in what concerns its actual existence, the understanding necessarily attains in an imperfect way a grasp however indirect of what the thing is that is, and it is this grasp that becomes the basis for further research. Consider the alternative: if in no way were there a grasp of *what* it is that is involved in the discovery *that* anything is, the one investigating, as Maritain put it (1959: 230; cf. 237n3), "would not know of what it was positing the existence" and would not have a clue as to how to follow up on the discovery. Situations even close to that occur but rarely, not as the normal situation in investigation, and never as the permanent situation.

Kantian commentators such as Schrader (1967: 188) are quite right in thinking that Kantian epistemology "cuts the nerve of philosophical inquiry"; but they are curiously reluctant to accept the full consequence of that realization, which ought to be the relegation of the "critical philosophy" in which modernity culminated to the museum for the history of discredited notions, along with the proofs that flying machines are impossible or that the human body would fly apart if subjected to speeds above sixty miles per hour.

61 Heidegger 1927: *Being and Time*, 175.

display[62] "such a knowledge of mediaeval philosophy as to put to shame any modern historian".

Without anywhere gaining clarity as to its principles, the influence of Hegelian thought is pervasive throughout the nineteenth century. But the confusion in Hegelianism nowhere demonstrates itself more effectively, perhaps, than in the failure of the Hegelians to isolate and develop the consequences of categorial relation with its ontological rationale. Hegel is in the modern period but not fully of it. He is *sui generis*, and the last word on him is far from said. He alone of the late moderns, together with some of his following, I expect to loom larger and with greater clarity in the advancing postmodern light.[63] To this end, as I discovered in work on the present book, a thorough "historical layering"[64] both of his writings and of the writings of his followers would be one of the most important initial steps.

The Anticipation of Semiotic Consciousness Signaled within Modernity: The Con-Venience ("Coming Together") of Philosophy and History

Hegel tried to restore a sense of history to philosophy. The actual influence of Descartes on the consciousness characteristic of modernity, to the contrary, was a spirit of contemning history, as we have seen, in favor of the reality of the individual consciousness as the *point de départ* of that systematic reasoning from experience which leads on the one side to the doctrinal development typical of philosophy and on the other side to the experimental development typical of science in the modern sense, both of which share in common the need to be internally consistent (that is to say, to resolve whatever inconsistencies come to light within experience on the supposition of this or that theoretical development). The problem was that, in the supposition that the individual consciousness attains at its base only its own productions, the reality of communication and a semiosis linking mind and nature was subtly precluded and shut down.

But abandon the presupposition – abandon, that is to say, the way of ideas – and a startling prospective shift of the horizon of interpretation immediately results. Instead of standing as an enemy of history in the search for philosophy and science, the Cartesian *cogito* suddenly appears as a vindication of the historical character of human understanding in the whole of its development and achievements. All we have to do is realize, in our terms, the correlativity of *Innenwelt* with *Umwelt*, together with the irreducible character of sensation as revelative of the physical environment in its impact on an organism of whatever type (including the human, wherein, through the modeling system of language, closed *Umwelt* becomes *Lebenswelt* open always in principle, if not always historically in fact, to the infinite both within and beyond

---

62 As Gilson put it, 1952: 99.
63 My own partial guess I have indicated in chapter 15 below, p. 658.
64 See the "Gloss on the References", p. 830 below, for the sense of the expression "historical layering".

experience), and the formula of Descartes becomes "the deepest and most fruitful expression" of the truth that "science presupposes history and can never get behind history" because "the fact of my actual present awareness", the *cogito* wherein "I am" (*sum*) for the purposes of whatever inquiry I may find myself motivated to undertake, is itself a "concrete historical fact". That is to say, my awareness as a dawn-of-the-21st-century American citizen is hardly the same as that of a dawn-of-the-5th-century citizen of Byzantium, a dawn-of-the-16th-century Turk, or even that of a dawn-of-the-21st-century citizen of the Republic of Ireland, Kazakhstan, or Istanbul.

Robin George Collingwood (1889–1943), from whom I have taken the foregoing quotes on this matter,[65] is not the only but easily the clearest illustration of semiotic consciousness inconscient of the name as modernity draws to closure. And through Bosanquet,[66] it was Hegel who begat Collingwood (as all the later idealists of significance) in this particular. The basic studies within semiotics of Collingwood and of this late-modern strain generally outside philosophy's mainstream – but adumbrative of the development of an explicitly semiotic consciousness in the sense we will take to be definitive of the positive essence of an immediately postmodern era or epoch in the history of philosophy – have been the large (if too compilative in tone) book by A. F. Russell entitled *Logic, Philosophy, and History*[67] together with the several minor essays by this same author,[68] and the more extended studies by Brooke Williams.[69]

Like Bertrand Russell, Collingwood came out of the British idealist atmosphere sustained by the works of Francis Herbert Bradley (1846–1924) and Bernard Bosanquet (1848–1923). But instead of losing the main intuition and true insight of idealism in the trajectory that developed after Hegel in order to affirm a realism as sterile as that of Cook Wilson (1849–1915),[70] Collingwood turned toward the very modern tradition itself in philosophy to suggest how it could be transformed into a true understanding of the historical nature of human understanding insofar as human understanding depends upon the action of signs. He well saw that indeed every individual thing we recognize is sustained in its objectivity by the whole network of affective and cognitive relations which contrast that type of thing with all the other individuals and types which we also know when we unconsciously say, as it were, "it is not that or those, but this (or one of these)".[71] But beyond this what

---

65 Collingwood 1924: 202. Cf. Collingwood 1939: 62–3, 72.
66 See A. Russell 1984: ch. 4, p. 75ff., text and refs.
67 Ibid.: see esp. ch. 9.
68 A. Russell 1981, 1982, 1987, and 1999.
69 B. Williams 1984, 1985a, 1985b, 1990, and 1991.
70 Or, we might add in hindsight, that of "analysis" in the wake of Russell, Wittgenstein, the Vienna Circle, and the Quinean nominalists dominating the American academies in logic and philosophy at the end of the 20th century.
71 The careful reader will realize that this is an insight logically subordinate to the Aquinian notion of the *primum cognitum* discussed in chapter 7 above. From this point of view, the error of idealism would appear as a consequence of taking a secondary insight as primary by losing sight of its ground, a consequence perhaps inevitable once the doctrine of sensation as prior to and independent

Collingwood clearly saw from the margins of modernity was that the destiny of the human animal to form a community of inquirers asymptotically approaching a "final opinion" concerning the "nature of things" requires the conscious apprehension of the abductive phase of logic itself, whence deductions and inductions result in the first place by being made possible: a "logic of question and answer", as Collingwood put it, wherein it is seen, in Anthony Russell's apposite summary,[72] that and why "the *medium of demonstration* in this interrogative reasoning is nothing other than *the investigator himself taken as a unique individual whole of structured subjectivity*", that is to say, the historical human individual probing from within the weave of experience the structure of the objective world in order to determine the various proportions and parts of it representing here the work of mind and there the work of nature. The "whole of experience" with its internal links of various levels and kinds to the physical surroundings thus exhibits an interconnectedness that cannot be observed from without "as if the whole and the part were independent entities whose sign relations to each other are only external", that is, mind-independent simply or mind-dependent simply. The whole is not simply relations of both orders, but of relations many of which pass back and forth between the two orders in a constantly changing mix determined by circumstances wholly external to the relations themselves, the very relations whose weave constitutes what is experienced as part of the objective world here and now.

Already with Collingwood we find (as we will find also in Peirce's self-consciously opening up as alternative to the way of ideas the way of signs and its supporting context of being grasped by the human understanding prior to and transcendent of the division within objects of their dimensions of what is and what is not independent of the activity of human thinking in this or that regard) the dissatisfaction with the forced choice between being a "realist" or "idealist".[73] But along with Collingwood we find not only the rich air of the logic of Bradley and Bosanquet,[74] in contrast to the stipulative logics which come after and all but obliterate their memory in the twentieth-century schools of Oxford and Cambridge, but also a significant number of thinkers marginalized with respect to the modern mainstream – such thinkers as Benedetto Croce (1866–1952) and Michael Polanyi (1891–1976) after – who similarly embody without the name and in a more groping fashion the postmodern reality of semiotic consciousness. This consciousness, as we will see, transcends from the outset the atmosphere of struggle between "realisms" and "idealisms" in which modernity breathes its dying gasps.

---

of mental images at its proper level in the constitution of experience was displaced by the modern presupposition that objects and the representative element in ideas are the same.

72 A. Russell 1981: 185.

73 Collingwood 1939: 56. See the extended discussion in Brooke Williams 1985: 57ff.

74 An air not only rich, but too rich in confusing the functional equivalence of real and unreal relations with the assumption that all external relations as such are ideal relations, resulting in a logic flawed by concealing the erroneous assumption that human understanding is unable to distinguish, within its grasp of being, particulars that are, as well as particulars, not instances of mind-dependent being.

Twilight on the Way of Ideas

But if we stick to the actual late-modern mainstream, after Hegel what do we encounter? In 1975, Schacht published a study entitled *Hegel and After*, in which he covers the side of the late-modern European development[75] in careful detail in order to demonstrate its relevance even for analytic philosophy. My aim in the rest of this chapter, however, is rather different; for the way to postmodernity does not open directly from Hegel's work, and the post-Hegel developments on the Continent and in Anglo-American circles alike, whether we are talking about phenomenology or so-called "analytic philosophy", from my point of view, remain under the trance of the modern assumption concerning the radically idealistic character of the objects of direct experience. From Hegel's death in 1831 to Peirce's publication of the semiotic categories in his "New List" of 1867 is a scant thirty-six years. Yet many who come long after that date chronologically, including many who fancy and label themselves "postmodern", yet remain conceptually wholly on the modern side of the historical development.

Since it is my conviction that, with Hegel, we are seeing, if not "the dawn's early light" of postmodernity, then at least some predawn glimmer, it would be natural to jump from Hegel directly to Peirce. But philosophy seldom develops in a logically straight line (the classical modern development from Descartes's idea of idea to Kant's unknowable *ding an sich* via Hume is the exception rather than the rule). In actual space and time the sun has first to set before it can rise, and the adherents to modern philosophy's underlying grand assumption will insist, largely unwittingly, on a long twilight for modernity. Yet with ideas we are more in a virtual than in a material reality; and one era's intellectual twilight can actually be the next era's light of dawn. But you have to know how the mind's eye in the given case is making use of and "seeing" with the light at hand. What needs to be traced is the long, slow fading of light and vitality from the classical modern enterprise, and that is my purpose in the remainder of this chapter.

Schacht mentions Sartre as a landmark figure. Yet Sartre was a child of "existentialism", that curious, fascinating, and powerful offspring of Hegelianism fathered by the pen of Søren Kierkegaard (1813–55), dramatically embodied in the very title of such works as *Either/Or*, *Fear and Trembling*, and *Sickness unto Death*. Kierkegaard, an intensely religious figure provoked by the writings of the religiously ambiguous author of *Das Leben Jesu* (Hegel's 1796 manuscript left unpublished till 1905),[76] begot a philosophical movement best known in the twentieth century for its atheist author Jean-Paul Sartre (1905–80), with literary protagonists as well, notably Albert Camus (1913–60).

---

75 "Continental philosophers between Kant and Sartre", as Schacht puts it (1975: xiv). But see also the fascinating work of Descombes 1981, which covers this same ground as a kind of sober tale of madness!

76 Not to be confused with the work of this same title authored by David Friedrich Strauss (1808–74) and published in 1835, four years after Hegel's death, by one of his followers of the so-called Hegelian Left. The work of Strauss was a full-scale attack upon the Gospel story of Christ.

Existentialism stressed the responsibility of the human individual for responses made to whatever circumstance, seeing in the interior side of those acts the constitution of the essence of the individual as human. Hence the famous existentialist maxim that "existence precedes essence", since it is from our actions as human beings that our essence is constituted, that we make of ourselves whatever we are as persons irreducible to the biology and physics of "bodies in motion". In the literature of existentialism, the author who most obviously contributes toward a doctrine of signs is Maurice Merleau-Ponty (1908–61).[77] His relevance to the development of the doctrine of signs has been most ingeniously and intricately advanced in a whole series of original writings by Richard Lanigan[78] – writings which, in defining the term and discipline of "communicology", carry Lanigan considerably beyond the status of "commentator" in making his own contributions to the doctrine of signs.[79] But in view of the whole history of philosophy out of which the doctrine of signs grows to its current position of central and dominant interest for the immediate future progress of philosophical understanding, I am of the opinion that Sartre's early book entitled *L'Étre et le Néant*, "Being and Nothingness",[80] is a major contribution to the concrete understanding of the distinction of *ens rationis* as "nonbeing" from *ens reale*, which we discussed at length in chapter 7.[81]

Here we reach the greatest point of danger for any historical introduction to or survey of philosophy: how to handle the time immediately precedent to and of the author's own present, the author's own milieu, the author's own historical ambience? For we begin now to traverse that final stretch of past terrain for which the author perforce lacks the perspective that a lengthy passage of time in part creates within human culture relatively independently of any personal vision on the author's part. The sands of time by their very accumulation bury the minor events and figures, to leave in the common view only the outline of the great occurrences, the world-historical events and figures, as landmarks to guide the remote historian. But to deal in a balanced and judicious fashion with the immediate past, that part of the history which verges on or is actually a part of the author's present life and intellectual formation, presents the greatest difficulty. One risks presenting a hundred years of philosophy as if it were ten thousand, or in such a way as to make it impossible for the reader to tell what is chaff and what is wheat, as happens in John Passmore's *A Hundred Years of Philosophy* (1966).

We reach the point where, if the utmost care is not taken, and perhaps even if it is, "a minute accumulation of circumstances must destroy the light and effect of those general pictures which compose the use and ornament of a remote history."[82]

---

77 Actually not in the late and eclectic collection bearing the name *Signs* (Merleau-Ponty 1960), but in the early systematic writings whose semiotic import is much greater: Merleau-Ponty 1942 and 1945.
78 Notably Lanigan 1972, 1977, 1988, and 1992.
79 E.g., Lanigan 1984, 1986, 1994, and 1995.
80 Sartre 1943.
81 See esp. the section "Nonbeing in Latin Philosophy", p. 350.
82 Gibbon 1788a: 180.

How to avoid this "minute accumulation" in treating of the recent past? Unless this can be done, the effect will indeed be to render the history all but worthless as a guide heuristic of the present scene respecting that which the history concerns, which is the immediate future of philosophy, the agenda that is or ought to be taken up as the twenty-first century commences. So "what the history concerns", in the present case, is the development and growth of philosophy beyond modernity, as the context of the doctrine of signs in particular. We have seen philosophy's birth as physics. We have seen its later Greek and especially Latin metamorphosis into a philosophy of being. We have seen its modern incarnation as an epistemology for which being turns out to be a foreign element. We must now try to see the metamorphosis of epistemology into a doctrine of signs wherein philosophy of being and philosophy of knowledge return to harmony. How, as part of a general history of philosophy's doctrinal or speculative development, shall we mark the transition accurately from "critical philosophy" to semiotics, from modern to postmodern times?

I know of no other solution than resolutely to adhere to the principles of selection which have succeeded in carrying us from Thales to Locke's proposal and naming of semiotic: to continue to concentrate alone on those speculative philosophical developments which enable us to understand more and more of the being and action unique to *signum*, and to brush to the margins all else, however fascinating some consideration might be on its own terms or when viewed from the perspective of another line of travel. We must keep in mind, too, that we are in the course of telling a story which has never more than provisional endings at any present moment, a story whose content always depends in part on players and developments yet to come. If we can stick to our own line of travel, and avoid the illusion that we are writing a finished history, then we should also be able to avoid that deadening accumulation of minutiae which buries in the sands of present time the elan of an inevitably surprising future. For the accumulation of minutiae tends mainly to dull readers' abductive sensibilities and hide from their eyes (if not quite to blind those eyes completely to) the possibility of seeing that there is more, even to the present, than future histories will be able to account for.

Passing over the details, then, not as unimportant but as not immediately germane to our present enterprise, suffice to say that, even after Hegel and the florescence of existentialism,[83] there is a long playing out of the consequences of the modern assumptions. This protracted playing out of consequences pertains not only to those assumptions specific and proper to the way of ideas as an epistemological paradigm,

---

83 Of Marxism, also an offspring of Hegel, I will say nothing, because it was essentially an expression of practical rather than of speculative thought in Aristotle's sense; and because, to the extent that it was at all an extension of speculative understanding, it was an extension of a speculative understanding excessively deformed and dogmatic, doctrinaire rather than doctrinal, which has left us as the last and most dangerous of its twisted offspring the political philosophy expressed by the guns of Tienanmen Square in 1988, and the missiles of 1996 in the straits of Taiwan sent as leaflets to the islanders suggesting how they should exercise their vote in any free elections.

but also to the pernicious influence Descartes had in convincing his colleagues and successors that to study the history of philosophy was a waste of time. This ahistorical attitude toward philosophy permeated the eighteenth, nineteenth, and twentieth centuries. Even today, you will find the successors to British empiricism, which transformed itself into "analytic philosophy" when it restricted its "data of sense" to logical formulae and linguistic expressions (and primarily current English ones at that), proudly and massively ignorant both of previous philosophy in general and of the Latin Age in particular.[84] When the analytic philosophers did study history, a great deal of damage frequently resulted, for they used their own fresh-minted view of philosophy as a Procrustean bed upon which to examine earlier philosophical works as verifications or anticipation of the latest fads of their own usage.

The successors of rationalism too continued to play out the consequences of the way of ideas. For a while, Edmund Husserl (1859–1938) thought he was doing something radically new with his phenomenology. But one day he realized what was up and renamed his planned lecture series, which became one of his most important books, the *Cartesian Meditations*.[85] Beyond that, he recommended a reading of the British empiricists as the best preparation for work in phenomenology. He was rationalism's answer to Locke, and the most important philosopher of the modern twilight.

Even the eighteenth-century split between empiricism as primarily British and rationalism as primarily Continental continued into late modernity. Occasionally an Englishman would show up in rationalist garb, as did Bertrand Russell (1872–1970) in some of his writing. Occasionally, too, a Continental would appear in empiricist garb, as did the later Wittgenstein, after his opening stint ("the early Wittgenstein") as a rationalist after Russell's heart and Frege's inspiration. Like Russell and Frege, the "early Wittgenstein" presented logic – reduced to the treatment of tautology – as the key to the very structure of the world.

Yet so ahistorical had philosophy become by the modern twilight that it was possible in the twentieth century for Bertrand Russell to market a best-selling history of philosophy in which the portraits even of such major figures as Aristotle and Aquinas bear almost no relation to historical actuality. In such a climate of historical obfuscation, his student Ludwig Wittgenstein succeeded in presenting the wholesale implementation of late Latin nominalism under the guise of a method without precedent for handling philosophical problems.

---

84 The general state of ignorance was such that individual authors who made public pretensions of appropriating Latin insights would often be lionized even by those who should know better. The case of Geach on abstraction, which I discussed in 1971, is illustrative of a situation from which many examples could be taken – as the discussion of "Analytical Thomism" by Shanley (1999) reminds us. But for quantity of illustrative examples of ignorant distortions ranging over all the periods of philosophy, the palm goes to Bertrand Russell's enormously popular *History of Western Philosophy* (1945, with many reprintings over the rest of the 20th century).

85 Consult Spiegelberg 1965.

The tale of this student, Ludwig Wittgenstein, of that professor, Bertrand Russell, is assuredly one of the most amazing in late-modern philosophy. Ludwig Wittgenstein (1889–1951), along with Russell, Frege, and perhaps Quine, is a figure of large sociological importance in so-called analytic philosophy and its sub-species, dubbed "logical positivism". Even granting that Wittgenstein was, within rather severe limits, a genius of sorts,[86] it needs also to be noted that he was an astonishingly ignorant one. His knowledge of ancient philosophy largely consisted of an acquaintance with Plato's *Dialogues*, while his knowledge of Latin thought was mainly confined to browsing in Augustine. Let us briefly recount the story.

First, with the thin little volume of his *Tractatus Logico-Philosophicus* (1922), he solved for us – in an "unassailable and definitive" fashion[87] – all the problems of philosophy. There being no more to be said, he dutifully retired from the field. It is true that, in his preface to the work, Wittgenstein had noted "how little is achieved when these problems are solved". The obvious conclusion to be drawn from this – that perhaps so little has been achieved because the conception of philosophy on which the achievement has been based was so narrow – only slowly occurred to Wittgenstein. Even without the aid of much reading in philosophy, further reflection, not surprisingly, convinced him he had been hasty.

He returned to Cambridge in January 1929, convinced that his *Tractatus* had been all wrong. He introduced "the later Wittgenstein" in the course of developing, with as little use of past resources as possible, an eccentric book that would appear posthumously (1953) under the title of *Philosophical Investigations*. In September 1943 Wittgenstein had proposed that the Cambridge University Press publish his new book, the *Investigations*, alongside a republication of his old book, the *Tractatus*. Monk tells[88] us that "he liked the idea of publishing a refutation of ideas in the *Tractatus* alongside the *Tractatus*". Cambridge University Press formally accepted this dual-publication plan in a letter dated 14 January 1944. But Wittgenstein never delivered a finished manuscript for the *Investigations*, and the plan came to nothing.

When the new book finally did appear, shortly after Wittgenstein's death, it set the movement of "analytic philosophy" on its heels and split off a following devoted to "ordinary language philosophy" wherein, as you might imagine, the whole of philosophy traditionally conceived is turned from a logistician's

---

86 So Monk announces in the subtitle of his excellent biography (1990), *Ludwig Wittgenstein: The Duty of Genius*.

87 Wittgenstein 1922: Preface. This remark is intersemiotic with that of Kant above, p. 568 at n55.

88 Monk 1990: 457. Kenny has argued (1984: ix–x, 24ff.) that Wittgenstein "tended systematically to exaggerate the inadequacies of his earlier work in a way which masks the underlying continuity" between the *Tractatus* and the *Investigations*, so that "what is attacked in Wittgenstein's later work, I maintain, is sometimes not the real *Tractatus* but a mere ghost of it." Of course, we can only guess how Wittgenstein himself would have responded to Kenny's argument. If correct, Kenny's argument is at once a vindication of the postmodern emphasis on the relative autonomy of any text as such from the psychological aims and states of its author and a bizarre underscoring of Wittgenstein's ignorance of philosophy's history no less within than before the time of his own life.

nightmare[89] into a nominalist's heaven. This split within the analytic movement endured for the remainder of the twentieth century.

According to Monk,[90] indeed, Wittgenstein saw himself as the "Antisocrates", meaning that "his method could be summed up by saying that it was the exact opposite of Socrates" in the matter of definition. The basis of this approach traces back to one thing Wittgenstein never did shake from his *Tractatus* days, namely, an ill-drawn distinction between "saying" and "seeing". This ghost both haunts and cripples the *Investigations*, often pushing the trapped author to try to show what needed rather to be said, and conversely. Cahalan[91] has wondered out loud what would have happened if Wittgenstein had read Poinsot. His reason for musing over this question is that the *Investigations*, along with the *Blue Book* and *Brown Book*, and the work of the "later Wittgenstein" generally, seems to be mainly an exploration of the consequences of the idea that there are only instrumental signs. From the point of view of rounding out modernity, this construal nicely complements the work of Kant, which, as we have already seen, was a systematization of the modern assumption that, from sensation to the heights of intellectual theorizing, objects and ideas in the broad sense of what the mind itself in knowing produces and directly attains, are the same; which precisely amounts to the reduction of formal to instrumental signs.

Cahalan's question, thus, is tantalizing but unanswerable. Not only is there little evidence that Wittgenstein read that much of anybody (and no evidence that he read Poinsot), there is further the insuperable obstacle that Wittgenstein took pride in having studied almost nothing of other philosophers. His was more a mathematical kind of genius, feeding off of its own imagination and, in the particular case of the *Investigations*, cleverness with words. That is one thing. But to parade ignorance of the work others have done in philosophy as his badge of authenticity as a philosopher was something else again, an abuse of the very historical circumstances that had allowed him to acquire a voice in the field, and a gross disservice, an intellectual injustice, to students who fell under his influence.

Two of Wittgenstein's students, D. A. T. Gasking and A. C. Jackson, report Wittgenstein as having compared his teaching philosophy to the work "of a guide showing you how to find your way around London":[92]

> Of course, a good guide will take you through the more important streets more often than he takes you down side streets; a bad guide will do the opposite. In philosophy, I'm a rather bad guide.

---

89 Logistician: a person skilled in symbolic logic.
90 Monk 1990: 337–8.
91 John C. Cahalan, "If Wittgenstein Had Read Poinsot: Recasting the Problem of Signs and Mental States" (1994).
92 "Wittgenstein as Teacher", in Fann ed. 1967: 51.

Well and truly spoken. But a good guide, of course, would have first himself to know the more important streets, and a man who boasted of having read not a word of Aristotle, and whose writing well demonstrated the same deficiency regarding practically everyone else who created the main avenues in philosophy's historical city, could hardly be expected to know the more important streets. Wittgenstein was like a cabbie who, on accepting a fare and being informed of a destination, proceeds to try to learn the city at the fare's expense. It is one way to learn philosophy: "You pays your money and you takes your chances".

In Wittgenstein, the solipsism and nominalism of modernity found their fullest incarnation, first the one, and then the other. Well past the crest of its own wave, late-modern thought had exhausted its resources, and was still determined not to reach beyond itself even on the off-chance that the older traditions might provide neglected or forgotten resources for discovering a way out of the dilemma of a thought trapped within itself. Mr Hyde may have been pathological, but he hated Dr Jekyll, and had yet to be convinced that a cure might not be worse than the disease.

For philosophy, modernity was a long winter. When did it end? Well, it hasn't entirely. You still find professors of philosophy contemptuous of its history and, when not contemptuous, ignorant of some of the historical discussion most pertinent to the evaluation of modern contributions. But almost no one is satisfied any more with the way of ideas, and the game is up for its proponents. Modern philosophy is over. The question is, Where do things go from here?

Journey's End, Journey's Beginning

The Latins liked to remark that the passing away of one thing is the coming into being of another.[93] Yet before we try our hand at divination by saying what is around the corner, there is at least one more question that needs to be asked about modernity: as a period, why did it end? For when we look at modern philosophy not on its terms from within but from outside the assumption of the way of ideas, and see it accordingly as one more period in the long history, we see right away that, in fact, it is one of the shorter of philosophy's periods. Why?

Actually, in the full scope of philosophy's near-three millennia, the brevity of the period of modern philosophy overall is not all that surprising. Given, on the one hand, the schizophrenic split between modern science and the consequences of the epistemological paradigm within which modern philosophy operated and, on the other hand, the total opposition to common sense necessitated by that same paradigm, what is surprising is that thinkers did not abandon the way of ideas considerably sooner. But, in the first place, they were unable readily to envision an alternative way to go, as they might have had the Hispanic late Latins been allowed a fuller participation in the early-modern dialogue. And, in the second

---

93 *Corruptio unius est generatio alterius.*

place, history is to philosophy what the laboratory is to science, as Gilson first said and in some ways best understood. Philosophy depends on discourse, and the contradictory implications of the most profound confusions may, in the psychology of human beings, take years or even centuries to become fully or generally apparent. So perhaps after all it is not so surprising that the way of ideas took about three centuries to traverse. We are at least lucky it took no longer.

From the point view of the "great conversation" which links philosophy across the graves of earlier generations, the seizure of philosophy's center-stage early in the 1600s by the classical modern authors effected a twofold disruption. First, the classical modern development definitively disrupted and temporarily consigned to oblivion the rich stirrings of a semiotic consciousness among the Latins, in the last Hispanic phase particularly. Second, modern epistemological theory, beginning with Descartes, as it was to culminate in Kant's synthesis of rationalism and empiricism, moved in a direction antithetical to a doctrine of signs. The modern development moved in such a direction because, within its guiding assumption, the carefully developed Hispanic Latin distinction between *representation* (in which an object may present itself) and *signification* (in which an object or a concept can only present something other than itself) remained undiscussed. From Hobbes to Wittgenstein as an extreme limit (the limit at which the pronouncement itself begins to crumble), with the limited exception of Hegel, as we remarked above, modern thought developed the consequences of its doctrinal pronouncement:[94] "Concerning relation, however, it must not be thought to exist in such a way as to be diverse from the other accidents of the related thing, but as one of them, namely, that very one according to which a comparison is made."

In this particular, precisely because both rationalism and empiricism took the equation of objects with ideas as their unchallenged point of departure, it must be said of the moderns that, as far as concerned the Latin doctrine of signs initiated by Augustine and culminated by Poinsot, the moderns quite literally knew not what they did. Equating ideas with objects does not simply make impossible the medieval notion of concepts as formal signs (that is to say, vehicles of signification in their proper being as founding and giving rise to relations of signification). It also makes undrawable the distinction (without which the action of signs is unintelligible) between objects partially inclusive of the physical environment as self-representative and signs as other-representative.

For what signs do specifically is to mediate between the physical and the objective, where the object represents itself in knowledge (both as partially including and as transcending the physical environment) and the sign always represents an object other than itself. The sign depends upon the object in that the object provides

---

94 Thomas Hobbes (1588–1679), "Philosophia Prima", in *Opera Philosophica, Quae Latine Scripsit, Omnia* (Amsterdam: Joannes Blaev, 1668), Vol. I, caput 11, ¶6, p. 71. Cf. Poinsot's *Treatise on Signs*, Second Preamble, Article 1, 8off. esp. 80/22–81/5 (= R I, 573b44–574a7), where this *ex cathedra* statement can be seen in a considerably larger framework of discussion.

the measure or content whereby and according to which the sign signifies. But the object in representing itself also depends upon the sign for being presented (the object determines *what* is presented, the sign *whether* it is presented), and the sign is, in its own being, indifferent to whether the object has also a physical existence. Hence, the sign is just as well able to include or to omit that physical existence, depending on the circumstance of the environment surrounding the significative action here and now.

The suppression of all of these basic doctrinal points follows in consequence of the modern adoption of the position of Ockham and the nominalists on the subject of relation, and of the position of Fonseca, Suárez, and the instrumentalists on the subject of signification. For in dropping out of the discussion the notion of ontological relation as indifferently real or unreal, but in every case superordinate to a subjective foundation or ground, the modern epistemologists precluded also the medieval notion of objects signified which may or may not also be things of nature.

When Kant distinguishes what is present in our awareness as "phenomena", in contrast to whatever may be there "in itself" as "unknowable", the phenomena accordingly can only exist as an opaque curtain *behind which* the "things-in-themselves" lie completely and forever concealed. Kant was able to make a synthesis of the two modern currents precisely because he saw that there was an assumption shared by both – the idea as the object which represents itself in knowledge – which could be used as the common ground for a higher synthesis in which the many differences otherwise could be fundamentally reconciled. That is why Kant dominates the landscape of modern thought as Aristotle or Plato the landscape of Greek thought, Aquinas and Scotus the landscape of Latin thought: Kant, more completely than any other, built from what was most fundamental in modernity.

Kant himself thought it was enough to acknowledge that there must be things in themselves to brush aside the idealism of the earlier moderns (from Descartes on) as an error. A few have agreed with him on this point, and so claimed for "transcendental idealism" the title of being, in the end, some variant of realism, an "empirical realism", in the expression of Arthur Collins[95] (that is to say, one that limits knowledge to the sensible world of common experience and science in the modern sense), but simply one so sophisticated in its account of "the ubiquitous subjectivity of our representation of reality"[96] that confusion of it with the subjective idealisms in the line of Descartes is almost invited and inevitable.

But far the majority of those who came after saw all too well that the full essence of modern idealism lies not in the denial or acceptance as necessary to experience of a world of mind-independent being, but rather in the denial or acceptance of an epistemological theory capable of providing a warrant for some direct access, however limited, to that "universe of things" sustaining the possibility within, and not just correlative to, behind, or apart from, the phenomenal world. And not even

---

95 Collins 1999: 143 and passim.
96 Ibid.

Collins, that most sophisticated and knowledgeable student of Kant, claims such an access in his determined effort to warrant a minority view of Kant as realist.[97] By this measure, Kant was, in the terms of his theory, simply the most unequivocal of all modern idealists; and his distinction of *transcendental* idealism[98] from *problematic* and *dogmatic* and *empirical* idealisms[99] proves to be without a difference that counts outside the technical framework of the putative "critique of pure reason". And even within that framework,[100] space and time "and with them all appearances, are not in themselves *things*; they are nothing but representations, and cannot exist outside [that is to say, apart from] our mind." Wherever things may stand, in our awareness for what they actually are (in *self-representations*, as Aquinas or Poinsot would put it consistently with their doctrine of sensation) as mind-independent beings known-in-themselves, however partially, is not one of the places possible – according to Kant. The Master of the Moderns stands before history as the principal theorist of the proposition that whatever the mind knows the mind itself makes, however sophisticated and constraining be the conditions under which that making occurs. That is why he stands before this same history, in spite of all the distinctions internal to his system whereby one classical modern idealism differs from another, as just one more figure, albeit the tallest one, in the idealist line-up.

For just as modern idealism developed as the notion of the universe of thought closed unto itself and ignorant in principle of any nature beyond thought, so all idealists share in common the view that the mind constitutes whatever the mind knows in whatever the mind knows of it. That some of the forms according to

---

97 "We will now say," Collins says (1999: 143–4) in summary of his theme of objects and empirical realism, "speaking of experience as a whole, only that *something* exists that we subjectively represent as a system of spatiotemporal objects in law-governed relations with one another. The fact that we represent this reality (which we do not create) as a system of objects is tied up with the fact that we have organized intuitive inputs so that they fit laws that come from the structure of our minds and not from the 'something'. That it is *objects* that we take to exist is traced entirely to our mental powers. In other words, even accepting the account of making objects possible given in the *Critique*, §14, we cannot say that Kant's view is that objects really do exist, but only that something exists that we inevitably represent as a system of objects." To emphasize "that the contrast between appearances or things considered as they appear to us and things considered as they are in themselves does not indicate two ontologically distinct sets of things, but, instead, two ways of considering the same things" hardly suffices "to dispel the atmosphere of idealism that Kant's terminology so easily generates" (ibid. 144), when the same interpreter concedes (p. 150) that "we never get to know anything about things considered as they are in themselves." To insist that "it is that realm of things that appears to us as a system of objects connected by laws" is no doubt Kant's doctrine, but it is further his doctrine that in knowing the objects we do not know the things in their own existence. Being and intelligibility are not convertible, only sensible being. There is the whole difference between ontology, whether ancient Greek or medieval Latin, and classical modern. For it is precisely mind-independent beings as the ground of appearances, and not just mind-dependent objects, that are in part grasped objectively according to the claims of the philosophy of being developed by the medievals after the principal ancient sketch worked out by Aristotle; and just this Kant no less than Descartes or Leibniz rules out in epistemology.
98 Kant 1787: 439.
99 Ibid.: 244, 440.
100 Ibid.: 440.

which sensations are organized are a-priori adds a variety within and likely is, as Collins argues, essential to a philosophy, like Kant's, that distinguishes scientific objectivity from delusions. But this is not sufficient for the preclusion of solipsism for the species *anthropos*, and hence for each individual within it; for whatever be the mechanism of representative consciousness, that does not change the basic situation admitted on all hands: nothing directly experienced has as such an existence also apart from our experiencing of it. This view is the hallmark of modernity. But the moderns never succeeded in figuring out *why* they were speculatively driven, over and over again, into a solipsistic corner from which, as Bertrand Russell summarized the modern dilemma in the historical twilight of its dominance in philosophy, there seems no way out. For only the sign in its proper being can effect the needed passage. And ideas *as representations* are emphatically not signs, but the mere vehicles and foundations through which the action of signs works to achieve, over and above individual subjectivity, the interweave of mind and nature that we call experience.

Bertrand Russell spoke in principle for the whole of modernity including Kant when, describing his own philosophical development, he confessed that he had never succeeded in moving beyond solipsism. This is the position that the self can know nothing but its own modifications. To put the matter in Russell's own words, which summarized his understanding of the logical outcome of the classical modern development of philosophy: "What I maintain is that we can witness or observe what goes on in our heads, and that we cannot witness or observe anything else at all."[101] To make a striking illustration of this general point, he contrasted the starry heavens we see with the starry heavens we believe in: according to Russell, the starry heavens that each of us sees (if there be an each of us, for technically the point remains unknown) is but an idea in our own mind, whereas the starry heavens that we believe in, beyond and, in main measure, independent of our minds, can never be directly touched or shown in knowledge. In sum:[102]

> The whole of what we perceive without inference belongs to our private world. In this respect, I agree with Berkeley. The starry heaven that we know in visual sensation is inside us. The external starry heaven that we believe in is inferred.

That monads, our thinking selves, have no windows was not the hard saying for the early moderns that it came to seem in late modernity. Still less had this view the character of a sophism too clever by half, as it appears in a postmodern light. Leibniz indeed, as mentioned earlier, spoke for the mainstream modern development when he adopted this view as the essence of his monadology, that little work which was itself the quintessence and summary modern statement about the nature of reality. What we call the physical universe is simply the totality of windowless monads, each locked in the living theater of its own representations.

---

101 B. Russell 1959: 26.
102 Ibid., 27.

But the moment people began to thematize their experience of communication and to think of communication as such as something real, the moment they began to think of *that* experience as a proper starting point for philosophy, the days of modern philosophy were numbered. For with the substitution of the experience of communication for ideas as the point of departure for considering "the nature and extent of humane understanding", with a belief in the occasional success of communication as the guiding notion for developing the consequences of that point of departure, postmodernism had begun.

Strangely, at the conclusion of his book launching empiricism as a main sub-current in the sea of modern idealism, Locke anticipated such a possibile turn of events. The anomaly of a founder of philosophical modernity prognosticating postmodernity, of an advocate of the way of ideas suggesting an alternative way of signs, has somehow escaped the notice of historians and philosophers heretofore – no doubt because the text in question appeared in its original time as a fossil did in the time of Albertus Magnus. Yet the importance of the text today can hardly be underestimated, providing, as it does, a key to what a contemporary philosopher[103] speaking from an authoritative post[104] well called "the delicate question of the demarcation of the different historical periods" to which this book has addressed itself, particularly in the matter of coalescing a consensus about how the designation "postmodern" ought to be received and established within "the philosophical field". Let us bring our inquiry into the modern period to close therefore with an interpretation of this Rosetta Stone that John Locke chiseled with a message for posterity to fathom.

---

103 Wojtyla 1998: ¶91: "A quibusdam subtilioribus auctoribus aetas nostra uti tempus 'post-modernum' est designata. Ita verbum idem ... in provinciam deinde philosophiae est translatum, at certa semper ambiguitate signatum, tum quia iudicium de iis quae uti 'post-moderna' appellantur nunc affirmans nunc negans esse potest, tum quia nulla est consensio in perdifficili quaestione de variarum aetatum historicarum terminis." ("Our age has been termed by some thinkers the age of 'postmodernity'. The term ... was finally transposed into the philosophical field, but has remained somewhat ambiguous, both because judgment on what is called 'postmodern' is sometimes positive and sometimes negative, and because there is as yet no consensus on the delicate question of the demarcation of the different historical periods.") The point is precisely that raised by Schmitz (1990: 153–4): "in determining the meaning of post-modernity, when is modernity supposed to have ended? ... And in what is modernity supposed to have consisted? These questions are of decisive importance since the meaning given to the term 'post-modernity' is parasitic upon the meaning given to the term 'modernity'." Exactly this matter we have been addressing throughout our work, and will bring to a head in part IV.

104 The papacy, to wit.

CHAPTER FOURTEEN

Locke Again:
The Scheme of Human Knowledge

Now here is a surprise: an unexpected answer from a non-logician to a question logicians had not been able to resolve satisfactorily for more than twenty-two centuries, and a decisive clarification of the role of logic in the tradition of liberal arts education some eleven centuries after that tradition was initiated.[1] Just such were the unwitting implications of the manner in which Locke brought his celebrated *Essay* of 1690 to a close with a proposal so anomalous with the body of the work it concluded and the times in which it was written that no one along the way of ideas, not even Locke himself, could see their way to taking the closing chapter full seriously.

That proposal was that there could well be unforeseeable consequences, upsetting to the whole enterprise of modern philosophy, were its basic premiss along the way of ideas, the equation of ideas with self-representing objects, to be rethought under the consideration that ideas might be other-representing signs rather than self-representing objects.

A modest proposal, received with considerably less notice, surprise, and consternation than would be accorded the modest proposal by Jonathan Swift (1667–1745) thirty-nine years later.[2] Such is the fate of philosophy, that satire normally eclipses the most revolutionary proposals of sound speculative thought, of which scarce notice is taken sometimes for centuries, sometimes never.

---

1 See chapter 5, p. 183ff.
2 Swift 1729: *A Modest Proposal for Preventing the Children of Poor People from Being a Burden to Their Parents or Country*, as follows: "I have been assured ... that a healthy young child well nursed, is, at a year old, a most delicious, nourishing, and wholesome food, whether stewed, roasted, baked, or boiled; and I make no doubt that it will equally serve in a fricassee or ragout. I do therefore humbly offer it for public consideration, that of the hundred and twenty thousand children already computed, twenty thousand may be reserved for breed, whereof only one fourth part to be males ... That the remaining hundred thousand may, at a year old, be offered in sale to the persons of quality and fortune throughout the Kingdom; always advising the mother to let them suck plentifully in the last month, so as to render them plump and fat for a good table. A child will make two dishes at an entertainment for friends; and when the family dines alone, the fore or hind quarter will make a reasonable dish, and, seasoned with a little pepper, will be very good .... Those

The actual basis which Locke's modest proposal presupposed was exactly the same as what Augustine's superficial learning confined to Latin had led him to suppose a thousand three hundred odd years before, namely, a *signum* which, as vehicle of communication, could cross the lines of every frontier encountered in experience and the organization of knowledge, most notably the frontier where phenomena and noumena meet in sensation – the very frontier marked "Unpassable" ninety-one years after Locke's *Essay* by Kant's *Critique of Pure Reason*. But Kant, in erecting his speculative barrier-critiques, had taken no notice of Locke's proposal, nor given a moment's thought to a way of signs as alternative to the way of ideas. Like Descartes, like all the moderns, like most men in most times, he saw the way of his tradition – the way of ideas – as the only way, and pushed forward accordingly, to what impasse we well know.

Augustine's proposal, which alone lent a basis for Locke's more modest one, had taken a long time to vindicate, as we saw – full well one thousand two hundred of the one thousand three hundred years separating the text of Augustine from the text of Locke's proposal. And even though the vindicating culmination of Latin discussions around Augustine's notion of *signum* as superior to the division between what is from nature and what is from the human mind had been achieved just fifty-eight years before Locke brought his *Essay concerning Humane Understanding* to publication, yet such were the distributions of national *Umwelten* within the political and intellectual Lebenswelt of seventeenth century life in the nations of the West that Locke knew nothing of it.

This fact makes all the more intriguing the subversive proposal with which Locke concluded the famous *Essay*, a proposal which his fellow moderns were all but completely to ignore, but which would have the privilege of giving to postmodernity the name for its most defining central element, "semiotics".

Locke's Modest Proposal Subversive of the Way of Ideas, Its Reception, and Its Bearing on the Resolution of an Ancient and a Modern Controversy in Logic

Locke opened his *Essay* with an embrace of the Cartesian assumption that ideas are objective self-representations. We have seen this,[3] and traced the consequences. In closing the *Essay*, however, he makes to his modern colleagues the suggestion that this "idea of idea" may perhaps be ill-considered. What if ideas are not objective self-representations? What if ideas are instead some species of what we all take

---

who are more thrifty may flay the carcass, the skin of which, artfully dressed, will make admirable gloves for ladies, and summer boots for fine gentlemen.

"[T]he advantages [of] the proposal are [that] it would greatly lessen the number of Papists with whom we are yearly overrun, ... the nation's stock will be thereby increased fifty thousand pounds per annum, besides the profit of a new dish introduced to the tables of all gentlemen of fortune ... who have any refinement in taste."

3 See in chapter 12 "The Nature of Ideas", p. 536.

words to be, namely, signs? And what if, instead of proceeding systematically from the assumption that ideas are objects, we were to proceed instead upon the assumption that ideas are signs? Would the speculative consequences for life, logic, and knowledge be the same, or would they be different? Perhaps this change of assumptions "would afford us another sort of Logic and Critic than what we have been hitherto acquainted" with[4] in the writings of either rationalism or empiricism, and hence different from any possible synthesis of the two based on their assumption shared in common.

Reception of the Proposal among the Moderns

Locke's modern confreres hardly gave the suggestion the time of day. Perhaps this is why, despite preparing carefully four subsequent editions of the *Essay* for publication (not to mention the French and Latin translations he supervised), and even a fifth one which he died before being able to bring to press, Locke never developed his concluding suggestion further. But neither did he withdraw it. There it stood, at the conclusion of every copy of the *Essay* published under Locke's own supervision,[5] for every reader to consider.

Berkeley[6] allowed it as an intriguing idea that ought to be pursued – as long as the pursuit is not too narrowly conceived, and as long, especially, as it does not depart from the truth of nominalism about the subjective or individual nature of reality. For signs "do not always suggest ideas signified to the mind", Berkeley noted, in a passage anticipatory of Peirce's array of interpretants as dynamic, emotional, and energetic as well as logical: "they have other uses besides barely standing for and exhibiting ideas, such as raising proper emotions, producing certain dispositions or habits of mind, and directing our actions in pursuit of that happiness, which is the ultimate end and design, the primary spring and motive, that sets rational agents at work". And when signs do suggest ideas, "they are not general abstract ideas", that great illusion of language to which Locke succumbed, which Berkeley considered the chief and almost sole cause of error and perplexity in the sciences and falsity in Locke's philosophy.

Leibniz[7] sees in Locke's discussion nothing more than "different ways in which one can organize the same truths, if one sees fit to express them more than once"; and as to the proposal for semiotics itself, Leibniz tells us, "really all it produces is a kind of Inventory", which is but another way of restating the original objection to Augustine's *signum*, that natural phenomena (*semeia*) and conventional signs (*symbola*) have no common denominator.

---

4 Locke 1690, penultimate paragraph.
5 Some of the later modern editors, in abridging the *Essay*, made this original concluding proposal the first part of the text to go; and indeed it has little or nothing to do with the reading or interpretation of the *Essay* in all that precedes the concluding page, so there was hardly reason to do otherwise in abridging the work.
6 *Alciphron, or The Minute Philosopher* (1732); see esp. Dialogue 7, sects. 12–15.
7 In *New Essays on Human Understanding* (1704), Book IV, ch. 21.

And even Condillac (1715–80), who began as a follower of Locke and ended with sweeping proposals on the role of signs in human knowledge, had only criticism for Locke's supposed failure to see the link between words as necessary to the development of thoughts. The point that words without thoughts are at least as empty as thoughts without words, and that, in Locke's proposal for semiotics, "ideas" are merely a synecdoche for the inner side of that for which "words" are a synecdoche for the outer side of, soared over his head like a three-base hit.[8]

Aside from these three passing discussions, Locke's concluding suggestion is met with a resounding silence that lasts as long as modernity itself. Even Locke's devoted late-modern editor, Alexander Campbell Fraser,[9] dismisses out of hand "this crude and superficial scheme of Locke".

So it is fitting that we should end our treatment of the modern period of philosophy with a consideration of that one part of Locke's *Essay* which was without serious influence in modern times, all the more so as it is the one place in the literature of mainstream early-modern writing where the way of ideas is subjected even to the suspicion of doubt, and all the more so as it provides us with what has proved the key term for an understanding of how postmodern thought contrasts with the thought of modern philosophy.

The Text of the Proposal

Like Anselm's original statement of the "ontological argument", the actual text of Locke's concluding proposal is quite brief, so that we may easily read it in full before discussing its details:[10]

CHAP. XX.

Of the Division of the Sciences.

§.1. All that can fall within the compass of humane Understanding, being either, *First*, The Nature of Things, as they are in themselves, their Relations, and their manner of Operations: Or, *secondly*, that which Man himself ought to do, as a rational and voluntary Agent, for the Attainment of any Ends, especially Happiness: Or, *Thirdly*, The ways and means, whereby the Knowledge of both the one and the other of these,

---

8 Windelband (1901: 478, text and n. 2) sees in Condillac a convergence of "the lines of the French and the English Enlightenment" which results in "a positivistic synthesis of sensualism and rationalism, which may be regarded as the most perfect expression of modern terminism. His *Logic* [Condillac 1778] and his posthumous *Langue des Calculs* [Condillac u.1779] developed this doctrine. It is built up essentially upon a theory of 'signs' (*signes*). After the *Langue des Calculs* became known, the Institute of Paris and the Berlin Academy gave out, almost at the same time, the theory of signs as the subject for their prizes. At both places a great number of elaborations were presented, mostly of very inferior quality." So there is room here for considerable more research.

9 Fraser 1894: II, 463n1.

10 Locke 1690, concluding chapter in full.

are attained and communicated; I think, *Science* may be divided properly into these *Three sorts.*

§.2. *First*, The Knowledge of Things, as they are in their own proper Beings, their Constitutions, Properties, and Operations, whereby I mean not only Matter, and Body, but Spirits also, which have their proper Natures, Constitutions, and Operations as well as Bodies. This in a little more enlarged Sense of the Word, I call φυσική, *or natural Philosophy*. The end of this, is bare speculative Truth, and whatsoever can afford the Mind of Man any such, falls under this branch, whether it be God himself, Angels, Spirits, Bodies, or any other of their Affections, as Number, and Figure, &c.

§.3. *Secondly*, πρακτική, The Skill of Right applying our own Powers and Actions, for the Attainment of Things good and useful. The most considerable under this Head, is *Ethicks*, which is the seeking out those Rules, and Measures of Humane Actions, which lead to Happiness, and the Means to practise them. The end of this is not bare Speculation, and the Knowledge of Truth; but Right, and a Conduct suitable to it.

§.4. *Thirdly*, The third Branch may be called σημιωτική, or *the Doctrine of Signs*, the most usual whereof being Words, it is aptly enough termed also λογική, Logick; the business whereof, is to consider the Nature of Signs, the Mind makes use of for the understanding of Things, or conveying its Knowledge to others. For since the Things, the Mind contemplates, are none of them, besides it self, present to the Understanding, 'tis necessary that something else, as a Sign or Representation of the thing it considers, should be present to it: And these are *Ideas*. And because the *Ideas* of one Man's Mind cannot immediately be laid open to the view of another; nor be themselves laid up any where, but in the Memory, which is apt to let them go and lose them: Therefore to communicate our *Ideas* one to another, as well as record them for our own use, Signs of our *Ideas* are also necessary. Those which Men have found most convenient, and therefore generally make use of, are articulate Sounds. The Consideration then of *Ideas* and Words, as the great Instruments of Knowledge, makes no despicable part of their Contemplation, who would take a view of humane Knowledge in the whole Extent of it. And, perhaps, if they were distinctly weighed, and duly considered, they would afford us another sort of Logick and Critick, than what we have been hitherto acquainted with.

§.5. *This* seems to me *the first and most general, as well as natural division* of the Objects of our Understanding. For since a Man can employ his Thoughts about nothing, but either the Contemplation of Things themselves for the discovery of Truth; Or about the Things in his own Power, which are his own Actions, for the Attainment of his own Ends; Or the Signs the Mind makes use of, both in the one and the other, and the right ordering of them for its clearer Information. All which three, *viz*. Things as they are in themselves knowable; Actions as they depend on us, in order to Happiness; and the right use of Signs in order to Knowledge, being *toto caelo* different, they seemed to me to be the three great Provinces of the intellectual World, wholly separate and distinct one from another.

Let us pass over as technical details discussed elsewhere[11] the many interesting peculiarities which attach to Locke's introduction here of an ostensibly Greek term, σημιωτική. It is enough here to note that the Latin transliteration of Locke's term is *semiotica*,[12] which becomes in English "semiotics". The division of human knowledge, you will remember, was one of the earliest proposals made in philosophy's morning light, first the one by Aristotle,[13] and, at almost the same time, the slightly different one of the Stoics.[14] With these two ancient divisions in mind, it will be easier to see what is novel about Locke's proposal, and what merely resumes or repeats well-established points of philosophical doctrine from the centuries of speculation that preceded modernity.

Resolution of the Ancient Quarrel between Stoics and Peripatetics over the Place of Logic among the Sciences and of the Late-Modern Quarrel over the Rationale of Logic as a Liberal Art

Perhaps no moment of great historical significance in the development of logic has received less recognition than Locke's resolution of the then almost twenty-four centuries old controversy between the Aristotelians and the Stoics[15] over whether logic should be conceived primarily as an instrument for use in other areas of intellectual inquiry or primarily as a science in its own right among the other sciences.

A number of factors have contributed to this lack of notice – besides the context and brevity of Locke's text. There is the fact that, in Locke's time, a somewhat stagnant Aristotelian conception of logic was regnant, and the Stoic alternative was little more than a vague memory. Being neither logician nor historian of philosophy, the resolution Locke achieved to the early-begun contestation between these two ancient schools was undoubtedly implicit and inadvertent. The text in question – Locke's text – was penned by an author who contributed nothing to the mainstream development of logic in its own right, and achieved its resolution of the ancient controversy in a passage that was peripheral even to the substance of its own author's philosophical work.

---

11 Deely 1994a: 111–14.
12 This transliteration was taken as the name of the official journal of the International Association for Semiotic Studies at its founding in January 1969 (see Sebeok 1971: 52). The journal became one of the largest international scholarly and interdisciplinary journals of the closing decades of the 20th century, a status it still holds as the 21st century opens.
13 See chapter 3, pp. 81ff.; discussion schematized on p. 91.
14 Chapter 4 above, beginning p. 97, with schema on p. 98.
15 See chapter 3, "The Instrument of All the Sciences", p. 87; chapter 4, "The Quarrel between the Stoics and Peripatetics", p. 98. Here I may repeat my observation on this quarrel from *Introducing Semiotic* (Deely 1982: 151n4): with the glibness that has become the hallmark of mainstream twentieth-century British academic philosophy where basic issues are concerned, the Kneales (1962: 737) see in this controversy a mere verbal quibble – in their own words, "little more than a quarrel about words". To the contrary, the very definition of philosophy and its relation to the order of mind-independent being was at stake in the quarrel. Cf. Bird 1963: 500–2.

Even so, it remains the case that the decisive distinction for clarifying the nature of logic's own subject matter in its relation to the other sciences was first suggested early in modern times in this concluding chapter of the *Essay concerning Humane Understanding* by John Locke, just as this same chapter is famous also for its successful suggestion of "semiotics" as the "logically proper name", so to speak, for the doctrine of signs – an indigenously Latin doctrine from the turn of the fifth century AD, as we have seen,[16] but one which Locke put forward as something for the future to envision, not knowing the actual provenance and past of what he was proposing under a novel name within a novel scheme for presenting the organization of human knowledge.

This final chapter in Locke's work, however, not only deserves to be famous among logicians for showing how the instrumentalist conception of logic advanced by the Aristotelians reconciles with rather than opposes the Stoic conception of logic as a discipline or science in its own right. The chapter, at the same time, anticipates and resolves a contemporary problem in the liberal arts curriculum that has festered since the mid-nineteenth century "logistic turn" of logical analysis toward mathematization of its techniques in the individual works of George Boole (1815–64), Gottlob Frege (1848–1925), and the 1910–13 joint work[17] of Alfred North Whitehead (1861–1947) and Bertrand Russell (1872–1970).

In the tradition of the liberal arts, logic was conceived from the beginning as a core requirement precisely because it was viewed, along Aristotelian lines, as instrumental to intellectual discourse in all areas of learning – that is to say, "across the curriculum". Since the middle of the nineteenth century, on the contrary, logic has developed along the quite different Stoic lines of a formal discipline conceived as a science in its own right concerned more with propositional patterns than with the terms and content of arguments. With respect to this "scientific" discipline, natural language functions only as a meta-language for the artificial system of symbols with which logic is conceived to be primarily concerned, logic being the working out of the consequences of the stipulations constitutive of the symbolic system as artificial.

To just this problem does the approach to logic outlined in the close of Locke's *Essay* suggest a resolution, by beginning with a semiotic reconceptualization of the foundations of traditional logic, Stoic *or* Aristotelian, that carries through to the conception of each of the parts of logic. For what an approach to logic that is based on Locke's sketch reveals is twofold. First, the sign-system of natural language must be regarded neither as peripheral nor as metalinguistic to logical concern, but as at the foundation of logic. Second, this primary relation of logic to the sign-system of species-specific natural language imposes the conception of logic as primarily a specific science within, rather than a perspective coextensive with, the doctrine of signs.

In short, adoption of Locke's proposal as the rationale for logic in the tradition of liberal arts, in place of the original Aristotelian rationale opposed to the Stoic

---

16 See "The First Latin Initiative in Philosophy: Sign in General", in chapter 6, p. 214.
17 Whitehead and Russell, *Principia Mathematica* (Cambridge, 1910–13), 3 vols.

conception, would bring about a reconciliation of the two proposals by the suggestion that the foundations of logic as a science ought be sought in logical relations as they occur within the structures of natural language, rather than in artificial languages parasitic upon or "metatheoretic" to natural language.

Such foundations go well below, without excluding, symbolic systems artificially substituted for the species-specifically human communication system whereby, consequent upon the exaptation of language, that cumulative transmission of learning that constitutes the cultural distinctiveness of the social organization of human animals is made possible. And while the resulting logic would in fact be closer to Aristotelian syllogistic than to any version of late-modern mathematical logic, such as predicate or propositional calculi, the reason for the correct pedagogical emphasis would be clear to all, making it much more likely to be implemented in the classroom at the level of core or general curriculum requirements.

We see the situation in considerably greater detail today than when Locke limned his initial sketch. Yet the logical implications behind the developments of detail remain in harmony with the framework of the initial sketch, which is why the text can embody such vast implications reaching in both directions – to an ancient past of which the text's author knew very little, and to a postmodern future which lay well beyond the lifetime of the text's author. There could hardly be a more striking confirmation of Peirce's semiotic thesis[18] that "the existence of thought now depends on what is to be hereafter; so that it has only a potential existence, dependent on the future thought of the community", than the confirmation provided by the first text in the history of philosophy to use semiotics as a proper name.

The Literary Device of Synecdoches in the Text of Locke's Proposal and His Initial Sketch for the Doctrine of Signs

Locke begins with Aristotle's distinction between knowledge we acquire of objects having as part of their objectivity an existence that obtains independently of, as well as extending outside of, our thinking ("speculative thought"), and knowledge of objects that precisely come into being as a result of human thought and action and would not exist as such apart from human action ("practical thought"). But to bring out the content of Locke's overly compressed proposal, the reader needs to attend to the role of the literary device of *synecdoche*, the figure of speech wherein a part is made to stand for a whole (as "wheels" for "car", "boards" for "stage", "a Croesus" for "a rich man", etc.) or, conversely, wherein the whole is made to stand for a part ("society" for "high society").

In the case of the present text, Locke employs five traditional terms familiar and well understood in his time, and even today – physics, ethics, words, ideas, logic. But each of these traditional words is made to play also an unfamiliar, synecdochic role which completely passed over the heads of his readership and his commentators,

---

18 "Some Consequence of Four Incapacities", 1868: CP 5.316.

down to the end of modern times. His proposal was brilliant, a stroke of genius; his
expression of the proposal, unfortunately, was so compressed and indirect that there
is plenty of reason to wonder if he himself had anything like a full grasp of its main
implications. Almost certainly not, for otherwise his persistence along the way of
ideas in all five of the editions he personally prepared for publication would be beyond
explanation. No clearer example of the postmodern point that a text never reduces
simply to its "author's intention" could be given than this text which, from within
the heart of modernity, sketches the postmodern project with an all-too-free hand.

To grasp the thrust of what is original in Locke's proposal, then, notice that he
begins, in effect, with Aristotle's distinction[19] between, on the one hand, knowledge
we acquire of objects having as part of their objectivity an existence that obtains
independently of, and extending outside of, our thinking ("speculative" thought);
and, on the other hand, knowledge of objects that precisely come into being as
a result of human thought and action and would not exist as such apart from the
context of human interaction ("practical" thought).

"Physics" and "Ethics" as Synecdoches

Drawing on classical terminology, then, Locke uses for the first division of his
proposal "Physics" as a synecdoche for the knowledge of mind-independent being,
or speculative thought, and "Ethics" as a synecdoche for the knowledge of mind-
dependent being, or practical thought. "Logic", which in Aristotle (as seen through
Latin eyes), remember,[20] was a study of mind-dependent being not as such but as
ordered to the study of mind-independent being, and in the Stoics was simply a
formal or speculative science in its own right,[21] Locke now uses in a synecdochic
way to name study of the means whereby *all* knowledge – *whether* speculative *or*
practical – is acquired, developed, and communicated. Thus, in each part of his
threefold division of knowledge – Physics, Ethics, Logic – Locke assigns a name
to the whole which is also the name for a specific part or subdivision within that
whole.

In each of the three cases, besides the synecdochal name, he gives an alternative
name for *the whole* area of knowledge (or "science") identified: "practica" in the
case of ethics, "natural philosophy" in the case of physics, "semiotics" in the case
of logic. There are critical details of this terminology that bear noting.

In the first case, "natural philosophy" as a synonym for physics in the synecdochal
sense of speculative knowledge *tout court* was itself already established by earlier
tradition as a synecdoche for speculative knowledge. This point was expressly made
by Aquinas[22] as a gloss on the Stoic use of the term "philosophia naturalis". The

---

19 Cf. the *Metaphysics* (c.348–7dBC) II, ch. 1, 993b19–23; and esp. the *Nicomachean Ethics* (c.335–4BC)
VI, chs. 3 8, 1139b14 1142a31.
20 See chapter 3, "The Instrument of All the Sciences", p. 87f.; and chapter 7, "Nonbeing in Latin
Philosophy", p. 350ff.
21 See "The Stoic Organization of Life and Knowledge" in chapter 4, p. 97f.
22 *Commentary on the Ten Books of Aristotle's Nicomachean Ethics* (c.1269) I, lect. 1, n. 2. Taking the
fourfold Stoic division of the sciences as his vehicle, Aquinas makes the following remarks: "Since

Stoic use, thus, appears to us in retrospect as anticipatory of Locke's usage in this particular. For our purposes, then, this second, embedded synecdoche says nothing new, but must be regarded rather as an already established and traditional usage. It has no bearing on what is novel in Locke's proposal for semiotics.

In the second case, "practica" as a synonym for ethics in the synecdochal sense of practical knowledge *tout court* was a usage new with Locke, but it was hardly a usage which clarified anything. On the contrary, it was more likely to create confusion – just the kind of confusion we encounter in late-modern times where the term "ethics" is taken to apply almost exclusively to individual behavior, quite missing the larger point of ethics which extends to business and politics, and where the idea of "art" quite disappears from the realm of manufacture, industry, and even, to some extent, architecture.[23]

Thus, in the case of the first two parts of Locke's scheme, each of the terms pertaining to the division of knowledge into physics and ethics, in whatever sense the term is taken, turns out either to be a traditional expression to which Locke adds no distinctively different sense, or a novel use of a traditional expression indeed, but one which clarifies nothing and confuses a great deal.

"Logic" as a Synecdoche

In the third case, however, the case of thus so-called "Logic", Locke is neither merely repeating a traditionally established distinction nor confusing something that was clearer in the traditional usage. In this case, when he gives an alternative name for the whole besides the formerly traditional but now synecdochical one of "logic", Locke is both saying something new and shedding a startlingly new light.

"Logic", he says, which *properly* names the study of conceptual relations among linguistic signs and only *synecdochically* names the study of sign relations in their totality (as including linguistic signs), may better be called SEMIOTICS in its total sense as the doctrine of signs. Logic in its full extent is not just alternatively but *better* so called.

The Explicit Initial Sketch

This may be represented in a schema, exhibiting both the generic or synecdochic sense of "logic", and "logic" in its specific sense as a part of semiotic. This schema, thus, embodies what may be called Locke's "initial sketch" for the doctrine of signs:

---

the human mind develops through disciplined exercise, there are as many kinds of knowledge as there are respects in which reason can be methodically employed. The first respect in which reason can be methodically and systematically employed concerns the *universe of nature* [ad philosophiam naturalem pertinet], to which pertains all deliberation about the order which the mind discerns as obtaining or able to obtain in things independently of the activity of our thinking. 'Nature' here must be understood in such a way as to include whatever there is of being [ita quod sub naturali philosophia comprehendamus et mathematicam et metaphysicam]."

23 See, in chapter 3, "Subdivisions of Speculative and Practical Thinking" and the place of art in human life, p. 85.

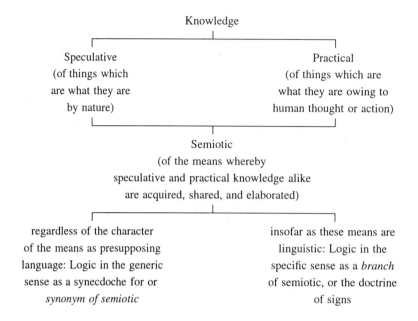

Knowledge

Speculative
(of things which
are what they are
by nature)

Practical
(of things which are
what they are owing to
human thought or action)

Semiotic
(of the means whereby
speculative and practical knowledge alike
are acquired, shared, and elaborated)

regardless of the character
of the means as presupposing
language: Logic in the generic
sense as a synecdoche for or
synonym of semiotic

insofar as these means are
linguistic: Logic in the
specific sense as a *branch*
of semiotic, or the doctrine
of signs

Locke's "Initial Sketch" for the Doctrine of Signs

Just as the realm of what exists independently of our thought and action is considerably wider than what we learn from physics as a specific science, and just as the realm of what comes about as a result of what we do and make is considerably broader than what we learn from ethics, so the study of the means whereby knowledge develops is considerably broader than the study of the species-specifically human logical forms within language.

We see, then, quite clearly, that in Locke's seminal scheme for semiotics (the part of the division that is new in his "division of knowledge"), the doctrine of signs taken as a whole not only occupies the instrumentalist place Aristotle conceived for logic as an analysis for the strictly intellectual dimension of species-specifically human discourse and the medieval Latins conceived for logic as a liberal art, but it also warrants on the same footing the Stoic idea that logic as the doctrine of signs is a "science" in its own right (as a whole and a-fortiori in logic in the traditional sense which now appears as a part within that whole) .

The Root of the Ancient Dispute in Logic as Unresolved Previously
What is, however, unique about the situation thus conceived is that this reconciliation of the formerly opposed views is achieved because the new division under which logic is now subsumed makes of it no longer, as the Stoics conceived, a speculative science *in contrast with* practical knowledge, which is what the Peripatetics objected to from the start. In the new scheme, logic appears rather *among* that whole panoply of studies concerned with the sign in its proper functioning as constitutive *equally*

of speculative and practical knowledge – which is to say, constitutive of human experience as a whole.

It turns out that the root of the dispute between the Peripatetics in following Aristotle and the Stoics in following Zeno of Citium and Chrysippus of Soli lay in the fact that neither school had any conception of the one doctrinal context in which the controversy could be resolved, namely, the context of a doctrine of signs – in no small part because neither school had a sufficient conception of sign to begin with.

The ancient dispute continued in the intellectual circles of medieval Arab civilization for exactly the same reason. In an effort to bring the controversy to clearer terms, the Arabs had introduced some new distinctions into the debate: to accommodate the instrumentalist view of logic as *organon*, they distinguished "logic as an art" (*logica utens*, or "applied logic") from "logic as a science" (*logica docens*, or the exposition of the principles themselves of logic) to accommodate the Stoic view. But this distinction, far from resolving or even really clarifying the dispute, simply begged the question over which the dispute first arose. As with the related distinction between "material logic" (*logica materialis*, or logic as concerned with proofs within a specific subject matter) and "formal logic" (*logica formalis*, or logic as concerned with the pattern of valid inference which alone makes any proof a proof regardless of subject matter), which the Latins had drawn on the basis of the difference between Aristotle's *Posterior* and *Prior Analytics*, the continuance of the discussion generated more heat than light.

In both the case of the Stoics versus the Peripatetics and the case of the Arab distinction between logic as a science (*logica docens*) and logic as an art (*logica utens*), the basic dispute went unresolved for exactly the same reason: the want of an adequate and explicit doctrinal context in which the sense of the proposed distinctions could find a clear ground of theoretical justification. What was wanting, in short, was a doctrine of signs. For even though, after Augustine, the Latins were the first to be in a position to envision the possibility of a doctrine of signs, they did not successfully bring that possibility to the ground of explicit achievement, as we saw in chapter 9, until a variety of cultural and political circumstances had made it too late to benefit the moderns. And even the author who finally did succeed in bringing the notion to ground never himself envisioned what he had achieved as the breakthrough it in fact was respecting the understanding of the traditional proposals for the right distribution of human knowledge. Precisely this breakthrough is what is envisioned in the text of Locke's concluding proposal.

"Words" and "Ideas" as Synecdoches

But now look what happens within this schema when we add the traditional terms "word" and "idea" to our list of synecdoches. Within this realm wherein knowledge of whatever type develops through signs, the terms "word" and "idea" take on a startlingly expansive sense – even though it is an open question to what extent Locke was aware of the full expansion.

In the ordinary and obvious sense, words mean words, the specifically human sub-units of linguistic communication orally and graphically articulable. Similarly, ideas mean what words stand for in linguistic exchanges among human beings, in the ordinary and obvious sense that Locke invokes when he says that "since the things the mind contemplates are none of them, besides itself, present to the understanding, 'tis necessary that something else, as a sign or representation of the thing it considers should be present to it".

These ordinary and obvious senses, however, are not the newly acquired semiotic sense of the terms in question. Chosen on the basis of their traditional sense in view of a new proposal, the further semiotic sense accrues to the key terms from their play within the proposal. That is to say, the terms in question take on their semiotic sense by becoming, in context, each in their own turn synecdoches.

In the case of "words", the sense of the term is expanded to represent that whole panoply of gestures, marks, and movements whereby one organism signals another or provides signals (wittingly or unwittingly) to another which manifest the interior states of the one signaling. *In the case of "ideas"*, the sense of the term is expanded to represent that whole panoply of interior or psychological states thanks to which one organism has "something to say" to another (again, wittingly or unwittingly) – its mood, "state of mind", attitudes, or intentions. Ideas and words taken semiotically become markers for the more general distinction between "inner" and "outer" as it applies especially to the cognitive activity of organisms. "If I see someone writhing in pain with evident cause I do not think: all the same, his feelings are hidden from me."[24]

So it becomes plain that "words" and "ideas" as semiotic is concerned with them (as belonging to the doctrine of signs) go well beyond the boundaries of the ordinary and obvious sense that readers of the *Essay* casually and customarily have attached to these expressions.

We have already noted that the semiotic sense of words and ideas is not only larger than, but actually at odds with, the specifically philosophical understanding of the terms Locke has developed in the main body of his *Essay*, because the main body of the essay travels the way of ideas in precisely the sense that the last Latins had been able to show as contradictory with and hence exclusive of the way of signs.

But what is to be immediately noted here is that the "semiotics" of which logic forms a part has to interpret much more than merely intellectual discourse. Semiotics has to make sense of experience as a whole, in all of its parts, and, ideally, in all of its biological manifestations. It has to deal with all those inner states on the basis of which the living, feeling, knowing being orients itself within the physical environment and interacts within and across species lines. And it has to deal with all those outer manifestations on the basis of which inner states are interpreted and

---

24 Wittgenstein c.1931–50: II, 223, if we may cite a remark by one who professed horror of theory in a context which gives the remark theoretical justification.

clues are taken as to the nature and activity generally of a living being as a part of the physical world.

Expanding upon Locke's Initial Sketch

Using terminology that has developed only in most recent times, we may spell out from Locke's initial sketch what we may call his larger *implied* sketch:

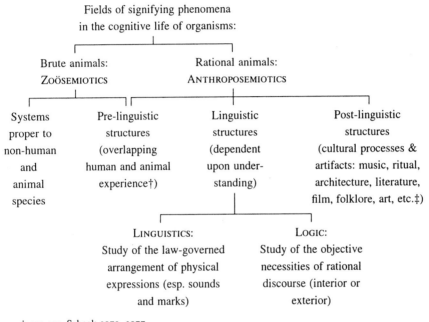

† see esp. Sebeok 1972, 1977

‡ terminology from Morris 1946: 49; Deely 1982: 199, 107–23 passim

Locke's Implied Sketch for the Doctrine of Signs Explicitated in the Terminology of Semiotics

From Semiotics as Knowledge of Signs to Semiosis as Action of Signs

If, however, now returning to the initial sketch of Locke's text, we take but one baby-step beyond Locke, we are in a position to contrast his *semiotics*, as a form of knowledge, to *the action of signs*, from the study of which action that knowledge specifically derives. For this we need a shorthand expression for the action of signs, and fortunately one has been provided us by Charles Sanders Peirce. He calls the action proper to signs, the action which follows upon the being proper to signs, "semiosis".[25] This term clearly derives from the ancient Greek name for natural

---

25 Sometimes also "semeiosy".

signs, *semeia*, but Peirce derived it more specifically from his reading of one of the Stoic fragments that has survived from the first century BC.[26] Semiosis and semiotics, thus, stand in the following relation:

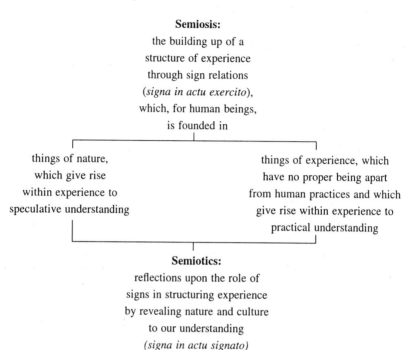

Semiosis:
the building up of a
structure of experience
through sign relations
(*signa in actu exercito*),
which, for human beings,
is founded in

things of nature,   things of experience, which
which give rise   have no proper being apart
within experience to   from human practices and which
speculative understanding   give rise within experience to
                                           practical understanding

Semiotics:
reflections upon the role of
signs in structuring experience
by revealing nature and culture
to our understanding
(*signa in actu signato*)

Semiosis and Semiotics Distinguished

Seeing how little further effort of thought is required to make explicit the scope of the vistas implicit in Locke's original proposal, we may consider it a pity that Locke himself did not develop his own proposal. That the principal modern authors did not see fit to develop the proposal themselves is perhaps even more a pity. No doubt the history of classical modern philosophy, the period from Descartes to Kant at least, and perhaps even with Hegel, would have been strikingly different in all that concerns what we now call epistemology had the semiotic turn suggested by Locke been taken by any influential philosopher prior to Peirce.

Be that as it may, despite the fact that Locke himself undertakes no full exposition of his synecdoches nor makes any particular adversion to their purport, as neither do his modern colleagues, we see now plainly that the "semiotics" of which logic forms a part has to interpret much more than the merely intellectual discourse to which the traditional conception of logic confines itself. Semiotics has to make sense

---

26 Philodemus i.54/40BC. See Fisch 1978: 40–1, for discussion of Peirce's derivation and coinage.

of experience as a whole, in all of its parts. In this comprehensive enterprise logic remains not just one subject-area among others but becomes also an indispensable tool for the organization (not of the whole itself, but) of the *knowledge within or about* the whole as rationally circumscribed.

The Semiotic Web

This whole of experience, which incorporates in principle the whole of nature as well – not "in itself" or insofar as it is prospectively knowable, indeed, but insofar as it is actually given for interpretation to any specified individual in any specified context of space and time – has never been better characterized than in Jakob von Uexküll's metaphor for experience as "a firm web which carries [the subject's] existence".[27] This metaphor has been deftly captured and fixed forever in the semiotic universe of today by T. A. Sebeok's expression of it as "the semiotic web".

This "semiotic web" of which Sebeok speaks is thus semiosic (or constructed by the action of signs) throughout. Every strand in the web – every relationship – is a product of the action of signs. But the web is hardly logical throughout. It is logical only in that small part of the web spun by language in the species-specifically human sense, and logic in the foundational sense – logic as an intellectual analysis of discourse – belongs to that small part as a subdivision thereof. The extension of logic to all other parts of the web was originally by way of synecdoche, indeed; but it was also through the extension of discourse whereby the understanding touches other parts of the web, and later also by way of a metaphor "unscientifically employed in two distinct senses"[28] – but now at great risk of confusion. This is a confusion into which Peirce himself, our lodestar in these matters, may well have fallen.

For semiotics names an area of investigation and knowledge much broader than logic names, if we are to speak properly and in a scientific sense. The broad-ranging contemporary development – as seen early, for example, in the mind-boggling description Sebeok gave in 1975,[29] which would already have to be much expanded upon – draws emphatic attention to what is unique about Locke's proposed division

---

27 Jakob von Uexküll 1934: 14.
28 As Peirce put it, c.1896: 1.444.
29 Sebeok 1975: 150: "This province of knowledge, variously cultivated in Antiquity, thoughtfully reexamined in the Middle Ages, scrutinized afresh during the Renaissance, elaborated into something like its contemporary forms under the impetus of the model of Saussure (1857–1913) and, above all, that of Peirce (1839–1914), begins to spread like wildfire, penetrating national borders and, at the same time, invading, like an infection, a range of human endeavor from anthropology (Clerk 1975) to more respectable culinary practices (Barthes 1964: 27f.), or from geomancy (Jaulin 1970) and fortune telling by tarot (Corti 1973) to abstract ideology (e.g., Veron 1971; Rastier 1972; Veltsos 1975), many of the crafts, such as those of the comic strip (Fresnault-Deruelle 1975) and the animated cartoon (Horanyi and Pleh 1975), all of the arts, a host of traditional academic disciplines, and not only a wide array of the nomothetic sciences of man (in the usage of Windelband [1894] and [Aldous] Huxley [1963: 7f.]) but, though to a lesser extent so far, certain natural sciences (notably ethology and genetics) as well."

of the sciences as including logic, when contrasted with the earlier proposals of Aristotle and the Stoics or with the divisions developed in the Arab world and Latin period.

A Distinction Which Unites

The uniqueness of Locke's proposal, what is usefully novel about it, consists in the fact that, whereas the earlier divisions separated logic in one way or another from the other branches of knowledge, Locke proposes in contrast *a distinction which unites*. Logic as semiotic – that is to say, as *a* semiotic,[30] a part within semiotics – is not just one among other, separated sciences or "bodies of knowledge". On the contrary, it is a discipline which affects all knowledge expressible in language, and explores the dimension common to all such forms of knowledge precisely as their objects enter into and form the substance of human experience through the ever growing and shifting network of sign relations in which experience consists and which language translates into discursive expression.

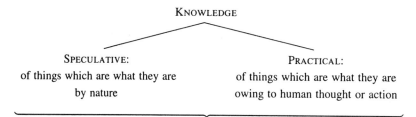

KNOWLEDGE

SPECULATIVE:
of things which are what they are
by nature

PRACTICAL:
of things which are what they are
owing to human thought or action

SEMIOTIC:
of the *means* whereby knowledge,
whether speculative or practical,
is acquired, elaborated, and shared

"A Distinction Which Unites"

---

30 E.g., B. Williams 1981: 309–10: "In speaking of a 'semiotic' beyond feminism, I am using a word in a way which, although common, has to my knowledge never been defined. It is a third-level spin-off of the original usage traceable to Locke. In his *Essay* of 1690, 'semiotic' means quite precisely the foundational doctrine of signs as these underlie and structure the whole of our experience and consciousness. Derivative from this usage but in contrast to it is the contemporary use of 'semiotics' as an umbrella term for that whole range of specialized and interdisciplinary inquiries which have stemmed from the inspiration of seeing things anew in the perspective of a doctrine of signs.

"In the interplay between these two terms, 'semiotic' and 'semiotics', a third term has arisen, a new use of 'semiotic' as a label for a given specialized study within the field of semiotics (such as the architectural semiotic of the Gothic cathedral). It is in this sense that feminist thought – like any other symbolic structure when viewed on its own and precisely in terms of its signifying – also constitutes a semiotic, not in the foundational sense, but in a sense which is aware of its foundations in knowledge and experience precisely as they are works of interpretation through signs."

This purview indeed was always the point in the study of logic in the classical Latin and modern developments of the tradition of liberal arts education.[31] Transdisciplinary by nature, a "liberal" education was always aimed to be an education which cultivated the powers and development of the mind for the sake of engendering sensitivity to the humane values of civilization, an education which cultivated proper appreciation of the human mind not just as a tool in the service of business and "earning a living", but as an end in itself in the search for truth (truth having its formal existence only in thought), and as the essential seat of the distinctively human in all of us. The mind finds its nobility in understanding and creating – in a word, by transcending the determination of what preceded its presence in the physical universe. Logic, whether one finds the subject "interesting" or not, provides the skeleton or structure of that understanding, and needs to be controlled – that is, artistically developed in use – in order to maximize the potential of reasoning, just as the athlete needs to train and discipline the body in order to achieve the best performances possible for the human frame.

Thus, logic in its most proper and fundamental conception is a *pars semeiotica*, a part of the doctrine of signs, that part, specifically, which is concerned with the use of language so far as it expresses the necessary relationships characteristic of rationality and of "being as thought". As a part of semiotic, logical analysis participates directly in the nature of the whole, which is to be inherently interdisciplinary, inasmuch as semiotics as such is concerned with the dimension common to every possible form of knowledge, namely, its sign character or structure.

That is how logic appears once the dispute between the Stoics and the Aristotelians, unresolved for over twenty-one centuries, received its casual and unwitting resolution in Locke's neglected text sent forth in the morning light of modern times. It is fitting, I think, most fitting, to be able to end our consideration of modern times with a text from the period which achieves just what modern philosophy in the mainstream mainly failed to achieve. For Locke's initial sketch for the place of the doctrine of signs within the organization of human knowledge not only makes a contribution to the effective resolution of one of the controversies from the earliest centuries of philosophic understanding. That sketch is also, at the same time, an indicator of the future of philosophic understanding as it expands itself once more, just as the ancients thought it should and Kant tried mightily to deny it could, to the whole universe of being, at once noumenal and phenomenal, but now newly understood as "perfused with signs".

---

31 See chapter 5, "The Origin of the Liberal Arts", p. 183.

PART FOUR

Postmodern Times

The Way of Signs

Charles Sanders Peirce (1839–1914)
Near the end of his 52nd year; photogravure from *Sun and Shade* of August 1892, vol. 4, no. 12, here reproduced on the basis of a photograph from the archives of the Peirce Edition Project housed at Indiana University–Purdue University, Indianapolis

CHAPTER FIFTEEN

Charles Sanders Peirce and the Recovery of *Signum*

There is a group of authors, mostly French at the core, with a surrounding cadre of literary types, who fancy themselves "postmodern", the inventors of the term, and proprietors of its copyright.[1] They tell us that postmodernism has done away with linear time and linear argument, and shows at the heart of every text a void. The argument of these authors comes down to a single insight, which, being thorough heirs of modernity, they hardly know how to express. If we were to loan them a term from the discussions of their Latin forebears, they might see that their founding insight comes down to a simple discovery which can seem revolutionary only in the context and against the immediate background of modern philosophy. The discovery might be put thus: not all signs are instrumental.

All the hoopla and pretensions surrounding literary postmodernism can be re-duced to a single statement in the writings of their principal high-priest: "the signified concept is never present in and of itself, in a sufficient presence that would refer only to itself".[2] We will leave to the next chapter the story of how these inheritors of modernity's idealism have tried to have it both ways: to revive the sign and yet leave epistemological matters to stand as they were when Kant left them; to revive the sign and yet maintain the illusion of Descartes that history counts for nothing and can be safely ignored.

The Last of the Moderns ...

Charles Sanders Peirce (1839–1914) was the man who fully introduced into the great conversation of philosophy the unconsidered assumption which had made the

---

1 A list is easy to draw, at least representatively, if not exhaustively (and without distinguishing "genuines" from "would-bes"): Jacques Lacan (1901–81), Maurice Blanchot (1907–), Jean François Lyotard (1924–), Gilles Deleuze (1925–95), Michel Foucault (1926–84), Jean Baudrillard (1929–), Pierre-Félix Guattari (1930–92); but there are such Eastern European precursors as György Lukács (1885–1971) and Mikhail Bakhtin (1895–1975); and even American offshoots or epigones such as Richard Rorty (1931–) and Fredric Jameson (1934–).

2 Jacques Derrida, "Différance", in *The Margins of Philosophy* (1982), 10.

way of ideas seem viable to the moderns, the assumption, to wit, that the direct objects of experience are wholly produced by the mind itself. In philosophy, he was raised on *The Critique of Pure Reason*. He claimed to know it by heart. When he said "No!" to Kant, it meant something.

Now why did he say no?

As a young teenager, Peirce read in his brother's room Whateley's *Elements of Logic*, a work which, between 1826 and 1857, went through nine editions. But it is not likely, and for sure we have no record, that another student was as inspired by Whateley as was Peirce. From those early days, he later told his correspondent friend Lady Welby, his whole life became one long meditation on the nature and action of signs, one long investigation of the question first left hanging in the air by Augustine.

And what a life. It was a tragedy, by any measure. It need not have been, but so it turned out. The first culprit was his father, but after that it was Peirce himself, with a few extra villains thrown in along the way. Notable in the cast was Simon Newcomb (1835–1909), whose reputation as a man of integrity is not likely to survive the coming to light of the details of the last years of Peirce's life.

Peirce's father taught him to indulge his genius and society be damned. But one would have expected Peirce at some point after fifty, if not sooner, to have unlearned so evil a lesson. He did not. But of all this and more you can read about to form your own impressions, thanks to the work of Joseph Brent, whose own career was almost wrecked by his work as a graduate student to write Peirce's biography. This biography[3] finally came to publication thanks to Thomas Sebeok, who tracked Brent down in his later years, and thanks to John Gallman who, as Director of the Indiana University Press, overcame the decades-long effort by Harvard University to prevent the Peirce biography from seeing the light of day. It is a sordid tale all around on the existential side, but on the side of thought and philosophy it becomes nonetheless a glorious one.

Here we will consider only the glorious side.

From the first, Peirce was a reader. He read everything, or tried to, particularly in the area of logic which, he tells us,[4] "in its general sense, is, as I believe I have shown, only another name for semiotic, the quasi-necessary, or formal, doctrine of signs". Probably, almost certainly, we have been repeatedly told, he took this notion and term from the end of Locke's 1690 *Essay*. Nearly everyone is content with the assurances; but when the matter is put under a microscope, it proves impossible to tell for sure. There emerge from the nineteenth-century mists of Peirce's childhood a debris of names and works from authors in England and America and Europe[5]

---

3 Joseph L. Brent, *Charles Sanders Peirce. A Life* (1993). With Brent's work the dam is broken, and we may expect a flood of works to follow in coming decades. The first of Ketner's three volumes of projected biography – or, as he bemusingly proposes, "autobiography" (Ketner 1998) – is promising harbinger of more, much more, to come.

4 Peirce c.1897a. A fragment on semiotics, partially printed in CP 2.227.

5 Thomas A. Sebeok has a beginning of the story in his *Semiotics in the United States* (Sebeok 1991). Yet more clues can be found in Zellweger 1990 and 1990a. In my own researches, embodied in a

from authors who were poking around in the semiotic wasteland which so many years on the way of ideas had created for the late moderns.

And Peirce violated the cardinal commandment of modernity: Thou shalt not learn from the Latins. He read even there, and what he found, more than any single influence, revolutionized his philosophy. From Scotus in particular, but also from Fonseca and the Conimbricenses,[6] he picked up the trail of the sign. He was never able to follow it as far as the text of Poinsot. This would have been only a question of time, no doubt; but in 1914 Peirce's time ran out.

Nonetheless, what he picked up from the later Latins was more than enough to convince him that the way of signs, however buried in the underbrush it had become since the moderns made the mistake of going the way of ideas instead, was the road to the future. And in this future Dr Jekyll and Mr Hyde might be cured of their schizophrenia, able together to live at last in a world where one could be a scientist whose self-image would be that of a student of nature without accusation of naïveté and, at the same time, that of a philosopher without having to sneer in private at the folly of naturalists and common sense in thinking that the mind could reach beyond itself and pull in from the depths something of nature herself in her mind-independent insouciance toward the practical world of human affairs. In other words, it was Peirce's suspicion that the Lebenswelt – into which culture (by the cumulative transmission of learning) had transformed the Umwelt of the linguistic animal – was yet not closed off from contact with and prospective knowledge about the mind-independent realities of the physical environment on which the linguistic animal, like any other, depends. The realm of what exists "in itself" and the realm of what exists "phenomenally" or "in appearances", he considered, are laced together in fact, in experience, and in cognition as such[7] by the action of signs in such a way

---

yet-unfinalized manuscript of some 52 pages under the title of "Why Semiotics?", developed over four days in the Library Congress in June of 1995, I have found the matter inconclusive. It may even be that Peirce took the term "semeiotic" from p. 22 of a book by Augustus Rauch, *Psychology, or a View of the Human Soul, including Anthropology* (1840), still to be found in the Harvard library, published coincidentally in the first year of Peirce's life (as Poinsot's *Treatise* was published in Locke's birth-year).

6 See chapter 9 above.

7 Peirce seems never to have realized the fact that the Latins had established a radical alternative to the treatment of sense qualities that modern philosophy adopted, as we saw in chapter 12 above. But he did clearly realize the necessity of finding a way to hold that a secondary quality "is just what it seems to be", as he put it (1907: EP 2.421) precisely in order to avoid blocking the way to holding that the primary qualities actually reveal to us something of the condition of nature as it is in itself. This problem, he thus tells us, was the inspiration to his drawing up of the "New List" of categories, so we may indeed consider it a "happy fault" that he did not think of the Latin alternative, in view of the result achieved. Yet Peirce's reasoning in this matter provides us both with an independent verification of the superiority of the Latin over the modern approach and with a reason for thinking that indeed Aquinas and those who followed him on the point were right in seeing proper sensibles as revelative in cognition of physical relations in nature, by virtue of the fact that, for example, in modern astrophysics, analysis of the spectrum of colors has proved indispensable to the determination of the physical composition of astronomical objects, which could not be the case if secondary qualities were

that we can come to distinguish and know the one as part of and through the other by the critical control of objectivity that is the heart of science and philosophy alike beyond their differences of orientation.

Fortunately, in setting off down his way of signs, Peirce did not have to reinvent the wheel. Drawing to a large extent on the same sources from which Poinsot had drawn, and being a man of scientific intelligence such as he had come to acknowledge the great scholastics also to have been – of which more anon – he quickly reached the substantially same conclusions that Poinsot had reached: that the sign consists not in a type of sensible thing but in a pure relation, irreducibly triadic, indifferent to the physical status of its object and to the source of its immediate provenance, nature or mind. Since all thought is in signs, and all signs are relations, the same bone which was related in nature to a dinosaur could come to be understood in thought as related to a dinosaur. The fact was inscribed in the being of the bone; thought had only to realize it.

He almost got a job at Johns Hopkins University as a tenured professor. Newcomb, playing on the Victorian conventions of the time, managed to turn that situation from victory to defeat. But in the five years he did have at Hopkins, Peirce had had in his class as a student John Dewey (1859–1952), as close to a household word as you can get in philosophy. And he had another friend of longer standing, every bit as celebrated as Dewey in the annals of American philosophy, William James (1842–1910), one of the heroes of the Peirce biography. Had it not been for James, and for Josiah Royce (1855–1916) as well, instead of pondering the way of signs today, we might all still be walking the way of ideas.

... and First of the Postmoderns

From Peirce, James and Dewey had picked up a new idea, "pragmatism". It seems to date back to the autumn of 1874, and the gatherings of the group called "The Metaphysical Club", meeting, Peirce tells us,[8] "sometimes in my study, sometimes in that of William James". The group was a minor "who's who" of the period, and, lest you entertain the illusion that our little historical survey of philosophy has been overly complete, I should mention that, in the particular of the idea for pragmatism, an especially influential source for the conception Peirce originally proposed was the Scottish philosopher Alexander Bain (1818–1903), with his definition of belief as "that upon which a man is prepared to act." It was Nicholas St John Green, a disciple of Jeremy Bentham (1748–1832), who, according to Peirce,[9] liked to push

---

as the modern empiricists had held them to be. Thus, progress in physical science even since Peirce's day shows that it is no longer possible to suppose, as Peirce's scheme of the semiotic categories allows (but, note, does not require) us to suppose, that (1907: EP 2.422) "the feelings of blue and red" could "be interchanged, without considerable (in fact, without enormous) disturbance of the general condition of nature, as well as a revolution in chemical physics, and other physical theories."

8 Peirce c.1906: CP 5.12.
9 Ibid.: CP 5.11.

this definition. In Peirce's view, Bain thus becomes the grandfather of pragmatism, for "from this definition, pragmatism is scarce more than a corollary."

In any event, Peirce tells us that from the discussions of this little group he drew up the first paper under the name pragmatism. In his view the basic idea had a long lineage, which he traced, or thought to trace, in every significant thinker, on the ground that "Any philosophical doctrine that should be completely new could hardly fail to prove completely false", which is assuredly so. "The rivulets at the head of the river of pragmatism", in Peirce's view,[10] "are easily traced back to almost any desired antiquity".

But that was not the way James and Dewey saw the matter, and they were the ones to put the new label into effective circulation. They were the ones who made it famous. After them the term came to be considered quintessentially American, expressive of all that "Can do!" spirit and down-to-earth thinking on which we like to pride ourselves. Americans are "pragmatists". They invented pragmatism, by showing that meaning consists in action, in doing.

But Peirce himself looked with a certain horror on what "pragmatism" became along this line, even if it happened at the hands of his dear friend William James and his old student John Dewey. For James and Dewey, however, pragmatism was a way to continue the modern dismissive attitude toward the past, and particularly toward Latin scholasticism. We have already had occasion to note this with regard to Dewey in particular.[11] But we have also noted that this was a general attitude of modernity at least since Descartes, whose whole approach to philosophizing made indifference to historical knowledge a matter of principle.

For Peirce, the matter was quite otherwise, and became the moreso as the years went by, as he became more and more clear about the centrality of a doctrine of signs for the future of philosophy. By 1905,[12] however, "after awaiting in vain, for a good many years, some particularly opportune conjuncture of circumstances that might serve to recommend his notions of the ethics of terminology," Peirce had had enough.

An ethics of terminology? What? An extraordinary notion. Not only did Peirce wait in vain for his contemporaries to take the point up, the point itself still waits in vain. Well, then, we shall take it up here. But not yet. Let us leave it to the end of the chapter, although we will note all along the way points where its rules would apply, to pique the reader's interest in this heretofore neglected topic. Should the reader find this method too frustrating, skip ahead to the final section of the chapter, where the ethical rules proposed by Peirce are stated in full.

Under the plan of making our chapter's end be the "particularly opportune conjuncture of circumstances that might serve to recommend his notions of the ethics of terminology," we will for the present stick to Peirce's own course of 1905,

10 Ibid.
11 See "John Dewey and the Influence of Darwinism on Philosophy" in chapter 11, p. 507.
12 See "What Pragmatism Is", *The Monist* 15 (April 1905), 161–81, as repr. in CP 5.411–37.

which was to drag the rules in, as he put it,[13] "over head and shoulders, on an occasion when he has no specific proposal to offer nor any feeling but satisfaction at the course usage has run without any canons or resolutions of a congress."

Taking *The Monist* for 1905 as his platform, and the proposition "What pragmatism is" as his lead, Peirce began the task of separating his views from those several contemporaries who, beginning with James, had commandeered in the public consciousness the banner of "Pragmatism". The body of that article, which the American philosophers united in refusing to hear, constituted a ringing statement to the effect that what pragmatism is, is not pragmaticism.

With the explicit treatment of the ethics of terminology reserved to the end of the chapter, then, our immediate task is to show the distance Peirce wishes to put between himself and what the usage of the term "pragmatism" came to signify.

Pragmaticism Is Not Pragmatism

The greatest American philosopher disowning the most famous American development in all of philosophy's history is a considerable embarrassment to those who cherish the idea of a home-grown philosophy, and prefer being able to cite their own to the constant deferral of philosophical greatness to the European past of the "colonies". So it is understandable that those desirous of promoting philosophy with a distinctively American accent have largely been discomfited or annoyed by Peirce's disavowal of "pragmatism", and have tried to pass it off as merely a verbal quibble, merely a far from isolated manifestation of the cantankerous primadonnaness of a notably eccentric individual. Even Corrington, who in writing the first *Introduction to C. S. Peirce*[14] with an explicitly semiotic consciousness should well know better (but who is also a devotee of "the American tradition in philosophy"), introduces this aspect of Peirce's own thought under the label Peirce repudiated.

Embarrassment or no, the fact remains that Peirce is the first figure in the history of American thought who enters into the grand history of philosophy as a whole on the merits of his speculative genius as embodied in the surviving texts we have from his pen. James and Dewey, by far the better known in popular consciousness, are by comparison on a second tier, and their main claim to a place in general histories of philosophy is that they have filled for a popular consciousness the previously empty niche of "American philosophers". But it is pragmaticism, not pragmatism, that properly fills that niche, and in the story of pragmaticism "pragmatism" is but a footnote.

Surveying the scene in 1905, Peirce considered that things had gone far enough:[15]

> ... at present, the word begins to be met with occasionally in the literary journals, where it gets abused in the merciless way that words have to expect when they fall into literary clutches. ... So then, the writer, finding his bantling "pragmatism" so

---

13 Peirce 1905: CP 5.414.
14 Corrington 1993.
15 Peirce 1905: CP 5.414–15.

promoted, feels that it is time to kiss his child good-by and relinquish it to its higher destiny; while to serve the precise purpose of expressing the original definition, he begs to announce the birth of the word "pragmaticism", which is ugly enough to be safe from kidnappers.

Much as the writer has gained from the perusal of what other pragmatists have written, he still thinks there is a decisive advantage in his original conception of the doctrine. From this original form every truth that follows from any of the other forms can be deduced, while some errors can be avoided into which other pragmatists have fallen. ...

In all the variants of pragmatism, practical, experimental effects are made the determination of truth. Three things distinguish pragmaticism from such a simple, positivistic doctrine, which is compatible with nominalism:[16] "first, its retention of a purified philosophy; secondly, its full acceptance of the main body of our instinctive beliefs; and thirdly, its strenuous insistence upon the truth of scholastic realism (or a close approximation to that)".

Pragmaticism and Metaphysics

Pragmatism prided itself on the demolition of "metaphysics". But what it understood by "metaphysics" had little or no connection to the "metaphysics" of Aristotle,[17] still less to that of the schoolmen of the Latin Age.[18] How could it? As Dewey inadvertently demonstrated in his famous essay on "The Influence of Darwinism on Philosophy",[19] these pragmatists knew nothing of metaphysics save what they had learned from the modern philosophers, and especially the British empiricists, where there is not that much of metaphysics to be learned. In the confines of the Metaphysical Club, Peirce tells us,[20] "the type of our thought was decidedly British. I, alone of our number, had come upon the threshing-floor of philosophy through the doorway of Kant, and even my ideas were acquiring the English accent." And for this modern metaphysics Peirce had no more use than his club fellows.

But Peirce, unlike his pragmatist colleagues, came well to learn that there was more to metaphysics than this. Let the pragmatists "wipe out metaphysics" in the sense of those "philosophers of very diverse stripes who propose that philosophy shall take its start from one or another state of mind in which no man, least of all a beginner in philosophy, actually is", such as we have seen espoused especially by Descartes, Berkeley, and Hume.[21]

---

16 Peirce 1905: CP 5.423.
17 Chapter 3, "'Metaphysics' by Any Other Name ...", p. 82.
18 See "The Glory of the Latins" in chapter 7, p. 253ff.
19 See "John Dewey (1859–1952) and 'The Influence of Darwinism on Philosophy'" in chapter 11, p. 507ff.
20 Peirce c.1906: CP 5.11.
21 Peirce 1905: CP 5.423: "all such rubbish being swept away, what will remain of philosophy will be a series of problems capable of investigation by the observational methods of the true sciences

There will still remain for pragmaticism, as not for pragmatism, the "retention of a purified philosophy" distinct from science, namely, that sense of philosophy capable of providing an explanation and consistent exposition in discourse of the general framework or horizon of human understanding within which alone scientific experiments of a particular type become possible in the first place. "Has it not occurred to you", Peirce asks his imaginary interlocutor who is trying to speak on behalf of the pragmatic interpretation of Peirce's original statements in the area,[22] "that every connected series of experiments constitutes a single collective experiment"? Or that "the unity of essence of the experiment lies in its purpose and plan"? So that when the pragmaticist speaks of experiment "he does not mean any particular event that did happen to somebody in the dead past, but what surely will happen to everybody in the living future who shall fulfill certain conditions."

Pragmaticism and Relations
In rejecting the nominalistic idea that an experiment reveals nothing more than that "something once happened to an individual object and that subsequently some other individual event occurred", Peirce cuts to the heart of the matter. Pragmaticism, in other words, is the contrary opposite to any view compatible with nominalism, and it is the very quintessence of nominalism, as our study of the Latin Age above finally showed, to deny the reality of relations outside of thought itself in the order of mind-independent being, *ens reale* as it pertains to the categorial scheme of Aristotle or, in Peirce's terms, to the "brute fact" of Secondness; and it is just this denial constitutive of nominalism (I mean, which makes the theoretical position of nominalism possible in the first place) that Peirce in turn denies[23] and indicates his "denial of nominalism's denial" to be the cornerstone of what we have come to see as postmodern philosophizing:[24]

– the truth about which can be reached without those interminable misunderstandings and disputes which have made the highest of the positive sciences a mere amusement for idle intellects, a sort of chess – idle pleasure its purpose, and reading out of a book its method. In this regard, pragmaticism is a species of prope-positivism." Here the reader is advised to advert to Peirce's adoption (e.g., c.1902: CP 1.242, 1.278) of a strange terminology from Jeremy Bentham (1748–1832, in a work of 1816), according to which Peirce divides science into *idioscopic* – what are ordinarily called the experimental sciences as requiring special experience to determine the sense of their propositions – and *cenoscopic* (also "coenoscopic"), what are dependent on observation only in that sense which is available to a mature human organism at any time. Thus Aristotelian physics is a coenoscopic science, and so was medieval metaphysics a coenoscopic science. But physics after Galileo, modern physics, is rather a definitely idioscopic science. The idioscopic sciences are scientific in the modern sense, but the coenoscopic or philosophical ones are, rather, doctrinal in the Latin sense which separates itself equally from theological dogma and scientific hypothesis to constitute the interpretive horizon of objectivity within which the relative autonomy of all three types of discourse can be verified and vindicated, both in general and as each admitting of a variety of further subdivisions.

22 Peirce 1905: CP 5.424.
23 Put positively, Peirce affirms what nominalism centrally denies, the *ens reale* status of some relations.
24 Peirce 1903d: EP 2.165.

if I were asked to say of what indisputable advantage to philosophy the exact study of the logic of relations had been, and if in answering the question I considered only the manner in which it presents itself to my own mind, I should unhesitatingly mention, as its first and most unquestionable service, that it had put, in the minds of every student of it, the Category of Reaction entirely beyond all doubt as an irreducible element of thought.

Suprasubjectivity in the very order of being as its exists independently of our opinions about it, which in turn proves to be the key to semiosis itself, Peirce identifies as the feature most distinctive of pragmaticism. For pragmaticism subscribes only to a view that[25] "meaning is undoubtedly general; and it is equally indisputable that the general is of the nature of a word or sign". But here the reader would be completely misled to think that "word" is being opposed to "sign" in the ancient Greek sense of *symbolon* opposed to *semeia*, or that Peirce is propounding some prenatal Wittgensteinian theory of meaning as linguistic. On the contrary, the "or" signifies *sign in general*, of which a word is but a well-known instance.

The "consideration that has escaped" the pragmatists is that individuality as such, as isolated in itself – substance in the rationalist sense[26] – is completely excluded by pragmaticism:[27]

> do not overlook the fact that the pragmaticist maxim says nothing of single experiments or of single experimental phenomena (for what is conditionally true *in futuro* can hardly be singular), but only speaks of general kinds of experimental phenomena. Its adherent does not shrink from speaking of general objects as real, since whatever is true represents a real. Now the laws of nature are true.

Good old "American individual conscience", for Peirce, is an empiricist heritage that is not sufficient to the requirements of a philosophy "purified" of the imaginary excesses of modern metaphysics. What is needed, on the contrary, is the older notion of substance as a *transcendental relative* as we have seen it introduced in the Latin Age to contrast with and provide the subjective ground for pure relations as suprasubjective in principle and actually intersubjective in fact when the circumstances of the environment dictate this (when the terminus of the relation as well as its ground in some subjective aspect of a subject of existence, an individual, physically exists).[28]

Peirce, as we saw, did not quite make it up to the point in his study of the Latin Age where this terminology of transcendental and ontological relatives became fully

---

25 Peirce 1905: CP 5.429.
26 See the citation in chapter 13, p. 556 above from Kant 1747.
27 Peirce 1905: CP 5.426.
28 See above, in chapters 3, 6, 9, and 12, pp. 72, 228, 423ff., & 556 respectively.

incorporated into the doctrine of signs itself.[29] Yet he leaves no doubt on the point of his own embrasure of what that terminology signified in the doctrinal context of Latin semiotic:[30]

> Whatever exists, ex-sists, that is, really acts upon other existents, so obtains a self-identity, and is definitely individual. As to the general, it will be a help to thought to notice that there are two ways of being general. A statue of a soldier on some village monument, in his overcoat and with his musket, is for each of a hundred families the image of its uncle, its sacrifice to the Union. That statue, then, though it is itself single, represents any one man of whom a certain predicate may be true. It is objectively general. The word 'soldier', whether spoken or written, is general in the same way; while the name, 'George Washington', is not so. But each of these two terms remains one and the same noun, whether it be spoken or written, and whenever and wherever it be spoken or written. This noun is not an existent thing: it is a type, or form, to which objects, both those that are externally existent and those which are imagined, may conform, but which none of them can exactly be. This is subjective generality. The pragmaticistic purport is general in both ways.

Only by acting and being acted upon, and through the network of relations that result from such interactions both in nature and in society, do the individual subjects of existence, the real substances, come into and maintain themselves in existence. To make the point as plain as possible, Peirce indicates that "two things here are all-important to assure oneself of and to remember":[31]

> The first is that a person is not absolutely an individual. His thoughts are what he is "saying to himself", that is, is saying to that other self that is just coming into life in the flow of time. When one reasons, it is that critical self that one is trying to persuade; and all thought whatsoever is a sign, and is mostly of the nature of language. The second thing to remember is that the man's circle of society (however widely or narrowly this phrase may be understood), is a sort of loosely compacted person, in some respects of higher rank than the person of an individual organism. It is these two things alone that render it possible for you – but only in the abstract, and in a Pickwickian[32] sense – to distinguish between absolute truth and what you do not doubt.

---

29 Krempel (1952: 668), the only one who has made anything like a complete survey of the terminology in question, leaves no room for doubt that John Poinsot, the author of the first *Treatise on Signs* systematically vindicating in doctrinal or speculative terms the general notion of sign posited by Augustine, was also the author in whom the notion of substance as transcendentally relative "found its true theoretician", and I suspect this was precisely because of the importance of the notion for stabilizing in a thematic way the distinction between representation and signification as such.

30 Peirce 1905: CP 5.429.

31 Peirce 1905: CP 5.421. On Peirce's approach to the self, Vincent Colapietro's 1989 monograph is an initial study that has already, and deservedly, achieved near-classic status.

32 Pickwickian, because "things as they appear to God" – the world as it would be seen by an omniscient intelligence present in awareness to the least details of the actual existence and

So we approach the heart of the matter. Generalities, relations which hold true over and above the subjectivities of individuality, are the heart and soul of pragmaticism. And, as if to emphasize the point, Peirce points out that: [33]

Not only may generals be real, but they may also be physically efficient, not in every metaphysical sense, but in the common-sense acception in which human purposes are physically efficient. Aside from metaphysical nonsense, no sane man doubts that if I feel the air in my study to be stuffy, that thought may cause the window to be opened. My thought, be it granted, was an individual event. But what determined it to take the particular determination it did, was in part the general fact that stuffy air is unwholesome, and in part other Forms. ... So, then, when my window was opened, because of the truth that stuffy air is malsain, a physical effort was brought into existence by the efficiency of a general and non-existent truth. ... Generality is, indeed, an indispensable ingredient of reality; for mere individual existence or actuality without any regularity whatever is a nullity.

It is not the individual actions and interactions as such that are significant but only those individual actions and interactions as they *further* relate to the "scheme in the observer's mind". The relations in physical nature are dyadic, but with this *further* element whereby they become *revelatory to* an observer, the physical environment itself is transformed into part of the objective world or Umwelt; and because that objective world in this case is a Lebenswelt, a species-specifically *human* objective world with language at its contemplative core and discursive center, at that moment the physical universe ceases to be merely physical. The realm of brute force and physical interaction as such at this moment becomes caught up in the semiotic web, and the universe becomes perfused with signs:[34]

The phenomenon consists in the fact that when an experimentalist shall come to act according to a certain scheme that he has in mind, then will something else happen, and shatter the doubts of sceptics, like the celestial fire upon the altar of Elijah.

Of the myriads of forms into which a proposition may be translated, what is that one which is to be called its very meaning? It is, according to the pragmaticist, that form in which the proposition becomes applicable to human conduct, not in these or those special circumstances, nor when one entertains this or that special design, but that form which is most directly applicable to self-control under every situation, and to every purpose. This is why he locates the meaning in future time; for future conduct is the only conduct that is subject to self-control. But in order that that form of the proposition

---

interactions of things at every level of the universe, such as is God according to Aquinas (and in contrast to Aristotle's God; see chapter 7, p. 284ff. above) – constitute absolute truth, without at all constituting that within our experience about which we have no doubt.

33 Peirce 1905: CP 5.431.
34 Peirce 1905: CP 5.425, 5.427.

which is to be taken as its meaning should be applicable to every situation and to every purpose upon which the proposition has any bearing, it must be simply the general description of all the experimental phenomena which the assertion of the proposition virtually predicts. For an experimental phenomenon is the fact asserted by the proposition that action of a certain description will have a certain kind of experimental result; and experimental results are the only results that can affect human conduct.

This is so even if we consider a certain truth to be an eternal and unchanging truth, such as the proposition that if God did not exist there could be no world, or whatever we might choose to cite as an instance of "unchanging truth":[35] "some unchanging idea may come to influence a man more than it had done; but only because some experience equivalent to an experiment has brought its truth home to him more intimately than before".

The Purpose of Human Life

The heart of the matter is the purpose of human life. Peirce saw that purpose to lie in so conducting oneself as to create of one's total self – the relative self in which we actually consist as a member of a community over a certain duration of time – something that is beautiful, an aesthetic whole. And for the individual life to be a beautiful life, Peirce, as one of the few moderns early or late to have any least familiarity with the medieval doctrine of the transcendentals,[36] according to which truth and goodness are convertible with being, required the human being so to live as to express over the time of one's life a commitment to truth on the side of thought and to goodness on the side of comportment.

An Ethics of Thinking as well as an Ethics of Doing

The heart of the difference between pragmaticism and pragmatism lies in the very notion of conduct itself. For the pragmatist, "conduct" means, mainly and ultimately, *outward behaviour*. This is a view which finds degenerate kin in the likes of the twentieth-century psychological doctrine of behaviorism espoused by such authors as B. F. Skinner (1904–90), or the doctrine of verification as a supposed theory of meaning in such authors as Rudolf Carnap (1891–1970) or A. J. Ayer (1910–89). Or, to the extent pragmatism encompasses *inward* behavior, it emphasizes the will, as in the writings of William James.

Pragmaticism avoids both these traps.[37] For the pragmaticist sees that "human conduct" is a complex of inner thought and outer social interaction; and that just as social interaction needs to be regulated by ethics so does thought need to be regulated

---

35 Peirce 1905: CP 5.427.
36 See chapter 7, p. 239, text and n10; chapter 9, p. 424n37.
37 Peirce 1905: CP 5.429. "if pragmaticism really made Doing to be the Be-all and the End-all of life, that would be its death. For to say that we live for the mere sake of action, as action, regardless of the thought it carries out, would be to say that there is no such thing as rational purport."

by logic. Logic, in fact, is nothing more nor less than the ethics of thinking – that is, the exercise of responsible self-control in the adoption of opinions and beliefs as our own:[38]

> Now, just as conduct controlled by ethical reason tends toward fixing certain habits of conduct, the nature of which (as to illustrate the meaning, peaceable habits and not quarrelsome habits) does not depend upon any accidental circumstances, and in that sense may be said to be destined; so, thought, controlled by a rational experimental logic, tends to the fixation of certain opinions, equally destined, the nature of which will be the same in the end, however the perversity of thought of whole generations may cause the postponement of the ultimate fixation [as happened to metaphysics, Peirce thought, in the classical modern mainstream on which the pragmatists almost exclusively drew in their reactive self-definitions].

Now "the real" for Peirce, exactly as for the Latin scholastics, is being in its character as independent of any finite mind. Not only does the human being have in thought contact with that which is independent of thought, Kant and all the epistemological theory of modern philosophy to the contrary notwithstanding. Further, to the extent that the human being succeeds in giving expression to that which "is" in this sense, human thought approximates to the truth. And, as Aristotle also noted, success in achieving such expression is not the work of the individual in isolation but of the individual as belonging to a community of inquirers; so that truth grows over time, even as the community of inquirers grows:[39]

> As to reality, one finds it defined in various ways; but if that principle of terminological ethics that was proposed be accepted, the equivocal language will soon disappear. For *realis* and *realitas* are not ancient words. They were invented to be terms of philosophy in the thirteenth century, and the meaning they were intended to express is perfectly clear. That is real which has such and such characters, whether anybody thinks it to have those characters or not. At any rate, that is the sense in which the pragmaticist uses the word.

As being is brought more and more into the objective sphere, the distinction between what is independently of human awareness and what exists objectively (that is,

---

Further (CP 5.436): "if one cares at all to know what the pragmaticist theory consists in, one must understand that there is no other part of it to which the pragmaticist attaches quite as much importance as he does to the recognition in his doctrine of the utter inadequacy of action or volition or even of resolve or actual purpose, as materials out of which to construct a conditional purpose or the concept of conditional purpose. ... continuity is an indispensable element of reality, and ... is simply what generality becomes in the logic of relatives, and thus, like generality, and more than generality, is an affair of thought, and is the essence of thought."

38 Peirce 1905: CP 5.430.
39 Ibid.

within human awareness) diminishes in fact. Part of this process consists in what exists only objectively coming to be more and more recognized as such, so that more and more the human community is in a position to avoid the mistake of saying that what is not is, or the opposite mistake of saying that what is is not. So more and more do human beings approach the state of the "ultimate opinion", that is, that opinion where what is objective will include the whole of the physical known as such, and whatever the objective includes which is of fiction will also be known as such. Exactly "the state of things which will be believed in that ultimate opinion is real", which is why truth as more than a partial achievement always lies in the future:[40]

> That which any true proposition asserts is real, in the sense of being as it is regardless of what you or I may think about it. Let this proposition be a general conditional proposition as to the future, and it is a real general such as is calculated really to influence human conduct; and such the pragmaticist holds to be the rational purport of every concept.

So precisely because and inasmuch as "the rational meaning of every proposition lies in the future", the pragmaticist, in contrast to every species of pragmatist, does not locate the highest human good in action. Action, for the human being as such, can be good only insofar as it is an embodiment of thought, an execution of some ideal plan to change the outer world, the "phenomenal" world, for the better:[41]

> Accordingly, the pragmaticist does not make the summum bonum to consist in action, but makes it to consist in that process of evolution whereby the existent comes more and more to embody those generals which were just now said to be destined, which is what we strive to express in calling them reasonable. In its higher stages, evolution takes place more and more largely through self-control, and this gives the pragmaticist a sort of justification for making the rational purport to be general.

Pragmaticism does not try to do away with the abstract in favor of the concrete, or to do away with speculative thought in order to concentrate on practical applications; nor does it tolerate a subordination of understanding to willing in decisions as to what is so. All such emphases can be left to the varieties of pragmatism; and left without loss, to the extent that such emphases tend to deform the nature of human understanding and interfere with the growth of truth in time. Pragmaticism finds general meanings in particular phenomena and abstracts these meanings as guides for future conduct, thought, and research:[42]

---

40 Peirce 1905: CP 5.432.
41 Peirce 1905: CP 5.432–3.
42 Peirce 1905: CP 5.428.

Pragmaticism does not intend to define the phenomenal equivalents of words and general ideas, but, on the contrary, eliminates their sential element, and endeavors to define the rational purport, and this it finds in the purposive bearing of the word or proposition in question.

The Line Separating Pragmaticism from Modern Philosophy

So we come to the bottom line. Pragmatism is, while pragmaticism is not, compatible with idealism in the modern sense. Peirce's own way of putting this was to say that "pragmaticism is at issue not only with English philosophy more particularly, but with all modern philosophy more or less, even with Hegel; and that is that it involves a complete rupture with nominalism".[43] That is why pragmatism belongs to late modern philosophy, while pragmaticism is determinately postmodern.

As the founder of the movement that came to be called pragmatism, Peirce may be said to be among the "last of the moderns". But in rejecting the interpretation of his earlier statements that gave rise to pragmatism as the distinctive movement of twentieth-century American philosophy, and in explaining those ideas instead in terms of pragmaticism, Peirce became the first of the postmoderns, the first to recover for human understanding the full scope of its doctrinal possibilities in the age of science.

Pragmaticism and the Doctrine of Signs

Pragmaticism, thus, is not itself a philosophical system but a way of thinking. Hence, "one of the faults that I think they" – the pragmatists – "might find with me is that I make pragmatism" – the original pragmatism, that is to say, what he resorts now to terming rather "pragmaticism", as we have seen – "to be a mere maxim of logic instead of a sublime principle of speculative philosophy".[44] Pragmaticism is not a theory of truth, as James and other pragmatists tried to have it be, but only of meaning as a way to truth, which alone, in the end, reality itself, *in collusion with thought*, can determine. Pragmaticism is a way of fostering and promoting the collusion.

Vincent Colapietro, in a telephone conversation, summarized Peirce's mind on the point excellently. Pragmaticism, he remarked,[45] is in Peirce's context "a maxim for how to conduct ourselves as investigators and a principle of translation for getting habits out of abstract concepts". If we wish to speak of pragmaticism in terms of a principle, Peirce tells us, he himself, "even in order to be admitted to better philosophical standing", has not succeeded in a formulation "any better than this":[46]

---

43 Peirce c.1905: CP 8.208, from an unsigned letter addressed to Signor Calderoni.
44 Peirce 1903b, Lecture I: "Pragmatism and the Normative Sciences", CP 5.18.
45 Colapietro on 24 May 1998.
46 Peirce 1903b, Lecture I: CP 5.18.

Pragmatism is the principle that every theoretical judgment expressible in a sentence in the indicative mood is a confused form of thought whose only meaning, if it has any, lies in its tendency to enforce a corresponding practical maxim expressible as a conditional sentence having its apodosis in the imperative mood.

Or, to put the matter as succinctly as possible:[47] "what a thing means is simply what habits it involves." And habits, engendered by things, involve beliefs about reality – beginning with the reality of the physical environment around us. Not only is Peirce's point of departure for philosophy far removed from the artificial "problem of the external world" which defeated the moderns. His very way of thinking, pragmaticism, construed as maxim or principle or both, is a way of thinking that succeeds precisely where modern philosophy failed dismally. For the pragmaticistic outlook brings together science and philosophy as complementary modes of knowledge bearing on the real, thus fulfilling the initial dream of modernity – before Descartes' dreams turned modernity into an epistemological nightmare as the inexorable logical consequences revealed themselves in thinker after thinker who pursued the way of ideas.

Thus did the first way of thinking in history to be conceived from the outset in function of the doctrine of signs overcome the schizophrenia of modern philosophy; but, by the late nineteenth century, that meant the overcoming of modern philosophy itself. For Jekyll to live a sane life, after all, Hyde had to die. It was radical therapy.

But let there be no mistake about it: in the thought of C. S. Peirce, it is semiotic that provides the framework within which pragmaticism is to be understood, not the other way around. If we may put the matter in light of the old scholastic distinction between the *ordo inventionis* ("order of discovery") and the *ordo disciplinae* ("order of exposition"), while it is pragmaticism into which Peirce "was forced by successive steps"[48] leading away from his Kantian beginnings in late-modern philosophy, inasmuch as it is the application of the pragmaticist maxim above all which assures us of the reality of the physical environment and of the nonsense of the "thing-in-itself" as "unknowable" yet conceivable if but indirectly as "behind the phenomena"; nonetheless, in the order of exposition, in order to found semiotics, we must go beyond pragmaticism. For "in cases like the present", the case being precisely the matter of achieving by analysis "the essential nature of a sign" such as can prove "applicable to everything which the most general science of semeiotic must regard as its business to study", we are "debarred from a direct appeal to the principle of pragmaticism".[49] So spoke Peirce in 1907. Nearer his end, in 1913,[50] he spoke more clearly still. Pragmaticism pertains principally to the *security* of our

---

47 Peirce 1901: from the entry "Pragmatic and Pragmatism" in Baldwin's *Dictionary of Philosophy and Psychology*, vol. I, as repr. in CP 5.4.
48 Peirce 1905a: EP 2.353.
49 Peirce 1907: EP 2.402–3.
50 Peirce 1913: "An Essay toward Reasoning in Security and Uberty", in EP 2.463ff.

reasoning; semiotics is rather our source of *uberty*[51] or "richness" of thought, without which security would stifle and reduce us to that very pure play of secondness which the old determinisms ever mistake for the whole truth about existence.

To understand how completely pragmaticism is, in Peirce's own thought, a function of semiotics conceived in terms of what is distinctive to the species-specifically human objective world, consider, first, how vast is the pragmaticistic notion of experience; and then consider how central this notion of experience as including real relations is to pragmaticism. Without the conception of experience distinctively human in a species-specific sense, there is no pragmaticism; but pragmaticism gives such expression to the conception as to remove itself at the outset from the climate and family of modern philosophy. Modern philosophy began with the universal doubt whereby Descartes had made being a function of his thinking. Pragmaticism begins rather from a belief in the reality of what is more than thought, and proceeds by continually putting to test the contrast between thought and what is more than thought, between merely objective being and objective being which reveals also something of the physical universe:[52]

if doubting were "as easy as lying" ... doubt has nothing to do with any serious business. But do not make believe; if pedantry has not eaten all the reality out of you, recognize, as you must, that there is much that you do not doubt, in the least. ... All you have any dealings with are your doubts and beliefs, with the course of life that forces new beliefs upon you and gives you power to doubt old beliefs. If your terms "truth" and "falsity" are taken in such senses as to be definable in terms of doubt and belief and the course of experience (as for example they would be, if you were to define the "truth" as that to a belief in which belief would tend if it were to tend indefinitely toward absolute fixity), well and good: in that case, you are only talking about doubt and belief. But if by truth and falsity you mean something not definable in terms of doubt and belief in any way, then you are talking of entities of whose existence you can know nothing, and which Ockham's razor would clean shave off. ...

Belief is not a momentary mode of consciousness; it is a habit of mind essentially enduring for some time, and mostly (at least) unconscious; and like other habits, it is (until it meets with some surprise that begins its dissolution) perfectly self-satisfied. Doubt is of an altogether contrary genus. It is not a habit, but the privation of a habit. Now a privation of a habit, in order to be anything at all, must be a condition of erratic activity that in some way must get superseded by a habit.

Among the things which the reader, as a rational person, does not doubt, is that he not merely has habits, but also can exert a measure of self-control over his future actions; which means, however, not that he can impart to them any arbitrarily assignable character, but, on the contrary, that a process of self-preparation will tend to impart to

---

51 A term from late middle English and old French, reflecting the Latin "ubertas": rich growth, fertility; copiousness.
52 Peirce 1905: CP 5.416–20.

action (when the occasion for it shall arise), one fixed character, which is indicated and perhaps roughly measured by the absence (or slightness) of the feeling of self-reproach, which subsequent reflection will induce. Now, this subsequent reflection is part of the self-preparation for action on the next occasion. Consequently, there is a tendency, as action is repeated again and again, for the action to approximate indefinitely toward the perfection of that fixed character, which would be marked by entire absence of self-reproach. ...

These phenomena seem to be the fundamental characteristics which distinguish a rational being. ... Now, thinking is a species of conduct which is largely subject to self-control. In all their features ... logical self-control is a perfect mirror of ethical self-control – unless it be rather a species under that genus. ...

... "thought", in what has just been said, should be taken ... as covering all rational life, so that an experiment shall be an operation of thought. ... that ultimate state of habit to which the action of self-control ultimately tends, where no room is left for further self-control, is, in the case of thought, the state of fixed belief, or perfect knowledge.

Now consider that, for Peirce, all thought is in signs. This means that all rational life is mediated through the action of signs, and "rational life" here embraces everything that tends in any way to fix or unsettle belief. That is why the "pragmatic maxim" pragmaticistically put can invoke explicitly semiotics: "The entire intellectual purport of any symbol consists in the total of all general modes of rational conduct which, conditionally upon all the possible different circumstances and desires, would ensue upon the acceptance of the symbol".[53] It is quite a notion. Without rational experience there is no pragmaticism. But without signs there is no experience of any kind. There is no thought at all. So, if we can but find out and follow "the right method of transforming signs, then truth can be nothing more nor less than the last result to which the following out of this method would ultimately carry us."[54] In this journey pragmaticism is but a step along the way, necessitated largely by the need to overcome the Kantian heritage by which the modern heritage in philosophy was both summarized and synthesized. Through pragmaticism, Peirce was able to free Dr Jekyll from the destructive darkness of Mr Hyde. It is a permanent achievement, integral to yet less than the grand vision that semiotics provides in revealing the true depth and compass of human understanding.

Peirce's Grand Vision

Yet Peirce has a vision even grander than that. He thinks that semiosis, as the action of signs, outruns the confines of experience. He thinks that experience itself, completely structured throughout by sign-relations, is yet itself but the expression of

53 Peirce 1905a: EP 2.346.
54 Peirce 1906: "The Basis of Pragmaticism in the Normative Sciences", EP 2.380.

a process with roots as deep as the being of rocks and stars. Not only human beings and other animals make use of signs. So do plants and inanimate substances:[55]

> The action of a sign generally takes place between two parties, the *utterer* and the *interpreter*. They need not be persons; for a chameleon and many kinds of insects and even plants make their living by uttering signs, and lying signs, at that. Who is the utterer of signs of the weather ...? However, every sign certainly conveys something of the general nature of thought, if not from a mind, yet from some repository of ideas, or significant forms, and if not to a person, yet to something capable of somehow 'catching on' ... that is, of receiving not merely a physical, nor even merely a psychical dose of energy, but a significant meaning. In that modified, and as yet very misty, sense, then, we may continue to use the italicized words [*utterer* and *interpreter*].

As we saw in the last chapter, contemporary philosophers at work on the development of the doctrine of signs according to the fullness of its possibilities have begun to speak, after Peirce, of the actions of signs as *semiosis*, and of the action of signs at each of the cosmological levels. At the broadest physical level of atoms, molecules, interstellar gases, galaxies, stars, planets, and geological development, the action of signs is called *physiosemiosis*. In the living world of plants, the action of signs is called *phytosemiosis*. Among animals generally, the action of signs has come to be called *zoösemiosis*. And the species-specifically human use of signs, rooted in language, as we have many times mentioned in crossing the centuries to this point, is an action of signs called *anthroposemiosis*. More recently, Jesper Hoffmeyer[56] has proposed the inclusive term *semiosphere* to express the penetration of the action of signs into all these dimensions of the cosmos, "a sphere just like the atmosphere, the hydrosphere, and the biosphere", but distinctive in that "it penetrates to every corner of these other spheres, incorporating all forms of communication: sounds, smells, movements, colors, shapes, electrical fields, thermal radiation, waves of all kinds, chemical signals, touching, and so on." Hoffmeyer generously notes discovering, after publishing the book in which he coined this term "semiosphere", that he found that the same lexical item in fact had been introduced earlier by Lotman;[57] but in fact Hoffmeyer's view of semiotics is so much more comprehensive than Lotman's that his deferral in point of coinage is perhaps uncalled for, and I would suggest *signosphere* as a term more appropriate for the narrower designation of semiosphere in Lotman's sense, leaving the broader coinage and usage to Hoffmeyer's credit.

Except for the generic term *semiosis*, all of this terminology develops well after Peirce.[58] But the vision for such a vast reach for the actions of signs was original

---

55 Peirce c.1907: ISP nos. 205–6.
56 Hoffmeyer 1996: vii.
57 Lotman 1990.
58 The term "physiosemiosis" comes from Deely 1990; "phytosemiotics" originates from Krampen 1981 (reprinted in Deely, Williams and Kruse eds 1986); "zoösemiotic" stems from Sebeok 1963, as

with Peirce, even though he himself was never able to bring it to ground in his lifetime. I have called it[59] "Peirce's Grand Vision", for that is what it is, one of the most grand visions to be found in all the annals of philosophy, with the added advantage of being rooted more in science than in mysticism.[60]

> [T]he problem of how genuine triadic relationships first arose in the world is a better, because more definite, formulation of the problem of how life first came about; and no explanation has ever been offered except that of pure chance, which we must suspect to be no explanation, owing to the suspicion that pure chance may itself be a vital phenomenon. In that case, life in the physiological sense would be due to life in the metaphysical sense. Of course, the fact that a given individual has been persuaded of the truth of a proposition is the very slenderest possible argument for its truth; nevertheless, the fact that I, a person of the strongest possible physicistic prejudices, should, as the result of forty years of questionings, have been brought to the deep conviction that there is some essentially and irreducibly other element in the universe than pure dynamism may have sufficient interest to excuse my devoting a single sentence to its expression. For you may be sure that I had reasons that withstood severe, not to say hostile criticism; and if I live to do it, I shall embody them in a volume.

If we had all the volumes philosophers had promised or hoped to write we would surely need many more libraries than we have. This volume Peirce hoped to live to write is yet one more of those ethereal volumes in the library of books that did not get written. In the case of this book, there was a special problem: its would-be author was on a bit of a wrong trail in trying to determine the type of causality proper to signs. He never fully got beyond the notion that some dressed-up version of final causality as teleology[61] might be the causality proper to the action of signs, although a careful analysis of his texts indeed reveals that he was at the same time on the scent of distinguishing final causality in all its forms from what he called "ideal" causality, which we are obliged by his own "ethics of terminology" to call rather *objective* or *extrinsic formal causality*.[62]

The trail was wrong, but not completely wrong, and certainly not as wrong as the direction that modern philosophy had pursued in shrinking the notion of

---

"anthroposemiotic" from Sebeok 1968. Of the first appearance of the expression "anthroposemiosis", widely used in the last two decades at least of the twentieth century, I am uncertain. My guess is that Sebeok originated it; and a full thematization of the notion was first undertaken in Deely 1994, a work for which the publisher at the last moment reversed the primary and secondary suggestions for title.

59 In Colapietro and Olshewsky eds 1996.
60 Peirce c.1909: CP 6.322.
61 Cf. "A Scheme of Causality", in chapter 3, p. 64.
62 See the "Excursus on Peirce and Poinsot" in the 1985 edition of Poinsot 1632a: 493–4, for a listing of texts in Peirce on this technical point.

causality down to dimensions that could be made to fit a thoroughgoing idealism. For pragmaticism, as we saw, requires us to think of human life as a growth and a development that it is up to us to make an aesthetic one, that is to say, one that is good and beautiful; and to do this requires the growing embodiment of rationality in our lives and in the world around us. Actually, European civilization in its political institutions – for example, as they have developed since the seventeenth century – provides a pretty good example of the sort of progress Peirce thought in store for humanity along pragmaticistic lines.[63]

So it was not surprising that the contemporary founder of the doctrine of signs, or semiotics, expressly "thought of semiotic as precisely the development of a concept of a final cause process and as a study of such processes".[64] Imbued with the modern prejudices against and misconceptions of the Latin tradition of natural philosophy, Peirce's would-be commentators seem to have found this fact, as Ransdell remarks,[65] "an embarrassment, a sort of intellectual club foot that one shouldn't be caught looking at, much less blatantly pointing out to others", which would explain "why the topic of final causation is so strangely absent in criticisms and explanations of Peirce's conception of semiotic and semiosis", despite its centrality in Peirce's own reflections and explanations.

As Ransdell rightly says,[66] "Peirce is talking about the overall form of a process, not about the relation of a process to something external to it.[67] He is talking about the tendency toward an end-state, and the general features of such a tendency in whatever medium the process may be realized." Thus, "the final causational form of a process can be realized only through efficient causation, and in that sense presupposes the possibility of a physical explanation as well". And in all this Peirce is thinking squarely within a mainstream of Latin thought,[68] even though eccentric, within that mainstream, to the line of causality immediately manifested in any action of signs consequent upon the being proper to signs as such.

This is one of those points in Peirce's semiotic where we have to regret that his researches among the Latins did not carry him as far as Poinsot's *Treatise on Signs* of 1632. For there in Poinsot's work[69] he would have found the clues he needed to make the sharp distinction between final causality and the formal specificative causality called by the scholastics "objective" or "extrinsic formal causality as specificative", as also to make the further distinction within extrinsic formal causality between its

---

63 Compare the situation described in chapter 5 under the heading "Islam Beheads Itself", p. 188ff.
64 Joseph Ransdell, "Some Leading Ideas of Peirce's Semiotic" (1977: 163).
65 Ibid.
66 Ibid.
67 Compare Poinsot 1633: 281a19.
68 Cf. Poinsot 1633: 282b17–19; Thomas Aquinas, *Disputed Questions on the Power of God* (c.1265–6), q. 5, art. 1. The articles by Ashley (1952, 1967, 1967a, 1973) are among the few sensible late-modern products on this topic.
69 See the references in n75 of this chapter, below, p. 633.

specificative and exemplificative exercises, the former of which is regulative, the latter comparative.[70] This last form of extrinsic formal causality, the exemplary, or "extrinsic formal causality as exemplar", the Latins also called "ideal causality". The Third and Fifth Rules of Peirce's "Ethics of Terminology",[71] as well as the Sixth, which proscribes introducing terms which interfere with an existing term, would have obliged him to adopt the name of *objective* or *specifying cause* to identify the action proper to signs, had he known of Poinsot's semiotic in particular.

Recall[72] Aristotle's successful identification of the notion of dependency in being as the central note in the concept of causality, and his further analysis showing that such dependency is fourfold in the case of the coming to be and passing away of material substances or individuals – namely, efficient, material, formal, and final. Building on this fourfold scheme, the later Latins were able to show that the scheme must be further refined to account for phenomena within the Umwelt or Lebenswelt as such, for the *objectivity as such* of phenomena, even when they are also physical.

To begin with, to account for works of art, "making" in the broadest sense, it was necessary to introduce two further distinctions. The first was a distinction between the intrinsic final causality observed in the maturation and growth of organisms, on the one hand, and an extrinsic final causality to explain an end intended by an intelligent agent but not itself part of the material used to achieve that end (as a fork is made *for* eating, although it is not the fork that will do the eating; or a dam is made by a beaver *for* a series of goals). The second was a distinction between the intrinsic formal causality observed in the cohesion and organization of material substances (again, organisms in particular) and an extrinsic *exemplary* formal causality, also called "ideal causality", to explain the plan or design (the idea) according to which an animal (rational or brute) executes the construction of a difference in its environment. This pattern or plan which is finally embodied in that construction as a formal pattern or series of relations which make it the kind of construction it is (such as the blueprint by comparison with which a house is built, or the outline according to which a paper is presented) is introduced from outside the materials manipulated, unlike the natural "formal cause" of Aristotle which unfolds by organizing its material from within.

But, in addition to these distinctions increasing the number of recognized fundamental types of causality, yet another is needed to explain how an observer or a thinker has attention directed to one feature rather than another of the objective world. This seventh (or eighth) mode of causality (depending on how one counts the

70 An exemplary cause, too, can function to regulate, but when it does it does so *through* a comparison, whereas an objective cause directly specifies the power in its knowing of this rather than that. Knowing this, it can advert to that, and so compare the two; but the knowing of this rather than that, or that rather than this, presupposes the specifying causality as more fundamental than the exemplary, which becomes possible only subsequently.
71 Peirce 1903: esp. 2.226; see below, p. 666f.
72 See chapter 3, p. 64.

distinctions[73]) is the causality required to explain cognition and psychological states in general. The later Latins called it *specificative* or *objective* causality, because it is from the object presented to the mind that attention is focused on this rather than that.[74] On the subjective side, a thinker may try to turn attention toward or away from triangles; but the measure of success lies not in the subjective effort but in the objective content surviving the effort. And since presenting objects is exactly the function of signs, the action of signs is a species of this last distinguished extrinsic formal causality, called "specificative", rather than a species of either final causality or exemplary causality.[75]

---

73 In Aristotle's original scheme (chapter 3, p. 64 above), remember, the factors identified were the agent or efficient cause; that upon which the agent acts, or the material cause; the result in or response of the material correlated with the action of the agent, called the formal cause; and the pattern of development which an effect once produced exhibits over time, called its "final cause". Thus were derived the famous "four causes" required for the investigation of nature. But to explain artefacts and cultural phenomena generally, later thinkers found it further necessary to distinguish, first, between the original formal cause as intrinsic to the effect and an extrinsic formal cause according to which, as a pattern or plan, such an internal formal cause might be introduced into matter by an intelligent agent, adding the *exemplary* or *ideal* cause as a fifth type of cause to the original four; and to distinguish, second, between the original final cause as the intrinsic pattern according to which a given effect sustains itself over time, and an *extrinsic* final cause representing the intention according to or purpose for which the artisan designs the material structure in the form that he or she gives it (as a fork is a certain ideal form embodied in a suitable material *for* conveying food to the mouth, speared if desired), adding the *extrinsic final cause* as a sixth type of cause to the original four. But the extrinsic formal cause as distinguished from the intrinsic formal cause, it turns out, is itself twofold, in one case as providing a pattern for fabrication, and in another case as specifying cognition as an awareness of this rather than that object or aspect of an object, adding *objective* or *specificative* cause to the original four. Extrinsic formal and final causes bring the original four to six; extrinsic formal causes further divided into exemplary and specificative bring the six to eight.

74 This is not as difficult to understand as first appears, when you consider that this is just how laws work in society (insofar as they do work): by the extrinsic specificative formal causality the scholastics called "objective". By contrast, "role models" are exercising rather the extrinsic exemplificative formal causality the scholastics called "ideal".

75 For a synoptic summary of the Latin discussions on efficient, material, intrinsic formal, and extrinsic exemplary formal causality, see Poinsot 1633: Questions 10–13, 197a11–287b43, where, however, extrinsic specificative formal causality ("objective causality") is mentioned only in response to an objection confusing it with exemplary causality (at 245a24–43, and 247a7–14).

The discussion of formal causality as extrinsic specification is to be found mainly as follows: in Poinsot 1632: Q. 17, arts. 5–7, 595b25–608b7 (included in the electronic but not in the print edition of the *Treatise on Signs*), Q. 21, arts. 4 and 5, 670a11–693a31, and Q. 22, arts. 1–4, 693a34–715a21 (= *Treatise on Signs*, Book I, questions 4 and 5, and Book II, questions 1–4, respectively); and in Poinsot 1635 – i.e., in the context of his discussion of cognitive organisms in the biological treatises – Q. 6., arts. 2–4, 177b1–198a16, Q. 8, art. 4, 265b1–271b20, Q. 10, arts. 1–5, 295b1–339a45, Q. 11, arts. 1 and 2, 344b1–366b34.

Notice that the contexts in which these questions mainly arise are generally biological and epistemological contexts, whence they inevitably come to a focus also in contexts specifically semiotic (Poinsot 1632a: Book I, questions 4 and 5; Book II, questions 1–4), where it is not too much to say that some of the most difficult and extended passages in Poinsot's attempt to systematize the foundations of semiotic inquiry arise from the need to make this heretofore peripheral topic of natural inquiry central to the establishment of semiotic.

Formal causality in the specificative sense best explains the action of signs from every point of view. This causality can be exercised through the intrinsic constitution of the sign-vehicle (in the case of a natural sign) or not (in the case of an arbitrary sign), as the situation calls for. It is more general than the final causality typical of vital powers, inasmuch as it specifies equally both vital activity and the chance interactions of brute secondness at the level of inorganic nature. This is the causality that enables the sign to achieve its distinctive function of making present what the sign-vehicle itself is not, regardless of whether the object signified enjoys a physical existence apart from the signification. Only extrinsic specificative formal causality is equally suited to the grounding of sign-behavior in chance occurrences (as when the implosion of a star leads to the discovery of a new law of physics, or when accidental scratches become the clue leading to the apprehension of the criminal) and planned happenings.

Once it is understood that the action proper to signs is explained by specificative causality, the central question for understanding the scope of semiosis turns out to be exactly the one asked by Peirce:[76] "What is the essential difference between a sign that is communicated to a mind, and one that is not so communicated?" On the one side of this line is the thirdness of experience, on the other side the thirdness of the laws of nature. How does semiosis link the two? The answer to this question is through the interpretant, which need not be anything mental, but must in every case provide the ground for objectivity. Hence Peirce elaborates on the central question thus:[77]

> If the question were simply what we *do* mean by a sign, it might soon be resolved. But that is not the point. We are in the situation of a zoölogist who wants to know what ought to be the meaning of "fish" in order to make fishes one of the great classes of vertebrates. It appears to me that the essential function of a sign is to render inefficient relations efficient, – not to set them into action, but to establish a habit or general rule whereby they will act on occasion ... A sign therefore is an object which is in relation to its object on the one hand and to an interpretant on the other, in such a way as to bring the interpretant into a relation to the object, corresponding to its own relation to the object.

Thus, the pieces to solve the puzzle of how to ground the Grand Vision are mostly there in Peirce himself, and only a little help is needed from the Latin semiotic tradition to complete the puzzle.

For want of this little extra assistance, Peirce sometimes was tempted to despair of his grand vision, or at least of its ever being established. In these moments, he

---

76 Peirce 1904: CP 8.332. Several interesting versions of this question occur in Poinsot, such as: Is the statue of a dead emperor still a sign of the emperor?; Are the letters in a closed book still signs?; etc. See Poinsot 1632a, passim.
77 Ibid.

could almost sympathize with those of his later critics who would persistently try to reduce the key notion of the *interpretant* to that of an *interpreter*. Thus, in his famous "sop to Cerberus" letter of December 1908, addressed to Lady Victoria Welby (EP 2.478):

> I define a sign as anything which is so determined by something else, called its object, and so determines an effect upon a person, which effect I call its interpretant, that the latter is thereby mediated by the former. My insertion of the term 'upon a person' is a sop to Cerberus, because I despair of making my own broader conception understood.

But in his calmer and more contemplative moments, he threw no such sops. For example:[78]

> Genuine mediation is the character of a Sign. A Sign is anything which is related to a Second thing, its Object, in respect to a Quality, in such a way as to bring a Third thing, its Interpretant, into relation to the same Object, and that in such a way as to bring a Fourth into relation to that Object in the same form, *ad infinitum*. If the series is broken off, the Sign, in so far, falls short of the perfect significant character. It is not necessary that the Interpretant should actually exist. A being *in futuro* will suffice.

Or again:[79]

> For the proper significate outcome of a sign, I propose the name, the interpretant of the sign. ... it need not be of a mental mode of being. Whether the interpretant be necessarily a triadic result is a question of words, that is, of how we limit the extension of the term "sign"; but it seems to me convenient to make the triadic production of the interpretant essential to a "sign" ....

Peirce's suggestion that semiosis is the fundamental process on which all the life forms depend has been taken up since Peirce principally by Thomas A. Sebeok in a variety of works. But Peirce's Grand Vision goes much further, to suggest that semiosis is perhaps the ultimate source of that general progress in physical nature from simple to complex forms that we have heretofore called "evolution".

Filling out this sketch is perhaps the greatest challenge in philosophy today, the over-reaching project, as we might say, for the postmodern era. It is a project well suited to a species on the frontiers of space. And it speaks well of Peirce's "Guess at the Riddle" of the universe that we are, after all, finally considering him in just the light that he hoped. Much criticism has been leveled, and justly leveled, at the way the Peirce papers were handled after his death. Even when parts of them were brought to print, those parts were butchered for presentation to those whose main

---

78 Peirce c.1902a: CP 2.92.
79 Peirce c.1907: CP 5.473.

interest was to understand his writings according to the categories already existing in modern philosophy so far as possible rather than on their own terms. Yet Hartshorne and Weiss, the principal early editors, certainly chose well their opening paragraph for the *Collected Papers* as a whole. For Peirce had for philosophy a postmodern dream to rival and surpass the dreams of Descartes:[80]

> To erect a philosophical edifice that shall outlast the vicissitudes of time, my care must be, not so much to set each brick with nicest accuracy, as to lay the foundations deep and massive. Aristotle built upon a few deliberately chosen concepts – such as matter and form, act and power – very broad, and in their outlines vague and rough, but solid, unshakable, and not easily undermined; and thence it has come to pass that Aristotelianism is babbled in every nursery, that "English Common Sense", for example, is thoroughly peripatetic, and that ordinary men live so completely within the house of the Stagyrite that whatever they see out of the windows appears to them incomprehensible and metaphysical. Long it has been only too manifest that, fondly habituated though we be to it, the old structure will not do for modern needs; and accordingly, under Descartes, Hobbes, Kant, and others, repairs, alterations, and partial demolitions have been carried on for the last three centuries. One system, also, stands upon its own ground; I mean the new Schelling-Hegel mansion, lately run up in the German taste, but with such oversights in its construction that, although brand new, it is already pronounced uninhabitable. The undertaking which this volume inaugurates is to make a philosophy like that of Aristotle, that is to say, to outline a theory so comprehensive that, for a long time to come, the entire work of human reason, in philosophy of every school and kind, in mathematics, in psychology, in physical science, in history, in sociology, and in whatever other department there may be, shall appear as the filling up of its details. The first step toward this is to find simple concepts applicable to every subject.

Nothing so applies to every subject as does the sign. All our knowledge of objects turns out to be in function of the actions of signs, yet pragmaticism was the first way of thinking conceived in recognition of this realization.

Semiotics as the Study of the Possibility of Being Mistaken
Peirce had another name for pragmaticism. He also called this way of thinking *fallibilism*;[81] and insofar as pragmaticism is conceived in function of the doctrine of signs, this alternative designation for it is truly excellent. For just as

---

80   From Peirce c.1898: CP 1.1. Lúcia Santaella-Braga (1992, 1993), perhaps with the dreams of Descartes in mind wherein the modern project of philosophy was explicitated (see chapter 12, p. 512), has even called this passage "the dream of Peirce".

81   Peirce c.1897. CP 1.13: "indeed the first step toward finding out is to acknowledge you do not satisfactorily know already; so that no blight can so surely arrest all intellectual growth as the blight of cocksureness; and ninety-nine out of every hundred good heads are reduced to impotence by that malady – of whose inroads they are most strangely unaware!".

the sign is that which every object presupposes,[82] so the study of signs and the action of signs, semiotics, is *eo ipso* the study of the possibility of being mistaken. The movement of human understanding from confusion in its first apprehension to clarity, unfortunately, is not a simple linear development from confusion to the clear grasp of truths. It is just as often a development from confusion to a clarity that is mistaken. Why it is that we have trouble telling what is real and what is not is rooted in the nature of experience itself, and for understanding this structure Peirce proposed his "New List of Categories" in 1867.

Categories and the Action of Signs

If we care to have an official date for the beginning of the postmodern era in philosophy, 14 May 1867, would suffice. Of course, like all official dates, it is but a fixed point in otherwise shifting sands, a landmark rather than an absolute beginning. The wintry winds of modernity would continue to blow long past this early date, but as the official beginning of spring does not by itself bring an end to winter's blasts, still, it signals that the end is near at hand.

Expanding the Semiotic Frontier

Peirce did not merely recover the Latin *signum*, he at once proceeded to develop it beyond anything to be found in the greatest of the Latin authors. He did not have to work his way to the arduous conclusion that the general notion of sign is no mere nominalism. That is the point at which the Latins had enabled his semiotic to begin. What were loose ends in the semiotic as first systematically realized in a speculative treatise became the threads of the new beginning for the doctrine of signs as Peirce introduced it in postmodern philosophy.

Peirce did not speak of "formal" and "instrumental signs". He did not have to. For him, the overcoming of the divide between nature and culture in the being of the sign was the point of departure, not the point of arrival. And, as we have seen,[83] in arriving at that point as the conclusion of semiotics in the Latin Age, the once-celebrated distinction had been but a stage along the way, and an equivocal one at that. This distinction was at best a terminological marking of analytic points in the doctrine of signs already achieved as early as the thirteenth century. At worst it was a diversion as well as an advance, since nothing in the terminology guaranteed that it needed to be understood as the modal expression of a single underlying or common way of being, as the nominalistic use to which the terminology was put in the work of the learned Fonseca proved.[84]

---

82 Chapter 9 above, p. 434.
83 See chapter 9, p. 432.
84 See "An Appearance to the Contrary Notwithstanding …" and "… Again the Ghost of Nominalism to Haunt Augustine", in chapter 9, p. 412 & 414.

Problems in the Latin Terminology

The defect of the Latin terminology on this point is worth dwelling on, for it helps to understand how it was possible for the moderns to get off on the way of ideas in the first place. We saw that, in the final clarification of the general notion of sign in the Latin Age, the calling of such physical structures as smoke and bones "natural signs" was justified by this fact, subsumed by the Latins, as we have seen over the course of the preceding chapters, under the rubric of transcendental relation: the very physical constitution of such signs serves to guide the formation in experience and cognition of objective relations which duplicate the essential structure of an intersubjectivity which at least at one time obtained independently of and prior to the experience in which such objective relations are here and now formed. But strictly, it is neither the smoke nor the bone but the relation itself so formed which constitutes the sign in its actual being as sign. Technically speaking, the smoke and bones are not signs, but rather *sign-vehicles*; they are signs *fundamentally* but not *formally*, in scholastic parlance.

The sign-vehicle, thus, in contrast to the sign-relation, is the representative element in the sign, while the relation arising *from* this foundation, obtaining (or obtainable) *over and above* the foundation, and *terminating* at a signified object, alone makes this representative element a representation of *something other than itself*. In the absence of this relation, hence, the foundation becomes merely virtual or material *as* a foundation and is then experienced instead simply as a *self*-representation or object.

But the concept or idea, too, the percept of a pure zoösemiosis no less, is a sign-vehicle in just this sense: it too is a subjective structure or modification which, according to its intrinsic being, guides the formation of a relation to an object signified, and as such (as a sign-vehicle) the idea is a sign fundamentally rather than formally. But, unlike the fossil bone or plume of smoke which can exist without being apprehended or known, the idea exists only insofar as it guides an apprehension to the awareness of this rather than that object. It is the knowing that forms the idea, so that the idea cannot be *except* as an idea *of* its object, as something "praecognitum formaliter" – something existing "as the rationale and form whereby an object is rendered known within a power, and so it is precognized formally, not denominatively and as a thing is cognized". In other words, the idea is not objectified as a self-representation.[85]

The bone, of course, which, even in order to signify, is objectified first as a self-representation, is the bone *of* some animal, as the smoke is *of* some fire. But here the *of* refers to the *productive source* of the bone, the animal whose bone it was, or to the fire whence the smoke arises, which is not necessarily an objective relation but only, as a relation, indifferent to the possibility of being objectified and duplicated or made to exist again now in cognition or even in cognition alone. By

85 Poinsot 1632a: Book II, "On the Divisions of Sign", Question 1, "Whether the Division of Sign into Formal and Instrumental Is Univocal and Sound", 226/43–5.

contrast, the *of* in the idea, which is objectified only through its other-representation, refers not to the mind as producing the idea but to *that of which the idea makes the mind aware in producing it*. In other words, the *of* distinctive of the idea as such refers not backward to the idea's productive source as *my* idea or *your* idea, but outward to the objective term of an experience in principle suprasubjective and, insofar, accessible to others besides the one here and now forming the idea that makes the object in question present.

It is necessary to be quite precise in symbolizing this situation, perhaps even more precise than whoever it was among the Latins who originally suggested the designation of the concept as a *signum formale*. For while this designation is justified by the fact that the idea cannot exist *without* founding a relation to an object, it is also a problematic designation inasmuch as the idea (or concept) in itself, that is, as a psychological mode of being, is not the *suprasubjective* referral or relation as such required for renvoi (as the irreducibly triadic relation constitutive of every sign has come to be known[86]). The idea or concept in itself as directly modifying and characterizing a knower is only the *subjective* referral or fundament (the transcendental relation) on which that (ontological sign) relation – in which alone the sign *formally* consists – is based. The existential inseparability of the two (of the transcendental relation of subjective foundation from the ontological relation of suprasubjective connection) in the case of the idea does not gainsay the modal real distinction of relation from its foundation. Nor does it gainsay the fact that the foundation as such is neither suprasubjective, nor (still less) intersubjective, but subjective. But this existential inseparability does explain why an idea, in contrast to, say, our fossil bone, has no existence apart from its semiosic one.

By speaking of *the concept*, the subjective quality or psychological state itself, as a "formal sign", the scholastic analysis did not foreclose the very confusion that surfaced in semiotics when Roman Jakobson proposed *aliquid stat pro aliquo*, "something that stands for something", as a correct formula for sign as such in general.[87] For this formula yet remains open to the interpretation of Fonseca, the interpretation which provides for the very reduction of sign to sign-vehicle that would become in Descartes and Locke the irredeemably solipsistic equation of objects with ideas. The correct formula is, then, rather, *aliquid stat pro alio*, "something that stands for another than itself"; something that may or may not present itself objectively, yet always presents objectively something that it itself is not.

Since the reality of relation and hence of general modes of being was his starting point, Peirce was able to begin more or less at the most advanced point reached in the earlier Latin conversation. He did not first have to consider what fossil bones and ideas of dinosaurs have in common with respect to the dinosaur as an object signified. He simply fastened at once on the fact that the sign in its proper being consists in a relation which is, like all relations, suprasubjective in principle and

---

86 See the essay by this name as chapter 8 in Deely 1994a: 201–44.
87 Jakobson, "A Glance at the Development of Semiotics" (1974), discussed in Deely 1993a.

often intersubjective in fact, but different from all other relations in the physical world in irreducibly involving in principle three and not just two terms. He began at once with the problem of tightening up the terminology of everyone else before him who, in speaking of the sign both strictly and loosely, had trod this ground.

Strictly, Peirce agreed with Poinsot that the sign in its proper and formal being consists not in a representation as such but in a representation only and insofar as it serves to found a relation to something other than itself, namely, an object signified as presented or presentable to and within the awareness of some organism, some observer. He saw also that, loosely, we, like our Latin forebears, speak of sign as that one of the three terms in the triadic relation from which the sign-relation – the sign formally – pointed toward its significate directly and the prospective observer indirectly. At once it was clear to Peirce that a further precision is called for, an improvement in the extant terminology, and "formal vs. instrumental sign", as we have just seen, will hardly do what is called for at this point.

Sign-Vehicle as Representamen

We have seen that that one of the three terms which is loosely called "sign", namely, the sign-vehicle, can be either a physical or a psychical structure. When this term (the sign-vehicle or "sign" loosely so-called) is a material mode of being – such as a sound, a mark, or a movement – it is also a perceptible object in its own right. As a perceptible object, however, the sign need not succeed as a sign. It remains perceptible whether it also functions as a sign (a sound heard and understood as a word) or whether it fails further so to function (a word heard but mistaken for a mere sound and not recognized as a linguistic expression at all, the footstep of a thief in the night heard but mistaken for a rustling of the leaves by wind), although even in such "failed cases" a signification is always virtually nascent, if only in the form of a question – "What?" – leading the mind to investigate further the status of this perceptible object which has intruded upon awareness to become part of a Lebenswelt. Yet all of this is beside the present point.

The present point is that whether the sign loosely so called is a material structure accessible to outer sense or a psychological structure accessible as such only inwardly (by feeling directly and cognition only indirectly, say), this in either case is the element in the sign formally considered that conveys the object signified to the observer, actual or prospective. We have come to call this sign loosely so called (indifferently formal or instrumental in the older parlance) the *sign-vehicle* in contrast to the *sign itself* as triadic relation linking this vehicle to its object signified and the interpretant through which the link is here and now actualized or verified. But Peirce had another name for the sign-vehicle, psychological or physical. He called it the *representamen*.[88]

----

88 Here I would like to repeat my quixotic note on the pronunciation of this Peircean term (Deely 1992: 157n1), which contemporary Peirceans, with the exception of Vincent Colapietro (who is unique among them in not being ignorant of Latin scholasticism), insist on mispronouncing with

"Ground"

And at once we land in yet another quagmire, that of the "ground":[89]

A sign, or representamen, is something which stands to somebody for something in some respect or capacity.[90] It addresses somebody, that is, creates in the mind of that person an equivalent sign, or perhaps a more developed sign. That sign which it creates I call the interpretant of the first sign. The sign stands for something, its object. It stands for that object, not in all respects, but in reference to a sort of idea, which I have sometimes called the ground of the representamen. ...

In consequence of every representamen being thus connected with three things, the ground, the object, and the interpretant, the science of semiotic has three branches.

What are we to understand by "ground" here? The difficulty arises from the fact that the term "ground" is often used to convey the Latin sense of *fundamentum*, the "foundation or ground" in a subject from which a relation springs and upon which the relation depends for its being correlative with a terminus. For example:[91]

though a cause is required for every entity and form, yet in a special sense a fundament is said to be required for a relation, because other forms require a cause only in order to be produced in being and exist, whereas relation – owing to its minimal entitative character and because in terms of its proper concept it is toward another – requires a fundament or ground not only in order to exist but also in order to be able to remain in existence, that is, in order to be a mind-independent rationale of physical being.

---

that insouciance with which Americans approach the sound-system of all languages outside of English. Since it is a question of pronunciation, an audial form, and here my sole medium is scriptal, my foray is perhaps doubly quixotic. Nonetheless, here goes. The term "representamen" is derived from the Latin for "to represent", or "a representation". In accordance with this etymology, the term should not be pronounced, as by the anglophile Peirceans, "represént-a-men", but rather as "represen-tá-men".

89 Peirce c.1897a: CP 2.228–9. See the extended discussion in Dco 2000: esp. 103–22.

90 "A sign, or representamen": the apparent equivalence should not be allowed to obscure the point that a "sign", loosely, Peirce uses to signify the one term in the three-term sign relation which stands for the object signified to the interpretant, the third term. A sign strictly is neither the one nor the other of these three terms but rather the triadic relation itself which unites them in a signification, or, better, through a semiosis. So "sign" in the sense of one of the three terms, namely, the representamen, is what is now coming rather to be called a "sign-vehicle". Whether this new usage will ever completely displace the customary loose usage according to which a "sign" is used as a name for the one of the three elements united in a sign relationship which directly founds the relation to the signified remains to be seen, but I deem it unlikely. Also, perhaps equally unlikely is the chance that the strict and technical sense of "sign" (whereby it names nothing sensible at all but rather a triadic relation as such) will completely supplant the loose sense of "sign" (whereby it names something sensible calling to mind something else).

91 Poinsot, *Tractatus de Signis* (1632a), Second Preamble, "On Relation", art. 2, "What Is Required for Any Relation to Be Categorial", 89/18–27.

But "ground" in this sense, in the case of a sign relation, would be identical with the representamen or sign-vehicle.

The mystery clarifies, however, if it be the case that what Peirce means by ground is exactly that extrinsic formal specification whereby the foundation of a relation gives rise to its relation as terminating at this rather than that aspect of an object signified. In other words, what Peirce means by "ground" is not at all the *foundation* of a relation but rather its strict formal *terminus* as such, very like the crucial Latin analytical concept of *formal object*, which we saw above was so essential to the Latin analysis of cognition[92] and so conspicuously absent from the modern analyses of the same phenomenological data of perception.[93] The ground, then, is that which is directly and immediately presented by a sign in its signified object, by reason of which whatever else is presented in the object as well is presented, as in the following description from the "New List of Categories":[94]

> the conception of a pure abstraction is indispensable, because we cannot comprehend an agreement of two things, except as an agreement in some respect, and this respect is such a pure abstraction as blackness. Such a pure abstraction, reference to which constitutes a quality or general attribute, may be termed a ground.
>
> Reference to a ground cannot be prescinded from being, but being can be prescinded from it.
>
> Empirical psychology has established the fact that we can know a quality only by means of its contrast with or similarity to another. By contrast and agreement a thing is referred to a correlate, if this term may be used in a wider sense than usual. The occasion of the introduction of the conception of reference to a ground is the reference to a correlate, and this is, therefore, the next conception in order.
>
> Reference to a correlate cannot be prescinded from reference to a ground; but reference to a ground may be prescinded from reference to a correlate.
>
> ... suppose we think of a murderer as being in relation to a murdered person; in this case we conceive the act of the murder, and in this conception it is represented that corresponding to every murderer (as well as to every murder) there is a murdered person; and thus we resort again to a mediating representation which represents the relate as standing for a correlate with which the mediating representation is itself in relation. Again, suppose we look up the word *homme* in a French[-English] dictionary; we shall find opposite to it the word *man*, which, so placed, represents *homme* as representing the same two-legged creature which *man* itself represents. By a further accumulation of instances, it would be found that every comparison requires, besides the related thing, the ground, and the correlate, also *a mediating representation which represents the relate to be a representation of the same correlate which this mediating representation itself represents*. Such a mediating representation may be termed an

---

92 See in chapter 7 "The 'Formal Object' of Latin Scholasticism", p. 343.
93 See "Sense and Understanding" in chapter 12, p. 535.
94 Peirce 1867: CP 1.551–3.

interpretant, because it fulfills the office of an interpreter, who says that a foreigner says the same thing which he himself says. The term representation is here to be understood in a very extended sense, which can be explained by instances better than by a definition. In this sense, a word represents a thing to the conception in the mind of the hearer, a portrait represents the person for whom it is intended to the conception of recognition, a weathercock represents the direction of the wind to the conception of him who understands it, a barrister represents his client to the judge and jury whom he influences.

Every reference to a correlate, then, conjoins to the substance the conception of a reference to an interpretant; and this is, therefore, the next conception in order in passing from being to substance.

Reference to an interpretant cannot be prescinded from reference to a correlate; but the latter can be prescinded from the former.

And the discussion continues, but let us leave it at this point. Representamen, we may say with Peirce,[95] is "that which refers to ground, correlate, and interpretant", and we have some definite notion as to what is being talked about.

For perhaps enough has been said to show both how "ground" may be best understood (though there may be some arguments to be made on this point in the framework of the ethics of terminology) and, at the same time, what is principally different about Peirce's semiotic as he picks it up from the Latins. This latter point holds even if we have quite missed the true import of "ground" as a technical term in the Peircean texts.

From the Being of Sign to the Action of Sign

What principally distinguishes the semiotic of Peirce in contrast with semiotics as the Latins left it is this. The Latins, for the most part, got only as far as establishing the being proper to signs, the common factor or element which justifies the notion of sign in general in Augustine's sense and removes it from every theoretical context of nominalism. But Peirce, in good medieval fashion, goes at once from this as established terrain to consider what immediately follows from it, namely, the action proper to signs. For as the Latins liked to say, *agere sequitur esse*, "action follows upon being, 'follows' logically, but is temporally simultaneous therewith and necessary thereto".[96]

Peirce gives his notion of sign in general in dynamic terms. From the first, he tries to keep his eye not on what the sign is as much as on how it acts as a result or consequence of what it is. Recall what Peirce said about the sign in its proper character as a genuine mediation:[97] anything is related to a second thing, its Object, in respect to a quality, its Ground, in such a way as to bring a third thing, its

---

95 Ibid.: CP 1.557.
96 For full discussion of the point, see *The Human Use of Signs* (Deely 1994), ¶3ff.
97 Peirce c.1902a: CP 2.92, cited above at p. 635.

Interpretant, into relation to the same Object, and that in such a way as to bring a fourth into relation to that Object in the same form, *ad infinitum*.

Infinite Semiosis

When an argument slipped off into infinite process, the scholastics, like Aristotle, at that moment jettisoned the argument; for by the fact of involving an infinite process, the argument was known to have skipped a cog in what was up for being explained, namely, some occurrence in the order of physical nature. Infinite process as such begged the question of any sought-for explanation in physical nature, because such a process was possible only by founding relation upon the basis of other relations, which cannot occur in the physical world but only in thought.[98] Indeed, as we saw, this point formed the linchpin in the cosmological form of argument to the existence of God.[99]

But when it comes to the sign, it is no longer a question of seeking for explanations determinately aimed at the order of *ens reale*, "mind-independent being". For the whole point of the sign is that, as mediating objectivity, it is not determinately located in that order, but equally, and, indeed, more fundamentally in a certain sense, in the order of mind-dependent being, inasmuch as outward signs depend upon inward signs, as we saw.[100] Infinite process, repugnant in physical explanations concerned with accounting for how the interactions of finite beings as such bring about this or that condition, are the normal condition with signs. This mind-dependent mediation of the sign as an infinite process is exactly why conspiracy theories, for example, can become irrefutable. The equivalence in objectivity of real and unreal relations make possible the attribution to objects by the mind of relations which, in the nature of the case, *could be* so. *Nothing prevents* their being so – though, on the other hand, nothing requires it. The problem is to decide not what relations could be, but which actually are or were. It is the whole problem of human understanding.

The human individual wakes up intellectually in the middle of a river of signs, for the most part hidden behind, below, and within the objects they present as "the way things are". Neither the banks of the river nor the bottom are in immediate reach. From the individual's point of view, there is neither a beginning point to the process in the past nor a foreseeable end to the process in the future. Once the human mind becomes aware of the role of signs in experience, the individual becomes aware also that he or she is caught up in precisely an infinite process – not a hopeless or self-defeating one, by any means, but neither is it one over which the individual can gain a complete critical control.

This is the situation Peirce found needed accounting for, and it was with this in mind that he devised his system of categories, the third such great system in the history of philosophy. The first great scheme of categories was that of Aristotle,

---

98 See chapter 7, p. 352.
99 See chapter 7, p. 271.
100 See chapter 7, p. 337.

intended to map out the basic irreducible modes of mind-independent being in terms of which we can make unequivocal predications.[101] The second great scheme of categories was that of Kant. We passed over Kant's categories without any discussion of their detail, except to point out that, in the nature of the case, they could provide no more than the essential categories of mind-dependent being insofar as it enters into discourse since, according to Kant, all phenomena are wholly the mind's own construct. Nonetheless, do not be deceived by this fact into thinking that the Kantian scheme is not worth studying. It is filled with triads, which Peirce found very suggestive in finally arriving at his own categories, even though Peirce's are categories of experience in precisely the sense that Kant tried to rule out and foreclose upon for all future philosophy.[102]

A New List of Categories

I call Peirce's "new list of categories" his *semiotic categories*, or the *categories of experience*, because precisely what they do is account for the transformation of the animal Umwelt into the human Lebenswelt. The simplicity of the scheme exhibits the same kind of genius we find in the history of semiotic at the point when Poinsot realized that, by framing the question of sign in terms of the contrast between transcendental and ontological relative, he had hit upon an exclusive and exhaustive alternative wherein the choice became a self-evident one.[103] Peirce gives his categories the names of Firstness, Secondness, and Thirdness.

The reason for the names becomes apparent as the manner in which the categories function unfolds. Experience moves the understanding from a confused total grasp wherein there is no difference between dream and reality, possibility and actuality —because all is wrapped up in one "blooming, buzzing confusion" – to definite experiences and conceptions wherein the determinate plurality intruded into the objective whole (Secondness) becomes intelligible through sign relations. Thus, Firstness is the *primum cognitum* of Aquinas left over as a free-floating problem from the thirteenth century,[104] but one now situated determinately at the base of the doctrine of signs.

The Peculiar Case of Firstness

Firstness is in several ways a particularly interesting case. Not only does the whole categorial scheme depend on its being well understood. It provides a striking exam-

---

101 See chapter 3, p. 73.
102 Mention could also be made of the Hegelian categories, but I think the devastating remark about them made by Peirce is enough for present purposes (1903a: CP 1.544): "Hegel's method has the defect of not working at all if you think with too great exactitude", for he seemed to think the very details of nature deducible by his method of dialectic; in which case we should not have had to wait till 1859 for the results Darwin achieved by mixing detailed observation in with his thinking.
103 See chapter 9, p. 430 above.
104 See chapter 7, p. 341.

ple of the importance of Peirce's ethics of terminology. This example gives a basis
for appreciating why Peirce was led to propose such an idea as a consequence of
his years of study of Latin philosophy in the course of working out his semiotic, or
contribution to the doctrine of signs.

Let us use the occasion to preface a look at the ethics of terminology, therefore,
by an examination of the categories, beginning at the beginning. We will see that
there is more of Latin history that bears on the idea of Firstness than even Peirce
realized. But the fact would not have surprised him in the least, except in the way
of delight. Such was the temper of his mind.

To begin with, there is a difference within experience between what is sensed and
what is understood regardless of whether or not it can also be sensed, especially with
reference to objects whose very understanding essentially excludes a proper sensory
instantiation, either because the object in question has never existed in the physical
environment, or, more radically, because the manner of existence postulated for the
object is *ex hypothesi* of its nature inaccessible to any sensory modality.

This is one way of making the point that there is something which can be
expressed through linguistic means that cannot be communicated in any other
way, something that differentiates human awareness as species-specifically as the
exaptation of language species-specifically differentiates human communication.
Something does so more primordially, since the apprehension in question antecedes
the exaptation of language and, moreover, seems to be of a piece with it. There is, to
refer back to Thomas Aquinas's characterization of the situation, something which is
to understanding (or "intellection") as sound is to hearing[105] and differentiated light
is to seeing.[106] There is, in short, a *primum intelligibile* or "primary intelligible",
just as there is a *primum visibile* or "primary visible" and a *primum audibile* or
"primary audible".

This is not a question that has often been posed in the history of philosophy, as
we have seen, for it is not easily faced. When we look at things, it is the diversity
of shapes and colors, not the omnipresent fact of the differentiation of light that we
call color as enabling seeing at all, that interests us. So too when we listen: it is the
particular sounds and combinations of sounds that interest us, not the general fact that
sound as such enables the particular hearings. So too in investigating what anything
is, it is the particulars of the case, the reason for this feature and that characteristic,
that interest us, not the fact that were things not intelligible in general, the particulars
of the case would both forever elude us and could not be inquired into in the first
place.

The first of all species-specifically human conceptions, therefore, is not a starting
point for intellectual knowledge in a temporal sense. That is to say, it is not a question
of a linear beginning which is left behind as understanding progresses. The question

---

105 Aquinas, *Summa theologiae* (c.1266), I, q. 5, art. 2, p. 191 (Busa vol. 2).
106 Aquinas c.1254/6, *In quattuor libros sententiarum Petri Lombardi* lib. 1, sent. dist. 19, q. 5, art. 1,
     ad 7, p. 55 (Busa vol. 1).

concerns what must be present throughout intellectual awareness whenever and as long as understanding occurs. Other particularized moments of understanding may proceed out of it, but it itself can proceed from nothing else, precisely because, respecting this object (this aspect or dimension of objectivity, let us say), there is no other preceding cognition as basis of its formation. The eye works together with the ear and with touch and taste, and so forth, in forming our perception of an object as sensible. Yet the contribution of each channel is distinct and irreducible. So also with the understanding, which contributes precisely intelligibility to what is directly perceived and sensed. What this intelligibility consists in is the objective world presented in perception apprehended in relation to itself.

The relation of an object to itself is a mind-dependent relation. Even if the object is in one or another aspect also a thing, that is, a mind-independent element of the physical environment, as is always in part the case with an Umwelt, any given thing "in itself" simply is what it is. It is not *related to* itself, it *is* itself. For a thing to be *related* to itself cognition must intervene, and cognition of a specifically intellectual type, able to construct and grasp relations independent of the related terms which, in the present case, are not even distinct mind-independently. Here, however, at the level of *primum intelligibile*, it is not a question of any given object of perception being cognized under a relation to itself. It is rather a question of the objective world as such, the Umwelt as the totality of objectification at any given moment, being grasped in relation to itself.[107] Peirce calls this "Firstness", "the Idea of that which is such as it is regardless of anything else";[108] "the positive internal characters of the subject in itself";[109] "the conception of being or existing independent of anything else";[110] "the present, in general", or "IT":[111]

> This is a conception, because it is universal. But as the act of *attention* has no connotation at all, but is the pure denotative power of the mind, that is to say, the power which directs the mind to an object, in contradistinction to the power of thinking any predicate of that object, – so the conception of *what is present in general*, which is nothing but the general recognition of what is contained in attention, has no connotation, and

---

107 See Poinsot 1635: 315b6–13, 315b30–40; Cajetan 1507: In I p. q. 79, art. 7. The point that Poinsot and Cajetan, and Aquinas before them, struggle to make is perhaps clarified in the contemporary formulation of Corrington (1992: 41): on the one hand, "embodiment radically limits the reach of the self and binds it to the fragmentary conditions of origin": this is the *virtus intellectus*; on the other hand, "the human process is not confined to its sheer embodiment but moves outward through its products and utterances": this is the *capacitas intellectus*, the asymptotic (or syncategorematic) "full reach of the human process" beyond its condition of embodiment – a reach doomed to fall short, to be sure, if actual achievement of infinity is the measure, but a reaching nonetheless ever-more-infinite in prospect and succession in time, according to the Peircean idea that the truth to which mankind has devotion ought not to be merely the "truth as we understand it", but precisely truths we do not yet understand, "truth as a symbolic growth in time".
108 Peirce 1903e: CP 5.66.
109 Peirce c.1906: CP 5.469.
110 Peirce 1891: CP 6.32.
111 Peirce 1867: CP 1.547.

therefore no proper unity. ... Before any comparison or discrimination can be made between what is present, what is present must have been recognized as such, as *it*, and subsequently the metaphysical parts which are recognized by abstraction are attributed to this *it*, but the *it* cannot itself be made a predicate.

Applying to "Firstness" the Ethics of Terminology

Peirce goes on to identify this "it", the objective world as the here and now present in general, with one of the meanings of the philosophical term substance. He excludes from "it" the conception of *being* as a predicative notion bound up with the copula. But his remarks show an ignorance of a main Latin tradition in one of its little explored particulars, the very one we are attempting to explore now, namely, the determination of the species-specifically human contribution to cognition from which language and the postlinguistic symbols of culture in general arise. Being in the sense Peirce rejects as inapplicable to the IT, the being wherein the junction of predicate to subject occurs, is only one of nine or so *derivative* senses Aquinas assigns to "being" as the "*primum cognitum*" of intellection.

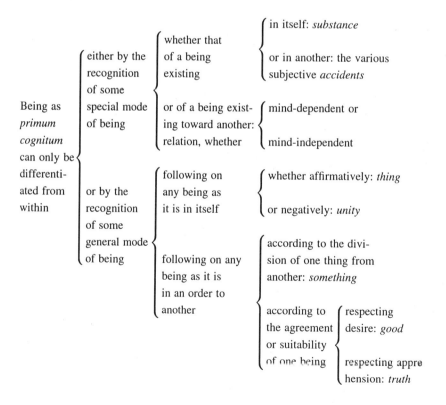

Differentiation from Within of "Being-as-First-Known"

The text in which Aquinas makes this point[112] is too long to cite here, but a diagrammatic summary of it should be useful (opposite page). Especially since the Latin Age, the term "being" is one of those most bandied about in the history of philosophy, whence it has been assigned a number of determinate meanings, including substance, which Peirce also assigns "in one of its meanings" to Firstness or the IT.[113] But in making this assignment Peirce is violating the Third as well as the Sixth Rule of the "Ethics of Terminology". Even the one sense of substance which partially fits the IT – Aristotle's "first substance", which is neither predicated of a subject nor in a subject – does not justify the identification of the two notions, for two reasons.

First, that which is first known by understanding in its difference from sense perception does not fail to be a predicate because it is identified with, or includes in itself, the notion of first substance. It fails because "in the first intellectual cognition of all things neither can the understanding apply itself nor the will the understanding, since there shall not have been another cognition by virtue of which such application could be made, and therefore there is only at work in the case the immediate proportion of object known with power knowing".[114]

Second, that which is first known by understanding is the prospectively definable structure or essence of perceptible objects. This "essence" is not by any means as restricted to "substance" as the being proper to individuals existing as such. "Definable structures" include equally "whatever can be conceived in the manner of some nature and essence, including characteristics of individuals and modes, and indeed singularity itself can be understood after the manner of an essence"[115] – such as the famous *haecceitas*, "thisness" or "form of individuality", in the writings of Scotus. The understanding investigates the properties of perceived objects through the concept of a definable unifying structure indicative of some principle. This structure has an order and dependence on the perception as on the abductive point of departure from which the sought for principle of unification can be derived. It provides also an inductive point of arrival against which the adequacy of the objectified principle can be verified.[116]

We can say, then, that that which is first apprehended intellectually, insofar as intellection differs from perception, is the objective world in relation to itself. In this apprehension the imperceptible "relation to itself" is the sole contribution of understanding. Yet this contribution is sufficient both to elevate the perceptible elements of the Umwelt to the level of intelligibility and, by the same stroke, to transform the Umwelt into a Lebenswelt, that is to say, an objective world perfused with

---

112 Aquinas c.1256/9: *De veritate* q. 1. art. 1 c.
113 Peirce 1867: CP 1.547.
114 Poinsot 1633a: 26b34–27a2. As mentioned in chapter 7 above, p. 355n231, Poinsot's discussion of "being as first known" is, as far as I know, the most extended treatment we have from the Latin Age after Aquinas.
115 Poinsot 1635: 318b7–19.
116 Poinsot 1633a: 33b5–17.

stipulable signs apprehended as such in the heart of otherwise naturally determined significations.

Making the Sensible World Intelligible

It was a very important and insufficiently understood insight of Latin scholasticism that the material elements of the physical environment, insofar as they enter into the cognitive structure constituting an Umwelt, are of themselves sensible but not of themselves intelligible. Understanding itself, taking the materials of sensation and perception as its base, has to make that material actually intelligible. This it does by first seeing the whole material of perception – the objective world or Umwelt in all its parts – in relation to itself, over and above the relations to biological needs and interests which are already factored into the structure of the Umwelt by virtue of the biological heritage of the cognitive organism.[117]

Hence the objective world, seen in relation to itself, already consists of a mixture of mind-independent and mind-dependent relations. But these relations are undistinguished as such. They are not explicitly recognized as mind-dependent, but simply function in accordance with their objective mutual equivalence as relations within the apprehension constitutive of Lebenswelt.[118] Thus, the first action of the

---

117 Poinsot 1635: 318b25–319a5. Poinsot speaks in this text of "abstraction" not as a scientific procedure, but as the simple negative process whereby a cognitive power – in this case, understanding or intellect – fastens on its proper object (i.e., the object which correlatively defines the power in its difference from what other channels of apprehension present or manifest) to the exclusion of all else that falls outside that formality. Guagliardo (1994: Section 3, 375ff.) has one of the few thematic discussions of negative abstraction. See Poinsot 1633a: 31a5–28, and compare this with Peirce's discussion of abstraction or "prescission" in his "New List of Categories" (1867: W 2.50 §5; 1867: CP 1.549).

Thus, the *ens ut primum cognitum*, contrary to common assumptions of the neoscholastics, as we mentioned in chapter 7 above (p. 341f.), is irreducible to *ens* as it is studied in any of the special sciences – *ens reale* or *ens mobile*, which is studied in physics; *ens quantitativum*, which is studied in mathematics; *ens commune* or *ens inquantum ens* or even *ens transcendentale*, such as is studied in Aristotelian or Thomistic metaphysics. *Ens ut primum cognitum* is a notion *sui generis*, prior to all predication as that which makes predication possible to begin with, from which all other notions of being, logical, scientific, or metaphysical, are derived *ab intra*, "from within", and on which all other specifically intellectual notions depend.

118 Aquinas c.1265/6: from the *Disputed Questions on the Power of God*, q. 9. art. 7. ad 6 (Busa 3, p. 258): "among these four transcendental concepts [namely, being, unity, truth, and good], the first by far is being. And for this reason [when, after the internal differentiation of being by nonbeing, predication becomes possible] being must be predicated positively, for negation or privation cannot be the first thing understanding conceives, because what is denied or deprived always belongs to the understanding of negation or privation. But the other three necessarily add over and above being something which being does not reduce to itself; for if they reduce to being they already would not be primitives. But this situation requires that they can add to being only something according to understanding alone: this is either a negation, which adds unity to being (as was said), or relation to something born to be referred to being in every instance ['quod natum sit referri universaliter']. And this last is either the understanding itself to which being conveys the relation of true, or desire, to which it conveys the relation of good." See, in chapter 7, the discussion of "Nonbeing in Latin Philosophy", p. 350, followed

understanding is to apprehend its objects in such a way that they *can eventually* be understood critically, and this is to apprehend the objective world under that mind-dependent relation which allows its contents to appear, truly or falsely, as present-at-hand and not merely ready-to-hand (as they appear to the animals which are not human).

Whence, to Heidegger's question,[119] "Why does Being get 'conceived' 'proximally' in terms of the present-at-hand *and not* in terms of the ready-to-hand, which indeed lies *closer* to us?", the answer lies in the difference between zoösemiosis as common to animals and anthroposemiosis as unique to linguistic animals. *Ens ut primum cognitum*, "Firstness", which constitutes the species-specifically human mode of apprehension underlying the exaptation of language for communicative purposes and at the root of the transformation of Umwelt into Lebenswelt, does no more than establish the foundation for the eventual arising thematically of questions of the form, "What is that?". Ready-to-handness neither requires nor admits of any such thematic development, for it contains no apprehension of otherness in the required sense. Thus:[120]

> The idea of the absolutely first must be entirely separated from all conception of or reference to anything else; for what involves a second is itself a second to that second. The first must therefore be present and immediate, so as not to be a second to a representation. It must be fresh and new, for if old it is second to its former state. It must be initiative, original, spontaneous, and free; otherwise it is second to a determining cause. It is also something vivid and conscious; *so only it avoids being the object of some sensation.* It precedes all synthesis and all differentiation; it has no unity and no parts. It cannot be articulately thought: assert it, and it has already lost its characteristic innocence; for assertion always implies a denial of something else.[121] Stop to think of it, and it has flown! What the world was to Adam on the day he opened his eyes to it, before he had drawn any distinctions, or had become conscious of his own existence – that is first, present, immediate, fresh, new, initiative, original, spontaneous, free, vivid, conscious, evanescent. Only, remember that every description of it must be false to it.

The animal aware of its objective world in such a fashion is alone positioned to form the conception, along with that of "reality", and of a piece with it, of *otherness*. Otherness (present-at-handness, in contrast to the ready-to-handness which reduces the environment within objectivity to the level of that extension of organismic

---

by the discussion of "The Order of Primitive Concepts" consequent upon being-as-first-known, p. 355.

119 Heidegger 1927: 487.
120 Peirce c.1890: CP 1.357, italics added.
121 See, in chapter 7, the discussion of "The Order of Primitive Concepts" consequent upon being-as-first-known, p. 355.

dispositions which is the essence of an Umwelt proportioned to the biological nature of the cognizing organism) arises precisely within experience through "brute actions of one subject or substance on another, regardless of law or of any third subject".[122] It is "the conception of being relative to, the conception of reaction with, something else".[123] It is, in a word, the conception of "something other", of one thing different from another thing within the play of objects of awareness. The experience of otherness within firstness is the motivation of every question of the form "What is that?"[124]

We have already seen that the ground of this question is established by the mind itself in presenting the objective world intellectually as relative to itself and, insofar, intelligible. "The formal rationale of knowing of the understanding", the Latins argued,[125] "in which understanding is distinguished from perception, is not the singularity itself of sensations, but the very definable structure of which singularity is a mode".

Sense perception and understanding work together as contraries within the genus of knowing. The former is primarily and essentially ordered to manifesting the individuating sensible characteristics of objects signified. The latter is primarily and essentially ordered to manifesting the relative structure which gives to the sensible properties their pattern of intelligibility as manifesting the underlying relations which give to the world as perceived its definable structures, both "natural" and "cultural".[126]

Relations and the Knowledge of Essences

We see, then, that the so-called "essences of material things" actually consist, so far as understanding is concerned, in *patterns of relationships* instantiated or verified in perceptible objectivities, but that the *relationships themselves*, in contrast to the elements of the system related, are never as such perceptible, though they can be understood. Thus, the grasping of the relationships themselves, in their distinction from the perceptible aspects of the objective world which manifest and sustain them, is precluded for an animal which has only sensation and perception to rely on, in their contrast with understanding.

Especially important to grasp at this juncture is a point made in passing by Thomas Aquinas quite early in his career,[127] in reflecting on the medieval doctrine that the intellect (in its difference from sense) is ordered to grasping the *quidditates*

---

122 Peirce c.1906: CP 5.469.
123 Peirce 1891: CP 6.32.
124 The fundamental awareness or apprehension is neither of existence as such nor of intelligibility – "essence" or "possibility" – as separate from existence, but simply of a *prospective intelligibility given in and through experience*. See Poinsot 1633a: 23b34–24a41.
125 Poinsot 1633a: 32b37–33a13.
126 See Aquinas c.1265/6: *Disputed Questions on the Power of God*, q. 9. art. 7. ad 15.
127 Aquinas c.1254/6: *Commentary on the Sentences of Peter Lombard*, lib. I. dist. 19. q. 5. art. 1. ad 7.

rerum sensibilium, "the definable structures of material being". "Even the being of an essence", he says, insofar as the human understanding lays hold of it, "is a kind of being of reason".[128] Essence "insofar as human understanding lays hold of it" is a kind of being of reason not simply because it is something known, for the known simply as such may equally be a being of nature. Essence as grasped by the understanding is a being of reason in the sense that the pattern of relations constituting what any given phenomenon – natural or cultural – is, so far as the understanding grasps that structure, is constructed by the understanding on the pattern of relations it has experienced as physically given and obtaining within the objective world.

Thus, the sensations elaborated within perception give us a structured world of embodied objects, and those aspects of the objects sensible as such coincide further with the physical surroundings as an environment common – as physical – to all the life forms.

On the basis of things as presented through the senses, the mind is provided with materials for the imagination to construct worlds which are not presented as such within perception, but "only imagined". Within these materials provided through perception, the understanding finds relations as well as related things, where perception finds only related things; and understanding constructs also relations of its own devising.

The relations constructed by the mind on the pattern of physical relations given in experience have this in common with the physical relations at their modular base: both the constructed relations and the physically given relations are truly relations, and both are experienced as such within the world of society, language, and culture. In contrast to these objective constructs are the objective constructs which are made on the basis of our experience of individuals and their characteristics, which are decidedly not themselves relations though they are involved in relations and are experienced, as we have seen, through these relations. Thus, we see not merely colors, shapes, and movements, but college presidents, diplomats, and policemen. The objects experienced are, from the standpoint of the physical environment as such, mixtures of mind-dependent and mind-independent relations. Both of these – the mind-dependent and the mind-independent, the relatively "unreal" and the relatively "real", relations – constitute the object of experience as such in its proper being and as "first intentions" thereof.[129]

---

128 Ibid. (Busa 1, p. 55, italics added): "etiam quidditatis esse est quoddam esse rationis, et secundum istud esse dicitur veritas in prima operatione intellectus: per quem etiam modum dicitur definitio vera. *sed huic veritati non adjungitur falsitas per se, quia intellectus habet verum judicium de proprio objecto in quod naturaliter tendit, quod est quidditas rei, sicut et visus de colore*".

129 Recall here the discussion of the notions of "first and second intentions" from chapter 7, p. 351ff. See further, in Poinsot's *Treatise on Signs*, First Preamble, Art. 2, 60/7–25; and Book I, Quest. 2, 141/12–14: "not every mind-dependent objective relation is a second intention, because even though every mind-dependent relation results from cognition, yet not every such relation denominates a

When we "invent" a character, such as Sherlock Holmes or Hamlet, in contrast to "real" characters such as Detective Tom Schaefer of the Dubuque Police Department or Cleopatra, the invented character is nothing besides a pattern of characteristics, nothing more than an objective nexus of mind-dependent relations. Some of these – the relations in which the character is involved, such as social roles, kinship, legal adversary, paternity – *are* themselves, as relations, just what that after which they are patterned are. Others of the characteristics – the size, weight, gender, and physiognomy of the character, say – consist in a being patterned after (consist in mind-dependent relations imitating) that which they themselves *are not*, namely, subjective characteristics of being given in our experience of objects as coincident with physical things. Thus, *the whole* of the invented creature is a pattern of relationships, both those of its features which are presented as if they were not mere relationships ("beings patterned after") and those of its features which are presented just as if they were physical relationships, even though all of the invented creature's features are "in reality" constituted by purely objective relations.

For this reason Poinsot, here following Aquinas and other major Latin authors, who in turn base themselves largely on texts of Aristotle,[130]divided being into natural (*ens naturale seu reale*) and mind-dependent, or *purely* objective being (*ens rationis*). Natural being is further subdivided into individuals with their characteristics and relations. Mind-dependent being is divided into relations formed on the pattern of natural relations and relations formed on the pattern of individuals with their subjective characteristics. This last class of mind-dependent relations the Latins called "negations", because – being relations – they were *not*, as relations, what their exemplars in nature *are*, namely, subjects (individuals) with their subjective characteristics. Negations and relations, thus, are both relations ontologically and objectively, and together they constitute the entire inventory of mind-dependent being – of being as *purely* objective.

In a word, *relations* constitute the entire inventory of mind-dependent being, both that part of it which diverges from the physical reality of the environment and that part of it which coincides with aspects and features of the physical surroundings. A synoptic diagram is useful here (opposite page).

From this we see that *objective* relations as such are neither physical (mind-independent) nor psychical (mind-dependent), but, although always determinately one or the other in a given case, are capable of being either, depending on changing circumstances. Hence, objective relations sometimes *pass back and forth within*

---

thing only in the state of a cognized being, which is a second state, but some also do so in the state of an existence independent of cognition, as, for example, the relations of being a doctor, being a judge. For the existing man, not the man as cognized, is a doctor or a judge, and so those mind dependent relations [being a doctor, judge, teacher, etc.] denominate a state of existence.

"You may gather from what has been said that even in the case of stipulated signs the rationale of sign must be explained by a relation to a signified."

130 See, in chapter 3, "The Categories", p. 73ff.; in chapter 7, "Nonbeing in Latin Philosophy", p. 350ff.

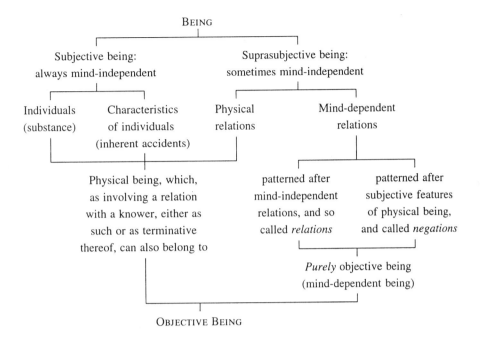

BEING

Subjective being:
always mind-independent

Suprasubjective being:
sometimes mind-independent

Individuals
(substance)

Characteristics
of individuals
(inherent accidents)

Physical
relations

Mind-dependent
relations

Physical being, which,
as involving a relation
with a knower, either as
such or as terminative
thereof, can also belong to

patterned after
mind-independent
relations, and so
called *relations*

patterned after
subjective features
of physical being,
and called *negations*

Purely objective being
(mind-dependent being)

OBJECTIVE BEING

The Interpenetration of Subjective and Suprasubjective Being in Objectivity

objectivity from a condition of being now mind-dependent, now mind-independent, and conversely.

An illustrative example. Two lovers travelling to meet one another at 1900 hours are involved in a whole network of physical and objective relations, and some of the physical relations in which they are involved are as such objective, that is, physical relations of which the parties are well aware. At precisely 1845 (i.e., 6:45 PM), unbeknownst to the young man who continues toward his appointed and agreed rendezvous, the young woman is struck by a meteor and instantly killed. At that moment, whatever physical relations she was involved in as such ceased, for physical relations require the existence of both terms in order to exist. The objective relations, of course, being sustained not by the dynamics of physical being as such but by semiosis, are, as objective, unaffected by the dramatic change in circumstances – except in this crucial particular: those of the objective relations which were *also* physical became, at 1845, *only* objective. Yet, for want of knowledge of the changed circumstances, the young man continued to rush on at 1850 hours just as he had been rushing at 1840 hours, so as not to keep his love waiting.

This example makes a quintessential point: the entitative character of a relation in its rationale as a relation is unaffected by the difference between being mind-dependent or mind-independent. One and the same relation, under different circumstances, can be one time only physical, one time both physical and objective, and another time only objective, in each case owing wholly to surrounding circumstances extrinsic to the being of the relation as such. Of course, the example could be used to make other points as well, existential as well as epistemic. One could concentrate on the tragedy of the situation, on how the continued implicit judgment "She is waiting for me now!" has been falsified and hopes crushed by a tragic loss soon to make itself known. Within the tragic transobjective subjectivity of individual being bound up with the objectivity of real and unreal relations by the action of signs or semiosis there is room for a whole "semiotic existentialism" and for novels to rival the best of Camus and Sartre. But while one example may make many points, any given use of the example, to be effective, needs to stick to one point as the "lesson of the moment".

The crucial point that one and the same relation, depending on circumstances alone, can exist with rationale unchanged, one time physically another time purely objectively, bears directly on the matter of supposed essences or "quiddities" of things insofar as they are *known* essences, that is to say, objective. There is no doubt that physical structures of the environment are internally determined and structured in their parts and in their relations to other physical structures – are "transcendentally relative", as the Latins said. Let us take again the example of the bone of a dinosaur. It is a physical structure. That structure can come to be known and, if respected, can even be made to tell us whether it is the bone of an apatosaurus, a pterodactyl, or indeed of some other of the great reptiles. The Greek and Latin doctrine of transcendental relation,[131] without using the name, was perfectly grasped by Cuvier (1769–1832), who made it the basis of modern paleontology and comparative anatomy:[132] "commencing our investigations by a careful survey of any one bone by itself, a person who is sufficiently master of the laws of organic structure may, as it were, reconstruct the whole animal to which that bone belonged", the environment essential to such an animal, and so on from part to part, one thing leading to another, to encompass eventually – in principle – the whole physical universe. For each bone, by its subjective structure, tells us where it fits and where it doesn't. The head-bone, for good reason, is connected to the neck-bone and not to the knee-bone! At the same time, the bones may be scattered about, their connection not obvious, their relation to an actual animal as dead as the species of which the animal once formed part of the genetic population. Yet each isolated bone contains the secret of the part of the animal to which it belonged and of the whole of the animal of which it was a part. Unlocking that secret of the dead is the work of the mind, should it be done.

Yet the finite mind needs that whereon and wherewith to work! It is the peculiar nature of relation, *first* as transcendental in the subjective structure of the bones,

---

131 See "Transcendental Relativity: Substance and Inherent Accidents" in chapter 3, p. 72; "Transcendental Relation" in chapter 6, p. 228; and the summary "Resuming the Ancient Discussion in Latin Terms" in chapter 9, p. 423.
132 From Cuvier's 1812–25 *Recherches sur les ossemens fossiles des quadrupèdes*, as cited from Cuvier 1818: 123f.

which enables those bones (or even forces them, in the right circumstances) to "tell their own story"; *then* as ontological in suprasubjective structure of referral wherein what is no longer physically is yet modeled and reconstituted objectively. For being able to tell a determinate story – not just any story, but the story true of these bones – is one thing, quite another actually to tell the story: "whence the thought of Aquinas forever distinguishes transcendental from ontological relation in the fact that what is principally signified by a transcendental relative is not a relation as such but rather that upon which a relation follows" when the circumstances dictate it (in which case the consequent relation is "categorial", that is to say, physical and provenates from nature) "or could follow" (as when the consequent relation, physical under other circumstances, under these circumstances here and now is only objective and provenates from thought).[133]

So in order to yield up its secrets of the physical world and the past, the bone must first of all be perceived. The transcendental relativity of things in the environment provides no more than the *prospective foundation*, a physical interpretant, for a scientific understanding to work with. The *"knowledge* of essences" arises, if at all, only in and through the ontological character of the objective relations that come to be founded on that transcendental relativity both in perception and (especially) understanding. The one perceiving the bone may be an ignorant human animal, or indeed an animal other than human. As a key to the past and to some scientific knowledge, the bone is in this case wasted, though it may be excellent to chew on or to use as a club. However, with luck, the one perceiving the bone, the one for whom the bone is objectified, may happen to be a paleontologist. In this circumstance the bone becomes a sign, not of a chew toy or of warfare, but of the age of the dinosaurs, and of some individual and type of individual dinosaur as well. A relation which was once physical between the bone and the dinosaur whose bone it was now has a chance of being reconstructed by the scientific mind. Should that happen, a relation once only physical comes to exist again, unchanged as a relation – that is to say, in its essential rationale and structure as a relation – but now existing only as purely objective.

The bone is not the bone of a shark. It is, and was all along, the bone of a dinosaur. That is its distinctive being, its subjectivity; that is its transcendental relativity, its subjectivity as a former part of the being "of a dinosaur"; that is what it is in itself. But for its *relation* to be realized, either the dinosaur had still to exist *or* a sufficiently knowledgeable observer had to objectify the bone. Either circumstance gives rise to the ontological relation "of a dinosaur",[134] whereas in the absence of

---

133 Poinsot, *Tractatus de Signis* (1632a), Second Preamble, "On Relation", Art. 2, "What is required for a relation to be physical", 89/21–90/30; also 99/6–42.

134 By contrast, as we have just seen, the bone as *"bone of* a dinosaur" is rather a transcendental relation, a subjective structure of physical being from which an ontological relation can arise, whether in nature or as the objective basis guiding the formation of a cognition. See Poinsot's *Treatise on Signs* (1632a), esp. 108/38–109/3.

both circumstances the *relation* as such, but not indeed *the bone* as such (the bone as a physical structure of calcium, etc.), wants for existence.

Nor is transcendental relativity restricted in its import to the world of nature. It applies also to the world of culture and the human self. Consider Russon's query,[135] which points directly to the need to understand not only substance, as we have seen, but the "substantial self" under the requirements of transcendental relativity:

> One of the ideas with which we are most comfortable in our everyday life is the idea that we are self-enclosed, independent beings. We strongly defend our claim to being self-possessed, insisting that "it's my view, and I have a right to it", or "that's mine", or "I'll do what I like". In each case, we identify ourselves as the "I" who is in charge of its own affairs, which means an "I" with a unique point of view, with a unique body, and with a unique will to initiate actions. On this view, it is up to each one of us to determine who we are and what we shall do. If this is what we are really like, then tradition has little intrinsic value: if we are in full self-possession, then traditions do not bind us or direct us or generate us, but are at most amusing objects of observation.

Nor is this surprising; for one of the best kept secrets of the modern attempt to sharply differentiate the *Naturwissenschaften* from the *Geisteswissenschaften*, and culture from nature in general, is that culture is a part of nature, albeit a distinctive part – whence Sebeok's imperial reference[136] to "that minuscule segment of nature some anthropologists grandly compartmentalize as culture."

Now since mind-dependent and mind-independent relations are univocal in their being as *objective* relations, just this circumstance arises: we can be deceived and cannot always tell when a relationship we have posited for the purpose of understanding some physical structure, or, indeed, some cultural structure, is real or unreal. We perforce rely on models in order to answer the question what something is, and models are systems of objective relations which may or may not be duplications of a system of *physical* relations as well. Insofar as the model is an accurate model, that is, insofar as it actually represents the physical structure we seek to understand, it provides us with the essence, the "quiddity", of the structure in question, whether

---

135 Russon 1997: 3. Indeed this remarkably unified collection which Russon introduces strongly suggests to me that one of the permanent values of the work of Hegel in the postmodern development will be a way of understanding the historical, cultural world traditionally seen in opposition to the world of nature as participating in the same requirements for intelligible discourse as physical being itself under the notion of transcendental relation as grounding and guiding ontological relations wherever and to the extent that they participate of *ens reale*. This suggestion strongly resonates with the pioneering work of A. F. Russell (1981, 1982, 1984) in bringing the work of R. G. Collingwood, one of the offshoots of Hegel's influence, into the mainstream development of the postmodern semiotic discourse; and the fact that Russell's work is pioneering in this regard is only another sign – yet another one – of how much remains to be done, how open the future is, how wide the path of inquiry.

136 Sebeok 1984a: 3.

that structure be natural or cultural. This need for models is nicely conveyed in a text Aquinas penned quite late in his lifelong series of reflections on *ens ut primum cognitum*:[137]

> It is impossible for the human mind ... actually to understand anything except by the use of models in the imagination. ... This is something that anyone can experience for themselves, namely, the fact that when one tries to understand something, one forms for the purpose some imaginary model to provide examples in which one can, as it were, inspect that which one desires to understand. And thence it is that even when we wish to make someone else understand something, we propose for that person examples on the basis of which he or she can form a model for understanding. ... And so reliance on imaginary models is necessary for the human mind to actually understand its proper object, for only in this way is the mind able to see a universal nature instantiated in a particular.

These models, Aquinas explains, in which our knowledge of "essences" (whether physical or cultural) principally, though not exclusively, consists, are not in

---

137 Thomas Aquinas, *Summa theologiae* (c.1266), I. q. 84. art. 7 c. (Busa vol. 2, p. 309): "... impossibile est intellectum nostrum, secundum praesentis vitae statum, quo passibili corpori coniungitur, aliquid intelligere in actu, nisi convertendo se ad phantasmata. ... hoc quilibet in seipso experiri potest, quod quando aliquis conatur aliquid intelligere, format aliqua phantasmata sibi per modum exemplorum, in quibus quasi inspiciat quod intelligere studet. et inde est etiam quod quando alium volumus facere aliquid intelligere, proponimus ei exempla, ex quibus sibi phantasmata formare possit ad intelligendum. huius autem ratio est, quia potentia cognoscitiva proportionatur cognoscibili. unde intellectus ... humani, qui est coniunctus corpori, proprium obiectum est quidditas sive natura in materia corporali existens; ... de ratione autem huius naturae [rei sensibilis] est, quod in aliquo individuo existat, quod non est absque materia corporali; ... unde de natura ... cuiuscumque materialis rei, cognosci non potest complete et vere, nisi secundum quod cognoscitur ut in particulari existens. particulare autem apprehendimus per sensum et imaginationem. et ideo necesse est ad hoc quod intellectus actu intelligat suum obiectum proprium, quod convertat se ad phantasmata, ut speculetur naturam universalem in particulari existentem."
His concluding remark of the article against Platonism and Neoplatonism bears citing as well: "si autem proprium obiectum intellectus nostri esset forma separata; vel si naturae rerum sensibilium subsisterent non in particularibus, secundum Platonicos; non oporteret quod intellectus noster semper intelligendo converteret se ad phantasmata." In this Kant's own idea of the noumenon finds precedent and resonance in the epistemology of Thomas Aquinas: see Kant 1783: §33, partially cited in chapter 13, p. 559n27. We can only wonder what Aquinas would have said of the "celestial hierarchy" of Dionysius had he known that the author was Pseudo-Dionysius. For surely we find there added to the house of experience "a much more extensive wing", furnished not only by transgressing the legitimate bounds of concepts based on experience but also by invoking an authority fictionally (not to say fraudulently: see the discussion in chapter 4 above, p. 132ff., text and notes) assumed. Take away the authority, remove the fiction, and then what are we to say of the "ecclesiastical hierarchy" modeled on the celestial one and embodied in historical structures originally justified by appeal to the legend of the authority and the fiction of the celestial hierarchy assumed as fact? It is a daunting task of theological deconstruction, as we have already had occasion to comment in passing (above, chapter 4, p. 134f.; chapter 5, p. 193ff.).

themselves true or false, though such a model can be said to be "true" insofar as it adequates the "reality" it has been constructed to explain by illustration.[138]

We see then that the grasp of being as first known (*ens ut primum cognitum*) is intimately related to the notion that the human mind can grasp the "essences" of material things (*quidditates rerum materialium*), but that this knowledge has nothing to do with a special intuition or immediate insight *into* what things are "beyond their sensible appearances". On the contrary, a "grasp of an essence" is normally those very sensible appearances themselves subsumed under the pattern of a set of relations abstractly taken apart from the instances and supposed or considered to exhibit the unique character of some object, whether real or fictional.

Two More Categories

The physical world "is what it is" when the individual human being is born into it as a part. That physical world intrudes itself through sensation at every point, sometimes brutally. That is why Peirce calls the physical interactions among the various parts of the physical environment, as including humans and other organisms,

---

138 See Aquinas c.1254/6: *Commentary on the Sentences of Peter Lombard*, Book I, dist. 19. q. 5. art. 1. ad 5 and 7 (Busa vol. 1, p. 55). Ad 5: "quamvis esse sit in rebus sensibilibus, tamen rationem essendi, vel intentionem entis, sensus non apprehendit, sicut nec aliquam formam substantialem, nisi per accidens, sed tantum accidentia sensibilia. ita etiam quamvis veritas sit in rebus sensibilibus, prout dicitur esse veritas in rebus, tamen intentio veritatis solo intellectu percipitur. vel dicendum, quod quamvis res sensibiles sensu comprehendantur, tamen earum adaequatio ad intellectum sola mente capitur, et pro tanto dicitur, quod veritas est sola mente perceptibilis.

Ad 7: "cum sit duplex operatio intellectus: una quarum dicitur a quibusdam 'imaginatio intellectus', quam philosophus nominat 'intelligentiam indivisibilium', quae consistit in apprehensione quidditatis simplicis, quae alio etiam nomine formatio dicitur; alia est quam dicunt fidem, quae consistit in compositione vel divisione propositionis: prima operatio respicit quidditatem rei; secunda respicit esse ipsius. et quia ratio veritatis fundatur in esse, et non in quidditate, ideo veritas et falsitas proprie invenitur in secunda operatione, et in signo ejus, quod est enuntiatio, et non in prima, vel signo ejus quod est definitio, nisi secundum quid; sicut etiam quidditatis esse est quoddam esse rationis, et secundum istud esse dicitur veritas in prima operatione intellectus: per quem etiam modum dicitur definitio vera. sed huic veritati non adjungitur falsitas per se, quia intellectus habet verum judicium de proprio objecto, in quod naturaliter tendit, quod est quidditas rei, sicut et visus de colore; sed per accidens admiscetur falsitas, scilicet ratione affirmationis vel negationis annexae, quod contingit dupliciter: vel ex comparationis definitionis ad definitum, et tunc dicitur definitio falsa respectu alicujus et non simpliciter, sicut definitio circuli est falsa de triangulo; vel in respectu partium definitionis ad invicem, in quibus implicatur impossibilis affirmatio; ... secundae autem operationi admiscetur falsitas etiam per se ... quantum ad consequentes: quia rationem inducendo contingit errare per applicationem unius ad aliud." To which, apropos of the *transcendentalia*, he adds this fascinating remark: "verum proprie loquendo, quod non invenitur tantum in complexis, non impedit conversionem veri et entis: quia quaelibet res incomplexa habet esse suum, quod non accipitur ab intellectu nisi per modum complexionis; et ideo ipsa ratione quam addit verum supra ens, scilicet ordinem ad intellectum, sequitur ista differentia, quod verum sit complexorum. et ens dicatur de re extra animam incomplexa".

The only contemporary work I am aware of as taking up fully this point of view Aquinas expresses is Wallace 1996.

"brute secondness". Firstness is as a dream out of which *ens reale*, the category of Secondness, inevitably at times awakens a sleeper.

But the realm of secondness is in itself also a structured realm, both subjectively and intersubjectively. Secondness comprises not only real individuals of various sorts, but myriads of real relations among them. To these the mind becoming aware of its surroundings adds relations of its own, to organize the objective world according to its own purposes and interests. This process, together with the assimilation of some of the environment's own relations and the sorting out of the whole network of relations constitutive of objectivity, constitutes Peirce's category of Thirdness.[139]

Thus, the categories are related not as building blocks but as compenetrating dimensions of human experience as the experience is developed, structured, and constantly modified by the action of signs. It is a question of "whether there be a life in Signs",[140] of accounting for the fact that "symbols grow".[141] The interpenetration of the categories in the constitution of experience as that through which the world becomes intelligible is the whole point of the "New List". "The world of fact contains only what is, and not everything that is possible of any description", Peirce points out,[142] and hence "the world of fact cannot contain a genuine triad. But though it cannot contain a genuine triad, it may be governed by genuine triads." So he describes his third category as marking a definite position, precisely one of the positions occupied by pragmaticism in the field of philosophical history:[143]

> a position which the pragmaticist holds and must hold, whether that cosmological theory be ultimately sustained or exploded, namely, that the third category – the category of thought, representation, triadic relation, mediation, genuine thirdness, thirdness as such – is an essential ingredient of reality, yet does not by itself constitute reality, since this category (which in that cosmology appears as the element of habit) can have no concrete being without action, as a separate object on which to work its government, just as action cannot exist without the immediate being of feeling on which to act. The truth is that pragmaticism is closely allied to the Hegelian absolute idealism, from

---

139 So the interaction of the subjectivity of environmental aspects of physical being with the mind in provenating a complex of ontological relations indifferently physical as well as objective or purely objective here and now, the ground of the convertibility of being and truth, as we have seen, is also the source of meaning even among those physical entities which, as artefacts, are *already* embodiments of finite mind and expressions of culture. Robert Wood has developed this consequence of medieval doctrine quite apart from the further question of its essentially semiotic structure (Wood 1966: 51): "the identification of this empirical object before us as an instance of universal paper finds meaning only insofar as paper in general is seen as related to writing implements in general, language in general, etc. – that is, paper finds meaning only as related to the world of communication as such. And each region of the world finds its significance in terms of the world as such, i.e., a view of being."

140 Peirce c.1902: CP 2.111.

141 Peirce 1893: CP 2.302.

142 Peirce c.1896: CP 1.478.

143 Peirce 1905: CP 5.436.

which, however, it is sundered by its vigorous denial that the third category (which Hegel degrades to a mere stage of thinking) suffices to make the world, or is even so much as self-sufficient. Had Hegel, instead of regarding the first two stages with his smile of contempt, held on to them as independent or distinct elements of the triune Reality, pragmaticists might have looked up to him as the great vindicator of their truth. ... For pragmaticism belongs essentially to the triadic class of philosophical doctrines, and is much more essentially so than Hegelianism is.

Peirce's categorial scheme is neither a scheme designed to express exclusively what is there in the objective world prior to the scheme and independently of it, as Aristotle's was, nor is it a scheme designed to express exclusively necessary aspects of the mind's own working in developing discursively the content of experience, as Kant's was. Peirce's scheme is designed to express the mixture and interweave of mind-dependent and mind-independent relations which constitute human experience in its totality as a network of sign relations, a semiotic web (or semiosic web). This web is a living tissue of relations. It not only ties together nature and culture, but it does so in a community of understanding, a "community of inquirers". As the spider depends on its web to catch its food, so the understanding sustains and nourishes itself from what its web of relations catches of reality and transforms into culture.

With the help of language, the web of understanding, spun of sign relations, keeps up contact over the centuries even with fellow workers of the life of the mind long dead in bodily form. For the community of inquirers making its way toward truth in the long run is not some isolated band, but includes all those human beings who have come before and will come after us, to the extent that they weave strands into the web that become part of our common heritage, reaching from the depths of the unconscious to the farthest reaches of human speculation in search of what is or what could be better.

It is not surprising that Peirce, in a play of musement, developed a "neglected argument for the existence of God",[144] the first serious advance in a cosmological argument since Aquinas, of whose "fifth way" the "neglected argument" can be considered a semiotic elaboration of much fuller and more credible form in a post-Darwinian universe.

The Ethics of Terminology

Who ever heard of such a thing? And who but Peirce among the moderns could even have dreamed of such a thing, let alone propose it? Next to his pragmaticism, of which it forms a piece, the ethics of terminology is, perhaps, the most postmodern idea in the Peircean corpus.

---

144 Peirce 1908a: CP 6.452–85.

General Discussion

I had known of Peirce's terminological canons as an odd idea, one of many such in Peirce, which I had no particular reason to ponder until I first posed for myself the question of how, exactly, *do* signs work? It was in the context of examining Sebeok's claim[145] that sign-science and life-science are co-extensive[146] that I first began to discover that Peirce himself, in this area, had run afoul of his own rules. Later, in trying to think through the whole matter of the species-specifically human use of signs whereby Umwelt becomes Lebenswelt,[147] I began to gain a serious appreciation for the terminological canons Peirce had proposed. I found myself using them enough times, in the end, to have to add an Appendix to that work[148] with the complete list of rules in order to enable readers to see for themselves "what the shooting was about".

I also came to see clearly why this, one of Peirce's most important ideas, is also his most neglected idea. It is the one feature of his thought which imposes on his would-be students or followers the obligation thoroughly to school themselves in the Latin scholasticism as it flourished before Descartes, an obligation which, for reasons not difficult to imagine, his admirers have been so far almost unanimous in finding ways to avoid. We are still close enough to modernity that its pernicious attitude of contempt for previous historical developments in philosophy breathes strong, even in the early postmodern air. On top of becoming aware of and getting some control over this pernicious attitude, there is the need to learn Latin to investigate with full seriousness Peirce's Latin sources in semiotics, and the several other Latin sources of even greater semiotic importance than the several Peirce heroically managed to rediscover. This is a challenge before which most hearts continue to sink (though it is not nearly so great a hurdle as they imagine[149]). Look at the bright side: since there was no general notion of sign before Augustine, at least you don't have to learn Greek as well (still, that is advisable).

In my own reading of Peirce, at first I thought that his "ethics of terminology" was surely some side or subsidiary point. Conversation with Ken Ketner soon disabused

---

145 Sebeok 1968, 1990, 1991.

146 See "Are Sign-Science and Life-Science Coextensive?" (Deely 1991).

147 Deely 1994.

148 See Deely 1994: 173–4.

149 See the encouraging and accurate remarks on the ease of learning the Latin of Aquinas in A. D. Sertillanges's classic discussion of *The Intellectual Life* (1948: 112): "A man who would allow himself to be deterred by the slight effort needed to make his way about a language that an ordinary mind can master in two months would not deserve to have interest wasted on his mental training"; for, as the translator explains (p. 112 n. 1), "the Thomist vocabulary is so limited, the turns of speech so often recur and are so free from the features that make Latin difficult that really only laziness can hesitate when a treasure is to be had at the price of so slight an effort." Be all that as it may, it remains that reading the Latin of Aquinas is like looking through miles of the clearest water, an experience well worth the having, and one never achieved in the comparatively muddy reading of even the best English "translations".

me of this notion, and Professor Ketner sent me his earlier essay on the point[150] which showed that, far from being some secondary issue in Peirce's mind, the matter of ethics in terminology had preoccupied him over most of his career as a thinker. I am sure that the issue took on the importance that it did for Peirce from his first-hand discovery of the Latin riches, on the one hand, contrasted, on the other hand, with the attitude of his late-modern contemporaries in general toward the Latins. This importance in Peirce's mind was compounded in particular by the attitude of present-minded dismissal of the pre-Descartes past of philosophy by those who considered him a "fellow pragmatist", but who had no understanding of scholastic realism nor, hence, of the pragmaticism to which such realism is essential. His peers wanted nothing to do with the results he had developed from the Latin past, still less did they want anything to do with the respect he had developed for that Latin past.

Looking into the matter further, I found that Peirce's ideas on the ethics of terminology, for depth and seriousness, really had no counterpart in previous philosophy. True, there are superficially similar formulations to be found in some early-modern authors, such as Francis Bacon (1561–1626)[151] and Locke himself;[152] but the operative term here is "superficial", as a comparative reading of the various proposals rapidly shows. Applications of such ideas were explicitly made in modern times in the development of biology and chemistry. To this extent, it can be said that Peirce's reflections on this question were "a culmination of scientific traditions antedating him by at least two centuries".[153] But the culmination so exceeds the forebears as to stand *sans pareil*.

Corrington[154] notes in regard to Peirce's view that the philosopher "must always be careful to shape a term so that its integrity and scope are truly commensurate with its subject matter", and "must always probe into the full connotation and denotation of any technical term". But these observations, while true, verge on platitudinous unless they are combined with a seriously historical temper of mind, and hence go not at all to the heart of Peirce's ethical claims in this matter. Putnam,[155] in an act of ritual symbolism in the politics of academe carried to the point of caricature, draws an analogy – as condescending in tone as it is otiose in substance – between Peirce's "charming section on the ethics of terminology" and Quine's "Mathematosis".[156]

So it became clear to me that Peirce must still be, after his 1905 try in *The Monist* to convince the pragmatists that they were far from pragmaticism, "awaiting in vain" – albeit now from afar – "some particularly opportune conjuncture of circumstances that might serve to recommend his notions of the ethics of terminology". Let us

---

150 "Peirce's Ethics of Terminology", Ketner 1981.
151 See Bacon 1620. See further "Francis Bacon" (Deely and Russell 1986).
152 Locke 1690: Book III, ch. X.
153 Ketner 1981: 327.
154 Corrington 1993: 51.
155 In Ketner ed. 1992: 93.
156 See Quine 1987: 127–9. The euphony with "halitosis" is probably without significance.

see if, between Ketner's lone essay[157] and the present book, such a conjuncture of circumstances might not yet soon come about.

In the extraordinary document crystallizing Peirce's reflections on the ethical obligations incumbent on philosophers in their use of terms, what needs to be specially attended to among the various strictures is the fact that care in choice of terms presupposes most fundamentally the recognition and acceptance of an *historical* obligation in *intellectual justice* to keep a kind of running account of the *decisive achievements of our predecessors*. This account must be kept with an eye "to keep the *essence* of every scientific term unchanged and exact", yet while meeting at the same time the duty, falling "upon the persons who introduce the new conception", of supplying new terms and families of cognate terms (as in the case of semiotics and its congeners). Balance in this twofold effort means that the duty of introducing new terms is "not to be undertaken without a thorough knowledge of the principles and a large acquaintance with the details and history of the special terminology in which it is to take place, nor without a sufficient comprehension of the principles of word-formation of the national language, nor without a proper study of the laws of symbols in general".[158]

In other words, Peirce would convince us that ethics in the use of terminology is of a piece with the communitarian nature of anthroposemiotic progress in the pursuit of truth. The effort is of a piece with his conviction that a semiotic view of logic presents that subject, cold and barren when taken narrowly, as the very ethics of understanding itself, performing for thought what moral principles perform for behavior.

This historical dimension of the growth of symbols in the species-specifically human communication system (*langue* as opposed to *parole*, we might say) Peirce saw as providing our main and often only safeguard against "arbitrary dictation in scientific matters". An example of such arbitrary dictation is the sort of short-sighted present-mindedness transmitted from classical modernity into twentieth-century philosophy by the early pretensions of Russell and Wittgenstein to have solved or dissolved all the problems of philosophical tradition, thus perpetuating the modern twilight well into the postmodern dawn.

In the case of philosophy as such (which, as I have both explained and illustrated over the preceding chapters, here means simply any foundational inquiry

---

157 There is some mention of Peirce's ethics of terminology in certain essays by Gérard Deledalle (1980, 1980a, 1981, 1990, 1992), but there discussion is limited to the development of terms within Peirce's own lifetime and to contrasting the context of Peircean terms with that of superficially similar Saussurean terms. Left unaddressed is the implication and application of the rules as a complete set, as Peirce himself emphasized the need, respecting the full historical dimension of human understanding embodied particularly in the Latin development of philosophical terminology between the advent of 12th-century scholasticism and the emergence of modern philosophy in the national languages after the 17th century.

158 From "The Ethics of Terminology" in Peirce 1903: 2.222.

of a doctrinal rather than hypothetical nature[159]) there is both "positive need of popular words in popular senses ... as objects of its study" (an example would be the subjective-objective dichotomy of modern parlance), and a "peculiar need of a language distinct and detached from the common speech ... so outlandish that loose thinkers will not be tempted to borrow its words".[160] With respect to this latter language, though it may indeed eventually influence the popular speech and in some measure become in turn part thereof (just as disastrously happened with Kant's use of 'subjective' and 'objective'), in the interim, "if a reader does not know the meaning of the words, it is infinitely better that he should know that he does not know" (which holds equally for the female reader, if we are to update in gender-neutral terms Peirce's nineteenth-century gender-specific phrases).

The Rules Themselves

So much by way of introduction. Here, then, in the form of seven rules,[161] with an eighth that I propose as needed in hindsight[162] to complete the list, are the final results of Peirce's reflections on terminology as he codified them eleven years before his death.

> *First.* To take pains to avoid following any recommendation of an arbitrary nature as to the use of philosophical terminology.
>
> *Second.* To avoid using words and phrases of vernacular origin as technical terms of philosophy.
>
> *Third.* To use the scholastic terms in their anglicised forms for philosophical conceptions, so far as these are strictly applicable; and never to use them in other than their proper senses.
>
> *Fourth.* For ancient philosophical conceptions overlooked by the scholastics, to imitate, as well as I can, the ancient expression.
>
> *Fifth.* For precise philosophical conceptions introduced into philosophy since the middle ages, to use the anglicised form of the original expression, if not positively unsuitable, but only in its precise original sense.
>
> *Sixth.* For philosophical conceptions which vary by a hair's breadth from those for which suitable terms exist, to invent terms with a due regard for the usages of philosophical terminology and those of the English language but yet with a distinctly technical appearance. Before proposing a term, notion, or other symbol, to

---

159 Or of a coenoscopic rather than an idioscopic character, as Peirce would say (see n21 in this chapter, p. 618 above).

160 Peirce 1903: 2.223. And here we see again the disdain that Peirce had acquired for literary pretensions paraded as philosophy. He was too early for deconstruction, but he anticipated its consequences in philosophy and, with his ethics of terminology, would have forestalled them – not completely, to be sure, but in the main.

161 From "The Ethics of Terminology", CP 2.226.

162 Needed for the speculative and historical reasons clear from the preceding fourteen chapters of the present work, and clear also in the more technical discussion in Deely 1994.

consider maturely whether it perfectly suits the conception and will lend itself to every occasion, whether it interferes with any existing term, and whether it may not create an inconvenience by interfering with the expression of some conception that may hereafter be introduced into philosophy.[163] Having once introduced a symbol, to consider myself almost as much bound by it as if it had been introduced by somebody else; and after others have accepted it, to consider myself more bound to it than anybody else.[164]

Seventh. To regard it as needful to introduce new systems of expression when new connections of importance between conceptions come to be made out, or when such systems can, in any way, positively subserve the purposes of philosophical study.

Eighth. To scrutinize contemporary epistemological problems in the light of late Latin developments which the moderns neglected, as an aid in determining the choices of terminology most suitable for postmodern considerations.

Conclusion

Let this complete our discussion of Peirce as the founder of postmodern times. His is the first philosophy to be conceived from start to finish in light of the doctrine of signs, and of what we have learned over the centuries about the central role that signs play in giving to our experience that part of its structure whence the intelligibility of the sensible world derives.

The one author after Peirce who contributes most to the consolidation and definitive establishment of a postmodern spirit in philosophy is Martin Heidegger (1889–1976). Although Heidegger's philosophy has neither the scope of Peirce's thought nor the clarity as to the being of sign as central to the development of human understanding, what Heidegger does contribute at the foundations of the postmodern age is an uncompromising clarity and rigor that exceeds Peirce's own in focusing on the central problem of human understanding vis-à-vis the notion of Umwelt. This heretofore neglected problem is what is central to the problematic of philosophy in a postmodern age. In Peirce's terms it is the problem of Firstness; in the language of Aquinas it is the problem of being-as-first-known; in the language of Heidegger it is the problem of the forgottenness of being, "*Seinsvergessenheit*". This problem is the ground and soil of the doctrine of signs. That is why I first brought it up in

---

163 I take this stricture in Rule 6 against employing terms that may "create an inconvenience by interfering with the expression of some conception that may hereafter be introduced into philosophy" to be a *monitum* against proposing terminology designed and intended to block further inquiry rather than a requirement, obviously preposterous, to divine the particulars of future developments of human understanding. Examples, then, of the sort of terminology this rule would militate against would be the 20th century analytic attempt to rule discussion of mind out of philosophy, the behaviorist attempt to rule discussion of consciousness out of psychology, or the attempt of the officers of the Linguistic Society of Paris by the Statutes of 1868 to rule out discussion of the origin of species-specifically human language, and so on.

164 So has Sebeok perforce had to stand by his coinage of zoösemiosis, now improved by the umlaut.

treating Aquinas,[165] and why I have focused on it in treating Peirce. As to Heidegger, Vincent Guagliardo (1944–95), in the time that he had, said enough to establish the historical connections for those with the good sense to look further.[166]

The original vindication or attainment of the ground of a semiotic consciousness in Poinsot's *Treatise on Signs* lay in the thematic realization that any division of sign proposed must first be understood in the light of what it is that is being divided. Any other procedure risks following the lines of this or that division down blind alleys and false byways, as the history of the pursuit of *signum* amply showed, first in the late Latin Age, then again in the semiological controversies on the frontier of modernity with postmodernity. In the spirit of that original realization, I have kept my consideration of Peirce strictly within the general purview of *signum* as a mode of being indifferent to the subjective source of its realization in what it has of pure relation. I have said nothing about Peirce's main proposal for the division of sign into icons (or sign-vehicles related to their significates on the basis of a resemblance), indices (sign-vehicles related to their significates on the basis of a connection in physical causality), and symbols (sign-vehicles related to their significates on the basis of a habit or stipulation), because I have been concerned exclusively with those parts of his semiotic necessary to understand the prior *general notion* of sign which is thus divided.

The older divisions of sign, such as into "natural" and "conventional", or into "formal" and "instrumental", turned out to be drawn more from considerations which were accidental to the sign's proper being,[167] which is not to say that they do not have plenty of merits that warrant, and will I am sure receive, further discussion in appropriate contexts as the postmodern age unfolds. Peirce's division has found greater currency than the older divisions, I suspect, not only because it is more recent, but also because it has the distinctive merit of being one more directly drawn from the being proper to sign than was the case with the historically prior divisions (even though this has not been the consciously stated motivation for adopting Peirce's proposal in the mind of a single commentator so far). We reach here one of the boundaries between history as a story of what has occurred or been accomplished by previous thinkers and history as it is something being accomplished. At the turn of the twenty-first century, much of what needs to be said in semiotics has yet to be said, and so can have as yet no place in a history currently written.

---

165 See, in chapter 7 above, "The Problem of Sign in Aquinas", p. 331ff.; and "The Problem of Being as First Known", p. 341ff.

166 See Guagaliardo 1994. Apart from this essay, Guagliardo's last major publication, I will mention only that, on his own terms today, Heidegger has a thousand epigones, among whom Professor Caputo is probably the best. See, e.g., the discussion of "Being and Esse Intentionale" in Caputo 1982: 229–37. Here is not the place directly to enter further into their fray, beyond the repetition of what has already been indicated, namely, the fact that Guagliardo alone appears to me seriously to have raised the level of historical consciousness in the understanding of Heidegger in relation to the previous ages of philosophy, the Latin Age in particular.

167 See chapter 9, "Reaching the Token Constituting Whatever Type", p. 432ff.

CHAPTER SIXTEEN

Semiology:
Modernity's Attempt to
Treat the Sign

Modern philosophy did not slip quietly into the night. As paganism took its final stand in Neoplatonism, so modern philosophy in the matter of the sign took a final stand in the one successful scientific treatment of signs produced in late-modern times, the *Cours de linguistique générale* of Ferdinand de Saussure (1857–1913), a work developed in a series of lectures only between 1906 and 1911, and then brought to a posthumous publication in 1916 by three of his students using from the lectures both Saussure's notes and their own.

This work from Saussure is a marvel. It is one of the handful of seminal writings from Northern Europe and Russia which established linguistics as a science after centuries of groping. The body of literature that has grown up around Saussure is enormous, indicating as clearly as could be the vast influence his ideas have had. What made Saussure's work so fateful to the twentieth-century development of a consciousness of signs in particular was the appropriation of his linguistic ideas by French structuralists and then by deconstructionists who raised and expanded his theories to the comprehensive and fundamental plane of philosophical discourse while maintaining a trenchant ignorance of the historical bearing and content of those theories within the doctrinal development of semiotics prior to Saussure, over the course of the Latin centuries in particular.

The Proposal of Semiology

In the matter of signs, by the time Saussure developed his *Cours*, thinking had come full-circle not from Augustine, but from ancient Greece. Remember that in the Hellenic world, there were only natural signs. Augustine proposed that the sign is higher than that, superior to the divide between nature and culture, and Latinity exhausted itself by the time it was able to establish the ground for such a notion. Modernity began by trying to forget Latinity, and in the matter of the sign, it succeeded almost completely. Even the ancient thesis that signs are natural phenomena was retained only as an antithesis. For by the time of the maturation of Saussure's influence, the most credible thesis was rather that there are only conventional signs – signs wholly of the mind's own making. And this was the thesis that Saussure took upon himself to propound under the banner of "semiology".

Background of Saussure's Proposal

By the time modern philosophy had achieved a self-awareness of the final consequence of travelling the way of ideas, it was very clear to all that even the ancients had been mistaken. Just as nominalism thought to have shown there can be no general notion of sign as a mode of being because there are no general modes of being at all, so modern philosophy, nominalistic in essence, was carried by the implications of its founding assumption even further on this point: neither is there a sign in general, nor is there a natural sign. Or at least if there is, we could never know it. For concerning nature there can only be an agnostic skepticism. Science may think it belongs to Jekyll, but philosophy knows that all of human knowledge belongs rather to Hyde.

Giovanni Manetti, in a rich and worthy book, yet seriously misleads his reader on this point.[1] He would have it be understood that the arrival of philosophy at a point in which "the model of the linguistic sign will end up as the semiotic model *par excellence*" is the result of a long evolution begun by Augustine. To read history after Augustine in this way is, in effect, to impose on him the systematic distortion that results not from semiotics properly so called but from *semiology*, as we will see, the general approach to the sign inspired by and borrowed from Saussure precisely because the general theory proposed by Saussure on the linguistic sign taken as model is the only approach consistent with the bias of modern idealism which is the heritage of modern philosophy: human thought has no access except to its own creations.

Modern philosophy, not Augustine, and, among the Latins, still not Augustine, but Ockham, the nominalists generally, Fonseca, and Suárez, prepared the way for a model of the linguistic sign to become – or try to become, for the attempt is failing on every hand, as we will see – the paradigm, *le patron général*, in Saussure's expression, for every approach to the study of signs in late-modern times.[2] But before there could be an idealist attempt at co-opting the irredentistly realist doctrine of

---

1 Manetti 1993: 160.

2 See how potent the Cartesian heritage remains. All history may be contemporary history, but it *remains* history. To read *the past* with contemporary eyes is inevitable. What Manetti does in this matter, however, is not read the past, at least not as it occurred between Augustine and Saussure. Instead, he reduces that Latin landscape to a flat extension of modern idealism, and incorporates Augustine into the present accordingly. Such a construal, on the theoretical side, from the outset begs the question Augustine's definition of sign posed for the medievals with such striking novelty: whether there is not a way of understanding the means of knowing so as to reveal in human experience how it is that nature and culture interpenetrate and mutually shape one another. On the historical side it ignores the actual development of semiotics first from Augustine to Aquinas, and then from Aquinas to Poinsot. To present the contemporary situation as Manetti tries to do, is to skip over completely the semiotic mainstream of the Latin Age. So it is hardly surprising that neither Aquinas, Roger Bacon, Duns Scotus, William of Ockham, Pierre d'Ailly, Dominic Soto, Pedro da Fonseca, the Conimbricenses, Francisco Araújo, nor John Poinsot make an appearance anywhere

signs that had developed after Augustine and then resumed and further developed by Peirce, there had first to be a systematically construed notion of the linguistic sign as such, and this is exactly what Saussure, the father of scientific linguistics, best first provided.

The Proposal Itself

In the course of laying the ground for a scientific linguistics, Saussure also proposed in passing a programmatic statement for a general study of signs. The name Saussure assigned for this new field of inquiry was "semiology". There is no reason to think that the first such statement, the one that John Locke had authored, was at all known to Saussure. He makes no mention of it. His semiology seems to come to his mind directly from his work in linguistics.

Like Locke, Saussure chose a name for his proposal derived from the ancient Greek name for natural signs, *sēmeîon*. His proposal is not quite as brief as Locke's, yet, like Locke's, it amounts to a very few paragraphs in a much larger work. The proposal has two parts. The first and longer part occurs early in the *Cours*, where, in ten paragraphs, most of them short, Saussure establishes the name "semiology" and outlines its program;[3] the second part consists of a single paragraph a little less than a third of the way through the *Cours*, where Saussure offers in a passing remark his guidance on how natural phenomena are to be incorporated into the semiological program, if at all.[4] Out of these eleven paragraphs, as from a seed, grows the whole movement of semiology culminating in contemporary deconstruction, where semiology "gets abused in the merciless way that words have to expect when they fall into literary clutches".[5] As we looked at Locke's proposal, so let us look at this one before proceeding further:[6]

[15]   PLACE OF LANGUAGE IN HUMAN FACTS. SEMIOLOGY.

The foregoing characteristics of language reveal an even more important characteristic. Language, once its boundaries have been marked off within the speech data, can be classified among human phenomena, whereas speech cannot.

We have just seen that language is a social institution; but several features set it apart from other political, legal, etc. institutions. [16] We must call in a new type of facts in order to illuminate the special nature of language.

Language is a system of signs that express ideas, and is therefore comparable to a system of writing, the alphabet of deaf-mutes, symbolic rites, polite formulas, military signals, etc. But it is the most important of all these systems.

---

in his text or references. Fortunately, the author is better when he sticks to classical antiquity, the world before Augustine. There the book is rich.

3 Saussure 1916 (=i.1906/11): pp. 15–17 in the Baskin translation.
4 Ibid.: p. 68 in the Baskin trans.
5 Peirce's lament over part of the fate of pragmatism, it will be remembered (see chapter 15, p. 616f.).
6 The page numbers inside brackets refer to the pagination of the original edition of the *Cours*.

A science that studies the life of signs within society is conceivable; it would be a part of social psychology and consequently of general psychology; I shall call it *semiology* (from the Greek *sēmeîon* 'sign'). Semiology would show what constitutes signs, what laws govern them. Since the science does not yet exist, no one can say what it would be; but it has a right to existence, a place staked out in advance. Linguistics is only a part of the general science of semiology; the laws discovered by semiology will be applicable to linguistics, and the latter will circumscribe a well-defined area within the mass of anthropological facts.

To determine the exact place of semiology is the task of the psychologist. The task of the linguist is to find out what makes language a special system within the mass of semiological data. This issue will be taken up again later; here I wish merely to call attention to one thing: if I have succeeded in assigning linguistics a place among the sciences, it is because I have related it to semiology.

Why has semiology not yet been recognized as an independent science with its own object like all the other sciences? Linguists have been going around in circles: language, better than anything else, offers a basis for understanding the semiological problem; but language must, to put it correctly, be studied in itself; heretofore language has almost always been studied in connection with something else, from other viewpoints.

There is first of all the superficial notion of the general public: people see nothing more than a name-giving system in language, thereby prohibiting any research into its true nature.

[17] Then there is the viewpoint of the psychologist, who studies the sign-mechanism in the individual; this is the easiest method, but it does not lead beyond individual execution and does not reach the sign, which is social.

Or even when signs are studied from a social viewpoint, only the traits that attach language to the other social institutions – those that are more or less voluntary – are emphasized; as a result, the goal is by-passed and the specific characteristics of semiological systems in general and of language in particular are completely ignored. For the distinguishing characteristic of the sign – but the one that is least apparent at first sight – is that in some way it always eludes the individual or social will.

In short, the characteristic that distinguishes semiological systems from all other institutions shows up clearly only in language where it manifests itself in the things which are studied least, and the necessity or specific value of a semiological science is therefore not clearly recognized. But to me the language problem is mainly semiological, and all developments derive their significance from that important fact. If we are to discover the true nature of language we must learn what it has in common with all other semiological systems; linguistic forces that seem very important at first glance (e.g., the role of the vocal apparatus) will receive only secondary consideration if they serve only to set language apart from the other systems. This procedure will do more than to clarify the linguistic problem. By studying rites, customs, etc. as signs, I believe that we shall throw new light on the facts and point up the need for including them in a science of semiology and explaining them by its laws.

···

[68] One remark in passing: when semiology becomes organized as a science, the question will arise whether or not it properly includes a mode of expression based on completely natural signs, such as pantomime. Supposing that the new science welcomes them, its main concern will still be the whole group of systems grounded on the arbitrariness of the sign. In fact, every means of expression used in society is based, in principle, on collective behavior or – what amounts to the same thing – on convention. Polite formulas, for instance (as in the case of a Chinese who greets his emperor by bowing down to the ground nine times), are nonetheless fixed by rule; it is this rule and not the intrinsic value of the gestures that obliges one to use them. Signs that are wholly arbitrary realize better than the others the ideal of the semiological process; that is why language, the most complex and universal of all systems of expression, is also the most characteristic; in this sense linguistics can become the master-pattern [*le patron général*] for all branches of semiology although language is only one particular semiological system.

The authorship of Saussure's statement is somewhat more ambiguous than was Locke's, in that it appeared in print only posthumously, as we said, and on the basis of class notes taken over the 1906–11 period and edited by Charles Bally and Albert Sechehaye with the collaboration of Albert Riedlinger for publication in 1916. Saussure's proposed name for the general study, "semiology", however, has been traced back to November 1894 in a note definitely from Saussure's own hand;[7] and Naville[8] reports an earlier version or outline for semiology essentially similar to what will appear in the *Cours* in 1916. Whether Saussure took the term "semiology" over, consciously or unconsciously, from some other source or, less probably, conceived it neologistically in his own mind, we know that the term has a history of its own among Protestant Latin authors of the late Latin–early modern period.[9] The decisive feature of the proposal so named in Saussure's writing, had the original paragraphs left any doubt, lies in the advice that natural signs are to be treated within semiology, if at all, only through an assimilation to the model of signs as conventional or "arbitrary" (unmotivated by anything in the vehicle's physical structure or subjectivity in their link between sign-vehicle and object signified).

---

7 Godel 1957: 275.
8 Naville 1901: 104.
9 Meier-Oeser 1997: 315: "Das Vorhandensein zumindest des Konzepts einer allgemeinen Zeichentheorie in der protestantischen Schulmetaphysik des 17. Jahrhunderts schlägt sich in dem begriffsgeschichtlichen Befund nieder, dass Terminus 'Semiologie' – anders als häufig zu lesen – älter ist als Saussures *Cours de linguistique générale* und auch hinter Hoffbauers *Tentamina semiologica* [1789] sowie Baumgartens Skizzierung einer als *Semiotica* oder *Semiologia philosophica* bezeichneten *scientia signorum* [1779] zurückdatiert. Denn bereits 1659 stellt Schultetus seine *Disputatio de Signo et Signato* unter den Obertitel Σημειολογία μεταφυσική."

Reception of Saussure's Proposal Compared with That of Locke

Saussure's proposal met with an immediate success. Whereas that of Locke had essentially fallen deadborn from the press in 1690 until it was resurrected in Peirce's time nearly two centuries later, Saussure's proposal was taken as a trumpet call heeded on all hands for the establishment of a new discipline. Writing in 1971, Sebeok noted of "semiology" that:[10]

> this is the term that, reinforced by the prestige of Parisian intellectual life, now turns up regularly in British newspapers and magazines, such as *The Times Literary Supplement*, and in an outpouring of volumes on the most diverse verbal and nonverbal arts, ranging from architecture to cinematography.

Only slowly, under the gradual but inexorable momentum being acquired by the mass of Peirce's literary corpus as Max Fisch in particular guided a whole new generation of students over the 1960s, '70s, and '80s, did the term "semiotics" begin to come seriously into play, and most of the twentieth-century history of semiotics took the form of a contest between these two original designations, "semiotics" as derived from Locke's late seventeenth-century proposal and "semiology" as derived from Saussure's independent turn-of-the-twentieth-century proposal. But, all the appearances of popular culture and intellectual media to the contrary notwithstanding, it was an unequal contest in which semiotics was bound to win. For being accumulates in language, and the term "semiotics" was in this case the "essence freighted with being",[11] the only legitimate heir to the traditional doctrinal development of the originally Augustinian Latin term.

By the closing decades of the twentieth century, so much ground had been lost by semiologists in the advance of semiotics that diehard adherents of the semiological standpoint resorted to the desperate nominalist ploy of pretending that no more was at stake in the contest of designations than a stipulable synonymy. Thus, we find the posthumously assembled collection of Barthes i.1962–1973, published in 1985 under the title *L'Aventure sémiologique*, rendered into English in 1988 as *The Semiotic Challenge*. The translator passes from "semiology" to "semiotic" without so much as a note of explanation, perhaps without an ounce of realization of how profoundly inept such a rendering actually is – as if to vindicate Peirce's contentious maxim[12] that words must expect merciless abuse when they fall into literary clutches! The translation ploy well suits the play of semiological fancy, but hardly fits with the actual doctrine of signs.

For despite their common etymological root in the Greek word σημεῖον

---

10 Sebeok, "'Semiotics' and Its Congeners" (1971: 55)
11 The *"seinsgeschichtliches Wesen"*.
12 Chapter 15, p. 616f.

("semeion") for "sign",[13] and notwithstanding their common recognition that a general study of signs would be a new departure in the organization of human knowledge, the two programmatic statements we inherit – the one concerning semiotics from Locke and the other concerning semiology from Saussure – are as radically different as scholastic realism and modern nominalism, and "the question between nominalism and realism is, in its nature, susceptible of but two answers: yes and no", as Peirce categorically pointed out[14] in the face of "that loose and slapdash style of thinking" (always with us) which would try to have it both ways.

In Locke's little-noticed earlier proposal, no definition of sign is given beyond its identification with the means whereby knowledge of whatever sort is acquired, developed, and communicated. Locke frankly admits that, so far as he was aware, ideas along with words had never yet been considered in such a perspective as he proposed, certainly not along the way of ideas; and, as we saw, he prophetically surmised that, were they to be so considered, we would arrive at "a different sort of Logick and Critick" than what modern times had accustomed us to. Yet despite his use of the pregnant Latin expression "doctrine of signs" as a synonym for semiotic in his proposal, Locke appears to have been mainly ignorant of the principal medieval Latin development of semiotic in the Hispanic world as it had taken place even in his life time, as we saw.

In Saussure's much bally-hooed proposal, by contrast, everything is made to turn on the specifically linguistic sign as the paradigm case for semiological analysis. "When semiology becomes organized as a science, the question will arise whether or not it properly includes modes of expression based on completely natural signs", says Saussure's proposal. By way of answer, he asserts that, even if the new science accepts to treat of so-called natural signs, "its main concern will still be the whole group of systems grounded on the arbitrariness of the sign" because "signs that are wholly arbitrary realize better than the others the ideal of the semiological process". For this reason, language, "the most complex and universal of all systems of expression, is also the most characteristic"; and linguistics, which takes language for its object, "can become the master-pattern for all branches of semiology". Thus was born Saussure's idea of linguistics and the linguistic sign as *le patron général* for any study of signs, the idea which, under a variety of minor transformations and modifications, remains the defining idea of semiology and the idea which links it determinately, despite the generation of much contrary rhetoric, to modernity and not to postmodernity. For that is exactly what was at stake in the contest between semiology and semiotics: the frontier between modern philosophy and postmodern times.

---

13 Or, more precisely, for *"natural* sign", since, as we have had repeated occasion to remind the reader, the Greeks had no term for a notion of sign generic to the cultural, especially linguistic, phenomena, and the phenomena of nature.

14 Peirce 1909: CP 1.27.

The sign as restricted to the realm of convention, especially as defined in terms of the conventional and arbitrary, as σύμβολον, is a conception as distinctively modern as the restriction of σημεῖον to natural events and propositional contexts of inference concerning φύσις was distinctively ancient. The sign as capacious enough to embrace both nature and culture in their constitution of and interpenetration within the objective world of experience, by contrast to both ancient and modern philosophy, is a conception of medieval Latin origin and distinctively postmodern development. That is why postmodern philosophy in its positive essence is, and will be for a long time to come, semiotics.

To the linguistic sign, the paradigm for semiological study, by contrast, Saussure assigns a very precise understanding. It is the arbitrary linkage – that is to say, again, a linkage unmotivated by any natural connection – of a concept with an acoustical image. Saussure is quite explicit on the point:[15] "I propose to retain the word *sign* to designate the whole and to replace concept and sound-image respectively by *signifié* and *signifiant*." But he is also careful to warn that "If I state simply that a word signifies something when I have in mind the association of a sound-image with a concept", I am making a statement that by no means expresses the linguistic fact in its essence and fullness.[16] The *signifiant* is not a mere sound but rather "the phonic differences that make it possible to distinguish this word from all others, for differences carry signification".[17]

The Essence of Semiology's Proposal

This point opens up the true vista of semiological analysis. What is central to the progress of semiology, it turns out, is not the linguistic sign as a positive fact, as if it were an entity in its own right, but, on the contrary, the fact that this sign is held together from without by the oppositions between words – that is, between linguistic signs. "The entire mechanism of language", Saussure says,[18] "is based on oppositions of this kind *and on the phonic and conceptual differences that they imply*" (emphasis added). Linguistic value is not the property of a (linguistic) sign (a word) standing for an idea (a signifié), it is the system of similarities and differences among *signifiants* and *signifiés* which keep the two in linkage despite the absence of any internal motivation for the linkage so maintained.

Here is what is crucial to the linguistic sign: that "in language there are only differences", differences *"without positive terms"*.[19] The linguistic sign, the pairing of signifiant and signifié, is indeed something "positive in its own class".[20] But the pairing is maintained by *nothing internal* either to the *signifiant* or the *signifié*.

---

15 Saussure 1916 (=i.1906/11): *Cours de linguistique générale*, Baskin trans., 67.
16 Baskin trans., 117.
17 Ibid., 118.
18 Ibid., p. 121.
19 Ibid., 120, italics added.
20 Ibid.

The pairing is what constitutes the elements of the linguistic (or any semiological) system as such, but the relations among the elements alone hold each element together as a positive unity. The content of the linguistic sign – its signification – "is really fixed only by the concurrence of everything that exists outside it" in the system of oppositions through which the differences – both phonic (*signifiant*) and psychological (*signifié*) – carry the signification.

A Logic of Similarities and Differences

The binary logic of similarities and differences thus opened up, applicable to all unities insofar as they consist of an intelligible content mind-dependently linked in social conventions to a sensible expression through a system of values obtaining among the elements so constituted, is what proves to be the heart of the idea of semiology. The linguistic sign is the key, but the system of values, and analysis in terms of them as a play of differences, is the vista this key opens.

Despite Saussure's insistence on the primacy not just of language but of language as spoken, further reflections revealed that the acoustic image is by no means the only way a semiological unit can be embodied. Derrida presented this discovery as the exposure of a great error on Saussure's part, an error which Derrida further presented as revelatory of a great fissure which runs through the whole of "Western metaphysics of sign" and renders it untenable. But this presentation is fraudulent, as empty of actual historical content as Manetti's presentation of a supposed "process of evolution" after Augustine that reaches its apex in Saussure. From a semiotic point of view, Peirce and Poinsot spoke as one on the point that "the rules of logic hold good of any symbols, of those which are written or spoken as well as of those which are thought".[21]

And let Saussure stand corrected on this point. It ultimately makes no more difference for semiology as a variant of modern idealism than it made for the way of ideas whether the material world evanesced à la Berkeley, was dismissed with a droll skepticism à la Hume, or was strenuously affirmed à la the Kant of the second edition of *The Critique of Pure Reason*: it remained that the mind dealt throughout only with the phantoms of its own construction. And so it is with semiology.

It is possible to substitute for the acoustic image any similarly mental image, visual or tactile. Nor is the concept the only psychological content that can be paired with a material image (of whatever sort – acoustic, visual, tactile, ...) as embodiment. It is possible to substitute for the concept an imagination or a feeling. The scope

---

21 Peirce, *Grand Logic: A Critick of Arguments*, 1893: CP 1.559. Poinsot (1632), *Treatise on Signs*, Preliminary Text, "The Definition of Term", 24/5–13, emphasis supplied: "following Aristotle, who defined noun, verb, and statement as spoken words (because they are the signs more known to us), the term is defined as 'A vocal expression significative by stipulation, from which a simple proposition or sentence is constructed'. *But in order to include the mental and the written term, it will be defined: 'A sign out of which a simple proposition is constructed'.*" A further consideration is that vocal and written terms depend in actual signifying on thought, even though their signification does not reduce to that of thought. See the early discussion of this point in chapter 7, p. 337 above.

of semiological analysis knows only one constraint: that the elements of the system it analyzes be constituted from without according to a mind-dependent relation determined by a community, that is to say, one which knows no intrinsic motivation either on the side of the *signifiant* (always a material or sensible "representamen" for semiology) or on the side of the *signifié* (always a mental creature for semiology). Any sign "linguistic" in this sense will serve as the vehicle for semiology. Thus, we can have a semiological analysis of art, architecture, music, and indeed of any cultural phenomenon.

Two Possible Construals of Semiology, One Broad, One Narrow

In this way, it is possible to see in Saussure's original proposal two distinct possibilities for semiology, one broad, the other narrow.

The broad view is implied in the following text:[22]

> All our proposals derive their rationale from this basic fact. If one wishes to discover the true nature of language systems, one must first consider what they have in common with all other systems of the same kind. *Linguistic factors which at first seem central ... must be relegated to a place of secondary importance if it is found that they merely differentiate language from other such systems.* In this way, light will be thrown not only upon the linguistic problem. By considering rites, customs, etc. as signs, it will be possible, we believe, to see them in a new perspective. The need will be felt to consider them as semiological phenomena and to explain them in terms of the laws of semiology.

One could argue from this that distinctive linguistic features, instead of providing the paradigm for semiology, merely serve to distinguish language as one among the many other semiological systems, whence it is possible to jettison the tie with spoken language, as just discussed, and expand the semiological perspective to whatever systems of culture, as in contemporary deconstruction.

In the narrow view, however, which Saussure himself more unmistakably championed, "linguistics serves as a model for the whole of semiology, even though languages represent only one type of semiological system".[23] For linguistic signs are of all the phenomena of culture the most arbitrary, that is, the least intrinsically motivated in terms of the unity of their elements; and the more arbitrary the sign the better the system to which it belongs illustrates "the ideal of the semiological process".

Both the broad and the narrow view enabled by Saussure's proposal for semiology have found protagonists who have carried the possibilities to their utmost extreme.

Representing the narrow view has been Roland Barthes. For Barthes,[24] "the world of signifieds is none other than the world of language". Though allowing that

---

22 Saussure's *Cours* of 1916: Harris trans., 35, emphasis supplied.
23 Harris trans., 101. Cf. Baskin trans., 68.
24 Barthes, *Elements of Semiology* (1964), 11.

language as the linguist conceives of it may perhaps have to be broadened through the perspective of semiology, Barthes[25] proposes that we must "face the possibility of inverting Saussure's declaration: linguistics is not a part of the general science of signs, even a privileged part, it is semiology which is part of linguistics".

Representing the broader view has been Jacques Derrida with his notion of *grammatology* and *différance*, arrived at by destroying Saussure's insistence on the primacy of spoken language in the paradigm for semiology, as we noted a few paragraphs above. Derrida's central notions are neither as recondite nor as profound as he would try to present them. Crucial to keep in mind here is the technical terminology of semiology inherited from Saussure: *concept* means always *signifié*; *word* means always an arbitrary *sign*, a sign which lacks any internal reason for the connection between a signifié and the signifiant with which it is nonetheless correlatively linked.

Thus, when Derrida says[26] that "every concept is inscribed in a chain or in a system within which it refers to the other, [i.e.,] to other concepts, by means of the systematic play of differences", and that such a play is "*différance*", despite the new word and change in emphasis it signals, we have advanced not a step beyond Saussure.

Saussure has already told us[27] that the concept (the *signifié*, remember, for we are still on the "way of ideas", even if pushing its margin) semiologically conceived "is only a value determined by its relations with other similar values", and so also for the *signifiant*, the sensible vehicle. But when Derrida repeatedly tells us that "différance", the play of semiological differences constituting and carrying the arbitrary significations, is "neither a concept nor a word among others",[28] like the attempted suicide who seems to be seeking death but in reality is crying out for assistance, Derrida seems to be saying something new and profound but in reality is crying out the inadequacy of the Saussurean notion of sign for the general problematic of semiotic.

For in saying that différance is neither a word nor a concept, Derrida is saying only that it is neither a sign nor a signifié, which is hardly an exclusive or an exhaustive enumeration of possible subject matters.[29] Similarly,[30] in saying "that the signified concept is never present in and of itself in a sufficient presence that would refer only to itself", Derrida is telling us no more than that the concept, unlike the exterior word within which it lives and for which it provides an interpretant, exists as a sign whether or not it is also objectified, and even objectified remains in its own being a sign (what the late medievals called a "formal sign", as we saw – a representation which cannot exist without giving rise to a relation which, over and

25 Ibid.
26 Derrida 1968: 11.
27 Baskin trans., 117.
28 Derrida 1968: 11.
29 See the discussion of "Signs without Objects" shortly below, p. 681ff.
30 Derrida 1968: 11.

above the concept as foundation, finds its terminus in an object other than itself) outside of and apart from the objectification.

All animals begin making use of signs without knowing that there are signs. When human animals discover that there are signs they may or may not realize that concepts are themselves signs. To do that, they have to objectify the concept according to its proper being. And if they objectify it according to its *proper* being, which is that of provenating objective relations sometimes physical and sometimes only objective, they discover that the concept is, in its proper being, and has been all along, a sign; and the concept does not cease to be a sign for having been discovered to be one. For unlike the objects which are discovered to be signs as well, the signification is not a *further* being for the concept but the *constitutive* being. If we wish to define the animal capable of discovering that there are signs, then, even though that animal is necessarily an animal endowed with language in the root sense, still, because the linguistic sign is but a species within a genus and one that presupposes for its coming into being through exaptation a whole prior array of nonlinguistic signs and nonlinguistic communicative modalities, we should not define that animal as a "linguistic animal" but more generically as the *semiotic animal*, the animal not only engaged in semiosis but capable of making that action of signs a distinctive object, a focal concern, a theme, the knowledge of which systematized has for its proper name, as we have seen, semiotics. If a lifeform ought to be defined by what is most distinctive of it, then the animal capable of becoming aware of the fact that there are signs and that the universe is perfused with them ought to be defined most properly as the semiotic animal.

Semiology, whether broadly or narrowly construed, turns all this on its head, and makes the linguistic sign its general and regulative concept. This makes of semiology in effect a semiotics which cannot take into account the fact that linguistic animals are animals and cannot take into account the concomitant fact that linguistic signs presuppose a broader semiosis in order to work at all. But a semiotics confined to the workings of the mind is in the end not a semiotics so much as it is a baroque filigree on the late modern development of idealism in philosophy. As pragmaticism is not pragmatism, and for isomorphic reasons, so must we say that semiology is not semiotics.

Points of Comparison between the Project of Semiotics and That of Semiology

If we compare the history of Locke's proposal for semiotics with that of Saussure's, apart from the fact that Locke's suggestion fell comparatively still-born from the press, other interesting points emerge.

A Foundational or a Subalternate Study?
Unlike Saussure, who proposed that the general study of signs would be a discipline or science subalternate to social psychology, as appears in the programmatic state-

ment reproduced above, Locke proposed the general study of signs as an independent science in its own right, co-ordinate with the sciences of nature, on the one hand, and the sciences of culture, on the other hand, but as investigating the means whereby knowledge in whatever area is acquired, developed, and communicated. And instead of the proposal being tied to one fully determinate and specific type of sign, the project of semiotics makes it clear that what is required is a general notion of sign able to cover equally internal and external expressions of knowledge, "words and ideas", as Locke quaintly and synecdochically put the matter.

The proposal of semiotics, thus, comes as a distinction which would unite nature and culture, the *Geisteswissenschaften* and *Naturwissenschaften*, and as a program which might well require abandonment of the way of ideas, as indeed it does. Saussure proposes a distinction which leaves nature and culture divided exactly as modern philosophy says they must be divided – divided, that is, so as to be kept forever separate.

At the Boundary of Modern and Postmodern
Semiology as proposed passingly in Saussure's lectures stands at the utmost extremity of the way of ideas. Later protagonists of the proposal come to look covetously at the prospects for postmodernity, but without coming to realize that to seize the fruit of those prospects it is necessary to abandon the way of ideas. To travel the way of signs a new departure is required. A nominal embarkation, à la Barthes or à la Derrida, cannot suffice. What separates the modern, early or late, from the postmodern *tout court*, is not at bottom a vocabulary but a being and the understanding of it, the being proper to the sign as navigating the ways both of nature and of culture, and the understanding of the semiotic web as made of strands spun through the action of signs in both those realms to constitute the garment of experience through which the sensible world acquires its intelligibility.

Until Charles Peirce read Locke's proposal in the late 1860s, it is true, no one had taken it at face value, perhaps not even Locke himself. But Peirce read Locke's outline in the context of his own knowledge of medieval semiotics as it had been developed in the Latin time just prior to Locke's own work. Peirce, as we saw, assigned to the notion of sign right from the outset the notion of a triadic relation in which there are three terms: what we ordinarily call the "sign" but which in reality is but the sign-vehicle and may be a psychological reality as well as an outwardly sensible, material structure; the object signified, which may but need not be also a material reality existing within the physical environment; and an interpretant on the basis of which the sign vehicle represents its significate to some mind, actually or only virtually.

Signs without Objects
If we compare this triadic notion of sign to the dyadic semiological notion of sign as the external linkage the mind provides (through conventions) between vehicle and content, *signifiant* and *signifié*, we find that precisely what is missing from the

semiological model of semiosis is the significate, in the sense of the *object signified*. This semiotic notion of objectivity, it is true, has yet to be fully developed.[31] Nonetheless, by opting for an irreducibly triadic model, Peirce picks up the ancient and medieval notion of a "semiotic triangle" which was common to ancient Greek and medieval Latin analyses, despite their many other differences (including the ancient restriction of signs to natural phenomena). In Peircean terms, the Saussurean or, more generally, the semiological notion of sign on its broadest possible construal is hopelessly deficient, on several counts, for developing any general science (doctrine, rather) of signs. To begin with, the *signifiant* corresponds more or less to the sign-vehicle, but the *signifié* corresponds only partially to the notion of interpretant;[32] and the notion of object signified is entirely wanting in the scheme.

In fact, the Saussurean terminology on this point has led to no end of confusion and analyses at cross-purpose. For the only plausible translation for *signifié*, Saussure's technical term for the concept, is significate or signified, *whereas a concept is not what is meant in any of the major semiotic writings* by the term *signatum* or *significatum*. The signified or significate has always been the *object* of some signification, be it the signification of a concept or the signification of a linguistic expression (written, spoken, or gestured). Derrida's "différance" indeed is (intended or coined to signify) no word or concept *on Saussure's terms*, but "différance" is indeed the very thing Saussure's vocabulary thoroughly omits to include – *an object in the semiotic sense, as is anything signified*, whether through language or through any other manifestation of semiosis; for an object is what anything, physical or psychical, becomes when and insofar as it is discoursed about or apprehended in any way.

We see how crucial the heritage of the Kantian subject-object dichotomy is theoretically. There is no "subject-object dichotomy" within semiotics as the doctrine of signs, for every object is but a significate confusedly spoken; and every significate is part of the sign-vehicle / object signified / interpretant trichotomy, never of a dichotomy, because no sign-relation can be binary in its proper being, and every object exists as the signified term of the three-term relation which constitutes the sign in its proper being.

Morevoer, we see how crucial the heritage of the Kantian appearance/thing-in-itself dichotomy is also for semiology. The "object" for Derrida is indefinitely postponed or deferred precisely because the "object" of which he speaks can never be or include, even aspectually, anything of the order of the physical surroundings in *their* proper being as subjectivity known, that is to say, objectified in and through sensation and perception prior to as well as within understanding. But in fact, what the doctrine of signs reveals is that a significate in principle, like the Oracle at Delphi, need neither be nor not be also a thing. Whether it is so or not depends on circumstances which bear on and can become known through, yet themselves remain other than, the sign relation as such.

---

31 See *The Human Use of Signs* (Deely 1994), Gloss 2, p. 136.
32 Merrell gives the best analyses of these points. See his *Deconstruction Reframed* (1985).

The "object deferred through différance" is not the object signified by the relation proper to any sign. Différance itself is a semiotic object, because what every signified in principle does is mediate between the subjectivity of the physical environment and the objectivity of the experienced world. Nor does différance defer indefinitely the signified, except that it *can* by an arbitrary exercise of will over understanding insist on pursuing a path of infinite process wherein the indifference of ontological relation to the mind-dependent and mind-independent orders can be used to found relations upon relations, not for the purpose of framing something or speaking intelligibly about it but rather for the narcissistic purpose of displaying a cleverness prospectively limitless or the nihilistic purpose of dissolving all frames by reducing the *indifference* of ontological relation to the difference between what is real and unreal to an *equivalence* of ontological relations with unreal relations. The equivalence is false, but it can be maintained; and precisely the indifference of ontological relation which enables semiosis and language in the first place enables this charade as well. For there is no end in principle to the building of castles in the air.

As soon as the semiotic character of sensation within perception is analyzed, however, and prescissed, we discover that sensation represents a limit case in which object and thing, in principle distinct, are in fact partially identified, and necessarily so by the absence of iconic structures in which the relations of sensation can terminate as in a pure object. At that moment the house of différance as Derrida portrays it comes crashing down. There may be narcissisms, nihilisms, paranoias so deep that nothing but death can terminate the semiosis underlying them. A human use of signs without sensation would be impossible. But a human use of signs which systematically and theoretically denies or mistakes what is distinctive about the semiosis of sensation is certainly possible. It may not be healthy philosophically, but neither is cancer physically. Yet nothing prevents the unhealthy from succeeding recurrently often. Just as there can be runaway growth of cells in the body, so can there be runaway growth of signs in the mind. Conspiracy theorists and paranoiacs have no monopoly on the cancerous forms of semiosis. Semiosis need not be healthy to be semiosis; but semiotics needs to be balanced in order to achieve the doctrine of signs. For sanity and insanity alike signs make possible; and how they do this is the business of semiotics to understand.

Signs Wanted: No Motives Accepted

The semiological insistence on systems of signification held together without any internal motivation binding their elementary units, while claiming an etymological derivation from the Greek notion of sign, is in fact, as we noted at the outset of this chapter, the polar opposite of the ancient notion. For while the ancient notion did not extend to cultural expression, so, inversely, the semiological notion precludes natural signs or, seeming to accept them, yet precludes in them the intrinsic motivation which constitutes them as genuinely natural events.

From this point of view, semiology is less a genuine move in the direction of a general doctrine of signs than it is an importing of the perspective of modern philosophy into the field of the sign – and one part of the field only, the part determinately having a cultural rather than any natural source. Semiology in this regard is what semiotics would be if it were reduced to a consideration of signs compatible with the idealist epistemologies of classical modern philosophy, according to which knowledge of nature in its proper being is precluded. Semiology, in short, is what semiotics would be if it were not semiotics, or, to use an analogy, what pragmaticism would be if it were pragmatism.

But semiotics, in Locke's programmatic statement, and in its Latin guise no less than in Peirce's contemporary proposals, precisely began from a general notion of sign respecting which natural and cultural signs, including language, are but species. In medieval terms, we saw, Augustine's original definition of sign as necessarily accessible to outward sense was criticized as too narrow, for excluding the "passions of the soul" which also serve to perform the essential sign-function of making present objectively that which they themselves are not. The Latins would criticize Saussure's definition of sign as similarly too narrow, for excluding in natural signs that which is proper to them, namely, a mind-independent, or intrinsically motivated, relation to the object signified.

Comparative Summary

For semiotics, in short, whether we consider the irretrievably dyadic character of the semiological sign or whether we consider the need for a general notion of sign to be superior to the division of being into natural and cultural, the semiological perspective simply will not do. It fails: at worst as hopelessly inadequate to the problematic which semiotics sets itself, at best as irredeemably restricted to one part of the semiotic field, namely, the part occupied by phenomena of culture considered only in what contrasts them to nature. In full contrast, semiotics insists on seeing nature and culture as compenetrative.

In either case, whether broadly or narrowly conceived, semiology transforms the project of the doctrine of signs by inappropriately anthropomorphizing the whole problematic into a general theory of cultural phenomena. Behind the veil of culture may lie *Dinge-an-sich*, but the veil cannot be parted. By contrast, if Peirce's notion of sign as taken over from the later Latins is anywhere near right, then semiology is less a proposal for a general study of signs than it is a Procrustean bed for such a study, a Kantian philosophy specifically applied. It is the last reach of modern idealism toward a future slipping through the fingers of modernity's heirs. For they have no way to hold on to a reality including more than pure constructs, and that is what is at stake.

Peirce latched on to semiotic from Locke's original proposal, and he fleshed it out with all the knowledge at his disposal. Saussure arrived at his proposal for semiology independently, and he bound it fast to his conception of the linguistic sign. Still, it is not without interest that these two thinkers so disparate took up at almost the same time – though Peirce was the earlier – the idea for a general science of sign, even though their conceptions for the project were so different in tendency.

As we saw, Saussure's proposal was an immediate success, and swept Europe. Paris lent its prestige to the notion; English literary outlets followed suit. Peirce's attempt to recover the resources of Latinity and to bring every intellectual resource to bear to implement Locke's proposal met with no such immediate success. Yet the last third or so of the twentieth century has seen a gradual reversal in the dominance of the two terms "semiotics" and "semiology", for reasons I have tried to suggest.

The Struggle for the Imagination of Popular Culture

In the popular consciousness of many in the 1990s, the two terms were deemed rough synonyms. We have seen that this is anything but the case. Saussure's proposal was too narrow for the project envisaged, and belonged definitively to the last stages of intellectual development adhering to the epistemological paradigm of classical modern philosophy. Peirce's implementation of Locke's proposal, by contrast, transcended the divide between modern and medieval, between national-language philosophy and Latin tradition, even as the sign itself transcends the divide between nature and culture. Semiotics does not fit the modern paradigm. In the popular culture of the turn of the twentieth century, the program of semiotics stood at a distinct disadvantage. It was the wave of the future, but only by being out of step with the then-present time.

The paradigm proper to semiotics requires at the outset from those who would develop it that they reject, consciously or unconsciously, explicitly or by implication, the epistemological paradigm of modernity. For the initial insight of semiotics is into the being proper to signs; and by that insight is captured again, wittingly or not, the heritage which was definitively rejected by modern philosophy as claiming the impossible, namely, the possibility of a knowledge of natural phenomena in their proper being from within human experience. Semiology is ultramodern, but semiotics is postmodern first. Naturally the ultramodern project of signs caught on first. It could rebel without really overthrowing the comfortable, deep assumptions of modern epistemology. It could propose a future without really having to leave the present.

Genuine versus Bogus Claims for Semiology
It is not that semiology cannot contribute to semiotics from within an inherently more limited perspective. The problems begin only when the semiological perspective is claimed to be equal to the general study of signs, which it is not. Presented in that way, which was not the main thrust of Saussure's work in linguistics, as we saw, but only a passing suggestion, semiology ties itself forever to modernity. To succeed in passing the frontier and become an active part of the postmodern development, however, the proponents of semiology need only to jettison the pretension of their paradigm to a completeness and governing role from which it is excluded in the nature of the case by the doctrine of signs itself. In other words, semiology can be admitted into the tradition of semiotics as a part thereof, a *pars semeiotica*, and its

protagonists as partners in the investigation of sign; but only on condition that the subordination of the linguistic sign to sign in general be well understood.

Saussure contributes to semiotics, in this way, a deepened understanding of the species-specifically human linguistic system. His failure to bring this understanding under the rubric of a general theory of signs as he hoped might be possible, by contrast, is a historical failure, one of the last demonstrations of the impotence of modernity before the future of philosophy. He was among the last of the true moderns, all those who, in philosophy, thought or still think that the way of ideas was a thoroughfare, when in fact it was a cul-de-sac. But, from Saussure through Barthes to Derrida, to see the possibilities of semiology in their true light, a larger and deeper understanding of the sign is necessary than the original semiologists had the intellectual resources or historical consciousness to allow as possible.

Positive Contributions from Semiology to the Doctrine of Signs

For the way of signs, the postmodern way, Saussure's proved an abortive proposal; but it helped create the climate and interest in which the deeper and fuller problematic of semiotic, already initiated in ways at the time little realized in the prodigious but difficult to access Peircean writings, could take hold generally in the contemporary intellectual consciousness. How linguistics as Saussure conceived it will finally be assimilated to that problematic remains to be seen in detail; but it will certainly not be in the way that Saussure or any of the principal semiological authors so far have envisioned. So yet another irony of history: that the first band of intellectuals to unfurl the banner of postmodernity did so under false colors, and not knowing what they did. The last stand of modern idealism concealed itself in the camouflage of one last nominalism, the labeling of the way of signs as "semiology".

Steps to a Postmodern Doctrine of Signs

Yet, properly assimilated to the doctrine of signs, a scientific understanding of the linguistic sign can be said to have come none too soon. In all previous epochs, the emergence of major philosophical systems happen to correspond, for profound reasons that have yet to be explored concerning the nature of the transformation of the objective world from generic animal Umwelt to species-specifically human Lebenswelt, with the major linguistic changes in civilizations. This has been especially true in the West, cradle in fact of all philosophy and science as existing in the self-conscious contrast and dynamic tension between *scientia* and *doctrina*, as we have seen. This fact has not been taken note of to the extent it needs to be, but the fact remains that the natural macro-units for the study of philosophy have been the major changes in the situation of the natural languages.

Up from the Past

The period of Greek philosophy extended from the pre-Socratics to the end of the dominance of Greek as the language of learning at the end of the Roman Empire in the fifth century. At that moment the Latin-speaking peoples were thrown back on their own resources, and the indigenous development of philosophy from a Latin linguistic base began. This development would dominate until the seventeenth century, when again a linguistic sea-change occurs with the emergence of the European national languages as the principal medium of mainstream philosophical discourse. Modern philosophy, not coincidentally, rose against Latin scholasticism on the tide of the emerging natural languages. The postmodern period, again, coincides with a breakdown of the modern national linguistic compartmentalizations, as a new global perspective begins to emerge beyond national differences of language.

But this time the old pattern gives way. Something radically different appears. The emerging postmodern perspective is based not on a radical change in the natural language serving as philosophical medium, as in the previous three epochs, but on the achievement of an epistemological perspective capable of taking into account the very mechanisms themselves of linguistic difference and change as part of the framework of philosophy in its semiotic guise. This is in part the profound contribution of semiology, properly understood in subordination to *signum*, to the development of the way of signs as the way of postmodernity.

The postmodern development may derive in a privileged way from the work of the American philosopher Charles Sanders Peirce, but it is based on this work precisely as that work takes up again and brings to higher levels of synthesis themes in logic and epistemology that developed especially strongly in the last two centuries or so of the Latin Age, but that began with Augustine, and were prepared for by the philosophical schemes of knowledge worked out in the ancient world before Augustine by Aristotle and the Stoics in particular. And Peirce's work itself in semiotics, as the anthropologist Richard Parmentier first pointed out to me,[33] cannot do without the addition of a theory of *codes* as the key to the action of signs specifically within culture, and the theory of codes was the principal development of semiology under the impetus given it by Saussure. So it was not merely by mistake or as a pure accident of chance that the first decades of postmodernity were filled with a kind of dust of semiological analysis.

It was not just air-pollution. It was the dust of researchers digging, in spite of themselves, for something deeper, something that lay at the very foundations of culture, and that tied those foundations to the larger physical universe of which culture, too, forms a part. We come to the last chapter that can be written today of

---

33 Originally in a personal letter, 1987a. But in *The Sacred Remains*, his superb anthropological study of that year, and yet more clearly since, first in *Signs and Society* (1994), then in *The Pragmatics of Culture* (1997), where he makes his own synthesis of Peircean semiotics and code as central to cultural anthropology, Parmentier gives plenty of public access to his point, which was, I may mention, my main provocation in writing *The Human Use of Signs* as a fundamental anthropology in the Heideggerian sense, but with an explicit semiotic consciousness from the start. Parmentier remains late modern only in his recalcitrance to acknowledging the historical layers on which present insights depend; yet so strong is the heritage of present-mindedness carrying over from modernity that this is hardly singular, one of the many Cartesian ghosts yet to be exorcised.

the history of philosophy as providing the context of the doctrine of signs, the story of how "that minuscule segment of nature some anthropologists grandly compart-mentalize as culture"[34] came to be seen in semiotic perspective for what it ultimately is, namely, itself a part of that grand whole which we call the physical universe, understanding "physical" in that large mainstream Latin sense outlined above[35] as including even God and, we now must add, even fictions in what they have of reality from the finite mind conceiving and normally confusing them objectively with the reality itself which is developing all around us.

On to the Future

As we will see in the next chapter, by way of the concept of code – the correlation of an idea "with some physical element within experience taken to serve as foundation or sign-vehicle for the relation in which the idea expressly consists"[36] – semiology found its entry into semiotics. What was assimilable of it became assimilated. Left behind were those idealistic developments which, by misconstruing the sign even while recognizing the effect of its action as irreducibly presenting what the sign itself is not, were destined to breathe the thin air of modernity unto death. The ultramodern protagonists of the adequacy of the semiological sign thus found themselves gazing all the while, with often visible envy, at those already walking the way of signs, those who had not mistaken that way for some nominalistic surrogate or who, having made such a mistake, recovered sufficiently to get on with the journey. We come, in our last chapter (for a closing "envoi" is not a chapter in the same sense), to the point where the past and future of philosophy meet in the actual making of that future in the current intellectual life. It is the last possible chapter, for the present moment, of a history of philosophy as bearing on the doctrine of signs; for it is the chapter which deals with the materials being prepared now for what history tomorrow will have to report.

---

34 Thomas A. Sebeok, "Vital Signs", 1984a: 3.
35 Chapter 8, p. 382.
36 See *The Human Use of Signs* (Deely 1994) on the full development and incorporation within semiotics proper of the notion of "code".

CHAPTER SEVENTEEN

At the Turn
of the Twenty-first Century

With semiology, the "tidal wave of nominalism"[1] was almost spent, and the doctrine of signs in its post-Latin guise could begin in earnest. Like every intellectual progression, this one too was ambiguous in the actual social life of the times incubating its progression. It took many years even for Peirce to realize clearly and definitely that pragmaticism was not pragmatism. So it took many years for the intellectual workers interested in sign to achieve a conscious realization that semiotics was not semiology.

We are, as we noted in closing the last chapter, standing here on the boundary of history as it can be written and history as it is yet being made. Not only is the story never finished, but we touch here almost on that part of it which cannot be written, at least not as a story. It is time, in short, to bring our history to a close, and to yield the stage for a while to the ones doing philosophy, shaping the doctrine of signs in the postmodern age, and so creating the materials which future historians of philosophy will have to sift as postmodern times in turn come to a twilight in some imprevisable future reorganization of discourse around problems that have yet to be sufficiently adumbrated.

Let us conclude with a detailed look barely twenty years past, but which already stands as a landmark in the shaping of postmodern consciousness along the way of signs, and as a transition in the awareness of the culture at large from semiology to semiotics. I am referring to the publication in English of Umberto Eco's book *A Theory of Semiotics*.

Trattato di semiotica generale

In 1976, Umberto Eco's *Trattato di semiotica generale*, published by Bompiani the year before, appeared in the English translation of David Osmond-Smith[2] under the

---

1 From Peirce's "Lessons from the History of Philosophy", 1903a: CP 1.19, cited in chapter 13, p. 544 above.
2 See Eco's comments in his "Prefazione" to the original volume (1975: 6).

title *A Theory of Semiotics*. This volume was the first in the Advances in Semiotics series begun with the Indiana University Press under the editorship of Thomas A. Sebeok. After twenty years, the series exceeded forty-six volumes, and the *Theory of Semiotics* had appeared in perhaps as many languages as the series has volumes. A general study heretofore pursued mostly by writers of solitary genius (such as Roger Bacon in the thirteenth century, John Poinsot in the seventeenth century, and Charles Peirce in the nineteenth) suddenly found in Eco's work a voice which would ring throughout the intellectual world of the late twentieth century, in practically every culture and every language. It was a giant leap for the doctrine of signs.

Here let us try to see this important book in three dimensions: as a work of transition in the emergence of semiotics as a contemporary intellectual movement, as a piece in the historical puzzle of how the way to contemporary semiotic consciousness was prepared, and as a theoretical proposal that needs to be met on its own terms.

A Work of Transition

If we juxtapose the title of Eco's 1975 book with the subtitle of his 1968 book, *Introduzione alla ricerca semiologica*, "Introduction to Semiological Research", the contrast in the choice of terms is of the greatest interest to the sophisticated reader; for, as we saw in chapter 16, the historical cargo of these two terms, "semiology" and "semiotics", is profoundly different.[3] Eco has become a giant of pop culture as well as of semiotics. After *The Name of the Rose* made him a best-selling novelist over and beyond his academic work, it is not surprising that the editors[4] and reviewers[5] of Eco's work persist in perpetuating the popular confusion that surrounds the derivation and destiny of these two profoundly different terms. As we shall see, not without some reason do Eco devotees, in particular, cling to this confusion. Yet is it well to note from the start that "the intellectual ambience evoked by each [of these two terms] is so different that Hill's dictum about synonymy" – that perfect synonyms do not exist[6] – "is reconfirmed once again".[7]

---

3 See also Sebeok 1971; and "Rectificando los terminos 'semiótica' y 'semiología'", in Deely 1996a: 300–17. "Arguments of the sixties" (Eco 2000: 341–2) may illustrate but hardly warrant today the confusion.

4 David Robey introduces English readers to *The Open Work* (Eco 1989) by assuring them glibly that "the terms 'semiotics' and 'semiology' can be used interchangeably".

5 Thus Michael Dirda, reviewing Eco's then-latest novel for the *Washington Post Book World* for 22 October 1995, ignorantly defines semiotics as "the study of cultural 'signs'" – a definition strictly applicable only to semiology as subalternate to, as a part only of, the much vaster study of sign action in the universe at large properly called semiotics.

6 Hill 1958: 412.

7 Sebeok 1971: 56. The author had preceded this remark by noting, in the same paragraph, that "While every contributor to *Semiotica*" – he names the journal of the International Association for Semiotic Studies, but the latinate formation will serve just as well to name "whatever matters semiotical", or "semiotic affairs" – "may indulge his personal taste [the text is pre-gender-neutral]

Perhaps the most noteworthy feature of this book is the immensity of Professor Eco's achievement in covering the range of the then-contemporary literature on signs, and in showing the semiotic import of a good deal more of the then-current writings in language, scientific linguistics, anthropology, aesthetics, ethology, and other 'traditional' specialized disciplines that had so far developed outside the orbit of an explicitly semiotic understanding. The degree of sophistication and comprehensiveness of the book put it in a class by itself. This book quickly became a book for every semiotician's bookshelf. Although more limited than its author imagined, as we now can assuredly say, *A Theory of Semiotics* was not only a classic of the period but made some vital and enduring contributions, especially with its notion of "code".

From a philosophical point of view, what we have learned about the nature and historical development of semiotics as an intellectual enterprise, both possible and more and more actual, enables us to see this landmark book of Eco's in quite a new light from that under which it was first able to be examined. The new light is no less favorable, but it brings out now the work's colors as a work of transition, colors that did not quite appear in the original light. This work not only reaches the boundary between late modernity and postmodernity, it actually straddles the frontier, but without completely crossing the line. While Eco's choice of title, in retrospect, signalled the end of the dominance of the Saussurean paradigm in the studies of sign, the work itself, in its text, notwithstanding its author's intentions to the contrary, remains within the orbit of an idealist understanding of sign as exclusively the work of human thought and culture.[8] This is what examination of the details of Eco's theoretical proposals will reveal in this penultimate chapter.

Some rectification of terms is in order before proceeding further.

By idealism I mean the distinctive epistemological position proper to modern philosophy as it developed from Descartes to Kant in revealing, by a series of logical consequences, that the common assumption of the early moderns (that ideas of the understanding are the direct objects of experience) leads inevitably to the conclusion that whatever the mind knows the mind itself constitutes or makes.

By postmodernism, or postmodernity, I do not mean that collection of quintessentially idealist writings which revel in deconstruction and Hermetic drift.[9] I mean quite

---

when attaching a label to the theory of signs, his terminology within the same piece of discourse will not oscillate *ad libitum*, for his initial selection will have signaled to his sophisticated readership whether he has chosen to align himself with the Locke-Peirce-Morris tradition, the Mead variation, or the Saussurean pattern of thought and action."

8 In this curious feature, as we shall have further occasion to note if but in passing, Eco achieves an authorial status parallel to that of Kant, who also could not realize the idealist status of his theory. See Kant 1787: "Preface to the Second Edition", esp. note *a*, pp. 34–5; discussion in chapter 13, p. 586ff. and passim.

9 Eco's wonderful term from 1990: 32, taken from the Greek figure, Hermes Trismegistus, "Mercury Thrice Great", legendary author of magical, astrological, and alchemical doctrines. In ancient Egypt known as Thoth, god of wisdom, who revealed to Egypt its laws and to her king the art of writing,

simply the development of the consequences for human thought of the demonstration that ideas as signs do not and cannot consist in being the direct objects of experience and apprehension, as the moderns assumed. Ideas serve merely to found relations to objects signified which, as such, are indifferent to physical existence without precluding such existence on any general or a-priori grounds.[10] This demonstration preceded modernity, but the founders of modernity had no cognizance of it. Since ideas are the principal form of sign, in the sense that all other signs depend, in differing ways, on the signs that are ideas, the realization that "all thought is in signs", as Peirce put it and as Poinsot earlier showed,[11] may be regarded as the beginning of semiotic consciousness.[12] This consciousness, vis-à-vis modernity, returns to the fork in the road where the moderns began their trek down the way of ideas, and follows rather the way previously less taken, the way of signs.[13]

By taking up where Latin thought left off on this point, semiotic consciousness constitutes a definitive break with modernity and, at the same time, manifests a continuity with the early-modern milieu out of which modernity first took rise. The doctrine of signs restores continuity to philosophical tradition and history, something that had been lost for three hundred years in the wake of Descartes. Postmodernity, in its positive content, consists first of all in that recovery, or rather, in the step outside the epistemological limits of modernity presupposed for fully entering upon the way of signs.

In taking this step semiotics definitively transcends modern idealism, something that Eco's *Theory of Semiotics* tried but, for reasons we shall here examine, did not quite manage to do. No more realist than idealist, and no less idealist than realist, to the extent that it achieves fully the perspective proper to itself and relies

---

this figure came to be known among the Greeks as a messenger god, signaled by his staff, the caduceus, and winged sandals, who conveyed and interpreted messages among the gods and from gods to mortals. From his name comes the term "hermeneutics", a word covering whatever relates to interpretation.

10 See Santaella-Braga 1994.

11 Peirce 1868a: CP 5.253; Poinsot 1632a: Book II, Question 2, 240/1–253/37, and Question 5, esp. 271/28–35.

12 This dates of course from Augustine. But not until the time of Aquinas and Bacon does the speculative development that will justify Augustine's notion begin, as we have seen in chapter 7, p. 336ff. "Firsts" in history, of course, are precarious to assert, though their assertion provides at once indispensable landmarks and targets of opportunity for later research to topple. As of now, this particular assertion of the date for the onset of the main speculative development is reflected also in the structure of Meier-Oeser's 1997 study of the Latin history (e.g., "Inhalt", p. ix ff.), to which I have had frequent helpful recourse in the final drafting of the present work.

And I should also like to endorse the abductive guess communicated to me in this area by Prof. Ken Schmitz, that were one to take a less rigorously doctrinal route through the riches of the Latin Age one would almost surely find in the turn to allegory of the 12th-century Victorines a rich adumbration and anticipation of speculative developments to come. The work of Gary Shank (1998) on the role of allegorical understanding in the formulation of medieval bestiaries as a medium coordinating epistemological stances which, in contemporary inquiry, are regarded as oppositional is highly suggestive in this regard.

13 For the historical details in particular, besides chapters 8 and 9 above, see also Deely 1994a.

on no previous philosophical paradigm in establishing its own paradigm rooted directly in the action and understanding of sign, semiotics begins from a standpoint superior to this classical and quintessentially late-modern opposition. The *Theory of Semiotics* does not quite achieve this standpoint, at least, so to speak, not "with both feet". Instead, from within the realist-idealist opposition, Eco's book develops, with consummate clarity[14] and rigor, the nature and role in human experience of that type of sign which the Latins called *ad placitum*, but fails to visualize the place and role of that other type of sign the Latins (with less clarity than one could wish) called, all too simply,[15] *naturale*.

So much for preliminary clarification of terms. We need now only to frame our discussion of the theoretical details of Eco's landmark book by a brief outline of what we have learned about the history of semiotics, almost entirely since 1976, an unfolding in which the continuing research of Eco and his students has been a decisive influence.

The History of Semiotics as It Appears Today (and When and Where Is That?[16])

Here we can conveniently summarize the way of signs as we have been able to trace it across the centuries in the preceding chapters. Semiotics is nothing more or other than the knowledge we develop by studying the action of signs, and it receives its various divisions from the various ways and regions in which that action is

---

14 I do not mean the clarity of easy reading. In this respect, my original characterization of the book as a "readable account" was quite misleading. The book is anything but that, as generations of students have learned. I mean the clarity of a theoretical conception rigorously formulated and adhered to in its logical consequences throughout. In my original review, I described Eco's book as a "more readable account of semiotics in the current market". More readable than what? At its time the work was *sui generis*, and "readable" means "able to be read easily" (*Webster's Collegiate Dictionary*), which cannot be truthfully said of this book. I have always wanted to correct this false characterization, and do so here.

15 We discussed some "Problems in the Latin Terminology" for signs in chapter 15, p. 638ff. Here we may further note that in the analytical inadequacy of their nomenclature for "natural sign", notwithstanding their later marker of the distinction between a "formal" and an "instrumental" sign (which, as we saw in chapter 9, was in basic respects superficial), the Latins had blurred the profound difference between the idea as sign and the dinosaur bone as sign, for example. In speaking of the *signum naturale* as both *formale* and *instrumentale*, and, as *instrumentale*, *ex consuetudine* as well, they had covered over (cf. Deely 1978a) – or glossed over – the profound need for what Eco calls a theory of sign-production, even though without losing a profound sense of the permeability of nature to culture and vice-versa (cf. esp. Poinsot 1632a: Book II, Questions 5 and 6; and see note 124 p. 718 below). And, connected with this last point, they had not developed at all their rudimentary understanding of the third term of the sign relation, what we now call the *interpretant*, even though their semiotic treatises had explicitly reached the point of demonstrating that the sign consists not only in a relationship as such, but in a relationship irreducibly triadic – the point where Peirce picked up the Ariadne's thread of late Latin–early modern discussion to give us what we call "semiotics" today (see Beuchot and Deely 1995).

16 What I call the "problem of the *hic et nunc*".

verified.[17] This study presupposes nothing more than a notion of sign as one thing standing for another in a relation of "renvoi",[18] that is to say, an irreducibly triadic relation, actual or virtual, but in the case of cognitive life, it seems, always actual. Such a general notion of sign is verified, at the extremes, in phenomena we call "natural" and in phenomena we call "cultural", as well as in the intermediary phenomena of social interaction (for example, such as sociology studies it). But – and this is one of the more surprising upshots of contemporary semiotic research – the actual proposal of such a general notion of sign appears to be no older than Augustine, and a creation of the specifically Latin Age of philosophical history.[19]

Proposed in the fourth century, the semiotic point of view did not receive a warrant until the early seventeenth century,[20] when it was for the first time demonstrated how the early Latin proposal for a general notion of sign, applicable in a single sense to the extremes of nature and culture, could be vindicated through the fact that relation according to the way it has being is indifferent to whether its subjective foundation or ground be taken from both the being of physical interaction and from cognitive activity, or from either alone. This establishment of a unified object or subject matter for semiotic investigation was in principle revolutionary for our understanding of human experience and the knowledge which derives therefrom. For it unified in a single instrument or medium the otherwise diverse products of speculative knowledge about the natures of things, on the one hand, and, on the other hand, practical knowledge about human affairs and the application thereto of speculative knowledge.[21]

The privilege of naming the idea of the doctrine of signs as a new and distinct philosophical discipline fell to John Locke.[22] But the first author who succeeded in giving voice to the underlying unity of the being in relation upon which all action of signs as such depends was John Poinsot (1589–1644), an Iberian philosopher of mixed Burgundian and Portuguese descent. In the text of his *Tractatus de Signis*, published in 1632,[23] the new beginning implicit in the adoption of the semiotic point of view was in two ways symbolized. First, the text expressly noted that the sign requires a standpoint superior to the division of being into what is and what is not independent of cognition, which translates, in modern parlance, into a standpoint superior to the confrontation of realism with idealism. Second, the compass of the *Tractatus de Signis* text united what were, in the then-traditional

---

17 E.g., see Diagram 10, "Semiotic condensation of the natural philosophy tradition", and Diagram 26 on "The place of structuralism in the study of signs", in *Introducing Semiotic* (Deely 1982: 41 and 197, respectively).
18 Jakobson 1974; Deely 1993a, 1994a: 201–44.
19 Deely 1982 and 1990: 108–14; Eco, Lambertini, Marmo, and Tabarroni 1986; and Manetti 1993.
20 Herculano de Carvalho 1969, 1970, 1973.
21 See "Locke's Proposal for Semiotic: What Was New and What Was Not", in Deely 1994a: 109ff ; see also the discussion of "a distinction which unites" in Deely 1982: 62–4.
22 Sebeok 1971; Romeo 1977; Deely 1986b, 1994a: 109ff.
23 Reviewed on the contemporary scene by Santaella-Braga 1991; Deely 1988; Bird 1987; FitzGerald 1986, 1986a; Sebeok 1986b; and Fisch 1986.

liberal arts curriculum of the European universities, the opening discussions of logic with the concluding discussions of the theory of knowledge.[24]

This new beginning, the way of signs, was not, however, the new beginning that the authors of what was to become the classical modern mainstream of philosophy actually undertook. Instead, they chose to follow what Leibniz summarily and accurately characterized[25] as the way of ideas. This historical path was predicated on the assumption that the very ideas formed by the human mind are as such the immediate and direct objects of experience at every level of cognitive activity – that is to say, in sensation no less than in intellection as the activity proper to human understanding. This assumption, the heart of the modern epistemological paradigm, is impossible in semiotic terms, because it depends upon a reduction of signification to representation.

The point is capital. Signification: the constitution of the relation proper to signs. Representation: the standing of one thing[26] for another, where "the other" might not really be *other* but be rather *the same* thing in a mind-dependent relation of partial self-identity (that it is one and the same thing is mind-independent, but that it is self-identical is a mind-dependent relation, as discussed above).[27] Whence representation is in the "genus" of subjectivity (or "transcendental relation"), whereas signification is in the "genus" of suprasubjectivity (or "ontological relation"). A representation can be of a thing by itself, but a sign must be of a thing by an other than itself.

Thus, a thing existing physically in the environment can enter into a relation with a cognitive organism through which relation the thing enters into the organism's awareness as an object. In this case the thing-in-itself exists independently of the relation to the knower as well as in the relation. Outside the relation it does not "represent" itself, it *is* itself; but in the relation it *both* represents itself *and* is itself. This self-representation in relation to the cognitive organism is what constitutes the thing as object. Existing physically as thing, it now exists objectively *as well*, that is, it both exists and, as existing, is known.

However, only in the case of sensation does physical and objective existence coincide or overlap of necessity. Beyond the involvement of external sense, the physical existence independent of the cognitive relation could cease without the objective existence ceasing (as in memory or false anticipation of a meeting with a partner who in fact unexpectedly has died in the meantime). In objective existence the "relation to the knower", originated in a physical activation of the senses wherein the knower was causally affected by and so really dependent upon the known, goes *from* the subjective modifications or states introduced into the cognitive organism via sensation *to* the thing-now-become-in-part-object as well. The thing as existing in itself is independent of the relation. But the thing as involved in the relation is not

---

24 See the fold-out Synoptic Table in Deely 1985: 371–5.
25 Leibniz 1704: 62.
26 And always assuming that "res est de transcendentalibus".
27 See chapter 15, p. 647. Full discussion in Deely 2000: chapter 7, note 5.

outside the relation, and, as *in* the relation, the difference is that the thing existing apart from the relation now exists *also* as the terminus of the relation of cognition *from* organism *to* it.

Now what exactly does it mean to be the terminus of a relation? How is a thing as terminus (a thing in relation not as founding but as terminating a relation subjectively founded elsewhere in the environment) any different from that same thing as thing in itself? Here we see one of the points of the Peircean notion of "ground" discussed above:[28] a relation as founded has as its correlate a terminus formally proportioned or proportionate thereto. In the case under consideration, the thing objectified is not *totally* cognized or known but only in and under that aspect according to which the cognizing organism as such (as cognizing) becomes aware of it. In other words, even though the thing in itself exists in the order of subjective being, the order of physical existence includes also the intersubjective dimension of physical relations, and in the case of sensation the conditions for such "real" (categorial or physical) relations are realized, making the relation of knower to known in this case a real relation, not merely a mind-dependent one. So the thing known insofar as it is known is an object which is *also* a thing intersubjectively tied, connected, and suprasubjectively related *to* a knower.

This "to a knower" on the side of the known is not a physical dependency; the physical dependency in the case before us is of the knower on the known. The "to a knower", moreover, is not even itself the aspect of terminus but rather a consequence of the terminus: *because* it is a terminus it can be said to be "related to its knower", but *this* is a mind-dependent relation created in and by discourse, and its foundation, the "being known" of the object, is what the scholastics called an "extrinsic denomination", hardly a feature of *ens reale*. The being of and as terminus is prior to both the extrinsic denomination "known" and to the mind-dependent relation *from* known object *to* organism knowing. The being of and as terminus is by a mind-dependent relation modally distinct from the thing and is mind-independently part and parcel of the relation. The relation of awareness or cognition, *founded* in the knower, is *terminated at* the thing known. The ground of the relation on the side of the terminus consists wholly and entirely in the opposition to the relation itself whereby it is this relation and not some other, the opposition, that is to say, whereby the relation is terminated under that aspect of the known which is proportioned and proportionate to, correlative with, the condition or state of the knower on the basis of which (as fundament) the knower is related to the known. The fundament gives to the relation its real being or existence; the terminus gives the relation only its specificity,

---

28 See chapter 15, p. 641ff. Here we deal also with the very matter that led me to expand the 1985 published edition of Poinsot's *Tractatus de Signis* to include also Art. 5, "Whether Relation Is Formally Terminated at Something Absolute or at Something Relative" from Quest. 17, "On the Category of Relation", from Poinsot's *Ars Logica* of 1632 when Intelex undertook to bring out the *Tractatus* in the 1992 electronic edition. See further Deely 1975 for an early wrestling with this matter; also Deely 1986d.

determining the type of relation it is, that is to say, the aspect, the "ground", under which the partially known thing is not merely as such ("in itself") but *as known*.[29]

In other words, in the case we are considering, there is a real ("mind-independent") relation from knower to known, but its opposite correlative relation from known to knower is an unreal ("mind-dependent") relation. There are other cases where a relation is the same on both sides; but in this case it is not the same on both sides. As in unrequited love, so at the basis of experience in sensation, we have a relation that, insofar as it is a real relation, is a one-sided relation. And what we are trying to understand is how from this side which is "real" is the terminus constituted, since as terminus it is a creature of the relation and so, like the relation, in some sense has its being from the foundation of the relation which is in a subjectivity other than the subjectivity of the object suprasubjectively existing as known.

The rationale of a terminus consists in the opposition to its correlative:[30] but the correlative in this case is the Innenwelt of the knower, the terminus the Umwelt (or some element thereof). We see therefore exactly why the Umwelt is distinct in principle from the physical environment even though it includes the environment partially through sensation, and why the Umwelt as based on the Innenwelt can reorganize and relate on a different basis than the causality proper to secondness even the elements of the physical environment objectively incorporated in the Umwelt. The Innenwelt *founds* the Umwelt, but the Umwelt *grounds* the Innenwelt. As so grounded, the Innenwelt is tied by real relations, including ones of causality as well as consequent ones of cognition and awareness, to the physical surroundings; and these very relations in turn can themselves be objectified in consequence of the peculiar being of relation whence it enjoys an indifference to its subjective ground, which is the root of semiosis itself, the reason for the very possibility of an "action of signs", thirdness, distinct from even though partially inclusive of the "action of things" at the level of secondness. The thing as thing, once the cognition rises above sensation in the *perception* and still more in any *understanding* of the object, is only fundamentally and proximally the terminus of the relation of cognition; formally as a self-representing object it is therefore aspectually distinct in a mind-dependent way from whatever of its being is not cognized, even though *that* being, its "real being in itself", is mind-independently continuous with and as such revealed within the aspect of the thing under which, in and through its physical impact on sense, be it remembered, it is *also* objectified.[31]

---

29 Poinsot 1632: Q. 17, Art. 5, 596b30–6: "Just as a relation cannot be understood other than as having an opposition to a terminus, so a terminus cannot be understood other than as opposed; but this opposition is relative; therefore insofar as it is a terminus a terminus is something relative."

30 Poinsot 1632: ibid., 597b20: "formalis ratio termini consistit in oppositione ad suum correlativum; haec autem oppositio non invenitur formaliter ex parte alterius extremi, quia non habet relationem realem et consequenter neque oppositionem relativam; ergo non est formaliter terminus in re".

31 This is the whole point of the most lengthy and complex discussions of Book III, Questions 1 & 2, in Poinsot's *Tractatus de Signis*.

We might say that what the difference between thing-as-object and thing-as-thing comes down to is no more nor less than the difference between a relation as truly a relation, *on the one hand*, and a relation as indifferently objective or physical, on the other. The Latins themselves, though they had of a certainty begun to address this point underneath the famous "literal appearances", had not reached a sufficient clarity to mark the point thematically and linguistically in a settled vocabulary. It is not that the same object cannot be both word ("sign") and object, as in the distinction between formal and material supposition ("man" is an organism, "man" is a three-letter word). No. The point of the distinction, I think, is that the sign as such can always be an unconscious element, wholly or at least partially; and, to the extent that it is not unconscious, it constitutes an object as such (which, of course, may *also be* a sign and, as such, *comparatively unconscious*). In other words, if the two in question, object as such and object as thing, are not distinct modally at the minimum,[32] then it is as impossible for the one to be a sign of the other as it is for a square to be a circle or for a circle to have corners.

Let us suppose that the distinction between representation as such and signification as such, in this way or in some other way, can be upheld to be irreducible, as the doctrine of signs requires. In any event, a reduction of the latter to the former had already been shown to be an implicit confusion by the work of a series of late Latin authors, principally Hispanic, as it seems, who had undertaken in the sixteenth century the initial exploration and development of the requirements of a semiotic consciousness. But their work in this regard was ignored by, perhaps unknown to, the authors who were destined to become known as the founders of philosophical modernity. In the glare of attention focused on the way of ideas, the way of signs, which had been barely adumbrated by authors of a waning Latinity, soon became lost in the shadows created by the new lights of modernity. The way of signs remained forgotten until a confluence of scholarly coincidences, themselves mostly occasioned by the contemporary interest of middle to late-twentieth-century academics in semiotic studies, brought them to light.[33]

In the ancient world dominated by Greek philosophy, the notion we translate as sign, σημεῖον ("semeion"), should actually be translated rather as "*natural* sign", for this term in antiquity referred only to natural phenomena such as meteorological occurrences and symptoms of disease. When attention was finally turned to the phenomena of signification in late modern times – in the very twilight of modernity in which mainstream philosophy of the twentieth century persists in dwelling – there was hardly any place left for a viable notion of natural phenomenon. It was therefore

---

32 See Deely 1986d.

33 Mauricio Beuchot and I are able at this time to name ten Latin authors of neglected semiotic treatises; when I arrived in México in September 1994 we knew only of four; and even more than we knew together are indicated in the rich work of Meier-Oeser 1997. Clearly we are talking of developments both in the revision of the history of philosophy, looking backward, and in the very doing itself of philosophy, looking around us today and forward into the 21st century in fact already begun, owing to the error in our calendrical system noted in chapter 5 above.

no accident that the original popular success of contemporary attempts to develop a theory of sign was not under the designation of *semiotics*, a name redolent of the natural origins of signification in physical processes anterior to human cognition. The attempts which caught the public eye went rather under the designation of *semiology*, a name taken from linguistic studies and intended to signify that the paradigm for any theory of signs should be not the early Latin general notion but a specifically modern notion of sign as determinately arbitrary and linguistic, that is, cultural, in derivation.

Only slowly and against the greatest resistance on all sides did semiotic research, indebted especially to the powerful impulse given it by the philosophical investigations in this area by Charles Sanders Peirce, compel the gradual recognition that any notion of sign as inherently arbitrary, however valid and necessary in specific areas, was incapable of providing an adequate foundation for the possible field of investigations opened up by the action of signs.[34] The progress of this grudging recognition was signalled in the literature on signs, iconically, as it were, by the shift in terminology from "semiology" to "semiotics" as the proper designation for the point of view under development.[35]

Thus, by the most unexpected of turns in philosophical history, semiotics as the way of signs puts us back at a point where modern philosophy began, and compels us to look anew at those late Latin–early modern texts, ignored by modernity, wherein was achieved the first establishment of the foundations for what we today call semiotics. From this curious standpoint, at once antiquarian and postmodern, as I have elsewhere explained,[36] Eco's book appears today as a definitive step in the muddled transition from semiology (as a final stage of the idealism of modernity) to semiotics proper and postmodern times.

Theoretical Heart of *Trattato di semiotica generale*

It remained for our own times effectively to recognize, in Saussure's words,[37] the "right to existence" and "place staked out in advance" for a unified approach to the phenomena of signification with their characteristic effect – communication, in whatever mode or on whatever levels it occurs. But we can no longer say with Saussure that "since it does not yet exist, one cannot say what form it will take". It will take the form of a definitely postmodern development, because it calls for

---

34 The earliest mapping of the terms at play was provided by Sebeok 1971, an essay we have already had occasion to quote. The clearest marking of the decisive paradigm-shift as such within contemporary sign studies was made in the anthology, *Frontiers in Semiotics* (Deely, Williams, and Kruse eds 1986). See in particular the editors' preface, "Pars Pro Toto", pp. xviii–xxii. Also Deely 1986a, and 1990: 1–8.

35 See Sebeok 1971; Beuchot and Deely 1995: 539–45; Deely 1995a. A more thorough investigation of the details of the terms and issues I hope to bring to publication soon under the title *Why Semiotics?*

36 Briefly in Deely 1984, at length in 1994a.

37 Saussure 1916: 16 (Baskin trans.).

an epistemological paradigm incompatible with that which defines modernity, and begins, as we saw, at a point beyond the quintessentially modern controversies between realism and idealism.

The characteristically contemporary attempt to realize such a perspective has emerged from nowhere, as it were, since the First World War, originally under the charismatic influence of the Swiss linguist Saussure, but more properly and later under the aegis of the American philosopher Charles Peirce, and along a truly supra-national front.[38] In a field burgeoning with such a bewildering array of pursuits as seemed to all but belie its claim to the possibility of an over-arching, systematic perspective or doctrine, the publication of Professor Eco's book provided a clarifying landmark.

For the purpose of discussing here the theoretical details of Eco's book, I will make use of Eco's own system of internal division and punctuation. Thus, all references to the work will be in terms of the chapters and numbered divisions within each chapter, usually followed by page numbers, or, occasionally, in terms of page numbers alone. "0", in Eco's numeration, is for "Introduction", followed by four chapters numbered 1 through 4, giving a total in effect of five major divisions or sections for the book. For reasons of space, I will here consider among these details only those which bear directly on the main concern of the present book, which conveniently overlap with the main concern of Eco's book, beginning with Eco's proposal that *signum* as the defining notion of semiotics can be adequately replaced by (or translated into) his notion of *sign function*.[39]

Field or Discipline?

What Professor Eco undertook in this work was not "to explore the theoretical possibility", such as Poinsot envisaged, "of a unified approach to every phenomenon of signification and/or communication" in an abstract and definitive way, but rather to make only "a *preliminary exploration* of such a theoretical possibility" in terms of "*the present state of the art*".[40]

I have emphasized this qualifying phrase in order to give it the sense and importance I think is due it in connection with the question Eco raises quite early, and in which any reader is certain to have an especial interest: "'Semiotics': field or discipline?"[41]

Eco himself, in 1976, did not attempt fully to settle this question – a prudent enough stance before the complexity and remaining obscurity shrouding the history of semiotics at that time. Even Sebeok, of whom Steiner[42] remarked that his

38 See the surveys of Sebeok 1974, 1975a, 1976.
39 For consideration of other technical details, notably the *ratio facilis* and *ratio difficilis*, which appears to me too theory-specific to Eco's work to be of general interest, I refer readers to my original review (Deely 1976).
40 0.1.1, p. 3; italics added.
41 0.2, pp. 7–8.
42 Steiner 1975: vii.

"knowledge of the whole range of current language studies may well be unrivalled", assumed at that period that Peirce "was heir to the entire tradition of philosophical analysis of signs".[43] What Eco did make clear was that his work had been conceived in view of semiotics more as a field than as a discipline. But this point was not as clear as might at first seem, since Eco's manner of making it gives the appearance of assuming, in line with the then-prevailing fashions in the analytic philosophy of science, that a discipline as such requires a deductive model at its center.

Yet even at the time such an assumption should not have passed unchallenged in a major work.[44] In subsequent years, within American semiotics at least, discussion shifted more from the "field–discipline" polarity, with its implied scientific model, to a discussion of the expression "doctrine" in the classical formula *doctrina signorum*.[45] This formula, "doctrine of signs", was used in common by Poinsot, Locke, and Peirce. It proved to have far more clarifying power with regard to the philosophical status of semiotics, in no small part because it avoided the trap into which Eco's discussion had fallen of buying into the regnant assumptions of an already stagnant, but institutionally dominant, school of late-modern philosophy, as Sebeok expressly noted in a work coeval with the book of Eco under discussion:[46]

> The expression *doctrine of signs*, for the title of this collection, was selected with deliberation to emblematically align the arguments embodied in these eleven essays with the semiotic tradition of Locke and Peirce rather more closely than with others that prefer to dignify the field – often with premature strategic intent – as a 'theory' or even a 'science'.

Yet the "field–discipline" polarity, like the medieval distinction between "material and formal logic" adopted from the Arabs, provoked much useful discussion without ever receiving a clear and agreed-upon sense, and still warrants further discussion today, since it both was one of the seminal points in Eco's book and directly contributes to a better situating and fuller understanding of that work. Let me try once again at giving this distinction its best sense.

When I reviewed this work in 1976, I proposed to use as semantic markers for the parts of this distinction the two terms "semiotic" and "semiotics", the former to name the foundational and philosophical disciplinary aspect, the latter to name the interdisciplinary field of studies to which the fundamental notion of sign as the medium of all thought (and therefore in whatever discipline) naturally gives rise. Like Russell's earlier attempt[47] to tie his theory of descriptions to the historical accident of the linguistic difference between "the" and "a" as definite and indefinite

---

43 Sebeok 1974: 220; see also Sebeok 1975a.
44 Cf. Deely 1973: 33n53, 49, and passim.
45 See Sebeok 1976; and Deely 1982a and 1986a.
46 Sebeok 1976: ix.
47 Russell, 1905, 1910, 1919.

articles of contemporary English (although I hope with better theoretical grounds), this attempt on my part soon enough proved to be too provincial from a linguistic point of view. Even though it worked quite well in English, it proved unworkable within the international context of the contemporary semiotic development.[48]

But the sense of the distinction as thus unsuccessfully marked still seems to me valid today, so I will try to represent it here under the auspices of some new semantic markers. Let us today speak rather of a difference between semiotics *theoretical* and *applied*,[49] where the qualifying terms have the Aristotelian sense of the difference between what cannot be and what can be brought under human control.[50] "Theoretical semiotics" refers to the doctrine of signs in its foundational sense. In this sense it authorizes, legitimizes, and gives rise to a whole field of investigations which follow the action of signs in carrying understanding across disciplinary lines as well as in establishing disciplines in the first place. But it also, and more importantly, establishes the structures of experience out of which the possibility of disciplines arises in the first place and against which disciplinary structures, like the structures of understanding in general, have constantly to recur for inductive verifications. "Applied semiotics", then, takes the results of such researches and tries to make use of them in various specific contexts of human thought and action, especially in those areas over which the human understanding has the relative maximum of voluntary control, which is to say in the areas of society and culture and the "arts" generally – whence "visual semiotics", "semiotics of film", "semiotics of gesture", "facial semiotics", "semiotics of culture", and so forth. Success in the former investigations would constitute semiotics as a discipline in the philosophical sense, while the play of the latter investigations would constitute the interdisciplinary and transdisciplinary field of semiotic inquiries, many of them "scientific" in the manner of the social and humanistic sciences.

Semiotics *as a discipline*, therefore, refers primarily to the development of what Peirce and Locke called the "doctrine" or theory of what a sign is, and the conditions for anything to be a sign.[51] *As a field*, on the other hand, semiotics consists in the development of attempts to isolate and pursue the implications of specifically signifying aspects and elements of phenomena that are studied in their own right by the range of traditional specialized pursuits (music, architecture, ethology, etc.), or

---

48 See Deely 1990: xi–xii, and 1992b; Figueiredo 1995: XIX note.
49 Compare Eco's remark, dated July 1974, in the "Prefazione" to the original edition of his *Trattato de semiotica generale*, p. 6: "Se qualcuno non avesse già avuto un'idea analoga, mi sarebbe piaciuto intitolarlo *Critica della semiotica pura e della semiotica practica*: tale titolo avrebbe reso abbastanza bene le mie intenzione, ma sfortunatamente timore reverenziale, senso dell misura e senso dell'umorismo si sono congiurati per sconsigliarmi tanta impudenza." The reverence for Kant is touching, but perhaps reveals more than was realized. Recall too Kant's own protestations (chapter 13, p. 586f.) that his work had escaped idealism.
50 See "Understanding the Distinction between Speculative and Practical Knowledge" in chapter 3, p. 81ff. Cf. the discussion of the point in Maritain 1921.
51 It was for naming the foundational area so conceived that the -ic form (semiot*ic*), in English at least, makes perhaps the most appropriate usage. See Deely 1976, 1978, and 1982.

that are involved in the specific production of signifying phenomena in the various areas.[52]

Thus, the 'field' conception of semiotics brings into focus the inherently interdisciplinary ramifications of the possibility of success in developing a unified theory of signs. Since all thought is in signs and, moreover, all the objects of our experience both presuppose and are themselves comprised of signs, the range of implications and applications of a theoretical semiotics successfully grounded are practically unlimited. Prior to semiotics, "interdisciplinary programs", so essential to compensating for the myopic tendencies of specializations in modern academe, have always required deliberate contrivance to develop, and, as a consequence, have had a rather tenuous (often "personality dependent") status vis-à-vis the specialties. Within the perspective of semiotics, this situation changes radically and for the better. For the first time an interdisciplinary outlook ceases to be something contrived or tenuous. Such an outlook appears now rather as something built into semiotics, simply by virtue of the universal role of signs as the vehicle of communication, within and between specialties, as everywhere else.

Clearly, theoretical and applied semiotics so understood are distinct but only imperfectly separable pursuits. Foundations call for superstructures as much as superstructures (if they are to endure) require foundations. But there is more than this. Unlike material constructions, which require that foundations be completely laid before superstructures are raised, the constructions of understanding are such that superstructures derive from foundational intuitions not only in advance of the perfect clarification (or "completed laying") of these foundations, but also in such a way that the foundational clarification itself proceeds (if at all) only by a backward glance (*Blickwendung*) from such superstructures as it enables. This is a Heideggerian point much more germane to the success of Eco's project than any disciplinary models to be found in the literature of analytic philosophy.

In this way, it becomes clear how and why the laying of foundations (in our case, theoretical semiotics, the establishment of what it is for anything to be a sign) and the study of a field (in our case, applied semiotics, the study of the production and functioning of particular signs and classes of signs) are only *relatively* independent. What also becomes clear is how and why this *relative* independence is such that the understanding of foundations must be achieved through a *preliminary* investigation of what those foundations have already made possible, namely, the interdisciplinary (or transdisciplinary[53]) field. Thus the prior, though independent of the posterior, is nonetheless *known* by its adumbration therein, and must be so approached, even

---

52 Again speaking in the strictly English-language context, for this – the study of how signs are produced and function in diverse contexts and areas – the -ics form (semio*tics*) makes a more appropriate designation. But as this way of putting the matter is not available within the semantic fields of many other contemporary languages, I no longer think much should be made of what amounts to an English provincialism.

53 For it is not only a question of the action of signs within and across anthroposemiotic structures, but of the action of signs in other species, both animal and plant, and even in nature as an evolutionary

though this epistemological dependence obtains only in a preliminary way, and by no means ties the foundational inquiry to the full grasp of the development of the field in all its possible ramifications. Were that the case foundational inquiry would be rendered impossible, since the grasp and development in question – being positive science – are an asymptotic affair in time. Heidegger's description of the process is still the best:[54]

> Basic concepts determine the way in which we get an understanding beforehand of the area of subject-matter underlying all the objects a science takes as its theme, and all positive investigation is guided by this understanding. Only after the area itself has been explored beforehand in a corresponding manner do these concepts become genuinely demonstrated and 'grounded'. But since every such area is itself obtained from the domain of entities themselves, this preliminary research, from which the basic concepts are drawn ... must run ahead of the positive sciences, and it *can*. ... Laying the foundations for the sciences in this way is different in principle from the kind of 'logic' that limps along after, investigating the status of some science as it chances to find it, in order to discover its 'method'. Laying the foundations, as we have described it, is rather a productive logic – in the sense that it leaps ahead, as it were, into some area of Being, discloses it in its constitution of Being, and, after thus arriving at the structures within it, makes these available to the positive sciences as transparent assignments for their inquiry.

Study of the field in its own right and, as it were, for its own sake (the case of semiotics as Eco principally envisages it for the present work) is thus tied to the state and diversity of the positive sciences (what Eco calls "the present state of the art") whose state and diversity are themselves functions of a *use of signs*.[55] Study of the discipline proper, on the other hand (also the case of semiotics, but envisaged now directly in terms of the action of signs as rooted in and stemming from the being proper to any sign), is *necessarily* first adumbrated in viewing the field in some overall sense, but is not itself tied through this adumbration to any permanent or thoroughgoing dependence upon the vagaries of scientific research. Semiotics adumbrates what it in turn springs from: the *Sein* proper to signs.

The distinction I have just outlined is not stated thus within Professor Eco's book. Yet it nonetheless applies thereto and is finally implied thereby. Understanding Eco's work in the light of the distinction between field and discipline taken in the manner just outlined demonstrates the appropriateness of his chosen title, while internal analysis of the book's structure leads toward a critical justification of the proposed distinction so grounded. Thus, as befits a new theory, Eco envisions no more than a

---

whole. See Sebeok 1963, 1972, 1975, 1977, 1978, and 1986a. Sebeok and Rosenthal eds 1981; Krampen 1981. Deely 1982b and 1990: 94–103; 1994a: 183–200; 1997, 1998. Hoffmeyer 1996.
54 Heidegger 1927: 10.
55 Cf. Locke 1690: 460–3.

preliminary exploration of the possibility of a unified approach to signification. He envisions not an exploration leading to *the proper foundation* of the very possibility of the field of semiotics, but a preliminary exploration rather of (or 'belonging to') *the field as such* – and as yet finally presupposing such a foundation as this book does not pretend to give.

By the de facto angling of his work in this way, Professor Eco is able to satisfy a need in some respects even more pressing at the time he wrote than the need for a purely philosophical establishment of the foundations of a doctrine of signs. What was at the time most sorely needed, and what this book magnificently supplied, was the need of a demonstration of the *common relevance* of the staggering array of writings that had proliferated in recent years under the banner of semiotics and its congeners (as including "semiology"). In achieving this much, Eco gave effective answer to those mistaken, but forgivably bemused, critics who so far had seen in semiotics only a nominal unity concealing a hopeless nest of jargon and equivocation, anything but the nascent form of a perspective and discipline of philosophy powerful and encompassing enough to achieve a major revolution in our understanding of the intellectual life and its diverse roles in nature and culture.

Sign or Sign-Function?

The theoretical difficulties which constitute the book's challenge are precisely what continues to be most interesting about the book. Of these various difficulties, one in particular is keyed to the book's overall structure. It crops up in the opening paragraphs of the very first chapter, as Professor Eco explains how he proposes to realize the aim of exploring in preliminary fashion "the theoretical possibility and the social function of a unified approach to every phenomenon of signification and/or communication".[56] "One must first take into account", Eco writes, "the all-purpose notion of 'sign'", not just to distinguish signs from objects signified, say, but, more importantly, "to translate the notion of 'sign' into the more flexible one of *sign-function* (which can be explained within the framework of a theory of codes)".[57] As we shall see over the course of this discussion, this amounts to proposing the elimination of semiotics in the name of semiotics, or, what amounts to the same thing, the restriction of semiotics to the horizon of semiology.

Sebeok had already commented,[58] approaching what proved to be the apogee of the transition from "semiology" to "semiotics", that "semiotics must surely be one of the rare provinces of knowledge the very practitioners of which have failed to reach a consensus even about what to call their discipline". He might have noted, more substantively and with even greater justice, that semiotics must surely be one

---

56 o.i.i, p. 3.
57 o.i.i, p. 34. I note that the terminology of "sign-function", though not its theoretcial baggage, is quietly dropped in Eco 2000.
58 Sebeok 1975a: 156.

of the rare provinces of knowledge the practitioners of which begin by denying the very existence of their proper subject matter. In July of that very year, at the First North American Semiotics Colloquium held at Tampa, Florida, on the campus of the University of South Florida,[59] I had listened to Professor Henry Hiz deliver the first presidential address of what was to become, in the following year at the Atlanta, Georgia, meeting, the Semiotic Society of America. In that memorable address, Professor Hiz, who, so far as I know, has not been heard from again on the American scene, solemnly proposed that the first *desideratum* for the nascent new society should be to do away with the notion of "sign". Here, then, in Eco's work, for the second time in a short interval, I found myself in the presence of an authority pronouncing, in the very name of semiotics (the *doctrina signorum*), elimination of *signum* as the basic theoretical and analytic category.

That such a translation as Eco proposed should truly be necessary is puzzling at first glance. Yet so radical a proposal from an author so prominent in the very field for which the proposal is made can be dismissed, if at all, only after examination in detail. This demand for examination in detail in the present case was all the more pressing as it became apparent that, though introduced with minimal preliminaries, the proposed "translation" doing away with *signum* as a theoretical notion is the key conceptual move for the book as a whole. The sequence of chapters in the book, as well as the boundary-definitions of Eco's research, are directly related to and largely consequent upon the substitution of sign-function for sign as the basic semiotic category.

Eco's Notion of Sign-Function

What, then, is a *sign-function*? Eco defines this term at a number of points. "A sign-function arises when an expression is correlated to a content";[60] "the sign-function is nothing more than the correspondence between a signifier and a signified".[61] But perhaps his fullest and most formal statement occurs on p. 191: "a sign-function is the correlation between an expression and a content based on a conventionally established code (a system of correlational rules)". Thus, the effort to understand signification, for Eco, "entails a theory of codes",[62] because "codes provide the rules that generate sign-functions".[63] And since communication "pre-supposes a signification system as its necessary condition",[64] it is clear both why the "discriminating categories" of semiotics are *signification* and *communication*, and why the theory of codes must precede the theory of sign (function) production as the instrument of communication's actual occurrence:[65]

---

59 See Sebeok Ed. 1976.
60 2.1, p. 48.
61 2.2, p. 52; see pp. 52–4.
62 0.1.1, p. 4.
63 3.5.1, p. 191.
64 0.3, p. 9.
65 0.1.1, p. 4.

... there is a signification system (and therefore a code) when there is the socially conventionalized possibility of generating sign-functions. ... There is on the contrary a communication process when the possibilities provided by a signification system are exploited in order to physically produce expressions for many practical purposes.

Hence the structure of Eco's book, as follows. After an introductory chapter stating the aim and bounds of the research (0.), there comes a first chapter (1.) on signification and communication, wherein an elementary communication model is proposed that serves mainly to clarify what is *properly* called a code (namely, a rule coupling a set of signals with a set either of notions or of behavioral responses[66]) as against what is – by homonymy – *commonly* called a code (namely, the notion of purely combinational systems, whether of signals, notions, behaviors, or whatever). This common notion of code, since it is *improperly* so called, Eco proposes to rename as an *s-code*. He proposes by this terminological clarification "to avoid the considerable theoretical damage" that can be produced by such homonymous equivocation[67] as obtains when both code properly so called (coupling rules, which are purely relational) and code improperly so called (an *s-code*, combinational systems of whatever elements founding relations, what the Latins called "transcendental relatives") are simply referred to by the same character-string "code":[68]

> I shall therefore call a system of elements such as the syntactic, semantic and behavioral ones ... an s-code (or code as system); whereas a rule coupling the items of one s-code with the items of another or several other s-codes ... will simply be called a code.

This clarification is followed by a second and much longer – 103- as opposed to 16-page – chapter (2.) on the theory of codes proper as the key to and basis for sign-functions, which leads to another lengthy 163-page chapter (3.) on the actual production of sign-functions in communicating. After this there is, in conclusion, only a very short – 5-page – chapter (4.) on the subject of semiotics. But "subject" here does not mean the subject-matter, but rather the "empirical subjects which display labor in order to physically produce expressions",[69] that is, you and me. This chapter seeks to make the purely methodological point that if "semiotics recognizes as the only testable subject matter of its discourse the social existence of the universe of signification",[70] then it "is entitled to recognize these subjects" – you and me – "only insofar as they manifest themselves through sign-functions". Whether, "by

---

66 1.2, pp. 36–7.
67 1.2, p. 37.
68 1.2, pp. 37–8.
69 4.0, p. 317.
70 Ibid. But if the author means the *actual* social existence of the universe of signification, we must demur from his formula; the formula holds only if what is meant is the *in principle* social existence of the universe of signification – i.e., the public-in-principle character of objects signified, whether in part physical also or objective only.

accepting this limit, semiotics fully avoids any risk of idealism", as Eco posits, is a point to which we shall have to return.

For the present, it is clear from the above that by far the bulk of Eco's work – 266 out of 318 pages, or, if we count the preliminary clarification of code as correlating rule in chapter 1, 282 out of 318 pages – is occupied with the discussion of topics whose importance is directly tied to the "translation" of the notion of *signum* into that of *sign-function*. Hence, equally for understanding and for criticizing Eco's transitional work, we must carefully look above all into this move.

In Eco's own framework, the importance of the move from sign to sign-function cannot be over stressed. "The notion of 'sign' is a fiction of everyday language", Eco asserts – just the sort of assertion that philosophers have gotten used to after Wittgenstein. This particular "linguistic fiction" is one "whose place should be taken by that of sign-function".[71] Or again, using Eco's own italics: *"it is the very notion of sign which is untenable"*.[72]

The Classical Notion of Sign
Claims such as these, however familiar in the context of analytic and "ordinary language" philosophy, are not obviously true, and should be argued for directly rather than simply posited as point of departure. Although short of a direct argument on this point, a remark Eco makes in passing about the supposed 'ordinary language' and 'classical' notion of sign provides important insight into his decision to replace *signum* with his conception of sign-function. The ordinary notion, he asserts, is "naive and non-relational",[73] whereas a sign-function is relational, "realized when two *functives* (expression and content) enter into a mutual correlation; the same functive can also enter into another correlation, thus becoming a different functive and therefore giving rise to a new sign-function".[74] Thus, "if the theory of codes and the theory of sign production succeed"[75] with the translation of sign into sign-function, "the classical notion of 'sign' *dissolves* itself into a highly complex network of changing relationships".[76]

That is all well and good, and certainly a complex network of changing relationships fits our experience of signifying incomparably better than any non-relational item or category possibly could. So true is this that, were it necessary to go from signs to sign-functions in order to achieve at the level of theory the identification of signification with some form of thoroughly relative being, Eco's translation would be ipso facto justified.

Such, however, is not the case. Let us suppose that there is, as Eco alleges, some "ordinary language" notion of sign that is "naive and non-relational". Even if that

71 3.1.3, p. 158.
72 3.5.10, p. 216
73 0.1.1, p. 4.
74 2.1, p. 49; Eco's italics.
75 P. 4.
76 2.1, p. 49; Eco's italics.

be true, such a notion can hardly be equated with anything that can credibly be called the "classical" notion of sign. Historical research has shown, on the contrary, that "a sign is something relative" is a proposition that has always been a point of common agreement wherever the notion has been thematized, certainly among the Latin discussants of signifying from Augustine (fifth century) and Boethius (sixth century) to Poinsot (seventeenth century) – the full extent of the Latin Age in philosophy.[77] So it is hard in the first place to know on what grounds Eco can speak of a "classical" notion of sign that is *non*-relational.[78]

In the sixteenth- and seventeenth-century scholastic discussions of *signum*, for example, which were commonplace in the Iberian world especially,[79] there was never any question as to *whether* signs were relative, "because nothing signifies itself, although something may represent itself", as Poinsot put it.[80] *That* signs are *aliquid relativum* was the starting point of discussion and controversy. So central was this realization in the Latin consciousness that Poinsot made it the point of departure for his epochal *Tractatus de Signis*,[81] which proved the first successful attempt historically, as we saw in chapter 9, to establish a unified subject matter for semiotic inquiry. The question has always been *how* signs are relative, what sort of relative being, precisely, belongs to signs as such. That signs are relative there was never any doubt.

Therefore I think that Eco is definitively moving in the right direction when he proposes that signs are neither physical nor fixed entities,[82] but wrong as a matter of historical fact in thinking that the classical notion of *signum* was not already pointed in this same direction. Moreover, any non-relational notion of sign, being a self-contradictory pseudo-notion, would prove no more suitable for colloquial than for technical semiotic discussions (except where irresolvable paradox were the subject being discussed). It would appear that, by opting for sign-functions to

---

77 Deely 1978, 1981, 1985, 1994a: 39–52; B. Williams 1985.
78 But, in the second place, it is also difficult to know on what grounds even a supposedly "ordinary" or "naive" notion of sign could be non-relational – unless it were very naive indeed – since such a notion would be self-contradictory, the semiotician's version of a square circle. Such a muddled notion, more than naive, would be pseudo. This predicament is not impossible in the play of common speech, but it should be *shown* rather than merely *asserted* to exist; and, even then, it would remain beside the point both for the history and the theory of semiotics.
79 "... recentiores ... quotidianis disputationibus agitare solent", Poinsot observed (1632a: 194/38–40). And see the anthology on this point by Beuchot ed. 1995.
80 Poinsot 1632a: 117/13–14: "quia nihil seipsum significat, licet se repraesentare possit". For fuller discussion of the point see further 116/14–117/11 and 121/19–123/32; also Deely 1980 and 1986d.
81 See Poinsot 1632a: Book I, Question 1, esp. 117/18–118/18.
82 Eco 2.1, p. 49 top. Compare Deely 1994: ¶32: "The first and most radical misconception to be addressed is the notion that there are other things besides signs, as if signs were an item within our experience which has its place among other things besides. For, when we speak from the strict standpoint of experience (which of course we must in all contexts where we hope to avoid delusion), the sign is not by any means one thing among many others: the sign is not any thing at all, nor is it even first of all a distinct class of objects. As a type of object or objective structure contrasting with other objective structures, the sign is singularly unstable and derivative, precisely because signs are not objects first of all. Signs are presupposed to there so much as being whatever objects there are in the content of experience in general and at any given time."

replace signs on this ground, Eco has either been frightened by or opted for the convenience of a straw man.

Overlaps and Differences in the Two Notions

An *indirect* argument in support of Eco's rejection of the notion of sign in favor of that of sign-function as the basic semiotic category can be construed from Eco's "Critique of iconism".[83] Yet, even considered as an indirect argument for the untenability of the very notion of sign, this critique of iconism (essential details of which we shall have occasion shortly to discuss) is so embedded in the code/sign-function theoretical context as to remain doubtful to one not already persuaded of the need for the suggested "translation".

The absence of detached argumentation for such an early and key conceptual move must be adjudged a serious flaw in the theoretical execution of this book. The flaw is underscored by Eco's own admission – tacitly in conflict with his insupportable claim that the "classical" notion of sign was non-relational – that "this notion [of] sign appears to be so suitable in ordinary language and in colloquial semiotic discussions that it should not be completely abandoned".[84] Accordingly, Eco writes, "I shall continue to use the word /sign/ every time the correlational nature of the sign-function may be presupposed",[85] even though "properly speaking there are not signs, but only sign-functions".[86] Thus, except where context clearly stipulates otherwise, as in the passages from pp. 158 and 216 quoted above, the word "sign" occurs in Eco's framework as a short-hand synonym for the expression "sign-function". For example: "… everything can be understood as a sign *if and only if* there exists a *convention* which allows it to stand for something else".[87] Or again: "I propose to define as a sign *everything* that, on the grounds of a previously established social convention, can be taken as *something standing for* something else".[88]

This centrality of *convention* as part and parcel of the notion of sign-function ("*every* pattern of signification is a cultural convention"[89]) – indeed, as its *essential ground* (*iff*: "if and only if") – by itself suffices to challenge not only the necessity of translating the notion of sign into that of sign-function, but even more the *adequacy* of such a translation. I shall explore this matter shortly. But first I want to conclude the discussion of a point made earlier.

Political or Natural Boundaries?

I have said that not only are the order and content of the main divisions or chapters of Eco's book basically consequent upon the adoption of sign-function in place of

---

83 3.5, pp. 191–217.
84 0.1.1, pp. 4–5.
85 0.1.1, p. 5.
86 1.1, p. 49.
87 0.7.1, p. 19; italics added.
88 0.5.2, p. 16; Eco's italics.
89 1.1, p. 32.

sign as the fundamental category of semiotics, but also that his conception of the *boundaries* of semiotics is in important ways tied to this same decision. We have already set out warrant for the first part of this claim. I would now like to extend that warrant to cover the rest of the assertion.

Eco distinguishes between *political* and *natural* boundaries for semiotics, that is to say, between the boundaries that people interested in semiotics must deal with as a consequence of the way academia currently has its "turf" apportioned, and the boundaries that are proper to semiotics as a consequence of the action of signs as a distinctive object of investigation. Political boundaries are more immediately important even if ultimately less interesting inasmuch as they are provisional and subject to change. They are chiefly the result, as Eco's discussion makes quite clear,[90] on the one hand, of the comparative infancy of the semiotic movement, and, on the other hand, of the fact that the great panoply of academic specialties – formal logic, analytic philosophy, linguistics, information theory, rhetoric, aesthetics, behavioral psychology, etc. – de facto arose and have come to relative maturity in a pre-semiotic environment of understanding.

Thus, "the semiotician may express the wish that one of these days there will be a general semiotic discipline of which all these researches and sciences can be recognized as particular branches";[91] but a more realistic interim approach would be the proposal of "a unified set of categories in order to make ... collaboration more and more fruitful",[92] keeping in view also the "whole group of phenomena which unquestionably have a semiotic relevance even though the various semiotic approaches have not yet completely succeeded in giving them a satisfactory definition".

Information Theory vs. Semiotics

In particular, information theory is one of the more immediate objects of Eco's concern to distinguish "politically" from semiotics, and for this his distinction between "codes" and "s-codes" serves nicely. At the "lower threshold" of semiotics, Eco points to the sort of "communicative process" improperly so called that involves merely the transmission or exchange of physical signals, in order to distinguish it from the sort of communication properly so-called that involves signification whereby one item not merely triggers but *stands for* another:[93]

> ... the elements of an informational 'grammar' explain the functioning not only of a syntactic system, but of every kind of structured system, such as for example a semantic or a behavioral one. What information theory does not explain is the functioning of a code as a correlating rule. In this sense information theory is neither a

90 Pp. 5–7, 9–14.
91 0.1.2, pp. 5–6.
92 P. 6.
93 1.3, p. 40, and 1.4.1, p. 41, respectively.

theory of signification nor a theory of communication but only a theory of the abstract combinational possibilities of an s-code.

> ... a theory of codes ... will use categories such as 'meaning' or 'content'. These have nothing to do with the category of 'information', since information theory is not concerned with the contents that the units it deals with can convey but, at best, with the internal combinational properties of the system of conveyed units, insofar as this too is an s-code.

In general, "the phenomena on the lower threshold" indicate "the point where semiotic phenomena rise from something non-semiotic".[94] Thus, in Eco's view, "neurophysiological and genetic phenomena", for example, "are not a matter for semioticians, but ... neurophysiological and genetic informational theories are so".[95]

Eco vs. Peirce

The *natural* boundaries of semiotics, more interesting for the long run, on the other hand, "those beyond which a semiotic approach cannot go",[96] precisely because of their definitive character, must be prescissed very carefully. In approaching this matter, Eco proceeds by way of a limited comparison of the basic thrust in the semiotic conceptions provided respectively by de Saussure and Peirce.[97] He concludes by preferring the conception of Peirce as far as it has been presented, because "it does not demand, as part of a sign's definition, the qualities of being intentionally emitted and artificially produced".[98] Yet he does not hesitate to part company with Peirce's conception in another respect: "It is incorrect to say that every act of inference is a 'semiosic' act – even though Peirce did so. ... straightforward identification of inference and signification ... needs to be corrected by adding the expression 'when this association is culturally recognized and systematically coded'."[99]

What is the reason this qualification "needs" to be added? Why must the identification of inference and signification be "corrected" in this way? It turns out that no reason is apparent *other than Eco's thesis* that a sign-function, the correlation between all expression and a content, must be based on a convention, that is, a cultural link.[100] The thesis requires it; therefore it must be – classic *petitio principii*.

---

94 0.7.2, p. 21.
95 0.7.3, p. 21; see also p. 47 n. 5. Even as a political matter, this particular boundary of semiotics has not survived in all respects over time, as the introduction of the notion of physiosemiosis may serve to illustrate. See Deely 1989, 1990: 83–95, 1997, and 1998. See also Sebeok 1968, 1974a.
96 0.1.2, p. 6.
97 0.5, pp. 14–16.
98 0.5.2, p. 15.
99 0.6.1, p. 17.
100 3.5.1, p. 191.

Conventional vs. Natural Correlations

Moreover, the dubiousness of Eco's refusal to acknowledge inference as a straight-forwardly semiosic act comes out clearly in his account of the sense in which events coming from a natural source must be listed as sign-functions:[101]

> [a] the first doctor who discovered a sort of constant relationship between an array of red spots on the patient's face and a given disease (measles) made an inference: but [b] insofar as this relationship has been made conventional and has been registered as such in medical treatises a *semiotic convention* has been established. There is a sign every time a human group decides to use and to recognize something as the vehicle of something else.

Apparently, we are to believe that in the initial inference [a] the red spots did not function as signs, whereas once this initial discovery had been coded and catalogued [b] they are enabled to function significantly, because now (ibid.) "there is a convention positing a coded correlation between an expression (the perceived event) and a content (its cause or its possible effect)".

But why should we deny sign status to the spots in the first instance of their recognition? Merely because they escape the *cor*relational definition of sign-function? But what about the fact that they exactly fit the basic *relational* definition of a sign as something standing for something else to a cognizing agent or, more generally, the notion of *renvoi* as the irreducible triadic relation constitutive of a signification,[102] *aliquid stans pro alio*?

Moreover, even when the originally inferred natural connection "has been registered as such in medical treatises" so that "a semiotic convention has been established" for present as for future generations of doctors, does it follow in any proper sense that "*this relationship* [of red spots to measles] has [*itself*] been made conventional"? It would hardly seem so. The verbal discourse whereby the symptoms are described and related to their cause is permeated by the conventions of natural language and stipulations of technical jargon, to be sure. But this does not gainsay the fact that *what the discourse is about, what is objectified as the core of the discourse*, transcends the conventions *and* the codes (to whatever extent these may or must be distinguished) of the verbal and cultural media. The relation crucial to the signifying in such a case is *recognized within but not itself based upon* the conventions of speech, no more after than during the initial inference. Thus, Eco's proposition that "factual beliefs, even if widespread, *must be coded* or in some way conventionally recognized by a society"[103] would better be stated: "factual beliefs, in order to become and insofar as widespread – precisely as widespread – must

---

101 0.6.1, p. 17; Eco's italics.
102 See Deely 1993a.
103 P. 99. Cf. the discussion of "alpha and beta modes" of perception in Eco 2000: 382–6.

be coded etc.", not in order to be *factual* beliefs but in order to be *widespread* or *readily accessible* beliefs.

Much later on, in discussing related matter,[104] Eco seems to sum up his position regarding natural signs with the formula "the correlation, first *proposed* as the result of an inference, was then *posited*".[105]

But this way of putting things risks involving a sophism. Red spots were first "proposed" as signs of measles consequent upon an inference, no doubt; but this proposal was subsequently verified inductively[106] as being the case in fact. Had the critical control of objectivity invalidated rather than validated the original inference and the original researcher still clung to his view, then indeed would we have had a posit in an unqualified sense. (But notice the relation of critical control to *public life*.) Yet the correlation obtained and was recognized as obtaining in critically specified senses independently of proposals and posits: and this 'relative independence of linguistic positing discovered and critically verified' not only for this or that culture, but for humanity *sub toto caelo* (for instance, as in the Viking Lander Mars probe of weather and possible life conditions) is what is crucial in all correlations of signifyings so far as they admit of being properly classified as in any sense "natural".

As Eco remarks,[107] an object "can be a fake or can be erroneously interpreted as an imprint, a symptom or a clue, when in fact it is the chance product of other physical agents." But the reason it can be "erroneously interpreted" is *precisely* because convention *didn't originally* posit or constitute it *on the side of what is crucial for the signifying*, namely, the physical status of the object signified in the aspect according to which it is signified with the help of, but not exclusively on the basis of, various conventions and codes. This point is decisive, and I will refine it further in the discussion following.

Illuminations vs. Anomalies

Thus, Eco's reasoning in his disagreement with Peirce over the semiosic status of inference is not sound, yet it explains a great deal in terms of the theoretical structure of the *Trattato di semiotica generale*. It explains why the claim is made that "the human addressee is the methodological (and not the empirical) guarantee of the existence of a signification",[108] for culture only exists among human beings. It also explains the claim that semiotics is not only "a general theory of culture", but, "in

---

104 3.6.2.: "Recognition".
105 P. 223.
106 "Inductively" in the triadic semiotic sense derived from Peirce, whereby ideas are applied to experienced objects pragmaticistically to determine the value of hypotheses abductively arrived at and deductively developed, not "inductively" in the simplistic, perhaps simply erroneous, dyadic (or dichotomous) sense of traditional logic, apparently accepted by Eco for the book under discussion (cf. pp. 131–3). This sense opposes induction to deduction as, in Eco's summary, a "contrast of opposite directions in the reasoning process between the same two points". See the discussion in Deely 1982: 70–5; 1985a.
107 P. 221.
108 0.5.2, p. 16.

the final analysis", "only a substitute for cultural anthropology",[109] with no mention of physical anthropology, a glaring omission in Eco's work.[110]

At the same time, these conclusions would seem[111] to be incompatible with Eco's earlier assignation[112] of *zoösemiotics*, the study of "the communicative behavior of non-human (and therefore non-cultural) communities",[113] a place within the "political" boundaries of semiotics.[114] Whereas zoösemiotics was originally proposed as a study of the action of signs insofar as such action proves to be *common* to human and other animals, or *species-specific* to other animals, if "the laws of signification are the laws of culture",[115] then *only* as anthroposemiotics is semiotics possible.

On the other hand, if it was a mistake to begin with to think that the notion of sign, adequately understood, translates into the notion of sign-function, if on the contrary the sign-function as Eco defines it is but a sub-class of the genus *signum* (namely, the sub-class of *signa* unique to the human being as the *animal culturale*), then the way is open to a semiotics that does *not* require a human addressee as its methodological guarantee; and nothing would be lost of Eco's fine work – save that it would have to be classed not as a *Trattato di semiotica generale* (p. viii), but as a special treatise in anthroposemiotics, or even in semiology become aware of its true status as a *pars semeiotica*.[116]

Iconism or Indexicality?

Eco is not unaware of the difficulty at the heart of his proposed translation, or substitution, of sign-function for sign. In his "critique of iconism" (3.5.1, p. 191), he attempts to meet the difficulty head-on:

> If there exist signs that are to some degree motivated by, similar to, analogous to, naturally linked with their object, then the definition given in 2.1[117] should no longer be tenable.

---

109 0.8.5, pp. 26–7.
110 Cf. Deely 1990: 49, concluding paragraph.
111 Though cf. 0.4, 2nd para.
112 In 0.4.
113 P. 9.
114 Of course, politics is not as such averse to contradictions. As Eco admitted in the Sunday, 5 November 1995, "roundtable discussion" on the interdisciplinary scope of semiotics held within the framework of the "Semiotics as a Bridge between the Humanities and the Sciences" conference organized by Marcel Danesi at Victoria College, University of Toronto, 2–5 November, he was hoping at the time to exclude from theoretical semiotics 'Sebeok with his many strange animals' (the single marks here indicate a recollection from a viva voce context which can claim at most approximate exactness). This perhaps was why Eco located zoösemiotics inside the *political* rather than the *natural* boundaries of the field.
115 0.8.5, p. 28; cf. 3.3.4, p. 166 top.
116 Deely 1986c, 1995a.
117 P. 48: "a sign is always an element of an *expression plane* conventionally correlated to one (or several) elements of a *content plane*"; "every time there is a correlation of this kind, recognized by human society, there is a sign" (Eco's italics).

The only way to maintain it is to demonstrate that even in these types of signs a correlational convention is in operation. The core of the problem is obviously the notion of convention, which is not co-extensive with that of arbitrary link, but which is co-extensive with that of *cultural* link.[118] If one examines the mode of production of signs one must not only analyze the mode of production of the signal in itself but also its mode of correlation to its content, the correlating operation being part of the production.

Careful choice of examples at this point is crucial, and the simpler the appropriate illustration the better, for the less chance there is of losing our way in the analysis of irrelevant variables.

Let us begin by noting that "motivated by, similar to, analogous to, naturally linked with", may be roughly equivalent expressions in the case of icons, but in themselves "similar to" and "analogous to" form one set of related terms, "motivated by" and "naturally linked with" quite another, such that it is possible to sharply detach the two sets. Images that function as representational signs are sometimes said to be "naturally linked with" the object signified by virtue of their similarity or analogicity (= correspondence) to that object. But this constitutes a case radically distinct from effects such as smoke or causes such as clouds that are also classically said to be "naturally linked with" an object signified, fire in the former instance, rain in the latter, despite their complete lack of similarity or analogicity to the signified objects in question, as appears in the following table:

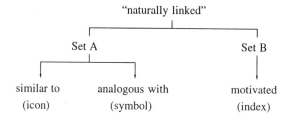

Table of Natural Linkage

---

118 Notice the parallel in Eco's theory, excepting only the expansion of "arbitrary link" to "cultural link", to Saussure's "remark in passing" (1916: 68, cited in chapter 16, p. 673 above): "when semiology becomes organized as a science, the question will arise whether or not it properly includes modes of expression based on completely natural signs, such as pantomime. Supposing that the new science welcomes them, its main concern will still be the whole group of systems grounded on the arbitrariness of the sign. In fact, every means of expression used in society is based, in principle, on collective behavior or – what amounts to the same thing – on convention. Polite formulas, for instance, though often imbued with a certain natural expressiveness (as in the case of a Chinese who greets his emperor by bowing down to the ground nine times), are nonetheless fixed by rule; it is this rule and not the intrinsic value of the gestures that obliges one to use them. Signs that are wholly arbitrary realize better than the others the ideal of the semiological process." The parallel runs all the way to the consideration of natural signs

Eco clarifies his notion of "motivates"[119] by indicating it has the basic sense of "determines": "For example the size of the imprinter determines (or motivates) the size of the imprint ...".[120] But this is the notion of a natural linkage which is primarily indexical, not of one that is primarily iconic or symbolic. In deciding, therefore, that the sign-function definition of 2.1 is tenable after effectively considering the role of culture only in the Set A sort of "natural linkage", or, as perhaps better put, after confounding and assimilating to the linkage of Set A the irreducibly different linkage proper to Set B, it can be said that Professor Eco is guilty of what he subsequently defines as a piece of "ideological discourse":[121]

> I mean by ideological discourse a mode of argument that, while using probable premises and considering only a partial section of a given semantic field, pretends to develop a 'true' argument, thus covering up the contradictory nature of the Global Semantic System and presenting its own point of view as the only possible conclusion (whether this attitude is deliberately and cynically adopted by a sender in order to deceive a naive addressee, or whether the sender is simply the victim of his own one-sidedness).

I suspect that the last is the case. But, in any event, with the above distinction of cases in mind, it is clear that the "critique of iconism" is a matter of special pleading so far as concerns the tenability of the definition from section 2.1.

Before proceeding further, it is crucial to note the feature of signs that underlies the possibility of such an assimilation and confusion as Eco seems here to have made, namely, the fact that "signs" are classified only indirectly, through their sign-vehicles, so that "it is not signs that are actually being classified", as Sebeok put it,[122] "but, more precisely, aspects of signs":[123]

> Aspects of a sign necessarily co-occur in an environment-sensitive hierarchy. Since all signs, of course, enter into complex syntagmatic as well as paradigmatic contrasts and oppositions, it is their place both in the web of a concrete text and the network of an abstract system that is decisive as to which aspect will predominate in a given context at a particular moment, a fact which leads directly to the problem of levels, so familiar to linguistics – being an absolute prerequisite for any typology – but as yet far from developed in the other branches of semiotics. This important issue ... cannot be dealt with here, beyond underlining it, and making an ancillary terminological assertion: that a sign is legitimately, if loosely, labeled after the aspect that ranks predominant.

---

primarily patterned on indexicality to the point of omission of indexicality as a distinctive base of connection. See further Eco 1972 and 1977 (with the comments in Deely 1994a: ¶168).

119 P. 221.

120 See also the usage context provided on pp. 188–9.

121 3.8.1., p. 278.

122 Sebeok 1975b: 120.

123 Ibid. 121.

Hence, in speaking of an "icon", an "index", or a "symbol", for example, along with the dominant aspect according to which the identification has been made, there are normally also subordinate aspects exhibiting differences in gradation which could also be emphasized to justify alternative cross-classifications legitimate from other points of view in conflict with the original one. There is probably no icon which is not *also* an index and *also* a symbol: yet it remains that, in cultural phenomena as such, a symbolic dimension preponderates; in physical occurrences, an indexical one; while icons more straddle both; and so forth.

Bearing in mind, then, that a hierarchic principle is inherent in the architectonic of any species of sign, let us proceed to consider the neglected sort of case of "natural linkage", namely, where that proper to Set B preponderates, in order to assess for ourselves the tenability of the definition in question and, more generally, of the proposed translation-without-loss of "sign" into "sign-function". I recognize some clouds as "signs" of rain: there is no doubt that certain clouds are *naturally linked with* rain. When I become aware of and *recognize* that link, I no doubt do so on the basis of experiences. In this sense, as Eco argues, the sign is something that always must be produced and, in the human case, is therefore always formed in terms that can be expressed also on the basis of a 'conventional code'.[124] But *what* I am recognizing, *what it is* that I become aware of in such a case, is *not fully* based on the code. To the contrary, *what* I am recognizing, *the linkage that constitutes what is properly described as natural about the signification*, is precisely antecedent to and independent of the "recognition codes" whereby I am here and now aware of it.

Moreover, it seems false to say in such a case, as Eco contends in the passage cited from p. 191, that "the correlating operation is a part of the production of the signal in itself". For the correlating operation resulting in signification which takes place is indeed wholly dependent upon my experience, but the production of the signal in itself takes place principally independently of my experience. What is needed is precisely an account of the manner in which what depends upon my experience

---

124 That the sign relation, the relation constituting a sign as such, is always different from physical relations of cause and effect, even in the case of signs called "natural", has long been a matter of explicit recognition is something we noted as early as 1267 in the Latin development: see "The Uniqueness of Sign Relations" in the discussion of Roger Bacon in chapter 8 above, p. 374. The late Latin sense on this question was expressly summarized by Poinsot in Book I, Question 2 of his *Tractatus de Signis*. See esp. 137/7, note 4. What no Latin author known to me went on to explain, however, was the exact manner in which the relation of effect to cause or cause to effect that arises as a result of the habilitation – the *motivation*, in recent terms – of sign-vehicle to object signified in the case of natural signs (e.g., smoke to fire or clouds to rain), and which relation is in itself a dyadic relation at the level of brute secondness, becomes incorporated into the triadic relation of renvoi in which alone any sign as such, whether natural or conventional, actually consists. For an explanation of this incorporation the topic of "the modes of sign production" is one of the essential topics to be thematized for the advance of semiotic consciousness. See the above remarks in this chapter, p. 693n15.

incorporates into my experience some things which as such do not depend upon my experience, and this Eco's theory does not provide for.[125]

The notion of sign-function as Eco employs it, therefore, fails to take account of a fundamental distinction among signs. All signs have the relation to what they signify here and now through experience. But some of these signs turn out, upon sufficiently controlled observation, to be connected with what they signify wholly due to the social action whereby they became signs (became assimilated as significantly relative within cognition) in the first place. Yet others, such as symptoms, clues, and imprints, in addition to being conjoined to something signified through experience (and therefore partly in terms of codes), also turn out to be conjoined – and knowable as so conjoined – independently of our experience of (and codes concerning) their conjunction. Recognition of the connection in every case depends upon our experience. But *the connection recognized* sometimes transcends that dependence and *is recognized so* to transcend. Part of what is recognized is the transcendence, the irreducibility to our experience.

Moreover, if culture functioned in the recognition of all natural structures and significations in the way that Professor Eco's definition of the sign-function requires it to do, then clouds could be signs of rain and smoke a sign of fire *only for humans*, whereas we have every reason to believe that they function as natural signs for many species of animals besides our own. It is not enough to show that culture *is at work* in the recognition of such signs as such, as Professor Eco does rightly and with little trouble.[126] It would be necessary to show further that it is at work *in the way required by the definition of the sign-function*, that is, as the sole essential ground of the correlation itself under every consideration, and not merely as the essential ground of the recognition of the correlation. Such a demonstration, to the extent that it might be possible, would be yet counterfactual.

Conclusions and Basic Problems
I conclude that the notion of sign-function is not an adequate – let alone necessary – substitute for the classical notion of *signum*, precisely inasmuch as the classical notion was proposed as a genus to which significant natural and cultural phenomena *alike* are species.

---

125 A remark Peirce made (c.1906a: CP 5.555) apropos of the relativizing of the true to the human by pragmatism (as opposed to pragmaticism, it should go without saying) would apply equally, *mutatis mutandis*, to the theory Eco would have us adopt: "there are certain mummified pedants who have never waked to the truth that the act of knowing a real object alters it. They are curious specimens of humanity, and as I am one of them, it may be amusing to see how I think. It seems that our oblivion to this truth is due to our not having made the acquaintance of a new analysis that the True is simply that in cognition which is Satisfactory [or, now, which conforms to our conventions]. As to this doctrine, if it is meant that True and Satisfactory [or true and conventionalized] are synonyms, it strikes me that it is not so much a doctrine of philosophy as it is a new contribution to English lexicography."
126 3.6.2: "Recognition", esp. pp. 222–4.

Mind-Dependent vs. Mind-Independent Relations

The basic problem in Eco's analysis of recognition and natural signs would seem
to devolve upon the irrelevance in his theory of mind-independent or physical
occurrences of relations and the role such relations play in signifying. Eco nowhere
discusses the subject of relation for its own sake. It is not that he denies the
existence of physical relations. Yet the irrelevance of such relations to semiosis
as he theorizes it is implicit in his definition of sign-function as dependent on a
"previously established social convention". The irrelevance of physical relativity to
semiosis is something required by his theory but gratuitous both in terms of the
historical development of Augustine's *signum* in the Latin Age and in terms of our
experience of the action of signs overall.

Sensation vs. Perception

The tacit failure to recognize the role of physical relations in semiosis is further borne out by Eco's reference[127] to "the vast problem of *perception as interpretation of sensory disconnected data* ... organized ... by a cognitive hypothesis based on previous experiences". This way of couching the problem profoundly confuses the phenomenologically interdependent but logically distinguishable (through prescission) and ontologically distinct levels of sensation and perception, what the Latins called *sentire* as distinct from (although presupposed to)
phantasiari.[128]

Eco states: "I connect together some stimuli coming from an as yet unstructured
field and I produce a *perceptum* based on a previously acquired experience".[129]
In so stating, he seems to take for granted the hoary empiricist and rationalist
conception of sense data as discrete and atomic in character (the "myth of the
given"), achieving any least measure of correlation and synthesis only and wholly
in the comparatively unreal constructions of perception and understanding, what the
Latins called "negationes et non entia".[130]

Yet a more careful analysis of what actually transpires in experience suggests that sensory data are never given in a simply disconnected way. For example, "a sense impression representing a colored thing also represents the profile and movement and other common sensibles there contained and adjoined,
yet does not on this account pass beyond simple cognition, even though the
thing cognized is not simple, but plural: otherwise, we would not be able to see
a plurality of objects by a simple vision. But if we are able to see many objects in a single vision, why not also an ordered plurality and one thing through

127 3.3.4, p. 165; Eco's italics.
128 See, in chapter 7, the sections on "Why Sensations Do Not Involve Mental Icons" and "Why
Perceptions Do Involve Mental Icons", p. 345ff ; and in chapter 12, "Sensation in the Perspective
of the Doctrine of Signs", p. 529ff. Further in Deely 1994: ¶s 41–3, 45, 120, 296, 298,
300.
129 3.5.2, p. 193.
130 Deely 2000. See chapter 7 above, p. 350ff.

another, and, consequently, a significate through a sign and as contained in the sign?"[131]

Sensation, analytically considered, differs from perception precisely in that it makes the organism aware only of the immediate physical surroundings insofar as they are proportioned to the biological cognitive powers or organs of the organism by a series of physical relationships introduced through the physical interaction of organism and environment. Perception will further structure this "data" according to the desires and needs specific to the organism, which may have no counterpart as such on the side of the environment. But to miss the fact that the data of sensation are already naturally structured through the determinate character of the stimulus acting on the determinate character of the cognitive dispositions of the organism is to miss a great deal that is important for understanding the dependency of anthroposemiosis on zoösemiosis and physiosemiosis generally.

We do not get sensory stimuli "from an as yet unstructured field" of simply "disconnected sensory data" subsequently organized *only* "on the basis of previous experience". *Already* in the sensory manifold as *here and now* stimulating, there is a *naturally determined* structure of objectivity – however minimal and under-determined respecting perception and understanding as gestalt wholes – which is 'then' *further* but *not wholly* structured by the intervention of constructive activities and previous experiences. And this naturally determined macrostructure, common across a broad range of biological species (e.g., the anthropoids), is precisely a system of relations physically relative to the constructive networks of perception and understanding based upon them and interwoven with them.

The "first interpretants" of phenomena thus are not ideas (percepts and concepts), but naturally determined patterns labile and in motion at the base and core (the "first immediate denotation", roughly, in Eco's terms) of the constructs that ideas elaborate in order further to interpret and give a "logical" sense to the larger phenomenal fields of unanalyzed experience. Whence the process of cultural semiosis is not an unlimited one in all directions.[132] It is susceptible of a "reality-check" through critical control exercised over variables in the direct experience and progressive objectifying of the environment,[133] including those various bubbles within the environment that semiotics has come to recognize as *Umwelten*, species-specific objective worlds distinct from the physical environs as common to all the life forms.

Invention vs. Invented

My analysis of the inadequacy of Eco's notion of sign-function as a full (let alone necessary) substitute for the classical notion of *signum* is borne out by Eco's own

---

131 Poinsot 1632a: 212/41–7; see also 208/34–47, 207/18–39, and Book I, Question 6 generally. See further Deely 1980a, 2000; chapter 12 above, p. 522ff.

132 Cf. ch. 2.7, pp. 68–72.

133 See Deely 1975b: esp. 96–9. Without raising them above the level of a Kantian "thing-in-itself", Eco 2000 (50ff. and passim) introduces "resistances" and a "grain" into the precultural continuum of "being".

analysis of *invention* as a mode of sign production. "How is it possible", he asks,[134] "to represent a man standing and a lady sitting under a tree, a calm landscape with clouds and a corn field behind them, a given light and a given mood – as happens in Gainsborough's *Mr. and Mrs. Andrews?*". I add some italics to Eco's own:[135]

> Nevertheless, *if such a phenomenon seems to escape the correlational definition of sign-function: it certainly does not escape the basic definition of a sign as something which stands for something else:* for Gainsborough's painting is exactly this, something physically *present* which conveys something *absent* and, in certain cases, could be used in order to mention a state of the world.

If something can escape the correlational definition of sign-function without escaping the basic definition of *signum*, however, what other conclusion is possible than the conclusion that sign is a more fundamental category for semiotic analysis than that of sign-function? Far from translating the notion of sign, the notion of sign-function is subordinate (inferior in the logical sense) to the notion of sign. "Sign-function" is but a partial transcription of *signum*, co-ordinate with but irreducibly distinct from the natural phenomena of signification which are also products of semiosis, but a semiosis more fundamental than the semiosis (and semiotics) of culture. Nor will it do, even within the semiotics of culture, to reduce the rich *entia realia* of experience to the poverty of "sensory data", particularly if the semiotic structure inherent and naturally determined with this "data", as we have seen,[136] is not well understood.

Modes of Sign-Production vs. Typologies of Sign

Here I should mention that, coupled with the attempted substitution of sign-function for sign, Eco proposed to substitute the identification of modes of sign production for the more traditional typologies of signs. Of course, in his text, this was a necessary move, inasmuch as everything began with the assumption that "there are not signs". But even in the absence of this assumption, counterfactual as it seems for the reasons stated, a study of the modes of sign-production is an essential development of semiotics. The initiation of such an inquiry is much to Eco's credit. For it is not enough simply to note, as we have seen among the Latins,[137] that in no case does a sign as such consist in the physical relation of cause to effect or effect to cause. It is further necessary to explain how such relations are incorporated through experience into the semiotic web of perception and understanding, and this is one of the most important tasks for the theory of sign production. For such a task, an account such as Eco's, *exclusively* in terms of socio-cultural convention, can hardly suffice.

---

134 3.6.7, pp. 249–50.
135 P. 250.
136 Chapter 12, "The Qualities Given in Sensation", p. 522ff.
137 See note 124 above.

We note, therefore, two things in Eco's undertaking to formulate an account of sign production: first, that the explicitation and thematization of this topic is an essential advance in the development of the doctrine of signs; second, that more is necessary than an account adequate exclusively to the *signum ad placitum* or sign as sign-function, for the sign in general extends to *signa naturalia* as well. To have taken the first step, nonetheless, is already an advance in the doctrine of signs, one of the several important advances signalized in Eco's pathmarking book.

Yet, granted the theoretical importance of this move toward a recognition of the necessity of developing a study of the modes of sign production, it is at the same time necessary to realize that this move is additional to, not, as Eco proposes, substitutive for, more traditional typologies of sign. The move is similar to that of Peirce in shifting the focus from the being of signs to their action.[138] For just as action follows from being, so a typology of signs is essential to the study of sign-production, in order that we might know what it is the production of which we seek to discover. To study a mode of production with no idea of what it is that the mode of production will produce would be a blind process indeed, incapable of being initiated for want of a clue in which direction to proceed.

Neglect of this basic point, at least as old as the *naturalia*, the "naturalist essays", of Aristotle,[139] leads Eco to commit a kind of howler, what Ryle might have termed a category mistake, in the context of his Gainsborough analysis. "If 'invention' were a category within a typology of signs ...", Eco writes.[140] But what would be a category within a typology of signs would be *invented signs*, not *invention* – that is, the product not the process. And *invented signs* belong to the subspecies *signum ad placitum* of the genus *signum*, coordinate with such other subspecies as the *signum ex consuetudine*, verified in zoösemiosis and anthroposemiosis alike, and *signa naturalia*, whose action is displayed further in phytosemiosis and physiosemiosis.

There are plenty of problems with traditional typologies,[141] but these are problems of the sort that semiotics cannot avoid. Improvement of the typologies and investigation of the modes of sign-production are lines of research that cannot proceed but in tandem. It is not fully clear, then, how Eco can think that, in this part of his work, "the idealistic fallacy is avoided",[142] especially as that fallacy is proper to modern philosophy, by the flight from typology to modes of production.

"Idealism" in modern philosophy, as stated above, is the thesis that everything the mind knows, in precisely what the minds knows of it, owes its basic constitution to the mind. Professor Eco goes out of his way, more than once, in an effort to avoid any risk of idealism.[143] Yet into idealism is precisely where his theory takes him with its claim that there are not signs but only sign-functions, inasmuch as these are

---

138 See Deely 1990: ch. 3, p. 22ff.
139 Deely 1965/6: notes.
140 3.6.8, p. 256.
141 Cf. Sebeok 1972a, 1974: 26–45, 1975b.
142 P. 256.
143 Pp. 22, 256, 317.

grounded entirely in cultural linkages. A giant step for the doctrine of signs in the terminological move from semiology to semiotics and on many particular points, Eco's theory as a whole is yet one small step within philosophy itself, because it does not succeed in leaping the chasm which separates the basic standpoint of semiotics from the pre-semiotic epistemological paradigms tied to the modern standpoint of idealism. It is not a question of any realism *versus* idealism. It is a question of a doctrine of signs which, when fully aware of its origins and proper standpoint, is able to begin at a point beyond the modern controversies. And this standpoint is the cognizance of the being in relation proper to signs as such, the *renvoi* by which every sign, natural, social, or cultural, is constituted.

Corrections and Subordinations

By correcting Eco's claim that there are no signs but only sign-functions we at the same time subordinate to the genus *signum* the sign-function. Sign-functions as Eco defines and presents them constitute the class of signifying phenomena most characteristic and typical of the human world or *Lebenswelt* in its contrast with the objective world – the *Umwelt* – of other organisms, which remains always tied to biological nature. But these sign-functions by no means constitute the whole of semiosis. With this simple correction the idealistic fallacy is truly avoided – a very great gain, at very little cost.

For the genius of semiotics is not to close the *Geisteswissenschaften* upon themselves, despite some trends in this direction.[144] On the contrary, the genius of semiotics is the adoption of a standpoint encompassing the intersections of culture and nature. This is why the first thinker who succeeded in divining the unity in relation of all signifying phenomena as such also set it as the semiotician's primary task to explain in the sign its way of being superior to the division between what depends upon and what is independent of our activities and our mechanisms of perception and conception, to discover how the workings of nature (*ens reale*) and culture (*ens rationis*) interweave in constituting the fabric of human experience and 'everyday life'. The best way for semiotics to avoid – and indeed vanquish – the legacy of idealism in post-seventeenth-century Western thought is by recognizing in the sign as its fundamental category a way of being superior to the classical division of being into what is dependent upon and what is independent of the workings of mind. And this feat is something the sign-function of Eco cannot perform, precisely because it is in nowise indifferent to such a division.

In many ways, the centrality of the sign-function in Professor Eco's book, with its entailment of codes, would seem to be a more or less direct consequence of his decision to condition his approach by the present state of the art. All but inevitably, this decision made of the work a kind of mirroring of the fact that semiotics

---

144 Cf. Rey-Debove ed. 1973: 8.

in its contemporary guise had developed principally at the hands of students of the language sciences, explicitly among linguists and inchoately among analytic philosophers steeped in the preoccupations and epistemological presuppositions of modernity. Eco himself tells us as much in connection with his supposed and proposed "translation" of the notion of sign into that of sign-function:[145] "Provided that my audience has read Katz, Fodor and Postal (and in the circle that I move in everybody has), the substitution is easily understood."[146] The situation of Eco's "theory of semiotics" is not unlike that of Russell's "theory of descriptions":[147] both depend on the *petitio principii* of a "translation" process in which everything that does not conform to the presuppositions of the one making the translation is omitted from the translated result.

There is, however, this great difference in the two cases: exposure of the sophism at the root of Eco's translation of signs into sign-functions does not vitiate his theory *tout court*. The exposure in this case merely serves to show the dependence of the notion of sign-function (the sign as it takes on a specifically cultural structure, as we might say) upon the more fundamental category of *signum*, while leaving sign-function intact as an analytical tool in its own right. The outstanding merit of Eco's achievement of a theory of codes capable of integrating the understanding of language within the larger cultural perspectives proper to anthroposemiosis appears, in this light, as the most important contribution of his book.

The Theory of Codes and Anthroposemiosis
The theory of codes at the heart of Eco's analysis of *signum* in its *ad placitum* guise, what he calls the "sign function", seen in its proper dimension, is an analytical tool of permanent importance for discriminating the more typically cultural elements at work in human experience, and especially the predominantly linguistic aspects of those elements. Parmentier's twin insistence – doubly correct – on the absence of a notion of code in Peirce and on the importance of the concept for anthropology doubly justifies the approach of Eco's tract. But his tract does not go far enough, for "cultural semiotics needs both Peirce's notion of indexicality and Saussure's notion of code".[148]

Eco's notion of code, unparalleled in sophistication, to be sure, is not simply that of Saussure. Still less is his notion of indexicality that of Peirce. But by drawing the Peircean notion of interpretant into the theory of codes, Eco accomplishes, especially by judicious illustrative passages, some interesting clarifications of what we might call the *experimental ground* of this difficult notion[149] so central to the doctrine of signs.

---

145 P. 282.
146 See also the discussion of ambiguity in 3.7.2, p. 262ff.
147 See Deely 1975.
148 Parmentier 1987; see further Parmentier 1994: xiii.
149 E.g., see the discussion of theological notions over pp. 61–8.

For the theory of codes is essential to an understanding of the distinctiveness of anthroposemiosis, the "human use of signs" as I called it in titling my 1994 book on the subject. And what the theory of the code is called upon to provide is precisely an account of the correlation of elements of the Innenwelt (affective and conative as well as cognitive) with physical elements experienced and accessible within the Umwelt (or Lebenswelt, more exactly) suchwise that these physical elements become, through and by virtue of the correlation, *representamina* or "sign-vehicles" in their own right respecting the larger organization of the objective world, in turn begetting interpretants (so that the original Innenwelt elements, beginning as signs, through the correlation with physical representamina come to function as interpretants respecting those representamina, and the objects signified through the representamina become in their turn interpretants measuring the understanding – the Innenwelt – of new participants who enter into the discourse, or old participants who re-enter at a later time). The manner in which signs, objects, and interpretants change place in what becomes a semiosis spiraling through time is what characterizes not only the action of signs as unlimited but also the very formation and identity of the individual as a "finite conscious self" through participation in the broader semiosis of which that self forms a temporary and local part.[150] The code, in other words, is needed to explain, at the linguistic level in particular and the symbolic level in general insofar as it is a postlinguistic sphere, how the unlimited character of semiosis there reveals itself.

Let us look first at the importance of Eco's notion of code in the contemporary context, and then look further at the notion of interpretant as Eco employs it.

Eco vis-à-vis "Logical Analysis" in Analytic Philosophy
and vis-à-vis Generative Grammar in Philosophy of Language
Eco's demonstration of the centrality of a theory of codes to the understanding of anthroposemiotics is an achievement of great merit. It may eventually displace and largely render untenable currently competing theoretical approaches to linguistic competence. Certainly the semiotic point of view renders nugatory the range of philosophical approaches to language inspired by Russell's theory of descriptions and the early (later repudiated) views of Wittgenstein, whereby the attempt is made[151] formally to restructure or replace natural languages with a sign-system directly correlated to "reality".[152]

For in every actual situation of discourse, "the *basic denotation* of a sign-vehicle can be understood just as the sender intended it to be, but different connotations can be attributed to it simply because the addressee *follows another path* on the compositional tree to which the sender referred (both paths being legitimately accepted by the

---

150 See the "semiotic spiral" diagram in *The Human Use of Signs* (Deely 1994), ¶224.
151 E.g., in Carnap 1937, as reported in Bochenski 1970: 31.
152 Cf. Eco, pp. 61, 161–2.

culture in which both sender and addressee live)".[153] Since such a "componential spectrum" as outlined in table 19 of Eco's text[154] "is a synchronico-diachronical one," the situation is enormously complicated in instances of cross-cultural communication. No less is it complicated in the transcultural instances of sign-production that critically controlled objectifications can circumscribe in the so-called "natural signifyings" – those significations whose roots, as discussed above, exhibit within experience an independence of that experience whereby they are exhibited (and always allowing for the possibility of being mistaken to a greater or lesser extent, inherent in all anthroposemiosis, *pace* Descartes), whether respecting only this or that individual, or respecting this or that species in some larger part of its totality.

Intra-culturally, of course, imaginative literature (perhaps poetry especially) compounds the complexity already inherent in the more literal, technical, controlled vocabularies of analytical reflection.[155] Thus, semiotics arrives independently at the basic discovery of Wittgenstein's *Philosophical Investigations* (the "later" as opposed to the "early" Wittgenstein): as Eco puts it,[156] "the universe of natural languages is a rather unformalized and 'primitive' one, and thus far from being scientific or highly formalized", to such an extent that a "theory of the ideal competence of an ideal speaker, carefully defended against the disturbances of historical and social intercourse, has a good chance of being a perfect formal construct, but has very poor chances of being useful to anyone".[157] Hence the marginal relevance to philosophical ontology or to epistemological investigations of mathematical and logical symbolisms.[158]

Perhaps the same can be said of the Chomskyan search for putative "innate structures" of the mind. "The labor of producing signs (and in particular code 'observing') consists in mapping the deep semantic representation in the surface structure by several rules or 'constraints'," writes Eco:[159] "These rules establish how vectorial devices may be realized and interpreted in surface structure. At this point the semantic representation (in terms of generative semantics) is an interpretant, or a compound of vectorial devices, which acts as a *metalinguistic* device able to explain the labor of choosing and producing signs".

Chomsky's approach from grammatical structures leads to the positing of the "innate structure" of mind enabling human beings to develop mastery of languages which "appears to be a species-specific capacity that is essentially independent of intelligence".[160] In sharp contrast with this, mastery of languages, as including

153 P. 139; italics added.
154 P. 113.
155 E.g., the discussion of Moby Dick on pp. 113 and 114.
156 P. 113.
157 P. 99; cf. Deely 1975.
158 Cf. Veatch 1969 for the same conclusion reached on different grounds.
159 P. 305 n. 29; original italics.
160 Chomsky 1968: 68–9; 1972: 79.

grammar (an aspect of coding), is, from Eco's semiotic viewpoint, a mastery of sign-systems. And inasmuch as "one can view intelligence and signification as a single process",[161] intelligence appears rather as *precisely* what enables human beings to develop mastery of languages in all that they comprise; so that, as Eco puts it,[162] "in the final analysis, what is needed is a theory of intelligence".

Chomsky views the grammatical approach as providing the key to the problem of knowledge. "Insofar as we have a tentative first approximation to a generative grammar for some language, we can for the first time formulate in a useful way the problem of the origin of knowledge", Chomsky states.[163] In semiotic perspective, especially when taking into account the many semiosical processes common to higher animals (which is not so easy in Eco's terms, however, as we have seen), such a view appears as an especially egregious version of what Eco terms a "verbo-centric fallacy",[164] and this view is contravened by the fundamental semiotic insight that a study of sign systems has no necessary dependence on linguistics.[165]

The rule of indeterminacy in matters of the cultural sciences, as contrasted to the sort of order that obtains in the natural sciences, and the role of *time* in both (especially as an ideal construct[166]), is also puzzling in the framework of the intelligence-independent, universal grammar of innate principles constituting the postulated species-specific capacity for organizing and syntactically sorting the linguistic data empirically encountered, say, in childhood. How is linguistic creativity – to be sure, Chomsky's *point de départ* from behaviorism – compatible with innate structures (a Kantian heritage more than a Cartesian one, after all[167]) when it comes to the problem of transcending in anthroposemiosis the divisions of *ens reale* and *non ens* alike?

As Eco accounts for linguistic competence (theory of competence = theory of codes), this problem easily assumes a proper place, open to the requirements of new foundations. "The semiotic approach is *ruled* by a sort of indeterminacy principle", Eco remarks,[168] for the reason "that not only do competences allow performances but that performances also establish new forms of competence".[169] It is *precisely* inasmuch as intelligence – human understanding in its species-specific difference from perceptual organizings – is involved in semiosis as the root of language "that every time a structure is described something occurs within the universe of

---

161 Eco, p. 31 n. 5; cf. Poinsot, 1632a: 642a 15–18.
162 P. 46.
163 Chomsky 1968: 68.
164 P. 303 n. 20. All the more remarkable is Eco's own later plunge (2000: chap 1, esp. 22) into just such a fallacy, to the point of confounding "language" with "speech" ("*dire*")!
165 *Pace* Barthes 1964; cf. Eco, p. 30 n.1.
166 Cf. Simon 1970: 89–111, esp. 91. See "Time and Space", chapter 3 above, p. 70ff.
167 Chomsky titled his 1966 work *Cartesian Linguistics*, but I have always suspected that this was the consequence of a shallow philosophical education, since the work is far more Kantian in its central thesis, and would have been far more aptly titled *Kantian Linguistics*.
168 0.9, p. 29; italics added.
169 P. 272. In Eco 2000 (esp. chap. 3), this is further articulated in terms of "Cognitive Types".

signification which no longer makes it [i.e., the described structure] completely reliable".[170]

Eco's Use of "Interpretant"

The notion of 'interpretant', of course, Eco takes over from Peirce. But he introduces, by judicious illustrative passages, some interesting clarifications of what we might call the *experimental ground* of this notion. For example, Eco observes[171] that "in order to understand the history of Christian theology, it is not necessary to know whether a specific actual phenomenon corresponds to the word /transubstantiation/ (even though for many people this belief was vitally important). But it is necessary to know which cultural unit ... corresponded to the content of that word". "Otherwise," he continues shortly, "there never would have been any thing like a theological discussion and believers would have continued to receive the Holy Communion without wondering about those who did not believe in it. Whereas it was, on the contrary, necessary to conceive a world so organized that a cultural unit corresponding to /transubstantiation/ ... could be a precisely segmented portion of the content of a given cultural background".[172] "An expression," in these terms, "does not in principle designate any object"[173] (though, of course, it *may* do so), "but on the contrary *conveys a cultural content*".[174]

"Recognition of the presence of these cultural units" as "the meaning to which the code makes the system of sign-vehicles correspond" – where "sign-vehicle" means precisely "a semantic unit posited in a precise 'space' within a semantic system"[175] – involves understanding language as a social phenomenon. Eco continues:[176]

> If I declare that /There are two natures in Christ, the human and the divine, and one Person/ a logician or scientist might observe to me that this string of sign-vehicles has neither extension nor referent, and that it could be defined as lacking meaning and therefore as a pseudo-statement. But they will never succeed in explaining why whole groups of people have fought for centuries over a statement of this kind or its denial. Evidently this happened because the expression conveyed precise contents which existed as cultural units within a civilization. Since they existed they became

---

170 2.13, p. 129. See further pp. 29 and 298; also Poinsot 1632a: "First Preamble," esp. 74/27–75/21; Maritain 1957; the discussion of infinite process in Deely 1994; and Deely 2000.

171 P. 62.

172 Ibid.

173 Here Eco falls into the trap of accepting the end-of-the-twentieth-century popular culture usage of the term "object" to designate in principle a physical referent of some kind, a usage inviable as philosophical doctrine. This was why, as the reader may recall, the first chapter of this book began by establishing an understanding of key terms to recur over the work as a whole, notably among them "objective" as meaning whatever exists as known regardless of its status as physical, and "subjective" as meaning whatever constitutes an individual as distinct or 'separate from' the rest of the universe.

174 P. 161; Eco's italics.

175 P. 84.

176 Pp. 67–8: the concluding italics only are in the original.

the supports for connotative developments[177] and opened up a whole range of semantic reactions of a type that directly affected behavior. *But behavioral reactions are not necessary in order to establish that the expression has a content*; the civilization itself elaborated a series of definitions and explanations of the terms involved (person, nature, etc.). Each definition was a new linguistic (or visual) message whose meaning had in turn to be clarified by means of other linguistic expressions which defined the cultural units carried by the preceding expression. The series of clarifications which circumscribed the cultural units carried by the preceding expression of a society in a continuous progression (always defining them in the form of sign-vehicles) represents the chain of what Peirce[178] called the *interpretants*.

The notion of the interpretant, at the time Eco wrote, was not a notion well understood in the secondary Peirce literature, thanks to the "many scholars who proceeded to exorcise it by misunderstanding it (interpretant = interpreter or receiver of the message)", as Eco well said.[179] In Eco's own understanding, "the idea of the interpretant makes a theory of signification a rigorous science of cultural phenomena, while detaching it from the metaphysics of the referent"[180] such as that appears in the philosophers and linguists inspired by Frege[181] and Ogden and Richards.[182] But, of course, these are very late authors in their own right, and very extraneous in their mode of conceptualizing to the Latin origins of semiotic consciousness in the sixteenth-century Hispanic authors traced by Beuchot.[183]

But, in the first place, the "metaphysics of the referent" about which Eco speaks amounts to little more than the modern blunder of confusing physical things and events with objects, whereas in fact the two concepts are as distinct in principle as is the Peircean category of brute force and secondness from the realm of thirdness constituted through signs. This is a terminological point of the greatest importance for semiotics, as we have seen at a number of points along our way.

And, in the second place, the notion of interpretant as we find it originally in the texts of Peirce may be used to help formulate a rigorous science of cultural

177 See 2.3, "Denotation and connotation," pp. 54–7.
178 Peirce c.1906: CP 5.470 *et alibi*.
179 Pp. 69–70. Nor, twenty years later, are the days of this gross misunderstanding yet past. Lecturing at Universidad Anáhuac in the winter of 1995, I introduced my audience to the notion of interpretant with the remark that this was a term invented by Peirce which had no previous counterpart in the modern languages. At this point my translator interrupted my remarks to inform me that I was mistaken, since the word already existed at least in Spanish, if not in English. Pray tell, I asked, what is this Spanish term which corresponds to Peirce's notion of interpretant. He replied, "Intérprete!" But I had not said that the word "Interpreter" did not exist in English! The incident well illustrates the mindset with which Eco's *Trattato di semiotica generale* had to contend already in the 1970s.
180 P. 70.
181 Frege 1892. Including Kripke 1980. On the semiotics of supposed "rigid designation", see Eco 2000: 292–303.
182 Ogden and Richards 1923. See Eco, 2.5.1 and 2.5.2, pp. 58–61.
183 Beuchot 1980 and 1995.

phenomena as phenomena of signification, but if this same theory does not by the same stroke demonstrate the permeability of culture as a human interface to the realities and forces of nature as providing culture's physical ambience overall, then it is no longer the original notion that is being deployed but a semiological diminution; for the interpretant, as we have seen, cannot by any means be restricted to cultural phenomena as closed unto themselves.

"*Differences of things* as things *are quite other than the differences of things* as objects"[184]

The basic insight of Eco's book on this point, probably even the motivating one for the theory of codes, is the fundamental contrast between *units of nature*, on the one hand ("things"), and *units of experience and of culture*, on the other:[185]

> ... codes, insofar as they are accepted by a society, set up a 'cultural' world which is neither actual nor possible in the ontological sense; its existence is linked to a cultural order, which is the way in which a society thinks, speaks and, while speaking, explains the 'purport' of its thought through other thoughts. Since it is through thinking and speaking that a society develops, expands or collapses, even when dealing with 'impossible' worlds (i.e., aesthetic texts, ideological statements), a theory of codes is very much concerned with the format of such 'cultural' worlds, and faces the basic problem of how *to touch* contents.

This insight belongs to the bedrock of Eco's book; and, if the earlier testimony of Poinsot on the point is accurate, it is an insight which belongs to the bedrock of semiotics itself.[186] "Units of nature" and "units of experience", what Poinsot would call "physical unities" and "objective unities", are by no means the same; and though they may occasionally coincide, and constantly intertwine in experience, the fact remains that, as Eco puts it,[187] "social life did not develop on the basis of things, but on the basis of cultural units", that is to say, objective as opposed to physical divisions. Thus, even at those points where the universe of objects and the universe of things intertwine, the significations in different phases or moments of anthroposemiosis – either within one culture or between different cultures – need be by no means the same. "The multiplicity of codes, contexts, and circumstances shows us that the same message can be decoded from different points of view and by reference to diverse systems of conventions".[188]

Of course, the simple notation of this *fact* is hardly new. To cite but a single classic example among many which could be given, any reader of

---

184 Poinsot, *Treatise on Signs*, 1632a: 270/39–40 and passim; and before that, Cajetan 1507: I. 1. 3.
185 Eco 1976: 2.5.3, pp. 61–6.
186 "Aliae differentiae rerum ut res, aliae ut obiecti et in esse obiecti", *Tractatus de Signis*, 270/39–41; see also 149/44–6, 187/32–5, and passim.
187 Eco 1976: 66.
188 2.15, p. 139.

Gibbon[189] will find in the notes dozens of concrete and colorful illustrations of the fact made in terms of the competing Lebenswelts of antiquity. But awareness of the fact is one thing; the attempt to assign express *reasons for* the fact quite another. This latter Eco achieves as yet another groundbreaking advance in the formulation of a doctrine of signs.[190] I think there can be no doubt of the need to work the notion of code into the fabric of the Peircean notion of semeiosy, and of the Latin notion of *signum* on which semiotics relies, to achieve a viable notion of textuality coextensive with the possibilities of objectification seen in the full scope of its dependence on the action of signs.[191]

Cultural units are, precisely, "the meaning to which the code makes the system of sign-vehicles correspond",[192] even though these units themselves first appear in the garb later known to be proper only to *res transcendentales*, environmental phenomena in their physical dimension. This is why language – the universe of discourse – is able to display a relative autonomy vis-à-vis so-called "facts" – the universe of being.[193] Eco's statement "that an expression does not, in principle, designate any object", where 'object' is taken to mean some actual existent or event, however, needs to be immediately qualified, for here our author has fallen into the trap of accepting the established usage of the term "object" to designate in principle a physical referent of some kind. This notion is inviable in semiotics, as I mentioned shortly above.[194] The expression "*does not*" should read "*need not*" to achieve an exactness which is not misleading. "The fact that *semiosis lives as a fact in a world of facts* limits the absolute purity of the universe of codes",[195] indeed, but Eco seems not to notice that it limits as well the proposition that "*semiosis explains itself by itself*".[196]

It remains that the relative independence of discourse from being stands as the first and most basic characteristic of signs to be reckoned with, and not only as including the sign-systems of species-specifically human language (I have argued this point in a variety of contexts since 1975, having first learned it from a *Tractatus*

---

189 Gibbon i.1776/88.
190 See the example of the case of whales in 2.11.3, and table 19, p. 113. But any comparison of this case where thing and object intertwine with the phoneme analysis of Jakobson and Halle 1956, such as Eco goes on to make (p. 114), is limited by the truth that phonemes as such are *primarily* within, whereas whales as such are only *secondarily* within, the universe of discourse as such (or, more generally, the human Lebenswelt in its contrast as objective with the physical environment as such). This point can well be generalized, and it is one that philosophical attempts at understanding language (such as that of Haas 1968) can ill afford systematically to avoid (we are back to the problem of the semiosis of sensation and the assimilation to perception of the physical relations involved as such in *signa naturalia*).
191 Eco 1972; Baer 1992; Deely 1994: part II.
192 Eco 1976: 2.6, p. 67.
193 2.5.2, pp. 60–1.
194 P. 732n133. See also Hjelmslev 1961: 22–3 – with whom, however, Eco is well familiar; and Deely 1996a.
195 P. 158; Eco's italics.
196 P. 71; Eco's italics. For relevant considerations on the notions of "fact" presupposed here, see the indexical entry in Deely and Nogar 1973.

de Signis antedating that of Eco by three hundred and forty-five years). This point, so central for semiotics, Eco trenchantly underscores by remarking: "The possibility of lying is the *proprium* of semiosis".[197] This is well put, if one sided, since the possibility of expressing any truth is equally the *proprium* of semiosis. Since the sign is that which every object presupposes, and since semiotics studies the action of signs, perhaps the best definition of semiotics would be: the study of the possibility of being mistaken.

The Line of Advance

Enough has been said to show that Eco's book set a standard of comprehensiveness fairly early in the game for further work in the field. I have concentrated in my remarks on this classic work on the critique of the alleged adequacy of the sign-function as a translation of the notion of *signum*, because, as a matter of fact, as our earlier chapters suffice to demonstrate, the notion of *signum* is broader and more fundamental than Eco's notion of sign-function, and nothing is more important in the long run than a proper clarification and laying of the foundations for the enterprises of semiotics.

Without such a clarification, the array of semiotics' pursuits would eventually become in fact just what it has always appeared to be in the eyes of obtuse critics: a disarray. Semiotics would risk dispersion and eventual assimilation of its pursuits back into the already established specialties for want of the critical awareness and development of its own foundation. The whole range of attempts to isolate and analyze the specifically *signifying* aspects and elements of disciplines as diverse as architecture, music, theater, ethology, and so on – the *field* of semiotics – must therefore never fail to reflect upon and succeed in grasping ever more surely the insight that underlies and gives justice to (*founds*) the entire panoply of semiotics' concerns. This is the realization that the sign is the universal instrument of communication, within oneself or with others equally.

Principally in this direction has Eco's work been "gone beyond", but without being "left behind", for the many reasons I have indicated. With such a focus, the inherently interdisciplinary character of semiotics is bound to reveal itself with increasing vitality and persuasive power. Professor Eco's fine study was one of the most important twentieth-century steps along the way. Albeit that it was one small step for philosophy, as appears from what we have since learned of the history of semiotics, including the lessons of Kant and the platypus. Even so, as a key text of an intellectual movement of contemporary culture, *A Theory of Semiotics* was one giant leap for the doctrine of signs, and a shaping influence as the reality of the postmodern era moved out of the shadows of modernity into the light of its own dawn.

---

197 P. 59; cf. pp. 7, 64, 116.

Maxim on Inquiry

Photograph of Carolyn Eisele (1902–2000) taken about 1976 at the former Peirce home, Arisbe, exhibiting over the mantel Peirce's maxim regarding the path of inquiry, together with Eisele's editions of Peirce's works; from the Peirce Edition Project archives

CHAPTER EIGHTEEN

Beyond Realism and Idealism: Resumé and Envoi

Bernard Lonergan, in describing the strategy I have followed in writing this book, but without suspecting that it was semiotics (and anthroposemiosis) about which he wrote, mused as follows: "Thoroughly understand what it is to understand, and not only will you understand the broad lines of all there is to be understood but also will you possess a fixed base, an invariant pattern, opening upon all further developments of understanding";[1] for "the known is extensive, but the knowing is a recurrent structure that can be investigated sufficiently in a series of strategically chosen instances", and while "the known is incomplete and subject to revision," our concern is "the knower that will be the source of the future additions and revisions".[2]

Rationale of This Work, in View of All That Could Be Said

What has been left out, what has not appeared along the route we have chosen from classical antiquity to the present? A great deal. Left out in particular is the whole of what Aristotle called "practical thought": the developments of art and technology; the developments of social and political thought; the transformation of human civilization (although we have seen important features of this last development along our way) by freeing the community of inquirers from the details of their investigations being subjected to a measure by external authorities, both civil and religious, who based their determinations on the exegesis of ancient texts which embodied neither philosophical nor scientific concerns properly understood.

I have chosen to lead the reader first by the route of speculative understanding, following the suggestion of Aquinas that speculative understanding "becomes practical by extension". That is to say, what is distinctively human about anthroposemiosis is not the practical world of social and political affairs of everyday life, but the manner in which this "practical world" is rooted in and grows out of an ultimately contemplative vision. This speculative vision is the *locus* of species-specifically

---

1 Bernard J. F. Lonergan, *Insight* (1965), xxviii and 748.
2 Ibid.: xviii.

human language, which is the transformative source whence, over the centuries, comes to be established that difference between the social world of animals and the social world of human beings that we call "civilization" and "culture".

In other words, I have tried to take the reader to an understanding of the heart of the matter, the reason for the difference between the objective world as species-specifically human, the Lebenswelt, and the objective world as it otherwise appears to any higher animal, the Umwelt, wherein no difference is made or can be made between how the physical universe is and how it appears in sensation and perception at any given time. From this difference everything else follows. If we get straight the understanding of this difference, our social and political thought, our artistic and technological thought, will rest on a firm foundation. Otherwise not. Not even science can provide the doctrinal foundation or framework for "understanding understanding"; only philosophy can. If all thought is in signs, which has been the thesis of this book, then the way of signs is the surest way "thoroughly to understand what it is to understand". This book has been about finding that way, or rather, about how the semiotic animal came to the point of finding this way and has now set upon it as the best hope of realizing the ancient advice of Socrates: "Know thyself."

The Semeiotic Animal

It is in and by the exercise of human understanding that the intrinsic indifference of the action of signs to the signification of what is or is not at any given moment is, through an explicit realization, brought to its highest exercise. In the exercise of human understanding, the intrinsic indifference to being and nonbeing that characterizes the action of signs finally reaches the level at which it can be itself thematized and explored on its own terms. These terms turn out to be the very terms of semiosis itself. Semiotics is that knowledge that arises from observation and reflection upon the action of signs, as biology is that knowledge that arises from observation and reflection upon the activity of organisms. Semiotics has as its principal upshot the realization that, together with the experiences upon which human knowledge depends, all of human knowledge in whatever field develops through this action which semiotics thematizes.

If the pursuit of this knowledge above all separates postmodern times from modernity, then we can see, in terms of genus and difference, the definition of human nature that the immediate future of philosophical thought calls for: the human animal, as the only animal that, besides making and making use of signs, knows that there are signs, is properly called *animal semeioticum*, the *semiotic animal*. Even as Descartes' definition of the human as a *res cogitans* served to mark the transition from ancient and medieval thought (inasmuch as the Greeks and Latins alike concurred in defining the human being as the "rational animal", *animal rationale*) to rationalistic and empiricist modern thought, so this definition will serve to mark for future generations the transition from modern to postmodern thought.

This new definition has a twofold symbolicity. It symbolizes the recovery of that possibility of an understanding of physical and natural being which the Greeks and the Latins prized but which the moderns had ruled out in consequence of their epistemological paradigm reducing ideas to representations. And it symbolizes at the same time the realization constitutive of semiotic consciousness: the action of signs as resulting in anthroposemiosis provides the sole means whereby the mind has the possibility of "becoming all things" – *anima est quodammodo omnia* – in that convertibility of being with truth that is the elusive, asymptotic goal of the community of inquirers. Such a community, in turn, needed to support intelligence in those scientific and literary aspects found as expressions only of semiotic animals.

In saying that the human being is the semiotic animal, we give voice to the realization that the human animal is the only animal that knows that there are signs as well as makes use of them. In such knowledge the human being realizes the source of its difference from the other life forms, the *humanitas* of the human animal, as well as the universality of the process on which all the life forms depend. It would now appear that this process is perhaps the ultimate source of that general progress in physical nature from simple to complex forms that we have heretofore called "evolution".

Resumé

Let us try to express, in a summary and synoptic fashion, the steps whereby we have arrived over this long journey at the distinctively postmodern understanding of ourselves as semiotic animals, the only ones on this planet, though probably not the only ones in the whole of the universe. For semiosis is not only criterial of life, as Thomas Sebeok first and best pointed out,[3] it also at once involves and exceeds the action of things as such. In the inorganic world and throughout the physical environment as such, the action of things as such, whether physical or psychic, is always subjective, restricted to the order of what exists here and now.[4] But wherever the future influences a present course of events, we are confronted by semiosis. And that has been from "the beginning"[5] of at least the present universe as we know it.

---

3 Sebeok 1968. See mention in chapter 15, p. 663, text and notes.
4 Peirce's way of putting this is obscure, outside the framework of his technical semiotic: thirdness, he says, always presupposes the brute interactions of secondness which also always presupposes the dream world which secondness differentiates, firstness. Thus, on the basis of his "recognition of ten respects in which Signs may be divided", Peirce concludes (1908: CP 8.343; see also 1904) that "since every one of them turns out to be a trichotomy, it follows that in order to decide what classes of signs result from them, I have 3^{10}, or 59049, difficult questions to carefully consider". For present purposes, and following the example of Peirce himself at this point (who did "not undertake to carry [his] systematical division of signs any further", but left that "for future explorers"), clarification of this technical way of phrasing the situation may safely be handed over to the exegetes of the Peircean texts. The aim here is to reach a more general audience.
5 See, in chapter 7, Aquinas's discussion of the meaning of "creation", p. 271; and, in chapter 11, the discussion of "creationism", p. 506.

Never confined to what has been or is, semiosis transpires at the boundary between what is and what might be or might have been, flourishing above all in the growth of inquiry as the food of human understanding.

For the realization of all of this, however, we had first to realize the being and action proper to signs. Let us bow to convention enough to agree, in this summary, that by "medieval" we mean the Latin Age; and by "medievals", therefore, we mean those who lived in any part of those twelve or so centuries between Augustine and Descartes, Augustine and Poinsot, the denizens of that philosophical epoch which began with the introduction and ended with the justification of the general notion of sign. To the medievals, then, we are mainly indebted for our current notion of "sign", and for the threads of semiotic consciousness that Charles S. Peirce picked up in his work, the weaving together of which would launch the postmodern and contemporary development of semiotics.

The word "medieval" here, then, designates the indigenous Latin Age in its entirety. Thus, "medieval" covers the period between the collapse of Greek as the language of learning with the fall of the Roman Empire in the fifth century AD, on the one hand, and, on the other hand, the emergence of the national languages in the seventeenth century as the principal vehicle of mainstream philosophical development for European civilization in the modern period. "Medieval" so taken is a synonym for the indigenous Latin interval of philosophical development separating the ancient Greek development from the classical modern development. Thus, roughly, the ancient Greek period extends from Thales of Miletus (c.625–545BC) to Proclus (c.AD410–485) and Pseudo-Dionysius (c.AD455–c.535). The medieval period extends from Augustine (AD354–430) to Poinsot (1589–1644). The modern period extends from Descartes (1596–1650) to Husserl (1859–1938), Russell (1872–1970), and Wittgenstein (1889–1950).

The word "semiotics" as qualifying "medieval" is taken in its contemporary sense of the study of signs in all their extent and variety, but particularly in the foundational sense established by Peirce. He based himself on the programmatic proposal given by Locke in the anomalous conclusion to his *Essay concerning Humane Understanding* of 1690. There semiotics was first outlined in the sense in which it is understood today, as an investigation of the essential nature and fundamental varieties according to which signs are capable of acting. In this understanding of semiotics, therefore, the term "sign" is not only the focal notion, but is also understood as applying to signification wherever it is to be found, within as well as outside of human culture.

The medieval expression equivalent to the term semiotics in the contemporary sense is *doctrina signorum* or "doctrine of signs". This medieval expression is used in Locke's early programmatic statement as a synonym for his proposed σημιωτική. So also is it used by C. S. Peirce, as well as in some of the best-informed discussions after Peirce. Thus, in speaking of "medieval semiotics", although we are using a term which was by no means medieval, we are looking back upon the Latin Age from a contemporary perspective congenial to medieval thought.

More than this: in looking back on the Latin Age from the perspective of contemporary semiotics, we are in fact seeing that age as whole, for the first time, from a point of view first made possible but only partially developed by the Latins. For the notion of sign in the contemporary sense, so far as written records go, was itself one of the earliest achievements of the Latin Age, and one of the last to be systematized. If we look back to the world and philosophers of ancient Greece, we find no equivalent, strictly speaking, of the Latin notion *signum*, whence is derived our contemporary term "sign". Even though "semiotics" as our contemporary term for the study of signs is in a haphazard way based upon the ancient Greek term for symptoms or what are sometimes called "natural" signs, namely, σημεῖον ("semeion"), it is important to realize that there is, strictly speaking, no ancient or even modern "semiotics" in the integral sense in which there is a contemporary and a medieval semiotics.

There is a symmetrical imbalance here, if we compare, from the point of view of semiotics in the contemporary sense, either the ancient period or the modern period with the medieval period. *In the ancient world*, the notion of sign (σημεῖον) did not extend to the world of culture. *In the modern period*, the notion of sign, even though taken over from the Latins, could not, for complex epistemological reasons best systematized by Kant, extend to the world of nature. But *in medieval times, as in contemporary semiotics*, the notion of sign is understood precisely as embracing the universe as a whole, the world of nature as well as the world of culture, precisely as the two come together in human experience semiotically understood.

Thus, though semiotics is an exclusively contemporary term, the *doctrina signorum* is a notion truly inclusive of medieval and postmodern thought alike. We can, of course, speak of an ancient as well as of a modern semiotics. But, in order to do so, we have to introduce restrictions on the term which do not apply either to contemporary or to medieval semiotics. Strictly speaking, the ancient period, from a semiotic point of view, is more properly termed presemiotic. The modern period, from the same point of view, is better termed "semiological" in its final stages, if we are to speak of it in terms of that anthropomorphically restricted part of the doctrine of signs to which the idealism of modern thought has properly contributed.

The *doctrina signorum*, by contrast, which was first introduced and developed in Latin times, has, in contemporary thought, been taken up anew and developed beyond the point where the Latins left it before their subtle achievements were obliterated by the mainstream modern development of philosophy in the wake of Descartes. Here we have traced the notion of sign in the contemporary sense of "the genus of which words (ὀνόματα) and natural symptoms (σημεῖα) are alike equally species"[6] from its first appearance in the i.AD397/426 work of Augustine of Hippo, *De doctrina Christiana*, through the writings of Thomas Aquinas (1225–74) and

---

6 Eco et al. 1986: 65.

Roger Bacon (c.1220–92), up to its establishment in the *Tractatus de Signis* of John Poinsot (1632). This contemporary notion of sign, thus, understands what it signifies as properly consisting in an irreducibly triadic relation as such, as distinct from that relation's foundation in an individual or characteristic of an individual, whether psychological or physical.

In modern times, after Descartes (1596–1650), the hard-won Latin notion of sign in general disappears, to be replaced by the notion of ideas as self-representing objects, until the Latin notion is taken up again in the writings of Charles Sanders Peirce (1839–1914) under the banner of "semiotics". Peirce brings an end to the notion of ideas as objects being the fundamental presupposition of philosophy and initiates a new way of philosophizing, "pragmaticism", or the way of signs.

Envoi: Beyond Realism and Idealism

From the first of his writings in which he takes a firm hold on the doctrine of signs (1867), Peirce's work, without peer in this regard over all the previous ages of understanding, best illustrates the range and complexity in detail of issues that need to be clarified in the perspective of semiotic. In equal measure, the *Tractatus de Signis* (1632) of the Latin-Iberian philosopher John Poinsot first expressed both the fundamental character of the issues and the ultimate simplicity of the standpoint determining them.

Now what was that standpoint? It was a vantage beyond being and nonbeing, as Poinsot put it,[7] or, as the point would be put in modern terms, a vantage transcending the contest between realism and idealism, even admitting, as both Peirce and Maritain said, that this contest in its own terms admits no third way between "yes" and "no".[8] In the terms the debate was couched, that is true; and, as Peirce well said, only "slap-dash thinking" has ever tried to have it otherwise. But the doctrine of signs changes exactly the terms of the debate. For the first time in philosophy's long history, it becomes possible thematically to dismantle "that final, most stubborn

---

7 *Tractatus de signis*, Book I, question 1, 118/2–8. See, in chapter 7, "Nonbeing in Latin Philosophy", p. 350ff., "nonbeing" being one of the Latin synonyms for *ens rationis*. The user of the Intelex electronic database version of Poinsot's *Tractatus* could instantly find 43 instances of this usage (or "hits") by entering "non-being" in the search engine, and 1 by entering "nonbeing".

   In modern times, the most famous use of nonbeing in this sense has been, without doubt, the incredible book of Jean-Paul Sartre, *Being and Nothingness* (Barnes trans. 1965).

8 For Maritain, see *The Degrees of Knowledge* (1959 trans.), p. 80; for Peirce on the same point, see above, pp. 246 & 387, where there is discussion around the following observation from Peirce 1909: CP 1.27: "Many philosophers call their variety of nominalism, 'conceptualism'; but it is essentially the same thing; and their not seeing that it is so is but another example of that loose and slapdash style of thinking that has made it possible for them to remain nominalists. Their calling their 'conceptualism' a middle term between realism and nominalism is itself an example in the very matter to which nominalism relates. For while the question between nominalism and realism is, in its nature, susceptible of but two answers: yes and no, they make an idle and irrelevant point which had been thoroughly considered by all the great realists; and instead of drawing a valid distinction, as they suppose, only repeat the very same confusion of thought which made them nominalists."

illusion that bedevils *realists*"9 – the illusion that they are free from illusions – without at all having to abandon or compromise the defining elements of *realism* as a philosophical claim concerning the scope and reach of human understanding.[10]

Peirce, though second to Poinsot as the first systematizer of semiotic foundations, was nonetheless the first to make of the full vision implied by the doctrine of signs a beacon and guideline for actually developing a new direction and general path for future philosophizing. Whence his famous description of himself on discovering the frontier separating postmodernity from the late-modern period in which he had cut his intellectual teeth:[11]

> I am, as far as I know, a pioneer, or rather, a backwoodsman, in the work of clearing and opening up what I call semiotic, that is, the doctrine of the essential nature and fundamental varieties of possible semiosis [or signifying]; and I find the field too vast, the labor too great, for a first-comer.

Beginning with his "New List of Categories" in 1867, and continuing until his death in 1914, semiotic provided the underlying thrust and unity for the whole of Peirce's philosophy. This fact came to be realized only gradually by later students of his thought (coming to it, as they generally did, from some pre-established perspective – such as realism, idealism, pragmatism, etc.). The belatedness of this realization has the effect of relegating all of the earlier publications concerning Peirce to the status of provisional enterprises at best, at worst to the dustbin of history.[12]

Even in the "New List of Categories" as originally drafted, Peirce labored overly under the influence of Kant as Master of the Moderns. He struggled between the horns of the dilemma set by the (false) dichotomy of the realism versus idealism controversy, a controversy which semiotic in principle begins by transcending. This is why Peirce has proved difficult to impossible to classify in realist-idealist terms, and why he had such a time of it classifying himself. Assuming naturally the terms of the controversy as it had developed over the course of modern thought, he only gradually came to critical terms with the fact that semiotic as such is a form neither of realism nor idealism, but beyond both.

Well, the future has begun. It is no longer a question of whether there is such a thing as a way of signs – the question thrown in the ring by Augustine. Nor is it any

---

9 As Peter Gay (1966: 27) so tartly put the matter. I italicize in the quotation the word "realists" in order to contrast (shortly in the text below) the abstract epistemological position of "realism" with those individuals who consider that position to be incarnate in their persons – the self-styled "realists", for whom to detect error is the same as to find opinions differing from their own.

10 To wit, as we remarked in chapter 13 above (pp. 565 & 586), that independently of our perceptions there exists a physical universe that we become aware of in our perceptions and consequently deal with in part in our everyday activities and apprehensions.

11 Peirce c.1906: CP 5.488.

12 Cf. esp. Fisch, Ketner, and Kloesel 1979; Ransdell 1966, 1976, 1977.

longer a question of rediscovering that path once found – for which we have Peirce to thank. The question now is exploring the path. "In the tradition of Peirce, Locke, and Poinsot", as Winance put it,[13] "logic becomes semiotic, able to assimilate the whole of epistemology and natural philosophy as well". In this tradition, 'natural philosophy' is understood in the general sense described by Aquinas "as including also mathematics and metaphysics".[14] "Metaphysics" particularly, in turn, is understood on Maritain's terms,[15] as a philosophy of being that is at once, and par excellence, a philosophy of mind. And within this "philosophy of mind", epistemology does not exist as a discipline distinct from, but as a part within, metaphysics.

Such is that ocean of signs called "semiotics", the fourth age of human understanding to which the history of previous speculative thought in its many rivers, streams, and hidden springs has conspired to lead us. For postmodern times and the immediate future of philosophy, the clear and central task is to come to terms with "a universe perfused with signs",[16] if not composed exclusively of them. In such a universe, as the most trenchant medieval critics of Augustine's definition and the most charismatic writer introducing postmodernity agreed, "the highest grade of reality is only reached by signs".[17]

To that future of philosophy I now leave the reader. *Vale!*

---

13 Winance 1983: 515.
14 Aquinas c.1269: Book I, lect. 1, n. 2: "ita quod sub naturali philosophia comprehendamus et mathematicam et metaphysicam" (Busa 4, p. 144).
15 Maritain 1959: ix.
16 Peirce 1905–6: CP 5.448n.
17 Peirce 1904: CP 8.327. For Aquinas on the same point see his *Summa* I. 3. 4 ad 2, discussed in chapter 7, p. 283; and Poinsot 1632a: Book III, Question 2, 308/7–13.

Historically Layered References

Note: See the *Gloss* at the end of the References, p. 834, for explanation of general style, sometime inclusion of author's birth and death dates, and abbreviations.

ABAELARD, Peter (often spelled "Abelard", also "Abailard"; c.1079–1142). *See also* Cousin, ed. 1836.

    Note on dating: Except for Abaelard's *Dialectica*, for which I rely on De Rijk (see the entry for i.1135/7 below), I have primarily relied on Buytaert 1969: xxiii–xxv for the dating of Abaelard's works. There Buytaert remarks that "the final word" on the chronological succession of Abaelard's works "– if that were possible, – is yet to be said"; yet in his particular introduction to Abaelard's *Theologia Christiana* (1969a: 43–4) he adds that "the problem of the chronology of Abelard's works poses itself so differently than before 1930 that it seems only fair to mention as little as possible of the authors who wrote about the problem before the said date"; a clear indication of just how much work on Abaelard remains to be done, as I have tried to indicate above (see chapter 6 above, p. 243nn84 & 85).

  a.1118. I have made use of #s 1, 2, and 3 from *Beiträge zur Geschichte der Philosophie des Mittelalters, Texte und Untersuchungen*, ed. Clemens Baumaker (Münster i. W.: Verlag der Aschendorffschen Verlagsbuchhandlung), Band XXI, *Peter Abaelards Philosophische Schriften*, ed. Bernhard Geyer, as follows:

    I. Die Logica 'Ingredientibus', in Heft 1 (1919), Heft 2 (1921), und Heft 3 (1927):

  #1. *Glossae secundum magistrum Petrum Abaelardum super Porphyrium*, in Heft 1 pp. 1–109. Pp. 1–32 of this text (i.e., only the general remarks, prior to taking up each of the five predicables in turn) have been trans. under the title "Glosses on Porphyry", in *Selections from Medieval Philosophers I*, ed. and trans. Richard McKeon (New York: Scribner's, 1929), 208–58.

  #2. *Glossae magistri Petri Abaelardi super Praedicamenta Aristotelis*, in Heft 2 pp. 111–305.

  #3. *Glossae magistri Petri Abaelardi super Peri ermenias*, in Heft 3 pp. 307–503. Further work on this text has been done by Minio-Paluello 1958.

i.1122/42. *Sic et Non. A Critical Edition*, prepared by Blanche Boyer and Richard McKeon (Chicago: University of Chicago Press, 1976–7).

c.1133. *Historia calamitatum mearum*, ed. J. Monfrin (3rd ed.; Paris, 1967). English trans. Henry Adams Bellows as *The Story of My Misfortunes, an Autobiography*, with intro. by Ralph Adams Cram (St. Paul, MN: Boyd, 1922).

i.1135/7. *Dialectica*, first complete edition of the Parisian ms. with Introduction by Lambert Marie de Rijk (2nd rev. ed.; Assen, Netherlands: Van Gorcum & Comp. N. V., 1970).

ABAELARD (= Abelard, 1079–1142), Peter, and HELOISE (c.1098–1164).

i.1114/17? *Epistolae Duorum Amantium, Briefe Abaelards und Heloises?* ed. Ewald Köngsen (Leiden: Brill, 1974); English trans. by Neville Chiavaroli and Constant J. Mews in Mews 1999: 189–289.

c.1120–41? "Petri Abaelardi et Heloissae conjugis Epistolae", in *Petri Abaelardi Opera Tomus Prior*, ed. Victor Cousin (Paris: Aug. Durand, 1849; photoprinted Hildesheim: Georg Olms, 1970), 1–236. See *The Letters of Abelard and Heloise*, trans. from the Latin by Betty Radice (Harmondsworth: 1974).

ADAMS, Henry (1838–1918).

1905. *Mont-Saint-Michel and Chartres* (Boston: Houghton Mifflin).

AERTSEN, Ian.

1985. "The Convertibility of Being and Good in St. Thomas Aquinas", *The New Scholasticism* LIX.4 (Autumn), 449–70.

1986. Review article: "Transzendental versus Kategorial: Die Zwiespältigkeit von Thomas' Philosophie? Eine kritische Studie", *Vivarium* XXIV.2 (November), 143–57.

1988. *Nature and Creature. Thomas Aquinas's Way of Thought* (Leiden: E. J. Brill).

1989. "Method and Metaphysics: The *via resolutionis* in Thomas Aquinas", *The New Scholasticism* LXIII.4 (Autumn), 405–18.

1991. "The Medieval Doctrine of the Transcendentals. The Current State of Research", *Bulletin de philosophie médiéval* 33, pp. 130–47.

1991a. "Good as Transcendental and the Transcendence of the Good", in *Being and Goodness*, ed. Scott MacDonald (Ithaca, NY: Cornell University Press), 56–73.

1992. "Ontology and Henology in Medieval Philosophy (Thomas Aquinas, Master Eckhart and Berthold of Moosburg", in Bos and Meijer eds 1992: 120–40.

1992a. "Truth as Transcendental in Thomas Aquinas", *Topoi* 11.2 (September; special issue on "The Transcendentals in the Middle Ages", guest-edited by Jorge J. E. Gracia), 159–71.

1993. "Was heisst Metaphysik bei Thomas von Aquin", in *Scientia und Ars im Hoch- und Spätmittelalter*, ed. Ingrid Craemer-Ruegenberg and Andreas Speer (Berlin: Walter de Gruyter), 217–39.

1995. "The Beginning of the Doctrine of the Transcendentals in Philip the Chancellor (ca.1230)", *Mediaevalia. Textos e Estudios* 7–8 (Porto, Portugal: Fundação Eng. Antônio de Almeida), 269–86.

1996. *Medieval Philosophy and the Transcendentals. The Case of Thomas Aquinas* (Leiden: E. J. Brill).

d'AILLY, Pierre (Petrus de Aliaco, 1350–1420).

    c.1372. *Concepts and Insolubles*, an annotated translation by Paul Vincent Spade (Dordrecht, Holland: D. Reidel Publishing Co., 1980).

    a.1396. *Destructiones modorum significandi (secundum viam nominalium)*, nach Inkunabelausgaben in einer vorlaufigen Fassung neu zusammengestellt und mit Anmerkungen versehen von Ludger Kaczmarek (Munster: Munsteraner Arbeitskreis fur Semiotik, 1980).

    1410. *Imago Mundi*, bilingual critical ed. (Latin original with French trans.) by J. P. Buron (Paris: Gembloux, 1930), 3 vols. A photostatic reproduction of the c.1474 ed. that Christopher Columbus (Cristóbal Colón) annotated (see p. 405n90 above) was issued by the Massachussets Historical Society (Boston, 1927). This work, notes Colisson (1966: 70), "is often mentioned mistakenly as an encyclopedia", but "is in fact an astronomical compendium of great importance", as evidenced in the use Columbus made of it toward his world-historical voyage to the Americas.

AKHTAR, Shabir.

    1996. "The Possibility of a Philosophy of Islam", being chapter 71 of Nasr and Leaman, eds 1996: 1162–9.

AL-GHAZALI (1058–1111).

    c.1095. *Tahafut al-Falasifah*, trans. as *The Incoherence of the Philosophers* by Sabih Ahmad Kamali (Lahore, Pakistan: Pakistan Philosophical Congress, 1958). One could wish for a more critical edition.

ALTANER, Berthold.

    1967. *Kleine patristische Schriften*, ed. G. Glockman (Texte und Untersuchungen 83; Berlin).

d'ALVERNY, Marie-Thérèse.

    1957. "Notes sur les Traductions Médiévales d'Avicenne", in *Archives d'Histoire doctrinale et littéraire du Moyen Age* XIX (1952), 337–58.

    1994. "Introduction" to *Avicenna Latinus Codices*, codices descripsit Marie-Thérèse d'Alverny, addenda collegerunt Simone van Riet et Pierre Jodogne (Leiden: E.J. Brill), 1–10.

AMMIANUS MARCELLINUS (c.AD330–c.395).

    c.AD363. The surviving books of the *Res Gestae* of Ammianus, being a history of the Roman state from the accession of Nerva in AD96 to the death of Valens in 378, of which only the last eighteen books covering AD353–8 survive; trans. by John C. Rolfe with facing Latin (Cambridge, MA: the Loeb Classical Library of Harvard University Press, 1935–1939), in 3 vols.

ANAXAGORAS of Clazomenae (c.500–428BC).

    Date for writing based on the prime assigned by Freeman 1966a: 261.

    c.460BC. Fragments in Freeman 1966: 82–6.

ANAXIMANDER (c.610–545BC).

Date for writing based on the prime assigned by Freeman 1966a: 55.

c.560BC. Fragments in Freeman 1966: 19.

ANAXIMENES (c.580–500BC).

Date for writing based on the prime assigned by Freeman 1966a: 64.

c.546BC. Fragments in Freeman 1966: 19.

ANGELELLI, Ignacio.

1992. "Logic in the Iberian Age of Discovery: Scholasticism, Humanism, Reformed Scholasticism", paper presented 15 October at the "Hispanic Philosophy in the Age of Discovery" conference held at the Catholic University of America 14–17 October.

ANONYMOUS 14TH-CENTURY ENGLISH MONK (c.1300–?).

Dating based on remarks in Hodgson 1967: 21, that the original manuscript dates from "30 years or more" after the death of Richard Rolle (c.1300–49), and Hodgson 1944: "It is generally assumed from its subject-matter that *The Cloud* is to be placed between the works of Rolle (†1349) and those of Hilton (†1395)".

c.1380. *The Cloud of Unknowing*, ed. James Walsh (New York: Paulist Press, 1981).

ANSELM of Canterbury (1033/4–1109).

Note: Dating based on Schmitt 1932.

c.1076. *De divinitatis essentia monologium*, complete Latin text in Migne (q.v.), PL 158: 141–242.

i.1077/8. *Proslogion seu Alloquium de Dei existentia*, complete Latin text in Migne (q.v.), PL 158: 223–42; English trans. of "Proslogion" chs. 2–4 in *Basic Writings*, trans. S. N. Deane, with an intro. by Charles Hartshorne (La Salle, IL: Open Court, 1962).

c.1079. *Sancti Anselmi Liber apologeticus contra Gaunilonem respondentem pro insipiente*, complete Latin text in Migne (q.v.), PL 158: 247–60.

ANSHEN, Ruth Nanda, editor.

1957. *Language: An Enquiry into Its Meaning and Function* (New York: Harper & Bros.).

APPIGNANESI, Lisa, and Sara MAITLAND, editors.

1990. *The Rushdie File* (Syracuse, NY: Syracuse University Press).

AQUINAS, Thomas (1224/5–74).

i.1252/73. *S. Thomae Aquinatis Opera Omnia ut sunt in indice thomistico*, ed. Roberto Busa (Stuttgart-Bad Cannstatt: Frommann-Holzboog, 1980), in septem volumina:

1. In quattuor libros Sententiarum;

2. Summa contra Gentiles, Autographi Deleta, Summa Theologiae;

3. Quaestiones Disputatae, Quaestiones Quodlibetales, Opuscula;

4. Commentaria in Aristotelem et alios;

5. Commentaria in Scripturas;

6. Reportationes, Opuscula dubiae authenticitatis;

7. Aliorum Medii Aevi Auctorum Scripta 61.

1244/5. *De fallaciis*, in *Opuscula Philosophica*, ed. R. Spiazzi (Turin: Marietti, 1954), pp. 225–40 (in Busa ed. vol. 6, 575–9). Dating based on Weisheipl 1974: 386. Since Weisheipl, opinion has moved to declare this work inauthentic and to assign its

composition toward the end of the 13th century, probably shortly after the death of
Aquinas. See Torrell 1996: 11. But Weisheipl's own conviction is that this work
"was written for former classmates in arts at the University of Naples, while Thomas
was in confinement at Roccasecca in 1244–45".

1251, or earlier? *De principiis naturae*, in Busa ed. vol. 3, 587–8.

c.1252/6. *De ente et essentia*, in Busa ed. vol. 3, 583–7. This early work is in effect the
commentary of Aquinas on Porphyry AD271.

> English trans. Armand Maurer, *On Being and Essence* (Toronto: Pontifical In-
> stitute, 1968); trans. with commentary by Joseph Bobik, *Aquinas on Being and
> Essence: A Translation and Interpretation* (Notre Dame, IN: University of Notre
> Dame Press, 1965).

c.1254/6. *In quattuor libros sententiarum Petri Lombardi*, in Busa ed. vol. 1.

c.1256/9. *Quaestiones disputatae de veritate*, in Busa ed. vol. 3, 1–186.

c.1257/8. *Super Boetium De Trinitate*, in Busa ed. vol. 4, 520–39.

c.1259. *Expositio in librum Boethii de Hebdomadibus*, in Busa ed. vol. 4, 539–42.

i.1259/65. *Summa contra gentiles,* in Busa ed. vol. 2, 1–152.

c.1265/6. *Quaestiones disputatae de potentia*, ed. R. P. Pauli M. Pession, in *Quaestiones
disputatae*, vol. II, 9th ed. rev. by P. Bazzi, M. Calcaterra, T. S. Centi, E. Odetto,
and P. M. Pession (Turin: Marietti, 1953), 7–276; in Busa ed. vol. 3, 186–269.

c.1265/6a. *Quaestio disputata de anima*, in Busa ed. vol. 3, 368–96.

c.1265/7. *Super librum Dionysii de divinis nominibus*, in Busa ed. vol. 4, 542–84.

c.1266/73. *Summa theologiae*, in Busa ed. vol. 2, 184–926.

i.1267/78. *In Aristotelis Libros de Anima Commentarium*, cura ac studio A. M. Pirotta
(Turin: Marietti, 1925); distributed in Busa ed. as follows: *In I de anima*, vol. 6,
5–15 (of dubious authenticity); *In II et III de anima*, vol. 4, 341–70.

c.1268/72. *In duodecim libros metaphysicorum Aristotelis expositio*, in Busa ed. vol. 4,
390–507.

c.1269. *Sententia libri ethicorum*, in Busa ed. vol. 4, 143–234.

c.1269/72. *Quaestiones quodlibetales, Quodlibet 4*, in Busa ed. 3, 457–65.

1270. *De unitate intellectus contra Averroistas*, in Busa ed. vol. 3, pp. 577–83. English
trans. with facing Latin followed by interpretive essays in Ralph M. McInerny,
Aquinas against the Averroists: On there being only one intellect (West Lafayette,
IN: Purdue University Press, 1993).

c.1270/1. *In libros posteriorum analyticorum*, in Busa ed. 3, 273–311.

c.1272. *In librum de causis*, in Busa ed. vol. 4, 507–20.

c.1272/3. *In libros de coelo et mundo*, in Busa ed. vol. 4, 1–49.

ARAÚJO, Francisco (1580–1664).

1617. *Commentariorum in universam Aristotelis Metaphysicam tomus primus* (Burgos
and Salamanca: J. B. Varesius, 1617). This rare, valuable survivor of the last Latin
century exists in very few copies. The work itself contains one of the most extensive
surveys we have, besides the *Disputationes Metaphysicae* of Francis Suárez, of late
Latin positions, including a thematic discussion of sign; and it has the advantage of
being later than Suárez. A summary exposition of the metaphysical doctrine of this

work has been published by Mauricio Beuchot (1987) as a stop-gap measure until an edition of the complete original can be published. But until now the huge size of Araújo's work – over 1000 pages – has posed an insuperable economic obstacle. Fortunately, Beuchot has published a Spanish translation of the section on sign (to wit, Book III, quest. 2, art. 2, dubia 1–4, in Beuchot ed. 1995: 51–106).

ARISTOTLE (384–322BC).

Note: Our citations here are from the 12-vol. Oxford edition prepared under W. D. Ross ed. 1928–52 (q.v.); for the convenience of the reader, after the abbreviation RM, we also give the pages where applicable to the more readily available 1-vol. edition of *The Basic Works of Aristotle* prepared by Richard McKeon using the Oxford translations (New York: Basic Books, 1941). Chronology for the works is based on Gauthier 1970, as follows:

c.360–330BC. *Organon*, i.e., Aristotle's writings on Logic, in Oxford vol. I (RM 1–212). The title "Organon", which means "instrument", seems to have originally been assigned as a general title for these writings by either Andronicus of Rhodes in the 1st century BC or Diogenes Laertius in the 3rd century AD, and has been retained ever since: see chapter 3 above, p89n66. The *Organon* consists of:

c.360BC. *Categories* (trans. E. M. Edghill; RM 1–37 complete).

c.353BC. *Topics* (trans. W. A. Pickard-Cambridge; RM 187–206 incomplete).

c.353aBC. *Refuting Sophisms* (trans. Pickard-Cambridge; RM 207–12 incomplete).

c.348–7BC. *Prior Analytics* (trans. Jenkinson; RM 62–107 incomplete).

c.348–7aBC. *Posterior Analytics* (trans. G. R. C. Mure; RM 108–86 complete).

c.330BC. *On Interpretation* (trans. Edghill; RM 38–61 complete).

As noted in chapter 3, Arabic Aristotelian tradition includes the *Rhetoric* (composed c.335–4BC) and the *Poetics* (c.335–4aBC) as part of the *Organon* itself, the part, specifically, pertaining to practical in contrast to theoretical discourse, i.e., discourse about what is to be made or done in contrast to discourse about the nature of things as transcending human action. Cfr. Lanigan 1969; Black 1987.

c.355BC. *On the Heavens (De Caelo)* (trans. Harold J. L. Stocks; RM 395–466, missing chs. 1–12 of Book II).

c.355aBC. *On Generation and Corruption* (trans. Harold H. Joachim; RM 467–531 complete).

c.353bBC. *Physics*, Book VII (further under c.348–7bBC).

c.348–7bBC. *Physics*, Books I–VI, VIII (further under c.353BC). Oxford vol. II, 184a9–267b26 (trans. Hardie and Gaye; RM 213–394 complete).

c.348–7cBC. *Politics*, Books VII–VIII.

c.348–7dBC. *Metaphysics*, Books I–IV, V(?), XIII chs. 9–10, XIV (further under c.330cBC).

c.345/4BC. *On the Parts of Animals*, Books II–IV (further under c.330aBC).

c.345/4aBC. *Politics*, Books II–III.

c.335/4BC. *Politics*, Books I & IV–VI.

c.335/4BC. *Nicomachean Ethics* (trans. W. D. Ross; RM 927–1112 complete).

c.330aBC. *On the Parts of Animals*, Book I (further under c.345/4BC).

c.330bBC. *On the Soul* (trans. J. A. Smith; RM 533–603 complete).

c.330cBC. *Metaphysics*, Books VI–X, XI(?), XII, XIII chs. 1–9; Oxford vol. VIII, 980a1–1093b29 (trans. Ross; RM 681–926 complete).

ARMSTRONG, Arthur Hilary.

1977. *An Introduction to Ancient Philosophy* (being a reprint of the 1957 3rd ed. with the addition of a Critical Introduction, pp. x–xviii, "to remove … the major misrepresentations and errors of judgement and to do something to bring the book up to date"; London: Methuen & Co. Ltd.).

1979. *Plotinian and Christian Studies* (London: ·Variorum Reprints).

ARMSTRONG, Robert L. (1926–).

1970. *Metaphysics and British Empiricism* (Lincoln: University of Nebraska Press).

ARNIM, Hans Friedrich August von (1859–1931).

i.1903/24. *Stoicorum Veterum Fragmenta* (Leipzig: B. G. Teubner), in 4 volumes.

ARNOLD, Duane W. H., and Pamela BRIGHT, editors.

1995. *De Doctrina Christiana. A Classic of Western Culture* (Notre Dame, IN: University of Notre Dame Press).

ARRIAN (Flavius Arrianus, c.AD85/90–c.175/80).

> *Note:* Dating is based mainly on Bosworth 1980. Arrian's work covers the military activity of Alexander the Great (356–323BC) from his accession in 336BC until his death.

a.AD125. *Anabasis of Alexander. Arrian's History of Alexander's Expedition*, trans. from Greek by Rooke (London: printed for R. Lea, 1814), in 2 vols. The most recent trans. by P. A. Brunt, *History of Alexander and Indica* [*Anabasis Alexandri et Indica*], in 2 vols. (Loeb Classical Library; Harvard: Harvard University Press, I 1976, II 1983), was consulted.

ASHLEY, Benedict.

1952. "Research into the Intrinsic Final Causes of Physical Things", *ACPA Proceedings* XXVI: 185–94.

1967. "Final Causality", in *The New Catholic Encyclopedia* (New York: McGraw-Hill), vol. V, 915–19, respectively, the first treating primarily of the Greek and Latin periods, the second treating of the modern period.

1967a. "Teleology", in *The New Catholic Encyclopedia* (New York: McGraw-Hill), vol. XIII, 979–81.

1973. "Change and Process", in *The Problem of Evolution*, ed. John N. Deely and Raymond J. Nogar (Indianapolis, IN: Hackett Publishing Co.), pp. 265–94.

ASHWORTH, Earline Jennifer

1974. *Language and Logic in the Post-Medieval Period* (Dordrecht, Holland: D. Reidel Publishing Co.).

1978. "Multiple Quantification and the Use of Special Quantifiers in Early Sixteenth Century Logic", *Notre Dame Journal of Formal Logic* XIX: 599–613.

1988. "The Historical Origins of John Poinsot's *Treatise on Signs*", *Semiotica* 69.1/2: 129–47.

1990. "Domingo de Soto (1494–1560) and the Doctrine of Signs", in *De Ortu Grammaticae: Studies in Medieval Grammar and Linguistic Theory in Memory of Jan*

Pinborg, ed. G. L. Bursill-Hall, Sten Ebbesen, and Konrad Koerner (Amsterdam: John Benjamins), 35–48.

1990a. "The Doctrine of Signs in Some Early Sixteenth-Century Spanish Logicians", in *Estudios de Historia de la Logica. Actas del II Simposio de Historia de la Logica: Universidad de Navarra Pamplona 25–27 de Mayo 1987*, ed. Ignacio Angelelli and Angel d'Ors (Pamplona: Ediciones EUNATE), 13–38.

1998. "Language, Renaissance Philosophy of", entry in the *Routledge Encyclopedia of Philosophy*, ed. in 10 vol. by Edward Craig (London: Routledge, 1998), vol. 5, 411–15.

1999. Review of McInerny 1996 in *Speculum* 74.1 (January): 215–17.

ATHENAEUS of Naucratis (fl.AD180–229).

No exact dates are known for this author. Grant (1980: 57) cites AD180 as the earliest possible date for the work; Gulick (1927: viii–ix, see within this entry below) dates its completion at "not long after 228". From these two we derive the *floruit*, using Gulick's date for the work itself.

c.AD228. *The Deipnosophists*, or *The Sophists at Dinner*, Greek text with English trans. by Charles Burton Gulick (Loeb Classical Library ed.; New York: G. P. Putnam, 1927–41), in 7 volumes.

According to M. Grant (1980: 56) the titular term "does not mean 'the professors at dinner' but 'the specialists on dining'," although, perhaps because it appears more dignified, some variant of the Gulick mistranslation has become customary.

AUGUSTINE of Hippo (AD354–430). Unless noted otherwise, I have used the *Sancti Aurelii Augustini Hipponensis Episcopi Opera Omnia*, opera et studio Monachorum Ordinis Sancti Benedicti e congreatione S. Mauri. Ed. Parisina altera, emendata et aucta (at the Xochimilco Dominican priory in Mexico City; Paris: Gaume Fratres, 1836), cited as follows:

i.AD397–426. *De doctrina christiana libri quattuor* ("Four Books on Christian Doctrine"), in Tomus Tertius Pars Prior, 13–151; also in *Patrologiae Cursus Completus*, ed. J. P. Migne, *Series Latina* (PL), vol. 34, cols. 15–122.

AD387. *Principia dialecticae*, Appendix Tomi Primae, 1312–29 (Chirii Fortunatiani nomine editum est Basileae anno 1558), the edition and text I used. This title for the work, used in 16th and 17th century eds of Augustine, is now considered, like the work itself, of dubious authenticity; the title Augustine himself mentions in his *Retractationes* of AD426/7 is rather *De Dialectica*, and this is the title Jan Pinborg uses in his ed. of the Latin text which appears, along with a facing English trans., intro., and notes by B. Darrell Jackson (Dordrecht, Holland: D. Reidl, 1975). Jackson, in his introduction, argues forcefully that both authorship and title of the work should now be considered authentic.

AD389. *De magistro liber unus* "in quo de verborum vi atque officino disputatur copiose, quo demum non verbis quae foris homo personat, sed aeterna veritate intus docente scientiam rerum obtineri evincatur", in Tomus Primus Pars Prior, 884–921; also in *Corpus Christianorum Series Latina* vol. XXXII, ed. Joseph Martin (Turnhout, Belgium: Brepols, 1962), 1–167.

AD390/1. *De vera religione liber unus*, in *Sancti Aurelii Augustini Hipponensis Episcopi Operum*, Maurist ed. (in the Loras College rare book collection; Antwerp, Belgium, 1700), tomus primus, cols. 557–90; also in *Corpus Christianorum Series Latina* vol. XXXII, ed. K.-D. Daur (Turnhout, Belgium: Brepols, 1962), 187–260.

AD397. *Aureli Augustini Confessionum libri tredecim*, Latin text in O'Donnell 1992: I, 1–205; English text *Confessions Books I–XIII*, trans. F. J. Sheed, introduced by Peter Brown (Indianapolis, IN: Hackett Publishing Co. 1993).

i.AD399 and 422/6. *De Trinitate libri XV*, ed W. J. Mountain with assistance from François Glorie (Corpus Christianorum Series Latina vols. L & LAVII; Turnholt: Brepols, 1968).

AD426/7. *Retractationum libri II*, ed. Almut Mutzenbecher (Corpus Christianorum Series Latina vol. LVII; Turnholt: Brepols, 1984).

AVERROES (ibn Rashd; 1126–98).

a.1198. *Commentarium Magnum in Aristotelis de Anima Libros*, ed. F. S. Crawford (Cambridge, MA: The Mediaeval Academy of America, 1953). See II, sect. 60, pp. 219–21 for origin of the term "intentional" as descriptive of cognition – Deely 1975: 293.

c.1180. *Averroes' Tahafut al-Tahafut (The Incoherence of the Incoherence)*, trans. from the Arabic with introduction and notes by Simon van den Bergh (London: E. J. W. Gibb Memorial Trust, 1954), in 2 vols.

Destructio destructionem philosophiae Algazelis, in the Latin version of Calo Calonymous, ed. with an introduction by Beatrice H. Zedler (Milwaukee, WI: Marquette University Press, 1961). For the dating of this work I have followed the suggestion of Bouyges as reported by Zedler in her introduction, p. 12.

AVICENNA (ibn Sina; AD980–1037).

Chronology based on Gutas 1988: 123–5.

i.1020/27. *The Cure (Kitāb al Shifā)*, a compendium of Logic, Physics, Mathematics, and Metaphysics (Gutas 1988: 101ff.), "a summa of philosophical wisdom … in his own style" (Houser 1999: 10), which appeared in Latin only by stages, between (very roughly) 1150 and 1306 (d'Alverny 1994: 4–80) . This work is cited here not in terms of any full edition I was able to consult, but to mark the important but as yet little-known point that Avicenna appears to be the single most important Arabic influence on the 13th-century work of Aquinas, far more than Averroes – yet another field rich and vast for the enterprising doctoral student in philosophy.

Here I want to add a gloss on Avicenna apropos of chapter 6, pp. 229–31 above, esp. 230n50. The Latin translation alleged by Krempel as the first explicit source of the notion of *relatio rationis* as over against *relatio realis seu categorialis seu praedicamentalis* is from an original part of the *Shifā* dated to c.1024, in a Latin trans. of a date p.1150. The passage in question can be found in *Avicenna Latinus Liber de Philosophia Prima sive Scientia Divina I–IV*, ed. critique de la traduction Latine médiévale par S. van Riet (Leiden: E. J. Brill, 1977), Tractatus Tertius, Capitulum Decimum, p. 178 – whether translated originally by Gerard of Cremona or Dominic Gundisalinus seemed undetermined (ed. cit. p. 123*n2).

c.1024, trans. into Latin p.1150, with earliest complete manuscript c.1240: *Avicenna Latinus. Liber de Philosophia Prima sive Scientia Divina I–IV*, édition critique de la traduction Latine médiévale, par S. van Riet (Louvain: E. Peeters, 1977).

BACON, Francis (1561–1626).

1620. *Novum Organum*, ed. Thomas Fowler (Oxford, 1889); English trans. and ed. Fulton H. Anderson, *The New Organon* (Indianapolis, IN: Bobbs-Merrill, 1960).

BACON, Roger (1214?–94).

c.1245. *Sumule dialectices magistri Rogeri Baconi*, in fascicle 15 of the 16 fascicles. *Opera hactenus inedita Rogeri Bacon*, ed. Robert Steele (Oxford: Clarendon Press, 1940), 191–359, with "Notes and Conjectural Emendations" on pp. 363–9. Steele's introduction, pp. x–xxiii, treats specifically of the *Sumule* beginning on p. xiii. Steele deems (p. xiv) that the *Sumule*, a work whose authenticity has often been challenged, "may now be ascribed with certainty to Roger Bacon".

c.1267. *De signis*, ed. Fredborg, Nielsen, and Pinborg in *Traditio*, vol. XXXIV (New York: Fordham University Press, 1978), 81–136.

1292. *Compendium studii theologiae*, trans. as *Compendium of the Study of Theology* in bilingual ed. by Thomas S. Maloney (Leiden: E. J. Brill, 1988), 31–119.

BADAWI, Abdurrahman.

1968. *La transmission de la philosophie grecque au monde arabe* (Paris: Vrin).

BAER, Eugen (1937–).

1977. "Things Are Stories: A Manifesto for a Reflexive Semiotics", *Semiotica* 25.3/4: 293–305.

1992. "Via Semiotica", *Semiotica* 92.3/4: 351–7.

BAILEY, Cyril (1871–1957).

1928. *The Greek Atomists and Epicurus* (New York: Russell & Russell).

BAIRD, Forrest E., and Walter KAUFMANN, editors.

1997. *Ancient Philosophy*, vol. I of *Philosophic Classics* (2nd ed.; Upper Saddle River, NJ: Prentice Hall).

BAKEWELL, Charles Montague (1867–1957).

1907. *Source Book in Ancient Philosophy* (New York: Charles Scribner's Sons).

BALDWIN, James M., editor (1861–1934).

1901–02. *Dictionary of Psychology and Philosophy*, "giving a terminology in English, French, German, and Italian. Written by many hands and edited by J. M. Baldwin", in 3 vols, vol. 3 being a bibliography of philosophy, psychology, and cognate subjects compiled by Benjamin Rand (original ed. New York: Macmillan; vols. 1 and 2 reissued by Peter Smith, New York, 1940, vol. 3 1949).

BAÑEZ, Domingo (1528–1604).

1584/8. *Scholastica commentaria in primam partem Summae Theologiae S. Thomae Aquinatis*, ed. L. Urbano (Madrid: Editorial F.E.D.A., 1934). For a partial English trans. which has tried to ameliorate the technical structure of the original commentary on Question 3, article 4, see Llamzon 1966.

1599. *Institutiones minoris dialecticae, quas summulae vocant* (Salamanca: Andreas Renaut); Book I, tract 1, cap. 2, pp. 15–18, trans. in Beuchot 1995: 103–6, which translation is cited in chapter 7, p. 360n245, of the present book.

BARTHES, Roland (1915–80).

  1964. *Éléments de sémiologie* (Paris: Éditions du Seuil), trans. Annette Lavers and Colin
      Smith as *Elements of Semiology* (New York: Hill and Wang, 1968). Page references
      here are to the English trans.

  i.1962/73 (posthumous assemblage of essays). *L'Aventure sémiologique* (Paris: Éditions
      du Seuil, 1985), grossly mistitled *The Semiotic Challenge* in the Richard Howard
      translation (New York: Farrar, Straus and Giroux, 1988). The French edition in-
      cludes a "Note de l'éditeur" signed only "F. W", but this editorial preface is silently
      omitted in the English edition. The Barthes 1964 entry, above, is included in the
      French publication but omitted from the English rendition.

BAUR, Michael (1954–), and John RUSSON (1960–), editors.

  1997. *Hegel and the Tradition: Essays in Honour of H. S. Harris* (Toronto: University of
      Toronto Press).

BAYLE, Pierre (1647–1706).

  1686/8. *Commentaire philosophique sur ces paroles de Jesus-Christ Contrain-les d'entrer:
      où l'on prouve par plusieurs raisons démonstratives qu'l n'y a rien de plus-
      abominable que de faire des conversions par la contrainte, & l'on refute tous les
      sophismes des convertisseurs à contrainte, & l'apologie que S. Augustin a faite des
      persécutions.* This work was issued pseudonymously as "Traduit de l'anglois du
      Jean Fox de Bruggs par M. J. F." and with a fictitions imprint: "A Cantorbery, Chez
      Thomas Litwel" (the actual publisher being Wolfgang of Amsterdam), details which
      serve to underline how fragile was the notion of "rights of conscience" as late as
      modernity's early years. The work appeared in four parts: Volumes I and II in October
      1686, Volume III in June 1687, with a "Supplement" that appeared in January 1688.

      The two volumes of 1686 only have been translated and commented upon, with
      scattered references to the "Supplement", by Amie Godman Tannenbaum, *Pierre
      Bayle's Philosophical Commentary: A modern translation and critical interpreta-
      tion* (New York: P. Lang, 1987).

  1710. *An Historical and Critical Dictionary* "translated into English, with many Additions
      and Corrections, made by the Author himself, that are not in the French Editions"
      (original French ed. 1697; London: Printed for C. Harper, D. Brown, J. Tonson,
      A. and F. Churchill, T. Horne, T. Goodwin, R. Knaplock, J. Taylor, A. Bell, B.
      Tooke, D. Midwinter, B. Lintott and W. Lewis). Edition in the Loras College Rare
      Book Collection; the cited text was checked against the French of the *Dictionnaire
      Historique et Critique par Monsieur Bayle, Tome Premier, Seconde Edition, Revue,
      corrigée & augmentée par l'Auteur* (Rotterdam: Reinier Leers, 1702), also in the
      same collection.

BELLARMINE, Robert (1542–1621).

  1615. Letter to Foscarini of April 12, trans. as Appendix VIII in Blackwell 1991: 265–7.

BÉNÉZIT, E. (1854–1920).

  1948–55. *Dictionnaire critique et documentaire des Peintres, Sculpteurs, Dessinateurs
      et Graveurs de tous les temps et de tous les pays par un groupe d'écrivains
      spécialistes français et étrangers* (nouvelle éd. entièrement refondue, rev. et cor.
      sous la direction des héritiers de Bénézit (Paris: Librairie Gründ), in 10 vols.

BENTHAM, Jeremy (1748–1832).

1816. *Chrestomathia: Being a Collection of Papers, Explanatory of the Design of an Institution Proposed to be Set on Foot Under the Name of the Chrestomathic Day School, or Chrestomathic School, for the Extension of the New System of Instruction to the Higher Branches of Learning, For the Use of the Middling and Higher Ranks in Life*, in *The Works of Jeremy Bentham*, ed. John Bowring (Edinburgh, 1838–43; reproduced 1962 by Russell & Russell, Inc., New York), vol. 8, pp. 1–191, esp. appendix IV, the "Essay on Nomenclature and Classification", 63–128.

BERGSON, Henri (1859–1941).

1909. *Creative Evolution*, authorized trans. Arthur Mitchell (New York: Modern Library, 1941).

BERKELEY, Bishop George (1685–1753).

1710. *The Principles of Human Knowledge*, in *The Works of George Berkeley, Bishop of Cloyne*, ed. A. A. Luce and T. E. Jessop (London: Nelson, 1948ff.).

1732. *Alciphron, or The Minute Philosopher*, vol. III of *The Works of George Berkeley, Bishop of Cloyne*, ed. T. E. Jessop (London: Thomas Nelson and Sons, 1950).

BEUCHOT, Mauricio (1950–).

1980. "La doctrina tomista clásica sobre el signo: Domingo de Soto, Francisco de Araújo y Juan de Santo Tomás", *Critica* XII.36 (México, diciembre): 39–60.

1983. "Los terminos y las categorías sintactico-semanticas en la lógica post-medieval", *Diánoia* 29, 175–96.

1986. "Signo y Lenguaje en San Agustín", *Dianoia* (anuario de filosofia) 32: 13–26.

1987. *Metafísica: La Ontología Aristotélico-Tomista de Francisco de Araújo* (México City: Universidad Nacional Autónoma de México).

1991. "El realismo cognoscitivo en Santo Tomás de Aquino. Sus condiciones metafísicas", *Diánoia* 37: 49–60.

1993. "La percepción sensible en Santo Tomás de Aquino", in *Percepción: Colores*, ed. Laura Benítez and José A. Robles (= La Filosofía y Sus Problemas; México City: Universidad Nacional Autónoma, Instituto de Investigaciones Filosóficas), 11–29.

1993a. "El argumento 'ontológico' de San Anselmo", *Medievalia* 15 (diciembre): 24–31.

1994. "Intentionality in John Poinsot", in *American Catholic Philosophical Quarterly* 68.3 (Summer 1994): 279–96.

1995. *Escolastica Ibérica Post-Medieval: Algunas Teorías del Signo*, selección de textos, introducción y traducción (Maracaibo y Caracas, Venezuela: Universidad del Zulia y Universidad Católica Andrés).

1998. "Bañez, Domingo (1528–1604)", entry in the *Routledge Encyclopedia of Philosophy*, ed. in 10 vols. by Edward Craig (London: Routledge, 1998), vol. 1, pp. 647–9.

BEUCHOT, Mauricio, editor and translator.

1995. *Algunas Teorías del Signo en la Escolastica Iberica Post-Medieval*, selección de textos, introducción y traducción (Maracaibo y Caracas, Venezuela: Universidad del Zulia y Universidad Católica Andrés).

BEUCHOT, Mauricio, and John DEELY.

1995. "Common Sources for the Semiotic of Charles Peirce and John Poinsot", *Review of Metaphysics* XLVIII.3 (March): 539–66.

BHAGAVAD-GITA, "The Song of God", a work of collective authorship.

i.499/199BC. The most popular Hindu religious text from the Smriti, the writings which comment upon and explain the revealed truths of Hindu faith recorded in the Sruti (the Scriptures proper, to wit, the *Vedas*). English trans. by Swami Prabhavanananda and Christopher Isherwood, with an Introduction by Aldous Huxley (New York: Mentor Books, 1954).

BIRD, Otto A. (1914–).

1963. "The History of Logic", *Review of Metaphysics* XVI.3 (March): 491–502. A gentlemanly, informed review of Kneale and Kneale 1962 and of the first English edition (Notre Dame 1960) of Bochenski 1970.

1987. "John of St. Thomas Redivivus ut John Poinsot", *The New Scholasticism* LXI.1 (Winter): 103–107.

BLACK, Deborah Louise.

1987. *The Logical Dimensions of Rhetoric and Poetics: Aspects of Non-Demonstrative Reasoning* (University of Toronto doctoral dissertation on microfilm from the National Library of Canada).

1989. "The 'Imaginative Syllogism' in Arabic Philosophy: A Medieval Contribution to the Philosophical Study of Metaphor", in *Mediaeval Studies* 51: 242–67.

1990. *Logic and Aristotle's* Rhetoric *and* Poetics *in Medieval Arabic Philosophy* (Leiden: E. J. Brill).

BLACKWELL, Richard J. (1929–).

1991. *Galileo, Bellarmine, and the Church* (Notre Dame, IN: University of Notre Dame Press).

BLUNDEVILLE, Thomas (fl. 1561).

1599. *The art of logike plainely taught in the English tongue … as well according to the doctrine of Aristotle, as of all other moderne and best accounted authors thereof …* (facsimile ed. no. 102; Amsterdam, Theatrum Orbis Terrarum; New York: Da Capo Press, 1969).

BOAS, George.

1953. Translation, with an Introduction of Bonaventure 1259 as *The Mind's Road to God* (New York: Bobbs-Merrill).

BOCHENSKI, I. M. (1902–95).

1970. *A History of Formal Logic* (2nd ed., with corrections; New York: Chelsea Publishing Co.), trans. and ed. "with the author's full concurrence" by Ivo Thomas from *Formale Logik* (Freiburg: Verlag Karl Alber, 1956).

BOETHIUS, Anicius Manlius Severinus (c.AD480–524).

Migne (q.v.) has presented in his PL vols. 63 & 64 the main *versiones Boethii* extant to our time, though not in the form of critical editions. The main works useful to the present study appear in vol. 64, *Manlii Severini Boetii opera omnia, non solum liberalium disciplinarum, sed etiam majorum facultatum studiosis utilissima, mo et sine quibus Aristoteles in praecipuis locis intelligi non potest*, etc. [Bibliothecae Cleri universae]. Dating of the works of Boethius is something of a scholarly nightmare. I have used for the works from PL 64 the dating worked out in Cappuyns 1937 (q.v.). Dating for nine of these works has been further examined in de Rijk 1964 (q.v.), and, for the convenience of other researchers, I have included the variant dates from de Rijk in brackets after the dates of Cappuyns.

Note that the *Liber de diffinitione* in PL 64 is spurious, authored in fact by Marius Victorinus (c.AD280/300–c.363).

a.AD509 [c.504/5]. *In Porphyrium dialogi a Victorino translati* (the text appears to date from sometime a.AD363); PL 64 cols. 9–70.

c.AD509–10 [c.507/9]. *Commentaria in Porphyrium a se translatum*; PL 64 cols. 71–158.

AD510 [c.509/11]. *In categorias Aristotelis libri quattuor*; PL 64 cols. 159–294.

c.AD511 [p.512: "not before 513" is how de Rijk puts it]. *In librum Aristotelis de interpretatione libri duo. Editio prima, seu Commentaria minor*; PL 64 cols. 293–392.

p.AD511. *Interpretatio priorum Analyticorum Aristotelis:* version ascribed by Cappuyns to James of Venice, c.1128; PL 64 cols. 639–712.

p.AD511a. *Interpretatio posteriorum Analyticorum Aristotelis libri octo*: allegedly also by James of Venice, c.1128; PL 64 cols. 711–62.

p.AD511b. *Interpretatio Topicorum Aristotelis libri octo*: also ascribed by Cappuyns to James of Venice, c.1128; PL 64 cols. 909–1008.

p.AD511c. *Interpretatio Elenchorum Sophisticorum Aristotelis libri duo*: version of James of Venice, c.1128; PL 64 cols. 1007–40.

c.AD511/13 [c.515/16]. *In librum Aristotelis de interpretatione libri sex. Editio secunda, seu Commentaria major*; PL 64 cols 394–638.

c.AD512–13 [c.505/6]. *De Syllogismo categorico libri duo*; PL 64 cols. 793–832.

c.AD512–13a. *Introductio ad Syllogismos categoricos* (in some mss., *Antepraedicamenta*). Perhaps a 2nd ed. of 512–13a, above; PL 64 cols. 761–94.

p.AD513. *Liber de divisione* (also probably soon after 513 in the estimation of Cappuyns); PL 64 cols. 875–92.

p.AD513a [i.516/22]. *De Syllogismo hypothetico libri duo* (Cappuyns deems this work completed soon after 513); PL 64 cols. 831–76.

c.AD513–15 [a.522]. *Commentaria in Topica Ciceronis libri sex*; PL 64 cols. 1039–1174.

c.AD515 [a.523]. *De differentiis topicis libri quattuor*; PL 64 cols. 1173–1216.

The two tracts following in the volume, namely, *Speculatio de rhetoricae cognitione* (cols. 1217–22) and *Locorum rhetoricorum distinctio* (cols. 1222–4), are only extracts from Book IV.

c.AD520. *De Trinitate*, or, properly, *Liber de Sancta Trinitate* (more fully: *Quomodo trinitas unus deus ac non tres dii*); PL 64 cols. 1247–1300.

c.AD523/4. *De consolatione philosophiae*; PL 63 cols. 547–862.

BOISSONNADE, Prosper (1862–1935).

1927. *Life and Work in Medieval Europe (Fifth to Fifteenth Centuries)*, trans. by Eileen Power (New York: A. A. Knopf) of *Le travail dans l'Europe chrétienne au moyen age* (Paris: Alcan, 1921).

BONAVENTURA of Bagnoregio (1217–74).

1259. (September–October). *Itinerarium mentis in Deum*, "Journey of the Mind to God"; Latin-English text by Philotheus Boehner, with introduction and commentary, *Saint Bonaventure's Itinerarium Mentis in Deum, Works of Saint Bonaventure Volume II* (Saint Bonaventure, NY: Saint Bonaventure University, The Franciscan Institute, 1956). Two additional English translations were consulted for the present work: see under Cousins 1978 and Boas 1953.

BONIFACE VIII, Pope (c.1225–1303).

1302. Bull "Unam Sanctam", English trans. in Thatcher and McNeal 1905: 314–17.

BOROWSKI, Ludwig Ernst (1740–1831).

1804. *Darstellung des Lebens und Charakters Immanuel Kants* (Königsberg: F. Nicolo Vius; repr. Brussels: Culture et Civilization, 1968 as vol. 40 in the series Aetas Kantiana).

BOS, E. P., and P. A. MEIJER, editors.

1992. *On Proclus and His Influence in Medieval Philosophy*, being the proceedings of the 7–8 September 1989 symposium held at the University of Leiden in celebration of the 65th birthday of L. M. de Rijk (Leiden: E. J. Brill).

BOSSEREL, J. B.

1615. *Synopses in quibus doctrina dialectica R.ᶦ P.ᶦ Petri Fonseca ad Ordinem Aristotelicum revocatur, Anno Domini 1615* (University of Graz MS 133; reprinted in Ferreira Gomes 1964: 779–861).

BOSSY, John.

1991. *Giordano Bruno and the Embassy Affair* (New Haven, CT: Yale University Press).

BOSWELL, James (1740–95).

1793. *The Life of Samuel Johnson, LL.D.* (rev. and augmented ed. of 1791 original publication; London: printed by Henry Baldwin for Charles Dilly).

BOSWORTH, A. B.

1980. "Introduction" to his *A Historical Commentary on Arrian's History of Alexander*, vol. 1 (Oxford: Clarendon Press), 1–41.

BOUISSAC, Paul, editor.

1998. *Encyclopedia of Semiotics* (Oxford, England: Oxford University Press).

BOYER, Blanche B., and Richard McKEON (1900–85).

1976/7. "Introduction" to Abaelard i.1122/42: 1–6.

BRAZILLER, George, editor & publisher.

1994. *For Rushdie: Essays by Arab and Muslim Writers in Defense of Free Speech*, a trans. of *Pour Rushdie: Cent intellectuels arabes et musulmans pour la liberté d'expression* (Paris: Éditions la Découverte, 1993) arr. by Braziller and executed by Kevin Anderson and Kenneth Whitehead (New York: George Braziller).

BRÉHIER, Émile (1876–1952).

1938. *Histoire de la philosophie: La Philosophie moderne. I: Le dix-septième siècle* (Presses Universitaires de France), trans. as *The Seventeenth Century* by Wade Baskin (Chicago: University of Chicago Press, 1966).

BREHIER, Émile, editor.

   1951. *Enneads*, edition of Greek text (Paris: Societé d'Édition "Les Belles Lettres"), vol. VI.

BRENNAN, Timothy (1953–).

   1989. *Salman Rushdie and the Third World* (New York: St Martin's Press).

BRENT, Joseph (1928–).

   1993. *Charles Sanders Peirce. A Life* (Bloomington: Indiana University Press).

BRENTANO, Franz (1838–1917).

   1874. *Psychologie von Empirischen Standpunkt*, trans. Linda McAlister, A. Rancurello, and D. B. Terrell as *Psychology from an Empirical Standpoint* (New York: Humanities Press, 1963).

BREZIK, Victor B. (1913–).

   1981. *One Hundred Years of Thomism: Aeterni Patris and Afterwards. A Symposium* [*held 4–5 October 1979*] (Houston, TX: University of St Thomas Center for Thomistic Studies).

BROWN, Peter.

   1967. *Augustine of Hippo. A Biography* (Berkeley: University of California Press).

BRUNO, Giordano (1548–1600).

   1591. *De Imaginum, Signorum et Idearum Compositione*, trans. as *On the Composition of Images, Signs, & Ideas* by Charles Doria, edited and annotated by Dick Higgins, with a foreword by Manfredi Piccolomini (New York: Willis, Locker & Owens, 1991).

BUCKLEY, Michael J. (1950–).

   1987. *At the Origins of Modern Atheism* (New Haven, CT: Yale University Press).

BURCKHARDT, Jacob (1818–97).

   1880. *Die Zeit Constantins des Grossen* (2nd ed.; Wien: Phaidon Verlag), trans. Moses Hadas as *The Age of Constantine the Great* (London: Routledge & Kegan Paul, 1949).

BURKS, Arthur W. (1915–).

   1958. "Bibliography of the Works of Charles Sanders Peirce", in *The Collected Papers of Charles Sanders Peirce, Volume VIII*, ed. Arthur W. Burks (Cambridge, MA: Harvard University Press, 1958), 249–330.

BURNET, J. (1863–1928).

   1914. *Greek Philosophy. Part I. Thales to Plato* (London: Macmillan and Co.).

   1930. *Early Greek Philosophy* (4th ed.; London: A. & C. Black).

BURRELL, David B.

   1986. *Knowing the Unknowable God: Ibn-Sina, Maimonides, Aquinas* (Notre Dame, IN: University of Notre Dame Press).

BURSILL-HALL, G. L.

   1972. *Speculative Grammars of the Middle Ages: The Doctrine of Partes Orationis of the Modistae* (= Approaches to Semiotics 11; The Hague: Mouton).

BURSILL-HALL, G. L., Sten EBBESEN, E. S. F. KOERNER, editors.

   1990. *De Ortu Grammaticae: Studies in Medieval Grammar and Linguistic Theory in Memory Jan Pinborg* (Amsterdam: J. Benjamins).

BURY, J. B. (1861–1927).

> 1911. Notes and critical apparatus to vol. 5 of 7 of his edition of Gibbon i.1776/88, which entry should be consulted for further bibliographical detail.
>
> 1911a. "Some Questions Connected with the Rise of the Papal Power in the Eighth Century", appendix 16, pp. 568–70, in vol. 5 of 7 of his edition of Gibbon i.1776/88, which entry should be consulted for further bibliographical detail.
>
> 1912. "Authorities", appendix 1, pp. 539–54, in vol. 5 of 7 of his edition of Gibbon i.1776/88, q.v.
>
> 1923. *History of the Later Roman Empire from the death of Theodosius I to the death of Justinian* (London: Macmillan & Co.), 2 vols.

BUYTAERT, Eligius.

> 1969. "General Introduction" to *Petri Abaelardi Opera Theologica*, in 2 vols. (= *Corpus Christianorum Continuatio Mediaevalis* XI–XII; Turnhout, Belgium: Brepols, 1969), ix–xxxviii.
>
> 1969a. "Introduction" to *Theologia Christiana*, pp. 7–68 of vol. 2 (=XII) immediately preceding.

CABANIS, Pierre Jean Georges (1757–1808).

> 1802. *On the Relations between the Physical and Moral Aspects of Man*, ed. George Mora with introductions by Sergio Moravia and George Mora, trans. by Margaret Duggan Saidi of the *Rapports du physique et du moral de l'homme* of 1802 (Baltimore, MD: Johns Hopkins University Press, 1981).

CAHALAN, John C.

> 1985. *Causal Realism: An Essay on Philosophical Method and the Foundations of Knowledge* (Lanham, MD: University Press of America).
>
> 1994. "If Wittgenstein Had Read Poinsot: Recasting the Problem of Signs and Mental States", *American Catholic Philosophical Quarterly* LXVIII (Summer): 297–319.

CAJETAN, Thomas de Vio (1469–1534).

> c.1493. *Commentaria in De Ente et Essentia*, ed. M. H. Laurent (Turin, Italy: Marietti, 1934).
>
> 1498. *De Nominum Analogia*, English trans. as *The Analogy of Names and the Concept of Being* by Edward A. Bushinski in collaboration with Henry J. Koren (2nd ed.; Louvain: Naulewaerts, 1959).
>
> 1498a. *Commentaria in Praedicamenta Aristotelis* (Pavia, 9 Jan.). The ed. of M.-H. Laurent (Rome: Angelicum, 1939) was used in preparing the present work.
>
> 1503. "On the Immortality of Souls", sermon delivered in the presence of Pope Julius II on the First Sunday of Advent; trans. James K. Sheridan in *Renaissance Philosophy. New Translations*, ed. Leonard A. Kennedy (The Hague: Mouton, 1973), 46–53.
>
> 1507. *Commentaria in summam theologicam. Prima pars.* (Rome: 2 May). Repr. in Leonine edition of the *Sancti Thomae Aquinatis Doctoris Angelici Opera Omnia*, vols. 4 and 5 (Rome, 1888–9), used in preparing the present work.
>
> 1509. "The Concept of Being", letter by Cajetan dated 27 Feb. 1509, included as an appendix in the Bushinski and Koren ed. of Cajetan 1498, above, pp. 79–83.
>
> 1509a. *Super libros de Anima* (Rome).

1519. *In Epistolas Pauli* (Paris, 1532).

1527. *In Evangelia Matthei* (Gaeta).

1534. *In Ecclesiasten* (Rome, 1542).

CAMBRIDGE MEDIEVAL HISTORY.

1924– (Cambridge University Press), 8 vols.

CAMERON, Averil.

1991. *Christianity and the Rhetoric of Empire. The Development of Christian Discourse* (Berkeley: University of California Press).

CANO, Melchior (1509–60).

1563 (posthumous). *De locis theologicis libri duodecim* (Salamanca: Mathias Gastius); there have been some 30 editions of this work, the most recent being that reproduced in Migne vol. 1, cols. 58–716.

CAPELLA, Martianus Minneus Felix (c.AD360–439).

i.AD410/29. *Liber de nuptiis Mercurii et Philologiae.* This is the title quoted in AD520 by Fabius Fulgentius Planciades; the work is also sometimes known as the *Disciplinae*, as the *Satiricon*, and as the *Satyra*. Trans. in Stahl, Johnson & Burge 1977, q.v.

CAPPUYNS, Maïeul (1901–?).

1933. *Jean Scot Érigène. Sa vie, son oeuvre, sa pensée* (Paris: Descleé de Brouwer).

1937. Entry "Boèce" in *Dictionnaire d'Histoire et de Géographie Ecclésiastiques*, tome 9ème (Paris: Librarie Letouzey), cols. 347–80.

CAPREOLUS, Johannes (c.1380–1444).

1483/4 (posthumous). *Quaestiones in IV libros Sententiarum seu Libri IV Defensionum theologiae Thomae Aquinatis*, ed. Thomas de S. Germano (Venice: Octavianus Scotus), in 3 vols. Modern edition entitled *Defensiones theologiae divi Thomae Aquinatis* by Ceslaus Paban and Thomas Pègues (Tours: A. Cattier, 1900–8), in 7 vols. (repr. Frankfurt am Main: Minerva, 1967).

CAPUTO, John D. (1946–).

1982. *Heidegger and Aquinas: An Essay on Overcoming Metaphysics* (New York: Fordham).

CARLYLE, Robert Warrand (1859–1934), and Alexander James CARLYLE (1861–1943).

1903–36. *A History of Mediaeval Political Theory in the West* (Edinburgh: W. Blackwood & Sons), 6 vols.

CARNAP, Rudolf (1891–1970).

1936/7. "Testability and Meaning", *Philosophy of Science* 3.4 (October 1936), 419–71; and 4.1 (January 1937), 1–40.

CARTLEDGE, Paul

1998. *Democritus* (London: Orion Phoenix).

CASSIODORUS (c.AD487–c.580).

i.AD544/5. *Institutiones divinarum et humanorum lectionum*, trans. as *An Introduction to Divine and Human Readings* by Leslie Weber Jones (= Records of Civilization: Sources and Studies, no. XL; New York: Columbia University Press, 1946).

CASSIRER, Ernst (1874–1945).

1921. *Kants Leben und Lehre* (2nd ed.; Berlin: Bruno Cassirer), trans. James Haden as

Kant's Life and Thought (New Haven, CT: Yale University Press, 1981). Page references are to the English trans.

CASSIRER, Ernst, Paul Oskar KRISTELLER, and John Herman RANDALL, Jr, editors.

1948. *The Renaissance Philosophy of Man: Petrarca, Valla, Ficino, Pico, Pomponazzi, Vives* (Chicago: University of Chicago Press).

CAVARNOS, Constantine.

1975. *The Classical Theory of Relations. A Study in the Metaphysics of Plato, Aristotle, and Thomism* (Belmont, MA: Institute for Byzantine and Modern Greek Studies).

1989. *The Hellenic-Christian Philosophical Tradition* (Belmont, MA: Institute for Byzantine and Modern Greek Studies).

CHASTAGNOL, André.

1966. *Le Sénate Romain sous le règne d'Odoacre* (Bonn: Habelt).

CHENU, Marie-Dominique (1895–1990).

1964. *Toward Understanding St. Thomas*, trans. with authorized corrections and bibliographical additions by A.-M. Landry and D. Hughes (Chicago: Henry Regnery Co.) from *Introduction à l'étude de Saint Thomas d'Aquin* (Paris: J. Vrin, 1950).

CHEVALIER, Philippe, editor (1884–?).

1937–50. *Dionysiaca. Recueil donnant l'ensemble des traductions latines des ouvrages attribués au Denys de l'Aréopage ...* (Paris: Desclées de Brouwer & Cie), 2 vols.

CHOMSKY, Noam (1928–).

1966. *Cartesian Linguistics* (New York: Harper & Row).

1968. *Language and Mind* (New York: Harcourt Brace Jovanovich).

1972. *Language and Mind* (enlarged edition; New York: Harcourt Brace Jovanovich).

CHROUST, Anton-Hermann (1907–).

1957. *Socrates, Man and Myth. The Two Socratic Apologies of Xenophon* (Notre Dame, IN: University of Notre Dame Press).

CIAPALO, Roman (1950–).

1987. *Life (ζωή) in Plotinus' Explanation of Reality* (Chicago, IL: Loyola University, unpub. diss.).

1998. "The Oriental Influences upon Plotinus' Thought: An Assessment of the Controversy between Bréhier and Rist on the Soul's Relation to the One", in *Neoplatonism and Indian Philosophy*, ed. Paulos Mar Gregorios (Ithaca, NY: SUNY Press).

CIAPALO, Roman, editor.

1997. *Postmodernism and Christian Philosophy* (a Proceedings of the American Maritain Association; Washington, DC: Catholic University of America Press).

CICERO, Marcus Tullius (106–43BC).

51BC. *De re publica* (Cambridge, MA: Loeb Classical Library of Harvard University Press, 1928).

45BC. *De finibus* (Cambridge, MA: Loeb Classical Library of Harvard University Press, 1914).

CLARKE, W. Norris (1915–).

1952. "The Limitation of Act by Potency", *The New Scholasticism* 26: 184–9.

1959. "Infinity in Plotinus: A Reply", *Gregorianum* 40: 75–98.

1992. "The 'We Are' of Interpersonal Dialogue as the Starting Point of Metaphysics", *The Modern Schoolman* 59: 357–68. Repr. in *Explorations in Metaphysics* (Notre Dame, IN: University of Notre Dame Press, 1994), chap. 2.

CLERK, Christian.

1975. "The Cannibal Sign", *Royal Anthropological Institute News* 8: 1–3.

THE CLOUD OF UNKNOWING. See entry above for Anonymous 14th Century English Monk.

CODEX THEODOSIANUS: see Theodosian Code.

COFFEY, Peter (1876–?).

1912. *The Science of Logic* (London: Longmans, Green and Co.), 2 vols.

COLAPIETRO, Vincent (1950–).

1989. *Pierce's Approach to the Self: A Semiotic Perspective on Human Subjectivity* (Albany: State University of New York).

COLAPIETRO, Vincent (1950–), and Thomas OLSHEWSKY (1934–), editors.

1996. *Peirce's Doctrine of Signs* (Berlin: Mouton de Gruyter).

COLISH, Marcia L.

1985. *The Stoic Tradition from Antiquity to the Early Middle Ages*, in 2 vols.: I. *Stoicism in Classical Latin Literature*; II. *Stoicism in Christian Latin Thought through the Sixth Century* (Leiden: E. J. Brill, 1985). The splendor of this fine work is marred by a completely uncritical use of the term "sign" throughout the discussion of the two volumes, as if it were a Stoic carry-over into the Latin Age, which is hardly the case.

1997. *Medieval Foundations of the Western Intellectual Tradition 400–1400* (New Haven, CT: Yale University Press).

COLISSON, Robert.

1966. *Encyclopedias: Their History throughout the Ages. A Bibliographical Guide with Extensive Historical Notes to the General Encyclopedias Issued throughout the World from 350 BC to the Present Day* (2nd ed.; New York: Hafner Publishing Co.).

COLLINGWOOD, R. G. (1889–1943).

1924. *Speculum Mentis* (Oxford: Clarendon Press).

1939. *An Autobiography* (London: Oxford University Press).

COLLINS, James Daniel (1917–85).

1947. *The Thomistic Philosophy of the Angels* (Washington: Catholic University of America Press).

1954. *A History of Modern European Philosophy* (Milwaukee, WI: Bruce).

COLLINS, Arthur W.

1999. *Possible Experience: Understanding Kant's Critique of Pure Reason* (Berkeley, CA: University of California Press).

COLLIS, Maurice (1889–?).

1954 *Cortes and Montezuma* (London: Faber and Faber).

COMAS DEL BRUGAR, Miguel ('Michael Comas').

1661. *Quaestiones minoris dialecticae* (Barcelona: Antonius Lacavalleria).

CONDILLAC, Étienne Bonnot de (1715–1780).

1778. *La Logique, ou Les premiers développemens de l'art de penser* (Paris: Chez Petit

Libraire, 1780); presented in bilingual format with facing French-English pages in the English trans. by W. R. Albury as *Logic* (New York: Abaris Books, Inc., 1980). Albury ("Introduction", p. 15) gives 1778 as the date of the sending of the completed ms. to the publisher, so I have used this as the reference date in preference to the publication date, which was in late August of 1780, Condillac having died on the 2nd of that same month.

u.1779. *La Langue des Calculs*, texte étabile et présenté par Anne-Marie Chouillet, introduction et notes de Sylvain Auroux (Lille, France: Presses Universitaires de Lille, 1981); based on Tome XXIII of the *Oeuvres Complètes de Condillac* (Paris: Houel, 1798). Auroux says, concerning the "*datation*" of the text (p. XXXVIII): "La question du *terminus ad quem* de la rédaction est aussi peu claire. ... Il est donc possible que Condillac ait abandonné la redaction ... dès le début 1779", whence I affix the "until" (*usque*) 1779 date used here for historically layering this reference.

CONIMBRICENSES.

1607. "De signis", being chapter 1 of their commentary on Aristotle's *De Interpretatione*, in *Commentarii Collegii Conimbricensis et Societatis Jesu. In Universam Dialecticam Aristotelis Stagiritae. Secunda Pars* (Lyons: Sumptibus Horatii Cardon, 1607), 4–67. An earlier edition minus the Greek text of Aristotle was published at Coimbra itself in 1606.

COOMBS, Jeffrey.

1996. "Modal Voluntarism in Descartes' Jesuit Predecessors", *ACPA Proceedings* LXXI (1996).

COPERNICUS (1473–1543).

c.1514. *Nicolai Copernici de hypothesibus motuum coelestium a se constitutis commentariolus*, circulated in ms. but never published in Copernicus' lifetime; in Rosen ed. 1939.

1543. Originally completed in 1530, the book was first published as *Nicolai Copernici revolutionum liber primus* (Nuremberg), with an unsigned preface inserted by Andreas Osiander; the work later came to be called *De revolutionibus orbium coelestium*. English trans. with commentary: Edward Rosen, *Nicholas Copernicus On the Revolutions* (Baltimore, MD: Johns Hopkins University Press, 1992).

CORRIGAN, Kevin.

1996. *Plotinus' Theory of Matter-Evil and the Question of Substance: Plato, Aristotle, and Alexander of Aphrodisias* (Leuven: Peeters).

CORRINGTON, Robert (1950–).

1992. *Nature and Spirit. An Essay in Ecstatic Naturalism* (New York: Fordham University Press).

1993. *An Introduction to C. S. Peirce: Philosopher, Semiotician, Ecstatic Naturalist* (Lanham, MD: Rowman & Littlefield).

1994. *Ecstatic Naturalism: The Signs of the World* (Bloomington: Indiana University Press).

CORTI, Maria.

1973. "Le jeu comme génération du texte: des tarots au récit", *Semiotica* 7.1: 33–48.

COTTINGHAM, John (1943–), Robert STOOTHOFF, and Dugald MURDOCH (1944–),
translators.

1985. *The Philosophical Writings of Descartes* (Cambridge, Eng.: Cambridge University
Press), 2 vols.

COURCELLE, Pierre (1912–).

1943. *Les lettres grecques en Occident de Macrobe à Cassiodore* (Paris: E. de Boccard),
trans. as *Late Latin Writers and Their Greek Sources* by H. E. Wedeck (Cambridge,
MA: Harvard University Press, 1969).

1950. *Recherches sur les Confessions de saint Augustine* (Paris: E. de Boccard).

1968. 2nd ed. of 1950; same publisher.

COUSIN, Victor, editor (1792–1867).

1836. *Ouvrages inédits d'Abélard pour servir a l'histoire de la philosophie scholastique
en France* (Paris: Imprimerie Royale).

COUSINS, Ewert.

1978. Translation and intro. to *Bonaventure: The Soul's Journey to God; The Tree of Life;
The Life of St. Francis* (New York: Paulist Press). In this work *The Soul's Journey*
(the *Itinerarum Mentis* of Bonaventure 1259) occupies pp. 51–116.

CROMBIE, I. M.

1962. *An Examination of Plato's Doctrine* (London: Routledge & Kegan Paul), 2 vols.
Vol. 1, 9–14, contains a discussion of the chronology of Plato's writings.

CROWLEY, B. (1914–).

1948. "The Life and Works of Bartholomew Mastrius, O.F.M. Conv. 1602–1673", *Franciscan Studies* 8: 97–152.

CUMMINS, Phillip D., and Guenter ZOELLER, editors.

1992. *Minds, Ideas, and Objects: Essays on the Theory of Representation in Modern
Philosophy* (Atascadero, CA: Ridgeview Publishing Co.).

CURD, Patricia.

1998. *The Legacy of Parmenides: Eleatic Monism and Later Presocratic Thought* (Princeton, NJ: Princeton University Press).

CURLEY, Edwin (1937–).

1988. "Editorial preface" to Spinoza i.1662/76: 401–5.

CURLEY, Edwin, editor and translator.

1988. *The Collected Works of Spinoza*, vol. 1, ed. and trans. Edwin Curley (corrected 2nd
printing; Princeton, NJ: Princeton University Press).

CUVIER, Baron George Leopold (1769–1832).

1818. *Essay on the theory of the earth* (New York: Kirk & Mercein), being the translation
by Robert Kerr (1755–1813) of *Discours sur les révolutions de la surface du globe*,
with mineralogical notes and an account of Cuvier's geological discoveries by
Robert Jameson (1774–1854), and observations on the geology of North America,
illustrated by the description of various organic remains found in that part of the
world by Samuel L. Mitchill (1764–1831); the French *Discours* was originally but
the introduction to Cuvier's much larger work, *Recherches sur les ossemens fossiles
des quadrupèdes, où l'on rétablit les caractères de plusieurs espèces d'animaux que*

les révolutions du globe paroissent avoir détruits (Paris, 1812; facsimile reprint, Brussels: Culture et Civilisation, 1969), in 4 vols, which grew ever larger in two subsequent editions.

Rudwick 1997: xi has criticized the Kerr translation as "often misleading and in places downright bad", and offers himself "a completely new translation into modern English" (see pp. 183–252). The passage quoted on p. 656 above at note 132 can be compared with the version in Rudwick 1997: 219.

DAVENPORT, Ernest Harold (1893–?).

1916. *The False Decretals* (Oxford: B. H. Blackwell).

DAVIDSON, Thomas (1848–1930).

1870. "Parmenides", historical article with original trans. of the fragments, *Journal of Speculative Philosophy*, ed. William T. Harris (St Louis) IV: 1–16.

DAWSON, Christopher (1889–1970).

1910. "Introduction" to Everyman's Library edition of Gibbon i.1776/88: v–xi.

1932. *The Making of Europe* (reprint ed.; New York: Barnes & Noble).

1954. *Medieval Essays* (New York: Sheed & Ward).

DE RIJK, Lambert Marie.

1964. "On the chronology of Boethius' works on logic I & II", *Vivarium* II.1 & 2 (May and November): 1–49 and 125–62, respectively.

1970. "Introduction" to the 2nd rev. ed. of Abaelard i.1135/7: vii–ciii.

DEANDREA, P. Marianus.

1957. *Praelectiones Metaphysicae juxt principia D. Thomae. II. De entis distinctione; De causis* (ad usum privatum auditorum; Rome: Angelicum).

DECKER, Bruno, editor.

1965. Critical apparatus, notes, etc. to *Sancti Thomae de Aquino Expositio super librum Boethii De Trinitate* (Leiden).

DEELY, John (1942–).

1965/6. "Evolution: Concept and Content", Part I, *Listening* vol. 0, No. 0 (Autumn 1965), 27–50; Part II, *Listening* 1.1 (Winter 1966): 35–66.

1966. "The Emergence of Man: An Inquiry into the Operation of Natural Selection in the Making of Man", *The New Scholasticism* XL.2 (April): 141–76.

1967. "Finitude, Negativity, and Transcendence: The Problematic of Metaphysical Knowledge", *Philosophy Today* XI.3/4 (Fall): 184–206.

1969. "The Philosophical Dimensions of the Origin of Species", *The Thomist* XXXIII (January and April) Part I, 75–149, Part II, 251–342.

1971. "Animal Intelligence and Concept-Formation", *The Thomist* XXXV.1 (January): 43–93.

1971a. *The Tradition via Heidegger* (The Hague: Martinus Nijhoff).

1973. "The Impact of Evolution on Scientific Method", in *The Problem of Evolution*, ed. J. N. Deely and R. J. Nogar (New York: Appleton-Century-Crofts; Indianapolis: Hackett Publishing Co.), 3–82; previously pub. in a two-part Italian trans. by P. Bonzani as "Evoluzione biologica e teoria della scienza", *Renovatio* V nos. 3 & 4 (Fall and Winter 1970), Part I, 404–18, Part II, 534–46.

1975. "Reference to the Non-Existent", *The Thomist* XXXIX.2 (April): 253–308.

1975a. "'Semeiotica': Dottrina dei segni", *Renovatio* X.4 (ottobre-dicembre): 472–90.

1975b. "Modern Logic, Animal Psychology, and Human Discourse", *Revue de l'Université d'Ottawa* 45.1 (janvier-mars): 80–100.

1976. "The Doctrine of Signs: Taking Form at Last", *Semiotica* 18.2: 171–93. Essay review of Eco 1976.

1977. "'Semiotic' as the Doctrine of Signs", *Ars Semeiotica* 1.3: 41–68.

1977a. "Metaphysics, Modern Thought, and 'Thomism'", *Notes et Documents* 8 (juillet-septembre): 12–18.

1978. "What's in a Name?", *Semiotica* 22.1–2: 151–181 (essay review of Sebeok 1976).

1978a. "Toward the Origin of Semiotic", in *Sight, Sound, and Sense*, ed. T. A. Sebeok (Bloomington: Indiana University Press), 1–30.

1978b. "Semiotic and the Controversy over Mental Events", *ACPA Proceedings* LII: 16–27.

1980. "Antecedents to Peirce's Notion of Iconic Signs", in *Semiotics 1980*, comp. Margot D. Lenhart and Michael Herzfeld (New York: Plenum), 109–20.

1980a. "The Nonverbal Inlay in Linguistic Communication", in *The Signifying Animal*, ed. Irmengard Rauch and Gerald F. Carr (Bloomington: Indiana University Press), 201–17.

1981. "Cognition from a Semiotic Point of View", in *Semiotics 1981*, ed. John N. Deely and Margot D. Lenhart (New York: Plenum), 21–8.

1982. *Introducing Semiotic: Its History and Doctrine* (Bloomington: Indiana University Press); trans. by Vivina de Campos Figueiredo as *Introdução à Semiótica: Historia e doutrina* (Lisbon, Portugal: Fundação Calouste Gulbenkian, 1995).

1982a. "On the Notion 'Doctrine of Signs'", appendix I in Deely 1982: 127–30.

1982b. "On the Notion of Phytosemiotics", in *Semiotics 1982*, ed. John Deely and Jonathan Evans (Lanham, MD: University Press of America, 1987), 541–54; repr. with minor revision in Deely, Williams, and Kruse eds 1986: 96–103.

1984. "Semiotic as Framework and Direction", paper presented at 1984 "Semiotics: Field or Discipline" State-of-the-Art Conference organized by Michael Herzfeld at the Bloomington campus of Indiana University, 8–10 October 1984, and subsequently pub. in Deely, Williams, and Kruse eds 1986: text 264–71, notes 287–8.

1985. "Editorial AfterWord" and critical apparatus to *Tractatus de Signis: The Semiotic of John Poinsot* (Berkeley: University of California Press), 391–514; electronic version hypertext-linked (Charlottesville, VA: Intelex Corp., 1992; see entry under Poinsot 1632a below).

1985a. *Logic as a Liberal Art* (Victoria College, University of Toronto: Toronto Semiotic Circle publication series, No. 3; prepub. of Part I of a 3-part monograph under contract with Indiana University Press).

1985b. "Semiotic and the Liberal Arts", *The New Scholasticism* LIX.3 (Summer), 296–322. The "second epsilon" mentioned in this work is a blunder, for the "first epsilon" in the Greek "semeiotic" is not an epsilon but an eta, thus: Σημειωτική.

1986. "Semiotic in the Thought of Jacques Maritain", *Recherche Sémiotique/Semiotic Inquiry* 6.2: 1–30.

1986a. "Doctrine", terminological entry for the *Encyclopedic Dictionary of Semiotics*, ed. Thomas A. Sebeok et al. (Berlin: Mouton de Gruyter), tome I, 214.

1986b. "John Locke's Place in the History of Semiotic Inquiry", in *Semiotics 1986*, ed. John Deely and Jonathan Evans (Lanham, MD: University Press of America), 406–18.

1986c. "A Context for Narrative Universals", *American Journal of Semiotics* 4.3/4, 53–68.

1986d. "Idolum. Archeology and Ontology of the Iconic Sign", in *Iconicity: Essays on the Nature of Culture*, Festschrift volume in honor of Thomas A Sebeok, ed. Paul Bouissac, Michael Herzfeld, and Roland Posner (Tübingen: Stauffenburg Verlag), 29–49.

1986e. "The Coalescence of Semiotic Consciousness", in Deely, Williams, and Kruse eds 1986: 5–34.

1987. "On the Problem of Interpreting the Term 'First' in the Expression 'First Philosophy'", in *Semiotics 1987*, ed. J. Deely (Lanham, MD: University Press of America), 3–14; "Maxim for Semiotics", pp. iii–vi.

1988. "The Semiotic of John Poinsot: Yesterday and Tomorrow", *Semiotica* 69.1/2 (April 1988): 31–128.

1989. "The Grand Vision", presented on 8 September at the 5–10 September Charles Sanders Peirce Sesquicentennial International Congress at Harvard University, in Colapietro and Olshewsky eds 1996: 45–67. This essay was first published in the *Transactions of the Charles S. Peirce Society* XXX.2 (Spring 1994): 371–400, but, inexplicably, after the submission of corrected proofs, the journal repaged the whole and introduced such extreme errors as to make the text unreadable at some points. The correct version has appeared as chap. 7 of Deely 1994a: 183–200.

1990. "Logic within Semiotics", in *Symbolicity*, ed. Jeff Bernard, John Deely, Terry Prewitt, Vilmos Voigt, and Gloria Withalm (Lanham, MD: University Press of America, 1993), 77–86; *Symbolicity* is bound together with *Semiotics 1990*, ed. Karen Haworth, John Deely, and Terry Prewitt, as a single vol.

1990a. *Basics of Semiotics* (Bloomington: Indiana University Press).

1991. "Semiotics and Biosemiotics: Are Sign-Science and Life-Science Coextensive?", in *Biosemiotics: The Semiotic Web 1991*, ed. Thomas A. Sebeok and Jean Umiker-Sebeok (Berlin: Mouton de Gruyter, 1992), 45–75. Since revised as chap. 6 "How Do Signs Work?" in Deely 1994a: 151–82.

1992. "From Glassy Essence to Bottomless Lake", in *Semiotics 1992*, ed. J. Deely (Lanham, MD: University Press of America), 151–8.

1992a. "Philosophy and Experience", *American Catholic Philosophical Quarterly* LXVI.4 (Winter): 299–319.

1992b. "The Supplement of the Copula", *Review of Metaphysics* 46.2 (December): 251–77.

1993. "Locke's Proposal for Semiotics and the Scholastic Doctrine of Species", *The Modern Schoolman* LXX.3 (March): 165–88.

1993a. "How Does Semiosis Effect Renvoi?", Thomas A. Sebeok Fellowship Inaugural Lecture delivered at the 18th Annual Meeting of the Semiotic Society of America, 22 Oct. 1993, St Louis, MO; published in *The American Journal of Semiotics* 11.1/2 (1994), 11–61; text available also as chap. 8 of Deely 1994a: 201–44.

1994. *The Human Use of Signs; or Elements of Anthroposemiosis* (Lanham, MD: Rowman & Littlefield).

1994a. *New Beginnings: Early Modern Philosophy and Postmodern Thought* (Toronto: University of Toronto Press).

1994b. "What Happened to Philosophy between Aquinas and Descartes?", *The Thomist* 58.4: 543–68.

1994c. "Why Investigate the Common Sources of Charles Peirce and John Poinsot?", in *Semiotics 1994*, ed. C. W. Spinks and John Deely (New York: Peter Lang Publishing, 1995), 34–50.

1994d. "Membra Ficte Disjecta (A Disordered Array of Severed Limbs)", editorial introduction to the electronic edition of Peirce i.1866/1913; see the *Note* on "the designation CP" beginning the PEIRCE entry, below (1 June; Charlottesville, VA: Intelex Corp.).

1995. "Quid Sit Postmodernismus?", in Ciapalo ed. 1997: 68–96. An essay on the work of Étienne Gilson and Jacques Maritain in relation to Poinsot.

1995a. "Ferdinand de Saussure and Semiotics", in *Ensaios em Homagem a Thomas A. Sebeok*, quadruple special issue of *Cruzeiro Semiótico*, ed. Norma Tasca (Porto, Portugal: Fundação Eng. António de Almeida), 75–85. Revised text appears under same title in *Semiotics 1995*, ed. C. W. Spinks and John Deely (New York: Peter Lang, 1996), 71–83.

1996. "The Seven Deadly Sins and the Catholic Church", pre-publication of the Centro Internazionale di Semiotica e di Linguistica (Università du Urbino, Italia; 250–1 gennaio-febbraio; serie A); definitive text in *Semiotica* 117.2/4 (1997), 67–102.

1996a. "A New Beginning for the Sciences", in *Semiotics as a Bridge between the Humanities and the Sciences*, ed. Paul Perron, Leonard G. Sbrocchi, Paul Colilli, John Wattanabee, and Marcel Danesi (proceedings of the 2–6 Nov. 1995 symposium organized at Victoria University by Prof. Danesi; Ottawa: Legas Press, 2000), pp. 103–16.

1996b. *Los Fundamentos de la Semiótica*, trans. José Luis Caivano (Mexico City, Mexico: Universidad Iberoamericana). An expanded text of Deely 1990a.

1996c. "The Four Ages of Understanding between Ancient Physics and Postmodern Semiotics", in *Semiotics 1996*, ed. C. W. Spinks and John Deely (New York: Peter Lang, 1997), 229–39.

1997. "How is the Universe Perfused with Signs?", in *Semiotics 1997*, ed. C. W. Spinks and John Deely (New York: Peter Lang, 1999), 389–94.

1998. "Physiosemiosis and Semiotics", in *Semiotics 1988*, ed. C. W. Spinks and John Deely (New York: Peter Lang, 1999), 191–7.

2000. *What Distinguishes Human Understanding* (South Bend, IN: St Augustine's Press).

DEELY, John N., and Raymond J. NOGAR.

   1973. *The Problem of Evolution: Philosophical Repercussions of Evolutionary Science*
   (New York: Appleton-Century-Crofts).

DEELY, John, and Anthony F. RUSSELL.

   1986. "Francis Bacon", bibliographical entry for *Encyclopedic Dictionary of Semiotics*,
   Thomas A. Sebeok, general editor (Berlin: Mouton de Gruyter), tome 1: 68–70.

DEELY, John N., Brooke WILLIAMS, and Felicia E. KRUSE, editors.

   1986. *Frontiers in Semiotics* (Bloomington: Indiana University Press). Preface, "Pars Pro
   Toto", viii–xvii; "Description of Contributions", xviii–xxii.

DEICHGRÄBER, Karl (1903–?).

   1933. "Hymnische Elemente in der philosophischen Prosa der Vorsokratiker", *Philologus*
   88: 347–61.

DeKONINCK, Charles (1905–63).

   1935. *Le problème de l'indéterminisme* (Québec: Académie Canadienne Saint-Thomas
   d'Aquin, sixième session), 65–159.

   1937. "Réflexions sur le problème de l'indéterminisme" *Revue Thomiste* XLIII nos. 2 &
   3, 227–52 & 393–409.

DELEDALLE, Gérard.

   1992. "Peirce's Sign: Its Concept and Its Use", *Transactions of the Charles S. Peirce
   Society* (Spring), XXVIII.2: 289–301.

   1990. "Traduire Charles S. Peirce. Le *signe*: le concept et son usage", *TTR: Traduction,
   Terminologie, Rédaction* 3.1 (Trois-Rivières: Université du Québec): 15–29.

   1987. "Quelle philosophie pour la sémiotique peircienne? Peirce et la sémiotique grecque",
   Semiotica 63.3/4: 241–51.

   1980. "Avertissement aux lecteurs de Peirce", *Langages* 58 (June): 25–7.

   1980a. "Les articles pragmatistes de Charles S. Peirce", *Revue philosophique* CLXX:
   17–29. See gloss on 1981 entry following.

   1981. English and French versions of C. S. Peirce's "The Fixation of Belief" and "How
   To Make Our Ideas Clear", *Transactions of the Charles S. Peirce Society* (Spring)
   XVII.2: 141–52. This article is substantially and essentially the English equivalent
   of the 1980a entry preceding.

DEMOCRITUS (c.460–c.362BC).

   Date for writing based on the prime assigned by Freeman 1966a: 289.

   c.420BC. Fragments in Freeman 1966: 91–120.

DERRIDA, Jacques (1930–).

   1967. *De Grammatologie* (Paris: Éditions de Minuit, trans. Gayatri Chakravorty Spivak
   as *Of Grammatology* (Baltimore, MD: Johns Hopkins University Press, 1974,
   1976.

   1968. "Différance", address to the Société Française de Philosophie, 27 Jan. 1968, as
   repr. in *The Margins of Philosophy* (New York: Harvester Wheatsheaf, 1982),
   3–27, being Alan Bass's trans. of *Marges de la Philosophie* (Paris: Éditions de
   Minuit, 1972).

DESCARTES, René (1596–1650).

1628. *Rules for the Direction of the Mind*, trans. Dugald Murdoch in Cottingham, Stoothoff, and Murdoch trans. 1985: I, 9–78.

1637. *Discourse on the Method of rightly conducting one's reason and seeking truth in the sciences*, trans. Robert Stoothoff in Cottingham, et al. 1985: I, 111–51.

1641. *Meditations on First Philosophy*, trans. John Cottingham in Cottingham, et al. 1985: II, 3–62.

1644. *Principles of Philosophy*, in Cottingham, et al. 1985: I, 179–291.

DESCOMBES, Vincent.

1981 *Le Même et l'Autre* (Paris: Minuit).

DEWEY, John (1859–1952).

1909. "Darwin's Influence upon Philosophy", in *Popular Science Monthly* LXXV (July–December; ed. J McKeen Cattell), 90–8.

1910. *The Influence of Darwin on Philosophy*, a collection of essays (New York: Henry Holt and Co.).

DIELS, Hermann (1848–1922), and Walther KRANZ (1884–1960), editors. (The first four editions of this work were edited by Diels alone.)

1951. *Die Fragmente der Vorsokratiker* (6th ed., rev., with additions and index by Kranz; Berlin: Weidmann), 3 vols.

DILL, Samuel (1844–1924).

1958. *Roman Society in the Last Century of the Western Empire* (2nd rev. ed.; New York: Meridian).

DIOGENES LAERTIUS: see under Laertius.

DIONYSIUS THE AREOPAGITE: see under Pseudo-Dionysius.

DIRDA, Michael.

1995. Review of novel by Umberto Eco, *The Island of the Day Before*, in *Washington Post Book World*, 22 October.

DITTMAR, Heinrich (1870–?).

1912. *Aischenes von Sphettos*, Studien zur Literaturgeschichte der Sokratiker; Untersuchungen und Fragmente ed. Heinrich Dittmar (Berlin: Weidmann).

DOBROLIUBOV, Aleksandr (1876–1944).

1895. *Natura Naturans. Natura Naturata*, as repr. together with *Sobranie Stixov* (1900) in *Sochineniia*, with intro. by Joan Delaney Grossman (Studies and Texts in Modern Russian Literature and Culture, vol. 10; Berkeley: Berkeley Slavic Specialties, 1981).

DODDS, Eric Robertson (1893–1979).

1963. Trans. of, intro. to, and commentary on Proclus c.450.

DONATUS, Aelius (c.AD310–c.380: see chapter 9 above, p. 436n62).

Dating based on Holtz 1981: esp. 18–19.

a.AD349. *Ars Donati Grammatici Urbis Romae Edition Prima, De Partibus Orationis (Ars Minor)*, critical ed. in Holtz 1981: 585–602; for English, see *De Partibus Orationis Ars Minor* ed. and trans. Wayland Johnson Chase as *The Ars Minor of Donatus* (Madison: University of Wisconsin Press, 1926).

p.AD349. *Ars Major I, II, II* in Holtz 1981: 603–74.

DOYLE, John P. (1930–).

1984. "The Conimbricenses on the Relations Involved in Signs", in *Semiotics 1984*, ed. John Deely (Proceedings of 9th annual meeting of Semiotic Society of America; Lanham, MD: University Press of America, 1985), 567–76.

1987. "Suárez on Beings of Reason and Truth (1)", *Vivarium* XXV.1: 47–76.

1988. "Suárez on Beings of Reason and Truth (2)", *Vivarium* XXVI.1; 51–72.

1990. "'Extrinsic Cognoscibility': A Seventeenth Century Supertranscendental Notion", *The Modern Schoolman* LXVIII (November): 57–80.

1994. "Poinsot on the Knowability of Beings of Reason", in *American Catholic Philosophical Quarterly* LXVIII. 3 (Summer 1994): 337–62.

1997. "Between Transcendental and Transcendental: The Missing Link?", *The Review of Metaphysics* 50 (June): 783–815.

1998. "The Conimbricenses on the Semiotic Character of Mirror Images", *The Modern Schoolman* LXXVI (November): 17–31.

DRAKE, Stillman, translator and editor.

1957. *Discoveries and Opinions* (Garden City, NY: Doubleday). Translations of selections from Galileo's chief works, with intros.

DRUART, Thérèse-Anne.

1994. "Averroes: The Commentator and the Commentators", in *Aristotle in Late Antiquity*, ed. Lawrence P. Schrenk (Washington: Catholic University of America Press, 1994), 184–202.

DRUART, Thérèse-Anne, guest-editor.

1991. *Medieval Islamic Thought*, a special issue of the *American Catholic Philosophical Quarterly* LXXIII.1 (Winter).

DUCHESNE, Louis (1843–1922).

1898. *Les premiers temps de l'état pontifical* (Paris: A. Fontemoing), authorized trans. Arnold Harris Matthew as *The Beginnings of the Temporal Sovereignty of the Popes, A.D. 754–1073* (London: Kegan Paul, Trench, Trubner & Co., 1908).

DURANT, Will (1885–1981).

1935. *Our Oriental Heritage. Being a history of civilization in Egypt and the Near East to the death of Alexander, and in India, China and Japan from the beginning to our own day; with an introduction on the nature and foundations of civilization* (= *The Story of Civilization: Part I*; New York: Simon and Schuster).

1944. *Caesar and Christ. A History of Roman Civilization and of Christianity from Their Beginnings to A.D. 325* (= *The Story of Civilization: Part II*; New York: Simon and Schuster).

1950. *The Age of Faith. A History of Medieval Civilization – Christian, Islamic, and Judaic – from Constantine to Dante: A.D. 325–1300* (= *The Story of Civilization: Part IV*; New York: Simon and Schuster).

EASTON, Stewart C. (1907–).

1952. *Roger Bacon and His Search for a Univocal Science: A reconsideration of the life and work of Roger Bacon in the light of his own stated purposes* (London; repr. New York: Russell and Russell, 1971).

ECO, Umberto (1932–).

   1968. *La Struttura Assente. Introduzione alla ricerca semiologica* (Milan: Casa editrice
       Valentino Bompiani & C. S.p.A.).

   1972. "Social Life as a Sign System", in *Structuralism: An Introduction*, ed. David Robey
       (Oxford: Clarendon Press), 57–72.

   1975. *Trattato di semiotica generale* (Milan: Bompiani).

   1976. *A Theory of Semiotics*, trans. David Osmond-Smith (Bloomington: Indiana Univer-
       sity Press). Reviewed in Deely 1976.

   1977. "The Code: Metaphor or Interdisciplinary Category?", in *Yale Italian Studies* 1.1
       (Winter): 24–52.

   1984. *Semiotics and the Philosophy of Language* (Bloomington: Indiana University
       Press).

   1984a. "On Fish and Buttons: Semiotics and Philosophy of Language", *Semiotica* 48.1/2,
       97–117.

   1989. *The Open Work*, trans. Anna Concogni (Cambridge, MA: Harvard University Press).

   1990. *The Limits of Interpretation* (Bloomington: Indiana University Press).

   2000. *Kant and the Platypus. Essays on Language and Cognition* (New York: Harcourt,
       Brace & Co.), English trans. in consultation with the author by Alastair McEwen
       of *Kant e l'ornitorinco* (Milano: Bompiani, 1997).

ECO, Umberto, Roberto LAMBERTINI, Costantino MARMO, and Andrea TABARRONI.

   1986. "Latratus Canis or: The Dog's Barking", in Deely, Williams, and Kruse eds 1986:
       63–73; see editorial note on provenance of this text, ibid. p. xix.

EERDMANN, J. E., and VOLLBRECHT, editors.

   1959. *Gottfried Wilhelm Leibniz Opera Philosohica quae extant latina gallica germanica
       Omnia*, Instruxit J. E. Eerdmann, Faksimiledruck der Ausgabe 1840 durch weitere
       Teststücke ergänzt und mit einem Vorwort versehen von Renate Vollbrecht, Mit
       einer Wiedergabe des einzigen signierten Originalporträts des Philosophen von
       Scheits (Germany: Scientia Aalen).

EISELEY, Loren (1907–77).

   1958. *The Immense Journey* (London: Gollancz).

EMPEDOCLES (c.495–c.435BC).

       Date for writing based on the prime assigned by Freeman 1966a: 172. But take
       note of the argument in Owens 1959: 417–419 (see chapter 2 above, p. 28n30) that
       the correct span should be earlier, to wit, 521–461BC.

   c.450BC. See *The Poem of Empedocles* in the edition of Inwood 1992. Fragments also in
       Freeman 1966: 51–69.

EPICURUS OF SAMOS (341–270BC).

       Note: Since I have made no detailed reference to this author's writings, I have made
       no breakdown of their dating, but indicate only the most readily available English
       version of his works.

   a.270BC. "The Extant Writings of Epicurus", trans. C. Bailey, in Oates ed. 1940: 1–66,
       q.v.

ERIGENA, John Scotus (c.AD810–c.877): see under Scotus Erigena.

ERIUGENA, John Scotus: see under Scotus Erigena.

ESCHBACH, Achim, and Jürgen TRABANT, editors.

1983. *History of Semiotics* (= Foundations of Semiotics, vol. 7) (Amsterdam: John Benjamins).

EUSEBIUS Pamphili (c.AD260–c.340).

i.AD312/24. *Historia Ecclesiastica*, in 10 books; Greek text with French trans. by Gustave Bardy *Histoire ecclésiastique* (Paris: Éditions du Cerf, 1952–71), in 4 vols. In English I consulted *The Church History of Eusebius*, trans. Arthur Cushman McGiffert in *A Select Library of Nicene and Post-Nicene Fathers of the Christian Church, Second Series*, under general editorship of Philip Schaff and Henry Wace, vol. I, *Eusebius* (New York: Charles Scribner's Sons, 1904), 73–404, incl. supplementary notes and tables after p. 387.

c.AD313. *The Martyrs of Palestine* (*Les Martyrs en Palestine*, in vol. 3 of Bardy, preceding entry, 121–74).

c.AD339. *The Life of the Blessed Emperor Constantine*, in 4 books, from AD306–37, rev. English trans. Ernest Cushing Richardson in Schaff and Wace 1904 vol. cited in first part of this entry, pp. 473–559. Of this *Vita* by Eusebius (which quietly suppresses without a mention Constantine's execution of his son Crispus and his wife Fausta, as it suppresses other murders of Constantine's later years), Ricciotti (1959: 67) well says: "It is not really a biography in the modern sense of the word but a panegyric which shows all the good points of its subject and omits everything which might be to its detriment. It was a common literary form of the times called an encomium, ἐγκώμιον .... Custom allowed works of this kind and Eusebius followed the custom."

FABRO, Cornelio.

1961. *Participation et Causalité selon S. Thomas d'Aquin* (Louvain & Paris: Nauwelarts).

FANN, K. T. (1937–), editor.

1967. *Ludwig Wittgenstein: The Man and His Philosophy* (New York: Dell).

FANTOLI, Annibale (1924–).

1996. *Galileo. For Copernicanism and for the Church*, trans. George V. Coyne (2nd ed., rev. and corr.; Rome: Vatican Observatory Publications).

FAVARO, Antonio (1847–1922).

1890–1909. *Le Opere di Galileo Galilei*, edizione nazionale sotto gli auspicii di Sau Maestà il re d'Italia (Firenze: Giunti Barèra; ristampa 1929–39).

FERRARIENSIS, Francisco de Sylvestris ("Francesco Silvestri", 1474–1528).

1524. *In libros s. Thomae Aquinatis Contra Gentiles Commentaria* (Venice); repr. in *Sancti Thomae Aquinatis Doctoris Angelici Opera Omnia*, ed. Leonine vols. XIII, XIV, and XV (Rome: Typis Riccardi Garroni, 1918–30).

FERRATER MORA, José (1912–).

1953. "Suárez and Modern Philosophy", *Journal of the History of Ideas* XIV.4 (October): 528–47.

FERREIRA GOMES, Joaquim.

1964. Introdução, Estabelecimento do Texto, Tradução e Notas for Fonseca 1564.

FIELD, G. C. (1887–1955).

1967. *Plato and His Contemporaries: A Study in Fourth-Century Life and Thought* (3rd ed.; London: Methuen & Co. Ltd.).

FIGUEIREDO, Vivino de Campos.

1995. Translator's note to *Introdução à Semiótica* (Lisbon: Fundação Calouste Gulbenkian), Portuguese version, rev. and expanded, of Deely 1982.

FISCH, Max H. (1900–95).

1967. "Peirce's Progress from Nominalism toward Realism", *The Monist* 51: 159–78; repr. in Fisch 1986a: 184–200.

1978. "Peirce's General Theory of Signs", in *Sight, Sound, and Sense*, ed. Thomas A. Sebeok (Bloomington: Indiana University Press), 31–70.

1986. Review of 1985 Deely edition of Poinsot's 1632 *Tractatus de Signis* in *New Vico Studies*, ed. Giorgio Tagliacozzo and Donald Phillip Verene (New York: Humanities Press International, Inc., for The Institute for Vico Studies), vol. IV, 178–82.

1986a. *Peirce, Semeiotic, and Pragmatism. Essays by Max H. Fisch*, ed. Kenneth L. Ketner and Christian J. W. Kloesel (Bloomington: Indiana University Press).

1986b. "Philodemus and Semeiosis (1879–1883)", sect. 5 (pp. 329–30) of the essay "Peirce's General Theory of Signs" reprinted Fisch 1986a (preceding entry): 321–56.

FISCH, Max H., Kenneth Laine KETNER, and Christian J. W. KLOESEL.

1979. "The New Tools of Peirce Scholarship, with Particular Reference to Semiotic", in *Peirce Studies* 1 (Lubbock, TX: Institute for Studies in Pragmaticism): 1–17.

FITZGERALD, Desmond J. (1924–).

1986. "The Semiotic of John Poinsot", paper on the *Tractatus* in *Semiotics 1986* (Proceedings of 11th annual meeting of Semiotic Society of America), ed. John Deely and Jonathan Evans (Lanham, MD: University Press of America, 1987), 430–33.

1986a. "John Poinsot's *Tractatus de Signis*", *Journal of the History of Philosophy* XXVI.1 (January): 146–9.

FLOSS, Henricus Josephus (1819–81), editor.

1853. *Joannis Scoti [Eriginae] Opera quae supersunt omnia ad fidem Italicorum, Germanicorum, Belgicorum, Franco-Gallicorum, Britannicorum Codicum, partim primus edidit, partim recognovit* (Paris: J.-P. Migne).

FONSECA, Petrus ("Pedro da").

1564. *Institutionum dialecticarum libri octo* (Coimbra: Apud haeredes Joannis Blauij). The most important edition of this work thus far is the bilingual presentation comparable to Poinsot 1632 of Joaquim Ferreira Gomes, *Instituicoes Dialecticas (Institutionum dialecticarum libri octo)*, 2 vols. (Instituto de Estudos Filosoficos da Universidad de Coimbra, 1964).

FOOTE, Edward T.

1940. "Anatomy of Analogy", *The Modern Schoolman* XVIII.1 (November): 12–16.

FORLIVESI, Marco.

1993. *Conoscenza e Affettività. L'incontro con l'essere secondo Giovanni di San Tommaso* (Bologna, Italia: Edizioni Studio Domenicano).

1994. "Le Edizioni del *Cursus Theologicus* di Joannes a Sancto Thoma", *Divus Thomas* 9.3 (Anno 97°, Settembre–Dicembre), 9–56.

FOSCARINI, Paolo (c.1565–1616).

1615. *Concerning the Opinion of the Pythagoreans and Copernicus About the Mobility of the Earth and the Stability of the Sun and the New Pythagorean System of the World, in which it is shown that that opinion agrees with, and is reconciled with, the passages of Sacred Scripture and theological propositions which are commonly adduced against it*, a letter to Fr. Sebastiano Fantone, General of the Franciscan Order, dated 6 January, published and circulated from Naples in booklet form; trans. and included as Appendix VI in Blackwell 1991: 217–51.

FOURNIER, Paul (1853–1935).

1906–7. "Etude sur les fausses décrétales", *Revue d'Histoire Ecclésiastique* VII (1906): 33–51, 301–16, 543–64, 761–84; VIII (1907): 19–56.

FRANKFORT, Henri (1897–1954), editor.

1946. *The Intellectual Adventure of Ancient Man* (Chicago: University of Chicago Press).

FRASER, Alexander Campbell (1819–1914).

1894. "Prolegomena", notes, and critical apparatus to edition of *John Locke, An Essay concerning Human Understanding* (Oxford).

FREDE, Michael.

1974. *Die Stoische Logik* (Göttingen: Vandenhoeck & Ruprecht).

FREEMAN, Kathleen (1897–1959).

> *Bibliographical note.* One would expect the publication record of a scholarly source book to be singularly clear, but that expectation is often bound to be disappointed, as in the present case. The two copies of Freeman, below, that I used bore the date and imprint as indicated; but the publishers of these works, neither the original British publishers nor the later American ones, anywhere indicate a convincing difference between what they call "editions" and simple reprints. I looked into this matter only after discovering that Freeman died in 1959, too late to modify all the "1966" mentions in final proof; so I report that, as far as I can tell, these posthumous editions that I used are simple reprints, not true editions, of what should therefore be Freeman 1948 (i.e., Freeman 1966 = Freeman 1948) and Freeman 1946 (i.e., Freeman 1966a = Freeman 1946, even though the 1949 printing claims "Second Edition" on the title page, and the 1953 printing claims "Third Edition").

1966. *Ancilla to the Presocratics. A complete translation of the Fragments in Diels,* Fragmente der Vorsokratiker (Cambridge, MA: Harvard University Press).

1966a. *The Pre-Socratic Philosophers. A companion to Diels,* Fragmente der Vorsokratiker (Cambridge, MA: Harvard University Press).

FREGE, Gottlob (1848–1925).

1892. "Uber Sinn und Bedeutung", *Zeitschrift für Philosophie und philosophische Kritik*, vol. C, 25–50. Trans. Herbert Feigl as "On Sense and Nominatum" for *Readings in Philosophical Analysis*, ed. Herbert Feigl and W. S. Sellars (New York, 1949), also repr. in *Translations from the Philosophical Writings of Gottlob Frege* by Peter

Geach and Max Black (Oxford, 1952), and in *Contemporary Readings in Logical Theory*, ed. I. M. Copi and J. A. Gould (New York: Macmillan, 1967); trans. by Max Black as "On Sense and Reference" in *The Philosophical Review* LVII (May 1948): 209–30.

FRESNAULT-DERUELLE, Pierre.

1975. "L'Espace interpersonnel dans les comics", in *Semiologie de la représentation: Théâtre, télévision, bande dessinée*, ed. Andre Helbo et al. (Brussels: Complexe), 129–50.

VON FRITZ, Kurt (1900–?).

1971. "The Philosophical Passage in the Seventh Platonic Letter and the Problem of Plato's 'Esoteric' Philosophy", in *Essays in Ancient Greek Philosophy*, ed. John P. Anton with George L. Kustas (Albany, NY: State University of New York Press, 1971), 408–47.

FROEHLICH, Karlfried.

1987. "Pseudo-Dionysius and the Reformation of the Sixteenth Century", in Luibheid et al. 1987: 33–46.

FROST, Robert Lee (1874–1963).

1915. "The Road Not Taken", poem from *The Atlantic Monthly*, vol. 116, no. 2 (August), 223. Text at p. 365n2.

FURTON, Edward J.

1987. Review of the 1985 Deely edition of Poinsot's 1632 *Tractatus de Signis*, in *The Review of Metaphysics* 40 (June): 766–7.

GALILEO Galilei (1546–1642).

Note: For the classic edition of Galileo's writings and related materials, see Favaro 1890–1909.

1610. *Sidereus nuncius*, trans. as *The Starry Messenger* in Drake 1957; Fantoli 1996: 150 n. 9 makes a point of correcting this to read *Starry Message*.

1613. *Letters on Sunspots* (Rome: Accademia dei Lincei), trans. in Drake 1957.

1623. *Il saggiatore* (Rome: Accademia dei Lincei), trans. as *The Assayer* in Drake 1957.

1632. *Dialogo ... dei due massimi sistemi del mundo*, trans. Stillman Drake as *Dialogue concerning the Two Chief World Systems* (Berkeley: University of California Press, 1953).

1638. *Discorsi e dimonstrazioni metematicheintorno adue nuove sicenze* (Leiden: Elsevir), trans. Henry Crew and Alfonso de Salvio as *Dialogues concerning Two New Sciences* (New York, 1914).

GALLOP, David.

1984. *Parmenides of Elea. Fragments. A Text and Translation with an Introduction* (Toronto: University of Toronto Press).

GANNON, Timothy J. (1904–91).

1991. *Shaping Psychology: How We Got Where We're Going* (Lanham, MD: University Press of America).

GARRIGOU-LAGRANGE, Reginald (1877–1964).

1909. *Le sens commun, la philosophie de l'être et les formules dogmatiques* (Paris: G. Beauchesne).

1936. *Le sens commun, la philosophie de l'être et les formules dogmatiques* (4th ed., rev. et aug.; Paris: Desclée de Brouwer).

GASKIN, Richard (1960–).

1997. "The Stoics on Cases, Predicates and the Unity of the Proposition", in *Aristotle and After*, ed. Richard Sorabji (London: Institute of Classical Studies, University of London), 91–107.

GASKING, D. A. T. (1911–94), and A. C. JACKSON (1903–).

1967. "Wittgenstein as Teacher", in Fann ed. 1967.

GAUNILON.

c.1079. *Liber pro Insipiente adversus S. Anselmi in proslogio ratiocinationem auctore Gaunilone Majoris Monasterii monacho*, complete Latin text in Migne (q.v.) PL 158: 241–8.

GAUTHIER, René Antoine.

1970. "Introduction", being tome I, vol. 1 ("Première Partie"), of *L'Éthique à Nicomaque*, traduction et commentaire par René Antoine Gauthier et Jean Yves Jolif (2nd ed. avec introduction nouvelle par Gauthier; Paris: Béatrice-Nauwelaerts), 2 tomes in 4 volumes (Introduction, Traduction, Commentaire livres I–V, Commentaire livres VI–X).

GAY, Peter (1927–).

1966. *The Enlightenment: An Interpretation*, vol. 1, *The Rise of Modern Paganism* (New York: Alfred A. Knopf)

GEBHARDT, C. (1881–1934), editor.

1925. *Spinoza Opera* (Heidelberg: Carl Winter, 1925), 4 vols.

GEIGER, Louis-Bertrand (1906–).

1947. "Abstractio et séparation d'après S. Thomas: in de trinitate, q. 5, a. 3.", *Revue des Sciences Philosophiques et Théologiques* XXXI: 3–40.

1953. *Participation dans la philosophie de saint Thomas* (2nd ed.; Paris: Vrin).

GERSH, Stephen.

1986. *Middle Platonism and Neoplatonism. The Latin Tradition* (Notre Dame, IN: Notre Dame University Press), 2 vols.

GERSHENSON, Daniel E., and Daniel A. GREENBERG.

1964. *Anaxagoras and the Birth of Physics* (New York: Blaisdell Publishing Co.).

GERSON, Lloyd P.

1994. *Plotinus* (London: Routledge).

1994a. "Plotinus and the Rejection of Aristotelian Metaphysics", in *Aristotle in Late Antiquity*, ed. Lawrence P. Schrenk (Washington: Catholic University of America Press, 1994), 3–21.

GERSON, Lloyd P., editor.

1996. *The Cambridge Companion to Plotinus* (Cambridge, England: Cambridge University Press).

GIBBON, Edward (1737–94).

Note. Page and note numbers to Gibbon are based on the text of the Bury ed. of

1909–14, with the equivalences to the chapters and years of the original publication of the Gibbon volumes as indicated below.

i.1776/88. *The Decline and Fall of the Roman Empire* (the work conceived, according to Gibbon, on 15 Oct. 1764), in the ed. of J. B. Bury (London: Methuen & Co., 1909–14), 7 vols. Original chs. 1–14 = Bury I (1909); chs. 15–24 = II (1909); chs. 25–35 = III (1909); chs. 36–44 = IV (1909); chs. 45–51 = V (1911); chs. 52–63 = VI (1912); chs. 64–71 = VII (1914).

1777. First printing of vol. I (in 1776, chs. 1–16); rev. in 3rd ed. of 1777 (= Bury I complete to II p. 148).

1781. First printing of vol. II (chs. 17–26; = Bury II after p. 148 to III p. 139)

1781a. First printing of vol. III (chs. 27–38; = Bury III after p. 139 to IV p. 181).

1788. First printing of vol. IV (1 March 1782–June 1784; chs. 39–47; = Bury IV after 181 to V p. 179).

1788a. First printing of vol. V (July 1784–1 May 1786; chs. 48–57; = Bury V after p. 179 to VI p. 268).

1788b. First printing of vol. VI (18 May 1786–27 June 1787; chs. 58–71; = Bury VI after p. 268 through VII).

GILSON, Étienne (13 June 1884–19 September 1978).

1922. *La philosophie au moyen age* (Paris: Payot), 2 vols; vol. I: *De Scot Érigène a S. Bonaventura*; vol. II: *De S. Thomas d'Aquin à G. d'Occam*.

1925. *La philosophie au moyen age de Scot Érigène a G. D'Occam* (Paris: Payot).

1937. *The Unity of Philosophical Experience* (New York: Scribner's).

1938. *Héloïse et Abélard* (Paris: J. Vrin).

1944. *La philosophie au moyen age: Des origines patristiques à la fin du XIVe siècle* (2nd ed., rev. et aug.; Paris: Payot).

1948. *L'être et l'essence* (1st ed.; Paris: J. Vrin).

1952. *Being and Some Philosophers* (2nd ed., corrected and enlarged; Toronto: Pontifical Institute of Mediaeval Studies).

1955. *History of Christian Philosophy in the Middle Ages* (New York: Random House).

1960. *The Christian Philosophy of Saint Augustine* (New York: Alfred A. Knopf).

1968. Personal letter to the author dated 28 August.

1974. Personal letter to the author dated 10 July.

GODEL, Robert.

1967. *Les Sources manuscrites du* Cours de linguistique générale *de F. de Saussure* (Geneva: Droz).

GORGIAS OF LEONTINI (c.481–c.375/2BC).

Date for writing is based on Freeman 1966a: 358.

c.444BC. Περὶ φύσεως ἢ περὶ τοῦ μὴ ὄντος, "On Nature, or On What Is Not". Fragments in Freeman 1966: 127–9.

Kirk et al. (1983: 103) refer to the title of this work of Gorgias as "sardonic" – bitter or mocking; and its intersemioticity inevitably suggests to the informed readers of later times the idea of a parody vis-à-vis the title of Melissus c.441/40BC below. But in fact, despite the inevitability of the suggestion, the status of the chronological framework within which we are currently able to situate the Presocratic writings is not sufficiently stable to warrant much in the way of safe conjecture on the point, historically speaking.

GOULD, Stephen J., and Elisabeth S. VRBA.

1982. "Exaptation – A Missing Term in the Science of Form", *Paleobiology* 8.1 (Winter): 4–15.

GRACIA, Jorge J. E.

1992. *Philosophy and Its History. Issues in Philosophical Historiography* (Albany: State University of New York Press).

1993. "Hispanic Philosophy: Its Beginning and Golden Age", *Review of Metaphysics* 46 (March 1993), 475–502. This paper was originally presented as the opening address at the 14–17 October "Hispanic Philosophy in the Age of Discovery" conference, Catholic University of America, Washington.

GRAESER, Andreas.

1978. "The Stoic Theory of Meaning", in *The Stoics*, ed. John M. Rist (Berkeley: University of California Press), 77–100.

GRANT, Michael.

1980. *Greek and Latin Authors, 800BC– AD1000* (New York: H. W. Wilson Co.).

GRANT, Robert M.

1970. *Theophilus of Antioch ad Autolycum*, Greek text with facing English trans. (Oxford: Clarendon Press).

GREDT, Josephus (1863–1940).

1899. *Elementa Philosophiae Aristotelico-Thomisticae* (Barcelona: Herder), 2 vols.

1936. 7th ed., last in author's lifetime.

1961. 13th (5th posthumous) ed. recognita et aucta ab Euchario Zenzen, O.S.B.

GRIFFITHS, Bede (1906–?).

1980. "Towards an Indian Christian Spirituality", in *Prayer and Contemplation*, ed. C. M. Vadakkekara (Bangalore, India: Asirvanam Benedictine Monastery), pp. 383–8.

GROSSMAN, Joan Delaney.

1981. Intro. to Dobroliubov 1895: 7–18.

GROTE, George (1794–1871).

1872. *Aristotle*, posthumous ed. by Alexander Bain and G. Croom Robinson (London: J. Murray), 2 vols.

GUAGLIARDO, Vincent (1944–95).

1992. "Hermeneutics: Deconstruction or Semiotics?", in *Symposium on Hermeneutics*, ed. Eugene F. Bales (private circulation; Conception, MO: Conception Seminary College, 1992), 63–74, followed by a discussion, 75–8. Dr Guagliardo was quite irritated that this essay was put into circulation without his knowledge or final revisions; but it is a valuable contribution to the literature of semiotics, an improbable and fascinating comparison of Poinsot and Derrida.

1993. "Being and Anthroposemiotics", in *Semiotics 1993*, ed. Robert Corrington and John Deely (Lanham, MD: University Press of America, 1994), 50–6.

1994. "Being-as-First-Known in Poinsot: A-Priori or Aporia?", *American Catholic Philo-sophical Quarterly* 68.3 "Special Issue on John Poinsot" (Summer 1994): 363–93.

1995. "Introduction" to special issue on Thomas Aquinas of *Listening* 30.1 (Winter): 3–6.

1995a. *An Introduction to the Metaphysics of St. Thomas Aquinas*, manuscript complete in 5 of a projected 10 chapters, with an additional intro. completed and conclusion projected, for 12 chapters in all.

1995b. "Introduction" to Guagliardo, Hess, and Taylor 1996.

GUAGLIARDO, Vincent, Charles R. HESS, and Richard C. TAYLOR, translators.

1996. *St. Thomas Aquinas Commentary on the Book of Causes* (Washington: Catholic University of America Press, 1996).

GUIZOT, M. François (1787–1874), with posthumous editing and additions by his daughter, Madame Guizot de Witt.

1832. *History of Civilization*, trans. William Hazlitt (London: George Bell & Sons, 1871–3), in 3 vols., vol. I to p. 268 being the "General History of Civilization in Europe" and vol. I, p. 269–end + vols. II & III being the "History of Civilization in France". Page reference in the present work is to this ed. of the Hazlitt trans., which in turn is based on the original French publication *Cours d'histoire moderne de M. Guizot* in 6 vols. (Paris: Pichon et Didier, 1829–32), subsequently repub. as separated into a one-vol. work titled *Histoire générale de la civilisation en Europe depuis la chute de l'Empire romain jusqu'en 1789*, and a multi-vol. work titled *Histoire de la civilisation en France depuis la chute de l'Empire romain jusqu'en 1789*. These are distributed in the Hazlitt English edition cited above in this entry.

1869. *History of France, from the earliest times to 1848*, trans. Robert Black (New York: John B. Alden, 1885), in 8 vols.; being *L'Histoire de France depuis les temps les plus reculés jusqu'en 1789* (Paris: Hachette & Cie, 1872–6) combined with *L'Histoire de France depuis 1789 jusqu'en 1848; leçons recueillies par madame de Witt, née Guizot* (Paris: Hachette & Cie, 1878–9); the reference date is based on Guizot's "letter to the publishers" of December 1869 submitting the mss. for their disposition.

GUTAS, Dimitri.

1988. *Avicenna and the Aristotelian Tradition. Introduction to reading Avicenna's philo-sophical works* (Leiden: E. J. Brill).

HAAS, Robert.

1968. "The Theory of Translation", in *The Theory of Meaning*, ed. G. H. R. Parkinson (London: Oxford), 86–108.

HAJDUKIEWICZ, Leszek.

1974. "Makowski, Szymon Stanislaw", entry in *Polski Słownik Biograficzny*, ed. Majdrowicz Eugeniusz and Malicki Bartłomiej (Warsaw, Poland: Polska Akademia Nauk), tome XIX/2, cahier 81, 244 6.

HALDANE, John.

1998. "Thomism", entry in *Routledge Encyclopedia of Philosophy*, ed. in 10 vols. by Edward Craig (London: Routledge, 1998), vol. 9, pp. 380–8.

HAMMAN, Adalbert (1910–).

1986. "The Turnabout of the Fourth Century", in *Patrology*, ed. Angelo di Berardino, vol. IV, *The Golden Age of Patristic Literature from the Council of Nicea to the Council of Chalcedon*, trans. from Italian ed. of *Patrologia* vol. III (Turin: Marietti, 1978) by Placid Solari (Westminster, MD: Christian Classics, Inc.).

HANDYSIDE, John (1883–1916).

a.1916. "Introduction" to Handyside trans. 1929: ix–xii.

HANDYSIDE, John, translator. *See further* Kemp Smith 1929, below.

1929 (posthumous). *Kant's Inaugural Dissertation and Early Writings on Space*, being an introduction to with translations of Kant 1768 and 1770, posthumously prepared for publication by Norman Kemp Smith (1872–1958), who added to Handyside's papers his own translation of selected passages from Kant 1747, included in the volume (Chicago: Open Court Publishing Co.).

HARDWICK, Charles S., editor, with assistance of James Cook.

1977. *Semiotics and Significs: The Correspondence between Charles S. Peirce and Victoria Lady Welby* (Bloomington: Indiana University Press).

HANKS, Patrick, and Flavia HODGES.

1988. *A Dictionary of Surnames* (Oxford, Eng.: Oxford University Press).

HARRIS, R. Baine, editor.

1982. *Neoplatonism and Indian Thought* (Norfolk, VA: International Society for Neoplatonic Studies).

HARRISON, James (1927–).

1992. *Salman Rushdie* (New York: Twayne Publishers).

HARTSHORNE, Charles (1897–2000).

1948. *The Divine Relativity: A Social Conception of God* (New Haven, CT: Yale University Press.

1962. *The Logic of Perfection* (La Salle, IL: Open Court).

1965. *Anselm's Discovery: A Re-Examination of the Ontological Proof for God's Existence* (La Salle, IL: Open Court).

1972. *Whitehead's Philosophy: Selected Essays, 1935–1970* (Lincoln, NB: University of Nebraska Press).

HASKINS, Charles Homer (1870–1937).

1957. *The Rise of Universities* (Ithaca, NY: Cornell University Press).

HAWKES, Terrence.

1977. *Structuralism and Semiotics* (Berkeley: University of California Press).

HEGEL, G. W. F. (1770–1831).

1802. "Glauben und Wissen oder die Reflexionsphilosophie der Subjektivität", from the *Journal der Philosophie*, Band II, Stück 1, as repr. in *Sämtliche Werke*, ed. Hermann Glockner (Stuttgart: Frommann, 1958), vol. I, 278–433.

1807. *Phänomenologie des Geistes*, trans A. V. Miller as *Phenomenology of Spirit*, analysis of the text and foreword by J. N. Findlay (Oxford: Clarendon Press, 1977).

1812. *Wissenschaft der Logik. Erster Teil: Die Objektive Logik*, in *Sämtliche Werke*, vol. 4 (Stuttgart: Frommann, 1958).

1817. *Enzyklopädie der philosophischen Wissenschaften*, ed. Georg Lasson (Leipzig: Felix Meiner, 1930), with a table, pp. v–vif., correlating all the elements of this original publication with what appears further in later editions, notably the two that appeared within Hegel's lifetime in 1827 and 1830, respectively.

1821. *Naturrecht und Staatswissenschaft im Grundrisse; Grundlinien der Philosophie des Rechts* ("Foreword" ["Vorrede"] completed 25 June 1820), trans. as *Hegel's Philosophy of Right* by T. M. Knox (Oxford: Clarendon Press, 1952, corrected sheets 1957).

1830. *Die Logik*, being the *Erster Teil* of *System der Philosophie*, in *Sämtliche Werke*, vol. 8 (Stuttgart: Frommann, 1964), i.e., part I of 3rd ed. of *Enzyklopädie der philosophischen Wissenschaften*, first pub. 1817.

1830a. *Die Philosophie des Geistes*, being the *Dritter Teil of System der Philosophie*, in *Sämtliche Werke*, vol. 10 (Stuttgart: Frommann, 1958), i.e., part III of *Enzyklopädie der philosophischen Wissenschaften*, first pub. 1817.

HEIDEGGER, Martin (1889–1976).

1927. *Sein und Zeit*, originally pub. in *Jahrbuch für Phänomenologie und phänomenologische Forschung*, ed. E. Husserl. Page references in present work are to 10th ed. (Tübingen: Niemeyer, 1963).

1929. *Vom Wesen des Grundes* (Frankfurt: Klostermann, 1955).

1943. *Vom Wesen der Wahrheit* (Frankfurt: Klostermann, 1954; actual composition 1930). The English translation by R. F. C. Hull and Alan Crick, "On the Essence of Truth", in *Existence and Being*, ed. Werner Brock (Chicago: Gateway, 1949), 292–324, was particularly consulted in preparing the present work.

1947. *Platons Lehre von der Wahrheit, mit einem Brief über den Humanismus* (Bern: Francke).

HENLE, Robert J. (1909–2000).

1956. *St. Thomas and Platonism: A Study of the* Plato *and* Platonici *Texts in the Writings of St. Thomas* (The Hague: Martinus Nijhoff). An exhaustive, definitive, and magisterial study.

1993. "Thomas Reid's Theory of Signs", in *Semiotics 1993*, ed. Jonathan Evans and John Deely (Lanham, MD: University Press of America, 1987), 155–68.

HENRY, Desmond Paul.

1987. "The Way to Awareness", review of Deely ed. of Poinsot's *Tractatus de Signis* in *The Times Literary Supplement* no. 4413 (30 October–5 November), p. 1201.

HENRY, P., and H.-R. SCHWYZER (1908–), editors.

Greek text of Plotinus:

1951. *Plotini Opera* (Paris: Desclée de Brouwer), vol. I.

1959. *Plotini Opera* (Paris: Desclée de Brouwer), vol. II.

HERACLITUS (c.540–c.480BC).

Date for writing based on the prime assigned by Freeman 1966a. 104.

c.500BC. See edition of Kahn 1979. Fragments also in Freeman 1966: 24–34.

HERCULANO DE CARVALHO, José G.

1969. "Segno e significazione in João de São Tomás", in *Estudos Linguísticos*, vol. 2

(Coimbra: Atlântida Editora). Pp. 129–53 are exposition; 154–68 reproduce selected passages of Latin text. This careful essay, a most important piece of work on Poinsot's semiotic, stands along with the essay of Maritain, 1938, 1943, as a first-hand presentation of Poinsot's views on the subject of signs. It is excerpted from Herculano de Carvalho 1970, following.

1970, 1973. *Teoria da linguagem. Natureza do fenómeno linguístico e a análise das línguas* (repr. with additions of 1967 work of same title, and now as "Tomo I" with 2nd vol. of same name pub. 1973; Coimbra: Atlântida).

HERODOTUS (c.484–425BC).

a.425BC. *The History of Herodotus*, trans. George Rawlinson (London: G. Murray, 1862), 4 vols.

HERREN, Michael W., editor, in collaboration with Shirley Ann BROWN.

1988. *The Sacred Nectar of the Greeks: The Study of Greek in the West in the Early Middle Ages* (King's College London: Medieval Studies).

HICK, John (1922–), and Arthur C. McGILL.

1967. *The Many-Faced Argument. Recent studies on the ontological argument for the existence of God* (New York: Macmillan).

HIGGINS, Dick (1938–), and Charles DORIA.

1991. "Introduction" to Bruno 1591: xxiii–xlviii.

HILL, Archibald A.

1948. "The Use of Dictionaries in Language Teaching", *Language Learning* 1: 9–13.

1958. *Introduction to Linguistic Structures. From sound to sentence in English* (New York: Harcourt, Brace).

HINSCHIUS, Paulus (1835–98).

1863. "Commentatio de Collectione Decretalium et Canonum Isidori Mercatoris", in Pseudo-Isidore c.849: xi–ccxxxviii (= 11–238).

HJELMSLEV, Louis (1899–1965).

1961. *Prolegomena to a Theory of Language*, being the 2nd, rev. trans. by Francis J. Whitfield of *Omkring sprogteoriens grundlæggelse* (Copenhagen: Ejnar Munksgaard, 1943), incorporating "several minor corrections and changes that have suggested themselves in the course of discussions between the author and the translator" (p. v).

HOBBES, Thomas (1588–1679).

1651. *Leviathan*, ed. Michael Oakeshott, repr. with intro. by Richard S. Peters (New York: Macmillan, 1962).

1668. *Opera Philosophica, Quae Latine Scripsit, Omnia* (Amsterdam: Joannes Blaev, 1668), 2 vols.

HODGSON, Phyllis.

1944. "Introduction" to *The Cloud of Unknowing and The Book of Privy Counselling*, ed. from the mss. with intro., notes, and glossary (London: Published for Early English Text Society by Oxford University Press).

1967. *Three 14th Century English Mystics* (London: Published for British Council and National Book League by Longmans, Green & Co.).

HÖFFDING, Harald (1843–1931).

> 1900. *A History of Modern Philosophy. A sketch of the history of philosophy from the close of the renaissance to our own day*, authorized trans. from the German by B. E. Meyer (London: Macmillan and Co.), in 2 vols.

HOFFMEYER, Jesper.

> 1996. *Signs of Meaning in the Universe* (Bloomington: Indiana University Press), trans. by Barbara J. Haverland of *En Snegl På Vejen: Betydningens naturhistorie* (Copenhagen: Rosinante, 1993).

HOLTZ, Louis.

> 1981. *Donat et la tradition de l'enseignement grammatical: Étude sur l'Ars Donati et sa diffusion (VIe–IXe siècle) et édition critique* (Paris: Centre national de la recherche scientifique, 1981), 585–674.

HOPKINS, Jasper.

> 1972. *A Companion to the Study of St. Anselm* (Minneapolis: University of Minnesota Press).

HORANYI, Ozseb, and Csaba PLEH.

> 1975. "Jelek a rajzfilmben", in *Tanulmanyok a magyar animacios filmrol* (Budapest: Magyar Filmtudomanyi Intezet es Filmarchivum), 246–8.

HOUSER, Nathan (1944–), et al., editor.

> See "The Designation EP" in the gloss on the entry for PEIRCE, below.

> 1992. *The Essential Peirce Volume 1 (1867–1893)* (Bloomington: Indiana University Press).

> 1998. *The Essential Peirce Volume 2 (1893–1913)* (Bloomington: Indiana University Press).

HOUSER, Rollen Edward (1946–).

> 1999. "Let Them Suffer into the Truth: Avicenna's Remedy for Those Denying the Axioms of Thought", in Druart ed. 1999: 107–33.

HOYLE, Fred (1915–).

> 1950. *The Nature of the Universe* (New York: Harper & Brothers).

HUGH OF ST VICTOR (1096?–1141).

> i.1120/30. *Hugonis de Sancto Victore Didascalion de studio legendi*, critical text ed. Charles Henry Buttimer (= studies in Mediaeval and Renaissance Latin X; Washington: Catholic University of America Press, 1939); first complete English trans., with critical apparatus, by Jerome Taylor, *The Didascalion of Hugh of St. Victor: A Mediaeval Guide to the Arts* (= Records of Civilization: Sources and Studies LXIV; New York: Columbia University Press, 1961).

HUME, David (1711–76).

> 1739–40. *A Treatise of Human Nature*, ed. in 1888 by Sir Lewis Amherst Selby-Bigge (1860–1950), 2nd ed. with text rev. and variant readings by P. H. Nidditch (Oxford: Clarendon, 1978).

> 1748. *An Enquiry Concerning Human Understanding* (originally pub. as *Philosophical Essays concerning the Human Understanding*, but retitled as of 1758 edition), ed. P. H. Nidditch (3rd ed.; Oxford, 1975).

1776 (18 April). "My Own Life", Hume's autobiography, repr. in *An Enquiry Concerning Human Understanding*, ed. and intro. Charles W. Hendel (New York: Bobbs-Merrill, 1955), 3–11.

HUSSERL, Edmund (1859–1938).

1900–1. *Logische Untersuchungen*, 2 vols. (Halle: Niemeyer). English trans. J. N. Findlay, *Logical Investigations*, also in 2 vols. (New York: Humanities Press, 1970).

1931. *Cartesianische Meditationen*, English trans. Dorian Cairns as *Cartesian Meditations* (The Hague: Martinus Nijhoff, 1960).

HUXLEY, Aldous (1894–1963).

1963. *Literature and Science* (New York: Harper and Row).

HUXLEY, Julian (1887–1975).

1953. *Evolution in Action* (New York: Mentor).

IBN DAUD, Abraham (c.1110–c.1180).

1160–1. *The Book of Tradition (Sefer ha-Qabbalah)*, critical ed. with trans. and notes by Gerson D. Cohen (Philadelphia: Jewish Publication Society of America).

INGE, Rev. W. R. (1860–1954).

1934. "Foreword" to Turnbull 1934: i–iv.

INWOOD, Brad.

1992. *The Poem of Empedocles*, text and trans. with an intro. (Toronto: University of Toronto Press).

JACKSON, B. Darrell.

1972. "The Theory of Signs in Augustine's *De Doctrina Christiana*", in *Augustine. A Collection of Critical Essays*, ed. R. A. Markus (Garden City, NY: Doubleday & Co.), 92–147.

1975. Translation, introduction, and notes to a bilingual edition of *Augustine: De Dialectica*, based on the "hand edition" of the Latin text established by Jan Pinborg (Dordrecht, Holland: D. Reidel).

JAKOBSON, Roman (1896–1982).

1974. "Coup d'oeil sur le développement de la sémiotique", in *Panorama sémiotique/A Semiotic Landscape*, Proceedings of First Congress of International Association for Semiotic Studies, Milan, June 1974, ed. Seymour Chatman, Umberto Eco, and Jean-Marie Klinkenberg (The Hague: Mouton, 1979), 3–18. Also pub. separately under same title by the Research Center for Language and Semiotic Studies as a small monograph (= Studies in Semiotics 3; Bloomington: Indiana University Publications, 1975); and in an English trans. by Patricia Baudoin titled "A Glance at the Development of Semiotics", in *The Framework of Language* (Ann Arbor: Michigan Studies in the Humanities, Horace R. Rackham School of Graduate Studies, 1980), 1–30.

JAKOBSON, Roman, and Morris HALLE.

1956. *Fundamentals of Language* (The Hague: Mouton).

JAMES, William (1842–1910).

1911. "Percept and Concept – The Import of Concepts", chap. IV of *Some Problems of Philosophy: A Beginning of an Introduction to Philosophy* (New York: Longmans

& Green), 47–74. This uncompleted book was worked on by James between March 1909 and his death in August 1910. It was edited and put into publishable form posthumously by Henry James, Jr, working with H. M. Kallen and R. B. Perry.

JASTROW, Joseph (1863–1944).

> 1900. *Fact and Fable in Psychology* (Boston: Houghton Mifflin & Co.).

JAULIN, Robert.

> 1970. "Formal Analysis of Geomancy", *Semiotica* 2.3: 195–246.

JEAUNEAU, Eduard A.

> 1979. "Jean Scot Erigène et le grec", *Archivum Latinitatis Medii Aevi* 41 (1977–8): 5–50.
>
> 1996. "Introduction" to his critical edition *Iohannis Scotti seu Eriugenae Periphyseon Liber Primus. Editionem nouam a suppositiciis quidem additamentis purgatam, ditatam uero appendice in qua uicissitudines operis synoptice exhibentur* (= Corpus Christianorum vol. 161 [CLXVI]; Turnhout, Belgium: Brepols), pp. v–xc.

JENKS, Edward (1861–1939).

> 1898. *Law and Politics in the Middle Ages* (New York: Henry Holt and Co.).

JOHN OF SALISBURY: see Salisbury, John of.

JOHNSON, Samuel (1709–84).

> 1755. *English Dictionary* (original ed. London: William Strahan; facsimile of original two folio vols. bound as one, London: Times Books, 1979).

KACZMAREK, Ludger.

> 1980. Intro., critical apparatus, and notes to d'Ailly a.1396.
>
> 1981. "Modi Significandi and Their Destructions: A 14th Century Controversy about Methodological Issues in the Science and Theory of Language", paper read at Seconde Conférence Internationale d'Histoire des Sciences du Langage (ICHOLS II), Lille, 2–5 September.
>
> 1983. "Significatio in der Zeichen- und Sprachtheorie Ockhams", in Eschbach and Trabant eds 1983: 87–104.

KAEPPELI, Th. (1900–?), and A. DONDAINE (1898–?), editors.

> 1941. *Monumenta Ordinis Fratrum Praedicatorum Historica*, vol. 20: *Acta Capitulorum Provincialium Provinciae Romanae (1243–1344)* (Rome).

KAHN, Charles H. (1921–).

> 1979. *The Art and Thought of Heraclitus. An edition of the fragments with translation and commentary* (Cambridge, Eng.: Cambridge University Press).

KANNENGIESSER, Charles.

> 1995. "The Interrupted *De Doctrina Christiana*", in Arnold and Bright eds 1995: 3–13.

KANT, Immanuel (1724–1804).

> 1747. Selected passages from Kant's first published writing, *Thoughts on the True Estimation of Living Forces*, trans. by Norman Kemp Smith and included in the posthumous ed. he prepared for press of the Handyside trans. 1929 (q.v.): 3–15.
>
> 1768. *On the First Ground of the Distinction of Regions of Space*, in Handyside trans. 1929: 19–29.
>
> 1770. *De Mundi Sensibilis atque Intelligibilis Forma et Principiis. Dissertatio pro loco professionis log. et metaph. ordinariae rite sibi vindicanda*, trans. as *Dissertation*

on the Form and Principles of the Sensible and Intelligible World, in Handyside trans. 1929: 33–85.

1781. *Kritik der reinen Vernunft* (Riga: Johann Friedrich Hartknoch).

1783. *Prolegomena zu einer jeden künftigen Metaphysik, die als Wissenschaft wird auftreten können*, ed. Rudolf Malter (Stuttgart: Philipp Reclam, 1989). I have used the English trans. *Prolegomena to Any Future Metaphysics [which will be able to come forth as science]* by Mahaffy (1872) after Richardson (1836), as edited in English by Carus (1902) and extensively revised, finally, by Lewis White Beck (Indianapolis, IN: Bobbs-Merrill Co., 1950); with intro. by Lewis White Beck.

1787. *Kritik der reinen Vernunft* (Zweite hin und wieder verbesserte Auflage; Riga: Johann Friedrich Hartknoch); English trans. Norman Kemp Smith, *Kant's Critique of Pure Reason* (New York: St Martin's Press, 1956).

1790. *Kritik der Urteilskraft*, 2 vols. in 1, trans. and ed. James C. Meredith as *Critique of Judgment* (Oxford, 1957).

KECKERMANN, Bartholomaeus (1573–1609).

Note: The c.1607 date here is a guess based on the date of the preface by Georgius Pauli in vol. 1.

c.1607. *Scientiae Metaphysicae Brevissima Synopsis et Compendium*, tomus primus in *D. Bartholomaei Keckermanni Operum Omnium quae extant ...* (Geneva: apud Petrum Aubertum, 1614), in 2 vols. In the matter of a doctrine of signs, Keckermann principally looks to Timpler, q.v.

KELLY, John Norman Davidson.

1968. *Early Christian Doctrines* (4th ed.; London: Adam & Charles Black).

KEMP SMITH, Norman (1872–1958).

1929. "Preface" to, and selected passages from, Kant 1747 in Handyside trans. 1929: v–vi and 1–15, respectively.

KENNY, Anthony (1942–).

1973. *Wittgenstein* (Cambridge, MA: Harvard University Press).

1984. *The Legacy of Wittgenstein* (Oxford: Basil Blackwell).

1989. *The Metaphysics of Mind* (Oxford: Clarendon Press).

KENNY, Anthony (1942–), editor.

1970. *Descartes. Philosohical Letters*, trans. and ed. Anthony Kenny (Oxford: Clarendon Press).

1994. *The Wittgenstein Reader* (Oxford: Blackwell).

KENYON, Frederic G. (1863–1952).

1951. *Books and Readers in Ancient Greece and Rome* (2nd ed.; Oxford: Clarendon Press).

KETNER, Kenneth Laine.

1981. "Peirce's Ethics of Terminology", *Transactions of the Charles S. Peirce Society* XVII.4 (Fall): 327–47.

1986. "Peirce's Most Lucid and Interesting Paper", *International Philosophical Quarterly* 26 (December): 375–92.

1989. "Hartshorne and the Basis of Peirce's Categories", in *Hartshorne, Process Philosophy, and Theology*, ed. Robert Kane and Stephen Phillips (Albany: State University of New York Press), 135–49.

1993. "Novel Science: or, How Contemporary Social Science Is Not Well and Why Literature and Semeiotic Provide a Cure", *Semiotica* 93: 33–59.

1998. *His Glassy Essence: An Autobiography* [sic] *of Charles Sanders Peirce* (Nashville, TN: Vanderbilt University Press).

KETNER, Kenneth Laine, editor.

1992. Text and apparatus for Peirce 1898, with joint "Introduction" with H. Putnam (pp. 1–19) and some other Putnam material included.

KIERKEGAARD, Søren (1813–55).

1843. *Either/or*, trans. of *Enten-Eller*, vol. 1 trans. David F. Swenson and Lillian Marvin Swenson, with revisions and foreword by Howard Albert Johnson, vol. 2 trans. Walter Lowrie with rev. and foreword by Johnson (Princeton, NJ: Princeton University Press, 1959–72).

1843a. *Fear and Trembling*, trans. of *Frygt og baeven* by Robert Payne (Garden City, NY: Doubleday, 1954).

1849. *The Sickness unto Death*, trans. of *Sygdommen til doden* by Walter Lowrie (Princeton, NJ: Princeton University Press, 1941).

KILWARDBY, Robert (c.1215–79). *See also* Kilwardby Adscriptus.

c.1250. *De Ortu Scientiarum*, ed. Albert G. Judy (London: The British Academy, 1976).

KILWARDBY ADSCRIPTUS, "The So-Called Kilwardby", or "The Work Ascribed to Kilwardby".

c.1250, i.1230/70. *The Commentary on "Priscianus Maior" Ascribed to Robert Kilwardby*, ed. K. M. Fredborg, N. J. Green-Pedersen, Lauge Nielsen, and Jan Pinborg, in (from book's spine) *Copenhagen Universitet. Institut for Graesk og Latinsk Middelal-Derfilologi. Cahiers 3*; (from the title page) *Cahiers de l'Institut du Moyen-Âge Grec et Latin* (Copenhagen: publiés par le directeur de l'Institut, 1975), No. 15, intro. material pp. 1+–20+ (incl. Pinborg 1975, Lewry 1975; and a constructed table of contents, pp. 18+–20+), followed by Latin text with some critical notes and apparatus pp. 1–143, and an "Index Nominum" pp 143–46.

KIRK, G. S. (1921–), J. E. RAVEN, and M. SCHOFIELD.

1983. *The Presocratic Philosophers. A critical history with a selection of texts* (2nd ed.; Cambridge, Eng.: Cambridge University Press).

KLUBERTANZ, George P. (1912–72).

1960. *St. Thomas Aquinas on Analogy: A Textual Analysis and Systematic Synthesis* (Chicago: Loyola University Press).

KNASAS, John F. X.

1990. *The Preface to Thomistic Metaphysics: A Contribution to the Neo-Thomist Debate on the Start of Metaphysics* (New York: Peter Lang).

KOCH, Hugo (1869–?).

1900. *Pseudo-Dionysius Areopagita in seinen Beziehungen zum Neoplatonismus und Mysterienwesen: eine litterarhistorische Untersuchungen* (Mainz: Franz Kirchheim).

KÖHLER, Wolfgang (1887–1967).

    1929. *Gestalt Psychology* (New York: H. Liveright).

KORN, Ernst R. (pseudonym for Heinz R. Schmitz).

    1973. "Preface" to Maritain 1973: vii–xxvii.

KOVACH, Francis Joseph.

    1974. *Philosophy of Beauty* (Norman: University of Oklahoma Press).

KNEALE, William, and Martha KNEALE.

    1962. *The Development of Logic* (London: Oxford University Press).

KRAMPEN, Martin (1928–).

    1981. "Phytosemiotics", *Semiotica*, 36.3/4: 187–209.

KRAUS, Heinrich.

    1911. *Aeschines Socratus*, Aeschinis Socratici reliquae, ed. et commentario instruxit Hein-rich Krauss (Leipzig, Germany: B. G. Teubner). (Available in photocopy from University Microfilms of Ann Arbor, MI.)

KREMPEL, A.

    1952. *La doctrine de la relation chez saint Thomas: Exposé historique et systématique* (Paris: J. Vrin).

KRETZMAN, Norman.

    1974. "Aristotle on Spoken Sound Significant by Convention", in *Ancient Logic and Its Modern Interpretations*, ed. John Corcoran (= *Synthese 9*; Dordrecht: D. Reidel), 3–21.

KRIPKE, Saul A. (1940–).

    1980. *Naming and Necessity* (rev. and enl. ed.; Oxford: Basil Blackwell).

LA METTRIE, Julien Offray de (1709–51).

    1748. *L'homme machine*, présentation et notes de Gérard Delaloye (Paris: J. J. Pauvert, 1966).

LACTANTIUS (c.AD240–c.320).

    c.AD314. *De mortibus persecutorum*, Latin-English ed. and trans. J. L. Creed (Oxford: Clarendon Press, 1984).

LAERTIUS, Diogenes (c.AD180–c.260).

    c.AD220. *Lives and Opinions of Eminent Philosophers*, facing Greek with English trans. by R. D. Hicks (rev. repr.; Cambridge, MA: Harvard University Press, 1942), in 2 vols.

LANGAN, Thomas.

    1996. *Being and Truth* (Columbia: University of Missouri Press).

LANGFORD, Jerome J.

    1992. *Galileo, Science and the Church* (3rd ed.; Ann Arbor: University of Michigan Press).

LANIGAN, Richard.

    1969. "Aristotle's Rhetoric: Addendum to the Organon", *Dialogue* 11.2 (November): 1–6.

    1972. *Speaking and Semiology: Maurice Merleau-Ponty's Phenomenological Theory of Existential Communication* (The Hague: Mouton).

    1977. *Speech Act Phenomenology* (The Hague: Martinus Nijhoff).

    1984. *Semiotic Phenomenology of Rhetoric: Eidetic Practice in Henry Grattan's Discourse on Tolerance* (Washington: University Press of America for the Center for Advanced Research in Phenomenology).

1986. "Semiotics, Communicology, and Plato's Sophist", in *Frontiers in Semiotics*, ed. J. Deely, B. Williams, and F. E. Kruse (Bloomington: Indiana University Press), text 199–216, notes 284–5.

1988. *Phenomenology of Communication: Merleau-Ponty's Thematics in Semiology and Communicology* (Pittsburgh, PA: Duquesne University Press).

1992. *The Human Science of Communicology: A Phenomenology of Discourse in Foucault and Merleau-Ponty* (Pittsburgh, PA: Duquesne University Press).

1994. "Capta versus Data: Method and Evidence in Communicology", *Human Studies: A Journal for Philosophy and the Social Sciences*, 17 (October): 109–30, with *erratum* for p. 119 on p. 285 of same vol.

1995. "From Enthymeme to Abduction: The Classical Law of Logic and the Postmodern Rule of Rhetoric", in *Recovering Pragmaticism's Voice*, ed. L. Langsdorf and A. R. Smith (Albany: State University of New York Press), 49–70.

LAO-TZU (LAO TSE, c.604–517BC), conventional principal author of the collective composition of the *Tao Te Ching*, q.v.

LAUGHLIN, Burgess.

1995. *The Aristotle Adventure. A guide to the Greek, Arabic, and Latin scholars who transmitted Aristotle's logic to the Renaissance* (Flagstaff, AZ: Albert Hale Publishing).

LAVAUD, M.-Benoît (1890–).

1928. "Jean de Saint-Thomas, l'homme et l'oeuvre", appendix II to *Introduction à la théologie de saint Thomas*, being Lavaud's French trans. of Poinsot's "Isagoge ad D. Thomae Theologiam" (in *Tomus Primus Cursus Theologici* [1637], Solesmes ed., 1931: 142–219) (Paris: André Blot), pp. 411–46.

LE GOFF, Jacques (1924–).

1988. *Medieval Civilization 400–1500*, trans. Julia Barrow (Oxford: Blackwell Publishers Ltd.), from *La civilisation de l'Occident médiéval* (Paris: B. Artaud, 1964).

LEBON, Joseph (1879–1957).

1930. "Le Pseudo-Denys l'Aréopagite et Sévère d'Antioche", *Revue d'histoire ecclésiastique* 26: 880–915.

LECLERQ, Jean (1911–).

1961. *The Love of Learning and the Desire for God: A Study of Monastic Culture* (esp. between AD800–1200), trans. Catharine Misrahi (New York: Fordham University Press).

1987. "Influence and Noninfluence of Dionysius in the Western Middle Ages", in Luibheid et al. 1987: 25–32.

LEIBNIZ, G. W. F. (1646–1716).

1704. *Nouveaux Essais sur l'entendement humain* (first published posthumously in Amsterdam, 1765), in Eerdmann and Vollbrecht eds 1959: 194–418. English trans. and ed. Peter Remnant and Jonathan Bennett, *New Essays on Human Understanding* (Cambridge University Press, 1981). An alternative English trans. of the preface to this work wherein Leibniz uses the expression "way of ideas" (p. 301) can be seen in *G. W. Leibniz. Philosophical Essays*, trans. and ed. Roger Ariew and Daniel Garber (Indianapolis, IN: Hackett, 1989), 291–305.

1714. *Monadologie*, in Eerdmann and Vollbrecht 1959: 705–12.

LEMONICK, Michael D. (1953–).

1996. "Dumping on Darwin", *Time* (18 March), 81.

LENFANT, F. David (1603–88), editor.

1665. *Concordantiae Augustinianae sive collectio omnium sententiarum quae sparsim reperiuntur in omnibus S. Augustini operibus ad instar concordantiarum sacrae scripturae* (Paris: Cramoisy & Mabre-Cramoisy), 2 vols.

LEO XIII, Pope (r.1878–1903; Vincenzo Gioacchino Pecci, 1810–1903).

1879, 4 August. *Aeterni Patris*, encyclical letter on scholastic philosophy (Rome, Italy: Vatican City). I have relied on the English text as printed in Brezik 1981: 173–97.

LEROY, M. V.

1949. "Le savoir spéculatif", in *Jacques Maritain, son oeuvre philosophique*, festschrift organized by editors of the *Revue Thomiste* (Paris: Desclée de Brouwer).

LESHER, J. H.

1992. *Xenophanes of Colophon. Fragments. A Text and Translation with a Commentary* (Toronto: University of Toronto Press).

LEUCIPPUS (c.470–390BC; fl.440–435).

Date for writing based on the prime assigned by Freeman 1966a: 285.

c.430BC. Fragments in Freeman 1966: 90–1.

LEVY, Leonard W. (1923–).

1993. *Blasphemy. Verbal Offense against the Sacred, from Moses to Salman Rushdie* (New York: Alfred A. Knopf).

LEWRY, Osmond (1929–).

1975. "The Problem of the Authorship" of Kilwardby Adscriptus c.1250.: 12+–17+.

1981. "Robert Kilwardby on Meaning: A Parisian Course on the *Logica Vetus*", in *Sprache und Erkenntnis im Mittelalter*, ed. Jan P. Beckman et al. (Berlin: Walter de Gruyter), pp. 376–84.

LIDDELL, Henry George (1811–98), and Robert SCOTT (1811–87).

1846. *Greek-English Lexicon, based on the German work of Francis Passow, by Henry George Liddell, M.A., and Robert Scott, M.A., with corrections and additions, and the insertion in alphabetical order of the proper names occurring in the principal Greek authors by Henry Drisler, LL.D.* (1st American ed.; New York: Harper & Brothers, 1846).

1940, 1968. *A Greek-English Lexicon*, comp. Henry George Liddell and Robert Scott (original ed. 1843), rev. and augmented throughout by Sir Henry Stuart Jones (1867–1939) with assistance of Roderick McKenzie (1887–1937) (9th ed., 1940) with a supplement (1968) by E. A. Barber with assistance of P. Maas, M. Scheller, and M. L. Left (Oxford University Press).

LINGUISTIC SOCIETY OF PARIS, STATUTES ("Statuts" de la Société de Linguistique de Paris).

1868. *Memoires de la Société de Linguistique de Paris* (Paris: Librairie A. Franck), vol. I, 3.

LITT, Thomas.

1963. *Les corps célestes dans l'univers de saint Thomas d'Aquin* (Paris: Nauwelaerts).

LIVINGSTONE, R. W. (1880–1960).

    1915. *The Greek Genius and Its Meaning to Us* (2nd ed.; Oxford: The Clarendon Press).

LIVINGSTONE, R. W., editor.

    1923. *The Legacy of Greece* (Oxford: Clarendon Press).

LLAMZON, B. S.

    1966. "Introduction" to *The Primacy of Existence in Thomas Aquinas*, a presentation by Llamzon in English of Question 3, Article 4 from Bañez 1584/8, without the technicalities of structure in the original text (Chicago: Regnery), 4–14.

LLEWELLYN, Peter (1937–).

    1971. *Rome in the Dark Ages* (London: Faber and Faber Ltd.).

LOCKE, John (1632–1704).

    1690. *An Essay Concerning Humane Understanding* (London: Printed by Elizabeth Holt for Thomas Basset). The concluding chapter introducing the term "semiotic" into the English language has been photographically reproduced from the copy of the original edition located at the Lilly Library of Indiana University, Bloomington, at least three times recently in Deely, Williams, and Kruse eds 1986: 2–4; Deely 1993; and Deely 1994a: 112.

    The most important modern editions of Locke's text are by Alexander Campbell Fraser (Oxford, 1894; Dover repr. 1959), in 2 vols.; and by P. H. Nidditch (Oxford: Clarendon Press, 1975; 1979 corrected paperback ed.), which restores the capitalization and spelling of the English in Locke's original. See entries under Fraser and Nidditch, respectively.

LOMBARD, Peter (1100–60).

    c.1150. *Libri Quattuor Sententiarum* ("The Four Books of the Sentences"), in PL 192 (Migne 1844ff.), cols. 522–963.

LONERGAN, Bernard J. F. (1904–84).

    1965. *Insight: A Study of Human Understanding* (New York: The Philosophical Library).

LOTMAN, Yuri (1922–93).

    1990. *Universe of the Mind: A Semiotic Theory of Culture* (London: I. B. Taurus).

LOZANO-MIRALLES, Helena.

    1988. "Signs and Language in Plato", *Versus* 50/51 (maggio-dicembre): 71–82.

LUCKS, Henry A (1901–).

    1935. "Natura Naturans – Natura Naturata", *The New Scholasticism* IX.1 (January): 1–24.

LUCRETIUS CARUS, Titus (c.99–55BC).

    a.55BC. *De Rerum Natura*, Latin text with facing English trans. by W. H. D. Rouse (2nd ed., rev.; Harvard: Loeb Classical Library, 1982). Trans. by Munro in Oates 1940: 67–219.

LUIBHEID, Colm, et al.

    1987. *Pseudo-Dionysius. The Complete Works*, trans. by Colm Luibheid; foreword, notes, and translation collaboration by Paul Rorem; preface by Rene Roques; with introductions by Jaroslav Pelikan, Jean Leclerq, and Karlfried Froehlich (New York: Paulist Press, 1987).

ŁUKASIEWICZ, Jan (1878–1956).

> 1935. "Zur Geschichte der Aussagenlogik", *Erkenntnis* 5 (1935): 111–31. According to Mates (1949: 290n1), "the best published account of Stoic logic" then available. A fuller account since has been essayed by Frede 1974.

LUTHER, Martin (1483–1546).

> 1518, 25 November. *Acta Augustana*, "Proceedings at Augsburg", in *Luther's Works* 31, *Career of the Reformer: I*, ed. and trans. Harold J. Grimm (Philadelphia: Fortress Press, 1957), 259–92.

> 1520. "De Captivitate Babylonica Ecclesiae Praeludium", in *D. Martin Luthers Werke, critische Gesamtausgabe* (Weimar: Herman Böhlau, 1888), 497–573, with an "Introduction" beginning on p. 484. Cf. "The Babylonian Captivity of the Church", trans. A. T. W. Steinhaüser and rev. Frederick C. Ahrens and Abdel Ross Wentz, in *Luther's Works* 36, *Word and Sacrament*, ed. Abdel Ross Wentz (Philadelphia: Fortress Press, 1959), 3–126.

> 1538–40. *D. Martin Luthers Werke, critische Gesamtausgabe, Tischreden, Vierter Band* (Weimar: Hermann Böhlaus Nachfolger, 1916). Cf. the entry no. 4638 for 4 June, 1539, titled "Luther Rejects the Copernican Cosmology", in *Luther's Works* 54, *Table Talk*, ed. and trans. Theodore G. Tappert (Philadelphia: Fortress Press, 1967), 358–9.

MacDONOGH, Steve (1949–), editor.

> 1993. *The Rushdie Letters. Freedom to Speak, Freedom to Write*, edited "in association with Article 19" of the United Nations Universal Declaration of Human Rights, text cited in chapter 5 above, p. 191 (Lincoln: University of Nebraska Press).

MAISONNEUVE, H.

> 1962. "Croyance religieuse et contrainte: la doctrine de S. Augustin", *Mélanges de science religieuse* XIX: 49–68.

MAKOWSKI, Simon Stanislaus.

> 1679. *Cursus Philosophicus* (Cracow, Poland: University of Cracow Press; available in the Lilly Library of Indiana University, Bloomington).

MALMESBURY, William of (c.1095/6–1143).

> *Note:* Dating based on Stubbs's preface, p. xxxi.

> i.1135/40. *Willelmi Malmesbiriensis Monachi De Gestis Regum Anglorum Libri Quinque*, ed. from the mss. by William Stubbs (London: Printed for Her Majesty's Stationery Office by Eyre and Spottiswoodie, 1887), in 2 vols. (vol. 2 to p. 522; pp. 523–96 being Malmesbury's *Historia Novella* of i.1140/2). Earlier trans. as *William of Malmesbury's Chronicle of the Kings of England, from the earliest period to the reign of King Stephen [incipit a.d. 1135]*, with notes and illustrations, by J. A. Giles (to p. 479, pp. 480–535 being the "Modern History" of i.1140/2; London: George Bell and Sons, 1847).

MALONEY, Thomas S.

> 1983. "The Semiotics of Roger Bacon", *Mediaeval Studies* 45: 120–54.

> 1988. "Introduction" and notes to trans. of R. Bacon 1292: 1–30 and 120–78, respectively.

MANDONNET, Pierre Felix (1858–1936).

  1905. "Cajétan (Thomas de Vio dit)", entry in the *Dictionnaire de théologie catholique*, vol. II (Paris: Letouzey et Ané), cols. 1313–29.

MANETTI, Giovanni.

  1993. *Theories of the Sign in Classical Antiquity* (Bloomington: Indiana University Press), trans. by Christine Richardson of *Le teorie del segno nell'antichità classica* (Milan: Bompiani, 1987).

MARC, André (1892–1961).

  1933. "L'Idée de l'être chez Saint Thomas et dans la scolastique postérieure", *Archives de philosophie* X, cahier 1.

  1933a. "L'Idée thomiste de l'être et les analogies d'attribution et de proportionalité", *Revue néo-scolastique de philosophie* XXXV: 157–89.

MARÉCHAL, Joseph (1878–1944).

  1922–47. *Le point de départ de la métaphysique: Leçons sur le développement historique du problème de la connaisance* (Bruges, Brussels: Éditions du Museum Lessianum). In 1944, a 3rd ed. of vols. I, II, and III was published (Brussels: L'Édition Universelle; Paris: Desclée de Brouwer); in 1947, vol. IV was reprinted (same publishers) with no edition mark; and in 1949 a 2nd ed. of vol. V.

MARENBON, John.

  1983. *Early Medieval Philosophy (480–1150): An Introduction* (London: Routledge & Kegan Paul).

  1987. *Later Medieval Philosophy (1150–1350): An Introduction* (London: Routledge & Kegan Paul).

  1991. *Later Medieval Philosophy (1150–1350): An Introduction* (London: Routledge & Kegan Paul), paperback ed., the "Preface" to which reads as follows: "The text of this paperback edition is exactly the same as that of the hardback, published in 1987, except for the correction of a number of minor verbal and typographical errors. I have, however, added a section of additional notes and bibliography, which lists some of the work on later medieval philosophy to have appeared since the original bibliography was compiled [I should rather say: 'constructed'] and, in the most important cases, notes briefly its bearing on the discussion in this Introduction. – Trinity College, Cambridge, 1991."

MARITAIN, Jacques (18 November 1882–1973 April 28).

  Note: The writings of Maritain are so diverse and have appeared in so many translations with so many modifications that it needs to be noted that in the 13 years spanning 1983 and 1995 the Cercle d'Etudes Jacques et Raïssa Maritain (in the persons of Jean-Marie Allion, Maurice Hany, Dominique and René Mougel, Michel Nurdin, and Heinz R. Schmitz) established the definitive text of all the writings and brought them to publication in 15 vols. entitled *Jacques et Raïssa Maritain. Oeuvres Complètes* (Éditions Universitaires Fribourg Suisse et Editions Saint-Paul Paris, 1983–95). In citing Maritain from various individual editions incorporated into this set, I will indicate their place in this set abbreviated to OC (for "*Oeuvres Complètes*") followed by vol. number in roman numerals and pages in arabic numbers. And where I have consulted only the OC text, I will note that page numbers so refer.

1920. *Introduction générale à la philosophie* (Paris: Librairie Pierre Téqui). In OC II 11–272.

1921. *Theonas, ou les Entretiens d'un Sage et de Deux Philosophes sur Diverses Matières Inégalement Actuelles* (Paris: Nouvelle Librarie Nationale). In OC II 765–921.

1924. "Á propos des 'cahiers' du R. P. Maréchal", *Revue Thomiste* N.S. VII (July–August), 416–25.

1932. *Distinguer pour Unir: Ou, les Degrés du Savoir* (Paris: Desclée de Brouwer). The definitive final edition of this work, OC IV 257–1110, was based on the 7th French ed. of 1963.

1932a. "De la notion de philosophie chrétienne", *Revue Néo-scolastique de Philosophie* XXXIV (May): 153–86; text of conference presented at Louvain University in December 1931.

1935. *Science et sagesse* (Paris: Laberge), in OC VI 9–250. English trans. Bernard Wall, *Science and Wisdom* (London: Geofrey Bles, 1940).

1938. *De la philosophie chrétienne* (2nd ed.; Paris: Desclée de Brouwer), the text made definitive in OC V 225–316. There exists an English trans. by Edward H. Flannery, *An Essay on Christian Philosophy* (New York: Philosophical Library, 1955).

1938a. "Signe et Symbole", *Revue Thomiste* XLIV (April), 299–330. Cf. OC VI 97–158.

1942. "On Human Knowledge", in *The Range of Reason* (New York: Charles Scribner's Sons), 3–18.

1943. "Sign and Symbol", English trans. by H. L. Binsse of 1938a entry above, but with footnotes separated from the text proper at the end of the volume, in *Redeeming the Time* (London: Geoffrey Bles), text pp. 191–224, Latin notes pp. 268–76.

1947. *Court Traité de l'Existence et de l'Existant* (Paris: Paul Hartmann); page nos. are to OC IX 9–140.

1951. "A Maritain Anthology on Art and Poetry", *Thought* XXVI (Autumn): 325–41.

1953, 1 November. Letter published as "Preface" to Simon et al. 1955: v–viii.

1953a. *Creative Intuition in Art and Poetry* (New York: Pantheon Books).

1954. "On Knowledge through Connaturality", *Review of Metaphysics* IV (June): 473–81.

1957. "Language and the Theory of Sign", originally published in English in Anshen ed. 1957: 86–101; repr. with the addition of a full technical apparatus explicitly connecting the essay to Maritain's work on semiotic begun in 1937 and to text of Poinsot 1632 on which Maritain centrally drew in Deely, Williams, and Kruse eds 1986: 51–62. Page refs. in this book are based on 1986 reprint as the most definitve English version.

1959. *Distinguish to Unite, or The Degrees of Knowledge*, trans. from 4th French ed. of original 1932 entry above under supervision of Gerald B. Phelan (New York: Scribner's).

1966. *God and the Permission of Evil* (Milwaukee: Bruce), trans. by Joseph Evans of *Dieu et la Permission du Mal* (Paris: Desclée de Brouwer, 1963); in OC XII 9–123.

1966a. *Le Paysan de la Garonne*, in OC XII 663–1035.

1970. *De l'Église du Christ* (Paris: Desclée de Brouwer); in OC XIII 9–411.

1973. *Approches sans entraves* (Paris: Librairie Arthème Fayard). I have used the original edition sent to me by Gilson; the final text is that of OC XIII 413–1223.

MARKUS, R. A. (1924–).

1972. "St. Augustine on Signs", in *Augustine: A Collection of Critical Essays*, ed. R. A. Markus (Garden City, NY: Doubleday & Co.), 61–91.

MARTIN, François Xavier (1762–1846), and John A. RICHMOND, editors.

1991. *From Augustine to Eriugena: Essays on Neoplatonism and Christianity in Honor of John O'Meara* (Washington: Catholic University of America Press).

MARTINDALE, J. R.

1980. "Odovacer", entry in *The Prosopography of the Later Roman Empire A.D. 395–527*, ed. A. H. M. Jones, J. R. Martindale, and J. Morris (Cambridge, Eng.: Cambridge University Press), vol. II, pp. 791–3.

MARQUAND, Allan (1853–1924).

1883. "The Logic of the Epicureans", in *Studies in Logic by Members of the Johns Hopkins University*, ed. C. S. Peirce (Boston: Little, Brown, and Co.), 1–11. Facsimile repr. with intro. essay by Max H. Fisch and preface by Achim Eschbach as vol. 1 in the series "Foundations in Semiotics" under general editorship of Eschbach (Amsterdam/Philadelphia: John Benjamins Publishing Co., 1983).

MASTRIUS, Bartholomeus (1602–73; "Bartolomeo Mastri"), and Bonaventura BELLUTUS (1600–76).

1639. *Disputationes in Organum Aristotelis quibus ab adversantibus tum veterum tum recentiorum iaculis Scoti logica vindicatur* (Venice: Typis Marci Ginammi).

1643. *Disputationes in Aristotelis Stagiritae libros De Anima. Quibus ab adversantibus tùm veterum, tùm recentiorum iaculis Scoti Philosophia vindicatur* (Vencie: Typis Marci Ginammi).

1646. *Disputationes in Organum Aristotelis quibus ab adversantibus tum veterum tum recentiorum iaculis Scoti logica vindicatur* (ed. sec., priori castigatior et auctior, novisque indicibus et additionibus exulta; Venice: Typis Marci Ginammi). I am indebted to Marco Forlivesi for the information that "this [1646 edition] isn't a reprint, but really a new edition".

1664. *Disputationes theologicae in quartum librum sententiarum; quibus ab adversantibus tum veterum tum recentiorum iaculis Scoti theologia vindicatur* (Venice: apud Valvasensem).

MATES, Benson (1919–).

1949. "Stoic Logic and the Text of Sextus Empiricus", *American Journal of Philology* LXX.3 (July): 290–8.

1961. *Stoic Logic* (Berkeley: University of California Press).

1996. *The Skeptic Way: Sextus Empiricus's Outlines of Pyrrhonism*, trans. (87–217) with intro. (3–85), commentary (219–314), glossary (315–20), bibliography (321–5), and index (327–35) (New York: Oxford University Press).

MATSON, Wallace I. (1921–).

1987. *A New History of Philosophy* (New York: Harcourt Brace Jovanovich), in 2 vols.

MAURER, Armand A. (1915–).

1958. "Introduction" to his trans. of St Thomas Aquinas, *The Division and Methods of the Sciences*, Questions V and VI of Aquinas, c.1257/8 (2nd rev. ed.; Toronto: Pontifical Institute of Medieval Studies), vii–xxxvi.

McCORD ADAMS, Marilyn.

1987. *William Ockham* (Notre Dame, IN: Notre Dame University Press), 2 vols.

McCORMICK, Michael (1941–).

1994. "Diplomacy and the Carolingian Encounter with Byzantium down to the Accession of Charles the Bald", in McGinn and Otten eds 1994: 15–84.

McDERMOTT, John J.

1998. *What Are They Saying about the Formation of Israel* [c.1250–1000BC] (New York: Paulist Press).

McGINN, Bernard (1937–).

1994. "Introduction" to McGinn and Otten eds 1994: 1–12.

McGINN, Bernard, and Willemien OTTEN, editors.

1994. *Eriugena: East and West* (Notre Dame, IN: Notre Dame University Press).

McINERNY, Ralph (1929–).

1961. *The Logic of Analogy: An interpretation of St. Thomas* (The Hague: Martinus Nijhoff).

1990. *Boethius and Aquinas* (Washington: Catholic University of America Press).

1996. *Aquinas and Analogy* (Washington: Catholic University of America Press).

McKEON, Richard (1900–85).

1929. *Selections from Medieval Philosophers I. Augustine to Albert the Great* (New York: Charles Scribner's Sons).

1930. *Selections from Medieval Philosophers II. Roger Bacon to William of Ockham* (New York: Charles Scribner's Sons).

MEIER-OESER, Stephan.

1995. Entry "Semiotik, Semiologie" in the *Historisches Wörterbuch der Philosophie*, ed. Joachim Ritter and Karlfried Gründer (Basel: Schwabe), band IX, cols. 601–8.

1997. *Die Spur des Zeichens. Das Zeichen und seine Funktion in der Philosohie des Mittelalters und der frühen Neuzeit* (Berlin: Walter de Gruyter).

MELANCTHON, Philipp (1497–1560).

1549. "Initia doctrinae physicae", in *Corpus Reformatorum*, ed. Bretshneider, XIII, 216ff.

MELISSUS OF SAMOS (c.481–c.401BC).

Date for writing based on the prime assigned in Freeman 1966a: 164.

c.441/40BC. Περὶ φύσεως ἢ περὶ τοῦ ὄντος, "On Nature, or On What Is". Fragments in Freeman 1966: 48–51.

Compare this title with that of Gorgias c.444BC, above.

MERGUET, Hugo (1841–1911).

1887. *Lexikon zu den Philosophischen Schriften Cicero's, mit Angabe sämtlicher Stellen* (2nd ed.; Hildesheim: Georg Olms Verlag, 1987 reproduction of 1887 Jena ed.), in 3 vols.

MERLEAU-PONTY, Maurice (1908–61).

1942. *La Structure de la comportement* (Paris: Presses Universitaires de France), ms. completed for the doctorate in 1938 but delayed in publication by World War II; trans. as *The Structure of Behavior* by Alden Fisher (Boston: Beacon Press, 1963).

1945. *Phénoménologie de la perception* (Paris: Éditions Gallimard), trans. as *Phenomenology of Perception* by Colin Smith, with corrections by Forrest Williams and David Guerrière (London: Routledge & Kegan Paul, 1981).

1960. *Signes* (Paris: Librairie Gallimard), trans. as *Signs* by Richard C. McCleary (Evanston, IL: Northwestern University Press, 1964).

MERRELL, Floyd (1937–).

1985. *Deconstruction Reframed* (West Lafayette, IN: Purdue University Press).

MERTON, Thomas (1915–68).

1951. *The Ascent to Truth* (New York: Harcourt, Brace and Co.).

MEWS, Constant J.

1999. *The Lost Love Letters of Heloise and Abelard. Perceptions of Dialogue in Twelfth-Century France* (New York: St Martin's Press).

MIGNE, J. P. (1800–75), editor.

c.1844–64. *Patrologiae Cursus Completus, Series Latina* (PL, customarily) (Paris), 221 vols.

c.1857–66. *Patrologiae Cursus Completus, Series Graeca* (PG, customarily) (Paris), 162 vols.

MILES, John Russiano ("Jack").

1985. Text of original announcement by University of California Press of the publication of *Tractatus de Signis: The Semiotic of John Poinsot*.

MINIO-PALUELLO, L., editor.

1958. *Twelfth Century Logic Texts and Studies II. Abaelardiana Inedita* (Rome: Edizione di Storia e Letteratura).

MOMMSEN, C. M. Theodor Ernst (1905–58).

1942. "Petrarch's Conception of the 'Dark Ages'", *Speculum* XVII: 226–42; repr. in Mommsen, *Medieval and Renaissance Studies*, ed. Eugene F. Rice, Jr (Ithaca, NY: Cornell University Press, 1959), 106–29.

MOMMSEN, Theodor (1817–1903), and Paul Martin MEYER (1865–), editors.

1905. *Theodosiani libri XVI cvm Constitutionibvs Sirmondianis. Edidit adsvmpto apparatv P. Krvegeri Th. Mommsen* (Berlin: Weidmann), 2 vols. bound as 3 (I.1 = Voluminis I Pars Prior; I.2 = Voluminis I Pars Posterior; II = Volumen 2).

MONK, Ray.

1990. *Ludwig Wittgenstein. The Duty of Genius* (New York: The Free Press).

MONTAGNES, Bernard.

1963. *La doctrine de l'analogie de l'être d'après saint Thomas d'Aquin* (Paris: Béatrice-Nauwelaerts).

MONTESQUIEU, Baron de La Brède et de (Charles-Louis de Secondat). (1689–1755).

c.1709. "Discours sur Cicéron", in *Oeuvres Complètes* in 2 vols, ed. Roger Callois (Paris: Gallimard, 1949), vol. I, 93–8.

MOORE, Thomas Verner (1877–).

1956. *The Life of Man with God* (New York: Harcourt, Brace).

MORA, José Ferrater (1912–).

1953. "Suárez and Modern Philosophy", in *Journal of the History of Ideas* XIV.4: 528–47.

MORRIS, Charles W. (1901–79).

    1946. *Signs, Language and Behavior* (New York: Prentice-Hall).

MUCKLE, J. T.

    1942. "Greek Works Translated Directly into Latin Before 1350; Part I – Before 1000", *Mediaeval Studies* IV: 33–42.

    1943. "Greek Works Translated Directly into Latin Before 1350 (Continuation); Part I – Before 1000 *(supplement)*", *Mediaeval Studies* V: 102–14.

MUÑOZ DELGADO, Vicente.

    1964. *Lógica formal y filosofía en Domingo de Soto* (Madrid: Revista "Estudios").

MURRAY, Gilbert (1866–1957).

    1927. *A History of Ancient Greek Literature* (New York: D. Appleton and Co.).

NASR, Seyyed Hossein.

    1996. "The Qur'ān and *Hadīth* as Source and Inspiration of Islamic Philosophy", being chap. 2 of Nasr and Leaman eds 1996: 27–39.

NASR, Seyyed Hossein, and Oliver LEAMAN, editors.

    1996. *History of Islamic Philosophy*, parts I & II (= Routledge History of World Philosophies, vol. 1; London: Routledge).

NATOLI, Joseph (1943–), and Linda HUTCHEON (1947–).

    1993. "Reading *A Postmodern Reader*", intro. to *A Postmodern Reader*, ed. Joseph Natoli and Linda Hutcheon (Albany: State University of New York Press), vii–xiv.

NAVILLE, Adrien (1845–1930).

    1901. *Nouvelle classification des sciences* (2nd ed.; Paris: Alcan).

NEWTON, Sir Isaac (1642–1727).

    1687. *Philosophiae Naturalis Principia Mathematica* (London: The Royal Society), newly trans. as *The Principia. Mathematical Principles of Natural Philosophy* by I. Bernard Cohen and Anne Whitman, assisted by Julia Budenz (Berkeley, CA: University of California Press, 1946), pp. 371–971; preceded by "A Guide to Newton's Principia" by I. Bernard Cohen, pp. 1-370.

NIDDITCH, Peter H. (1928–83).

    1975, 1979. Foreword, notes, and critical apparatus to new ed. of John Locke, *An Essay concerning Human Understanding* (Cambridge).

NOGAR, Raymond ("Cosmic Ray") J. (19 November 1916–1967 November 17).

    1963. *The Wisdom of Evolution* (New York: Doubledy).

NUCHELMANS, Gabriel.

    1987. Review of John Poinsot: *Tractatus de Signis: The Semiotic of John Poinsot*, ed. John N. Deely with Ralph A. Powell, in *Renaissance Quarterly* XL.1 (Spring): 146–9.

OATES, Whitney J. (1904–?), editor.

    1940. *The Stoic and Epicurean Philosophers: The Complete Extant Writings of Epicurus, Epictetus, Lucretius, Marcus Aurelius*, with an intro. (New York: Random House).

OCKHAM, William of (c.1285–c.1349).

    Note 1: I have followed McCord Adams's general *monitum* (1987: I, xvi) that "the exact chronological order of Ockham's works is not known" while ignoring her specific claim (since historical layering was clearly a point of minimal interest in her dominantly synchronic perspective) as to what "groupings are clear"; for I find that the editors of the critical edition of Ockham's writings, in their series of Introductions, consider that they have been able to give an absolute date in fact to every work "give or take a year". Hence I have based my dating on the editorial materials of the critical edition *Guillelmi de Ockham: Opera Philosophica et Theologica*, complete in 17 volumes (St Bonaventure, NY: Editions of the Franciscan Institute of the University of St Bonaventure, 1974–88).

Of the 17 volumes, the *Opera Philosophica* (or OP) are numbered vols. I through VII, published between 1974 and 1988; the *Opera Theologica* (or OT) again begin with vol. I and continue to X, published between 1967 and 1986. Accordingly, each reference herein conforms to the following pattern: after the date and title of each work, I will indicate by OP or OT the respective series within which the named work falls, followed by the vol. no., a parenthesis indicating year of publication (together with specific page nos. when the vol. contains more than one work), then the editor(s) of the vol., and finally (again in parentheses) the place of their discussion of the date of the work.

i.1317/19. *Scriptum in librum primum sententiarum ordinatio*, as follows: OT I (1967), Prologus et Distinctio Prima, ed. Gedeon Gál with Stephanus Brown (time of composition discussed on pp. 34*–36*); OT II (1970), Distinctiones ii–iii, ed. idem; OT III (1977), Distinctiones iv–xviii, ed. Girardus I. Etzkorn; OT IV (1979), Distinctiones xix–xlviii, ed. Girardus I. Etzkorn and Franciscus E. Kelley.

i.1317/19a. *Quaestiones in librum secundum sententiarium (Reportatio)*, OT V (1981), ed. Gedeon Gál and Rega Wood.

i.1317/19b. *Quaestiones in librum tertium sententiarium (Reportatio)*, OT VI (1982), ed. Franciscus E. Kelley and Girardus I. Etzkorn.

i.1317/19c. *Quaestiones in librum quartum sententiarium (Reportatio)*, OT VII (1984), ed. Rega Wood and Gedeon Gál with Romualdo Green.

c.1318/19. *Quaestiones Variae* [1. De necessitate caritatis; 2. Utrum anima sit subiectum scientiae; 3. Quaestio disputata de aeternitate mundi; 4. Quaestio disputata de fine; 5. Quaestio disputata de intellectu agente; 6. Notabilia, dubitationes, determinationes, in 11 articles; 7. De connexione virtutum, in 4 articles; 8. De actu virtuoso et de intellectu erroneo), OT VIII (1984), ed. Girardus I. Etzkorn, Franciscus E. Kelley, and Josephus C. Wey (time of composition discussed on p. 5*: "… forsitan exortae sunt quaedam quidem simul cum *Reportatione*, aliae vero post, sed ante redactionem completam *Scripti* seu *Ordinationis*"; and on p. 22* re Q. 7: "… si eam ad autumnum anni 1319 adsignemus, haud longe a veritate aberimus").

i.1319/21. *Summula Philosophiae Naturalis*, in OP VI (1984: 135–394), ed. Stephanus Brown (time of composition discussed on pp. 28*–30*).

i.1321/4. *Ars Vetera*, in OP II ed. Ernestus A. Moody, Gedeon Gál, Angelus Gambatese, and Stephanus Brown (time of composition discussed on pp. 13*–16*, esp. 15*), as follows:

1321a, October–December. *Expositionis in libros artis logicae prooemium et Expositio in librum Porphyrii de Praedicabilibus*, in OP II (1978: 1–16, 16–131, respectively), ed. Ernestus A. Moody.

1321b, October–December. *Expositio in librum praedicamentorum Aristotelis*, in OP II (1978: 133–339), ed. Gedeon Gál.

1322, January–April. *Expositio in librum perihermenias Aristotelis*, in OP II (1978: 341–504), ed. Angelus Gambatese and Stephanus Brown.

1322a, January–April. *Tractatus de praedestinatione et de praescientia Dei respectu futurorum contingentium*, in OP II (1978: 505–39), ed. Philotheus Boehner with Stephanus Brown (time of composition discussed on pp. 13*–16*, esp. 15*).

1322b, April–October. *Expositio super libros elenchorum*, OP III (1979), ed. Franciscus del Punta (time of composition discussed on pp. 13*–16*, esp. 15*).

i.1322/3. *Brevis summa libri physicorum*, in OP VI (1984: 1–134), ed. Stephanus Brown (time of composition discussed on pp. 10*–13*).

i.1322/4. *Expositio in libros physicorum Aristotelis*, as follows: OP IV (1985), Prologus et libri i–iii, ed. Vladimirus Richter et Gerhardus Leibold; OP V (1985), libri iv–viii, ed. R. Wood, R. Green, G. Gál, J. Giermek, F. Kelley, G. Leibold, and G. Etzkorn. (Time of composition for work as a whole discussed in OP IV pp. 8*–9*).

i.1322/4a. *Quodlibeta Septem* (1322 fall: Q. I; 1323, winter & spring: Qq. II & III; 1323, fall: Q. IV; 1324, winter & spring: Qq. V, VI, VII), OT IX (1980), ed. Joseph C. Wey (time of composition discussed on pp. 36*–38*).

1323. *Summa Logicae*, OP I (1974), ed. Philotheus Boehner, Gedeon Gál, and Stephanus Brown (time of composition discussed on pp. 47*–56*, esp. 50* and 56*).

1323a. *Tractatus de quantitate*, in OT X (1986: 1–85), ed. Carolus A. Grassi (time of composition discussed on pp. 23*–28*, esp. pp. 24*, 26*, & 27*).

1323b. *Tractatus de corpore christi*, in OT X (1986: 87–234), ed. Carolus A. Grassi (time of composition discussed on pp. 23*–28*, esp. pp. 24*, 26*, & 27*).

i.1323/4. *Quaestiones in libros physicorum Aristotelis*, in OP VI (1984: 395–813), ed. Stephanus Brown (time of composition discussed on p. 41*).

Note 2: OP VII contains 6 works, of which the first 3 are dubious but probably authentic, the next 2 dubious but probably spurious, and one which is certainly spurious but (according to the editors) certainly expressive of Ockham's doctrine. Following the editors, I chronologize these "dubia et spuria" separately as follows:

PROBABLY AUTHENTIC

a.1323 if authentic; i.1394/1427 if spurious. *Tractatus de praedicamentis*, in OP VII (1988: 305–32), ed. G. I. Etzkorn (time of composition discussed on pp. 14*–15*).

1345. *Tractatus Minor Logicae*, in OP VII (1988: 1–57), ed. E. M. Buytaert and rev. G. Gál and J. Giermak (time of composition discussed on pp. 5*–11*, esp. p. 11*).

1346/7. *Elementarium Logicae*, in OP VII (1988: 59–304), ed. E. M. Buytaert and rev. G. Gál and J. Giermak (time of composition discussed on pp. 5*–11*, esp. p. 11*).

PROBABLY SPURIOUS

c.1323. *Quaestio de relatione*, in OP VII (1988: 333–69), ed. G. Mohan and rev. G. I. Etzkorn (time of composition discussed on p. 16*).

a.1400. *Centiloquium*, in OP VII (1988: 371–505), ed. Ph. Boehner and rev. G. I. Etzkorn (time of composition discussed on p. 20*).

CERTAINLY SPURIOUS IN AUTHOR, CERTAINLY AUTHENTIC IN DOCTRINE

i.1328/50. *Tractatus de Principiis Theologiae*, in OP VII (1988: 507–639), ed. L. Baudry and rev. F. E. Kelley (time of composition discussed on p. 26*).

O'DONNELL, James J. (1850–1934).

1992. *Augustine Confessions*, in 3 vols.: vol. I *Introduction and Text*; vol. II *Commentary on Books 1–7*; vol. III *Commentary on Books 8–13, Indexes* (Oxford: Clarendon Press).

OESTERLE, John (1912–1977).

1943. "The Problem of Meaning", *The Thomist* VI.2 (July): 180–229.

1944. "Another Approach to the Problem of Meaning", *The Thomist* VII.2 (April): 233–63.

OGDEN, Charles K. (1889–1957), and Ivor A. RICHARDS (1893–1979).

1923. *The Meaning of Meaning: A Study of the Influence of Language upon Thought and of the Science of Symbolism* (New York: Harcourt, Brace).

OGG, Frederic Austin (1878–1951).

1908. *A Source Book of Medieval History: Documents Illustrative of European Life and Institutions from the German Invasions to the Renaissance* (New York: American Book Co.).

O'MEARA, Dominic J.

1996. "The Hierarchical Ordering of Reality in Plotinus", in *The Cambridge Companion to Plotinus*, ed. Lloyd P. Gerson (Cambridge, Eng.: Cambridge University Press), 66–81.

O'MEARA, Thomas F. (1935–).

1997. *Thomas Aquinas, Theologian* (Notre Dame, IN: University of Notre Dame Press).

d'ORS, Angel.

1997. "Petrus Hispanus O.P., Auctor Summularum", *Vivarium* 35.1: 21–71.

OSBORN, Eric Francis (1911–).

1967. "Pseudo-Dionysius", entry for *The Encyclopedia of Philosophy*, ed. Paul Edwards (New York: Macmillan & The Free Press), vol. 6, 510–11.

OWENS, Joseph (1908–).

1959. *A History of Ancient Western Philosophy* (Englewood Cliffs, NJ: Prentice-Hall).

1963. *An Elementary Christian Metaphysics* (Milwaukee, WI: Bruce Publishing Co.)

1968. *An Interpretation of Existence* (Milwaukee, WI: Bruce Publishing Co.)

PARKINSON, G. H. R.

1993. "Introduction" to Parkinson ed. 1993: 1–15.

PARKINSON, G. H. R., editor.

1993. *The Renaissance and Seventeenth-Century Rationalism*, vol. IV of *Routledge History of Philosophy* (London: Routledge). The promising title of this volume proves a disappointment in the end, for the construction of the volume breaks no new ground but follows only the received outlines of the period from c.1350 to Descartes, outlines which screen out the developments of greatest philosophical interest for the contemporary scene.

PARMENIDES (c.515–c.450BC).

Date for writing based on the prime assigned by Freeman 1966a: 140.

c.475BC. See edition of Gallop 1984. Fragments also in Freeman 1966: 41–6.

PARMENTIER, Richard (1948–).

  1987. *The Sacred Remains: Myth, History, and Polity in Belau* (Chicago: University of Chicago Press).

  1987a. Letter to the author dated 19 August.

  1994. *Signs in Society: Studies in Semiotic Anthropology* (Bloomington: Indiana University Press).

  1997. "The Pragmatic Semiotics of Culture", *Semiotica* 116–1 (1997), a monograph special issue.

PARSONS, Edward Alexander (1878–1962).

  1952. *The Alexandrian Library. Glory of the Hellenic World. Its Rise, Antiquities, and Destruction* (Amsterdam: Elsevier).

PASSMORE, John (1914–).

  1966. *A Hundred Years of Philosophy* (2nd ed., rev.; New York: Basic Books).

PEIRCE, Charles Sanders (1838–1914).

  Note: **The designation CP** abbreviates *The Collected Papers of Charles Sanders Peirce*, vols. I–VI ed. Charles Hartshorne and Paul Weiss (Cambridge, MA: Harvard University Press, 1931–35), vols. VII–VIII ed. Arthur W. Burks (same publisher, 1958); all 8 vols. in electronic form ed. John Deely (Charlottesville, VA: Intelex Corporation, 1994). Dating within the CP (which covers Peirce's life 1866–1913) is based principally on the Burks bibliography at the end of CP 8 (see Burks 1958 above). The abbreviation followed by volume and paragraph numbers with a period between follows the standard CP reference form.

  The designation EP followed by volume and page numbers with a period in between abbreviates the 2-vol. set of *The Essential Peirce*, a selection of those essays from the complete Peirce corpus (that is, unpublished as well as previously published) deemed most seminal and central to Peirce's propriate perspective (pragmaticism or semiotic) made by the personnel of the Peirce Edition Project under the general editorship of Nathan Houser. EP 1 covers 1867–93, EP 2 1893–1913 (Bloomington: Indiana University Press, 1992, 1998, respectively).

  The designation NEM abbreviates *The New Elements of Mathematics*, ed. Carolyn Eisele (The Hague: Mouton, 1976), 4 vols. bound as 5.

  The designation W followed by volume and page numbers with a period in between abbreviates the ongoing *Writings of Charles S. Peirce: A Chronological Edition*, initiated as the Peirce Edition Project at Indiana University–Purdue University/Indianapolis by Edward C. Moore under the general editorship of Max H. Fisch, succeeded first by Christian Kloesel in late 1984, then in late 1993 by Nathan Houser (Bloomington: Indiana University Press, 6 vols. – [1982, 1984, 1986, 1989, 1993, 2000] – of a projected 20 published so far).

  Unpublished mss. are cited by number, using pagination made by the Institute for Studies in Pragmaticism at Texas Tech University in Lubbock.

  Chronology and identification of Peirce materials is based on Burks 1958, Fisch et al. 1979, Hardwick 1977, and Robin 1967, 1971, as indicated at specific points.

1867. "On a New List of Categories", *Proceedings of the American Academy of Arts and Sciences* 7 (presented 14 May 1867), 287–98; in CP 1.545–59, with "notes on the preceding" continuing to 1.567 (Burks p. 261); and in W 2.49–59.

1868. "Some Consequence of Four Incapacities", *Journal of Speculative Philosophy* 2: 140–57, repr. in CP 5.264–317.

1868a. "Questions concerning Certain Faculties Claimed for Man", *Journal of Speculative Philosophy* 2: 103–14; repr. in CP 5.213–63; and in W 2.193–211.

1871. Review of *The Works of George Berkeley*, in *The North American Review* 113 (Oct 1871): 449–72, as repr. in CP 8.7–38.

c.1890. *A Guess at the Riddle*, uncompleted work printed in CP 1.354–68, 1.373–5, 1.379–416. See also c.1898 entry following.

1891. "The Architecture of Theories", *The Monist* 1 (January): 161–76; repr. in CP 6.7–34 (Burks p. 276).

1893. *Grand Logic or How to Reason: A Critick of Arguments* (G-1893-5), a completed but unpublished book "ficte disiecta" throughout CP (1.545–59, except 549n1; 2.281, 2.285, 2.297–302; 2.391–426; 2.427–30; 2.445–60; 2.517n; 2.517–31; 2.532–5; 2.645–60; 3.328–58; 3.345n; 4.21–52; 4.53–79; 4.80–4; 4.85–152; 4.88n*; 5.358–87; 5.388–410; 6.278n1; 6.278–86; 7.388–450 except 392n7; 7.559–64; 7.463–7): see Burks 278–80 for details.

c.1896. "The Logic of Mathematics; An Attempt to Develop My Categories from Within" (first 4 ms. pages missing), in CP 1.417–520 (Burks p. 287).

c.1897. A fragment on Peirce's philosophy, partially printed in CP 1.8–14.

c.1897a. A fragment on semiotics, partially printed in CP 2.227–9, 2.244n1.

1898. *Reasoning and the Logic of Things*, lectures delivered in series of Cambridge Conferences, 10 February–7 March; ed. Kenneth Laine Ketner (Cambridge, MA: Harvard University Press).

c.1898. Alternative version of c.1890: sect. 1, in CP 1.1–2.

1901. From the entry "Pragmatic and Pragmatism" in vol. I of Baldwin's *Dictionary of Philosophy and Psychology* (1901–2), CP 5.4.

1902. "Universal (and Universality)", entry for Baldwin 1901–02, vol. 2, 737–41; CP 2.367–71 (deletions) (Burks p. 293).

1902a. "Premise (and Premiss)", entry for Baldwin 1901–02, vol. 2, 330–1; CP 2.582–3.

1902b. "Sign", entry for Baldwin 1901–02, vol. 2, 527.

c.1902. "Minute Logic", draft for a book complete consecutively only to chap. 4. Published in CP in extracts scattered over 6 of the 8 vols., incl. 1.203–83, 1.575–584; 2.1–202; 4.227–323; 6.349–52; 7.279, 7.374n10, 7.362–87 except 381n19. (For fuller detail, see Burks pp. 293–4.)

1903. "The Ethics of Terminology", from *A Syllabus of Certain Topics of Logic* (Boston: Alfred Mudge & Son), pp. 10–14; repr. in CP 2.219–26 continuing 1.202 (Burks p. 295).

1903a. Lowell Lectures, "Some Topics of Logic Bearing on Questions Now Vexed", esp.: lect. IIIA, "Lessons from the History of Philosophy", CP 1.15–26; draft 3 of lect. 3 entitled "Degenerate Cases", in CP 1.521–44; lect. 8, "How To Theorize", CP

5.590–604 (Burks p. 295); and the section published in CP 4.510–29 under the title "The Gamma Part of Existential Graphs".

1903b. Materials for the series of lectures on pragmatism delivered at Harvard, March–May (fuller detail in Burks pp. 294–5):

Lecture I, "On Pragmatism and the Normative Sciences", in CP 5.14–40;

Lecture II, "On Phenomenology", Draft 1 CP 1.322–3 are from it, Draft 2 CP 5.41–56 and 541n* are from it, Draft 3 (adding "or the Categories" to the title) CP 5.59–65;

Lecture III, "On the Categories" (cf. CP 5.66n* and 5.82n*), Version "a", "The Categories Continued" CP 5.71n1 and 5.82–7 are from it, Version "b", "The Categories Defended" CP 5.66–81 (except 5.71n1 and 5.77n1) and 5.88–92 are from it;

Lecture IV, "The Seven Systems of Metaphysics", CP 5.77.1n1, 5.93–119, 5.57–8, 5.57n*, 1.314–6, 1.314n*, 5.118n*;

Lecture V, "On Three Kinds of Goodness", CP 5.120–50;

Lecture VI, "On Three Types of Reasoning", CP 5.151–79;

Lecture VII, "On Pragmatism and Abduction", CP 5.180–212.

1903c. "On Phenomenology, or The Categories", Draft 3 of Lecture 2 for the March–May Harvard lecture series on Pragmatism, in CP 5.59–65 (Burks p. 294).

1903d. "The Categories Defended", ms. 308 as printed in EP 2.160–78. This is the text of the third of the Harvard Lectures of 1903 (entry 1903b above), delivered on April 3.

1903e. "Degenerate Thirdness", from version b of the third Harvard Lecture of 1903 (entry 1903b above).

c.1903. "Nomenclature and Divisions of Dyadic Relations, as far as they are determined", CP 2.233–72 (Burks p. 296).

1904. "On Signs and the Categories", from a letter to Lady Welby dated 12 October, in CP 8.327–41 (Burks p. 321).

1904a. Letter of 12 October from Peirce to Lady Welby, in *Semiotics and Significs. The correspondence between Charles S. Peirce and Victoria Lady Welby*, ed. Charles S. Hardwick (Bloomington: Indiana University Press, 1977), 22–36.

1905. "What Pragmatism Is", *The Monist* 15 (April): 161–81; repr. in CP 5.411–37, with 5.414–35 being editorially headed "Pragmaticism" in CP.

1905a. "Issues of Pragmaticism", *The Monist* 15 (October): 481–99; repr. in CP 5.438–63, except 448n1, which is from 1906 [see Burks, entry for 1905(d), p. 298] (Burks p. 297). Also repr. in EP 2.346–59.

c.1905. Unsigned letter addressed to Signor Calderoni, in CP 8.205–13.

1905–06. Ms. 283, partially published under the title "The Basis of Pragmaticism" in CP 1.573–4 (= ms. pp. 37–45), 5.549–54 (= ms. pp. 45–59), and 5.448n. (= ms. pp. 135–48) (Burks p. 328 and 298).

1906. "The Basis of Pragmaticism in the Normative Sciences", in EP 2.371–97.

c.1906. Partially printed under the title, "The Founding of Pragmatism", in *The Hound and the Horn* 2 (April–June, 1929), and repr. under the title, "Historical Affinities and Genesis [of Pragmatism]", in CP 5.11–13; both are from "Pragmatism (Editor [3])", which continues 5.13, under the title "A Survey of Pragmaticism", in CP 5.464–96.

c.1906a. "Reflexions upon Pluralistic Pragmatism and upon Cenopythagorean Pragmaticism", CP 5.555–64.

1907. "Pragmatism", Reading 28 in EP 2.398–433.

c.1907. Ms. 318 in Robin 1967: 36–7, numbered ISP 00002–00350: one of the most important of Peirce's literary remains, this many-layered ms. has never been published in full. Where I have drawn on unpublished sections I have used a photocopy bearing the sheet numbers stamped by the Texas Tech Institute for Studies in Pragmatism (hence: ISP nos.) on the electroprint copy Ketner with associates had made from microfilm, and then checked against the original in the Harvard archives. Further subdivisions and rearrangements have been made since. Originally an untitled letter-article to the editor of *The Nation*, this ms has several partial draft endings signed "Charles Santiago Peirce", but no single, consecutive, complete draft as a whole. Part appears in CP 5.464–96 under a title supplied by the editors of the volume, "A Survey of Pragmaticism" (cf. Burks p. 299). A small segment appears under the title "From Pragmatism" in NEM III.I: 481–94. The most complete, but still partial, presentation of this document is in EP 2.398–433, under the title "Pragmatism" (the 1907 entry immediately above).

1908. Draft of a letter dated 24, 25, 28 December "On the Classification of Signs", CP 8.342–79 except 368n23 are from it (Burks p. 321 para. 20.b). In Hardwick ed. 1977: 73–86; and EP 2.478–83.

1908a. "A Neglected Argument for the Reality of God", CP 6.452–85 (Burks p. 300).

1909. A set of mss. all with "Meaning" and the date in the upper left-hand corner of the pages, from which CP 1.27 derives (Burks p. 300).

c.1909. "Some Amazing Mazes, Fourth Curiosity", CP 6.318–48.

1913. "An Essay toward Reasoning in Security and Uberty", in EP 2.463–74.

PEIRCE, Charles S., editor.

1883. *Studies in Logic by Members of the Johns Hopkins University* (Boston: Little, Brown, and Co.).

PELIKAN, Jaroslav (1923–).

1971–89. *The Christian Tradition: A History of the Development of Doctrine* (Chicago: University of Chicago Press), in 5 vols.:

1971. Vol. 1, *The Emergence of the Catholic Tradition (100–600)*

1974. Vol. 2, *The Spirit of Eastern Christendom (600–1700)*

1978. Vol. 3, *The Growth of Medieval Theology (600–1300)*

1984. Vol. 4, *Reformation of Church and Dogma (1300–1700)*

1989. Vol. 5, *Christian Doctrine and Modern Culture (since 1700)*

1987. "The Odyssey of Dionysian Spirituality", in Luibheid et al. 1987: 11–24.

1993. *Christianity and Classical Culture: The Metamorphosis of Natural Theology in the Christian Encounter with Helenism* (New Haven, CT: Yale University Press).

PETRARCA ("Petrarch"), Francesco (1304–74).

  1367/8. *De suiipsius et multorum ignorantia*, in *Francisci Petrarchae Operum* (Basle,
    Switzerland: 1554), vol. II, pp. 1141–68. An English trans. by Hans Nachod appears
    in Cassirer, Kristeller, and Randall eds 1948: 47–133.

PETRUS HISPANUS ("Peter of Spain").

  c.1245. *Summulae Logicales*, ed. I. M. Bochenski (Rome: Marietti, 1947).

PHARR, Clyde (1883–?), in collaboration with Theresa Sherrer DAVIDSON and Mary Brown
    PHARR.

  1952. *The Theodosian Code and Novels and the Sirmondian Constitutions. A Translation
    with Commentary, Glossary, and Bibliography* (Princeton, NJ: Princeton University
    Press); being the compilation of the laws of the Roman Empire between AD313 and
    438, and of the bulk of those in the Western Empire between AD438 and 468.

PHELAN, Gerald B. (1892–1965).

  1941. *Saint Thomas and Analogy* (Milwaukee, WI: Marquette University Press).

  1957. "The Being of Creatures", in *Proceedings of the American Catholic Philosophical
    Association* XXXI: 118–125.

PHERECYDES OF SYROS (c.585/4–c.500/498BC).

    Date for writing based on the prime assigned by Schibli 1990: 2.

  c.544/1BC. Fragments in Freeman 1966: 13–15.

PHILIP CANCELLARIUS (c.1160/1185–1236, "Philip the Chancellor").

  c.1225/8. *Philippi Cancellarii Parisiensis Summa de Bono*, critical ed. by N. Wicki (Bern:
    Corpus philosophorum medii aevi II, 1985).

PHILO Judaeus (Philo of Alexandria, c.30BC–AD50/54).

  a.AD54. "De confusione linguarum", trans. F. H. Colson in *Philo*, vol. IV of 10 vols.
    (Cambridge, MA: Loeb Classical Library of Harvard University Press, 1932), 8–
    119. (According to Colson, "Preface", p. v, G. H. Whitaker, despite his name being
    on the volume, died before becoming involved enough to be considered a translator
    of the text in question.)

PHILODEMUS (c.110–c.40BC).

  i.54/40BC. Περὶ σημειώσεων (*De Signis*), trans. as *On the Methods of Inference* in ed.
    of Phillip Howard De Lacy and Estelle Allen De Lacy, rev. with collaboration
    of Marcello Gigante, Francesco Longo Auricchio, and Adele Tepedino Guerra
    (Naples: Bibliopolis, 1978), Greek text pp. 27–87, English 91–131.

PINBORG, Jan (1937–82).

  1975. "Introduction to the Text" of Kilwardby Adscriptus c.1250: 1+–11+.

  1975a. "Introduction to the Text" of Augustine AD387: see Jackson 1975.

PINNER, H. L. (1892–1964).

  1958. *The World of Books in Classical Antiquity* (2nd ed.; Leiden, Netherlands: A. W.
    Sijthoff).

PIPES, Daniel (1949–).

  1990. *The Rushdie Affair: The Novel, the Ayatollah, and the West* (New York: Birch Lane
    Press).

PITTENDRIGH, Colin S.

  1958. "Adaptation, Natural Selection, and Behavior", in *Behavior and Evolution*, ed. Anne Roe and George Gaylord Simpson (New Haven, CT: Yale University Press), 390–416.

PLATO (c.427–c.347BC).

  i.399/347BC. *The Dialogues of Plato*, which I have consulted in the trans. of B. Jowett (4th ed., rev.; Oxford, 1953) and in the ed. of Edith Hamilton and Huntington Cairns, including the Letters (Pantheon Books: Bollingen Series LXXI, 1961). References to translators of Plato other than Jowett will be found in this Hamilton & Cairns collection. The dialogues are chronologized as follows, on the general basis of Crombie 1962: I, 9–14:

    c.399–390BC, early dialogues presenting the life and teaching of Socrates: *Apology, Charmides, Cratylus, Crito, Euthydemus, Euthyphro, Gorgias, Hippias I ("Minor") and II ("Major"), Ion, Laches, Lysis, Menexenus, Meno, Protagoras*

    c.391–360BC, middle dialogues presenting Plato's own thought through the vehicle of Socrates: *Parmenides, Phaedo, Phaedrus, Republic, Symposium, Theaetetus*

    c.359–347BC, late dialogues, treating sophisticated and 'semi-professional' issues: *Laws, Philebus, Sophist, Statesman, Timaeus, Critias*

  c.353BC. Letter VII: "Plato to the relatives and friends of Dion", in *The Platonic Epistles*, trans. with introduction and notes by J. Harward (Cambridge, Eng.: Cambridge University Press, 1932), text of letter pp. 115–47 (= 324a–52a), introductory remarks pp. 188–92, notes pp. 198–222; date assigned on p. 192. In the Hamilton & Cairns ed., the text of Letter VII is on pp. 1574–98 in the trans. of Post, q.v.

PLOTINUS (AD205–270/1).

  Note: We have, as far as we know, most or all that Plotinus wrote. The best contemporary scholarship suggests that in fact he left 45 separate treatises (Gerson 1994: xiv), but that these 45 treatises were divided up so that they could be presented in 6 groups of 9 treatises (6 and 9 being in Porphyry's mind "perfect" numbers), whence the title of the work, *Enneads* (= "The Nines"). The arrangement within the *Enneads* of the treatises artificially expanded to number 54 is again to some extent the posthumous devising of Porphyry. He arranges them according to themes, beginning with the "earthly" themes, which are supposedly easier, and moving to the "heavenly" themes, more difficult. (Thus he anticipated the blunder of Peirce's editors in the creation of the so-called *Collected Papers*, but at least did not remove the means of correcting the blunder.)

    Fortunately, in his *Life* of Plotinus, Porphyry he tells us what the chronological sequence of the treatises was overall, the first twenty-one having been composed prior to Porphyry's arrival as a pupil in AD263 and probably beginning only around 255 (i.255/63, therefore); the next 23 being composed during the period of Porphyry's discipleship, that is, between 263 and 268 (i 263/8); and the final 9 having been composed between the time of Porphyry's departure and the death of Plotinus (i.AD269 and 270/1). We use this threefold main dating system and retain the numbered sequence of 54 treatises subordinate to it, because this is how the student will find the treatises divided in all editions of the *Enneads*. Nonetheless, despite the "anti-developmentalist position" dominant among Plotinus scholars today (Gerson 1994: xvii) – an attitude unable to cause too much harm in this case in view of the lateness of the beginning of the writings, combined with the comparatively short span of time, some 16 years in all, over which developments could occur – it would be desirable to see a chronological edition of Porphyry's text restored to what was most probably its author's own division, toward which we note that the following combinations would be made to reach a probable 45 actual treatises: #s22+23; #s27+28+29; #s35+31+32+33; #s42+43+44; #s47+48. The resulting text of 45 treatises could still be titled *Enneads* ("The Nines"), but would have 5 groups instead of the traditional 6.

In our entry, the arabic numbers used for the chronological order are followed by a roman numeral to indicate the main *Ennead* entry (I–VI), followed by a period and an arabic number (1–9) to indicate the substatus within the main entry. For Greek editions used, see under Henry and Schwyzer eds, and under Bréhier ed., respectively.

i.AD255/63

1 = I.6	*On Beauty*	
2 = IV.7	*On the Immortality of the Soul*	
3 = III.1	*On Destiny*	
4 = IV.2	*On the Essence of the Soul (II)*	
5 = V.9	*On Intellect, the Forms, and Being*	
6 = IV.8	*On the Descent of the Soul into Bodies*	
7 = V.4	*How That Which Is After the First Comes from the First, and On the One*	
8 = IV.9	*If All Souls Are One*	
9 = VI.9	*On the Good or the One*	
10 = V.1	*On the Three Primary Hypostases*	
11 = V.2	*On the Origin and Order of the Beings Which Come after the First*	
12 = II.4	*On Matter*	
13 = III.9	*Various Considerations*	
14 = II.2	*On the Movement of Heaven*	
15 = III.4	*On Our Allotted Guardian Spirit*	
16 = I.9	*On Going out of the Body*	
17 = II.6	*On Substance, or On Quality*	
18 = V.7	*On the Question Whether There Are Ideas of Particulars*	
19 = I.2	*On Virtues*	
20 = I.3	*On Dialectic*	
21 = IV.1	*On the Essence of the Soul (I)*	

i.AD263/8

22 = VI.4	*On the Presence of Being, One and the Same, Everywhere as a Whole (I)*	
23 = VI.5	*On the Presence of Being, One and the Same, Everywhere as a Whole (II)*	
24 = V.6	*On the Fact That That Which Is Beyond Being Does Not Think, and On What Is the Primary and What the Secondary Thinking Principle*	

25 = II.5   *On What Exists Potentially*

26 = III.6   *On the Impassibility of Things without Body*

27 = IV.3   *On Difficulties about the Soul (I)*

28 = IV.4   *On Difficulties about the Soul (II)*

29 = IV.5   *On Difficulties about the Soul (III), or On Sight*

30 = III.8   *On Nature and Contemplation and the One*

31 = V.8   *On the Intelligible Beauty*

32 = V.5   *That the Intelligibles Are Not Outside the Intellect, and On the Good*

33 = II.9   *Against the Gnostics*

34 = VI.6   *On Numbers*

35 = II.8   *On Sight, or On How Distant Objects Appear Small*

36 = I.5   *On Whether Well-Being Increases with Time*

37 = II.7   *On Complete Transfusion*

38 = VI.7   *How the Multitude of the Forms Came into Being, and On the Good*

39 = VI.8   *On Free Will and the Will of the One*

40 = II.1   *On Heaven*

41 = IV.6   *On Sense Perception and Memory*

42 = VI.1   *On the Kinds of Being (I)*

43 = VI.2   *On the Kinds of Being (II)*

44 = VI.3   *On the Kinds of Being (III)*

45 = III.7   *On Eternity and Time*

i.AD269 and 270/71

46 = I.4   *On Well-Being*

47 = III.2   *On Providence (I)*

48 = III.3   *On Prividence (II)*

49 = V.3   *On the Knowing Hypostases and That Which Is Beyond*

50 = III.5   *On Love*

51 = I.8   *On What Are Evils*

52 = II.3   *On Whether the Stars Are Causes*

53 = I.1   *What Is the Living Being and What Is Man?*

54 = I.7   *On the Primal Good and Other Goods*

PLUTARCH (c.AD46–120).

a.AD120. *Lives* (New York: Everyman's Library), 3 vols.

POINSOT, John (1589–1644).

> *Note:* A complete table of all the editions, complete and partial, and in whatever language, of Poinsot's systematic works in philosophy and theology is provided in Deely 1985: 396–7. A complete breakdown of the contents of the original volumes of Poinsot's *Cursus Theologicus* and of the relation of that content to the volumes of the principal modern editions is provided in Deely 1994a: 284. The principal modern editions referred to in this work are abbreviated as follows:
>
> R followed by a volume number (I, II, or III) and pages, with column (a or b) and line indications as needed = the *Cursus Philosophicus Thomisticus*, ed. B. Reiser in 3 vols. (Turin: Marietti, 1930, 1933, 1937).

S followed by a volume number (I–IV) and page numbers = the 5 volumes of the incomplete critical edition of the *Cursus Theologicus* ed. at Solesmes (Paris: Desclée, 1931, 1934, 1937, 1946; Matiscone: Protat Frères, 1953).

V followed by a volume number (I–IX) = the complete edition, ed. Ludovicus Vivès, published in Paris 1883–86.

1631. *Artis Logicae Prima Pars* (Alcalá, Spain). The opening pages 1–11a14 of this work and the "Quaestio Disputanda I. De Termino. Art. 6. Utrum Voces Significant per prius Conceptus an Res" pages 104b31–108a33, relevant to the discussion of signs in the *Secunda Pars* of 1632 (entry following), have been incorporated in the 1632a entry (2nd entry following, pp. 4–30 and 342–51 "Appendix A. On the Signification of Language", respectively), for the independent edition of that discussion published by University of California Press. From R I: 1–247.

1632. *Artis Logicae Secunda Pars* (Alcalá, Spain). From R I: 249–839.

1632a. *Tractatus de Signis*, subtitled *The Semiotic of John Poinsot*, extracted from the *Artis Logicae Prima et Secunda Pars* of 1631–32 (above 2 entries) using the text of the emended second impression (1932) of the 1930 Reiser edition (Turin: Marietti), and arranged in bilingual format by John Deely in consultation with Ralph A. Powell (1st ed.; Berkeley: University of California Press, 1985), as explained in Deely 1985.

This work is also available as a text database, stand-alone on floppy disk or combined with an Aquinas database, as an Intelex Electronic Edition (Charlottesville, VA: Intelex Corp., 1992).

Pages in this volume are set up in matching columns of English and Latin, with intercolumnar numbers every fifth line. (Thus, references to the volume are by page number, followed by a slash and the appropriate line number of the specific section of text referred to: e.g., 287/3–26.)

1633. *Naturalis Philosophiae Prima Pars* (Madrid, Spain). In R II: 1–529.

1633a. By reason of its importance for the contemporary discussion of semiotic categories, I give a separate listing here to Poinsot's treatment *De primo cognito*, "of being-as-first-known", within his *Philosophiae naturalis prima pars* (*Part I of Natural Philosophy*), as follows: Quaestio 1, "De Scientia Philosophiae et Ordine Cognoscendi" ("On Philosophical Knowledge and the Order of Knowing"), articulus 3, "Utrum magis universale, atque adeo ipsum ens ut sic, sit primo cognitum ab intellectu nostro" ("Whether the more universal, and therefore being itself as such, is primarily known by human understanding"), Reiser ed. vol. II, 20a2–33b38.

The most important commentary on this text is to be found in Guagliardo 1994.

1634. *Naturalis Philosophiae Tertia Pars* (Alcalá, Spain); in R II: 533–888.

1635. *Naturalis Philosophiae Quarta Pars* (Alcalá, Spain); in R III: 1–425.

1637. *Tomus Primus Cursus Theologici* (Alcalá, Spain). V I & II; S I complete & II through p. 529. (Contents: *Three Introductory Treatises* for beginners in theology: *First*, discussion of the complete text of Lombard's sentences, *Second*, an explanation of the order of the questions and the subject matter in the *Summa* of St. Thomas Aquinas, *Third*, an examination of the purity, exactness, and unique authority of

St. Thomas's doctrine; *Commentary* on the First Part of the *Summa theologiae* of Thomas Aquinas, 'Concerning God', Questions 1–14; and finally a *Treatise on the Days of the Creation*".)

In this volume, specific citation has been made from disp. VIII, "De Immensitate et Contactu Divino ad Res", S II 3–40, particularly Art. 6, "Utrum specialis modus existendi Dei per gratiam, sit bene assignatus", S II pp. 36–9.

1643. *Tomus Secundus Cursus Theologici* (Lyons, France). V III; S II 531–end + III. (Contents: continuation of the *Commentary* on the First Part of Aquinas's *Summa*, Questions 15–26 "Concerning God".)

In this volume, specific citation has been made from disp. XXII, "De Veritate Transcendentali et Formali", S II 589–638.

1667 (posthumously edited). *Tomus Octavus Cursus Theologici*, ed. Franciscus Combefis (Paris). The Vivès edition of this work (Vol. IX; Paris, 1885) is the best modern edition. (Contents: *In Illam Partem, de Sacramentis in genere, de Eucharistia, de Poenitentia*).

POJMAN, Louis P., editor.

1998. *Classics of Philosophy* (Oxford: Oxford University Press).

POMPONAZZI, Pietro (1462–1524).

1516. *De Immortalitate Animae*, editio princeps with an English trans. by William Henry Hay II (Haverford, PA: Haverford College, 1938). Hay trans., with revisions by J. H. Randall, printed separately in Cassirer, Kristeller, and Randall eds 1948: 280–381, to which separate printing of the English page references are made, with Latin taken from the princeps facsimile.

POPPER, Karl (1902–94).

1963. *The Open Society and Its Enemies* (4th ed., rev.; Princeton, NJ: Princeton University Press).

PORPHYRY the Phoenician (c.AD232–301/6).

c.271. *Porphyrii Isagoge et in Aristotelis Categorias Commentarium* (Greek text), ed. A. Busse (Berlin, 1887); English trans. Edward W. Warren, *Porphyry the Phoenician: Isagoge* (Toronto: Pontifical Institute of Mediaeval Studies, 1975).

c.AD300. *Porphyry on the Life of Plotinus and the Order of His Books*, Greek text with English trans. A. H. Armstrong in vol. 1 of the 6-vol. Loeb Classical Library ed. (Cambridge, MA: Harvard University Press, 1961), 1–85.

POST, L. A.

1925. *Thirteen Epistles of Plato*, introduction, translation, and notes, by L. A. Post 1925 (Oxford: Clarendon Press, 1925).

POTTER, Jean A.

1976. Introduction to Uhlfelder trans. 1976: ix–xli.

POUILLON, H.

1930. "Le premier traité des propriétés transcendantales. La 'Summa de Bono' du Chancelier Philippe", *Revue néoscolastique de philosophie* 42: 40–77.

POWELL, Philip Wayne.

1971. *Tree of Hate: Propaganda and Prejudices Affecting United States Relations with the Hispanic World* (New York: Basic Books; repr., with new "Introduction" by the author, Vallecito, CA: Ross House Books, 1985).

POWELL, Ralph A. (1914–).

1960. "Etiam in sua tractatione acatholicorum probatur solum statum catholicum adimplere altissima desideria humanae naturae in hac vita" ("Only in its treatment of non-Catholics is it proved that even the Catholic state can fulfill the highest desires of human nature in this life" – Powell's trans.), in *Thomistica Morum Principia* (Rome: Officium Libri Catholici), Vol. I, 442–51.

2000. "That a State Establishment of Any Religion Claiming Divine Revelation Is Contrary to Natural Law", in *Semiotics 2000*, ed. Scott Simpkins, C. W. Spinks, and John Deely (New York: Peter Lang), in preparation.

PREVITÉ-ORTON, C. W. (1877–1947).

1952. *The Shorter Cambridge Medieval History* (Cambridge, Eng.: Cambridge University Press), in 2 vols.

PREZIOSI, Donald (1941–).

1979. *The Semiotics of the Built Environment* (Bloomington: Indiana University Press).

PRISCIAN ("Priscianus Caesariensis", c.AD480–c.560/70: but see chapter 9 above, p. 436 on the matter of dates).

c.AD526–7. *Institutiones Grammaticae ("Foundations of Grammar")*; ed. Martin Hertz in vols. 2 (1855) and 3 (1859) of the *Grammatici Latini* in 7 vols. + 1 suppl., ed. Heinrich Keil (Leipzig: Teubner, 1855–1923).

PROCLUS (AD410–85).

Note on dating: Dodds (1963: xiv–xviii) sees no basis for a firm dating scheme within the Proclean corpus beyond affirming that the *Elements* is a "relatively early work". The approximate date assigned, therefore, represents a guess trying to balance what "relatively early" might mean in the life of the author with the maturity of thought the work nonetheless embodies. And, in any event, it remains certain that none of the writings post-dated AD485!

c.AD450. *The Elements of Theology*, a revised text with trans., intro., and commentary by E. R. Dodds (2nd ed.; Oxford: Clarendon Press, 1963).

PROTAGORAS OF ABDERA (c.490/84–414/11BC).

The writing date assigned here reflects no more than the best guess that can be made as to the *floruit* of Protagoras.

c.444/1BC. *On Truth*. Fragment in Freeman 1966: 125.

The title of this work we have from Plato in the *Theaetetus*, 161BC. Sextus Empiricus (a.AD225b: VII, 60) refers to it under the title of *Refutatory Arguments*; but it would seem that a mid-4th-century BC entitling should be given more weight than an early 3rd-century AD one.

PRZYWARA, Erich (1889–1972).

1962. *Analogia Entis: Metaphysik* (Einsiedeln: Johannes-Verlag).

PSEUDO-DIONYSIUS THE AREOPAGITE.

Dating of this work is based on the earliest mention we have of this author's works (AD532), which should be considered in connection with the fact that they presuppose the work of Proclus in particular and were composed within about a generation of Proclus' death in AD485.

a.AD532. *Pseudo-Dionysius. The Complete Works*, trans. Colm Luibheid; foreword, notes, and trans. collaboration by Paul Rorem; preface by Rene Roques; with intros. by Jaroslav Pelikan, Jean Leclerq, and Karlfried Froehlich (New York: Paulist Press, 1987). The works break down as follows:

1. *The Divine Names*, 47–131
2. *The Mystical Theology*, 134–41
3. *The Celestial Hierarchy*, 143–91.
4. *The Ecclesiastical Hierarchy*, 193–259
5. *The [Ten] Letters*, 261–91

PSEUDO-ISIDORE.

c.AD849. *Decretales Pseudo-Isidorianae et Capitula Angilramni*, ed. with intro. by Paulus Hinschius (Leipzig: Bernard Tauchnitz, 1863).

PSEUDO-KILWARDBY, Robert: see Kilwardby Adscriptus.

PTOLEMY, Claudius (c.AD1000–c.175).

c.AD150. *Almagest (Mathematike Syntaxis)*, trans. and annotated G. J. Toomer with a foreword by Owen Gingerich (Princeton, NJ: Princeton University Press, 1998).

PYTHAGORAS OF CROTONA (c.570–c.495BC).

Date for writing based on the prime assigned by Freeman 1966a: 73.

c.530BC. No known writings; Freeman 1966: 20.

QUASTEN, Johannes (1900–).

1950. *Patrology vol. I. The Beginnings of Christian Literature* (Westminster, MD: The Newman Press).

QUINE, Willard Van Orman (1908–2000).

1987. "Mathematosis", in *Quiddities* (Cambridge, MA: Harvard University Press), 127–9.

RAHNER, Karl (20 March 1904–30 March 1984).

1939. *Geist in Welt: zur Metaphysik der endlichen Erkenntnis bei Thomas von Aquin* (doctoral diss. completed in May 1936; Innsbruck: Felizian Rauch).

1957. *Geist in Welt* (2. Auflage im Auftrage des Verfassers überarbeitet und ergänzt von Johannes Baptist Metz; Munich: Kösel-Verlag), trans. William Dych as *Spirit in the World* (from 2nd German ed. prepared by John Baptist Metz; New York: Herder and Herder, 1968). In his "Preface" to this 2nd ed. Rahner tells us that "whatever distinguishes the second from the first edition is due to Dr. Metz" with whom in the matter Rahner professes himself "in complete agreement".

RAMIREZ, Didacus.

1645. "Vita Rmi P. Joannis a Sto Thoma", earliest biography of Poinsot, originally published at beginning of 1st posthumous vol., i.e., *Tomus Quartus*, of *Cursus Theologicus*; repr. as Appendix I to Solesmes 1931: xxv–xliij, to which reprinting page refs. in this work are made.

RAMIREZ, J. M. (1891–?).

1924. "Jean de St. Thomas", *Dictionnaire de théologie catholique* (Paris: Letouzey), vol. 8, 803–8. (Note: This work is not reliable for chronology. See Reiser 1930: xv, ¶c.).

RANDALL, John Herman, Jr. (1871–1946).

1962. *The Career of Philosophy*. vol. I: *From the Middle Ages to the Enlightenment* (New York: Columbia University Press).

RANSDELL, Joseph.

1966. *Charles Peirce: The Idea of Representation* (unpub. doctoral diss.; New York: Columbia University).

1976. "Another Interpretation of Peirce's Semiotic", *Transactions of the Charles S. Peirce Society* 12: 97–110.

1977. "Some Leading Ideas of Peirce's Semiotic", *Semiotica* 19.3/4: 157–78.

RAPOSA, Michael.

1994. "Poinsot on the Semiotics of Awareness", *American Catholic Philosophical Quarterly* 68.3, "Special Issue on John Poinsot" (Summer 1994): 395–408.

RASMUSSEN, Douglas B.

1980. "Deely, Wittgenstein, and Mental Events", *The New Scholasticism* LIV.1 (Winter 1980), 60–7.

1982. "Wittgenstein and the Search for Meanings", in *Semiotics 1982*, ed. John Deely and Jonathan Evans (Lanham, MD: University Press of America 1987), 577–90.

1983. "Rorty, Wittgenstein, and the Nature of Intentionality", *ACPA Proceedings* 57 (1983), 157–62.

RASTIER, François.

1972. *Idéologie et théorie des signes* (The Hague: Mouton).

RAUCH, Augustus.

1840. *Psychology, or a View of the Human Soul, including Anthropology* (New York: M. W. Dodd).

REDONDI, Pietro.

1983. *Galileo eretico* (Torino: Giulio Einaudi); trans. as *Galileo Heretic* by R. Rosenthal (Princeton: Princeton University Press, 1987).

REDPATH, Peter.

1997. *Cartesian Nightmare: An Introduction to Transcendental Sophistry* (Amsterdam: Rodopi).

1997a. *Wisdom's Odyssey. From Philosophy to Transcendental Sophistry* (Amsterdam: Rodopi).

1998. *Masquerade of the Dream Walkers: Prophetic Theology from the Cartesians to Hegel* (Amsterdam: Rodopi).

REID, Thomas (1710–96).

1764. *An Inquiry into the Human Mind on the Principles of Common Sense*, in *Thomas Reid, Philosophical Works*, ed. with notes and suppl. dissertations by Sir William Hamilton (Edinburgh, 1852), 2 vols.

REILLY, John P.

1971. *Cajetan's Notion of Existence* (The Hague: Mouton).

RENAN, Ernest (1823–92).

1882. *Averroès et l'Averroïsme* (4th ed., rev. and enlarged, of 1852 original; Paris: Calman Lévy).

REY-DEBOVE, Josette, editor.

    1973. *Recherches sur les systèmes signifiants: Symposium de Varsovie 1968* (The Hague: Mouton).

REYNOLDS, L. D., and N. G. WILSON.

    1974. *Scribes and Scholars: A Guide to the Transmission of Greek and Latin Literature* (2nd ed., rev. and enlarged; Oxford: Clarendon Press).

RHEES, Rush (1860–1939).

    1984. *Recollections of Wittgenstein* (Oxford).

RICCIOTTI, Giuseppe (1890–?).

    1953. *Era dei Martiri*, trans. as *The Age of the Martyrs: Christianity from Diocletian to Constantine* (Milwaukee: Bruce, 1959).

RIST, John M.

    1967. *Plotinus: The Road to Reality* (Cambridge, Eng.: Cambridge University Press).

    1969. *Stoic Philosophy* (Cambridge, Eng.: Cambridge University Press).

RIST, John M., editor.

    1978. *The Stoics* (Berkeley: University of California Press).

ROBERT, J. D. (1910–).

    1947. "La métaphysique, science distincte de toute autre discipline philosophique selon Saint Thomas d'Aquin", *Divus Thomas* (Piacenza) L: 206–23.

ROBEY, David.

    1989. "Introduction" to Eco 1989: vii–xxxii.

ROBIN, Richard S.

    1967. *Annotated Catalogue of the Papers of Charles S. Peirce* (Worcester, MA: The University of Massachusetts Press).

    1971. "The Peirce Papers: A Supplementary Catalogue", *Transactions of the Charles S. Peirce Society* VII.1 (Winter), 37–57.

ROBINSON, T. M. (1936–).

    1987. Heraclitus *Fragments: A Text and Translation with a Commentary* (Toronto: University of Toronto Press).

ROENSCH, Frederick J.

    1964. *The Early Thomistic School* (Dubuque, IA: The Priory Press).

ROLT, C. E.

    1920. "Dionysius the Areopagite. Introduction" to *Dionysius the Areopagite on the Divine Names and the Mystical Theology*, trans. C. E. Rolt (London: Macmillan), 1–49.

ROMEO, Luigi.

    1976. "Heraclitus and the Foundations of Semiotics", *Versus* 15.5 (dicembre): 73–90. Repr. without brief section on philological sources (pp. 75–9) in Deely, Williams, and Kruse eds 1986: 224–34.

    1977. "The Derivation of 'Semiotics' through the History of the Discipline", in *Semiosis* 6, Heft 2: 37–49.

    1979. "Pedro da Fonseca in Renaissance Semiotics: A Segmental History of Footnotes", *Ars Semeiotica* II.2 (1979): 187–204.

ROREM, Paul.

    1993. *Pseudo-Dionysius: A Commentary on the Texts and an Introduction to Their Influence* (Oxford: Oxford University Press).

ROSEN, Edward (1906–78), editor.

    1939. *Three Copernican Treatises* (New York: Columbia University Press).

ROSS, W. D. (1877–?).

    1928–52. *The Works of Aristotle Translated into English*, in XII vols. (Oxford: The Clarendon Press).

RUDWICK, Martin J. S.

    1997. *Georges Cuvier, Fossil Bones, and Geological Catastrophes. New Translations and Interpretations of the Primary Texts* (Chicago: University of Chicago Press).

RUSHDIE, Salman (1947–).

    1988. *The Satanic Verses* (London: Viking Penguin).

RUSSELL, Anthony F. (1922–99).

    1981. "The Logic of History as a Semiotic Process of Question and Answer in the Thought of R. G. Collingwood", in *Semiotics 1981*, ed. John N. Deely and Margot D. Lenhart (New York: Plenum, 1983), 179–89.

    1982. "The Semiosis Linking the Human World and Physical Reality", in *Semiotics 1982*, ed. John Deely and Jonathan Evans (Lanham, MD: University Press of America, 1987), 591–600.

    1984. *Logic, Philosophy, and History: A Study in the Philosophy of History of R. G. Collingwood*, with foreword by Brooke Williams (Lanham, MD: University Press of America).

    1987. "The Semiotic of Causality and Participation: A New Perspective on the Cajetan–Fabro–Montagnes Controversy over the Analogy of Being", in *Semiotics 1987*, ed. John Deely (Lanham, MD: University Press of America, 1988), 467–72.

    1999. "In Response to G. E. Moore: A Semiotic Perspective on R. G. Collingwood's Concrete Universal", in *Semiotics 1999*, ed. C. W. Spinks, Scott Simpkins, and John Deely (New York: Peter Lang Publishing, 2000).

RUSSELL, Bertrand (1872–1970).

    1905. "On Denoting", *Mind* XIV: 479–93 (see gloss on 1919 entry below). Repr. in collection of Russell's essays 1901–50, *Logic and Knowledge,* ed. Robert C. Marsh (London: Allen & Unwin, 1956), 41–56.

    1910. "Incomplete Symbols", 3rd intro. chapter of Whitehead and Russell 1910–13: I, 66–84. See gloss on 1919 entry following.

    1919. *Introduction to Mathematical Philosophy* (London: George Allen & Unwin Ltd.). Russell's so-called "Theory of Descriptions" first appeared in 1905 (q.v.) under the title "On Denoting". The most technical and 'logically simple' exposition of the theory is perhaps the version incorporated into the third introductory chapter of his work with Whitehead, *Principia Mathematica* (1910–13: I, 66–84), under the title "Incomplete Symbols": see entry for 1910 above. But insofar as philosophy is more concerned with underlying assumptions and principles than with the resolution of problems into definite conclusions, the most philosophically important exposition of the theory is probably that found in chapters 15–17 of this 1919 book. Discussion in Deely 1975: 262ff.

1945. *A History of Western Philosophy* (New York: Simon & Schuster).

1959. *My Philosophical Development* (New York: Simon & Schuster).

RUSSON, John (1960–).

1997. "Hegel and Tradition", Intro. to *Hegel and Tradition: Essays in Honour of H. S. Harris*, ed. Michael Baur and John Russon (Toronto: University of Toronto Press), 3–13.

SALISBURY, John of (c.1115/20–80).

1159. *Metalogicus*, first printed in Paris in 1610, trans. with intro. and notes by Daniel D. McGarry as *The Metalogicon of John of Salisbury: A Twelfth-Century Defense of the Verbal and Logical Arts of the Trivium* (Berkeley: University of California Press).

SANTAELLA, Lúcia (= Santaella-Braga).

1991. "John Poinsot's Doctrine of Signs: The Recovery of a Missing Link", *Journal of Speculative Philosophy*, new ser., 5.2 (1991), 151–9.

1992. *A Assinatura das Coisas* (Rio de Janeiro: Imago Editora).

1993. "El Dialogismo entre la Semiótica General y las Semióticas Especiales", in *Escritos. Semiótica de la Cultura*, ed. Adrián S. Gimate-Welsh (Segundo Encuentro Nacional de Estudiosos de la Semiótica, Noviembre de 1993; Oaxaca, México: Universidad Autónoma Benito Juárez de Oaxaca, 1994), 43–55.

1994. "The Way to Postmodernity", in Deely 1994a: xi–xiii.

SANTILLANA, Giorgio de (1902–74).

1955. *The Crime of Galileo* (Chicago: University of Chicago Press).

SARTRE, Jean-Paul (1905–).

1943. *L'Etre et le Néant: Essai d'ontologie phénoménologique* (Paris: Gallimard); trans. Hazel E. Barnes, *Being and Nothingness* (New York: The Philosophical Library, 1956).

SAUSSURE, Ferdinand de (1857–1913).

1916. *Cours de linguistique général* (Paris: Payot, 1916). Lectures delivered at University of Geneva i.1906/11 and posthumously published from auditors' notes by Charles Bally and Albert Sechehaye with collaboration of Albert Riedlinger.

    Four subsequent Payot editions were published (1922, 1931, 1949, 1955), the second of which was slightly revised and has become the basis of the "standard pagination" incorporated, e.g., into the Harris trans. mentioned later in this gloss. Two critical editions have been prepared, one by Tullio de Mauro (Paris: Payot, 1972) and one by R. Engler (publishing in full the lecture notes taken by Saussure's pupils on which the original Payot edition was based; Wiesbaden: Otto Harrassowitz, 1967–74). My main reference has been to the de Mauro edition.

    The work has been translated into English twice under the same title, *Course in General Linguistics*, first by Wade Baskin (New York: McGraw-Hill, 1959), then by Roy Harris (London: Duckworth, 1983). The Harris trans. is based on the Payot editions but provides a fuller index and corrects printers' errors repeated in the series of Payot editions; yet the Baskin trans. is perhaps superior as an English text.

SCHACHT, Richard (1941–).

1975. *Hegel and After. Studies in Continental Philosophy between Kant and Sartre* (Pittsburgh, PA: University of Pittsburgh Press).

SCHEIBLER, Christoph (1589–1653).

1617. *Opus Metaphysicum, Duobus Libris* (Glessae Hessorum: Typis Nicholai Hampelii), esp. I, 776–826, for the discussion of signs.

SCHIBLI, Hermann S.

1990. *Pherekydes of Syros* (Oxford: Clarendon Press).

SCHILLACI, Anthony (a.k.a. Peter P.; 1927–).

1961. *Separation: Starting Point of Metaphysics* (unpub. doctoral diss.; Rome: International Pontifical Athenaeum "Angelicum"), 2 vols.

SCHMITT, F. S.

1932. "Zur Chronologie der Werke des hl. Anselm von Canterbury", *Revue Bénédictine* 44: 322–50.

SCHMITZ, Kenneth L. (1922–).

1953. *The Problem of the Immortality of the Human Soul in the Works of Cajetan (1469–1534)* (unpub. doctoral diss.; University of Toronto).

1982. *The Gift: Creation* (Milwaukee, WI: Marquette University Press).

1990. "Postmodern or Modern-plus?", *Communio* 17 (Summer): 152–66.

SCHOFIELD, Malcolm.

1980. *An Essay on Anaxagoras* (Cambridge, Eng.: Cambridge University Press).

SCHRADER, George.

1967. "The Thing in Itself in Kantian Philosophy", in *Kant: A Collection of Critical Essays*, ed. Robert Paul Wolff (Notre Dame, IN: University of Notre Dame Press), 172–88.

SCHRENK, Lawrence P., editor.

1994. *Aristotle in Antiquity* (Washington: Catholic University of America Press).

SCOTT-MONCRIEFF, C. K. (1889–1930).

i.1133/44. *The Letters of Abelard and Heloise* (New York: A. A. Knopf, 1926).

SCOTUS, Joannes Duns (c.1266–1308).

Note: I have used the *Joannis Duns Scoti Doctoris Subtilis, Ordinis Minorum Opera Omnia*, editio nova juxta editionem Waddingi XII tomos (at Dominican priory in Xochimilco, Mexico City; Lyons 1639) continentem a patribus Franciscanis de observantia accurate recognita, apud Ludovicum Vivès, Bibliopolam Editorem Via Vulgo Dicta Delambre, 13 (Paris, 1891–95), 26 vols.

c.1300. *Opus Oxoniense (=Ordinatio)*, vols. 8–21.

c.1302–03. *Reportata Parisiensia*, vols. 22–4.

a.1308. *Quaestiones aureae et subtiles super libros Elenchorum Aristotelis* (Venice: Joannes Hertzog, 1495).

a.1308a. *In Perihermenias, opus secundum*, in vol. I.

a.1308b. *Super libros Elenchorum*, in vol. II.

SCOTUS ERIGENA, Joannes (c.AD810–c.877).

c.AD840/60. *Iohannis Scotti Annotationes in Marcianum* [*Commentary on Capella i.AD410–429, The Marriage of Philology and Mercury*], ed. C. Lutz (Cambridge, MA: Medieval Academy of America, 1939).

c.AD867. *Periphyseon*, or *The Division of Nature (De divisione naturae)*, ed. and trans. Myra I. Uhlfelder with summaries of untrans. text by Jean A. Potter (Indianapolis: Bobbs-Merrill, 1976). *See further* Floss ed. 1853, and Jeauneau 1996, for the best Latin editions of this text.

SCRUTON, Roger.

1980. "Possible Worlds and Premature Sciences", in *London Review of Books*, 7 Feb. 1980, reviewing Preziosi 1979 and Eco 1976.

SEBEOK, Thomas A. (1920–).

1963. Book review article of M. Lindauer, *Communication among Social Bees*; W. N. Kellog, *Porpoises and Sonar*; and J. C. Lilly, *Man and Dolphin*, *Language* 39: 448–66.

1968. "Goals and Limitations of the Study of Animal Communication", in Sebeok ed. 1968: 3–14, q.v.; repr. in Sebeok 1985: 59–69, to which page reference is made.

1971. "'Semiotic' and Its Congeners", in *Linguistic and Literary Studies in Honor of Archibald Hill, I: General and Theoretical Linguistics*, ed. Mohammed Ali Jazayery, Edgar C. Polomé, and Werner Winter (Lisse, the Netherlands: Peter de Ridder Press), 283–95; repr. in Sebeok 1985: 47–58, and in Deely, Williams, and Kruse eds 1986: 255–63.

1972. *Perspectives in Zoosemiotics* (The Hague: Mouton).

1972a. "Problems in the Classification of Signs", in *Studies for Einar Haugen*, ed. Evelyn Scherabon Finchow et al. (The Hague: Mouton), 511–21, as repr. in Sebeok 1985: 71–81.

1974. "Semiotics: A Survey of the State of the Art", in *Linguistics and Adjacent Arts and Sciences*, vol. 12 of *Current Trends in Linguistics* series, ed. Sebeok (The Hague: Mouton), 211–64. Repr. in Sebeok 1985: 1–45: page refs. here are to this reprint.

1974a. "La dynamique des signes", impromptu remarks and discussion repr. in Sebeok 1985: 95–110.

1975. "The Semiotic Web: A Chronicle of Prejudices", *Bulletin of Literary Semiotics* 2: 1–63; repr. "with essential corrections and additions" in Sebeok 1976: 149–88, to which reprint page nos. in the present monograph are keyed.

1975a. "Zoosemiotics: At the Intersection of Nature and Culture", in *The Tell-Tale Sign*, ed. T. A. Sebeok (Lisse, the Netherlands: Peter de Ridder Press), 85–95.

1975b. "Six Species of Signs: Some Propositions and Strictures", *Semiotica* 13.3: 233–60, repr. in Sebeok 1985: 117–42.

1976. *Contributions to the Doctrine of Signs* (Indiana University, Bloomington, and Peter De Ridder Press, Lisse).

1977. "Zoosemiotic Components of Human Communication", in *How Animals Communicate*, ed. Thomas A. Sebeok (Bloomington: Indiana University Press), 1055–77.

1978. "'Talking' with Animals: Zoosemiotics Explained", *Animals* 111.6 (December): 20ff.

1978a. "Looking in the Destination for What Should Have Been Sought in the Source", *Diogenes* 104: 112–38; repr. in Sebeok 1989: 272–9.

1979. "Semiosis in Nature and Culture", as repr. in *The Sign & Its Masters* (= Sources in Semiotics VIII; Lanham, MD: University Press of America, 1989), 3–26.

1983. "On the History of Semiotics", in *Semiotics Unfolding*, ed. Tasso Borbé (Berlin: Mouton de Gruyter), 353–4.

1984. "Signs of Life", *International Semiotic Spectrum* 2 (June): 1–2.

1984a. "Vital Signs", presidential address delivered 12 October to the 9th annual meeting of Semiotic Society of America, Bloomington, IN, 11–14 October; subsequently printed in *American Journal of Semiotics* 3.3: 1–27, and repr. in Sebeok 1986: 59–79.

1984b, 3 June. "The Evolution of Communication and the Origin of Language", lecture in the 1–3 June ISISSS 1984 colloquium "Phylogeny and Ontogeny of Communication Systems". Published as "Communication, Language, and Speech. Evolutionary Considerations", in Sebeok 1986: 10–16.

1984c. "Symptom", chap. 10 of *New Directions in Linguistics and Semiotics*, ed. James E. Copeland (Houston: Rice University Studies), 212–30.

1985. *Contributions to the Doctrine of Signs* (= Sources in Semiotics IV; reprint of 1976 original with extended preface by Brooke Williams, "Challenging Signs at the Crossroads" [Williams 1985], evaluating the book in light of major reviews; Lanham, MD: University Press of America).

1986. *I Think I Am a Verb: More Contributions to the Doctrine of Signs* (New York: Plenum Press).

1986a. "The Doctrine of Signs", in Deely, Williams, and Kruse eds 1986: 35–42.

1986b. "A Signifying Man", feature review of *Tractatus de Signis* in *New York Times Book Review* for Easter Sunday, 30 March 1986, pp. 14–15; German trans. by Jeff Bernard appears in *Semiotische Berichte* Jg. 11 2/1987: 234–9, with translator's "Anmerkung", p. 240.

1989. *The Sign & Its Masters* (= Sources in Semiotics VIII; Lanham, MD: University Press of America). Corrected reprint with new author's preface and editor's intro. of University of Texas Press 1979 original imprint.

1990. "The Sign Science and the Life Science", in *"Symbolicity"*, ed. Jeff Bernard, John Deely, Vilmos Voigt, and Gloria Withalm (Lanham, MD: University Press of America, 1993), 243–52. This volume is bound together with *Semiotics 1990*, ed. Karen Haworth, John Deely, and Terry Prewitt.

1991. *Semiotics in the United States* (Bloomington: Indiana University Press).

1996. "Galen in Medical Semiotics", *Interdisciplinary Journal for Germanic Linguistics and Semiotic Analysis* 1.1 (Spring): 89–111.

SEBEOK, Thomas A., editor.

1968. *Animal Communication: Techniques of Study and Results of Research* (Bloomington, IN: Indiana University Press).

1976. *A Perfusion of Signs. Transactions of the First North American Semiotics Collo- quium, University of South Florida, Tampa, 28–30 July 1975* (Bloomington: Indiana University Press).

SEBEOK, Thomas A., general editor; Paul BOUISSAC, Umberto ECO, Jerzy PELC, Roland POSNER, Alain REY, Ann SHUKMAN, editorial board.

1986. *Encyclopedic Dictionary of Semiotics* (Berlin: Mouton de Gruyter), in 3 vols.

SEBEOK, Thomas A., and Robert ROSENTHAL, editors.

1981. *The Clever Hans Phenomenon: Communication with Horses, Whales, Apes, and People* (New York: New York Academy of Sciences).

SERTILLANGES, A. D. (1863–1948).

1945. *L'Idée de Creation* (Paris: Aubier).

1948. *The Intellectual Life: Its Spirit, Conditions, Methods*, trans. Mary Ryan (Westmin- ster, MD: Newman Press) of *La Vie intellectuelle: Son esprit, ses conditions, ses méthodes* (nouvelle ed., rev. et aug.; Paris: Desclée, 1934).

SEXTUS EMPIRICUS (c.150–c.225AD).

The reference here to Sextus Empiricus uses the traditional twofold division, dated as prior to ("a." = *ante* or "before") the guesstimated demise of the author in AD225 and arranged as "a" and "b", with further explanation following:

a.AD225a. *Outlines of Pyrrhonism*, in 3 books (= Bury vol. 1). Alternate trans. in Mates 1996: 87–217.

a.AD225b. *Adversus Mathematicos*, in 11 books (= Bury vols. 4, 3, and 2, respectively) as follows:

Introductory section "Against the Professors" in general, Book I, §s 1–40, Bury vol. 1, 1–25.

Book I = "Against the Grammarians", §s 41–end, Bury vol. 4, 25–187.

Book II = "Against the Rhetoricians", Bury vol. 4, 188–243.

Book III = "Against the Geometers", Bury vol. 4, 244–303.

Book IV = "Against the Arithmeticians", Bury vol. 4, 304–21.

Book V = "Against the Astrologers", Bury vol. 4, 322–71.

Book VI = "Against the Musicians", Bury vol. 4, 372–405.

Book VII = "Against the Logicians Book I" ('on the criterion of truth'), in Bury vol. 2, 2–239.

Book VIII = "Against the Logicians Book II" ('on Truth itself'), in Bury vol. 2, 240–489.

Book IX = "Against the Physicists Book I", in Bury vol. 3, 2–209.

Book X = "Against the Physicists Book II", in Bury vol. 3, 210–381.

Book XI = "Against the Ethicists", in Bury vol. 3, 384–509.

The extant works of this author are of three titles: (1) *Outlines of Pyrrhonism* in 3 books, i.e., *Outlines of Skepticism*, Pyrrho having founded the ancient school now called "Skepticism", as we saw in chapter 4, p. 99 above; (2) *Against the Dogmatists* in 5 books, to wit, logicians, physicists, and ethicists; and (3) *Against the Professors* or "Mathematici", i.e., the professors of the arts of grammar, rhetoric, geometry, arithmetic, astronomy (or "astrology"), and music. (How the grammarians and rhetoricians came to be called "mathematicists" is unclear, whereas the others are self-explanatory.)

For whatever reason, perhaps because logic and ethics along with natural philosophy were taught in the faculty of arts in Latin universities, these three works of Sextus Empiricus came to be divided simply into two: the *Outlines*, which summarizes the skeptical position and contrasts it with dogmatism, especially that ascribed to the Stoics; and the *Adversus Mathematicos*, formed into 11 books by appending the 5 books of work (2) above to the 6 books of work (3) to give in one handy compendium a comprehensive attack in detail against all the professors of arts and sciences. It is this later, twofold division that came to be most customarily used in citing the author.

The only full English translation of Sextus Empiricus, that of R. G. Bury, fortunately appears along with the Greek text in 4 volumes (Cambridge, MA: Harvard University Press, 1935–53, in the copies before me). But, less fortunately (cf. the remarks in Mates 1996: 220), Bury presents the writings according to the inner divisions of the three works rather than using for his main title pages *either* the threefold title and subdivisions we have apparently from Sextus himself *or* the twofold title and subdivisions which subsequently became customary. As a result, Bury in effect constructs his own presentation for the writings, one which creates sufficient confusion to require a great deal of sorting out for anyone coming to his 4 volumes on the basis of any reference to or familiarity with the more customary twofold presentation of the *Outlines* in 3 books followed by *Adversus Mathematicos* in 11 books.

Accordingly, for the ease of the reader and especially to facilitate anyone using this present volume in connection with any research involving Sextus Empiricus, I here present the contents of the volumes containing Bury's translation along with the Greek text, and show how Bury's contents correlate with the original threefold division of Sextus Empiricus's writings, the correlation with the traditional twofold division being given in the main reference entry above.

First, then, the Bury presentation itself: vol. 1 (1939), *Outlines of Pyrrhonism*; vol. 2 (1935), *Against the Logicians*, in 2 books; vol. 3 (1953), *Against the Physicists*, in 2 books, 1–381, and *Against the Ethicists*, pp. 383–509; vol. 4 (1949), *Against the Professors*, in 6 books. This correlates with Sextus Empiricus' own threefold division of his works as follows: the *Outlines of Pyrrhonism*, in 3 books = Bury vol. I; the 5 books *Against the Dogmatists* (logicians, physicists, and ethicists) = Bury vols. 2 and 3; the 6 books *Against the Professors* or "Schoolmasters" (grammarians, rhetoricians, geometricians, arithmeticists, astronomers, and musicians) = Bury vol. 4. The correlation of the Bury presentation with the traditional twofold division, wherein the 5 books against the dogmatists are added to the 6 books against the arts professors under the one contrarian title of the latter work, then, is as set out in the main reference entry above.

SHANK, Gary.

1998. "The Lesson of the Bestiary", in *New Approaches to Medieval Textuality*, ed. Michael D. Ledgerwood (New York: Peter Lang), 140–51.

SHANLEY, Brian J.

1999. "Analytical Thomism", *The Thomist* 63.1 (January): 125–37.

SHIRCEL, Cyril L.

1942. *The Univocity of the Concept of Being in the Philosophy of John Duns Scotus* (published diss.; Washington: Catholic University of America).

SIEBECK, Hermann (1842–1921).

1890. "Ueber die Enstehung der Termini natura naturans und natura naturata", *Archiv für Geschichte der Philosophie* III Band, 3 Heft (see p. 347 for the Heft opening; Berlin: G. Reimer): 370–78.

SIKES, J. G.

1932. *Peter Abailard* (Cambridge, Eng.: Cambridge University Press).

SIMON, Yves R. (1903–1961).

1955. "Foreword" and "Notes" to *The Material Logic of John of St. Thomas*, trans. Yves R. Simon, John J. Glanville, and G. Donald Hollenhorst (Chicago: University of Chicago Press), ix–xxiii and 587–625.

1970. *The Great Dialogue of Nature and Space* (posthumous), ed. Gerard J. Dalcourt (New York: Magi Books).

1971. "An Essay on the Classification of Action and the Understanding of Act", *Revue de l'Université d'Ottawa* 41 (octobre–décembre), 518–41.

SIMON, Yves R., John J. GLANVILLE, and G. Donald HOLLENHORST.

1955. *The Material Logic of John of St. Thomas*, selections trans. from Poinsot's *Artis Logicae Secunda Pars* of 1632 (Reiser ed.; Turin: Marietti, 1930). Detailed discussions of the Simon trans. in the context of Poinsot's doctrine of signs are in Deely 1985: 117 n. 6, 406 n. 15, 459 n. 93.

SIMONIN, H.-D.

1930. "Review" of 1930 Reiser ed. of Poinsot's *Ars Logica* of 1631–32, in *Bulletin Thomiste* III (septembre), 140–8.

SOLESMES.

1931. "Editorum Solesmensium Praefatio" to Joannes a Sancto Thoma (Poinsot 1637) *Cursus Theologici Tomus Primus* (Paris: Desclée), i–cviij.

SOMMERVOGEL, Carlos (1834–1902).

1891. *Bibliothèque de la Compagnie de Jésus* (Bruxelles: Oscar Schepens).

SOTO, Dominicus ("Domingo de") (1494–1560).

1529, 1554. *Summulae* (1st ed., Burgos; 2nd ed., Salamanca; 3rd rev. ed., Salamanca; facsimile of 3rd ed., Hildesheim, New York: Georg Olms Verlag).

1570. *Summularum* editio postrema, nunc denuo in Summulistarum gratiam ab innumeris diligenter repurgata mendis Salamanca in aedibus Dominici à Portonariis, S.C.M. Typographi (en 200 maravedis), 1570.

SOUTHERN, Richard William (1912–).

1962. *Western Views of Islam in the Middle Ages* (Cambridge, MA: Harvard University Press).

SOZOMEN, Salamon Hermias (c.AD400–c.450).

i.AD443/50. *Ecclesiastical History: A History of the Church in Nine Books, from A.D. 324* to A.D. *440*, a new trans. from the Greek, with a memoir of the author (= *The Greek Ecclesiastical Historians of the First Six Centuries of the Christian Era*, vol. 5 of 6; London: Samuel Bagster and Sons, 1846).

SPIEGELBERG, Herbert (1904–).

  1965. *The Phenomenological Movement* (2nd ed., rev.; The Hague: Martinus Nijhoff), 2 vols.

SPINOZA, Benedict (1632–77).

  i.1662/76. *Ethica ordine geometrico demonstrata* (Amsterdam, 1677), trans. as *Ethics Demonstrated in Geometric Order and Divided into Five Parts, Which Treat: I. Of God; II. Of the Nature and Origin of the Mind; III. Of the Origin and Nature of the Affects; IV. Of Human Bondage, or of the Powers of the Affects; V. Of the Power of the Intellect, or of Human Freedom*; in Curley ed. 1988: 408–615.

  1663. *Parts I and II of Descartes' Principles of Philosophy Demonstrated in the Geometric Manner*, by Benedictus de Spinoza, of Amsterdam. To which are added his Metaphysical Thoughts in which are briefly explained the more difficult problems which arise both in the general and in the special part of Metaphysics (Amsterdam: Johannes Riewerts); in trans. and ed. of Curley 1988: 222–345.

STAHL, William Harris, Richard JOHNSON (1929–), and Evan Laurie BURGE (1933–).

  1971. *Martianus Capella and the Seven Liberal Arts* I: *The Quadrivium of Martianus Capella. Latin Traditions in the Mathematical Sciences 50 B.C. to A.D. 1250, with a Study of the Allegory and the Verbal Disciplines* (New York: Columbia University Press).

  1977. *Martianus Capella and the Seven Liberal Arts*, II: *The Marriage of Philology and Mercury* (New York: Columbia University Press). (Note that Stahl and Johnson invert the names from "Mercury and Philology", as they appear in Latin.)

STEGMULLER, Friedrich (1902–).

  1959. *Filosofia e Teologia nas Universidades de Coimbra e Évora no seculo XVI* (Coimbra: Universidade de Coimbra).

STEINER, George (1929–).

  1975. *After Babel: Aspects of Language in Translation* (Oxford: Oxford University Press).

STEVENSON, Robert Louis (1850–1894).

  1885/6. *Strange Case of Dr. Jekyll and Mr. Hyde* (London: Longman). The first edition was actually prepared late in December 1885, but deemed too late for the Christmas book trade and therefore postponed to a January 1886 release. On the original printed copies from Longman, the date is actually hand-corrected from 1885 to read 1886. Note the absence of *The* at the beginning of the original title, commonly inserted in later editions. I have used the text of Michael Hulse, *Strange Case of Dr. Jekyll and Mr. Hyde and Other Stories* (Cologne: Könemann Verlagsgesellshcaft mbH, 1995), 5–78, which is based in turn on the Edmund Gosse London ed. of 1906.

STIGLMAYR, Joseph (1851–1934).

  1895. "Der Neuplatoniker Proclus als Vorlage des sogen. Dionysius Areopagita in der Lehre vom Uebel", *Historisches Jahrbuch* 16: 253–73, 721–48.

1895a. *Das Aufkommen der Pseudo-Dionysischen Schriften und ihr Eindringen in die Christliche Literatur bis zum Literanconcil 649. Ein zweiter Beitrag zur Dionysios-Frage* (Feldkirch: L. Sausgruber).

1900. "Der 'Vater der Mystik' im Lichte des Neoplatonismus", in *Historisch-Politische Blätter für das Catholische Deutschland*, ed. Edmund Jörg und Franz Binder (München), 541–50 and 613–27.

1909. "Dionysius the Pseudo-Areopagite" entry in *The Catholic Encyclopedia* ed. Charles G. Herbermann et. al. (New York: Robert Appleton Company), vol. V of XV vols., 13–18.

1928. "Der Sogenannte Dionysius Areopagita und Severus von Antiochien", *Scholastik* 3: 1–27, 721–48.

STOCK, Brian.

1996. *Augustine the Reader: Meditation, Self-Knowledge, and the Ethics of Interpretation* (Cambridge, MA: Belknap Press).

STOCK, St George (1850–?).

1908. *Stoicism* (London: Kennikat Press).

STOOTHOFF, Robert.

1985. "Translator's Preface" to *Discourse and Essays* in Cottingham, Stoothoff, and Murdoch trans. 1985: I, 109–10, q.v.

STRASSER, Stephen.

1963. *Phenomenology and the Human Sciences: A Contribution to a New Scientific Ideal* (Pittsburgh: Duquesne University Press).

SUÁREZ, Francis.

1597. *Disputationes Metaphysicae* (Salamanca), vols. 25–6 of the *Opera Omnia*, new ed. by Carolus Berton (Paris: Vivès, 1861).

1605. *De Sacramentis* (Venice: apud Societatem Minimam); being vol. 20 of the *Opera Omnia*, ed. Carolus Berton (Paris: Vivès, 1860).

SULLIVAN, John Edward (1922–81).

1963. *The Image of God: The Doctrine of St. Augustine and Its Influence* (Dubuque, IA: Priory Press).

1970. *Prophets of the West* (New York: Harcourt).

SURIG, H. W. J.

1951. *De betekenis van Logos bij Herakleitos volgens de traditie en de fragmenten* (Nijmegen dissertaton).

SWEENEY, Leo (1918–).

1961. "Basic Principles in Plotinus's Philosophy", *Gregorianum* 52: 506–16.

SWIFT, Jonathan (1667–1745).

1729. *A Modest Proposal for Preventing the Children of Poor People from Being a Burden to Their Parents or Country* (Dublin: printed by S. Harding); repr. in *Jonathan Swift. Irish Tracts 1728–1733*, ed. Herbert Davis (Oxford. Basil Blackwell, 1964), 109–18.

SYMONDS, John Addington (1840–93).

1893. *Studies of the Greek Poets* (3rd ed.; London: A. & C. Black 1-vol. reprint, 1920).

TACHAU, Katherine H.

1988. *Vision and Certitude in the Age of Ockham: Optics, Epistemology, and the Foundations of Semantics 1250–1345* (Leiden, the Netherlands: E. J. Brill, 1988).

TAO TE CHING, "THE BOOK OF THE WAY", a work of collective authorship deemed to reflect especially Lao Tse (c.604–517BC) as its main historical source.

i.550/399BC. New English version with foreword and notes by Stephen Mitchell (New York: Harper Perennial, 1988).

TATAKIS, Basile (1896–).

1949. *La Philosophie Byzantine* (Paris: Presses Universitaires de France).

TAYLOR, Henry Osborn (1856–1941).

1911. *The Classical Heritage of the Middle Ages* (3rd ed.; Macmillan). There is a putative 4th ed. of this work, but in fact it is a posthumous reproduction of the 1901 1st ed. text, with an appendix tacked on by the publisher – very close to a fraud.

THALES OF MILETUS (c.625–c.545BC).

Date for writing based on the prime assigned by Freeman 1966a: 49.

c.585BC. No work or even genuine fragments survive.

THATCHER, Oliver J. (1857–1937), and Edgar H. McNEAL.

1905. *A Source Book for Medieval History: Selected Documents Illustrating the History of Europe in the Middle Age* (New York: Charles Scribner's Sons).

THEODOSIAN CODE: *see* Mommsen and Meyer eds 1905, and Pharr trans. 1952.

THEOPHILUS OF ANTIOCH (c.AD120–c.185/191).

c.AD181. Τὸ Αὐτόλυκον, in the bilingual ed. titled *Theophilus of Antioch Ad Autolycum*, text and trans. Robert M. Grant (Oxford: Clarendon Press, 1970).

THORNDIKE, Lynn (1882–1965).

1965. *Michael Scot* (London: Thomas Nelson and Sons).

THORBURN, William.

1918. "The Myth of Occam's Razor", *Mind* 27: 345–53, incl. an appendix (pp. 352–3) of 17 quotations of maxim formulae Ockham actually used.

TIMPLER, Clemens (1563/4–1624).

1604. *Metaphysicae Systema Methodicum, Libris Quinque* (Steinfurt).

1612. *Logica Systema Methodicum* (Hanover).

TIPTON, Ian.

1992. "'Ideas' and 'Objects': Locke on Perceiving 'Things'", in Cummins and Zoeller eds 1992: 97–110.

TIXERONT, Joseph (1856–1925).

1920. *Précis de Patrologie* (4th ed.; Paris: J. Gabalda), authorized trans. as *A Handbook of Patrology* (St Louis, MO: B. Herder Book Co.).

TODOROV, Tzvetan (1939–).

1982. *Theories of the Symbol* (Oxford: Oxford University Press); trans. by C. Porter of *Théories du symbole* (Paris: Éditions du Seuil, 1977).

TORNAY, Stephen C. (1889–).

1938. *Ockham: Studies and Sketches* (La Salle, IL: Franciscan Institute).

TORRELL, Jean-Pierre.

>1996. *Saint Thomas Aquinas*, vol. 1, *The Person and His Work*, trans. Robert Royal (Washington: Catholic University of America Press) from *L'Initiation à Saint Thomas d'Aquin: Sa personne et son oeuvre* (Paris: Éditions du Cerf, 1993).

TREDENNICK, Hugh.

>1933. "Introduction" to his trans. of Aristotle's *Metaphysics*, in vol. 1 (Cambridge, MA: Loeb Classical Library of Harvard University Press, 1933).

TRENDELENBURG, F. A. (1802–72).

>1846. *Geschichte der Kategorienlehre. Zwei Abhandlungen (I. Aristoteles Kategorienlehre. II. Die Kategorienlehre der Philosophie* (Berlin: G. Berthge; reproduced Hildesheim: G. Olms, 1963), being vol. 1 of Trendelenburg's 3-vol. *Historische Beiträge zur Philosophie* (Berlin: G. Berthge, 1846–67).

TRITHEMIUS, Johannes (1462–1516).

>a.1516. *Opera pia et spiritualia* (Moguntiae [= Mayence]; G. Albini, 1605; microfiche Zug, Switzerland, Inter Documentation).

TURNBULL, Grace H. (1880–), compiler.

>1934. *The Essence of Plotinus. Extracts from the six Enneads and Porphyry's Life of Plotinus based on the translation by Stephen MacKenna, with an appendix giving some of the most important Platonic and Aristotelian sources on which Plotinus drew, and an annotated bibliography; Foreword by W. R. Inge* (New York: Oxford University Press).

TURNBULL, Robert G.

>1998. *The* Parmenides *and Plato's Late Philosophy. Translation of and commentary on the* Parmenides *with Interpretative Chapters on the* Timaeus, *the* Theaetetus, *the* Sophist, *and the* Philebus (Toronto: University of Toronto Press).

UCCELLI, Peter Anthony (?–1880).

>1880. *S. Thomae Aquinatis in Boetium de Trinitate Expositiones* (Rome).

VON UEXKÜLL, Jakob (1864–1944).

>1934. *Streifzuge durch die Umwelten von Tieren und Menschen*, with illustrations by Georg Kriszat (=Verstandliche Wissenschaft, Bd. 21) (Berlin). English trans. by Claire H. Schiller, "A Stroll through the World of Animals and Men; A Picture Book of Invisible Worlds", in *Instinctive Behavior: The Development of a Modern Concept*, ed. Claire H. Schiller (New York: International Universities Press, Inc., 1957), 5–80.

UHLFELDER, Myra I., translator.

>1976. Partial trans. of Scotus Erigena c.867, q.v.

ULLMANN, Walter (1910–).

>1962. *The Growth of Papal Government in the Middle Ages: A Study in the Ideological Relation of Clerical to Lay Power* (2nd ed.; London: Methuen).

USENER, Hermann, editor (1834–1905).

>1887. *Epicurea* (Leipzig: B. G. Teubner). Greek text with Latin preface and commentary.

VAN FLETEREN, Frederick.

>1995. "St. Augustine, Neoplatonism, and the Liberal Arts: The Background to *De Doctrina Christiana*", in Arnold and Bright eds 1995: 14–24.

VEATCH, Henry.

  1952. *Intentional Logic* (New Haven: Yale University Press).

  1969. *Two Logics* (Evanston: Northwestern University Press).

VELTSOS, Giorgos S.

  1975. *Semeiologia tonpolitikon thesmon* (Athens: Ekdoseis Papazisis).

VERON, Eliseo.

  1971. "Ideology and Social Sciences: A Communicational Approach", *Semiotica* 3.1: 59–76.

VICO, Giambattista (1668–1744).

  1744. *Scienza Nuova* (3rd ed.; Naples), as edited by Fausto Nicolini (Bari: Laterza, 1928), and presented in rev. trans. by Thomas Goddard Bergin and Max Harold Fisch, *The New Science of Giambattista Vico* (Ithaca, NY: Cornell University Press, 1968).

VILLIEN, A. (1867–?).

  1911. "Décrétales (les Fausses)", entry in *Dictionnaire de Théologie Catholique*, ed. A. Vacant and E. Mangenot (Paris: Letouzey et Ané), tome 4, cols. 212–22.

VILLOSLADA, Ricardo G.

  1938. *La Universidad de Paris durante los Estudios de Francisco de Vitoria* (= Analecta Gregoriana XIV; Rome: Gregorian University).

VOGT, Joseph.

  1967. *The Decline of Rome. The Metamorphosis of Ancient Civilisation*, trans. Janet Sondheimer (London: Weidenfeld and Nicolson) from *Der Niedergang Roms. Metamorphose der antiken Kultur* (Zürich, Switzerland: Kindler, 1965); covering the period c.AD284–476.

VON FRITZ: see Fritz

VON UEXKÜLL: see Uexküll

WALLACE, William A.

  1972. *Causality and Scientific Explanation I. Medieval and Early Classical Science* (Ann Arbor: University of Michigan Press).

  1974. *Causality and Scientific Explanation II. Classical and Contemporary Science* (Ann Arbor: University of Michigan Press).

  1977. *Galileo's Early Notebooks: The Physical Questions*, trans. from the Latin with historical and paleographical commentary (Notre Dame, IN: Notre Dame University Press).

  1980. "Albertus Magnus on Suppositional Necessity in the Natural Sciences", in *Albertus Magnus and the Sciences. Commemorative Essays 1980*, ed. James A. Weisheipl (Toronto: Pontifical Institute of Mediaeval Studies), 103–28. Wallace documents a remarkable discussion in Albert's *De Praedicabilibus*, tract. 7, ch. 2, and tract. 8, ch. 10 (in vol. I of the *Opera Omnia*, Borgnet ed., pp. 122a–b and 140a, respectively) of the conditions of egg-formation under which a crow that was not black would be produced.

  1981. *Prelude to Galileo*, essays on medieval and 16th-century sources of Galileo's thought (= Boston Studies in the Philosophy of Science 62; Dordrecht, Holland: D. Reidel Publishing Co.).

1984. *Galileo and His Sources*, the heritage of the Collegio Romano in Galileo's science (Princeton, NJ: Princeton University Press).

1991. *Galileo, the Jesuits, and the Medieval Aristotle* (= Collected Studies 346; Hampshire, UK: Variorum Publishing).

1992. *Galileo's Logic of Discovery and Proof*, the background, content, and use of his appropriated treatises on Aristotle's Posterior Analytics (= Boston Studies in the Philosophy of Science 137; Dordrecht, Holland: Kluwer Academic Publishing).

1992a. *Galileo's Logical Treatises*, translation with notes and commentary, of his appropriated treatises on Aristotle's Posterior Analytics (= Boston Studies in the Philosophy of Science 138; Dordrecht, Holland: Kluwer Academic Publishers).

1996. *The Modeling of Nature: Philosophy of Science and Philosophy of Nature in Synthesis* (Washington: Catholic University of America Press).

WALLACE, William A., editor.

1986. *Reinterpreting Galileo* (= Studies in Philosophy and the History of Philosophy 15; Washington: Catholic University of America Press).

WALLACE, William A., guest editor.

1996. Special issue on Albertus Magnus ("Albert the Great") of *American Catholic Philosophical Quarterly* LXX.1 (Winter).

WALLACE, William A., and W. F. EDWARDS, editors.

1988. *Galileo Galilei, "Tractatio de praecognitionibus et praecognitis" and "Tractatio de demonstratione"* (Padua, Italy: Editrice Antenore).

WEIJERS, Olga.

1978. "Contribution à l'histoire des termes 'natura naturans' et 'natura naturata' jusqu'à Spinoza", *Vivarium* XVI.1: 70–80.

WEISHEIPL, James A. (1923–84).

1965. "Classification of the Sciences in Mediaeval Thought", *Mediaeval Studies* XXVII: 54–90.

1967. "Cajetan (Tommaso de Vio)", entry for *The New Catholic Encyclopedia* (New York: McGraw-Hill), vol. 2, 1053–5.

1967a. "Robert Kilwardby", entry for *The New Catholic Encyclopedia* (New York: McGraw-Hill), vol. 12, 533.

1974. *Friar Thomas d'Aquino, His Life, Thought, and Works* (Garden City, NY: Doubleday & Co.).

1980a, b. "Life and Works of Albert the Great", and "Appendix I. Albert's Work on Natural Science (*libri naturales*) in Probable Chronological Order", in *Albertus Magnus and the Sciences. Commemorative Essays 1980*, ed. James A. Weisheipl (Toronto: Pontifical Institute of Mediaeval Studies), 13–51 and 565–77.

WELLS, Norman J.

1994. "Poinsot on Created Eternal Truths vis-à-vis Suárez, Vazquez, and Descartes", in *American Catholic Philosophical Quarterly* LXVIII.3 (Summer 1994). 425–46.

1998. "Descartes and Suárez on Secondary Qualities: A Tale of Two Readings", *Review of Metaphysics* 51 (March): 565–604.

WERTHEIMER, Max (1880–1943).

   1912. "Experimentelle Studien über das Sehen von Bewegung" ("Experimental Studies on the Viewing of Motion"), *Zeitschrift für Psychologie* 60: 321–78.

WEST, M. L. (1937–).

   1971. *Early Greek Philosophy and the Orient* (Oxford: Clarendon Press).

WHATELY, Richard (1787–1863).

   1857. *Elements of Logic* (9th ed. revised of 1826 orig.; Cambridge: James Munroe and Company).

WHITEHEAD, Alfred North (1861–1947).

   1925. *Science and the Modern World* (New York: Macmillan).

   1929. *Process and reality, an essay in cosmology* (the Gifford lectures delivered at the University of Edinburgh during the session 1927–28; Cambridge, Eng.: Cambridge University Press).

WHITEHEAD, Alfred North (1861–1947), and RUSSELL, Bertrand (1872–1970).

   1910–13. *Principia Mathematica* (Cambridge), 3 vols.

WILLIAMS, Brooke (1941–).

   1981. "The Feminist Revolution in 'Ultramodern' Perspective", *Cross Currents* XXXI.3: 307–18.

   1982. "The Historian as Observer", in *Semiotics 1982*, ed. John Deely and Jonathan Evans (Lanham, MD: University Press of America, 1987), 13–25.

   1983. "History as a Semiotic Anomaly", in *Semiotics 1983*, ed Jonathan Evans and John Deely (Lanham, MD: University Press of America, 1987), 409–19.

   1984. "Preface" to *Logic, Philosophy, and History* (A. F. Russell 1984: xiii–xx).

   1985. "Challenging Signs at the Crossroads", prefatory essay to Sebeok 1985: xv–xlii.

   1985a. *History and Semiotic* (Toronto Semiotic Circle Monograph, No. 4; Victoria University, University of Toronto).

   1985b. "What Has History To Do with Semiotic??", *Semiotica* 54.3/4: 267–333.

   1986. "History in Relation to Semiotic", in Deely, Williams, and Kruse 1986: 217–23.

   1987. "Opening Dialogue between the Discipline of History and Semiotic", in *The Semiotic Web*, ed. Thomas A. Sebeok and Jean Umiker-Sebeok (Berlin: Mouton de Gruyter, 1998), 821–34.

   1987a. "Historiography as a Current Event", in *Semiotics 1987*, ed. John Deely (Lanham, MD: University Press of America), 479–86.

   1990. "Uma década de debates: História e Semiótica nos annos 80", *Face* 3.1 (janeiro/junho), 11–28.

   1991. "History and Semiotics in the 1990s", *Semiotica* 83.3/4: 385–417.

WILLIAMS, C. Dickerman.

   1952. "Introduction" to Pharr et al. (q.v.), xvii–xxii.

WILLIAMS, Henry Smith (1863–1943).

   1904. *History of Science* (New York: Harper & Bros.), 5 vols.

WILLIAMS, Schafer (1910–).

   1964. "The Oldest Text of the *Constitutum Constantini*", in *Traditio* XX: 448–61.

WILSON, Margaret D. (1939–).

1992. "History of Philosophy in Philosophy Today; and the Case of the Sensible Qualities", *The Philosophical Review* 101.1 (January): 191–243.

WILSON, Thomas (c.1525–81).

1551. *The rule of reason, conteinyng the arte of logique, set forth in Englishe* (London;
facsimile ed. no. 261; Amsterdam: Theatrum Orbis Terrarum; New York: Da Capo
Press, 1970).

WINANCE, Eleuthère (1909–).

1983. Review article of Deely 1982 in *Revue Thomiste* LXXXIII.3: 514–16.

WINDELBAND, Wilhelm (1848–1915).

1894. *Geschichte und Naturwissenschaft* (Strasbourg: Heitz).

1901. *A History of Philosophy with especial reference to the formation and development
of its problems and conceptions*, authorized trans. by James H. Tufts (2nd ed., rev.
and enlarged; New York: Macmillan).

1910. *Lehrbuch der Geschichte der Philosophie* (Tübingen: Mohr, 1928 reprint).

WITTGENSTEIN, Ludwig (1889–1951).

1922 (completed in the summer of 1918). *Tractatus Logico-Philosophicus*, trans. C. K.
Ogden and F. P. Ramsey (London: Routledge, 1922); retrans. by D. F. Pears and
B. F. McGuinness (same publisher, 1961).

c.1931–1950. *Philosophical Investigations*, published posthumously in the edition of
G. E. M. Anscombe and R. Rhees (London: Blackwell, 1953).

WOJTYLA, Karol Jósef (1920–; r.1978– as "Pope John-Paul II").

1998, September 14. *Fides et Ratio*, encyclical letter on the relationship between faith and
reason (Rome: Vatican City).

WOLTER, Allan B. (1913–).

1946. *The Transcendentals and Their Function in the Metaphysics of Duns Scotus* (St
Bonaventure, NY: Franciscan Institute).

1978. "An Oxford Dialogue on Language and Metaphysics", Part I, *Review of Metaphysics*
31 (June): 615–48.

1978a. "An Oxford Dialogue on Language and Metaphysics", Part II, *Review of Metaphysics* 32 (December): 323–48.

WOLTERS, Albert M.

1982. "A Survey of Modern Scholarly Opinion on Plotinus and Indian Thought", in Harris
ed. 1982: 293–308.

WOOD, Oscar P., and George PITCHER, editors.

1971. *Ryle* (New York: Macmillan).

WOOD, Robert E. (1934–).

1966. "Toward a Reinterpretation of the Transcendentals. The Self and the Other", *Philosophy Today* X (Spring): 48–63.

1990. *A Path into Metaphysics* (Albany: State University of New York Press).

XENOPHANES OF COLOPHON (c.570–475BC).

Date for writing based on the prime assigned by Freeman 1966a: 88.

c.530BC. See edition of Lesher 1992. Fragments also in Freeman 1966: 20–4.

ZELLER, E. (1814–1908).

　1870. *The Stoics, Epicureans, and Skeptics*, trans. from German by Oswald J. Reichel (London: Longmans, Green, and Co.).

ZELLWEGER, Shea.

　1990. "John James Van Nostrand and Sematology: Another Neglected Figure in American Semiotics", in *Semiotics 1990*, ed. Karen Haworth, John Deely, and Terry Prewitt (bound together with *"Symbolicity"*, ed. Jeff Bernard, John Deely, Vilmos Voigt, and Gloria Withalm; Lanham, MD: University Press of America, 1993), 224–40.

　1990a. "Before Peirce and Icon/Index/Symbol", in *Semiotic Scene* n.s. 2.1 (Spring): 3 (2 cols.).

ZEMAN, Jay (1934–).

　1997. "Peirce and Philo", in *Studies in the Logic of Charles Sanders Peirce*, ed. Nathan Houser, Don D. Roberts, and James van Evra (Bloomington: Indiana University Press), 402–17.

ZENO OF ELEA (c.490–c.430BC).

　Date for writing based on the prime assigned by Freeman 1966a: 153.

　c.450BC. Fragments in Freeman 1966: 47–51.

ZIMMERMANN, Albert (1928–).

　1966. *Ontologie oder Metaphysik? Die Diskussion über den Gegenstand der Metaphysik in 13. und 14. Jahrhundert* (Leiden: E. J. Brill).

Gloss on the References

The reference section of this book has been constructed using the principle of "historical layering of sources" first outlined in the *Style Manual* of the Semiotic Society of America, a principle which merits universal bibliographical adoption, because it makes explicit the historical levels on which any given discourse draws while at the same time making explicit the relation of any text or edition used to the original source work actually produced within the lifetime of each author cited. For the details of this style sheet, I refer readers to its full published form, "Semiotic Society of America Style Sheet", *The American Journal of Semiotics* 4.3–4 (1986), 193–215.

In this application of the SSA Style, I have added life dates in parentheses after the name of authors when we were able to find this information. Simple absence of a death date after a birth date indicates a presumption that, as this book went to press, the author was yet living. Birth dates with only a question mark in place of a death date indicate a presumption that the author is no longer living, though we were not able to find the death date. The general presumption regarding names without dates (mostly contemporary writers), according to the principle of historical layering as explained above, is that they were alive at least as of the date used in citation of their work.

Here I wish mainly to direct attention to the fact that, under the authors of cited sources arranged alphabetically, the dates when those sources first came into existence can be seen at a glance, like geological layers in a rock or the age rings in a tree trunk. For a historical work the advantage of this system should be obvious at once. But in fact human understanding itself is a historical achievement, and the value of this bibliographical principle is just as great even in purely speculative and theoretical works in any field.

With the exception of two cases that come to mind, Plotinus and Sextus Empiricus, where the internal organization of the reference itself makes necessary the full citation of the works of the author, and the cases of Boethius and Ockham, again because of dating difficulties, I have aimed to restrict this list of references to those works actually cited in the course of the chapters; and, without exception, the works included in this final list are the books and articles which I had in hand as this book was written and its bibliography compiled. I have tried so to record them that the interested researcher could easily take in hand exactly what I had in hand, and go from there. Eschewing bibliography for bibliography's sake, the list is not a list of secondary sources relied on third-hand, or an inflated list of works known, but an effort to provide the reader with an inventory of the actual bookshelf, as it were, utilized in order to write this particular book. The intention is to provide the interested reader with as accurate a basis as possible for evaluating the sources the author employed, without prejudging other works which the reader might find useful or necessary in further research into topics touched upon.

Finally, the specific conventions concerning the dating of works and authors that can be assigned only an approximate time frame needs to be made explicit. In such cases the following prefixes are attached to assigned dates:

a.   = *ante* or "before"

c.   = *circa* or "approximately"

fl.   = *floruit* or "the prime of life", "the time of flourishing"

i.   = *inter* or "between"

p.   = *post* or "after"

r.   = the beginning of the period of occupation of an office; so = *regnat* or "rules"

u.   = *usque* or "until", "up to the time of"; used to indicate the outside date on which an author worked on a manuscript left uncompleted.

Within references, the following abbreviations are used:

cf.   = confer or consult

q.v.   = *quod vide* or "which see", a cross-reference.

Index

RERUM ET PERSONARUM

Conventions of the Index. The nine main-entry Greek terms are grouped at the beginning as a separate list, though Greek terms within subentries are alphabetized according to Roman alphabetization. Individuals and expressions which play significant roles in the narrative are set off by bold face SMALL CAPITAL letters in the main alphabetical list. Small capitals ALONE are used to set off terms of less than central but more than passing interest to the narrative. In the alphabetizing of the main list, hyphenated names or terms are treated as if they were single expressions not containing a hyphen (e.g., "al-Farabi" is alphabetized as "alf…"), the same is true for expressions with parts separated (or joined) by "/" (e.g., OBJECT/THING DISTINCTION) and names with prefixes (such as "D" or "von", etc.) are alphabetized without regard to the prefix.

A lower case letter "n" after a page number indicates *footnote*. If the "n" is immediately followed by a further number (e.g., 433n58) that further number indicates the footnote number. If the "n" has no number following (e.g., 618n) the point indexed occurs in footnote text carried over from a note whose number lies on a preceding page. As in the book proper (see the Gloss on the References, pp. 834–5), "q.v." indicates a cross-reference to consult, "cf." a comparison to be made.

Subentries under the main entries of the alphabetized list are of various levels, signified by number of indents preceding each. In cases where an entry takes more than one line, the subsequent line(s) are double indented to signal they are continuations rather than subentries in their own right (see, e.g., the first entry under ABDUCTION). Each subentry, in turn, is arranged alphabetically within its level, with a *caveat*.

The subentries had to be treated overall as complex terms. Sometimes it was possible to begin the subentry with a keyword most important to the entry, and alphabetize accordingly. Othertimes it was necessary to use the subentry as a complex whole establishing a context for the keyword or keywords, a context which could not be maintained if the keyword itself were moved to the beginning. In such cases alphabetization was perforce according to the first expression within the complex whole (including use of an adverb or, rarely, preposition, as alphabetization base) required as a unit to display the central point.

Finally, by way of grasping Hill's dictum that there are no perfect synonyms, take note that, since the construction of an index is to be guided by logical considerations as they arise within the actual flow of the discourse, even terms which supposedly translate one another (e.g., *"ens rationis"*; *"ens reale"*, and "mind-dependent being", "nonbeing"; "mind-independent being", etc.) prove in context to require independent entries to approximate full coverage.

The overall result is an alphabetized list of key terms, figures, and sources used in the work, with an outline structure under the main entries of a quasi-narrative form but alphabetically keyed throughout. Nothing in the structure of such an index is novel, except in the sense that, despite the proven scholarly value of an index that approximates completeness for any work, such indexes seldom accompany the work in its first edition. Without the editorial encouragement of Ron Schoeffel of the University of Toronto Press, the assistance of Mary Catherine Sommers and Sheila Waggoner of the University of St. Thomas, Houston, and of Osmo Vartiainen of Helsinki University, this work too might have followed the usual path of author exhaustion and appeared without an index at all or with one limited to proper names.

3. *third degree*: to constitute object of metaphysics by developing doctrinal consequences of notion
     of being as able to be realized existentially in or apart from matter 309, 309n124, 310, 328
   sometimes opposed unwarrantably to "separation" 310–13

prescissive or *negative*: focus for analytical purposes on certain aspect 78n45, 310n125, 650n117

importance of for understanding relation as distinct category 228

as kind of awareness contrasted with awareness of objects physically at hand ("intuitive") 381, 648

perceptual abstraction alone recognized among modern mainstream founders before Peirce 381,
     527n39, 581n184

positive not applicable to Firstness of *primum cognitum* 647–8

as psychological or epistemological theory on formation of ideas 81, 113, 380

removal from here and now 24, 380

abstractive 206, 378–82, 567

Academy of Plato 42, 60, 79, 93, 96, 99–101, 113, 143, 203, 251, 510

ACCIDENT

  as category (as division of *ens reale*, q.v.) 73–8, 226–31

  commonality of every 74

  debate over number of 145

  dependency upon substance twofold 75

  diagram 145

  difference of relation as accident from other accidents 74

  differential status and importance of relation among accidents 74

  as form 72

  inherent

    accidents within Porphyry's Tree 152, 352n34

    as part of transcendental relativity 72, 226–31, 424n27, 656

  as intersubjective 73–7

  as predicable 144–50

  as prior to knowing being 341

  and property 145, 152, 352n34

  quantity as first of 78, 300, 423

    see also Quantity

  subjective (inherent) 389, 425, 463

  superstructural to substance 76, 442

  suprasubjective vs. subjective (inherent) 73, 227–31, 353, 426, 470, 546, 648, 655

  See also INHERENT ACCIDENT

accidental change 72, 80, 123

ACTION OF SIGNS

  in ancient thought 156–7

  in Aquinas 336

  Augustine, in connection with 336, 378

  basic doctrinal issue concerning 369

  and being 226

  causality proper to (*see* OBJECTIVE CAUSALITY) 472, 631–7

  circumstances of give rise to different types of sign-vehicle 391

  and codes, theory of 687, 732

  in Collingwood 576–7

  communication as effect of 429, 479

  as connection of being with appearances 613–14

  consequent upon being proper to sign 383, 643

  distinction basic to explanation of 585

realized:

 cause-effect relations in nature are distinct from relations of signification 374, 388–9, 718n124

 traditional focus in logic on intellectual interpretation was too narrow, but didn't follow through 367

"religious studies", rationale for replacing "theology" with anticipated by 366

repeats Augustine's pattern of too narrow a focus for understanding being proper to sign 367

scholastic realism, still wrote within epistemological perspective of too narrow for being of sign 391,
  407, 417

unwitting foreclosure on zoösemiosis (a self-referential inconsistency) 372–3

 works by and on 752, 771, 793, 797

Badawi, Abdurrahman 188n52, 752

Baer, Eugen 732, 752

Baghdad, one of principal Arabic centers for medieval Latin renderings of Aristotle 186, 189, 197

Bailey, Cyril 106, 752, 772

BAIN, Alexander (1818–1903), author of notion of belief from which Peirce reached original proposal
  of pragmaticism under label ("pragmatism") later misappropriated by James and Dewey in
  perpetuating nominalism 614, 615, 779

Bakewell, Charles Montague 28, 39, 752

Bakhtin, Mikhail (1895–1975) 611n1

the Bald: see Charles the Bald

Baldric, early 12th cent. Archbishop of Dol, Christian Epicurean 101

Baldwin, James Mark (1861–1934), ed. of 1901–2 *Dictionary of Psychology and Philosophy* 752

Bally, Charles 673, 675, 818

Bañez, Domingo (1528–1604), important Latin expositor of Aquinas 360–2, 752, 792

baptism 166, 195, 196

barbarisms of Latin grammar 436n62

Barbarossa, Frederick (c.1123–1190), ruler who, at mid-12th cent., inserted "holy" into title of "Roman
  empire" as revived by Pope Leo III in his dawn of 9th cent. crowning of Charlemagne 198

Barthes, Roland (1915–1980) 605, 674, 678, 679, 681, 686, 728, 753

Baskin, Wade, translator of Saussure 671, 676, 678, 679, 699, 757, 818, 819

Baudrillard, Jean (1929–) 611n1

Baumaker, Clemens 743

Baur, Michael 753, 818

Bayle, Pierre (1647–1706), author of "first book of the Enlightenment" (1697) and first systematic
  response (1686/8) to Augustine in matters of using police power to enforce religious
  orthodoxy 175n25, 245, 753

beans, prohibited food for Pythagoreans 33, 33n49

 why proscribed 33n49

 beauty 120, 254, 330, 364, 789, 809, 810

Beck, Lewis White 787

behaviorism 622, 728

BEING, semiotic quality of in general 348–9

 in another (*esse in*, inherent accident, subjective modification) 75

 in itself (*esse in se*, substance, subjectivity of individual) 75, 347n217, 454n28, 534, 697

 toward another (*esse ad aliud*, linking accident, suprasubjective characteristic) 73, 75, 77, 228,
  264n34, 346, 425, 462–3, 470, 474, 478, 563–4, 648, 655

 way it must be expressed in discourse (transcendental relation, q.v.) 226, 423–45, 424n37, 563–4, 656

BEING-AS-FIRST-KNOWN (also without hyphens)

 differentiation of from within 648

 horizon against which things first appear in difference from objects 348, 651

signs, doctrine of, grounded in 358, 363, 424n37, 473

species-specifically human awareness is tied to 347, 355n232, 469, 651

as unity of being prior to categorial schemes of whatever kind 483

See also BEING-AS-FIRST-KNOWN

ENS RATIONIS (= mind-dependent being)

analogy of proportionality illustrated by 321

animals without language too form and use without recognizing as such 472

attained objectively in "second degree of abstraction" (mathematics) 310, 314

Avicenna first introduced idea of as relation 229–30, 751

categorial relation excluded from according to existence but not according to essence 426, 475

complexity of needs to be studied 470

considered in context of transcendental properties of being 424n37

conventional signs and 428

creation of distinguished from prescissions 310n125

creature or construct of mind, fiction xxxi, 217

debate over whether all relations are (position of nominalism) 425

dependent upon experience 469

division of:

   into negation and relation 469

   reduces to ontological relation 470

early medieval interest in was logical 426–7

essential to notion of essence as known 653

as fiction of language not recognized as such 324n192

fictum as opposed to *factum* 279

first intentions too can be purely objective 470

infinite regress, home of 352–3, 353n226

logical being 230

modistae and 435

nonbeing (*non ens*), complementary opposite of being (*ens*) 248, 290, 350, 356, 469n82, 740n7

   nonbeing and being co-ordinate to one another within experience 356, 724

   presupposed to grasping principle of contradiction 356, 469n82

   theme of 20th cent. existentialism 290, 579

notion in Kant divorced from correlativity in awareness with *ens reale* known but not distinguished as such 559

noumenon in Kant would be single subspecies of for Latins (scil. *ens rationis sine fundamento in re*) 559

ontological relation transcends distinction of *ens rationis* from *ens reale* 244n89, 473, 474–5

as part of original problem of sign 388

perceptual as well as conceptual 351–2

precluded from any Aristotelian category (i.e., any category of what can be apart from thought) 425, 425n38, 426

presupposed along with relation for discussing being proper to sign 457, 473

purely objective being 350, 654

second intentions as conceptual examples 352–3

   distinction of from first intentions as subject of formal logical study main medieval interest 470

   second intentions, however, can assume social reality and existence 353

signs:

   can be mind-dependent beings depending upon circumstance 476

   can neither be excluded from nor reduced to mind-dependent being 476–8

in semiology (Saussure) 112, 157
and soul as form 301n106
as substantial form:
  alone 82, 291
  correlated with prime matter 68, 291
of thought 622n37
two ways of having 284–5
ultimate irreducibility of 361n246
of Umwelt 650–1
as unchanging, development of doctrine of 81, 152
unknowable according to Kant 560
Unmoved Mover and 271
of way of ideas 564
as what is regardless of what appears to be 60
of world according to Spinoza 139n138
essentia 38, 239, 281, 282, 284, 288, 291, 293, 296, 297, 308, 315, 318, 330, 339, 361, 444, 746, 747,
    759
ETHICS
book of Spinoza 519, 597–600
business ethics 85
emotional interpretant part of 332n172
foundations in natural philosophy and metaphysics 208
narrow sense of rules for individual behavior 54, 86–7
in plan of this book 736
politics in full sense 54
practical science of what human beings ought to do 84–5, 91, 98
  subdivisions of 85, 185
synecdoche in Locke for whole of practical thought 481
synonym for moral philosophy, esp. as developed by Socrates 44, 441
of terminology: *see* ETHICS OF TERMINOLOGY
of thinking (logic) 622–3
ETHICS OF TERMINOLOGY
applied to:
  discussion of Firstness 645–6, 648–9
  naming causality involved in actions of signs as such 630, 631–2
  usage of term:
    "ground" to single out "formal object" of an apprehension 343, 643
    "pragmatism" 616
    "*realis*" and "*realitas*" 623
    "sign" 640
logical thought historically informed essential to 622–3
modernity never provided circumstances recommending it 615
part of doctrine of signs which pertains to critical expression of understanding in science and
    philosophy 323
postmodern basis for progress in philosophy 369
the rules themselves:
  eight specific guidelines 666–7
  in general 663–6
  gloss on rule six 667n160

general meaning of expression 223–4, 223n33

"great fathers" so-called 223n32

invoked by Bellarmine and inquisition against accommodating Scripture to emergence of idioscopic
science 496, 497n16

and Lombard's *Sentences* 249–50, 258, 262–3, 262n31

early modern reaction against 543

late modern revival of similar perspective ("religious studies" vis-à-vis "theology") 258, 366

in *Summa* of Aquinas 264n34

See also patristic thought

"fatwa", Islamic religious denunciation or curse, sentence 191

Fausta, second wife of Constantine, murdered by same 167, 773

felix culpa "happy fault", said of original sin for bringing redeemer, here applied to Augustine's
ignorance which brought sign 216

feminism 606

Ferrara 203, 386

Ferrariensis (Francisco de Sylvestris, c.1474–1528), second in importance only to Cajetan re analogy
328, 359, 773

Ferrater Mora, José 500, 773

Ferreira Gomes, Joaquim, principal modern editor of FONSECA, q.v. 416, 757, 773, 774

Feuerbach, Ludwig Andreas (1804–1872) 572

Fichte, Johann Gottlieb (1762–1814) 572

Ficino, Marsilio (1433–1499), led revival of Greek learning and study of Plato in Renaissance Italy
141, 203, 761

FICTION, fictional

Augustine's proposal of sign and 368, 708

and being as first known (*ens primum cognitum*) 119

being of signs equally at home in fact and 217

belongs always to *esse ad*, never *esse in* 230n52, 426

and development of "reality" 688

environmental support for doctrine of fixity of species proved to be 80, 265

and essences 660

and fact contrasted 230n52, 426

and "final opinion" 624

and God 275

and Holy Roman Empire 196

and noumenal constructs 659n137

Pseudo-Dionysius used to promote belief in authenticity of his writings 133n118, 659

and "second intentions", logical meaning of 352

of secondary qualities implies same of primary 547

sign superior to contrast between fact and 244n89

symbolizing relation between doctrine of modern philosophy and development of modern science 540

transcendentals not reducible to 424n37

Figueiredo, Vivino de Campos 702n48, 766, 764

figures of speech 436

filioque, Latin-Greek controversy over Trinity 180, 181, 199, 203, 204

final causality, final cause 64, 65, 255, 472, 630–4

See further CAUSALITY; CAUSE; OBJECTIVE CAUSALITY

Findlay, John Niemayer 781, 785

first florescence of nominalism 154, 161, 243, 244, 386

of convertibility of being and truth 661n139
of correlation distinguished from ground of recognition 719
cover obscuring later Latin development of doctrine of signs 369, 371, 465
of denying:
    common denominator in natural and conventional signs 481
    mind-independent reality according to Berkeley 527
of dependence of *scientia* upon *doctrina* respecting fundamental conceptual frames of objectivity
    704–5
of development from Kant to Sartre "as a kind of sober tale of madness" (Descombs) 578n75
of dietary preferences 85n57
of difference in view of soul between Augustine on one hand and on other hand Plotinus and Plato 52
of discussion in *Meno* of *primum cognitum* of Aquinas 52
of dissatisfaction with Cajetan's interpretation of doctrine of analogy in Aquinas 328–9
of distinction
    between demonstrative and hypothetical reason 264–5, 265n35
    between physical environment and objective world 350
    of regions of space discussed by Kant 1768 786
    between signs as formal and instrumental 392, 433
        can be interpreted either realistically or nominalistically 392, 403–4, 417
of doctrine of:
    divine names (*see* NAMES OF GOD) in experience 316, 321
    signs and Heidegger 667–8
of eliminating gods from traditional Porphyrian Tree 151–2
of endurance of Peripatetic/Stoic dispute over place of logic 601
in experience of reason as species-specifically human 12, 41, 157, 189
    as relatively autonomous by right vis-à-vis scriptural interpretations 189–91, 202, 278, 304
of external sense cognition
    thinkable as attaining certain aspects of mind-independent being objectified 454n28, 531–5, 576n71
    transcended in abstractive awareness perceptual or intellectual 381
of fame of Heraclitus 36
held by Arianism at outset of dark ages 187
of human knowledge in structures of cognition shared with other animal forms 5
for idea of "reality" 3, 5
for identifying spiritual substances as physical beings 382, 475n110
of infinite process within discourse 352n226, 356
of inherently interdisciplinary character of semiotics 703
of intellectual judgments as intersubjectively communicable 356–7
of interpretant in experience 729
of knowledge shared among animal forms 5, 505
of late-modern shift to anthropocentric notion of theology's subject-matter 299
literal and "nose of wax" fallacy 465
lost by semiology to advance of semiotics 674
of medieval notion between "theology" as sacred and philosophy as "handmaid" thereto 261–2
of metaphysics as distinct mode of knowing 310–11n128
of mystical experience in relation to philosophy 127
of nominalism 246
    of nominalism's dispute with semiotics xxxi, 254n, 387–8, 417n21, 481, 566, 586
of objectifications scientific in modern sense 505
of objective universe in *primum cognitum* 350

clear beginnings of astronomy as distinguished from astrology 65–6, 494n10, 555

early idea of as unchanging ("celestial matter") 79, 79n47

    fixity of species associated with 80, 502, 508

    reservations of Aquinas concerning hypothetical character of celestial matter 80, 264–6, 265n35, 499

focus of philosophical interest from earliest times 22, 25

movements of bodies in earliest focus for successful mathematical interpretations of nature 22, 187, 555

    motion as phenomenon transcended distinction between celestial and terrestrial changes 270

to be reconstituted at end of time ("Parousia") 303, 338–9

reduced in modern philosophy to prospective fictions of our own mind's making:

    in Descartes 514

    in Kant 567

    in B. Russell 588

thought to provide proof for existence of disembodied intelligences as cause of their regular motion 255, 264, 308

    Cajetan needlessly entangles arguments concerning existence of God with cosmological imagery 499

Hecataeus of Miletus, 7th cent. BC visit to Egypt (Herodotus) 12

HEGEL, Georg Wilhelm Friedrich (1770–1831)

abortive attempt at a postmodern doctrine of categories 571, 571n89, 645n102

attack on Kantian doctrine of Ding-an-sich (thing-in-itself, q.v.) as unknowable 571–2n59, 573n60

    on untenability of Kantian full separation of phenomena from things-in-themselves 573n60

and Christianity 578, 578n76

"Circle of Friends of the Eternal One" 573

counters Cartesian bias against studying philosophy in its history 574, 575

definition of being misses problem of *primum cognitum*, precategorial unity of being 483n126, 574

idealism, his influence over speculative twilight of 575

    in anticipating semiotic: Collingwood 576, 578, 658n135

    in existentialism: Kirkegaard 578, 580

    in Marxism 580n83

"last true giant on way of ideas" 572

metaphor attributed to for illustrating difference between philosophy and science 186, 490

"a nominalist of realistic yearnings" according to Peirce 544

owl of wisdom, saying concerning xxxii

political theory, influence in 573

and possibility of integrating culture with nature 658n135

and postmodernity 578, 604, 658n135

and pragmaticism 625, 636, 661–2

rejecting Kant rejects modernity 521, 543, 556n22, 562n39, 574, 585

works on and by 753, 781–2, 815, 818, 819

Hegelian categories 571, 571n89, 645n102

HEIDEGGER, Martin (1889–1976)

basic thought unconnected with Thomistic metaphysics of *esse* 287n76, 290, 330n166, 342, 668n166

and Eco's semiotic project 703

and fundamental anthropology 687n33

and Maritain's dissociation with expression "Christian philosophy" 343

and possibility of conformity truth 357n237, 483

and postmodern era of philosophy 508–9, 521, 667

INFINITE SEMIOSIS

openness of understanding in contrast with sense perception to interpretations of being not biologically
        determined 306, 644
possibility of rendering nugatory opening of Lebenswelt to mind-independent being by
        mind-dependently structuring objectivity in ways alternative to what either cenoscopy or
        idioscopy suggests relative to sense-perception 189–90, 644
process whereby more and more of reality is incorporated into Lebenswelt 471–2, 472n92
rooted in relation as being proper to sign in general 435, 573n60
shorthand expression for discovery that all knowledge involves action of signs 644–5
    Cf. BEING-AS-FIRST-KNOWN; INFINITE REGRESS; INTELLECT; MIND-DEPENDENT BEING
Inge, Rev. William Ralph (1860–1954), pessimistic Christian Neoplatonist who was national figure in
        Britain 143, 785, 828

INHERENT ACCIDENT

aspect of subjectivity:
    considered precisely in view of relation it does or could support is called "fundament" 226, 231,
        424n37
    which serves to support relation to other individuals 75, 425
intrinsic individualizing characteristic, aspect of subjectivity 72–3, 75, 386–7, 546
    whole point of as such is to distinguish and individualize 389, 426, 655
sign-vehicles but not signs as signs belong to class of 546, 717–18
    See ACCIDENT; SUBJECTIVITY; TRANSCENDENTAL RELATION

INITIAL SKETCH FOR SEMIOTICS 597, 599, 603, 607

innate
    principles of grammar (Chomsky) 727, 728, 728n167
    idea of God (Descartes) 240n76, 520
    ideas rejected (Locke, Poinsot) 454n28, 521

INNENWELT

codes essential to exaptation of language to linguistic communication 726
cognitive and affective states on basis of which organism transforms surroundings into objective
        world 6, 7
    cognitive elements called ideas, affective elements feelings 7
cognitive map orientating organism to surroundings 6, 7
contrasts as private to correlated Umwelt as public 8
foundation of relations terminating or "grounded" (q.v.) in objects experienced 697
integration of things within as founding Umwelt focus of Heideggerean *Sein* 290
language is ability to reorganize elements of in ways only indirectly tied to biological heritage 9,
        306, 575
Latin anticipations of notion 347
logic pertains to as species-specifically human 90
one of three factors essential to constitution of objective world 7
original elements of begin as signs and become interpretants consequent upon success of codes 726
sign mediates with Umwelt, within Umwelt, and between Umwelts 340, 411
source of "histories" discursively established 350
states of are "subjective" as belonging intrinsically to distinct physical entity 6
subjective elements of are correlated with objective elements of Umwelt 6, 8, 126, 340, 575
    sensation, perception, understanding distinct levels within 379, 575
tied by real relations within sensation to physical aspects of environment 697
Tinker-toy structure is unique to human 11, 306, 697
underlies possibilities of communication and error 8

subjective being to maintain itself in actual existence 72–3, 523n27

requires that both foundation and terminus have subjective being in nature (order of *ens reale*) 73

is suprasubjective being a-fortiori 426

See also MIND-DEPENDENT; MIND-INDEPENDENT; SUPRASUBJECTIVE

intuition 125, 206, 282, 418, 536, 558, 563, 567, 576, 660, 795

intuitive 206, 378–82, 531, 587

invention 13, 206, 721–3

Ipsum Esse Subsistens 63, 124, 272, 282, 283, 294, 316, 318, 340, 349, 463

See ESSE; EXISTENCE OF GOD; GOD

Iran 191

Irene (AD752–803), Eastern Roman Empress (r.780–802) to whom Charlemagne in vain proposed
    marriage; restored icons 198

Irish philosophy 135

IRONIES OF HISTORY 100, 129, 130, 143, 241n74, 275, 324, 345n215, 390, 414n9, 436, 544, 552, 558n26

irony 27, 131, 172, 219, 345, 390, 392, 686

Isaac Comnenus (1005–1061), Eastern Emperor crowned (1057) by Cerularius, Patriarch who
    precipitated Greek-Latin schism 203n84

Isagoge (Porphyry), thematic treatment of five logical terms involved in defining 144, 147, 148, 150,
    153, 208, 812

Isidore, scholarly associate of Proclus (5th cent. AD) 144

ISIDORE MERCATOR, 9th cent. forger of papal decretals exposed in early 17 cent. esp. by reformed
    theologian David Blondel 201, 783

Isidore of Seville (c.AD560–636) 183, 185, 223n33

Islam 12, 164, 174, 186–90, 202, 205, 244, 257, 492, 509, 824

Islamic philosophy (cf. "Eastern" philosophy; "Christian philosophy") 189–90n53

Istanbul 167, 202, 205, 576

Italy 33, 165, 169, 171–4, 178, 181–3, 185, 196, 197, 199, 202–5, 263, 324, 455, 493, 496, 759, 791,
    830, 832

ivy, symbol of sobriety in pagan world, of everlasting life in early Christianity 414, 414n9

Jackson, A. C. 583, 777

Jackson, B. Darrell 111nn59 & 60, 217n16, 220n27, 750, 785, 807

Jackson Park, Dubuque, Iowa vii

Jakobson, Roman (1896–1982) 639, 694, 732, 785

James, the Apostle 133n116

James, Henry (1843–1916) 786

James of Venice (?–1148) 756

James de Vio, name by Christening of Cardinal CAJETAN, q.v. 355

James, William (1842–1910) 355, 355n230, 508, 614–16, 622, 625

Jameson, Fredric (1934–) 611n1

Jameson, Robert 764

Japan 12, 128, 164, 771

"jaskrave", Ukrainian term for light so sharp as to force squinting 448

Jastrow, Joseph 347, 786

Jaulin, Robert 605, 786

Jean de Meung (c.1240–1305), made public correspondence claiming to being that of Heloïse and
    Abaelard 243

Jean de Saint-Thomas (= POINSOT, q.v.) 481

Jeauneau, Eduard A 135, 136, 786, 820

Koerner, E. S. F. 440, 758
Koerner, Konrad 750
Köhler, Wolfgang 347, 788
Köngsen, Ewald 744
Königsberg, Germany 554, 757
de Koninck, Charles: *alphabetized under* DeKoninck
Koran (Qu'ran), revealed Scripture of Islam 187–91, 234, 244
Korn, Ernst R., pen-name of Heinz R. Schmitz (q.v.), secretary and executor for Jacques Maritain
          260n24, 343nn202 & 203, 789, 794
Kovach, Francis Joseph 254, 789
Krampen, Martin 629n58, 704n, 789
Kranz, Walther 21, 26, 36, 770
Krempel, A. 75, 226, 230, 444, 464, 620, 751, 789
Kretzman, Norman 406, 789
Kristeller, Paul Oskar 761, 807, 812

La Fleche, Jesuit college where Descartes received intellectual formation, with Dominican authors
          interdicted at time 450n10
La Mettrie, Julien Offray de (1709–1751) 523, 789
Lacan, Jacques (1901–1981) 611n1
Lactantius, Lucius Caecilius Firminianus, 4th cent. Christian apologist, later tutor to Crispus, q.v. 789
Lady Welby, Victoria (1837–1912), British aristocrat who was correspondent with C. S. Peirce in
          semiotics 612, 635, 781, 805
Laertius, Diogenes (c.AD180–c.260) 23, 33, 43, 53, 89, 94, 95, 99, 102, 103, 109, 110, 748, 770, 789
Lamarck Jean-Baptiste-Pierre-Antoine de Monet, Chevalier de (1744–1829) 85
Lambertini, Roberto 216n15, 772
Lampsacus, remote city of ancient Asia 101, 103
Lanfranc (c.1005–1089), Archbishop of Canterbury 1079–1089 194
Langan, Thomas 529n43, 789
von Langenstein, Heinrich (c.1325–1397), important participant in 14th-cent. conciliar controversy 401
Langford, Jerome J. 493, 496, 789
LANGUAGE
    ability to reorganize Innenwelt in ways not tied to biological constitution as are both sensation and
          perception 9, 10–11, 12, 301n106, 488
    analogy as phenomenon of 313, 314, 315, 324–5, 329
      rule for analogous usage of 319–20
    in ancient world not considered semiotically 108–9, 111, 155–6, 216–17, 342–3, 417n21
    of Aquinas, ease of learning 663n149
    capacity to deal with relations as such, enables human organism to model objects as prospective
          "things in themselves", subject to verification and test 8n7, 9, 488
    and categories of Aristotle 227, 227n47
    and changes of age in philosophy 92, 115, 134, 144, 161, 164, 165, 174, 175n25, 203, 210–11, 213,
          450–1, 492, 574, 665n157, 686–7, 738
    Cicero first to fashion Latin philosophically 163
    deals with relations as such in their difference from objects as perceptible 9, 488
    depends upon and does not supplant perceptual modalities of Umwelt 9–10, 57n16, 110n49
      yet constitutes semiosically distinct level respecting 107, 217, 417n21
    as discourse about God 278, 279, 281, 284
    distinguished from communication and speech 11–12, 728n164

MacDonough, Steve 191, 793

Macedon, King Philip of (382–336BC, r.359–336), father to Alexander the Great 87

machine, dominant image in early modern science of nature 523, 555, 789

MacKenna, Stephen 118n71, 828

macroexperience 535

de Magelhães, Cosmas (1551–1624), member of Conimbricenses 420

Mahaffy, Sir John Pentland (1839–1919), late 19th century Kant scholar 787

Maimonides, Moses (Moses Ben Maimon, 1135–1204), principal Jewish intellectual of Latin Age 251,
    274n48, 297, 302n107, 386, 758

Maisonneuve, H. 175n25, 793

Maitland, Sara 192, 746

Majorian, briefly mid-5th cent. Western Roman Emperor, by sufferance of Ricimer, q.v. 171

Makowski, Simon Stanislaus (c.1612–1683), author of minor interest in waning of Latin semiotic
    consciousness 444, 793

malice 54, 202

Maloney, Thomas S. 250, 366, 367, 372, 373, 376, 752, 793

Malter, Rudolf 787

Manetti, Giovanni 17, 57, 107, 110, 111, 215, 218, 418, 670, 694, 794

Marc, André 329, 794

Marcus Aurelius (AD121–180) 97, 225, 799

Maréchal, Joseph (1878–1944), font of so-called "transcendental Thomism" within 20th cent.
    Neothomist revival 289, 312n133, 794, 795

Marenbon, John 138, 162, 205, 206, 794

MARITAIN, Jacques (1882–1973) 14, 729, 761, 767, 768, 783, 791, 794–5

on abstraction as path into metaphysics 309, 309n24, 312–13

among leading figures of Neothomism 289

on angels 339, 339n196, 403n85

on "common sense" as philosophical doctrine 552n12

"Christian philosophy" so-called, need to face embarrassments of history in matter of 437n65

on primitive confusions essential to idea of philosophy as denominational 190n, 257–8, 257n19,
    260n24, 298n101, 305, 343

and confessional contexts, rights of reason in 298n101

on Cyclopean Thomism 360n245

on Descartes and attempt to distinguish "ideosophy" from philosophy proper 511n1

idiosyncratic proposal thematized and advanced by Redpath 511–12n1

on distinction between speculative and practical knowledge 702n50

on importance of nonbeing in philosophy of being 360n245

on impossibility of knowing "that something is" divorced from all access to "what" that is that is
    573n60

intersemioticity of Sebeok with 480n118

on knowability and unknowability of God 274–5, 275n50, 317, 317n140

and label "Neothomist" 342n200

and Poinsot 406n95, 450n8, 473n102

modern rediscovery of his *Treatise on Signs* 209n100, 371n25, 443, 445, 450

on place of among Thomist authors 362

on realism

vs. idealism as *sic et non* 740, 740n8

in philosophy, authentic source of 345–6, 565, 5734n60

on relation of work of Aquinas to that of his commentators 362

Mews, Constant J., produced English ed. of purported lost early letters of Heloise and Abaelard 243, 744, 798

Mexico (México) xxvii, 263n33, 301n106, 422n28, 698n33, 750

Michael Scot (c.1175–c.1234/5) 139n41, 140

Michael "the Stammerer", Byzantine emperor from AD820–829 through whom Greek ms. of Pseudo-Dionysius came to reside at monastery of St. Denis (Dionysius) awaiting Scotus Erigena 135

Migne, Jacques-Paul (1800–1875) 746, 750, 755, 760, 774, 777, 792, 798

Milan, erstwhile capitol of Western Roman Empire 165, 168–72, 401, 772, 785, 794

Miles, Jack (John Russiano) 209, 209n100, 482–3, 798

Miletus, ancient Greek city of western Anatolia 12, 20–2, 29, 738, 827

Miller, Arnold V. 781

Miltiades: *under* POPES

MIND-DEPENDENT BEING (*ens rationis, non ens*)

   abstraction can give rise to objects not capable of transfer directly into order of mind-independent being 310, 423, 425

   analogy necessarily involves mind-dependent relations but is indifferent to also involving mind-independent relations 322

   animals as cognitive organisms

      form objects by interweaving mind-dependent with mind-independent relations 351, 354, 448, 472, 577, 650

      make use of mind-dependent relations without knowing their difference from objects related 472, 577n74, 650–1

   and being as first known (*primum cognitum*) 347–57, 647, 648

   binary distinctions tacitly based upon 677–8

   circumstance, role of in determining mind-dependent status of sign relation

      decisive for doctrinal unity of semiotic 371, 409, 463, 476

      irrelevant to distinction between sign as this or that type 476–7

   divisions of mind-dependent being not restricted to intellectual order of understanding 351, 354

   in Eco 720

   experience in light of being reveals its structure to be interweave of mind-dependent with mind-independent relations sustaining objects 340, 351, 354, 448, 472, 577, 650, 653, 662

      at base of difference between Umwelt as such and as Lebenswelt 650–1

      Peirce's categories designed to catch interweaving 662

   and extrinsic denomination of "being known" 696

   incorporation of actual relations into objectivity by semiosis heart of, multiplication of mind-dependent surrogate for, inquiry 193, 354

   indifference of relation as being to mind-dependent/mind-independent distinction key to understanding:

      being of sign in general 244n89, 371, 409, 434, 457–8, 463, 476–8, 696

      nature of mind-dependent in contrast to mind-independent being 457, 457n45, 463

   indifference of relation in positive structure to its subjective ground:

      called after Boethius *secundum esse* or "ontological" 230, 423, 425, 427, 475

      determines prior possibility for relation as suprasubjective to become in fact intersubjective 429, 478, 562, 562n39, 696

   infinite process, relations based directly on other relations, is distinctive to order of mind-dependent being 189, 533, 683

   intersubjectivity of depends upon circumstance 429, 463, 476

   mind-dependent relations:

      are called "rational" because only "reason" (language in contrast to perception) can distinguish between mind-dependent & mind-independent in being 229, 351, 472, 577n74, 697

can enter into social structure of reality and become part of public experience as such 353, 448,
    650–1
have same essence or positive structure in being as mind-independent relations 230, 425, 655
negation has positive structure of relation 469–70, 654
as nonbeing:
    integral to study of semiotic 368, 473–5, 598, 644
    root of problem along way of ideas 528, 556–7, 561n37, 562, 562n39, 569, 587n97, 645
objects viewed comparatively give rise to mind-dependent relations 229–30, 351
positive structure of relation, as such always and unexceptionably has 457n45, 469–70, 652, 654–5
received no comprehensive study in Latin Age 469–70, 598
relation constituting formal being of natural signs becomes mind-dependent according to circumstance
    370n24, 371
and relation objectively considered 654–5, 658
"second intentions":
    arise within objective order but not always restricted to order of mind-dependent relations 353, 577
    not simply mind-dependent beings 470–2
self-identity, like relation of known to knower, is mind-dependent relation 647, 695–7
    key to difference between objects and signs 695
sign:
    divided into
        natural/conventional not by its being as sign formally but by being of its fundament 370n24, 476
        formal/instrumental not by its being as sign formally but by fundament being interior or external
            to psychological constitution of sign user 370n24, 435, 476
        icon/index/symbol according to type of sign-vehicle rather than being proper to sign as such
            668, 717–18
    in general posited mode of being indifferent to difference between mind-dependent &
        mind-independent 226, 371
space is constituted by physical differences mind-dependently related 71
subject matter of logical investigation restricted to 351–2, 470
subjectivity is excluded from order of mind-dependent being 463, 561
suprasubjectivity is common essence of all relations as such 231, 425, 429
terminates objectively relations *founded* on subjective reality of psychological states 435, 561, 696
textual interpretation risks interpreter substituting mind-dependent for actual relations resulting in
    pure or principally fictions 189, 533, 683
that two things are separated is mind-independent but which is to right or left mind-dependent 71
time is constituted by physical regularities preserved and linked by mind-dependent relations 71
in time & space mind-dependence is formal, mind-independence fundamental 71
"where" and "when" express objective mixture of mind-dependent and mind-independent elements 71
See also , ENS RATIONIS; NONBEING
MIND-INDEPENDENT or physical
advance in knowledge of depends upon use of models 658
Augustine's *signum* poses question of how indifference to difference in objectivity between
    mind-dependent and mind-independent being is possible 409
being:
    respecting sign:
        not determinately constituted by relation in this order 371
        motivation in being proper to depends upon connection of signs with order of 684, 720
        posited by Augustine and explained by Poinsot as irreducible to 226, 474, 477–8

sometimes is and sometimes not part of objective being 534–5

status:

    of relation as within this order or not depends not upon relation itself but upon circumstance 370, 370n24, 658

    of sense qualities cannot be

        maintained without analysis of relation 527, 528, 570

        presupposed apart from analysis of relation 526–7

subjectivity (*inesse*) is synonym for all mind-independent being except categorial relation 73–4

synonyms for: categorial, predicamental, real 423

terminology of Boethius to mark uniqueness of mind-independent applies equally to mind-dependent relation 230

theories developed to explain mind-independent dimensions of objective world provide conceptual tools necessary to explain action of signs within objectivity 18

transcendental relation is synonym for subjective being as dependent upon environmental interactions 72

uniqueness of relation as mode of mind-independent being proves basis for explaining semiosis from God to sub-atomic particles 344n89

whatever is known that lacks mind-independent counterpart exists purely objectively 425

See further ENS REALE

Minerva, ancient goddess of wisdom xxxii

minimal sign function 222n31, 391

Minio-Paluello, Lorenzo 743, 798

MISSION:

    of Apollo XIII 265

    of Christianity as regards late-modern situation of theology 299

    of Descartes in philosophy 512–13

    of philosophy 14

    of Poinsot respecting intellectual culture of his day 455

Mitchill, Samuel Latham (1765–1831), associated with work of Cuvier 764

Moby Dick 727

modal 637, 639

models 658, 659, 703

MODERN, MODERNITY: period of development and institutionalization of science as idioscopic enterprise and of mainstream development in philosophy of nominalist paradigm for epistemology xxxi, 544, 740 and *passim* (cf. *entry for* DR. JEKYLL AND MR. HYDE)

modistae 435, 436, 440, 758

Moerbeke, William of (c.1215–c.1286), Aquinas's preferred translator of Aristotle 142, 366

Mohammed (AD570–632), first prophet and founder of Islam 12, 205, 820

Mommsen, Christian Matthias Theodor (1905–1958) 179n38, 798

Mommsen, Theodor Ernst (1817–1903) 213n1, 798

Mommsen, T.E. and Meyer (Theodosian Code) 179n38, 798, 827

monad, Leibniz's name for fundamental natural unit 512, 569, 588

Monadologie (*Monadology*), title from one of Leibniz's books often used to designate his distinctive doctrine 519, 544, 588, 791

"monads have no windows", maxim from Leibniz best summative of modern philosophy 512

monism 21, 23, 24, 29, 41, 67, 69, 764

monist 25, 615, 616, 664, 774, 804, 805

monistic 23

monotheism vs. polytheism, metaphysical resolution of issue 283–4

object/thing distinction
  being vs. seeming is version of this distinction 10
  see also separate entries for OBJECT, THING
organization of environment into objects to be sought and avoided is perception 7, 346, 346–7,
        347n216, 379, 661
perceived depends upon subjective psychological states functioning as sign-vehicles 223, 404–5,
        406n95, 412, 432–4
as perceptible differ from relations as such 9, 488
of perception modeled in their difference from things as independent of perception results from
        difference between understanding and sense perception, between linguistic and nonlinguistic
        animals 9, 652–4, 657
physical objects distinguished:
  from material objects 382, 646
  from sensible objects 9
presupposes sign for existing as complex item within experience 733
problem of being proper to things as objects of experience beginning of philosophy xxx, 3, 14
related objects can be perceived, but relations as such can only be understood 9, 351
to say "object" is to say "significate" or "object signified" 7, 378, 384, 451
sciences are differentiated by their objects of investigation 81, 186, 225–6, 261, 261n26, 308,
        309–10, 343
sensory selectivity together with network of relations constituting objects comprises objective world
        or Umwelt 6
sign proves to be that which every object presupposes xxx, 19, 155n172, 434, 709n82
things are encountered only in and with objects 14, 19, 230n51, 341, 349–50, 644
time and space exist objectively but not wholly physically 70
and truth 454
within Umwelt acquires further relations to other objects whereby one becomes sign of others 7,
        413, 416, 456, 703
understanding, or language, is capacity to model world in ways that do not reduce to perceptual
        appearances, according to relations without bearing on our biological constitution 9, 488
  See also LEBENSWELT; SIGN; THING-IN-ITSELF; UMWELT
OBJECTIVE CAUSALITY, PROPER TO ACTION OF SIGNS
  extrinsic formal causality ("objective", or "specificative" causality) 472, 565, 630–3
    exemplary ("ideal") distinguished form specificative ("objective") 632–4
      Latin discussions of 633n75
  mistakenly identified with final causality by Peirce 631
    ethics of terminology applies to question of name for this causality 472, 632
  See further CAUSALITY
OBJECTIVE RELATION
  and knowledge of essences 657–8
  relation obtaining:
    as able to pass back and forth within experience between mind-dependent and mind-independent
        654–5, 658
    so as to constitute entire reality of fictive objects 654
    among objects as expressing reality of things 434, 638
    among objects only 229, 231, 561–2
    among objects regardless of whether also obtaining or able to obtain among things 253n10,
        371n25, 423, 474, 654
    among things as well as among objects 424, 426, 653n129, 658

restores to philosophy continuity:
  with common sense 8n6, 468, 636
  with Latin tradition 157, 211, 215, 377–8, 380–1, 435, 445, 481, 508–9, 637, 646, 663–4, 671, 681, 687, 738
role of sign in details of its full extent first actually to undertake study of 216, 456n37, 462, 667, 740, 741
scientific intelligence, requirements of for community support 192–3, 213n1
Scotus favorite writer of Peirce among Latins 385
Secondness, category of:
  anticipated in Roger Bacon's discussion of sign relation 374
  physical reality manifests itself within 14, 660–1, 737, 737n4
  transcendental relation falls within 429
  why called "brute" 660
and semiology 670–1, 674–5, 682, 684, 686, 689, 699
"semiosis" name coined by (c.1883) for action of signs 109, 110n51, 383, 603–4, 604n26, 629
  arbitrariness of sign inadequate to requirements of 699
  and evolution 637
  scope of, central question concerning 634
  terms more specific coined by others subsequently 629
and semiotic triangle 682
"semiotics", main influence in opening of 21st century currency of term 362, 605n29, 674, 685, 690n, 699–700, 738, 740
sign in Peirce:
  being of more fundamental than divisions of 668
  division into formal and instrumental, why not discussed 637, 640, 668
    comparative merit of Peirce's own division of sign 668
  dynamically conceived 643–4
  main figure in restoring general notion of as mode of being verifiable in nature equally with culture 57n16
  needs to be supplemented by theory of code 687, 687n33, 725, 732
  strictly so called is triadic relation, *loosely* is sign-vehicle or representamen 639–40, 641n90, 643, 681
sign vehicles can be indifferently physical or psychical, material or psychological 407
and "speculative grammar", idea for 435, 435n61
"all thought is in signs", import of formula 534, 628, 692
"type/token" distinction analogous with traditional "universal type/particular instance" distinction 60
Thirdness, category of, how constituted 661
  anticipated in Roger Bacon's discussion of sign relation 374
triadic character of sign relation known before Peirce, though third term of never named as such 442, 463–4, 683, 693n15
unification in semiotics of epistemology with knowledge of nature
  cures modern split between Mr. Hyde and Dr. Jekyll xxxi, 449–50, 628
  ties view of with Locke and Poinsot 481n120, 482, 684, 742
uniqueness of action of signs in transcending distinction between mind-dependent and mind-independent being 476, 740
  "why we have trouble telling what is real and what is not" 637
why last of moderns & first of postmoderns 625
works by and on 755, 758, 762, 763, 766–9, 774, 781, 784, 787–8, 796, 803–6, 808, 815–16, 833
Peirce Edition Project 609, 734, 803

Stoic view of logic as on footing with 97

synonymous originally with NATURAL PHILOSOPHY, q.v. 21

theology, connection with original idea of 83, 256, 261, 283

translation of Averroes' version of creates Latin distinction between *natura naturans* and *natura naturata* 138–9

Unmoved Mover and, original idea for distinguished from further implications of 83–4, 255–7, 310

See also NATURAL PHILOSOPHY

physiosemiosis 629, 712, 721, 723

phytosemiosis 629, 723

phytosemiotics (Krampen) 629n58

Picot, Abbé Claude, man on whom Descartes relied to translate his *Principles of Philosophy* from Latin to French 518

Pickwickian 620, 620n32

Pinborg, Jan (1937–1982) 439, 440, 750, 752, 758, 785, 788, 807

Pinner, Harry Leo 20, 807

Pipes, Daniel 192, 807

Pitcher, George 832

Pittendrigh, Colin S., coiner of term "TELEONOMY", q.v., to displace "teleology" 66, 808

Pius VII: *under* POPES

Placidia, sister of Eastern Roman Emperor Honorius who herself became Empress for a quarter century 171

PLATO (c.427–348/7BC)

Aristotle in relation to 60–1, 73

and Aristotle after Neoplatonism 187, 251

astronomical theory, best worked out early in Academy of 80

Athens birthplace only of Socrates and Plato among philosophers 43

Augustine and 213, 257, 257n19

congenial to mystical and religious views 113–14, 116–17

context for understanding 18, 35

contraries in Plato and pre-Socratics compared by Aristotle 24n20

dialectic, place of in 55, 58

dominated:

Byzantine thought always 142n156, 164n

early Latin Age indirectly, Aristotle directly later Latin Age 92, 108, 182, 185, 213

earliest figure with some writings to survive intact 32

on education 56, 58

elitist view of philosophy 55

Epicurus and 101, 107–8

exoteric teachings alone committed to writing 42, 55

distrusted writing 55–6

Forms or "Ideas", reality supra-sensible in true being of 54, 58, 122

Aristotle main source for knowledge of theory of, together with Plato's *Dialogues* 60

early medieval versions of:

in Anselm 233

in William of Champeaux 245, 387

criticism of theory:

in Abaelard 245

in Aristotle 113

and Galileo 523

QUIA ("that"), demonstration that something exists preparatory to exploration of why it is way that it is found to be 267, 270, 274, 315

Quine, Willard Van Orman (1908–2000) 576n70, 582, 664, 814

QUINTESSENCE, QUINTESSENTIAL

dualism of mind and body quintessentially modern 523

Hermetic drift and deconstruction quintessentially idealist tendencies 691

idealism, quintessence of modern 561

indifference of relation to difference between mind-dependent and mind-independent quintessential point 655

Kant's philosophy quintessentially modern 557n24

Leibniz's monadology captured quintessence of modern view of subjectivity 588

nominalism, quintessence of, to deny reality of relations outside of thought 618

Poinsot was quintessential scholastic 454

"pragmatism" expresses quintessentially American spirit 615

realist vs. idealist opposition quintessentially modern controversy 692–3

standpoint of semiotics transcends quintessentially modern oppositions 700

QUINQUE VERBA, Latin name sometimes given to Porphyry's *Isagoge*, q.v. 144, 154, 208

QUINQUE VIAE, "the five ways" which Aquinas presents to manifest dependency of universe on God 241, 267, 270, 275, 280, 281, 284, 293, 317, 330, 352, 499

"the Rabbi" or "Teacher", honorific title used in later Latin Age for Moses Maimonides 302n107, 386

Radcliffe-Brown, Alfred Reginald (1881–1955) 11n11

Rahner, Karl (1904–1984), major theological figure of 20th cent. "transcendental Thomism" 289, 299, 299n102, 814

Rainalducci, Pietro: *under* POPES, Nicholas V

Ramirez, Didacus, friend, biographer, and editor of Poinsot who preserved only known likeness of his face 159, 814

Ramirez, Jaime Maria 362n247, 814

Randall, Jr., John Herman (1899–1980) 162, 761, 807, 812, 815

Ransdell, Joseph 302, 631, 741, 815

Raposa, Michael 431, 815

Rasmussen, Douglas B. 410n100, 815

Rastier, François 605, 815

ratio difficilis, technical term in Eco's theory of semiotics 700

rational animal ("*animal rationale*"), oldest known attempt at species-specific definition of human being 151, 259

rational relation 430

RATIONALISM, modern mainstream current presupposing reason both fundamentally independent of and different in kind from sense 41, 126, 141, 222, 404, 450, 481, 501, 518–21, 524, 526, 536, 547, 548, 553, 565, 566, 572, 581, 585, 592, 593, 802

Rauch, Augustus 612

Rauch, Felzian, publisher of first edition of Rahner's *Geist in Welt* 814, 815

Rauch, Irmengard 766

Raven, John Earle 22, 26, 29, 31, 38, 788

Ravenna, early 4th cent. imperial capital, late 4th cent. site of Odoacer's assassination by Theodoric the Ostrogoth, q.v. 171–3, 181

ready-to-hand, ready-to-handness (*cf.* present-at-hand) 651

real relations (*see* CATEGORIAL RELATION; ENS REALE; MIND-INDEPENDENT BEING) 389, 419, 539, 573, 627, 661, 697

interpretant, some adumbration of notion 382–3
involved in network or system 383
role of nonbeing within 384–5
use among angels contrasted with humans 383
sign, definition of:
joined Aquinas in criticism of Augustine's formula as too narrow to cover concepts 222
terminology "formal/instrumental" not used by Scotus, and will prove ambiguous 391, 392,
403, 409, 414, 417, 432
own definition mirrored that of Roger Bacon as inversely too narrow to cover percepts 378, 385
corrected by Fonseca on this point three centuries later 412
signification of existence:
intuitive/abstractive distinction of semiotic import in this regard 378–9, 381, 382
nonbeing, role of in clearly recognized 378, 384–5, 431
recognized as circumstantial 378, 384–5, 384n59, 431
"thisness" (haecceitas) and essence 649
works on and by 819, 824, 832
zoösemiosis, weak on 378, 385
SCOTUS ERIGENA, Joannes (c.810–875/7), "only star in the night of Irish philosophy"
death, reported (probably apocryphally) to have been stabbed by student pens 137, 137n21
"Eriugena" variant of name technically more correct 135n122
main influence in Latin Age was as first translator of Pseudo-Dionysius 135, 232, 242n80
brought from Ireland to teach in Charlemagne's school, also accepted task of translation 135–6,
135n127, 242n80
work made of Proclus a Latin phoenix and of Neoplatonism a renewed force 136
own masterpiece, Periphyseon or De divisione naturae, not well received in its time 136
attempts to show positive influence of work in Latin Age have so far failed 137–8
aim of work may yet be realized 136
denounced by 9th cent. Pope, condemned by 13th cent. Council, and described by then-Pope as
"swarming with worms of heretical perversity" 136, 491
dispute over title 136
"oblique influence" at best argued through intersemioticity of Erigena's fourfold division of nature
collapsed into twofold natura naturans/naturata from translators of Averroes, and oblique
pattern of influence indeed 138–40
structure of work 136
philosophy, deemed by Erigena essential for salvation 137, 137n131
singular case in story of Latin philosophy 127, 135
works by and on 774, 786, 820, 828
SCRIPTURE, SCRIPTURES: writings taken as divinely revealed 12, 131, 189, 201, 202, 220–1, 223, 236,
250, 258, 259, 264, 285, 297, 299, 304, 331, 338, 366, 367, 372, 494, 496, 497, 507, 543,
775
scrolls 20n5, 214n8
Scruton, Roger 419, 820
SEBEOK, Thomas Albert (1920–)
biosemiotics, study of action of signs throughout biosphere, special interest of 635, 663, 703n53, 737
Charles S Peirce, first scholarly biography of, brought to publication through instrumentality of 612
"Clever Hans phenomenon", drew attention to semiotic character of as source of methodological
fallacy 111n56
Eco's main work brought into English by 690
editor-in-chief (1969) involved in establishment and naming of journal Semiotica 595n12

transcends opposition of mind-independent to mind-dependent being 728, 736, 738

understanding highest flowering of 306, 348–9, 738

unlimited in growth of symbols expressing human understanding of God 274–5

when not degenerate guarantees both contact with physical being in sensation and growth of apprehension 468, 471, 575, 721

semiosphere, Hoffmeyer's sense distinguished from that of Lotman 629

semiotic animal, postmodern definition of human being 158, 680, 736, 737

SEMIOTIC CONSCIOUSNESS

analysis of triadic incorporation of dyadic physical relations in sign crucial to advance of 718n124

definitive break with modernity 692

explicit attainment of begun with Augustine extends to overcoming inner/outer split 407, 692, 692n12

figures marking historical path to:

Abaelard 247–8, 248n97

d'Ailly 670n2

Aquinas 331, 336, 362, 382, 404, 414, 430, 670n2, 742n17

Araújo 432, 432n55, 670n2

Aristotle 157, 157n178, 529

Augustine 217, 219n22, 220, 224, 247, 362, 378, 388, 411, 417–18n21, 418–19, 422, 443, 445, 585, 669–70, 670n2, 684, 694

Bacon, Roger 365, 367, 367nn13&14, 374–5, 404

Berkeley 592

Brentano 404, 404n87

Collingwood 576, 658n135

Comas del Brugar 444, 444n85

Condillac 593

Conimbricenses 422, 428, 670n2

Croce 577

Descartes 450, 450n10, 481

Donatus 436

Eco 548n7, 689–90, 699–700, 702, 706, 710, 712, 714–15, 715n114, 725, 728, 729–31

Epicurus 106, 108–10

Fonseca 378, 411, 414, 417–20, 428, 670, 670n2

Fraser, Alexander Campbell 481

Hegel 575

Heraclitus 35

Husserl 222n30

Jakobson 639

Kilwardby Adscriptus 439–41

Kilwardby, Roger 437–9

Leibniz 592

Locke 215–16, 362, 440, 441, 450, 480–1, 482, 547–8, 580, 591, 596, 604, 612, 681, 684, 694, 742

Lonergan 735

Maritain 443, 445, 450

Merleau-Ponty 579, 579n77

modistae 435

Neothomism 445

Ockham 388, 403–4, 428, 481

Peirce 220, 362, 377–8, 435, 445, 450, 467–8, 481–3, 578, 604, 616, 619–20, 628, 637, 662, 677, 684, 692, 699, 712, 737n4, 740–2

representative factor as perceptible by outer sense in dividing of signs seen as subordinate to question of relation as mode of being constituting every sign as sign, which relation as such is never perceptible apart from elements related chs. 9–10, e.g., 432, 440–1, 473–8

sign as such constituted in every case by relation necessarily involving three elements or terms: element representing, element represented, and element to which representation is made chs. 8–10, e.g., 374–5, 463–4

strict sense of being of sign is triadic relation (like every relation never directly perceptible) distinguished from loose sense of sign as representative element within triadic relation, whether or not sense perceptible chs. 9–10, e.g., 433, 476–8, 640

"to" representation, making of in action proper to signs identified and named "semiosis"; third term of sign relation distinguished and named as such "interpretant"; role of three terms united by sign-relation recognized as interchangeable in process of semiosis as spiral of interpretations grounded in interactions among finite beings ch. 15, e.g., 629, 635, 640, 643–4, 653–4

triadic relations as being of signs strictly presupposed to every object in being known, are engendered by semiosis incorporating physical relations among their terms and recognized as essential means by which whole of experience, perception, and understanding is developed, maintained, and communicated e.g., 434, 640, 709n82, 716, 720–1

   See further entries under BEING; DEFINITION OF SIGN; ENS; OBJECT; PERFUSION OF SIGNS; THING
sign function, sign-function 391, 700, 705
sign vehicle: see SIGN-VEHICLE
signa naturalia (*see* NATURAL SIGN) 413, 723, 732
signature 335, 433, 463, 476, 589, 682
signifiant 112, 676–9, 681, 682, 816
significare formaliter 405
significare instrumentaliter 405
SIGNIFICATION
   action of sign 156
   Anselm's view on within his ontological argument 236
   consequences of reduction to representation 563–5
   in conventional signs or culture 419–20, 477n112, 649–50, 677, 705–7, 710, 715, 811
   and Derridean *différance* 679, 682
   in discourse about God 274–5, 280, 280n58, 320
   distinction of from representation 430–2, 695
      basis of distinguishing between things and objects 431, 585, 695
   distinguished from representation key to doctrine of signs 620n29, 695–8
   failure of reduction of to representation 443, 565
   formal vs. instrumental 404, 409, 415–17, 419, 433, 444, 447, 585
   in general sense Augustine proposed depends upon doctrine of relation developed after Aristotle 369–71, 419, 427, 467–8, 586
   indifferent:
      to reality of object signified 434
      to subjective or objective status of its vehicle 427, 430–2, 634
   and inference 712–13, 714
   influence of syntax on 435–6
   and intelligence 728
   and intentionality in late modern discussions 404
   and interpretants 730–1
   at intersection of nature and culture 731, 738
   as involved in process 434, 641n90, 707, 729

Timetable of Figures

First evidence of great civilizations:
Sumeria, Egypt, Babylonia, Assyria,
Persia, India, China (c.4000BC)

Sumerian *Epic of Gilgamesh* composed
(a.2000BC)

"Israel" becomes collective name (c.1050–
1000BC)

Vedas composed in India (i.1000/500BC)

Hebrew *Old Testament* (i.1000/200BC)

Jewish prophets (c.800–700BC)

Upanishads written (i.800/500BC)

Homer, esp. *Iliad* (c.790–c.710BC,
fl.750BC)

Conventional "founding of Rome" (753BC)

Hesiod, *Theogony* and *Works and Days*
(c.740–c.660BC; fl.700BC)

The Ancient Age of Philosophy

Thales of Miletus (c.625–c.545BC)

Anaximander (c.610–c.545BC)

Lao-tzu (c.604–517BC)

Pherecydes of Syros (c.585/4–c.500/498BC)

Pythagoras of Crotona (c.582/570–
c.507/495BC)

Anaximenes (c.580–c.500BC)

Xenophanes of Colophon (c.570–475BC)

Buddha (c.563–483BC)

Confucius (c.551–479BC)

Compilation of the *Tao Te Ching*,
i.550/399BC

Heraclitus the Obscure, of Ephesus
(c.540/535–c.480/475BC)

Alcmaeon of Croton (c.530–c.450BC;
fl. c.490BC)

Parmenides of Elea (c.515–c.450BC)

Polygnotus (c.500–c.440BC)

Anaxagoras of Clazomenae (c.500–428BC)

Bhagavad-Gita composed (i.499/199BC)

Empedocles of Acragas (c.495–c.435BC)

Zeno of Elea (c.495/490–c.430BC)

Protagoras of Abdera (c.490/84–414/11BC,
fl.444/41BC)

Gorgias of Leontini (c.481–c.375/72BC,
fl. a.400BC)

Herodotus (c.484–430/20BC)

Melissus of Samos (c.481–c.401BC)

Leucippus (c.470–390; fl. 440–435BC)

Socrates (c.469–399BC)

Hippocrates (c.460–377BC)

Democritus (c.460–370/362BC)

Cratylus (c.450–c.393BC)

Eucleides of Megara (c.450–374BC)

Aristophanes (c.448–c.388BC)

Xenophon (445–355BC)

Antisthenes of Cyrene (444–365BC)

Plato (c.427–348/7BC)

Diogenes the Cynic (c.412–323BC)

Eudoxus of Cnidus (c.400–c.350BC)

Aristotle (384–322BC)

Stilpo of Megara (c.380–300BC)

Theophrastus (c.371–287/6BC)

Xenocrates (c.365–c.284BC; fl. 339–314BC)

Pyrrho of Ellis (c.365–275BC)

Alexander the Great (356–323BC)

Epicurus of Samos (341–270BC)

Polemo (c.338–c.260BC; fl. 313–270BC)

Zeno of Citium (c.366–260BC)

Metrodorus of Lampsacus (c.330–277BC)

Timon of Phlius (320–230BC)

Arcesilaus (316–241BC)

Composition of the Dead Sea Scrolls
    (c.300BC–50AD)

Archimedes (c.290/80–212/11BC)

Chrysippus of Soli (c.280–c.206BC)

Philodemus of Gadara (c.110–c.40BC)

Cicero (106–43BC)

Andronicus of Rhodes (c.100–c.25BC)

Lucretius (c.99–55BC)

Caesar Augustus (63BC–AD14)

Philo of Alexandria (Philo Judaeus,
    20/15BC–AD50/54)

Jesus Christ (i.7/4BC–c.AD30)

Diocles the Magnesian (c.AD30–90;
    fl. a.AD100)

New Testament written (c.AD50–110/20)

Epictetus (c.AD50–130)

Ptolemy (Claudius Ptolemaeus, c.AD100–
    175; fl. AD127–151)

Marcus Aurelius (AD121–180)

Galen (AD129–c.199/215)

Sextus Empiricus (c.AD150–225)

Ammonias Saccas (c.AD175–p.242)

Diogenes Laertius (c.AD180–c.260,
    fl. c.AD210–230)

Origen (c.AD185–254)

Plotinus (AD203–270)

Porphyry the Phoenecian (c.AD233–304)

Diocletian (AD245–313)

Iamblichus (c.AD250–330)

Aedesius (c.AD275–355)

Marius Victorinus (c.AD280/300–c.363)

Athanasius (AD297–373)

Aelius Donatus (c.AD310–a.380)

Gregory of Nyssa (c.AD331–c.396)

Julian the Polytheist (Flavius Claudius
    Julianus, AD331/2–363)

Ambrose (c.AD340–397)

Proclus (c.AD410–485)

Pseudo-Dionysius (c.AD455–c.535;
    fl. c.490–500)

Simplicius of Cilicia (AD490–560)

The Latin Age

Jerome (Eusebius Hieronymous, c.AD347–
    419/20)

Augustine of Hippo (354–430)

Martianus Capella (c.360–439)

Boethius (c.480–524/5)

Priscian ("Priscianus Caesariensis";
    c.480–560/70)

Cassiodorus (480/90–573/585)

Dionysius Exiguus ("Dennis the Short",
    c.486–a.566)

Isidore of Seville (c.560–636)

Mohammed (570–632)

Qur'an dictation begun (c.AD625)

Alcuin of York (732–804)

Charlemagne (c.742–814)

Hilduin (c.775–855)

al-Kindi (c.803–870)

John Scotus Erigena (c.810–c.875/7)

Pseudo-Isidore (c.805–c.885; fl. c.840–850)

al-Farabi (c.878–c.950)

Avicenna (ibn Sina, 980–1037)

Berengar of Tours (c.1000–1088)

Peter Damian (1007–1072)

Anselm of Canterbury (c.1033–1109)

Jean Roscelin (1050–1120)

al-Ghazali (1058 1111)

William of Champeaux (c.1070–1121)

Gilbert de la Porrée (1070–1154)

Peter Abaelard (c.1079–1142)

William of Conches (c.1080–1154)

Peter Lombard (c.1095–1160)

William of Malmesbury (c.1095/6–1143)

Hugh of St Victor (1096–1141)

Heloise (c.1098–1164)

Hildegard of Bingen (1098–1179)

ibn Daud (c.1110–c.1180)

Gerard of Cremona (c.1114–1187)

John of Salisbury (1115–1180)

Averroes (ibn Rushd, 1126–1198)

Moses Maimonides (1135–1204)

Dominic Guzman (c.1170–1221)

Michael Scot (c.1175–c.1234/5)

Francis of Assisi (c.1182–1226)

Albertus Magnus (c.1201–1280)

Petrus Hispanus (Peter of Spain, c.1210–1277)

Roger Bacon (c.1214/20–1292)

Robert Kilwardby (c.1215–1279)

Kilwardby Adscriptus (fl. i.1230/70)

Bonaventure of Bagnoregio (1217/21–1274)

Thomas of Aquino (1224/5–1274)

Siger of Brabant (c.1235/40–1281/84)

Giles of Rome (1243–1316)

Meister Eckhart (c.1260–1327/28)

Dante Alighieri (1265–1321)

Duns Scotus (c.1266–1308)

John of Jandun (c.1275–1328)

Marsilius of Padua (c.1280–1343)

William of Ockham (c.1285–1349)

John Tauler (c.1290–1361)

Jan Ruysbroeck (1293–1381)

Henry Suso (1295–1365)

Francesco Petrarch (1304–1374)

Heinrich von Langenstein (c.1325–1397)

John Wycliffe (c.1328–1384)

Juliana of Norwich (c.1342–c.1423)

Catherine of Siena (1347–1380)

Vincent Ferrer (1350–1419)

Petrus de Aliaco (Pierre d'Ailly, 1350–1420)

Gemistus Pletho (c.1356–1450)

Jan Hus (c.1369–1415)

Joannes Capreolus (c.1380–1444)

Nicolas of Cusa (Nicolaus Cusanus, 1401–1464)

John Bessarion (1403–1472)

Lorenzo Valla (1406–1457)

Marsilio Ficino (1433–1499)

Cristóbal Colon (Christopher Columbus, 1451–1506)

Johannes Trithemius (1462–1516)

Pietro Pomponazzi (1462–1525)

Cajetan (Tommaso de Vio, 1469–1534)

Nicolaus Copernicus (1473–1543)

Sylvester Ferrariensis (c.1474–1528)

Ferdinand Magellan (c.1480–1521)

Martin Luther (1483–1546)

Ulrich Zwingli (1484–1521)

Ignatius Loyola (1491–1556)

Francisco de Vitoria (1492–1536)

Dominic Soto (1494–1560)

Philipp Melancthon (1497–1560)

Andreas Osiander (1498–1552)

Melchior Cano (1509–1560)

John Calvin (1509–1564)

Teresa of Avila (1515–1582)

Pedro da Fonseca (1528–1599)

Domingo Bañez (1528–1604)

John of the Cross (Juan de la Cruz, 1542–1591)

Emmanuel de Goes (1542–1597)

Robert Bellarmine (1542–1621)

Tycho Brahe (1546–1601)

Francisco Suárez (1548–1617)

Cosmas de Magelhães (1551–1624)

Balthasar Alvarez (1561–1630)

Clemens Timpler (1563/4–1624)

Paolo Antonio Foscarini (c.1565–1616)

Sebastian de Couto (1567–1639)

Bartholomaeus Keckermann (c.1571–1608/9)

João Baptista Bosserel (1583–1648)

Francisco Araújo (1580–1664)

John Poinsot (1589–1644)

Christoph Scheibler (1589–1653)

The *Conimbricenses* (publ. i.1592/1606)

Pierre Gassendi (1592–1655)

Bartholomaeus Mastrius (1602–1673)

Simon Stanislaus (Szymon Stanisław) Makowski (c.1612–1683)

The Modern Age

Giordano Bruno (c.1548–1600)

Francis Bacon (1561–1626)

Galileo Galilei (1564–1642)

Johannes Kepler (1571–1630)

Thomas Hobbes (1588–1679)

René Descartes (1596–1650)

Benedict Spinoza (1632–1677)

John Locke (1632–1704)

Isaac Newton (1642–1727)

Gottfried Wilhelm von Leibniz (1646–1716)

Pierre Bayle (1647–1706)

Jonathan Swift (1667–1745)

Giambattista Vico (1668–1744)

Christian Wolff (1679–1754)

George Berkeley (1685–1753)

John Wesley (1703–1791)

Georges Louis Buffon (1707–1788)

Julien Offroy de La Mettrie (1709–1751)

Samuel Johnson (1709–1784)

Thomas Reid (1710–1796)

David Hume (1711–1776)

Jean-Jacques Rousseau (1712–1778)

Étienne Bonnot de Condillac (1715–1780)

Immanuel Kant (1724–1804)

Edward Gibbon (1737–1794)

Jean-Baptiste de Monet Lamarck (1744–1829)

Jeremy Bentham (1748–1832)

Pierre-Simon Laplace (1749–1827)

Pierre-Jean-Georges Cabanis (1757–1808)

Johann Gottlieb Fichte (1762–1814)

Friedrich D. E. Schleiermacher (1768–1834)

Napoleon Bonaparte (1769–1821)

George Léopold Cuvier (1769–1832)

Georg Wilhelm Friedrich Hegel (1770–1831)

Jakob Friedrich Fries (1773–1843)

Friedrich Wilhelm Joseph von Schelling (1775–1854)

Arthur Schopenhauer (1788–1860)

Leopold von Ranke (1795–1886), father of scientific history

Ludwig Andreas Feuerbach (1804–1872)

John Stuart Mill (1806–1873)

David Friedrich Strauss (1808–1874)

Charles Darwin (1809–1882)

Søren Kierkegaard (1813–1855)

George Boole (1815–1864)

Karl Marx (1818–1883)

Friedrich Engels (1820–1895)

Simon Newcomb (1835–1909)

Franz Brentano (1838–1917)

William James (1842–1910)

Friedrich Wilhelm Nietzsche (1844–1900)

F. H. Bradley (1846–1924)

Bernard Bosanquet (1848–1923)

Gottlob Frege (1848–1925)

Robert Louis Stevenson (1850–1894)

Désiré-Joseph Mercier (1851–1926)

Josiah Royce (1855–1916)

Sigmund Freud (1856–1939)

Edmund Husserl (1859–1938)

Henri Bergson (1859–1941)

John Dewey (1859–1952)

Alfred North Whitehead (1861–1947)

Lenin (Vladimir Ilich Ulyanov, 1870–1924)

Bertrand Russell (1872–1970)

Ernst Cassirer (1874–1945)

Robert Frost (1874–1963)

Carl Gustav Jung (1875–1961)

Joseph Maréchal (1878–1944)

Albert Einstein (1879–1955)

Jacques Maritain (1882–1973)

Raïssa Maritain (Raïssa Oumançoff, 1883–1960)

Étienne Gilson (1884–1978)

Ludwig Wittgenstein (1889–1951)

Georges Lemaitre (1894–1966); "Big Bang" theory, 1927

Charles Hartshorne (1897–2000)

Bernard Lonergan (1904–1984)

Karl Rahner (1904–1984)

B. F. Skinner (1904–1990)

Jean-Paul Sartre (1905–1980)

Simone de Beauvoir (1908–1986)

Maurice Merleau-Ponty (1908–1961)

A. J. Ayer (1910–1989)

Albert Camus (1913–1960)

Willard Van Orman Quine (1908–2000)

Noam Chomsky (1928–)

Ralph McInerny (1929–)

Postmoderns, Real and Would-Be

Charles Sanders Peirce (1839–1914)

Ferdinand de Saussure (1857–1913)

Jakob von Uexküll (1864–1944)

György Lukács (1885–1971)

Robin George Collingwood (1889–1943)

Martin Heidegger (1889–1976)

Rudolf Carnap (1891–1970)

Mikhail Bakhtin (1895–1975)

Suzanne Langer (1895–1985)

Roman Jakobson (1896–1982)

Jacques Lacan (1901–1981)

Maurice Blanchot (1907–)

Roland Barthes (1915–1980)

Jean-François Lyotard (1924–)

Gilles Deleuze (1925–1995)

Michel Foucault (1926–1984)

Jean Baudrillard (1929–)

Pierre-Félix Guattari (1930–1992)

Jacques Derrida (1930–)

Richard Rorty (1931–)

Umberto Eco (1932–)

Fredric Jameson (1934–)

Floyd Merrell (1937–)